The University of Chicago Spanish Dictionary

Universidad de Chicago

Diccionario
Inglés-Español *y* Español-Inglés

Tercera Edicion, Revisada y Ampliada

Un Diccionario Manual Nuevo y Conciso que
Contiene las Voces y Locuciones Básicas de
Ambos Idiomas y Además una Lista de 1000
Modismos y Refranes Españoles con Variantes
y Traducción al Inglés

Recopilación de
Carlos Castillo *y* **Otto F. Bond**

Con la ayuda de
Barbara M. García

Revisado por
D. Lincoln Canfield

The University of Chicago Press
Chicago & London

The University of Chicago

Spanish Dictionary

Third Edition, Revised and Enlarged

A New Concise Spanish-English and English-Spanish
Dictionary of Words and Phrases Basic to the Written
and Spoken Languages of Today, plus a List
of 1000 Spanish Idioms and Sayings, with Variants
and English Equivalents

Compiled by
Carlos Castillo & Otto F. Bond

With the Assistance of
Barbara M. García

Revised by
D. Lincoln Canfield

The University of Chicago Press
Chicago & London

The University of Chicago Press, Chicago 60637
The University of Chicago Press, Ltd., London

© 1948, 1972, 1977 by The University of Chicago
All rights reserved
First Edition published 1948
Third Revised Edition 1977

Printed in the United States of America

81 80 79   987654

Library of Congress Cataloging in Publication Data

Main entry under title:

The University of Chicago Spanish dictionary.

Added t.p. in Spanish: Diccionario inglés-
español-y español-inglés.
Includes index.
1. Spanish language—Dictionaries—English.
2. English language—Dictionaries—Spanish.
I. Castillo, Carlos, 1890-   II. Bond,
Otto Ferdinand, 1885-   III. García, Barbara M.
IV. Canfield, Delos Lincoln, 1903-
V. Chicago. University.
PC4640.U5 1977 463'.21 76-449

ISBN 0-226-09673-4
ISBN 0-226-09674-2 pbk.

Contents

Foreword to the Third Edition

The University of Chicago Spanish Dictionary has been compiled for the general use of the American learner of Spanish and the Spanish-speaking learner of English, with special reference to New World usages as found in the United States and in Spanish America.

With this purpose in mind, the editors and the author of the revisions and additions of this new third edition have selected the words to be defined, first according to the relative frequency of their occurrence, secondly in keeping with dialectal variants of the New World, both Anglo and Hispanic, and thirdly in accordance with the increase in technological lexicon during the past two decades.

The Spanish-English section of the Dictionary contains all the items listed in Juilland and Chang Rodriguez's *Frequency Dictionary of Spanish Words* (The Hague: Mouton & Co., 1964). The hundreds of dialectal variants which appeared in the 1972 edition as well as the entries related to developments in the fields of aviation, atomic energy, linguistics, and so forth, have been augmented. More than 1000 new entries have been added to the Spanish-English section and in the English-Spanish section some 500 new entries—in addition to the 1500 items new to the second edition—have been added. No attempt has been made to add an equal number of entries in both parts for the simple reason that in the past three decades many more new terms of universal usage have been coined in English than in Spanish. Many of these new English terms have been assimilated into Spanish.

One of the outstanding features of the third edition is the list of 1000 Spanish idioms and sayings that follows the Spanish-English section. Dialectal variants and English equivalents, also with variants, are listed for these idioms, and an English index makes locating them easy.

Also new to the third edition is syllabication of all the entries in both parts as well as a new phonetic transcription of the Spanish entries. (The English entries had been transcribed phonetically in the first edition.) In keeping with the New World application of the Dictionary, the phonetic transcriptions of the Spanish entries have been made to represent "Highland American" usage (Mexico, Guatemala, Costa Rica, Highland Colombia, Ecuador, Peru, Bolivia). Local variations have been disregarded.

Regional Spanish-American usage is still identified by abbreviations of country or area, and parenthetical identifying expressions continue to be employed to facilitate distinction among several possible definitions of a particular word.

The extensive auxiliary data of the second edition has been retained, including the list of monetary units, the adjectives of nationality, and the extensive discussion of American-Spanish and its regional dialects.

A dictionary should be an instrument for better understanding between peoples. It is the earnest wish of the editors of this one that it may serve that end.

Part One Spanish-English

List of Abbreviations

adj.	adjective	*math.*	mathematics
adv.	adverb	*neut.*	neuter
arith.	arithmetic	*num.*	numeral
conj.	conjuction	*p.p.*	past participle
contr.	contraction	*pers.*	personal
def.	definite	*pers. pron.*	personal pronoun
def. art.	definite article	*pl.*	plural
dem.	demonstrative	*poss.*	possessive
dem. adj.	demonstrative adjective	*prep.*	preposition
dem. pron.	demonstrative pronoun	*pron.*	pronoun
etc.	et cetera	*refl.*	reflexive
f.	feminine noun	*refl. pron.*	reflexive pronoun
fam.	familiar	*rel.*	relative
indef.	indefinite	*rel. adv.*	relative adverb
indef. art.	indefinite article	*rel. pron.*	relative pronoun
inf.	infinite	*sing.*	singular
interj.	interjection	*subj.*	subjunctive
interr.	interrogative	*v.*	verb
irr.	irregular	*v. irr.*	irregular verb
m.	masculine noun		

Special Words and Abbreviations Used to Indicate Regional Occurrence

Am.[1]	Spanish-American
Andalusia	
Andes	(Ecuador, Peru, Bolivia)
Arg.	Argentina
Bol.	Bolivia
Carib.	(Cuba, Puerto Rico, Dominican Republic)
C.A.	Central America (Guatemala, El Salvador, Honduras, Nicaragua, Costa Rica)
Ch.	Chile
Col.	Colombia
C.R.	Costa Rica
Cuba	
Ec.	Ecuador
Guat.	Guatemala
Hond.	Honduras
Mex.	Mexico
Nic.	Nicaragua
N.Sp.	Northern Spain
Pan.	Panama
Par.	Paraguay
Peru	
P.R.	Puerto Rico
Riopl.	Rio de la Plata region (Eastern Argentina, Uruguay)
S.A.	South America
Sal.	El Salvador
Spain	
Ur.	Uruguay
Ven.	Venezuela

Spanish Pronunciation

The Spanish of Spain (except the southwest) has 24 phonemes, or minimum units of sound-meaning distinction. The Spanish of southwest Spain and most of Spanish America has 22 phonemes. These minimum units of sound are indicated in the following charts and descriptions by slashes, /b/, /e/, /č/, and stand for

---

[1] This abbreviation is employed to indicate general Spanish-American usage, usually with the implication of obsolescence in Spain. It is also used to identify words that are currently little used but which may occur in literary works of bygone days.

1

Phonetic Manifestations of the Phonemes of Spanish

	Bilabial		Labiodental		Interdental		Dental		Alveolar		Palatal		Velar		Glottal	
Voice	vs	vd	vs	vd	vs	vd	vs	vd	vs	vd	vs	vd	vs	vd	vs	vd
Occlusive	p	b			t	d	t	d					k	g		
Fricative	φ	ƀ	f		θ	đ						y	x	ǥ	h	
Sibilant							s	z	S	Z	(š)	(ž)				
Affricate											č	ŷ				
Nasal										n		ñ		ŋ		
Lateral										l		ļ				
Vibrant										r rr						
Semiconsonant		w										j				

an abstract representation of a group or class of sounds, the individual members of which are variants or allophones. The latter are indicated by brackets: [b̵], [e], [ŷ]. Some of the phonemes of Spanish have two or three variants, depending on position within the phrase.

The two principal characteristics of Spanish pronunciation as contrasted with English are tenseness of articulation and continuity in transition from word to word within the breath group. Thus all the vowels have a clear nondiphthongal character and sound "clipped" to the English-speaking person. The consonants, especially /p/, /t/, /k/, /l/, /r/, /rr/, have much less vocalic interference than in English, and the first three have no aspiration. The glottal stop, so common in the Germanic languages, including English, is very rare in Spanish. The transition between vowels of contiguous words is smooth. **El hado, helado, el lado** sound very much alike. **Para hacerlo** is [paraasèrlo] or in rapid speech [parasèrlo]. So marked is the continuity that following sounds influence the preceding ones: **los dos niños** [lozdózniños]; **un peso** [umpèso] **en que** [èŋke].

The Consonantal Phonemes of the Spanish of Northern Spain

/p/	/b/	/t/	/d/	/k/	/g/
	/f/	/θ/	/S/	/y/	/x/
			/č/		
/m/			/n/	/ñ/	24
			/l/	/l̬/	
		/r/	/rr/		

The Vocalic Phonemes of Spanish

$$i \qquad\qquad u$$
$$e \qquad o$$
$$a$$

The Consonantal Phonemes of Andalusian and Latin American Spanish

/p/	/b/	/t/	/d/	/k/	/g/
	/f/		/s/	/y/	/x/
			/č/		
/m/			/n/	/ñ/	22 or 23
			/l/	(/l̬/)	[Bolivia, Paraguay, Perú]
			/r/	/rr/	

The Spanish Spelling System and the Sounds Represented

I. The Vowels

1. **i** as a single vowel always represents [i], similar to the second vowel of *police*. Examples: **hilo, camino, piso**. As a part of a diphthong, it represents [j], much like English /y/ in *yes, year*. Examples: **bien** [bjen], **diablo** [djab̵lo], **ciudad, baile, reina, boina.** The first syllable of **baile** is much like *by* in English.

2. **e** represents [e], which has no exact equivalent in most English dialects. It is higher than the /e/ of *get* but without the diphthong of *they*. It is

much more tense in articulation than either English sound. It varies slightly
according to adjacent sounds. The vowel of **perro** is more open than that of
pero. Generally it is more open in a closed syllable. Examples: **mesa, del,
hablé, en, tres.**

3. **a** represents [a], which is similar to the first vowel of *mama*, stressed on the
   first syllable. Examples: **caso, cano, ¡ah!, América.** Even when not stressed,
   it has the same clear sound. English *America* has at least two neutral or
   schwa sounds [ə].

4. **o** represents [o], which is more like the Scotch-English sound of *auld* than
   the British or American *old*. It has no off-glide or diphthongal character
   such as is heard in the latter. It varies slightly according to adjacent sounds:
   the first syllable of **corro** is slightly more open than the first of **coro**. **Sol** is
   slightly more open than **no**. Examples: **boto, modo, señor, oso, amó.**

5. **u** represents [u], which always has the value of the sound indicated by
   English *oo* in *boot, fool*, never that of *book*, nor that of the *u* in *union*.
   Examples: **cura, agudo, uno.**
   a. Note that the spelling combinations **qui, que, gui, gue** represent [ki],
      [ke], [gi], [ge].
   b. **u** is used to represent the semiconsonant [w] in a diphthong: **cuida,
      cuento, cuadro, cuota** [kwíḍa], [kwénto], [kwáḍro], [kwóta].
   c. Likewise **u** is used to represent the semivocalic element of a diphthong:
      bou, deuda, causa [bow], [déwḍa], [káwsa].

II. The Consonants

1. **p** represents [p], which never has the aspiration of English /p/ (*pill, papa*),
   but is like that of *spot*. Examples: **padre, capa, apuro, punto.**

2. **b** and **v** represent /b/, which has two variants, according to position in the
   phrase: [b], [ƀ]. These do not depend on spelling, which goes back centuries.
   Either letter represents [b] at the beginning of a breath group or when
   preceded by [m] (spelled either **m** or **n**), and is much like English /b/.
   Examples: **bomba, burro, en vez de, vine, invierno.** In spite of spelling, the
   last three examples are [embézḍe], [bíne], [imbjérno]. Either letter represents
   [ƀ] in all other situations. English has no equivalent. It is a /b/ with the
   lips slightly open. Examples: **haba, uva, Cuba, la vaca, habla, la barba.**

3. **m** represents [m], which is essentially the same as English /m/ (*much*).
   Examples: **madre, mano, cama.** [m] does not occur syllable final in Spanish.
   Álbum is pronounced [álƀun].

4. **f** represents [f], which is similar to the /f/ of English. In some areas and
   among certain strata of Hispanic society the articulation is bilabial rather
   than labiodental.

5. **t** represents [t], which never has the aspiration of English /t/ in prevocalic
   stressed position (*tea, two, ten*). It is more similar to the English /t/ of the
   cluster [st] (*stop, step*). Examples in Spanish: **tela, tino, tinta.** The point of
   articulation is dental.

6. **d** represents /d/, which has three variants according to position in the
   phrase: [d], [ḍ], [Ø]. At the beginning of the breath group or after /n/ and

/l/, **d** represents [d], which is similar to the English /d/ of *dame, did, darn.* Examples: **donde, falda, conde.** In all other situations the letter represents [đ], or even [Ø]. There is a tendency in modern Spanish to move from the fricative [đ] (similar to the sound represented by the *th* in *mother, this, then*) to zero articulation [Ø]. Examples: **hado, cuerda, es de, dos dados, cuadro, padre, abad, usted, Madrid.** The last two words are usually pronounced without final consonant, and the consonant tends to be very weak in the ending /-ado/: **hablado, estado, mercado.**

7. **s** In Spain, except the southwest, this letter represents [S], an apicoalveolar sibilant, similar to the /s/ of southern Scotland and that of older speakers of the Midland dialect of the United States. Examples: **solo, casa, es.** Before a voiced consonant within the phrase it usually represents [Z]. Examples: **desde, mismo, es verde, los labios, las manos.**

In southwestern Spain and in all of Spanish America except a small area of Colombia, this letter represents [s], a dental sibilant of high resonance similar to the usual "feminine" sibilant of much of the United States. In some areas it is actually lisped. Before a voiced consonant within the phrase it usually represents [z], a voiced sibilant similar to the /z/ of English *razor, ooze,* Examples: **desde, mismo, es verde, los labios, las manos.** In the Caribbean and in coastal Spanish generally, there is a strong tendency to aspirate the /s/ syllable final, and the above voicing does not occur.

8. **z,** and **c** before **e** and **i** represent in Spain, except the southwest, [θ], an interdental fricative of tenser and more prolonged articulation than that represented by English *th* in *thin, cloth, ether.* Examples: **zagal, zorro, luz** [θagál], [θórro], [luθ]; or **luces, ciento, cerro** [lúθes], [θjento], [θerro]. In southwestern Spain and in Spanish America, these letters represent [s] (see paragraph 7). Examples: **zagal, zorro, luz, luces, ciento, cerro** [sagál], [sórro], [lus], [lúses], [sjènto], [sèrro]. Before a voiced consonant in the phrase, the **z** represents [z] (see paragraph 7). Examples: **en vez de, mayorazgo, la luz de.**

9. **l** always represents [l], a clear alveolar lateral that is rarely heard in English, except in Irish and Scottish dialects. It is never velar as in English *bell, full.* Examples: **lado, ala, el, al, sol.**

10. **n** represents /n/, which has variants according to the following consonants. It stands for [n] in all cases except before /b/, /p/, /m/, where it represents [m], and before /k/, /g/, /x/, where it represents [ŋ] (similar to the final consonant of *sing*). Examples of [n]: **no, nada, mano, aman;** of [m]: **en vez de, en Barcelona, un peso;** of [ŋ]: **anca, banco, en que, tengo, naranja.**

11. **ll** represents [l] (a palatal lateral) in northern Spain and in Bolivia, Paraguay, and most of Peru, as well as in the Bogotá area of Colombia. This sound is similar to that heard in English *million.* In other parts of the Spanish-speaking world, *ll* represents [y]. Examples: **calle, llano, olla.**

12. **ñ** represents [ñ] among all speakers of Spanish. It is similar to the sound heard in English *canyon,* but is more one articulation than the English. Examples: **cañnón, año, ñato.**

13. **ch** represents [č], which is similar to English /č/ (*church, cheek, reach*). Examples: **chato, chaleco, mucho.**

14. **y** represents [y], which varies regionally from [y] to [ž] (as in *azure*), and in most regions it represents [ŷ] (similar to *just* of English) in initial position in the phrase and after /l/ and /n/. Examples: **ayer, mayo** [ayér], [máyo]; **¡yo! un yugo, el yerno** [ŷo], [unŷúgo], [elŷérno]. In nearly all areas, Spanish /y/ has more palatal friction than English /y/.

15. a. **x** represents between vowels [gs] or simply [S] in Spain (see paragraph 7) and [ks] in Spanish America. Examples: **examen, próximo.**

    b. Before a consonant **x** represents [S] in Spain and [s] in Spanish America, except in affected speech, when one hears [ks]. Examples: **extranjero, experiencia.**

    c. In several Indian words of Mexico and Central America **x** represents [x] (see paragraph 20). **México** is one of these and is spelled **Méjico** in most of the Spanish-speaking world.

16. a. **c** represents [k] before **a, o, u, l,** or **r.** The [k] of Spanish does not have the aspiration of English /k/ in the unprotected prevocalic position (*can, quill, coal*) but is more like the sound in *scan*. Examples: **casa, cosa, cuna, quinto, queso, crudo, aclamar.** Note that **quinto** and **queso** are [kínto] and [kèso]. The syllable final [k] in Spanish occurs only in "learned" terms and is dealt with in various ways by the people. In Spain generally it tends to voice to [g]: **técnico, acto, doctor** [tégnico], [ágto], [dogtór], but today in Madrid and farther north, the latter becomes [doθtór]. In Central America, Cuba, Venezuela, and Colombia [kt] often becomes [pt] and vice versa; [ps] is [ks]: **Pepsi Cola** [péksi kóla].

    b. **c** before **e** and **i** represents [θ] in Spain, except the southwest, and [s] in Spanish America (see paragraph 8).

17. **k** represents [k] in certain words of foreign origin, mainly Greek, German, and English: **kilo, kilómetro, kermesse, kiosko.**

18. **q** combined with **u** represents [k]. Examples: **queso, aquí, quien** [késo], [akí], [kjen]. **qu** occurs only before **e** and **i.**

19. a. **g** represents [g] before **a, o, u** when initial in the breath group or after /n/. Examples: **ganga, goma, guarda, tengo. gue, gui** represents [ge], [gi], **güe, güi** represent [gwe], [gwi].
    Before **a, o, u** under other circumstances, **g** represents [g], a voiced velar fractive. Examples: **la guerra** [lagérra], **lago** [lágo], **la goma** [lagóma], **agrado** [agrádo].

    b. **g** before **e, i,** represents [x], a palatal or velar fricative, which is also represented by **j.** Examples: **gente, giro** [xénte], [xíro]. In the Caribbean and Central America, as well as in southern Spain, the /x/ is simply [h].

20. **j** always represents /x/. The usual manifestation of this phoneme is [x], but in some areas (see paragraph 19) it is [h]. Examples: **jamás, jugo, jota** [xamás], [xúgo], [xóta].

21. **h** represents a former aspiration that is no longer present except in some rural areas of southern Spain and Spanish America. Examples: **hoja** [óxa], **humo** [úmo], **harto** [árto].

22. **r** represents [r], an alveolar single flap, similar to the sound represented by
tt in American English *kitty* in rapid speech. However, at the beginning of a
word or after **n, l, s,** it represents [rr], a multiple vibrant (trill). Examples
of [r]: **caro, farol, mero, tren, comer.** Examples of [rr] written **r: rosa, rana,
Enrique, Israel, alrededor.**
rr represents [rr] under all circumstances. Examples: **carro, correr, guerrero.**

The Noun

I. Gender[2]

A. *Masculine Gender*

1. Names of male beings are naturally masculine: **el hombre** the man; **el
muchacho** the boy; **el tío** the uncle; **el rey** the king; **el buey** the ox.

2. Nouns ending in **-o** are masculine: **el libro** the book; **el banco** the bank.
Exception: **la mano** the hand.

3. Days of the week, months, rivers, oceans, and mountains are masculine:
el martes Tuesday; **enero** January; **el Pacífico** the Pacific; **el Rin** the Rhine;
los Andes the Andes.

4. Many nouns in **-1** or **-r,** and nouns of Greek origin ending in **-ma** are
masculine: **el papel** the paper; **el azúcar** the sugar; **el favor** the favor;
el drama the drama. *Common exceptions*: **la miel** the honey; **la sal** the salt;
la catedral the cathedral; **la flor** the flower. Note that **mar** is both masculine
and feminine.

B. *Feminine Gender*

1. Names of female persons or animals are naturally feminine: **la mujer** the
woman; **la muchacha** the girl; **la tía** the aunt; **la vaca** the cow.

2. Nouns ending in **-a** are feminine: **la pluma** the pen; **la carta** the letter;
la casa the house. *Common exceptions*: **el día** the day; **el mapa** the map;
nouns of Greek origin ending in **-ma: el dogma** the dogma; **el programa**
the program.

3. Letters of the alphabet are feminine: **la** *e*, **la** *s*, **la** *t*.

4. Nouns ending in **-ión, -tad, -dad, -tud, -umbre** are feminine: **la canción** the
song; **la facultad** the faculty; **la ciudad** the city; **la virtud** the virtue;
la muchedumbre the crowd. *Exceptions*: **el gorrión** the sparrow; **el sarampión**
the measles.

C. *Formation of the Feminine*

1. Nouns ending in **-o** change **-o** to **-a: tío** uncle, **tía** aunt; **niño** boy, **niña** girl.

2. Nouns ending in **-ón, -or,** and **-án** add **-a: patrón** patron, **patrona** patroness;
pastor shepherd, **pastora** shepherdess; **holgazán** lazy man, **holgazana** lazy
woman.

---

[2] There is no general gender rule for the type of nouns not treated in this section.

3. Certain nouns have a special form for the feminine: **el poeta, la poetisa; el cantante, la cantatriz; el sacerdote, la sacerdotisa; el emperador, la emperatriz; el abad, la abadesa; el conde, la condesa; el duque, la duquesa.**

Note that (a) some nouns have different genders according to their meanings: **el corte** the cut or the cutting edge; **la corte** the court; **el guía** the guide; **la guía** the guidebook; **el capital** the capital (money); **la capital** the capital (city); (b) some nouns have invariable endings which are used for both the masculine and the feminine: **artista** (and all nouns ending in -ista), **amante, mártir, testigo, reo, demócrata, aristócrata, intérprete, consorte, comensal, homicida, suicida, indigena, cómplice, cliente.**

II. Plural of Nouns[3]

1. Nouns ending in an unaccented vowel add -s to form the plural: **el libro, los libros; la casa, las casas.**

2. Nouns ending in a consonant, in **-y,** or in an accented vowel add **-es: el papel, los papeles; la canción, las canciones: la ley, las leyes; el rubí, los rubíes.** The accepted plural, however, of **papá** is **papás,** and of **mamá** is **mamás.**

3. Nouns ending in unaccented **-es** and **-is** do not change in the plural: **el lunes** Monday, **los lunes** Mondays; **la tesis** the thesis, **las tesis** the theses.

The Adjective and the Adverb

I. The Adjective

A. *Agreement.* The adjective in Spanish agrees in gender and number with the noun it modifies: **el lápiz rojo** the red pencil; **la casa blanca** the white house; **los libros interesantes** the interesting books; **las muchachas hermosas** the beautiful girls.

B. *Formation of the plural.* Adjectives follow the same rules as nouns for the formation of the plural: **pálido, pálidos** pale; **fácil, fáciles** easy; **cortés, corteses** courteous; **capaz, capaces** capable.

C. *Formation of the feminine.*

1. Adjectives ending in -o change -o to -a: **blanco, blanca.**

2. Adjectives ending in other vowels are invariable: **verde** green; **fuerte** strong; **indígena** indigenous, native; **pesimista** pessimistic; **baladí** trivial.

3. Adjectives ending in a consonant are invariable: **fácil** easy; **cortés** courteous. *Exceptions:* (a) adjectives ending in **-ón, -án, -or** (except comparatives) add **-a** to form the feminine: **holgazán, holgazana** lazy; **preguntón, preguntona** inquisitive; **hablador, habladora** talkative (Note that **mayor, mejor, menor, peor, superior, inferior, exterior, interior, anterior,** and **posterior** are invariable). **Superior** adds an **-a** when it is used as a noun meaning ("mother superior"). (b) adjectives of nationality ending in a consonant add **-a** to form the feminine: **francés, francesa** French; **español, española** Spanish; **alemán, alemana** German; **inglés, inglesa** English.

Note that (a) nouns ending in -z change z to c before -es: **lápiz, lápices;** (b) nouns ending in -ión lose the written accent in the plural: **canción, canciones.**

[3] The plurals of certain masculine nouns may include the masculine and feminine genders: **los padres** the father(s) and mother(s), the parents; **los tíos** the uncle(s) and aunt(s); **los reyes** the king(s) and queen(s).

II. The Adverb

Many adverbs are formed by adding **-mente** to the feminine form of the adjective: **claro, claramente; lento, lentamente; fácil, fácilmente.**

III. Comparison of Adjectives and Adverbs

A. *Comparative of inequality.* The comparative of inequality is formed by placing **más** or **menos** before the positive form of the adjective or adverb: **más rico que** richer than; **menos rico que** less rich than; **más tarde** later; **menos tarde** less late. The superlative is formed by placing the definite article **el** before the comparative: **el más rico** the richest; **el menos rico** the least rich. Note the position of the article in the following examples: **la niña más linda** or **la más linda niña** the prettiest girl.

The following adjectives and adverbs have in addition irregular forms of comparison:

Positive	Comparative	Superlative
bueno	mejor	el (la) mejor
malo	peor	el (la) peor
grande	mayor	el (la) mayor
pequeño	menor	el (la) menor
alto	superior	supremo
bajo	inferior	ínfimo
mucho	más	
poco	menos	

B. *Comparative of equality.* With adjectives and adverbs the comparative of equality is formed with **tan ... como: tan fácil como** as easy as; **tan bien como** as well as; with nouns the comparative of equality is formed with **tanto (tanta, tantos, tantas) ... como: tanto dinero como** as much money as; **tantas personas como** as many people as.

C. *Absolute superlative of adjectives.* The absolute superlative of adjectives is formed by placing **muy** (very) before the adjective or by adding the suffix **-ísimo:**

Positive	Absolute Superlative
feliz	muy feliz, felicísimo
fácil	muy fácil, facilísimo
importante	muy importante, importantísimo
limpio	muy limpio, limpísimo
feo	muy feo, feísimo
rico	muy rico, riquísimo
largo	muy largo, larguísimo
notable	muy notable, notabilísimo

A few adjectives have, in addition, other forms derived from the Latin superlatives:

bueno	muy bueno, bonísimo[4], óptimo
malo	muy malo, malísimo, pésimo
grande	muy grande, grandísimo, máximo
pequeño	muy pequeño, pequeñísimo, mínimo

Some adjectives ending in -ro or -re revert to the corresponding Latin superlative:

acre	muy acre, acérrimo
célebre	muy célebre, celebérrimo
mísero	muy mísero, misérrimo
salubre	muy salubre, salubérrimo

D. *Absolute superlative of adverbs.* The absolute superlative of adverbs not ending in -mente is formed in the same manner as that of adjectives:

tarde	muy tarde, tardísimo
pronto	muy pronto, prontísimo
mucho	muchísimo
poco	poquísimo
cerca	muy cerca, cerquísima
lejos	muy lejos, lejísimos

Superlative adverbs ending in -mente are formed by adding the suffix -ísima to the corresponding feminine adjective:

claramente	muy claramente, clarísimamente
noblemente	muy noblemente, nobilísimamente

Common Spanish Suffixes

I. Diminutives

The most common diminutive endings in Spanish are:

-ito, -ita	(-cito, -cita, -ecito, -ecita). Examples: **librito** (from **libro**), **casita** (from **casa**), **corazoncito** (from **corazón**), **mujercita** (from **mujer**), **cochecito** (from **coche**), **florecita** (from **flor**).
-illo, -illa	(-cillo, -cilla, -ecillo, -ecilla). Examples: **corderillo** (from **cordero**), **dolorcillo** (from **dolor**), **viejecillo** (from **viejo**), **piedrecilla** (from **piedra**).
-ico, -ica	(-cico, -cica, -ecico, -ecica). Examples: **niñico** (from **niño**), **hermanica** (from **hermana**), **corazoncico** (from **corazón**), **mujercica** (from **mujer**), **pobrecico** (from **pobre**).
-uelo, -uela	(-zuelo, -zuela, -ezuelo, -ezuela). Examples: **arroyuelo** (from **arroyo**), **mozuela** (from **moza**), **mujerzuela** (from **mujer**), **reyezuelo** (from **rey**), **piedrezuela** (from **piedra**).
-ete, -eta	Examples: **vejete** (from **viejo**), **vejeta** (from **vieja**).
-uco, -uca	Example: **casuca** (from **casa**).
-ucho, -ucha	Examples: **serrucho** (from **sierra**), **casucha** (from **casa**).

[4] Also **buenísimo**.

II. Augmentatives

The most common augmentative endings in Spanish are:

-acho, -acha	Example: **ricacho** (from **rico**).
-azo, -aza	Examples: **gigantazo** (from **gigante**), **bribonazo** (from **bribón**), **manaza** (from **mano**), **bocaza** (from **boca**).
-on, -ona	Examples: **hombrón** (from **hombre**), **mujerona** (from **mujer**), **almohadón** (from **almohada**), **borrachón** (from **borracho**).
-ote, -ota	Examples: **grandote** (from **grande**), **muchachote** (from **muchacho**), muchachota (from **muchachà**).

III. Depreciatives

The most common depreciative endings in Spanish are:

-aco, -aca	Example: **pajarraco** ugly bird.
-ejo, -eja	Example: **librejo** old, worthless book.

Note that a depreciative or ironic connotation is often conveyed by many of the augmentatives and by the diminutive endings **-uelo, -ete, -uco, -ucho, -illo**.

IV. Other Suffixes

-ada
    a. is sometimes equal to the English suffix *-ful:* **cucharada** spoonful; **palada** shovelful;
    b. often indicates a blow: **puñada** blow with the fist; **puñalada** stab or blow with a dagger; **topetada** butt, blow with the head;
    c. indicates a group or a crowd of: **peonada** a group or crowd of peons; **indiada** a group or crowd of Indians.

-al, -ar
    denote a grove, field, plantation or orchard: **naranjal** orange grove; **cauchal** rubber plantation; **pinar** pine grove.

-azo
    indicates a blow or explosion: **puñetazo** blow with the fist; **topetazo** butt, blow with the head; **escobazo** blow with a broom; **cañonazo** cannon shot.

-dad, -tad
    are suffixes forming many abstract nouns and are usually equivalent to the English suffix *-ty:* **fraternidad** fraternity; **facultad** faculty; **cantidad** quantity; **calidad** quality.

-dizo
    is an adjective-forming suffix which means sometimes *tending to*, or *in the habit of:* **resbaladizo** slippery; **olvidadizo** forgetful; **enojadizo** irritable, easily angered; **asustadizo** easily frightened, scary, timid; **movedizo** movable.

-ería
    a. denotes a place where something is made or sold: **panadería** bakery; **librería** bookstore; **zapatería** shoestore; **pastelería** pastry shop;
    b. indicates a profession, business or occupation: **carpintería** carpentry; **ingeniería** engineering;

                    c. means sometimes a collection: **pastelería** pastry, pastries;

d. is sometimes equivalent to English suffix *-ness*; it also suggests a single act or action: **tontería** foolishness; foolish act; **niñería** childishness; childish act.

-ero
  a. indicates a person who makes, sells, or is in charge of: **panadero** baker; **librero** bookseller; **zapatero** shoemaker, **carcelero** jailer; **cajaro** cashier;

b. is an adjective-forming suffix; **parlero** talkative; **guerrero** warlike.

-ez, -eza
  are used to make abstract nouns: **vejez** old age; **niñez** childhood; **viudez** widowhood; **grandeza** greatness.

-ía
  a. is the ending of the names of many arts and sciences: **geología** geology; **geometría** geometry; **biología** biology;

b. see **-ería.**

-iento
  indicates a *resemblance,* or a *tendency to*: **ceniciento** ashlike; **soñoliento** sleepy, drowsy.

-ísimo
  is the ending of the absolute superlative: **hermosísimo** very beautiful.

-izo
  is a suffix meaning *tending to* or *somewhat*: **rojizo** reddish. See **-dizo.**

-mente
  is the adverbal ending attached to the feminine form of the adjective: **generosamente** generously; **claramente** clearly.

-ón
  a. is an augmentative suffix;

b. is also a suffix without an augmentative force, meaning *in the habit of,* or *full of*: **juguetón** playful; **preguntón** full of questions, inquisitive; **llorón** tearful; crybaby;

c. indicates suddenness or violence of an action: **estirón** pull, tug, jerk; **apretón** squeeze.

-or, -dor
  a. are equivalent to the English suffixes *-or*, *-er*, and indicate the agent or doer: **hablador** talker; **regulador** regulator;

b. may also be used as adjectives: **hablador** talkative; **regulador** regulating.

-oso
  is an adjective-forming suffix which usually means *having, full of,* or *characterized by*: **rocoso** rocky; **tormentoso** stormy; **fangoso** muddy; **herboso** grassy; **lluvioso** rainy; **maravilloso** marvelous; **famoso** famous.

-udo
  is an adjective-forming suffix meaning *having* or *characterized by*: **zancudo** long-legged; **peludo** hairy; **panzudo** big-bellied; **caprichudo** stubborn.

-ura
  is a suffix forming many abstract nouns: **negrura** blackness; **blancura** whiteness; **altura** height; **lisura** smoothness.

-uzco   indicates *resemblance* or *a tendency to*; it is akin to the
                              English suffix *-ish*: **blancuzco** whitish; **negruzco** blackish.

Spanish Irregular and Orthographic Changing Verbs

The superior number, or numbers, after a verb entry indicate that it is conjugated
like the model verb in this section which has the corresponding number. Only
the tenses which have irregular forms or spelling changes are given. The
irregular forms and spelling changes are shown in bold-face type.

1. pensar (if stressed, the stem vowel e becomes ie)
    Pres. Indic. **pienso, piensas, piensa**, pensamos, pensáis, **piensan.**
    Pres. Subj.   **piense, pienses, piense**, pensemos, penséis, **piensen.**
    Imper.   **piensa** tú, **piense** Vd., pensemos nosotros, pensad vosotros,
                    piensen Vds.

2. contar (if stressed, the stem vowel o becomes ue)
    Pres. Indic. **cuento, cuentas, cuenta**, contamos, contáis, **cuentan.**
    Pres. Subj.   **cuente, cuentes, cuente**, centemos, contèis, **cuenten.**
    Imper.   **cuenta** tú, **cuente** Vd. contemos nosotros, contad vosotros,
                    cuenten Vds.

3.*a.* sentir (if stressed, the stem vowel e becomes ie; if unstressed, the stem
       vowel e becomes i when the following syllable contains stressed a, ie, or ió)
    Pres. Indic. **siento, sientes, siente**, sentimos, sentís, **sienten.**
    Pres. Subj.   **sienta, sientas, sienta, sintamos, sintáis, sientan.**
    Pret. Indic. **sentí**, sentiste, **sintió**, sentimos, sentisteis, **sintieron.**
    Imp. Subj.   **sintiera** or **sintiese, sintieras** or **sintieses, sintiera** or **sintiese,
                    sintiéramos** or **sintiésemos, sintierais** or **sintieseis, sintieran** or
                    sintiesen.
    Imper.   **siente** tú, **sienta** Vd., **sintamos** nosotros, sentid vosotros,
                    sientan Vds.
    Pres. Part.   **sintiendo.**

  b. erguir (this verb has same vowel changes as *sentir*, but the initial i of the
       diphthong ie is changed to y. For regular spelling changes see No. 12,*a*)
    Pres. Indic. **yergo, yergues, yergue**, erguimos, erguís, **yerguen.**
    Pres. Subj.   **yerga, yergas, yerga, irgamos, irgáis, yergan.**
    Pret. Indic. erguí, erguiste, **irguió**, erguimos, erguisteis, **irguieron.**
    Imp. Subj.   **irguiera** or **irguiese, irguieras** or **irguieses, irguiera** or **irguieses,
                    irguiéramos** or **irguiésemos, irguierais** or **irguieseis, irguieran** or
                    irguiesen.
    Imper.   **yergue** tú, **yerga** Vd., **irgamos** nosotros, erguid vosotros, **yergan**
                    Vds.
    Pres. Part.   **irguiendo.**

4. dormir (if stressed, the stem vowel o becomes ue; if unstressed, the stem
    vowel o becomes u when the following syllable contains stressed a, ie, or
    ió)
    Pres. Indic. **duermo, duermes, duerme**, dormimos, dormís, **duermen.**
    Pres. Subj.   **duerma, duermas, duerma, durmamos, durmáis, duerman.**
    Pret. Indic. dormí, dormiste, **durmió**, dormimos, dormisteis, **durmieron.**

Imp. Subj.	**durmiera** or **durmiese, durmieras** or **durmieses, durmiera** or **durmiese, durmiéramos** or **durmiésemos, durmierais** or **durmieseis, durmieran** or **durmiesen.**
Imper.	**duerme** tú, **duerma** Vd., **durmanos** nosotros, dormid vosotros, **duerman** Vds.
Pres. Part.	**durmiendo.**

5. pedir (if stressed, the stem vowel **e** becomes **i**; if unstressed, the stem vowel **e** becomes **i** when the following syllable contains stressed **a, ie,** or **ió**)

Pres. Indic.	**pido, pides, pide,** pedimos, pedís, **piden.**
Pres. Subj.	**pida, pidas, pida, pidamos, pidáis, pidan.**
Pret. Indic.	**pedí,** pediste, **pidió,** pedimos, pedisteis, **pidieron.**
Imp. Subj.	**pidiera** or **pidiese, pidieras** or **pidieses, pidiera** or **pidiese, pidiéramos** or **pidiésemos, pidierais** or **pidieseis, pidieran** or **pidiesen.**
Imper.	**pide** tú, **pida** Vd., **pidamos** nosotros, pedid vosotros, **pidan** Vds.
Pres. Part.	**pidiendo.**

6. buscar (verbs ending in **car** change **c** to **qu** before **e**)

Pres. Subj.	**busque, busques, busque, busquemos, busquéis, busquen.**
Pret. Indic.	**busqué,** buscaste, buscó, buscamos, buscasteis, buscaron.
Imper.	busca tú, **busque** Vd., **busquemos** nosotros, buscad vosotros, **busquen** Vds.

7. llegar (verbs ending in **gar** change the **g** to **gu** before **e**)

Pres. Subj.	**llegue, llegues, llegue, lleguemos, lleguéis, lleguen.**
Pres. Indic.	**llegué,** llegaste, llegó, llegamos, llegasteis, llegaron.
Imper.	llega tú, **llegue** Vd., lleguemos nosotros, llegad vosotros, **lleguen** Vds.

8. averiguar (verbs ending in **guar** change the **gu** to **gü** before **e**)

Pres. Subj.	**averigüe, averigües, averigüe, averigüemos, averigüéis, averigüen.**
Pret. Indic.	**averigüé,** averiguaste, averiguó, averiguamos, averiguasteis, averiguaron.
Imper.	averigua tú, **averigüe** Vd., **averigüemos** nosotros, averiguad vosotros, **averigüen** Vds.

9. abrazar (verbs ending in **zar** change **z** to **c** before **e**)

Pres. Subj.	**abrace, abraces, abrace, abracemos, abracéis, abracen.**
Pret. Indic.	**abracé,** abrazaste, abrazó, abrazamos, abrazasteis, abrazaron.
Imper.	abraza tú, **abrace** Vd., **abracemos** nosotros, abrazad vosotros, **abracen** Vds.

10.*a.* convencer (verbs ending in **cer** preceded by a consonant change **c** to **z** before **a** and **o**)

Pres. Indic.	**convenzo,** convences, convence, convencemos, convencéis, convencen.
Pres. Subj.	**convenza, convenzas, convenza, convenzamos, convenzáis, convenzan.**
Imper.	convence tú, **convenza** Vd., **convenzamos** nosotros, convenced vosotros, **convenzan** Vds.

b. esparcir (verbs ending in **cir** preceded by a consonant change **c** to **z** before **a** and **o**)

Pres. Indic.	**esparzo,** esparces, esparce, esparcimos, esparcís, esparcen.
Pres. Subj.	**esparza, esparzas, esparza, esparzamos, esparzáis, esparzan.**
Imper.	esparce tú, **esparza** Vd., **esparzamos** nosotros, esparcid vosotros, **esparzan** Vds.

c. mecer (some verbs ending in **cer** preceded by a vowel change **c** to **z** before **a** and **o**; see No. 13.*a*)

Pres. Indic.	**mezo,** meces, mece, mecemos, mecéis, mecen.
Pres. Subj.	**meza, mezas, meza, mezamos, mezáis, mezan.**
Imper.	mece tú, **meza** Vd., **mezamos** nosotros, meced vosotros, **mezan** Vds.

11.*a.* dirigir (verbs ending in **gir** change **g** to **j** before **a** and **o**)

Pres. Indic.	**dirijo,** diriges, dirige, dirigimos, dirigís, dirigen.
Pres. Subj.	**dirija, dirijas, dirija, dirijamos, dirijáis, dirijan.**
Imper.	dirige tú, **dirija** Vd., **dirijamos** nosotros, dirigid vosotros, **dirijan** Vds.

b. coger (verbs ending in **ger** change **g** to **j** before **o** and **a**)

Pres. Indic.	**cojo,** coges, coge, cogemos, cogéis, cogen.
Pres. Subj.	**coja, cojas, coja, cojamos, cojáis, cojan.**
Imper.	coge tú, **coja** Vd., **cojamos** nosotros, coged vosotros, **cojan** Vds.

12.*a.* distinguir (verbs ending in **guir** drop the **u** before **o** and **a**)

Pres. Indic.	**distingo,** distingues, distingue, distinguimos, distinguís, distinguen.
Pres. Subj.	**distinga, distingas, distinga, distingamos, distingáis, distingan.**
Imper.	distingue tú, **distinga** Vd., **distingamos** nosotros, distinguid vosotros, **distingan** Vds.

b. delinquir (verbs ending in **quir** change **qu** to **c** before **o** and **a**)

Pres. Indic.	**delinco,** delinques, delinque, delinquimos, delinquís, delinquen.
Pres. Subj.	**delinca, delincas, delinca, delincamos, delincáis, delincan.**

13.*a.* conocer (verbs ending in **cer** when preceded by a vowel insert **z** before **c** when **c** is followed by **o** or **a**; see No. 10.*c*)

Pres. Indic.	**conozco,** conoces, conoce, conocemos, conocéis, conocen.
Pres. Subj.	**conozca, conozcas, conozca, conozcamos, conozcáis, conozcan.**
Imper.	conoce tú, **conozca** Vd., **conozcamos** nosotros, conoced vosotros, **conozcan** Vds.

b. lucir (verbs ending in **cir** when preceded by a vowel insert **z** before **c** when **c** is followed by **o** or **a**; see No. 25)

Pres. Indic.	**luzco,** luces, luce, lucimos, lucís, lucen.
Pres. Subj.	**luzca, luzcas, luzca, luzcamos, luzcáis, luzcan.**
Imper.	luce tú, **luzca** Vd., **luzcamos** nosotros, lucid vosotros, **luzcan** Vds.

14. creer (unstressed **i** between vowels is regularly changed to **y**)

Pret. Indic.	creí, creíste, **creyó,** creímos, creísteis, **creyeron.**
Imp. Subj.	**creyera** or **creyese, creyeras** or **creyeses, creyera** or **creyese, creyéramos** or **creyésemos, creyerais** or **creyeseis, creyeran** or **creyesen.**
Pret. Part.	**creyendo.**

15. reír (like No. 5, except that when the **i** of the stem would be followed by **ie** or **ió** the two **i**'s are reduced to one)

Pres. Indic.	**río, ríes, ríe,** reímos, reís, **ríen.**
Pres. Subj.	**ría, rías, ría, riamos, riáis, rían.**
Pret. Indic.	reí, reíste, **rió,** reímos, reísteis, **rieron.**
Imp. Subj.	**riera** or **riese, rieras** or **rieses, riera** or **riese, riéramos** or **riésemos, rierais** or **rieseis, rieran** or **riesen.**
Imper.	**ríe** tú, **ría** Vd., **ríamos** nosotros, reíd vosotros, **rían** Vds.
Pres. Part.	**riendo.**

16. podrir or pudrir

Pres. Indic.	**pudro, pudres, pudre,** podrimos or pudrimos, podrís or pudrís, **pudren.**
Pres. Subj.	**pudra, pudras, pudra, pudramos pudráis, pudran.**
Imp. Indic.	pudría or podría, etc. (Seldom *podría* because of confusion with *poder*)
Pret. Indic.	podrí or pudrí, podriste or pudriste, **pudrió,** podrimos or pudrimos, podristeis or pudristeis, **pudrieron.**
Imp. Subj.	**pudriera** or **pudriese, pudrieras** or **pudrieses, pudriera** or **pudriese, pudriéramos** or **pudriésemos, pudrierais** or **pudrieseis, pudrieran** or **pudriesen.**
Fut. Indic.	pudriré or podriré, etc.
Cond.	pudriría or podriría, etc.
Pres. Part.	**pudriendo.**
Past Part.	podrido or pudrido.

17. enviar

Pres. Indic.	envío, envías, envía, enviamos, enviáis, envían.
Pres. Subj.	envíe, envíes, enviemos, enviéis, envíen.
Imper.	envía tú, envíe Vd., enviemos nosotros, enviad vosotros, envíen Vds.

18. continuar

Pres. Indic.	continúo, continúas, continúa, continuamos, continuáis, continúan.
Pres. Subj.	continúe, continúes, continúe, continuemos, continuéis, continúen.
Imper.	continúa tú, continúe Vd., continuemos nosotros, continuad vosotros, continúen Vds.

19. gruñir (**i** of the diphthong **ie** or **ió** is lost after **ñ**)

Pret. Indic.	gruñi, gruñiste, **gruñó,** gruñisteis, **gruñeron.**
Imp. Subj.	**gruñera** or **gruñese, gruñeras** or **gruñeses, gruñera** or **gruñese, gruñéramos** or **gruñésemos, gruñerais** or **gruñeseis, gruñeran** or **gruñesen.**
Pres. Part.	**gruñendo.**

20. bullir (**i** of the diphthong **ie** or **ió** is lost after **ll**)

Pret. Indic.	bullí, bulliste, **bulló,** bullimos, bullisteis, **bulleron.**
Imp. Subj.	**bullera** or **bullese, bulleras** or **bulleses, bullera** or **bullese, bulléramos** or **bullésemos, bullerais** or **bulleseis, bulleran** or **bullesen.**

	Pres. Part.	**bullendo.**
21.	andar	
	Pret. Indic.	**anduve, anduviste, anduvo, anduvimos, anduvisteis, anduvieron.**
	Imp. Subj.	**anduviera** or **anduviese, anduvieras** or **anduvieses, anduviera** or **anduviese, anduviéramos** or **anduviésemos, anduvierais** or **anduvieseis, anduvieran** or **anduviesen.**
22.	asir	
	Pres. Indic.	**asgo,** ases, ase, asimos, asís, asen.
	Pres. Subj.	**asga, asgas, asga, asgamos, asgáis, asgan.**
	Imper.	ase tú, **asga** Vd., **asgamos** nosotros, asid vosotros, **asgan** Vds.
23.	caber	
	Pres. Indic.	**quepo,** cabes, cabe, cabemos, cabéis, caben.
	Pres. Subj.	**quepa, quepas, quepa, quepamos, quepáis, quepan.**
	Pret. Indic.	**cupe, cupiste, cupo, cupimos, cupisteis, cupieron.**
	Imp. Subj.	**cupiera** or **cupiese, cupieras** or **cupieses, cupiera** or **cupiese, cupiéramos** or **cupiésemos, cupierais** or **cupieseis, cupieran** or **cupiesen.**
	Fut. Indic.	**cabré, cabrás, cabrá, cabremos, cabréis, cabrán.**
	Cond.	**cabría, cabrías, cabría, cabríamos, cabríais, cabrían.**
	Imper.	cabe tú, **quepa** Vd., **quepamos** nosotros, cabed vosotros, **quepan** Vds.
24.	caer	
	Pres. Indic.	**caigo,** caes, cae, caemos, caéis, caen.
	Pres. Subj.	**caiga, caigas, caiga, caigamos, caigáis, caigan.**
	Pret. Indic.	caí, caiste, **cayó,** caímos, caísteis, **cayeron.**
	Imp. Subj.	**cayera** or **cayese, cayeras** or **cayases, cayera** or **cayese, cayéramos** or **cayésemos, cayerais** or **cayeseis, cayeran** or **cayesen.**
	Imper.	cae tú, **caiga** Vd., **caigamos** nosotros, caed vosotros, **caigan** Vds.
	Pres. Part.	**cayendo.**
25.	conducir (all verbs ending in **ducir** have the irregularities of conducir)	
	Pres. Indic.	**conduzco,** conduces, conduce, conducimos, conducís, conducen.
	Pres. Subj.	**conduzca, conduzcas, conduzca, conduzcamos, conduzcáis, conduzcan.**
	Pret. Indic.	**conduje, condujiste, condujo, condujimos, condujisteis, condujeron.**
	Imp. Subj.	**condujera** or **condujese, condujeras** or **condujeses, condujera** or **condujese, condujéramos** or **condujésemos, condujerais** or **condujeseis, condujeran** or **condujesen.**
	Imp.	conduce tú, **conduzca** Vd., **conduzcamos** nosotros, conducid vosotros, **conduzcan** Vds.
26.	dar	
	Pres. Indic.	**doy,** das, da, damos, dais, dan.
	Pres. Subj.	dé, des, dé, demos, deis, den.
	Pret. Indic.	**dí, diste, dió, dimos, disteis, dieron.**

| *Imp. Subj.* | **diera** or **diese, dieras** or **dieses, deira** or **diese, diéramos** or **diésemos, dierais** or **dieseis, dieran** or **diesen.** |

27. decir

Pres. Indic.	**digo, dices, dice,** decimos, decís, **dicen.**
Pres. Subj.	**diga, digas, diga, digamos, digáis, digan.**
Pret. Indic.	**dije, dijiste, dijo, dijimos, dijisteis, dijeron.**
Imp. Subj.	**dijera** or **dijese, dijeras** or **dijeses, dijera** or **dijese, dijéramos** or **dijésemos, dijerais** or **dijeseis, dijeran** or **dijesen.**
Fut. Indic.	**diré, dirás, dirá, diremos, deréis, dirán.**
Cond.	**diría, dirías, diría, diríamos, diríais, dirían.**
Imper.	**di** tú, **diga** Vd., **digamos** nosotros, decid vosotros, **digan** Vds.
Pres. Part.	**diciendo.**
Past Part.	**dicho.**

NOTE. The compound verbs of *decir* have the same irregularities with the exception of the following:
a. The future and conditional of the compound verbs *bendecir* and *maldecir* are regular: *bendeciré, maldeciré,* etc.; *bendeciría, maldeciría,* etc.
b. The familiar imperative is regular: *bendice tu, maldice tu, contradice tu,* etc.
c. The past participles of *bendecir* and *maldecir* are regular when used with *haber:* *bendecido, maldecido;* when used as an adjective with *estar,* the forms are: *bendito, maldito.*

28. errar (like No. 1, except that the initial **ie** is spelled **ye**)

Pres. Indic.	**yerro, yerras, yerra,** erramos, erráis, **yerran.**
Pres. Subj.	**yerre, yerres, yerre,** erremos, erréis, **yerren.**
Imper.	**yerra** tú, **yerre** Vd., erremos nosotros, errad vosotros, **yerren** Vds.

29. estar

Pres. Indic.	**estoy, estás, está,** estamos, estáis, **están.**
Pres. Subj.	**esté, estés, esté,** estemos, estéis, **estén.**
Pret. Indic.	**estuve, estuviste, estuvo, estuvimos, estuvisteis, estuvieron.**
Imp. Subj.	**estuviera** or **estuviese, estuvieras** or **estuvieses, estuviera** or **estuviese, estuviéramos** or **estuviésemos, estuvierais** or **estuvieseis, estuvieran** or **estuviesen.**
Imper.	**está** tú, **esté** Vd., estemos nosotros, estad vosotros, **estén** Vds.

30. .haber

Pres. Indic.	**he, has, ha, hemos,** habéis, **han.**
Pres. Subj.	**haya, hayas, haya, hayamos, hayáis, hayan.**
Pret. Indic.	**hube, hubiste, hubo, hubimos, hubisteis, hubieron.**
Imp. Subj.	**hubiera** or **hubiese, hubieras** or **hubieses, hubiera** or **hubiese, hubiéramos** or **hubiésemos, hubierais** or **hubieseis, hubieran** or **hubiesen.**
Fut. Indic.	**habré, habrás, habrá, habremos, habréis, habrán.**
Cond.	**habría, habrías, habría, habríamos, habríais, habrían.**

31. hacer

Pres. Indic.	**hago,** haces, hace, hacemos, hacéis, hacen.
Pres. Subj.	**haga, hagas, haga, hagamos, hagáis, hagan.**
Pret. Indic.	**hice, hiciste, hizo, hicimos, hicisteis, hicieron.**
Imp. Subj.	**hiciera** or **hiciese, hicieras** or **hicieses, hiciera** or **hiciese,**

	hiciéramos or hiciésemos, hicierais or hicieseis, hicieran or hiciesem.
Fut. Indic.	haré, harás, hará, haremos, haréis, harán.
Cond.	haría, harías, haría, haríamos, haríais, harían.
Imper.	haz tú, haga Vd., hagamos nosotros, haced vosotros, hagan Vds.
Past Part.	hecho.

32.*a.* huir

Pres. Indic.	huyo, huyes, huye, huimos, huís, huyen.
Pres. Subj.	huya, huyas, huya, huyamos, huyáis, huyan.
Pret. Indic.	huí, huiste, huyó, huimos, huisteis, huyeron.
Imp. Subj.	huyera or huyese, huyeras or huyeses, huyera or huyese, huyéramos or huyésemos, huyerais or huyeseis, huyeran or huyesen.
Imper.	huye tú, huya Vd., huyamos nosotros, huid vosotros, huyan Vds.
Pres. Part.	huyendo.

b. argüir

Pres. Indic.	arguyo, arguyes, arguye, argüimos, argüís, arguyen.
Pres. Subj.	arguya, arguyas, arguya, arguyamos, arguyáis, arguyan.
Pret. Indic.	argüí, argüiste, arguyó, argüimos, argüisteis, arguyeron.
Imp. Subj.	arguyera or arguyese, arguyeras or arguyeses, arguyera or arguyese, arguyéramos or arguyésemos, arguyerais or arguyeseis, arguyeran or arguyesen.
Imper.	arguye tú, arguya Vd., arguyamos nosotros, agrüid vosotros, arguyan Vds.
Pres. Part.	arguyendo.

33. ir

Pres. Indic.	voy, vas, va, vamos, vais, van.
Pres. Subj.	vaya, vayas, vaya, vayamos, vayáis, vayan.
Imp. Indic.	iba, ibas, iba, íbamos, ibais, iban.
Pret. Indic.	fui, fuiste, fué, fuimos, fuisteis, fueron.
Imp. Subj.	fuera or fuese, fueras or fueses, fuera or fuese, fuéramos or fuésemos, fuerais or fueseis, fueran or fuesen.
Imper.	ve tú, vaya Vd., vayamos (vamos) nosotros, id vosotros, vayan Vds.
Pres. Part.	yendo.

34. jugar (cf. Nos. 2 and 7)

Pres. Indic.	juego, juegas, juega, jugamos, jugáis, juegan.
Pres. Subj.	juegue, juegues, juegue, juguemos, juguéis, jueguen.
Pret. Indic.	jugué, jugaste, jugó, jugamos, jugasteis, jugaron.
Imper.	juega tú, juegue Vd., jueguemos nosotros, jugad vosotros, jueguen Vds.

35. adquirir

Pres. Indic.	adquiero, adquieres, adquiere, adquirimos, adquirís, adquieren.
Pres. Subj.	adquiera, adquieras, adquiera, adquiramos, adquiráis, adquieran.
Imper.	adquiere tú, adquiera Vd., adquiramos nosotros, adquirid vosotros, adquieran Vds.

36. oír
   Pres. Indic. **oigo, oyes, oye,** oímos, oís, **oyen.**
   Pres. Subj. **oiga, oigas, oiga, oigamos, oigáis, oigan.**
   Pret. Indic. oí, oíste, **oyó,** oímos, oísteis, **oyeron.**
   Imp. Subj. **oyera** or **oyese, oyeras** or **oyeses, oyera** or **oyese, oyéramos** or **oyésemos, oyerais** or **oyeseis, oyeran** or **oyesen.**
   Imper. **oye** tú, **oiga** Vd., **oigamos** nosotros, oíd vosotros, **oigan** Vds.
   Pres. Part. **oyendo.**

37. oler like No. 2, except that initial **ue** is spelled **hue)**
   Pres. Indic. **huelo, hueles, huele,** olemos, oléis, **huelen.**
   Pres. Subj. **huela, huelas, huela,** olamos, oláis, **huelan.**
   Imper. **huele** tú, **huela** Vd., olamos nosotros, oled vosotros, **huelan** Vds.

38. placer
   Pres. Indic. **plazco,** places, place, placemos, placéis, placen.
   Pres. Subj. **plazca, plazcas, plazca, plazcamos, plazcáis, plazcan.** (There are also the antiquated forms, **plegue** and **plega,** used now only in the third person in poetic language.)
   Pret. Indic. In addition to the regular forms, there is the antiquated form **plugo,** used now only in poetic language.
   Imp. Subj. In addition to the regular forms, there are the antiquated forms, **pluguiera** and **pluguiese,** used now only in poetic language.

39. poder
   Pres. Indic. **puedo, puedes, puede,** podemos, podéis, **pueden.**
   Pres. Subj. **pueda, puedas, pueda,** podamos, podáis, **puedan.**
   Pret. Indic. **pude, pudiste, pudo, pudimos, pudisteis, pudieron.**
   Imp. Subj. **pudiera** or **pudiese, pudieras** or **pudieses, pudiera** or **pudiese, pudiéramos** or **pudiésemos, pudierais** or **pudieseis, pudieran** or **pudiesen.**
   Fut. Indic. **podré, podrás, podrá, podremos, podréis, podrán.**
   Cond. **podría, podrías, podría, podríamos, podríais, podrían.**
   Pres. Part. **pudiendo.**

40. poner
   Pres. Indic. **pongo,** pones, pone, ponemos, ponéis, ponen.
   Pres. Subj. **ponga, pongas, ponga, pongamos, pongáis, pongan.**
   Pret. Indic. **puse, pusiste, puso, pusimos, pusisteis, pusieron.**
   Imp. Subj. **pusiera** or **pusiese, pusieras** or **pusieses, pusiera** or **pusiese, pusiéramos** or **pusiésemos, pusierais** or **pusieseis, pusieran** or **pusiesen.**
   Fut. Indic. **pondré, pondrás, pondrá, pondremos, pondréis, pondrán.**
   Cond. **pondría, pondrías, pondría, pondríamos, pondríais, pondrían.**
   Imper. **pon** tú, **ponga** Vd., **pongamos** nosotros, poned vosotros, **pongan** Vds.
   Past Part. **puesto.**

41. querer
   Pres. Indic. **quiero, quieres, quiere,** queremos, queréis, **quieren.**
   Pres. Subj. **quiera, quieras, quiera,** queramos, queráis, **quieran.**

Pret. Indic.	quise, quisiste, quiso, quisimos, quisisteis, quisieron.	
Imp. Subj.	quisiera or quisiese, quisieras or quisieses, quisiera or quisiese, quisiéramos or quisiémos, quisierais or quisieseis, quisieran or quisiesen.	
Fut. Indic.	querré, querrás, querrá, querremos, querréis, querrán.	
Cond.	querría, querrías, querría, querríamos, querríais, querrían.	
Imper.	quiere tú, quiera Vd., queramos nosotros, quered vosotros, quieran Vds.	

42. saber

Pres. Indic.	sé, sabes, sabe, sabemos, sabéis, saben.
Pres. Subj.	sepa, sepas, sepa, sepamos, sepáis, sepan.
Pret. Indic.	supe, supiste, supo, supimos, supisteis, supieron.
Imp. Subj.	supiera or supiese, supieras or supieses, supiera or supiese, supiéramos or supiésemos, supierais or supieseis, supieran or supiesen.
Fut. Indic.	sabré, sabrás, sabrá, sabremos, sabréis, sabrán.
Cond.	sabría, sabrías, sabría, sabríamos, sabríais, sabrían.
Imper.	sabe tú, sepa Vd., sepamos nosotros, sabed vosotros, sepan Vds.

43. salir

Pres. Indic.	salgo, sales, sale, salimos, salís, salen.
Pres. Subj.	salga, salgas, salga, salgamos, salgáis, salgan.
Fut. Indic.	saldré, saldrás, saldrá, saldremos, saldréis, saldrán.
Cond.	saldría, saldrías, saldría, saldríamos, saldríais, saldrían.
Imper.	sal tú, salga Vd., salgamos nosotros, salid vosotros, salgan Vds.

NOTE. The compound *sobresalir* is regular in the familiar imperative: sobresale tú.

44. ser

Pres. Indic.	soy, eres, es, somos, sois, son.
Pres. Subj.	sea, seas, sea, seamos, seáis, sean.
Imp. Indic.	era, eras, era, éramos, erais, eran.
Pret. Indic.	fui, fuiste, fué, fuimos, fuisteis, fueron.
Imp. Subj.	fuera or fuese, fueras or fueses, fuera or fuese, fuéramos or fuésemos, fuerais or fueseis, fueran or fuesen.
Imper.	sé tú, sea Vd., seamos nosotros, sed vosotros, sean Vds.

45. tener

Pres. Indic.	tengo, tienes, tiene, tenemos, tenéis, tienen.
Pres. Subj.	tenga, tengas, tenga, tengamos, tengáis, tengan.
Pret. Indic.	tuve, tuviste, tuvo, tuvimos, tuvisteis, tuvieron.
Imp. Subj.	tuviera or tuviese, tuvieras or tuvieses, tuviera or tuviese, tuviéramos or tuviésemos, tuvierais or tuvieseis, tuvieran or tuviesen.
Fut. Indic.	tendré, tendrás, tendrá, tendremos, tendréis, tendrán.
Cond.	tendría, tendrías, tendría, tendríamos, tendríais, tendrían.
Imper.	ten tú, tenga Vd., tengamos nosotros, tened vosotros, tengan Vds.

46. traer

Pres. Indic.	traigo, traes, trae, traemos, traéis, traen.
Pres. Subj.	traiga, traigas, traiga, traigamos, traigáis, traigan.

Pret. Indic.	**traje, trajiste, trajo, trajimos, trajisteis, trajeron.**
Imp. Subj.	**trajera** or **trajese, trajeras** or **trajeses, trajera** or **trajese, trajéramos** or **trajésemos, trajerais** or **trajeseis, trajeran** or **trajesen.**
Imper.	trae tú, **traiga** Vd., **traigamos** nosotros, traed vosotros, **traigan** Vds.
Pres. Part.	**trayendo.**

47. valer

Pres. Indic.	**valgo,** vales, vale, valemos, valéis, valen.
Pres. Subj.	**valga, valgas, valga, valgamos, valgáis, valgan.**
Fut. Indic.	**valdré, valdrás, valdrá, valdremos, valdréis, valdrán.**
Cond.	**valdría, valdrías, valdría, valdríamos, valdríais, valdrían.**
Imper.	**val** or vale tú, **valga** Vd., **valgamos** nosotros, valed vosotros, **valgan** Vds.

48. venir

Pres. Indic.	**vengo, vienes, viene,** venimos, venís, **vienen.**
Pres. Subj.	**venga, vengas, venga, vengamos, vengáis, vengan.**
Pret. Indic.	**vine, viniste, vino, vinimos, vinisteis, vinieron.**
Imp. Subj.	**viniera** or **viniese, vinieras** or **vinieses, viniera** or **viniese, viniéramos** or **viniésemos, vinierais** or **vinieseis, vinieran** or **viniesen.**
Fut. Indic.	**vendré, vendrás, vendrá, vendremos, vendréis, vendrán.**
Cond.	**vendría, vendrías, vendría, vendríamos, vendríais, vendrían.**
Imper.	**ven** tú, **venga** Vd., **vengamos** nosotros, venid vosotros, **vengan** Vds.
Pres. Part.	**viniendo.**

49. ver

Pres. Indic.	**veo,** ves, ve, vemos, veis, ven.
Pres. Subj.	**vea, veas, vea, veamos, veáis, vean.**
Imp. Indic.	**veía, veías, veía, veíamos, veíais, veían.**
Imper.	ve tú, **vea** Vd., **veamos,** nosotros, ved vosotros, **vean** Vds.
Past Part.	**visto.**

50. yacer

Pres. Indic.	**yazco** or **yazgo,** yaces, yace, yacemos, yacéis, yacen.
Pres. Subj.	**yazca** or **yazga, yazcas** or **yazgas, yazca** or **yazga, yazcamos** or **yazgamos, yazcáis** or **yazgáis, yazcan** or **yazgan.**
Imper.	yace tú, **yazca** or **yazga** Vd., **yazcamos** or **yazgamos** nosotros, yaced vosotros, **yazcan** or **yazgan** Vds.

51. Defective Verbs

a. The following verbs are used only in the forms that have an **i** in the ending: abolir, agredir, aterirse, empedernir, transgredir.

b. atañer
This verb is used only in the third person. It is most frequently used in the present indicative: atañe, atañen.

c. concernir
This verb is used only in the third person of the following tenses:

Pres. Indic.	**concierne, conciernen.**
Pres. Subj.	**concierna, conciernan.**
Imp. Indic.	concernía, concernían.
Imp. Subj.	concerniera or concerniese, concernieran or concerniesen.
Pres. Part.	concerniendo.

d. soler

This verb is used most frequently in the present and imperfect indicative. It is less frequently used in the present subjunctive.

Pres. Indic.	**suelo, sueles, suele,** solemos, soléis, **suelen.**
Pres. Subj.	**suela, suelas, suela,** solamos, soláis, **suelan.**
Imp. Indic.	solía, solías, solía, solíamos, solíais, solían.

The preterit is seldom used. Of the compound tenses, only the present perfect is commonly used: he solido, etc. The other tenses are very rare.

e. roer

This verb has three forms in the first person of the present indicative: **roo, royo, roigo,** all of which are infrequently used. In the present subjunctive the perferable form is **roa, roas, roa,** etc., although the forms **roya** and **roiga** are found.

52. *Irregular Past Participles*

abrir—**abierto**
absorber—absorbido, **absorto**
bendecir—bendecido, **bendito**
componer—**compuesto**
cubrir—**cubierto**
decir—**dicho**
deponer—**depuesto**
descomponer—**descompuesto**
describir—**descrito**
descubrir—**descubierto**
desenvolver—**desenvuelto**
deshacer—**deshecho**
devolver—**devuelto**
disolver—**disuelto**
encubrir—**encubierto**
entreabrir—**entreabierto**
entrever—**entrevisto**
envolver—**envuelto**

escribir—**escrito**
freir—**frito,** freído
hacer—**hecho**
imprimir—**impreso**
inscribir—**inscrito, inscripto**
maldecir—maldecido, **maldito**
morir—**muerto**
poner—**puesto**
prescribir—**prescrito, prescripto**
proscribir—**proscrito, proscripto**
proveer—proveído, **provisto**
resolver—**resuelto**
revolver—**revuelto**
romper—rompido, **roto**
satisfacer—**satisfecho**
subscribir—**subscrito**
ver—**visto**
volver—**vuelto**

The Spanish Language in America

Introduction

In a sense Latin is not dead. The speech of Roman soldiers, merchants, and colonists, the Latin of another day, was taken bodily to Iberia, to Gaul, to Dacia, and to many other regions. As it developed under some influence from the languages previously spoken in these areas, it became known eventually by several other names—Spanish, Portuguese, French, Italian, Romanian, etc.

The Latin of northern Spain came to be called Castilian since its speakers were from the province of Castilla (Latin *Castella*, "castles"), and although later it was often called Spanish (**español**), to this day the people of many regions of Spanish speech refer to their language as **castellano,** and the children of Argentina and Chile, for instance, study **composición castellana.**

Castilian, among other Latin dialects, became prominent in the Iberian peninsula because of the hegemony of north central Spain in the reconquest of the peninsula from the Moors during the Middle Ages and subsequently in the discovery and settlement of America. Thus its predominance over other manifestations of Latin is not due to its own nature but rather to nonlinguistic factors: political and military power and organization, church-state relations, and finally literary ascendance.

The Spanish of Latin America, like most "colonial" speech, tends to be conservative in its structural changes compared with that of the mother country. In addition, it reflects regional traits of the southwestern part of Spain, notably Andalusia and adjacent areas, from where a large part of the sailors, conquistadores, and colonists came. In other words, the Spanish of America would seem to be Andalusian Castilian of the sixteenth and seventeenth centuries, as far as pronunciation and grammar are concerned. But in vocabulary hundreds of Indian words have entered the language, especially in Mexico, Guatemala, the Andes (Ecuador, Peru, and Bolivia), and in the Río de la Plata region. The Indian words of the Caribbean islands were taken to other parts of Latin America by the original Spanish settlers and often form a part of the general Spanish lexicon. It should be noted that these Indian languages belong to distinct, unrelated families, so that an **ahuacate** (avocado) in Mexico and Central America becomes a **palta** in the Andes. Although Spanish Americans generally have little difficulty understanding each other, the following variants represent rather extreme divergences:

	Little boy	*bus*	*blond*
Mexico	**chamaco**	**camión**	**güero**
Guatemala	**patojo**	**camioneta**	**canche**
El Salvador	**cipote**	**camioneta**	**chele**
Panamá	**chico**	**chiva**	**fulo**
Colombia	**pelado**	**autobús**	**mono**
Argentina	**pibe**	**colectivo**	**rubio**
Chile	**cabro**	**micro**	**rubio**
Cuba	**chico**	**guagua**	**rubio**

Although most of these words are actually Spanish (of Latin origin), several are from the Indian languages of the respective areas. The fact that there are differences of this sort is to be expected in a general culture that contains so many national boundaries.

Today Spanish (**castellano**) is the most extensive manifestation of the former spoken Latin. Those who think and express themselves in this language number about 200,000,000, and they live in some twenty countries, most of which have rapidly growing populations. It is estimated as of 1977 that by A.D. 2000 Spanish will be the language of nearly 500,000,000 people, most of whom will be **hispanoamericanos.** It is one of the principal languages of the world.

The Pronunciation of Latin-American Spanish

The fundamental phonological traits of American Spanish are to be found in Castilla, but only changes that have taken place in the Andalusian dialect of Castilian have become established in America. Furthermore, these changes apparently took place between the fifteenth and the eighteenth centuries, during the settlement of Latin America. Evidence indicates that inaccessible areas of Spanish America (the mountainous regions of Mexico, Guatemala, Colombia, Ecuador, Peru, Bolivia, as well as Paraguay, inland Venezuela, and northern Argentina) received only the early changes of Andalusian Castilian, while the accessible coastal areas and port cities tend to reflect both early changes and those of the late colonial period. Thus it is that Cuban and Panamanian Spanish resemble that of present-day Sevilla more than does Mexican Spanish or that of Bogotá. In the meantime Madrid Spanish (called Castilian by many North Americans) developed one or two features that never reached America.

The outstanding common feature of American-Spanish pronunciation that goes back to the early colonial period is the so-called **seseo.** About the time of Columbus the people of southwestern Spain began to confuse the two sibilant sounds of **casa** [KáSa] ("house") and **caza** [kása] ("hunt") (the capital [S] representing a "thick" alveolar sound and the [s] representing a "normal" dental sound), with the result that only the dental sound survived. Since most settlers of America were from the south, this became the general Spanish-American tendency. **Coser** and **cocer** are alike in southern Spain and in Latin America. The sibilant is a delicate dental one. In northern and central Spain a distinction between these two sounds is still maintained, and the second or dental one has become interdental [θ], similar to the voiceless *th* of English. The former [S] is still apicoalveolar, and to the foreigner approaches the sound represented by English *sh.*

In the seventeenth and eighteenth centuries other changes occurred in the pronunciation of southern Spanish. As has been indicated, these became part of the Spanish of the accessible areas of America, but most did not reach the high mountains and plateaus. The first of these was the aspiration or even the loss of /s/ syllable final. **Estos** becomes (éhtoh] or even [éto], the result of what might be termed a "relaxed" articulation. About the same time the /l̦/ (written **ll**) tended to be "relaxed" to the extent that it coincided with the /y/ (written **y**), so that **valla** and **vaya** were levelled to [báya] in Andalusia and parts of America. Today Bolivia, Paraguay, and much of Peru and Ecuador still maintain a distinction. One of the latest levelings of Andalusia was the confusion of /l/ and /r/ syllable final. This is heard today in Puerto Rico, Panama, and Venezuela, and to a certain extent in Cuba, the Dominican Republic, and central Chile. **Puerta** sounds like [pwelta], **mar** like [mal] and the infinitives seem to end in /l/. A final Andalusian trait is the velar /n/ [ŋ] as a sign of open transition. **Enamora** is [enamóra], but **en amor** is [eŋamór]. English-speakers think of *ng* when they hear **son** and **pan** pronounced [soŋ] and [paŋ].

Perhaps the only oustanding feature of American Spanish that is not traceable to Andalusia is the assibilation of /rr/ [r̃r̃] and /r/ [r̃] final and postconsonantal. This occurs in vast areas of America: Guatemala, Costa Rica, in the eastern cordillera of Colombia, highland Ecuador, Bolivia, Chile, western and northern Argentina, and Paraguay.

Map 1

 Vos used instead of tú in informal address.

In Chile the distinction is one of class: vos is used in the
lower economic levels.

Map 2

Aspiration or loss of /s/ syllable final.

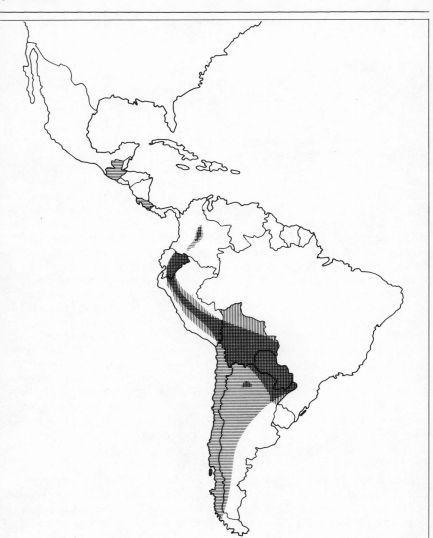

Map 3

 Distinction between /ʎ/ and /y/.

Assibilation of /rr/ and /tr/.

The maps show the distribution of the distinguishing features of Spanish-American pronunciation.

Syntactic Features

The familiar form of address in Spanish, **tú,** is a direct descendant of the Latin *tu.* The Latin plural form *vos* also came down to Spanish, but by the late Middle Ages it had assumed the function of polite singular as well as familiar plural. To make the distinction, people began to say **vosotros** (you others) for the plural. In the sixteenth century there came into being a very polite form of address: **vuestra merced** (your mercy), used with the third person of the verb, as one might say, "Does his majesty wish to enter?" It has been shortened to **usted.** With this new polite form, **vos,** the former polite singular, lost prestige and became a familiar form. This was the state of affairs when the colonists came to America. As a result, vast sections of Latin America use **vos** instead of **tú** as the singular familiar form of address. All of Spanish America uses **ustedes** for the familiar plural as well as the polite plural. It will be noted in the map on page 26 that the **vos** areas are generally far from the old Viceroyalties of Mexico and Lima. Only in Chile is there a social distinction.

The verb used with **vos** is the modified plural of Old Spanish: **hablás, comés, vivís;** the imperative is **hablá, comé, viví.** The object pronoun and the possessive are from the singular, the object of the preposition, **vos: LLevate tu perro con vos.** Since the imperative of **ir** would be simply **i,** the verb **andar** is used instead: ¡**andate!** Another interesting syntactic trait is the general tendency to differentiate gender of nouns of occupation and status of people and to create feminine forms where they may not have existed in so-called standard Spanish. **Presidenta, ministra, dependienta, liberala, abogada,** and **arquitecta** have been heard. Equally general are the tendencies to use adjectives as adverbs (**corre ligero, toca el piano lindo**) and to make certain adverbs "agree" with adjectives they modify (**media muerta; medias locas**) as well as to use the impersonal **haber** in the plural (**habían dos; ¿cuántos habrán?**).

The Vocabulary of Spanish America

There are three main tendencies in the development of Hispanic-American lexical elements: (1) to use words that were popular at the time of the settlement of America, especially maritime terms or rural expressions, often out of popular etymology; (2) to adopt Indian words, especially those related to the domestic scene; and (3) to borrow directly from English and to develop cases of correlative analogy due to English influence.

Of the first category are such terms as **flota** for a bus line, **amarrar** for **atar; botar** for **echar; virar** for **volverse.** In the tropical zone of America (from Guatemala south through Peru), where there are no seasons of heat and cold, since these depend on altitude, the Spaniards began to call the wet periods **invierno** (winter) and the dry, **verano** (summer). The custom continues to this day in Guatemala, El Salvador, Honduras, Nicaragua, Costa Rica, Panama, Colombia, Venezuela, Ecuador, and Peru. One may ask, ¿**qué tal el invierno?** ("How was the winter?") and receive the answer ¡**copioso!** ("copious").

Indian words entered the Spanish of America by the hundreds. In the Caribbean the Spaniards learned **tabaco, canoa, huracán, maíz, ají;** in Mexico, from Náhuatl, **chocolate, tomate, coyote, chicle, cacao;** in the Andes, from Quechua, **pampa, quinina, cóndor, puma, poncho;** and in the Río de la Plata region, from Guaraní, **ananás, ñandú, ombú, yajá, tapioca.**

During the twentieth century the influence of English has been strong in Latin America, and the direct borrowings in some areas could be counted in the hundreds: **control, lonche, lonchería, sandwich, jaibol** ("highball"), **cóctel, ponche, bar, twist, chance, fútbol, béisbol, fildear** ("to field"), **jonrón** ("home run"), **noquear** ("to knock out"), **lobista,** and even such verbs as **taipear** ("to type") and **blofear** ("to bluff"). In the realm of correlative analogy or sense loans, English has tremendous influence, and **educación** ("upbringing") takes the place of **pedagogía, instrucción,** and **enseñanza; argumento** ("plot of a story") moves into the slot of **discusión; atender** ("to wait on") into that of **asistir; audiencia** into that of **concurrencia; acta** ("minutes") takes the place of **ley; complexión** ("physical constitution") takes the place of **tez.**

Regional Features: Mexico

Among speakers of Spanish, a Mexican is recognized by his intonation and by his tendency to lengthen the articulation of his /s/ and by his general preference for the consonant over the vowel. If intonation of Spanish is represented in a pattern of four levels, Mexicans, especially males in a "man-about-town" mood, tend to strike a terminal point between standard statement and emphatic statement, giving the utterance a "minor-key" effect. The tensely-grooved /s/ of Mexican Spanish leads to the virtual elimination of unstressed vowels, especially /e/, in rapid speech: **accidentes de coches** may tend to be [aksiɗénts ɗe kočs].

Typical adjectives of Mexico are **mero** and **puro.** The first of these is so popular that it means not only "mere" but "very," "real," "just," "same," and many other things, and is even used adverbially: **ya merito** ("It won't be long now").

As has been noted, Mexico is the center of Aztec vocabulary that has entered Spanish and eventually many languages of the world; **tomate, chocolate, cacao, coyote, chicle,** and hundreds of less common terms.

Guatemala

The Spanish of Guatemala is characterized by a strong assibilated /rr/ [řř] and by [ř] for /r/ except in intervocalic position. The **jota** tends to be [h] rather than [x], and velar /n/ marks open transition. Along with those of other Central-American areas, Guatemalan speakers tend to weaken intervocalic /y/ to the extent that **silla** sounds like [sía] and **bella** like [bea]. Through a process of ultracorrection, **vea** may become [béya]. Guatemalans generally pronounce their /s/ syllable final with clarity and tension.

A fairly universal feature of the Spanish of Guatemala is the **voseo,** or use of **vos** as the subject form of familiar address in the singular. The verb used with this is the plural familiar, but the pronoun objects and possessives are always singular. **Ceando te vayas, llévate tu perro contigo,** as one might say in Spain or in Mexico, would be **Cuando te vayás, llevate tu perro con vos** in Guatemala.

Little boys are **patojos** in Guatemala, and blonds are **canches.**

El Salvador, Honduras, Nicaragua

Perhaps more than any other group of independent countries, these three form a linguistic unity in most respects. They represent in phonology a middle point between the highland conservatism (Mexico and the Andes, for instance) and the later trends of the lowlands (Cuba and Panamá, for example). The inhabitants of these countries call each other **guanacos, catrachos,** and **nicas** respectively, and are always talking of Central-American union.

The phonological phenomenon of recent discovery—although it is probably an "archaic" trait—is the occlusive pronunciation of /b/, /d/, /g/ after another consonant, a situation in which they would be fricative in "standard" Spanish.

It is in this region of Central America that one hears a lisped /s/ that approaches [θ] among many residents, and especially among the working classes. As in northern Mexico, the intervocalic /y/ (representing orthographic **y** and **ll**) tends to be a semivowel or even disappears. The **jota** /x/ is [h] in all speakers, and there is a strong tendency to aspirate syllable final /s/.

The Salvador-Honduras-Nicaragua region is rich in forms of combinative analogy, especially noun formation on the basis of other nouns. The suffixes **-ada** and **-ón** are of extensive application: **babosada, pendejada, lambida, atolada, paisanada, perrada, barbón, narizón, pistón, quemazón;** and the longer diminutive form **-ecito** that might be used in Spain and in Mexico is simply **-ito: llavita, lucita, crucita, piedrita.** The place where things grow or are to be found is indicated by the suffix **-al: cañal, guacal, platanal, cafetal, piñal, pinal.**

Along with Guatemala and the other Central-American countries, except Panama, this region uses the **vos** form of familiar address, and in the way described for Guatemala: **Vení y decime, ¿son vos y tu padre ladrones?**

Many indigenous words are used in everyday conversation, most of them from the Pipil, a sublanguage of the Náhuatl. A blond is a **chele,** a boy is a **cipote, pushco** is dirty, **peche** is slender, and there is the usual stock of Aztec terms that were imported after the conquest of Mexico.

Costa Rica

Like Guatemala, Costa Rica is noted for its assibilated /rr/, along with assibilated /r/ syllable final. It also shares with Guatemala a fairly conservative articulation of /s/ syllable final. As in all Central-American and Caribbean countries, the /n/ is velar when final, as a sign of open juncture: [eŋ amor] but [enamorár], and intervocalic /y/ weakens to the point of elimination through vocalization.

As a part of the syntactic structure of the dialect, **vos** and related forms operate where **tú** would prevail in Spain or Mexico today, and lexically, Costa Rica shows less Aztec influence than Guatemala, El Salvador, or Honduras.

Panama

The Spanish of Panama might be termed "trade route Spanish," in that it has the phonological character of parts of America that were in constant communication with Spain at the grass-roots level and yet were removed from the courtly influences of the viceregal centers (Mexico and Lima). It resembles strongly the Spanish of Cuba, Puerto Rico, an Venezuela and the northern coast of Colombia.

Along with other Caribbean residents, the Panamanians tend to aspirate their /s/ at the end of a syllable, or to eliminate it entirely.

Colombia

The development of the language in Colombia, which has three high mountain ranges and several important ports, might serve as an example of how American Spanish grew in disparate ways from Peninsular models. The relative inaccessibility of the high sierras and valleys makes it possible to find at least five distinct linguistic zones in the former Nueva Granada. The "dialects" therefore represent stages in the historical development of southern Peninsular Spanish, the most inaccessible regions generally representing the earliest and the most accessible in general representing the latest in Andalusian vogues, before independence.

Strange as it may seem, Colombian Spanish has two general traits in common with that of El Salvador, Honduras, and Nicaragua: the /x/ is [h] in all regions, and the /b/, /d/, /g/ are occlusive after any consonant. Thus **pardo, barba, algo, desde, las vacas,** all have occlusives where a Spaniard or a Mexican would use fricatives.

The Spanish of Bogotá has the conservative distinction of /l/ and /y/ and, like that of Costa Rica and Guatemala, tends to assibilate the /rr/, the /tr/, and the /r/ final.

Pastuso Spanish (of Nariño) is in many ways Ecuadorean, and like the Spanish of highland Mexico, slights the vowel in favor of the consonant, tends to pronounce the /d/ od **-ado,** and uses an apicodental /s/, strong and well defined.

Antioquia's Spanish is unique in America in one way. The /s/ is apicoalveolar [S], like that of Spain, and although no distinction is made between **casa** and **caza,** the Colombian ambassador to Spain, an **antioqueño,** gave the impression of "talking like a Spaniard." The second distinguishing feature of this region's Spanish is the /y/ of such tenseness that it even becomes affricate intervocalically [maŷo, kabaŷo].

Colombia is unusually formal in most sections as far as direct address is concerned. Many speakers use **usted** almost exclusively—even to cats and dogs. Not only is this the case within the family, but some relatives speak to each other as **su merced.** The **voseo** prevails in Antioquia and in Santander and in the **Valle,** while Bogotá and the Coast always employ the **tuteo.**

Typical of Colombia are the idiomatic expressions ¡**siga**! and ¡**a la orden**! The first is said to invite one to enter, and the other to ask, "What can I do for you?" Black coffee, especially the demitasse, is a **tinto,** and to invite one to partake, one says: ¿**Le provoca un tinto?** This same sentence to a Spaniard might mean, "Does red wine make you fight?" Instead of sending regards with **saludos,** Colombians use **saludes** ("healths").

Venezuela

The speech pattern of Venezuela is for the most part that of the Caribbean, and therefore late Andalusian. One "eats" his final /s/; /l/ and /r/ are confused at syllable end; /n/ is velar as a sign of finality; and as in El Salvador, Honduras, and Nicaragua, many people pronounce the /s/ as [θ].

As far as address is concerned, most of Venezuela is **tuteo** country, but sections near the Colombian frontier are **vos** areas.

Ecuador

In a country where thousands speak Quechua (the language of the Incas) in preference to Spanish and where many are bilingual, the Spanish language of the upper inter-Andean region is very conservative in its phonological evolution. Ecuadoreans (except those of the coast) still distinguish /l̯/ and /y/ as [ž] and [y], still pronounce /s/ with deliberate tenseness and, like many Mexicans, slight the vowel in favor of the consonant. Because Quechua is so widely spoken, and because this language has a simple three-vowel system, the Spanish of the highlands tends to heighten /o/ to /u/ and /e/ to /i/. Unique in Latin America is the final /s/ as [z] before a vowel in the following word: [laz aǵwas].

Peru

About 11,000,000 **peruanos,** or as their neighbors may say, **peruleros** or **cholos,** occupy the territory of the central Inca Empire of preconquest days. Their money is counted in **soles** and their babies are **guaguas.** Along with Ecuador and Bolivia, Peru belongs to heavily populated Andean Spanish America, and besides having many Quechua-speaking inhabitants, the region boasts a clear Spanish that gives evidence of sixteenth-century origin and viceregal nurture.

Except in Lima and along the northern coast, Peruvians still distinguish the /l̯/ and /y/, and the general impression of Peruvian Spanish is similar to that of Mexico, Bolivia, and Ecuador.

Nearly all of Peru uses the **tú** form of familiar address, and as one might expect, hundreds of Quechua words have entered the Spanish of everyday life. In fact, several **quechismos** have become universal terms: **pampa, cóndor, puma, puna, quinina, llama, alpaca, gaucho, china** ("sweetheart"), **poncho,** and many others.

Chile

Linguistically, Chile can be divided into three sections, north, middle, and south. The north and the south resemble each other more than they do the middle. The heavily populated central valley partakes of many of the traits of late Andalusian, through the port of Valparaiso and the city of Santiago. Final /s/ is aspirated, /l/ and /r/ are confused in the syllable final situation, and /l̯/ and /y/ are not distinguished. Chiloé still distinguishes these latter two, and in the north there are vowel-heightening influences of Quechua. Two features that seem to characterize all Chilean Spanish are the /č/ of alveolar articulation rather than palatal and the /x/ with a palatal element of semiconsonantal nature before /e/. One seems to hear **la gente de Chile** as [la xjénte de tSíle].

Argentina, Uruguay, Paraguay

The Spanish of this vast territory is of two main types, according to the direction from which the settlers came. The western and northwestern sections were settled from Peru and Chile from about 1590. Although Buenos Aires and the humid Pampa were first settled about 1535, it was not until 1580 that a permanent settlement was established. The important factor producing the differences of today was the accessibility of Buenos Aires and surrounding country to constant influences from the ports of southern Spain in the colonial period. Thus the interior shows more conservative features: an /s/ of more tense articulation, a distinction between /ļ/ and /y/ in some areas, and the assibilated /rr/ of Costa Rica, Bogotá, and Guatemala.

The **porteño** of the Río de la Plata region is noted for his /y/ with strong [ž] articulation: **bayo, calle** [bážo], [káže].

Both Argentina and Uruguay are **voseo** territories, and the style has been recorded extensively in gaucho poetry. As a cattle region, the pampas have a lexicon that is rich in the terminology of the ranch and of horses. English and French are contributors to the vocabulary of the area, and one hears of **five o'clock tea a todas horas,** and the frequency of **chau** for "good-by" attests the influence of Italian, the original language of more than half of the inhabitants of Argentina. **Argentinos** are often called **che,** since they use this term to attract attention.

Paraguay, being more inaccessible, has two conservative features in its phonology: the distinction of /ļ/ and /y/, and the assibilation of /rr/. It is unique in that nearly all its inhabitants are bilingual. They speak the original Indian language, Guaraní, and Spanish. The occasion usually dictates which will be used, and speakers will often shift from one to the other in the same utterance.

Cuba, The Dominican Republic, and Puerto Rico

The Spanish of the Caribbean, like that of Panama, could be termed "trade route" Spanish, since it shows rather typically the American evolution of Andalusian trends of the seventeenth and eighteenth centuries, trends that do not seem to be present in the more inaccessible hinterland. Add to this the Afro-Cuban influences of slave days and the many American English loans of the twentieth century, and we have perhaps the least "conservative" Castilian.

Cubans tend to aspirate their syllable final /s/ or drop it altogether, and the tendency is as marked or more so in Puerto Rico and Santo Domingo. In all three, syllable final /l/ and /r/ are confused, most of all in Puerto Rico, where the /l/ is favored: **puerta, izquierdo** [pwélta], [ihkjéldo]. In contrast to Mexico, Ecuador, Peru, and Bolivia, where the vowel may be slighted, those of the Caribbean tend to slight the consonant in favor of the vowel. In Puerto Rico /rr/ is now velar in about half of the population. It resembles the **jota** of Spain: [x].

Cuba, Puerto Rico, and the Dominican Republic are **tuteo** countries.

This brief description of some of the features of the Castilian of America may help to show that distinctive features do not correspond to geographical or political entities to the extent that has been believed, and one might indicate as many as a hundred dialects—and yet it is all Spanish.

Numerals—Números

Cardinal Numbers	Números Cardinales	Ordinal Numbers	Números Ordinales[5]
1........ one	uno, una	first	primero
2....... two	dos	second	segundo
3....... three	tres	third	tercero
4....... four	cuatro	fourth	cuarto
5....... five	cinco	fifth	quinto
6....... six	seis	sixth	sexto
7....... seven	siete	seventh	séptimo
8....... eight	ocho	eighth	octavo
9....... nine	nueve	ninth	noveno, nono
10...... ten	diez	tenth	décimo
11...... eleven	once	eleventh	undécimo
12...... twelve	doce	twelfth	duodécimo
13...... thirteen	trece	thirteenth	décimotercio
14...... fourteen	catorce	fourteenth	décimocuarto
15...... fifteen	quince	fifteenth	décimoquinto
16...... sixteen	dieciseis, diez y seis	sixteenth	décimosexto
17...... seventeen	diecisiete, diez y siete	seventeenth	décimoséptimo
18...... eighteen	dieciocho, diez y ocho	eighteenth	décimoctavo
19...... nineteen	diecinueve, diez y nueve	nineteenth	décimonono
20...... twenty	veinte	twentieth	vigésimo
21...... twenty-one	veintiuno, veinte y uno	twenty-first	vigésimo primero
30...... thirty	treinta	thirtieth	trigésimo
40...... forty	cuarenta	fortieth	cuadragésimo
50...... fifty	cincuenta	fiftieth	quincuagésimo
60...... sixty	sesenta	sixtieth	sexagésimo
70...... seventy	setenta	seventieth	septuagésimo
80...... eighty	ochenta	eightieth	octogésimo
90...... ninety	noventa	ninetieth	nonagésimo
100..... one hundred	ciento	(one) hundredth	centésimo
101..... one hundred and one	ciento (y) uno	(one) hundred and first	centésimo primo
200..... two hundred	doscientos	two-hundredth	ducentésimo
300..... three hundred	trescientos	three-hundredth	tricentésimo

[5] The ordinals beyond the "tenth" are less used in Spanish than in English. They are often replaced by the cardinals: *Alfonso the Thirteenth* **Alfonso trece.**

Cardinal Numbers	Números Cardinales	Ordinal Numbers	Números Ordinales[5]
400...... four hundred	cuatrocientos	four-hundredth	cuadringentésimo
500...... five hundred	quinientos	five-hundredth	quingentésimo
600...... six hundred	seiscientos	six-hundredth	sexagésimo
700...... seven hundred	setecientos	seven-hundredth	septingentésimo
800...... eight hundred	ochocientos	eight-hundredth	octingentésimo
900...... nine hundred	novecientos	nine-hundredth	noningentésimo
1000..... one thousand	mil	(one thousandth	milésimo
100,000... one hundred thousand	cien mil	(one) hundred thousandth	cienmilésimo
1,000,000 one million	un millón	(one) millionth	millonésimo

Nations, Cities, and Adjectives of Nationality

Afganistán	afgano
Albania	albanés
Alto Volta	voltaico
Arabia Saudita	árabe saudita
Argelia	argelino
Argentina	argentino
Asunción	asunceño
Basutolandia	basutolandés
Bechuanalandia	bechuanalandés
Bélgica	belga
Birmania	birmano
Bogotá	bogotano
Bolivia	boliviano
Brasil	brasileño
Bruselas	bruselense
Buenos Aires	bonaerense or porteño
Bulgaria	búlgaro
Burundi	burundi
Camboya	camboyano
Camerún	camerunés
Canadá	canadiense
Caracas	caraqueño
Ceilán	ceilanés
Colombia	colombiano
Congo (both)	congoleño
Costa de Marfil	marfileño
Costa Rica	costarricense
Cuba	cubano
Chad	chadiano
Checoslovaquia	checoslovaco
Chile	chileno
China	chino
Chipre	chipriota

Dahomey	dahomeyano
Dinamarca	dinamarqués or danés
Ecuador	ecuatoriano
El Salvador	salvadoreño
España	español
Estados Unidos de América	estadounidense
Etiopía	etíope
Filipinas	filipino
Finlandia	finlandés or finés
Francia	francés
Gabón	gabonés
Gambia	gambio
Ghana	ghanés
Ginebra	ginebrino
Grecia	griego
Guatemala	guatemalteco
Guayaquil	guayaquileño
Guinea	guineo
Haití	haitiano
Honduras	hondureño
Hungría	húngaro
Ifni	ifneño
India	indio
Indonesia	indonesio
Irak	iraqués
Irán	iranio
Irlanda	irlandés
Islandia	islandés
Israel	israelí
Italia	italiano
Jamaica	jamaicano
Japón	japonés
Jordania	jordanio
Jerusalém	jerosolimitano
Kenia	kenio
Kuwait	kuwaiteño
Laos	laosiano
La Paz	paceño
Líbano	libanés
Liberia	liberiano
Liberia	
Libia	libio
Lima	limeño
Lisboa	lisboeta or lisbonense
Londres	londinense

Luxemburgo	luxemburgués
Madagascar	malache
Madrid	madrileño
Malasia	malayo
Malavi	malavio
Malí	maliense
Managua	managüense
Marruecos	marroquí
Mauritania	mauritano
México (Mejico)	mejicano (mexicano)
Mongolia	mongol
Montevideo	montevideño or montevideano
Nepal	nepalés
Nicaragua	nicaragüense
Níger	nigerino
Nigeria	nigeriano
Noruega	noruego
Nueva York	neoyorquino
Nueva Zelandia	neozelandés
Paises Bajos	holandés
Pakistán	pakistano
Panamá	panameño
Paraguay	paraguayo
París	parisiense
Perú	peruano
Polonia	polaco
Portugal	portugués
Puerto Rico	puertorriqueño
	or portorriqueño
Reino Unido de Gran Bretaña e	
Irlanda del Norte	británico
República Arabe Unida	egipcio
República Centroafricana	centroafricano
República Dominicana	dominicano
República Socialista Soviética de	
Bielorrusia	bieloruso
República Socialista Soviética de	
Ucrania	ucranio
Río de Janeiro	carioca
Río Muni	ríomuniense
Rodesia	rodesio
Rumania	rumano
Rwanda	rwandés
San José	josefino
São Paulo	paulistano

Santa Cruz	cruceño
Santiago	santiagueño or santiaguino
Senegal	senegalés
Sierra Leona	leonense
Siria	sirio
Somalia	somalí
Suazilandia	suazilandés
Sudáfrica	sudafricano
Sudán	sudanés
Suecia	sueco
Tailandia	tailandés
Tanganyica	tanganyikano
Tanzania	tanzanio
Tegucigalpa	tegucigalpense
Tenerife	tinerfeño
Tetuán	tetuaní
Togo	togolés
Trinidad y Tobago	trinitario
Túnez	tunecí
Turquía	turco
Uganda	ugandés
Unión de Repúblicas Socialistas Soviéticas	ruso
Uruguay	uruguayo
Venecia	veneciano or véneto
Venezuela	venezolano
Viena	vienés
Yemen	yemenita
Yugoslavia	yugoslavo
Washington	washingtoniano
Zambia	zambio
Zanzíbar	zanzibareño

Monetary Units and Exchange Rates

Country	Basic Unit	Standard Subdivision	Exchange Rate as of Jan. 1976*
Argentina	peso nuevo	100 centavos	$ .0255
Bolivia	peso	100 centavos	$b .0468
Brazil	cruzeiro	100 centavos	Cr$ .1200
Chile	peso	100 centésimos	$ .1400
Colombia	peso	100 centavos	$ .0330
Costa Rica	colón	100 céntimos	¢ .1160
Cuba	peso	100 centavos	$ 1.000 (official)

* U.S. dollar = 1.000

Country	Basic Unit	Standard Subdivision	Exchange Rate as of Jan. 1976*
Dominican Republic	peso	100 centavos	$ 1.000
Ecuador	sucre	100 centavos	S/ .045
El Salvador	colón	100 centavos	¢ .400
Guatemala	quetzal	100 centavos	Q 1.000
Haiti	gourde	100 centimes	G .200
Honduras	lempira	100 centavos	L .500
Mexico	peso	100 centavos	$ .0801
Nicaragua	córdoba	100 centavos	C$ .142
Panama	balboa	100 centésimos	B 1.000
Paraguay	guaraní	100 céntimos	G .0098
Peru	sol	100 centavos	S/ .0230
Spain	peseta	100 céntimos	Pts. .0172
Uruguay	peso	100 centésimos	N$ .41
Venezuela	bolívar	100 céntimos	Bs .2340

A:a **a** [a] *prep.* to; in, into; on; by.
abacería [a·b̶a·se·rí·a] *f.* grocery;
grocery store; **abacero**
[a·b̶a·sé·ro] *m.* grocer.
abad [a·b̶áḏ] *m.* abbot; **abadía** [a·b̶a·ḏí·a] *f.* abbey.
abadejo [a·b̶a·ḏé·xo] *m.* *N.Sp.* codfish.
abadesa [a·b̶a·ḏé·sa] *f.* abbess.
abajarse [a·b̶a·xár·se] *v.* to lower oneself,
humiliate oneself.
abajeño [a·b̶a·xé·ño] *adj. Mex., C.A.* lowland; *n.*
lowlander.
abajo [a·b̶á·xo] *adv.* down, below; downstairs.
abalanzar[9] [a·b̶a·lan·sár] *v.* to balance; to hurl,
impel, **-se** to hurl oneself; to rush (upon), swoop
down (upon); *Am.* to rear, balk.
abalear [a·b̶a·le·ár] *v.* to "shoot up"; *Am.* to
winnow.
abanderado [a·b̶an·de·rá·ḏo] *adj.* standard-bearing;
n. standard-bearer.
abandonamiento [a·b̶an·do·na·mjén·to] =
abandono.
abandonar [a·b̶an·do·nár] *v.* to abandon, desert;
to give up.
abandono [a·b̶an·dó·no] *m.* abandon; desertion;
neglect.
abanicar[6] [a·b̶a·ni·kár] *v.* to fan.
abanico [a·b̶a·ní·ko] *m.* fan.
abaratar [a·b̶a·ra·tár] *v.* to cheapen, lower the
price of.
abarcar[6] [a·b̶ar·kár] *v.* to embrace, contain,
include; *Carib., Ríopl.* to buy up, monopolize.
abarrancarse[6] [a·b̶a·rran·kár·se] *v.* to fall into an
opening; to get into a difficult situation.
abarrotería [a·b̶a·rro·te·rí·a] *f. Mex., C.A., Andes*
grocery, grocery store; **abarrotero**
[a·b̶a·rro·té·ro] *m. Mex., C.A., Andes* grocer.
abarrotes [a·b̶a·rró·tes] *m. pl.* small packages (*in
hold of a ship*); *Mex., C.A., Andes* groceries;
tienda de — *Mex., C.A., Andes* grocery store.
abastecer[13] [a·b̶as·te·sér] *v. irr.* to supply.
abastecimiento [a·b̶as·te·si·mjén·to] *m.* supply;
provisions.
abasto [a·b̶ás·to] *m.* supply; **no dar — a** to be
unable to cope with.
abatido [a·b̶a·tí·ḏo] *adj.* dejected, depressed,
crestfallen, humbled; fallen; lowered.
abatimiento [a·b̶a·ti·mjén·to] *m.* discouragement,
dejection, depression; descent, swoop, drop.
abatir [a·b̶a·tír] *v.* to lower; to knock down; to
depress; to humble, **-se** to become discouraged;
to swoop down.
abdicar[6] [ab·ḏi·kár] *v.* to abdicate.
abdomen [ab·ḏó·men] *m.* abdomen.
abecedario [a·b̶e·se·ḏá·rjo] *m.* alphabet; primer.
abedul [a·b̶e·ḏúl] *m.* birch.
abeja [a·b̶é·xa] *f.* bee; **abejera** [a·b̶e·xé·ra] *f.*
beehive; **abejón** [a·b̶e·xón] *m.* drone; bumblebee;
abejorro [a·b̶e·xó·rro] *m.* bumblebee.
aberración [a·b̶e·rra·sjón] *f.* aberration, mental or
moral deviation.
abertura [a·b̶er·tú·ra] *f.* aperture, opening, hole,
slit.
abeto [a·b̶é·to] *m.* fir (*tree and wood*).
abierto [a·b̶jér·to] *p.p. of* **abrir** opened; *adj.* open;
frank; *Am.* proud, self-satisfied; *Am.* generous.
abigarrado [a·b̶i·ga·rrá·ḏo] *adj.* motley;
multicolored; variegated.
abigeato [a·b̶i·xe·á·to] *m.* cattle stealing.
abismado [a·b̶iz·má·ḏo] *p.p.* absorbed, buried in
thought; overwhelmed.
abismal [a·b̶iz·mál] *adj.* abysmal.

abismar [a·b̶iz·már] *v.* to overwhelm; to depress;
-se to be plunged (into); to bury oneself (*in
thought, grief, etc.*).
abismo [a·b̶íz·mo] *m.* abyss, precipice, chasm.
abjurar [ab·xu·rár] *v.* to abjure; to renounce
solemnly.
ablandar [a·b̶lan·dár] *v.* to soften.
ablativo [a·b̶la·tí·b̶o] *m.* ablative.
abnegación [ab·ne·ḏa·sjón] *f.* abnegation, self-
denial, self-sacrifice.
abnegado [ab·ne·ga·ḏo] *adj.* self-sacrificing.
abnegarse[7] [ab·ne·gár·se] *v.* to deny oneself,
sacrifice oneself.
abobado [a·b̶o·b̶á·ḏo] *adj.* stupid, silly.
abocar[6] [a·b̶o·kár] *v.* to bite; to bring near; to flow
into.
abocinar [a·b̶o·si·nár] *v.* to flare; to fall on one's
face.
abochornar [a·b̶o·čor·nár] *v.* to overheat; to
embarrass; **-se** to get overheated; to blush;
to be embarrassed.
abofetear [a·b̶·fe·te·ár] *v.* to slap.
abogacía [a·b̶o·ga·sí·a] *f.* the legal profession; a
law career.
abogado [a·b̶o·gá·ḏo] *m.* lawyer.
abogar[7] [a·b̶o·gár] *v.* to advocate, plead in favor
of; to intercede.
abolengo [a·b̶o·léŋ·go] *m.* lineage, ancestry;
inheritance, patrimony.
abolición [a·b̶o·li·sjón] *f.* abolition.
abolir[51] [a·b̶o·lír] *v.* to abolish; to repeal.
abolsarse [a·b̶ol·sár·se] *v.* to bag (*said of trousers,
skirts, etc.*).
abollado [a·b̶o·yá·ḏo] *p.p. & adj.* dented; bumped;
bruised.
abolladura [a·b̶o·ya·ḏú·ra] *f.* dent, bump.
abollar [a·b̶o·yár] *v.* to dent; to bump; to crush,
crumple; to bruise.
abombar [a·b̶om·bár] *v.* to make bulge; **-se** *Ríopl.*
to get drunk.
abominable [a·b̶o·mi·ná·b̶le] *adj.* abominable,
detestable.
abominar [a·b̶o·mi·nár] *v.* to abominate, abhor,
detest.
abonado [a·b̶o·ná·ḏo] *m.* subscriber; *p.p. of* **abonar.**
abonar [a·b̶o·nár] *v.* to credit with; to make a
payment; to endorse, back (*a person*); to fertilize
(*soil*); **-se** to subscribe.
abonaré [a·b̶o·na·ré] *m.* promissory note; I.O.U.
abono [a·b̶ó·no] *m.* (*monetario*) payment;
installment; endorsement; guarantee; (*del suelo*)
fertilizer; (*suscripción*) subscription.
abordar [a·b̶or·dár] *v.* to board (*a ship*); to dock,
put into port; to approach; to undertake, take
up (*a matter, problem, etc.*).
aborigen [a·b̶o·rí·xen] *adj.* aboriginal, indigenous,
native; **aborígenes** [a·b̶o·rí·xe·nes] *m. pl.*
aborigines, primitive inhabitants.
aborrascarse[6] [a·b̶o·rras·kár·se] *v.* to become
stormy.
aborrecer[13] [a·b̶o·rre·sér] *v. irr.* to abhor, hate,
detest.
aborrecible [a·b̶o·rre·sí·b̶le] *adj.* abominable,
hateful.
aborrecimiento [a·b̶o·rre·si·mjén·to] *m.* abhorrence;
hatred.
abortar [a·b̶or·tár] *v.* to miscarry, have a
miscarriage; to give birth prematurely; to fail.
aborto [a·b̶ór·to] *m.* abortion, miscarriage;
monster.
abotagarse[7] [a·b̶o·ta·gár·se] *v.* to bloat; to swell.

abotonador [a·ƀo·to·na·dór] *m.* buttonhook.
abotonar [a·ƀo·to·nár] *v.* to button, button up;
to bud; **-se** to button up.
abovedar [a·ƀo·ƀe·ɖár] *v.* to vault, cover with a
vault; to arch.
abozalar [a·ƀo·sa·lár] *v.* to muzzle.
abra [á·ƀra] *f.* cove; mountain gap or pass; dale;
Am. breach (*in the jungle*); *Am.* leaf (*of a door*).
abrasador [a·ƀra·sa·dór] *adj.* burning, very hot.
abrasar [a·ƀra·sár] *v.* to burn; to parch; **-se** to
burn up, be consumed.
abrazar[9] [a·ƀra·sár] *v.* to hug, embrace; to include.
abrazo [a·ƀrá·so] *m.* hug, embrace.
abrebotellas [a·ƀre·ƀo·té·yas] *m.* bottle opener.
abrelatas [a·ƀre·lá·tas] *m.* can opener.
abrevadero [a·ƀre·ƀa·ɖé·ro] *m.* drinking trough;
watering place for cattle.
abrevar [a·ƀre·ƀár] *v.* to water (*livestock*).
abreviación [a·ƀre·ƀja·sjón] *f.* abbreviation.
abreviar [a·ƀre·ƀjár] *v.* to abbreviate, shorten,
condense.
abreviatura [a·ƀe·ƀja·tú·ra] *f.* abbreviation.
abrigar[7] [a·ƀri·gár] *v.* to shelter, cover, protect;
to wrap up; to harbor (*fear*), cherish (*hope*);
-se to find shelter; to wrap oneself up.
abrigo [a·ƀrí·go] *m.* shelter, cover, protection;
wrap; overcoat.
abril [a·ƀríl] *m.* April.
abrillantar [a·ƀri·yan·tár] *v.* to polish, shine; to
glaze.
abrir[52] [a·ƀrír] *v.* to open; to unlock.
abrochar [a·ƀro·čár] *v.* to button; to clasp; to
fasten.
abrogación [a·ƀro·ga·sjón] *f.* repeal.
abrogar[7] [a·ƀro·gár] *v.* to abrogate, repeal, annul.
abrojo [a·ƀró·xo] *m.* thistle, thorn; **-s** reef.
abrumador [a·ƀru·ma·ɖór] *adj.* crushing,
overwhelming; oppressive; fatiguing.
abrumar [a·ƀru·már] *v.* to crush, overwhelm; to
trouble, annoy; **-se** to become foggy.
abrupto [a·ƀrúp·to] *adj.* abrupt, steep.
absceso [aƀ·sé·so] *m.* abscess.
absolución [aƀ·so·lu·sjón] *f.* absolution; acquittal.
absoluto [aƀ·so·lú·to] *adj.* absolute; unconditional.
absolver[2, 52] [aƀ·sol·ƀér] *v. irr.* to absolve, free
from guilt; to pardon, acquit.
absorbente [aƀ·sor·ƀén·te] *adj. & m.* absorbent.
absorber[52] [aƀ·sor·ƀér] *v.* to absorb.
absorción [aƀ·sor·sjón] *f.* absorption.
absorto [aƀ·sór·to] *p.p. irr. of* **absorber** *& adj.*
absorbed, engrossed; amazed.
abstenerse[45] [aƀs·te·nér·se] *v. irr.* to abstain,
refrain.
abstinencia [aƀs·ti·nén·sja] *f.* abstinence; fasting.
abstracción [aƀs·trak·sjón] *f.* abstraction, reverie.
abstracto [aƀs·trák·to] *adj.* abstract.
abstraer[46] [aƀs·tra·ér] *v. irr.* to abstract; to
withdraw, remove; **-se** to be lost in thought.
abstraído [aƀs·tra·í·ɖo] *adj.* lost in thought, absent-
minded; aloof.
absuelto [aƀ·swél·to] *p.p. of* **absolver** absolved,
acquitted.
absurdo [aƀ·súr·ɖo] *adj.* absurd, ridiculous,
senseless; *m.* absurdity.
abuela [a·ƀwé·la] *f.* grandmother.
abuelo [a·ƀwé·lo] *m.* grandfather; **-s** grandparents;
ancestors.
abulia [a·ƀú·lja] *f.* abulia, loss of will power.
abultado [a·ƀul·tá·ɖo] *adj.* bulky, bulgy.
abultar [a·ƀul·tár] *v.* to bulge; to be bulky; to
enlarge.

abundancia [a·ƀun·dá·sja] *f.* abundance, plenty.
abundante [a·ƀun·dán·te] *adj.* abundant, plentiful.
abundar [a·ƀun·dár] *v.* to abound, be plentiful.
aburrido [a·ƀu·rrí·ɖo] *p.p. & adj.* bored; boring,
tiresome; weary.
aburrimiento [a·ƀu·rri·mjén·to] *m.* weariness,
dullness, boredom.
aburrir [a·ƀu·rrír] *v.* to bore, vex; **-se** to become
bored or vexed.
abusar [a·ƀu·sár] *v.* to abuse, mistreat; to misuse;
— de to take unfair advantage of; to impose
upon.
abuso [a·ƀú·so] *m.* abuse; misuse.
abyecto [aƀ·yék·to] *adj.* abject.
acá [a·ká] *adv.* here, over here; this way, hither.
acabado [a·ka·ƀá·ɖo] *m.* a finishing material: paint,
varnish.
acabamiento [a·ka·ƀa·mjén·to] *m.* finish,
completion, end; death; *Am.* exhaustion,
physical decline.
acabar [a·ka·ƀár] *v.* to end, finish, complete; **—
de** (+ *inf.*) to have just; **— por** (+ *inf.*) to end
by; **— con** to put an end to, make short work
of; to destroy; **-se** to be over, finished; to be
consumed; *Am.* to wear oneself out; *Ríopl.,
Mex., C.A.* to age or decline in health.
academia [a·ka·ɖé·mja] *f.* academy; a special
school; a scientific, literary, or artistic society.
académico [a·ka·ɖé·mi·ko] *adj.* academic; *m.*
academician, member of an academy.
acaecer[13] [a·ka·e·sér] *v. irr.* to happen, occur.
acaecimiento [a·ka·e·si·mjén·to] *m.* event,
happening.
acalorado [a·ka·lo·rá·ɖo] *adj.* heated, excited,
angry.
acaloramiento [a·ka·lo·ra·mjén·to] *m.* heat, ardor,
excitement.
acalorar [a·ka·lo·rár] *v.* (*calentar*) to heat, warm;
(*emocionar*) to excite.
acallar [a·ka·yár] *v.* to silence; to calm, quiet.
acampar [a·kam·pár] *v.* to encamp; to camp.
acanalar [a·ka·na·lár] *v.* to groove; to flute (*as a
column*); to form a channel in.
acantilado [a·kan·ti·lá·ɖo] *adj.* sheer, steep (*cliff*);
m. bluff, cliff.
acantonar [a·kan·to·nár] *v.* to quarter (*troops*).
acaparar [a·ka·pa·rár] *v.* to corner (*the market*);
to monopolize; to gather in (*for one's gain or
profit*).
acarear [a·ka·re·ár] *v.* to bring face to face; to
confront.
acariciar [a·ka·ri·sjár] *v.* to caress, pet; to cherish
(*a hope or illusion*).
acarreador [a·ka·rre·a·ɖór] *m.* carter; carrier.
acarrear [a·ka·rre·ár] *v.* to cart, transport; to bring
about (*harm, disaster*).
acarreo [a·ka·rré·o] *m.* cartage, carriage, transport,
haul.
acaso [a·ká·so] *adv.* perhaps; by chance; **por si —**
just in case; *m.* chance, accident.
acatamiento [a·ka·ta·mjén·to] *m.* homage,
reverence, respect.
acatar [a·ka·tár] *v.* to revere, respect; to pay
homage to; *Mex., C.A., Ven.* to realize; *Mex.,
C.A., Ven.* to notice, pay attention.
acatarrar [a·ka·ta·rrár] *v.* to chill; *Mex. Ven.* to
bother, annoy; **-se** to get chilled, catch cold;
Ríopl. to get tipsy.
acaudalado [a·kaw·ɖa·lá·ɖo] *adj.* wealthy.
acaudillar [a·kaw·ɖi·yár] *v.* to lead, command.
acceder [ak·se·ɖér] *v.* to accede.

accesible [ak·se·sí·ƀle] *adj.* accessible; approachable.

acceso [ak·sé·so] *m.* access; entrance, admittance; attack; fit (*of madness, anger, etc.*).

accesorio [ak·se·só·rjo] *adj. & m.* accessory.

accidentado [ak·si·ɗen·tá·ɗo] *adj.* seized with a fit; in a swoon; rough, uneven (*ground*).

accidental [ak·si·ɗen·tál] *adj.* accidental, casual.

accidentarse [ak·si·ɗen·tár·se] *v.* to have a seizure or fit; to swoon, faint.

accidente [ak·si·ɗén·te] *m.* accident, mishap; chance; sudden fit, swoon.

acción [ak·sjón] *f.* (*física*) action; act; gesture; (*militar*) battle; (*de bolsa*) share of stock; — **de gracias** thanksgiving.

accionar [ak·sjo·nár] *v.* to gesticulate, make gestures; *Am.* to act, be active.

accionista [ak·sjo·nís·ta] *m. & f.* shareholder, stockholder.

acecinar [a·se·si·nár] *v.* to dry-cure; to salt down.

acechanza [a·se·čán·sa] *f.* snare; ambush.

acechar [a·se·čár] *v.* to lurk; to spy.

acecho [a·sé·čo] *m.* ambush; spying; **al** (*or* **en**) — waiting in ambush, lying in wait.

acedo [a·sé·ɗo] *adj.* rancid; acid; sour; harsh, disagreeable.

aceitar [a·sej·tár] *v.* to oil, grease.

aceite [a·séj·te] *m.* oil; — **alcanforado** camphorated oil; — **de hígado de bacalao** cod-liver oil; — **de oliva** olive oil; — **de ricino** castor oil.

aceitera [a·sej·té·ra] *f.* oil can; oil cruet (*bottle for the table*).

aceitoso [a·sej·tó·so] *adj.* oily.

aceituna [a·sej·tú·na] *f.* olive; **aceitunado** *adj.* olive green.

aceituno [a·sej·tú·no] *m.* olive tree.

aceleración [a·se·le·ra·sjón] *f.* acceleration.

acelerador [a·se·le·ra·ɗór] *m.* accelerator.

acelerar [a·se·le·rár] *v.* to accelerate, speed up; to quicken; to hurry, hasten.

acémila [a·sé·mi·la] *f.* pack mule.

acendrado [a·sen·drá·ɗo] *adj.* pure, without blemish; purified.

acendrar [a·sen·drár] *v.* to refine (*metals*); to purify, cleanse.

acento [a·sén·to] *m.* accent; emphasis.

acentuar[18] [a·sen·twár] *v.* to accentuate, emphasize; to accent; -**se** to become worse (*as an illness*).

acepción [a·sep·sjón] *f.* acceptation, usual meaning.

acepillar [a·se·pi·yár] *v.* to brush; to plane.

aceptación [a·sep·ta·sjón] *f.* acceptance; approval.

aceptar [a·sep·tár] *v.* to accept; to approve; to admit.

acequia [a·sé·kja] *f.* irrigation canal or ditch; *Peru, Ch.* small stream; *Ven., Mex., Andes* sewer.

acera [a·sé·ra] *f.* sidewalk.

acerado [a·se·rá·ɗo] *adj.* steely, made of steel; steel-like; sharp.

acerar [a·se·rár] *v.* to steel.

acerbo [a·sér·ƀo] *adj.* bitter; harsh, cruel.

acerca de [a·sér·ka·ɗe] *prep.* about, concerning.

acercamiento [a·ser·ka·mjén·to] *m.* approach; approaching; rapprochement (*coming together*).

acercar[6] [a·ser·kár] *v.* to bring near, draw up; -**se** to get near, approach.

acero [a·sé·ro] *m.* steel.

acérrimo [a·sé·rri·mo] *adj.* very sour, very tart; very harsh; very strong, stanch, stalwart, steadfast.

acertado [a·ser·tá·ɗo] *adj.* accurate; right; sure.

acertar[1] [a·ser·tár] *v. irr.* to hit (*the mark*); to hit upon; find by chance; to guess right; — **a** (+ *inf.*) to happen to.

acertijo [a·ser·tí·xo] *m.* riddle.

acetileno [a·se·ti·lé·no] *m.* acetylene.

aciago [a·sjá·go] *adj.* ill-fated, unlucky.

acicalado [a·si·ka·lá·ɗo] *p.p. & adj.* polished; dressed up; adorned; trim, neat.

acicalar [a·si·ka·lár] *v.* to polish; to adorn; -**se** to dress up, doll up.

acicate [a·si·ká·te] *m.* spur; incentive.

acidez [a·si·dés] *f.* acidity, sourness.

ácido [á·si·ɗo] *m.* acid; *adj.* acid, sour.

acierto [a·sjér·to] *m.* right guess; lucky hit; good aim; good judgment; **con** — effectively, successfully.

aclamación [a·kla·ma·sjón] *f.* acclamation, applause.

aclamar [a·kla·már] *v.* to acclaim, cheer, hail; applaud.

aclaración [a·kla·ra·sjón] *f.* explanation.

aclarar [a·kla·rár] *v.* to clarify, explain; to clear up; to rinse; to dawn.

aclimatar [a·kli·ma·tár] *v.* to acclimatize, accustom to a climate or new environment.

acobardar [a·ko·ƀar·ɗár] *v.* to frighten, intimidate.

acogedor [a·ko·xe·ɗór] *adj.* friendly; hospitable.

acoger[11] [a·ko·xér] *v.* to receive; to give shelter; -**se** to take refuge.

acogida [a·ko·xí·ɗa] *f.* reception, welcome; refuge.

acogimiento [a·ko·xi·mjén·to] *m.* reception, welcome.

acojinar [a·ko·xi·nár] *v.* to cushion; to quilt.

acolchar [a·kol·čár] *v.* to quilt.

acólito [a·kó·li·to] *m.* acolyte, altar boy.

acometer [a·ko·me·tér] *v.* to attack; to undertake.

acometida [a·ko·me·tí·ɗa] *f.* **acometimiento** [a·ko·me·ti·mjén·to] *m.* attack, assault.

acomodadizo [a·ko·mo·ɗa·ɗí·so] *adj.* obliging; accommodating.

acomodado [a·ko·mo·ɗá·ɗo] *adj.* well-off, wealthy; suitable, convenient; *p.p. of* **acomodar.**

acomodador [a·ko·mo·ɗa·ɗór] *m.* usher (*in a theater*).

acomodar [a·ko·mo·ɗár] *v.* (*cosa*) to arrange, adjust; (*a una persona*) to lodge; to give employment to; -**se** to make oneself comfortable; to adapt oneself.

acomodo [a·ko·mó·ɗo] *m.* occupation, employment; arrangement.

acompañador [a·kom·pa·ña·ɗór] *m.* companion; accompanist.

acompañamiento [a·kom·pa·ña·mjén·to] *m.* accompaniment; retinue, company.

acompañante [a·kom·pa·ñán·te] *m.* companion; escort; attendant; accompanist.

acompañar [a·kom·pa·ñár] *v.* to accompany; to escort; to be with; to enclose (*in a letter*).

acompasado [a·kom·pa·sá·ɗo] *adj.* rhythmical; measured; slow, deliberate.

acondicionado [a·kon·di·sjo·ná·ɗo] *adj.* conditioned; comfortable; air-conditioned; *Am.* adequate, suitable.

acondicionar [a·kon·di·sjo·nár] *v.* to condition; to prepare; to arrange; -**se** to become conditioned or prepared.

acongojar [a·koŋ·go·xár] *v.* to grieve; -**se** to grieve; to be distressed.

aconsejar [a·kon·se·xár] *v.* to advise, counsel.

acontecer[13] [a·kon·te·sér] *v. irr.* to happen, occur.

acontecimiento [a·kon·te·si·mjén·to] *m.* event, happening.

acopiar [a·ko·pjár] *v.* to gather, accumulate, store up.

acopio [a·kó·pjo] *m.* storing; accumulation; stock, store, supply.

acoplamiento [a·ko·pla·mjén·to] *m.* coupling; joint, connection.

acoplar [a·ko·plár] *v.* to couple, connect; to fit or join together; to yoke; to pair, mate.

acorazado [a·ko·ra·sá·đo] *m.* armored ship, battleship.

acorazar⁹ [a·ko·ra·sár] *v.* to armor.

acordar [a·kor·đár] *v. irr. (estar conforme)* to arrange, to decide; *(instrumento)* to tune, put in harmony *(stringed instrument)*; *Peru, Ch., Ríopl., Mex., Cuba* to grant; **-se** to remember.

acorde [a·kór·đe] *adj.* in harmony; in tune; *m.* chord.

acordelar [a·kor·đe·lár] *v.* to measure with a cord; to rope off, put a cord around.

acordeón [a·kor·đe·ón] *m.* accordion.

acordonar [a·kor·đo·nár] *v.* to tie with a cord, string, or rope; to rope off, tie a rope around *(a place)*; to mill *(a coin)*.

acornear [a·kor·ne·ár] *v.* to gore, wound with a horn; to butt.

acorralar [a·ko·rra·lár] *v.* to corral; to surround.

acortamiento [a·kor·ta·mjén·to] *m.* shortening.

acortar [a·kor·tár] *v.* to shorten, diminish; **-se** to shrink; to be shy, bashful.

acosar [a·ko·sár] *v.* to pursue, harass.

acostado [a·kos·tá·đo] *adj.* reclining, lying down, in bed; tilted.

acostar² [a·kos·tár] *v. irr.* to put to bed; to lay down; **-se** to lie down, go to bed; to tilt.

acostumbrado [a·kos·tum·brá·đo] *adj.* accustomed, used, usual, habitual.

acostumbrar [a·kos·tum·brár] *v.* to accustom, train; to be used to, be accustomed to; **-se** to get accustomed.

acotación [a·ko·ta·sjón] *f.* marginal note; stage directions *(for a play)*; boundary mark; mark on a map showing altitude.

acotar [a·ko·tár] *v.* to mark off *(with boundary marks)*; to make marginal notes or citations; to put the elevation marks on *(maps)*.

acre [á·kre] *adj.* sour, tart, sharp; rude, harsh; *m.* acre.

acrecentamiento [a·kre·sen·ta·mjén·to] *m.* growth, increase.

acrecentar¹ [a·kre·sen·tár] *v. irr.* to increase; to advance, promote.

acreditar [a·kre·đi·tár] *v.* to credit; to bring fame or credit to; to accredit, authorize; **-se** to win credit or fame.

acreedor [a·kre·e·đór] *adj.* worthy, deserving; *m.* creditor.

acribillar [a·kri·bi·yár] *v.* to riddle; to perforate; to pierce.

acriollar [a·krjo·yár] *v.* to make Spanish American; **-se** to become Spanish American like; to take on Spanish-American customs.

acróbata [a·kró·ba·ta] *m. & f.* acrobat.

acra [ák·ta] *f.* minutes *(of a meeting)*; document; **levantar** — to write the minutes.

actitud [ak·ti·túđ] *f.* attitude; posture, pose.

activar [ak·ti·bár] *v.* to activate, make active; to speed up, hasten.

actividad [ak·ti·bi·đađ] *f.* activity; energy.

activista [ak·ti·bís·ta] *m. & f.* activist.

activo [ak·tí·bo] *adj.* active, lively; *m.* assets.

acto [ák·to] *m.* act; action, deed; ceremony; — **continuo** (or **seguido**) immediately after; **en el** — immediately.

actor [ak·tór] *m.* actor; **actriz** *f.* actress.

actuación [ak·twa·sjón] *f.* action; intervention, participation, performance; **-es** legal proceedings.

actual [ak·twál] *adj.* present *(time)*; of the present month; **-mente** *adv.* at present, nowadays.

actualidad [ak·twa·li·đađ] *f.* present time; **-es** latest news, fashions, or events; **de** — current, up-to-date.

actuar¹⁸ [ak·twár] *v.* to act, perform a function or act; to set in motion, cause to act.

acuarela [a·kwa·ré·la] *f.* water color.

acuario [a·kwá·rjo] *m.* aquarium.

acuartelar [a·kwar·te·lár] *v.* to quarter *(troops)*.

acuático [a·kwá·ti·ko] *adj.* aquatic; **deportes -s** water sports.

acuchillar [a·ku·či·yár] *v.* to knife; to stab; to slash.

acudir [a·ku·đír] *v.* to go or come *(to aid, or in response to a call)*; to attend, be present; to resort or turn to for help.

acueducto [a·kwe·đúk·to] *m.* aqueduct, water channel or pipe.

acuerdo [a·kwér·đo] *m.* agreement; decision, resolution; opinion; remembrance; **estar de** — to be in agreement; **ponerse de** — to come to an agreement; **tomar un** — to take a decision.

acullá [a·ku·yá] *adv.* yonder, over there.

acumulación [a·ku·mu·la·sjón] *f.* accumulation.

acumulador [a·ku·mu·la·đór] *m.* storage battery.

acumular [a·ku·mu·lár] *v.* to accumulate, gather, pile up.

acuñación [a·ku·ña·sjón] *f.* coinage, minting; wedging.

acuñar [a·ku·ñár] *v.* to mint, coin, to wedge.

acuso [a·kwó·so] *adj.* watery.

acurrucarse⁶ [a·ku·rru·kár·se] *v.* to cuddle, nestle; to huddle.

acusación [a·ku·sa·sjón] *f.* accusation, charge.

acusado [a·ku·sá·đo] *p.p. & adj.* accused; *m.* defendant.

acusar [a·ku·sár] *v.* to accuse, denounce; to acknowledge *(receipt)*.

acusativo [a·ku·sa·tí·bo] *adj.* accusative.

acuse [a·kú·se] *m.* acknowledgment *(of receipt)*.

acústica [a·kús·ti·ka] *f.* acoustics *(science of sound)*.

acústico [a·kús·ti·ko] *adj.* acoustic.

achacar⁶ [a·ča·kár] *v.* to impute, attribute.

achacoso [a·ča·kó·so] *adj.* sickly.

achaparrado [a·ča·pa·rrá·đo] *adj.* shrub, of shrub size; squat, squatty.

achaque [a·čá·ke] *m.* slight chronic illness; excuse; pretext; infirmity.

achicar⁶ [a·či·kár] *v.* to shorten; to make small; to bail *(water)*; to humiliate; *Col.* to kill; *Ríopl.* to tie, fasten; **-se** to get smaller; to shrink.

achicoria [a·či·kó·rja] *f.* chicory.

adagio [a·đá·xjo] *m.* adage, proverb, wise saying; adagio *(musical Spanish America)*.

adaptar [a·đap·tár] *v.* to adapt, fit, adjust.

adecuado [a·đe·kwá·đo] *adj.* adequate, fit, suitable.

adecuar [a·đe·kwár] *v.* to fit, adapt.

adefesio [a·đe·fé·sjo] *m.* absurdity, nonsense; ridiculous sight, dress, or person.

adelantado [a·đe·lan·tá·đo] *p.p. & adj.* anticipated; advanced; ahead; forward, bold; **por** — in advance; *m.* govenor of a province (*in colonial Spanish America*).

adelantamiento [a·ðe·lan·ta·mjén·to] *m.* advancement, progress, betterment.

adelantar [a·ðe·lan·tár] *v.* to advance; to move forward; to progress; to better; **-se** to get ahead.

adelante [a·ðe·lán·te] *adv.* forward, ahead; **en —** from now on.

adelanto [a·ðe·lán·to] *m.* advance; advancement, progress; betterment.

adelfa [a·ðél·fa] *f.* oleander.

adelgazar[9] [a·ðel·ga·sár] *v.* to thin out, taper; **-se** to get thin, slender.

ademán [a·ðe·mán] *m.* gesture, gesticulation; attitude.

además [a·ðe·más] *adv.* moreover, besides; **— de** *prep.* in addition to, besides.

adentro [a·ðén·tro] *adv.* within, inside; **tierra —** inland; **mar —** out to sea; **hablar para sus -s** to talk to oneself.

aderezamiento [a·ðe·re·sa·mjén·to] *m.* dressing; adornment, decoration.

aderezar [a·ðe·re·sár] *v.* (*embellecer*) to fix up, adorn, beautify, garnish; (*condimentar*) to season, prepare; (*almidonar*) to starch, stiffen.

aderezo [a·ðe·ré·so] *m.* (*adorno*) adornment, garnish, trappings, finery, set of jewels; (*alimento*) seasoning; (*almidón*) starch, stiffener, filler (*used in cloth*).

adestrado [a·ðes·trá·ðo] *adj.* trained, skilled.

adestrar[1] [a·ðes·trár] *v. irr.* to train; to guide.

adeudado [a·ðew·ðá·ðo] *adj.* indebted; in debt; *p.p. of* **adeudar.**

adeudar [a·ðew·ðár] *v.* to owe; to debit, charge; **-se** to run into debt.

adeudo [a·ðéw·ðo] *m.* debt, indebtedness; duty (*on imports*); debit, charge.

adherencia [a·ðe·rén·sja] *f.* adherence; attachment)

adherir[3] [a·ðe·rír] *v. irr.* to adhere, stick.

adhesión [a·ðe·sjón] *f.* adhesion; attachment.

adicto [a·ðík·to] *adj.* addicted; devoted; *m.* addict; follower.

adiestrado [a·ðjes·trá·ðo] = **adestrado.**

adiestramiento [a·ðjes·tra·mjén·to] *m.* training; drill.

adiestrar [a·ðjes·trár] = **adestrar.**

adinerado [a·ði·ne·rá·ðo] *adj.* wealthy.

¡adiós! [a·ðjós] *interj.* good-bye!; farewell!; hello!; *Am.* you don't say!

aditamento [a·ði·ta·mén·to] *m.* addition; annex.

adivinación [a·ði·ϐi·na·sjón] *f.* divination, prediction; guess.

adivinanza [a·ði·ϐi·nán·sa] *f.* conundrum, riddle.

adivinar [a·ði·ϐi·nár] *v.* to guess.

adivino [a·ði·ϐí·no] *m.* fortuneteller; soothsayer.

adjetivo [að·xe·tí·ϐo] *m. & adj.* adjective.

adjudicar[6] [að·xu·ði·kár] *v.* to adjudge, award, assign; **-se** to appropriate.

adjuntar [að·xun·tár] *v.* to put with; to bring together; to enclose (*in a letter*).

adjunto [að·xún·to] *adj.* adjoining; attached, enclosed.

adminículo [að·mi·ní·ku·lo] *m.* accessory; gadget.

administración [að·mi·nis·tra·sjón] *f.* administration, management; headquarters; *Ven., Mex., Cuba* extreme unction, last sacrament.

administrador [að·mi·nis·tra·ðór] *m.* administrator, manager.

administrar [að·mi·nis·trár] *v.* to administer; to

manage; **-se** *Ven., Mex., Cuba* to receive the extreme unction or last sacrament.

administrativo [að·mi·nis·tra·tí·ϐo] *adj.* administrative.

admirable [að·mi·rá·ϐle] *adj.* admirable, wonderful.

admiración [að·mi·ra·sjón] *f.* admiration, wonder; **punto de —** exclamation point.

admirador [að·mi·ra·ðór] *m.* admirer.

admirar [að·mi·rár] *v.* to admire; **-se** to be astonished or amazed; to wonder.

admisible [að·mi·sí·ϐle] *adj.* admissible, allowable.

admisión [að·mi·sjón] *f.* admission; acceptance; acknowledgment.

admitir [að·mi·tír] *v.* to admit; to let in; to accept; to allow, permit.

adobar [a·ðo·ϐár] *v.* to fix, cook, prepare (*food*); to tan (*hides*); to pickle (*meats, fish*).

adobe [a·ðó·ϐe] *m.* adobe, sun-dried mud brick.

adobo [a·ðó·ϐo] *m.* mending; sauce for seasoning or pickling; mixture for dressing skins or cloth; rouge.

adoctrinamiento [a·ðok·tri·na·mjén·to] *m.* indoctrination, teaching, instruction.

adoctrinar [a·ðok·tri·nár] *v.* to indoctrinate, teach, instruct.

adolecer[13] [a·ðo·le·sér] *v. irr.* to suffer (*from an illness, defect, etc.*).

adolescencia [a·ðo·le·sén·sja] *f.* adolescence.

adolescente [a·ðo·le·sén·te] *adj.* adolescent.

adonde [a·ðón·de] *rel. adv.* where; **¿adónde?** *interr. adv.* where to?; where?

adoptar [a·ðop·tár] *v.* to adopt; to accept (*an opinion*)

adoptivo [a·ðop·ti·ϐo] *adj.* adoptive, related by adoption; adopted.

adoración [a·ðo·ra·sjón] *f.* adoration, worship.

adorar [a·ðo·rár] *v.* to adore, worship.

adormecer[13] [a·ðor·me·sér] *v. irr.* to make sleepy or drowsy; to lull; **-se** to get sleepy; to get numb; to fall asleep.

adormilado [a·ðor·mi·lá·ðo] *adj.* drowsy.

adornar [a·ðor·nár] *v.* to adorn, decorate, ornament.

adorno [a·ðór·no] *m.* adornment, ornament, decoration.

adquirir[35] [að·ki·rír] *v. irr.* to acquire, gain, win, obtain.

adquisición [að·ki·si·sjón] *f.* acquisition; attainment.

adrede [a·ðré·ðe] *adv.* on purpose, intentionally.

aduana [a·ðwá·na] *f.* customhouse.

aduanero [a·ðwa·né·ro] *m.* customhouse officer; *adj.* customhouse.

aduar [a·ðwár] *m.* gypsy camp; *Ríopl.* Indian camp or ranch.

aducir[25] [a·ðu·sír] *v. irr.* to cite, allege, offer as proof.

adueñarse [a·ðwe·ñár·se] *v.* to take possession.

adulación [a·ðu·la·sjón] *f.* flattery.

adulador [a·ðu·la·ðór] *m.* flatter.

adular [a·ðu·lár] *v.* to flatter.

adulterar [a·ðul·te·rár] *v.* to adulterate, corrupt, make impure.

adulterio [a·ðul·té·rjo] *m.* adultery.

adúltero [a·ðúl·te·ro] *m.* adulterer.

adulto [a·ðúl·to] *m. & adj.* adult.

adusto [a·ðús·to] *adj.* stern, severe, austere.

advenedizo [að·ϐe·ne·ðí·so] *m.* newcomer, stranger; upstart; *Mex., Carib., Andes* novice, beginner; *adj.* newly arrived; upstart; *Mex., Carib., Andes* inexperienced.

advenimiento [aḏ·ḇe·ni·mién·to] *m.* advent, arrival, coming.

adverbio [aḏ·ḇér·ḇjo] *m.* adverb.

adversario [aḏ·ḇer·sá·rjo] *m.* adversary, opponent; foe.

adversidad [aḏ·ḇer·si·ḏáḏ] *f.* adversity; calamity.

adverso [aḏ·ḇér·so] *adj.* adverse; contrary; unfavorable.

advertencia [aḏ·ḇer·tén·sja] *f.* notice; warning; advice.

advertir[3] [aḏ·ḇer·tír] *v. irr.* to notice; to warn; to advise.

adyacente [aḏ·ya·sén·te] *adj.* adjacent.

aéreo [a·é·re·o] *adj.* aerial; airy; **correo** — air mail.

aerodinámico [a·e·ro·ḏi·ná·mi·ko] *adj.* aerodynamic; *f.* aerodynamics.

aeródromo [a·e·ró·ḏro·mo] *m.* airport.

aerofluyente [a·e·ro·flu·yén·te] *adj.* streamlined.

aeronautica [a·e·ro·náw·ti·ka] *f.* aeronautics.

aeronave [a·e·ro·ná·ḇe] *f.* airship.

aeropista [a·e·ro·pís·ta] *f.* landing strip; runway.

aeroplano [a·e·ro·plá·no] *m.* airplane.

aeropuerto [a·e·ro·pwér·to] *m.* airport.

aerosol [a·e·ro·sól] *m.* aerosol.

afabilidad [a·fa·ḇi·li·ḏáḏ] *f.* friendliness, pleasantness, courtesy; **afable** [a·fá·ḇle] *adj.* affable, pleasant, courteous.

afamado [a·fa·má·ḏo] *adj.* famous.

afán [a·fán] *m.* eagerness, anxiety, ardor.

afanar [a·fa·nár] *v.* to urge, press; **-se** to hurry; to worry; to work eagerly; to toil.

afanoso [a·fa·nó·so] *adj.* laborious; hardworking.

afasia [a·fá·sja] *f.* aphasia.

afear [a·fe·ár] *v.* to make ugly; to disfigure; to blame, censure, condemn.

afección [a·fek·sjón] *f.* affection, fondness; disease.

afectado [a·fek·tá·ḏo] *p.p. & adj.* affected; *Am.* hurt, harmed; *Am.* **estar — del corazón** to have heart trouble.

afectar [a·fek·tár] *v. (promover)* to affect, move; *(fingir)* to pretend to have or feel; *Am.* to hurt, to harm, to injure.

afecto [a·fék·to] *m.* affection; *adj.* fond; — **a** fond of; given to; prone to.

afectuoso [a·fek·twó·so] *adj.* affectionate, tender.

afeitada [a·fej·tá·ḏa] *f. Am.* shave, shaving.

afeitar [a·fej·tár] *v.* to shave; **-se** to shave oneself; to put on make-up.

afeite [a·féj·te] *m.* make-up, cosmetics.

afeminado [a·fe·mi·ná·ḏo] *adj.* effeminate.

aferrado [a·fe·rrá·ḏo] *adj.* stubborn, obstinate; *p.p. of* **aferrar.**

aferramiento [a·fe·rra·mjén·to] *m.* grasping, seizing; attachment; stubbornness, tenacity.

aferrar [a·fe·rrár] *v.* to seize, grasp, grapple; **-se** to take or seize hold of; to cling; **-se a una opinión** to cling to an opinion.

afianzar[9] [a·fjan·sár] *v.* to fasten, secure; to steady; to give bail or bond.

afición [a·fi·sjón] *f.* taste, inclination; fondness; affection.

aficionado [a·fi·sjo·ná·ḏo] *adj.* fond; *m.* amateur, fan.

aficionar [a·fi·sjo·nár] *v.* to inspire a liking or fondness; **-se a** to become fond of.

afiche [a·fi·če] *m. Ríopl.*, poster.

afijo [a·fí·xo] *m.* affix.

afilador [a·fi·la·ḏór] *m.* grinder, sharpener.

afilar [a·fi·lár] *v.* to sharpen; to grind; *Am.* to make love to, woo; *Am.* to flatter; *Am.* — **con** to flirt with.

afín [a·fín] *adj.* kindred, related; **ideas afines** related ideas.

afinador [a·fi·na·ḏór] *m.* piano tuner.

afinar [a·fi·nár] *v.* to refine, polish; to tune.

afinidad [a·fi·ni·ḏáḏ] *f.* affinity; similarity; relationship.

afirmación [a·fir·ma·sjón] *f.* affirmation, assertion.

afirmar [a·fir·már] *v.* to affirm, assert; to make firm; *Am.* — **un golpe** to deal a blow.

afirmativa [a·fir·ma·ti·ḇa] *f.* affirmative.

afirmativo [a·fir·ma·tí·ḇo] *adj.* affirmative.

aflicción [a·flik·sjón] *f.* affliction, trouble, pain, grief.

afligir[11] [a·fli·xír] *v.* to afflict, trouble, grieve; *Ríopl.*, *Ven.* to mistreat, harm, beat, strike; **-se** to worry, grieve.

aflojar [a·flo·xár] *v.* to slacken; to loosen, unfasten; to let go; *Mex. Ríopl.*, *Carib.* to let go of money, spend easily; *Mex. Ríopl.*, *Carib.* — **un golpe** to give a blow.

afluente [a·flwén·te] *m.* tributary; *adj.* abundant.

afluir[32] [a·flwír] *v. irr.* to flow (into).

afortunado [a·for·tu·ná·ḏo] *adj.* fortunate; lucky.

afrenta [a·frén·ta] *f.* affront, offense, insult.

afrentar [a·fren·tár] *v.* to insult, offend, dishonor.

afrentoso [a·fren·tó·so] *adj.* outrageous, shameful, disgraceful.

africado [a·fri·ká·ḏo] *adj.* affricative; *f.* affricate.

africano [a·fri·ká·no] *adj. & m.* African.

afrontar [a·fron·tár] *v.* to face; to confront.

afuera [a·fwé·ra] *adv.* out, outside; **-s** *f. pl.* outskirts.

agachar [a·ga·čár] *v.* to lower; to bend down; **-se** to stoop, bend down, duck; to crouch; *Am.* to give in, yield; *Col.* **-se con algo** to make away with or steal something.

agalla [a·gá·ya] *f.* gill; tonsil; *Col.*, *Ven.* greed; **tener -s** to have guts, have courage; *Ríopl.*, *Ch.*, *Carib.* to be unscrupulous and bold in business deals; *Ríopl.*, *Ch.*, *Carib.* to be greedy or stingy; *C.A.* to be smart, astute, cunning.

agarrar [a·ga·rrár] *v.* to seize, grasp, grab; **-se** to cling, hold on.

agarro [a·gá·rro] *m.* clench, clutch, grasp, grip, grab; **agarrón** *m.* tight clench, sudden grasp, grab; *Mex.*, *Col.*, *Ven.*, *C.A.* pull, tug.

agasajar [a·ga·sa·xár] *v.* to entertain; to flatter.

agasajo [a·ga·sá·xo] *m.* entertainment, kind reception; friendliness; flattery.

agazapar [a·ga·sa·pár] *v.* to nab, seize *(a person)*; **-se** to crouch; to squat.

agencia [a·xén·sja] *f.* agency; *Ch.* pawnshop.

agenciar [a·xen·sjár] *v.* to negotiate; to procure by negotiation; to promote.

agente [a·xén·te] *m.* agent; *Am.* officer, official.

ágil [á·xil] *adj.* agile, nimble, limber.

agilidad [a·xi·li·ḏáḏ] *f.* agility, nimbleness.

agitación [a·xi·ta·sjón] *f.* agitation; excitement.

agitador [a·xi·ta·ḏór] *m.* agitator; *adj.* agitating; stirring.

agitar [a·xi·tár] *v.* to agitate, excite; to stir; to wave; to shake.

aglomeración [a·glo·me·ra·sjón] *f.* conglomeration, heap, pile, mass.

aglomerar [a·glo·me·rár] *v.* to mass together; to cluster; **-se** to crowd together, pile up.

aglutinante [a·glu·ti·nán·te] *adj.* agglutinative.

agobiar [a·go·ḇjár] *v.* to oppress, weigh down; to overwhelm.

agolparse [a·gol·pár·se] *v.* to crowd together, jam.

agonía [a·go·ní·a] *f.* agony.

agonizante [a·go·ni·sán·te] *adj.* dying; *m.* dying person.

agonizar[9] [a·go·ni·sár] *v.* to be dying.

agorero [a·go·ré·ro] *adj.* ominous, of bad omen; prophetic; *m.* augur, prophet, fortune-teller.

agostar [a·gos·tár] *v.* to parch, dry up; to pasture; to plow (*in August*).

agosto [a·gós·to] *m.* August; harvest; **hacer su —** to make hay while the sun shines.

agotado [a·go·tá·ḍo] *adj. & p.p.* exhausted; out-of-print.

agotamiento [a·go·ta·mjén·to] *m.* exhaustion; draining.

agotar [a·go·tár] *v.* to exhaust, use up; to drain off; -se (*acabarse*) to be exhausted, used up; (*terminarse la edición*) to go out of print.

agraciado [a·gra·sjá·ḍo] *adj.* graceful; *m.* winner (*of a favor, prize, etc.*).

agraciar [a·gra·sjár] *v.* to grace; to adorn.

agradable [a·gra·ḍá·ḅle] *adj.* agreeable, pleasant.

agradar [a·gra·ḍár] *v.* to please, be agreeable (to).

agradecer[13] [a·gra·ḍe·sér] *v. irr.* to thank for; to be grateful for.

agradecido [a·gra·ḍe·si·ḍo] *adj.* thankful, grateful.

agradecimiento [a·gra·ḍe·si·mjén·to] *m.* gratitude, thankfulness.

agrado [a·gra·ḍo] *m.* agreeableness; liking, pleasure; **de su —** to his liking.

agrandar [a·gran·dár] *v.* to enlarge; to aggrandize, make greater.

agravar [a·gra·ḅár] *v.* to aggravate, make worse; to make heavier; to oppress; -se to get worse.

agraviar [a·gra·ḅjár] *v.* to offend, insult, affront.

agravio [a·grá·ḅjo] *m.* offense, insult, affront.

agredir[51] [a·gre·ḍír] *v.* to assail, assault, attack.

agregado [a·gre·ḡá·ḍo] *m.* attaché, person attached to a staff; aggregate, collection.

agregar[7] [a·gre·ḡár] *v.* to add; to join; to attach.

agresivo [a·gre·si·ḅo] *adj.* aggressive, offensive.

agresor [a·gre·sór] *m.* aggressor; assailant.

agreste [a·grés·te] *adj.* rustic; wild (*fruit, flower, etc.*).

agriar[17] [a·grjár] *v.* to sour, make sour; -se to sour, turn sour, become sour.

agrícola [a·grí·ko·la] *adj.* agricultural.

agricultor [a·gri·kul·tór] *m.* agriculturist, farmer.

agricultura [a·gri·kul·tú·ra] *f.* agriculture.

agridulce [a·gri·ḍúl·se] *adj.* bittersweet, tart.

agrietarse [a·grje·tár·se] *v.* to crack; to chap (*said of the skin*).

agrimensura [a·gri·men·sú·ra] *f.* survey, surveying (*of land*).

agrio [á·grjo] *adj.* sour; disagreeable.

agropecuario [a·gro·pe·kwá·rjo] *adj.* farming (*crops and cattle*).

agrupación [a·gru·pa·sjón] *f.* group; bunch; grouping; gathering.

agrupar [a·gru·pár] *v.* to group, bunch up.

agrura [a·grú·ra] *f.* sourness.

agua [á·ḡwa] *f.* water; rain; **— abajo** downstream; **— arriba** upstream; **aguas inmundas** *f.* sewage.

aguacate [a·ḡwa·ká·te] *m. Am.* avocado, alligator pear; *Am.* avocado tree; *Am.* phlegmatic person.

aguacero [a·ḡwa·sé·ro] *m.* shower.

aguada [a·ḡwá·ḍa] *f.* watering place; supply of drinking water; flood in a mine; wall wash; water color.

aguadero [a·ḡwa·ḍé·ro] *m.* watering place.

aguado [a·ḡwá·ḍo] *adj.* watery; watered; *Am.* soft, unstarched; *Am.* weak, limp; *Andes* insipid,

uninteresting, dull; **sopa aguada** thin soup; *p.p. of* **aguar.**

aguaitar [a·ḡwaj·tár] *v. Col., Ven., Andes, Ch.* to spy; to watch; to wait for.

aguantar [a·ḡwan·tár] *v.* to endure, bear; to resist; -se to be silent, restrain oneself.

aguante [a·ḡwán·te] *m.* endurance, fortitude, resistance.

aguar[9] [a·ḡwár] *v.* to water, dilute with water; to spoil (*pleasure*); *Ríopl., Ven., C.A.* to water (*livestock*); -se to become diluted; to get watery; to fill up with water; **se aguó la fiesta** the party was spoiled.

aguardar [a·ḡwar·ḍár] *v.* to wait; to wait for.

aguardentoso [a·ḡwar·ḍen·tó·so] *adj.* alcoholic; hoarse, raucous.

aguardiente [a·ḡwar·ḍjén·te] *m.* brandy, hard liquor; **— de caña** rum.

aguarrás [a·ḡwa·rrás] *m.* turpentine, oil of turpentine.

aguazal [a·ḡwa·sál] *m.* marsh, swamp.

agudeza [a·ḡu·ḍé·sa] *f.* sharpness; keenness; wit; witty remark or saying.

agudo [a·ḡú·ḍo] *adj.* sharp; sharp-pointed; keen, witty; acute; shrill.

agüero [a·ḡwé·ro] *m.* augury, prediction; sign, omen; *Ríopl., Mex., Carib.* fortune-teller.

aguijar [a·ḡi·xár] *v.* (*picar*) to prick, goad, spur; (*animar*) to encourage, excite.

aguijón [a·ḡi·xón] *m.* prick; sting; spur, goad.

aguijonear [a·ḡi·xo·ne·ár] *v.* to goad; to prick.

águila [á·ḡi·la] *f.* eagle; **es un —** he is a shark.

aguileño [a·ḡi·lé·ño] *adj.* aquiline; eaglelike.

aguinaldo [a·ḡi·nál·ḍo] *m.* Christmas or New Year's gift; bonus.

aguja [a·ḡú·xa] *f.* needle; crochet hook; watch hand; church spire; railroad switch.

agujerear [a·ḡu·xe·re·ár] *v.* to pierce, perforate; to riddle.

agujero [a·ḡu·xé·ro] *m.* hole; needle peddler; needle box; pincushion.

aguzar[9] [a·ḡu·sár] *v.* to sharpen; to goad, stimulate; **— las orejas** to prick up one's ears.

ahí [a·í] *adv.* there; **por —** over there.

ahijado [a·i·xá·ḍo] *m.* godchild.

ahijar [a·i·xár] *v.* to adopt.

ahinco [a·ín·ko] *m.* effort, eagerness, zeal.

ahogar[7] [a·o·ḡár] *v.* to drown; to choke, strangle; to smother; to quench, extinguish.

ahogo [a·ó·ḡo] *m.* suffocation; breathlessness; anguish, grief.

ahondar [a·on·dár] *v.* to deepen; to dig; to penetrate, go deep into.

ahora [a·ó·ra] *adv.* now; **— mismo** right now; **por —** for the present; **— que** *Am.* as soon as; **ahorita** [a·o·rí·ta] instantly, this very minute; **ahoritica** [a·o·ri·tí·ka], **ahoritita** [a·o·ri·tí·ta] *Am.* this very second, in a jiffy.

ahorcar[6] [a·or·kár] *v.* to hang, kill by hanging.

ahorrar [a·o·rrár] *v.* to save; to spare; to avoid.

ahorro [a·ó·rro] *m.* saving, economy; **caja de -s** savings bank.

ahuecar[6] [a·we·kár] *v.* to make hollow; to hollow out; **— la voz** to speak in a hollow voice; *Am.* **¡ahueca!** get out of here!; -se to become puffed up, get conceited.

ahuehuete [a·we·wé·te] *m. Am.* a Mexican cypress.

ahumado [a·u·má·ḍo] *adj.* smoked; smoky.

ahumar [a·u·már] *v.* to smoke; to fume.

ahuyentar [a·u·yen·tár] *v.* to drive away; to scare away; -**se** to go away, flee; *Ven., Carib., Mex.* to stop frequenting a place.
aindiado [ajn·djá·d̶o] *adj.* Indian-like.
airado [aj·ra·d̶o] *adj.* irate; angry.
airar [aj·rár] *v.* to annoy, irritate; -**se** to get angry.
aire [áj·re] *m.* air; wind; tune; appearance; conceit; -**cito** *m.* breeze; a little tune; a certain air or appearance.
ariear [aj·re·ár] *v.* to air, ventilate.
airoso [aj·ró·so] *adj.* windy; airy; graceful, elegant; lively, spirited.
aislador [ajz·la·d̶ór] *m.* insulator; isolator; *adj.* insulating; isolating.
aislamiento [ajz·la·mjén·to] *m.* isolation; insulation.
aislar [ajz·lár] *v.* to isolate, place apart; to insulate.
¡aja! [a·xá] *interj.* great! fine!
ajar [a·xár] *v.* to crumple, wither.
ajedrez [a·xe·d̶rés] *m.* chess.
ajenjo [a·xén·xo] *m.* absynthe.
ajeno [a·xé·no] *adj.* (*de otro*) another's; (*inconciente*) unaware; (*extranjero*) alien; **— a mi voluntad** beyond my control; **— de cuidados** free from cares.
ajetrearse [a·xe·tre·ár·se] *v.* to hustle and bustle; to get tired out.
ajetreo [a·xe·tré·o] *m.* bustle, hustle; hubbub; fuss; fatigue.
ají [a·xí] *m. S.A., Carib.* chili pepper, chili sauce.
ajo [a·xo] *m.* garlic; garlic clove; garlic sauce; swear word.
ajuar [a·xwár] *m.* furniture set; trousseau, bride's outfit; bride's portion or dowry.
ajustado [a·xus·tá·d̶o] *adj.* tight, fitting tight; agreed upon (*as a price*); **— a la ley** in accordance with the law; *p.p. of* **ajustar.**
ajustamiento [a·xus·ta·mjén·to] *m.* adjustment.
ajustar [a·xus·tár] *v.* to adjust; to fit tight; to regulate; to tighten; to settle (*accounts*); to hire (*a person*); *Col.* to stint, scrimp, save; *C.A.* **— una bofetada** to give a good slap; *C.A., Mex.* **hoy ajusta quince años** he is just fifteen years old today; -**se** to come to an agreement.
ajuste [a·xús·te] *m.* adjustment, fit; agreement; settlement (*of accounts*).
ajusticiar [a·xus·ti·sjár] *v.* to execute, put to death.
al [al] = **a** + **el** to the.
ala [á·la] *f.* wing; hat brim.
alabanza [a·la·bán·sa] *f.* praise.
alabar [a·la·bár] *v.* to praise.
alabastro [a·la·bás·tro] *m.* alabaster.
alacena [a·la·sé·na] *f.* cupboard; closet: *Am.* booth, stall, market stand.
alacrán [a·la·krán] *m.* scorpion.
alado [a·la·d̶o] *adj.* winged.
alambicado [a·lam·bi·ka·d̶o] *p.p. & adj.* distilled; over-refined, over-subtle (*applied to style*).
alambique [a·lam·bí·ke] *m.* still.
alambrada [a·lam·brá·d̶a] *f.* wire, entanglement.
alambrado [a·lam·brá·d̶o] *m.* wire fence; wire screening; wiring.
alambre [a·lám·bre] *m.* wire.
alameda [a·la·mé·d̶a] *f.* poplar grove; park.
álamo [á·la·mo] *m.* poplar.
alancear [a·lan·se·ár] *v.* to lance, spear.
alano [a·lá·no] *m.* mastiff.
alarde [a·lár·d̶e] *m.* boast, bluff, brag.
alardear [a·lar·d̶e·ár] *v.* to boast, brag.

alargar[7] [a·lar·gár] *v.* to lengthen; to prolong; to stretch out, extend.
alarido [a·la·rí·d̶o] *m.* shout, scream, howl.
alarma [a·lár·ma] *f.* alarm.
alarmar [a·lar·már] *v.* to alarm.
alazán [a·la·sán] *adj.* chestnut-colored; sorrel.
alba [ál·b̶a] dawn; alb (*white robe worn by priest*).
albacea [al·b̶a·sé·a] *m.* executor.
albañal [al·b̶a·ñál] *m.* sewer.
albañil [al·b̶a·ñíl] *m.* mason, brickmason; **albañilería** [al·b̶a·ñi·le·rí·a] *f.* masonry.
albaricoque [al·b̶a·ri·kó·ke] *m.* apricot; **albaricoquero** [al·b̶a·ri·ko·ke·ro] *m.* apricot tree.
abayalde [a·b̶a·yál·de] *m.* white lead.
albazo [al·b̶á·so] *m. Mex.* early morning serenade; *Mex.* bad surprise, surprise attack at dawn.
albear [al·b̶e·ár] *v.* to show white (*in the distance*); *Am.* to rise at dawn.
albedrío [al·b̶e·d̶rí·o] *m.* free will.
albéitar [al·b̶éj·tar] *m.* veterinary.
alberca [al·b̶ér·ka] *f.* water reservoir, tank; *Mex.* swimming pool.
albergar[7] [al·b̶er·gár] *v.* to house, shelter, lodge; -**se** to take shelter; to lodge.
albino [al·b̶í·no] *m. & f.* albino.
albo [ál·b̶o] *adj.* white; *Am.* white-footed (*horse*).
albóndiga [al·b̶ón·di·ga] *f.* meat ball; fish ball.
albor [al·b̶ór] *f.* dawn; whiteness.
alborada [al·b̶o·rá·d̶a] *f.* dawn; reveille (*morning bugle call*).
alborear [al·b̶o·re·ár] *v.* to dawn.
alborotador [al·b̶o·ro·ta·d̶ór] *m.* agitator, troublemaker.
alborotar [al·b̶o·ro·tár] *v.* to disturb, upset; *Am.* to excite, arouse enthusiasm; -**se** to get upset; to mutiny; to riot; *Am.* to get excited; *Am.* to rear, balk (*said of a horse*).
alboroto [al·b̶o·ró·to] *m.* uproar, disturbance; riot; *Am.* excitement, enthusiasm; *Col., C.A.* popcorn; candied popcorn ball.
alborozado [al·b̶o·ro·sá·d̶o] *adj.* elated, excited.
alborozar[9] [al·b̶o·ro·sár] *v.* to gladden; -**se** to rejoice.
alborozo [al·b̶o·ró·so] *m.* joy, delight.
albricias [al·b̶rí·sjas] *f. pl.* good news; reward (*for good news*).
alcachofa [al·ka·có·fa] *f.* artichoke; *Ch.* sock, blow.
alachuete [al·ka·wé·te] *m.* procurer, pander; go-between; **alcahueta** *f.* bawd, procuress, go-between.
alcaide [al·káj·d̶e] *m.* warden (*of a fortress, prison, etc.*).
alcalde [al·kál·de] *m.* mayor; justice of the peace; **— mayor** mayor.
alcance [al·kán·se] *m.* (*extensión*) reach, scope; (*capacidad*) talent, capacity; (*noticas*) last minute news, newspaper extra; **cortos -s** meagre intellect; **dar — a** to catch up with
alcancía [al·kan·sí·a] *f.* money box (*with slit for coin*); savings bank.
alcanfor [al·kan·fór] *m.* camphor.
alcantarilla [al·kan·ta·rí·ya] *f.* conduit; drain.
alcantarillado [al·kan·ta·ri·yá·d̶o] *m.* sewage system.
alcanzado [al·kan·sá·d̶o] *adj.* needy; broke, short of funds.
alcanzar[9] [al·kan·sár] *v.* to reach; to overtake; to obtain; to befall; to be enough; *Am.* to hand, pass, put within reach.
alcayata [al·ka·yá·ta] *f.* wall hook; meat hook.
alcázar [al·ká·sar] *m.* castle, fortress.

alcoba [al·kó·ƀa] *f.* alcove, bedroom.
alcohol [al·ko·ól] *m.* alcohol; **alcoholico**
[al·ko·ó·li·ko] *adj.* alcoholic.
alcor [al·kór] *m.* hill.
alcornoque [al·kor·nó·ke] *m.* cork tree; cork wood;
blockhead, dunce.
alcuza [al·kú·sa] *f.* oil can; cruet, oil bottle.
aldaba [al·dá·ƀa] *f.* knocker (*of a door*); crossbar,
bolt, latch; handle (*of a door, chest, etc.*);
tener buenas -s to have "pull", influential
connections.
aldabón [al·da·ƀón] *m.* large iron knocker; large
handle; **aldabonazo** [al·da·ƀo·ná·so] *m.* knock,
knocking.
aldea [al·dé·a] *f.* village; **aldehuela** [al·de·wé·la]
f. little village, hamlet.
aldeano [al·de·á·no] *adj.* rustic, countrified; *m.*
villager; peasant.
aleación [a·le·a·sjón] *f.* alloy; alloying.
alear [a·le·ár] *v.* to alloy, mix (*metals*); to flutter;
to flap (*wings, arms, etc.*).
aleccionar [a·lek·sjo·nár] *v.* to coach; to teach,
instruct; to train; to drill.
aledaños [a·le·ɖá·ños] *m. pl.* borders, frontiers.
alegar[7] [a·le·ɡár] *v.* to allege, assert; *Am.* to argue,
dispute.
alegato [a·le·ɡá·to] *m.* allegation; assertion.
alegrar [a·le·ɡrár] *v.* to cheer up, gladden; to
brighten; **-se** to be glad, rejoice; to get tipsy.
alegre [a·lé·ɡre] *adj.* merry, gay, joyful, cheerful,
bright; tipsy.
alegría [a·le·ɡrí·a] *f.* joy mirth, gaiety,
merriment.
alejamiento [a·le·xa·mjén·to] *m.* withdrawal;
retirement, aloofness.
alejar [a·le·xár] *v.* to remove, move away from;
-se to move away; to withdraw, be aloof.
alelado [a·le·lá·ɖo] *adj.* stupefied, open-mouthed;
silly.
alemán [a·le·mán] *adj. & m.* German.
alentar[1] [a·len·tár] *v. irr.* to breathe; to encourage,
cheer, cheer up; **-se** to take heart; *Am.* to
recover (*from illness*).
alergia [a·lér·xja] *f.* allergy.
alero [a·lé·ro] *m.* eaves; projecting edge.
alerón [a·le·rón] *m.* aileron; flap.
alerto [a·lér·to] *adj.* alert; watchful; **¡alerta!**
attention! look out!; **estar alerta** to be on the
alert.
aleta [a·lé·ta] *f.* small wing; flap; fin (*of a fish*).
aletargado [a·le·tar·ɡá·ɖo] *adj.* drowsy, sluggish.
aletargarse[7] [a·le·tar·ɡár·se] *v.* to fall into a state
of lethargy; to become drowsy.
aletazo [a·le·tá·so] *m.* flap, blow with a wing.
aletear [a·le·te·ár] *v.* to flap, flutter.
aleteo [a·le·té·o] *m.* flapping, flutter (*of wings*).
aleve [a·lé·ƀe] *adj.* treacherous.
alevosía [a·le·ƀo·sí·a] *f.* treachery.
alevoso [a·le·ƀó·so] *adj.* treacherous.
alfabeto [al·fa·ƀé·to] *m.* alphabet.
alfalfa [al·fál·fa] *f.* alfalfa; **alfalfar** [al·fa·fár] *m.*
alfalfa field.
alfarería [al·fa·re·rí·a] *f.* pottery; **alfarero**
[al·fa·ré·ro] *m.* potter.
alfeñicar[6] [al·fe·ñi·kár] *v.* to frost with sugar (*a
cake, cookie, etc.*); **-se** to get frail, delicate; to act
affectedly.
alfeñique [al·fe·ñí·ke] *m.* sugar paste; delicate
person.
alférez [al·fé·res] *m.* ensign; second lieutenant.
alfil [al·fíl] *m.* bishop (*in chess*).

alfiler [al·fi·lér] *m.* pin; brooch; **-es** pin money;
ponerse de veinticinco -es to doll up, dress up.
alfombra [al·fóm·bra] *f.* carpet; **alfombrilla**
[al·fom·brí·ya] *f.* (*para el suelo*) carpet, rug;
(*enfermedad*) measles; *Mex.* plant of the vervain
family; *Carib.* black smallpox; *Carib.* skin
eruption.
alforja [al·fór·xa] *f.* saddlebag; knapsack; food
provisions for a trip; *Am.* **pasarse a la otra —**
to take undue liberties.
alforza [al·fór·sa] *f.* tuck, fold, pleat; scar.
alga [ál·ɡa] *f.* seaweed; alga.
algarabía [al·ɡa·ra·ƀí·a] *f.* jargon; chatter; uproar.
algarrobo [al·ɡa·rró·ƀo] *m.* locust tree; carob tree.
algazara [al·ɡa·sá·ra] *f.* clamor; shouting; uproar.
álgebra [ál·xe·ƀra] *f.* algebra.
algo [ál·ɡo] *pron.* something; *adv.* somewhat.
algodón [al·ɡo·ɖón] *m.* cotton; **algodonal**
[al·ɡo·ɖo·nál] *m.* cotton plantation.
alguacil [al·ɡwa·síl] *m.* policeman, constable.
alguien [ál·gjen] *pron.* somebody, someone.
algún(o) [al·ɡún(o)] *adj.* some; any; *pron.* someone.
alhaja [a·lá·xa] *f.* jewel.
alharaca [a·la·rá·ka] *f.* rumpus, clamor, racket.
aliado [a·ljá·ɖo] *adj.* allied; *m.* ally.
alianza [a·lján·sa] *f.* alliance, union; *Andes*
wedding ring; *Am.* mixture of liquors.
aliar[17] [a·ljár] *v.* to ally; to unite; **-se** to form
an alliance; to unite.
alicaído [a·li·ka·í·ɖo] *adj.* crestfallen, downcast,
discouraged; drooping.
alicates [a·li·ká·tes] *m. pl.* pliers, small pincers.
aliciente [a·li·sjén·te] *m.* inducement, incentive,
attraction.
alienista [a·lje·nís·ta] *m.* alienist (*doctor who treats
mental diseases*).
aliento [a·ljén·to] *m.* (*de los pulmones*) breath;
(*ánimo*) encouragement.
aligerar [a·li·xe·rár] *v.* to lighten; to hasten.
alimentación [a·li·men·ta·sjón] *f.* nourishment,
food, nutrition; feeding.
alimentar [a·li·men·tár] *v.* to feed, nourish.
alimenticio [a·li·men·tí·sjo] *adj.* nutritious,
nourishing.
alimento [a·li·mén·to] *m.* food.
alinear [a·li·ne·ár] *v.* to line up, put into line; to
range; **-se** to fall in line; form into a line.
aliño [a·lí·ño] *m.* ornament, decoration; neatness;
condiment, dressing, seasoning.
alisar [a·li·sár] *v.* to smooth; to polish; to plane.
alistamiento [a·lis·ta·mjén·to] *m.* enlistment;
enrollment.
alistar [a·lis·tár] *v.* to enlist; to enroll; to make
ready, **-se** to enlist; to get ready; *Am.* to dress
up.
aliviar [a·li·ƀjár] *v.* to lighten; to alleviate, relieve,
remedy, soothe; **-se** to get better, recover.
alivio [a·lí·ƀjo] *m.* relief, remedy; aid, help;
improvement.
aljibe [al·xi·ƀe] *m.* cistern, reservoir, tank; water
tanker; *Riopl.* well, artesian well, spring.
alma [ál·ma] *f.* soul, spirit; inhabitant.
almacén [al·ma·sén] *m.* warehouse; department
store; store.
almacenaje [al·ma·se·ná·xe] *m.* storage.
almacenar [al·ma·se·nár] *v.* to store, store up; to
put in storage.
almacenista [al·ma·se·nís·ta] *m. & f.* department
store owner; warehouse owner or manager;
wholesale merchant.
almanaque [al·ma·ná·ke] *m.* almanac, calendar.

almeja [al·mé·xa] *f.* clam.
almendra [al·mén·dra] *f.* almond; **almendrado**
[al·men·drá·do] *m.* almond paste; **almendro**
[la·mén·dro] *m.* almond tree.
almíbar [al·mí·bar] *m.* syrup.
almidón [a·mi·dón] *m.* starch; *Col., Ven.* paste
(*for gluing*).
almidonar [al·mi·do·nár] *v.* to starch.
alminar [al·mi·nár] *m.* turret.
almirante [al·mi·rán·te] *m.* admiral.
almirez [al·mi·rés] *m.* metal mortar.
almohada [al·mo·á·da] *f.* pillow; **almohadón** *m.*
large cushion or pillow.
almohaza [al·mo·á·sa] *f.* currycomb (*for grooming
horses*).
almoneda [al·mo·ne·da] *f.* auction.
almorzar[2, 9] [al·mor·sár] *v. irr.* to lunch, eat lunch.
almuerzo [al·mwér·so] *m.* lunch.
alojamiento [a·lo·xa·mjén·to] *m.* lodging.
alojar [a·lo·xár] *v.* to lodge; to house; to quarter
(*troops*); **-se** to lodge, room.
alondra [a·lón·dra] *f.* lark.
alpaca [al·pá·ka] *f.* alpaca (*sheeplike animal of
South America*); alpaca wool; alpaca cloth.
alpargata [al·par·gá·ta] *f.* sandal (*usually of canvas
and with hemp sole*).
alpinismo [al·pi·níz·mo] *m.* mountain climbing.
alpinista [al·pi·nís·ta] *m. & f.* mountain climber.
alquería [al·ke·rí·a] *f.* farmhouse.
alquilar [al·ki·lár] *v.* to rent; to hire; **-se** to hire
out.
alquiler [al·ki·lér] *m.* rent, rental; **de** — for rent,
for hire.
alquitrán [al·ki·trán] *m.* tar.
alrededor [al·rre·de·dór] *adv.* about, around; — **de**
prep. around; **-es** *m. pl.* environs, outskirts.
altanería [al·ta·ne·rí·a] *f.* haughtiness.
altanero [al·ta·né·ro] *adj.* haughty, proud.
altar [al·tár] *m.* altar; — **mayor** high altar.
altavoz [al·ta·bós] *m.* loud-speaker.
alteración [al·te·ra·sjón] *f.* alteration, change;
disturbance.
alterar [al·te·rár] *v.* to alter, change; to disturb.
altercar[6] [al·ter·kár] *v.* to argue, dispute; to
quarrel.
alternador [al·ter·na·dor] *m.* alternator.
alternar [al·ter·nár] *v.* to alternate; to take turns;
— **con** to rub elbows with, be friendly with.
alternativa [al·ter·na·tí·ba] *f.* alternative, choice,
option.
alternativo [al·ter·na·tí·bo] *adj.* alternating,
alternative.
alterno [al·tér·no] *adj.* alternate.
alteza [al·té·sa] *f.* highness (*title*); lofty height.
altibajo [al·ti·bá·xo] *m.* downward thrust (*in
fencing*); **-s** ups and downs; uneven ground.
altiplanicie [al·ti·pla·ní·sje] *f.* upland; high
plateau.
altiplano [al·ti·plá·no] *m. Am.* high plateau.
altisonante [al·ti·so·nán·te] *adj.* high-sounding.
altitud [al·ti·túd] *f.* altitude.
altivez [al·ti·bés] *f.* haughtiness, arrogance.
altivo [al·ti·bo] *adj.* haughty, proud, arrogant.
alto [ál·to] *adj.* (*tamaño*) high; *m.* height; upper
story (*of a building*); *Am.* heap, pile; **-s** *Am.*
upper floors; *v.* **hacer** — to halt, stop; **pasar por**
— to omit, overlook; **¡**—**!** halt!
altoparlante [al·to·par·lán·te] *m.* loud-speaker.
altura [al·tú·ra] *f.* height, altitude.
alud [a·lúd] *m.* avalanche.
aludir [a·lu·dír] *v.* to allude, refer indirectly.

alumbrado [a·lum·brá·do] *m.* lighting; *adj.* lit,
lighted; tipsy.
alumbramiento [a·lum·bra·mjén·to] *m.* childbirth;
lighting.
alumbrar [a·lum·brár] *v.* to light, give light; to
enlighten; to give birth; **-se** to get tipsy.
aluminio [a·lu·mí·njo] *m.* aluminum.
alumnado [a·lum·ná·do] *m.* student body.
alumno [a·lúm·no] *m.* student.
alusión [a·lu·sjón] *f.* allusion.
alveolar [al·be·o·lár] *adj.* alveolar.
alza [ál·sa] *f.* rise; lift (*for shoes*).
alzada [al·sá·da] *f.* height (*of a horse*).
alzamiento [al·sa·mjén·to] *m.* raising, lifting;
uprising, insurrection.
alzar[9] [al·sár] *v.* to lift, raise; to cut (*cards*); **-se** to
rebel, rise up in arms; *Col., Ven., C.A., Mex.,
Andes* to puff up with pride; **-se con algo** to
run off with something, steal something.
allá [a·yá] *adv.* there, over there; **más** — farther.
allanar [a·ya·nár] *v.* to level, even off; to invade,
break into (*a house*); to raid; — **una dificultad**
to smooth out a difficulty.
allegado [a·ye·gá·do] *adj.* near; related; allied; *m.*
relative; partisan, follower.
allegar[7] [a·ye·gár] *v.* to accumulate, heap up,
gather.
allende [a·yén·de] *adv.* on the other side; beyond;
— **el mar** across the sea, overseas.
allí [a·yí] *adv.* there; **por** — through that place,
around there.
ama [á·ma] *f.* mistress, owner; — **de leche** wet
nurse; — **de llaves** housekeeper.
amabilidad [a·ma·bi·li·dád] *f.* kindness, courtesy.
amable [a·má·ble] *adj.* kind, amiable.
amador [a·ma·dór] *m.* lover.
amaestrar [a·ma·es·trár] *v.* to teach, coach,
train.
amagar[7] [a·ma·gár] *v.* to threaten; to feint, make
a threatening motion; to strike at.
amago [a·má·go] *m.* threat; indication.
amalgamar [a·mal·ga·már] *v.* to amalgamate,
combine, mix, blend.
amamantar [a·ma·man·tár] *v.* to nurse, suckle.
amanecer[13] [a·ma·ne·sér] *v. irr.* to dawn; — **malo**
to wake up ill; *m.* dawn, sunrise.
amanecida [a·ma·ne·sí·da] *f.* dawn, sunrise.
amansar [a·man·sár] *v.* to tame; to subdue; to
pacify.
amante [a·mán·te] *m.* lover; — **de** fond of.
amañarse [a·ma·ñár·se] *v. Ec., Col., Ven.* to be
accustomed; to acclimate oneself.
amapola [a·ma·pó·la] *f.* poppy.
amar [a·már] *v.* to love.
amargar[7] [a·mar·gár] *v.* to embitter, make
bitter.
amargo [a·már·go] *adj.* bitter; *m.* bitters; *Am.* mate
(*Paraguayan tea*) without sugar.
amargor [a·mar·gór] *m.* bitterness.
amargura [a·mar·gú·ra] *f.* bitterness; grief.
amarillear [a·ma·ri·ye·ár] *v.* to show or have a
yellowish tinge; to turn yellow.
amarillento [a·ma·ri·yén·to] *adj.* yellowish.
amarillo [a·ma·rí·yo] *adj.* yellow.
amarra [a·má·rra] *f.* cable; rope; strap.
amarrar [a·ma·rrár] *v.* to tie, fasten, rope; to moor
(*a ship*); *Am.* **amarrárselas** [a·ma·rrár·se·las] to
get "tight," drunk.
amasar [a·ma·sár] *v.* to knead, mix; to mash; *Am.*
to amass, accumulate (*a fortune*).
amatista [a·ma·tís·ta] *f.* amethyst.

ambages [am·bá·xes] *m. pl.* circumlocutions;
hablar sin — to go straight to the point, speak
plainly, not to beat about the bush.

ámbar [ám·bar] *m.* amber; **ambarino** [am·ba·rí·no]
adj. amber; like amber.

ambición [am·bi·sjón] *f.* ambition; aspiration.

ambicionar [am·bi·sjo·nár] *v.* to seek, aspire after;
to covet.

ambicioso [am·bi·sjó·so] *adj.* ambitious, eager;
greedy, grasping.

ambiente [am·bjén·te] *m.* atmosphere, environment.

ambigüedad [am·bi·gwe·ðáð] *f.* ambiguity.

ambiguo [am·bí·gwo] *adj.* ambiguous; uncertain,
doubtful.

ámbito [ám·bi·to] *m.* precinct, enclosure.

ambos [ám·bos] *adj. & pron.* both.

ambulancia [am·bu·lán·sja] *f.* ambulance; field
hospital.

ambulante [am·bu·lán·te] *adj.* walking; itinerant;
moving; wandering.

amedrentar [a·me·ðren·tár] *v.* to scare, frighten.

amenaza [a·me·ná·sa] *f.* menace, threat.

amenazador [a·me·na·sa·ðór], **amenazante**
[a·me·na·sán·te] *adj.* threatening.

amenazar [a·me·na·sár] *v.* to menace, threaten.

amenguar [a·meŋ·gwár] *v.* to lessen, diminish; to
defame, dishonor.

amenidad [a·me·ni·ðáð] *f.* pleasantness.

amenizar [a·me·ni·sár] *v.* to make pleasant, cheer,
brighten.

ameno [a·mé·no] *adj.* pleasant, agreeable.

americana [a·me·ri·ká·na] *f.* suit coat.

americanismo [a·me·ri·ka·níz·mo] *m.*
Americanism; characteristic of any part of
America.

americano [a·me·ri·ká·no] *adj. & m.* American.

ametrallador [a·me·tra·ya·ðór] *m.* gunner;
ametralladora [a·me·tra·ya·ðó·ra] *f.* machine
gun.

amigable [a·mi·gá·ble] *adj.* friendly; affable,
pleasant.

amígdala [a·míg·ða·la] *f.* tonsil; **amigdalitis**
[a·mig·ða·lí·tis] *f.* tonsilitis.

amigo [a·mí·go] *m.* friend; — **de** fond of.

aminorar [a·mi·no·rár] *v.* to lessen.

amistad [a·mis·táð] *f.* friendship; friendliness.

amistoso [a·mis·tó·so] *adj.* friendly.

amistía [am·nis·tí·a] *f.* amnesty.

amo [á·mo] *m.* master, owner, boss.

amodorrado [a·mo·ðo·rrá·ðo] *adj.* drowsy.

amodorrar [a·mo·ðo·rrár] *v.* to make drowsy; **-se**
to become drowsy.

amolador [a·mo·la·ðór] *m.* grinder, sharpener; *adj.*
grinding, sharpening.

amolar [a·mo·lár] *v. irr.* to grind, hone, sharpen;
to annoy; *Col., Mex., C.A.* to ruin, harm; **-se**
Mex., C.A., Col. to go to rack and ruin.

amoldar [a·mol·dár] *v.* to mold; to shape; to
adjust; to adapt.

amonestación [a·mo·nes·ta·sjón] *f.* admonition,
advice, warning; **-es** marriage bans (*or* banns).

amonestar [a·mo·nes·tár] *v.* to admonish, advise,
warn.

amoníaco [a·mo·ní·a·ko] *m.* ammonia.

amontonamiento [a·mon·to·na·mjén·to] *m.*
accumulation, pile, heap.

amontonar [a·mon·to·nár] *v.* to heap up, pile up,
crowd up.

amor [a·mór] *m.* love; — **propio** self-esteem.

amoratado [a·mor·tá·ðo] *adj.* livid, bluish,
purplish.

amordazar[9] [a·mor·ða·sár] *v.* to gag; to muzzle.

amorío[a·mo·rí·o] *m.* love affair; love-making.

amoroso [a·mo·ró·so] *adj.* loving, tender,
affectionate.

amortajar [a·mor·ta·xár] *v.* to shroud.

amortiguador [a·mor·ti·gwa·ðór] *m.* shock
absorber; silencer, muffler.

amortiguar[8] [a·mor·ti·gwár] *v.* to muffle; to deafen
(*a sound*); to deaden (*a blow or sound*); to soften,
tone down (*a color or sound*).

amortizar[9] [a·mor·ti·sár] *v.* to pay on account; to
liquidate, pay (*a debt*); to provide a sinking
fund.

amoscarse[6] [a·mos·kár·se] *v.* to get peeved,
annoyed; *Am.* to blush, be inhibited or
embarrassed.

amostazar[9] [a·mos·ta·sár] *v.* to anger, irritate; **-se**
to get angry or irritated.

amotinar [a·mo·ti·nár] *v.* to incite to rebellion; **-se**
to mutiny; to riot.

amparar [am·pa·rár] *v.* to protect; to defend; *Am.*
to grant mining rights; **-se** to seek protection or
refuge; to protect oneself.

amparo [am·pá·ro] *m.* protection; habeas corpus
(*protection against imprisonment*); *Am.* mining
rights.

ampliación [am·plja·sjón] *f.* enlargement, widening.

ampliar[17] [am·pljár] *v.* to enlarge, widen.

amplificador [am·pli·fi·ka·ðór] *m.* amplifier.

amplificar[6] [am·pli·fi·kár] *v.* to amplify, expand,
extend, enlarge; to magnify.

amplio [ám·pljo] *adj.* ample; wide, large, roomy.

amplitud [am·pli·túð] *f.* breadth, extent, width.

ampolla [am·pó·ya] *f.* (*condición*) blister, water
bubble; (*vasija*) narrow-necked bottle or vase,
cruet.

ampollar [am·po·yár] *v.* to blister; **-se** to blister.

ampuloso [am·pu·ló·so] *adj.* inflated, wordy,
bombastic, pompous.

amputar [am·pu·tár] *v.* to amputate, cut off.

amueblar [a·mwe·blár] *v.* to furnish (*with
furniture*).

ánade [á·na·ðe] *m. & f.* duck; **anadeja** [a·na·ðé·xa]
f. duckling.

anadear [a·na·ðe·ár] *v.* to waddle.

anales [a·ná·les] *m. pl.* annals, historical records.

analfabeto [a·na·fa·bé·to] *adj. & m.* illiterate;
analfabetismo [a·na·fa·be·tíz·mo] *m.* illiteracy.

analgésico [a·nal·xé·si·ko] *adj.* analgesic.

analisis [a·ná·li·sis] *m.* analysis.

analítico [a·na·lí·ti·ko] *adj.* analytical.

analizar[9] [a·na·li·sár] *v.* to analyze, examine.

analogía [a·na·lo·xí·a] *f.* analogy, similarity.

análogo [a·ná·lo·go] *adj.* analogous, similar,
comparable.

ananá [a·na·ná], **ananás** [a·na·nás] *f.* pineapple. *See*
pina.

anaquel [a·na·kél] *m.* shelf; bookshelf; **anaquelería**
[a·na·ke·le·rí·a] *f.* shelves, bookshelves, library
stacks.

anaranjado [a·na·raŋ·xá·ðo] *adj.* orange-colored;
m. orange color.

anarquía [a·nar·ki·a] *f.* anarchy.

anatomía [a·na·to·mí·a] *f.* anatomy.

anatómico [a·na·tó·mi·ko] *adj.* anatomical.

anca [áŋ·ka] *f.* haunch, hind quarter, rump; *Andes*
popcorn.

ancianidad [an·sja·ni·ðáð] *f.* old age.

anciano [an·sjá·no] *adj.* old, aged; *m.* old man.

ancla [áŋ·kla] *f.* anchor.

anclar [aŋ·klár] *v.* to anchor.

AL

ancho [án·čo] *adj.* wide, broad; loose; roomy; *Col., Ven.* self-satisfied, conceited; **a sus anchas** at one's ease; comfortable; leisurely; *m.* width.

anchoa [an·čó·á], **anchova** [an·čó·ƀa] *f.* anchovy.

anchura [an·čú·ra] *f.* width, breadth; comfort, ease.

anchuroso [an·ču·ró·so] *adj.* vast, extensive; spacious.

andada [an·dá·ɖa] *f. Mex., Ven.* walk, stroll; **-s** track, footprints; **volver a las -s** to fall back into one's old ways or habits.

andadura [an·da·ɖú·ra] *f.* gait, pace.

andaluz [an·da·lús] *adj.* Andalusian, of or pertaining to Andalusia, Spain; *m.* Andalusian, native or Andalusia.

andamiada [an·da·mjá·ɖa] *f.* **andamiaje** [an·da·mjá·xe] *m.* scaffolding; framework.

andamio [an·dá·mjo] *m.* scaffold, scaffolding.

andanada [an·da·ná·ɖa] *f.* (*localidad*) grandstand; (*descarga*) broadside; **soltar una —** to discharge a broadside; to reprimand.

andante [an·dán·te] *adj.* walking; errant, wandering; moderately slow (*music*); **caballero — knight-errant.**

andanzas [an·dán·sas] *f. pl.* rambles, wanderings.

andar[21] [an·dár] *v. irr.* to walk; to go, go about; to run (*as a watch or machinery*); **— con cuidado** to be careful; **anda en quince años** he is about fifteen; **a todo —** at full (walking) speed; **a más —** walking briskly; **¡anda!** move on!; **¿qué andas haciendo?** what are you doing?; *Am.* **— andando** to be walking around; *Am.* **¡ándale!** hurry!

andariego [an·da·rjé·go] *adj.* fond of walking; roving; *m.* walker.

andas [án·das] *f. pl.* portable platform; litter.

andén [an·dén] *m.* railway station platform; *C.A., Col., Ven.,* sidewalk.

andino [an·dí·no] *adj.* Andean, of or from the Andes.

andrajo [an·drá·xo] *m.* rag.

andrajoso [an·dra·xó·so] *adj.* ragged, in rags.

anécdota [a·nék·ɖo·ta] *f.* anecdote, story.

anegar[7] [a·ne·ǵár] *v.* to drown; to flood.

anejo [a·né·xo] *adj.* annexed, attached.

anestesia [a·nes·té·sja] *f.* anesthesia.

anestésico [a·nes·té·si·ko] *m. & adj.* anesthetic.

anexar [a·nek·sár] *v.* to annex.

anexo [a·nék·so] *m.* annex; *adj.* annexed, joined.

anfibio [an·fí·bjo] *adj.* amphibian.

anfiteatro [an·fi·te·á·tro] *m.* amphitheater.

anfitrión [an·fi·trjón] *m.* generous host.

ángel [án̄·xel] *m.* angel.

angélico [an̄·xé·li·ko] *adj.* angelic.

angina [an̄·xí·na] *f.* angina, inflammation of the throat; *Mex., Ven.* tonsil; **— del pecho** angina pectoris.

anglosajón [an̄·glo·sa·xón] *adj. & m.* Anglo-Saxon.

angostar [an̄·gos·tár] *v.* to narrow; **-se** to narrow, become narrow; to contract.

angosto [an̄·gós·to] *adj.* narrow.

angostura [an̄·gos·tú·ra] *f.* narrowness; narrows (*narrow part of a river, valley, strait, etc.*).

anguila [an̄·gí·la] *f.* eel.

angular [an̄·gu·lár] *adj.* angular; **piedra —** cornerstone.

ángulo [án̄·gu·lo] *m.* angle, corner.

anguloso [an̄·gu·ló·so] *adj.* angular, sharp-cornered.

angustia [an̄·gús·tja] *f.* anguish, sorrow, grief, worry.

angustiar [an̄·gus·tjár] *v.* to distress, grieve, worry.

angustioso [an̄·gus·tjó·so] *adj.* anguished, worried, grievous; distressing.

anhelante [a·ne·lán·te] *adj.* anxious, desirous, longing; panting.

anhelar [a·ne·lár] *v.* to long for; to breathe hard; to pant.

anhelo [a·né·lo] *m.* longing.

anheloso [a·ne·ló·so] *adj.* anxious; eager.

anidar [a·ni·ɖár] *v.* to nest; to nestle; to dwell; to shelter.

anillo [a·ní·yo] *m.* ring.

ánima [á·ni·ma] *f.* soul, spirit.

animación [a·ni·ma·sjón] *f.* animation, liveliness, life.

animal [a·ni·mál] *m.* animal; *adj.* animal; stupid; beastly; **animalejo** *m.* little animal; **animalucho** *m.* insignificant animal; hideous little beast.

animar [a·ni·már] *v.* to animate, give life to; to inspire, encourage.

ánimo [á·ni·mo] *f.* spirit, mind; courage, valor; intention.

animosidad [a·ni·mo·si·ɖáɖ] *f.* animosity, ill will; courage, energy.

animoso [a·ni·mó·so] *adj.* spirited; courageous.

aniñado [a·ni·ñá·ɖo] *adj.* boyish; childish; **aniñada** girlish.

aniquilar [a·ni·ki·lár] *v.* to annihilate, wipe out, destroy completely.

aniversario [a·ni·ƀer·sá·rjo] *m.* anniversary.

anoche [a·nó·če] *adv.* last night.

anochecer[13] [a·no·če·sér] *v. irr.* to grow dark; to be or arrive at nightfall; *m.* nightfall.

anochecida [a·no·če·sí·ɖa] *f.* nightfall.

anonadar [a·no·na·ɖár] *v.* to annihilate; to humiliate.

anónimo [a·nó·ni·mo] *adj.* anonymous; nameless; *m.* anonymous letter or note.

anormal [a·nor·mál] *adj.* abnormal.

anotación [a·no·ta·sjón] *f.* annotation; note.

anotar [a·no·tár] *v.* to annotate, provide with notes; to write down.

anquilosado [an̄·ki·lo·sa·ɖo] *adj.* stiff-jointed; gnarled.

anquilosarse [an̄·ki·lo·sár·se] *v.* to become stiff in the joints; to become metally stagnant.

ansia [án·sja] *f.* anxiety, anguish; longing, eagerness; **-s** anguish; *Col., Ven., P.R.* nausea.

ansiar[17] [an·sjár] *v.* to long for, desire eagerly.

ansiedad [an·sje·ɖáɖ] *f.* anxiety; worry.

ansioso [an·sjó·so] *adj.* anxious, troubled; eager.

antagonismo [an·ta·go·níz·mo] *m.* antagonism.

antagonista [an·ta·go·nís·ta] *m. & f.* antagonist, adversary, opponent.

antaño [an·tá·ño] *adv.* yesteryear, formerly; **días de —** days of old.

ante [án·te] *prep.* before, in the presence of; **— todo** above all; *m.* elk; buckskin.

anteanoche [an·te·a·nó·če] *adv.* night before last.

anteayer [an·te·a·yér] *adv.* day before yesterday.

antebrazo [an·te·ƀrá·so] *m.* forearm.

antecámara [an·te·ká·ma·ra] *f.* antechamber, waiting room.

antecedente [an·te·se·ɖén·te] *m.* antecedent; *adj.* antecedent, preceding.

antecesor [an·te·se·sór] *m.* ancestor; predecessor.

antedicho [an·te·dí·čo] *adj.* aforesaid.

antelación [an·te·la·sjón] *f.* precedence, priority (*in time*).

antemano [an·te·má·no] *de* **—** beforehand.

antena [an·té·na] *f.* antenna (*of a radio or wireless*); lateen yard (*of a ship*); **-s** antennae, feelers;

— **emisora** *f.* broadcasting antenna; — **receptora**
f. receiving antenna; — **parabólica** *f.* parabolic
(*T V*) antenna.
antenoche [an·te·nó·če] = **anteanoche.**
anteojera [an·te·o·xé·ra] *f.* blinder.
anteojo [an·te·ó·xo] *m.* spyglass; small telescope;
eyeglass; **-s** spectacles; **-s de larga vista** field
glasses.
antepasado [an·te·pa·sá·ɗo] *adj.* passed; **año** —
year before last; *m.* ancestor.
antepecho [an·te·pé·čo] *m.* sill, railing.
anteponer⁴⁰ [an·te·po·nér] *v. irr.* to place before;
to prefer.
antepuesto [an·te·pwés·to] *p.p. of* **anteponer.**
anterior [an·te·rjór] *adj.* front, toward the front;
earlier, previous; **el día** — the day before.
antes [án·tes] *adv.* before, formerly; — **de** *prep.*
before; — (**de**) **que** *conj.* before.
antesala [an·te·sá·la] *f.* anteroom, waiting room.
antiaéreo [an·tja·é·re·o] *adj.* antiaircraft.
antibiótico [an·ti·ƀjó·ti·ko] *adj. & m.* antibiotic.
anticipación [an·ti·si·pa·sjón] *f.* anticipation,
advance consideration; **con** — in advance.
anticipado [an·ti·si·pa·ɗo] *adj.* early, ahead of time;
advanced (*payment*); **por** — in advance; *p.p. of*
anticipar anticipated.
anticipar [an·ti·si·pár] *v.* to anticipate; to advance,
pay in advance; **-se** to get ahead (of).
anticipo [an·ti·sí·po] *m.* advance, advance
payment.
anticlericalismo [an·ti·kle·ri·ka·líz·mo] *m.*
anticlericalism (*opposition or antagonism of the
clergy*).
anticoncepción [an·ti·kon·sep·sjón]
contraconception; birth control.
anticuado [an·ti·kwá·ɗo] *adj.* antiquated,
out-of-date.
antídoto [an·tí·ɗo·to] *m.* antidote.
antigualla [an·ti·gwá·ya] *f.* antique; anything old.
antigüedad [an·ti·gwe·ɗáɗ] *f.* antiquity, ancient
times; **-es** antique objects, antiques.
antiguo [an·tí·gwo] *adj.* ancient, old; antique.
antílope [an·tí·lo·pe] *m.* antelope.
antimonio [an·ti·mó·njo] *m.* antimony.
antiparras [an·ti·pá·rras] *f. pl.* goggles; spectacles.
antipatía [an·ti·pa·tí·a] *f.* antipathy, dislike; mutual
antagonism.   ˋ
antipático [an·ti·pá·ti·ko] *adj.* disagreeable;
unlikeable, unpleasant.
antipoliomielítico [an·ti·po·lio·mje·lí·ti·ko] *adj.*
antipolio.
antiséptico [an·ti·sép·ti·ko] *adj. & m.* antiseptic.
antisocial [an·ti·so·sjál] *adj. & m.* antisocial;
criminal.
antojadizo [an·to·xa·ɗí·so] *adj.* fanciful, whimsical.
antojarse [an·to·xar·se] *v.:* **antojársele a uno** to
take a notion or fancy to; to strike one's fancy;
to want, desire.
antojo [an·tó·xo] *m.* whim, notion, fancy.
antorcha [an·tór·ča] *f.* torch.
antracita [an·tra·sí·ta] *f.* anthracite, hard coal.
antropología [an·tro·po·lo·xí·a] *f.* anthropology.
antropólogo [an·tro·pó·lo·go] *m.* anthropologist.
anual [a·nwál] *adj.* annual, yearly.
anuario [a·nwá·rjo] *m.* annual, yearbook.
anublar [a·nu·ƀlár] *v.* to cloud; to dim, abscure;
-se to become cloudy.
anudar [a·nu·ɗár] *v.* to knot; **anudársele a uno la
garganta** to choke up with emotion.
anulación [a·nu·la·sjón] *f.* voiding, cancellation.
anular [a·nu·lár] *v.* to annul, void, cancel, abolish.

anunciador [a·nun·sja·ɗór] *m.* announcer;
advertiser; *adj.* announcing; advertising.
anunciante [a·nun·sján·te] *m. & f.* announcer,
advertiser.
anunciar [a·nun·sjár] *v.* to announce; to advertise.
anuncio [a·nún·sjo] *m.* announcement;
advertisement.
anzuelo [an·swé·lo] *m.* fishhook; lure, attraction.
añadidura [a·ña·ɗi·ɗú·ra] *f.* addition.
añadir [a·ña·ɗír] *v.* to add.
añejado [a·ñe·xá·ɗo] *adj.* aged (*wine, cheese, etc.*).
añejo [a·ñé·xo] *adj.* old; of old vintage; stale.
añicos [a·ñí·kos] *m. pl.* bits, shatters, fragments;
hacer(se) — to shatter, break into a thousand
pieces.
añil [a·ñíl] *m.* indigo (*plant*); indigo blue.
año [a·ño] *m.* year; — **bisiesto** leap year;
¿**cuántos -s tiene Vd?** how old are you?
añoranza [a·ño·rán·sa] *f.* nostalgia, longing.
añorar [a·ño·rár] *v.* to long for, yearn for, be
homesick for; to make reminiscences.
añoso [a·ñó·so] *adj.* old, aged.
aojar [a·o·xár] *v.* to bewitch; to cast the evil eye.
apabullar [a·pa·ƀu·yár] *v.* to crush, crumple.
apacentar¹ [a·pa·sen·tár] *v. irr.* to graze, pasture;
to feed (*the spirit, desires, passions, etc.*); **-se** to
graze, pasture.
apacibilidad [a·pa·si·ƀi·li·ɗáɗ] *f.* gentleness,
mildness, pleasantness; **apacible** [a·pa·sí·ƀle]
adj. pleasant, quiet, gentle.
apaciguamiento [a·pa·si·gwa·mjén·to] *m.*
appeasement.
apaciguar⁸ [a·pa·si·gwár] *v.* to pacify, calm,
appease; **-se** to calm down.
apachurrar [a·pa·ču·rrár] *v. Mex., C.A., Carib.,
Andes* to crush. *See* **despachurrar.**
apadrinar [a·pa·dri·nár] *v.* to sponsor; to act as a
godfather; to act as a second in a duel.
apagar⁷ [a·pa·gár] *v.* to put out, extinguish; to
deafen (*a sound*).
apagón [a·pa·gón] *m.* blackout.
apalabrar [a·pa·la·ƀrár] *v.* to speak for, engage,
reserve; **-se con** to make a verbal agreement
with.
apalear [a·pa·le·ár] *v.* to beat up, thrash; to thresh.
aparador [a·pa·ra·ɗór] *m.* sideboard; cupboard;
showcase; show window; workshop.
aparato [a·pa·rá·to] *m.* apparatus; pomp.
aparatoso [a·pa·ra·tó·so] *adj.* pompous,
ostentatious.
aparcero [a·par·sé·ro] *m.* co-owner of land; *Am.*
pal, comrade.
aparear [a·pa·re·ár] *v.* to mate; to match; to pair;
-se to mate; to match; to pair.
aparecer¹³ [a·pa·re·sér] *v. irr.* to appear, show up.
aparecido [a·pa·re·sí·ɗo] *m.* ghost, specter,
phantom.
aparejar [a·pa·re·xár] *v.* to prepare; to harness; to
rig; to equip.
aparejo [a·pa·ré·xo] *m.* harness; packsaddle;
rigging (*of a boat*); preparation; fishing tackle;
-s equipment, tools.
aparentar [a·pa·ren·tár] *v.* to appear, seem; to
pretend, feign, affect.
aparente [a·pa·rén·te] *adj.* apparent.
aparición [a·pa·ri·sjón] *f.* apparition, ghost;
appearance.
apariencia [a·pa·rjén·sja] *f.* appearance.
apartado [a·par·tá·ɗo] *m.* compartment; — **postal**
post office letter box; *p.p. of* **apartar.**
apartamento [a·par·ta·mén·to] *m.* apartment.

apartamiento [a·par·ta·mjén·to] *m.* separation; retirement; aloofness; retreat, refuge; *Am.* apartment, flat.

apartar [a·par·tár] *v.* to set apart, separate; to remove; *Am.* — **las reses** to sort out cattle; -se to withdraw; to step aside; to go away.

aparte [a·pár·te] *adv.* apart; aside; *m.* aside (*in a play*); new paragraph; *Am.* sorting out of cattle.

apasionado [a·pa·sjo·ná·đo] *adj.* passionate; very fond (of); impassioned, emotional.

apasionar [a·pa·sjo·nár] *v.* to arouse passion; to fill with passion; -se to become impassioned; to fall ardently in love.

apatía [a·pa·tí·a] *f.* apathy, indolence, indifference.

apático [a·pá·ti·ko] *adj.* apathetic, indifferent, indolent.

apear [a·pe·ár] *v.* (*de caballo*) dismount; (*bajar*) to lower, take down; to shackle (*a horse*); to fell (*a tree*); *Ríopl.* to fire, dismiss from a position; — **el tratamiento** to omit the title (*in addressing a person*); -se to get off, alight; *Am.* -se **por la cola** (*or* **por las orejas**) to go off at a tangent, make an irrelevant remark.

apechugar [a·pe·ču·gár] *v.* to push with the chest; to push ahead; — **con** to accept reluctantly; to go through with (*something*) courageously; *P.R.* to snatch, take possession of.

apedrear [a·pe·dre·ár] *v.* to stone, hit with stones.

apegado [a·pe·ga·đo] *adj.* devoted, attached; *p.p. of* **apegarse.**

apegarse [a·pe·gár·se] *v.* to become attached (to); to become fond (of).

apego [a·pé·go] *m.* attachment, fondness.

apelación [a·pe·la·sjón] *f.* appeal.

apelar [a·pe·lár] *v.* to appeal.

apelotonar [a·pe·lo·to·nár] *v.* to form or roll into a ball; to pile up, bunch together.

apellidar [a·pe·yi·đár] *v.* to call, name; -se to be named; to have the surname of.

apellido [a·pe·yí·đo] *m.* surname.

apenar [a·pe·nár] *v.* to grieve, afflict; -se to be grieved; *Col., Ven., C.A., Carib.* to feel embarrassed, feel ashamed.

apenas [a·pé·nas] *adv.* hardly, scarcely; *conj.* as soon as.

apéndice [a·pén·di·se] *m.* appendix.

apercibir [a·per·si·bir] *v.* to prepare beforehand; to supply; to warn, advise; to perceive; -se **a la pelea** to get ready to fight; *Am.* -se **de** to notice.

apergaminado [a·per·ga·mi·ná·đo] *adj.* parchment-like; dried up.

aperitivo [a·pe·ri·tí·bo] *m.* aperitif, appetizer; cocktail.

aperlado [a·per·lá·đo] *adj.* pearly, pearl-colored.

apero [a·pé·ro] *m.* farm equipment; -s tools, implements; *Ríopl., Ch., Mex., Ven., Andes* saddle and trappings.

apertura [a·per·tú·ra] *f.* opening (*act of opening or beginning*).

apestar [a·pes·tár] *v.* to infect; to corrupt; to sicken; to stink; -se to turn putrid, become corrupted; *Am.* to catch cold.

apestoso [a·pes·tó·so] *adj.* putrid, foul-smelling.

apetecer [a·pe·te·sér] *v. irr.* to desire, crave.

apetecible [a·pe·te·sí·ble] *adj.* desirable; appetizing.

apetencia [a·pe·tén·sja] *f.* hunger, appetite; desire.

apetito [a·pe·tí·to] *m.* appetite; hunger.

apetitoso [a·pe·ti·tó·so] *adj.* appetizing; gluttonous.

apiadarse [a·pja·đár·se] *v.* to pity; — **de** to pity, take pit on.

ápice [á·pi·se] *m.* apex, top, summit.

apilar [a·pi·lár] *v.* to pile up, stack, heap.

apiñado [a·pi·ñá·đo] *p.p. of* **apiñar** & *adj.* crowded, jammed; cone-shaped, shaped like a pine cone.

apiñamiento [a·pi·ña·mjén·to] *m.* crowd, jam (*of people or animals*); crowding together.

apiñar [a·pi·ñár] *v.* to cram together; to crowd; -se to pile up, crowd together.

apio [á·pjo] *m.* celery.

apisonadora [a·pi·so·na·đó·ra] *f.* road roller.

apisonar [a·pi·so·nár] *v.* to pack down, flatten by pounding.

aplacar [a·pla·kár] *v.* to appease, pacify, soothe.

aplanamiento [a·pla·na·mjén·to] *m.* flattening, leveling; dejection, depression.

aplanar [a·pla·nár] *v.* to level; to flatten; to astonish; *Am.* — **las calles** to tramp the streets; -se to be flattened out; to be leveled to the ground; to lose one's strength; *Col.* to give in, yield.

aplastar [a·plas·tár] *v.* to squash, crush, flatten; *Am.* to tire out, break (*a horse*); -se *Am.* to plump oneself down; *Col., Andes* to overstay a call (*remaining seated*).

aplaudir [a·plaw·đir] *v.* to applaud, clap; to approve, praise.

aplauso [a·pláw·so] *m.* applause; praise, approval.

aplazamiento [a·pla·sa·mjén·to] *m.* postponement; adjournment.

aplazar [a·pla·sár] *v.* to postpone; to adjourn.

aplicable [a·pli·ká·ble] *adj.* applicable, suitable, fitting.

aplicación [a·pli·ka·sjón] *f.* application; effort, diligence; -es appliqué (*trimming laid on a dress*).

aplicado [a·pli·ká·đo] *adj.* industrious, diligent.

aplicar [a·pli·kár] *v.* to apply; to put on, lay on; -se to apply oneself, work hard.

aplomado [a·plo·má·đo] *adj.* gray, lead-colored; *p.p. of* **aplomar.**

aplomar [a·plo·már] *v.* to plumb (*a wall*); to make vertical; to make heavier; -se *Am.* to become ashamed or embarrassed; *Am.* to be slow.

aplomo [a·pló·mo] *m.* assurance, confidence, self-possession, serenity; **estar** — to be plumb, vertical.

apocado [a·po·ká·đo] *adj.* cowardly; timid; *p.p. of* **apocar.**

apocamiento [a·po·ka·mjén·to] *m.* timidity; bashfulness; belittling.

apocar [a·po·kár] *v.* to lessen; to belittle, give little importance to; -se to humble oneself.

apodar [a·po·đár] *v.* to nickname.

apoderado [a·po·đe·rá·đo] *m.* attorney; proxy, substitute.

apoderar [a·po·đe·rár] *v.* to empower, give power of attorney; -se **de** to take possession of, seize.

apodo [a·pó·đo] *m.* nickname.

apogeo [a·po·xé·o] *m.* apogee (*point at which a planet, satellite, or rocket is at the greatest distance from the earth*); highest point, height (*of glory, fame, etc.*).

apolillado [a·po·li·yá·đo] *adj.* moth-eaten; worm-eaten.

apología [a·po·lo·xí·a] *f.* praise, apologia.

apoplejía [a·po·ple·xí·a] *f.* apoplexy, stroke.

aporrear [a·po·rre·ár] *v.* to beat; to maul; *Am.* to beat (*in a game*), defeat.

aportación [a·por·ta·sjón] *f.* contribution.

aportar [a·por·tár] *v.* to bring; to contribute; to arrive in port; to reach an unexpected place (*after having gone astray*); **-se** *Am.* to appear, approach.

aporte [a·pór·te] *m.* contribution.

aposento [a·po·sén·to] *m.* room; lodging.

apostar² [a·pos·tár] *v. irr.* to bet; to post, station.

apóstol [a·pós·tol] *m.* apostle; religious leader.

apostólico [a·pos·tó·li·ko] *adj.* apostolic (*pertaining to the apostles, or to the Pope and his authority*).

apostura [a·pos·tú·ra] *f.* elegant bearing, graceful carriage.

apoyar [a·po·yár] *v.* to lean, rest; to back, support; to aid, favor; to confirm; **-se** to lean (on).

apoyo [a·pó·yo] *m.* support; favor, protection.

apreciable [a·pre·sjá·ble] *adj.* estimable, esteemed; valuable; appraisable; noticeable.

apreciación [a·pre·sja·sjón] *f.* appreciation; valuation; estimation.

apreciar [a·pre·sjár] *v.* to appreciate, value, esteem; to price, fix the price of; to appraise.

aprecio [a·pré·sjo] *m.* esteem, high regard; appraisal, valuation, estimate; *Mex., Ven., Cuba* **hacer —** to notice, pay attention.

aprehender [a·pre·en·dér] *v.* to apprehend, seize, arrest.

aprehensión [a·pre·en·sjón], **aprensión** [a·pren·sjón] *f.* apprehension; fear, dread; seizure, arrest; *Am.* prejudice.

aprehensor [a·pre·en·sór], **aprensor** [a·pren·sór] *m.* captor.

apremiante [a·pre·mján·te] *adj.* pressing, urgent.

apremiar [a·pre·mjár] *v.* to press, urge onward, hurry.

apremio [a·pré·mjo] *m.* pressure; urgency.

aprender [a·pren·dér] *v.* to learn.

aprendiz [a·pren·dís] *m.* apprentice.

aprendizaje [a·pren·di·sá·xe] *m.* apprenticeship; learning (*act of learning*).

apresar [a·pre·sár] *v.* to seize, grab; to capture; to imprison.

aprestar [a·pres·tár] *v.* to prepare, make ready; **-se** to get ready.

apresto [a·prés·to] *m.* preparation; readiness.

apresurado [a·pre·su·rá·do] *adj.* hasty.

apresurar [a·pre·su·rár] *v.* to hurry, hasten; **-se** to hurry, hasten.

apretado [a·pre·tá·do] *adj.* tight; compact; stingy, miserly; difficult, dangerous; *p.p. of* **apretar.**

apretar¹ [a·pre·tár] *v. irr.* to press, squeeze, tighten; to urge on; *Am.* to increase in strength or intensity (*as rain, wind, etc.*); *Am.* to redouble one's effort; **— a correr** to start to run; **-se** *Col.* to gorge, overeat.

apretón [a·pre·tón] *m.* sudden pressure; squeeze; dash, short run; **— de manos** hand-shake.

apretura [a·pre·tú·ra] *f.* jam, crush; tight squeeze, narrow place; difficulty, predicament; dire poverty.

aprieto [a·prjé·to] *m.* tight spot, difficulty.

aprisa [a·prí·sa] *adv.* quickly, fast, speedily.

aprisco [a·prís·ko] *m.* sheepfold.

aprisionar [a·pri·sjo·nár] *v.* to imprison; to tie, fasten.

aprobación [a·pro·ba·sjón] *f.* approbation, approval; consent; pass, passing grade.

aprobar² [a·pro·bár] *v. irr.* to approve; to pass (*in an examination*).

aprontar [a·pron·tár] *v.* to make ready; to expedite; to hand over without delay; *Am.* to pay in advance.

apropiación [a·pro·pja·sjón] *f.* appropriation; confiscation.

apropiado [a·pro·pjá·do] *adj.* appropriate, proper, fitting, suitable; *p.p. of* **apropiar.**

apropiar [a·pro·pjár] *v.* to fit; to adapt; **-se** to take possession (of); to confiscate.

aprovechable [a·pro·be·čá·ble] *adj.* available; usable, fit to use.

aprovechado [a·pro·be·čá·do] *adj.* diligent, industrious; *p.p. of* **aprovechar.**

aprovechamiento [a·pro·be·ča·mjén·to] *m.* use, utilization; exploitation; profit, benefit; progress.

aprovechar [a·pro·be·čár] *v.* to profit, be profitable; to progress, get ahead; to utilize; **-se de** to take advantage of; **¡que aproveche!** may you enjoy it!

aproximado [a·prok·si·má·do] *adj.* approximate; near; nearly correct.

aproximar [a·prok·si·már] *v.* to place or bring near; to approximate; **-se** to get near, approach.

aproximativo [a·prok·si·ma·tí·bo] *adj.* approximate.

aptitud [ap·ti·túd] *f.* aptitude, capacity, ability.

apto [áp·to] *adj.* apt; competent.

apuesta [a·pwés·ta] *f.* bet, wager.

apuesto [a·pwés·to] *adj.* smart, stylish; good-looking.

apuntación [a·pun·ta·sjón] *f.* note; memorandum; musical notation, set of musical symbols or signs.

apuntalar [a·pun·ta·lár] *v.* to prop; to shore up.

apuntar [a·pun·tár] *v.* (*señalar*) to point; (*arma*) to aim; (*escribir*) to write down; (*a un actor*) to prompt; (*remendar*) to mend, to stitch; to sharpen; (*brotar*) to begin to show; **— el día** to begin to dawn; **-se** to sprout.

apunte [a·pún·te] *m.* note, memorandum.

apuñalar [a·pu·ña·lár] *v.* to stab.

apuración [a·pu·ra·sjón] *f.* worry; trouble.

apurado [a·pu·rá·do] *adj.* worried; needy; difficult; dangerous; in a hurry.

apurar [a·pu·rár] *v.* (*acabar*) to exhaust, to drain to the last drop; (*preocupar*) to worry, annoy; (*acelerar*) to hurry, press; **-se** to be or get worried; to hurry up.

apuro [a·pú·ro] *m.* need; worry; predicament; *Am.* rush, hurry.

aquejar [a·ke·xár] *v.* to grieve, afflict.

aquel [a·kél], **aquella** [a·ké·ya] *dem. adj.* that (*at a distance*); **aquellos** [a·ké·yos], **aquellas** [a·ké·yas] those; **aquél, aquélla** *m., f. dem. pron.* that one; the former; **aquello** [a·ké·yo] that, that thing; **aquéllos, aquéllas** *m., f. pl.* those; the former.

aquí [a·kí] *adv.* here; **por —** this way; through here; around here.

aquietar [a·kje·tár] *v.* to quiet, calm; to hush; **-se** to calm down, become calm.

aquilón [a·ki·lón] *m.* north wind.

ara [á·ra] *f.* altar.

árabe [á·ra·be] *adj. & m.* Arab; Arabic.

arado [a·rá·do] *m.* plow; *Am.* plowed land, piece of cultivated land.

aragonés [a·ra·go·nés] *adj.* Aragonese, of or from Aragón, Spain; *m.* Aragonese.

arancel [a·ran·sél] *m.* tariff; **— de aduanas** customs, duties; **arancelario** [a·ran·se·lá·rjo] *adj.* pertaining to tariff.

arándano [a·rán·da·no] *m.* cranberry.

araña [a·rá·ña] *f.* spider; chandelier.

arañar [a·ra·ñár] *v.* to scratch; to claw.

araño [a·rá·ño] *m.* scratch; **arañazo** [a·ra·ñá·so] *m.* big scratch.

arar [a·rár] *v.* to plow.

arbitración [ar·bi·tra·sjón] *f.* arbitration.
arbitrador [ar·bi·tra·dór] *m.* arbitrator; referee, umpire.
arbitraje [ar·bi·trá·xe] *m.* arbitration.
arbitrar [ar·bi·trár] *v.* to arbitrate; to umpire.
arbitrario [ar·bi·trá·rjo] *adj.* arbitrary.
arbitrio [ar·bí·trjo] *m.* free will; scheme, means; compromise, arbitration; sentence (*of a judge*); judgment.
árbitro [ár·bi·tro] *m.* arbitrator, sole judge, umpire.
ábol [ár·bol] *m.* tree; mast; **arbolado** [ar·bo·lá·do] *adj.* wooded; *m.* grove of trees.
arboleda [ar·bo·le·da] *f.* grove.
arbusto [ar·bús·to] *m.* shrub.
arca [ár·ka] *f.* ark; chest, coffer; **arcón** [ar·kón] *m.* large coffer or chest; bin.
arcada [ar·ka·da] *f.* arcade; archway.
arcaico [ar·káj·ko] *adj.* archaic.
arcano [ar·ká·no] *adj.* hidden, secret; *m.* secret, mystery.
arce [ár·se] *m.* maple, maple tree.
arcilla [ar·sí·ya] *f.* clay.
arco [ár·ko] *m.* arc; arch; bow; violin bow; — **iris** rainbow.
archipiélago [ar·či·pjé·la·go] *m.* archipelago (*group of many islands*).
archisabido [ar·či·sa·bí·do] *adj.* very well-known.
archivo [ar·čí·bo] *m.* archives; file; public records; *Am.* office, business office; **archivero** [ar·či·bé·ro] *m.* keeper of archives; city clerk.
arder [ar·dér] *v.* to burn; to be consumed (*with fever or passion*); *Col., Carib.* to smart, sting.
ardid [ar·did] *m.* trick, scheme.
ardiente [ar·djén·te] *adj.* ardent, burning, fervent; passionate; fiery.
ardilla [ar·dí·ya] *f.* squirrel.
ardite [ar·dí·te] *m.* ancient coin of small value; bit, trifle; **no valer un** — not to be worth a penny.
ardor [ar·dór] *m.* ardor; heat; fervor, eagerness.
ardoroso [ar·do·ró·so] *adj.* ardent, fiery.
arduo [ár·dwo] *adj.* arduous, hard, difficult.
área [á·re·a] *f.* area.
arena [a·ré·na] *f.* sand; arena; **-s** kidney stones; **arenal** [a·re·nál] *m.* sand pit.
arenga [a·rén·ga] *f.* address, speech.
arenisco [a·re·nís·ko] *adj.* sandy; gritty; **piedra arenisca** sandstone.
arenoso [a·re·nó·so] *adj.* sandy; gritty.
arenque [a·rén·ke] *m.* herring.
arepa [a·ré·pa] *f. Col., Ven., Carib.* a fried (*griddle*) cake made of corn meal that corresponds to the Mexican tortilla.
arete [a·ré·te] *m.* earring.
argamasa [ar·ga·má·sa] *f.* mortar.
argentar [ar·xen·tár] *v.* to plate (*with silver*); to polish.
argentino [ar·xen·tí·no] *adj.* silvery; Argentine; *m.* Argentine; Argentine gold coin worth 5 pesos.
argolla [ar·gó·ya] *f.* large iron ring; *Am.* plain finger ring, engagement ring; *Am.* **tener** — to be lucky.
argón [ar·gón] *m.* argon.
argucia [ar·gú·sja] *f.* cunning, astuteness; scheme; subtlety.
argüir[32] [ar·gwír] *v. irr.* to argue; to deduce; infer.
argumentación [ar·gu·men·ta·sjón] *f.* argumentation, argument, reasoning.
argumento [ar·gu·mén·to] *m.* reasoning; substance, subject matter, resumé (*of a play or story*).
aridez [a·ri·dés] *f.* barrenness; dryness; drought.

árido [á·ri·do] *adj.* arid, dry, barren; **-s** *m. pl.* grains and dry vegetables; **medida para -s** dry measure.
ariete [a·rjé·te] *m.* ram, battering ram; — **hidráulico** hydraulic ram.
arisco [a·rís·ko] *adj.* gruff, harsh, unsociable; *Am.* shy, distrustful.
arista [a·rís·ta] *f.* sharp edge; ridge; beard (*of wheat or corn*).
aristocracia [a·ris·to·krá·sja] *f.* aristocracy.
aristócrata [a·ris·tó·kra·ta] *m. & f.* aristocrat.
aristocrático [a·ris·to·krá·ti·ko] *adj.* aristocratic.
aritmética [a·rit·mé·ti·ka] *f.* arithmetic.
arma [ár·ma] *f.* arm, weapon; branch (*of the army*); **-s** armed forces; — **arrojadiza** missile weapon; — **blanca** sword or knife; **de -s tomar** ready for any emergency; ready to fight.
armada [ar·má·da] *f.* armada, fleet.
armador [ar·ma·dór] *m.* shipbuilder; assembler.
armadura [ar·ma·dú·ra] *f.* armor; armature (*of a generator or dynamo*); framework; mounting.
armamento [ar·ma·mén·to] *m.* armament; equipment.
armar [ar·már] *v.* to arm; to set up, assemble, rig up; — **una pendencia** to start a quarrel; *Col.* — **un trique** to lay a snare, set a trap; *Am.* **-se** to balk, to be stubborn; *Ven., Mex.* **-se con alguna cosa** to refuse to return something.
armario [ar·má·rjo] *m.* wardrobe, clothes closet; cabinet.
armatoste [ar·ma·tós·te] *m.* unwieldy object or machine; clumsy thing; heavy, clumsy fellow.
armazón [ar·ma·són] *f.* framework, skeleton; *m.* skeleton (*of an animal*); *Am.* shelf, set of shelves.
armella [ar·mé·ya] *f.* staple; screw eye.
armiño [ar·mí·ño] *m.* ermine.
armisticio [ar·mis·tí·sjo] *m.* armistice.
armonía [ar·mo·ní·a] *f.* harmony.
armónico [ar·mó·ni·ko] *adj.* harmonic; harmonious.
armonioso [ar·mo·njó·so] *adj.* harmonious, musical.
armonizar[9] [ar·mo·ni·sár] *v.* to harmonize.
arnés [ar·nés] *m.* harness; coat of mail; **-es** harness and trappings; equipment, outfit.
aro [á·ro] *m.* hoop; rim (*of a wheel*); *Am.* finger ring; *Ch., Riopl.* earring.
aroma [a·ró·ma] *f.* aroma, scent, perfume.
aromático [a·ro·má·ti·ko] *adj.* aromatic, fragrant, spicy; **sales aromáticas** smelling salts.
arpa [ár·pa] *f.* harp.
arpía [ar·pí·a] *f.* shrew.
arpón [ar·pón] *m.* harpoon, spear.
arqueado [ar·ke·á·do] *adj.* arched.
arquear [ar·ke·ár] *v.* to arch.
arquitecto [ar·ki·ték·to] *m.* architect.
arquitectónico [ar·ki·tek·tó·ni·ko] *adj.* architectural.
arquitectura [ar·ki·tek·tú·ra] *f.* architecture.
arrabal [a·rra·bál] *m.* outlying district; **-es** outskirts, suburbs.
arracada [a·rra·ká·da] *f.* earring.
arraigar[7] [a·rraj·gár] *v.* to root, take root; **-se** to become rooted, attached.
arrancado [a·rraŋ·ká·do] *adj. Mex., Carib., C.A., Andes* without money, broke.
arrancar[6] [a·rraŋ·kár] *v.* to uproot; to pull out; to start, start out; *Ch., Mex.* to flee, run away.
arranque [a·rraŋ·ke] *m.* start; pull; uprooting; automobile starter; — **de ira** fit or outburst of anger; **punto de** — starting point.

arras [á·rras] *f. pl.* earnest money; pledge; dowry.

arrasar [a·rra·sár] *v.* to level; to tear down, raze; to fill to the brim; **-se** to clear up (*said of the sky*); **-se de lágrimas** to fill up with tears.

arrastrado [a·rras·trá·ḏo] *adj.* poor, destitute; mean, vile; wretched; rascally; **llevar una vida arrastrada** to lead a dog's life.

arrastrar [a·rras·trár] *v.* to drag, haul; *Ven.* to harrow (*land*); **-se** to drag along, crawl.

arrayán [a·rra·yán] *m.* myrtle.

¡arre! [á·rre] *interj.* gee! get up there!

arrear [a·rre·ár] *v.* to drive (*mules, cattle*); *Guat.* to rustle, steal cattle; *Am.* **-le a uno una bofetada** to give a person a slap.

arrebatamiento [a·rre·ḇa·ta·mjén·to] *m.* snatch; ecstasy; rage.

arrebatar [a·rre·ḇa·tár] *v.* to snatch away; **-se de cólera** to have a fit of anger.

arrebatiña [a·rre·ḇa·tí·ña] *f.* grab, snatch; scramble; **arrebatón** [a·rre·ḇa·tón] *m.* quick or violent grab.

arrebato [a·rre·ḇá·to] *m.* rage; rapture, ecstasy; fit.

arrebol [a·rre·ḇól] *m.* red color of the sky; rouge; **-es** red clouds.

arreciar [a·rre·sjár] *v.* to increase in intensity, get stronger.

arrecife [a·rre·sí·fe] *m.* reef.

arredrar [a·rre·ḏrár] *v.* to frighten, intimidate; **-se** to be or get scared.

arreglar [a·rre·ǥlár] *v.* to arrange, put in order; to regulate; to fix; to adjust, settle; *Am.* to pay (*a debt*); *Am.* to correct, punish; **-se** to doll up, fix oneself up; to settle differences, come to an agreement.

arreglo [a·rré·ǥlo] *m.* arrangement; adjustment; settlement; conformity, agreement; **con — a** according to.

arrellanarse [a·rre·ya·nár·se] *v.* to sprawl, lounge; to be self-satisfied.

arremangado [a·rre·maŋ·gá·ḏo] *adj. & p.p.* turned up; **nariz arremangada** turned up nose.

arremangar[7] a·rre·maŋ·gár] *v.* to tuck up, turn up, roll up (*the sleeves, trousers, etc.*); **-se** to roll up one's sleeves; **-se los pantalones** to roll up one's trousers.

arremeter [a·rre·me·tér] *v.* to attack, assail, assault.

arremetida [a·rre·me·tí·ḏa] *f.* thrust, push, attack.

arremolinarse [a·rre·mo·li·nár·se] *v.* to whirl, swirl; to eddy; to mill around.

arrendamiento [a·rren·da·mjén·to] *m.* renting; lease; rental, rent.

arrendar[1] [a·rren·dár] *v. irr.* to rent, lease, let; to hire; to tie (*a horse*); to bridle; *Am.* to head for.

arrendatario [a·rren·da·tá·rjo] *m.* renter, tenant.

arreo [a·rré·o] *m.* raiment; ornament; *Am.* driving of horses or mules; *Ríopl., Ch., Mex., Ven.* drove of horses or mules; **-s** trappings; equipment; finery; *adv.* uninterruptedly, without interruption.

arrepentido [a·rre·pen·tí·ḏo] *adj.* repentant; *p.p. of* **arrepentirse.**

arrepentimiento [a·rre·pen·ti·mjén·to] *m.* repentance, regret.

arrepentirse[3] [a·rre·pen·tír·se] *v. irr.* to repent, regret.

arrestado [a·rres·ta·ḏo] *adj.* daring, rash; *p.p. of* **arrestar.**

arrestar [a·rres·tár] *v.* to arrest; *Am.* to return, strike back (*a ball*); *Peru* to reprimand; **-se** to dare, venture.

arresto [a·rrés·to] *m.* arrest, imprisonment; detention; daring, rashness; rash act.

arriar[17] [a·rrjár] *v.* to haul down, lower (*the flag*); to lower (*the sails*); to slacken (*a rope*).

arriba [a·rrí·ḇa] *adv.* above; upstairs; **de — abajo** from top to bottom; up and down; **rio —** upstream; **¡ — !** hurrah!

arribada [a·rri·ḇá·ḏa] *f.* arrival; *Am.* back talk, impudent answer.

arribar [a·rri·ḇár] *v.* to arrive; to put into port; *Am.* to prosper, better one's lot.

arribo [a·rrí·ḇo] *m.* arrival.

arriendo [a·rrjén·do] = **arrendamiento.**

arriero [a·rrjé·ro] *m.* muleteer.

arriesgado [a·rrjez·gá·ḏo] *adj.* risky, daring.

arriesgar[7] [a·rrjez·gár] *v.* to risk; **-se** to dare, run a risk.

arrimar [a·rri·már] *v.* to bring or place near; to lay aside; to strike (*a blow*); **-se** to lean (on); to get near; to seek shelter.

arrinconar [a·rriŋ·ko·nár] *v.* to corner; to put in a corner; to lay aside; to slight, neglect; **-se** to retire; to live a secluded life.

arriscado [a·rris·ká·ḏo] *adj.* bold; daring; brisk; spirited (*horse*); craggy, rugged.

arriscar[6] [a·rris·kár] *v.* to risk, venture; *Mex.* to roll up, curl up, tuck up, fold back; *Col.* to have vim and vigor; *Am.* **— a** to reach, amount to; **-se** to get angry; *Peru., C.A.* to dress up, doll up.

arroba [a·rró·ḇa] *f.* weight of 25 pounds.

arrobamiento [a·rro·ḇa·mjén·to] *m.* trance, rapture.

arrobarse [a·rro·ḇár·se] *v.* to be entranced; to be in a trance; to be enraptured.

arrodillarse [a·rro·ḏi·yár·se] *v.* to kneel.

arrogancia [a·rro·gán·sja] *f.* arrogance, pride.

arrogante [a·rro·gán·te] *adj.* arrogant, haughty, proud.

arrogarse[7] [a·rro·gár·se] *v.* to appropriate, usurp, assume (*power or rights*).

arrojadizo [a·rro·xa·ḏí·so] *adj.* missile; **arma arrojadiza** missile weapon.

arrojado [a·rro·xá·ḏo] *adj.* daring, rash, fearless; *p.p. of* **arrojar.**

arrojar [a·rro·xár] *v.* to throw, hurl, cast; to expel; *Am.* to throw up, vomit; **— un saldo de** to show a balance of; **-se a** to hurl oneself upon or at; to dare to.

arrojo [a·rró·xo] *m.* boldness, daring.

arrollador [a·rro·ya·ḏór] *adj.* sweeping, overwhelming, violent; winding (*that serves to wind or roll up*).

arrollar [a·rro·yár] *v.* to roll up; to sweep away; to trample upon; to destroy.

arropar [a·rro·pár] *v.* to wrap, cover; *Col.* to snap up, accept on the spot (*a deal*); **-se** to wrap up, cover up.

arrostrar [a·rros·trár] *v.* to face, defy; **-se** to dare, dare to fight face to face.

arroyada [a·rro·yá·ḏa] *f.* gully, valley of a stream; bed (*formed by a stream*); river flood.

arroyo [a·rró·yo] *m.* brook, small stream, rivulet; gutter; **arroyuelo** [a·rro·ywé·lo] *m.* rivulet.

arroz [a·rrós] *m.* rice; **arrozal** [a·rro·sál] *m.* rice field.

arruga [a·rrú·ǥa] *f.* wrinkle.

arrugar[7] [a·rru·gár] *v.* to wrinkle; *Carib.* to bother, annoy; **-se** to get wrinkled; *Mex., Col.* to crouch with fear, be afraid.

arruinar [a·rrwi·nár] *v.* to ruin, destroy; **-se** to become ruined; *Am.* to go "broke", lose all one's fortune.

arrullar [a·rru·yár] *v.* to lull; to coo.
arrullo [a·rrú·yo] *m.* lullaby; cooing.
arrumbar [a·rrum·bár] *v.* to lay aside (*as useless*), put away in a corner, discard; to dismiss, remove (*from office or a position of trust*); to take bearings; — **a su adversario** to corner one's opponent, overpower him.
arsenal [ar·se·nál] *m.* arsenal; navy yard.
arsénico [ar·sé·ni·ko] *m.* arsenic.
arte [ár·te] *m. & f.* art; skill, ability; cunning; craft; **por — de** by way or means of **bellas -s** fine arts.
artefacto [ar·te·fák·to] *m.* piece of workmanship, manufactured object; handiwork; contrivance.
arteria [ar·té·rja] *f.* artery.
artero [ar·té·ro] *adj.* crafty, astute.
artesa [ar·té·sa] *f.* trough.
artesano [ar·te·sá·no] *m.* artisan, craftsman; **artesanía** [ar·te·sa·ní·a] *f.* arts and crafts; workmanship, craftsmanship.
artesonado [ar·te·so·ná·ɗo] *m.* ceiling decorated with carved panels.
ártico [ár·ti·ko] *adj.* arctic.
articulación [ar·ti·ku·la·sjón] *f.* articulation; pronunciation; joint.
articular [ar·ti·ku·lár] *v.* to articulate; to join, unite.
artículo [ar·tí·ku·lo] *m.* article; — **de fondo** editorial.
artífice [ar·tí·fi·se] *m.* artisan, craftsman.
artificial [ar·ti·fi·sjál] *adj.* artificial.
artificio [ar·ti·fi·sjo] *m.* artifice, clever device; craft, skill; cunning, deceit.
artificioso [ar·ti·fi·sjó·so] *adj.* cunning, astute, deceitful; skilful.
artillería [ar·ti·ye·rí·a] *f.* artillery, gunnery; — **de plaza** (*or* **de sitio**) heavy artillery; — **de montaña** light mountain artillery.
artillero [ar·ti·yé·ro] *m.* artilleryman, gunner.
artimaña [ar·ti·má·ña] *f.* trick.
artista [ar·tís·ta] *m. & f.* artist.
artístico [ar·tís·ti·ko] *adj.* artistic.
arveja [ar·ɓé·xa] *f. C.A., Col., Ven.* pea. *Also referred to as* **alverja** [al·ɓér·xa].
arzobispo [ar·so·ɓis·po] *m.* archbishop.
arzón [ar·són] *m.* saddletree.
as [as] *m.* ace.
asa [á·sa] *f.* handle.
asado [a·sá·ɗo] *m.* roast; *p.p. & adj.* roasted.
asador [a·sa·ɗór] *m.* spit (*for roasting*).
asaltador [a·sal·ta·ɗór] *m.* assailant; highway robber.
asaltar [a·sal·tár] *v.* to assault, attack; **-le a uno una idea** to be struck by an idea; *Ríopl., Carib.* — **la casa de un amigo** to give a surprise party.
asalto [a·sál·to] *m.* assault, attack; *Am.* surprise party.
asamblea [a·sam·blé·a] *f.* assembly, legislature; meeting.
asar [a·sár] *v.* to roast; **-se** to roast; to feel hot.
asaz [a·sás] *adv.* enough, very.
ascendencia [a·sen·dén·sja] *f.* ancestry; origin.
ascendente [a·sen·dén·te] *adj.* ascendant, ascending, upward, rising.
ascender[1] [a·sen·dér] *v. irr.* to ascend, climb; to promote; to amount (to).
ascendiente [a·sen·djén·te] *m.* ancestor; influence.
ascensión [a·sen·sjón] *f.* ascension; ascent.
ascenso [a·sén·so] *m.* ascent, rise; promotion.
ascensor [a·sen·sór] *m.* elevator.
asco [ás·ko] *m.* digust, loathing; nausea; **me da —**

it makes me sick; it disgusts me; *Mex., Ven.* **poner a uno del —** to call a person all kinds of bad names; to soil.
ascua [ás·kwa] *f.* ember.
aseado [a·se·á·ɗo] *adj.* clean, neat; *p.p. of* **asear**.
asear [a·se·ár] *v.* to adorn; to make neat and clean; **-se** to clean oneself up.
asechanza [a·se·čán·sa] = **acechanza**.
asediar [a·se·ɗjár] *v.* to besiege, attack.
asedio [a·sé·ɗjo] *m.* siege.
asegurar [a·se·gu·rár] *v.* to assure; to secure; to affirm; to insure; **-se** to make sure; to hold on; to get insured.
asemejar [a·se·me·xár] *v.* to liken, compare; **-se a** to resemble.
asentaderas [a·sen·ta·ɗé·ras] *f. pl.* buttocks.
asentador [a·sen·ta·ɗór] *m.* razor strop.
asentar [a·sen·tár] *v.* (*poner*) to set; to put down in writing; (*afirmar*) to assert; to iron out; to establish; (*afilar*) to hone; strop; **-se** to settle.
asentimiento [a·sen·ti·mjén·to] *m.* assent, acquiescence, agreement.
asentir[3] [a·sen·tír] *v. irr.* to assent, agree.
aseo [a·sé·o] *m.* neatness, cleanliness.
asequible [a·se·kí·ɓle] *adj.* obtainable, available.
aserción [a·ser·sjón] *f.* assertion, affirmation.
aserradero [a·se·rra·ɗé·ro] *m.* sawmill.
aserrar[1] [a·se·rrár] *v. irr.* to saw.
aserrín [a·se·rrín] *m.* sawdust.
aserto [a·sér·to] *m.* assertion.
asesinar [a·se·si·nár] *v.* to assassinate, murder.
asesinato [a·se·si·ná·to] *m.* assassination, murder.
asesino [a·se·sí·no] *m.* assassin, murderer; *adj.* murderous.
asestar [a·ses·tár] *v.* to point, aim, direct; — **un golpe** to deal a blow; — **un tiro** to fire a shot.
aseveración [a·se·ɓe·ra·sjón] *f.* assertion, affirmation, contention.
aseverar [a·se·ɓe·rár] *v.* to assert, affirm.
asfalto [as·fál·to] *m.* asphalt.
asfixia [as·fík·sja] *f.* suffocation.
asfixiar [as·fik·sjár] *v.* to suffocate, smother.
así [a·sí] *adv.* so, thus, like this; therefore; — — so-so; — **que** so that; — **que** (*or* **como**) *conj.* as soon as; *Ríopl., Ch., Ven., Mex., Andes* — **no más** so-so; just so.
asiático [a·sjá·ti·ko] *adj. & m.* Asiatic.
asidero [a·si·ɗé·ro] *m.* handle; hold.
asiduo [a·sí·ɗwo] *adj.* assiduous, diligent, persevering.
asiento [a·sjén·to] *m.* seat; site, location; bottom; entry (*in bookkeeping*); **-s** dregs, sediment.
asignación [a·sig·na·sjón] *f.* assignment; allowance.
asignar [a·si·gnár] *v.* to assign; to allot; to attribute; to appoint.
asilado [a·si·lá·ɗo] *m.* inmate (*of an asylum*).
asilar [a·si·lár] *v.* to house, shelter; to put in an asylum.
asilo [a·sí·lo] *m.* asylum, refuge, shelter.
asimilar [a·si·mi·lár] *v.* to assimilate, digest, absorb; to liken, compare.
asimismo [a·si·míz·mo] *adv.* likewise, also.
asir[22] [a·sir] *v. irr.* to seize, take hold of.
asistencia [a·sis·tén·sja] *f.* presence; attendance; assistance, help; *Mex.* sitting room; **-s** allowance; *Col., Ven., Mex.* **casa de —** boarding house.
asistente [a·sis·tén·te] *m.* assistant; helper; military orderly; *Col., Ven., P.R.* servant; **los -s** those present.

asistir [a·sis·tír] *v.* to attend, be present; to help; *Am.* to board, serve meals.
asno [áz·no] *m.* ass, donkey.
asociación [a·so·sja·sjón] *f.* association.
asociado [a·so·sjá·đo] *m.* associate.
asociar [a·so·sjár] *v.* to associate; **-se** to join; to associate.
asolamiento [a·so·la·mjén·to] *m.* devastation, ravage, havoc, destruction.
asolar² [a·so·lár] *v. irr.* to raze; to lay waste; to parch; **-se** to dry up, become parched; to settle (*as liquids*).
asoleado [a·so·le·á·đo] *adj.* sunny; *p.p. of* **asolear.**
asolear [a·so·le·ár] *v.* to sun; **-se** to bask in the sun; to get sunburnt.
asomar [a·so·már] *v.* to show, appear; — **la cabeza** to stick one's head out; **-se** to look out (*of a window*); to peep out (*or* into); *Peru* to draw near, approach.
asombrar [a·som·brár] *v.* (*hacer sombra*) to cast a shadow, darken; (*asustar*) to astonish, amaze, frighten; **-se** to be astonished, amazed.
asombro [a·sóm·bro] *m.* astonishment, amazement; fright.
asombroso [a·som·bró·so] *adj.* astonishing, amazing.
asomo [a·só·mo] *m.* sign, indication; conjecture, suspicion; **ni por** — by no means.
aspa [ás·pa] *f.* wing of a windmill; blade (*of a propeller*); reel (*for winding yarn*).
aspecto [as·pék·to] *m.* aspect, look, appearance.
aspereza [as·pe·ré·sa] *f.* roughness, ruggedness; harshness; severity.
áspero [ás·pe·ro] *adj.* rough, uneven, harsh; gruff.
aspiración [as·pi·ra·sjón] *f.* aspiration, ambition, longing; inhalation, breathing in.
aspiradora [as·pi·ra·đó·ra] *f.* vacuum cleaner.
aspirante [as·pi·rán·te] *m. & f.* applicant; candidate.
aspirar [as·pi·rár] *v.* (*anhelar*) to aspire, long for, seek; (*inspirar*) to breathe in, to inhale; to aspirate (*a sound*).
asquear [as·ke·ár] *v.* to disgust, nauseate, sicken.
asqueroso [as·ke·ró·so] *adj.* loathsome, disgusting, sickening, filthy.
asta [ás·ta] *f.* horn; antler; mast, pole, staff, flagstaff; lance; **a media** — at half mast.
asterisco [as·te·rís·ko] *m.* asterisk, star (*used in printing*).
astilla [as·tí·ya] *f.* chip; splinter; splint.
astillar [as·ti·yár] *v.* to chip; to splinter; **-se** to splinter, break into splinters.
astillero [as·ti·yé·ro] *m.* dry dock; shipyard; lumber yard; rack (*for lances or spears*).
astringente [as·triŋ·xén·te] *adj. & m.* astringent.
astro [ás·tro] *m.* star; planet.
astronauta [as·tro·náw·ta] *m. & f.* astronaut.
astronomía [as·tro·no·mía·a] *f.* astronomy; **astrónomo** *m.* astronomer.
astucia [as·tú·sja] *f.* shrewdness, cunning; trick.
asturiano [as·tu·rjá·no] *adj.* Asturian, of or from Asturias, Spain; *m.* Asturian.
astuto [as·tú·to] *adj.* astute, shrewd, wily, crafty.
asueto [a·swé·to] *m.* recess, vacation; **día de** — holiday.
asumir [a·su·mír] *v.* to assume.
asunto [a·sún·to] *m.* topic, subject matter; business; affair.
asustadizo [a·sus·ta·đí·so] *adj.* shy, scary, easily frightened, jumpy.
asustar [a·sus·tár] *v.* to frighten, scare.

atacante [a·ta·kán·te] *m.* attacker; *adj.* attacking.
atacar⁶ [a·ta·kár] *v.* to attack; to tighten, fasten; to ram; to plug, wad (*a gun*).
atadura [a·ta·đú·ra] *f.* tie, knot; fastening.
atajar [a·ta·xár] *v.* to intercept; to interrupt, cut off; to take a short cut; to cross out.
atajo [a·tá·xo] *m.* short cut; interception; *Am.* drove. *See* **hatajo.**
atalaya [a·ta·lá·ya] *f.* lookout, watchtower; *m.* lookout, watchman, guard.
atañer¹⁹, ⁵¹ [a·ta·ñér] *v.* to concern.
ataque [a·tá·ke] *m.* attack; fit.
atar [a·tár] *v.* to tie, fasten; **-se** to get tied up; to be puzzled or perplexed.
atardecer [a·tar·đe·sér] *m.* late afternoon.
atareado [a·ta·re·á·đo] *adj.* busy, over-worked.
atarear [a·ta·re·ár] *v.* to overwork, load with work; **-se** to toil, work hard; to be very busy.
atascadero [a·tas·ka·đé·ro] *m.* muddy place; obstruction.
atascar⁶ [a·tas·kár] *v.* to stop up; to jam, obstruct; **-se** to get stuck; to stick; to jam, get obstructed; to stall.
ataúd [a·ta·úđ] *m.* coffin.
ataviar¹⁷ [a·ta·ƀjár] *v.* to attire, deck, adorn; **-se** to dress up, doll up.
atavío [a·ta·ƀí·o] *m.* attire, costume; ornaments, finery.
atemorizar⁹ [a·te·mo·ri·sár] *v.* to frighten, scare.
atención [a·ten·sjón] *f.* attention, care, thought; courtesy; **-es** business, affairs; **en** — **a** having in mind, considering.
atender¹ [a·ten·dér] *v. irr.* to heed, pay attention; to attend to, take care of; to take into account or consideration.
atendido [a·ten·dí·đo] *adj. Am.* attentive, courteous.
ateneo [a·te·né·o] *m.* literary forum.
atenerse⁴⁵ [a·te·nér·se] *v. irr.* to rely (on); to accept, abide (by).
atenido [a·te·ní·đo] *adj. Mex., Carib., C.A., Andes* habitually dependent on another; *p.p. of* **atenerse.**
atentado [a·ten·tá·đo] *m.* offense, violation; crime, violence.
atentar¹ [a·ten·tár] *v. irr.* to attempt, try; — **contra la vida de alguien** to attempt the life of someone.
atento [a·tén·to] *adj.* attentive; courteous, polite.
atenuar¹⁸ [a·te·nwár] *v.* to attenuate, lessen; to tone down; to dim; to make thin or slender.
ateo [a·té·o] *m.* atheist; *adj.* atheistic.
aterciopelado [a·ter·sjo·pe·lá·đo] *adj.* velvety.
aterido [a·te·rí·đo] *adj.* stiff, numb from cold.
aterirse³, ⁵¹ [a·te·rír·se] *v. irr.* to become numb with cold.
aterrador [a·te·rra·đór] *adj.* terrifying, appalling.
aterrar [a·te·rrár] *v.* to terrify, frighten.
aterrizaje [a·te·rri·sá·xe] *m.* landing (*of a plane*); **pista de** — landing strip.
aterrizar⁹ [a·te·rri·sár] *v.* to land (*said of a plane*).
aterronar [a·te·rro·nár] *v.* to make lumpy, form into lumps; **-se** to lump, form into lumps, become lumpy.
aterrorizar⁹ [a·te·rro·ri·sár] *v.* to terrify, frighten, appal.
atesorar [a·te·so·rár] *v.* to treasure; to hoard, lay up, accumulate.
atestado [a·tes·tá·đo] *adj.* crowded, jammed, stuffed; witnessed; *p.p. of* **atestar.**
atestar [a·tes·tár] *v.* (*legal*) to attest, testify, witness; (*llenar*) to fill up, cram, stuff, crowd; **-se de** to stuff oneself with, to get stuffed with.

atestiguar[8] [a·tes·ti·ǵwár] *v.* to testify, witness; to attest.

atiborrar [a·ti·b̌o·rrár] *v.* to stuff; **-se** to stuff oneself.

atiesar [a·tje·sár] *v.* to stiffen.

atildado [a·til·dá·ďo] *adj.* spruce, trim; painstaking in dress or style.

atinar [a·ti·nár] *v.* to hit the mark; to guess right.

atisbar [a·tiz·b̌ár] *v.* to spy, look cautiously; to watch, pry; to catch a glimpse of; to peek.

atisbo [a·tíz·b̌o] *m.* glimpse; insight; peek; spying.

atizar[9] [a·ti·sár] *v.* to poke, stir (*the fire*); to kindle, rouse; to trim (*a wick*); — **un bofetón** to give a wallop.

atlántico [aď·lán·ti·ko] *adj.* Atlantic; **el Atlántico** the Atlantic.

atlas [áď·las] *m.* atlas.

atleta [aď·lé·ta] *m. & f.* athlete.

atlético [aď·lé·ti·ko] *adj.* athletic.

atletismo [aď·le·tíz·mo] *m.* athletics.

atmósfera [aď·mós·fe·ra] *f.* atmosphere, air.

atmosférico [aď·mos·fé·ri·ko] *adj.* atmospheric.

atole [a·tó·le] *m. Mex.* Mexican drink made of corn meal; **atol** in C.A.

atolondrado [a·to·lon·drá·ďo] *p.p. & adj.* confused, muddled; stunned; heedless, harebrained, thoughtless.

atolondramiento [a·to·lon·dra·mjén·to] *m.* thoughtlessness, recklessness; confusion, perplexity.

atolondrar [a·to·lon·drár] *v.* to confuse, muddle, perplex; to stun; **-se** to get muddled, confused; to get stunned.

atómico [a·tó·mi·ko] *adj.* atomic.

átomo [á·to·mo] *m.* atom; small particle, tiny bit.

atónito [a·tó·ni·to] *adj.* astonished, amazed.

átono [á·to·no] *adj.* unstressed.

atontado [a·ton·tá·ďo] *adj.* stupefied, stupid, stunned.

atontar [a·ton·tár] *v.* to stupefy, stun; to confuse.

atorar [a·to·rár] *v.* to jam; to stop up, clog; *Am.* to hold up, stop; **-se** to get stuck (*in the mud*); to get clogged; to get jammed; to choke (*with food*).

atormentar [a·tor·men·tár] *v.* to torment; to worry, afflict; to tease, bother, vex.

atornasolado [a·tor·na·so·lá·ďo] = **tornasolado**.

atornillar [a·tor·ni·yár] *v.* to screw; *Am.* to bother, torment.

atorrante [a·to·rrán·te] *m. & f. Col., Ch. Ríopl., Bol.* vagabond, tramp.

atrabancar[6] [a·tra·b̌aŋ·kár] *v.* to rush awkwardly; to run over; **-se** to get involved in difficulties; *Ríopl.* to rush into things.

atrabiliario [a·tra·b̌i·ljá·rjo] *adj.* melancholy; bad-tempered.

atracar [a·tra·kár] *v.* (*llenar*) to cram, stuff; (*amarrar*) to moor, to approach land; (*atacar*) to hold up, assault; *Am.* to seize; *Col.* to pursue, harass; *Am.* to treat severely; *Mex., C.A.* to thrash, beat; — **al muelle** to dock, moor to the wharf; **-se** to stuff oneself, overeat; *Ch.* to have a fist fight; *Ríopl.* to falter, stutter; **-se a** to come alongside of (*a ship*).

atracción [a·trak·sjón] *f.* attraction.

atraco [a·trá·ko] *m.* holdup, assault; *Am.* **darse un** — **de comida** to stuff oneself, gorge.

atracón [a·tra·kón] *m.* stuffing, gorging; *C.A.* violent quarrel; **darse un** — **de comida** to stuff oneself, gorge.

atractivo [a·trak·ti·b̌o] *adj.* attractive; *m.* attractiveness, charm.

atraer[46] [a·tra·ér] *v. irr.* to attract.

atragantarse [a·tra·gan·tár·se] *v.* to gobble up; to choke (*with food*).

atrancar[6] [a·traŋ·kár] *v.* to bolt, fasten with a bolt; *Am.* **-le a una cosa** to face something, stand up against something; **-se** to get crammed, obstructed; *Am.* to be stubborn, stick to one's opinion; *Col.* to stuff oneself, choke (*with food*).

atrapar [a·tra·pár] *v.* to trap, ensnare; to seize, grab; to overtake.

atrás [a·trás] *adv.* back; behind; backward; *Am.* **echarse** — (*or* **para** —) to back out, go back on one's word.

atrasado [a·tra·sá·ďo] *adj.* late; behind time; backward; behind (*in one's work, payments, etc.*); slow (*said of a clock*); *p.p. of* **atrasar**.

atrasar [a·tra·sár] *v.* to delay; to be slow or behind time; **-se** to get behind, lose time; *Am.* to suffer a setback (*in one's health or fortune*).

atraso [a·trá·so] *m.* backwardness; delay; setback; **-s** arrears.

atravesar[1] [a·tra·b̌e·sár] *v. irr.* to cross; to walk across; to go through; to pierce; *Am.* to buy wholesale.

atreverse [a·tre·b̌ér·se] *v.* to dare, risk; to be insolent, saucy.

atrevido [a·tre·b̌í·ďo] *adj.* bold, daring; insolent.

atrevimiento [a·tre·b̌i·mjén·to] *m.* boldness, daring; insolence.

atribuir[32] [a·tri·b̌wír] *v. irr.* to attribute, ascribe, impute.

atribular [a·tri·b̌u·lár] *v.* to grieve, distress; **-se** to grieve; to be distressed.

atributo [a·tri·b̌ú·to] *m.* attribute, quality.

atril [a·tríl] *m.* lectern, reading desk; book stand; music stand.

atrincherar [a·trin·če·rár] *v.* to entrench, fortify with trenches; **-se** to entrench oneself.

atrio [á·trjo] *m.* court, patio in front of a church; entrance hall.

atrocidad [a·tro·si·ďáď] *f.* atrocity.

atronador [a·tro·na·ďór] *adj.* thunderous, deafening.

atronar[2] [a·tro·nár] *v. irr.* to deafen; to stun.

atropellar [a·tro·pe·yár] *v.* to run over, run down, knock down; to trample upon; to insult; — **por** to knock down, overcome with violence; **-se** to rush.

atropello [a·tro·pé·yo] *m.* violent act; insult; outrage; trampling.

atroz [a·trós] *adj.* atrocious, awful; inhuman.

atún [a·tún] *m.* tunny fish, tuna fish.

aturdido [a·tur·ďí·ďo] *adj. & p.p.* stupid, awkward; stunned, bewildered.

aturdimiento [a·tur·ďi·mjé·to] *m.* daze, bewilderment, confusion.

aturdir [a·tur·ďír] *v.* to stun; to deafen; to bewilder.

atusar [a·tu·sár] *v.* to trim.

audacia [aw·ďá·sja] *f.* daring, boldness.

audaz [aw·ďás] *adj.* daring, bold.

audiencia [aw·ďjén·sja] *f.* audience, hearing; court of justice.

auditor [aw·ďi·tór] *m.* judge advocate.

auditorio [aw·ďi·tó·rjo] *m.* audience.

auge [áw·xe] *f.* boom (*in the market*); boost (*in prices*); topmost height (*of fortune, fame, dignity, etc.*); **estar** (*or* **ir**) **en** — to be on the increase.

augurar [aw·gu·rár] *v.* to fortell, predict.

augusto [aw·gús·to] *adj.* venerable; majestic.
aula [áw·la] *f.* schoolroom, classroom; lecture hall.
aullar [aw·yár] *v.* to howl; to shriek; to bawl.
aullido [aw·yí·ɗo] *m.* howl.
aumentar [aw·men·tár] *v.* to augment, increase.
aumento [aw·mén·to] *m.* increase, advance, rise.
aun [awn] **(aún)** [a·un] *adv.* even, still, yet.
aunque [áwn·ke] *conj.* though, although.
aura [áw·ra] *f.* breeze; favor, applause; *Am.* bird of prey, buzzard, vulture.
áureo [áw·re·o] *adj.* golden.
aureola [aw·re·ó·la] *f.* aureole, halo.
aureomicina [aw·re·o·mi·sí·na] *f.* Aureomycin (*trademark for chlortetracycline*).
aurora [aw·ró·ra] *f.* dawn; beginning; — **boreal** aurora borealis, northern lights.
auscultar [aws·kul·tár] *v.* to sound, examine by listening to (*the chest, lungs, heart, etc.*).
ausencia [aw·sén·sja] *f.* absence.
ausentarse [aw·sen·tár·se] *v.* to absent oneself; to be absent; to leave.
ausente [aw·sén·te] *adj.* absent.
auspicios [aws·pí·sjos] *m. pl.* auspices, patronage; omens.
austeridad [aws·te·ri·ɗáɗ] *f.* austerity, severity, sternness, harshness.
austero [aws·té·ro] *adj.* austere, stern, strict; harsh.
austral [aws·trál] *adj.* southern.
austríaco [aws·trí·a·ko] *adj. & m.* Austrian.
austro [áws·tro] *m.* south wind.
auténtico [aw·tén·ti·ko] *adj.* authentic, true, genuine.
auto [áw·to] *m.* auto, automobile; one-act play; writ, order; — **sacramental** one-act religious play; **-s** proceedings.
autobús [aw·to·bús] *m.* bus, autobus.
autóctono [aw·tók·to·no] *adj.* indigenous, native.
autogiro [aw·to·xí·ro] *m.* autogiro.
automático [aw·to·má·ti·ko] *adj.* automatic.
automotriz [aw·to·mo·tríz] *adj.* automotive, self-moving.
automóvil [aw·to·mó·bil] *m.* automobile, auto.
automovilista [aw·to·mo·bi·lis·ta] *m. & f.* motorist.
autonomía [aw·to·no·mí·a] *f.* autonomy.
autopista [aw·to·pís·ta] *f.* expressway, superhighway, freeway, throughway, turnpike.
autor [aw·tór] *m.* author.
autoridad [aw·to·ri·ɗáɗ] *f.* authority.
autoritario [aw·to·ri·tá·rjo] *adj.* authoritative; authoritarian, domineering; bossy.
autorización [aw·to·ri·sa·sjón] *f.* authorization, sanction.
autorizar[9] [aw·to·ri·sár] *v.* to authorize, give power (to).
autoservicio [aw·to·ser·bí·sjo] *m.* self-service.
auxiliar [awk·si·ljár] *v.* to aid, help; *adj.* auxiliary, helping, assisting; *m.* assistant.
auxilio [aek·si·ljo] *m.* aid, help.
avaluación [a·ba·lwa·sjón] *f.* valuation, appraisal, assessment.
avaluar[18] [a·ba·lwár] *v.* to value, appraise.
avalúo [a·ba·lú·o] *f.* valuation, appraisal.
avance [a·bán·se] *m.* advance, progress, headway; advanced payment; attack.
avanzada [a·ban·sá·ɗa] *f.* advance guard; outpost; advanced unit, spearhead.
avanzar[9] [a·ban·sár] *v.* to advance.
avaricia [a·ba·rí·sja] *f.* avarice, greed.
avariento [a·ba·rjén·to] *adj.* avaricious, miserly; *m.* miser.
avaro [a·bá·ro] *adj.* miserly, greedy; *m.* miser.

avasallar [a·ba·sa·yár] *v.* to subject, dominate, subdue.
ave [á·be] *f.* bird; fowl; — **de corral** domestic fowl; — **de rapiña** bird of prey.
avecindarse [a·be·sin·dár·se] *v.* to settle, locate, establish oneself, take up residence (*in a community*).
avellana [a·be·yá·na] *f.* hazelnut; **avellano** [a·be·yá·no] *m.* hazel; hazelnut tree; **avellanado** [a·be·ya·ná·ɗo] *adj.* hazel, light brown.
avena [a·bé·na] *f.* oats.
avenencia [a·be·nēn·sja] *f.* harmony, agreement; conformity.
avenida [a·be·ní·ɗa] *f.* avenue; flood.
avenir[48] [a·be·nír] *v. irr.* to adjust; to reconcile; **-se a** to adapt oneself to; **-se con alguien** to get along with someone.
aventador [a·ben·ta·ɗór] *m.* fan (*for fanning a fire*); ventilator; winnower (*machine for separating wheat from chaff*).
aventajar [a·ben·ta·xár] *v.* to excel; to be ahead (of); **-se a** to get ahead of.
aventar[1] [a·ben·tár] *v. irr.* to fan; to winnow, blow chaff from grain; to throw out, expel; *Am.* to pitch, throw; *Am.* to dry sugar (*in the open*); *Am.* to rouse (*game*); **-se** to be full of wind; to flee, run away; *Am.* to attack, hurl oneself (*on someone*).
aventura [a·ben·tú·ra] *f.* adventure; risk, danger; chance.
aventurado [a·ben·tu·rá·ɗo] *adj.* adventurous, risky; bold, daring.
aventurar [a·ben·tu·rár] *v.* to venture, risk; **-se a** to risk, run the risk of; to dare.
aventurero [a·ben·tu·ré·ro] *adj.* adventurous; *m.* adventurer.
avergonzar[2, 9] [a·ber·gon·sár] *v. irr.* to shame; **-se** to feel ashamed.
avería [a·be·rí·a] *f.* damage; aviary, birdhouse; *Am.* misfortune; *Mex., Cuba* mischief.
averiar[17] [a·be·rjár] *v.* to damage, spoil, hurt; **-se** to become damaged; to spoil.
averiguar[8] [a·be·ri·gwár] *v.* to find out; to investigate.
aversión [a·ber·sjón] *f.* aversion, dislike; reluctance.
avestruz [a·bes·trús] *m.* ostrich.
avezado [a·be·sá·ɗo] *p.p. & adj.* accustomed; trained, practiced.
aviación [a·bja·sjón] *f.* aviation.
aviador [a·bja·ɗór] *m.* aviator, flyer; purveyor, provider; *Am.* moneylender (*to miners or laborers*), promoter.
aviar[17] [a·bjár] *v.* to equip; to supply; to prepare, make ready; *Am.* to lend money or equipment; **estar aviado** to be surrounded by difficulties; to be in a fix.
ávido [á·bi·ɗo] *adj.* eager; greedy.
avinagrado [a·bi·na·grá·ɗo] *adj.* sour; acid; cross.
avinagrar [a·bi·na·grár] *v.* to sour, make sour or acid; **-se** to sour, become sour.
avío [a·bí·o] *m.* provision, supply; preparation; *Cuba, Mex.* loan of money or equipment; **-s** equipment; **-s de pescar** fishing tackle.
avión [a·bjón] *m.* airplane; martin (*a bird similar to a swallow*).
avisar [a·bi·sár] *v.* to inform, give notice, advise; to announce; to warn.
aviso [a·bí·so] *m.* notice, advice, announcement; warning.
avispa [a·bís·pa] *f.* wasp; **avispero** [a·bis·pé·ro] *m.* wasp's nest; **avispón** [a·bis·pón] *m.* hornet.

AT

avispado [a·bis·pa·do] *adj.* lively, keen, clever, wide-awake; *Am.* frightened, scared.

avispar [a·bis·pár] *v.* to spur, incite; **-se** to be on the alert; to be uneasy; *Am.* to become frightened, scared.

avistar [a·bis·tár] *v.* to glimpse, catch sight of; **-se** to see each other, meet.

avivar [a·bi·bár] *v.* to enliven, give life to; to revive; to brighten; to quicken.

avizor [a·bi·sór] *adj.* alert, watchful.

avizorar [a·bi·so·rár] *v.* to spy, watch closely.

aya [á·ya] *f.* child's nurse, governess; **ayo** [á·yo] *m.* tutor guardian.

ayer [a·yér] *adv.* yesterday.

ayuda [a·yú·da] *f.* aid, help.

ayudante [a·yu·dán·te] *m.* assistant.

ayudar [a·yu·dár] *v.* to aid, help.

ayunar [a·yu·nár] *v.* to fast.

ayunas [a·yú·nas]: **en — fasting; en — de** totally ignorant of.

ayuno [a·yú·no] *m.* fast; **— de** wholly ignorant of.

ayuntamiento [a·yun·ta·mjén·to] *m.* municipal government; town hall.

azabache [a·sa·bá·če] *m.* jet; **-s** jet ornaments.

azada [a·sá·da] *f.* spade; hoe; **azadón** [a·sa·dón] *m.* hoe.

azafata [a·sa·fá·ta] *f.* airline hostess.

azafrán [a·sa·frán] *m.* saffron.

azahar [a·sa·ár] *m.* orange or lemon blossom.

azar [a·sár] *m.* hazard; chance; accident; disaster.

azogue [a·só·ge] *m.* quicksilver.

azolvar [a·sol·bár] *v.* to clog, obstruct; **-se** to clog, get clogged.

azorar [a·so·rár] *v.* to disturb, startle; to bewilder; **-se** to be startled, astonished; to be bewildered, perplexed; to be uneasy.

azotaina [a·so·táj·na] *f.* flogging, lashing, beating.

azotar [a·so·tár] *v.* to whip, lash, beat; *Am.* to thresh (*rice*); **— las calles** to "beat the pavement", walk the streets.

azote [a·só·te] *m.* whip; lash with a whip; scourge; affliction, calamity.

azotea [a·so·té·a] *f.* flat roof.

azteca [as·té·ka] *adj., m. & f.* Aztec.

azúcar [a·sú·kar] *m.* sugar.

azucarar [a·su·ka·rár] *v.* to sugar; to sweeten; **-se** to become sweet; *Am.* to crystallize, turn to sugar.

azucarera [a·su·ka·ré·ra] *f.* sugar bowl; sugar mill.

azucarero [a·su·ka·ré·ro] *adj.* sugar (*used as adj.*); *m.* sugar manufacturer, producer or dealer; sugar bowl.

azucena [a·su·sé·na] *f.* white lily.

azufre [a·sú·fre] *m.* sulphur.

azul [a·súl] *adj.* blue; **— celeste** sky-blue; **— marino** navy blue; **— turquí** indigo; *Am.* **tiempos -es** hard times.

azulado [a·su·lá·do] *adj.* bluish.

azular [a·su·lár] *v.* to dye or color blue.

azulejo [a·su·lé·xo] *m.* glazed tile; *Am.* bluebird; *adj.* bluish.

azuzar[9] [a·su·sár] *v.* to urge, egg on; to incite.

B:b

baba [bá·ba] *f.* drivel, slaver, saliva; slime, slimy secretion; *Am.* small alligator.

babear [ba·be·ár] *v.* to drivel; to slobber.

babero [ba·bé·ro] *m.* baby's bib.

babor [ba·bór] *m.* port, port side (*of a ship*).

babosear [ba·bo·se·ár] *v.* to slaver, drivel; to keep one's mouth open; to act like a fool.

baboso [ba·bó·so] *adj.* driveling, slobbering; slimy; foolishly sentimental; *Am.* silly, idiotic, foolish;

babosa [*f.* slug (*creature like a snail, but without a shell*).

babucha [ba·bú·ča] *f.* slipper; *Ríopl.* **a —** pickaback, on the back or shoulders.

bacalao [ba·ká·lá·o], **bacallao** *m. Andalusia, Am.* codfish.

bacía [ba·sí·a] *f.* basin.

bacilo [ba·sí·lo] *m.* bacillus.

bacín [ba·sín] *m.* pot, chamber pot; **bacinica** [ba·si·ní·ka] *f.* chamber pot.

bacteria [bak·té·rja] *f.* bacterium; **-s** bacteria.

bacteriología [bak·te·rjo·lo·xí·a] *f.* bacteriology.

bacteriológico [bak·te·rjo·ló·xi·ko] *adj.* bacteriological, pertaining to bacteriology.

báculo [bá·ku·lo] *m.* staff, cane; aid, support.

bache [bá·če] *m.* rut, hole in the road.

bachiller [ba·či·yér] *m.* bachelor (*one who holds degree*); talkative person; **bachillerato** [ba·či·ye·rá·to] *m.* bachelor's degree; studies for the bachelor's degree.

badajo [ba·dá·xo] *m.* clapper of a bell; foolish talker.

badana [ba·dá·na] *f.* sheepskin.

bagaje [ba·gá·xe] *m.* baggage; army pack mule.

bagatela [ba·ga·té·la] *f.* trifle.

bagazo [ba·gá·so] *m.* waste pulp (*of sugarcane, olives, grapes, etc.*).

bagual [ba·gwál] *adj. Ríopl.* wild, untamed, unruly; *Ríopl.* rude, discourteous; *Ríopl.* lanky, awkward; *m. Ríopl.* wild horse.

bahía [ba·í·a] *f.* bay, harbor.

bailador [baj·la·dór] *m.* dancer; *adj.* dancing.

bailar [baj·lár] *v.* to dance; to spin around.

bailarín [baj·la·rín] *m.* dancer; **bailarina** [baj·la·rí·na] *f.* dancer.

baile [báj·le] *m.* dance; ball; ballet.

bailotear [baj·lo·te·ár] *v.* to jig, jiggle; to dance poorly; to dance around.

baja [bá·xa] *f.* fall (*of prices*); war casualty; **dar de —** to discharge, muster out.

bajá [ba·xá] *m.* pasha.

bajada [ba·xá·da] *f.* descent; slope, dip (*on a road*); **de —** on the way down; **subidas y -s** ups and downs.

bajar [ba·xár] *v.* to go down; to drop (*as price or value*); to lower; to take or carry down; to humble; **-se** to get down or off; to alight; *Am.* to stop at a hotel.

bajel [ba·xél] *m.* boat, ship.

bajeza [ba·xé·sa] *f.* vile act or remark; meanness; baseness; degradation.

bajío [ba·xí·o] *m.* shoal, sand bank; *Am.* lowland.

bajo [bŏ·xo] *adj.* low; short; soft, bass (*tone or voice*); shallow (*water*); subdued (*color*); humble; base; **— piso — first** floor, ground floor; *prep.* under, underneath; *m.* bass.

bala [bá·la] *f.* bullet, shot, ball; bale (*of cotton*).

balada [ba·lá·da] *f.* ballad.

baladí [ba·la·dí] *adj.* trivial; flimsy.

balance [ba·lán·se] *m.* balance; equilibrium; balance sheet; rocking, rolling.

balancear [ba·lan·se·ár] *v.* to balance; to rock, roll; to swing, sway; to waver.

balanceo [ba·lan·séo] *m.* rocking, rolling; swinging; balancing; wavering; wobbling.

balanza [ba·lán·sa] *f.* balance, scale.

balar [ba·lár] *v.* to bleat.

balaustrada [ba·laws·trá·ḍa] *f.* balustrade, banister, railing.

balaustre [ba·láws·tre] *m.* banister.

balazo [ba·lá·so] *m.* shot; bullet wound; *adj. Ch.* clever, cunning.

balbucear [bal·bu·se·ár] *v.* to stammer, stutter; to babble.

balbuceo [bal·bu·sé·o] *m.* babble.

balcón [bal·kón] *m.* balcony.

baldado [bal·dá·ḍo] *m.* cripple; *adj. & p.p.* crippled.

baldar [bal·dár] *v.* to cripple; to trump (*a card*).

balde [bál·de] *m.* pail; bucket; **de** — free of charge; **en** — in vain.

baldío [bal·dí·o] *adj.* barren; fallow, uncultivated; *m.* fallow land; wasteland.

baldón [bal·dón] *m.* infamy, insult.

baldosa [bal·dó·sa] *f.* floor tile; paving stone.

balido [ba·lí·ḍo] *m.* bleat, bleating.

balneario [bal·ne·á·rjo] *m.* bathing resort; *adj.* pertaining to bathing resorts or medicinal springs.

balompié [ba·lom·pjé] *m.* football

balota [ba·ló·ta] *f.* ballot.

balotar [ba·lo·tár] *v.* to ballot, vote.

balsa [bál·sa] *f.* (*de agua*) pond, pool; (*embarcación*) raft; *Am.* marsh; *Am.* a species of ceiba (*a tropical tree*).

bálsamo [bál·sa·mo] *m.* balsam, balm.

baluarte [bal·wár·te] *m.* bulwark.

ballena [ba·yé·na] *f.* whale; whalebone.

bambolear [bam·bo·le·ár] *v.* to sway, swing, rock; **-se** to stagger; to sway.

bambú [bam·bú] *m.* bamboo.

banana [ba·ná·na] *f.* banana; **banano** [ba·ná·no] *m.* banana tree.

banasta [ba·nás·ta] *f.* large basket.

banca [báŋ·ka] *f.* bench; card game; banking; banking house.

bancario [baŋ·ká·rjo] *adj.* bank, pertaining to a bank.

bancarrota [baŋ·ka·rró·ta] *f.* bankruptcy; failure, collapse.

banco [báŋ·ko] *m.* bank; bench, stool; school (*of fish*); *Mex.* pile of grain; *Am.* small hill on a plain.

banda [bán·da] *f.* (*musical*) band; (*cinta*) ribbon, sash; (*grupo*) gang, group, party; flock; (*lindero*) side, edge, border.

bandada [ban·dá·ḍa] *f.* flock of birds; *Am.* gang.

bandeja [ban·dé·xa] *f.* tray; *Mex., Ven., Col.* bowl.

bandera [ban·dé·ra] *f.* banner, flag; *Ríopl., Cuba, Mex.* **parar uno** — to take the lead, be a gangleader.

banderilla [ban·de·rí·ya] *f.* dart with a small flag or streamers (*used in bullfights*); **clavar a uno una** — to goad or taunt someone; **tercio de** — the **banderilla** phase of the bullfight; *Am.* **pegar una** — to touch for a loan.

banderillero [ban·de·ri·yé·ro] *m.* bullfighter who sticks the **banderillas** into the bull.

banderín [ban·de·rín] *m.* small flag; signal flag; pennant; recruiting office.

banderola [ban·de·ró·la] *f.* streamer, small banner or flag; pennant.

bandidaje [ban·di·ḍá·xe] *m.* banditry, highway robbery; bandits.

bandido [ban·dí·ḍo] *m.* bandit, gangster.

bando [bán·do] *m.* (*decreto*) decree, proclamation; (*partido*) party, faction.

bandolero [ban·do·lé·ro] *m.* bandit.

bandurria [ban·dú·rrja] *f.* bandore (*stringed instrument*); *Am.* a species of wading bird.

banquero [baŋ·ké·ro] *m.* banker.

banqueta [baŋ·ké·ta] *f.* bench (*without a back*); stool; footstool; *Mex.* sidewalk.

banquete [baŋ·ké·te] *m.* banquet.

banquetear [baŋ·ke·te·ár] *v.* to banquet, feast.

banquillo [baŋ·kí·yo] *m.* bench, stool.

bañada [ba·ñá·ḍa] *f.* shower, spray; dip, bath.

bañar [ba·ñár] *v.* to bathe, wash; to dip; **-se** to take a bath.

bañera [ba·ñé·ra] *f.* bathtub.

bañista [ba·ñís·ta] *m. & f.* bather.

baño [bá·ño] *m.* (*aseo*) bath; bathtub; (*acabado*) cover, coating; **— de María** double boiler; *Am.* **— ruso** steam bath.

baqueta [ba·ké·ta] *f.* rod; whip; **-s** drumsticks; **tratar a la** — to treat scornfully, despotically.

baquiano [ba·kjá·no], **baqueano** [ba·ke·á·no] *m. Ríopl., Ven., Andes* native guide (*through the wilderness, pampas, etc.*); *adj. Ríopl., Andes* having an instinctive sense of direction.

bar [bar] *m.* bar, taproom, tavern.

baraja [ba·rá·xa] *f.* pack of cards.

barajar [ba·ra·xár] *v.* to shuffle; to mix, jumble together; to scuffle, wrangle; *Am.* to hinder, obstruct.

baranda [ba·rán·da] *f.* railing; **barandal** [ba·ran·dál] *m.* banister, railing.

barandilla [ba·ran·dí·ya] *f.* balustrade, rail, railing.

barata [ba·rá·ta] *f.* barter, exchange; *Am.* bargain sale; *Peru, Ch.* cockroach.

baratear [ba·ra·te·ár] *v.* to sell cheap; to cheapen; to cut the price of.

baratija [ba·ra·tí·xa] *f.* trinket, trifle.

barato [ba·rá·to] *adj.* cheap; *m.* bargain sale; money given by the winning gambler.

baratura [ba·ra·tú·ra] *f.* cheapness.

baraúnda [ba·ra·ún·da] *f.* clamor, uproar, clatter.

barba [bár·ba] *f.* chin; beard; **-s** whiskers.

barbacoa [bar·ba·kó·a] *f. Am.* barbecue; barbecued meat.

barbado [bar·bá·ḍo] *adj.* bearded.

barbaridad [bar·ba·ri·ḍáḍ] *f.* cruelty, brutality; rudeness; **una — de** a lot of; **¡que —!** what nonsense!; what an atrocity!

barbarie [bar·bá·rje] *f.* barbarousness; savagery; lack of culture, ignorance; cruelty, brutality.

bárbaro [bár·ba·ro] *adj.* barbarous, cruel, savage; crude, coarse; *m.* barbarian.

barbechar [bar·be·čár] *v.* to plow; to fallow.

barbecho [bar·bé·čo] *m.* first plowing; plowed land; fallow, fallow land.

barbería [bar·be·rí·a] *f.* barbershop.

barbero [bar·bé·ro] *m.* barber; flatterer.

barbilla [bar·bí·ya] *f.* point of the chin.

barbón [bar·bón], **barbudo** [bar·bú·ḍo] *adj.* bearded.

barca [bár·ka] *f.* boat, launch, barge.

barco [bár·ko] *m.* boat, ship.

bardo [bár·ḍo] *m.* bard, minstrel, poet.

bario [bá·rjo] *m.* barium.

barítono [ba·rí·to·no] *m.* baritone.

barlovento [bar·lo·ben·to] *m.* windward.
barniz [bar·nís] *m.* varnish; glaze; printer's ink.
barnizar[9] [bar·ni·sár] *v.* to varnish; to glaze.
barómetro [ba·ró·me·tro] *m.* barometer.
barquero [bar·ké·ro] *m.* boatman; bargeman.
barquillo [bar·kí·yo] *m.* rolled wafer; ice-cream cone.
barquinazo [bar·ki·ná·so] *m.* tumble, bad fall, hard bump, somersault; *Am.* lurch (*of a vehicle or boat*).
barra [bá·rra] *f.* bar; rod; railing; sand bar; claque, audience; — **de jabón** bar of soap.
barrabasada [ba·rra·ba·sá·da] *f.* mischief, mean prank; rash, hasty act.
barraca [ba·rrá·ka] *f.* hut, cabin; *Andes* large shed, warehouse.
barranca [ba·rráŋ·ka] *f.*, **barranco** [ba·rráŋ·ko] *m.* ravine, gorge; *Am.* cliff.
barreminas [ba·rre·mí·nas] *m.* mine-sweeper.
barrena [ba·rré·na] *f.* auger, drill; gimlet (*small tool for boring holes*); spinning dive (*of a plane*).
barrenar [ba·rre·nár] *v.* to drill, bore; to scuttle (*a ship*); to blast (*a rock*).
barrendero [ba·rren·dé·ro] *m.* sweeper.
barrer [ba·rrér] *v.* to sweep; to sweep away; *Am.* to defeat; *Am.* **al** — altogether, as a whole.
barrera [ba·rré·ra] *f.* barrier; obstacle.
barreta [ba·rré·ta] *f.* small iron bar; *Mex., Cuba, Col.* pick, pickaxe.
barrica [ba·rrí·ka] *f.* cask, keg.
barrida [ba·rrí·da] *f. Am.* sweep, sweeping.
barrido [ba·rrí·do] *m.* sweep, sweeping; sweepings; *p.p. of* **barrer**.
barriga [ba·rrí·ga] *f.* belly; bulge.
barrigón [ba·rri·gón], **barrigudo** [ba·rri·gú·do] *adj.* big-bellied.
barril [ba·rríl] *m.* barrel, keg.
barrilete [ba·rri·lé·te] *m.* clamp.
barrio [bá·rrjo] *m.* district, neighborhood, quarter; **-s bajos** slums.
barro [bá·rro] *m.* (*tierra*) mud, clay; (*granillo*) pimple; *Am.* **hacer** (*or* **cometer**) **un** — to commit a blunder.
barroso [ba·rró·so] *adj.* muddy; pimply; reddish.
barrote [ba·rró·te] *m.* short, thick bar; brace; rung (*of a ladder or chair*).
barruntar [ba·rrun·tár] *v.* to foresee; to have a presentiment; to conjecture.
barrunto [ba·rrún·to] *m.* foreboding, presentiment; guess; hint, indication, sign.
bártulos [bár·tu·los] *m. pl.* household goods; implements, tools.
barullo [ba·rú·yo] *m.* hubbub, racket, disorder.
basa [bá·sa] *f.* base, pedestal; basis, foundation.
basar [ba·sár] *v.* to base; to put on a base.
basca [bás·ka] *f.* nausea, sickness to one's stomach; **tener -s** to be nauseated, sick to one's stomach.
báscula [bás·ku·la] *f.* scale (*for weighing*), platform scale.
base [bá·se] *f.* base, basis, foundation.
básico [bá·si·ko] *adj.* basic.
basquear [bas·ke·ár] *v.* to heave, try to vomit; to be nauseated, sick to one's stomach.
basquetbol [bas·ke·ból] *m.* basketball.
bastante [bas·tán·te] *adj.* enough, sufficient; *adv.* enough.
bastar [bas·tár] *v.* to be enough; to suffice.
bastardilla [bas·tar·dí·ya] *f.* italic type, italics.
bastardo [bas·tár·do] *adj.* bastard.
bastidor [bas·ti·dór] *m.* wing (*of a stage*); frame; embroidery frame; window sash; easel (*support*

for a picture, blackboard, etc.); **entre -es** behind the scenes, off stage.
bastilla [bas·tí·ya] *f.* hem.
bastimento [bas·ti·mén·to] *m.* supply, provisions; vessel, ship.
basto [bás·to] *adj.* coarse; *m.* club (*in cards*); *Am.* saddle pad.
bastón [bas·tón] *m.* cane, walking stick.
basura [ba·sú·ra] *f.* rubbish, scraps; garbage; refuse.
basurero [ba·su·ré·ro] *m.* garbage or rubbish dump; manure pile; garbage man, rubbish man; street cleaner.
bata [bá·ta] *f.* lounging robe; housecoat, wrapper, dressing gown; smock; **batín** [ba·tín] *m.* smock.
batahola [ba·ta·ó·la] *f.* hubbub, racket, uproar.
batalla [ba·tá·ya] *f.* battle; struggle.
batallar [ba·ta·yár] *v.* to battle, fight, struggle.
batallón [ba·ta·yón] *m.* battalion.
batata [ba·tá·ta] *f. Caribe, Sp.* sweet potato.
bate [bá·te] *m.* baseball bat.
batea [ba·té·a] *f.* tray; trough; bowl; barge; *Am.* washtub.
bateador [ba·te·a·dór] *m.* batter (*in baseball*).
batear [ba·te·ár] *v.* to bat.
batería [ba·te·rí·a] *f.* battery (*military, naval, or electric*); — **de cocina** set of kitchen utensils; — **de jazz** a jazz combo; *Mex.* **dar** — to raise a rumpus; to plod, work hard.
batidor [ba·ti·dór] *m.* beater; scout.
batintín [ba·tin·tín] *m.* gong.
batir [ba·tír] *v.* (*combatir*) to beat, whip, defeat; (*reconocer*) reconnoiter, explore; (*mover*) to flap; *Ch.* to rinse (*clothes*); *Ríopl.* to denounce; **-se** to fight; — **palmas** to clap, applaud.
batisfera [ba·tis·fé·ra] *f.* bathysphere.
baturrillo [ba·tu·rrí·yo] *m.* medley, mixture; hodgepodge.
batuta [ba·tú·ta] *f.* orchestra conductor's baton or wand; **llevar la** — to lead; to be the leader.
baúl [ba·úl] *m.* trunk, chest; — **mundo** large trunk.
bautismo [baw·tíz·mo] *m.* baptism, christening; **nombre de** — Christian name.
bautista [baw·tís·ta] *m. & f.* Baptist; baptizer.
bautizar[9] [baw·ti·sár] *v.* to baptize, christen.
bautizo [baw·tí·so] *m.* christening, baptism.
baya [bá·ya] *f.* berry.
bayeta [ba·yé·ta] *f.* flannel; flannelette; **bayetón** *m.* thick wool cloth; *Col.* long poncho lined with flannel.
bayo [bá·yo] *adj.* bay, reddish-brown.
baza [bá·sa] *f.* trick (*cards played in one round*); **meter** — to meddle; to butt into a conversation; **no dejar meter** — not to let a person put a word in edgewise.
bazar [ba·sár] *m.* bazaar; department store.
bazo [bá·so] *m.* spleen.
bazofia [ba·só·fja] *f.* scraps, refuse, garbage; dregs.
beatitud [be·a·ti·túd] *f.* bliss, blessedness.
beato [be·á·to] *adj.* blessed; beatified; devout; overpious; hypocritical.
bebé [be·bé] *m.* baby.
bebedero [be·be·dé·ro] *m.* drinking trough; watering place; spout.
bebedor [be·be·dór] *m.* drinker; drunkard.
beber [be·bér] *v.* to drink; to drink in, absorb.
bebida [be·bí·da] *f.* drink, beverage; **dado a la** — given to drink.
beca [bé·ka] *f.* scholarship, fellowship; sash worn over the academic gown.

BA

becario [be·ká·rjo] *m.* scholar, fellow, holder of a scholarship.

becerro [be·sé·rro] *m.* young bull (*less than a year old*); calf; calfskin.

becuadro [be·kwá·dro] *m.* natural sign (*in music*).

bedel [be·dél] *m.* beadle.

befa [bé·fa] *f.* scoff, jeer.

befar [be·fár] *v.* to scoff, jeer at, mock.

bejuco [be·xú·ko] *m.* reed; **silla de —** cane chair.

beldad [bel·dád] *f.* beauty.

belga [bél·ga] *adj., m. & f.* Belgian.

bélico [bé·li·ko] *adj.* warlike.

beligerante [be·li·xe·rán·te] *adj., m. & f.* belligerent.

bellaco [be·yá·ko] *adj.* sly, deceitful; *m.* villain; rascal.

bellaquear [be·ya·ke·ár] *v.* to cheat; to play tricks; *Am.* to rear, stand up on the hind legs; *Am.* to balk; *Am.* to be touchy, oversensitive.

bellaquería [be·ya·ke·rí·a] *f.* cunning, trickery; sly act or remark.

belleza [be·yé·sa] *f.* beauty.

bello [bé·yo] *adj.* beautiful.

bellota [be·yó·ta] *f.* acorn.

bemol [be·mól] *adj.* flat (*in music*); **tener -es** to have difficulties.

bendecir[27, 52] [ben·de·sír] *v. irr.* to bless.

bendición [ben·di·sjón] *f.* benediction, blessing; *Mex., C.A., Col., Ven.* **echarle la — a una cosa** to give something up for lost.

bendito [ben·dí·to] *adj.* blessed; saintly; **es un —** he is a saint, he is a simple soul; *p.p. of* **bendecir**.

benefactor [be·ne·fak·tór] *m.* benefactor; patron.

beneficencia [be·ne·fi·sén·sja] *f.* beneficence, kindness, charity; **— pública** welfare.

beneficiar [be·ne·fi·sjár] *v.* to benefit, do good; to cultivate (*land*); to exploit (*a mine*); to treat (*metals*); *Col., Ven.* to slaughter (*cattle*) for marketing.

beneficio [be·ne·fí·sjo] *m.* (*provecho*) benefit, profit; exploitation of a mine; (*cultivo*) cultivation of land; *Am.* fertilizer; *Am.* slaughtering (*of cattle*).

benéfico [be·né·fi·ko] *adj.* beneficent, good, kind.

benemérito [be·ne·mé·ri·to] *m.* worthy, notable; *adj.* worthy.

benevolencia [be·ne·ßo·len·sja] *f.* benevolence, kindness.

benévolo [be·né·ßo·lo] *adj.* benevolent, good, kindly.

benigno [be·níg·no] *adj.* benign, gentle, mild, kind.

beodo [be·ó·do] *adj.* drunk; *m.* drunkard.

berbiquí [ber·ßi·kí] *m.* carpenter's brace.

berenjena [be·ren·xí·na] *f.* eggplant; *Mex., C.A.* kind of squash; **berenjenal** *m.* egg-plant patch; **meterse uno en un —** to get into a mess.

bergantín [ber·gan·tín] *m.* brigantine, brig (*square-rigged ship with two masts*).

beriberi [be·ri·bé·ri] *m.* beriberi.

berilio [be·rí·ljo] *m.* beryllium.

bermejo [ber·mé·xo] *adj.* crimson, bright red.

bermellón [ber·me·yón] *adj.* vermilion (*bright red*).

berrear [be·rre·ár] *v.* to bellow; to scream; to sing off key.

berrido [be·rrí·do] *m.* bellow, bellowing; scream.

berrinche [be·rrín·če] *m.* fit of anger; tantrum.

berro [bé·rro] *m.* water cress.

berza [bér·sa] *f.* cabbage.

besar [be·sár] *v.* to kiss.

beso [bé·so] *m.* kiss.

bestia [bés·tja] *f.* beast.

bestialidad [bes·tja·li·dád] *f.* bestiality, brutality.

besugo [be·sú·go] *m.* sea bream (*a fish*).

besuquear [be·su·ke·ár] *v.* to kiss repeatedly.

betabel [be·ta·ßél] *f. Mex.* beet.

betún [be·tún] *m.* bitumen (*combustible mineral*); black pitch; shoeblacking.

Biblia [bí·ßlja] *f.* Bible.

bíblico [bí·ßli·ko] *adj.* Biblical.

biblioteca [bi·ßljo·té·ka] *f.* library; set of volumes; bookcase.

bibliotecario [bi·ßljo·te·ká·rjo] *m.* librarian.

bicarbonato [bi·kar·ßo·ná·to] *m.* bicarbonate.

bicicleta [bi·si·klé·ta] *f.* bicycle; **biciclista** [bi·si·klís·ta], **bicicletista** [bi·si·kle·tís·ta] *m. & f.* bicyclist, bicycle rider.

bicho [bí·čo] *m.* insect, bug; any small animal; an insignificant person.

biela [bjé·la] *f.* connecting rod (*of an engine*).

bien [bjen] *adv.* well; **— que** although; **ahora —** now then; **más —** rather; **si —** although; *m.* good, benefit; **-es** property; **-es inmuebles** real estate; **-es raíces** real estate.

bienaventurado [bje·na·ßen·tu·rá·do] *adj.* blessed, happy.

bienaventuranza [bje·na·ßen·tu·ran·sa] *f.* blessedness; beatitude; bliss.

bienestar [bje·nes·tár] *m.* well-being, comfort, welfare.

bienhechor [bje·ne·čór] *m.* benefactor.

bienvenida [bjem·be·ní·da] *f.* welcome.

bienvenido [bjem·be·ní·do] *adj.* welcome.

biftec [bif·ték], **bistec** [bis·ték], **bisté** [bis·té] *m.* beefsteak.

bifurcación [bi·fur·ka·sjón] *f.* fork, forking, branching out; railway junction; branch railroad.

bifurcarse[6] [bi·fur·kár·se] *v.* to fork, branch off, divide into two branches.

bigamía [bi·ga·mí·a] *f.* bigamy.

bigote [bi·gó·te] *m.* mustache.

bikini [bi·ki·ni] *m.* bikini bathing suit.

bilabial [bi·la·ßjál] *adj.* bilabial.

bilingüe [bi·lĩ·gwe] *adj.* bilingual.

bilingüismo [bi·lĩ·gwíz·mo] *m.* bilingualism.

bilis [bí·lis] *f.* bile.

billar [bi·yár] *m.* billiards; billiard room.

billete [bi·yé·te] *m.* ticket; note; bill, banknote.

billón [bi·yón] *m.* billion.

bimestre [bi·més·tre] *m.* two-month period; bi-monthly salary, rent, etc.; *adj.* bi-monthly; **bimestral** [bi·mes·trál] *adj.* bimonthly.

biografía [bjo·gra·fí·a] *f.* biography.

biología [bjo·lo·xí·a] *f.* biology.

biombo [bjóm·bo] *m.* folding screen.

birlar [bir·lár] *v.* to snatch away; to steal; to kill or knock down with one blow.

birrete [bi·rré·te] *m.* academic cap; mortarboard.

bisabuelo [bi·sa·ßwé·lo] *m.* great-grandfather; **bisabuela** *f.* great-grandmother.

bisagra [bi·sá·gra] *f.* hinge.

bisel [bi·sél] *m.* bevel.

bisiesto [bi·sjés·to] *adj.* leap (*year*).

bismuto [biz·mú·to] *m.* bismuth.

bisojo [bi·só·xo] *adj.* squint-eyed.

bisonte [bi·són·te] *m.* bison; the American buffalo.

bisturí [bis·tu·rí] *m.* bistoury, surgical knife.

bitoque [bi·tó·ke] *m.* barrel plug, stopper; *Am.* faucet; *Col., Cuba, Mex.* injection point (*of a syringe*).

bizarría [bi·sa·rrí·a] *f.* gallantry, bravery; generosity.

bizarro [bi·sá·rro] *adj.* gallant, brave; generous.

bizco [bís·ko] *adj.* cross-eyed.
bizcocho [bis·kó·čo] *m.* hardtack, hard biscuit;
cake; cookie; — **borracho** cake dipped in wine.
biznieto [biz·njé·to] *m.* great-grandson; **biznieta** *f.*
great-granddaughter.
blanco [bláŋ·ko] *adj.* (*color*) white; *m.* white man;
(*nada escrito*) blank, blank sheet; (*objeto de tiro*)
target, goal.
blancura [blaŋ·kú·ra] *f.* whiteness.
blancuzco [blaŋ·kús·ko], **blanquecino**
[blaŋ·ke·sí·no], **blanquizco** [blaŋ·kís·ko] *adj.*
whitish.
blandir [blan·dír] *v.* to brandish, flourish, swing.
blando [blán·do] *adj.* bland, smooth; soft;
  blanducho *adj.* flabby; soft.
blandura [blan·dú·ra] *f.* softness; mildness,
gentleness.
blanquear [blaŋ·ke·ár] *v.* to whiten, bleach; to
whitewash; to show white; to begin to turn
white.
blanqueo [blaŋ·ké·o] *m.* whitening, bleach,
bleaching.
blanquillo [blaŋ·kí·yo] *adj.* whitish; white (*flour*);
  m. Mex., C.A. egg; *Peru, Ch., Andes* white peach.
blasfemar [blas·fe·már] *v.* to blaspheme, curse,
swear.
blasfemia [blas·fé·mja] *f.* blasphemy.
blasón [bla·són] *m.* coat of arms; honor, glory.
blasonar [bla·so·nár] *v.* to boast.
blindaje [blin·dá·xe] *m.* armor, armor plating.
blindar [blin·dár] *v.* to armor.
bloc [blok] *m. Am.* tablet, pad of paper.
blocaje [blo·ká·xe] *m.* action of blocking.
blondo [blón·do] *adj.* blond.
bloque [bló·ke] *m.* block (*of stone, wood, etc.*); *Am.*
tablet, pad of paper; *Cuba, Mex., Ríopl.* political
bloc.
bloquear [blo·ke·ár] *v.* to blockade.
bloqueo [blo·ké·o] *m.* blockade.
blusa [blú·sa] *f.* blouse.
boato [bo·á·to] *m.* pomp, ostentation.
bobada [bo·bá·ḍa] *f.* foolishness, folly.
bobalicón [bo·ba·li·kón] *adj.* foolish, silly; *m.*
simpleton, blockhead, dunce.
bobear [bo·be·ár] *v.* to act like a fool; to fool
around; to gawk, stare foolishly.
bobería [bo·be·rí·a] *f.* foolishness, folly; nonsense;
foolish remark.
bobina [bo·bí·na] *f.* bobbin, reel; electric coil;
  — **distribuidora** feeding reel; — **receptora** rewind
reel (*on a tape recorder*).
bobo [bo·bo] *adj.* simple, foolish, stupid; *m.* booby,
fool, dunce.
boca [bó·ka] *f.* mouth; opening; — **abajo** face
downward; — **arriba** face upward; **a — de jarro**
at close range; **bocaza** *f.* large mouth.
bocacalle [bo·ka·ká·ye] *f.* street intersection.
bocado [bo·ká·ḍo] *m.* mouthful, morsel, bite; bit
(*of a bridle*); **bocadillo** [bo·ka·ḍí·yo], **bocadito**
[bo·ká·ḍí·to] *m.* snack; sandwich; tidbit; *Am.*
piece of candy.
bocanada [bo·ka·ná·ḍa] *f.* mouthful; puff (*of
smoke*).
boceto [bo·sé·to] *m.* sketch; outline; skit.
bocina [bo·sí·na] *f.* horn; trumpet; automobile
horn; speaking tube; megaphone.
bochorno [ba·čór·no] *m.* sultry weather; suffocating
heat; blush, flush; embarrassment.
bochornoso [bo·čor·nó·so] *adj.* sultry;
embarrassing.
boda [bó·ḍa] *f.* marriage, wedding; — **de negros**

a noisy party; **-s de Camacho** lavish feast,
banquet.
bodega [bo·ḍé·ga] *f.* cellar; wine cellar; storeroom;
warehouse; *Cuba, Ven., Col.* grocery store;
bodeguero *m.* keeper of a wine cellar; liquor
dealer; *Cuba, Ven., Col.* grocer.
bodoque [bo·ḍó·ke] *m.* wad; lump; dunce; *Am.*
bump, swelling.
bofe [bó·fe] *m.* lung; *P.R.* snap, easy job; **echar
uno los -s** to throw oneself into a job; to work
hard; *Am.* **ser un** — to be a bore; to be
repulsive.
bofetada [bo·fe·tá·ḍa] *f.* slap; **bofetón** *m.* big slap,
blow, hard sock, wallop.
boga [bó·ga] *f.* vogue, fashion; rowing; *m.*
rower.
bogar[7] [bo·gár] *v.* to row.
bohemio [bo·é·mjo] *adj. & m.* Bohemian.
bohío [bo·í·o] *m. Carib., Ven.* cabin, shack, hut.
boina [bó·i·o] *f.* cap.
bola [bó·la] *f.* (*esfera*) ball, bowling; (*mentira*) fib,
lie; (*betún*) shoe polish; *Am.* disturbance, riot,
false rumor; **no dar pie con** — not to do things
right; not to hit the mark; to make mistakes;
Am. **darle a la** — to hit the mark.
boleada [bo·le·á·ḍa] *f. Ríopl.* lassoing with
boleadoras; *Ríopl.* hunting expedition (*with
boleadoras*); *Mex.* shoeshine; *Col.* affront, insult.
boleadoras [bo·le·a·ḍó·ras] *f. pl. Ríopl.* throwing
weapon made of three united thongs with balls
at the ends.
bolear [bo·le·ár] *v.* to play billiards; to bowl; to
lie, fib; *Am.* to lasso with **boleadoras**; *Am.* to
entangle; *Am.* to polish (*shoes*); *Am.* to dismiss;
Am. to blackball, vote against; *Am.* to flunk;
-se *Am.* to rear, balk (*said of a horse*); *Am.* to
blush, be ashamed.
boleta [bo·lé·ta] *f.* certificate; pass; pay order;
Mex., C.A. ballot; *Ch.* first draft of a deed.
boletín [bo·le·tín] *m.* bulletin.
boleto [bo·lé·to] *m. Am.* ticket; **boletería** *f. Am.*
ticket office.
boliche [bo·lí·če] *m.* bowl (*wooden ball for bowling*);
bowling alley; *Ríopl.* cheap tavern; *Ch.* gambling
joint; *Ríopl.* cheap store or shop, notions store,
variety store.
bolígrafo [bo·lí·gra·fo] *m.* ball point pen.
bolillo *m. Mex., C.A.* hard roll.
bolita [bo·li·ta] *f.* small ball; *Am.* ballot (*small ball
used in voting*); *Col., Ven.* marble; *Am.*
armadillo.
bolo [bó·lo] *m.* one of the ninepins (*used in
bowling*); dunce, stupid fellow; **-s** bowls,
bowling; **jugar a los -s** to bowl.
bolsa [ból·sa] *f.* bag, purse; stock exchange; *Ríopl.*
pocket.
bolsillo [bol·sí·yo] *m.* pocket; pocketbook.
bolsista [bol·sís·ta] *m.* stockbroker; market
operator.
bollo [bó·yo] *m.* bun, muffin; bump, lump; puff
(*in a dress*); tuft (*on upholstery*); *Andes* loaf of
bread; *Am.* a kind of tamale; **-s** *Am.* difficulties,
troubles.
bomba [bóm·ba] *f.* pump; lamp globe; bomb;
  — **atómica** atomic bomb; — **de hidrógeno**
hydrogen bomb; *Carib.* false news; *Am.* stanza
improvised by a dancer; *Ríopl.* firecracker,
skyrocket; *Mex., Col.* satirical remark; *Am.* large
drum; — **para incendios** fire engine; *Am.* **estar
con una** — to be drunk; **bombita** *f.* soap bubble;
Col. shame, embarrassment.

bombachas [bom·bá·čas] *f. pl. Ríopl.* loose-fitting breeches.

bombacho [bom·bá·čo] *adj.* loose-fitting (*trousers or breeches*).

bombardear [bom·bar·đe·ár] *v.* to bomb.

bombardeo [bom·bar·đé·o] *m.* bombardment, bombing; **avión de —** bomber, bombing plane.

bombardero [bom·bar·đé·ro] *m.* bombardier; bomber.

bombear [bom·be·ár] *v.* (*echar bombas*) to bomb; (*alabar*) to praise, extol; *Am.* to pump; *Col.* to fire, dismiss; *Am.* to puff hard on a cigar or cigarette.

bombero [bom·bé·ro] *m.* fireman; pumper.

bombilla [bom·bí·ya] *f.* electric-light bulb; *Am.* kerosene lamp tube; *Am.* small tube for drinking mate.

bombo [bóm·bo] *m.* large drum; bass drum; player on a bass drum; *Mex., Col., Ch.* pomp, ostentation; *Ríopl.* buttocks, rump; **dar —** to praise, extol (*in the press or newspapers*); *Col., Ríopl.* **darse —** to put on airs; *Am.* **irse uno al —** to fail; *adj.* stunned; *Am.* lukewarm; *Am.* slightly rotten; *Am.* stupid, silly, simple; *Cuba* **fruta bomba** papaya (*tropical fruit*).

bombón [bom·bón] *m.* bonbon, candy; **— de altea** marshmallow.

bonachón [bon·na·čón] *adj.* good-natured; naïve, simple.

bonanza [bo·nán·sa] *f.* fair weather; prosperity; rich vein of ore.

bondad [bon·dáđ] *f.* goodness.

bondadoso [bon·da·đó·so] *adj.* good, kind.

boniato [bo·njá·to] *m. Am.* sweet potato.

bonito [bo·ní·to] *adj.* pretty; *m.* striped tunny (*a fish*).

bono [bó·no] *m.* certificate; bond.

boñiga [bo·ñí·ga] *f.* dung, manure.

boqueada [bo·ke·á·đa] *f.* gape, gasp.

boquear [bo·ke·ár] *v.* to open one's mouth; to gape, gasp; to be dying.

boquete [bo·ké·te] *m.* breach, gap, hole, opening.

boquiabierto [bo·kja·bjér·to] *adj.* openmouthed.

boquilla [bo·kí·ya] *f.* (*abertura*) little mouth; small opening; (*de cigarro*) holder; tip; (*de instrumento*) mouthpiece.

borbollón [bor·bo·yón], **borbotón** [bor·bo·tón] *m.* spurt; spurting; big bubble; bubbling up; **a -es** in spurts.

borbotar [bor·bo·tár] *v.* to bubble up; to spurt, gush forth; to boil over.

bordado [bor·đá·đo] *m.* embroidery.

bordadura [bor·đa·đú·ra] *f.* embroidery.

bordar [bor·đár] *v.* to embroider.

borde [bór·đe] *m.* border, edge.

bordear [bor·đe·ár] *v.* to skirt, go along the edge of; *Am.* to trim with a border; *Am.* to make a **bordo** (*small, temporary dam*); **-se** *Ch., Mex., Ven.* to approach, get near.

bordo [bór·đo] *m.* board, side of a ship; tack (*of a ship*); *Mex., Ven.* ridge (*of a furrow*); *Mex.* small dam; **a —** on board.

borla [bór·la] *f.* (*indumentaria*) tassel; doctor's cap; (*título*) doctor's degree; (*cosmético*) powder puff; tuft; **tomar uno la —** to get a doctor's degree.

borlarse [bor·lár·se] *v. Am.* to get a doctor's degree.

boro [bó·ro] *m.* boron.

borrachera [bo·rra·čé·ra] *f.* drunkenness; drunken spree.

borrachín [bo·rra·čín] *m.* toper.

borracho [bo·rrá·čo] *adj.* drunk; *m.* drunkard; **borrachón** [bo·rra·čón] *m.* drunkard, heavy drinker.

borrador [bo·rra·đór] *m.* rough draft; *Am.* rubber eraser.

borrar [bo·rrár] *v.* to blot out; to erase.

borrasca [bo·rrás·ka] *f.* storm, tempest.

borrascoso [bo·rras·kó·so] *adj.* stormy.

borrego [bo·rré·go] *m.* lamb; fool, simpleton; *Mex., C.A.* false news.

borrico [bo·rrí·ko] *m.* donkey, ass; fool; sawhorse.

borrón [bo·rrón] *m.* blotch (*of ink*), blot.

borronear [bo·rro·ne·ár] *v.* to blot, blotch; to scribble; to blur; to make a rough sketch.

boruca [bo·rú·ka] *f.* racket, noise.

boscaje [bos·ká·xe] *m.* grove, thicket, woods; landscape (*picture of natural scenery*).

bosque [bós·ke] *m.* forest, woods; **bosquecillo** *m.* small forest, grove.

bosquejar [bos·ke·xár] *v.* to sketch; to outline.

bosquejo [bos·ké·xo] *m.* sketch, plan, outline, rough draft.

bostezar[9] [bos·te·sár] *v.* to yawn.

bostezo [bos·té·so] *m.* yawn.

bota [bó·ta] *f.* (*calzado*) boot; (*bolsa*) leather wine bag; *adj. Am.* stupid, clumsy; *Mex.* drunk.

botar [bo·tár] *v.* (*echar*) to launch; to fling; to throw away; (*rebotar*) to bounce; *Ven.* to waste, squander; *Am.* to fire, dismiss; **-se** *Am.* to lie down.

botarate [bo·ta·rá·te] *m.* fool; braggart; *Mex., Carib.* spendthrift.

bote [bó·te] *m.* (*jarro*) small jar; (*embarcación*) boat; (*rebote*) bounce; (*golpe*) blow; jump; *Ríopl.* liquor bottle; *Mex., C.A.* jail; **estar de en —** to be crowded, completely filled up.

botella [bo·té·ya] *f.* bottle.

botica [bo·tí·ka] *f.* drugstore.

boticario [bo·ti·ká·rjo] *m.* druggist.

botija [bo·tí·xa] *f.* earthen jug; fat person; *Am.* buried treasure; *Am.* belly; *Col.* **poner a uno como — verde** to dress down, scold, insult a person.

botijo [bo·tí·xo] *m.* earthen jar with spout and handle.

botín [bo·tín] *m.* booty, plunder; high shoe; *Am.* sock.

botiquín [bo·ti·kín] *m.* medicine cabinet; medicine kit; *Am.* liquor store, wine shop.

botón [bo·tón] *m.* bud; button; knob; handle; **-es** bellboy.

bóveda [bó·be·đa] *f.* arched roof; vault, underground cellar; burial place.

boxeador [bok·se·a·đór] *m.* boxer.

boxear [bok·se·ár] *v.* to box, fight with the fists.

boxeo [bok·sé·o] *m.* boxing.

boya [bó·ya] *f.* buoy; float net; *Am.* crease, dent; *Am.* rich mineral vein; *Am.* **estar en la buena —** to be in good humor.

bozal [bo·sál] *m.* (*de animal*) nuzzle; (*cascabel*) bells on a harness; (*novicio*) novice; (*negro*) Negro native of Africa; *Am.* headstall (*of a halter*); *Spain* person (*especially a Negro*) who speaks broken Spanish; *Am.* coarse, crude individual; *adj.* green, inexperienced; wild, untamed; stupid.

bozo [bó·so] *m.* down (*on the upper lip*); mustache; outside part of the mouth; headstall (*of a halter*).

bracear [bra·se·ár] *v.* to swing one's arms; to struggle; to crawl, swim with a crawl.

bracero [bra·sé·ro] *m.* laborer; **de** — arm in arm; **servir de** — **a una señora** to serve as an escort, give a lady one's arm.

bracete [bra·sé·te]: **de** — arm in arm.

bramante [bra·mán·te] *m.* hemp cord, hemp string; Brabant linen; *adj.* roaring, bellowing.

bramar [bra·már] *v.* to bellow, roar, howl; to rage.

bramido [bra·mí·ďo] *m.* roar; howl; bellow.

brasa [brá·sa] *f.* red-hot coal.

brasero [bra·sé·ro] *m.* brazier (*pan for burning coal*), grate; hearth; *Ríopl.* brick cooking stove.

bravata [bra·ḃá·ta] *f.* bravado, boastfulness, defiance.

bravear [bra·ḃe·ár] *v.* to bluster; to bully.

bravío [bra·ḃí·o] *adj.* savage, wild; rustic.

bravo [brá·ḃo] *adj.* (*agresivo*) wild, ferocious, harsh; ill-tempered; (*valiente*) brave; *Carib.*, *C.A.*, *Andes* angry; *Am.* hot, highly seasoned.

bravura [bra·ḃú·ra] *f.* fierceness; courage; bravado, show of boldness.

braza [brá·sa] *f.* fathom; stroke.

brazada [bra·sá·ďa] *f.* armful; movement of the arms (*swimming stroke*); **a una** — at arm's length.

brazalete [bra·sa·lé·te] *m.* bracelet.

brazo [brá·so] *m.* arm; branch; **-s** day laborers; *Ríopl.*, *Cuba* **de** — arm in arm; **luchar a** — **partido** to wrestle; to fight hand to hand.

brea [bré·a] *f.* pitch; tar; canvas.

brecha [bré·ča] *f.* breach, gap.

brega [bré·ga] *f.* fight, scrap.

bregar[7] [bre·gár] *v.* to struggle; to fight.

breña [bré·ña] *f.* rough, craggy ground covered with brambles; bramble; **breñal** *m.* brambles; bush country.

breve [bré·ḃe] *adj.* brief, short; **en** — shortly.

brevedad [bre·ḃe·ďáď] *f.* brevity, shortness.

bribón [bri·ḃón] *adj.* idle, indolent; *m.* rascal, rogue; **bribonazo** *m.* scoundrel, cheat.

brida [brí·ďa] *f.* bridle; rein.

brigada [bri·gá·ďa] *f.* brigade.

brillante [bri·yán·te] *adj.* brilliant, bright; *m.* diamond.

brillantez [bri·yan·tés] *f.* brilliance, dazzle.

brillar [bri·yár] *v.* to shine.

brillo [brí·yo] *m.* luster, sparkle, shine.

brincar[6] [brin·kár] *v.* to hop, skip, jump, bounce.

brinco [brín·ko] *m.* hop, skip, bounce, leap.

brindar [brin·dár] *v.* to toast, drink to the health of; to offer.

brindis [brín·dis] *m.* toast (*to a person's health*).

brío [brí·o] *m.* vigor, liveliness; valor, courage.

brioso [brjó·so] *adj.* lively; brave.

brisa [brí·sa] *f.* breeze.

británico [bri·tá·ni·ko] *adj.* British.

brizna [bríz·na] *f.* particle, chip, fragment; blade of grass.

brocal [bro·kál] *m.* curb, curbstone (*of a well*).

brocha [bró·ča] *f.* painter's brush; loaded dice; **cuadro de** — **gorda** badly done painting; **pintor de** — **gorda** house painter **brochada** *f.* stroke of the brush, brush stroke; **brochazo** *m.* blow with a brush; brush stroke.

broche [bró·če] *m.* brooch; clasp, clip, fastener; hook and eye.

broma [bró·ma] *f.* jest, joke; fun, merriment; *Am.* disappointment, irritation; **de** — in jest; **fuera de** — all joking aside.

bromear [bro·me·ár] *v.* to joke, jest.

bronca [brón·ka] *f.* quarrel, dispute, wrangle;

armar una — to cause a disturbance, raise a rumpus.

bronce [brón·se] *m.* bronze.

bronceado [bron·se·áďo] *adj.* bronzed; bronze-colored; *m.* bronze finish.

bronco [brón·ko] *adj.* hoarse; raspy, harsh; coarse, rough; uncouth; wild, untamed (*horse*).

bronquio [brón·kjo] *m.* bronchus, bronchial tube.

broquel [bro·kél] *m.* buckler, shield (*worn on the arm*).

brotar [bro·tár] *v.* to shoot forth; to bud; to break out (*on the skin*); to gush, flow; to spring forth.

broza [bró·sa] *f.* brushwood, underbush; rubbish, refuse, trash; coarse, hard brush.

bruces [brú·ses]: **de** — face downward.

bruja [brú·xa] *f.* witch; hag; owl; *adj. Mex.* broke, poor; **brujo** *m.* sorcerer, magician, wizard.

brújula [brú·xu·la] *f.* (*compás*) compass; magnetic needle; (*mira*) peephole; gunsight.

bruma [brú·ma] *f.* mist, fog; **brumoso** *adj.* foggy, misty, hazy.

bruñir[19] [bru·ñír] *v. irr.* to burnish, polish; to put on make-up.

brusco [brús·ko] *adj.* blunt, rude, abrupt.

brutal [bru·tál] *adj.* brutal, beastly, savage.

brutalidad [bru·ta·li·ďáď] *f.* brutality.

bruto [brú·to] *adj.* (*tonto*) stupid, brutal; (*burdo*) coarse, rough; **peso** — gross weight; **diamante en** — diamond in the rough, unpolished diamond; *m.* brute, beast.

bucal [bu·kál] *adj.* oral, pertaining to the mouth.

bucear [bu·se·ár] *v.* to dive; to dive into, plunge into; to explore thoroughly a subject.

bucle [bú·kle] *m.* curl, ringlet.

buche [bú·če] *m.* crop (*of a bird*); mouthful (*of water*); wrinkle, bag (*in clothes*); *Ríopl. Mex.*, *Ven.* goiter.

budín *m.* pudding.

buen(o) [bwé·n(o)] *adj.* good; kind; useful; well, in good health; **de buenas a primeras** all of a sudden, unexpectedly, on the spur of the moment; **por la(s) buena(s) o por la(s) mala(s)** willingly or unwillingly, by hook or crook.

buey [bwej] *m.* ox.

búfalo [bú·fa·lo] *m.* buffalo.

bufanda [bu·fán·da] *f.* muffler, scarf.

bufar [bu·fár] *v.* to snort; to puff with anger; **-se** *Mex.* to swell, bulge (*as a wall*).

bufete [bu·fé·te] *m.* desk, writing table; lawyer's office.

bufido [bu·fí·ďo] *m.* snort.

bufón [bu·fón] *m.* buffoon, jester, clown; *adj.* comical, funny; **bufonada** [bu·fo·ná·ďa] *f.* wisecrack; jest.

bufonear [bu·fo·ne·ár] *v.* to clown; to jest.

buhardilla [bu·ar·ďi·ya], [bwar·ďi·ya] *f.* garret, attic; skylight.

buho [bú·o] *m.* owl.

buhonero [bu·o·né·ro] *m.* peddler.

buitre [bwí·tre] *m.* vulture.

buje [bú·xe] *m.* bushing; axle box.

bujía [bu·xí·a] *f.* candle; candle power; candlestick; spark plug.

bula [bú·la] *f.* bull (*papal document*); papal seal.

buldózer [bul·dó·ser] *m.* bulldozer.

bulevar [bul·le·ḃár] *m.* boulevard.

bulto [búl·to] *m.* (*cuerpo*) body, bundle, shadow, lump, swelling; (*tamaño*) bulk, volume; **a** — haphazardly, by guess; **escurrir el** — to dodge; **imagen de** — statue, sculpture; **una verdad de** — an evident truth.

bulla [bú·ya] *f.* shouting, uproar; noisy crowd.
bullicio [bu·yí·sjo] *m.* noise, uproar.
bullicioso [bu·yi·sjó·so] *adj.* boisterous, noisy; gay, lively; turbulent, stormy.
bullir[20] [bu·yír] *v. irr.* to boil; to buzz about; to bustle; to stir, move; *Am.* to deride.
buñuelo [bu·ñwé·lo] *m.* fritter; botch, poor piece of work.
buque [bú·ke] *m.* ship, boat.
burbuja [bur·bú·xa] *f.* bubble.
burdo [búr·do] *adj.* coarse.
burgués [bur·gés] *adj.* bourgeois, middle-class.
burla [búr·la] *f.* jest, mockery; **de** — in jest.
burlador [bur·la·dór] *m.* practical joker; jester; scoffer; seducer.
burlar [bur·lár] *v.* to mock, ridicule, deceive; **-se de** to scoff at; to make fun of
burlón [bur·lón] *m.* jester, teaser.
burocracia [bu·ro·krá·sja] *f.* bureaucracy.
burócrata [bu·ró·kra·ta] *m.* bureaucrat.
burro [bú·rro] *m.* ass, donkey; *Mex., Cuba, Ríopl.* stepladder; *adj.* stupid; **burrito** *m.* small donkey; *Am.* saddle rack.
busca [bús·ka] *f.* search; hunting party; *Am.* **-s** profit on the side; graft.
buscar[6] [bus·kár] *v.* to seek, search, look for; *Andes* to provoke.
búsqueda [bús·ke·da] *f.* search.
busto [bús·to] *m.* bust (*upper part of body*).
butaca [bu·tá·ka] *f.* armchair; orchestra seat; **butacón** [bu·ta·kón] *m.* large armchair.
buzo [bú·so] *m.* diver; deep-sea or "skin" diver.
buzón [bu·són] *m.* mailbox; letter drop.

C·c **cabal** [ka·bál] *adj.* complete, entire; exact; **estar uno en sus -es** to be in one's right mind.
cabalgar[7] [ka·bal·gár] *v.* to ride, mount (*a horse*); to ride horseback.
caballa [ka·bá·ya] *f.* horse mackerel.
caballada [ka·ba·yá·da] *f.* herd of horses; *Am.* nonsense, stupidity, blunder.
caballejo [ka·ba·yè·xo] *m.* nag; poor horse.
caballeresco [ka·ba·ye·rés·ko] *adj.* gentlemanly; knightly; chivalrous, gallant.
caballería [ka·ba·ye·rí·a] *f.* cavalry; horsemanship; mount, horse; knighthood; chivalry.
caballeriza [ka·ba·ye·rí·sa] *f.* stable; horses of a stable.
caballerizo [ka·ba·ye·rí·so] *m.* groom, stableman.
caballero [ka·ba·yé·ro] *m.* gentleman; knight, horseman; *adj.* gentlemanly.
caballerosidad [ka·be·ye·ro·si·dád] *f.* chivalry, gentlemanly conduct.
caballeroso [ka·ba·ye·ró·so] *adj.* chivalrous, gentlemanly.
caballete [ka·ba·yé·te] *m.* (*de casa*) ridge of a roof; (*madero*) sawhorse; (*de la cara*) bridge of the nose.
caballo [ka·bá·yo] *m.* horse; knight (*in chess*); *Am.* stupid or brutal person; **a** — on horseback; **caballuco** [ka·ba·yú·ko] *m.* nag.
cabaña [ka·bá·ña] *f.* hut, cabin; *Am.* cattle ranch.
cabecear [ka·be·se·ár] *v.* to nod; to shake the head; to pitch (*as a boat*); *Am.* to begin to rise or fall (*said of a river*).
cabeceo [ka·be·sé·o] *m.* nodding; pitching (*of a boat*).

cabecera [ka·be·sé·ra] *f.* head (*of bed or table*); seat, chief city (*of a district*).
cabecilla [ka·be·si·ya] *f.* small head; *m.* ringleader.
cabellera [ka·be·yé·ra] *f.* head of hair, long hair; wig; tail of a comet.
cabello [ka·bé·yo] *m.* hair; **traer algo por los -s** to bring in a far-fetched fact or quotation; **-s de ángel** cotton candy.
cabelludo [ka·be·yú·do] *adj.* hairy; **cuero** — scalp.
caber[23] [ka·bér] *v. irr.* to fit into, go into; to have enough room for; to befall; **no cabe duda** there is no doubt; **no cabe más** there is no room for more; **no — uno en sí** to be puffed up with pride; **no cabe en lo posible** it is absolutely impossible.
cabestro [ka·bés·tro] *m.* halter; leading ox; *Carib., Mex.* rope, cord; *Am.* advance payment; **cabestrillo** [ka·bes·trí·yo] *m.* sling (*for an arm*).
cabeza [ka·bé·sa] *f.* (*parte superior*) head; upper part; (*director*) chief, leader; capital (*of a district*); *Carib.* source (*of a river*); — **de playa** beachhead; — **de puente** bridgehead; — **sonora** recording head.
cabezada [ka·be·sá·da] *f.* butt (*with the head*); bump on the head; nod; shake of the head; pitching (*of a ship*); headgear (*of a harness*).
cabezazo [ka·be·sá·so] *m.* butt (with the head); bump on the head.
cabezudo [ka·be·súdo] *adj.* big-headed; hard-headed, pig-headed, stubborn, headstrong.
cabezón [ka·be·són] *adj.* big-headed; pig-headed, stubborn; *Ch.* strong (*liquor*); *m.* large head; cavesson (*iron noseband used in breaking a horse*); *Col.* rapids or whirlpool in a river.
cabida [ka·bí·da] *f.* space, room, capacity; **tener — con alguien** to have influence with someone.
cabildo [ka·bíl·do] *m.* cathedral chapter; municipal council; council room; town hall.
cabina [ka·bí·na] *f.* cabin (*of an airplane*).
cabizbajo [ka·biz·bá·xo] *adj.* crestfallen, downcast; pensive.
cable [ká·ble] *m.* cable.
cablegrafiar[17] [ka·ble·gra·fjár] *v.* to cable.
cablegrama [ka·ble·grá·ma] *m.* cablegram.
cabo [ká·bo] *m.* (*cosa*) end, tip, handle; piece of rope; (*geográfico*) cape, headland; (*persona*) foreman, corporal; **al** — finally; **al fin y al** — anyway, in the long run; **de** — **a rabo** from beginning to end; **estar al** — **de** to be well informed about; **llevar a** — to carry out, finish.
cabotaje [ka·bo·tá·xe] *m.* coastal trade or traffic.
cabra [ká·bra] *f.* goat; *Col.* fraud, trick; *Am.* loaded dice; *Am.* light two-wheeled carriage; **cabrillas** [ka·brí·yas] *f. pl.* whitecaps (*small waves with white crests*); Pleiades (*constellation*); game of skipping stones on the water.
cabrero [ka·bré·ro] *m.* goatherd.
cabrío [ka·brí·o] *adj.* goatish; **macho** — he-goat; *m.* herd of goats.
cabriola [ka·brjó·la] *f.* caper, leap, hop, skip; somersault; **hacer -s** to cut capers; to prance.
cabriolar [ka·brijo·lár] *v.* to prance; to caper; to romp, frolic, frisk.
cabrito [ka·brí·to] *m.* kid; **cabritilla** [ka·bri·tí·ya] *f.* kid, kidskin.
cabrón [ka·brón] *m.* he-goat; cuckold (*man whose wife is unfaithful*).
caca [ká·ka] *f.* excrement (popular children's expression).

cacahuate [ka·ka·wá·te] *m. Mex., C.A.* peanut; *Spain* **cacahuete** [ka·ka·wé·te], **cacahuey** ka·ka·wéj].

cacao [ka·ká·o] *m.* cocoa.

cacarear [ka·ka·re·ár] *v.* to cackle; to boast; *Am.* to run away from a fight.

cacareo [ka·ka·ré·o] *m.* cackle.

cacería [ka·se·rí·a] *f.* hunt, hunting.

cacerola [ka·se·ró·la] *f.* saucepan.

cacique [ka·sí·ke] *m.* chief; political boss; *Mex.* tyrant; *Ch., Ven.* one who leads an easy life.

caciquismo [ka·si·kíz·mo] *m.* political bossism (*rule by political bosses*).

cacofonía [ka·ko·fo·ní·a] *f.* cacophony.

cacto [kák·to] *m.* cactus.

cacumen [ka·kú·men] *m.* acumen, keen insight.

cacha [ká·ča] *f.* handle (*of a knife or pistol*); *Am.* the horns of a bull; *C.A.* **hacer la** — to complete a task, to get.

cacharro [ka·čá·rro] *m.* earthen pot or vase; broken piece of a pot; crude utensil; *Am.* cheap trinket.

cachaza [ka·čá·sa] *f.* slowness; calm; rum.

cachazudo [ka·ča·sú·đo] *adj.* slow, easy going.

cachetada [ka·če·tá·đa] *f. Am.* slap on the face.

cachete [ka·čé·te] *m.* cheek; slap on the cheek.

cachimbo [ka·čím·bo] *m. Am.* pipe (*for smoking*); *Cuba* small sugar mill; also **cachimba** [ka·čím·ba].

cachivache [ka·či·bá·če] *m.* piece of junk; worthless fellow; *Mex., Carib., Ven.* trinket.

cacho [ká·čo] *m. Am.* horn (of an animal); *adj.* bent, crooked.

cachorro [ka·čó·rro] *m.* cub; small pistol; *Am.* rude, ill-bred person.

cachucha [ka·čú·ča] *f.* cap; rowboat; popular Andalusian dance, song and music; *Am.* slap.

cada [ká·đa] *adj.* each, every; — **uno** each one; — **y cuando que** whenever; *Am.* **a** — **nada** every second.

cadalso [ka·đal·so] *m.* gallows; scaffold, platform.

cadáver [ka·đá·ber] *m.* corpse; **cadavérico** [ka·đa·bé·ri·ko] *adj.* deadly, ghastly, pale, like a corpse.

cadena [ka·đé·na] *f.* chain.

cadencia [ka·đen·sja] *f.* cadence.

cadencioso [ka·đen·sjó·so] *adj.* rhythmical.

cadera [ka·đé·ra] *f.* hip.

cadete [ka·đé·te] *m.* cadet.

cadmio [kađ·mjo] *m.* cadmium.

caducar[6] [ka·đu·kár] *v.* to dote, be in one's dotage; to lapse, expire; to become extinct, fall into disuse.

caduco [ka·đú·ko] *adj.* decrepit, very old, feeble; perishable.

caer[24] [ka·ér] *v. irr.* to fall; to fall down; to fall off; **-se** to fall down, tumble; — **a** to face, overlook; — **bien** to fit, be becoming; — **en cama** to fall ill; — **en la cuenta** to catch on, get the point; — **en gracia** to please; **al** — **de la noche** at nightfall; **dejar** — to drop.

café [ka·fé] *m.* coffee, café; *Am.* annoyance, bad time.

cafeína [ka·fe·í·na] *f.* caffein.

cafetal [ka·fe·tál] *m.* coffee plantation.

cafetera [ka·fe·té·ra] *f.* coffeepot; woman café owner, coffee vendor or merchant; coffee-bean picker.

cafetería [ka·fe·te·rí·a] *f.* café, bar, lunchroom.

cafetero [ka·fe·té·ro] *adj.* pertaining to coffee; *m.*

coffee grower; coffee merchant; owner of a café or coffee-house; *Am.* coffee drinker.

cafeto [ka·fé·to] *m.* coffee bush.

cagar[7] [ka·gár] *v. irr.* to defecate (*popular term*).

caída [ka·í·đa] *f.* fall, drop; descent; **a la** — **del sol** (*or* **de la tarde**) at sunset.

caimán [kaj·mán] *m.* cayman, alligator.

caja [ká·xa] *f.* case, box; — **de ahorros** savings bank; — **de cambios** transmission (*automobile*); — **de píldora** pillbox; — **fuerte** safe; **echar a uno con -s destempladas** to give someone the gate.

cajero [ka·xé·ro] *m.* cashier; box maker.

cajetilla [ka·xe·tí·ya] *f.* small box; package of cigarettes.

cajón [ka·xón] *m.* large box, chest; drawer; vendor's booth or stand; *Ch., Mex.* narrow conyon; — **de muerto** coffin; *Mex.* — **de ropa** dry-goods and clothing store.

cal [kal] *f.* lime (*mineral*).

calabaza [ka·la·ba·sa] *f.* pumpkin, squash; gourd; an ignorant person; **dar -s** to jilt, turn down (*a suitor*); to flunk; fail.

calabozo [ka·la·bó·so] *m.* dungeon; prison cell.

calado [ka·lá·đo] *m.* drawn work; openwork (*in wood, metal linen, etc.*), fretwork; draft (*of a ship*).

calamar [ka·la·már] *m.* squid, cuttlefish.

calambre [ka·lám·bre] *m.* cramp.

calamidad [ka·la·mi·đáđ] *f.* calamity, misfortune.

calandria [ka·lan·drja] *f.* lark, skylark.

calar [ka·lár] *v.* (*penetrar*) to pierce, penetrate; to soak through; to make openwork (*in cloth, metal*); (*probar*) to probe, search into; **-se el sombrero** to put on one's hat; to pull down one's hat.

calavera [ka·la·bé·ra] *f.* skull; *m.* madcap, rounder, reckless fellow; *Mex.* taillight.

calcar[6] [kal·kár] *v.* to trace; to copy, imitate.

calceta [kal·sé·ta] *f.* hose, stocking; **hacer** — to knit; **calcetería** [kal·se·te·rí·a] *f.* hosiery shop; hosiery (*business of making hose*).

calcetín [kal·se·tín] *m.* sock.

calcinar [kal·si·nár] *v.* to burn, char, heat.

calcio [kál·sjo] *m.* calcium.

calco [kál·ko] *m.* tracing, traced copy; exact copy; imitation.

calculadora [kal·ku·la·đó·ra] *f.* calculator (*machine for performing mathematical operations*); — **electrónica** computer.

calcular [kal·ku·lár] *v.* to calculate, figure, estimate.

cálculo [kál·ku·lo] *m.* calculation, estimate; calculus; gravel (*in the gall bladder, kidney, etc.*).

caldear [kal·de·ár] *v.* to heat; to weld; **-se** *Am.* to become overheated, excited; *Am.* to get "lit up", get drunk.

caldera [kal·dé·ra] *f.* boiler; caldron, kettle; **calderilla** [kal·de·rí·ya] *f.* copper coin.

caldo [kál·do] *m.* broth; gravy.

calefacción [ka·le·fak·sjón] *f.* heat, heating.

calendario [ka·len·dá·rjo] *m.* calendar; almanac.

caléndula [ka·lén·du·la] *f.* marigold.

calentador [ka·len·ta·đór] *m.* heater.

calentar[1] [ka·len·tár] *v. irr.* to warm, heat; to spank; *Am.* to annoy, bother; **-se** to warm oneself; to become heated, excited; to be in heat; *Am.* to become angry.

calentura [ka·len·tú·ra] *f.* fever; *Col.* fit of temper; — **de pollo** feigned illness; **calenturón** [ka·len·tu·rón] *m.* high fever.

calenturiento [ka·len·tu·rjén·to] *adj.* feverish; *Ch.* tubercular.

caletre [ka·lé·tre] *m.* judgment, acumen, keen insight.

calibrar [ka·li·b́rár] *v.* to gauge, measure; to measure the caliber of.

calibre [ka·li·b́re] *m.* caliber; bore, gauge (*of a gun*); diameter (*of a pipe, tube, wire*).

calicanto [ka·li·kán·to] *m.* stone masonry.

calicó [ka·li·kó] *m.* calico, cotton cloth.

calidad [ka·li·d́á́d́] *f.* quality.

cálido [ká·li·d́o] *adj.* warm, hot.

caliente [ka·lién·te] *adj.* warm, hot; heated; fiery; *Am.* angry; *Col.* bold brave; *m. Am.* brandy in hot water; **calientito** *adj.* nice and warm.

calificación [ka·li·fi·sjón] *f.* qualification; grade, mark (*in a course or examination*); judgment.

calificar[6] [ka·li·fi·kár] *v.* to qualify; to rate, consider, judge; to grade; *Am.* to compute (*election returns*); **-se** *Ch.* to qualify or register (*as a voter*).

caligrafía [ka·li·gra·fí·a] *f.* penmanship.

calina [ka·lí·na] *f.* haze, mist.

cáliz [ká·lis] *m.* chalice, communion cup; cup, goblet; calyx (*of a flower*).

calma [kál·ma] *f.* calm, quiet.

calmante [kal·mán·te] *adj.* soothing; *m.* sedative.

calmar [kal·már] *v.* to calm, quiet, soothe.

calmo [kál·mo] *adj.* calm, quiet.

calmoso [kal·mó·so] *adj.* calm; soothing; phlegmatic, slow.

caló [ka·ló] *m.* underworld slang.

calor [ka·lór] *m.* heat, warmth; ardor.

caloría [ka·lo·rí·a] *f.* calorie.

calorífero [ka·lo·rí·fe·ro] *m.* heater, radiator; furnace.

calosfrío [ka·los·frí·o], **calofrío** [ka·lo·frí·o] *m.* chill.

calumnia [ka·lúm·nja] *f.* slander.

calumniar [ka·lum·njár] *v.* to slander.

caluroso [ka·lu·ró·so] *adj.* (*literal*) hot, warm; (*figurado*) heated, excited; cordial, enthusiastic.

calva [kál·b́a] *f.* bald head; bald spot; barren spot.

calvario [kal·b́á·rjo] *m.* Calvary, place of the Cross; suffering, tribulation.

calvo [kál·b́o] *adj.* bald; barren.

calza [kál·sa] *f.* wedge; shoehorn; *Col., Ven.* gold inlay, tooth filling; **-s** breeches.

calzada [kal·sá·d́a] *f.* paved road; highway; *Mex., Carib.* wide avenue.

calzado [kal·sá·d́o] *m.* footwear.

calzador [kal·sa·d́ór] *m.* shoehorn.

calzar[9] [kal·sár] *v.* to put on (*shoes, gloves, spurs*); to put a wedge under a wheel; *Am.* to fill (*a tooth*).

calzón [kal·són] *m.* (*or* **calzones** [kal·só·nes]) breeches, short trousers; *Mex., Ven.* drawers; *Mex.* white cotton trousers; **calzoncillos** [kal·son·sí·yos] *m. pl.* drawers, men's shorts; **calzoneras** [kal·so·né·ras] *f. pl. Mex.* trousers open down the sides.

callado [ka·yá·d́o] *adj.* silent, quiet.

callar [ka·yár] *v.* to be silent; to hush; **-se** to be or keep silent.

calle [ká·ye] *f.* street.

calleja [ka·yé·xa] *f.* small street, alley, lane; **callejuela** [ka·ye·xwé·la] *f.* small, narrow street; lane.

callejear [ka·ye·xe·ár] *v.* to walk the streets, ramble.

callejero [ka·ye·xé·ro] *m.* street-rambler, street-stroller; street-loiterer; *adj.* fond of walking the streets; rambling.

callejón [ka·ye·xón] *m.* alley; lane; narrow pass; **— sin salida** blind alley.

callo [ká·yo] *m.* callus, corn; *Spain* **-s** tripe (*food*).

calloso [ka·yó·so] *adj.* callous, hard.

cama [ká·ma] *f.* bed, couch, cot; litter **caer en —** to fall ill; **guardar —** to be confined to bed; *Am.* **tenderle uno la — a otro** to help one in his love affairs; to set a trap for someone; **camastro** [ka·más·tro] *m.* poor, uncomfortable bed.

camada [ka·má·d́a] *f.* litter; brood.

camaleón [ka·ma·le·ón] *m.* chameleon.

cámara [ká·ma·ra] *f.* chamber, hall, parlor; house (*of a legislative body*); cabin, stateroom; chamber (*of a gun*); **— de aire** inner tube; **— fotográfica** camera.

camarada [ka·ma·rá·d́a] *m.* comrade; **camaradería** [ka·ma·ra·d́e·rí·a] *f.* comradeship, companionship.

camarera [ka·ma·ré·ra] *f.* waitress; chambermaid; stewardess.

camarero [ka·ma·ré·ro] *m.* waiter; chamberlain; steward; valet.

camarilla [ka·ma·rí·ya] *f.* political lobby; small group of politicians, "kitchen cabinet", group of unofficial advisers; small room.

camarón [ka·ma·rón] *m.* shrimp.

camarote [ka·ma·ró·te] *m.* cabin, stateroom.

cambalache [kam·ba·lá·če] *m.* swap, barter, exchange.

cambalachear [kam·ba·la·če·ár] *v.* to swap, barter, exchange.

cambiador [kam·bja·d́ór] *m.* barterer; money changer; *Am.* switchman.

cambiante [kam·bján·te] *adj.* changing; exchanging; **-s** *m. pl.* iridescent colors.

cambiar [kam·bjár] *v.* to change; to exchange; to shift; **— de marcha** to shift gears.

cambiavía [kam·bja·b́í·a] *m. Carib., Mex., Andes* railway switchman. *See* **guardagujas** *and* **cambiador.**

cambio [kám·bjo] *m.* change; exchange; railway switch; **libre — free** trade; **en —** on the other hand; in exchange.

cambista [kam·bís·ta] *m.* exchange broker, banker; *Am.* railway switchman.

camello [ka·mé·yo] *m.* camel.

camilla [ka·mí·ya] *f.* stretcher; cot; **camillero** [ka·mi·yé·ro] *m.* stretcher bearer.

caminante [ka·mi·nán·te] *m. & f.* walker, traveler.

caminar [ka·mi·nár] *v.* to travel; to walk; *Am.* to progress, prosper.

caminata [ka·mi·ná·ta] *f.* long walk; hike; jaunt.

camino [ka·mí·no] *m.* road; course; *Ríopl.* table runner; *Am.* hall runner; **— de hierro** railroad; **— real** highway; **de —** on the way.

camión [ka·mjón] *m.* truck; wagon; *Mex.* bus; **camionero** [ka·mjo·né·ro] *m.* truck driver; **camioneta** [ka·mjo·né·ta] *f.* small truck; station wagon; *C.A.* bus.

camisa [ka·mí·sa] *f.* shirt; **— de fuerza** straitjacket; **meterse en — de once varas** to attempt more than one can manage, bite off more than one can chew; **camiseta** [ka·mi·sé·ta] *f.* undershirt.

camisón [ka·mi·són] *m.* long shirt; *Am.* nightgown; *Am.* gown, dress.

camote [ka·mó·te] *m. Am.* a kind of sweet potato.

campamento [kam·pa·mén·to] *m.* encampment; camp.

campana [kam·pá·na] *f.* bell; *Ríopl., Andes* spy, lookout (*for thieves*); **campanada**

[kam·pa·ná·ɗa] *f.* stroke of a bell; *Am.* **por — de vacante** once in a blue moon, very seldom.
campanario [kam·pa·ná·rjo] *m.* bell tower.
campanilla [kam·pa·ní·ya] *f.* small bell; bubble; uvula; tassel; bell-flower.
campanillazo [kam·pa·ni·yá·so] *m.* loud ring of a bell.
campanilleo [kam·pa·ni·yé·o] *m.* ringing; tinkling.
campaña [kam·pá·ña] *f.* level, open country; campaign; period of active service.
campear [kam·pe·ár] *v.* to pasture; to grow green (*said of the fields*); to excel; to be prominent, stand out; to be in the field; *Ríopl.* to search the plains for lost cattle; *Col., Ven.* to act the bully.
campechano [kam·pe·čá·no] *adj.* frank, open.
campéon [kam·pe·ón] *m.* champion; defender.
campeonato [kam·pe·o·ná·to] *m.* championship.
campero [kam·pé·ro] *adj.* out in the open; related to the country.
campesino [kam·pe·si·no] *adj.* rural, rustic; *m.* peasant, countryman; farmer.
campestre [kam·pés·tre] *adj.* rural, rustic.
campiña [kam·pí·ña] *f.* large field; open country.
campo [kám·po] *m.* country; field; camp; **a — raso** in the open; **a — traviesa** (*or* **travieso**) cross-country.
camposanto [kam·po·sán·to] *m.* churchyard, cemetery.
camuesa [ka·mwé·sa] *f.* pippin (*a variety of apple*).
camuflaje [ka·mu·flá·xe] *m.* camouflage.
can [kan] *m.* dog; trigger (*of a gun*).
cana [ká·na] *f.* white hair, grey hair; *Carib.* a kind of palm; **echar una — al aire** to go out for a good time; to go out on a fling.
canadiense [ka·na·ɗjén·se] *adj., m. & f.* Canadian.
canal [ka·nál] *m.* canal, channel; *f.* eaves trough.
canalla [ka·ná·ya] *f.* rabble, mob; *m.* mean fellow.
canana [ka·ná·na] *f.* cartridge belt; **-s** *Col., Ven.* handcuffs.
canapé [ka·na·pé] *m.* couch, lounge, sofa; settee.
canario [ka·ná·rjo] *m.* canary; native of the Canary Islands; *interj.* great Scott!
canasta [ka·nás·ta] *f.* basket; crate.
cancelación [kan·se·la·sjón] *f.* cancellation.
cancelar [kan·se·lár] *v.* to cancel.
canciller [kan·si·yór] *m.* chancellor.
canción [kan·sjón] *f.* song; a kind of lyric poem; **volver a la misma —** to repeat, harp on the same thing.
cancha [kán·ča] *f.* court (*for tennis, etc.*); sports ground or field; cockpit, enclosure for cockfights; *Peru* roasted corn or beans; *Am.* ¡**abran —**! gangway!; make room!
candado [kan·dá·ɗo] *m.* padlock; *Col.* goatee.
candela [kan·dé·la] *f.* candle; fire, forest fire; light.
candelabro [kan·de·lá·βro] *m.* candelabrum.
candelero [kan·de·lé·ro] *m.* candlestick.
candente [kan·dén·te] *adj.* incandescent, white-hot, red-hot.
candidato [kan·di·ɗá·to] *m.* candidate.
candidatura [kan·di·ɗa·tú·ra] *f.* candidacy.
candidez [kan·di·ɗés] *f.* candor, simplicity.
cándido [kán·di·ɗo] *adj.* candid, simple, innocent; white.
candil [kan·díl] *m.* lamp; *Ríopl., Mex.* chandelier; **candileja** [kan·di·lé·xa] *f.* small oil lamp; oil receptacle (*of a lamp*); **-s** footlights (*of a stage*).
candor [kan·dór] *m.* candor, simplicity, innocence; frankness, sincerity.
canela [ka·né·la] *f.* cinnamon; an exquisite thing.

caney [ka·nej] *m. Caribe* hut; crude structure (*often without walls*).
cangrejo [kan·gré·xo] *m.* crab.
canguro [kan·gú·ro] *m.* kangaroo.
caníbal [ka·ní·βal] *m.* cannibal.
canica [ka·ní·ka] *f.* marble (*small glass or marble ball*).
canilla [ka·ní·ya] *f.* long bone (*of the arm or leg*); cock (*of a barrel*), faucet; spool (*for a sewing machine*); *C.A.* slender leg; *Ch., Col., Ríopl.* calf (*of the leg*); *Mex., Ven.* **tener — to** have physical strength; **canillita** [ka·ni·yí·ta] *m. Ríopl., Ch., C.A., Andes* newspaper boy.
canino [ka·ní·no] *adj.* canine; **tener un hambre canina** to be ravenous; to be hungry as a dog.
canje [kán·xe] *m.* interchange, exchange.
canjear [kaŋ·xe·ár] *v.* to exchange, interchange.
cano [ká·no] *adj.* grey-headed, grey-haired.
canoa [ka·nó·a] *f.* canoe.
canon [ká·non] *m.* canon; precept, rule, principle.
canónigo [ka·nó·ni·ɡo] *m.* canon (*churchman*).
canonizar[9] [ka·no·ni·sár] *v.* to canonize, saint.
canoso [ka·nó·so] *adj.* grey, grey-haired.
cansado [kan·sá·ɗo] *adj.* tired; tiresome, boring.
cansancio [kan·sán·sjo] *m.* fatigue, weariness.
cansar [kan·sár] *v.* to tire, fatigue; **-se** to get tired.
cantar [kan·tár] *v.* to sing; to squeal, confess; *Am.* **— alto** to ask a high price; **— claro** (*or* **-las claras**) to speak with brutal frankness; *m.* song, epic poem.
cántaro [kán·ta·ro] *m.* pitcher, jug.
cantatriz [kan·ta·trís] *f.* singer.
cantera [kan·té·ra] *f.* quarry; *Ríopl., Mex., Carib.* stone block.
cántico [kán·ti·ko] *m.* canticle, religious song.
cantidad [kan·ti·ɗáɗ] *f.* quantity.
cantilena [kan·ti·lé·na] *f.* song, ballad; monotonous repetition.
cantimplora [kan·tim·pló·ra] *f.* canteen; metal vessel for cooling water; *Col.* flask for carrying gunpowder.
cantina [kan·tí·na] *f.* mess hall; wine cellar; wine shop; canteen; *Carib., Mex., Ríopl.* barroom, tavern; *Col.* saddlebag.
cantinela [kan·ti·né·la] = **cantilena**.
cantinero [kan·ti·né·ro] *m.* bartender; tavern keeper.
canto [kán·to] *m.* song; singing; canto (*division of a long poem*); stone; edge; *Col.* lap; *Am.* piece.
cantón [kan·tón] *m.* canton, region; corner; *Am.* cotton cloth.
cantor [kan·tór] *m.* singer; song bird.
canturrear [kan·tu·rre·ár], **canturriar** [kan·tu·rrjár] *v.* to hum, sing softly.
canturreo [kan·tu·rré·o] *m.* hum, humming.
caña [ká·ña] *f.* cane, reed; tall, thin glass; stem; *Ríopl., Col., Ven.* sugar-cane brandy; *Am.* a kind of dance; *Am.* bluff, boast.
cañada [ka·ñá·ɗa] *f.* narrow canyon, dale, dell, gully, ravine; *Am.* brook.
cáñamo [ká·ña·mo] *m.* hemp; hemp cloth; *Am.* hemp cord, rope; **cañamazo** [ka·ña·má·so] *m.* canvas.
cañaveral [ka·ña·βe·rál] *m.* cane field; reed patch; sugar-cane plantation.
cañería [ka·ñe·rí·a] *f.* conduit, pipe line; tubing; piping; gas or water main.
caño [ká·ño] *m.* pipe, tube; spout; sewer; narrow channel; *Ven.* branch of a river, stream.
cañón [ka·ñón] *m.* (*arma*) cannon, gun; barrel (*of a gun*); (*topográfico*) ravine, gorge, canyon;

(*tubo*) pipe, tube; (*figurado*) beard stubble;
pinfeather; quill (*of a feather*); chimney shaft;
cañonazo [ka·ño·ná·so] *m.* cannon shot.
cañonear [ka·ño·ne·ár] *v.* to cannonade, bombard.
cañoneo [ka·ño·né·o] *m.* cannonade;
bombardment.
cañonero [ka·ño·né·ro] *m.* gunboat; gunner; **lancha
cañonera** gunboat.
caoba [ka·ó·ƀa] *f.* mahogany.
caos [ká·os] *m.* chaos, confusion.
capa [ká·pa] *f.* (*ropa*) cape, cloak; (*cubierta*)
covering, coating; layer; scum; **so — de** under
the guise of, under pretense of.
capacidad [ka·pa·si·ɗáɗ] *f.* capacity; ability.
capacitar [ka·pa·si·tár] *v.* to enable, prepare, fit,
qualify; *Col.* to empower, authorize.
capataz [ka·pa·tás] *m.* boss, foreman, overseer.
capaz [ka·pás] *adj.* capable, able, competent;
spacious, roomy.
capellán [ka·pe·yán] *m.* chaplain, priest,
clergyman.
caperuza [ka·pe·rú·sa] *f.* pointed hood.
capicúa [ka·pi·kú·a] *f.* a number which reads the
same from right to left as from left to right.
capilla [ka·pí·ya] *f.* chapel; hood.
capirote [ka·pi·ró·te] *m.* hood; **tonto de —** dunce,
plain food.
capital [ka·pi·tál] *m.* capital, funds; *f.* capital,
capital city; *adj.* capital; **capitalismo**
[ka·pi·ta·líz·mo] *m.* capitalism; **capitalista**
[ka·pi·ta·lís·ta] *m. & f.* capitalist; *adj.*
capitalistic.
capitalino [ka·pi·ta·lí·no] *adj.* relative to the capital
city; *m.* a resident of the capital.
capitalizar[9] [ka·pi·ta·li·sár] *v.* to capitalize.
capitán [ka·pi·tán] *m.* captain.
capitanear [ka·pi·ta·ne·ár] *v.* to command, lead.
capitolio [ka·pi·tó·ljo] *m.* capitol.
capitular [ka·pi·tu·lár] *v.* to surrender; to come to
an agreement.
capítulo [ka·pí·tu·lo] *m.* chapter.
caporal [ka·po·rál] *m.* boss, leader; *Am.* foreman
in a cattle ranch.
capote [ka·pó·te] *m.* cloak (*with sleeves*);
bullfighter's cape; *Ch.* thrashing, beating; **decir
para su —** to say to oneself; *Am.* **de —** in an
underhanded way; *Ven., Carib.* **dar —** to get
ahead; to deceive.
capricho [ka·prí·čo] *m.* caprice, whim, notion.
caprichoso [ka·pri·čó·so] *adj.* capricious, whimsical;
changeable, fickle.
caprichudo [ka·pri·čú·ɗo] *adj.* whimsical; stubborn,
willful.
cápsula [káp·su·la] *f.* capsule; percussion cap,
cartridge shell; metal cap (*on bottles*).
captar [kap·tár] *v.* to win, attract; to capitivate;
Am. to get, tune in on (*a radio station*).
captura [kap·tú·ra] *f.* capture.
capturar [kap·tu·rár] *v.* to capture, arrest.
capucha [ka·pú·ča] *f.* hood.
capullo [ka·pú·yo] *m.* cocoon; bud; acorn cup.
cara [ká·ra] *f.* face; expression, countenance; front;
de — opposite; **echar** (*or* **dar**) **en —** to reproach,
blame; **sacar la — por alguien** to take
someone's part, defend him.
carabina [ka·ra·ƀí·na] *f.* carbine, rifle.
caracol [ka·ra·kól] *m.* snail; winding stairs; *Am.*
embroidered blouse; *Am.* curl.
caracolear [ka·ra·ko·le·ár] *v.* to caper, prance
around (*said of horses*); *Col., Ven.* to muddle,
entangle; *Am.* to sidestep an obligation.

caracoleo [ka·ra·ko·lé·o] *m.* prancing around;
winding, turn.
carácter [ka·rák·ter] *m.* character; temper.
característico [ka·rak·te·rís·ti·ko] *adj.*
characteristic; **característica** [ka·rak·te·rís·ti·ka]
f. characteristic, trait.
caracterizar[9] [ka·rak·te·ri·sár] *v.* to characterize.
¡caramba! [ka·rám·ba] *interj.* great guns! great
Scott!
carámbano [ka·rám·ba·no] *m.* icicle.
caramelo [ka·ra·mé·lo] *m.* caramel.
caramillo [ka·ra·mí·yo] *m.* reed pipe, small flute;
armar un — to raise a rumpus, create a
disturbance.
carancho [ka·rán·čo] *m. Ríopl.* hawk, buzzard.
carátula [ka·rá·tu·la] *f.* mask; *Col., Ven., Ríopl.,
Carib., Andes* title page of a book; *C.A., Mex.,
Andes* dial, face of a watch.
caravana [ka·ra·ƀá·na] *f.* caravan.
caray [ka·ráj] *m.* tortoise shell; *interj.* gosh!
carbólico [kar·ƀó·li·ko] *adj.* carbolic.
carbón [kar·ƀón] *m.* carbon; coal; **— de leña**
charcoal; **carbono** [kar·ƀó·no] *m.* carbon.
carbonera [kar·ƀo·né·ra] *f.* coal bin; coal cellar;
woman coal or charcoal vendor; *Am.* coal mine;
carbonero [kar·ƀo·né·ro] *m.* coal dealer;
charcoal vendor; *adj.* coal, relating to coal or
charcoal.
carburador [kar·ƀu·ra·ɗór] *m.* carburetor.
carajada [kar·ka·xá·ɗa] *f.* loud laughter, peal of
laughter.
cárcel [kár·sel] *f.* jail, prison.
carcelero [kar·se·lé·ro] *m.* jailer; *adj.* relating to a
jail.
carcomido [kar·ko·mí·ɗo] *adj.* worm-eaten;
decayed.
cardán [kar·ɗán] *m.* universal joint.
cardar [kar·ɗár] *v.* to card, comb (*wool*).
cardenal [kar·ɗe·nál] *m.* cardinal; cardinal bird;
bruise.
cárdeno [kár·ɗe·no] *adj.* dark-purple.
cardo [kár·ɗo] *m.* thistle; a kind of cactus.
carear [ka·re·ár] *v.* to confront, bring face to face;
to compare; **-se** to meet face to face.
carecer[13] [ka·re·sér] *v. irr.* to lack, be in need of.
carencia [ka·rén·sja] *f.* lack, want.
carente [ka·rén·te] *adj.* lacking.
carero [ka·ré·ro] *adj.* overcharging; profiteering;
m. profiteer.
carestía [ka·res·tí·a] *f.* dearth, scarcity; high
price.
careta [ka·ré·ta] *f.* mask.
carga [kár·ga] *f.* load, burden; freight; cargo;
charge or gunpowder; **volver a la —** to insist
again and again.
cargado [kar·gá·ɗo] *p.p. & adj.* loaded; strong (*as
tea or coffee*); cloudy, sultry; **— de espaldas**
round-shouldered, stoop-shouldered.
cargador [kar·ga·ɗór] *m.* loader; stevedore; *Am.*
carrier, errand boy, mover.
cargamento [kar·ga·mén·to] *m.* cargo.
cargar[6] [kar·gár] *v.* (*poner carga*) to load; to
charge; (*atacar*) to charge; (*molestar*) to bother,
annoy; *Am.* to carry, lug; *Am.* to punish;
— con to carry away; to assume (*responsibility*);
— con el muerto to get the blame (*unjustly*).
cargo [kár·go] *m.* charge, position, duty, burden;
loading; accusation; **hacerse — de** to take
charge of; to realize.
carguero [kar·gé·ro] *adj.* load-carrying; freight-
carrying; *m. Am.* beast of burden; *Am.* skilled

loader of pack animals; *Am.* patient, long-suffering person.
caribe [ka·ri·ße] *adj.* Caribbean; *m.* Carib, Caribbean Indian; cannibal; savage.
caricatura [ka·ri·ka·tú·ra] *f.* caricature; cartoon.
caricia [ka·rí·sja] *f.* caress.
caridad [ka·ri·đáđ] *f.* charity; alms.
caries [ká·rjes] *f.* decay (*of a bone*); tooth cavity.
cariño [ka·rí·ño] *m.* affection, love; *Am.* gift.
cariñoso [ka·ri·ñó·so] *adj.* affectionate, loving.
caritativo [ka·ri·ta·tí·ßo] *adj.* charitable.
cariz [ka·rís] *m.* aspect, appearance.
carmesí [kar·me·sí] *adj. & m.* crimson.
carmín [kar·mín] *m.* crimson.
carnal [kar·nál] *adj.* carnal, sensual.
carnaval [kar·na·ßál] *m.* carnival.
carne [kár·ne] *f.* meat; flesh; — **de gallina** "goose flesh", "goose pimples"; **echar -s** to put on weight, get fat; *Am.* — **de res** beef.
carneada [kar·ne·á·đa] *f. Ríopl.* butchering, slaughtering.
carnear [kar·ne·ár] *v. Ríopl.* to butcher; *Ríopl.* to kill.
carnero [kar·né·ro] *m.* (*animal*) ram, male sheep; (*carne*) mutton; *Am.* a weak-willed person; *Am.* waste basket; *Am.* — **de la tierra** llama (*or any fleece-bearing animal*); *Am.* **cantar uno el** — to die.
carnet [kar·né] *m.* identification card; notebook.
carnicería [kar·ni·se·rí·a] *f.* (*tienda*) meat market; (*matanza*) butchery, slaughter; *C.A., Ec.* slaughterhouse.
carnicero [kar·ni·sé·ro] *m.* butcher; *adj.* carnivorous, flesh-eating; cruel.
carnívoro [kar·ní·ßo·ro] *adj.* carnivorous.
carnosidad [kar·no·si·đáđ] *f.* fleshiness, fatness; abnormal growth (*on animal or plant tissues*).
carnoso [kar·nó·so] *adj.* fleshy; meaty; pulpy.
caro [ká·ro] *adj.* expensive; dear; *adv.* at a high price.
carona [ka·ró·na] *f.* saddle pad.
carozo [ka·ró·so] *m.* cob, corncob.
carpa [kár·pa] *f.* carp (*fresh-water fish*); *Am.* canvas tent, circus tent; — **dorada** goldfish.
carpeta [kar·pé·ta] *f.* (*cubierta*) table cover; desk pad; (*cartera*) portfolio, letter case or file; *Andes* office desk; *Am.* bookkeeping department; **carpetazo** [kar·pe·tá·so]: **dar** — to table (*a motion*); to set aside, pigeonhole or dismiss.
carpintería [kar·pin·te·rí·a] *f.* carpentry; carpenter's workshop.
carpintero [kar·pin·té·ro] *m.* carpenter; **pájaro** — woodpecker.
carraspear [ka·rras·pe·ár] *v.* to cough up; to clear one's throat; to be hoarse.
carraspera [ka·rras·pé·ra] *f.* hoarseness.
carrera [ka·rré·ra] *f.* career; race, run; course; stocking run.
carreta [ka·rré·ta] *f.* long narrow wagon; cart; *Col., Ven.* wheelbarrow.
carretaje [ka·rre·tá·xe] *m.* cartage (*transporting by cart, truck, etc.*); price paid for cartage.
carrete [ka·rré·te] *m.* spool; reel — **distribuidor** feeding reel; — **receptor** take-up reel (*tape recorder*).
carretel [ka·rre·tél] *m.* reel, spool, bobbin; fishing reel; log reel (*of a boat*).
carretera [ka·rre·té·ra] *f.* highway.
carretero [ka·rre·té·ro] *m.* carter, teamster; cart maker; **camino** — highway.
carretilla [ka·rre·tí·ya] *f.* wheelbarrow; small cart;

baggage truck; *Ríopl.* wagon; *Am.* jaw; *Col.* string, series (*of lies, blunders, etc.*); *Am.* firecracker; **repetir de** — to rattle off, repeat mechanically.
carretón [ka·rre·tón] *m.* truck; wagon, cart.
carril [ka·rríl] *m.* rail; rut; furrow.
carrillo [ka·rrí·yo] *m.* (*de la cara*) cheek; (*mecánico*) pulley; cart.
carrizo [ka·rrí·so] *m.* reed; reed grass.
carro [ká·rro] *m.* cart; cartload; *Am.* car, auto, streetcar, coach; *Am.* **pararle a uno el** — to restrain someone; *Am.* **pasarle a uno el** — to suffer an injury or misfortune; **carroza** [ka·rró·sa] *f.* large and luxurious carriage; chariot; *Am.* hearse.
carrocería [ka·rro·se·rí·a] *f.* chassis; frame for a parade float.
carroña [ka·rró·ña] *f.* dead and decaying flesh; putrid, decaying carcass.
carruaje [ka·rrwá·xe] *m.* carriage, vehicle.
carta [kár·ta] *f.* (*misiva*) letter; (*naipe*) card; (*documento*) charter; map; — **blanca** full authority, freedom to act; — **de naturaleza** naturalization papers; — **de venta** bill of sale; *Ch.* **retirar** — to repent, back down; *Am.* **ser la última** — **de la baraja** to be the worst or most insignificant person or thing.
cartearse [kar·te·ár·se] *v.* to correspond, write to each other.
cartel [kar·tél] *m.* poster, handbill; cartel, written agreement; **cartela** [kar·té·la] *f.* tag, slip of paper, small card, piece of cardboard; **cartelera** [kar·te·lé·ra] *f.* billboard; **cartelón** [kar·te·lón] *m.* large poster.
cartera [kar·té·ra] *f.* (*objeto*) wallet; briefcase; desk pad; (*puesto*) portfolio, cabinet post; **carterista** [kar·te·rís·ta] *m. & f.* pickpocket.
cartero [kar·té·ro] *m.* mailman, letter carrier, postman.
cartilla [kar·tí·ya] *f.* primer; note, short letter; **leerle a uno la** — to scold, lecture someone concerning his duties.
cartografiar[17] [kar·to·gra·fjár] *v.* to chart; to make charts.
cartón [kar·tón] *m.* cardboard; pasteboard; **cartulina** [kar·tu·lí·na] *f.* fine cardboard.
cartuchera [kar·tu·čé·ra] *f.* cartridge belt.
cartucho [kar·tú·čo] *m.* cartridge; roll of coins; paper cone or bag.
casa [ká·sa] *f.* (*doméstica*) house, home; household; (*negocio*) business firm; square (*of a chessboard*); *Am.* bet, wager; — **de empeños** pawnshop; — **de huéspedes** boardinghouse; **echar la** — **por la ventana** to spend recklessly, squander everything; **poner** — to set up housekeeping.
casabe [ka·sá·ße], **cazabe** *m. Am.* cassava; *Am.* cassava bread.
casaca [ka·sá·ka] *f.* long military coat; **volver** — to be a turncoat, change sides or parties.
casamiento [ka·se·mjén·to] *m.* wedding; marriage.
casar [ka·sár] *v.* to marry; to match; *Am.* to graft (*trees*); **-se** to get married.
cascabel [kas·ka·ßél] *m.* jingle bell, tinkle bell; snake's rattle; *Am.* rattlesnake; **cascabela** [kas·ka·ße·la] *f. C.R.* rattlesnake.
cascada [kas·ká·đa] *f.* cascade, waterfall.
cascajo [kas·ká·xo] *m.* coarse gravel; crushed stone; pebble; fragment; rubbish.
cascanueces [kas·ka·nwé·ses] *m.* nutcracker.
cascar[6] [kas·kár] *v.* to crack, break; **-se** to crack or break open.

cáscara [kás·ka·ra] *f.* shell, husk, hull, rind; bark of a tree; *Ríopl.* **dar a uno — de novillo** to give someone a whipping; **cascarudo** [kas·ka·rú·đo] *adj.* having a thick husk; having a thick rind.

cascarrabias [kas·ka·rrá·ƀjas] *m. & f.* crab, grouch, ill-tempered person; *adj.* grouchy, cranky, irritable.

casco [kás·ko] *m.* helmet; hoof; skull; broken piece of earthenware; cask; empty bottle; hull of a ship; *Mex., Ríopl.* compound, main buildings of a farm; **caliente de -s** hot-headed; **ligero de -s** light-headed, frivolous; **romperse los -s** to rack one's brain.

caserío [ka·se·rí·o] *m.* hamlet, small settlement.

casero [ka·sé·ro] *adj.* domestic; homemade; *m.* landlord; janitor, caretaker; *Ch.* customer; *Col., Peru, Ven.* delivery boy; **casera** [ka·sé·ra] *f.* landlady; housekeeper.

caseta [ka·sé·ta] *f.* small house, cottage; booth, stall.

casi [ká·si] *adv.* almost.

casilla [ka·sí·ya] *f. (puesto)* stall, booth; *(apartado)* post office box; pigeonhole; **sacarle a uno de sus -s** to change someone's way of life or habits; to irritate, annoy, try someone's patience; **salirse de sus -s** to lose one's temper; to do something out of the way.

casino [ka·sí·no] *m.* club, society; clubhouse; recreation hall.

caso [ká·so] *m.* case; point; matter; event — **que** *(or* **en — de que)** in case that; **dado —** supposing; **hacer — de** to pay attention to; **hacer — omiso de** to omit; **no viene al — that** is not to the point.

casorio [ka·só·rjo] *m.* wedding, marriage.

caspa [kás·pa] *f.* dandruff.

casta [kás·ta] *f.* race, breed; caste, distinct class; quality, kind.

castaña [kas·tá·ña] *f.* chestnut; jug; knot or roll of hair; *Am.* small barrel; *Mex.* trunk, large suitcase.

castañetear [kas·ta·ñe·te·ár] *v.* to rattle the castanets; to chatter *(said of the teeth)*; to crackle *(said of the knees or joints)*; — **con los dedos** to snap one's fingers.

castañeteo [kas·ta·ñe·té·o] *m.* rattle or sound of castanets; chatter, chattering *(of the teeth).*

castaño [kas·tá·ño] *m.* chestnut *(tree and wood)*; *adj.* chestnut-colored.

castañuela [kas·ta·ñwé·la] *f.* castanet.

castellano [kas·te·yá·no] *adj. & m.* Castilian, Spanish.

castidad [kas·ti·đáđ] *f.* chastity.

castigar[7] [kas·ti·gár] *v.* to chastise, punish.

castigo [kas·tí·go] *m.* punishment; correction.

castillo [kas·tí·yo] *m.* castle.

castizo [kas·tí·so] *adj.* pure, correct *(language)*; pure-blooded.

casto [kás·to] *adj.* chaste, pure.

castor [kas·tór] *m.* beaver; beaver cloth.

casual [ka·swál] *adj.* casual, accidental.

casualidad [ka·swa·li·đáđ] *f.* chance, accident.

casuca [ka·sú·ka] *f.* little house; hut, shanty.

casucha [ka·sú·ča] *f.* hut, hovel, shack.

catadura [ka·ta·đú·ra] *f.* aspect, appearance.

catalán [ka·ta·lán] *adj.* Catalan, Catalonian, of or from Catalonia, Spain; *m.* Catalan.

catalejo [ka·ta·lé·xo] *m.* telescope.

catalogar[7] [ka·ta·lo·gár] *v.* to catalogue.

catálogo [ka·tá·lo·go] *m.* catalogue.

catar [ka·tár] *v.* to look at, examine; to taste, sample.

catarata [ka·ta·rá·ta] *f.* cataract; waterfall.

catarro [ka·tá·rro] *m.* catarrh, cold.

catástrofe [ka·tás·tro·fe] *f.* catastrophe, mishap.

catear [ka·te·ár] *v.* to explore, look around; *Ch., C.A., Mex.* to search or raid *(a home)*; *Am.* to explore for ore; *Col., Ríopl.* to test, try.

catecismo [ka·te·síz·mo] *m.* catechism.

cátedra [ká·te·đra] *f.* class; subject; chair, professorship.

catedral [ka·te·đrál] *f.* cathedral.

catedrático [ka·te·đrá·ti·ko] *m.* professor.

categoría [ka·te·go·rí·a] *f.* category, rank; kind, class.

categórico [ka·te·gó·ri·ko] *adj.* categorical, positive.

catequizar[9] [ka·te·ki·sár] *v.* to catechize, give religious instruction (to); to induce, persuade.

católico [ka·tó·li·ko] *adj.* Catholic; universal; *m.* Catholic; **catolicismo** [ka·to·li·síz·mo] *m.* Catholicism.

catre [ká·tre] *m.* cot, small bed; *Am.* raft, float; *C.A.,* camp stool, folding stool; **— de tijera** folding cot.

catrín [ka·trín] *m. Am.* dandy; *adj. Mex., C.A.* over-elegant, dressy.

cauce [káw·se] *m.* river bed.

caución [kaw·sjón] *f.* precaution; security, guarantee; bail.

cauchero [kaw·cé·ro] *m. Am.* rubber gatherer; *Am.* rubber producer; *adj. Am.* rubber, pertaining to rubber.

caucho [káw·čo] *m.* rubber; **— sintético** [synthetic rubber; *Am.* rubber tree; *Col.* rubber raincoat or cloak; **cauchal** [kaw·čál] *m.* rubber grove or plantation.

caudal [kaw·đál] *m. (monetario)* wealth; *(torrente)* river current; volume of water.

caudaloso [kaw·đa·ló·so] *adj.* wealthy; abundant.

caudillaje [kaw·đi·yá·xe] *m.* military leadership; *Am.* political bossism; *Am.* tyranny.

caudillo [kaw·đi·yo] *m.* leader, chief; *Am.* political boss.

causa [káw·sa] *f.* cause; case, lawsuit; *Am.* light lunch, snack; **a causa de** on account of.

causar [kaw·sár] *v.* to cause.

cautela [kaw·té·la] *f.* caution; cunning, craftiness; trick, deception.

cauteloso [kaw·te·ló·so] *adj.* cautious; crafty.

cautivar [kaw·ti·ƀár] *v.* to capture; to charm, fascinate.

cautiverio [kaw·ti·ƀé·rjo] *m.* captivity.

cautivo [kaw·tí·ƀo] *m.* captive, war prisoner.

cauto [káw·to] *adj.* cautious.

cavar [ka·ƀár] *v.* to dig, spade; to excavate.

caverna [ka·ƀér·na] *f.* cavern, cave.

cavernoso [ka·ƀer·nó·so] *adj.* cavernous, like a cavern; hollow; **voz cavernosa** deep, hollow voice.

cavidad [ka·ƀi·đáđ] *f.* cavity.

cayado [ka·yá·đo] *m.* shepherd's crook, staff.

cayo [ká·yo] *m.* key, island reef.

caza [ká·sa] *f.* hunt, hunting; wild game; *m.* attack plane; **dar —** to pursue, track down.

cazador [ka·sa·đór] *adj.* hunting; *m.* hunter.

cazar[9] [ka·sár] *v.* to chase, hunt; to track down.

cazatorpedero [ka·sa·tor·pe·đé·ro] *m.* destroyer, torpedo-boat.

cazo [ká·so] *m.* dipper; pot, pan.

cazuela [ka·swé·la] *f.* stewing pan; earthenware cooking pan; topmost theatre gallery; *Ven.*

stewed hen; *P.R.* candied sweet potatoes with spices.

cebada [se·bá·da] *f.* barley; *Am.* brewing of **mate**; **cebadal** [se·ba·dál] *m.* barley field.

cebar [se·bár] *v.* to feed, fatten (*animals*); to encourage, nourish (*a passion*); to prime (*a gun, pump, etc.*); to bait (*a fishhook*); *Ríopl.* to brew and serve **mate** or tea; **-se** to vent one's fury.

cebo [sé·bo] *m.* feed (*for animals*); bait; incentive.

cebolla [se·bó·ya] *f.* onion.

cebollar [se·bo·yár] *m.* onion patch.

cecear [se·se·ár] *v.* to lisp.

ceceo [se·sé·o] *m.* lisp, lisping.

cecina [se·sí·na] *f.* dried beef, jerked beef.

cedazo [se·dá·so] *m.* sieve.

ceder [se·dér] *v.* to cede, transfer; to yield, surrender, submit; to diminish, abate.

cedilla [se·dí·ya] *f.* cedilla.

cedro [sé·dro] *m.* cedar.

cédula [sé·du·la] *f.* slip of paper; certificate; — **de vecindad** (*or* — **personal**) official identification card.

céfiro [sé·fi·ro] *m.* zephyr, soft breeze; *Am.* fine muslin.

cegar[1, 7] [se·gár] *v. irr.* to blind; to become blind; to confuse; to fill up, stop up (*a hole*).

ceguedad [se·ge·dád], **ceguera** [se·gé·ra] *f.* blindness.

ceiba [séj·ba] *f. Am.* ceiba, silk-cotton tree.

ceja [sé·xa] *f.* eyebrow; brow of a hill.

cejar [se·xár] *v.* to go backward; to back; to back down, give in, yield; to slacken.

cejijunto [se·xi·xún·to] *adj.* frowning; with knitted eyebrows.

celada [se·lá·da] *f.* ambush, snare, trap.

celaje [se·lá·xe] *m.* colored clouds; skylight; presage, portent; *P.R.* shadow, ghost; *Am.* **como un** — like lightning.

celar [se·lár] *v.* to guard, watch; to watch over jealously; to conceal.

celda [sél·da] *f.* cell.

celebración [se·le·bra·sjón] *f.* celebration.

celebrar [se·le·brár] *v.* to celebrate; to praise, honor; to be glad.

célebre [sé·le·bre] *adj.* famous; funny, witty; *Col.* graceful, pretty (*woman*).

celebridad [se·le·bri·dád] *f.* fame, renown; celebrity, famous person; celebration.

celeridad [se·le·ri·dád] *f.* swiftness, speed.

celeste [se·lés·te] *adj.* celestial, heavenly.

celestial [se·les·tjál] *adj.* celestial, heavenly, divine.

celibe [sé·li·be] *adj.* unmarried; *m. & f.* unmarried person.

celo [sé·lo] *m.* (*humano*) zeal, ardor; envy; (*animal*) heat (*sexual excitement in animals*); **-s** jealousy, suspicion; **tener -s** to be jealous.

celosía [se·lo·sí·a] *f.* window lattice; Venetian blind.

celoso [se·ló·so] *adj.* jealous; zealous, eager; suspicious.

célula [sé·lu·la] *f.* cell.

celuloide [se·lu·lój·de] *m.* celluloid.

cellisca [se·yís·ka] *f.* sleet; rain and snow.

cementar [se·men·tár] *v.* to cement.

cementerio [se·men·té·rjo] *m.* cemetry.

cemento [se·mén·to] *m.* cement; — **armado** reinforced concrete.

cena [sé·na] *f.* supper.

cenagal [se·ne·gál] *m.* quagmire, muddy ground, swamp.

cenagoso [se·na·gó·so] *adj.* muddy, miry.

cenar [se·nár] *v.* to eat supper.

cencerrada [sen·se·rrá·da] *f.* racket, noise (*with cowbells, tin cans, etc.*); tin pan serenade.

cencerrear [sen·se·rre·ár] *v.* to make a racket (*with cowbells, tin cans, etc.*).

cencerro [sen·sé·rro] *m.* cowbell.

cendal [sen·dál] *m.* gauze; thin veil.

cenicero [se·ni·sé·ro] *m.* ash tray; ash pit; ash pan.

cenicienta [se·ni·sjén·ta] *f.* a Cinderella.

ceniciento [se·ni·sjén·to] *adj.* ashen, ash-colored.

cenit [sé·nit] *m.* zenith.

ceniza [se·ní·sa] *f.* ashes, cinders.

cenizo [se·ní·so] *adj.* ash-colored.

censo [sén·so] *m.* census.

censor [sen·sór] *m.* censor.

censura [sen·sú·ra] *f.* censure, criticism, disapproval; censorship.

censurador [sen·su·ra·dór] *m.* censor, critic; critical person; *adj.* critical.

censurar [sen·su·rár] *v.* to censure, criticize, reprove; to censor.

centavo [sen·tá·bo] *m.* cent.

centella [sen·té·ya] *f.* lightning, flash; spark.

centelleante [sen·te·ye·án·te] *adj.* sparkling, flashing.

centellear [sen·te·ye·ár] *v.* to twinkle; to sparkle, glitter; to flash.

centelleo [sen·te·yé·o] *m.* glitter, sparkle.

centenar [sen·te·nár] *m.* one hundred; field of rye.

centenario [sen·te·ná·rjo] *m.* centennial, one hundredth anniversary; *adj.* centennial; old, ancient.

centeno [sen·té·no] *m.* rye.

centésimo [sen·té·si·mo] *adj. & m.* hundredth.

centímetro [sen·tí·me·tro] *m.* centimeter (*one hundredth part of a meter*).

céntimo [sén·ti·mo] *m.* one hundredth part of a **peseta**.

centinela [sen·ti·né·la] *m.* sentry, sentinel.

central [sen·trál] *adj.* central; *f.* main office; headquarters; *Am.* main sugar mill or refinery.

centrar [sen·trár] *v.* to center.

céntrico [sén·tri·ko] *adj.* central.

centrífugo [sen·trí·fu·go] *adj.* centrifugal.

centrípeto [sen·trí·pe·to] *adj.* centripetal.

centro [sén·tro] *m.* center, middle.

ceñidor [se·ñi·dór] *m.* girdle, belt, sash.

ceñir[5, 19] [se·ñír] *v. irr.* (*redear*) to gird, girdle; to tighten; to encircle; (*abreviar*) to diminish; to limit; **-se a** to limit oneself to.

ceño [sé·ño] *m.* frown; scowl; **fruncir el** — to frown; to scowl.

cepa [sé·pa] *f.* stump, stub (*of a tree or plant*); vinestock; origin, stock (*of a family*); *Am.* mass of plants growing from a common root; *Am.* excavation (*for a building*), hole, pit (*for planting trees*); **de buena** — of good stock.

cepillo [se·pi·yo] *m.* brush; alms box; carpenter's plane; flatterer; — **de dientes** toothbrush.

cepo [sé·po] *m.* branch, stock.

cera [sé·ra] *f.* wax.

cerámica [se·rá·mi·ka] *f.* ceramics, pottery.

cerca [sér·ka] *adv.* near, near by; — **de** *prep.* near, nearly; *f.* fence, low wall.

cercado [ser·ká·do] *m.* enclosure; fenced-in garden; fence; *Am.* Peruvian political division; *p.p. of* **cercar.**

cercanía [ser·ka·ní·a] *f.* proximity; **-s** surroundings, vicinity.

cercano [ser·ká·no] *adj.* near; neighboring.

cercar[6] [ser·kár] *v.* to fence, enclose; to surround; to besiege.

cercenar [ser·se·nár] *v.* to clip off; to curtail, diminish, reduce.

cerciorar [ser·sjo·rár] *v.* to assure, affirm; **-se** to ascertain, find out.

cerco [sér·ko] *m.* fence enclosure; siege; circle; *Ch.* small farm or orchard.

cerda [sér·d̶a] *f.* bristle; *Am.* **ir en -s** to go halves or share in a deal.

cerdo [sér·d̶o] *m.* hog; pig; pork.

cerdoso [ser·d̶ó·so] *adj.* bristly.

cereal [se·re·ál] *m.* cereal, grain.

cerebro [se·ré·b̶ro] *m.* brain.

ceremonia [se·re·mó·nja] *f.* ceremony.

ceremonial [se·re·mo·njál] *adj. & m.* ceremonial.

ceremonioso [se·re·mo·njó·so] *adj.* ceremonious.

cereza [se·ré·sa] *f.* cherry; **cerezo** [se·ré·so] *m.* cherry tree; cherry wood.

cerilla [se·rí·ya] *f.* wax taper; wax match; earwax.

cerillo [se·rí·yo] *m. Mex., C.A., Ven., Andes* match.

cerner[1] [ser·nér] *v. irr.* to sift; to drizzle; *Am.* to strain through a sieve; **-se** to hover (*as a bird or plane*).

cero [sé·ro] *m.* zero; nothing.

cerquita [ser·kí·ta] *adv.* quite near, nice and near.

cerrado [se·rrá·d̶o] *adj.* closed; cloudy; thick (*beard*); reserved (*person*); dull; *Am.* stubborn.

cerradura [se·rrá·d̶ú·ra] *f.* locking, closing; lock; **— de golpe** spring lock.

cerrajería [se·rra·xe·rí·a] *f.* locksmith's shop; locksmith's trade.

cerrajero [se·rra·xé·ro] *m.* locksmith.

cerrar[1] [se·rrár] *v. irr.* to close, shut, lock; **-se** to close; **-se el cielo** to become overcast or cloudy.

cerrazón [se·rra·són] *f.* cloudiness, darkness.

cerro [sé·rro] *m.* hill.

cerrojo [se·rró·xo] *m.* latch, bolt.

certamen [ser·tá·men] *m.* contest, literary contest; debate; competition.

certero [ser·té·ro] *adj.* accurate, exact; well-aimed; **tirador —** good shot.

certeza [ser·té·sa] *f.* certainty.

certidumbre [ser·ti·d̶úm·bre] *f.* certainty.

certificado [ser·ti·fi·ká·d̶o] *adj.* certified, registered; *m.* certificate.

certificar[6] [ser·ti·fi·kár] *v.* to certify; to register (*a letter*).

cervato [ser·b̶á·to] *m.* fawn, young deer.

cerveza [ser·b̶é·sa] *f.* beer; **cervecería** [ser·b̶e·se·rí·a] *f.* beer tavern; brewery.

cerviz [ser·b̶ís] *f.* cervix.

cesante [se·sán·te] *adj.* unemployed.

cesar [se·sár] *v.* to cease, stop; to quit.

cesio [sé·sjo] *m.* cesium.

cesta [sés·ta] *f.* basket; a kind of racket for playing jai alai (*Basque ball game*).

cesto [sés·to] *m.* large basket, hamper.

cetrino [se·trí·no] *adj.* greenish-yellow, lemon-colored; citronlike; melancholy, gloomy.

cetro [sé·tro] *m.* scepter, staff.

cibernética [si·b̶er·né·ti·ka] *f.* cybernetics, computer science.

cicatero [si·ka·té·ro] *adj.* miserly, stingy.

cicatriz [si·ka·trís] *f.* scar.

cicatrizar[9] [si·ka·tri·sár] *v.* to heal, close (*a wound*).

ciclo [sí·klo] *m.* cycle; period of time; school term.

ciclón [si·klón] *m.* cyclone.

ciclotrón [si·klo·trón] *m.* cyclotron.

ciego [sjé·g̶o] *adj.* blind; **a ciegas** blindly; *m.* blindman.

cielo [sjé·lo] *m.* sky; heaven; **— de la boca** palate; **poner en el —** to praise, extol; **poner el grito en el —** to "hit the ceiling"; **cielito** *m. Am.* gaucho group dance and tune.

ciempiés [sjem·pjés], **cientopiés** [sjen·to·pjés] *m.* centipede.

ciénaga [sjé·na·g̶a] *f.* swamp, bog, quagmire, marsh.

ciencia [sjén·sja] *f.* science; learning; skill; **a** (*or* **de) — cierta** with certainty.

cieno [sjé·no] *m.* mud, mire.

científico [sjen·tí·fi·ko] *adj.* scientific; *m.* scientist.

cierre [sjé·rre] *m.* clasp, fastener; zipper; closing. fastening, locking; method of closing.

cierto [sjér·to] *adj.* certain, true, sure; **por —** certainly; *Col., C.A.* **ciertas hierbas** so-and-so (*person not named*).

ciervo [sjér·b̶o] *m.* deer; **cierva** [sjér·b̶a] *f.* doe, hind, female deer.

cierzo [sjér·so] *m.* north wind.

cifra [sí·fra] *f.* cipher, number; figure; abridgment, summary; code; monogram; emblem.

cifrar [si·frár] *v.* to write in code; to summarize; **— la esperanza en** to place one's hope in.

cigarra [si·g̶á·rra] *f.* cicada, locust.

cigarrera [si·g̶a·rré·ra] *f.* cigar or cigarette case; woman cigar maker or vendor.

cigarrillo [si·g̶a·rrí·yo] *m.* cigarette.

cigarro [si·g̶á·rro] *m.* cigar, cigarette.

cigüeña [si·g̶wé·ña] *f.* stork; crank, handle (*for turning*).

cigüeñal [si·g̶we·ñál] *m.* crankshaft.

cilíndrico [si·lín·dri·ko] *adj.* cylindrical.

cilindro [si·lín·dro] *m.* cylinder; *Mex.* hand organ.

cima [sí·ma] *f.* peak, summit, top; **dar —** to complete, carry out.

cimarrón [si·ma·rrón] *adj. Ríopl., Mex., Carib., Ven., Andes* wild, untamed; *Ríopl.* **mate —** black, bitter **mate**.

cimarronear [si·ma·rro·ne·ár] *v. Ríopl.* to drink **mate** without sugar.

cimbrar [sim·brár], **cimbrear** [sim·bre·ár] *v.* to brandish, flourish, swing; to shake; to bend; *Am.* to swing around, change suddenly one's direction, **— a uno de un golpe** to knock a person down with a blow; **-se** to swing, sway; to vibrate, shake.

cimiento [si·mjén·to] *m.* foundation, base; source, root; **abrir los -s** to break ground for a building.

cinc [siŋk] *m.* zinc.

cincel [sin·sél] *m.* chisel.

cincelar [sin·se·lár] *v.* to chisel; to engrave.

cincha [sín·č̶a] *f.* cinch, girth; *Am.* blows with the flat of a sword; *Col., Ríopl.* **a revienta -s** unwillingly; hurriedly; at breakneck speed.

cinchar [sin·č̶ár] *v.* to cinch, tighten the saddle girth; *Am.* to hit with the flat of a sword.

cine [sí·ne], **cinema** [si·né·ma] *m.* cinema, motion picture, movie; **cinematógrafo** [si·ne·ma·tó·g̶ra·fo] *m.* motion picture.

cinematografía [si·ne·ma·to·g̶ra·fí·a] *f.* cinematography, the science of motion picture photography.

cíngulo [síŋ·g̶u·lo] *m.* girdle, cord, belt.

cínico [sí·ni·ko] *adj.* cynical, sarcastic, sneering; *m.* cynic.

cinta [sín·ta] *f.* ribbon, band; tape; strip; movie film; coarse fishing net; *Am.* tin can.

cintarada [sin·ta·rá·d̶a] *f.* beating, flogging; **cintarazo** *m.* blow with the flat of a sword.

CE

cintilar [sin·ti·lár] *v.* to sparkle, twinkle; to glimmer.

cinto [sín·to] *m.* belt; girdle.

cintura [sin·tú·ra] *f.* waist; **meter en** — to subdue, subject.

cinturón [sin·tu·rón] *m.* belt; — **de seguridad** safety belt.

ciprés [si·prés] *m.* cypress.

circo [sír·ko] *m.* circus.

circonio [sir·kó·njo] *m.* zirconium.

circuito [sir·kwí·to] *m.* circuit.

circulación [sir·ku·la·sjón] *f.* circulation; traffic.

circular [sir·ku·lár] *v.* to circulate; to circle; *adj.* circular; *f.* circular letter, notice.

círculo [sír·ku·lo] *m.* circle; group; club; clubhouse.

circundante [sir·kun·dán·te] *adj.* surrounding.

circundar [sir·kun·dár] *v.* to surround.

circunferencia [sir·kun·fe·rén·sja] *f.* circumference.

circunlocución [sir·kun·lo·ku·sjón] *f.* circumlocution, roundabout expression.

circunspección [sir·kun·spek·sjón] *f.* circumspection, decorum, prudence, restraint.

circunspecto [sir·kuns·pék·to] *adj.* circumspect, prudent.

circunstancia [sir·kuns·tán·sja] *f.* circumstance.

circunstante [sir·kuns·tán·te] *adj.* surrounding; present; **-s** *m. pl.* bystanders, onlookers, audience.

circunvecino [sir·kum·be·sí·no] *adj.* neighboring, surrounding.

cirio [sí·rjo] *m.* wax candle; saguaro cactus.

ciruela [si·rwé·la] *f.* plum; prune; — **pasa** prune, dried prune; **ciruelo** *m.* plum tree.

cirugía [si·ru·xi·a] *f.* surgery.

cirujano [si·ru·xá·no] *m.* surgeon.

cisne [síz·ne] *m.* swan; *Ríopl.* powder puff.

cisterna [sis·tér·na] *f.* cistern.

cita [sí·ta] *f.* date, appointment; citation; summons; quotation.

citación [si·ta·sjón] *f.* citation, quotation; summons.

citar [si·tár] *v.* (*convocar*) to make a date or appointment with; (*referir*) to cite, quote; (*incitar*) incite, provoke; to summon.

cítrico [sí·tri·ko] *adj.* citric.

ciudad [sju·ɗáɗ] *f.* city.

ciudadano [sju·ɗa·ɗá·no] *m.* citizen; resident of a city; *adj.* of or pertaining to a city; **ciudadanía** [sju·ɗa·ɗa·ní·a] *f.* citizenship.

ciudadela [sju·ɗa·ɗé·la] *f.* citadel.

cívico [sí·bi·ko] *adj.* civic.

civil [si·bíl] *adj.* civil; polite, courteous.

civilidad [si·bi·li·ɗáɗ] *f.* civility, courtesy.

civilización [si·bi·li·sa·sjón] *f.* civilization.

civilizador [si·bi·li·sa·ɗór] *adj.* civilizing; *m.* civilizer.

civilizar[9] [si·bi·li·sár] *v.* to civilize.

cizaña [si·sá·ña] *f.* weed; vice; discord; **sembrar** — to sow discord.

clamar [kla·már] *v.* to clamor, shout; to whine.

clamor [kla·mór] *m.* clamor, shout; whine; knell.

clamoreo [kla·mo·ré·o] *m.* clamoring; shouting.

clamorear [kla·mo·re·ár] *v.* to clamor, shout; to toll, knell.

clandestino [klan·des·tí·no] *adj.* clandestine, underhanded, secret.

clara [klá·ra] *f.* white of egg; bald spot; thin spot (*in a fabric*); **a las -s** clearly, openly, frankly.

claraboya [kla·ra·bó·ya] *f.* skylight.

clarear [kla·re·ár] *v.* (*poner claro*), to clarify, make

clear; (*haber más luz*) to grow light, begin to dawn; to clear up; *Am.* to pierce through and through; **-se** to become transparent; to reveal oneself.

claridad [kla·ri·ɗáɗ] *f.* clarity, clearness; blunt remark, slam; fame.

claridoso [kla·ri·ɗó·so] *adj. Mex., Ven., C.A.* blunt, outspoken, plainspoken.

clarificar[6] [kla·ri·fi·kár] *v.* to clarify, make clear.

clarín [kla·rín] *m.* bugle; bugler; organ stop; *Am.* song bird.

clarinete [kla·ri·né·te] *m.* clarinet; clarinet player.

clarito [kla·rí·to] *adj. & adv.* quite clear, nice and clear.

clarividencia [kla·ri·bi·ɗén·sja] *f.* clairvoyance; keen insight.

claro [klá·ro] *adj.* clear; light (*color*); illustrious; *adv.* clearly; *m.* skylight; space, gap; clearing (*in a forest*); **pasar la noche de** — **en** — not to sleep a wink; *Mex., Carib.* **en** — without eating or sleeping; *Am.* **poner en** — to copy (*a rough draft*).

clase [klá·se] *f.* class; classroom; kind, sort.

clásico [klá·si·ko] *adj.* classic, classical.

clasificación [kla·si·fi·ka·sjón] *f.* classification.

clasificar[6] [kla·si·fi·kár] *v.* to classify.

claustro [kláws·tro] *m.* cloister; meeting of a university faculty; — **de profesores** university faculty.

cláusula [kláw·su·la] *f.* clause.

clausura [klaw·sú·ra] *f.* closing; seclusion, monastic life.

clavado [kla·bá·ɗo] *m. Mex.* a dive.

clavar [kla·bár] *v.* to nail; to fix; to deceive, cheat; **-se** to be deceived; *Mex.* to fall into a trap; *Mex.* to dive.

clave [klá·be] *f.* key, code; keystone; clef.

clavel [kla·bél] *m.* carnation, pink.

clavetear [kla·be·te·ár] *v.* to nail; to stud with nails.

clavícula [kla·bí·ku·la] *f.* collarbone.

clavija [kla·bí·xa] *f.* peg; electric plug; peg (*of a stringed instrument*).

clavijero [kla·bi·xé·ro] *m.* hat or clothes rack.

clavo [klá·bo] *m.* nail; clove (*spice*); sharp pain or grief; sick headache; *Mex.* rich mineral vein; *Am.* bother, worry; *Col.* surprise, disappointment; *Ríopl.* drug on the market (*unsaleable article*); **dar en el** — to hit the nail on the head; *Am.* **meter a uno en un** — to put a person in a predicament; *Am.* **ser un** — to be punctual, exact.

clemencia [kle·mén·sja] *f.* mercy; **clemente** [kle·mén·te] *adj.* merciful.

clerical [kle·ri·kál] *adj.* clerical, of a clergyman or the clergy.

clérigo [klé·ri·go] *m.* clergyman.

clero [klé·ro] *m.* clergy.

cliché [kli·čé] *m.* photographic plate; also **clisé**.

cliente [kljén·te] *m. & f.* client; customer; **clientela** [kljen·té·la] *f.* clientele, clients; customers.

clima [klí·ma] *m.* climate.

clímax [klí·maks] *m.* climax.

clínica [klí·ni·ka] *f.* clinic.

clíper [klí·per] *m.* clipper.

cloaca [klo·á·ka] *f.* sewer.

cloquear [klo·ke·ár] *v.* to cluck.

cloqueo [klo·ké·o] *m.* cluck, clucking.

cloro [kló·ro] *m.* chlorine.

clorofila [klo·ro·fí·la] *f.* chlorophyll.

cloruro [klo·rú·ro] *m.* chloride.
club [kluḃ] *m.* club, society.
clueca [klwé·ka] *f.* brooding hen.
coacción [ko·ak·sjón] *f.* compulsion, force; enforcement.
coagular [ko·a·ḡu·lár] *v.* to coagulate, thicken, clot; to curd, curdle; -se to coagulate, clot; to curd, curdle.
coágulo [ko·á·ḡu·lo] *m.* coagulation, clot.
coartar [ko·ar·tár] *v.* to restrain, limit.
coba [kó·ḃa] *f.* flattery; fib; dar — to flatter; to tease.
cobalto [ko·ḃál·to] *m.* cobalt.
cobarde [ko·ḃár·ḋe] *adj.* cowardly; timid; weak; *m.* coward.
cobardía [ko·ḃar·ḋí·a] *f.* cowardice.
cobertizo [ko·ḃer·tí·so] *m.* shed; shanty.
cobertor [ko·ḃer·tór] *m.* bedcover, quilt.
cobertura [ko·ḃer·tú·ra] *f.* cover, covering.
cobija [ko·ḃí·xa] *f.* cover; shelter; roof; *Am.* blanket; *Am.* shawl, serape, poncho; -s *Am.* bedclothes.
cobijar [ko·ḃi·xár] *v.* to cover; to shelter.
cobrador [ko·ḃra·ḋór] *m.* collector; ticket collector.
cobranza [ko·ḃrán·sa] *f.* collection (*of a sum of money*); cashing.
cobrar [ko·ḃrár] *v.* to collect (*bills, debts*); to charge; to cash (*a draft, check, etc.*); to recover, regain; to gain, acquire; *Am.* to demand payment; — cariño a to take a liking to.
cobre [kó·ḃre] *m.* copper; copper kitchen utensils; *Am.* copper coin; -s brass musical instruments; batir el — to hustle, work with energy; *Am.* mostrar el — to show one's worse side.
cobrizo [ko·ḃrí·so] *adj.* coppery, copper-colored.
cobro [kó·ḃro] *m.* collection (*of bills*); poner en — to put in a safe place; ponerse en — to take refuge, get to a safe place.
coca [kó·ka] *f.* *Am.* coca (*South American shrub and its leaves*); *Am.* cocaine; *Am.* coca tea; *Am.* eggshell; *Am.* fruit skin or rind; *Am.* de — free of charge; in vain.
cocaína [ko·ka·í·na] *f.* cocaine.
cocear [ko·se·ár] *v.* to kick.
cocer [2, 10] [ko·sér] *v. irr.* to cook; to boil; to bake.
cocido [ko·sí·ḋo] *m.* Spanish stew; *p.p. of* cocer.
cociente [ko·sjén·te] *m.* quotient.
cocimiento [ko·si·mjén·to] *m.* cooking; baking; liquid concoction (*generally made of medicinal herbs*).
cocina [ko·sí·na] *f.* kitchen; cuisine, cooking; — económica stove, range.
cocinar [ko·si·nár] *v.* to cook.
cocinero [ko·si·né·ro] *m.* cook.
coco [kó·ko] *m.* coconut; coconut palm; bogeyman, goblin; *Am.* derby hat; *Mex., Carib., Ríopl.* head; *Am.* blow on the head; hacer -s a to make eyes at, flirt with; *Col., Ven., Andes* pelar a — to crop the hair; cocotal [ko·ko·tál] *m.* grove of coconut palms; coconut plantation; cocotero [ko·ko·té·ro] *m.* coconut palm.
cocodrilo [ko·ko·ḋrí·lo] *m.* crocodile.
coche [kó·če] *m.* coach; car; taxi.
cochero [ko·čé·ro] *m.* coachman; cabman; taxi driver.
cochinada [ko·či·ná·ḋa] *f.* filth, filthiness; filthy act or remark; dirty trick; herd of swine.
cochinilla [ko·či·ní·ya] *f.* cochineal (*insect*).
cochino [ko·čí·no] *m.* hog, pig; dirty person; *Ch.* stingy person; *Am.* — de monte wild boar; *adj.* filthy, dirty; *Ch.* miserly, stingy.

codazo [ko·ḋá·so] *m.* nudge; poke (*with the elbow*).
codear [ko·ḋe·ár] *v.* to elbow; to nudge; -se con alguien to rub elbows with someone.
códice [kó·ḋi·se] *m.* codex.
codicia [ko·ḋi·sja] *f.* greed; greediness.
codiciar [ko·ḋi·sjár] *v.* to covet.
codicioso [ko·ḋi·sjó·so] *adj.* covetous, greedy.
código [kó·ḋi·ḡo] *m.* code of laws.
codo [kó·ḋo] *m.* elbow; bend; alzar (*or* empinar) el — to drink too much; hablar por los -s to talk too much; meterse (*or* estar metido) hasta los -s to be up to the elbows, be very busy.
codorniz [ko·ḋor·nís] *f.* partridge.
coetáneo [ko·e·tá·ne·o] *adj.* contemporary.
cofrade [ko·frá·ḋe] *m. & f.* fellow member (*of a brotherhood, club, society, etc.*).
cofradía [ko·fra·ḋí·a] *f.* brotherhood; sisterhood; guild; trade union.
cofre [kó·fre] *m.* coffer, jewel box; chest, trunk.
coger [11] [ko·xér] *v.* to seize; to catch; to grasp; to gather; *Am.* -se una cosa to steal something.
cogollo [ko·ḡó·yo] *m.* heart (of lettuce), head (of cabbage).
cogote [ko·ḡó·te] *m.* nape, back of the neck.
cohechar [ko·e·čár] *v.* to bribe.
coheredero [ko·e·re·ḋé·ro] *m.* joint heir.
coherente [ko·e·rén·te] *adj.* coherent; connected.
cohete [ko·é·te] *m.* skyrocket; rocket; *Ríopl.* al — in vain, uselessly.
cohetería [ko·e·te·rí·a] *f.* rocketry; rocket weaponry; shop for making fireworks.
cohibición [koj·ḃi·sjón] *f.* repression, inhibition, restraint.
cohibido [koj·ḃí·ḋo] *p.p. & adj.* inhibited; embarrassed, uneasy.
cohibir [koj·ḃír] *v.* to restrain, repress; to inhibit.
coincidencia [kojn·si·ḋén·sja] *f.* coincidence.
coincidir [kojn·si·ḋír] *v.* to coincide.
cojear [ko·xe·ár] *v.* to limp; cojeamos del mismo pie we both have the same weakness.
cojera [ko·xé·ra] *f.* limp, lameness.
cojín [ko·xín] *m.* cushion; pad; cojincillo *m.* pad.
cojinete [ko·xi·né·te] *m.* small pillow or cushion, pad; bearing, ball bearing.
cojo [kó·xo] *adj.* lame, crippled; one-legged.
col [kol] *f.* cabbage; — de Bruselas Brussels sprouts.
cola [kó·la] *f.* (*rabo*) tail; train of a dress; (*hilera de gente*) line of people; piano de — grand piano; piano de media — baby grand; hacer — to stand in line; *Am.* comer — to be the last one in a contest.
colaboración [ko·la·ḃo·ra·sjón] *f.* collaboration, mutual help.
colaborar [ko·la·ḃo·rár] *v.* to collaborate, work together.
coladera [ko·la·ḋé·ra] *f.* colander, strainer, sieve; *Mex., Ven.* drain.
colar [2] [ko·lár] *v. irr.* to strain, filter; to bleach with lye; -se to slip in or out, sneak in.
colcha [kól·ča] *f.* quilt; bedspread; -s *Ríopl.* saddle and trappings; *Ríopl.* gaucho clothing.
colchón [kol·čón] *m.* mattress.
colear [ko·le·ár] *v.* to wag the tail; to grab a bull by the tail and throw him over; *Am.* to flunk (*a student*); *Am.* to trail, tag behind (*a person*); *Col.* to bother, nag, harass; *Am.* to smoke one cigarette after another.
colección [ko·lek·sjón] *f.* collection; set; gathering.
coleccionar [ko·lek·sjo·nár] *v.* to collect, make a collection.

coleccionista [ko·lek·sjo·nís·ta] *m. & f.* collector (*of stamps, curios, etc.*).

colecta [ko·lék·ta] *f.* collection of voluntary gifts; assessment; collect (*a short prayer of the mass*).

colectivo [ko·lek·tí·ƀo] *adj.* collective; *m.* small bus.

colector [ko·lek·tór] *m.* collector; water pipe, drain.

colega [ko·lé·ǵa] *m. & f.* colleague, fellow worker.

colegiatura [ko·le·xja·tú·ra] *f.* college fellowship or scholarship; *C.A.* tuition in a college.

colegio [ko·lé·xjo] *m.* boarding school; school, academy; college, body of professional men.

colegir[5, 11] [ko·le·xír] *v.* to gather; to conclude, infer.

cólera [kó·le·ra] *f.* anger, rage; *m.* cholera (*disease*).

colérico [ko·lé·ri·ko] *adj.* irritable; angry.

coleto [ko·lé·to] *m.* leather jacket; one's inner self; *Am.* impudence, shamelessness; **decir para su —** to say to oneself; **echarse al —** to drink down; to devour.

colgadero [kol·ga·ðé·ro] *m.* hanger; hook, peg; hat or clothes rack.

colgadura [kol·ga·ðú·ra] *f.* drape, hanging; drapery; tapestry.

colgante [kol·gán·te] *adj.* hanging; dangling; **puente —** suspension bridge.

colgar[2, 7] [kol·gár] *v. irr.* (*suspender*) to hang, suspend; to dangle; to drape (*walls*); (*achacar*) to impute, attribute; *Cuba* to flunk, fail (*a student*); *Col.* **-se** to fall behind.

colibrí [ko·li·ƀrí] *m.* hummingbird.

coliflor [ko·li·flór] *f.* cauliflower.

coligarse[7] [ko·li·ǵár·se] *v.* to league together, band together.

colilla [ko·lí·ya] *f.* small tail; butt (*of a cigarette*), stub (*of a cigar*).

colina [ko·lí·na] *f.* hill.

colindante [ko·lin·dán·te] *adj.* contiguous, neighboring, adjacent.

colindar [ko·lin·dár] *v.* to border (on); to be adjoining.

colisión [ko·li·sjón] *f.* collision, clash.

colmar [kol·már] *v.* to fill to the brim; **— de** to fill with; to shower with (*gifts, favors, etc.*); **-le a uno el plato** to exhaust one's patience.

colmena [kol·mé·na] *f.* beehive; *Mex.* bee.

colmillo [kol·mí·yo] *m.* eyetooth, canine tooth; tusk; fang.

colmo [kól·mo] *m.* overfullness; limit; **— de la locura** height of folly; **¡eso es el —!** that's the limit! *adj.* overfull, filled to the brim.

colocación [ko·lo·ka·sjón] *f.* placing, arrangement; position, job.

colocar[6] [ko·lo·kár] *v.* to place; to put in place, arrange; to give employment to.

colocho [ko·ló·čo] *m. C.A.* curly hair; wood shavings.

colombiano [ko·lom·bjá·no] *adj.* Colombian, of or pertaining to Colombia, South America.

colon [kó·lon] *m.* colon (*of the large intestine*).

colonia [ko·ló·nja] *f.* colony; silk ribbon; *Mex., Carib.* city district; *Am.* sugar plantation.

coloniaje [ko·lo·njá·xe] *m. Am.* colonial period.

colonial [ko·lo·njál] *adj.* colonial.

colonización [ko·lo·ni·sa·sjón] *f.* colonization.

colonizador [ko·lo·ni·sa·ðór] *m.* colonizer, colonist; *adj.* colonizing.

colonizar[9] [ko·lo·ni·sár] *v.* to colonize.

colono [ko·ló·no] *m.* colonist, settler; tenant farmer; *Carib.* owner of a sugar plantation; *Am.* bootlicker, flatterer.

coloquio [ko·ló·kjo] *m.* conversation, talk; literary dialogue; *Col.* street comedy farce.

color [ko·lór] *m.* color; coloring; paint; rouge; **so — de** under the pretext of.

coloración [ko·lo·ra·sjón] *f.* coloring.

colorado [ko·lo·ra·ðo] *adj.* red, reddish; colored; **ponerse —** to blush.

colorante [ko·lo·rán·te] *adj. & m.* coloring.

colorar [ko·lo·rár] *v.* to color; to stain; to dye.

colorear [ko·lo·re·ár] *v.* to color; to redden; to give color to.

colorete [ko·lo·ré·te] *m.* rouge.

colorido [ko·lo·rí·ðo] *m.* coloring; color; *adj.* colored; colorful.

colosal [ko·lo·sál] *adj.* colossal, huge.

columbrar [ko·lum·brár] *v.* to see faintly; to glimpse.

columna [ko·lúm·na] *f.* column.

columpiar [ko·lum·pjár] *v.* to swing; **-se** to swing; to sway.

columpio [ko·lúm·pjo] *m.* swing.

collado [ko·yá·ðo] *m.* hillock, knoll.

collar [ko·yár] *m.* necklace; dog collar; *Am.* collar (*of a draft horse*); **collera** [ko·yé·ra] *f.* collar (*for draft animals*).

coma [kó·ma] *f.* comma; *m.* coma, stupor, prolonged unconsciousness.

comadre [ko·má·ðre] *f.* (*amiga*) woman friend; (*chismosa*) gossip; (*partera*) midwife; (*alcahueta*) go-between; *name used to express kinship between mother and godmother*; **comadrona** [ko·ma·ðró·na] *f.* midwife.

comadreja [ko·ma·ðré·xa] *f.* weasel.

comandancia [ko·man·dán·sja] *f.* command; position and headquarters of a commander.

comandante [ko·man·dán·te] *m.* major; commander.

comandar [ko·man·dár] *v.* to command (*troops*).

comandita [ko·man·dí·ta] *f.* silent partnership; **sociedad en —** limited company.

comando [ko·mán·do] *m.* military command.

comarca [ko·már·ka] *f.* district, region.

comba [kóm·ba] *f.* bulge, warp.

combar [kom·bár] *v.* to warp, bend, twist; **-se** to warp; to sag; to bulge.

combate [kom·bá·te] *m.* combat, battle, fight.

combatiente [kom·ba·tjén·te] *m.* combatant, fighter.

combatir [kom·ba·tír] *v.* to combat; to fight.

combinación [kom·bi·na·sjón] *f.* combination.

combinar [kom·bi·nár] *v.* to combine, unite.

comburente [kom·bu·rén·te] *m.* the chemical agent that causes combustion, e.g., oxygen; *adj.* causing combustion.

combustible [kom·bus·tí·ƀle] *adj.* combustible; *m.* fuel.

combustión [kom·bus·tjón] *f.* combustion.

comedero [ko·me·ðé·ro] *m.* trough (*for feeding animals*); *adj.* edible, eatable.

comedia [ko·mé·ðja] *f.* comedy; farce.

comediante [ko·me·ðján·te] *m.* actor, comedian.

comedido [ko·me·ðí·ðo] *adj.* courteous, polite; obliging; *p.p.* of **comedirse**.

comedirse[5] [ko·me·ðír·se] *v. irr.* to be civil, polite, obliging; *Ec.* to meddle; *Am.* **— a hacer algo** to volunteer to do something.

comedor [ko·me·ðór] *m.* dining room; great eater.

comején [ko·me·xén] *m.* termite.

comelón [ko·me·lón] *m. Am.* big eater. *See* **comilón.**

comendador [ko·men·da·ðór] *m.* commander (*of certain military orders*).

comensal [ko·men·sál] *m.* & *f.* table companion; dinner guest.

comentador [ko·men·ta·ðór] *m.* commentator.

comentar [ko·men·tár] *v.* to comment.

comentario [ko·men·tá·rjo] *m.* commentary, explanation.

comentarista [ko·men·ta·rís·ta] *m.* & *f.* commentator.

comenzar[1, 9] [ko·men·sár] *v. irr.* to begin.

comer [ko·mér] *v.* to eat; to dine; to take (*in chess or checkers*); **dar de —** to feed; **ganar de —** to earn a living; **-se** to eat; to eat up; to skip (*a letter, syllable, word, etc.*); *Riopl., Col.* **-se uno a otro** to deceive each other.

comercial [ko·mer·sjál] *adj.* commercial.

comerciante [ko·mer·sján·te] *m.* merchant; storekeeper.

comerciar [ko·mer·sjár] *v.* to trade; to have dealings (with).

comercio [ko·mér·sjo] *m.* commerce, trade.

comestible [ko·mes·tí·ƀle] *adj.* edible, eatable; **-s** *m. pl.* food, groceries.

cometa [ko·mé·ta] *m.* comet; *C.A.* person seldom seen; *f.* kite.

cometer [ko·me·tér] *v.* to commit; to entrust; to use (*a figure of speech*).

cometido [ko·me·tí·ðo] *m.* commission, assignment, charge; task, duty.

comezón [ko·me·són] *f.* itch.

comicios [ko·mí·sjos] *m. pl.* primaries, elections.

cómico [kó·mi·ko] *adj.* comic, of comedy; comical, funny, amusing; *m.* comedian, actor.

comida [ko·mí·ða] *f.* meal; dinner; good; **comidilla** *f.* small meal; gossip; **la comidilla de la vecindad** the talk of the town.

comienzo [ko·mjén·so] *m.* beginning; origin.

comilitona [ko·mi·li·tó·na] *f.* spread, big feast.

comilón [ko·mi·lón] *m.* big eater.

comillas [ko·mí·yas] *f. pl.* quotation marks.

comino [ko·mí·no] *m.* cuminseed.

comisario [ko·mi·sá·rjo] *m.* commissary, deputy, delegate; manager; *Am.* police inspector.

comisión [ko·mi·sjón] *f.* commission; committee.

comisionado [ko·mi·sjo·ná·ðo] *adj.* commissioned, charged, delegated; *m.* commissioner; *Am.* constable.

comisionar [ko·mi·sjo·nár] *v.* to commission.

comistrajo [ko·mis·trá·xo] *m.* mess, strange food concoction, mixture.

comité [ko·mi·té] *m.* committee, commission.

comitiva [ko·mi·tí·ƀa] *f.* retinue, group of attendants or followers.

como [kó·mo] *adv.* & *conj.* as, like, such as; if, provided that, since, when; *Mex., Ven.* about, approximately; **¿cómo?** [kó·mo] *interr. adv.* how?; what (did you say)?; *Am.* **¡cómo no!** yes, of course!

cómoda [kó·mo·ða] *f.* bureau, chest of drawers.

comodidad [ko·mo·ði·ðáð] *f.* comfort; convenience.

comodín [ko·mo·ðín] *m.* joker, wild card.

cómodo [kó·mo·ðo] *adj.* comfortable; convenient; *m. Am.* bedpan.

compacto [kom·pák·to] *adj.* compact.

compadecer[13] [kom·pa·ðe·sér] *v. irr.* to pity, sympathize with; **-se con** to be in harmony with; **-se de** to take pity on.

compadrazgo [kom·pa·ðráz·go] *m.* compaternity (*spiritual affinity between the godfather and the parents of a child*); friendship; relationship; clique, group of friends.

compadre [kom·pá·ðre] *m.* (*amigo*) pal, crony,

comrade; (*padrino*) cosponsor; *name used to express kinship between father and godfather*.

compañero [kom·pa·ñé·ro] *m.* companion; partner; **mate; compañerismo** [kom·pa·ñe·ríz·mo] *m.* companionship.

compañía [kom·pa·ñí·a] *f.* company; *Am.* **— del ahorcado** silent companion, poor company.

comparación [kom·pa·ra·sjón] *f.* comparison.

comparar [kom·pa·rár] *v.* to compare.

comparativo [kom·pa·ra·tí·ƀo] *adj.* comparative.

comparecer[13] [kom·pa·re·sér] *v. irr.* to appear (*before a judge or tribunal*).

compartimiento [kom·par·ti·mjén·to] *m.* compartment.

compartir [kom·par·tír] *v.* to share; to divide into shares.

compás [kom·pás] *m.* compass; measure; beat; **llevar el —** to beat time.

compasión [kom·pa·sjón] *f.* compassion, pity.

compasivo [kom·pa·sí·ƀo] *adj.* compassionate, sympathetic.

compatible [kom·pa·tí·ƀle] *adj.* compatible, in harmony.

compatriota [kom·pa·trjó·ta] *m.* & *f.* compatriot, fellow countryman.

compeler [kom·pe·lér] *v.* to compel, force.

compendiar [kom·pen·djár] *v.* to abstract, summarize, condense.

compendio [kom·pén·djo] *m.* summary, condensation.

compensación [kom·pen·sa·sjón] *f.* compensation; recompense.

compensar [kom·pen·sár] *v.* to balance; to make equal; to compensate, recompense.

competencia [kom·pe·tén·sja] *f.* competition, rivalry; competence, ability.

competente [kom·pe·tén·te] *adj.* competent; capable; adequate.

competidor [kom·pe·ti·ðór] *m.* competitor; rival; *adj.* competing.

competir[5] [kom·pe·tír] *v. irr.* to compete, vie.

compilar [kom·pi·lár] *v.* to compile.

compinche [kom·pín·če] *m.* chum, pal, comrade.

complacencia [kom·pla·sén·sja] *f.* complacency, satisfaction, contentment.

complacer[38] [kom·pla·sér] *v. irr.* to please, humor; to comply; **-se** to take pleasure or satisfaction (in).

coplaciente [kom·pla·sjén·te] *adj.* obliging, agreeable, willing to please.

complejidad [kom·ple·xi·ðáð] *f.* complexity.

complejo [kom·plé·xo] *adj.* & *m.* complex.

complemento [kom·ple·mén·to] *m.* complement; object (*of a verb*).

completamiento [kom·ple·ta·mjén·to] *m.* completion.

completar [kom·ple·tár] *v.* to complete; to finish.

completo [kom·plé·to] *adj.* complete, full, perfect.

complexión [kom·plek·sjón] *f.* constitution, make-up.

complicar[6] [kom·pli·kár] *v.* to complicate.

cómplice [kóm·pli·se] *m.* & *f.* accomplice, companion in crime.

complot [kom·plót], [kom·pló] *m.* plot, conspiracy; intrigue.

componenda [kom·po·nén·da] *f.* adjustment; compromise.

componente [kom·po·nén·te] *adj.* component, constituent; *m.* component, essential part.

componer[40] [kom·po·nér] *v. irr.* to fix, repair; to

fix up; to adorn, trim; to compose; to set up
(*type*); to settle (*a dispute*); *Col.* to set (*bones*).
comportamiento [kom·por·ta·mjén·to] *m.* conduct,
behavior.
composición [kom·po·si·sjón] *f.* composition;
settlement.
compositor [kom·po·si·tór] *m.* composer.
compostura [kom·pos·tú·ra] *f.* (*arreglo*) repair;
settlement, adjustment; (*aseo*) neatness,
composition; (*dignidad*) composure, dignity.
compota [kom·pó·ta] *f.* fruit preserves; — **de
manzana** applesauce.
compra [kóm·pra] *f.* purchase; buying; **ir de -s** to
go shopping.
comprador [kom·pra·dór] *m.* buyer, purchaser.
comprar [kom·prár] *v.* to buy, purchase.
comprender [kom·pren·dér] *v.* to understand,
grasp, comprehend; to comprise, embrace.
comprensible [kom·pren·sí·ble] *adj.*
comprehensible, understandable.
comprensión [kom·pren·sjón] *f.* understanding;
comprehension; keenness.
comprensivo [kom·pren·sí·bo] *adj.* comprehensive;
understanding.
compresión [kom·pre·sjón] *f.* compression.
compresor [kom·pre·sór] *m.* compressor.
comprimido [kom·pri·mí·do] *adj.* compressed; *m.*
medicinal tablet.
comprimir [kom·pri·mír] *v.* to compress; to
repress.
comprobación [kom·pro·ba·sjón] *f.* confirmation,
check, proof, test.
comprobante [kom·pro·bán·te] *adj.* proving,
verifying; *m.* proof; evidence; certificate;
voucher; warrant.
comprobar[2] [kom·pro·bár] *v. irr.* to verify; to
check; to prove.
comprometer [kom·pro·me·tér] *v.* (*exponer*) to
compromise; to endanger; to bind; to force;
(*concordar*) to come to an agreement; *-se* to
promise, bind oneself; to become engaged; to
compromise oneself.
compromiso [kom·pro·mí·so] *m.* (*convenio*)
compromise; (*obligación*) engagement;
appointment; (*dificultad*) predicament,
trouble.
compuerta [kom·pwér·ta] *f.* sluice (*gate to control
the flow of water*), floodgate.
compuesto [kom·pwés·to] *p.p. of* **componer** & *adj.*
repaired; fixed, adorned; composed; composite;
compound; *m.* composite; compound.
compungirse[11] [kom·pun·xír·se] *v.* to feel regret or
remorse.
computadora electrónica [kom·pu·ta·dó·ra
e·lek·tró·ni·ka] *f.* electronic computer.
computar [kom·pu·tár] *v.* to compute, calculate.
cómputo [kóm·pu·to] *m.* computation, calculation.
comulgar[7] [ko·mul·gár] *v.* to commune, take
communion.
común [ko·mún] *adj.* common; **por lo —**
generally; *m.* toilet; **el — de las gentes** the
majority of the people; the average person.
comunero [ko·mu·né·ro] *adj.* common, popular;
Am. pertaining to a community; *m.* commoner
(*one of the common people*); *Col., Ven., Andes*
member of an Indian community.
comunicación [ko·mu·ni·ka·sjón] *f.*
communication.
comunicar[6] [ko·mu·ni·kár] *v.* to communicate; to
notify; *-se* to communicate; to correspond; to be
in touch (with); to connect.

comunicativo [ko·mu·ni·ka·tí·bo] *adj.*
communicative, talkative.
comunidad [ko·mu·ni·dád] *f.* community;
commonwealth; the common people;
commonness; guild.
comunión [ko·mu·njón] *f.* communion; political
party.
comunismo [ko·mu·níz·mo] *m.* communism;
comunista [ko·mu·nís·ta] *m.* & *f.* communist;
adj. communistic, communist.
con [kon] *prep.* with; — **ser** in spite of being;
— **tal que** provided that; — **todo** however.
conato [ko·ná·to] *m.* attempt, effort; assault (*law*).
concavidad [koŋ·ka·bi·dád] *f.* hollow, cavity;
hollowness.
cóncavo [kóŋ·ka·bo] *adj.* concave, hollow.
concebible [kon·se·bí·ble] *adj.* conceivable.
concebir[5] [kon·se·bír] *v. irr.* to conceive; to
imagine; to understand, grasp.
conceder [kon·se·dér] *v.* to concede, grant; to
admit.
concejal [kon·se·xál] *m.* councilman, alderman.
concejo [kon·sé·xo] *m.* town council.
concentración [kon·sen·tra·sjón] *f.* concentration.
concentrar [kon·sen·trár] *v.* to concentrate.
concepción [kon·sep·sjón] *f.* conception.
concepto [kon·sép·to] *m.* concept, idea, thought.
concernir[51] [kon·ser·nír] *v. irr.* to concern.
concertar[1] [kon·ser·tár] *v. irr.* (*arreglar*) to arrange,
plan, settle; to conclude (*a treaty or business
deal*); (*concordar*) to harmonize; to agree.
concesión [kon·se·sjón] *f.* concession, grant;
granting; acknowledgment.
conciencia [kon·sjén·sja] *f.* conscience.
concienzudo [kon·sjen·sú·do] *adj.* conscientious.
concierto [kon·sjér·to] *m.* concert; harmony;
agreement; **de —** by common agreement.
conciliar [kon·si·ljár] *v.* to conciliate, win over; to
reconcile, bring into harmony; — **el sueño** to get
to sleep.
concilio [kon·sí·ljo] *m.* council.
concisión [kon·si·sjón] *f.* conciseness, brevity.
conciso [kon·sí·so] *adj.* concise, brief.
conciudadano [kon·sju·da·dá·no] *m.* fellow citizen,
fellow countryman.
concluir[32] [koŋ·klwír] *v. irr.* to conclude, finish; to
infer.
conclusión [koŋ·klu·sjón] *f.* conclusion.
concordancia [koŋ·kor·dán·sja] *f.* concord,
agreement, harmony.
concordar[2] [koŋ·kor·dár] *v. irr.* to agree; to be in
harmony; to put in harmony.
concordia [koŋ·kór·dja] *f.* concord, harmony,
agreement.
concretar [koŋ·kre·tár] *v.* to summarize, condense;
to limit; *-se a* to limit oneself to.
concreto [koŋ·kré·to] *adj.* concrete, real, specific;
en — concretely; to sum up; *m. Am.* concrete.
concupiscente [koŋ·ku·pi·sen·te] *adj.* sensual.
concurrencia [koŋ·ku·rrén·sja] *f.* gathering,
audience; concurrence, simultaneous meeting or
happening; competition.
concurrido [koŋ·ku·rrí·do] *adj.* well-patronized,
well-attended, much frequented.
concurrir [koŋ·ku·rrír] *v.* to concur, meet together;
to happen at the same time or place; to
attend; to agree.
concurso [koŋ·kúr·so] *m.* gathering; contest;
competitive examination; assistance.
concha [kón·ča] *f.* shell; shellfish; prompter's box;
Mex. **tener —** to be indifferent, unruffled, tough.

conchabar [kon·ča·ḃár] *v.* to unite, join; *Mex., S.A.* to hire (*labor*); **-se** to join, gang together; to conspire; *Ríopl.* to hire oneself out, get a job.
conchabo [kon·čá·ḃo] *m. Am.* hiring of a laborer or servant; *Ríopl.* job, menial job.
conde [kón·de] *m.* count; **condesa** *f.* countess.
condecoración [kon·de·ko·ra·sjón] *f.* decoration; badge, medal.
condecorar [kon·de·ko·rár] *v.* to decorate (*with a badge or medal*).
condena [kon·dé·na] *f.* term in prison, sentence, penalty.
condenación [kon·de·na·sjón] *f.* condemnation; conviction (*of a prisoner or criminal*); damnation.
condenar [kon·de·nár] *v.* to condemn; to sentence; *Am.* to annoy, irritate; **-se** to be damned, go to hell.
condensar [kon·den·sár] *v.* to condense.
condescendencia [kon·de·sen·dén·sja] *f.* condescension, patronizing attitude.
condescender[1] [kon·de·sen·dér] *v. irr.* to condescend; to comply, yield.
condición [kon·di·sjón] *f.* condition.
condimentar [kon·di·men·tár] *v.* to season.
condimento [kon·di·mén·to] *m.* condiment, seasoning.
condiscípulo [kon·di·sí·pu·lo] *m.* schoolmate, classmate.
condolerse[2] [kon·do·lér·se] *v. irr.* to condole (with), sympathize (with), be sorry (for).
cóndor [kón·dor] *m. Am.* condor, vulture; *Am.* gold coin of Ecuador, Chile and Colombia.
conducir[25] [kon·du·sír] *v. irr.* to conduct, lead; to drive (*an auto*); **-se** to behave, act.
conducta [kon·dúk·ta] *f.* conduct; behavior; convoy, escort; management.
conducto [kon·dúk·to] *m.* conduit, pipe, channel; **por — de** through.
conductor [kon·duk·tór] *adj.* conducting; *m.* leader; chauffeur; guide; conductor (*electrical*); *Am.* conductor, ticket collector (*on trains, buses, streetcars*); *Am.* teamster, driver.
conectar [ko·nek·tár] *v.* to connect.
conejera [ko·ne·xé·ra] *f.* burrow; rabbit warren (*piece of land for breeding rabbits*); den, joint, dive (*of ill repute*).
conejo [ko·nè·xo] *m.* rabbit; *Am.* guinea pig; **conejillo de Indias** [ko·ne·xí·yo đe in·djas] guinea pig.
conexión [ko·nek·sjón] *f.* connection.
conexo [ko·nék·so] *adj.* connected; coherent.
confección [kon·fek·sjón] *f.* making; confection; manufactured article; workmanship; concoction, compound.
confeccionar [kon·fek·sjo·nár] *v.* to make; to manufacture; to mix, put up (*a prescription*).
confederación [kon·fe·đe·ra·sjón] *f.* confederation, alliance, league.
confederar [kon·fe·đe·rár] *v.* to confederate; **-se** to confederate, form into a confederacy.
conferencia [kon·fe·rén·sja] *f.* lecture; conference, meeting.
conferenciante [kon·fe·ren·sján·te] *m. & f.* lecturer.
conferencista [kon·fe·ren·sís·ta] *m. & f.* lecturer.
conferir[3] [kon·fe·rír] *v. irr.* to confer; to give, bestow.
confesar[1] [kon·fe·sár] *v. irr.* to confess.
confesión [kon·fe·sjón] *f.* confession.
confesionario [kon·fe·sjo·ná·rjo] *m.* confessional, confessional box.

confesor [kon·fe·sór] *m.* confessor.
confiado [kon·fjá·đo] *adj.* confident, trusting, credulous; presumptuous, self-confident.
confianza [kon·fján·sa] *f.* confidence, trust; familiarity; informality; **reunión de —** informal gathering or party.
confianzudo [kon·fjan·sú·đo] *adj.* over-friendly, over-familiar; *Am.* meddlesome.
confiar[17] [kon·fjár] *v.* to confide, entrust; to trust, hope firmly.
confidencia [kon·fi·đén·sja] *f.* confidence, trust; secret, confidential remark; **confidencial** [kon·fi·đen·sjál] *adj.* confidential.
confidente [kon·fi·đén·te] *m.* confidant; spy, secret agent; settee or sofa for two people, love seat; *adj.* faithful, trustworthy.
confín [kon·fín] *m.* limit, border, boundary; *adj.* bordering, limiting.
confinar [kon·fi·nár] *v.* to border (upon); to confine, exile to a specific place.
confirmación [kon·fir·ma·sjón] *f.* confirmation.
confirmar [kon·fir·már] *v.* to confirm.
confiscar[6] [kon·fis·kár] *v.* to confiscate.
confitar [kon·fi·tár] *v.* to candy (*with sugar syrup*); to make into candy or preserves; to sweeten.
confite [kon·fí·te] *m.* candy, bonbon; **confitería** [kon·fi·te·rí·a] *f.* confectionery; candy shop; **confitura** [kon·fi·tú·ra] *f.* confection.
conflicto [kon·flík·to] *m.* conflict.
confluencia [kon·flwén·sja] *f.* junction (*of two rivers*).
conformar [kon·for·már] *v.* to adapt, adjust; **-se** to conform, comply; to agree; to be resigned (to); to be satisfied.
conforme [kon·fór·me] *adj.* in agreement; resigned, satisfied; alike, similar; **— a** in accordance with.
conformidad [kon·for·mi·đáđ] *f.* conformity; agreement, harmony; compliance; **— con la voluntad de Dios** resignation to the will of God; **en — con** in compliance with; **estar de — con** to be in accordance or agreement with.
confortar [kon·for·tár] *v.* to comfort, console.
confraternidad [kon·fra·ter·ni·đáđ] *f.* brotherhood.
confrontar [kon·fron·tár] *v.* to confront; to face; to compare, check.
confundir [kon·fun·dír] *v.* to confound, confuse, mix up; to bewilder; to shame.
confusión [kon·fu·sjón] *f.* confusion.
confuso [kon·fú·so] *adj.* confused, bewildered; blurred; vague.
congelado [koŋ·xe·lá·đo] *p.p. & adj.* frozen; icy.
congelar [koŋ·xe·lár] *v.* to congeal, freeze.
congenial [koŋ·xe·njál] *adj.* congenial.
congeniar [koŋ·xe·njár] *v.* to be congenial (with); to harmonize, be in harmony (with).
congoja [koŋ·gó·xa] *f.* anguish, grief, anxiety.
congratular [koŋ·gra·tu·lár] *v.* to congratulate.
congregación [koŋ·gre·ga·sjón] *f.* congregation, assembly; religious fraternity.
congregar[7] [koŋ·gre·gár] *v.* to congregate, call together; to assemble; **-se** to congregate, assemble.
congresista [koŋ·gre·sís·ta] *m.* congressman; conventionite; *f.* congresswoman.
congreso [koŋ·gré·so] *m.* congress, assembly; convention; **— de los Diputados** House of Representatives.
conjetura [koŋ·xe·tú·ra] *f.* conjecture, guess, surmise.
conjeturar [koŋ·xe·tu·rár] *v.* to conjecture, guess, surmise.

CO

conjugación [koŋ·xu·ga·sjón] *f.* conjugation; coupling, joining together.
conjugar[7] [koŋ·xu·gár] *v.* to conjugate.
conjunción [koŋ·xun·sjón] *f.* conjunction; union, combination.
conjunto [koŋ·xún·to] *m.* total, whole, entirety; **en** — as a whole; *adj.* joined; related, allied.
conjuración [koŋ·xu·ra·sjón] *f.* conspiracy, plot.
conjurado [koŋ·xu·rá·đo] *m.* conspirator.
conjurar [koŋ·xu·rár] *v.* to conspire, plot; to join a conspiracy; to entreat; to conjure; to ward off.
conjuro [kon·xu·ro] *m.* conspiracy; exorcism.
conmemorar [kom·me·mo·rár] *v.* to commemorate.
conmemorativo [kom·me·mo·ra·tí·bo] *adj.* memorial, serving to commemorate.
conmigo [kom·mí·go] with me.
conminación [kom·mi·na·sjón] *f.* threat.
conminatorio [kom·mi·na·tó·rjo] *adj.* threatening.
conmoción [kom·mo·sjón] *f.* commotion.
conmovedor [kom·mo·be·đór] *adj.* moving, touching; stirring.
conmover[2] [kom·mo·bér] *v. irr.* to move, touch, affect (*with emotion*); to stir (*emotions*).
conmutador [kom·mu·ta·đór] *m.* electric switch; **cuadro** — switchboard.
connatural [kon·na·tu·rál] *adj.* inborn.
cono [kó·no] *m.* cone; pine cone.
conocedor [ko·no·se·đór] *adj.* knowing, aware, expert; *m.* connoisseur, judge, expert; **ser** — **de** to be judge of.
conocer[13] [ko·no·sér] *v. irr.* (*tener idea de*) to know, be acquainted with; to recognize; (*llegar a conocer*) to meet; **se conoce que** it is clear or evident that.
conocido [ko·no·sí·đo] *p.p. & adj.* known; well-known; *m.* acquaintance.
conocimiento [ko·no·si·mjén·to] *m.* (*inteligencia*) knowledge, understanding; acquaintance; (*documento*) bill of lading; **-s** knowledge, learning; **poner en** — to inform.
conque [kóŋ·ke] *conj.* so then, well then, and so.
conquista [koŋ·kís·ta] *f.* conquest.
conquistador [koŋ·kis·ta·đór] *m.* conqueror; *adj.* conquering, victorious.
conquistar [koŋ·kis·tár] *v.* to conquer, defeat; to win.
consabido [kon·sa·bí·đo] *adj.* aforementioned, aforesaid.
consagración [kon·sa·gra·sjón] *f.* consecration.
consagrar [kon·sa·grár] *v.* to consecrate.
consciencia [kon·sjén·sja] *f.* consciousness.
consciente [kon·sjén·te] *adj.* conscious.
consecución [kon·se·ku·sjón] *f.* attainment.
consecuencia [kon·se·kwén·sja] *f.* consequence; result; **a** — **de** as a result of; **por** (*or* **en**) — therefore; consequently.
consecuente [kon·se·kwén·te] *adj.* consequent, logical; consistent; *m.* consequence, result.
consecutivo [kon·se·ku·tí·bo] *adj.* consecutive, successive.
conseguir[5, 12] [kon·se·gír] *v. irr.* to get, obtain; to reach, attain.
conseja [kon·sé·xa] *f.* old wives' tale, fable.
consejero [kon·se·xé·ro] *m.* adviser counselor.
consejo [kon·sé·xo] *m.* counsel, advice; council; council hall.
consentimiento [kon·sen·ti·mjén·to] *m.* consent.
consentir[3] [kon·sen·tír] *v. irr.* to consent, permit; to pamper, spoil.
conserje [kon·sér·xe] *m.* janitor, caretaker.

conserva [kon·sér·ba] *f.* preserve; pickled fruit or vegetables; *Ch.* filling (*for tarts or candy*).
conservación [kon·ser·ba·sjón] *f.* conservation.
conservador [kon·ser·ba·đór] *m.* conservative; preserver; guardian; *adj.* conservative.
conservar [kon·ser·bár] *v.* to conserve, keep; to preserve.
considerable [kon·si·đe·rá·ble] *adj.* considerable.
consideración [kon·si·đe·ra·sjón] *f.* consideration.
considerado [kon·si·đe·rá·đo] *adj.* considerate, thoughtful; respected; prudent.
considerar [kon·si·đe·rár] *v.* to consider; to treat with consideration.
consigna [kon·sig·na] *f.* watchword, password; *Am.* checkroom.
consignar [kon·sig·nár] *v.* to consign; to deliver; to deposit; to assign; to check (*baggage*).
consigo [kon·sí·go] with oneself; with himself (herself, themselves).
consiguiente [kon·si·gjén·te] *adj.* consequent; *m.* consequence; **por** — consequently.
consistente [kon·sis·tén·te] *adj.* firm, substantial.
consistir [kon·sis·tír] *v.* to consist; to be based on; **¿en qué consiste?** why?; what is the explanation for it?
consocio [kon·só·sjo] *m.* associate, partner.
consolación [kon·so·la·sjón[*f.* consolation.
consolar[2] [kon·so·lár] *v. irr.* to console, cheer.
consolidar [kon·so·li·đár] *v.* to consolidate, make solid; to unite, combine.
consonante [kon·so·nán·te] *m.* perfect rhyme; *f.* consonant; *adj.* in harmony.
consorte [kon·sór·te] *m. & f.* consort; mate; companion.
conspicuo [kons·pí·kwo] *adj.* conspicuous.
conspiración [kons·pi·ra·sjón] *f.* conspiracy, plot.
conspirador [kons·pi·ra·đór] *m.* conspirator, plotter.
conspirar [kons·pi·rár] *v.* to conspire, plot.
constancia [kons·tán·sja] *f.* (*firmeza*) constancy; perseverance; (*certeza*) evidence, certainty; *Am.* documentary proof, record.
constante [kons·tán·te] *adj.* constant; continual; firm, faithful.
constar [kons·tár] *v.* to be evident, clear; to consist (of), be composed (of); to be on record.
constatación [kons·ta·ta·sjón] *f. Am.* proof, check, evidence.
constelación [kons·te·la·sjón] *f.* constellation.
constipado [kons·ti·pá·đo] *adj.* suffering from a cold; *m.* cold in the head.
constipar [kons·ti·pár] *v.* to stop up (*the nasal passages*); to cause a cold; **-se** to catch cold.
constitución [kons·ti·tu·sjón] *f.* constitution.
constitucional [kons·ti·tu·sjo·nál] *adj.* constitutional.
constituir[32] [kons·ti·twír] *v. irr.* to constitute, form; to set up, establish; **-se en** to set oneself up as.
constitutivo [kons·ti·tu·tí·bo] = **constituyente**.
constituyente [kons·ti·tu·yén·te] *adj.* constituent.
constreñir[5, 19] [kons·tre·ñír] *v. irr.* to constrain; to compel, oblige.
construcción [kons·truk·sjón] *f.* construction; structure; building.
construir[32] [kons·trwír] *v. irr.* to construct, build.
consuelo [kon·swé·lo] *m.* consolation, comfort; relief; cheer.
consuetudinario [kon·swe·tu·đi·ná·rjo] *adj.* habitual, customary; **derecho** — common law.
cónsul [kón·sul] *m.* consul.
consulado [kon·su·lá·đo] *m.* consulate.

consulta [kon·súl·ta] *f.* consultation; opinion.
consultar [kon·sul·tár] *v.* to consult.
consultorio [kon·sul·tó·rjo] *m.* office for consultation; doctor's office or clinic.
consumado [kon·su·má·đo] *p.p. of* **consumar**; *adj.* consummate, perfect, complete; accomplished.
consumar [kon·su·már] *v.* to consummate, complete.
consumidor [kon·su·mi·đór] *m.* consumer; *adj.* consuming.
consumir [kon·su·mír] *v.* to consume; to waste; **-se** to be consumed; to burn out; to be exhausted; to waste away.
consumo [kon·sú·mo] *m.* consumption (*of food, provisions, etc.*).
consunción [kon·sun·sjón] *f.* consumption (*illness*).
contabilidad [kon·ta·ƀi·li·đáđ] *f.* accounting; bookkeeping.
contacto [kon·ták·to] *m.* contact.
contado [kon·tá·đo]: **al** — in cash; **de** — immediately; **por de** — of course; **contados** *adj.* few, scarce, rare.
contador [kon·ta·đór] *m.* accountant; purser, cashier; counter; meter (*for water, gas, or electricity*); — **geiger** Geiger counter; Geiger-Müller counter.
contaduría [kon·ta·đu·rí·a] *f.* accountant's or auditor's office; box office; cashier's office; accounting.
contagiar [kon·ta·xjár] *v.* to infect; to corrupt; to contaminate.
contagio [kon·tá·xjo] *m.* contagion; infection.
contagioso [kon·ta·xjó·so] *adj.* contagious; infectious.
contaminar [kon·ta·mi·nár] *v.* to contaminate, defile; to corrupt.
contar[2] [kon·tár] *v. irr.* to count; to tell, relate; — **con** to count on, rely on; **a** — **desde** starting from, beginning with.
contemplación [kon·tem·pla·sjón] *f.* contemplation; gazing; meditation.
contemplar [kon·tem·plár] *v.* to contemplate, gaze at; to examine; to meditate.
contemporáneo [kon·tem·po·rá·ne·o] *adj.* contemporary.
contender[1] [kon·ten·dér] *v. irr.* to contend, fight; to compete.
contener[45] [kon·te·nér] *v. irr.* to contain; to restrain, check; **-se** to refrain; to restrain oneself.
contenido [kon·te·ni·đo] *m.* contents; *adj.* restrained, moderate.
contentamiento [kon·ten·ta·mjén·to] *m.* contentment, joy.
contentar [kon·ten·tár] *v.* to give pleasure, make happy; **-se** to be satisfied, pleased; *Am.* to make up, renew friendship.
contento [kon·tén·to] *adj.* content, contented, satisfied, glad; *m.* gladness, contentment.
contera [kon·té·ra] *f.* metal tip (*of a cane, umbrella, etc.*); tip, end; refrain of a song; **por** — as a finishing touch.
contertulio [kon·ter·tú·ljo] *m.* fellow-member.
contestación [kon·tes·ta·sjón] *f.* answer, reply; argument.
contestar [kon·tes·tár] *v.* to answer, reply.
contextura [kon·tes·tú·ra] *f.* texture, composition; structure (*of animal or vegetable tissues*).
contienda [kon·tjén·da] *f.* fight; dispute; contest.
contigo [kon·ti·ǵo] with you (with thee).
contiguo [kon·ti·gwo] *adj.* contiguous, next, neighboring.

continental [kon·ti·nen·tál] *adj.* continental.
continente [kon·ti·nén·te] *m.* continent; countenance; *adj.* continent, moderate, sober.
contingencia [kon·tiŋ·xén·sja] *f.* contingency, possibility; risk.
contigente [kon·tiŋ·xén·te] *adj.* contingent, accidental; *m.* quota; military contingent.
continuación [kon·ti·nwa·sjón] *f.* continuation; continuance; **a** — below, as follows.
continuar[18] [kon·ti·nwár] *v.* to continue; to last.
continuidad [kon·ti·nwi·đáđ] *f.* continuity.
continuo [kon·tí·nwo] *adj.* continuous, connected; continual; steady, constant.
contonearse [kon·to·ne·ár·se] *v.* to strut, swagger; to waddle.
contoneo [kon·to·né·o] *m.* strut; waddle.
contorno [kon·tór·no] *m.* (*circuito*) environs, surrounding country (*usually used in plural*); (*línea*) contour, outline.
contra [kón·tra] *prep.* against; **el pro y el** — the pro and con; *f.* opposition; *Am.* antidote, remedy; **-s** *Am.* play-off, final game (*to determine the winner*); **llevar a uno la** — to contradict a person, take the opposite view.
contraalmirante [kon·tra·al·mi·rán·te] *m.* rear admiral.
contrabajo [kon·tra·ƀá·xo] *m.* bass fiddle, string bass.
contrabandear [kon·tra·ƀan·de·ár] *v.* to smuggle.
contrabandista [kon·tra·ƀan·dís·ta] *m.* smuggler.
contrabando [kon·tra·ƀán·do] *m.* contraband; smuggled goods; smuggling.
contracción [kon·trak·sjón] *f.* contraction; *Ch., Peru* diligence, application, devotion.
contradecir[27] [kon·tra·đe·sír] *v. irr.* to contradict.
contradicción [kon·tra·đik·sjón] *f.* contradiction.
contradictorio [kon·tra·đik·tó·rjo] *adj.* contradictory, contrary, opposing.
contradicho [kon·tra·đí·čo] *p.p. of* **contradecir**.
contraer[46] [kon·tra·ér] *v. irr.* to contract; — **matrimonio** to get married; **-se** to shrink; to contract.
contrafuerte [kon·tra·fwér·te] *m.* buttress; spur (*of a mountain*); **-s** secondary chain of mountains.
contrahacer[31] [kon·tra·a·sér] *v. irr.* to counterfeit; to forge; to copy, imitate; to mimic.
contrahecho [kon·tra·é·čo] *p.p. of* **contrahacer** & *adj.* counterfeit; forged; deformed.
contralor [kon·tra·lór] *m. Am.* controller or comptroller (*of accounts or expenditures*). *See* **controlador**.
contraorden [kon·tra·ór·đen] *f.* countermand; cancellation of an order.
contrapelo [kon·tra·pé·lo]: **a** — against the grain.
contrapesar [kon·tra·pe·sár] *v.* to counterbalance, balance; to offset.
contrapeso [kon·tra·pé·so] *m.* counterpoise, counterweight, counterbalance; *Am.* fear, uneasiness.
contrariar[17] [kon·tra·rjár] *v.* to oppose; to contradict; to irritate, vex.
contrariedad [kon·tra·rje·đáđ] *f.* opposition; contradiction; bother, irritation; disappointment.
contrario [kon·trá·rjo] *adj.* contrary; opposite; *m.* opponent.
contrarrestar [kon·tra·rres·tár] *v.* to counteract; to resist, oppose; to strike back (*a ball*).
contrarrevolución [kon·tra·rre·ƀo·lu·sjón] *f.* counterrevolution.
contraseña [kon·tra·sé·ña] *f.* password, watchword.

CO

mark; check (*for baggage*); — **de salida** theatre check (*to re-enter during the performance*).
contrastar [kon·tras·tár] *v.* (*contrapesar*) to contrast; to test (*scales, weights, measures, etc.*); to assay (*metals*); (*resistir*) to resist, oppose.
contraste [kon·trás·te] *m.* contrast; assay, test; assayer, tester; assayer's office.
contrata [kon·trá·ta] *f.* contract, bargain, agreement.
contratar [kon·tra·tár] *v.* to contract for; to trade; to engage, hire (*men*); **-se** to come to, or make, an agreement.
contratiempo [kon·tra·tjém·po] *m.* accident, mishap.
contratista [kon·tra·tís·ta] *m. & f.* contractor.
contrato [kon·trá·to] *m.* contract.
contraventana [kon·tra·ɓen·tá·na] *f.* shutter.
contribución [kon·tri·ɓu·sjón] *f.* contribution; tax.
contribuir[32] [kon·tri·ɓwír] *v. irr.* to contribute.
contribuyente [kon·tri·ɓu·yén·te] *m.* contributor; tax-payer; *adj.* contributing.
control [kon·tról] *m. Am.* control.
controlador [kon·tro·la·ɗór] *m. Am.* controller.
controlar [kon·tro·lár] *v. Am.* to control.
controversia [kon·tro·ɓér·sja] *f.* controversy.
contumacia [kon·tu·má·sja] *f.* stubbornness, obstinacy; contempt of court, failure to appear in court; rebelliousness.
contumaz [kon·tu·más] *adj.* stubborn; rebellious.
contusión [kon·tu·sjón] *f.* bruise.
convalecer[13] [kom·ba·le·sér] *v. irr.* to convalesce, recover from an illness.
convecino [kom·be·sí·no] *adj.* near, neighboring; *m.* neighbor.
convencedor [kom·ben·se·ɗór] *adj.* convincing.
convencer[10] [kom·ben·sér] *v.* to convince.
convencimiento [kom·ben·si·mjén·to] *m.* conviction, belief; convincing.
convención [kom·ben·sjón] *f.* convention, assembly; pact, agreement; *Ríopl., Col., Ven., Mex., Carib.* political convention; **convencional** [kom·ben·sjo·nál] *adj.* conventional.
convenido [kom·be·ní·ɗo] *adj.* agreed; O.K., all right; *p.p. of* **convenir**.
conveniencia [kom·be·njén·sja] *f.* convenience; comfort; utility, profit.
conveniente [kom·be·njén·te] *adj.* convenient, useful, profitable; fit, proper, suitable; opportune.
convenio [kom·bé·njo] *m.* pact, agreement.
convenir[48] [kom·be·nir] *v. irr.* to agree; to convene, assemble; to be suitable, proper, advisable; to suit, fit; **-se** to agree.
conventillo [kom·ben·tí·yo] *m. Ríopl., Ch.* tenement house.
convento [kom·bén·to] *m.* convent.
convergente [kom·ber·xén·te] *adj.* convergent, coming together.
converger[11] [kom·ber·xér], **convergir**[11] [kom·ber·xir] *v.* to converge.
conversación [kom·ber·sa·sjón] *f.* conversation.
conversar [kom·ber·sár] *v.* to converse.
conversión [kom·ber·sjón] *f.* conversion.
convertir[3] [kom·ber·tír] *v. irr.* to convert.
convicción [kom·bik·sjón] *f.* conviction.
convicto [kom·bík·to] *p.p. irr. of* **convencer**; convicted, guilty.
convidado [kom·bi·ɗá·ɗo] *m.* guest; *Am.* — **y con ollita** guest who abuses hospitality.
convidar [kom·bi·ɗár] *v.* to invite; **-se** to volunteer one's services; to invite oneself.

convincente [kom·bin·sén·te] *adj.* convincing.
convite [kom·bí·te] *m.* invitation; banquet.
convocación [kom·bo·ka·sjón] *f.* convocation.
convocar[6] [kom·bo·kár] *v.* to convoke, call together.
convoyar [kom·bo·yár] *v.* to convoy, escort.
convulsión [kom·bul·sjón] *f.* convulsion.
convulsivo [kom·bul·sí·ɓo] *adj.* convulsive; **tos convulsiva** whooping cough.
conyugal [kon·ŷu·gál] *adj.* conjugal, pertaining to marriage or a married couple; **vida** — married life.
cónyuge [kón·yu·xe] *m.* husband; *f.* wife.
cooperación [ko·o·pe·ra·sjón] *f.* cooperation.
cooperador [ko·o·pe·ra·ɗór] *adj.* cooperating, cooperative; *m.* cooperator, co-worker.
cooperar [ko·o·pe·rár] *v.* to cooperate.
cooperativo [ko·o·pe·ra·tí·ɓo] *adj.* cooperative; **cooperativa** *f.* cooperative, cooperative society.
coordinación [ko·or·ɗi·na·sjón] *f.* coordination.
coordinar [ko·or·ɗi·nár] *v.* to coordinate.
copa [kó·pa] *f.* (*vaso*) goblet; (*de árbol*) treetop; (*de sombrero*) crown; (*palo de la baraja*) card in the suit of copas (*Spanish deck of cards*); *Am.* **empinar la** — to drink, get drunk.
copartícipe [ko·par·tí·si·pe] *adj.* participant; *m. & f.* joint partner.
copete [ko·pé·te] *m.* tuft; crest; top, summit; ornamental top on furniture; **de** — of high rank, important; proud; **estar uno hasta el** — to be stuffed; to be fed up; **tener mucho** — to be arrogant, haughty.
copia [kó·pja] *f.* copy; imitation; abundance.
copiar [ko·pjár] *v.* to copy.
copioso [ko·pjó·so] *adj.* copious, abundant.
copita [ko·pí·ta] *f.* little glass; little drink.
copla [kó·pla] *f.* couplet; stanza (*of variable length and meter*); popular song.
copo [kó·po] *m.* (*de nieve*) snowflake; (*mechón*) wad, tuft (*of wool or cotton*).
copularse [ko·pu·lár·se] *v.* to have sexual relations.
coqueta [ko·ké·ta] *f.* coquette, flirt.
coquetear [ko·ke·te·ár] *v.* to flirt.
coquetería [ko·ke·te·rí·a] *f.* coquetry, flirting.
coraje [ko·rá·xe] *m.* courage, valor; anger.
coral [ko·rál] *m.* coral; *Am.* red poisonous snake; **-es** coral beads; *adj.* choral, pertaining to a choir; **coralino** [ko·ra·lí·no] *adj.* coral, like coral.
coraza [ko·rá·sa] *f.* cuirass, armor; armor plate or plating; shell (*of a turtle*).
corazón [ko·ra·són] *m.* heart; core, center.
corazonada [ko·ra·so·ná·ɗa] *f.* presentiment, foreboding; hunch.
corbata [kor·bá·ta] *f.* necktie; cravat; *Am.* colorful kerchief, scarf.
corcel [kor·sél] *m.* charger, steed.
corcova [kor·kó·ba] *f.* hump, hunch; **corcovado** [kor·ko·ɓá·ɗo] *adj.* hunchbacked; *m.* hunchback.
corcovear [kor·ko·ɓe·ár] *v.* to prance about, leap; *Am.* to kick, protest against.
corchete [kor·čé·te] *m.* hook and eye.
corcho [kór·čo] *m.* cork; beehive; *adj. Am.* cork-like, spongy.
cordel [kor·dél] *m.* cord, rope.
cordero [kor·ɗé·ro] *m.* lamb; lambskin.
cordial [kor·djál] *adj.* cordial, friendly; **dedo** — middle finger.
cordialidad [kor·dja·li·ɗáɗ] *f.* cordiality, friendliness, warmth.
cordillera [kor·ɗi·yé·ra] *f.* mountain range.
cordobés [kor·ɗo·ɓés] *adj.* Cordovan, of or

pertaining to Cordova; *m.* native of Cordova.
cordón [kor·dón] *m.* cord; braid; cordon, line of
soldiers; *Riopl.* — **de la acera** curb, curbstone
of the sidewalk; **cordonería** [kor·do·ne·rí·a] *f.*
lace or cord maker's shop; collection of cords
and laces; cordmaker's work; braiding.
cordoncillo [kor·don·sí·yo] *m.* small cord,
drawstring, lace, lacing; braid; mill (*ridged edge
of a coin*); ridge, rib (*of certain fabrics*).
cordura [kor·dú·ra] *f.* good judgment, wisdom;
sanity.
cornada [kor·ná·da] *f.* goring; butt with the horns;
dar -s to gore, horn, butt with the horns.
corneta [kor·né·ta] *f.* cornet; bugle; horn; *m.*
bugler.
cornisa [kor·rí·sa] *f.* cornice.
coro [kó·ro] *m.* choir; chorus.
corona [ko·ró·na] *f.* crown; wreath.
coronar [ko·ro·nár] *v.* to crown; to top.
coronel [ko·ro·nél] *m.* colonel.
coronilla [ko·ro·ní·ya] *f.* small crown; crown of the
head; **estar uno hasta la** — to be fed up, be
satiated.
corpanchón [kor·pan·čón] *m.* large body; carcass.
corpiño [kor·pí·ño] *m.* bodice.
corporación [kor·po·ra·sjón] *f.* corporation.
corporal [kor·po·rál] *adj.* corporal, of the body;
m. corporal (*small piece of linen used at Mass*).
corpóreo [kor·pó·re·o] *adj.* corporeal, bodily;.
tangible, material.
corpulento [kor·pu·lén·to] *adj.* corpulent, fat, stout.
corral [ko·rrál] *m.* yard; corral, cattle yard;
corralón [ko·rra·lón] *m.* large corral; *Am.* lumber
warehouse.
correa [ko·rré·a] *f.* leather strap; resistance; *Ch.*
-s leather blanket carrier; *Am.* **tener muchas -s**
to be phlegmatic, calm.
corrección [ko·rrek·sjón] *f.* correction; correctness.
correcto [ko·rrék·to] *adj.* correct, proper.
corredizo [ko·rre·dí·so] *adj.* sliding, slipping; **nudo**
— slip knot.
corredor [ko·rre·dór] *m.* (*que corre*) runner, racer;
(*pasillo*) corridor; gallery around a patio;
(*revendedor*) broker; *Carib., Andes* covered
porch; *Am.* beater of wild game; *adj.* running;
speedy.
corregidor [ko·rre·xi·dór] *m.* corrector; Spanish
magistrate.
corregir[5, 11] [ko·rre·xír] *v. irr.* to correct; to
reprove; to punish; **-se** to mend one's ways.
correligionario [ko·rre·li·xjo·ná·rjo] *adj.* of the
same religion; of the same political party or
sympathies; *m.* coreligionist.
correntada [ko·rren·tá·da] *f. Ch., Riopl., C.A.,
Carib.* strong river current.
correo [ko·rré·o] *m.* mail; mail service; postman;
post office; — **aéreo** air mail.
correón [ko·rre·ón] *m.* large strap.
correoso [ko·rre·ó·so] *adj.* flexible; leathery, tough;
correosidad [ko·rre·o·si·dád] *f.* toughness;
flexibility.
correr [ko·rrér] *v.* (*caminar*) to run; to blow (*said
of the wind*); (*encarrera*) to race; to chase;
(*pasar*) to pass, elapse (*time*); to draw (*a
curtain*); *Am.* to dismiss, throw out; **-se** to slip
through; to slide; to be embarrassed.
correría [ko·rre·rí·a] *f.* foray, raid for plunder;
excursion, short trip; **-s** wanderings, travels;
raids.
correspondencia [ko·rres·pon·dén·sja] *f.*
correspondence; letters, mail; agreement;

interchange.
corresponder [ko·rres·pon·dér] *v.* to reciprocate,
return (*love, favors*); to belong; to concern; to
correspond (*one thing with another*).
correspondiente [ko·rres·pon·djén·te] *adj.*
corresponding, agreeing; respective; *m.*
correspondent.
corresponsal [ko·rres·pon·sál] *m.* correspondent;
agent; newspaper reporter.
corretear [ko·rre·te·ár] *v.* to run around; to roam,
rove; *Am.* to pursue, chase.
corrida [ko·rrí·da] *f.* race; *Ch.* row, file; *P.R.* night
spree; *Am.* beating up of game; — **del tiempo**
swiftness of time; — **de toros** bullfight; **de** —
without stopping.
corrido [ko·rrí·do] *adj.* embarrassed, ashamed;
worldly-wise; flowing, fluent; **de** — without
stopping; *m. Mex., Col., Ven., Riopl., Andes*
popular ballad.
corriente [ko·rrjén·te] *adj.* (*que corre*) running;
flowing, fluent; (*común*) usual, common,
ordinary; *Am.* frank, open; **¡** — **!** all right!
O.K.!; **el ocho del** — the eighth of the current
month; **estar al** — to be up-to-date; to be
well-informed (*about current news*); **poner a uno
al** — to keep someone posted or well
informed; *f.* current; flow; course; *Am.* **hay que
llevarle la** — one must humor him.
corrillo [ko·rrí·yo] *m.* circle or group of gossipers.
corro [kó·rro] *m.* group of talkers or spectators.
corroer[51] [ko·rro·ér] *v. irr.* to corrode.
corromper [ko·rrom·pér] *v.* to corrupt; to seduce;
to bribe; **-se** to rot; to become corrupted.
corrompido [ko·rrom·pi·do] *adj.* corrupt; rotten,
spoiled; degenerate; *p.p. of* **corromper.**
corrupción [ko·rrup·sjón] *f.* corruption.
corrupto [ko·rrúp·to] *adj.* corrupt, rotten.
corsé [kor·sé] *m.* corset.
cortada [kor·tá·da] *f. Col., Ven., Carib.* cut, slash.
cortador [kor·ta·dór] *m.* cutter.
cortadura [kor·ta·dú·ra] *m.* cut; gash; slash.
cortante [kor·tán·te] *adj.* cutting; sharp.
cortaplumas [kor·ta·plú·mas] *m.* penknife.
cortar [kor·tár] *v.* to cut; to cut off; to cut out;
to cut down; to interrupt; *Ven.* to harvest,
pick (*fruit*); to gossip, speak ill of someone;
-se to be embarrassed, ashamed; to sour, curdle
(*said of milk*); *Am.* to become separated, cut off;
Mex., Cuba to leave in a hurry; *Am.* to die.
corte [kór·te] *m.* cut; cutting; cutting edge; fit,
style; *Carib., Mex., Riopl.* cut (*in cards*); *Am.*
harvest; *Am.* weeding; *Am.* gracefulness in
dancing; *f.* royal court; retinue; *P.R., Ven.* court
of justice; **-s** Spanish parliament; **hacer la** —
to court, woo; *Am.* **darse uno** — to put on airs.
cortedad [kor·te·dád] *f.* smallness; timidity;
bashfulness, shyness.
cortejar [kor·te·xár] *v.* to court, woo.
cortejo [kor·té·xo] *m.* cortege, procession; retinue;
courtship; suitor.
cortés [kor·tés] *adj.* courteous, polite.
cortesana [kor·te·sá·na] *f.* courtesan, prostitute.
cortesano [kor·te·sá·no] *m.* courtier; *adj.* courtlike;
courteous.
cortesía [kor·te·sí·a] *f.* courtesy, politeness.
corteza [kor·té·sa] *f.* bark; crust; peel.
cortijo [kor·tí·xo] *m.* farmhouse.
cortina [kor·tí·na] *m.* curtain.
corto [kór·to] *adj.* short; scanty; bashful.
corveta [kor·bé·ta] *f.* buck, leap, bound (*of a
horse*); **hacer -s** to prance.

CO

corvo [kór·ƀo] *adj. see* **curvo**.

cosa [kó·sa] *f.* thing; — **de** approximately, about; **no es** — it is not worth anything; **otra** — something else; **como si tal** — serene, as if nothing had happened; *Am.* **ni por una de estas nueve -s** absolutely not, not for anything in the world.

cosecha [ko·sé·ča] *f.* crop; harvest.

cosechar [ko·se·čár] *v.* to reap; to harvest.

coser [ko·sér] *v.* to sew; to stitch.

cosmético [koz·mé·ti·ko] *m. & adj.* cosmetic.

cosquillas [kos·kí·yas] *f. pl.* ticklishness; tickling; **hacer** — to tickle; to excite (*one's desire or curiosity*); **tener** — to be ticklish.

cosquillear [kos·ki·ye·ár] *v.* to tickle; to excite (*one's curiosity or desire*).

cosquilleo [kos·ki·yé·o] *m.* tickle, tickling sensation.

cosquilloso [kos·ki·yó·so] *adj.* ticklish; touchy.

costa [kós·ta] *f.* coast; cost, expense, price; **a toda** — at all costs, by all means.

costado [kos·tá·ɖo] *m.* side; flank.

costal [kos·tál] *m.* sack; **estar hecho un** — **de huesos** to be nothing but skin and bones; to be very thin.

costanero [kos·ta·né·ro] *adj.* coastal, relating to a coast; sloping.

costar[2] [kos·tár] *v. irr.* to cost; — **trabajo** to be difficult.

costarricense [kos·ta·rri·sén·se] *adj., m. & f.* Costa Rican.

coste [kós·te], **costo** [kós·to] *m.* cost; expense.

costear [kos·te·ár] *v.* (*pagar*) to defray or pay costs; to pay, be profitable; (*pasar junto a*) to navigate along the coast; to go along the edge of; **no costea** it does not pay.

costero [kos·té·ro] *adj.* coastal; **navegación costera** coastal navigation.

costilla [kos·tí·ya] *f.* rib; chop, cutlet.

costoso [kos·tó·so] *adj.* costly, expensive.

costra [kós·tra] *f.* crust; scab.

costroso [kos·tró·so] *adj.* crusty, scabby.

costumbre [kos·túm·bre] *f.* custom, habit.

costura [kos·tú·ra] *f.* sewing; stitching; seam.

costurera [kos·tu·ré·ra] *f.* seamstress.

costurero [kos·tu·ré·ro] *m.* sewing table or cabinet; sewing box; sewing room.

costurón [kos·tu·rón] *m.* coarse stitching; large seam; patch, mend; big scar.

cotejar [ko·te·xár] *v.* to confront, compare.

cotejo [ko·té·xo] *m.* comparison.

contense [ko·tén·se] *m. Ch., Mex.* burlap.

cotidiano [ko·ti·ɖjá·no] *adj.* daily.

cotizable [ko·ti·sá·ƀle] *adj.* quotable (*price*).

cotización [ko·ti·sa·sjón] *f.* quotation of prices; current price.

cotizar[9] [ko·ti·sár] *v.* to quote (*prices*); *Ch.* to contribute one's share or quota; *Am.* to prorate, distribute proportionally.

coto [kó·to] *m.* enclosure; landmark; limitation; limit, boundary; **poner** — **a** to set a limit to; to put an end to.

cotón [ko·tón] *m. Mex., C.A.* shirt of cheap fabric.

cotorra [ko·tó·rra] *f.* small parrot; magpie; talkative person, chatterbox.

cotorrear [ko·to·rre·ár] *v.* to chatter; to gossip.

covacha [ko·ƀá·ča] *f.* small cave; grotto; *Mex., Cuba, Andes* hut, shanty; *Col.* cubbyhole, small dark room.

coyote [ko·yó·te] *m. Am.* coyote, prairie wolf; *Mex.* shyster, tricky, lawyer; *C.A.* agent, broker (*often illegal*).

coyuntura [ko·yun·tú·ra] *f.* joint; articulation; occasion; precise moment.

coz [kos] *f.* kick; recoil of a gun; butt of a firearm; **dar** (*or* **tirar**) **coces** to kick.

cráneo [krá·ne·o] *m.* cranium, skull.

craso [krá·so] *adj.* fat; thick, coarse, gross; **ignorancia crasa** gross ignorance.

cráter [krá·ter] *m.* crater of a volcano.

creación [kre·a·sjón] *f.* creation.

creador [kre·a·ɖór] *m.* creator; *adj.* creating, creative.

crear [kre·ár] *v.* to create.

crecer[13] [kre·sér] *v. irr.* to grow; to increase; **-se** to swell (*as a river*); to become or feel important.

crecida [kre·sí·ɖa] *f.* river flood.

crecido [kre·sí·ɖo] *adj.* grown, increased; large; swollen.

creciente [kre·sjén·te] *adj.* growing, increasing; crescent (*moon*); *f.* river flood; *m.* crescent.

crecimiento [kre·si·mjén·to] *m.* growth, increase.

credenciales [kre·ɖen·sjá·les] *f. pl.* credentials.

crédito [kré·ɖi·to] *m.* credit; credence, belief; fame, reputation; letter of credit; **dar a** — to loan on credit.

credo [kré·ɖo] *m.* creed; **en un** — in a jiffy, in a minute.

crédulo [kré·ɖu·lo] *adj.* credulous, too ready to believe.

creencia [kre·én·sja] *f.* belief, faith.

creer[14] [kre·ér] *v.* to believe; to think, suppose; **¡ya lo creo!** I should say so!; yes, of course!

creíble [kre·í·ƀle] *adj.* credible, believable.

crema [kré·ma] *f.* cream; custard; cold cream.

cremallera [kre·ma·yé·ra] *f.* rack (*rack and pinion*).

crepitar [kre·pi·tár] *v.* to crackle, snap; to creak; to rattle.

crepuscular [kre·pús·ku·lár] *adj.* twilight.

crepúsculo [kre·pús·ku·lo] *m.* twilight.

crespo [krés·po] *adj.* curly; artificial (*style*); angry; crisp.

crespón [kres·pón] *m.* crepe.

cresta [krés·ta] *f.* crest; top, summit; tuft, comb (*of a bird*).

cretona [kre·tó·na] *f.* cretonne.

creyente [kre·yén·te] *m. & f.* believer; *adj.* believing.

creyón [kre·yón] *m. Am.* crayon.

cria [krí·a] *f.* brood; suckling; breeding.

criadero [krja·ɖé·ro] *m.* tree nursery; breeding place; hotbed; rich mine.

criado [krjá·ɖo] *m.* servant; *adj.* bred; **mal** — ill-bred; **criada** *f.* maid, servant.

criador [krja·ɖór] *m.* breeder, raiser, rearer; creator; *adj.* creating, creative; breeding; nourishing.

crianza [krján·sa] *f.* breeding; nursing; manners.

criar[17] [krjar] *v.* to breed; to bring up, rear, educate; to nurse.

criatura [krja·tú·ra] *f.* creature; baby, child.

criba [krí·ƀa] *f.* sieve.

cribar [kri·ƀár] *v.* to sift.

crimen [krí·men] *m.* crime.

criminal [kri·mi·nál] *adj., m. & f.* criminal.

crin [krin] *f.* mane.

crinudo [kri·nú·ɖo] *adj. Am.* with a long or thick mane.

criollo [krjó·yo] *m. Am.* Creole; native of America (*especially Spanish America*); *adj. Am.* national, domestic (*not foreign to Spanish America*).

criptón [krip·tón] *m.* krypton.

crisantema [kri·san·té·ma] *f.*, **crisantemo** [kri·san·té·mo] *m.* chrysanthemum.
crisis [krí·sis] *f.* crisis.
crisol [kri·sól] *m.* crucible, melting pot; hearth of a blast furnace.
crispar [kris·pár] *v.* to contract (*muscles*); to clench (*fists*); to put (*nerves*) on edge.
cristal [kris·tál] *m.* crystal; glass; mirror; lens.
cristalería [kris·ta·le·rí·a] *f.* glassware shop or factory; glassware.
cristalino [kris·ta·lí·no] *adj.* crystalline, transparent, clear; *m.* lens of the eye.
cristalizar[9] [kris·ta·li·sár] *v.* to crystallize.
cristiandad [kris·tjan·đáđ] *f.* Christianity; Christendom.
cristianismo [kris·tja·níz·mo] *m.* Christianity.
cristiano [kris·tjá·no] *m.* Christian; person; **hablar en —** to speak clearly; *adj.* Christian.
criterio [kri·té·rjo] *m.* criterion, rule, standard; judgment.
crítica [krí·ti·ka] *f.* criticism; censure; gossip.
criticador [kri·ti·ka·đór] *adj.* critical; *m.* critic, faultfinder.
criticar[6] [kri·ti·kár] *v.* to criticize; to censure; to find fault with.
crítico [krí·ti·ko] *adj.* critical; *m.* critic, judge; *Am.* faultfinder, slanderer; **criticón** [kri·ti·kón] *m.* critic, knocker, faultfinder; *adj.* critical, over-critical, faultfinding.
croar [kro·ár] *v.* to croak.
cromo [kró·mo] *m.* chromium.
cromosoma [kro·mo·só·ma] *m.* chromosome.
crónica [kró·ni·ka] *f.* chronicle, history; **cronista** [kro·nís·ta] *m. & f.* chronicler.
crónico [kró·ni·ko] *adj.* chronic.
cronómetro [kro·nó·me·tro] *m.* chronometer, timepiece.
croquis [kró·kis] *m.* rough sketch.
cruce [krú·se] *m.* crossing; crossroads; crossbreeding.
crucero [kru·sé·ro] *m.* (*cruciforme*) crossing; crossbearer; crossroads; transept (*of a church*); crossbeam; cross (*a constellation*); (*buque*) cruiser.
cruceta [kru·sé·ta] *f.* crosspiece; crosstree; universal joint (*automobile*).
crucificar[6] [kru·si·fi·kár] *v.* to crucify.
crucifijo [kru·si·fí·xo] *m.* crucifix.
crucigrama [kru·si·grá·ma] *m.* crossword puzzle.
crudo [krú·đo] *adj.* raw; uncooked; unripe; harsh; **agua cruda** hard water; **petróleo —** crude oil; *Mex.* **estar —** to have a hang-over; **cruda** *f. Mex.* hang-over.
cruel [krwel] *adj.* cruel.
crueldad [krwel·dáđ] *f.* cruelty.
crujido [kru·xí·đo] *m.* creak, crack, creaking; rustle.
crujir [kru·xír] *v.* to creak, crackle; to grate (*one's teeth*); to rustle; to crunch.
cruz [krus] *f.* cross.
cruzada [kru·sá·đa] *f.* crusade; holy war; campaign.
cruzado [kru·sá·đo] *m.* crusader; *adj.* crossed; cross, crosswise, transverse.
cruzamiento [kru·sa·mjén·to] *m.* crossing; crossroads.
cruzar[9] [kru·sár] *v.* to cross; *Am.* to fight, dispute; **-se con** to meet.
cuaco [kwá·ko] *m. Mex.* horse; *Am.* cassava flour.
cuaderno [kwa·đér·no] *m.* notebook; memorandum book; booklet; *Mex., Ven.* pamphlet.
cuadra [kwá·đra] *f.* hall, large room; stable;

hospital or prison ward; *Am.* city block; *Am.* reception room.
cuadrado [kwa·đrá·đo] *adj.* square; *m.* square; square ruler; die, metal block or plate.
cuadrante [kwa·đrán·te] *m.* dial, face of a clock or watch; sundial; quadrant (*fourth part of circle*; *instrument used in astronomy*).
cuadrar [kwa·đrár] *v.* (*cuadriforme*) to square; to form into a square; (*agradar*) to please; to conform; to harmonize; to set well; *Am.* to be becoming (*said of clothes*); *Am.* to be ready; *Am.* to contribute a large sum; *Am.* to come out well, succeed; **-se** to stand at attention.
cuadricular [kwa·đri·ku·lár] *v.* to square off, divide into squares.
cuadrilla [kwa·đrí·ya] *f.* group, troupe, gang; armed band; quadrille, square dance.
cuadro [kwá·đro] *m.* square; picture; scene; frame; flower bed; *Am.* blackboard; *Ch.* slaughterhouse.
cuajada [kwa·xá·đa] *f.* curd.
cuajado [kwa·xá·đo] *p.p. & adj.* coagulated, curdled; filled, covered; **— de** full or covered with (*flowers, dew, etc.*).
cuajar [kwa·xár] *v.* to coagulate, thicken, curd, curdle; to turn out well; to jell; to please; *Am.* to chatter, prattle; **-se** to coagulate, curd; to become crowded, be filled; **la cosa no cuajó** the thing did not work, did not jell.
cuajarón [kwa·xa·rón] *m.* clot.
cual [kwal] *rel. pron.* which; **cada —** each one; **— más — menos** some people more, others less; **el —, la —, los -es, las -es** which; who; **lo —** which; *adv.* as, like; **¿cuál?** *interr. pron.* which one? what?
cualidad [kwa·li·đáđ] *f.* quality; trait.
cualquier(a) [kwal·kjér(a)] *indef. adj. & pron.* any, anyone; whichever; **un hombre cualquiera** any man whatever.
cuando [kwán·do] *rel. adv. & conj.* when; **aun —** even though; **¿cuándo?** *interr. adv.* when?
cuantía [kwan·tí·a] *f.* quantity; rank, importance.
cuantioso [kwan·tjó·so] *adj.* plentiful, abundant; numerous.
cuanto [kwán·to] *rel. adj. & pron.* as much as, as many as; all that; **— antes** as soon as possible, immediately; **en — conj.** as soon as; **en — a** as for, with regard to; **unos -s** a few; **¿cuánto?** *interr. adj. & pron.* how much?; **¿cuántos?** how many?
cuaquerismo [kwa·ke·ríz·mo] *m.* the Quaker sect, or doctrine.
cuáquero [kwá·ke·ro] *m.* Quaker.
cuarentena [kwa·ren·té·na] *f.* quarantine; forty units of anything; period of forty days, months, or years.
cuarentón [kwa·ren·tón] *m.* man in his forties; **cuarentona** [kwa·ren·tó·na] *f.* woman in her forties.
cuaresma [kwa·réz·ma] *f.* Lent.
cuarta [kwár·ta] *f.* fourth, fourth part; span of a hand; *Am.* horse whip; *P.R.* **echar —** to beat, flog.
cuartear [kwar·te·ár] *v.* to quarter, divide into quarters; *P.R.* to whip; **-se** to crack, split (*said of walls or ceilings*); *Mex.* to back down, go back on one's word.
cuartel [kwar·tél] *m.* quarter, one fourth; quarters, barracks; district; quarter, mercy; **no dar —** to give no quarter.
cuartelada [kwar·te·lá·đa] *f.* military coup d'état, uprising, insurrection.

cuartelazo [kwar·te·lá·so] *m. Am.* military coup d'état, insurrection.

cuarterón [kwar·te·rón] *m.* quarter, fourth part; fourth of a pound; panel (*of a door or window*); *adj. & m.* quarter-breed (*one fourth Indian and three fourths Spanish*); quadroon (*person of quarter negro blood*).

cuarteto [kwar·té·to] *m.* quartet; quatrain (*stanza of four lines*).

cuartilla [kwar·tí·ya] *f.* (*hoja*) sheet of paper; (*medida*) about 4 quarts; about 1½ pecks; fourth of an **arroba** (about 6 pounds); *Am.* three cents' worth; *Am.* **no valer uno** — not to be worth a penny.

cuartillo [kwar·tí·yo] *m.* fourth of a peck; about a pint; fourth of a **real**.

cuarto [kwár·to] *m.* room; quarter, one fourth; **tener -s** to have money; *adj.* fourth.

cuarzo [kwár·so] *m.* quartz.

cuate [kwá·te] *adj., m. & f. Mex.* twin; pal, buddy.

cuatrero [kwa·tré·ro] *m.* horse thief, cattle thief; *Am.* Indian who speaks "broken" Spanish.

cuba [kú·ba] *f.* cask, barrel; tub, vat; big-bellied person; drunkard.

cubano [ku·bá·no] *adj. & m.* Cuban.

cubeta [ku·bé·ta] *f.* small barrel or keg; bucket, pail.

cúbico [kú·bi·ko] *adj.* cubic.

cubierta [ku·bjér·ta] *f.* cover; covering; envelope; deck (*of a ship*); *Am.* sheath.

cubierto [ku·bjér·to] *p.p. of* **cubrir**; *m.* cover; place setting for one person at a table.

cubismo [ku·bíz·mo] *m.* cubism.

cubo [kú·bo] *m.* cube; bucket, pail; hub of a wheel; mill pond; *Am.* finger bowl.

cubremesa [ku·bre·mé·sa] *f.* table cover.

cubrir[52] [ku·brír] *v.* to cover; to hide; to coat; to settle, pay (*a bill*); **-se** to cover oneself; to put on one's hat.

cucaracha [ku·ka·rá·ča] *f.* cockroach.

cuclillas [ku·klí·yas] **en** — in a squatting position; **sentarse en** — to squat.

cuclillo [ku·klí·yo] *m.* cuckoo.

cuco [kú·ko] *adj.* dainty, cute; sly, shrewd; *m.* cuckoo; a kind of caterpillar; card game; *Ríopl.* peach, peach tree; *Am.* **hacer — a** to make fun of; to fool.

cucurucho [ku·ku·rú·čo] *m.* paper cone; *Am.* peak, summit; *Peru, C.A., Mex.* cowl, cloak with a hood (*worn by penitents in Holy Week processions*).

cuchara [ku·čá·ra] *f.* spoon; scoop; *Am.* mason's trowel; **media** — mediocre person; *Am.* mason's helper; *Am.* **hacer** — to pout; *Am.* **meter uno su** — to butt into a conversation; to meddle;

cucharada [ku·ča·rá·da] *f.* spoonful; scoop;

cucharón [ku·ča·rón] *m.* large spoon; ladle; dipper; scoop.

cuchichear [ku·či·če·ár] *v.* to whisper.

cuchicheo [ku·či·čé·o] *m.* whispering, whisper.

cuchillo [ku·čí·yo] *m.* knife; gore (*in a garment*); — **de monte** hunting knife; **cuchillería** *Mex., P.R.* mountain ridge; *Am.* gore (*in a garment*); *Am.* narrow tract of land.

cuchillada [ku·či·yá·da] *f.* thrust with a knife, stab, slash; cut, gash.

cuchillo [ku·čí·yo] *m.* knife; gore (*in a garment*); — **de monte** hunting knife; **cuchillería** [ku·či·ye·rí·a] *f.* cutlery; cutlery shop.

cueca [kwé·ka] *f. Am.* a Chilean dance.

cuello [kwé·yo] *m.* neck; collar.

cuenca [kwén·ka] *f.* river basin; narrow valley; wooden bowl; socket of the eye.

cuenco [kwén·ko] *m.* earthen bowl.

cuenta [kwén·ta] *f.* (*cálculo*) count, calculation; bill; account; (*bolita*) bead (*of a rosary or necklace*); **a fin de -s** in the final analysis; **caer en la** — to see, get the point; **darse** — to realize; *Col.* **de toda** — anyway; **eso corre de mi** — that is my responsibility; I'll take charge of that; **eso no me tiene** — that does not pay me; it is of no profit to me; **en resumidas -s** in short; *P.R.* **hacerle** — **una cosa a uno** to be useful or profitable for one; **tomar en** — to take into account; **tomar una cosa por su** — to take charge of something, take the responsibility for it; **vamos a -s** let's understand or settle this.

cuentagotas [kwen·ta·gó·tas] *m.* dropper (*for counting drops*).

cuento [kwén·to] *m.* story, tale; — **de nunca acabar** never-ending tale; **déjese de -s** come to the point; **no viene a** — it is not opportune or to the point.

cuerda [kwér·da] *f.* cord, string, rope; chord; watch spring; **dar — a** to wind (*a watch*).

cuerdo [kwér·do] *adj.* sane; wise.

cuereada [kwe·re·á·da] *f. Mex., C.A., Col., Ven.* flogging, whipping; *Am.* skinning of an animal.

cuerear [kwe·re·ár] *v. Am.* to flog, whip; *Am.* to harm, dishonor; *Am.* to beat (*in a game*); *Am.* to skin (*an animal*).

cuerno [kwér·no] *m.* horn; antenna, feeler; **poner -s a** to be unfaithful to, deceive (*a husband*); *Am.* **mandar al** — to send to the devil.

cuero [kwé·ro] *m.* hide, skin; leather; wineskin; *Col., Ven.* whip; **en -s** naked.

cuerpeada [kwer·pe·á·da] *f. Ríopl.* dodge; evasion.

cuerpo [kwér·po] *m.* body; bulk; corps; **en** — without hat or coat; **luchar — a** — to fight in single combat; *Am.* **sacar el** — to dodge; to escape, avoid doing something.

cuervo [kwér·bo] *m.* crow; raven; *Ven.* buzzard; *Am.* dishonest priest; *Ríopl., Ch.* **hacer uno la del** — to leave abruptly and not return.

cuesta [kwés·ta] *f.* hill, slope; **a -s** on one's shoulders or back; in one's care; — **abajo** downhill; — **arriba** uphill.

cuestión [kwes·tjón] *f.* question; controversy, dispute; problem, matter.

cuestionario [kwes·tjo·ná·rjo] *m.* questionnaire, list of questions.

cueva [kwé·ba] *f.* cave, cavern; cellar.

cuico [kwí·ko] *m. Mex.* cop, policeman; *Am.* gossiper, tattletale, "squealer"; *Ch., Bol., Peru* half-breed; *Ríopl.* short, chubby person.

cuidado [kwi·dá·do] *m.* care, attention; worry, misgiving; **al — de** in care of; **tener — to be** careful; **¡ — !** look out!; be careful! **¡cuidadito!** be very careful!

cuidadoso [kwi·da·dó·so] *adj.* careful; attentive; anxious.

cuidar [kwi·dár] *v.* to take care of, look after, keep; to make or do carefully.

cuita [kwí·ta] *f.* grief, care, anxiety; misfortune; *C.A.* bird dung.

cuitado [kwi·tá·do] *adj.* unfortunate; timid, shy.

culata [ku·lá·ta] *f.* haunch, buttock; rear; butt (*of a firearm*).

culatazo [ku·la·tá·so] *f.* blow with the butt of a rifle; recoil, kick of a firearm.

culebra [ku·le·bra] *f.* snake; coil; *Mex.* money belt.

culebrear [ku·le·bre·ár] *v.* to zigzag; to twist,

wriggle.
culminación [kul·mi·na·sjón] *f.* culmination, climax.
culminar [kul·mi·nár] *v.* to culminate; to come to a climax.
culo [kú·lo] *m.* anus, behind.
culpa [kúl·pa] *f.* fault; guilt; blame; **echar la — a** to blame; **tener la — to be to blame.
culpabilidad [kul·pa·ƀi·li·đáđ] *f.* guilt; **culpable** [kul·pá·ƀle] *adj.* guilty.
culpar [kul·pár] *v.* to blame; to declare guilty.
cultivación [kul·ti·ƀa·sjón] *f.* cultivation.
cultivador [kul·ti·ƀa·đór] *m.* cultivator; **máquina cultivadora** cultivator.
cultivar [kul·ti·ƀár] *v.* to cultivate.
cultivo [kul·ti·ƀo] *m.* cultivation, culture.
culto [kúl·to] *adj.* cultured; *m.* cult, worship; religious sect; **rendir — a** to pay homage to; to worship.
cultura [kul·tú·ra] *f.* culture; cultivation.
cumbre [kúm·bre] *f.* summit; top.
cumpleaños [kum·ple·á·ños] *m.* birthday.
cumplido [kum·plí·đo] *adj. (completo)* complete, full; perfect; *(cortés)* courteous; *p.p.* fulfilled; due, fallen due; **tiene tres años -s** he is just over three years old; *m.* courtesy, attention; compliment.
cumplimentar [kum·pli·men·tár] *v.* to compliment; to congratulate; to pay a courtesy visit.
cumplimiento [kum·pli·mjén·to] *m.* fulfilment; courtesy; completion; compliment; **de — formal,** ceremonious.
cumplir [kum·plír] *v.* to fulfill; to comply; to carry out; to fall due; **— año,** to have a birthday; to be *(so many)* years old.
cúmulo [kú·mu·lo] *m.* pile, heap; accumulation; cumulus *(mass of clouds).*
cuna [kú·na] *f.* cradle; origin; *Am.* coffin for the poor; *Am.* dive, den *(for gambling and dancing).*
cundir [kun·dír] *v.* to spread *(as news, disease, liquids);* to propagate, extend, multiply.
cuña [kú·ña] *f.* wedge; splinter; *Ch., Ríopl.* influential person.
cuñado [ku·ñá·đo] *m.* brother-in-law; **cuñada** [ku·ñá·đa] *f.* sister-in-law.
cuota [kwó·ta] *f.* quota; dues, fee; **— de entrada** admission fee.
cuotidiano [kwo·ti·đjá·no] *adj.* everyday, daily.
cupé [ku·pé] *m.* coupé.
cupo [kú·po] *m.* quota; *Col.* place, seat *(on a plane or train).*
cupón [ku·pón] *m.* coupon.
cúpula [kú·pu·la] *f.* dome.
cura [kú·ra] *f.* cure; *m.* curate, priest.
curación [ku·ra·sjón] *f.* cure.
curandero [ku·ran·dé·ro] *m.* healer *(not a doctor);* quack; medicine man *(among Indians).*
curar [ku·rár] *v.* to cure, heal; to treat; to cure *(meats, tobacco);* to tan *(skins); Am.* to load *(dice),* fix *(cards);* **— de** to take care of; **-se** to cure oneself; to get well; *Ríopl.* to get drunk.
curiosear [ku·rjo·se·ár] *v.* to snoop, peek, peer, pry; to observe with curiosity.
curiosidad [ku·rjo·si·đáđ] *f.* curiosity; neatness, daintiness.
curioso [ku·rjó·so] *adj.* curious; neat, dainty; **libros raros y -s** rare books.
curro [kú·rro] *adj.* showy, gaudy, flashy; *m.* dandy.
currutaco [ku·rru·tá·ko] *m.* fop, dandy; *adj.* affected *(in one's dress).*
cursi [kúr·si] *adj.* common, in bad taste; cheap,

ridiculous; **cursilería** [kur·si·le·rí·a] *f.* bad taste, cheapness, false elegance; group of cheap, ridiculous people.
curso [kúr·so] *m.* course, direction; scholastic year; course of study.
curtidor [kur·ti·đór] *m.* tanner.
curtiduría [kur·ti·đu·rí·a] *f.* tannery.
curtir [kur·tír] *v.* to tan; to harden, accustom to hardships; *Col., Ven.* to dirty, soil; **-se** to get tanned or sunburned; to become accustomed to hardships.
curva [kúr·ƀa] *f.* curve.
curvo [kúr·ƀo] *adj.* curved; bent, crooked; arched.
cúspide [kús·pi·đe] *f.* summit, peak, top; spire, steeple.
custodia [kus·tó·đja] *f.* custody; guard, guardian; monstrance *(vessel in which the consecrated Host is exposed).*
custodiar [kus·to·đjár] *v.* to guard, watch; to keep in custody.
custodio [kus·tó·đjo] *m.* guardian, keeper.
cutícula [ku·tí·ku·la] *f.* cuticle.
cutis [kú·tis] *m.* skin; complexion.
cuyo [kú·yo] *rel. poss. adj.* whose, of whom, of which.
cuz! [kus] *interj.* come here! here! *(to a dog).*

CH:ch

chabacano [ča·ƀa·ká·no] *adj.* crude, unpolished; inartistic; cheap, in bad taste; *m. Mex.* a variety of apricot.
chacota [ča·kó·ta] *f.* fun; jest; **echar a —** to take as a joke; **hacer — de** to make fun of.
chacotear [ča·ko·te·ár] *v.* to frolic, joke, make merry; to be boisterous; to show off.
chacra [čá·kra] *f. Ec., Peru, Ch.* small farm; *Col., Ec.* cultivated field.
chagra [čá·gra] *f. Col., Ec.* farm, piece of farm land; *m. & f. Ec.* peasant; *adj.* uncivilized, unrefined.
chal [čal] *m.* shawl.
chalán [ča·lán] *m.* horse trader; *Am.* broncobuster, horse breaker.
chaleco [ča·lé·ko] *m.* waistcoat, vest.
chalupa [ča·lú·pa] *f.* sloop, sailboat; launch; *Mex., Col., Ven., Ríopl.* canoe; *P.R.* raft; *Mex.* Mexican tortilla with sauce.
chamaco [ča·má·ko] *m. Mex., C.A.* boy; **chamaquito** *m. Mex., C.A.* little boy.
chamarra [ča·má·rra] *f.* coarse wool jacket or sweater; *Mex.* sheepskin jacket, leather jacket; *Am.* heavy wool blanket.
chamarreta [ča·ma·rré·ta] *f.* short loose jacket; *Am.* square poncho.
chambergo [čam·bér·go] *m.* gaucho sombrero.
chambón [čam·bón] *adj.* clumsy, awkward. unskillful; *m.* bungler, clumsy performer, awkward workman; clumsy player.
champaña [čam·pá·ña] *f.* champagne.
champú [čam·pú] *m.* shampoo.
champurrado [čam·pu·rrá·đo] *m. Mex.* a mixed drink of chocolate and **atole;** *Col.* a mixed alcoholic beverage.
champurrar [čam·pu·rrár], *Am.* **champurrear** [čam·pu·rre·ár] *v.* to mix *(drinks).*
chamuscada [ča·mus·ká·đa], **chamuscadura** [ča·mus·ka·đú·ra] *f. Am.* singe, scorch.

CU

chamuscar[6] [ča·mus·kár] *v.* to scorch; to singe; to sear; *Am.* to sell at a low cost; **-se** to get scorched, singed, or seared; *Am.* to get peeved, offended.

chamusquina [ča·mus·kí·na] *f.* singe, scorch.

chancear [čan·se·ár] *v.* to fool, joke, jest.

chancero [čan·sé·ro] *m.* jester, joker; *adj.* jolly.

chancla [čáŋ·kla] *f.* slipper; old shoe; **chancleta** *f.* slipper; *m. Am.* good-for-nothing.

chanclo [čáŋ·klo] *m.* galosh, overshoe; clog; rubber overshoe; **-s** rubbers.

chancho [čán·čo] *m. S.A.* pig, pork.

changador [čaŋ·ga·ďór] *m. Ríopl.* carrier, porter; *Am.* handy man, person who does odd jobs.

chango [čáŋ·go] *m. Mex.* monkey; **ponerse** — to be alert, wary.

chantaje [čan·tá·xe] *m.* blackmail, blackmailing.

chanza [čán·sa] *f.* joke, jest.

chapa [ča·pa] *f.* metal plate; veneer (*thin leaf of wood*); rosy spot on the cheeks; *Mex., C.A., Andes* lock; *Am.* Indian spy; **-s** game of tossing coins; **hombre de** — serious, reliable man.

chapado [ča·pá·ďo] *adj.* veneered (*covered with a thin layer of wood or other material*); — **a la antigua** old-fashioned.

chapalear [ča·pa·le·ár] = **chapotear**.

chapapote [ča·pa·pó·te] *m.* tar; asphalt.

chaparro [ča·pá·rro] *m.* scrub oak; short, chubby person; *Am.* a kind of tropical shrub with rough leaves; *Am.* short whip; *adj. Mex., C.A.* short, squatty.

chaparrón [ča·pa·rrón] *m.* downpour, heavy shower.

chapetón [ča·pe·tón] *m.* red spot on the cheek; *Col.* nickname for a Spaniard.

chapitel [ča·pi·tél] *m.* spire, steeple; capital (*of a column*).

chapotear [ča·po·te·ár] *v.* to splash, paddle in the water.

chapoteo [ča·po·té·o] *m.* splash.

chapucear [ča·pu·se·ár] *v.* to fumble; to botch, bungle, do or make clumsily; *Am.* to deceive, trick.

chapulín [ča·pu·lín] *m. Mex., C.A.* grasshopper.

chapurrar [ča·pu·rrár] *v.* to speak (*a language*) brokenly; to mix (*drinks*).

chapuz [ča·pús] *m.* dive, duck, ducking.

chapuza [ča·pú·sa] *f.* botch, clumsy piece of work; *Am.* foul trick, fraud.

chapuzar[9] [ča·pu·sár] *v.* to duck; to dive.

chaqueta [ča·ké·ta] *f.* jacket; **chaquetón** [ča·ke·tón] *m.* long jacket, coat.

charamusca [ča·ra·mús·ka] *f. Mex.* twisted candy stick or cane; *Col., Ven.* brushwood, firewood; *C.A.* hubbub, uproar.

charamusquero [ča·ra·mus·ké·ro] *m. Am.* candy-stick maker or vendor.

charca [čár·ka] *f.* pond.

charco [čár·ko] *m.* puddle, pool; **pasar el** — to cross the pond, cross the ocean.

charla [čár·la] *f.* chat, chatter, prattle.

charladuría [čar·la·ďu·rí·a] *f.* chatter, gossip.

charlar [čar·lár] *v.* to chat, chatter, prate.

charlatán [čar·la·tán] *m.* chatterer, prater; gossiper; charlatan, quack.

charol [ča·ról] *m.* varnish; patent leather; *Col.* tray; **charola** *f. Mex.* tray.

charolar [ča·ro·lár] *v.* to varnish, polish.

charqui [čár·ki] *m.* jerky, jerked beef.

charro [čá·rro] *m. Spain* a villager of Salamanca province; *Mex.* Mexican horseman of special

costume and cultural status.

charrúa [ča·rrú·a] *m.* & *f. Am.* Charruan Indian (*Indian of Uruguay*).

chascarrillo [čas·ka·rri·yo] *m.* joke, funny story.

chasco [čás·ko] *m.* joke, prank; surprise; disillusionment, disappointment; **llevar-se** — to be disappointed, surprised or fooled; *adj. Am.* thick, curly (*hair*); *Am.* ruffled (*plumage*).

chasquear [čas·ke·ár] *v.* to play a trick on; to disappoint; to crack (*a whip*); to smack (*the lips*); to click (*the tongue*); to crack, snap; *Col., Ven.* to chatter (*said of the teeth*); *Am.* to munch (*food*); **-se** to be disappointed or disillusioned; to be tricked or fooled.

chasqui [čás·ki] *m. Andes, Ríopl.* courier, messenger.

chasquido [čas·kí·ďo] *m.* crack of a whip; crackle; smack (*of the lips*); click (*of the tongue*).

chata [čá·ta] *f.* bedpan; scow, barge, flat-bottomed boat; *Am.* platform wagon, platform car, flatcar; **chatita** [ča·tí·ta] *f. Mex.* "honey", "cutie", "funny face".

chato [čá·to] *adj.* snub-nosed, flat-nosed; flat; flattened; squatty; *Mex.* **quedarse uno** — to be left flat or in the lurch; to be disappointed.

chaval [ča·bál] *m.* lad; young man.

chayote [ča·yó·te] *m. Am.* vegetable pear (*a tropical fruit growing on a vine*); *Am.* dunce, silly fool.

che [če] *interj. Ríopl.* word used to attract attention among intimates; say! listen! hey!; nickname for citizens of Argentina.

cheque [čé·ke] *m.* check, bank check.

chica [čí·ka] *f.* little girl; girl, maid, servant.

chicle [čí·kle] *m. Am.* chicle; *Am.* chewing gum.

chico [čí·ko] *adj.* small, little; *m.* child, boy; *Col.* each game of billiards; *Am.* = **chicozapote** [čí·ko·sa·pó·te] (*tropical fruit and tree from which chicle is extracted*).

chicote [či·kó·te] *m.* cigar; piece of rope; *Am.* whip; *Col., Ven.* cigar butt.

chicotear [či·ko·te·ár] *v. Ríopl., Col., Peru* to lash, whip, flog; *Am.* to fight, quarrel; *Am.* to kill.

chicoteo [či·ko·té·o] *m. Ríopl.* whipping; *Am.* shooting, killing; *Am.* crackling, rattling (*as of machine guns*); *Am.* quarreling.

chicha [čí·ča] *f. Peru, Col., Ch., Ríopl., C.A.* chicha (*a popular alcoholic beverage*); *Peru* thick-soled shoe; **no ser ni** — **ni limonada** to be worth nothing, be neither fish nor fowl.

chícharo [čí·ča·rro] *m.* pea; *Col.* bad cigar; *Am.* apprentice.

chicharra [či·čá·rra] *f.* cicada, locust; talkative person; *Mex.* person with a shrill voice; *Am.* rickety, squeaky car; *Ch.* harsh-sounding musical instrument or bell; *C.A., Mex., Cuba* piece of fried pork skin.

chicharrón [či·ča·rrón] *m.* crackling, crisp piece of fried pork skin; burned piece of meat; sunburnt person; *Am.* dried-up, wrinkled person; *Am.* bootlicker, flatterer.

chiche [čí·če] *m. Mex., C.A.* breast, teat; wet nurse.

chichón [či·čón] *m.* bump, lump; *Am.* joker, jester; **chichona** [či·čó·na] *adj. Mex., C.A.* large-breasted.

chiflado [či·flá·ďo] *adj. Am.* "cracked", "touched", crazy; *p.p.* of **chiflar**.

chifladura [či·fla·ďú·ra] *f.* craziness, mania; mockery, jest.

chiflar [či·flár] *v.* to whistle; to hiss; *Am.* to sing (*said of birds*); **-se** to lose one's head; to become unbalanced, crazy.

chiflido [či·flí·d̄o] *m.* whistle; hiss; *Am.* **en un** — in a jiffy, in a second.

chile [čí·le] *m.* chili, red pepper.

chileno [či·lé·no] *adj. & m.* Chilean.

chillante [či·yán·te] *adj.* flashy, bright, showy, loud; shrieking.

chillar [či·yár] *v.* to shriek, scream; to hiss; *Am.* to shout, protest, moan; *Am.* to "squeal," turn informer; *Ríopl., Ven., C.A., P.R.* **no** — not to say a word; *Mex.* **-se** to be piqued, offended.

chillido [či·yí·d̄o] *m.* shriek, scream.

chillón [či·yón] *adj.* shrieking, screaming; shrill; loud, gaudy; *Col., Andes* whining, discontented; *Ríopl.* touchy.

chimenea [či·me·né·a] *f.* chimney; fireplace, hearth.

china [čí·na] *f. (de la China)* Chinese woman; China silk or cotton; porcelain; *(piedra)* pebble; marble; *Andes, Ch., Ríopl., Col.* girl, young woman *(usually half-breed or Indian); Am.* servant girl; *P.R.* sweet orange; *Col.* spinning top; **chinita** [či·ní·ta] *f. Am.* little Indian girl; darling.

chinche [čín·če] *f.* bedbug; thumbtack; tiresome person, bore; *Col., Ven., Ríopl.* touchy or irritable person; *Am.* plump, squatty person.

chinchilla [čin·čí·ya] *f.* chinchilla.

chinchorro [čin·čó·rro] *m. Ven., Col.* hammock.

chino [čí·no] *adj.* Chinese; *Mex.* curly; *m. Ríopl.* Chinese; Chinaman; *Am.* pig; *Am.* half-breed *(Negro and Indian, white and Indian); Am.* Indian; *Col.* house servant; *Am.* coarse, rough, ugly person; *Col.* straight, coarse hair.

chiquero [či·ké·ro] *m.* pigsty, pigpen; pen for bulls; goat shelter.

chiquilín [či·ki·lín] *m. Am.* tot, little boy; **chiquilina** [či·ki·lí·na] *f. Am.* little girl.

chiquito [či·kí·to] *adj.* tiny, very small; *m.* tiny tot, tiny child; **chiquitico** [či·ki·tí·ko] *adj.* tiny.

chiripa [či·rí·pa] *f.* stroke of good luck.

chiripá [či·ri·pá] *m. Ríopl.* loose riding trousers *(square of cloth draped from the waist and between the legs).*

chirola [ĕi·ró·la] *f. Mex., Ven., Ríopl.* "jug", jail; *Am.* coin of low value.

chirona [či·ró·na] *f.* "jug", jail.

chirriado [či·rrjá·d̄o] *adj. Col.* attractive; lively.

chirriar[17] [či·rrjár] *v.* to squeak, creak; to sizzle; to chirp; to sing out of tune; *Col.* to go on a spree.

chirrido [či·rrí·d̄o] *m.* creak, squeak; chirp; squeaking, creaking; chirping.

chisguete [čiz·gé·te] *m.* squirt.

chisme [číz·me] *m.* gossip, piece of gossip; trifle, trinket, knickknack, gadget.

chismear [čiz·me·ár] *v.* to gossip; to tattle.

chismería [čiz·me·rí·a] *f.* gossiping, talebearing.

chismero [čiz·mé·ro] *adj.* gossiping; *m.* gossip.

chismoso [čiz·mó·so] *adj.* gossiping; *m.* gossip, talebearer, tattletale.

chispa [čís·pa] *f.* spark; small diamond; wit; *Col.* false rumor, lie; *Am.* two-wheeled cart; *Mex.* brazen, shameless woman; *Am.* **da** — it clicks, works, functions; *Am.* **ponerse** — to get drunk.

chispeante [čis·pe·án·te] *adj.* sparkling.

chispear [čis·pe·ár] *v.* to spark; to sparkle; to twinkle; to drizzle.

chisporrotear [čis·po·rro·te·ár] *v.* to sputter, throw off sparks.

chiste [čís·te] *m.* joke, jest; **dar en el** — to guess right, hit the nail on the head.

chistera [čis·té·ra] *f.* top hat; fish basket.

chistoso [čis·tó·so] *adj.* funny, amusing, humorous.

¡chito! [čí·to] **¡chitón!** [čí·tón] *interj.* hush!

chiva [či·β̄a] *f.* female goat; *Am.* goatee; *Pan., Col.* flivver, small bus; **chivo** *m.* he-goat; *Am.* fit of anger; *Am.* insulting remark; *Am.* **estar hecho un** — to be very angry; *adj. Am.* angry; **chivato** [či·β̄á·to] *m. Cuba* informer, squealer.

chocante [čo·kán·te] *adj.* striking, surprising; shocking; disgusting; *Col., Andes* tiresome, annoying, impertinent.

chocar[6] [čo·kár] *v.* to bump, collide, clash; to fight; to shock, surprise, disgust; **me choca ese hombre** I loathe that man.

chocarrear [čo·ka·rre·ár] *v.* to tell coarse jokes; to clown.

chocarrería [čo·ka·rre·rí·a] *f.* coarse joke; **chocarrero** [čo·ka·rré·ro] *adj.* coarse, vulgar; clownish.

choclo [čó·klo] *m.* overshoe; clog; *Mex.* low shoe or slipper; *Andes, Col., Ch., Ríopl.* ear of corn; *Am.* corn stew; *Am.* spike, ear of wheat.

chocolate [čo·ko·lá·te] *m.* chocolate.

chochear [čo·če·ár] *v.* yo be in one's dotage, act senile.

chochera [čo·čé·ra], **chochez** [čo·čés] *f.* senility, dotage; **chocheras** [čo·čé·ras], **chocheces** [čo·čé·ses] senile actions or habits.

chocho [čó·čo] *adj.* doting; *m.* childish old man.

chófer [čó·fer], [čo·fér] *m.* chauffeur.

cholo [čó·lo] *m. Andes, Ríopl., Ch.* half-breed; *Am.* half-civilized Indian; *adj. Am.* coarse, rude; *C.R.* dark-skinned; *Ch.* black *(dog).*

chopo [čó·po] *m.* black poplar; *adj. Am.* stupid.

choque [čó·ke] *m.* collision, bump; shock; clash, conflict; dispute.

chorizo [čo·rí·so] *m.* sausage; *Am.* string of things; *Am.* fool.

chorrasco [čo·rrá·so] *m.* spurt, large stream or jet.

chorrear [čo·rre·ár] *v.* to drip; to spout.

chorro [čó·rro] *m.* spurt, jet; stream, flow; *Am.* strand of a whip; *Am.* river rapids.

choteador [čo·te·a·d̄ór] *m. Am.* joker, jester.

chotear [čo·te·ár] *v. Cuba* to make fun of, jeer, jest, mock, kid; *Mex., C.A.* to idle, fool around; *Am.* to pamper.

choteo [čo·té·o] *m. Cuba* joking, jeering, kidding.

choza [čó·sa] *f.* hut, cabin.

chubasco [ču·bás·ko] *m.* squall, sudden shower; **aguantar el** — to weather the storm.

chuchería [ču·če·rí·a] *f.* trifle, trinket; knick-knack; tidbit.

chueco [čwé·ko] *adj. Am.* crooked, bent; *Col.* crook-legged, bow-legged, knock-kneed; *Am.* worn-out, dejected; *Mex.* disgusted, annoyed; *Am.* **commerciar en** — to trade in stolen goods.

chuleta [ču·lé·ta] *f.* cutlet, chop; blow, slap.

chulo [ču·lo] *m.* dandy; effeminate man; clownish fellow; bullfighter's assistant; *Col.* buzzard; *Am.* coarse, thick brush; *adj. C.A., Col., Mex.* goodlooking pretty.

chumpipe [čum·pí·pe] *m. C.A.* turkey; also **chompipe.**

chupada [ču·pá·d̄a] *f.* sucking; suction; suck, sip; *Mex., C.A., Ven., Andes* puff from a cigarette; *Ríopl.* big swallow of liquor.

chupador [ču·pa·d̄ór] *m.* sucker; teething ring; *Am.* toper, heavy drinker; *Am.* smoker.

chupaflor [ču·pa·flór], **chuparrosa** [ču·pa·rró·sa] *m. Am.* hummingbird.

chupar [ču·pár] *v.* to suck; to sip; to absorb,

take in; *Am.* to smoke; *C.A., Ríopl., Andes* to drink, get drunk; **-se** to shrivel up.

churrasco [ču·rrás·ko] *m. Ríopl., Andes* roasted meat; *Ríopl., Andes* barbecued meat; *Ríopl., Andes* large piece of meat for barbecuing.

churrasquear [ču·rras·ke·ár] *v. Ríopl., Andes* to barbecue, roast over coals; *Ríopl., Andes* to prepare (*meat*) for barbecuing; *Ríopl., Andes* to eat barbecued meat.

churrasquito [ču·rras·kí·to] *m.* small piece of roast.

churrigueresco [ču·rri·ge·rés·ko] *adj.* baroque, ornate (*architecture*).

churro [čú·rro] *adj.* coarse; *m. Spain* doughnut-like fritter.

chuscada [čus·ká·ɖa] *f.* jest, joke.

chusco [čús·ko] *adj.* funny, witty; ridiculous; *Peru* **perro** — mongrel dog.

chusma [čúz·ma] *f.* rabble, mob.

chuzo [čú·so] *m.* pike or cane carried by the watchman (*sereno*).

D:d

dable [dá·ble] *adj.* feasible, possible.

daca [dá·ka] = **da acá**.

dávida [dá·ɖi·ba] *f.* gift.

dadivoso [da·ɖi·bó·so] *adj.* liberal, generous.

dado [dá·ɖo] *m.* die; **-s** dice.

dador [da·ɖór] *m.* giver.

daga [dá·ga] *f.* dagger.

dama [dá·ma] *f.* lady; **jugar a las -s** to play checkers.

damajuana [da·ma·xwá·na] *f.* demijohn.

damasquinado [da·mas·ki·ná·ɖo] *m.* damascene (*incrustation of gold in steel*).

damisela [da·mi·sé·la] *f.* damsel, girl.

danza [dán·sa] *f.* dance.

danzante [dan·sán·te] *m. & f.* dancer.

danzar[9] [dan·sár] *v.* to dance.

danzarina [dan·sa·rí·na] *f.* dancer.

dañar [da·ñár] *v.* to harm, hurt, damage; **-se** to spoil, rot; to get hurt; to get damaged.

dañino [da·ñí·no] *adj.* harmful; destructive.

daño [dá·ño] *m.* damage, harm, loss.

dañoso [da·ñó·so] *adj.* harmful.

dar[26] [dar] *v. irr.* (*hacer don*) to give, confer; (*golpear*) to strike, hit; (*emitir*) give off, emit; **— a luz** to give birth to; to publish; **— con** to encounter, find; **— de comer** to feed; **— de si** to give, stretch; **— en** to hit upon; to persist in; **— largas a un asunto** to prolong or postpone a matter; *C.A., Ven., Col.* **— cuero** (guasca, **puños**) to beat, thrash, lash; **lo misma da** it makes no difference; **-se** to give up; **dárselas de** to boast of.

dardo [dár·ɖo] *m.* dart, arrow.

dares y tomares [dá·res·i·to·má·res] *m. pl.* give-and-take, dispute; dealings.

dársena [dár·se·na] *f.* dock, wharf.

datar [da·tár] *v.* to date; **— de** to date from.

dátil [dá·til] *m.* date (*fruit of the date palm*).

dato [dá·to] *m.* datum, fact; **-s** data.

de [de] *prep.* of, from; about, concerning; in (*after a superlative*); if (*before inf.*); **— no llegar** if he does not arrive; **el — la gorra azul** the one with the blue cap; **el mejor — América** the best in America; **más — lo que dice** more than he says.

debajo [de·bá·xo] *adv.* under, underneath; **— de** *prep.* under.

debate [de·bá·te] *m.* debate; dispute, quarrel.

debatir [de·ba·tír] *v.* to debate, argue, discuss; to fight; **-se** to struggle.

debe [de·be] *m.* debit.

debelar [de·be·lár] *v.* to subdue, defeat.

deber [de·bér] *v.* to owe; to have to (must, should, ought); **debe de ser** it must be, probably is; **ime la debes!** I have an account to settle with you!

deber [de·bér] *m.* duty, obligation; debt; debit, debit side (*in bookkeeping*).

debido [de·bí·ɖo] *adj.* due, owing; just, appropriate.

débil [dé·bil] *adj.* weak, feeble.

debilidad [de·bi·li·ɖáɖ] *f.* debility, weakness.

debilitación [de·bi·li·ta·sjón] *f.*, **debilitamiento** [de·bi·li·ta·mjén·to] *m.* weakening; weakness.

debilitar [de·bi·li·tár] *v.* to weaken.

débito [dé·bi·to] *m.* debt; debit.

debutar [de·bu·tár] *v.* to make a debut, make a first public appearance.

década [dé·ka·ɖa] *f.* decade, ten years; series of ten.

decadencia [de·ka·ɖén·sja] *f.* decadence, decline, falling off.

decaer[24] [de·ka·ér] *v. irr.* to decay, decline, wither, fade; to fall to leeward.

decaimiento [de·kaj·mjén·to] *m.* decline, decay; dejection; weakness.

decano [de·ká·no] *m.* dean; senior member of a group.

decantado [de·kan·tá·ɖo] *p.p. & adj.* much talked about; overrated.

decapitar [de·ka·pi·tár] *v.* to behead.

decencia [de·sén·sja] *f.* decency; **decente** [de·sén·te] *adj.* decent; respectable; fair.

decenio [de·sé·njo] *m.* decade.

decepción [de·sep·sjón] *f.* disillusion, disappointment.

decepcionante [de·sep·sjo·nán·te] *adj.* disappointing.

decepcionar [de·sep·sjo·nár] *v.* to disillusion, disappoint.

decibel [de·si·bél] *m.* decibel (*unit for the measurement of the intensity of sound*).

decidir [de·si·ɖír] *v.* to decide, resolve; **-se a** to make up one's mind to; to decide to.

décima [dé·si·ma] *f.* tenth; tithe; stanza of ten octosyllabic lines.

décimo [dé·si·mo] *adj.* tenth.

decir[27] [de·sír] *v. irr.* to say; to tell; to speak; **es** — that is; **querer** — to mean, signify.

decisión [de·si·sjón] *f.* decision.

decisivo [de·si·si·bo] *adj.* decisive, final.

declamar [de·kla·már] *v.* to declaim, recite.

declaración [de·kla·ra·sjón] *f.* declaration; statement; deposition, testimony.

declarar [de·kla·rár] *v.* to declare, state, affirm; to testify; **-se** to propose, declare one's love; to give one's views or opinion.

declinar [de·kli·nár] *v.* to decline; to go down; to lose vigor, decay; to bend down.

declive [de·klí·be] *m.* declivity, slope.

decoración [de·ko·ra·sjón] *f.* decoration, ornament; stage setting.

decorar [de·ko·rár] *v.* to decorate, adorn.

decorativo [de·ko·ra·tí·bo] *adj.* decorative, ornamental.

decoro [de·kó·ro] *m.* decorum, propriety, dignity; honor.

decoroso [de·ko·ró·so] *adj.* decorous, becoming, proper, decent.

decrépito [de·kré·pi·to] *adj.* decrepit, old, feeble.

decretar [de·kre·tár] *v.* to decree.
decreto [de·kré·to] *m.* decree; decision, order.
dechado [de·čá·ďo] *m.* model, pattern, example.
dedal [de·ďál] *m.* thimble.
dedicar[6] [de·ďi·kár] *v.* to dedicate; to devote; **-se** to apply oneself.
dedicatoria [de·ďi·ka·tó·rja] *f.* dedication, inscription.
dedo [dé·ďo] *m.* (*de la mano*) finger; (*del pie*) toe; **— del corazón** middle finger; **— meñique** little finger; **— pulgar** thumb; **no mamarse el —** not to be easily fooled; **dedillo** *m.* small finger; **saber al dedillo** to know perfectly, know by heart.
deducción [de·ďuk·sjón] *f.* deduction; inference.
deducir[25] [de·ďu·sír] *v. irr.* to deduce, conclude; to deduct.
defecar[6] [de·fe·kár] *v. irr.* to defecate.
defecto [de·fék·to] *m.* defect, fault.
defectuoso [de·fek·twó·so] *adj.* defective, faulty.
defender[1] [de·fen·dér] *v. irr.* to defend.
defensa [de·fén·sa] *f.* defense; *Am.* automobile bumper.
defensivo [de·fen·sí·ḃo] *adj.* defensive; *m.* defense, safeguard; **defensiva** [de·fen·si·ḃa] *f.* defensive.
defensor [de·fen·sór] *m.* defender.
deficiencia [de·fi·sjén·sja] *f.* deficiency; **deficiente** [de·fi·sjén·te] *adj.* deficient.
déficit [dé·fi·sit] *m.* deficit, shortage.
definición [de·fi·ni·sjón] *f.* definition.
definido [de·fi·ní·ďo] *adj.* definite; *p.p. of* **definir**.
definir [de·fi·nír] *v.* to define, explain; to determine.
definitivo [de·fi·ni·tí·ḃo] *adj.* definitive, conclusive, final; **en definitiva** in short, in conclusion; definitely.
deformación [de·for·ma·sjón] *f.* deformation, deformity.
deformar [de·for·már] *v.* to deform; **-se** to become deformed; to lose its shape or form.
deforme [de·fór·me] *adj.* deformed; ugly.
deformidad [de·for·mi·ďáď] *f.* deformity.
defraudar [de·fraw·ďár] *v.* to defraud, cheat, rob of.
defunción [de·fun·sjón] *f.* death, decease.
degenerado [de·xe·ne·rá·ďo] *adj. & m.* degenerate.
degenerar [de·xe·ne·rár] *v.* to degenerate.
deglución [de·glu·sjón] *f.* swallowing.
deglutir [de·glu·tír] *v.* to swallow.
degollar[2] [de·ġo·yár] *v. irr.* to behead; to slash the throat; to cut (*a dress*) low in the neck.
degradar [de·gra·ďár] *v.* to degrade; to debase.
degüello [de·ġwé·yo] *m.* beheading; throat-slashing.
dehesa [de·é·sa] *f.* pasture, grazing ground.
deidad [dej·ďáď] *f.* deity.
dejadez [de·xa·ďés] *f.* lassitude, languor, listlessness; self-neglect, slovenliness.
dejado [de·xá·ďo] *adj.* indolent, listless; slovenly.
dejar [de·xár] *v.* (*abandonar*) to leave; to quit; to abandon; to omit; (*permitir*) to permit, let; (*soltar*) to let go; **— de** to stop, cease; **— caer** to drop; *Am.* **no -se** not to be an easy mark, not to let others pick on one.
dejo [dé·xo] *m.* (*sabor*) aftertaste; slight taste; (*acento*) slight accent, peculiar inflection.
del [del] **= de + el** of the.
delantal [de·lan·tál] *m.* apron.
delante [de·lán·te] *adv.* before, in front; **— de** *prep.* in front of.
delantera [de·lan·té·ra] *f.* lead, forepart, front.
delantero [de·lan·té·ro] *adj.* front, foremost, first.
delatar [de·la·tár] *v.* to denounce, accuse, inform against.

delator [de·la·tór] *m.* accuser, informer.
delegación [de·le·ga·sjón] *f.* delegation.
delegado [de·le·gá·ďo] *m.* delegate.
delegar[7] [de·le·gár] *v.* to delegate.
deleitable [de·lej·tá·ḃle] *adj.* delightful, enjoyable.
deleitar [de·lej·tár] *v.* to delight, please.
deleite [de·léj·te] *m.* delight, joy, pleasure.
deleitoso [de·lej·tó·so] *adj.* delightful.
deletrear [de·le·tre·ár] *v.* to spell.
deleznable [de·lez·ná·ḃle] *adj.* perishable; brittle.
delfín [del·fín] *m.* dolphin; dauphin.
delgadez [del·ga·ďés] *f.* thinness; slimness; fineness.
delgado [del·gá·ďo] *adj.* thin, slender, slim.
deliberado [de·li·ḃe·rá·ďo] *adj.* deliberate; *p.p. of* **deliberar**.
deliberar [de·li·ḃe·rár] *v.* to deliberate, consider, ponder.
delicadeza [de·li·ka·ďé·sa] *f.* fineness; delicacy; softness, exquisiteness.
delicado [de·li·ká·ďo] *adj.* delicate; weak, frail; exquisite, dainty; tender.
delicia [de·lí·sja] *f.* delight.
delicioso [de·li·sjó·so] *adj.* delicious, delightful.
delincuente [de·lin·kwén·te] *adj., m. & f.* deliquent.
delineación [de·li·ne·a·sjón] *f.*, **delineamiento** [de·li·ne·a·mjén·to] *m.* delineation, design, outline, drawing; portrayal.
delinear [de·li·ne·ár] *v.* to delineate, sketch, outline.
delirante [de·li·rán·te] *adj.* delirious, raving.
delirar [de·li·rár] *v.* to be delirious; to rave, talk wildly or foolishly.
delirio [de·lí·rjo] *m.* delirium, temporary madness; wild excitement; foolishness.
delito [de·lí·to] *m.* crime; misdemeanor.
demacrado [de·ma·krá·ďo] *adj.* scrawny, emaciated, thin.
demanda [de·mán·da] *f.* demand; petition; question; claim; complaint; lawsuit.
demandado [de·man·dá·ďo] *m.* defendant; *p.p. of* **demandar**.
demandante [de·man·dán·te] *m. & f.* plaintiff.
demandar [de·man·dár] *v.* to demand; to petition; to sue, file a suit; to indict.
demás [de·más] *indef. adj. & pron.:* **los —** the rest; the others; **las — personas** the other people; **lo —** the rest; **por —** useless; uselessly; **por lo —** as to the rest; moreover.
demasía [de·ma·sí·a] *f.* excess; boldness, insolence; offense, outrage; **en —** excessively.
demasiado [de·ma·sjá·ďo] *adv.* too much, excessively; too; *adj.* too much, excessive.
demente [de·mén·te] *adj.* demented, insane, crazy.
democracia [de·mo·krá·sja] *f.* democracy; **demócrata** [de·mó·kra·ta] *m. & f.* democrat; **democrático** [de·mo·krá·ti·ko] *adj.* democratic.
demoler[2] [de·mo·lér] *v. irr.* to demolish, tear down.
demonio [de·mó·njo] *m.* demon, devil; evil spirit.
demontre [de·món·tre] *m.* devil; **¡ — !** the deuce!
demora [de·mó·ra] *f.* delay.
demorar [de·mo·rár] *v.* to delay; to retard; **-se** to linger; to be delayed.
demostración [de·mos·tra·sjón] *f.* demonstration; proof, explanation.
demostrar[2] [de·mos·trár] *v. irr.* to demonstrate, show, prove, explain.
demostrativo [de·mos·tra·tí·ḃo] *adj.* demonstrative.
demovilizar[9] [de·mo·ḃi·li·sár] *v.* to demobilize.
demudar [de·mu·ďár] *v.* to change, alter; to disguise; **-se** to change color or one's facial expression; to turn pale.
dengoso [deŋ·gó·so], **denguero** [deŋ·gé·ro] *adj.*

CH

affected; finicky.

dengue [déŋ·ge] *m.* primness; coyness, affectation; dengue, breakbone fever; *Am.* marigold; *Col.* zigzag; *Am.* swagger **hacer -s** to act coy, make grimaces.

denigrar [de·ni·grár] *v.* to blacken, defame, revile, insult.

denodado [de·no·dá·do] *adj.* dauntless, daring.

denominación [de·no·mi·na·sjón] *f.* denomination; name, title, designation.

denominar [de·no·mi·nár] *v.* to name, call, entitle.

denostar[2] *v. irr.* to insult, outrage, revile.

denotar [de·no·tár] *v.* to denote, indicate, mean.

densidad [den·si·dád] *f.* density.

denso [dén·so] *adj.* dense, compact; thick.

dentado [den·tá·do] *adj.* toothed, notched.

dentadura [den·ta·dú·ra] *f.* set of teeth.

dentar[1] [den·tár] *v. irr.* to tooth, furnish (a saw) with teeth; to indent; to cut teeth, grow teeth (*referring to a child*).

dentellada [den·te·yá·da] *f.* bite; tooth mark; **a -s** with big bites.

dentición [den·ti·sjón] *f.* teething.

dentífrico [den·tí·fri·ko] *m.* dentrifice, tooth cleanser; **pasta dentífrica** toothpaste; **polvos dentífricos** toothpowder.

dentista [den·tís·ta] *m.* dentist.

dentro [dén·tro] *adv.* inside, within; **— de** *prep.* inside of; **por —** on the inside.

denuedo [de·nwé·do] *m.* spirit, courage, daring.

denuesto [de·nwés·to] *m.* affront, insult.

denuncia [de·nún·sja] *f.* denunciation; condemnation, accusation; miner's claim.

denunciar [de·nun·sjár] *v.* to denounce, accuse; to proclaim, advise, give notice; to claim (a mine).

deparar [de·pa·rár] *v.* to furnish, offer, supply.

departamento [de·par·ta·mén·to] *m.* department; compartment; apartment.

departir [de·par·tír] *v.* to talk, converse.

dependencia [de·pen·dén·sja] *f.* dependence; dependency; branch office.

depender [de·pen·dér] *v.* to depend, rely (on).

dependiente [de·pen·djén·te] *m.* clerk; dependent, subordinate; *adj.* dependent.

depilar [de·pi·lár] *v.* to depilate.

depilatorio [de·pi·la·tó·rjo] *adj. & m.* depilatory.

deplorar [de·plo·rár] *v.* to deplore, lament, regret.

deponer[40] [de·po·nér] *v. irr.* to set aside; to depose, remove (*an official*); to testify, declare; to have a bowel movement; *Am.* to vomit.

deportar [de·por·tár] *v.* to deport, banish.

deporte [de·pór·te] *m.* sport; pastime, recreation.

deportista [de·por·tís·ta] *m.* sportsman; *f.* sportswoman.

deportivo [de·por·ti·bo] *adj.* sport, sports (*used as an adj.*); **copa deportiva** loving cup.

deposición [de·po·si·sjón] *f.* declaration, assertion; testimony; dismissal, removal (*from office or power*); bowel movement.

depositar [de·po·si·tár] *v.* to deposit; to deliver, intrust.

depositario [de·po·si·tá·rjo] *m.* receiver, trustee.

depósito [de·pó·si·to] *m.* deposit; storage; warehouse; **— de agua** reservoir.

depravado [de·pra·bá·do] *adj.* depraved, corrupt, degenerate.

depravar [de·pra·bár] *v.* to corrupt, pervert, contaminate.

depreciar [de·pre·sjár] *v.* to depreciate, lessen the value of.

depresión [de·pre·sjón] *f.* depression; dip, sag.

deprimente [de·pri·mén·te] *adj.* depressing.

deprimir [de·pri·mír] *v.* to depress; to press down; to humiliate, belittle.

depuesto [de·pwés·to] *p.p. of* **deponer**.

depurar [de·pu·rár] *v.* to purify.

derecha [de·ré·ča] *f.* right hand; right side; right wing (*in politics*); **a la —** to the right; **derechazo** [de·re·čá·so] *m.* a blow with the right hand, a right (*boxing*).

derechista [de·re·čís·ta] *adj. & m. f.* rightist.

derecho [de·ré·čo] *adj.* right; straight; *m.* law; duty, tax; fee.

derechura [de·re·čú·ra] *f.* straightness.

deriva [de·rí·ba] *f.* drift (*of a boat or plane*); **irse** (*or* **andar**) **a la —** to drift, be drifting.

derivar [de·ri·bár] *v.* to derive; to come (from).

derogar[7] [de·ro·gár] *v.* to revoke, repeal, abolish.

derramamiento [de·rra·ma·mjén·to] *m.* spill, spilling, shedding; overflow; scattering; **— de sangre** bloodshed.

derramar [de·rra·már] *v.* to spill; to spread, scatter; to shed.

derrame [de·rrá·me] *m.* spill, spilling, shedding; overflow; discharge (*of secretion, blood, etc.*); slope.

derredor [de·rre·dór] *m.* circuit; contour; **al —** around; **en —** around.

derrengado [de·rreŋ·ga·do] *p.p. & adj.* lame, crippled; dislocated (*said of hip or spine*).

derrengar[1, 7] [de·rreŋ·gár] *v. irr.* to dislocate or sprain (*hip or spine*); to cripple; to bend.

derretimiento [de·rre·ti·mjén·to] *m.* thaw, thawing, melting.

derretir[5] [de·rre·tír] *v. irr.* to melt, dissolve; **-se** to be consumed; to melt.

derribar [de·rri·bár] *v.* to demolish, knock down, fell; to overthrow; **-se** to lie down, throw oneself down.

derrocamiento [de·rro·ka·mjén·to] *m.* overthrow.

derrocar[6] [de·rro·kár] *v.* to fling down; to fell; to overthrow.

derrochador [de·rro·ča·dór] *m.* squanderer, spendthrift; *adj.* wasteful, extravagant.

derrochar [de·rro·čár] *v.* to waste; to squander.

derroche [de·rró·če] *m.* waste; dissipation, lavish spending.

derrota [de·rró·ta] *f.* rout, defeat; ship's route or course.

derrotar [de·rro·tár] *v.* to defeat; to squander; to destroy, ruin; to lose or shift its course (*said of a ship*).

derrotero [de·rro·té·ro] *m.* course, direction; ship's course; book of marine charts.

derrumbadero [de·rrum·ba·dé·ro] *m.* precipice.

derrumbamiento [de·rrum·ba·mjén·to] *m.* landslide; collapse.

derrumbar [de·rrum·bár] *v.* to fling down; *Am.* to knock down; *Am.* to go down in a hurry; **-se** to crumble away; to topple over; *Col., Ven.* to dwindle (*as a business*).

derrumbe [de·rrúm·be] *m.* landslide; collapse.

desabotonar [de·sa·bo·to·nár] *v.* to unbutton.

desabrido [de·sa·brí·do] *adj.* tasteless, insipid; harsh; sour.

desabrigar[7] [de·sa·bri·gár] *v.* to uncover; **-se** to uncover oneself.

desabrimiento [de·sa·bri·mjén·to] *m.* tastelessness; harshness; sourness.

desabrochar [de·sa·bro·čár] *v.* to unfasten, unbutton, unclasp; **-se** to unbutton oneself, unfasten one's clothes.

desacato [de·sa·ká·to] *m.* irreverence, disrespect; profanation.

desacierto [de·sa·sjér·to] *m.* mistake, error.

desacoplar [de·sa·ko·plár] *v.* to uncouple, disconnect.

desacostumbrado [de·sa·kos·tum·brá·đo] *adj.* unaccustomed; unusual; *p.p. of* **desacostumbrar**.

desacostumbrar [de·sa·kos·tum·brár] *v.* to disaccustom, rid of a habit; **-se** to become unaccustomed; to lose a custom.

desacreditar [de·sa·kre·đi·tár] *v.* to discredit; to disgrace.

desacuerdo [de·sa·kwér·đo] *m.* disagreement; discord; blunder; forgetfulness.

desafiar[17] [de·sa·fjár] *v.* to challenge; to compete; to defy.

desafinado [de·sa·fi·ná·đo] *adj.* out of tune.

desafinar [de·sa·fi·nár] *v.* to be discordant; to be out of tune; **-se** to get out of tune.

desafío [de·sa·fí·o] *m.* challenge, defiance; duel; contest.

desafortunado [de·sa·for·tu·ná·đo] *adj.* unfortunate, unlucky.

desafuero [de·sa·fwé·ro] *m.* violation; outrage, abuse.

desagradable [de·sa·gra·đá·ƀle] *adj.* disagreeable, unpleasant.

desagradar [de·sa·gra·đár] *v.* to displease.

desagradecido [de·sa·gra·đe·sí·đo] *adj.* ungrateful.

desagrado [de·sa·grá·đo] *m.* displeasure; discontent.

desagraviar [de·sa·gra·ƀjár] *v.* to make amends; to compensate for a damage or injury; to right a wrong; to apologize; to vindicate.

desagravio [de·sa·grá·ƀjo] *m.* reparation; compensation for a wrong or injury; vindication; apology.

desaguadero [de·sa·gwa·đé·ro] *m.* drain, drain, pipe, water outlet.

desaguar[8] [de·sa·gwár] *v.* to drain, draw off; to flow (into); *Ch.* to wash (something) two or more times; *Am.* to extract the juice from; *Col., Ven., Mex.* to urinate; **-se** to drain.

desagüe [de·sá·gwe] *m.* drainage; drain.

desaguisado [de·sa·gi·sá·đo] *m.* outrage, violence, wrong.

desahogado [de·sa·o·gá·đo] *p.p. & adj.* (aliviado) relieved; (espacioso) roomy, spacious; **estar —** to be in easy or comfortable circumstances; to be well-off.

desahogar[7] [de·sa·o·gár] *v.* to relieve from pain or trouble; **-se** to find relief or release; to unbosom oneself, disclose one's feelings.

desahogo [de·sa·ó·go] *m.* relief from pain or trouble; release; ease, comfort, relaxation; freedom, unrestraint.

desairar [de·saj·rár] *v.* to slight, snub, disdain; to rebuff; to disappoint; to neglect.

desaire [de·sáj·re] *m.* rebuff, snub, slight, disdain.

desajustar [de·sa·xus·tár] *v.* to put out of order.

desalentar[1] [de·sa·len·tár] *v. irr.* to put out of breath; to discourage; **-se** to get discouraged.

desaliento [de·sa·ljén·to] *m.* discouragement, dejection.

desaliñado [de·sa·li·ñá·đo] *adj.* disheveled, slovenly, unkempt, untidy; disorderly.

desaliño [de·sa·li·ño] *m.* slovenliness, untidiness; neglect, carelessness; disorder.

desalmado [de·sal·má·đo] *adj.* soulless, cruel, inhuman.

desalojar [de·sa·lo·xár] *v.* to dislodge; to evict,

expel from a lodging; to vacate.

desamarrar [de·sa·ma·rrár] *v.* to untie, unfasten; to unmoor (a ship).

desamparar [de·sam·pa·rár] *v.* to abandon, forsake.

desamparo [de·sam·pá·ro] *m.* desertion, abandonment.

desamueblado [de·sa·mwe·ƀlá·đo] *adj.* unfurnished.

desangrar [de·saŋ·grár] *v.* to bleed, draw blood from; to drain; **-se** to bleed, lose blood.

desanimado [de·sa·ni·má·đo] *adj.* discouraged; lifeless; dull (said of a party, meeting, etc.).

desanimar [de·sa·ni·már] *v.* to dishearten, discourage.

desaparecer[13] [de·sa·pa·re·sér] *v. irr.* to disappear; to hide; **-se** to disappear, vanish.

desaparición [de·sa·pa·ri·sjón] *f.* disappearance.

desapasionado [de·sa·pa·sjo·ná·đo] *adj.* dispassionate; free from passion; calm; impartial.

desapego [de·sa·pe·go] *m.* aloofness, indifference, detachment.

desapercibido [de·sa·per·si·ƀí·đo] *adj.* unprepared; unprovided; unnoticed.

desaprobación [de·sa·pro·ƀa·sjón] *f.* disapproval.

desaprobar[2] [de·sa·pro·ƀár] *v. irr.* to disapprove.

desarmar [de·sar·már] *v.* to disarm; to dismount, take apart.

desarme [de·sár·me] *m.* disarmament.

desarraigar[7] [de·sa·rraj·gár] *v.* to root out, uproot.

desarreglado [de·sa·rre·glá·đo] *p.p. & adj.* disordered; disorderly; slovenly.

desarreglar [de·sa·rre·glár] *v.* to disarrange, disorder, disturb, upset.

desarreglo [de·sa·rré·glo] *m.* disorder, confusion.

desarrollar [de·sa·rro·yár] *v.* to unroll, unfold; to develop, explain; **-se** to develop; to unfold.

desarrollo [de·sa·rró·yo] *m.* development.

desaseado [de·sa·se·á·đo] *adj.* unkempt, untidy.

desaseo [de·sa·sé·o] *m.* slovenliness, untidiness.

desasir[22] [de·sa·sir] *v. irr.* to loosen, unfasten; **-se** to get loose (from); to let go (of).

desasosiego [de·sa·so·sjé·go] *m.* unrest, uneasiness, restlessness.

desastrado [de·sas·trá·đo] *adj.* unfortunate, unhappy; ragged, dirty, untidy.

desastre [de·sás·tre] *m.* disaster.

desastroso [de·sas·tró·so] *adj.* disastrous, unfortunate.

desatar [de·sa·tár] *v.* to untie, loosen; to dissolve; to unravel, clear up; **-se** to let loose, let go; to break loose; **-se en improperios** to let out a string of insults.

desatascar[6] [de·sa·tas·kár] *v. irr.* to extricate, dislodge; to pull out of the mud.

desatención [de·sa·ten·sjón] *f.* inattention, lack of attention; discourtesy.

desatender[1] [de·sa·ten·dér] *v. irr.* to disregard, pay no attention (to); to slight, neglect.

desatento [de·sa·tén·to] *adj.* inattentive; discourteous.

desatinado [de·sa·ti·ná·đo] *adj.* senseless; reckless.

desatinar [de·sa·ti·nár] *v.* to act foolishly; to talk nonsense; to blunder; to rave; to lose one's bearings.

desatino [de·sa·tí·no] *m.* blunder, error; folly, nonsense.

desatracar[6] [de·sa·tra·kár] *v.* to push off (from shore or from another ship); to cast off, unmoor.

desavenencia [de·sa·ƀe·nén·sja] *f.* disagreement, discord; dispute, misunderstanding.

desayunarse [de·sa·yu·nár·se] *v.* to eat breakfast;

—con la noticia to hear a piece of news for the first time.

desayuno [de·sa·yú·no] *m.* breakfast.

desazón [de·sa·són] *f.* uneasiness, anxiety; insipidity, flatness, tastelessness; displeasure.

desbandarse [dez·ƀan·dár·se] *v.* to disband, scatter, disperse; to desert the army or a party.

desbaratar [dez·ƀa·ra·tár] *v.* to destroy, ruin; to upset, disturb; to disperse, put to flight; to talk nonsense; **-se** to be upset, be in disorder; to fall to pieces.

desbocado [dez·ƀo·ká·ɖo] *adj.* runaway (*horse*), dashing headlong; foul-mouthed, abusive; broken-mouthed (*jar, pitcher, etc.*).

desbordamiento [dez·ƀor·ɖa·mjén·to] *m.* overflow, flood.

desbordante [dez·ƀor·ɖán·te] *adj.* overflowing; *Am.* frantic.

desbordar [dez·ƀor·ɖár] *v.* to overflow, flood; **-se** to spill over; to get overexcited.

desbravar [dez·ƀra·ƀár] *v.* to tame; **-se** to calm down.

descabalar [des·ka·ƀa·lár] *v.* to break (*a given amount, making it thereby incomplete*).

descabello [des·ka·ƀé·yo] *m.* the act of killing the bull by piercing the brain with the sword.

descabezado [des·ka·ƀe·sá·ɖo] *p.p.* beheaded; *adj.* headless; harebrained, thoughtless.

descabezar[9] [des·ka·ƀe·sár] *v.* to behead; to chop off the head or tip of; **—el sueño** to take a nap; **-se** to break one's head; to rack one's brain.

descaecido [des·ka·e·sí·ɖo] *adj.* feeble, weak; **—de ánimo** depressed, dejected, despondent.

descaecimiento [des·ka·e·si·mjén·to] *m.* languor, weakness; depression, dejection.

descalabradura [des·ka·la·ƀra·ɖú·ra] *f.* blow or wound on the head; scar on the head.

descalabrar [des·ka·la·ƀrár] *v.* to wound on the head; to hurt, injure; to damage; **-se** to suffer a head wound or skull fracture.

descalabro [des·ka·lá·ƀro] *m.* loss, misfortune.

descalzar[9] [des·kal·sár] *v.* to take off (*someone's*) shoes or (and) stockings; **-se** to take off one's shoes or (and) stockings; to lose a shoe (*said of horses*).

descalzo [des·kál·so] *adj.* barefoot; shoeless.

descaminar [des·ka·mi·nár] *v.* to mislead, lead astray; **-se** to go astray.

descamisado [des·ka·mi·sá·ɖo] *adj.* shirtless; in rags; *m.* ragamuffin, ragged fellow.

descansar [des·kan·sár] *v.* to rest.

descanso [des·kán·so] *m.* rest; staircase landing.

descarado [des·ka·rá·ɖo] *adj.* shameless, impudent, brazen.

descarga [des·kár·ga] *f.* discharge; unloading.

descargar[7] [des·kar·gár] *v.* to discharge; to unload.

descargo [des·kár·go] *m.* discharge (*of a duty or obligation*); unloading; relief.

descargue [des·kár·ge] *m.* unloading; discharge.

descarnado [des·kar·ná·ɖo] *adj.* fleshless, scrawny.

descarnar [des·kar·nár] *v.* to pull the flesh from the bone; to corrode, eat away; **-se** to become thin, emaciated.

descaro [des·ká·ro] *m.* effrontery, shamelessness, impudence, audacity.

descarriar[17] [des·ka·rrjár] *v.* to mislead, lead astray; to separate (*cattle*) from the herd; **-se** to stray; to go astray.

descarrilar [des·ka·rri·lár] *v.* to derail (*cause a train to run off the track*); to wreck (*a train*);

-se to get or run off the track; to go astray.

descartar [des·kar·tár] *v.* to discard; to put aside.

descascarado [des·kas·ka·rá·ɖo] *p.p. & adj.* peeled off; chipped off.

descascarar [des·kas·ka·rár] *v.* to shell, hull, husk; to peel; to chip off (*plaster*); *Am.* to defame, discredit; *Col.* to flay; **-se** to chip off, peel off.

descendencia [de·sen·dén·sja] *f.* descent, lineage; descendants, offspring.

descendente [de·sen·dén·te] *adj.* descending, downward.

descender[1] [de·sen·dér] *v. irr.* to descend, go down; to get down; to come (from), originate.

descendiente [de·sen·djén·te] *m. & f.* descendant; *adj.* descending.

descendimiento [de·sen·di·mjén·to] *m.* descent.

descenso [de·sén·so] *m.* descent; fall.

descifrar [de·si·frár] *v.* to decipher, puzzle out, figure out.

descolgar[2, 7] [des·kol·gár] *v. irr.* to unhang, take down; to let down; **-se** to climb down (*a rope, tree, etc.*); to drop in, appear unexpectedly.

descolorar [des·ko·lo·rár] *v.* to discolor; to fade; **-se** to fade, lose its color; to discolor.

descolorido [des·ko·lo·rí·ɖo] *adj.* pale.

descollar[2] [des·ko·yár] *v. irr.* to excel; to stand out; tower (above).

descomedido [des·ko·me·ɖí·ɖo] *adj.* rude, discourteous, impolite; unobliging.

descompletar [des·kom·ple·tár] *v.* to make incomplete, break (*a unit, sum, set, etc.*)

descomponer[40] [des·kom·po·nér] *v. irr.* (*estorbar*) to upset, disturb; (*echar a perder*) to put out of order; to decompose; **-se** to decompose, rot; to become upset, ill; to get out of order; *Col., Ven., C.A., Carib., Mex.* **se me descompuso el brazo** I dislocated my arm, my arm got out of joint.

descomposición [des·kom·po·si·sjón] *f.* decomposition; decay, corruption; disorder, confusion.

descompuesto [des·kom·pwés·to] *p.p. of* **descomponer;** *adj.* out of order; insolent; brazen; immodest.

descomunal [des·ko·mu·nál] *adj.* colossal, enormous, monstrous.

desconcertante [des·kon·ser·tán·te] *adj.* disconcerting, disturbing, confusing, baffling, embarrassing.

desconcertar[1] [des·kon·ser·tár] *v. irr.* to disconcert, bewilder, confuse; to disturb; **-se** to be confused, perplexed.

desconcierto [des·kon·sjér·to] *m.* disorder; confusion; disagreement; feeling of discomfort.

desconchadura [des·kon·ča·ɖú·ra] *f.* chip (*chipped off place*); chipping off, peeling off (*of plaster, varnish, etc.*).

desconchar [des·kon·čár] *v.* to scrape off (*plaster or stucco*); **-se** to peel off, chip off (*as plaster*).

desconectar [des·ko·nek·tár] *v.* to disconnect.

desconfiado [des·kon·fjá·ɖo] *adj.* distrustful, suspicious.

desconfianza [des·kon·fján·sa] *f.* mistrust, distrust.

desconfiar[17] [des·kon·fjár] *v.* to distrust; to lose confidence.

desconocer[13] [des·ko·no·sér] *v. irr.* to fail to recognize or remember; to disown; to disregard, slight; not to know.

desconocido [des·ko·no·sí·ɖo] *adj.* unknown; unrecognizable; *m.* stranger.

desconocimiento [des·ko·no·si·mjén·to] *m.*

disregard; ignorance.
desconsolado [des·kon·so·lá·ḍo] *p.p & adj.*
disconsolate, forlorn; disheartened, grieved.
desconsolador [des·kon·so·la·ḍór] *adj.*
disheartening, saddening.
desconsolar[2] [des·kon·so·lár] *v. irr.* to sadden,
grieve; to discourage; **-se** to become
disheartened, grieved.
desconsuelo [des·kon·swé·lo] *m.* dejection, sadness,
distress.
descontar[2] [des·kon·tár] *v. irr.* to discount, deduct;
to allow for.
descontentadizo [des·kon·ten·ta·ḍí·so] *adj.*
discontented, fretful, hard to please.
descontentar [des·kon·ten·tár] *v.* to displease.
descontento [des·kon·tén·to] *adj.* discontent,
displeased; *m.* discontent, displeasure.
descorazonado [des·ko·ra·so·ná·ḍo] *adj.*
disheartened, discouraged, depressed.
descorchar [des·kor·čár] *v.* to uncork; to remove
the bark from (*a cork tree*); to force or break
open.
descortés [des·kor·tés] *adj.* discourteous, rude,
impolite.
descortesía [des·kor·te·sí·a] *f.* discourtesy, rudeness,
impoliteness.
descortezar[9] [des·kor·te·sár] *v.* to bark, strip the
bark from (*trees*); to remove the crust or shell
from; to peel; to civilize, remove the rough
manners from.
descoser [des·ko·sér] *v.* to rip, unsew, unstitch;
-se to rip, come unstitched; to talk too much
or indiscreetly.
descosido [des·ko·sí·ḍo] *m.* rip; *adj.* too talkative,
indiscreet; disorderly; *p.p. of* **descoser.**
descostrar [des·kos·trár] *v.* to flake; to scale off;
to remove the crust from; **-se** to flake, scale off.
descoyuntado [des·ko·yun·tá·ḍo] *p.p. & adj.*
dislocated, out of joint.
descoyuntar [des·ko·yun·tár] *v.* to dislocate, put
out of joint; **-se** to get out of joint.
descrédito [des·kré·ḍi·to] *m.* discredit.
descreído [des·kre·í·ḍo] *adj.* incredulous,
unbelieving; *m.* unbeliever.
descreimiento [des·krej·mjén·to] *m.* unbelief, lack
of faith.
describir[52] [des·kri·ƀír] *v.* to describe.
descripción [des·krip·sjón] *f.* description.
descriptivo [des·krip·ti·ƀo] *adj.* descriptive.
descrito [des·krí·to] *p.p. irr. of* **describir.**
descuartizar[9] [des·kwar·ti·sár] *v.* to quarter (*an
animal*; to tear or cut into parts.
descubierto [des·ku·ƀjér·to] *p.p. of* **descubrir** & *adj.*
(*sin cubierta*) uncovered; hatless, bareheaded;
(*hallado*) discovered; *m.* deficit, shortage; **al**—
openly, in the open; **en**— uncovered, unpaid.
descubridor [des·ku·ƀri·ḍór] *m.* discoverer.
descubrimiento [des·ku·ƀri·mjén·to] *m.* discovery;
find; invention.
descubrir[52] [des·ku·ƀrír] *v.* to discover; to uncover;
-se to uncover; to take off one's hat.
descuento [des·kwén·to] *m.* discount; deduction.
descuidado [des·kwi·ḍá·ḍo] *adj.* careless, negligent;
untidy, slovenly; unaware; thoughtless.
descuidar [des·kwi·ḍár] *v.* to neglect; to overlook;
to be careless or negligent; **-se** to be careless
or negligent.
descuido [des·kwí·ḍo] *m.* carelessness; neglect;
oversight; disregard; inattention; slip, error.
desde [déz·ḍe] *prep.* from; since; **—luego** of
course; **—que** *conj.* since, ever since.

desdecir[27] [dez·ḍe·sir] *v. irr.* to be out of harmony
(with); to detract (from); **-se** to retract; to
contradict oneself.
desdén [dez·ḍén] *m.* disdain, scorn.
desdentado [dez·ḍen·tá·ḍo] *adj.* toothless.
desdeñar [dez·ḍe·ñár] *v.* to disdain, scorn.
desdeñoso [dez·ḍe·ñó·so] *adj.* disdainful, scornful.
desdicha [dez·ḍí·ča] *f.* misfortune; misery; poverty.
desdichado [dez·ḍí·čá·ḍo] *adj.* unfortunate;
unhappy, wretched; miserable; *m.* wretch.
desdoblamiento [dez·ḍo·ƀla·mjén·to] *m.* unfolding.
desdoblar [dez·ḍo·ƀlár] *v.* to unfold; to spread out.
desdorar [dez·ḍo·rár] *v.* to remove the gilt from;
to tarnish; to dishonor.
desdoro [dez·ḍó·ro] *m.* tarnish, blemish; dishonor.
deseable [de·se·á·ƀle] *adj.* desirable.
desear [de·se·ár] *v.* to desire, want.
desecación [de·se·ka·sjón] *f.*, **desecamiento**
[de·se·ka·mjén·to] *m.* drying; drainage.
desecar[6] [de·se·kár] *v.* to dry; to dry up; to drain
(*land*).
desechar [de·se·čár] *v.* to discard; to reject; to
refuse, decline; *Col.* to cut across, take a short
cut.
desecho [de·sé·čo] *m.* remainder, residue; waste
material; piece of junk; discard; **-s** refuse, scraps,
junk; **hierro de**—scrap iron; **papel de**—
wastepaper, scraps of paper.
desembalar [de·sem·ba·lár] *v.* to unpack.
desembarazar[9] [de·sem·ba·ra·sár] *v.* to rid, free,
clear; *Ch.* to give birth; **-se** to get rid of.
desembarazo [de·sem·ba·rá·so] *m.* freedom, ease,
naturalness; *Ch.* childbirth.
desembarcadero [de·sem·bar·ka·ḍé·ro] *m.* dock,
wharf, pier.
desembarcar[6] [de·sem·bar·kár] *v.* to disembark,
land; to unload; to go ashore.
desembarco [de·sem·bár·ko], **desembarque**
[de·sem·bár·ke] *m.* landing; unloading.
desembocadura [de·sem·bo·ka·ḍú·ra] *f.* mouth (*of a
river, canal, etc.*); outlet.
desembocar[6] [de·sem·bo·kár] *v.* to flow (into); to
lead (to).
desembolsar [de·sem·bol·sár] *v.* to disburse, pay
out.
desembolso [de·sem·ból·so] *m.* disbursement,
outlay, expenditure.
desembragar[7] [de·sem·bra·gár] *v.* to throw out the
clutch; to disconnect.
desemejante [de·se·me·xán·te] *adj.* unlike.
desempacar[6] [de·sem·pa·kár] *v.* to unpack.
desempañar [de·sem·pa·ñár] *v.* to wipe clean; to
remove steam or smudge (*from glass*).
desempeñar [de·sem·pe·ñár] *v.* to recover, redeem,
take out of pawn; **—un cargo** to perform the
duties of a position; **—un papel** to play a part;
-se to get out of debt.
desempeño [de·sem·pé·ño] *m.* fulfillment, carrying
out, discharge; performance (*of a duty*); acting
(*of a role*); redeeming (*of a thing pawned*).
desempleado [de·sem·ple·á·ḍo] *adj.* unemployed.
desempleo [de·sem·plé·o] *m.* unemployment.
desempolvar [de·sem·pol·ƀár] *v.* to dust, remove
the dust from.
desencadenar [de·sen·ka·ḍe·nár] *v.* to unchain, free
from chains; to loosen, set free; **-se** to free
oneself; to break loose.
desencajado [de·seŋ·ka·xá·ḍo] *p.p. & adj.* disjointed;
disfigured; sunken (*eyes*); emaciated.
desencajar [de·seŋ·ka·xár] *v.* to dislocate; **-se** to
become dislocated.

DE

desencantar [de·seŋ·kan·tár] *v.* to disillusion. disappoint.

desencanto [de·seŋ·kán·to] *m.* disillusion, disappointment.

desenfadar [de·sen·fa·ḍár] *v.* to free of anger; **-se** to calm down.

desenfado [de·sen·fá·ḍo] *m.* ease, freedom; calmness.

desenfrenado [de·sen·fre·ná·ḍo] *p.p. & adj.* unbridled; wanton, reckless; loose, immoral.

desenganchar [de·seŋ·gan·čár] *v.* to unhitch; to unhook; to unfasten.

desengañador [de·seŋ·ga·ña·ḍór] *adj.* disappointing, disillusioning.

desengañar [de·seŋ·ga·ñár] *v.* to undeceive, disillusion, disappoint.

desengaño [de·seŋ·gá·ño] *m.* disillusion, disappointment, blighted hope.

desengranar [de·seŋ·gra·nár] *v.* to throw out of gear.

desenmarañar [de·sem·ma·ra·ñár] *v.* to untangle; to unravel.

desenmascarar [de·sem·mas·ka·rár] *v.* to unmask.

desenredar [de·sen·rre·ḍár] *v.* to disentangle, unravel.

desenrollar [de·sen·rro·yár] *v.* to unroll.

desensartar [de·sen·sar·tár] *v.* to unstring; to unthread; to unfasten from a ring.

desensillar [de·sen·si·yár] *v.* to unsaddle.

desentenderse[1] [de·sen·ten·dér·se] *v. irr.* to neglect, ignore, pay no attention to; to pretend not to see, hear or understand.

desentendido [de·sen·ten·dí·ḍo] *adj.* unmindful, heedless; *p.p. of* **desentenderse; hacerse el**—to pretend not to notice.

desenterrar[1] [de·sen·te·rrár] *v. irr.* to unearth, dig up.

desentonado [de·sen·to·ná·ḍo] *adj.* inharmonious, out of tune.

desentonar [de·sen·to·nár] *v.* to be out of tune; to be out of harmony; to sing off key, play out of tune.

desenvoltura [de·sem·bol·tú·ra] *f.* freedom, ease, abandon; boldness, impudence.

desenvolver[2, 52] [de·sem·bol·ḅér] *v. irr.* to unroll, unfold; to unwrap; to develop.

desenvolvimiento [de·sem·bol·ḅi·mjén·to] *m.* development, unfolding.

desenvuelto [de·sem·bwél·to] *adj.* free, easy; forward, bold; shameless, brazen; *p.p. of* **desenvolver.**

deseo [de·sé·o] *m.* desire, wish.

deseoso [de·se·ó·so] *adj.* desirous, eager.

desequilibrado [de·se·ki·li·ḅrá·ḍo] *adj.* unbalanced; *p.p. of* **desequilibrar.**

desequilibrar [de·se·ki·li·ḅrár] *v.* to unbalance; to derange.

desequilibrio [de·se·ki·lí·ḅrjo] *m.* lack of balance; derangement, mental disorder.

deserción [de·ser·sjón] *f.* desertion.

desertar [de·ser·tár] *v.* to desert; to abandon; **-se de** to desert.

desertor [de·ser·tór] *m.* deserter; quitter.

desesperación [de·ses·pe·ra·sjón] *f.* despair; desperation; fury.

desesperado [de·ses·pe·rá·ḍo] *adj.* desperate; despairing; hopeless; *p.p. of* **desesperar.**

desesperanzado [de·ses·pe·ran·sá·ḍo] *p.p. & adj.* discouraged; hopeless; desperate, in despair.

desesperanzar[9] [de·ses·pe·ran·sár] *v.* to discourage, deprive of hope; **-se** to be discouraged; to despair, lose one's hope.

desesperar [de·ses·pe·rár] *v.* to despair, lose hope; to make (*someone*) despair; **-se** to despair, be desperate; to be furious.

desfachatez [des·fa·ča·tés] *f.* shamelessness, effrontery, impudence.

desfalcar[6] [des·fal·kár] *v.* to embezzle; to remove a part of.

desfalco [des·fál·ko] *m.* embezzlement; diminution, decrease.

desfallecer[13] [des·fa·ye·sér] *v. irr.* to grow weak; to faint.

desfallecimiento [des·fa·ye·si·mjén·to] *m.* faintness; weakness; languor; swoon, faint.

desfavorable [des·fa·ḅo·rá·ḅle] *adj.* unfavorable.

desfigurar [des·fi·ǵu·rár] *v.* to disfigure; to deface; to distort.

desfiladero [des·fi·la·ḍé·ro] *m.* narrow passage, narrow gorge; road on the edge of a precipice.

desfilar [des·fi·lár] *v.* to march, parade, pass by.

desfile [des·fí·le] *m.* parade.

desgana [dez·ǵá·na] *f.* lack of appetite; reluctance.

desgarrado [dez·ǵa·rrá·ḍo] *p.p.* torn; *adj.* shameless; impudent.

desgarradura [dez·ǵa·rra·ḍú·ra] *f.* tear.

desgarrar [dez·ǵa·rrár] *v.* to tear, rend; to expectorate, cough up; **-se** to tear; to separate oneself (from).

desgastar [dez·ǵas·tár] *v.* to waste, consume, wear away, **-se** to waste away, lose one's strength or vigor; to wear off.

desgaste [dez·ǵás·te] *m.* waste; wear and tear.

desgracia [dez·ǵrá·sja] *f.* misfortune, mishap; disgrace.

desgraciado [dez·ǵra·sjá·ḍo] *adj.* unfortunate, wretched.

desgranar [dez·ǵra·nár] *v.* to thrash, thresh (*grain*); to remove the grain from; to shell (*peas, beans, etc.*).

desgreñado [dez·ǵre·ñá·ḍo] *adj.* disheveled.

desgreñar [dez·ǵre·ñár] *v.* to dishevel; **-se** to muss up one's own hair.

deshabitado [de·sa·ḅi·li·tá·ḍo] *adj.* uninhabited, deserted; empty, vacant.

deshacer[31] [de·sa·sér] *v. irr.* to undo; to dissolve; to destroy; to untie; **-se** to dissolve; to melt; to waste away; **-se de** to get rid of.

desharrapado, desarrapado [de·sa·rra·pá·ḍo] *adj.* ragged, shabby, tattered.

deshecha [de·sé·ča] *f.* simulation, pretense; **hacer la**—to feign, pretend.

deshecho [de·sé·čo] *p.p. of* **deshacer** & *adj.* undone; ruined, destroyed, in pieces; violent (*said of rainstorms*); worn-out, fatigued; *Am.* disorderly, untidy.

deshelar[1] [de·se·lár] *v. irr.* to melt; to thaw; **-se** to melt; to thaw.

desherbar[1] [de·ser·ḅár] *v. irr.* to weed.

deshielo [dez·yé·lo] *m.* thaw.

deshierbe [dez·yér·ḅe] *m.* weeding.

deshilachar [de·si·la·čár] *v.* to ravel, fray.

deshilar [de·si·lár] *v.* to unravel, **-se** to unravel; to fray.

deshojar [de·so·xár] *v.* to strip off the leaves, petals, or pages; **-se** to lose its leaves (*said of a plant or book*); to lose petals.

deshollejar [de·so·ye·xár] *v.* to husk, hull; to peel, pare, skin; to shell (*beans*).

deshonesto [de·so·nés·to] *adj.* immodest; unchaste, lewd.

deshonra [de·són·rra] *f.* dishonor; disgrace.

deshonrar [de·son·rrár] *v.* to dishonor, disgrace; to insult, offend; to seduce.

deshonroso [de·son·rró·so] *adj.* dishonorable; shameful.

deshora [de·só·ra] *f.* inopportune time; **a —** (*or* **a -s**) unexpectedly; **comer a —** to piece, eat between meals.

deshuesar [dez·we·sár] *v.* to stone, remove the pits or stones from (*fruits*); to bone, remove the bones from (*an animal*).

deshumanizar [9] [de·su·ma·ni·sár] *v. irr.* to dehumanize.

desidia [de·si·ɖja] *f.* indolence, laziness.

desidioso [de·si·ɖjó·so] *adj.* indolent, negligent, lazy; listless.

desierto [de·sjér·to] *adj.* deserted, uninhabited; alone; lonely; *m.* desert, wilderness.

designación [de·siɡ·na·sjón] *f.* designation; appointment.

designar [de·siɡ·nár] *v.* to designate, appoint, select; to design, plan, intend.

designio [de·siɡ·njo] *m.* design, plan, purpose.

desigual [de·si·ɡwál] *adj.* unequal; uneven; variable, changeable.

desigualdad [de·si·ɡwa·li·ɖáɖ] *f.* inequality; unevenness; roughness (*of the ground*).

desilusión [de·si·lu·sjón] *f.* disillusion, disappointment.

desilusionar [de·si·lu·sjo·nár] *v.* to disillusion, disappoint; **-se** to become disillusioned; to lose one's illusions.

desinencia [de·si·nén·sja] *f.* termination, ending (*of a word*).

desinfectante [de·sin·fek·tán·te] *adj.* disinfecting; *m.* disinfectant.

desinfectar [de·sin·fek·tár] *v.* to disinfect.

desinflado [de·sin·flá·ɖo] *adj.* deflated, not inflated, flat.

desinflar [de·sin·flár] *v.* to deflate.

desinterés [de·sin·te·rés] *m.* disinterestedness, unselfishness, impartiality.

desinteresado [de·sin·te·re·sá·ɖo] *adj.* disinterested, unselfish, fair, impartial.

desistir [de·sis·tír] *v.* to desist, stop, cease.

deslavado [dez·la·ba·ɖo] *p.p. & adj.* half-washed; weakened; faded; pale; saucy.

deslavar [dez·la·bár] *v.* to wash away; to fade; to wash superficially.

desleal [dez·le·ál] *adj.* disloyal, faithless.

desleír [15] [dez·le·ír] *v. irr.* to dissolve; to dilute, make thin or weak; **-se** to become diluted.

deslindar [dez·lin·dár] *v.* to mark off, mark the boundaries of.

desliz [dez·lís] *m.* slip, slide; error.

deslizador [dez·li·sa·ɖór] *m.* glider.

deslizamiento [dez·li·sa·mjén·to] *m.* slip, slipping; glide; sliding, skidding.

deslizar [9] [dez·li·sár] *v.* to slip, slide; **-se** to slip; to skid; to glide; to slip out.

deslucido [dez·lu·sí·ɖo] *p.p. & adj.* tarnished; dull; discredited; dingy, shabby; awkward, ungraceful; inelegant.

deslucir [13] [dez·lu·sír] *v. irr.* to tarnish, dull the luster of; to discredit.

deslumbrador [dez·lum·bra·ɖór] *adj.* dazzling, glaring.

deslumbramiento [dez·lum·bra·mjén·to] *m.* dazzle, glare; daze, confusion.

deslumbrar [dez·lum·brár] *v.* to dazzle.

deslustrado [dez·lus·trá·ɖo] *adj. & p.p.* tarnished; dim, dull; opaque.

deslustrar [dez·lus·trár] *v.* to tarnish; to soil, stain (*one's honor or reputation*).

deslustre [dez·lús·tre] *m.* tarnish; disgrace.

desmadejado [dez·ma·ɖe·xá·ɖo] *p.p. & adj.* enervated, exhausted; depressed.

desmadejar [dez·ma·ɖe·xár] *v.* to enervate, weaken.

desmán [dez·mán] *m.* misconduct, abuse, insult; calamity, disaster.

desmantelar [dez·man·te·lár] *v.* to dismantle, strip of furniture, equipment, etc.

desmañado [dez·ma·ñá·ɖo] *adj.* unskillful, awkward, clumsy.

desmayar [dez·ma·yár] *v.* to dismay; to lose strength, courage; **-se** to faint.

desmayo [dez·má·yo] *m.* faint, swoon; dismay, discouragement.

desmazalado [dez·ma·sa·lá·ɖo] *adj.* dejected, depressed.

desmedido [dez·me·ɖí·ɖo] *adj.* limitless; excessive.

desmejorar [dez·me·xo·rár] *v.* to impair; to make worse; **-se** to grow worse; to waste away, lose one's health.

desmentir [3] [dez·men·tír] *v. irr.* to contradict; to give the lie; **-se** to contradict oneself; to retract, take back one's word.

desmenuzar [9] [dez·me·nu·sár] *v.* to crumble, break into bits; to mince; to shred; **-se** to crumble, fall to pieces.

desmerecer [13] [dez·me·re·sér] *v. irr.* to become unworthy of; to deteriorate, lose merit or value; to be inferior to.

desmigajar [dez·mi·ɡa·xár] *v.* to crumb (*bread*); to crumble; **-se** to crumble.

desmochar [dez·mo·čár] *v.* to cut off, chop off (*the top or tip*).

desmolado [dez·mo·lá·ɖo] *adj.* toothless, without molars.

desmontar [dez·mon·tár] *v.* to dismount; to cut down (*a forest*); to clear or level off (*ground*); to dismantle, take apart; to tear down; **-se** to dismount, alight, get off.

desmoronar [dez·mo·ro·nár] *v.* to crumble; **-se** to crumble down, fall gradually to pieces.

desnatar [dez·na·tár] *v.* to skim, take the cream from (*milk*).

desnaturalizado [dez·na·tu·ra·li·sá·ɖo] *adj.* unnatural, cruel; **alcohol —** denatured alcohol (*made unfit for drinking*); **madre desnaturalizada** unnatural mother (*one without motherly instincts*).

desnudar [dez·nu·ɖár] *v.* to undress, uncover; **-se** to undress.

desnudez [dez·nu·ɖés] *f.* nudity, nakedness.

desnudo [dez·nú·ɖo] *adj.* nude, naked, bare.

desobedecer [13] [de·so·be·ɖe·sér] *v. irr.* to disobey.

desobediencia [de·so·be·ɖjén·sja] *f.* disobedience; **desobediente** [de·so·be·ɖjén·te] *adj.* disobedient.

desocupación [de·so·ku·pa·sjón] *f.* unemployment; idleness; vacationing.

desocupado [de·so·ku·pá·ɖo] *adj.* unoccupied; unemployed, idle; empty, vacant.

desocupar [de·so·ku·pár] *v.* to empty, vacate; **-se de un negocio** to get rid of, or not pay attention to, a business.

desoír [36] [de·so·ír] *v. irr.* to turn a deaf ear to, not to heed; to refuse (*a petition*).

desolación [de·so·la·sjón] *f.* desolation; ruin; loneliness; anguish, affliction, grief.

desolado [de·so·lá·ɖo] *adj.* desolate; *p.p. of* **desolar.**

desolar [2] [de·so·lár] *v. irr.* to lay waste, ruin; **-se** to

DE

be in anguish; to grieve.
desollar[2] [de·so·yár] *v. irr.* to skin, flay; to fleece,
extort money from.
desorbitado [de·sor·ƀi·tá·ḍo] *adj.* out of its orbit;
out of place or proportion; decentered;
Ch. Andes popeyed, with bulging eyes; *Am.*
crazy, eccentric.
desorden [de·sór·ḍen] *m.* disorder, confusion.
desordenado [de·sor·ḍe·ná·ḍo] *adj.* disorderly;
lawless; unsettled; *p.p. of* **desordenar.**
desordenar [de·sor·ḍe·nár] *v.* to disturb, confuse,
upset.
desorientar [de·so·rjen·tár] *v.* to throw off one's
bearings; to lead astray; to misdirect, mislead;
to confuse; **-se** to lose one's bearings; to go
astray, get lost.
desoxidar [de·sok·si·ḍár] *v.* to deoxidize.
despabilado [des·pa·ƀi·lá·ḍo] *adj.* wakeful;
wide-awake; bright, lively.
despabilar [des·pa·ƀi·lár] *v.* to snuff, trim the wick
of (*a candle*); to enliven, awaken (*the mind*),
sharpen (*the wits*); **-se** to wake up, rouse oneself,
shake off drowsiness.
despacio [des·pá·sjo] *adv.* slowly.
despacioso [des·pa·sjó·so] *adj.* slow.
despachar [des·pa·čár] *v.* to dispatch; to send; to
facilitate; to ship.
despacho [des·pá·čo] *m.* (*oficina*) office, bureau;
salesroom; (*comunicación*) dispatch; (*envío*)
sending; shipment; (*sin demora*) promptness; *Ch.*
country store, farm store.
despachurrar [des·pa·ču·rrár] *v.* to crush, squash.
desparejo [des·pa·ré·xo] *adj.* unequal, uneven.
desparpajar [des·par·pa·xár] *v.* to upset,
disarrange; to rant, talk too much; *Mex.* to
disperse, scatter.
desparpajo [des·par·pá·xo] *m.* ease, freedom of
manner; freshness, pertness; *Col.* dispersion,
scattering; *Am.* disorder, jumble.
desparramar [des·pa·rra·már] *v.* to scatter, spread;
to spill; to squander; **-se** to "spread" oneself,
spend lavishly; to scatter; to spill.
desparramo [des·pa·rrá·mo] *m. Ch., C.A.*
scattering, spreading, spilling; *Riopl., Carib.*
disorder, commotion.
despatarrarse [des·pa·ta·rrár·se] *v.* to sprawl; to
fall sprawling to the ground.
despecho [des·pé·čo] *m.* spite; grudge; despair;
weaning; **a — de** in spite of.
despedazar[9] [des·pe·ḍa·sár] *v.* to break, cut, tear
into pieces.
despedida [des·pe·ḍí·ḍa] *f.* farewell; departure;
dismissal.
despedir[5] [des·pe·ḍír] *v. irr.* (*cesar*) to discharge,
dismiss; (*emitir*) emit, throw off, give off; to see
(*a person*) off (*at a station, airport, etc.*); **-se** to
take leave, say good-bye.
despegar[7] [des·pe·gár] *v.* to detach; to unfasten;
to take off (*said of a plane*); *Am.* to unhitch;
no — los labios not to say a word, not to
open one's mouth; **-se** to grow apart; to come
loose or become detached.
despego [des·pé·go] = **desapego.**
despegue [des·pé·ge] *m.* takeoff (*of an airplane*).
despejado [des·pe·xá·ḍo] *adj.* clear, cloudless;
smart, bright; *p.p. of* **despejar.**
despejar [des·pe·xár] *v.* to clear; to remove
obstacles from; **-se** to clear up (*as the sky*); to
clear one's mind.
despellejar [des·pe·ye·xár] *v.* to skin, flay.
despensa [des·pén·sa] *f.* pantry; storeroom (*for

food); food provisions.
despensero [des·pen·sé·ro] *m.* butler; steward.
despeñadero [des·pe·ña·ḍé·ro] *m.* steep cliff,
precipice.
despeñar [des·pe·ñár] *v.* to fling down a
precipice; **-se** to fall down a precipice; to throw
oneself down a cliff.
despepitar [des·pe·pi·tár] *v.* to seed, remove the
seeds from; **-se** to talk or shout vehemently;
to rave, talk wildly; **-se por una cosa** to long
for something; to be crazy about something.
desperdiciado [des·per·ḍi·sjá·ḍo] *adj.* wasteful; *p.p.*
of **desperdiciar.**
desperdiciar [des·per·ḍi·sjár] *v.* to squander; to
waste.
desperdicio [des·per·ḍí·sjo] *m.* waste; extravagance;
-s leftovers, garbage; residue.
desperdigar[7] [des·per·ḍi·gár] *v.* to disperse; to
scatter; to strew.
desperezarse[9] [des·pe·re·sár·se] *v.* to stretch oneself.
desperfecto [des·per·fék·to] *m.* damage; flaw, defect.
despertador [des·per·ta·ḍór] *m.* alarm clock.
despertar[1] [des·per·tár] *v. irr.* to awaken; to wake
up; **-se** to wake up.
despiadado [des·pja·ḍá·ḍo] *adj.* pitiless, heartless,
cruel.
despierto [des·pjér·to] *adj.* awake; wide-awake.
despilfarrado [des·pil·fa·rrá·ḍo] *adj.* wasteful,
extravagant; ragged; *p.p. of* **despilfarrar.**
despilfarrar [des·pil·fa·rrár] *v.* to squander; to
waste.
despilfarro [des·pil·fá·rro] *m.* extravagance,
squandering; waste.
despistar [des·pis·tár] *v.* to throw off the track.
desplantador [des·plan·ta·ḍór] *m.* garden trowel.
desplante [des·plán·te] *m.* arrogance; impudent
remark or act.
desplazar[9] [des·pla·sár] *v.* to displace.
desplegar[1, 7] [des·ple·gár] *v. irr.* to unfold; to
unfurl; to show, manifest.
desplomar [des·plo·már] *v.* to cause (*a wall*) to
lean; **-se** to slump; to topple over, tumble
down, collapse.
desplome [des·pló·me] *m.* collapse; toppling over;
landslide.
desplumar [des·plu·már] *v.* to pick, pluck (*a fowl*);
to fleece, skin, rob, strip; **-se** to molt, shed the
feathers.
despoblado [des·po·ƀlá·ḍo] *adj.* uninhabited,
desolate; **— de árboles** treeless; *m.* open
country; uninhabited place; wilderness.
despojar [des·po·xár] *v.* to despoil, rob; to strip
(of), deprive (of); **-se** to undress; to deprive
oneself.
despojo [des·pó·xo] *m.* plundering, robbery; spoil,
booty; leftover, scrap; **-s** remains.
desportilladura [des·por·ti·ya·ḍú·ra] *f.* chip; nick.
desportillar [des·por·ti·yár] *v.* to chip; to nick.
desposar [des·po·sár] *v.* to marry; **-se** to become
formally engaged; to get married.
déspota [dés·po·ta] *m & f.* despot, tyrant.
despótico [des·pó·ti·ko] *adj.* despotic, tyrannical.
despotismo [des·po·tíz·mo] *m.* despotism, tyranny.
despreciable [des·pre·sjá·ƀle] *adj.* contemptible;
worthless; insignificant, negligible.
despreciar [des·pre·sjár] *v.* to despise, scorn.
desprecio [des·pré·sjo] *m.* scorn, contempt.
desprender [des·pren·dér] *v.* to unfasten, loosen; to
detach; **-se** to get loose, come unfastened; to
climb down; to get rid (of); to be inferred, be
deduced.

desprendimiento [des·pren·di·mjén·to] *m.*
detachment; generosity; unfastening; landslide.
despreocupado [des·pre·o·ku·pá·đo] *p.p. & adj.*
unbiased; liberal, broadminded; unconventional,
carefree; *Am.* careless, slovenly; *Am.* indifferent
to criticism.
desprestigiar [des·pres·ti·xjár] *v.* to discredit, harm
the reputation of; **-se** to lose one's prestige.
desprestigio [des·pres·tí·xjo] *m.* discredit, loss of
prestige.
desprevenido [des·pre·ƀe·ní·đo] *adj.* unprepared;
unaware.
despropósito [des·pro·pó·si·to] *m.* absurdity,
nonsense.
desprovisto [des·pro·ƀís·to] *adj.* destitute; lacking;
devoid.
después [des·pwés] *adv.* after, afterward; then,
later; — **de** *prep.* after; — **(de) que** *conj.* after.
despuntado [des·pun·tá·đo] *adj.* blunt, dull; *p.p. of*
despuntar.
despuntar [des·pun·tár] *v.* (*quitar la punta*) to
blunt; to cut off (*a point*); nip; (*brotar*) to bud
or sprout; (*sobresalir*) to excel; to be clever,
witty; — **el alba** to begin to dawn.
desquiciar [des·ki·sjár] *v.* to unhinge; to perturb.
desquitar [des·ki·tár] *v.* to retrieve, restore (*a loss*);
-se to get even, take revenge; to win back one's
money; to make up (for).
desquite [des·kí·te] *m.* retaliation, revenge; getting
even; recovery of a loss; return game or match.
desrazonable [des·rra·so·ná·ƀle] *adj.* unreasonable.
destacado [des·ta·ká·đo] *adj.* outstanding; *p.p. of*
destacar.
destacamento [des·ta·ka·mjén·to] *m.* military
detachment.
destacar[6] [des·ta·kár] *v.* to detach (*troops*); to
make stand out; to stand out; **hacer** — to
emphasize; to make stand out; **-se** to stand out.
destapar [des·ta·pár] *v.* to uncover; to uncork;
Am. to start running; **-se** to uncover, get
uncovered; to get uncorked; *Am.* to burst out
talking.
destartalado [des·tar·ta·la·đo] *adj.* in disorder; in
rack and ruin; dismantled, stripped of
furniture.
destechado [des·te·čá·đo] *adj.* roofless.
destellar [des·te·yár] *v.* to flash; to sparkle,
twinkle; to gleam.
destello [des·té·yo] *m.* flash, sparkle, gleam.
destemplado [des·tem·plá·đo] *adj.* out of tune, out
of harmony; immoderate; **sentirse** — not to feel
well; to feel feverish.
desteñir[5, 19] [des·te·ñír] *v. irr.* to discolor; to fade;
to bleach; **-se** to become discolored; to fade.
desternillarse [des·ter·ni·yár·se] *v.* — **de risa** to
split one's sides with laughter.
desterrado [des·te·rrá·đo] *m.* exile; outcast; *p.p. &
adj.* exiled, banished.
desterrar[1] [des·te·rrár] *v. irr.* to exile, banish; to
remove earth (from).
destetar [des·te·tár] *v.* to wean.
destierro [des·tjé·rro] *m.* exile.
destilación [des·ti·la·sjón] *f.* distillation,
destiladera [des·ti·la·đé·ra] *f.* still; *Am.* filter.
destilar [des·ti·lár] *v.* to distill; to drip, trickle; to
filter.
destilería [des·ti·le·rí·a] *f.* distillery.
destinación [des·ti·na·sjón] *f.* destination.
destinar [des·ti·nár] *v.* to destine; to employ.
destinatario [des·ti·na·tá·rjo] *m.* addressee.
destino [des·tí·no] *m.* destiny, fate; destination;

employment, job.
destituido [des·ti·twí·đo] *adj.* destitute; *p.p. of*
destituir.
destituir[32] [des·ti·twír] *v. irr.* to deprive.
destorcer[10] [des·tor·sér] *v. irr.* to untwist.
destornillador [des·tor·ni·ya·đór] *m.* screwdriver.
destornillar [des·tor·ni·yár] *v.* to unscrew.
destrabar [des·tra·ƀár] *v.* to unlock, unfasten; to
untie; to separate; to unfetter.
destreza [des·tré·sa] *f.* dexterity, skill, ability.
destronar [des·tro·nár] *v.* to dethrone, depose,
overthrow.
destrozar[9] [des·tro·sár] *v.* to shatter, cut to pieces;
to destroy; to squander.
destrozo [des·tró·so] *m.* destruction; ruin.
destrucción [des·truk·sjón] *f.* destruction.
destructivo [des·truk·tí·ƀo] *adj.* destructive.
destructor [des·truk·tór] *adj.* destructive; *m.*
destroyer.
destruir[32] [des·trwír] *v. irr.* to destroy; to ruin.
desunir [de·su·nír] *v.* to divide, separate.
desusado [de·su·sá·đo] *adj.* unusual,
unaccustomed; obsolete, out of use.
desuso [de·sú·so] *m.* disuse; obsoleteness.
desvaído [dez·ƀa·í·đo] *adj.* lanky, tall and
awkward; gaunt; dull, faded.
desvainar [dez·ƀaj·nár] *v.* to shell (*peas, beans, etc.*).
desvalido [dez·ƀa·lí·đo] *adj.* abandoned; destitute;
helpless.
desvalijar [dez·ƀa·li·xár] *v.* to ransack the contents
of a valise; to rob.
desván [dez·ƀán] *m.* garret, attic.
desvanecer[13] [dez·ƀa·ne·sér] *v. irr.* to fade,
dissolve; to make vain; to make dizzy; **-se** to
evaporate; to vanish; to fade out, disappear; to
get dizzy.
desvanecido [dez·ƀa·ne·sí·đo] *adj.* (*desmayado*)
dizzy, faint; (*orgulloso*) proud, haughty; *p.p. of*
desvanecer.
desvanecimiento [dez·ƀa·ne·si·mjén·to] *m.* dizziness,
faintness; vanity.
desvariar[17] [dez·ƀa·rjár] *v.* to rave, be delirious;
to rant, talk excitedly; to talk nonsense.
desvarío [dez·ƀa·rí·o] *m.* raving; delirium;
madness; inconstancy.
desvelado [dez·ƀe·lá·đo] *adj.* sleepless, awake;
watchful; *p.p. of* **desvelar.**
desvelar [dez·ƀe·lár] *v.* to keep (*another*) awake;
-se to keep awake; to have insomnia, lose sleep;
to be worried, anxious.
desvelo [dez·ƀé·lo] *m.* lack of sleep; restlessness;
vigilance, watchfulness; worry, anxiety.
desvencijado [dez·ƀen·si·xá·đo] *adj.* tottering,
rickety, shaky, falling apart.
desventaja [dez·ƀen·tá·xa] *f.* disadvantage.
desventura [dez·ƀen·tú·ra] *f.* misfortune,
unhappiness.
desventurado [dez·ƀen·tu·rá·đo] *adj.* unfortunate,
unhappy, miserable, wretched.
desvergonzado [dez·ƀer·ǥon·sá·đo] *adj.* shameless,
brazen.
desvergüenza [dez·ƀer·ǥwén·sa] *f.* shamelessness;
disgrace; shame; insolence; impudent word.
desvestir[5] [dez·ƀes·tír] *v. irr.* to undress; **-se** to
undress.
desviación [dez·ƀja·sjón] *f.* deviation, turning aside,
shift; detour.
desviar[17] [dez·ƀjár] *v.* to deviate, turn aside; to
swerve; **-se** to shift direction; to branch off, turn
off the main road; to swerve.
desvío [dez·ƀí·o] *m.* deviation, turning aside;

DE

indifference, coldness; side track, railroad siding; detour.

desvirtuar[18] [dez·ḅir·twár] v. to impair, diminish the value or quality of.

desvivirse [dez·ḅi·ḅír·se] v. — **por** to long for; to be excessively fond of, be crazy about, make a fuss over; to do one's best for; **ella se desvive por complacerme** she does her utmost to please me.

desyerbar [dez·yer·ḅár] = **desherbar**.

detallar [de·ta·yár] v. to detail, report in detail; to retail.

detalle [de·tá·ye] m. detail; retail; **¡ahí está el — !** that's the point.

detallista [de·ta·yís·ta] m. & f. retailer; detailer, person fond of detail.

detective [de·tek·tí·ḅe], **detectivo** [de·tek·tí·ḅo] m. detective.

detención [de·ten·sjón] f. detention, arrest; stop, halt; delay.

detener[45] [de·te·nér] v. irr. to detain, stop; to arrest; **-se** to halt; to delay oneself, stay.

detenimiento [de·te·ni·mjén·to] m. detention; delay; care, deliberation.

deteriorar [de·te·rjo·rár] v. to deteriorate, damage; **-se** to deteriorate, become impaired or damaged; to wear out.

deterioro [de·te·rjó·ro] m. deterioration, impairment.

determinación [de·ter·mi·na·sjón] f. determination; firmness.

determinar [de·ter·mi·nár] v. to determine; to decide; **-se** to resolve, decide.

detestable [de·tes·tá·ḅle] adj. detestable; hateful.

detestar [de·tes·tár] v. to detest.

detonación [de·to·na·sjón] f. detonation, report (of a gun), loud explosion; pop.

detonar [de·to·nár] v. to detonate, explode with a loud noise; to pop.

detrás [de·trás] adv. behind; — **de** prep. behind; **por** — from the rear, by the rear, from behind.

deuda [déw·ḍa] f. debt; indebtedness.

deudo [déw·ḍo] m. relative, kinsman.

deudor [dew·ḍór] m. debtor; adj. indebted, obligated.

devanar [de·ḅa·nár] v. to spool, wind on a spool; **-se los sesos** to rack one's brain.

devaneo [de·ḅa·né·o] m. frenzy; dissipation; wandering; idle pursuit; giddiness.

devastar [de·ḅas·tár] v. to devastate, lay waste, destroy.

devenir[48] [de·ḅe·nír] v. irr. to befall; to become, be transformed into.

devoción [de·ḅo·sjón] f. devotion; piety; attachment.

devocionario [de·ḅo·sjo·ná·rjo] m. prayer book.

devolución [de·ḅo·lu·sjón] f. return, giving back; replacement.

devolver[2, 52] [de·ḅol·ḅér] v. irr. to return, give back, pay back.

devorador [de·ḅo·ra·ḍór] adj. devouring; absorbing; ravenous; m. devourer.

devorar [de·ḅo·rár] v. to devour, gobble up.

devoto [de·ḅó·to] adj. devout, religious, pious; very fond (of).

devuelto [de·ḅwél·to] p.p. of **devolver**.

día [dí·a] m. day; **al otro** — on the next day; **hoy** — nowadays; **un** — **sí y otro no** every other day.

diablo [djá·ḅlo] m. devil, demon.

diablura [dja·ḅlú·ra] f. deviltry, mischief, devilish prank.

diabólico [dja·ḅó·li·ko] adj. diabolic, devilish, fiendish.

diácono [djá·ko·no] m. deacon.

diadema [dja·ḍé·ma] f. diadem, crown.

diáfano [djá·fa·no] adj. transparent, clear; sheer.

diagnosticar[6] [djag·nos·ti·kár] v. to diagnose.

diagrama [dja·grá·ma] m. diagram; graph.

dialecto [dja·lék·to] m. dialect.

dialectología [dja·lek·to·lo·xi·a] f. dialectology.

dialogar[7] [dja·lo·gár] v. to dialogue.

diálogo [djá·lo·go] m. dialogue.

diamante [dja·mán·te] m. diamond.

diámetro [djá·me·tro] m. diameter.

diantre [dján·tre] m. devil.

diapasón [dja·pa·són] m. pitch (of a sound); tuning fork.

diapositiva [dja·po·si·tí·ḅa] f. Spain slide, lantern slide.

diario [djá·rjo] adj. daily; m. newspaper; daily expense; journal, diary.

diarrea [dja·rré·a] f. diarrhea.

dibujante [di·ḅu·xán·te] m. & f. draftsman; designer.

dibujar [di·ḅu·xár] v. (diseñar) to draw, make a drawing of; (describir) depict, portray; describe; **-se** to appear, show.

dibujo [di·ḅú·xo] m. drawing; delineation, portrayal, picture; — **natural** drawing of the human figure, drawing from life.

dicción [dik·sjón] f. diction; word; choice of words, style.

diciembre [di·sjém·bre] m. December.

dictado [dik·tá·ḍo] m. dictation; title; dictate; **escribir al** — to take dictation.

dictador [dik·ta·ḍór] m. dictator.

dictadura [dik·ta·ḍú·ra] f. dictatorship.

dictamen [dik·tá·men] m. opinion, judgment.

dictaminar [dik·ta·mi·nár] v. to give an opinion or judgment.

dictar [dik·tár] v. to dictate.

dicha [dí·ča] f. happiness; good luck.

dicharachero [di·ča·ra·čé·ro] adj. fond of making wisecracks; witty.

dicharacho [di·ča·rá·čo] m. wisecrack, smart remark; malicious remark.

dicho [dí·čo] p.p. of **decir** said; — **y hecho** no sooner said than done; m. saying, popular proverb.

dichoso [di·čó·so] adj. happy, lucky.

diente [djén·te] m. tooth; tusk; — **de león** dandelion; **de -s afuera** insincerely; Am. **pelar el** — to smile affectedly.

diéresis [djé·re·sis] f. diaeresis (as in **vergüenza**).

diesel [dí·sel] m. diesel; diesel motor.

diestra [djés·tra] f. right hand.

diestro [djés·tro] adj. skillful; right; m. matador; skillful swordsman; halter.

dieta [djé·ta] f. diet; assembly; salary, fee.

diezmo [djéz·mo] m. tithe.

difamación [di·fa·ma·sjón] f. libel, slander.

difamador [di·fa·ma·ḍór] m. slanderer.

difamar [di·fa·már] v. to defame, libel, malign, slander.

difamatorio [di·fa·ma·tó·rjo] adj. scandalous, slandering.

diferencia [di·fe·rén·sja] f. difference.

diferencial [di·fe·ren·sjál] m. differential.

diferenciar [di·fe·ren·sjár] v. to differentiate, distinguish; to differ, disagree; **-se** to distinguish oneself; to become different.

diferente [di·fe·rén·te] adj. different.

diferir[3] [di·fe·rír] v. irr. to defer, put off, delay;

to differ, disagree; to be different.
difícil [di·fí·sil] *adj.* difficult.
dificultad [di·fi·kul·tád] *f.* difficulty.
dificultar [di·fi·kul·tár] *v.* to make difficult; — **el paso** to impede or obstruct the passage; -**se** to become difficult.
dificultoso [di·fi·kul·tó·so] *adj.* difficult, hard.
difteria [dif·té·rja] *f.* diphtheria.
difundir [di·fun·dír] *v.* to diffuse, spread out, scatter; to broadcast by radio.
difunto [di·fún·to] *adj.* deceased, dead; *m.* corpse.
difusión [di·fu·sjón] *f.* diffusion, spreading. scattering; wordiness; broadcasting.
difuso [di·fú·so] *adj.* diffuse; diffused, widespread.
digerible [di·xe·rí·ḅle] *adj.* digestible.
digerir[3] [di·xe·rír] *v. irr.* to digest.
dignarse [dig·nár·se] *v.* to deign, condescend.
dignatario [dig·na·tá·rjo] *m.* dignitary (*person in a high office*).
dignidad [dig·ni·ḍáḍ] *f.* dignity.
digno [díg·no] *adj.* worthy; dignified.
digresión [di·gre·sjón] *f.* digression.
dije [dí·xe] *m.* trinket, small piece of jewelry; locket; woman of fine qualities, a "jewel"; *Am.* locket or charm.
dilación [di·la·sjón] *f.* delay.
dilatado [di·la·tá·ḍo] *adj.* vast, spacious; extensive; *p.p. of* **dilatar.**
dilatar [di·la·tár] *v.* to dilate, widen, enlarge; to expand; to lengthen, extend; to spread out; to defer, put off, retard; -**se** to expand; to be diffuse, wordy; *Am.* to delay oneself, take long.
diligencia [di·li·xén·sja] *f.* diligence, care, industry; speed; stagecoach; business, errand.
diligente [di·li·xén·te] *adj.* diligent; quick, speedy.
diluir[32] [di·lwír] *v. irr.* to dilute.
diluvio [di·lú·ḅjo] *m.* flood.
dimensión [di·men·sjón] *f.* dimension.
dimes: — **y diretes** [dí·mes·i·ḍi·ré·tes] quibbling, arguing; **andar en** — **y diretes** to quibble, argue.
diminución [di·mi·nu·sjón] *f.* diminution. decrease.
diminutivo [di·mi·nu·tí·ḅo] *adj.* diminutive, tiny; diminishing; *m.* diminutive.
diminuto [di·mi·nú·to] *adj.* tiny, little.
dimisión [di·mi·sjón] *f.* resignation (*from an office*).
dimitir [di·mi·tír] *v.* to resign, give up (*a position, office, etc.*).
dinámica [di·ná·mi·ka] *f.* dynamics; **dinámico** *adj.* dynamic.
dinamismo [di·na·míz·mo] *m.* vigor, forcefulness; dynamic force or energy.
dinamita [di·na·mí·ta] *f.* dynamite.
dínamo [dí·na·mo] *m.* dynamo.
dinastía [di·nas·tí·a] *f.* dynasty.
dineral [di·ne·rál] *m.* a lot of money.
dinero [di·né·ro] *m.* money; currency; *Peru* Peruvian silver coin equivalent to about ten cents; — **contante y sonante** ready cash, hard cash.
dios [djos] *m.* god: **Dios** God; **a la buena de** — without malice; without plan, haphazard, at random.
diosa [djó·sa] *f.* goddess.
diplomacia [di·plo·má·sja] *f.* diplomacy; tact.
diplomático [di·plo·má·ti·ko] *adj.* diplomatic; tactful; *m.* diplomat.
diputación [di·pu·ta·sjón] *f.* deputation; committee.
diputado [di·pu·tá·ḍo] *m.* deputy, representative.
diputar [di·pu·tár] *v.* to depute, delegate,

commission.
dique [dí·ke] *m.* dike; barrier; — **de carena** dry dock.
dirección [di·rek·sjón] *f.* direction, course; advice, guidance; management; board of directors; office of the board of directors; address.
directivo [di·rek·tí·ḅo] *adj.* directive, directing, guiding; **mesa directiva** board of directors.
directo [di·rék·to] *adj.* direct, straight.
director [di·rek·tór] *m.* director, manager; *adj.* directing.
directorio [di·rek·tó·rjo] *adj.* directory, directive, directing; *m.* directory, book of instructions; directorate, board of directors.
dirigente [di·ri·xén·te] *adj.* directing, leading; *m.* leader, director.
dirigible [di·ri·xí·ḅle] *adj. & m.* dirigible.
dirigir[11] [di·ri·xír] *v.* to direct, manage, govern; to guide; to address (*letters, packages*); to dedicate; -**se a** to address (*a person*); to go to or toward.
discernimiento [di·ser·ni·mjén·to] *m.* discernment, keen judgment, insight, discrimination.
discernir[3] [di·ser·nír] *v. irr.* to discern; to distinguish; to discriminate.
disciplina [di·si·plí·na] *f.* discipline, training; rule of conduct; order; any art or science; scourge, whip.
disciplinar [di·si·pli·nár] *v.* to discipline; train; to drill, -**se** to discipline oneself; to scourge oneself.
discípulo [di·sí·pu·lo] *m.* pupil; disciple.
disco [dís·ko] *m.* disk; discus; phonograph record.
díscolo [dís·ko·lo] *adj.* unruly, disobedient; unfriendly.
discordancia [dis·kọr·ḍán·sja] *f.* discord, disagreement.
discordia [dis·kór·ḍja] *f.* discord.
discreción [dis·kre·sjón] *f.* discretion; keenness; wit; **darse** (*or* **rendirse**) **a** — to surrender unconditionally; **discrecional** [dis·kre·sjo·nál] *adj.* optional.
discrepancia [dis·kre·pán·sja] *f.* discrepancy.
discreto [dis·kré·to] *adj.* discreet, prudent; clever.
disculpa [dis·kúl·pa] *f.* excuse; apology.
disculpable [dis·kul·pá·ḅle] *adj.* excusable.
disculpar [dis·kul·pár] *v.* to excuse, free from blame; -**se** to excuse oneself, apologize.
discurrir [dis·ku·rrír] *v.* (*charlar*) to discuss; (*recorrer*) to ramble about; (*imaginar*) to invent, think out.
discursear [dis·kur·se·ár] *v.* to make speeches.
discurso [dis·kúr·so] *m.* discourse; speech; reasoning; lapse of time.
discusión [dis·ku·sjón] *f.* discussion.
discutible [dis·ku·tí·ḅle] *adj.* debatable, questionable.
discutir [dis·ku·tír] *v.* to discuss.
disecar[6] [di·se·kár] *v.* to dissect; to stuff and mount (*the skins of animals*).
diseminación [di·se·mi·na·sjón] *f.* dissemination, spread, scattering.
diseminar [di·se·mi·nár] *v.* to disseminate, scatter, spread.
disensión [di·sen·sjón] *f.* dissension, dissent, disagreement.
disentería [di·sen·te·rí·a] *f.* dysentery.
disentir[3] [di·sen·tír] *v. irr.* to dissent, differ, disagree.
diseñador [di·se·ña·ḍór] *m.* designer.
diseñar [di·se·ñár] *v.* to design; to sketch, outline.
diseño [di·sé·ño] *m.* design; sketch, outline.

disertar [di·ser·tár] *v.* to discourse, discuss.
disforme [dis·fór·me] *adj.* deformed; ugly, hideous; out of proportion.
disfraz [dis·frás] *m.* disguise, mask; masquerade costume.
disfrazar[9] [dis·fra·sár] *v.* to disguise, conceal; **-se** to disguise oneself; to masquerade.
disfrutar [dis·fru·tár] *v.* to enjoy; to reap benefit or advantage; to make use of.
disfrute [dis·frú·te] *m.* enjoyment, benefit, use.
disgustar [diz·gus·tár] *v.* to disgust, displease; **-se** to get angry; to get bored.
disgusto [diz·gús·to] *m.* displeasure; unpleasantness; annoyance; quarrel; grief; disgust.
disidente [di·si·dén·te] *m. & f.* dissident; protester.
disimulado [di·si·mu·lá·do] *adj.* underhanded, sly, cunning; *p.p. of* **disimular.**
disimular [di·si·mu·lár] *v.* to feign, hide, mask; to overlook, excuse.
disimulo [di·si·mú·lo] *m.* dissimulation, feigning, pretense; slyness; reserve.
disipación [di·si·pa·sjón] *f.* dissipation; waste, extravagance.
disipar [di·si·pár] *v.* to dissipate, scatter; to squander; **-se** to vanish.
dislocar[6] [diz·lo·kár] *v.* to dislocate, put out of joint; **-se** to become dislocated, get out of joint.
disminución [diz·mi·nu·sjón] = **diminución.**
disminuir[32] [diz·mi·nwír] *v. irr.* to diminish, decrease, lessen.
disociación [di·so·sja·sjón] *f.* dissociation, separation.
disociar [di·so·sjár] *v.* to dissociate, separate.
disolución [di·so·lu·sjón] *f.* dissolution, breaking up; dissoluteness, lewdness.
disoluto [di·so·lú·to] *adj.* dissolute, loose, immoral, dissipated.
disolver[2, 52] [di·sol·bér] *v. irr.* to dissolve; to melt.
disonancia [di·so·nán·sja] *f.* discord.
disparada [dis·pa·rá·da] *f. C.A., Mex., Carib., Ríopl.* rush, run.
disparar [dis·pa·rár] *v.* to shoot, fire, discharge; to throw; **-se** to run away, dart out.
disparatado [dis·pa·ra·tá·do] *adj.* absurd, foolish, senseless.
disparatar [dis·pa·ra·tár] *v.* to talk nonsense; to blunder; to act foolishly.
disparate [dis·pa·rá·te] *m.* nonsense, blunder.
disparidad [dis·pa·ri·dád] *f.* inequality.
disparo [dis·pá·ro] *m.* shooting, discharge, explosion; shot; sudden dash, run.
dispensa [dis·pén·sa] *f.* dispensation; exemption.
dispensar [dis·pen·sár] *v.* to excuse, absolve, pardon; to grant, give.
dispensario [dis·pen·sá·rjo] *m.* dispensary; pharmaceutical laboratory; pharmacopoeia (*book containing list and description of drugs*).
dispersar [dis·per·sár] *v.* to disperse, scatter.
dispersión [dis·per·sjón] *f.* dispersion, dispersal.
displicencia [dis·pli·sén·sja] *f.* displeasure, discontent, dislike.
displicente [dis·pli·sén·te] *adj.* unpleasant, disagreeable, cross.
disponer[40] [dis·po·nér] *v. irr.* (*arreglar*) to dispose; to arrange, put in order; to prepare; (*mandar*) to order, command; **-se** to get ready; to make one's will and testament.
disponible [dis·po·ní·ble] *adj.* spare, available; on hand.
disposición [dis·po·si·sjón] *f.* disposition;

arrangement; order, command; aptitude; disposal.
dispuesto [dis·pwés·to] *p.p. of* **disponer** & *adj.* disposed; ready; fit; smart, clever.
disputa [dis·pú·ta] *f.* dispute.
disputar [dis·pu·tár] *v.* to dispute.
distancia [dis·tán·sja] *f.* distance.
distante [dis·tán·te] *adj.* distant.
distar [dis·tár] *v.* to be distant, far (from).
distender[1] [dis·ten·dér] *v. irr.* to distend, stretch; to inflate; **-se** to distend, expand.
distinción [dis·tin·sjón] *f.* distinction.
distinguido [dis·tin·gi·do] *adj. & p.p.* distinguished.
distinguir[12] [dis·tin·gír] *v.* to distinguish; **-se** to distinguish oneself, excel; to differ, be different.
distintivo [dis·tin·ti·bo] *adj.* distinctive, distinguishing; *m.* distinguishing characteristic; mark, sign; badge.
distinto [dis·tín·to] *adj.* distinct, plain, clear; different.
distracción [dis·trak·sjón] *f.* distraction; diversion; amusement; lack of attention.
distraer[46] [dis·tra·ér] *v. irr.* to distract; to divert, amuse; to lead astray; to divert (*funds*); **-se** to have a good time; to be absentminded; to be inattentive.
distraído [dis·tra·í·do] *adj.* distracted; inattentive; absentminded; *Am.* slovenly, untidy.
distribución [dis·tri·bu·sjón] *f.* distribution, apportionment.
distribuidor [dis·tri·bwi·dór] *m.* distributor; *adj.* distributing.
distribuir[32] [dis·tri·bwír] *v. irr.* to distribute; to sort; classify.
distrito [dis·trí·to] *m.* district; region.
disturbio [dis·túr·bjo] *m.* disturbance.
disuadir [di·swa·dír] *v.* to dissuade.
disuelto [di·swél·to] *p.p. of* **disolver.**
diurno [djúr·no] *adj.* day, of the day.
divagación [di·ba·ga·sjón] *f.* rambling, digression.
divagar[7] [di·ba·gár] *v.* to ramble; to digress.
diván [di·bán] *m.* divan, sofa.
divergencia [di·ber·xén·sja] *f.* divergence; difference (*of opinion*).
divergir[11] [di·ber·xir] *v.* to diverge; to differ.
diversidad [di·ber·si·dád] *f.* diversity; variety.
diversión [di·ber·sjón] *f.* amusement.
diverso [di·bér·so] *adj.* diverse; different; **-s** several, various.
divertido [di·ber·tí·do] *adj.* amusing, funny.
divertir[3] [di·ber·tír] *v. irr.* to amuse, entertain; to divert, turn aside; **-se** to have a good time, amuse oneself.
dividendo [di·bi·dén·do] *m.* dividend.
dividir [di·bi·dír] *v.* to divide, split.
divinidad [di·bi·ni·dád] *f.* divinity, deity; ¡qué—! what a beauty!
divino [di·bí·no] *adj.* divine.
divisa [di·bí·sa] *f.* device, emblem; foreign exchange.
divisar [di·bi·sár] *v.* to sight; to make out, distinguish.
división [di·bi·sjón] *f.* division.
divisorio [di·bi·só·rjo] *adj.* dividing.
divorciar [di·bor·sjár] *v.* to divorce; to separate.
divorcio [di·bór·sjo] *m.* divorce.
divulgar[7] [di·bul·gár] *v.* to divulge, spread, make public, give out.
diz [dis] = **dice; dizque** [dís·ke] they say that . . .
do [do] *m.* the first note of the diatonic scale in solfeggio.

dobladillar [do·bla·di·yár] *v.* to hem.
dobladillo [do·bla·dí·yo] *m.* hem; — **de ojo** hemstitch.
doblar [do·blár] *v.* to bend, fold; to double; to toll, knell; *Ríopl.* to knock down; — **la esquina** to turn the corner; **-se** to stoop; to bend down; to give in.
doble [dó·ble] *adj.* double, twofold; double-faced, hypocritical; *Am.* broke, poor; *m.* fold; toll, tolling of bells, knell.
doblegar [7] [do·ble·gár] *v.* to bend; to fold; **-se** to bend over; to stoop; to submit, yield.
doblete [do·blé·te] *m.* doublet; a two-base hit.
doblez [do·blés] *m.* fold, crease; duplicity, hypocrisy.
docena [do·sé·na] *f.* dozen.
docente [do·sén·te] *adj.* teaching; educational; **cuerpo** — faculty (*of a school*).
dócil [dó·sil] *adj.* docile, obedient, manageable, meek; flexible; **docilidad** [do·si·li·dád] *f.* obedience, meekness, gentleness; flexibility.
docto [dók·to] *adj.* learned; expert.
doctor [dok·tór] *m.* doctor.
doctorar [dok·to·rár] *v.* to grant a doctor's degree to; **-se** to get a doctor's degree.
doctrina [dok·trí·na] *f.* doctrine.
documentar [do·ku·men·tár] *v.* to document.
documento [do·ku·mén·to] *m.* document.
dogal [do·gál] *m.* halter; noose.
dogma [dóg·ma] *m.* dogma; **dogmático** [dog·má·ti·ko] *adj.* dogmatic, pertaining to dogma; positive.
dolencia [do·lén·sja] *f.* ailment; ache, aching.
doler [2] [do·lér] *v. irr.* to ache, hurt, cause pain; to cause grief; **-se de** to feel pity for, feel sorry for; to repent from.
doliente [do·ljén·te] *adj.* sorrowful; suffering; aching; *m.* sick person, patient; mourner.
dolor [do·lór] *m.* pain, ache; sorrow, grief.
dolorido [do·lo·rí·do] *adj.* aching, sore; afflicted; repentant; doleful.
doloroso [do·lo·ró·so] *adj.* painful; sorrowful.
doma [dó·ma] *f.* breaking of horses.
domador [do·ma·dór] *m.* horsebreaker, broncobuster.
domar [do·már] *v.* to tame, subdue.
domeñar [do·me·ñár] *v.* to tame; to subdue; to dominate.
domesticar [6] [do·mes·ti·kár] *v.* to domesticate, tame.
doméstico [do·més·ti·ko] *adj.* domestic; *m.* house servant.
domiciliar [do·mi·si·ljár] *v.* to house, lodge; *Ríopl.* to address (*a letter*); **-se** to take up residence; to settle down; to dwell, reside.
domicilio [do·mi·sí·ljo] *m.* home, dwelling.
dominación [do·mi·na·sjón] *f.* domination, rule, authority.
dominador [do·mi·na·dór] *adj.* dominant, dominating; domineering, bossy; *m.* ruler, boss.
dominante [do·mi·nán·te] *adj.* dominant; domineering; tyrannical; prevailing, predominant.
dominar [do·mi·nár] *v.* to dominate, rule, lead; to stand out, tower above; to master.
dómine [dó·mi·ne] *m.* teacher; pedagogue; pedant.
domingo [do·mín·go] *m.* Sunday; — **de ramos** Palm Sunday.
dominio [do·mi·njo] *m.* domain; dominion; authority; mastery (*of a science, art, language, etc.*).

dominó [do·mi·nó] *m.* domino.
don [don] *m.* gift; ability, knack; Don (*title used only before Christian names of men*).
donación [do·na·sjón] *f.* donation; grant.
donador [do·na·dór] *m.* donor, giver.
donaire [do·náj·re] *m.* grace, elegance; wit; humor; witty remark.
donairoso [do·naj·ró·so] *adj.* elegant, graceful; witty.
donar [do·nár] *v.* to donate.
doncella [don·sé·ya] *f.* virgin, maiden; maidservant; *Col.* felon (*sore or inflammation near a finger or toenail*).
donde [dón·de] *rel. adv.* where, in which; **a** — **(adonde)** where, to which; *C.A., Ríopl.* to the house of; **de** — from where, from which; **en** — where, in which; **por** — where, through which; wherefore; — **no** otherwise; if not; ¿**dónde**? *interr. adv.* where?; ¿**por** —? which way?
dondequiera [don·de·kjé·ra] *adv.* wherever; anywhere.
donjuanismo [don·xwa·níz·mo] *m.* Don Juanism, conduct reminiscent of Don Juan Tenorio.
donoso [do·nó·so] *adj.* witty, gay; graceful.
doña [dó·ña] *f.* Doña (*title used only before Christian names of women*).
dorada [do·rá·da] *f.* gilthead (fish).
dorado [do·rá·do] *p.p. & adj.* gilded, gilt; golden; *m.* gilding; *Am.* a kind of hummingbird; **doradillo** [do·ra·dí·yo] *adj. Am.* honey-colored, golden (*applied to horses*).
dorar [do·rár] *v.* to gild.
dormir [4] [dor·mír] *v. irr.* to sleep; **-se** to go to sleep, fall asleep; to become numb.
dormitar [dor·mi·tár] *v.* to doze.
dormitorio [dor·mi·tó·rjo] *m.* dormitory; bedroom.
dorso [dór·so] *m.* back, reverse.
dosel [do·sél] *m.* canopy.
dosis [dó·sis] *f.* dose.
dotación [do·ta·sjón] *f.* endowment, endowing; donation, foundation; dowry; complement (*personnel of a warship*); office force.
dotar [do·tár] *v.* to endow; to provide with a dowry.
dote [dó·te] *m. & f.* dowry; *f.* natural gift, talent, or quality.
draga [drá·ga] *f.* dredge, dredging machine.
dragado [dra·gá·do] *m.* dredging.
dragaminas [dra·ga·mí·nas] *m.* mine sweeper.
dragar [7] [dra·gár] *v.* to dredge.
dragón [dra·gón] *m.* dragon.
drama [drá·ma] *m.* drama.
dramático [dra·má·ti·ko] *adj.* dramatic; *m.* dramatic actor; playwright, dramatist.
dramatizar [9] [dra·ma·ti·sár] *v.* to dramatize.
dramaturgo [dra·ma·túr·go] *m.* playwright, dramatist.
drenaje [dre·ná·xe] *m. Am.* drainage.
drenar [dre·nár] *v. Am.* to drain.
dril [dril] *m.* drill (*strong cotton or linen cloth*).
droga [dró·ga] *f.* (*medicina*) drug, medicine; (*mentira*) lie, fib; trick; (*molestia*) bother, nuisance; *Peru, Carib.* bad debt; *Ríopl.* drug on the market unsalable article.
droguería [dro·ge·rí·a] *f.* drugstore; drug business.
droguero [dro·gé·ro] *m.* druggist; *Am.* cheat, debt evader.
droguista [dro·gís·ta] *m. & f.* druggist; cheat, crook.
dúctil [dúk·til] *adj.* ductile.
ducha [dú·ča] *f.* shower bath; douche.

ducho [dú·čo] *adj.* expert, skillful.
duda [dú·da] *f.* doubt.
dudable [du·dá·ƀle] *adj.* doubtful.
dudar [du·dár] *v.* to doubt; to hesitate.
dudoso [du·dó·so] *adj.* doubtful; uncertain.
duela [dwé·la] *f.* stave (*of a barrel*); *Mex., Andes* long, narrow floor board.
duelo [dwé·lo] *m.* (*luto*) grief, sorrow; mourning; mourners; (*pleito*) duel; **estar de** — to be in mourning; to mourn.
duende [dwén·de] *m.* goblin.
dueña [dwé·ña] *f.* owner, landlady; duenna, chaperon or governess.
dueño [dwé·ño] *m.* owner; master.
dueto [dwé·to], **dúo** [dú·o] *m.* duet.
dulce [dúl·se] *adj.* sweet; pleasant, agreeable; fresh (*water*); soft (*metal*); *m.* sweetmeat; candy; preserves; *Am.* sugar, honey; **dulcería** [dul·se·rí·a] *f.* candy shop.
dulcificar[6] [dul·si·fi·kár] *v.* to sweeten; to soften.
dulzón [dul·són] *adj.* over-sweet, sickeningly sweet.
dulzura [dul·sú·ra] *f.* sweetness; meekness.
duna [dú·na] *f.* dune, sand dune.
duplicado [du·pli·ká·do] *adj. & m.* duplicate; **por** — in duplicate; *p.p.* of **duplicar.**
duplicar[6] [du·pli·kár] *v.* to duplicate, double; to repeat.
duplicidad [du·pli·si·dád] *f.* duplicity, deceit, deceitfulness, treachery.
duque [dú·ke] *m.* duke.
duquesa [du·ké·sa] *f.* duchess.
durabilidad [du·ra·ƀi·li·dád] *f.* durability, durable quality, wear.
durable [du·rá·ƀle] *adj.* durable.
duración [du·ra·sjón] *f.* duration.
duradero [du·ra·dé·ro] *adj.* durable, lasting.
durante [du·rán·te] *prep.* during, for.
durar [du·rár] *v.* to last, endure; to wear well.
durazno [du·ráz·no] *m.* peach; peach tree; **duraznero** [du·raz·né·ro] *m.* peach tree.
dureza [du·ré·sa] *f.* hardness; harshness.
durmiente [dur·mjén·te] *adj.* sleeping; *m.* sleeper; crossbeam; *Col., Ven., Mex., Ch.* railroad tie.
duro [dú·ro] *adj.* (*sólido*) hard; firm, solid; untiring; (*cruel*) cruel; harsh; rigid; (*tacaño*) stubborn; stingy; **a duras penas** with difficulty; *Am.* — **y parejo** eagerly, tenaciously; *Am.* **hacer** — to resist stubbornly; *m.* **duro** (*Spanish dollar*).

E·**e** **e** [e] *conj.* and (*before words beginning with* i *or* hi).
ebanista [e·ƀa·nís·ta] *m.* cabinetmaker.
ébano [é·ƀa·no] *m.* ebony.
ebrio [é·brjo] *adj.* drunk.
ebullición [e·ƀu·yi·sjón] *f.* boiling, bubbling up.
eclesiástico [e·kle·sjás·ti·ko] *adj.* ecclesiastic, belonging to the church; *m.* clergyman.
eclipsar [e·klip·sár] *v.* to eclipse; to outshine, surpass.
eclipse [e·klíp·se] *m.* eclipse.
écloga [é·klo·ga] *f.* eclogue, pastoral poem, idyll.
eco [é·ko] *m.* echo.
economía [e·ko·no·mi·a] *f.* economy; — **política** economics, political economy.
económico [e·ko·nó·mi·ko] *adj.* economic;

economical, saving; **economista** [e·ko·no·mís·ta] *m.* economist.
economizar[9] [e·ko·no·mi·sár] *v.* to economize, save.
ecuación [e·kwa·sjón] *f.* equation.
ecuador [e·kwa·dór] *m.* equator.
echar [e·čár] *v.* (*tirar*) to throw, cast; to expel; to throw out; (*emitir*) to give off; to sprout; — **a correr** to run away; **-(se) a perder** to spoil; — **a pique** to sink; **-(se) a reír** to burst out laughing; — **carnes** to get fat; — **de menos** to miss; — **de ver** to notice; to make out; — **mano** to seize; — **papas** to fib; — **raíces** to take root; — **suertes** to draw lots; **-se** to lie down; *Am.* **echársela** [e·čár·se·la] to boast.
edad [e·dád] *f.* age.
edecán [e·de·kán] *m.* aide-de-camp.
edén [e·dén] *m.* Eden; paradise.
edición [e·di·sjón] *f.* edition; publication.
edificación [e·di·fi·ka·sjón] *f.* edification (*moral or spiritual uplift*); construction.
edificar[6] [e·di·fi·kár] *v.* to construct, build; to edify, uplift.
edificio [e·di·fí·sjo] *m.* edifice, building.
editar [e·di·tár] *v.* to publish.
editor [e·di·tór] *m.* publisher; *adj.* publishing.
editorial [e·di·to·rjál] *adj.* publishing, editorial; *m.* editorial; *f.* publishing house.
edredón [e·dre·dón] *m.* down quilt, comforter, quilted blanket.
educación [e·du·ka·sjón] *f.* education, training; breeding, manners.
educador [e·du·ka·dór] *m.* educator; *adj.* educating.
educando [e·du·kán·do] *m.* pupil; inmate (*of an orphanage, boarding school, etc.*).
educar[6] [e·du·kár] *v.* to educate, teach, train, raise, bring up.
educativo [e·du·ka·tí·ƀo] *adj.*— educational.
efectivo [e·fek·tí·ƀo] *adj.* effective; real; in operation, active; *m.* cash.
efecto [e·fék·to] *m.* (*resultado*) effect, result; (*fin*) end, purpose, **-s** goods, personal property; **en** — in fact, actually; **llevar a** — to carry out; **surtir** — to come out as expected; to give good results.
efectuar[18] [e·fek·twár] *v.* to effect, bring about.
eficacia [e·fi·ká·sja] *f.* efficacy; efficiency; effectiveness.
eficaz [e·fi·kás] *adj.* effective; active; efficient.
eficiencia [e·fi·sjén·sja] *f.* efficiency; **eficiente** [e·fi·sjén·te] *adj.* efficient.
efímero [e·fí·me·ro] *adj.* ephemeral, short-lived, brief.
efluvio [e·flú·ƀjo] *m.* emanation, exhalation, vapors.
efusión [e·fu·sjón] *f.* effusion, unrestrained expression of feeling, gushy manner; — **de sangre** bloodshed.
efusivo [e·fu·sí·ƀo] *adj.* effusive, too demonstrative, over-emotional.
egipcio [e·xíp·sjo] *adj. & m.* Egyptian.
egocéntrico [e·go·sén·tri·ko] *adj.* egocentric, self-centered.
egoísmo [e·go·íz·mo] *m.* selfishness.
egoísta [e·go·ís·ta] *adj.* selfish; *m. & f.* selfish person.
egolatría [e·go·la·trí·a] *f.* self-worship.
eje [é·xe] *m.* axis; axle.
ejecución [e·xe·ku·sjón] *f.* execution; carrying out.
ejecutar [e·xe·ku·tár] *v.* to execute; to carry out; to perform, do.

ejecutivo [e·xe·ku·tí·βo] *adj.* executive; active; *m.* executive.

ejecutor [e·xe·ku·tór] *m.* executor; — **de la justicia** executioner.

ejemplar [e·xem·plár] *adj.* exemplary, model; *m.* copy; specimen.

ejemplo [e·xém·plo] *m.* example; model, pattern.

ejercer[10] [e·xer·sér] *v.* to practice (*a profession*); to exert.

ejercicio [e·xer·sí·sjo] *m.* exercise; practice; military drill; exercise (*of authority*); **hacer** — to take exercise.

ejercitar [e·xer·si·tár] *v.* to practice, exercise; to drill, train; **-se** to train oneself; to practice.

ejército [e·xér·si·to] *m.* army.

ejido [e·xí·đo] *m.* public land, common.

ejote [e·jó·te] *m. Mex., Guat.* string bean.

el [el] *def. art. m.* the; — **de** the one with, that one with; — **que** *rel. pron.* he who, the one that; **él** *pers. pron.* he; him, it (*after a prep.*).

elaboración [e·la·βo·ra·sjón] *f.* manufacture, making; development.

elaborar [e·la·βo·rár] *v.* to elaborate.

elasticidad [e·las·ti·si·đáđ] *f.* elasticity.

elástico [e·lás·ti·ko] *adj.* elastic; flexible; *m.* elastic; elastic tape; wire spring; **-s** *Am.* suspenders.

elección [e·lek·sjón] *f.* election; choice.

electo [e·lék·to] *adj.* elect, chosen; *m.* elect, person chosen.

elector [e·lek·tór] *m.* elector, voter; *adj.* electoral, electing.

electoral [e·lek·to·rál] *adj.* electoral.

electricidad [e·lek·tri·si·đáđ] *f.* electricity.

electricista [e·lek·tri·sís·ta] *m.* electrician; electrical engineer.

eléctrico [e·lék·tri·ko] *adj.* electric, electrical.

electrizar[9] [e·lek·tri·sá] *v.* to electrify; to thrill, excite; *Am.* to anger, irritate.

electrocardiógrafo [e·lek·tro·kar·đjó·gra·fo] *m.* electrocardiograph.

electroimán [e·lek·troj·mán] *m.* electromagnet.

electrólisis [e·lek·tró·li·sis] *f.* electrolysis.

electromagnético [e·lek·tro·mag·né·ti·ko] *adj.* electromagnetic.

electrón [e·lek·trón] *m.* electron.

electrónico [e·lek·tró·ni·ko] *adj.* electronic; **electrónica** [e·lek·tro·ni·ka] *f.* electronics.

elefante [e·le·fán·te] *m.* elephant.

elegancia [e·le·gán·sja] *f.* elegance, grace, distinguished manner.

elegante [e·le·gán·te] *adj.* elegant, graceful, polished; stylish.

elegir[5, 11] [e·le·xír] *v. irr.* to elect, choose.

elemental [e·le·men·tál] *adj.* elementary; elemental, fundamental.

elemento [e·le·mén·to] *m.* element; **-s** elements, fundamentals; personnel; — **químicos** chemical elements, simple substances; *Am.* **ser** (*or* **estar**) **hecho un** — to be an idiot, a fool.

elevación [e·le·βa·sjón] *f.* elevation; height; rise; rapture.

elevador [e·le·βa·đór] *m. Am.* elevator, hoist.

elevar [e·le·βár] *v.* to elevate, raise, lift; **-se** to go up; to soar.

eliminación [e·li·mi·na·sjón] *f.* elimination, removal.

eliminar [e·li·mi·nár] *v.* to eliminate.

elocuencia [e·lo·kwén·sja] *f.* eloquence.

elocuente [e·lo·kwén·te] *adj.* eloquent.

elogiar [e·lo·xjár] *v.* to praise.

elogio [e·ló·xjo] *m.* praise.

elote [e·ló·te] *m. Mex., C.A.* ear of corn, corn on the cob.

elucidación [e·lu·si·đa·sjón] *f.* elucidation, explanation.

elucidar [e·lu·si·đár] *v.* to elucidate, illustrate, explain.

eludir [e·lu·đír] *v.* to elude, avoid, dodge.

ella [é·ya] *pers. pron.* she; her, it (*after a prep.*).

ello [é·yo] *pron.* it; — **es que** the fact is that.

emanación [e·ma·na·sjón] *f.* emanation, flow; fumes, vapor, odor; manifestation.

emanar [e·ma·nár] *v.* to emanate, spring, issue.

emancipación [e·man·si·pa·sjón] *f.* emancipation.

emancipar [e·man·si·pár] *v.* to emancipate, set free; **-se** to become free.

embajada [em·ba·xá·da] *f.* embassy; errand, mission.

embajador [em·ba·xá·dor] *m.* ambassador.

embalador [em·ba·la·đór] *m.* packer.

embalaje [em·ba·lá·xe] *m.* packing.

embalar [em·ba·lár] *v.* to pack; to bale, crate.

embaldosar [em·bal·do·sár] *v.* to pave with flagstones or tiles.

embalsamar [em·bal·sa·már] *v.* to embalm; to scent, perfume.

embarazar[9] [em·ba·ra·sár] *v.* (*impedir*) to hinder, to obstruct; (*preñar*) to make pregnant; **-se** to become pregnant; to become embarrassed.

embarazo [em·ba·rá·so] *m.* (*obstáculo*) impediment, obstacle; (*preñez*) pregnancy; (*timidez*) bashfulness, awkwardness.

embarazoso [em·ba·ra·só·so] *adj.* embarrassing; cumbersome, unwieldly.

embarcación [em·bar·ka·sjón] *f.* ship, boat; embarkation.

embarcadero [em·bar·ka·đé·ro] *m.* wharf, pier.

embarcador [em·bar·ka·đór] *m.* shipper.

embarcar[6] [em·bar·kár] *v.* to embark; to ship; *Am.* to ship by train or any vehicle; **-se** to embark, sail; to engage (in); *Am.* to board, get on a train.

embarco [em·bár·ko] *m.* embarkation.

embargar[7] [em·bar·gár] *v.* to impede; to restrain; to attach, confiscate; to lay an embargo on; **estar embargado de emoción** to be overcome with emotion.

embargo [em·bár·go] *m.* embargo, restriction on commerce; attachment, confiscation; **sin** — nevertheless.

embarque [em·bár·ke] *m.* shipment.

embarrado [em·ba·rrá·do] *p.p. & adj.* smeared: plastered; muddy.

embarrar [em·ba·rrár] *v.* to smear, daub.

embaucador [em·baw·ka·đór] *m.* cheat, impostor.

embaucar[6] [em·baw·kár] *v.* to fool, trick, swindle, deceive.

embebecido [em·be·βe·sí·đo] *p.p. & adj.* absorbed; amazed.

embebecimiento [em·be·βe·si·mjén·to] *m.* absorption; rapture.

embeber [em·be·βér] *v.* to imbibe, absorb; to soak; to shrink; **-se** to be fascinated; to be absorbed.

embelesar [em·be·le·sár] *v.* to enrapture, delight, charm.

embeleso [em·be·lé·so] *m.* delight, ectasy.

embellecer[13] [em·be·ye·sér] *v. irr.* to embellish, beautify, adorn.

embestida [em·bes·tí·đa] *f.* sudden attack, onset, assault.

embestir[5] [em·bes·tír] *v. irr.* to attack, assail.

embetunar [em·be·tu·nár] *v.* to cover with pitch; to black.

emblanquecer[13] [em·blaŋ·ke·sér] *v. irr.* to whiten; to bleach; to become white; **-se** to whiten, become white.

emblema [em·blé·ma] *m.* emblem.

embobar [em·bo·bár] *v.* to fool; to amuse; to fascinate; to amaze; **-se** to be amazed; to be fascinated.

embobinado [em·bo·bi·ná·do] *m.* reel assembly (*of a tape recorder or computer*).

embocadura [em·bo·ka·dú·ra] *f.* mouth (*of a river*); entrance (*through a narrow passage*); mouthpiece (*of a wind instrument*); bit (*of a bridle*); taste, flavor (said of *wines*).

embolado [em·bo·lá·do] *m.* bull whose horns have been tipped with balls; impotent, ineffectual person; *p.p. of* **embolar.**

embolar [em·bo·lár] *v.* (*al toro*) to tip a bull's horns with balls; (*dar lustre*) to polish, to black; **-se** *C.A.* to get drunk.

émbolo [ém·bo·lo] *m.* piston; plunger (*of a pump*); embolus (*clot in a blood vessel*).

embolsar [em·bol·sár] *v.* to put into a pocket or purse; **-se** to pocket, put into one's pocket.

emborrachar [em·bo·rra·čár] *v.* to intoxicate; **-se** to get drunk.

emborronar [em·bo·rro·nár] *v.* to blot; to scribble.

emboscada [em·bos·ká·da] *f.* ambush.

emboscar[6] [em·bos·kár] *v.* to ambush; **-se** to lie in ambush; to go into a forest.

embotado [em·bo·tá·do] *adj.* dull, blunt; *p.p. of* **embotar.**

embotamiento [em·bo·ta·mjén·to] *m.* dullness, bluntness; dulling, blunting.

embotar [em·bo·tár] *v.* to dull, blunt; to enervate, weaken.

embotellador [em·bo·te·ya·dór] *m.* bottling machine; **embotelladora** [em·bo·te·ya·dó·ra] bottling works.

embotellar [em·bo·te·yár] *v.* to bottle; to bottle up; *Am.* to jail.

embozado [em·bo·sá·do] *adj.* cloaked; muffled, covered up to the face.

embozar[7] [em·bo·sár] *v.* to muffle; to cloak, conceal, disguise; to muzzle; **-se** to muffle oneself, wrap oneself.

embragar[7] [em·bra·gár] *v.* to engage or throw in the clutch.

embrague [em·brá·ge] *m.* clutch (*of a machine*); coupling.

embriagar[7] [em·brja·gár] *v.* to intoxicate; **-se** to get drunk, intoxicated.

embriaguez [em·brja·gés] *f.* intoxication; drunkenness.

embrión [em·brjón] *m.* embryo.

embrollar [em·bro·yár] *v.* to involve, ensnare, entangle; to confuse.

embrollo [em·bró·yo] *m.* confusion, tangle; trickery, lie, deception.

embromar [em·bro·már] *v.* to chaff, make fun of "kid"; *Am.* to bother, molest; *Am.* to delay unnecessarily; *Col., Ven.* to ruin, harm; **-se** *Am.* to be bothered, disgusted; *Mex.* to get delayed.

embrujar [em·bru·xár] *v.* to bewitch, enchant.

embrujo [em·brú·xo] *m.* charm, enchantment; glamour.

embrutecer[13] [em·bru·te·sér] *v. irr.* to stupefy, render brutish; to dull the mind, make insensible.

embudo [em·bú·do] *m.* funnel; trick.

embuste [em·bús·te] *m.* lie, fraud; trinket.

embustero [em·bus·té·ro] *m.* liar; *adj.* deceitful, tricky.

embutido [em·bu·tí·do] *m.* sausage; inlaid work; *Am.* insertion of embroidery or lace; *p.p. of* **embutir.**

embutir [em·bu·tír] *v.* to insert, inlay; to stuff.

emerger[11] [e·mer·xér] *v.* to emerge, come out.

emigración [e·mi·gra·sjón] *f.* emigration.

emigrante [e·mi·grán·te] *m. & f.* emigrant.

emigrar [e·mi·grár] *v.* to emigrate; to migrate.

eminencia [e·mi·nén·sja] *f.* eminence; height.

eminente [e·mi·nén·te] *adj.* eminent, high, lofty.

emisión [e·mi·sjón] *f.* issue (*of bonds, money, etc.*); radio broadcast.

emisor [e·mi·sór] *adj.* emitting; broadcasting; *m.* radio transmitter; **emisora** [e·mi·só·ra] *f.* broadcasting station.

emitir [e·mi·tír] *v.* to emit, give off; to utter; to send forth; to issue; to broadcast.

emoción [e·mo·sjón] *f.* emotion.

emocional [e·mo·sjo·nál] *adj.* emotional.

emocionante [e·mo·sjo·nán·te] *adj.* moving, touching, thrilling.

emocionar [e·mo·sjo·nár] *v.* to cause emotion, touch, move; **-se** to be touched, moved, stirred.

emotivo [e·mo·tí·bo] *adj.* emotional.

empacador [em·pa·ka·dór] *m.* packer.

empacar[6] [em·pa·kár] *v.* to pack up, wrap up, bale, crate; *Ríopl.* to goad, irritate (*an animal*); **-se** to be stubborn; to get angry; *Ríopl.* to balk; *Ríopl.* to put on airs.

empachado [em·pa·čá·do] *p.p. & adj.* (*relleno*) clogged; stuffed; upset from indigestion; (*tímido*) embarrassed; bashful.

empachar [em·pa·čár] *v.* to stuff, cram; to cause indigestion; **-se** to get upset; to get clogged; to be stuffed; to suffer indigestion; to get embarrassed.

empacho [em·pá·čo] *m.* indigestion; bashfulness; **no tener — en** to have no objection to; to feel free to.

empalagar[7] [em·pa·la·gár] *v.* to cloy; to pall on, become distasteful; to disgust.

empalagoso [em·pa·la·gó·so] *adj.* cloying; sickeningly sweet; boring, wearisome.

empalizada [em·pa·li·sá·da] *f.* stockade, palisade.

empalmar [em·pal·már] *v.* to splice; to join; **— con** to join (*as railroads or highways*).

empalme [em·pál·me] *m.* junction; joint, connection; splice.

empanada [em·pa·ná·da] *f.* pie, meat pie; swindle, fraud.

empanizar[9] [em·pa·ni·sár] *v. Carib., C.A., Mex.* to bread.

empañado [em·pa·ñá·do] *adj. & p.p.* tarnished; dim, blurred.

empañar [em·pa·ñár] *v.* to blur, dim, tarnish.

empapada [em·pa·pá·da] *f. Am.* drenching, soaking.

empapar [em·pa·pár] *v.* to soak, drench, saturate.

empapelador [em·pa·pe·la·dór] *m.* paper hanger.

empapelar [em·pa·pe·lár] *v.* to paper; to wrap in paper.

empaque [em·pá·ke] *m.* (*bulto*) packing; (*parecer*) looks, appearance, air; airs, importance; *Am., Peru* impudence.

empaquetar [em·pa·ke·tár] *v.* to pack; to pack in; to make a package; **-se** to dress up, doll up.

emparedado [em·pa·re·dá·do] *adj.* shut up, confined between walls; *m.* sandwich; prisoner confined in a narrow cell.

emparejar [em·pa·re·xár] *v.* to even up, level off; to match; to pair off; to overtake, catch up with.
emparentado [em·pa·ren·tá·đo] *adj. & p.p.* related by marriage.
emparentar [em·pa·ren·tár] *v.* to become related by marriage.
emparrado [em·pa·rrá·đo] *m.* vine arbor.
empastar [em·pas·tár] *v.* to paste; to fill (*a tooth*); to bind (*books*); **-se** *Ch.* to get lost in the pasture; *Mex.* to become overgrown with grass.
empaste [em·pás·te] *m.* tooth filling; binding (*of a book*).
empatar [em·pa·tár] *v.* (*igualar*) to tie (*in a game*), have an equal score; to have an equal number of votes; (*impedir*) to hinder, obstruct; *Col., Ven., Carib.* to tie, join.
empate [em·pá·te] *m.* tie, draw, equal score, equal number of votes; hindrance, obstruction; *Am.* joint, junction.
empecinado [em·pe·si·ná·đo] *adj. Am.* stubborn.
empedernido [em·pe·đer·ní·đo] *adj.* hardened, hardhearted.
empedernir[51] [em·pe·đer·nír] *v.* to harden, toughen; **-se** to become hardened.
empedrado [em·pe·đrá·đo] *m.* cobblestone pavement; *p.p. & adj.* paved with stones.
empedrar[1] [em·pe·đrár] *v. irr.* to pave with stones.
empeine [em·péj·ne] *m.* instep; groin (*hollow between lower part of abdomen and thigh*).
empellón [em·pe·yón] *m.* push, shove; **a -es** by pushing.
empeñar [em·pe·ñár] *v.* (*dar en prenda*) to pawn; (*obligar*) to oblige, compel; **-se** to persist, insist; to apply oneself; to go into debt; **-se por** to plead for, intercede for; **se empeñaron en una lucha** they engaged in a fight.
empeño [em·pé·ño] *m.* (*fianza*) pledge, pawn; (*deseo*) persistence, insistence; eagerness; perseverance; *Am.* pawnshop; **tener — en** to be eager to.
empeorar [em·pe·o·rár] *v.* to impair; to make worse; to grow worse; **-se** to grow worse.
empequeñecer[13] [em·pe·ke·ñe·sér] *v. irr.* to diminish, make smaller; to belittle.
emperador [em·pe·ra·đór] *m.* emperor; **emperatriz** [em·pe·ra·trís] *f.* empress.
emperifollar [em·pe·ri·fo·yár] *v.* to decorate, adorn; **-se** to dress up, deck out, doll up.
empero [em·pé·ro] *conj.* however, nevertheless.
empezar[1, 9] [em·pe·sár] *v. irr.* to begin.
empiezo [em·pjé·so] *m. Carib., Mex., C.A.* beginning.
empinado [em·pi·ná·đo] *adj.* steep; lofty.
empinar [em·pi·nár] *v.* to raise, lift; to incline, bend; **— el codo** to drink; **-se** to stand on tiptoes; to rear (*said of horses*); to rise high; *Am.* to overeat.
empiojado [em·pjo·xá·đo] *adj.* lousy, full of lice.
emplasto [em·plás·to] *m.* plaster, poultice.
empleado [em·ple·á·đo] *m.* employee; *p.p. of* **emplear.**
emplear [em·ple·ár] *v.* to employ; to invest, spend; **-se en** to be employed in.
empleo [em·plé·o] *m.* employment, position, job; employ; occupation; aim; investment.
emplumar [em·plu·már] *v.* to feather; to adorn with feathers; to tar and feather; *C.A.* to deceive; *Ec.* to send away to a house of correction or prison; *Am.* **— con algo** to run away with something, steal it; *Ch., Col., Ven.* **-las** (*or* **emplumárselas** [em·plu·már·se·las]) to

take to one's heels, flee, escape.
empobrecer[13] [em·po·ḃre·sér] *v. irr.* to impoverish; **-se** to become poor.
empobrecimiento [em·po·ḃre·si·mjén·to] *m.* impoverishment.
empolvado [em·pol·ḃá·đo] *adj.* dusty, covered with dust or powder.
empolvar [em·pol·ḃár] *v.* to sprinkle powder; to cover with dust; **-se** to get dusty; to powder one's face.
empollar [em·po·yár] *v.* to hatch, brood.
emponzoñar [em·pon·so·ñár] *v.* to poison.
emprendedor [em·pren·de·đór] *adj.* enterprising.
emprender [em·pren·dér] *v.* to undertake.
empreñar [em·pre·ñár] *v.* to impregnate, make pregnant.
empresa [em·pré·sa] *f.* enterprise, undertaking; symbol; company, management.
empresario [em·pre·sá·rjo] *m.* manager; impresario, promoter.
empréstito [em·prés·ti·to] *m.* loan.
empujar [em·pu·xár] *v.* to push, shove.
empuje [em·pú·xe] *m.* push; shove; impulse; energy.
empujón [em·pu·xón] *m.* shove, push.
empuñar [em·pu·ñár] *v.* to grasp, grab, clutch, seize.
émulo [é·mu·lo] *m.* rival, competitor.
en [en] *prep.* in, on, upon.
enaguas [e·ná·ǥwas] *f. pl.* underskirt, petticoat; short skirt.
enajenamiento [e·na·xe·na·mjén·to] *m.* trance; abstraction, absence of mind; transfer (*of property*); **— mental** mental disorder; **— de los sentidos** loss of consciousness.
enajenar [e·na·xe·nár] *v.* (*distraer*) to enrapture, charm; to deprive (*of one's sense*); (*trasladar*) to transfer property; to dispossess; **— el afecto de** to alienate the affection of; **-se** to be enraptured, be in a trance.
enaltecer[13] [e·nal·te·sér] *v.* to extol, exalt.
enamorado [e·na·mo·rá·đo] *adj.* in love; *m.* lover.
enamorar [e·na·mo·rár] *v.* to make love, woo, court; to enamor; **-se** to fall in love.
enano [e·ná·no] *m.* dwarf; *adj.* dwarfish, tiny, little.
enarbolar [e·nar·ḃo·lár] *v.* to hoist, lift, raise on high; to brandish (*a sword, cane, etc.*); **-se** to rear, balk.
enarcado [e·nar·ká·đo] *p.p.* arched.
enarcar[6] [e·nar·kár] *v.* to arch; to hoop (*barrels, kegs, etc.*); **— las cejas** to arch one's eyebrows.
enardecer[13] [e·nar·de·sér] *v. irr.* to excite, kindle, fire with passion; **-se** to become excited; to become passionate; to get angry.
enardecimiento [e·nar·de·si·mjén·to] *m.* ardor, passion, unbridled enthusiasm; inflaming.
encabezado [eŋ·ka·ḃe·sá·đo] *m.* headline; heading.
encabezamiento [eŋ·ka·ḃe·sa·mjén·to] *m.* heading; headline; list or roll of taxpayers; registration of taxpayers.
encabezar[9] [eŋ·ka·ḃe·sár] *v.* to give a heading or title to; to head; to lead; to make up (*a list or tax roll*); to strengthen (*wine*).
encabritarse [eŋ·ka·ḃri·tár·se] *v.* to rear, rise up on the hind legs.
encadenar [eŋ·ka·đe·nár] *v.* to chain; to link together.
encajar [eŋ·ka·xár] *v.* to thrust in, fit into, insert; **-se** to squeeze into; to intrude, meddle.
encaje [eŋ·ká·xe] *m.* lace; adjustment; fitting

EM

together; socket, groove, hole; inlaid work.

encajonar [eŋ·ka·xo·nár] *v.* to box (*put or pack in a box*).

encallar [eŋ·ka·yár] *v.* to strand, run aground; to get stuck.

encamado [eŋ·ka·má·ḍo] *p.p.* confined in bed.

encaminar [eŋ·ka·mi·nár] *v.* to direct, guide; -se to betake oneself, go (toward); to start out on a road.

encanecer[13] [eŋ·ka·ne·sér] *v. irr.* to get grey, get grey-haired.

encanijado [eŋ·ka·ni·xá·ḍo] *adj.* emaciated, thin, sickly.

encanijarse [eŋ·ka·ni·xár·se] *v.* to get thin, emaciated.

encantado [eŋ·kan·tá·ḍo] *p.p. & adj.* delighted, charmed; enchanted.

encantador [eŋ·kan·ta·ḍór] *adj.* charming; *m.* charmer, enchanter.

encantamiento [eŋ·kan·ta·mjén·to] *m.* enchantment.

encantar [eŋ·kan·tár] *v.* to charm, enchant.

encanto [eŋ·kán·to] *m.* charm, enchantment, delight.

encapillar [eŋ·ka·pi·yár] *v. P.R.* to confine in the death cell.

encapotado [eŋ·ka·po·tá·ḍo] *p.p. & adj.* cloaked; overcast, cloudy; in a bad humor.

encapotarse [eŋ·ka·po·tár·se] *v.* to become overcast, cloudy; to cover up, put on a cloak or raincoat; to frown.

encapricharse [eŋ·ka·pri·čár·se] *v.* to persist in one's whims; to get stubborn.

encaramar [eŋ·ka·ra·már] *v.* to raise; to elevate; to extol; -se to climb; to climb upon, get upon, perch upon; *Ch.* to be ashamed; *Carib.* to go to one's head (*said of liquor*).

encarar [eŋ·ka·rár] *v.* to face; to aim; -se con to face; to confront.

encarcelación [eŋ·kar·se·la·sjón] *f.* imprisonment.

encarcelamiento [eŋ·kar·se·la·mjén·to] = **encarcelación.**

encarcelar [eŋ·kar·se·lár] *v.* to imprison, jail.

encarecer[13] [eŋ·ka·re·sér] *v. irr.* (*alzar precio*) to go up in value; to make dear, raise the price of; (*ponderar*) to exaggerate; to extol; to recommend highly, to enhance.

encarecidamente [eŋ·ka·re·si·ḍa·mén·te] *adv.* earnestly.

encargar[7] [eŋ·kar·ǵár] *v.* (*dar cargo*) to put in charge; to entrust; to commission; (*aconsejar*) to recommend, advise; (*pedir*), to order; to beg; -se de to take charge of.

encargo [eŋ·kár·ǵo] *m.* recommendation, advice; charge; order; commission; errand.

encariñado [eŋ·ka·ri·ñá·ḍo] *adj. & p.p.* attached, fond, enamored.

encariñamiento [eŋ·ka·ri·ña·mjén·to] *m.* affection, fondness, attachment.

encariñar [eŋ·ka·ri·ñár] *v.* to awaken love or affection; -se to become fond (of), attached (to).

encarnado [eŋ·kar·ná·ḍo] *adj.* flesh-colored; red; *p.p. of* **encarnar.**

encarnar [eŋ·kar·nár] *v.* to incarnate, embody; to bait (*a fishhook*).

encarnizado [eŋ·kar·ni·sá·ḍo] *adj.* bloody; hard-fought, fierce.

encarnizar[9] [eŋ·kar·ni·sár] *v.* to infuriate, enrage; -se to get furous, enraged; to fight with fury.

encasillar [eŋ·ka·si·yár] *v.* to pigeonhole, put in a pigeonhole or compartment; to put in a stall; to classify, sort out.

encender[1] [en·sen·dér] *v. irr.* to light, kindle; to set on fire; -se to take fire, be on fire; to get red.

encendido [en·sen·di·ḍo] *adj.* red; *p.p. of* **encender;** *m.* ignition (*of a motor*).

encerado [en·se·rá·ḍo] *m.* blackboard; oilcloth; wax coating; *p.p. & adj.* waxed; wax-colored; **papel** — wax paper.

encerar [en·se·rár] *v.* to wax; to thicken (*lime*).

encerramiento [en·se·rra·mjén·to] *m.* enclosure, confinement; locking up; retreat; prison.

encerrar[1] [en·se·rrár] *v. irr.* to enclose; to lock up; to contain; -se to lock oneself up, go into seclusion.

encía [en·sí·a] *f.* gum (*of the teeth*).

enciclopedia [en·si·klo·pé·ḍja] *f.* encyclopedia.

encierro [en·sjé·rro] *m.* confinement; retreat; prison.

encima [en·sí·ma] *adv.* above, overhead, over, on top; besides, in addition; — **de** on top of; **por** — **de** over; *Am.* **de** — besides, in addition; *Col., C.A., Riopl., Carib.* **echárselo todo** — to spend everything on clothes.

encina [en·sí·na] *f.* live oak.

encinta [en·sín·ta] *adj.* pregnant.

encintado [en·sin·tá·ḍo] *m.* curb (*of a sidewalk*).

enclaustrar [eŋ·klaws·trár] *v.* to cloister.

enclavar [eŋ·kla·ḅár] *v.* to nail, fix, fasten.

enclenque [eŋ·klén·ke] *adj.* sickly, wan; weak, feeble.

enclítico [eŋ·klí·ti·ko] *adj.* enclitic.

encobar [eŋ·ko·ḅár] *v.* to brood.

encoger[11] [eŋ·ko·xér] *v.* to shrink, shrivel, shorten, contract; -se to shrink; to shrivel; -se de hombros to shrug one's shoulders.

encogido [eŋ·ko·xí·ḍo] *p.p. & adj.* shrunk, shrivelled; timid, shy.

encogimiento [eŋ·ko·xi·mjén·to] *m.* shrinking; timidity; — de hombros shrug.

encolerizar[9] [eŋ·ko·le·ri·sár] *v.* to anger; -se to get angry.

encomendar[1] [eŋ·ko·men·dár] *v. irr.* (*encargar*) to charge, advise; to entrust; (*recomendar*) to recommend, commend; -se to put oneself in the hands (of); to send regards; to pray (to).

encomiar [eŋ·ko·mjár] *v.* to extol, praise.

encomienda [eŋ·ko·mjén·da] *f.* charge, commission; recommendation; royal land grant (*including Indian inhabitants*); *Am.* warehouse (*for agricultural products*); *Am.* parcel-post package.

encomio [eŋ·kó·mjo] *m.* encomium, high praise.

enconado [eŋ·ko·ná·ḍo] *p.p. & adj.* inflamed; infected; sore; angry.

enconar [eŋ·ko·nár] *v.* to inflame; to infect; to irritate; -se to become inflamed, infected; to get irritated.

encono [eŋ·kó·no] *m.* rancor, animosity, ill will; *Cuba, Mex.* inflammation, swelling.

encontrado [eŋ·kon·trá·ḍo] *adj.* opposite; opposing; contrary; *p.p. of* **encontrar.**

encontrar[2] [eŋ·kon·trár] *v. irr.* to encounter, meet; to find; -se to meet; to coincide; to be; to be found, be situated; to collide; to conflict; -se con to come across, meet up with.

encontrón [eŋ·kon·trón], **encontronazo** [eŋ·kon·tro·ná·so] *m.* bump, collision; **darse un** — to collide (with) bump (into); to bump into each other.

encordelar [eŋ·kor·ḍe·lár] *v.* to string; to tie with strings.

encorvar [eŋ·kor·ḅár] *v.* to curve, bend; -se to bend down; to stoop.

encrespar [eŋ·kres·pár] v. (rizar) to curl; to ruffle; (agitar) to irritate; -se to curl; to get ruffled; to become involved or entangled (a matter or affair); to become rough (said of the sea).
encrucijada [eŋ·kru·si·xá·ḍa] f. crossroads, street intersection; ambush.
encuadernación [eŋ·kwa·ḍer·na·sjón] f. binding (of books).
encuadernar [eŋ·kwa·ḍer·nár] v. to bind (books).
encuadrar [eŋ·kwa·ḍrár] v. to enclose in a frame; to encompass; to fit (into); Am. to suit; Ven. to summarize briefly, give a synthesis of.
encubierto [eŋ·ku·ḅjér·to] p.p. of **encubrir.**
encubrir⁵² [eŋ·ku·ḅrír] v. to cover, hide.
encuentro [eŋ·kwén·tro] m. (hallazgo) encounter, meeting; find, finding; (conflicto) conflict, clash; collision; **salir al — de** to go out to meet; to make a stand against, oppose; Am. **llevarse de —** to run over, knock down; to drag along.
encuerado [eŋ·kwe·rá·ḍo] adj. Am. naked.
encuerar [eŋ·kwe·rár] v. Am. to strip of clothes; Am. to skin, fleece, strip of money; -se Am. to strip, get undressed.
encuesta [eŋ·kwés·ta] f. search, inquiry, investigation; survey.
encumbrado [eŋ·kum·brá·ḍo] p.p. & adj. elevated; exalted; high, lofty.
encumbramiento [eŋ·kum·bra·mjén·to] m. elevation; exaltation; height; eminence.
encumbrar [eŋ·kum·brár] v. to elevate; to exalt, extol; -se to climb to the top; to rise up; to hold oneself high; to soar.
encurtido [eŋ·kur·tí·ḍo] m. pickle; p.p. of **encurtir.**
encurtir [eŋ·kur·tír] v. to pickle.
enchilada [en·či·lá·ḍa] f. Mex. C.A. rolled **tortilla** served with chili.
enchuecar⁶ [en·čwe·kár] v. to bend, twist; -se Col., Ven., Mex., Ríopl. to get bent or twisted.
enchufar [en·ču·fár] v. to plug in; to telescope; to fit (a tube or pipe) into another.
enchufe [en·čú·fe] m. socket; plug; electric outlet; Spain influence; position obtained through influence.
ende [én·de]: **por —** hence, therefore.
endeble [en·dé·ḅle] adj. weak, feeble; flimsy.
endemoniado [en·de·mo·njá·ḍo] adj. possessed by the devil; devilish, fiendish; mischievous.
endentar¹ [en·den·tár] v. irr. to indent, form notches in; to furnish (a saw, wheel, etc.) with teeth; to mesh.
enderezar⁹ [en·de·re·sár] v. to straighten; to set upright; to right, correct; to direct; to address; -se to go straight (to); to straighten up.
endeudado [en·dew·ḍá·ḍo] p.p. & adj. indebted; in debt.
endeudarse [en·dew·ḍár·se] v. to get into debt, become indebted.
endiablado [en·dja·ḅlá·ḍo] adj. devilish; possessed by the devil; ugly; mean, wicked; Col., Ven., Mex., Ríopl. dangerous, risky.
endomingado [en·do·miŋ·gá·ḍo] p.p. & adj. dressed up in one's Sunday, or best, clothes.
endosante [en·do·sán·te] m. endorser.
endosar [en·do·sár] v. to endorse (a check, draft, etc.).
endose [en·dó·se], **endoso** [en·dó·so] m. endorsement.
endulzar⁹ [en·dul·sár] v. to sweeten; to soften.
endurecer¹³ [en·du·re·sér] v. irr. to harden; -se to get hardened; to get cruel.
enebro [e·né·ḅro] m. juniper.

enemigo [e·ne·mí·ǧo] m. enemy; devil; adj. hostile; unfriendly; **ser — de una cosa** to dislike a thing.
enemistad [e·ne·mis·táḍ] f. enmity, hatred.
enemistar [e·ne·mis·tár] v. to cause enmity between; -se con to become an enemy of.
energía [e·ner·xí·a] f. energy; **— nuclear** nuclear energy.
enérgico [e·nér·xi·ko] adj. energetic.
enero [e·né·ro] m. January.
enervar [e·ner·ḅár] v. to enervate, weaken.
enfadar [en·fa·ḍár] v. to anger; -se to get angry.
enfado [en·fá·ḍo] m. anger, disgust.
enfadoso [en·fa·ḍó·so] adj. annoying.
enfardar [en·far·ḍár] v. to bale, pack.
énfasis [én·fa·sis] m. emphasis; **enfático** [en·fá·ti·ko] adj. emphatic.
enfermar [en·fer·már] v. to become ill; to make ill; to weaken; -se to become ill.
enfermedad [en·fer·me·ḍáḍ] f. sickness, illness.
enfermería [en·fer·me·rí·a] f. infirmary.
enfermero [en·fer·mé·ro] m. male nurse; **enfermera** [en·fer·mé·ra] f. nurse (for the sick).
enfermizo [en·fer·mí·so] adj. sickly; unhealthy.
enfermo [en·fer·mo] adj. sick, ill; feeble; m. patient.
enflaquecer¹³ [en·fla·ke·sér] v. irr. to become thin; to make thin; to weaken.
enfocar⁶ [en·fo·kár] v. to focus.
enfrenar [en·fre·nár] v. to bridle; to brake, put the brake on; to check, curb.
enfrentar [en·fren·tár] v. to put face to face; -se con to confront, face, meet face to face.
enfrente [en·frén·te] adv. in front, opposite; **— de** in front of, opposite.
enfriamiento [en·frja·mjén·to] m. cooling; chill; refrigeration.
enfriar¹⁷ [en·frjár] v. to cool, chill; Carib. to kill; -se to cool, cool off; to get chilled.
enfurecer¹³ [en·fu·re·sér] v. irr. to infuriate, enrage; -se to rage; to get furious; to get rough, stormy (said of the sea).
enfurruñarse [en·fu·rru·ñár·se] v. to get angry; to grumble.
engalanar [eŋ·ga·la·nár] v. to adorn, decorate; -se to dress up, primp.
enganchamiento [eŋ·gan·ča·mjén·to] = **enganche.**
enganchar [eŋ·gan·čár] v. to hitch; to hook; to ensnare; to draft; to attract into the army; Col., Ven., Mex., Ríopl. to hire (labor with false promises); -se to engage, interlock; to get hooked; to enlist in the army.
enganche [eŋ·gán·če] m. hooking; coupling; draft (into the army); Col., Ven., Mex., Ríopl. enrolling of laborers (for a rubber plantation or other risky business under false promises); Mex. down payment.
engañador [eŋ·ga·ña·ḍór] adj. deceitful, deceiving; m. deceiver.
engañar [eŋ·ga·ñár] v. to deceive; to while away (time); to ward off (hunger or sleep); -se to deceive oneself; to be mistaken.
engaño [eŋ·gá·ño] m. deceit, trick, fraud; mistake, misunderstanding; Ch., C.A. bribe.
engañoso [eŋ·ga·ñó·so] adj. deceitful; tricky; misleading.
engastar [eŋ·gas·tár] v. to mount, set (jewels).
engaste [eŋ·gás·te] m. setting (for a gem or stone).
engatusar [eŋ·ga·tu·sár] v. to coax, entice; to fool.
engendrar [eŋ·xen·drár] v. to engender, beget, produce; to cause.
engolfarse [eŋ·gol·fár·se] v. to get deep (into); to go deeply (into); to become absorbed, lost in

thought.

engomar [eŋ·go·már] *v.* to gum; to glue.

engordar [eŋ·gor·ḍár] *v.* to fatten; to get fat; to get rich.

engorroso [eŋ·go·rró·so] *adj.* cumbersome; bothersome.

engranaje [eŋ·gra·ná·xe] *m.* gear, gears, gearing.

engranar [eŋ·gra·nár] *v.* to gear, throw in gear; to mesh gears.

engrandecer[13] [eŋ·gran·de·sér] *v. irr.* to aggrandize, make greater; to magnify; to exalt.

engrane [eŋ·grá·ne] *m.* engagement (*of gears*); gear.

engrasar [eŋ·gra·sár] *v.* to lubricate, grease; to stain with grease; to fertilize, manure; to dress (*cloth*).

engrase [eŋ·grá·se] *m.* grease job.

engreído [eŋ·gre·í·ḍo] *adj. & p.p.* conceited, vain; *Col.* attached, fond.

engreír[15] [eŋ·gre·ír] *v. irr.* to make vain, conceited; -se to puff up, get conceited; *Col.* to become fond (of), become attached (to).

engrosar[2] [eŋ·gro·sár] *v. irr.* to enlarge; to thicken; to fatten; to get fat.

engrudo [eŋ·grú·ḍo] *m.* paste (*for gluing*).

engullir[20] [eŋ·gu·yír] *v.* to gobble, devour; to gorge.

enhebrar [en·e·ḅrár] *v.* to thread (*a needle*); to string (*beads*).

enhiesto [en·jés·to] *adj.* straight, upright, erect.

enhorabuena [en·o·ra·ḅwé·na] *f.* congratulation; *adv.* safely; well and good; all right; with much pleasure.

enigma [e·níg·ma] *m.* enigma, riddle, puzzle.

enjabonar [en·xa·ḅo·nár] *v.* to soap; to soft-soap, flatter.

enjaezar[9] [eŋ·xa·e·sár] *v.* to harness.

enjalbegar[7] [eŋ·xal·ḅe·ǥar] *v.* to whitewash; -se to paint (*one's face*).

enjambre [eŋ·xám·bre] *m.* swarm of bees; crowd.

enjaular [eŋ·xaw·lár] *v.* to cage; to confine; to jail.

enjuagar[7] [eŋ·xwa·ǥár] *v.* to rinse, rinse out.

enjuague [eŋ·xwá·ǥe] *m.* mouth wash; rinse; rinsing; scheme, plot.

enjugar[7] [eŋ·xu·ǥár] *v.* to dry; to wipe; -se to dry oneself.

enjuiciar [eŋ·xwi·sjár] *v.* to indict; to prosecute, bring suit against; to try (*a case*); to judge.

enjundia [eŋ·xún·dja] *f.* substance, essence; fat; force, strength.

enjuto [en·xú·to] *adj.* dried; thin, skinny; -s *m. pl.* dry kindling.

enlace [en·lá·se] *m.* link; tie, bond; marriage.

enladrillado [en·la·ḍri·yá·ḍo] *m.* brick pavement or floor.

enladrillar [en·la·ḍri·yár] *v.* to pave with bricks.

enlatar [en·la·tár] *v.* to can; *Col.* to roof with tin.

enlazar[9] [en·la·sár] *v.* to join, bind, tie; to rope; *Ven., Mex.* to lasso; -se to join; to marry; to become related through marriage.

enlodar [en·lo·ḍár] *v.* to cover with mud; to smear, sully, soil, dirty; -se to get in the mud; to get muddy.

enloquecer[13] [en·lo·ke·sér] *v. irr.* to make crazy; to drive mad; to lose one's mind; -se to go crazy.

enlosado [en·lo·sá·ḍo] *m.* flagstone pavement; *p.p.* of **enlosar.**

enlosar [en·lo·sár] *v.* to pave with flagstones.

enmantecado [em·man·te·ká·ḍo] *m. Am.* ice cream. See **mantecado.**

enmantecar[6] [em·man·te·kár] *v.* to butter; to grease (*with lard or butter*).

enmarañar [emma·ra·ñár] *v.* to entagle; to snarl; to confuse, mix up.

enmascarar [em·mas·ka·rár] *v.* to mask; -se to put on a mask; to masquerade.

enmendar[1] [em·men·dár] *v. irr.* to amend, correct; to indemnify, compensate; -se to reform, mend one's ways.

enmienda [em·mjén·da] *f.* correction; amendment; reform; indemnity, compensation.

enmohecer[13] [em·mo·e·sér] *v.* to rust; to mold; -se to rust, become rusty; to mold.

enmudecer[13] [em·mu·ḍe·sér] *v. irr.* to silence; to remain silent; to lose one's voice; to become dumb.

ennegrecer[13] [en·ne·ǥre·sér] *v. irr.* to blacken; to darken; -se to become dark; to get cloudy.

ennoblecer[13] [en·no·ḅle·sér] *v. irr.* to ennoble, dignify.

enojadizo [e·no·xa·ḍí·so] *adj.* irritable, ill-tempered.

enojado [e·no·xá·ḍo] *adj.* angry.

enojar [e·no·xár] *v.* to make angry, vex, annoy; -se to get angry.

enojo [e·nó·xo] *m.* anger; annoyance.

enojoso [e·no·xó·so] *adj.* annoying, bothersome.

enorgullecer[13] [e·nor·ǥu·ye·sér] *v. irr.* to fill with pride; -se to swell up with pride; to be proud.

enorme [e·nór·me] *adj.* enormous.

enramada [en·rra·má·ḍa] *f.* arbor, bower; shady grove.

enrarecer[13] [en·rra·re·sér] *v. irr.* to rarefy, thin, make less dense (*as air*); -se to become rarefied; to become scarce.

enrarecimiento [en·rra·re·si·mjén·to] *m.* rarity, thinness (*of the air*); rarefaction (*act of making thin, rare or less dense*).

enredadera [en·rre·ḍa·ḍé·ra] *f.* climbing vine.

enredar [en·rre·ḍár] *v.* (*enmarañar*) to entangle, snare; to snarl; to mix up; to wind (*on a spool*); (*enemistar*) to raise a rumpus; -se to get tangled up, mixed up; to get trapped; -se con to have an affair with.

enredista [en·rre·ḍís·ta] *m. Am.* liar; *Am.* talebearer.

enredo [en·rré·ḍo] *m.* tangle; confusion; lie; plot.

enredoso [en·rre·ḍó·so] *adj.* tangled up; *Am.* tattler.

enrejado [en·rre·xá·ḍo] *m.* trellis; grating.

enrevesado [en·rre·ḅe·sá·ḍo] *adj.* turned around; intricate, complicated; unruly.

enriquecer[13] [en·rri·ke·sér] *v. irr.* to enrich; to become rich; -se to become rich.

enrojecer[13] [en·rro·xe·sér] *v.* to redden; -se to get red, blush.

enrollar [en·rro·yár] *v.* to roll, roll up; to coil.

enronquecer[13] [en·rroŋ·ke·sér] *v. irr.* to make hoarse; to become hoarse; -se to become hoarse.

enroscar[6] [en·rros·kár] *v.* to coil; to twist, twine; -se to coil; to curl up.

ensacar[6] [en·sa·kár] *v.* to sack, bag, put in a bag or sack.

ensalada [en·sa·lá·ḍa] *f.* salad; hodgepodge, mixture.

ensalmo [en·sál·mo] *m.* incantation.

ensalzar[9] [en·sal·sár] *v.* to exalt, praise.

ensanchar [en·san·čár] *v.* to widen, enlarge; -se to expand; to puff up.

ensanche [en·sán·če] *m.* widening, expansion, extension.

ensangrentado [en·saŋ·gren·tá·ḍo] *adj.* gory, bloody; *p.p.* of **ensangrentar.**

ensangrentar [en·saŋ·gren·tár] *v.* to stain with blood; -se to be covered with blood; to get red with anger.

ensartar [en·sar·tár] *v.* to string; to thread; to link; to rattle off (*tales, stories, etc.*); *Ch.* to tie to a ring; *Am.* to swindle, trick; **-se** *Andes* to fall into a trap.

ensayar [en·sa·yár] *v.* to try; to attempt; to test; to rehearse; **-se** to practice, train oneself.

ensayo [en·sá·yo] *m.* trial, attempt; rehearsal; test; experiment; essay.

ensenada [en·se·ná·ḍa] *f.* small bay, cove.

enseñanza [en·se·ñán·sa] *f.* teaching; education, training.

enseñar [en·se·ñár] *v.* to show; to teach; to train; to point out.

enseres [en·sé·res] *m. pl.* household goods; utensils; implements; equipment.

ensillar [en·si·yár] *v.* to saddle; *Ch.* to abuse, mistreat, domineer; *Ríopl.* — **el picazo** to get angry.

ensimismarse [en·si·miz·már·se] *v.* to become absorbed in thought; *Col., Ven., Ch.* to become conceited or vain.

ensoberbecer[13] [en·so·ḅer·ḅe·sér] *v. irr.* to make proud or haughty; **-se** to puff up with pride; to become haughty; to get rough, choppy (*said of the sea*).

ensordecer[13] [en·sor·ḍe·sér] *v. irr.* to deafen; to become deaf.

ensortijar [en·sor·ti·xár] *v.* to curl; to ring the nose of (*an animal*); **-se** to curl.

ensuciar [en·su·sjár] *v.* to dirty, soil; to stain; **-se** to get dirty; to soil oneself.

ensueño [en·swé·ño] *m.* illusion, dream.

entablar [en·ta·ḅlár] *v.* to board up; to plank; to splint; — **una conversación** to start a conversation; — **un pleito** to bring a lawsuit.

entablillar [en·ta·ḅi·yár] *v.* to splint; *Mex.* to cut (*chocolate*) into tablets or squares.

entallar [en·ta·yár] *v.* to fit closely (*a dress*); to carve.

entapizar[9] [en·ta·pi·sár] *v.* to cover with tapestry; to drape with tapestries; to upholster.

entarimar [en·ta·ri·már] *v.* to floor (*with boards*).

ente [én·te] *m.* entity, being; queer fellow.

enteco [en·té·ko] *adj.* sickly, skinny.

entender[1] [en·ten·dér] *v. irr.* to understand; — **de** to know, be an expert in; — **en** to take care of; to deal with; **-se con** to have dealings or relations with; to have an understanding with.

entendido [en·ten·dí·ḍo] *p.p.* understood; *adj.* wise, prudent; well-informed; able, skilful; **no darse por** — to pretend not to hear or understand; not to take the hint.

entendimiento [en·ten·di·mjén·to] *m.* understanding; intellect; mind.

enterado [en·te·rá·ḍo] *p.p. & adj.* informed; aware.

enterar [en·te·rár] *v.* to inform, acquaint; **-se** to know, learn, find out; to understand, get the idea.

entereza [en·te·ré·sa] *f.* entirety; integrity; fortitude; serenity; firmness; perfection.

enternecedor [en·ter·ne·se·ḍór] *adj.* touching, moving, pitiful.

enternecer[13] [en·ter·ne·sér] *v. irr.* to soften, touch, stir, move; **-se** to become tender; to be touched, stirred.

entero [en·té·ro] *adj.* (*completo*) entire, whole; (*justo*) just, right; firm; *m.* integer, whole number; *Col.* payment, reimbursement; *Ch.* balance of an account; **caballo** — stallion.

enterramiento [en·te·rra·mjén·to] *m.* burial.

enterrar[1] [en·te·rrár] *v. irr.* to bury; *Am.* to sink,

stick into.

entibiar [en·ti·ḅjár] *v.* to make lukewarm; **-se** to become lukewarm.

entidad [en·ti·ḍáḍ] *f.* entity; unit, group, organization; **de** — of value or importance.

entierro [en·tjé·rro] *m.* burial; funeral; grave; *Am.* hidden treasure.

entintar [en·tin·tár] *v.* to ink; to stain with ink; to dye.

entoldar [en·tol·ḍár] *v.* to cover with an awning; **-se** to puff up with pride; to become overcast, cloudy.

entonación [en·to·na·sjón] *f.* intonation.

entonar [en·to·nár] *v.* to sing in tune; to start a song (*for others to follow*); to be in tune; to harmonize; **-se** to put on airs.

entonces [en·tón·ses] *adv.* then, at that time; **pues** — well then.

entornado [en·tor·ná·ḍo] *adj.* half-open; half-closed, ajar.

entornar [en·tor·nár] *v.* to half-open.

entorpecer[13] [en·tor·pe·sér] *v. irr.* to stupefy; to be numb, make numb; to delay, obstruct; to thwart, frustrate.

entorpecimiento [en·tor·pe·si·mjén·to] *m.* numbness; dullness; delay, obstruction.

entrada [en·trá·ḍa] *f.* (*apertura*) entrance; entry; gate; opening; (*acción o privilegio*) entering, admission; entrée (*dish or dinner course*); *Am.* attack, assault, goring; *Mex.* beating; **-s** cash receipts.

entrambos [en·trám·bos] *adj. & pron.* both.

entrampar [en·tram·pár] *v.* to trap, ensnare; to trick; to burden with debts; **-se** to get trapped or entangled; to run into debt.

entrante [en·trán·te] *adj.* entering; incoming; **el año** — next year.

entraña [en·trá·ña] *f.* entrail; innermost recess; heart; disposition, temper; **-s** entrails, "innards", insides; **hijo de mis -s** child of my heart; **no tener -s** to be cruel.

entrar [en·trár] *v.* to enter, go in, come in; to attack; **me entró miedo** I became afraid; **-se** to slip in, get in, sneak in; to enter.

entre [én·tre] *prep.* between; among; **dijo — sí** he said to himself; — **tanto** meanwhile; *Am.* — **más habla menos dice** the more he talks the less he says.

entreabierto [en·tre·a·ḅjér·to] *p.p. of* **entreabrir**; *adj.* ajar, half-open, partly open.

entreabrir[52] [en·tre·a·ḅrír] *v.* to half-open.

entreacto [en·tre·ák·to] *m.* intermission; intermezzo (*entertainment between the acts*); small cigar.

entrecano [en·tre·ká·no] *adj.* greyish.

entrecejo [en·tre·sé·xo] *m.* space between the eyebrows; **fruncir el** — to wrinkle one's brow.

entrecortado [en·tre·kor·tá·ḍo] *adj.* hesitating, faltering (*speech*); breathless, choking; *p.p.* interrupted.

entrecortar [en·tre·kor·tár] *v.* to cut halfway through or in between; to interrupt at intervals.

entrecruzar[9] [en·tre·kru·sár] *v.* to intercross, cross; to interlace; **-se** to cross.

entredicho [en·tre·ḍí·čo] *m.* prohibition, injunction.

entrega [en·tré·ga] *f.* (*acto de ceder*) delivery; surrender; (*parte suelta*) installment (*of a book*); **novela por -s** serial novel.

entregar[7] [en·tre·gár] *v.* to deliver, hand over; **-se** to surrender, submit, give up; to devote oneself (to); to abandon oneself (to).

entrelazar[9] [en·tre·la·sár] *v.* to interlace; to weave together.

entremés [en·tre·més] *m.* relish, side dish (*of olives, pickles, etc.*); one-act farce (*formerly presented between the acts of a play.*)

entremeter [en·tre·me·tér] *v.* to insert; to place between; **-se** to meddle; to intrude.

entremetido [en·tre·me·tí·đo] *adj.* meddlesome; *m.* meddler; intruder.

entremetimiento [en·tre·me·ti·mjén·to] *m.* intrusion, meddling.

entremezclar [en·tre·mes·klár] *v.* to intermix, intermingle.

entrenador [en·tre·na·đór] *m. Am.* trainer.

entrenamiento [en·tre·na·mjén·to] *m. Am.* training, drill.

entrenar [en·tre·nár] *v. Am.* to train, drill; **-se** *Am.* to train.

entresacar[6] [en·tre·sa·kár] *v.* to pick out, select.

entresuelo [en·tre·swé·lo] *m.* mezzanine; second floor.

entretanto [en·tre·tán·to] *adv.* meanwhile.

entretejer [en·tre·te·xér] *v.* to weave together; to intertwine.

entretener[45] [en·tre·te·nér] *v. irr.* to delay, detain; to amuse, entertain; **-se** to amuse oneself; to delay oneself; **— el tiempo** to while away the time.

entretenido [en·tre·te·ní·đo] *adj.* entertaining, amusing; *p.p. of* **entretener.**

entretenimiento [en·tre·te·ni·mjén·to] *m.* entertainment; pastime; delay.

entrever[49] [entre·ɓér] *v.* to glimpse, catch a glimpse of; to half-see, see vaguely.

entreverar [en·tre·ɓe·rár] *v.* to intermingle, intermix.

entrevista [en·tre·ɓís·ta] *f.* interview; date, appointment.

entrevistar [en·tre·ɓis·tár] *v.* to interview; **-se con** to have an interview with.

entrevisto [en·tre·ɓís·to] *p.p. of* **entrever.**

entristecer[13] [en·tris·te·sér] *v. irr.* to sadden, make sad; **-se** to become sad.

entrometer [en·tro·me·tér] = **entremeter.**

entrometido [en·tro·me·tí·đo] = **entremetido.**

entumecer[13] [en·tu·me·sér] *v. irr.* to make numb; **-se** to get numb; to surge; to swell.

entumido [en·tu·mí·đo] *adj.* numb, stiff; *Am.* timid, shy, awkward.

entumirse [en·tu·mír·se] *v.* to get numb.

enturbiar [en·tur·ɓjár] *v.* to make muddy; to muddle; to disturb; to obscure; **-se** to get muddy; to get muddled.

entusiasmar [en·tu·sjaz·már] *v.* to excite, fill with enthusiasm; **-se** to get enthusiastic, excited.

entusiasmo [en·tu·sjáz·mo] *m.* enthusiasm.

entusiasta [en·tu·sjás·ta] *m. & f.* enthusiast; **entusiástico** *adj.* enthusiastic.

enumeración [e·nu·me·ra·sjón] *f.* enumeration, counting.

enumerar [e·nu·me·rár] *v.* to enumerate.

enunciar [e·nun·sjár] *v.* to express, state, declare.

envainar [em·baj·nár] *v.* to sheathe.

envalentonar [em·ba·len·to·nár] *v.* to make bold or haughty; **-se** to get bold; to brag, swagger.

envanecer[13] [em·ba·ne·sér] *v. irr.* to make vain; **-se** to become vain.

envasar [em·ba·sár] *v.* to pack, put up in any container; to bottle; to can.

envase [em·bá·se] *m.* packing; container, jar, bottle, can (*for packing*).

envejecer[13] [em·be·xe·sér] *v. irr.* to make old; to

grow old, get old; **-se** to grow old, get old.

envenenamiento [em·be·ne·na·mjén·to] *m.* poisoning.

envenenar [em·be·ne·nár] *v.* to poison; to infect.

envergadura [em·ber·ga·đú·ra] *f.* span (*of an airplane*); spread (*of a bird's wings*); breadth (*of sails*).

envés [em·bés] *m.* back or wrong side.

enviado [em·bjá·đo] *m.* envoy.

enviar[17] [em·bjár] *v.* to send; **— a uno a paseo** to give someone his walking papers.

enviciar [em·bi·sjár] *v.* to vitiate, corrupt; **-se** to become addicted (to), overly fond (of).

envidar [em·bi·đjár] *v.* to bid (*in cards*); to bet.

envidia [em·bi·đja] *f.* envy.

envidiable [em·bi·đjá·ɓle] *adj.* enviable, desirable.

envidiar [em·bi·đjár] *v.* to envy.

envidioso [em·bi·đjó·so] *adj.* envious.

envilecer[13] [em·bi·le·sér] *v. irr.* to revile, malign, degrade; **-se** to degrade or lower oneself.

envilecimiento [em·bi·le·si·mjén·to] *m.* degradation, humiliation, shame.

envío [em·bí·o] *m.* remittance, sending; shipment.

envite [em·bí·te] *m.* bid; stake (*in cards*); offer; push.

envoltorio [em·bol·tó·rjo] *m.* bundle, package.

envoltura [em·bol·tú·ra] *f.* wrapping, cover; wrapper.

envolver[2, 52] [em·bol·ɓér] *v. irr.* to involve, entangle; to wrap; to wind (*a thread, rope, etc.*); to surround; **-se** to become involved, entangled; to cover up, wrap up.

envuelto [em·bwél·to] *p.p. of* **envolver.**

enyesar [en·ỹe·sár] *v.* to plaster; to chalk.

enzolvar [en·sol·ɓár] *v. Am.* to clog, obstruct; *Am.* **-se** to clog, get clogged. *See* **azolvar.**

¡epa! [é·pa] *interj. Riopl., Ven., Col., Mex.* hey! listen! stop! look out!

épico [é·pi·ko] *adj.* epic.

epidemia [e·pi·đe·mja] *f.* epidemic.

episodio [e·pi·só·đjo] *m.* episode.

epístola [e·pís·to·la] *f.* epistle; letter.

epitafio [e·pi·tá·fjo] *m.* epitaph.

época [é·po·ka] *f.* epoch.

epopeya [e·po·pé·ya] *f.* epic poem.

equidad [e·ki·đáđ] *f.* equity, justice, fairness.

equidistante [e·ki·đis·tán·te] *adj.* equidistant, equally distant, halfway, midway.

equilibrar [e·ki·li·ɓrár] *v.* to balance, poise.

equilibrio [e·ki·lí·ɓrjo] *m.* equilibrium, balance; poise.

equilibrista [e·ki·li·ɓrís·ta] *m. & f.* acrobat.

equipaje [e·ki·pá·xe] *m.* baggage, luggage; equipment, outfit; crew.

equipar [e·ki·pár] *v.* to equip, fit out; to man, equip and provision (*a ship*).

equipo [e·kí·po] *m.* (*materiales*) equipment, equipping; outfit; (*grupo*) work crew; sport team; **— de novia** trousseau.

equitación [e·ki·ta·sjón] *f.* horsemanship; horseback riding.

equitativo [e·ki·ta·tí·ɓo] *adj.* fair, just.

equivalente [e·ki·ɓa·lén·te] *adj.* equivalent.

equivaler[47] [e·ki·ɓa·lér] *v. irr.* to be equivalent.

equivocación [e·ki·ɓo·ka·sjón] *f.* error, mistake.

equivocado [e·ki·ɓo·ká·đo] *p.p. & adj.* mistaken.

equivocar[6] [e·ki·ɓo·kár] *v.* to mistake; **-se** to be mistaken; to make a mistake.

equívoco [e·kí·ɓo·ko] *adj.* equivocal, ambiguous, vague; *Am.* mistaken; *m.* pun, play on words; *Am.* mistake, error.

era [é·ra] *f.* era, age; threshing floor.
erario [e·rá·rjo] *m.* public treasury.
erguido [er·ǵi·đo] *adj.* erect; *p.p. of* **erguir**.
erguir[3] [er·ǵir] *v. irr.* to erect, set upright; to lift (*the head*); **-se** to sit up or stand erect; to become proud and haughty.
erial [e·rjál] *m.* uncultivated land; *adj.* unplowed, untilled.
erigir[11] [e·ri·xír] *v.* to erect, build; to found.
erizado [e·ri·sá·đo] *adj.* bristly, prickly; — **de** bristling with.
erizar[9] [e·ri·sár] *v.* to set on end, make bristle; **-se** to bristle; to stand on end (*hair*).
erizo [e·rí·so] *m.* hedgehog, porcupine; thistle; — **de mar** sea urchin; **ser un** — to be irritable, harsh.
ermitaño [er·mi·tá·ño] *m.* hermit.
erosion [e·ro·sjón] *f.* erosion.
errabundo [e·rra·ƀún·do] *adj.* wandering.
errado [e·rrá·đo] *adj.* mistaken, wrong, in error; *p.p. of* **errar**.
errante [e·rrán·te] *adj.* errant, roving, wandering.
errar[28] [e·rrár] *v. irr.* to err, make mistakes; to miss (*target, road*); to rove, wander.
errata [e·rrá·ta] *f.* misprint, printer's error.
erróneo [e·rró·ne·o] *adj.* erroneous, mistaken, wrong, incorrect.
error [e·rrór] *m.* error, fault, mistake.
eructar [e·ruk·tár] *v.* to belch.
eructo [e·rúk·to] *m.* belch.
erudición [e·ru·đi·sjón] *f.* erudition, learning.
erudito [e·ru·đí·to] *adj.* erudite, scholarly, learned; *m.* scholar.
erupción [e·rup·sjón] *f.* eruption; outburst; rash.
esbelto [ez·ƀel·to] *adj.* slender.
esbozar[9] [ez·ƀo·sár] *v.* to sketch, outline.
esbozo [ez·ƀó·so] *m.* sketch, outline.
escabechar [es·ka·ƀe·čár] *v.* to pickle.
escabeche [es·ka·ƀé·če] *m.* pickled fish; pickle (*solution for pickling*).
escabel [es·ka·ƀél] *m.* stool; footstool.
escabrosidad [es·ka·ƀro·si·đáđ] *f.* roughness, unevenness; harshness; improper word or phrase.
escabroso [es·ka·ƀró·so] *adj.* rough; rugged; scabrous, rather indecent.
escabullirse[20] [es·ka·ƀu·yír·se] *v. irr.* to slip away; to slip through; to scoot, scamper, scurry.
escala [es·ká·la] *f.* ladder; scale; port of call; stopover; **hacer — en** to stop over at; **escalafón** [es·ka·la·fón] *m.* army register.
escalar [es·ka·lár] *v.* to scale; to climb.
escaldar [es·kal·dár] *v.* to scald; to make red-hot; **-se** to get scalded.
escalera [es·ka·lé·ra] *f.* stairs, staircase; ladder; — **mecánica** escalator.
escalfar [es·kal·fár] *v.* to poach (*eggs*).
escalinata [es·ka·li·ná·ta] *f.* flight of stairs (*usually on the outside*).
escalofriarse[17] [es·ka·lo·frjár·se] *v.* to become chilled.
escalofrío [es·ka·lo·frí·o] *m.* chill; **-s** chills and fever.
escalón [es·ka·lón] *m.* step (*of a ladder or staircase*); stepping stone; *Am.* **-es** tribe of quichua Indians.
escalonar [es·ka·lo·nár] *v.* to echelon (*arrange in step-like formation*); to terrace; **-se** to rise in terraces.
escama [es·ká·ma] *f.* scale, fish scale; flake.
escamoso [es·ka·mó·so] *adj.* scaly.

escamotear [es·ka·mo·te·ár] *v.* to whisk out of sight; to steal or snatch away with cunning; to conceal by a trick of sleight of hand.
escampar [es·kam·pár] *v.* to clear (*weather*).
escandalizar[9] [es·kan·da·li·sár] *v.* scandalize, shock; **-se** to be shocked.
escándalo [es·kán·da·lo] *m.* scandal; bad example.
escandaloso [es·kan·da·ló·so] *adj.* scandalous, shocking; *Mex., C.A., Col., Andes* showy, loud (*color*).
escandio [es·kán·djo] *m.* scandium.
escapada [es·ka·pá·đa] *f.* escape, flight.
escapar [es·ka·pár] *v.* to escape, flee, avoid; **-se** to run away, escape.
escaparate [es·ka·pa·rá·te] *m.* show window; glass case, glass cabinet or cupboard.
escapatoria [es·ka·pa·tó·rja] *f.* escape, loophole, excuse.
escape [es·ká·pe] *m.* escape; vent, outlet; exhaust; **a** — rapidly, at full speed.
escarabajo [es·ka·ra·ƀá·xo] *m.* black beetle.
escaramuza [es·ka·ra·mú·sa] *f.* skirmish; quarrel.
escarbar [es·kar·ƀár] *v.* to scrape, scratch; to dig out; to pry into, investigate.
escarcear [es·kar·se·ár] *v. Ch., Ríopl.* to prance.
escarcha [es·kár·ča] *f.* frost; frosting.
escarchar [es·kar·čár] *v.* to frost; to freeze.
escardar [es·kar·đár] *v.* to weed; to weed out.
escarlata [es·kar·lá·ta] *f.* scarlet; scarlet fever; scarlet cloth; **escarlatina** [es·kar·la·tí·na] *f.* scarlet fever.
escarmentar[1] [es·kar·men·tár] *v. irr.* to punish (*as an example or warning*); to profit by one's misfortunes, punishment, etc.; — **en cabeza ajena** to profit by another's mistake or misfortune.
escarmiento [es·kar·mjén·to] *m.* lesson, example, warning; punishment.
escarnecer[13] [es·kar·ne·sér] *v. irr.* to jeer, insult, mock.
escarnio [es·kár·njo] *m.* scoff, jeer.
escarpa [es·kár·pa] *f.* steep slope, bluff, cliff; scarp (*of a fortification*).
escarpado [es·kar·pá·đo] *adj.* steep; rugged.
escarpia [es·kár·pja] *f.* hook (*for hanging something*).
escasear [es·ka·se·ár] *v.* to be scarce; to grow less, become scarce; to stint.
escasez [es·ka·sés] *f.* scarcity, lack, scantiness.
escaso [es·ká·so] *adj.* scarce, limited; scant; scanty; stingy.
escatimar [es·ka·ti·már] *v.* to stint, skimp; to curtail.
escena [e·sé·na] *f.* scene; scenery, theatre, stage.
escenario [e·se·ná·rjo] *m.* stage.
escenificación [e·se·ni·fi·ka·sjón] *f.* dramatization, stage adaptation.
escepticismo [e·sep·ti·síz·mo] *m.* scepticism; doubt, unbelief.
escéptico [e·sép·ti·ko] *m. & adj.* sceptic.
esclarecer[13] [es·kla·re·sér] *v. irr.* to lighten, illuminate; to elucidate, make clear, explain.
esclarecimiento [es·kla·re·si·mjén·to] *m.* clarification, illumination, illustration; worth, nobility.
esclavitud [es·kla·ƀi·túđ] *f.* slavery.
esclavizar[9] [es·kla·ƀi·sár] *v.* to enslave.
esclavo [es·klá·ƀo] *m.* slave.
esclusa [es·klú·sa] *f.* lock (*of a canal*); sluice, floodgate.
escoba [es·kó·ƀa] *f.* broom.
escobazo [es·ko·ƀá·so] *m.* blow with a broom.

EN

escobilla [es·ko·ƀí·ya] *f.* whisk broom; small broom.

escobillón [es·ko·ƀi·yón] *m.* swab; push broom.

escocer[2,10] [es·ko·sér] *v. irr.* to sting, smart.

escocés [es·ko·sés] *adj.* Scottish; Scotch; *m.* Scot; Scotchman.

escoger[11] [es·ko·xér] *v.* to choose, select, pick out.

escolar [es·ko·lár] *adj.* scholastic, academic; *m.* scholar, student.

escolástico [es·ko·lás·ti·ko] *adj. & m.* scholastic.

escolta [es·kól·ta] *f.* escort; convoy.

escoltar [es·kol·tár] *v.* to escort; to convoy.

escollo [es·kó·yo] *m.* reef; danger; obstacle.

escombro [es·kóm·bro] *m.* debris, rubbish; mackerel.

esconder [es·kon·dér] *v.* to hide, conceal; -se to hide, go into hiding.

escondidas [es·kon·dí·ðas]: **a** — on the sly, under cover; *Am.* **jugar a las** — to play hide-and-seek.

escondite [es·kon·dí·te] *m.* hiding place; *Spain* **jugar al** — to play hide-and-seek.

escondrijo [es·kon·dri·xo] *m.* hiding place.

escopeta [es·ko·pé·ta] *f.* shotgun.

escopetazo [es·ko·pe·tá·so] *m.* gunshot; gunshot wound; sudden bad news; *Am.* offensive or ironic remark.

escoplo [es·kó·plo] *m.* chisel.

escoria [es·kó·rja] *f.* slag; scum; **escorial** [es·ko·rjál] *m.* dump, dumping place; pile of slag.

escorpión [es·kor·pjón] *m.* scorpion.

escote [es·kó·te] *m.* low neck; **convite a** — Dutch treat (*where everyone pays his share*).

escotilla [es·ko·tí·ya] *f.* hatchway; **escotillón** *m.* hatch, hatchway; trap door.

escozor [es·ko·zór] *m.* smarting sensation, sting.

escribano [es·kri·ƀá·no] *m.* court clerk; lawyer's clerk; notary.

escribiente [es·kri·ƀjén·te] *m.* clerk, office clerk.

escribir[52] [es·kri·ƀír] *v.* to write.

escritc [es·krí·to] *p.p. of* **escribir** written; *m*— writing; manuscript.

escritor [es·kri·tór] *m.* writer.

escritorio [es·kri·tó·rjo] *m.* desk; office.

escritura [es·kri·tú·ra] *f.* writing, handwriting; deed, document; **Sagrada Escritura** Holy Scripture.

escrúpulo [es·krú·pu·lo] *m.* scruple, doubt.

escrupuloso [es·kru·pu·ló·so] *adj.* scrupulous; particular, exact.

escrutador [es·kru·ta·ðór] *adj.* scrutinizing, examining; peering; penetrating; *m.* scrutinizer, examiner; inspector of election returns.

escrutar [es·kru·tár] *v.* to scrutinize.

escrutinio [es·kru·tí·njo] *m.* scrutiny, careful inspection.

escuadra [es·kwá·ðra] *f.* squadron; fleet; square (*instrument for drawing or testing right angles*).

escuadrón [es·kwa·ðrón] *m.* squadron.

escualidez [es·kwa·li·ðés] *f.* squalor.

escuálido [es·kwá·li·ðo] *adj.* squalid, filthy; thin, emaciated.

escuchar [es·ku·čár] *v.* to listen; to heed.

escudar [es·ku·ðár] *v.* to shield.

escudero [es·ku·ðé·ro] *m.* squire.

escudo [es·kú·ðo] *m.* shield; escutcheon, coat of arms; gold crown (*ancient coin*); *Am.* Chilean gold coin.

escudriñar [es·ku·ðri·ñár] *v.* to scrutinize, search, pry into.

escuela [es·kwé·la] *f.* school.

escuelante [es·kwe·lán·te] *m. & f. Col.* schoolboy; schoolgirl.

escueto [es·kwé·to] *adj.* plain, unadorned, bare.

esculcar[6] [es·kul·kár] *v. Am.* to search; *Carib., Col., Ven.* to frisk (*a person's pockets*).

esculpir [es·kul·pír] *v.* to sculpture; to engrave.

escultor [es·kul·tór] *m.* sculptor.

escultura [es·kul·tú·ra] *f.* sculpture.

escupidera [es·ku·pi·ðé·ra] *f.* cuspidor.

escupir [es·ku·pír] *v.* to spit.

escurridero [es·ku·rri·ðé·ro] *m.* drain pipe; drainboard.

escurrir [es·ku·rrír] *v.* to drip; to drain; to trickle; -se to ooze out, trickle; to slip out, sneak out.

ese [é·se], **esa** [é·sa] *dem. adj.* that; **esos** [é·sos], **esas** [é·sas] those; **ése, ésa** *m., f. dem. pron.* that one; **ésos, ésas** *m., f. pl.* those.

esencia [e·sén·sja] *f.* essence.

esencial [e·sen·sjál] *adj.* essential.

esfera [es·fé·ra] *f.* sphere; clock dial.

esférico [es·fé·ri·ko] *adj.* spherical.

esforzado [es·for·sá·ðo] *adj.* strong; valiant; courageous.

esforzar[2,9] [es·for·sár] *v. irr.* to give or inspire strength; to encourage; -se to make an effort; to strive, try hard.

esfuerzo [es·fwér·so] *m.* effort; spirit, courage, vigor; stress.

esfumar [es·fu·már] *v.* to shade, tone down; -se to vanish, disappear.

esgrima [ez·grí·ma] *f.* fencing.

esgrimir [ez·gri·mír] *v.* to fence; to brandish; to wield (*the sword or pen*).

eslabón [ez·la·ƀón] *m.* link of a chain; steel knife sharpener; black scorpion.

eslabonar [ez·la·ƀo·nár] *v.* to link; to join; to connect.

esmaltar [ez·mal·tár] *v.* to enamel; to beautify; adorn.

esmalte [ez·mál·te] *m.* enamel; enamel work; smalt (*a blue pigment*).

esmerado [ez·me·rá·ðo] *adj.* painstaking, careful, conscientious; *p.p. of* **esmerar**.

esmeralda [ez·me·rál·da] *f.* emerald; *Am.* an eel-like fish; *Col.* hummingbird; *Mex.* variety of pineapple.

esmerar [ez·me·rár] *v.* to polish, clean; -se to strive, take special pains, use great care.

esmero [ez·mé·ro] *m.* care, precision.

esmoquin [ez·mó·kin] *m.* tuxedo, dinner coat.

eso [é·so] *dem. pron.* that, that thing, that fact; — **es** that is it; **a** — **de** at about (*referring to time*); *Am.* ¡**eso**! that's right!

espaciar[17] [es·pa·sjár] *v.* to space; to spread; to expand; -se to enlarge (*upon a subject*): to relax, amuse oneself.

espacio [es·pá·sjo] *m.* space; interval; slowness, delay; *adv. Mex.* slowly.

espacioso [es·pa·sjó·so] *adj.* spacious; slow.

espada [es·pá·ða] *f.* sword; skilled swordsman; matador (*bull-fighter who kills the bull*); -s swords (*Spanish card suit*).

espalda [es·pál·da] *f.* back, shoulders; -s back, back part; **a** -s behind one's back; **de** -s on one's back; **dar la** — **a** to turn one's back on; **espaldilla** [es·pal·dí·ya] *f.* shoulder blade.

espaldar [es·pal·dár] *m.* back (*of a chair*); trellis (*for plants*); backplate of a cuirass (*armor*).

espantadizo [es·pan·ta·dí·so] *adj.* scary, shy, timid.

espantajo [es·pan·tá·xo] *m.* scarecrow.

espantapájaros [es·pan·ta·pá·xa·ros] *m.* scarecrow.

espantar [es·pan·tár] *v.* to frighten, scare; to scare away; *Col.* to haunt; **-se** to be scared; to be astonished; *Mex.* **espantárselas** [es·pan·tár·se·las] to be wide-awake, catch on quickly.

espanto [es·pán·to] *m.* fright, terror; astonishment; *Col., Ven., Mex.* ghost.

espantoso [es·pan·tó·so] *adj.* frightful, terrifying; wonderful.

español [es·pa·ñól] *adj.* Spanish; *m.* Spaniard; Spanish language.

esparadrapo [es·pa·ra·ḍrá·po] *m.* court plaster, adhesive tape. *See* **tela adhesiva.**

esparcir[10] [es·par·sír] *v.* to scatter, spread; **-se** to relax, amuse oneself.

espárrago [es·pá·rra·ḡo] *m.* asparagus.

esparto [es·pár·to] *m.* esparto grass (*used for making ropes, mats, etc.*).

espasmo [es·páz·mo] *m.* spasm; horror.

espátula [es·pá·tu·la] *f.* spatula.

especia [es·pé·sja] *f.* spice.

especial [es·pe·sjál] *adj.* special; **en** — in particular. specially.

especialidad [es·pe·sja·li·ḍáḍ] *f.* specialty.

especialista [es·pe·sja·lís·ta] *m.* & *f.* specialist.

especializar[9] [es·pe·sja·li·sár] *v.* to specialize; **-se en** to specialize in.

especie [es·pé·sje] *f.* species; kind, sort; pretext; idea.

especificar[6] [es·pe·si·fi·kár] *v.* to specify; to name.

específico [es·pe·sí·fi·ko] *adj.* specific; *m.* specific (*medicine*).

espécimen [es·pé·si·men] *m.* specimen, sample.

espectacular [es·pek·ta·ku·lár] *adj.* spectacular.

espectáculo [es·pek·tá·ku·lo] *m.* spectacle.

espectador [es·pek·ta·ḍór] *m.* spectator.

espectro [es·pék·tro] *m.* spectre, ghost; spectrum.

espectrógrafo [es·pek·tró·ḡra·fo] *m.* spectrograph.

especulación [es·pe·ku·la·sjón] *f.* speculation.

especulador [es·pe·ku·la·ḍór] *m.* speculator.

especular [es·pe·ku·lár] *v.* to speculate.

especulativo [es·pe·ku·la·tí·ƀo] *adj.* speculative.

espejismo [es·pe·xíz·mo] *m.* mirage; illusion.

espejo [es·pé·xo] *m.* mirror; model; — **de cuerpo entero** full-length mirror.

espeluznante [es·pe·luz·nán·te] *adj.* hair-raising, terrifying.

espeluznarse [es·pe·luz·nár·se] *v.* to be terrified; to bristle with fear.

espera [es·pé·ra] *f.* wait; stay (*granted by judge*), delay; extension of time (*for payment*); **sala de** — waiting room; **estar en** — **de** to be waiting for; to be expecting.

esperanza [es·pe·rán·sa] *f.* hope; expectation.

esperanzado [es·pe·ran·sá·ḍo] *adj.* hopeful.

esperanzar[9] [es·pe·ran·sár] to give hope to.

esperar [es·pe·rár] *v.* (*tener esperanza*) to hope; to expect; to trust; (*permanecer*) to wait, wait for; — **en alguien** to place hope or confidence in someone.

esperezarse [es·pe·re·sár·se] = **desperezarse.**

esperma [es·pér·ma] *f.* sperm.

esperpento [es·per·pén·to] *m.* ugly thing; nonsense.

espesar [es·pe·sár] *v.* to thicken; to make dense; **-se** to thicken; to become thick or dense.

espeso [es·pé·so] *adj.* thick, dense; compact; slovenly; *Ríopl.* bothersome, boring.

espesor [es·pe·sór] *m.* thickness.

espesura [es·pe·sú·ra] *f.* density, thickness; thicket; thickest part (*of a forest*).

espetar [es·pe·tár] *v.* to spring (*a joke, story, etc.*)

on (*a person*), surprise with (*a joke, speech, story, etc.*); to pop (*a question*); to run a spit through (*meat, fish, etc. for roasting*); to pierce; **-se** to be stiff, pompous.

espía [es·pí·a] *m.* & *f.* spy.

espiar[17] [es·pjár] *v.* to sp‎̥; *Col., Mex.* **-se** to bruise the hoofs, get lame (*said of horses*).

espiga [es·pí·ḡa] *f.* ear of wheat; peg; spike.

espigar[7] [es·pi·ḡár] *v.* to glean; to grow spikes (*said of corn or grain*); **-se** to grow tall and slender.

espina [es·pí·na] *f.* thorn; sharp splinter; fish bone; spine; fear, suspicion; **darle a uno mala** — to arouse one's suspicion.

espinaca [es·pi·ná·ka] *f.* spinach.

espinazo [es·pi·ná·so] *m.* spine, backbone.

espinilla [es·pi·ní·ya] *f.* shin (*front part of leg*); blackhead (*on the skin*).

espino [es·pí·no] *m.* hawthorn; thorny shrub; thorny branch.

espinoso [es·pi·nó·so] *adj.* thorny; difficult, dangerous.

espionaje [es·pjo·ná·xe] *m.* espionage, spying.

espiral [es·pi·rál] *adj.* & *f.* spiral.

espirar [es·pi·rár] *v.* to exhale; to emit, give off; to die. *See* **expirar.**

espíritu [es·pí·ri·tu] *m.* spirit; soul; courage; vigor; essence; ghost.

espiritual [es·pi·ri·tuál] *adj.* spiritual.

espita [es·pí·ta] *f.* spigot, faucet, tap; toper, drunkard.

esplendidez [es·plen·di·ḍés] *f.* splendor.

espléndido [es·plén·di·ḍo] *adj.* splendid.

esplendor [es·plen·dór] *m.* splendor.

esplendoroso [es·plen·do·ró·so] *adj.* resplendent, shining.

espliego [es·pljé·ḡo] *m.* lavender (*plant*).

espolear [es·po·le·ár] *v.* to spur; to incite.

espoleta [es·po·lé·ta] *f.* bomb fuse.

espolón [es·po·lón] *m.* spur (*on a cock's leg*); ram (*of a boat*); spur; buttress.

espolvorear [es·pol·ƀo·re·ár] *v.* to powder, sprinkle with powder.

esponja [es·pón·xa] *f.* sponge, sponger, parasite; *Col., Peru, Ch., Ríopl.* souse, habitual drunkard.

esponjado [es·poŋ·xá·ḍo] *adj.* fluffy; spongy; puffed up; *p.p. of* **esponjar.**

esponjar [es·poŋ·jár] *v.* to fluff; to make spongy or porous; **-se** to fluff up; to become spongy or porous; to swell, puff up; to puff up with pride.

esponjoso [es·poŋ·xó·so] *adj.* spongy.

esponsales [es·pon·sá·les] *m. pl.* betrothal.

espontaneidad [es·pon·ta·nej·ḍáḍ] *f.* spontaneity, ease, naturalness.

espontáneo [es·pon·tá·ne·o] *adj.* spontaneous.

esposa [es·pó·sa] *f.* wife; **-s** handcuffs.

esposo [es·pó·so] *m.* husband.

espuela [es·pwé·la] *f.* spur.

espulgar[7] [es·pul·ḡár] *v.* to delouse, remove lice or fleas from; to scrutinize.

espuma [es·pú·ma] *f.* foam, froth; scum; — **de jabón** suds.

espumar [es·pu·már] *v.* to skim; to froth, foam.

espumarajo [es·pu·ma·rá·xo] *m.* froth, foam (*from the mouth*); **echar -s** to froth at the mouth; to be very angry.

espumoso [es·pu·mó·so] *adj.* foamy.

esputo [es·pú·to] *m.* sputum, spit, saliva.

esquela [es·ké·la] *f.* note, letter; announcement.

esqueleto [es·ke·lé·to] *m.* skeleton; carcass; framework; *Mex., C.A., Col., Ven.* blank (*to fill*

ES

out); *Am.* outline.

esquema [es·ké·ma] *f.* scheme, outline.

esquí [es·kí] *m.* ski, skiing; — **náutico,** — **acuático** water ski.

esquiar[17] [es·kjár] *v.* to ski.

esquila [es·kí·la] *f.* small bell; cow bell; sheep-shearing.

esquilar [es·ki·lár] *v.* to shear; to clip; to crop.

esquina [es·kí·na] *f.* corner, angle; **esquinazo** [es·ki·ná·so] *m.* corner; *Am.* serenade; **dar esquinazo** to avoid meeting someone; to "ditch" someone.

esquivar [es·ki·βár] *v.* to avoid, dodge; to shun; **-se** to withdraw, shy away.

esquivez [es·ki·βés] *f.* shyness; aloofness; disdain.

esquivo [es·kí·βo] *adv.* reserved, unsociable; shy; disdainful, aloof.

estabilidad [es·ta·βi·li·ðáð] *f.* stability.

estable [es·tá·βle] *adj.* stable, firm, steady.

establecer[13] [es·ta·βle·sér] *v. irr.* to establish; to found; to decree, ordain.

establecimiento [es·ta·βle·si·mjén·to] *m.* establishment; foundation; statute, law.

establo [es·tá·βlo] *m.* stable; **establero** [es·ta·βlé·ro] *m.* groom.

estaca [es·tá·ka] *f.* stake, club; stick; picket.

estacada [es·ta·ká·ða] *f.* stockade; picket fence; *Am.* predicament.

estacar[6] [es·ta·kár] *v.* to stake; to tie on a stake; to stake off, mark with stakes; *Am.* to fasten down with stakes; **-se** to remain stiff or rigid.

estación [es·ta·sjón] *f.* station; season; railway station.

estacionar [es·ta·sjo·nár] *v.* to station; to place; to park (*a car*); **-se** to remain stationary; to park.

estacionario [es·ta·sjo·ná·rjo] *adj.* stationary; motionless.

estada [es·tá·ða] *f.* sojourn, stay.

estadía [es·ta·ðí·a] *f.* detention, stay; stay in port (*beyond time allowed for loading and unloading*); *C.A., Carib.* sojourn, stay (*in any sense*).

estadio [es·tá·ðjo] *m.* stadium.

estadista [es·ta·ðís·ta] *m.* statesman.

estadística [es·ta·ðís·ti·ka] *f.* statistics.

estado [es·tá·ðo] *m.* state, condition; station, rank; estate; — **mayor** army staff; **hombre de** — statesman; *Am.* **en** — **interesante** pregnant.

estadounidense [es·ta·ðow·ni·ðén·se] *adj.* from the United States, American.

estafa [es·tá·fa] *f.* swindle, fraud, trick.

estafador [es·ta·fa·ðór] *m.* swindler, crook.

estafar [es·ta·fár] *v.* to swindle, defraud, cheat.

estalactita [es·ta·lak·tí·ta] *f.* stalactite.

estalagmita [es·ta·laǥ·mí·ta] *f.* stalagmite.

estallar [es·ta·yár] *v.* to explode, burst; to creak, crackle.

estallido [es·ta·yí·ðo] *m.* explosion, outburst; crash; creaking; crack (*of a gun*), report (*of a gun or cannon*).

estambre [es·tám·bre] *m.* woolen yarn; stamen (*of a flower*).

estampa [es·tám·pa] *f.* image; print; stamp; cut, picture; footprint; figure, appearance.

estampado [es·tam·pá·ðo] *m.* print, printed fabric; printing.

estampar [es·tam·pár] *v.* to stamp, print.

estampida [es·tam·pí·ða] *f.* crack, sharp sound; *Col., Ven., C.A.* stampede (*sudden scattering of a herd of cattle or horses*).

estampido [es·tam·pí·ðo] *m.* crack, sharp sound; report of a gun.

estampilla [es·tam·pí·ya] *f.* stamp, seal; *Mex., C.A., Andes* postage stamp.

estancar[6] [es·taŋ·kár] *v.* to stem; to stanch; to stop the flow of; to corner (*a market*); **-se** to stagnate, become stagnant.

estancia [es·tán·sja] *f.* (*permanencia*) stay; (*lugar*) hall, room; mansion; *Ríopl.* farm, cattle ranch; *Carib.* main building of a farm or ranch.

estanciero [es·tan·sjé·ro] *m. Ríopl.* rancher, ranch-owner, cattle raiser; *adj.* pertaining to an estancia.

estanco [es·táŋ·ko] *m.* monopoly; government store (*for sale of monopolized goods such as tobacco, stamps and matches*); tank, reservoir; *Ec., C.A.* liquor store.

estándar [es·tán·dar] *m. Am.* standard, norm.

estandardizar [es·tan·dar·ði·sár], **estandarizar**[9] [es·tan·da·ri·sár] *v. Am.* to standardize.

estandarte [es·tan·dár·te] *m.* standard, flag, banner.

estanque [es·táŋ·ke] *m.* pond, pool, reservoir.

estanquillo [es·táŋ·kí·yo] *m.* tobacco store; *Am.* small store; *C.A., Mex.* small liquor store, tavern.

estante [es·tán·te] *m.* shelf; bookshelf; *Am.* prop, support; **estantería** [es·tan·te·rí·a] *f.* shelves; bookcases.

estaño [es·tá·ño] *m.* tin.

estaquilla [es·ta·kí·ya] *f.* peg; spike.

estar[29] [es·tár] *v. irr.* to be; **-le bien a uno** to be becoming to one; — **de prisa** to be in a hurry; **¿a cuántos estamos?** what day of the month is it today?; **-se** to keep, remain.

estático [es·tá·ti·ko] *adj.* static; **estática** [es·tá·ti·ka] *f.* statics; radio static.

estatua [es·tá·twa] *f.* statue.

estatura [es·ta·tú·ra] *f.* stature, height.

estatuto [es·ta·tú·to] *m.* statute.

este [és·té], **esta** [és·ta] *dem. adj.* this; **estos** [és·tos], **estas** [és·tas] these; **éste, ésta** *m., f. dem. pron.* this one, this thing; the latter; **esto** [és·to] this, this thing; **éstos, éstas** *m., f. pl.* these; the latter.

este [és·te] *m.* east; east wind.

estela [es·té·la] *f.* wake of a ship.

estenógrafo [es·te·nó·ǥra·fo] *m.* stenographer.

estentóreo [es·ten·tó·re·o] *adj.* loud, thundering (*voice*).

estepa [es·té·pa] *f.* steppe, treeless plain.

estera [es·té·ra] *f.* matting; mat.

estercolar [es·ter·ko·lár] *v.* to manure, fertilize with manure.

estercolero [es·ter·ko·lé·ro] *m.* manure pile, manure dump; manure collector.

estereoscopio [es·te·re·os·kó·pjo] *m.* stereoscope.

estereotipo [es·te·re·o·tí·po] *m.* stereotype.

estéril [es·té·ril] *adj.* sterile, barren.

esterilidad [es·te·ri·li·ðáð] *f.* sterility, barrenness.

esterilizar[9] [es·te·ri·li·sár] *v.* to sterilize.

esterlina [es·te·ri·li·na] *adj.* sterling; **libra** — pound sterling.

estero [es·té·ro] *m.* estuary.

estertor [es·ter·tór] *m.* death-rattle; snort.

estético [es·té·ti·ko] *adj.* aesthetic; **estética** [es·té·ti·ka] *f.* aesthetics.

estetoscopio [es·te·tos·kó·pjo] *m.* stethoscope.

estibador [es·ti·βa·ðór] *m.* stevedore, longshoreman.

estibar [es·ti·βár] *v.* to stow (*in a boat*); to pack down, compress.

estiércol [es·tjér·kol] *m.* manure; fertilizer.

estigma [es·tíǥ·ma] *m.* stigma; brand, mark of disgrace; birthmark.

estilar [es·ti·lár] v. to use, be accustomed to using; -se to be in style (said of clothes).

estilete [es·ti·lé·te] m. stiletto, narrow-bladed dagger; stylet (instrument for probing wounds); long, narrow sword.

estilo [es·tí·lo] m. style; fashion.

estima [es·ti·ma] f. esteem.

estimación [es·ti·ma·sjón] f. esteem, regard; valuation.

estimar [es·ti·már] v. to esteem, regard highly; to estimate, appraise; to judge, think.

estimulante [es·ti·mu·lán·te] adj. stimulant, stimulating; m. stimulant.

estimular [es·ti·mu·lár] v. to stimulate, excite, goad.

estímulo [es·tí·mu·lo] m. stimulation, incitement; stimulus.

estío [es·tí·o] m. summer.

estipulación [es·ti·pu·la·sjón] f. stipulation, specification, provision, proviso.

estipular [es·ti·pu·lár] v. to stipulate, specify.

estirado [es·ti·rá·ḍo] p.p. & adj. stretched; extended, drawn out; stuck-up, conceited.

estirar [es·ti·rár] v. to stretch, extend; — la pata to die; -se to stretch out; Am. to die.

estirón [es·ti·rón] m. hard pull, tug; stretch; dar un — to grow suddenly (said of a child).

estirpe [es·tir·pe] f. lineage, family, race.

estival [es·ti·ḅál] adj. summer, relating to the summer.

estocada [es·to·ká·ḍa] f. thrust, stab; stab wound.

estofa [es·tó·fa] f. stuff, cloth; class, quality; gente de baja — low class people, rabble.

estofado [es·to·fá·ḍo] m. stew, stewed meat; p.p. of estofar.

estofar [es·to·fár] v. to quilt; to stew.

estoico [es·tój·ko] adj. & m. stoic.

estola [es·tó·la] f. stole; — de visón mink wrap.

estómago [es·tó·ma·/go] m. stomach.

estopa [es·tó·pa] f. burlap; oakum (loose fiber of old ropes).

estoque [es·tó·ke] m. long, narrow sword.

estorbar [es·tor·ḅár] v. to hinder; to obstruct.

estorbo [es·tór·ḅo] m. hindrance; nuisance, bother.

estornudar [es·tor·nu·ḍár] v. to sneeze.

estornudo [es·tor·nú·ḍo] m. sneeze.

estrado [es·trá·ḍo] m. dais (platform for a throne, seats of honor, etc.); main part of a parlor or drawing room.

estragado [es·tra·gá·ḍo] p.p. & adj. corrupted; spoiled; ruined; tired, worn out.

estragar[7] [es·tra·gár] v. to corrupt, contaminate; to spoil; to ruin.

estrago [es·trá·go] m. havoc, ruin; massacre.

estrangulador [es·traŋ·gu·la·ḍór] m. strangler, choke (of an automobile); adj. strangling.

estrangular [es·traŋ·gu·lár] v. to strangle; to choke, throttle.

estratagema [es·tra·ta·xé·ma] f. stratagem, scheme.

estrategia [es·tra·té·xja] f. strategy.

estratégico [es·tra·té·xi·ko] adj. strategic; m. strategist, person trained or skilled in strategy.

estrato [es·trá·to] m. stratum, layer (of mineral).

estratorreactor [es·tra·to·rre·ak·tór] m. supersonic jet plane.

estratosfera [es·tra·tos·fé·ra] f. stratosphere.

estrechar [es·tre·čár] v. to tighten; to narrow down; to embrace, hug; — la mano to squeeze, grasp another's hand; to shake hands.

estrechez [es·tre·čés], **estrechura** [es·tre·čú·ra] f. narrowness; tightness; austerity; dire straits;

poverty; closeness.

estrecho [es·tré·čo] adj. narrow; tight; m. strait, narrow passage.

estrella [es·tré·ya] f. star; — de mar starfish.

estrellado [es·tre·yá·ḍo] adj. starry; spangled with stars; huevos -s fried eggs.

estrellar [es·tre·yár] v. to shatter; to dash to pieces; to star, spangle with stars; -se to shatter, break into pieces; to fail.

estremecer[13] [es·tre·me·sér] v. irr. to shake; -se to shiver, shudder; to vibrate.

estremecimiento [es·tre·me·si·mjén·to] m. shiver, shudder; vibration; shaking.

estrenar [es·tre·nár] v. to wear for the first time; to perform (a play) for the first time; to inaugurate; to begin.

estreno [es·tré·no] m. début, first appearance or performance.

estreñimiento [es·tre·ñi·mjén·to] m. constipation.

estreñir[5, 19] [es·tre·ñír] v. irr. to constipate; -se to become constipated.

estrépito [es·tré·pi·to] m. racket, noise, crash.

estrepitoso [es·tre·pi·tó·so] adj. noisy; boisterous.

estriado [es·trjá·ḍo] p.p. & adj. fluted, grooved; streaked.

estriar[17] [es·trjár] v. to groove; to flute (as a column).

estribación [es·tri·ḅa·sjón] f. spur (of a mountain or mountain range).

estribar [es·tri·ḅár] v. to rest (upon); eso estriba en que . . . the basis or reason for it is that . . .

estribillo [es·tri·ḅí·yo] m. refrain.

estribo [es·tri·ḅo] m. (de caballo o vehículo) stirrup; footboard, running board; (apoyo) support; brace; spur (of a mountain); perder los -s to lose one's balance; to lose control of oneself.

estribor [es·tri·ḅór] m. starboard.

estricto [es·trík·to] adj. strict.

estrofa [es·tró·fa] f. strophe, stanza.

estroncio [es·trón·sjo] m. strontium.

estropajo [es·tro·pá·xo] m. fibrous mass (for scrubbing); tratar a uno como un — to treat someone scornfully.

estropear [es·tro·pe·ár] v. to spoil, ruin, damage; to cripple.

estructura [es·truk·tú·ra] f. structure.

estructural [es·truk·tu·rál] adj. structural.

estruendo [es·trwén·do] m. clatter; clamor, din, racket.

estruendoso [es·trwen·dó·so] adj. thunderous, uproarious, deafening.

estrujamiento [es·tru·xa·mjén·to] m. crushing, squeezing.

estrujar [es·tru·xár] v. to squeeze, press, crush.

estrujón [es·tru·xón] m. squeeze, crush; smashing.

estuario [es·twá·rjo] m. estuary.

estuco [es·tú·ko] m. stucco.

estuche [es·tú·če] m. jewel box; instrument case, kit; small casket; sheath.

estudiantado [es·tu·ḍjan·ta·ḍo] m. the student body (of a school or college).

estudiante [es·tu·ḍján·te] m. & f. student.

estudiantil [es·tu·ḍjan·tíl] adj. pertaining to students.

estudiar [es·tu·ḍjár] v. to study.

estudio [es·tú·ḍjo] m. study; studio.

estudioso [es·tu·ḍjó·so] adj. studious; m. learner.

estufa [es·tú·fa] f. heater; stove; hothouse; steam room; steam cabinet.

estupefacto [es·tu·pe·fák·to] adj. stunned; speechless.

ES

estupendo [es·tu·pén·do] *adj.* stupendous, marvelous.

estupidez [es·tu·pi·déś] *f.* stupidity.

estúpido [es·tú·pi·do] *adj.* stupid.

esturión [es·tu·rjón] *m.* sturgeon.

etapa [e·tá·pa] *f.* stage, lap (*of a journey or race*); army food rations; epoch, period.

éter [é·ter] *m.* ether.

etéreo [e·té·re·o] *adj.* ethereal; heavenly.

eternidad [e·ter·ni·dáḍ] *f.* eternity.

eternizar[9] [e·ter·ni·sár] *v.* to prolong excessively; to perpetuate, make eternal.

eterno [e·tér·no] *adj.* eternal, everlasting.

ética [é·ti·ka] *f.* ethics; **ético** *adj.* ethical, moral.

etimología [e·ti·mo·lo·xí·a] *f.* etymology.

etiqueta [e·ti·ké·ta] *f.* etiquette; formality; tag; **de** — formal (*dress, function, etc.*).

étnico [ét·ni·ko] *adj.* ethnic.

eucalipto [ew·ka·líp·to] *m.* eucalyptus.

Eucaristía [ew·ka·ris·tí·a] *f.* Eucharist.

euforia [ew·fó·rja] *f.* euphoria.

europeo [ew·ro·pé·o] *adj. & m.* European.

evacuación [e·ḅa·kwa·sjón] *f.* evacuation; bowel movement.

evacuar[18] [e·ḅa·kwár] *v.* to evacuate, empty; to vacate.

evadir [e·ḅa·ḍír] *v.* to evade, elude; **-se** to slip away, escape.

evaluar[18] [e·ḅa·lwar] *v.* to evaluate, appraise.

evangelio [e·ḅaŋ·xé·ljo] *m.* gospel.

evaporar [e·ḅa·po·rár] *v.* to evaporate; **-se** to evaporate; to vanish, disappear.

evasión [e·ḅa·sjón] *f.* evasion, dodge, escape.

evasiva [e·ḅa·sí·ḅa] *f.* evasion, dodge, escape.

evasivo [e·ḅa·sí·ḅo] *adj.* evasive.

evasor [e·ḅa·sór] *m.* evader, dodger.

evento [e·ḅén·to] *m.* event.

evidencia [e·ḅi·dén·sja] *f.* evidence.

evidenciar [e·ḅi·den·sjár] *v.* to prove, show, make evident.

evidente [e·ḅi·ḍén·te] *adj.* evident.

evitable [e·ḅi·tá·ḅle] *adj.* avoidable.

evitar [e·ḅi·tár] *v.* to avoid, shun.

evocar[6] [e·ḅo·kár] *v.* to evoke, call forth.

evolución [e·ḅo·lu·sjón] *f.* evolution.

evolucionar [e·ḅo·lu·sjo·nár] *v.* to evolve; to perform maneuvers; to go through changes.

exacerbar [ek·sa·ser·ḅár] *v.* to exasperate, irritate; to aggravate, make worse.

exactitud [ek·sak·ti·túḍ] *f.* exactness, precision; punctuality.

exacto [ek·sák·to] *adj.* exact, precise; punctual.

exagerar [ek·sa·xe·rár] *v.* to exaggerate.

exaltación [ek·sal·ta·sjón] *f.* exaltation; excitement.

exaltado [ek·sal·tá·ḍo] *adj.* elated; excited; hotheaded.

exaltar [ek·sal·tár] *v.* to exalt, elevate, glorify; to praise; **-se** to get excited; to become upset emotionally.

examen [ek·sá·men] *m.* examination; inspection.

examinar [ek·sa·mi·nár] *v.* to examine; to inspect.

exangüe [ek·sáŋ·gwe] *adj.* lacking blood; anemic; exhausted.

exánime [ek·sá·ni·me] *adj.* lifeless, motionless; weak, faint.

exasperar [ek·sas·pe·rár] *v.* to exasperate, irritate, annoy.

excavar [es·ka·ḅár] *v.* to excavate, dig, dig out.

excedente [ek·se·ḍén·te] *m.* surplus; *adj.* exceeding, extra.

exceder [ek·se·ḍér] *v.* to exceed, surpass; to

overdo; **-se** to go beyond the proper limit; to misbehave.

excelencia [ek·se·lén·sja] *f.* excellence, superiority; excellency (*title*).

excelente [ek·se·lén·te] *adj.* excellent.

excelso [ek·sél·so] *adj.* lofty, elevated; sublime; **El Excelso** the Most High.

excéntrico [ek·sén·tri·ko] *adj.* eccentric; queer, odd.

excepción [ek·sep·sjón] *f.* exception.

excepcional [ek·sep·sjo·nál] *adj.* exceptional, unusual.

excepto [ek·sép·to] *adv.* except, with the exception of.

exceptuar[18] [ek·sep·twár] *v.* to except.

excesivo [ek·se·sí·ḅọ] *adj.* excessive.

exceso [ek·sé·so] *m.* excess; crime; — **de equipaje** excess baggage; **en** — in excess, excessively.

excitación [ek·si·ta·sjón] *f.* excitement.

excitante [ek·si·tán·te] *adj.* exciting; stimulating.

excitar [ek·si·tár] *v.* to excite, stir; **-se** to get excited.

exclamación [es·kla·ma·sjón] *f.* exclamation.

exclamar [es·kla·már] *v.* to exclaim.

excluir[32] [es·klwír] *v. irr.* to exclude.

exclusivo [es·klu·sí·ḅo] *adj.* exclusive.

excomunicar[6] [es·ko·mu·ni·kár] *v.* to excommunicate.

excomunión [es·ko·mu·njón] *f.* excommunication.

excrecencia [es·kre·sén·sja], **excrescencia** [es·kre·sén·sja] *f.* excrescence (*abnormal growth or tumor*).

excremento [es·kre·mén·to] *m.* excrement.

excursión [es·kur·sjón] *f.* excursion, tour, outing.

excusa [es·kú·sa] *f.* excuse.

excusado [es·ku·sá·ḍo] *p.p. & adj.* excused; exempt; superfluous; unnecessary; reserved, private; *m.* toilet.

excusar [es·ku·sár] *v.* (*disculpar*) to excuse; to exempt; (*evitar*) to avoid, shun; **-se** to excuse oneself, apologize; to decline.

exención [ek·sen·sjón] *f.* exemption.

exentar [ek·sen·tár] *v.* to exempt. See **eximir**.

exento [ek·sén·to] *adj.* exempt, freed; free, unobstructed.

exequias [ek·sé·kjas] *f. pl.* obsequies, funeral rites.

exhalar [ek·sa·lár] *v.* to exhale; to emit, give off; to breathe forth; **-se** to evaporate; to run away.

exhibición [ek·si·ḅi·sjón] *f.* exhibition; exposition; *Mex.* payment of an installment.

exhibir [ek·si·ḅír] *v.* to exhibit; *Mex.* to pay for in installments (*stocks, policies, etc.*); **-se** to exhibit oneself, show off.

exhortar [ek·sor·tár] *v.* to exhort, admonish.

exigencia [ek·si·xén·sja] *f.* demand; urgent want; emergency.

exigente [ek·si·xén·te] *adj.* demanding, exacting; urgent.

exigir[11] [ek·si·xír] *v.* to require; to demand; to exact.

exiguo [ek·sí·gwo] *adj.* scanty, meager.

eximio [ek·si·mjo] *adj.* very distinguished.

eximir [ek·si·mír] *v.* to exempt, except, excuse; **-se de** to avoid, shun.

existencia [ek·sis·tén·sja] *f.* existence; **-s** stock on hand, goods; **en** — in stock, on hand.

existente [ek·sis·tén·te] *adj.* existent, existing; in stock.

existir [ek·sis·tír] *v.* to exist.

éxito [ék·si·to] *m.* outcome, result; success; **tener buen (mal)** — to be successful (unsuccessful).

éxodo [ék·so·ḍo] *m.* exodus, emigration.

exonerar [ek·so·ne·rár] *v.* to exonerate, free from blame; to relieve of a burden or position; to dismiss.

exorbitante [ek·sor·þi·tán·te] *adj.* exorbitant, excessive, extravagant.

exótico [ek·só·ti·ko] *adj.* exotic, foreign, strange; quaint.

expansión [es·pan·sjón] *f.* expansion; relaxation; recreation.

expansivo [es·pan·si·þo] *adj.* expansive; demonstrative, effusive.

expatriar [es·pa·trjár] *v.* to expatriate, exile; **-se** to expatriate oneself, renounce one's citizenship; to emigrate.

expectación [es·pek·ta·sjón] *f.* expectation.

expectativa [es·pek·ta·tí·þa] *f.* expectation; hope, prospect; **estar en — de algo** to be expecting, or on the lookout for, something.

expectorar [es·pek·to·rár] *v.* to expectorate, cough up.

expedición [es·pe· di·sjón] *f.* expedition; dispatch, promptness; papal dispatch or bull.

expedicionario [es·pe·di·sjo·ná·rjo] *adj.* expeditionary; *m.* member of an expedition; explorer.

expediente [es·pe·djén·te] *m.* certificate; papers pertaining to a business matter; expedient, means; dispatch, promptness.

expedir[5] [es·pe·dír] *v. irr.* to dispatch; to issue officially; to remit, send.

expeler [es·pe·lér] *v.* to expel, eject.

experiencia [es·pe·rjén·sja] *f.* experience; experiment.

experimentado [es·pe·ri·men·tá·do] *adj. & p.p.* experienced.

experimental [es·pe·ri·men·tál] *adj.* experimental.

experimentar [es·pe·ri·men·tár] *v.* to experiment, try, test; to experience, feel.

experimento [es·pe·ri·mén·to] *m.* experiment, trial.

experto [es·pér·to] *adj.* expert, skillful; *m.* expert.

expiación [es·pja·sjón] *f.* expiation, atonement.

expiar[17] [es·pjár] *v.* to atone for; to make amends for; to purify.

expirar [es·pi·rár] *v.* to die; to expire, come to an end.

explayar [es·pla·yár] *v.* to extend; **-se** to become extended; to relax in the open air; to enlarge upon a subject; **-se con un amigo** to unbosom oneself, speak with utmost frankness with a friend.

explicable [es·pli·ká·þle] *adj.* explainable.

explicación [es·pli·ka·sjón] *f.* explanation.

explicar[6] [es·pli·kár] *v.* to explain; **— una cátedra** to teach a course; **-se** to explain oneself; to account for one's conduct.

explicativo [es·pli·ka·tí·þo] *adj.* explanatory, explaining.

explícito [es·plí·si·to] *adj.* explicit, express, clear, definite.

exploración [es·plo·ra·sjón] *f.* exploration.

explorador [es·plo·ra·dór] *m.* explorer, scout; *adj.* exploring.

explorar [es·plo·rár] *v.* to explore.

explosión [es·plo·sjón] *f.* explosion.

explosivo [es·plo·si·þo] *adj. & m.* explosive.

explotación [es·plo·ta·sjón] *f.* exploitation; operation of a mine; development of a business; plant.

explotar [es·plo·tár] *v.* to exploit, operate, develop; to utilize, profit by; to make unfair use of; *Am.* to explode.

exponer[40] [es·po·nér] *v. irr.* (*dejar ver*) to expose, reveal; to show, exhibit; to display; (*sin protección*) to leave unprotected, to expose (*film*); (*explicar*) to expound; to explain; **-se a** to expose oneself to; to run the risk of.

exportación [es·por·ta·sjón] *f.* exportation; export.

exportar [es·por·tár] *v.* to export.

exposición [es·po·si·sjón] *f.* exposition; exhibition; explanation; exposure.

exprés [es·prés] *m. Am.* express; *Am.* express company.

expresar [es·pre·sár] *v.* to express; **-se** to express oneself, speak.

expresión [es·pre·sjón] *f.* expression; utterance; **-es** regards.

expresivo [es·pre·si·þo] *adj.* expressive; affectionate.

expreso [es·pré·so] *adj.* expressed; express, clear, exact; fast; *m.* express train.

exprimir [es·pri·mír] *v.* to squeeze, extract (*juice*); to wring out; to express, utter.

expuesto [es·pwés·to] *p.p. of* **exponer** & *adj.* exposed; expressed; displayed; risky, dangerous; **lo —** what has been said.

expulsar [es·pul·sár] *v.* to expel, eject.

expulsión [es·pul·sjón] *f.* expulsion, expelling.

exquisitez [es·ki·si·tés] *f.* exquisiteness.

exquisito [es·ki·sí·to] *adj.* exquisite.

extasiado [es·ta·sjá·do] *adj.* rapt, in ecstasy; *p.p. of* **extasiar.**

extasiar[17] [es·ta·sjár] *v.* to delight; **-se** to be in ecstasy; to be entranced.

éxtasis [és·ta·sis] *m.* ecstasy.

extender[1] [es·ten·dér] *v. irr.* to extend; to spread; to unfold; to draw up (*a document*); **-se** to extend, spread; to expatiate, be too wordy.

extensión [es·ten·sjón] *f.* extension; extent; expanse; expansion.

extensivo [es·ten·sí·þo] *adj.* extensive.

extenso [es·tén·so] *p.p. irr. of* **extender** extended; *adj.* extensive, vast, spacious; **por —** extensively, in detail.

extenuado [es·te·nwá·do] *adj.* wasted, weak, emaciated.

exterior [es·te·rjór] *adj.* exterior, outer; *m.* exterior; outside; outward appearance.

exterminar [es·ter·mi·nár] *v.* to exterminate.

exterminio [es·ter·mí·njo] *m.* extermination, destruction.

externo [es·tér·no] *adj.* external, outward.

extinguir[12] [es·tiŋ·gír] *v.* to extinguish, put out; to destroy.

extinto [es·tín·to] *adj.* extinct.

extintor [es·tin·tór] *m.* extinguisher; **— de espuma** fire extinguisher.

extirpar [es·tir·pár] *v.* to eradicate, pull out by the roots, root out, remove completely; to destroy completely.

extorsión [es·tor·sjón] *f.* extortion.

extorsionar [es·tor·sjo·nár] *v. Am.* to extort, extract money, blackmail.

extorsionista [es·tor·sjo·nís·ta] *m. Am.* extortioner, profiteer, racketeer.

extracto [es·trák·to] *m.* extract; abstract, summary.

extraer[46] [es·tra·ér] *v. irr.* to extract.

extranjero [es·tran·xé·ro] *adj.* foreign; *m.* foreigner.

extrañamiento [es·tra·ña·mjén·to] *m.* wonder, surprise, amazement.

extrañar [es·tra·ñár] *v.* to wonder at; to banish; *Am.* to miss (*a person or thing*); **-se** to marvel, be astonished.

extrañeza [es·tra·ñé·sa] *f.* strangeness; surprise,

astonishment; oddity, odd thing.
extraño [es·trá·ño] *adj.* strange; rare; odd; *m.* stranger.
extraordinario [es·tra·or·ḍi·ná·rjo] *adj.* extraordinary.
extravagancia [es·tra·ḅa·ǵán·sja] *f.* extravagance; folly.
extravagante [es·tra·ḅa·ǵán·te] *adj.* extravagant, fantastic; queer, odd.
extraviar[17] [es·tra·ḅjár] *v.* to lead astray; to strand; to misplace; **-se** to lose one's way; to get stranded; to get lost; to miss the road.
extravío [es·tra·ḅí·o] *m.* deviation, straying; error; misconduct; damage.
extremado [es·tre·má·ḍo] *adj.* extreme; extremely good or extremely bad; *p.p. of* **extremar.**
extremar [es·tre·már] *v.* to carry to an extreme; **-se** to take great pains, exert great effort.
extremidad [es·tre·mi·ḍáḍ] *f.* extremity; extreme degree; remotest part; **-es** extremities, hands and feet.
extremo [es·tré·mo] *adj.* extreme, last; farthest; excessive; utmost; *m.* extreme, highest degree or point; end, extremity; extreme care; **con (en** *or* **por) —** very much, extremely.
exuberante [ek·su·ḅe·rán·te] *adj.* exuberant; luxuriant.

F:f

fa [fa] *m.* fourth note of the musical scale (*solfa syllables*).
fabada [fa·ḅá·ḍa] *f.* a bean and bacon soup popular in Spain.
fábrica [fá·ḅri·ka] *f.* manufacture; factory, mill; structure.
fabricación [fa·ḅri·ka·sjón] *f.* manufacture.
fabricante [fa·ḅri·kán·te] *m.* manufacturer, maker.
fabricar[6] [fa·ḅri·kár] *v.* to manufacture, make; to construct, build; to fabricate, make up, invent.
fabril [fa·ḅríl] *adj.* manufacturing.
fábula [fá·ḅu·la] *f.* fable, tale; falsehood.
fabuloso [fa·ḅu·ló·so] *adj.* fabulous; false, imaginary.
facción [fak·sjón] *f.* faction, band, party; battle; **-es** features; **estar de —** to be on duty.
faceta [fa·se·ta] *f.* facet.
faceto [fa·sé·to] *adj. Am.* cute, funny; *Am.* affected.
fácil [fá·sil] *adj.* easy; docile, yielding, manageable; likely; probable.
facilidad [fa·si·li·ḍáḍ] *f.* facility, ease; opportunity.
facilitar [fa·si·li·tár] *v.* to facilitate, make easy; to furnish; give; **— todos los datos** to furnish all the data.
facón [fa·kón] *m. Riopl., Bol.* dagger, large knife; **faconazo** [fa·ko·ná·so] *m. Riopl., Bol.* stab.
factible [fak·tí·ḅle] *adj.* feasible.
factor [fak·tór] *m.* factor; element, joint cause; commercial agent; baggage man.
factoría [fak·to·rí·a] *f.* trading post; *Am.* factory.
factura [fak·tú·ra] *f.* (*cuenta*) invoice, itemized bill; (*hechura*) make; workmanship, form; *Am.* roll, biscuit, muffin; **— simulada** temporary invoice, memorandum.
facturar [fak·tu·rár] *v.* to invoice, bill; to check (*baggage*).
facultad [fa·kul·táḍ] *f.* faculty; ability, aptitude; power, right; permission; branch of learning; school or college of a university.
facultativo [fa·kul·ta·tí·ḅo] *m.* doctor, physician.

facundia [fa·kún·dja] *f.* eloquence, fluency, facility in speaking, gift of expression.
facha [fá·ča] *f.* appearance, figure, aspect, looks.
fachada [fa·čá·ḍa] *f.* façade, front (*of a building*); title page.
fachenda [fa·čén·da] *f.* ostentation, vanity.
fachendoso [fa·čen·dó·so] *adj.* vain, boastful, ostentatious.
faena [fa·é·na] *f.* task, job, duty; *Carib., Mex., C.A.* extra job; *Ch.* work crew, labor gang.
faja [fá·xa] *f.* sash; girdle; band; *Am.* belt, waist band.
fajar [fa·xár] *v.* to girdle; to bind, wrap, or bandage with a strip of cloth; *Am.* to beat, strike, thrash; *Am.* **— un latigazo a uno** to whip, thrash someone; **-se** to put on a sash or belt; to tighten one's sash or belt; *Am.* **-se con** to have a fight with, come to blows with.
fajo [fá·xo] *m.* bundle; sheaf.
falaz [fa·lás] *adj.* illusive, illustory; deceitful, deceiving.
falda [fál·da] *f.* skirt; lap; hat brim; foothill, slope; **faldón** [fal·dón] *m.* coattail; shirttail.
faldear [fal·de·ár] *v.* to skirt (*a hill*).
falsario [fal·sá·rjo] *m.* crook, forger; liar.
falsear [fal·se·ár] *v.* to falsify, misrepresent; to counterfeit; to forge; to pick (*a lock*); to flag, grow weak; to hit a wrong note.
falsedad [fal·se·ḍáḍ] *f.* falsehood, lie; deceit.
falsificación [fal·si·fi·ka·sjón] *f.* falsification, forgery; counterfeit.
falsificar[6] [fal·si·fi·kár] *v.* to falsify, make false; to counterfeit; to forge.
falso [fál·so] *adj.* false; untrue, unreal; deceitful; counterfeit; sham; *C.A.* cowardly; *m.* inside facing of a dress; lining; *Mex.* false testimony, slander; **en —** upon a false foundation; without proper security; *Am.* **coger a uno en —** to catch one lying.
falta [fál·ta] *f.* (*defecto*) lack, want; fault, mistake; defect; absence; (*infracción*) misdemeanor, offense; **a — de** for want of; **hacer —** to be necessary; to be missing; **me hace —** I need it; **sin —** without fail.
faltar [fal·tár] *v.* to be lacking, wanting; to be absent or missing; to fail, be of no use or help; to fail to fulfill (*a promise or duty*); to die; *Mex., C.A.* to insult; **— poco para las cinco** to be almost five o'clock; **¡no fáltaba más!** that's the last straw!; why, the very idea!
falto [fál·to] *adj.* lacking; deficient, short; *Am.* foolish, stupid.
faltriquera [fal·tri·ké·ra] *f.* pocket.
falla [fá·ya] *f.* fault, defect; failure; fault (*fracture in the earth's crust*); *Riopl.* baby's bonnet; **-s** popular *fiestas* of Valencia, Spain.
fallar [fa·yár] *v.* (*juzgar*) to render a verdict; (*fracasar*) to fail, be deficient; to default; to miss; to fail to hit; to give way, break; to trump.
fallecer[13] [fa·ye·sér] *v. irr.* to die.
fallecimiento [fa·ye·si·mjén·to] *m.* decease, death.
fallido [fa·yí·do] *adj.* frustrated; bankrupt.
fallo [fá·yo] *m.* verdict, judgment; decision; *adj.* lacking (*a card, or suit, in card games*); *Ch.* silly, foolish.
fama [fá·ma] *f.* fame, reputation; rumor, report; *Ch.* bull's-eye, center of a target.
famélico [fa·mé·li·ko] *adj.* ravenous, hungry, starved.
familia [fa·mi·lja] *f.* family.
familiar [fa·mi·ljár] *adj.* domestic, homelike;

familiar, well-known; friendly, informal; colloquial (*phrase or expression*); *m.* intimate friend; member of a household; domestic servant; familiar spirit, demon; *Am.* relative.
familiaridad [fa·mi·lja·ri·ḍáḍ] *f.* familiarity, informality.
familiarizar[9] [fa·mi·lja·ri·sár] *v.* to familiarize, acquaint; **-se** to acquaint oneself, become familiar (with).
famoso [fa·mó·so] *adj.* famous; excellent.
fanal [fa·nál] *m.* beacon, lighthouse; lantern; headlight; bell jar, glass cover.
fanático [fa·ná·ti·ko] *adj.* & *m.* fanatic.
fanatismo [fa·na·tíz·mo] *m.* fanaticism.
fanega [fa·né·ḡa] *f.* Spanish bushel; — **de tierra** land measure (*variable according to region*).
fanfarrón [fan·fa·rrón] *m.* braggart, boaster; bluffer.
fanfarronada [fan·fa·rro·ná·ḍa] *f.* boast, brag, swagger, bluff.
fanfarronear [fan·fa·rro·ne·ár] *v.* to bluff, brag; to swagger.
fango [fáŋ·go] *m.* mud, mire.
fangoso [faŋ·gó·so] *adj.* muddy, miry.
fantasear [fan·ta·se·ár] *v.* to fancy; to imagine.
fantasía [fan·ta·sí·a] *f.* fantasy, imagination, fancy, whim; **-s** string of pearls; *Ven.* **tocar por** — to play by ear.
fantasma [fan·táz·ma] *m.* phantom, image; vision, ghost; *f.* scarecrow.
fantasmagórico [fan·taz·ma·ḡó·ri·ko] *adj.* fantastic, unreal, illusory.
fantástico [fan·tás·ti·ko] *adj.* fantastic.
fardel [far·ḍél] *m.* knapsack, bag; bundle.
fardo [fár·ḍo] *m.* bundle; bale, *Riopl., Andes* **pasar el** — to "pass the buck", shift the responsibility to someone else.
faringe [fa·ríŋ·xe] *f.* pharynx.
faríngeo [fa·ríŋ·xe·o] *adj.* pharyngeal.
farmacéutico [far·ma·séw·ti·ko] *m.* pharmacist, druggist; *adj.* pharmaceutical (*pertaining to a pharmacy or pharmacists*).
farmacia [far·má·sja] *f.* pharmacy; drugstore.
faro [fá·ro] *m.* lighthouse; beacon; *Am.* headlight.
farol [fa·ról] *m.* (*linterna*) lantern; street lamp; (*fachendoso*) conceit, self-importance; *Riopl.* balcony; *Am.* presumptuous man; *Am.* bluff; **darse** — to show off; to put on airs.
farola [fa·ró·la] *f.* street light; lamppost.
farolero [fa·ro·lé·ro] *adj.* vain, ostentatious; *m.* lamp maker or vendor; lamplighter (*person*).
farra [fá·rra] *f.* *Riopl., Ch., Col., Ven., Andes* spree, revelry, wild party, noisy merrymaking; *Riopl., Ch., Col., Ven., Andes* **ir de** — to go on a spree.
farsa [fár·sa] *f.* farce; company of actors; sham, fraud.
farsante [far·sán·te] *m.* charlatan, bluffer; quack; comedian; wag.
fascinación [fa·si·na·sjón] *f.* fascination; glamour.
fascinador [fa·si·na·ḍór] *adj.* fascinating, glamorous; charming.
fascinar [fa·si·nár] *v.* to fascinate, bewitch, charm; to allure.
fascismo [fa·síz·mo] *m.* fascism.
fascista [fa·sís·ta] *m.* & *f.* fascist.
fase [fá·se] *f.* phase, aspect.
fastidiar [fas·ti·djár] *v.* to annoy, bother; to bore; *Col., P.R.* to hurt, harm, ruin.
fastidio [fas·tí·ḍjo] *m.* boredom; disgust; nuisance, annoyance.
fastidioso [fas·ti·ḍjó·so] *adj.* annoying, bothersome; boring, tiresome.

fatal [fa·tál] *adj.* fatal; mortal, deadly; unfortunate.
fatalidad [fa·ta·li·ḍáḍ] *f.* fatality, destiny; calamity, misfortune.
fatalismo [fa·ta·líz·mo] *m.* fatalism.
fatiga [fa·tí·ḡa] *f.* fatigue, weariness; toil; **-s** hardships.
fatigar[7] [fa·ti·ḡár] *v.* to fatigue, weary; to bother.
fatigoso [fa·ti·ḡó·so] *adj.* fatiguing, tiring.
fatuo [fá·two] *adj.* foolish, stupid; vain; **fuego** — will-o'-the-wisp.
favor [fa·ḅór] *m.* favor; kindness; help, aid; protection; *Am.* ribbon bow; **a** — **de** in favor of; **hágame el** — please.
favorable [fa·ḅó·rá·ḅle] *adj.* favorable.
favorecer[13] [fa·ḅo·re·sér] *v. irr.* to favor, help, protect.
favoritismo [fa·ḅo·ri·tíz·mo] *m.* favoritism.
favorito [fa·ḅo·rí·to] *adj.* & *m.* favorite.
faz [fas] *f.* face.
fe [fe] *f.* faith; — **de bautismo** baptismal certificate.
fealdad [fe·al·dáḍ] *f.* ugliness, homeliness; foulness, foul or immoral action.
febrero [fe·ḅré·ro] *m.* February.
febril [fe·ḅríl] *adj.* feverish.
fécula [fé·ku·la] *f.* starch.
fecundar [fe·kun·dár] *v.* to fertilize.
fecundo [fe·kún·do] *adj.* fruitful, fertile, productive.
fecha [fé·ča] *f.* date.
fechar [fe·čár] *v.* to date.
fechoría [fe·čo·rí·a] *f.* misdeed, misdemeanor.
federación [fe·ḍe·ra·sjón] *f.* federation, union.
federal [fe·ḍe·rál] *adj.* federal.
felicidad [fe·li·si·ḍáḍ] *f.* happiness; **i-es!** congratulations.
felicitación [fe·li·si·ta·sjón] *f.* congratulation.
felicitar [fe·li·si·tár] *v.* to congratulate.
feligrés [fe·li·grés] *m.* parishioner.
feliz [fe·lís] *adj.* happy; lucky.
felpa [fél·pa] *f.* plush.
felpudo [fel·pú·ḍo] *adj.* plushy, like plush; *m.* small plushlike mat; door mat.
femenil [fe·me·níl] *adj.* womanly, feminine.
femenino [fe·me·ní·no] *adj.* feminine.
fementido [fe·men·tí·ḍo] *adj.* false; treacherous.
fenecer[13] [fe·ne·sér] *v. irr.* to die; to finish, end.
fénico [fé·ni·ko] *adj.* carbolic; **acido** — carbolic acid.
fénix [fé·nis] *m.* phoenix (*mythical bird*).
fenómeno [fe·nó·me·no] *m.* phenomenon.
feo [fé·o] *adj.* ugly, homely; *Am.* bad (*referring to taste or odor*); **feote** [fe·ó·te] *adj.* hideous, very ugly.
féretro [fé·re·tro] *m.* bier; coffin.
feria [fé·rja] *f.* fair; market; *Mex.* change (*money*); *Am.* tip; **-s** *Am.* present given to servants or the poor during holidays.
feriante [fe·rján·te] *m.* & *f.* trader at fairs; trader; peddler.
feriar [fe·rjár] *v.* to trade.
fermentar [fer·men·tár] *v.* to ferment.
fermento [fer·mén·to] *m.* ferment; yeast, leaven.
ferocidad [fe·ro·si·ḍáḍ] *f.* ferocity, fierceness.
feroz [fe·rós] *adj.* ferocious, wild, fierce.
férreo [fé·rre·o] *adj.* ferrous (*pertaining to or derived from iron*); ironlike; harsh; **vía férrea** railroad.
ferretería [fe·rre·te·rí·a] *f.* hardware shop; hardware.
ferrocarril [fe·rro·ka·rríl] *m.* railroad.
ferroviario [fe·rro·ḅjá·rjo] *adj.* railway, railroad (*used as adj.*); *m.* railroad man; railroad

employee.

fértil [fér·til] *adj.* fertile, productive; **fertilidad** [fer·ti·li·ḍaḍ] *f.* fertility.

fertilizar[9] [fer·ti·li·sár] *v.* to fertilize.

ferviente [fer·ḅjén·te] *adj.* fervent, ardent.

fervor [fer·ḅór] *m.* fervor, zeal, devotion.

fervoroso [fer·ḅo·ró·so] *adj.* fervent, ardent; pious, devout; zealous.

festejar [fes·te·xár] *v.* to feast, entertain; to celebrate; to woo; *Mex.* to thrash, beat.

festejo [fes·té·xo] *m.* entertainment, festival, celebration; courtship; *Am.* revelry.

festín [fes·tín] *m.* feast; banquet.

festividad [fes·ti·ḅi·ḍáḍ] *f.* festival; holiday; holy day; festivity, gaiety, rejoicing.

festivo [fes·ti·ḅo] *adj.* festive, gay; **día** — holiday.

fétido [fé·ti·ḍo] *adj.* foul, foul-smelling.

fiado [fjá·ḍo] *p.p. of* **fiar**; **al** — on credit.

fiador [fja·ḍór] *m.* guarantor, backer, bondsman; *Ec., Ch.* chin strap, hat guard.

fiambre [fjám·bre] *m.* cold meat; cold or late news; *Riopl., Mex., Col., Ven.* cold meat salad; *Am.* flop, failure (*referring to a party*).

fianza [fján·sa] *f.* bond, security, surety, guarantee; bail.

fiar[17] [fjar] to trust; to guarantee, back; *Am.* to borrow on credit; **-se de** to place confidence in.

fibra [fí·ḅra] *f.* fiber; **fibroso** *adj.* fibrous.

ficción [fik·sjón] *f.* fiction.

ficticio [fik·tí·sjo] *adj.* fictitious.

ficha [fí·ča] *f.* (*pieza*) chip; token; domino; (*tarjeta*) file card; *Am.* check (*used in barbershops and stores*); *Am.* rascal, scamp; **fichero** [fi·čé·ro] *m.* file, card index, filing cabinet.

fidedigno [fi·ḍe·ḍiġ·no] *adj.* trustworthy, reliable.

fidelidad [fi·ḍe·li·ḍáḍ] *f.* fidelity, faithfulness.

fideo [fi·ḍé·o] *m.* vermicelli, thin noodle; thin person.

fiebre [fjé·ḅre] *f.* fever; excitement, agitation; *Ch.* astute person.

fiel [fjel] *adj.* faithful; true, accurate; *m.* public inspector; pointer of a balance or scale; pin of the scissors; **los -es** the worshipers, the congregation.

fieltro [fjél·tro] *m.* felt; felt hat; felt rug.

fiera [fjé·ra] *f.* wild beast; *Am.* go-getter, hustler; **ser una — para el trabajo** to be a demon for work.

fiereza [fje·ré·sa] *f.* ferocity, fierceness; cruelty; ugliness.

fiero [fjé·ro] *adj.* fierce, ferocious, wild; cruel; ugly, horrible; huge; *m.* threat; **echar** (*or* **hacer**) **-s** to threaten; to boast.

fierro [fjé·rro] *m. Am.* iron; *Am.* iron bar; *Am.* cattle brand; **-s** *Am.* tools, implements. *See* **hierro.**

fiesta [fjés·ta] *f.* festivity, celebration, entertainment; holiday; **estar de** — to be in a holiday mood; **hacer -s a uno** to fawn on a person.

fiestero [fjes·té·ro] *adj.* fond of parties, fond of entertaining; gay, festive; playful; *m.* merrymaker.

figón [fi·ġón] *m.* cheap eating house, "joint."

figura [fi·ġú·ra] *f.* figure; shape, form; countenance; face card.

figurado [fi·ġu·rá·ḍo] *adj.* figurative.

figurar [fi·ġu·rár] *v.* to figure; to form; to represent, symbolize; **-se** to imagine; **se me figura** I think, guess, or imagine.

figurín [fi·ġu·rín] *m.* fashion plate; dandy.

fijar [fi·xár] *v.* to fix, fasten; to establish; **-se** to settle; **-se en** to notice, pay attention to.

fijeza [fi·xé·sa] *f.* firmness, solidity, steadiness.

fijo [fí·xo] *adj.* fixed; firm; secure.

fila [fí·la] *f.* row, tier; rank.

filamento [fi·la·mén·to] *m.* filament.

filatelia [fi·la·té·lja] *f.* philately.

filete [fi·lé·te] *m.* (*moldura*) edge, rim; (*carne*) fillet, tenderloin; (*freno*) snaffle bit (*for horses*); hem; screw thread.

filial [fi·ljál] *adj.* filial.

filigrana [fi·li·ġrá·na] *f.* filigree.

filmar [fil·már] *v.* to film, screen (*a play or novel*).

filo [fí·lo] *m.* cutting edge; *Andes* hunger; **por** — exactly; *Am.* **de** — resolutely.

filología [fi·lo·lo·xí·a] *f.* philology.

filólogo [fi·ló·lo·ġo] *m.* philologist.

filón [fi·lón] *m.* seam, layer (*of metallic ore*).

filoso [fi·ló·so] *adj. Am.* sharp, sharp-edged.

filosofía [fi·lo·so·fí·a] *f.* philosophy.

filosófico [fi·lo·só·fi·ko] *adj.* philosophic, philosophical.

filósofo [fi·ló·so·fo] *m.* philosopher.

filtrar [fil·trár] *v.* to filter; **-se** to leak through, leak out; to filter.

filtro [fíl·tro] *m.* filter.

filudo [fi·lú·ḍo] *adj. Am.* sharp, sharp-edged.

fin [fin] *m.* end, ending; purpose; **al** — at last; **al — y al cabo** at last; anyway; in the end; **a — de que** so that; **a -es del mes** toward the end of the month; **en** — in conclusion; well; in short.

finado [fi·ná·ḍo] *m.* the deceased.

final [fi·nál] *adj.* final.

finalizar[9] [fi·na·li·sár] *v.* to finish; to end.

financiamiento [fi·nan·sja·mjén·to] *m. Am.* financing.

financiar [fi·nan·sjár] *v. Am.* to finance.

financiero [fi·nan·sjé·ro] *adj.* financial; *m.* financier.

financista [fi·nan·sis·ta] *m. Am.* financier.

finanza [fi·nán·sa] *f. Am.* finance; **-s** *Am.* public treasury, government funds.

finca [fíŋ·ka] *f.* real estate; property; country house; *Am.* ranch, farm.

fincar [fiŋ·kár] *v.* to buy real estate; *Am.* to rest (on), be based (on); *Am.* to build a farmhouse or country house.

fineza [fi·né·sa] *f.* fineness; nicety; courtesy; favor, kindness; present.

fingimiento [fiŋ·xi·mjén·to] *m.* pretense, sham.

fingir[11] [fiŋ·xír] *v.* to feign, pretend, fake; to imagine.

finiquito [fi·ni·ki·to] *m.* settlement (*of an account*); quittance, final receipt; **dar** — to finish up.

fino [fí·no] *adj.* fine; nice; delicate; sharp; subtle; refined.

finura [fi·nú·ra] *f.* fineness; nicety; subtlety; courtesy, good manners.

fiordo [fjór·ḍo] *m.* fjord.

firma [fír·ma] *f.* signature; firm, firm name.

firmamento [fir·ma·mén·to] *m.* firmament, sky.

firmante [fir·mán·te] *m. & f.* signer.

firmar [fir·már] *v.* to sign.

firme [fír·me] *adj.* firm; solid, hard; **de** — without stopping, hard, steadily.

firmeza [fir·mé·sa] *f.* firmness.

fiscal [fis·kál] *m.* public prosecutor, district attorney; *adj.* fiscal.

fisgar[7] [fiz·ġár] *v.* to pry; to snoop; to spy on.

fisgón [fiz·ġón] *m.* snoop, snooper; *adj.* snooping; curious.

fisgonear [fiz·ǵo·ne·ár] v. to pry about; to snoop.

física [fí·si·ka] f. physics.

físico [fí·si·ko] adj. physical; Am. vain, prudish, affected; Am. real; m. physicist.

fisiología [fi·sjo·lo·xía] f. physiology.

fisiológico [fi·sjo·ló·xi·ko] adj. physiological.

fisionomía [fi·sjo·no·mí·a] f. face, features.

flaco [flá·ko] adj. lean, skinny; frail, weak; **su lado** — his weak side, his weakness.

flacura [fla·kú·ra] f. thinness.

flama [flá·ma] f. flame.

flamante [fla·mán·te] adj. bright, shiny; brand-new.

flameante [fla·me·án·te] adj. flaming, flashing.

flamear [fla·me·ár] v. to flame; to flap, flutter (in the wind).

flamenco [fla·méŋ·ko] adj. Flemish; C.A., P.R. skinny; m. Flemish, Flemish language; flamingo; Andalusian dance.

flan [flan] m. custard.

flanco [fláŋ·ko] m. flank, side.

flanquear [flaŋ·ke·ár] v. to flank.

flaps [fla(p)s] m. pl. flaps (of an airplane).

flaquear [fla·ke·ár] v. to weaken, flag.

flaqueza [fla·ké·sa] f. thinness, leanness; weakness, frailty.

flauta [fláw·ta] f. flute; **flautista** [flaw·tís·ta] m. & f. flute player.

fleco [flé·ko] m. fringe; bangs, fringe of hair.

flecha [flé·ča] f. arrow, dart.

flechar [fle·čár] v. to dart, shoot (an arrow); to strike, wound or kill with an arrow; to cast an amorous or ardent glance; Ven. to prick, sting; Am. to burn (said of the sun).

flechazo [fle·čá·so] m. arrow shot; wound from an arrow.

flema [flé·ma] f. phlegm.

fletamento [fle·ta·mén·to] m. charter, charter party (of a ship).

fletar [fle·tár] v. to charter (a ship); to freight; Ch. to hire (pack animals); Peru to let loose (strong words); Am. to scatter (false rumors); -**se** Col., Mex., Carib., Ch. to run away, slip away; Am. to slip in uninvited; Am. **salir fletado** to leave on the run.

flete [flé·te] m. freight, freightage; cargo; load; Am. fine horse, race horse; Am. bother, nuisance; Col., Ven. **salir sin -s** to leave in a hurry.

flexibilidad [flek·si·ḅi·li·ḍáḍ] f. flexibility; **flexible** [flek·sí·ḅle] adj. flexible.

flexión [flek·sjón] f. bending, bend; sag.

flojear [flo·xe·ár] v. to slacken; to weaken; to idle, to be lazy.

flojedad [flo·xe·ḍáḍ] f. laxity, looseness; slackness; laziness; slack.

flojera [flo·xé·ra] = **flojedad.**

flojo [fló·xo] adj. (mal atado) lax; loose, slack; (sin fuerza) lazy; weak.

flor [flor] f. flower, blossom; compliment; — **de la edad** prime; — **de lis** iris (flower); — **y nata** the best, the cream, the chosen few; **a** — **de** flush with; **echar -es** to throw a bouquet; to compliment, flatter.

floreado [flo·re·á·ḍo] p.p. & adj. flowered; made of the finest wheat.

florear [flo·re·ár] v. to decorate with flowers; to brandish, flourish; to make a flourish on the guitar; to flatter, compliment; to bolt, sift out (the finest flour); Am. to flower, bloom; Am. to choose the best; -**se** C.A. to shine, excel; Am. to burst open like a flower.

florecer[13] [flo·re·sér] v. irr. to flower, bloom; to flourish, thrive.

floreciente [flo·re·sjén·te] adj. flourishing, thriving; prosperous.

florecimiento [flo·re·si·mjén·to] m. flourishing, flowering, bloom.

floreo [flo·ré·o] m. flourish; idle talk; flattery, compliment.

florería [flo·re·rí·a] f. florist's shop.

florero [flo·ré·ro] m. florist; flower vase; flatterer; adj. flattering.

floresta [flo·rés·ta] f. wooded place, grove; arbor.

florete [flo·ré·te] m. fencing foil.

florido [flo·rí·ḍo] adj. flowery.

flota [fló·ta] f. fleet; Col., **echar -s** to brag, boast.

flotador [flo·ta·ḍór] m. floater; float; pontoon (of a hydroplane); adj. floating.

flotante [flo·tán·te] adj. floating; m. Col., Ven. bluffer, braggart.

flotar [flo·tár] v. to float.

flote [fló·te]: **a** — afloat.

fluctuación [fluk·twa·sjón] f. fluctuation; wavering, hesitation.

fluctuar[18] [fluk·twár] v. to fluctuate; to waver; to hesitate.

fluente [flwén·te] adj. fluent, flowing.

fluidez [flwi·ḍés] f. fluidity, easy flow, fluency.

flúido [flú·i·ḍo] adj. fluid, flowing, fluent; m. fluid.

fluir[32] [flwir] v. irr. to flow.

flujo [flú·xo] m. flux; flow; flood tide.

flúor [flú·or] m. fluorin.

fluorescente [flwo·re·sén·te] adj. fluorescent.

flux [flus] f. flush (in cards); P.R., Col., Ven. suit of clothes; **hacer** — to use up one's funds, lose everything; Am. **tener uno** — to be lucky.

foca [fó·ka] f. seal, sea lion.

foco [fó·ko] m. focus, center; Am. electric-light bulb.

fofo [fó·fo] adj. spongy, porous; light (in weight); soft.

fogata [fo·ǵa·ta] f. fire, blaze, bonfire.

fogón [fo·ǵón] m. hearth, fireplace; grill (for cooking); vent of a gun; C.A., Mex. fire, bonfire; **fogonazo** [fo·ǵo·ná·so] m. flash (of gunpowder).

fogoso [fo·ǵó·so] adj. fiery, ardent; lively, spirited.

follaje [fo·yá·xe] m. foliage.

folletín [fo·ye·tín] m. small pamphlet; serial story.

folleto [fo·yé·to] m. pamphlet.

fomentar [fo·men·tár] v. to foment, encourage, promote, foster.

fomento [fo·mén·to] m. promotion, encouragement; encouragement; aid.

fonda [fón·da] f. inn; restaurant.

fondear [fon·de·ár] v. to cast anchor; to sound, make soundings; to search (a ship); to sound out; -**se** Cuba to save up for the future.

fondero [fon·dé·ro] m. Am. innkeeper.

fondillos [fon·dí·yos] m. pl. seat of trousers.

fondista [fon·dís·ta] m. & f. innkeeper.

fondo [fón·do] m. (hondura) bottom; depth; background; back, rear end; (esencia) mature, heart, inner self; fund; Cuba, Ven. underskirt; **-s funds; a** — thoroughly; **echar a** — to sink.

fonducho [fon·dú·čo] m. cheap eating place.

fonema [fo·né·ma] m. phoneme.

fonética [fo·né·ti·ka] f. phonetics, study of pronunciation.

fonógrafo [fo·nó·ǵra·fo] m. phonograph.

fonología [fo·no·lo·xí·a] f. phonology.

forajido [fo·ra·xí·ḍo] m. outlaw, fugitive; highwayman, bandit.

FE

foráneo [fo·rá·ne·o] *adj.* foreign; *m.* outsider, stranger.

forastero [fo·ras·té·ro] *m.* stranger; foreigner; outsider; *adj.* foreign.

forcejear [for·se·xe·ár], **forcejar** [for·se·xar] *v.* to struggle; to strive; to oppose, resist.

forja [fór·xa] *f.* forge; forging; blacksmith's shop.

forjador [for·xa·ḍór] *m.* forger (*of metals*); smith, blacksmith; inventor (*of lies, stories, tricks, etc.*).

forjar [for·xár] *v.* to forge; to form, shape; to invent, feign, fake.

forma [fór·ma] *f.* form, shape, figure; manner; format (*size and shape of a book*); host (*unleavened bread for communion*).

formación [for·ma·sjón] *f.* formation.

formal [for·mál] *adj.* formal; serious, trustworthy, punctual; reliable.

formalidad [for·ma·li·ḍáḍ] *f.* formality; seriousness, reliability; gravity, dignity; punctuality; red tape.

formalismo [for·ma·líz·mo] *m.* formality, red tape (*excess of formalities*); **formalista** [for·ma·lís·ta] *adj.* fond of excessive formalities, fond of red tape.

formalizar[9] [for·ma·li·sár] *v.* to give proper form to; to legalize; to make official; -se to settle down, become serious.

formar [for·már] *v.* to form; to shape, mold; -se to get into line; to be molded, educated; to take form.

fórmico [fór·mi·ko] *adj.* formic.

formidable [for·mi·ḍá·ḅle] *adj.* formidable; fearful.

formón [for·món] *m.* wide chisel.

fórmula [fór·mu·la] *f.* formula.

formular [for·mu·lár] *v.* to formulate, word.

fornido [for·ní·ḍo] *adj.* stout, strong, sturdy.

foro [fó·ro] *m.* stage; back, rear (*of a stage*); forum, court; bar (*profession of law*).

forraje [fo·rrá·xe] *m.* forage, green grass, fodder, feed.

forrajear [fo·rra·xe·ár] *v.* to forage, gather forage.

forrar [fo·rrár] *v.* to line; to cover, put a sheath, case, or covering on; -se *Ríopl., C.A.* to eat well; *Am.* to supply oneself with provisions; *Ríopl., Mex., Cuba* to save money.

forro [fó·rro] *m.* lining; sheathing, casing; covering; book cover.

fortalecer[13] [for·ta·le·sér] *v. irr.* to fortify; to strengthen.

fortaleza [for·ta·lé·sa] *f.* fortress; fortitude; strength, vigor; *Ch.* stench, stink.

fortificación [for·ti·fi·ka·sjón] *f.* fortification; fort.

fortificar[6] [for·ti·fi·kár] *v.* to fortify.

fortuito [for·twí·to] *adj.* fortuitous, accidental, unexpected.

fortuna [for·tú·na] *f.* fortune; fate, chance; wealth; **por —** fortunately.

forzar[9] [for·sár] *v. irr.* to force; to compel; to take (*a fort*); to rape; **— la entrada en** to break into.

forzoso [for·só·so] *adj.* compulsory; necessary.

fosa [fó·sa] *f.* grave; cavity.

fosco [fós·ko] *adj.* dark; cross, irritable, frowning; *see* **hosco.**

fosfato [fos·fá·to] *m.* phosphate.

fosforecer[13] [for·fo·re·sér], **fosforescer** [fos·fo·re·sér] *v.* to glow.

fósforo [fós·fo·ro] *m.* phosphorus; match.

fósil [fó·sil] *adj. & m.* fossil.

foso [fó·so] *m.* hole, pit; stage pit; ditch.

foto [fó·to] *f.* snapshot.

fotoeléctrico [fo·to·e·lék·tri·ko] *adj.* photoelectric.

fotograbado [fo·to·gra·ḅá·ḍo] *m.* photoengraving.

fotografía [fo·to·gra·fí·a] *f.* photograph; photography.

fotografiar[17] [fo·to·gra·fjár] *v.* to photograph.

fotógrafo [fo·tó·gra·fo] *m.* photographer.

fotosíntesis [fo·to·sín·te·sis] *f.* photosynthesis.

fracasado [fra·ka·sá·ḍo] *adj.* failed; *m.* failure.

fracasar [fra·ka·sár] *v.* to fail; to come to ruin; to crumble to pieces.

fracaso [fra·ká·so] *m.* failure, ruin; calamity; crash.

fracción [frak·sjón] *f.* fraction.

fractura [frak·tú·ra] *f.* fracture; break, crack.

fracturar [frak·tu·rár] *v.* to fracture, break.

fragancia [fra·gán·sja] *f.* fragrance, scent, perfume.

fragante [fra·gán·te] *adj.* fragrant; **en —** in the act.

fragata [fra·gá·ta] *f.* frigate.

frágil [frá·xil] *adj.* fragile, breakable; frail, weak.

fragmento [frag·mén·to] *m.* fragment.

fragor [fra·gór] *m.* clang, din; crash.

fragoroso [fra·go·ró·so] *adj.* deafening, thunderous.

fragoso [fra·gó·so] *adj.* rugged, craggy, rough, uneven; noisy.

fragua [frá·gwa] *f.* forge; blacksmith's shop.

fraguar [fra·gwár] *v.* to forge; to scheme, hatch (*a plot*).

fraile [fráj·le] *m.* friar; priest; **frailuco** [fraj·lú·ko] *m.* little old friar.

frambuesa [fram·bwé·sa] *f.* raspberry; **frambueso** [fram·bwé·so] *m.* raspberry bush.

francés [fran·sés] *adj.* French; *m.* Frenchman; French language.

franco [fráŋ·ko] *adj.* (*sincero*) frank, open, candid, sincere; (*exento*) free; *m.* franc; **francote** [fraŋ·kó·te] *adj.* very frank, blunt, outspoken.

franela [fra·né·la] *f.* flannel.

franja [fráŋ·xa] *f.* fringe, border; stripe; braid.

franquear [fraŋ·ke·ár] *v.* to exempt; to free; to frank (*a letter*); to dispatch, send; to make grants; **— el paso** to permit the passage (of); -se to unbosom oneself, disclose one's innermost thoughts and feelings.

franqueo [fraŋ·ké·o] *m.* postage; franking (*of a letter*); freeing (*of slaves or prisoners*).

franqueza [fraŋ·ké·sa] *f.* frankness; freedom.

franquicia [fraŋ·kí·sja] *f.* franchise, grant, privilege; freedom or exemption (*from fees*).

frasco [frás·ko] *m.* flask, vial, small bottle.

frase [frá·se] *f.* phrase; sentence.

fraternal [fra·ter·nál] *adj.* fraternal, brotherly.

fraternidad [fra·ter·ni·ḍáḍ] *f.* fraternity; brotherhood.

fraude [fráw·ḍe] *m.* fraud.

fraudulento [fraw·ḍu·lén·to] *adj.* fraudulent, tricky, deceitful, dishonest.

fray [fraj] *m.* (*contr. of* **fraile** [fráj·le], *used before Christian name*) friar.

frazada [fra·sá·ḍa] *f.* blanket.

frecuencia [fre·kwén·sja] *f.* frequency; **con —** frequently.

frecuentar [fre·kwen·tár] *v.* to frequent.

frecuente [fre·kwén·te] *adj.* frequent.

fregadero [fre·ga·ḍe·ro] *m.* sink.

fregado [fre·gá·ḍo] *m.* scrub, scrubbing; *p.p. of* **fregar**; *adj. Ch., Andes* bothersome, annoying; *Col.* stubborn; *Mex., C.A.* brazen.

fregar[7] [fre·gár] *v. irr.* to scour; to scrub; to rub; to wash (*dishes*); *Am.* to molest, annoy.

fregona [fre·gó·na] *f.* scrub woman; dishwasher, kitchen maid.

freír[15] [fre·ír] *v. irr.* to fry; to tease, bother.

frenar [fre·nár] *v.* to apply the brakes; to restrain.

frenesí [fre·ne·sí] *m.* frenzy, madness.
frenético [fre·né·ti·ko] *adj.* frantic; furious; in a frenzy.
freno [fré·no] *m.* bridle; brake; control; bit (*for horses*).
frente [frén·te] *f.* forehead; countenance; *m.* front; **en — de** in front of; **— a** in front of, facing; **hacer —** to face.
fresa [fré·sa] *f.* strawberry.
fresca [frés·ka] *f.* fresh air; fresh remark.
fresco [frés·ko] *adj.* (*bastante frío*) fresh; cool, (*sereno*) calm, serene; (*descarado*) forward, bold; *m.* coolness; cool air; fresco (*painting*); *C.A., Col.* refreshment; **al —** in the open air; **pintura al —** painting in fresco.
frescor [fres·kór] *m.* freshness, coolness.
frescura [fres·kú·ra] *f.* (*temperatura baja*) freshness; coolness; (*serenidad*) calm; freedom; ease; (*insolencia*) boldness, impudence; impudent remark.
fresno [fréz·no] *m.* ash, ash tree.
fresquecillo [fres·ke·sí·yo] *adj.* nice and cool; cool air, fresh breeze; **fresquecito** [fres·ke·sí·to], **fresquito** [fres·kí·to] *adj.* nice and cool.
frialdad [frjal·dáḍ] *f.* coldness; coolness, indifference.
fricativo [fri·ka·tí·ƀo] *adj.* fricative.
fricción [frik·sjón] *f.* friction, rub, rubbing.
friccionar [frik·sjo·nár] *v.* to rub; to massage.
friega [frjé·ga] *f.* rub, rubbing; *Am.* bother, nuisance, irritation; *Am.* flogging, beating.
frigorífico [fri·go·rí·fi·ko] *adj.* freezing; *m. Spain* refrigerator, icebox; *Riopl.* meatpacking house.
frijol [fri·xól] *m.* bean; kidney bean, navy bean.
frío [frí·o] *adj.* cold; frigid; cool, indifferent; *m.* cold; **-s** *Mex.* chills and fever; *Col., C.A., Ven.* malaria.
friolento [frjo·lén·to] *adj.* cold-blooded, sensitive to cold; chilly.
friolera [frjo·lé·ra] *f.* trifle.
fritada [fri·tá·ḍa] *f.* dish of fried food.
frito [frí·to] *p.p. irr. of* **freír** fried; *m.* fry, dish of fried food.
fritura [fri·tú·ra] *f.* fry, dish of fried food; fritter.
frivolidad [fri·ƀo·li·ḍáḍ] *f.* frivolity; **frívolo** [frí·ƀo·lo] *adj.* frivolous.
fronda [frón·da] *f.* leaf; fern leaf; foliage.
frondoso [fron·dó·so] *adj.* leafy.
frontera [fron·té·ra] *f.* frontier, border; **fronterizo** [fron·te·rí·so] *adj.* frontier (*used as an adj.*); opposite, facing.
frontero [fron·té·ro] *adj.* facing, opposite.
frontis [frón·tis] *m.* façade, front (*of a building*).
frontispicio [fron·tis·pí·sjo] *m.* front, façade (*front of a building*); title page.
frontón [fron·tón] *m.* main wall of a handball court; handball court; jai alai court; game of *pelota*.
frotación [fro·ta·sjón] *f.* friction, rubbing.
frotar [fro·tár] *v.* to rub; to scour.
frote [fró·te] *m.* rubbing; friction.
fructificar[6] [fruk·ti·fi·kár] *v.* to fruit, bear or produce fruit; to yield profit.
fructuoso [fruk·twó·so] *adj.* fruitful.
frugal [fru·gál] *adj.* frugal, economical, saving, thrifty; **frugalidad** [fru·ga·li·ḍáḍ] *f.* frugality, thrift.
fruncir[10] [frun·sír] *v.* to wrinkle; to gather in pleats; to contract, shrivel; **— las cejas** to frown; to knit the eyebrows; **— los labios** to purse or curl the lips.

fruslería [fruz·le·rí·a] *f.* trifle, trinket.
frustración [frus·tra·sjón] *f.* frustration; failure.
frustrar [frus·trár] *v.* to frustrate, thwart, foil; **-se** to fail, be thwarted.
fruta [frú·ta] *f.* fruit (*not a vegetable*); **frutería** [fru·te·rí·a] *f.* fruit store.
frutero [fru·té·ro] *m.* fruit vendor; fruit dish; *adj.* fruit (*used as adj.*); **buque —** fruit boat; **plato —** fruit dish.
fruto [frú·to] *m.* fruit (*any organic product of the earth*); result; benefit, profit.
¡fuche! [fú·če] *interj. Mex.* phew! ugh! pew! phooey!
fuego [fwé·go] *m.* (*incendio*) fire; (*pasión*) passion; (*erupción*) skin eruption; *Am.* cold sore; **-s artificiales** fireworks; **hacer —** to fire, shoot; **estar hecho un —** to be very angry; **romper —** to begin to fire, start shooting.
fuelle [fwé·ye] *m.* (*instrumento*) bellows; (*arruga*) pucker, wrinkle, fold; (*hablador*) tattletale, windbag, gossiper.
fuente [fwén·te] *f.* fountain; source, origin; spring; platter, serving dish.
fuera [fwé·ra] *adv.* outside, out; **— de** *prep.* outside of; in addition to.
fuereño [fwe·ré·ño] *m. Mex., Ven., Andes* outsider, stranger.
fuero [fwé·ro] *m.* law, statute; power, jurisdiction; code of laws; exemption, privilege.
fuerte [fwér·te] *adj.* (*robusto*) strong; loud; secure, fortified; (*grave*) grave, serious; (*áspero*) excessive; *Ch.* stinking; *m.* fort; forte, strong point; forte (*music*); *Mex.* alcohol, liquor; *adv.* strongly; excessively; loud; hard.
fuerza [fwér·sa] *f.* force; power, strength; violence, compulsion; **a — de** by dint of; **a la — (por —, por la —, de por —)**, *Am.* **de —)** by force, forcibly; necessarily; **ser —** to be necessary.
fuete [fwé·te] *m. Col., Cuba, Ríopl., Mex., Ven., Andes* whip; **fuetazo** [fwe·tá·so] *m. Am.* lash.
fuga [fú·ga] *f.* flight, escape; leak, leakage; fugue (*musical composition*).
fugarse[7] [fu·gár·se] *v.* to flee, escape.
fugaz [fu·gás] *adj.* fleeing; fleeting, brief, passing.
fugitivo [fu·xi·tí·ƀo] *adj.* fugitive; fleeting, passing; perishable; *m.* fugitive.
fulano [fu·lá·no] *m.* so-and-so (*referring to person*).
fulgor [ful·gór] *m.* radiance, brilliance.
fulgurar [ful·gu·rár] *v.* to gleam, flash, shine.
fulminar [ful·mi·nár] *v.* to thunder, thunder forth; to utter (*threats*).
fulo [fú·lo] *m. Pan.* blond.
fullero [fu·yé·ro] *m.* cardsharp; crooked gambler; cheat.
fumada [fu·má·ḍa] *f.* puff, whiff (*of smoke*).
fumadero [fu·ma·dé·ro] *m.* smoking room.
fumador [fu·ma·ḍór] *m.* smoker, habitual smoker.
fumar [fu·már] *v.* to smoke (*tobacco*); *Am.* **-se a uno** to swindle or cheat someone.
fumigar[7] [fu·mi·gár] *v.* to fumigate.
función [fun·sjón] *f.* (*actividad*) function; functioning; (*empleo*) office; occupation; (*espectáculo*) show, performance; religious festival.
funcionamiento [fun·sjo·na·mjén·to] *m.* functioning, action, working, operation.
funcionar [fun·sjo·nár] *v.* to function; to work, run (*said of machines*).
funcionario [fun·sjo·ná·rjo] *m.* public employee, officer or official.
funda [fún·da] *f.* cover, case; *Col.* skirt; **— de**

FO

almohada pillowcase.

fundación [fun·da·sjón] *f.* foundation.

fundador [fun·da·ḍór] *m.* founder.

fundamental [fun·da·men·tál] *adj.* fundamental.

fundamento [fun·da·mén·to] *m.* foundation, groundwork; basis; *Col.* skirt.

fundar [fun·dár] *v.* to found, establish; to erect; to base, ground.

fundición [fun·di·sjón] *f.* foundry; smelting.

fundir [fun·dír] *v.* to smelt, fuse, melt; to cast, mold; *Am.* to ruin; **-se** to fuse, melt together; to unite; *Ríopl., Mex.* to be ruined.

fundo [fún·do] *m.* farm, country estate; property, land.

fúnebre [fú·ne·ḅre] *adj.* funeral; funereal, gloomy, dismal.

funeral [fu·ne·rál] *adj. & m.* funeral.

funeraria [fu·ne·rá·rja] *f.* undertaking establishment, funeral parlor.

funesto [fu·nés·to] *adj.* ill-fated, unlucky; sad, unfortunate.

fungosidad [fun·go·si·ḍáḍ] *f.* fungus, fungous growth.

funicular [fu·ni·ku·lár] *adj. & m.* funicular.

furgón [fur·ɡón] *m.* freight car, boxcar; baggage car; **furgonada** [fur·ɡo·ná·ḍa] *f.* carload.

furia [fú·rja] *f.* fury, rage; speed.

furibundo [fu·ri·ḅún·do] *adj.* furious.

furioso [fu·rjó·so] *adj.* furious.

furor [fu·rór] *m.* fury, rage, anger; frenzy.

furtivo [fur·ti·ḅo] *adj.* furtive, sly, secret.

fuselaje [fu·se·lá·xe] *m.* fuselage (*of an airplane*).

fusible [fu·sí·ḅle] *adj.* fusible; *m.* electric fuse.

fusil [fu·síl] *m.* gun, rifle.

fusilar [fu·si·lár] *v.* to shoot, execute.

fusión [fu·sjón] *f.* fusion; melting; — **nuclear** nuclear fusion.

fustigar[7] [fus·ti·ɡár] *v.* to lash, whip; to censure severely, scold sharply.

fútbol [fú·ḅol] *m.* soccer.

fútil [fú·til] *adj.* futile, useless; trivial; **futilidad** [fu·ti·li·ḍáḍ] *f.* futility, uselessness.

futuro [fu·tú·ro] *adj.* future; *m.* fiancé, future husband; future.

G·g

gabacho [ga·ḅá·čo] *adj.* from or of the Pyrenees; Frenchlike; *Am.* **me salió** — it turned out wrong; *m.* Frenchman (*used depreciatively*).

gabán [ga·ḅán] *m.* overcoat.

gabeta [ga·ḅé·ta] = **gaveta.**

gabinete [ga·ḅi·né·te] *m.* cabinet (*of a government*); studio; study, library room; dressing room; sitting room; private room; dentist's office; laboratory; *Am.* glassed-in **mirador.**

gaceta [ga·sé·ta] *f.* gazette, official newspaper; professional periodical; *Am.* any newspaper.

gacetilla [ga·se·tí·ya] *f.* short newspaper article; column of short news items; gossip column; *m. & f.* newsmonger, tattletale; **gacetillero** [ga·se·ti·yé·ro] *m.* newspaper reporter; newsmonger.

gacha [gá·ča] *f.* watery mass or mush; *Col.* china or earthenware bowl; **-s** porridge, mush; caresses; **-s de avena** oatmeal.

gacho [gá·čo] *adj.* drooping; bent downward; turned down; stooping; slouching; with horns

curved downward; **sombrero** — slouch hat; **a gachas** on all fours; **con las orejas gachas** with drooping ears; crestfallen, discouraged.

gafas [gá·fas] *f. pl.* spectacles; grappling hooks.

gaita [gáj·ta] *f.* flageolet, a kind of flute; *Am.* good-for-nothing, lazy bum; — **gallega** bagpipe; **sacar la** — to stick out one's neck; **gaitero** [gaj·té·ro] *m.* piper, bagpipe player.

gaje [gá·xe] *m.* fee; **-s** wages, salary; fees.

gajo [gá·xo] *m.* broken branch; bunch.

gala [gá·la] *f.* elegance; full dress or uniform; ostentation; *Am.* award, prize, tip; **-s** finery, regalia, best clothes; **-s de novia** trousseau; **hacer — de** to boast of.

galán [ga·lán] *m.* gallant, lover; leading man (*in a play*).

galante [ga·lán·te] *adj.* gallant, attentive to ladies; polite.

galanteador [ga·lan·te·a·ḍór] *m.* gallant, lady's man; flatterer.

galantear [ga·lan·te·ár] *v.* to court, woo; to make love.

galanteo [ga·lan·té·o] *m.* wooing, courtship.

galantería [ga·lan·te·rí·a] *f.* gallantry, compliment, attention to ladies; courtesy; gracefulness; generosity.

galardón [ga·lar·ḍón] *m.* recompense, reward.

galeote [ga·le·ó·te] *m.* galley slave.

galera [ga·lé·ra] *f.* galley; large wagon; women's jail; printer's galley; *Mex.* jail; *Ch., Ríopl.* tall hat.

galerada [ga·le·rá·ḍa] *f.* galley, galley proof; wagon load, van load.

galería [ga·le·rí·a] *f.* gallery; corridor.

galgo [gál·ɡo] *m.* greyhound; *adj. Col.* gluttonous, always hungry.

galicismo [ga·li·síz·mo] *m.* gallicism.

galillo [ga·lí·yo] *m.* uvula.

galio [gá·ljo] *m.* gallium.

galón [ga·lón] *m.* galloon, braid, trimming; gallon.

galoneado [ga·lo·ne·á·ḍo] *adj.* gallooned, trimmed with braid.

galopada [ga·lo·pá·ḍa] *f.* gallop; **pegar una** — to break into a gallop.

galopar [ga·lo·pár] *v.* to gallop.

galope [ga·ló·pe] *m.* gallop; **a (al** *or* **de)** — at a gallop; speedily.

galopear [ga·lo·pe·ár] = **galopar.**

galpón [gal·pón] *m. Ríopl., Andes* large open shed.

galvanómetro [gal·ḅa·nó·me·tro] *m.* galvanometer.

gallardete [ga·yar·ḍé·te] *m.* streamer.

gallardía [ga·yar·ḍí·a] *f.* elegance; gracefulness; bravery.

gallardo [ga·yár·ḍo] *adj.* elegant, graceful; brave.

gallego [ga·yé·ɡo] *adj.* Galician, from or of Galicia, Spain; *m.* Galician; *Carib., Ríopl.* Spaniard (*used as a nickname*).

galleta [ga·yé·ta] *f.* cracker; hardtack, hard biscuit; hard cookie; blow, slap; small pot; *Ríopl.* bread of coarse meal or bran; *Ch.* reproof; *Am.* **colgarle la — a uno** to fire, dismiss someone; *Am.* **tener** — to have strength, muscle.

gallina [ga·yi·na] *f.* hen; *m. & f.* chickenhearted person.

gallinero [ga·yi·né·ro] *m.* chicken coop, house, or yard; flock of chickens; basket for carrying chickens; poultryman; noisy gathering; top gallery of a theater.

gallo [gá·yo] *m.* cock, rooster; aggressive, bossy person; cork float; false note (*in singing*); frog (*in one's throat*); *Am.* secondhand clothing; *Am.*

fire wagon; *Mex., Riopl.* serenade.
gamba [gám·ba] *f. Spain* large shrimp.
gamo [gá·mo] *m.* buck, male deer.
gamonal [ga·mo·nál] *m. Am.* boss; overseer.
gamuza [ga·mú·sa] *f.* chamois, chamois skin (*soft leather made from the skin of sheep, goats, deer, etc.*).
gana [gá·na] *f.* desire, appetite; **de buena (mala)** — willingly (unwillingly); **tener** — (*or* **-s**) to feel like, want to; **no me da la** — I don't want to.
ganadero [ga·na·dé·ro] *m.* cattleman; cattle dealer; *adj.* cattle, pertaining to cattle.
ganado [ga·ná·do] *m.* cattle; herd; livestock; — **mayor** cattle; horses; mules; — **menor** sheep; — **de cerda** swine.
ganador [ga·na·dór] *m.* winner; *adj.* winning.
ganancia [ga·nán·sja] *f.* profit, gain; *Am.* something to boot, something extra.
ganancioso [ga·nan·sjó·so] *adj.* winning; profitable; *m.* winner.
ganar [ga·nár] *v.* to win; to profit, gain; to earn; to get ahead of.
gancho [gán·čo] *m.* hook; hooked staff; *Mex., Cuba, Riopl., Col., C.A.* hairpin; *Am.* bait, lure, trick; **aguja de** — crochet hook; **echar a uno el** — to hook someone; **tener** — to be attractive, alluring.
gandul [gan·dúl] *m.* bum, loafer.
ganga [gáŋ·ga] *f.* bargain; snap, easy job; kind of prairie hen.
gangoso [gáŋ·gó·so] *adj.* twangy, nasal (*voice*).
gangrena [gaŋ·gré·na] *f.* gangrene.
gangrenar [gaŋ·gre·nár] *v.* to gangrene, cause gangrene; **-se** to gangrene.
ganguear [gaŋ·ge·ár] *v.* to talk "through the nose."
ganoso [ga·no·so] *adj.* desirous; *Am.* lively, spirited (*horse*).
ganso [gán·so] *m.* goose, gander; lazy, slovenly person; dunce.
ganzúa [gan·sú·a] *f.* hook; picklock (*tool for picking locks*); *m. & f.* burglar.
garabato [ga·ra·bá·to] *m.* hook; scrawl, scribble; **hacer -s** to scribble, write poorly.
garaje [ga·rá·xe] *m.* garage.
garantía [ga·ran·tí·a] *f.* to guaranty; security; bail, bond.
garantizar[9] [ga·ran·ti·sár] *v.* to guarantee, vouch for.
garañón [ga·ra·ñón] *m.* jackass, male ass; male camel (*for breeding*); *Riopl., Mex., C.A.* stallion.
garapiñar [ga·ra·pi·ñár] *v.* to candy (*almonds, fruits, etc.*).
garbanzo [gar·bán·so] *m.* chickpea.
garbo [gár·bo] *m.* elegance, graceful air, good carriage.
garboso [gar·bó·so] *adj.* graceful; elegant; sprightly.
garduña [gar·dú·ña] *f.* marten.
garfio [gár·fjo] *m.* hook.
garganta [gar·gán·ta] *f.* throat, neck; gorge, ravine; **gargantilla** [gar·gan·tí·ya] *f.* necklace.
gárgara [gár·ga·ra] *f.* gargling; **-s** *Am.* gargle, gargling solution; **hacer -s** to gargle.
gargarear [gar·ga·re·ár] *v. Am.* to gargle.
gargarismo [gar·ga·riz·mo] *m.* gargling; gargle, gargling solution.
gargarizar[9] [gar·ga·ri·sár] *v.* to gargle.
garita [ga·rí·ta] *f.* sentry box; watchman's booth; *Col.* vendor's booth.
garito [ga·rí·to] *m.* gambling house, gambling joint; gambler's winnings.
garra [gá·rra] *f.* claw, paw; hook; *Am.* strength;

Col. leather or cloth remnant; *Am.* skinny person or animal; *Am.* margin of profit in a business deal; **echar la** — to arrest; to grab; *Mex., C.A., Ven., Andes* **hacer -s** to tear to pieces.
garrafa [ga·rrá·fa] *f.* decanter; **garrafón** [ga·rra·fón] *m.* large decanter; demijohn.
garrapata [ga·rra·pá·ta] *f.* tick (*an insect*).
garrapatear [ga·rra·pa·te·ár] *v.* to scribble, scrawl, write poorly.
garrocha [ga·rró·ča] *f.* pole; iron-pointed staff; **salto de** — pole vault; *Am.* goad (*for goading oxen*).
garrote [ga·rró·te] *m.* club, cudgel, heavy stick; *Mex., Ur.* brake; **dar** — to strangle; *Am.* to brake, set the brakes; **garrotazo** [ga·rro·tá·so] *m.* blow with a club; huge stick.
garrotero [ga·rro·té·ro] *m. Mex., Ven.* brakeman; *Am.* beater (*one who beats with a club*); *adj. Am.* stingy.
garrucha [ga·rrú·ča] *f.* pulley.
garúa [ga·rú·a] *f. C.A., Riopl., Ven., Andes* drizzle.
garza [gar·sa] *f.* heron; egret.
garzo [gár·so] *adj.* blue, bluish; blue-eyed.
gas [gas] *m.* gas, vapor; *Col., Riopl., Ven.* gasoline; — **lacrimógeno** tear gas.
gasa [gá·sa] *f.* gauze.
gaseosa [ga·se·ó·sa] *f.* soda water; soda pop.
gaseoso [ga·se·ó·so] *adj.* gaseous.
gasolina [ga·so·lí·na] *f.* gasoline.
gastador [gas·ta·dór] *adj.* lavish, extravagant, wasteful; *m.* spendthrift, lavish spender.
gastar [gas·tár] *v.* to spend; to wear; to use; to waste; **-se** to wear out; to get old.
gasto [gás·to] *m.* expense, expenditure; wear.
gatas : [gá·tas] **a** — on all fours; **andar a** — to creep, crawl; **salir a** — to crawl out of a difficulty.
gateado [ga·te·á·do] *adj.* catlike; veined, streaked; *m. Am.* light-colored horse with black streaks.
gatear [ga·te·ár] *v.* to creep, crawl; to walk on all fours; to claw, scratch; to steal.
gatillo [ga·tí·yo] *m.* kitten; trigger; forceps (*for extracting teeth*); petty thief.
gato [gá·to] *m.* cat; moneybag; jack (*for lifting weights*); sneak thief; sly fellow; *Am.* trigger; *Am.* outdoor market; *Am.* hot-water bottle; *Am.* a gaucho song and tap dance (*by extension, the dancer*); *Am.* blunder.
gatuperio [ga·tu·pé·rjo] *m.* fraud, intrigue.
gauchada [gaw·čá·da] *f. Riopl.* gaucho deed or exploit.
gauchaje [gaw·čá·xe] *m. Riopl.* band of Gauchos, Gaucho folk.
gauchesco [gaw·čés·ko] *adj. Am.* relating to Gauchos.
gaucho [gáw·čo] *m. Am.* Gaucho, Argentine and Uruguayan cowboy; *Riopl., Ven.* good horseman; *adj. Am.* relating to Gauchos, Gaucho-like; *Am.* sly, crafty.
gaveta [ga·bé·ta] *f.* drawer.
gavilla [ga·bí·ya] *f.* sheaf; gang, band (*of rogues, thieves, etc.*).
gaviota [ga·bjó·ta] *f.* sea gull.
gaza [gá·sa] *f.* loop; *Carib.* noose of a lasso.
gazmoñería [gaz·mo·ñe·rí·a] *f.* prudery, affected modesty; **gazmoño** [gaz·mó·ño] *adj.* prudish, affected, coy.
gaznate [gaz·ná·te] *m.* windpipe; a kind of fritter; *Andes* a sweetmeat made a pineapple or coconut.
gazpacho [gas·pá·čo] *m. Spain* cold vegetable soup.

gelatina [xe·la·tí·na] *f.* gelatin; jelly.
gema [xé·ma] *f.* gem, jewel; bud.
gemelo [xe·mé·lo] *m.* twin; **-s** twins; binoculars,
opera glasses, field glasses; cuff links.
gemido [xe·mí·do] *m.* moan; wail, cry.
gemir [xe·mír] *v. irr.* to moan; to wail, cry.
gendarme [xen·dár·me] *m. Mex., Ven., Riopl., C.A.*
policeman.
genealogía [xe·ne·a·lo·xí·a] *f.* genealogy.
generación [xe·ne·ra·sjón] *f.* generation.
generador [xe·ne·ra·dór] *m.* generator; — **molecular**
atom smasher.
general [xe·ne·rál] *adj. & m.* general; **por lo** —
generally.
generalidad [xe·ne·ra·li·dád] *f.* generality; majority.
generalizar[9] [xe·ne·ra·li·sár] *v.* to generalize; **-se** to
spread, become general.
genérico [xe·né·ri·ko] *adj.* generic.
género [xé·ne·ro] *m.* (*clase*) kind, sort, class; gender;
(*tela*) goods, material, cloth; — **humano** human
race.
generosidad [xe·ne·ro·si·dád] *f.* generosity.
generoso [xe·ne·ró·so] *adj.* generous; best (*wine*).
genial [xe·njál] *adj.* genial, jovial, pleasant.
genio [xé·njo] *m.* genius; temperament, disposition;
spirit.
gente [xén·te] *f.* (*personas*) people; crowd; (*pueblo*)
race, nation; clan; *Am.* — **bien** upper-class or
important person; *Am.* **ser** — to be a somebody;
to be cultured; to be socially important.
gentil [xen·tíl] *adj.* graceful; genteel; courteous;
gentile; *m.* pagan; gentile.
gentileza [xen·ti·lé·sa] *f.* grace, courtesy; nobility;
gavor.
gentilicio [xen·ti·lí·sjo] *adj.* national; *m.* name used
to identify national or local origin.
gentío [xen·tí·o] *m.* crowd, throng.
gentuza [xen·tú·sa] *f.* rabble.
genuino [xe·nwí·no] *adj.* genuine.
geofísica [xe·o·fí·si·ka] *f.* geophysics.
geografía [xe·o·gra·fí·a] *f.* geography; **geográfico**
[xe·o·grá·fi·ko] *adj.* geographical.
geología [xe·o·lo·xí·a] *f.* geology; **geológico**
[xe·o·ló·xí·ko] *adj.* geological.
geometría [xe·o·me·trí·a] *f.* geometry; **geométrico**
[xe·o·mé·tri·ko] *adj.* geometric.
geranio [xe·rá·njo] *m.* geranium.
gerencia [xe·rén·sja] *f.* management, administration.
gerente [xe·rén·te] *m.* manager.
germen [xér·men] *m.* germ; origin, source.
germinar [xer·mi·nár] *v.* to germinate.
gerundio [xe·rún·djo] *m.* gerund; present participle.
gesticular [xes·ti·ku·lár] *v.* to gesticulate.
gestión [xes·tjón] *f.* action, step, maneuver;
intervention; **-es** negotiations.
gestionar [xes·tjo·nár] *v.* to manage; to take steps;
to negotiate or carry out (*a deal, transaction,
etc.*).
gesto [xés·to] *m.* face, expression; grimace; gesture;
estar de buen (*or* **mal**) — to be in a good (*or*
bad) humor; **hacer -s** a to make faces at.
giba [xí·ba] *f.* hump, hunch.
gigante [xi·gán·te] *adj.* gigantic; *m.* giant.
gigantesco [xi·gan·tés·ko] *adj.* gigantic.
gimnasia [xim·ná·sja] *f.* gymnastics; **gimnasio**
[xim·ná·sjo] *m.* gymnasium; German institute
(*for secondary instruction*).
gimotear [xi·mo·te·ár] *v.* to whimper, whine.
gimoteo [xi·mo·té·o] *m.* whimper, whining.
ginebra [xi·né·bra] *f.* gin (*liquor*).
ginecología [xi·ne·ko·lo·xí·a] *f.* gynecology.

gira [xí·ra] *f.* excursion, tour; outing, picnic.
girador [xi·ra·dór] *m.* drawer (*of a check or draft*).
girar [xi·rár] *v.* to revolve, rotate, whirl; to send,
issue, or draw (*checks, drafts, etc.*); to manage (*a
business*).
girasol [xi·ra·sól] *m.* sunflower.
giratorio [xi·ra·tó·rjo] *adj.* rotary, revolving.
giro [xí·ro] *m.* (*movimiento circular*) rotation; bend,
turn; (*dirección*) direction, trend; (*estructura*)
turn of phrase; (*monetario*) draft; — **postal**
money order; *adj.* yellowish (*rooster*); *Am.* black
and white (*rooster*); *Am.* cocky.
gitano [xi·tá·no] *adj.* gypsy; gypsylike; sly, clever;
m. gypsy.
gitomate [xi·to·má·te] *Am.* = **jitomate.**
glacial [gla·sjál] *adj.* glacial, icy, very cold.
glaciar [gla·sjár] *m.* glacier.
glándula [glán·du·la] *f.* gland.
glasear [gla·se·ár] *v.* to glaze (*paper, fruits, etc.*),
make glossy.
glaucoma [glaw·kó·ma] *m.* glaucoma.
globo [gló·bo] *m.* globe, sphere; world; balloon.
glóbulo [gló·bu·lo] *m.* globule; corpuscle.
gloria [gló·rja] *f.* glory; gloria (*song of praise to
God*).
gloriarse[17] [glo·rjár·se] *v.* to glory (in), delight (in),
be proud (of); to boast (of).
glorieta [glo·rjé·ta] *f.* arbor, bower; secluded nook
in a park (*with benches*).
glorificar[6] [glo·ri·fi·kár] *v.* to glorify; **-se** to glory
(in), take great pride (in).
glorioso [glo·rjó·so] *adj.* glorious.
glosa [gló·sa] *f.* gloss.
glosar [glo·sár] *v.* to gloss, comment upon, explain
(*a text*).
glosario [glo·sá·rjo] *m.* glossary.
glotal [glo·tál] *adj.* glottal.
glotis [gló·tis] *f.* glottis.
glotón [glo·tón] *adj.* gluttonous; *m.* glutton.
glotonería [glo·to·ne·rí·a] *f.* gluttony.
gobernador [go·ber·na·dór] *adj.* governing; *m.*
governor, ruler.
gobernante [go·ber·nán·te] *adj.* governing, ruling;
m. governor, ruler.
gobernar[1] [go·ber·nár] *v. irr.* to govern, rule; to
lead, direct; to steer (*a boat*).
gobierno [go·bjér·no] *m.* government; management;
control; helm, rudder.
goce [gó·se] *m.* enjoyment; joy.
goleta [go·lé·ta] *f.* schooner, sailing vessel.
golfo [gól·fo] *m.* gulf; open sea; faro (*gambling
game*); vagabond, bum, ragamuffin.
golondrina [go·lon·drí·na] *f.* swallow; swallow fish.
golosina [go·lo·sí·na] *f.* sweet, dainty, tidbit; trifle;
appetite, desire.
goloso [go·ló·so] *adj.* sweet-toothed, fond of
sweets; gluttonous.
golpazo [gol·pá·so] *m.* bang, whack, heavy blow,
hard knock.
golpe [gól·pe] *m.* blow, hit, stroke; knock; beat;
Col. facing (*of a garment*); *Am.* sledge hammer;
— **de fortuna** stroke of good luck; — **de gente**
crowd, throng; — **de gracia** death blow; finishing
stroke; **de** — suddenly; **de un** — all at once;
pestillo de — spring latch; *Am.* **al** — instantly,
at once; *Am.* **al** — **de vista** at one glance.
golpear [gol·pe·ár] *v.* to strike, hit; to knock; to
beat; *Am.* to knock at a door.
golpetear [gol·pe·te·ár] *v.* to tap, knock or pound
continuously; to flap; to rattle.
golpeteo [gol·pe·té·o] *m.* tapping, pounding,

knocking; flapping; rattling.

gollería [go·ye·rí·a] *f.* dainty, delicacy; superfluous thing.

goma [gó·ma] *f.* gum; rubber; elastic; eraser; tire; — **de repuesto** spare tire; *Am.* **estar de** — to have a hang-over (*after excessive drinking*).

gomero [go·mé·ro] *adj.* rubber, pertaining to rubber; *m. Riopl.* gum or rubber tree; *Am.* rubber producer; *Am.* rubber-plantation worker; *Ven.* glue container or bottle.

gomífero [go·mí·fe·ro] *adj.* rubber-bearing, rubber-producing.

gomoso [go·mó·so] *adj.* gummy, sticky; *m.* dandy.

gordiflón [gor·di·flón] *adj.* fat; chubby.

gordo [gór·do] *adj.* fat; plump; *m.* suet, fat; **gorda** [gór·da] *f. Mex.* thick tortilla or cornmeal cake; **se armó la gorda** all hell broke loose; there was a big rumpus.

gordura [gor·dú·ra] *f.* fatness; stoutness; fat.

gorgojo [gor·gó·xo] *m.* weevil; puny person; *Am.* wood borer, wood louse; **gorgojoso** *adj.* infested with weevils.

gorila [go·rí·la] *m.* gorilla.

gorjeador [gor·xe·a·dór] *m.* warbler; *adj.* warbling; **pájaro** — warbler.

gorjear [gor·xe·ár] *v.* to warble; to chirp.

gorjeo [gor·xé·o] *m.* warble; warbling.

gorra [gó·rra] *f.* cap; bonnet; **de** — at another's expense; **vivir de** — to sponge, live at another's expense.

gorrino [go·rrí·no] *m.* sucking pig.

gorrión [go·rrjón] *m.* sparrow.

gorro [gó·rro] *m.* cap; bonnet.

gorrón [go·rrón] *m.* sponge, parasite; bum; rake (*dissolute fellow*).

gota [gó·ta] *f.* (*líquido*) drop; (*enfermedad*) gout; **sudar la** — **gorda** to sweat profusely, toil, work hard.

gotear [go·te·ár] *v.* to drip; to leak; to dribble,

gotear [go·te·ár] *v.* to drip; to leak; to dribble, trickle; to sprinkle, begin to rain; **-se** to leak.

goteo [go·té·o] *m.* trickle, drip.

gotera [go·té·ra] *f.* leak, hole (*in the roof*); eaves, trough; **-s** *Mex.* surroundings, outskirts.

gotero [go·té·ro] *m. Carib., Mex.* dropper (*for counting drops*).

gótico [gó·ti·ko] *adj.* Gothic; *m.* Goth; Gothic language.

gozar [go·sár] *v.* to enjoy; to possess, have; **-se** to rejoice.

gozne [góz·ne] *m.* hinge.

gozo [gó·so] *m.* pleasure, joy

gozoso [go·só·so] *adj.* joyful, glad, merry.

gozque, [gós·ke] **gozquejo,** [gos·ké·xo] **gozquecillo** [gos·ke·sí·yo] *m.* a small dog.

grabación [gra·ba·sjón] *f.* recording (*tape*).

grabado [gra·bá·do] *adj.* engraved; recorded; *m.* engraving; woodcut, print; — **al agua fuerte** etching.

grabadora [gra·ba·dó·ra] *f.* tape recorder; *Spain* **grabadora magnetofónica.**

grabar [gra·bár] *v.* to engrave; to carve; to fix, impress; to record on tape; — **al agua fuerte** to etch.

gracejada [gra·se·xá·da] *f. C.A.* clownish act or expression.

gracejo [gra·sé·xo] *m.* grace; cuteness; humor, wit.

gracia [grá·sja] *f.* (*humorismo*) witty remark; joke; humor; (*garbo*) grace; gracious act; (*favor*) favor; pardon; **caer en** — to please; **hacer** — to amuse, make (*someone*) laugh; **¡-s!** thanks!; **dar -s** to

thank.

gracioso [gra·sjó·so] *adj.* (*chistoso*) amusing; funny; witty; (*con garbo*) graceful, attractive; *m.* comedian, clown.

grada [grá·da] *f.* step of a staircase; harrow; **-s** steps; seats of an amphitheater; bleachers.

gradación [gra·da·sjón] *f.* gradation.

gradería [gra·de·rí·a] *f.* series of steps; rows of seats (*in an amphitheater or stadium*); — **cubierta** grandstand; **-s** bleachers.

grado [grá·do] *m.* (*medida*) degree; step; (*título*) degree; **de (buen)** — willingly, with pleasure; **de mal** — unwillingly; **de** — **en** — by degrees, gradually.

graduación [gra·dwa·sjón] *f.* graduation; military rank.

gradual [gra·dwál] *adj.* gradual; *m.* response sung at mass.

graduar[18] [gra·dwár] *v.* to graduate, give a diploma, rank or degree to; to gauge; to classify, grade; **-se** to graduate, take a degree.

gráfico [grá·fi·ko] *adj.* graphic; vivid, lifelike; **gráfica** *f.* graph, diagram, chart.

grafito [gra·fí·to] *m.* graphite.

grajo [grá·xo] *m.* rook; crow.

grama [grá·ma] *f.* grama grass.

gramática [gra·má·ti·ka] *f.* grammar; **gramatical** [gra·ma·ti·kál] *adj.* grammatical; **gramático** [gra·má·ti·ko] *adj.* grammatical; *m.* grammarian.

gramo [grá·mo] *m.* gram.

gran [gran] *contr. of* **grande.**

grana [grá·na] *f.* cochineal, kermes (*insects used for producing a red dye*); scarlet color; scarlet cloth; any small seed.

granada [gra·ná·da] *f.* pomegranate; grenade, shell, small bomb; — **de mano** hand grenade.

granado [gra·ná·do] *m.* pomegranate tree; *adj.* notable; illustrious; select.

grande [grán·de] *adj.* large, big; great, grand; *Mex., C.A., Ven., Andes* **mamá (papá)** — grandmother (grandfather); *m.* grandee (*Spanish or Portuguese nobleman*); **en** — on a large scale.

grandeza [gran·dé·sa] *f.* greatness; grandeur, splendor; bigness; size; grandeeship; body of grandees.

grandiosidad [gran·djo·si·dád] *f.* grandeur, grandness; greatness; **grandioso** [gran·djó·so] *adj.* grandiose, great, grand, magnificent.

granero [gra·né·ro] *m.* granary; grain bin; country or region rich in grain.

granito [gra·ní·to] *m.* granite; small grain; small pimple.

granizada [gra·ni·sá·da] *f.* hailstorm; shower, volley.

granizar[9] [gra·ni·sár] *v.* to hail.

granizo [gra·ní·so] *m.* hail; hailstorm; web or film in the eye; *adj. Mex.* spotted (*horse*).

granja [grán·xa] *f.* grange, farm; country house.

granjear [gran·xe·ár] *v.* to earn, gain; to acquire, obtain; *Ch., C.A.* to steal; **-se** to win for oneself (*favor, goodwill, esteem, etc.*).

granjería [gran·xe·rí·a] *f.* farming; business profit.

granjero [gran·xé·ro] *m.* farmer.

grano [grá·no] *m.* (*cereal*) grain; seed; grain (*unit of measure*); **ir al** — to come to the point.

granuja [gra·nú·xa] *m.* ragamuffin, urchin; scamp.

granular [gra·nu·lár] *v.* to granulate; **-se** to become granulated; to break out with pimples.

grapa [grá·pa] *f.* clamp; staple; (*carbunclo*) pimple.

grasa [grá·sa] *f.* grease; fat; tallow; *Mex., Riopl., Ven.* shoe polish; *Am.* **dar** — to polish (*shoes*).

GE

grasiento [gra·sjén·to] *adj.* greasy, oily.

grasoso [gra·só·so] *adj.* greasy, oily.

gratificación [gra·ti·fi·ka·sjón] *f.* gratuity, bonus, tip; recompense, reward.

gratis [grá·tis] *adv.* gratis, for nothing, free of charge.

gratitud [gra·ti·túḏ] *f.* gratitude.

grato [grá·to] *adj.* pleasing, pleasant; gratuitous; **su grata** your favor, your letter.

gratuito [gra·twí·to] *adj.* gratuitous, free, free of charge.

grava [grá·ḇa] *f.* gravel.

gravamen [gra·ḇá·men] *m.* burden; mortgage.

grave [grá·ḇe] *adj.* grave; serious; weighty, heavy; grievous; deep, low (*in pitch*).

gravedad [gra·ḇe·ḏáḏ] *f.* (*fuerza*) gravity; (*seriedad*) seriousness, gravity; (*tono*) depth (*of a sound*).

gravoso [gra·ḇó·so] *adj.* burdensome; **serle a uno —** to be burdensome; to weigh on one's conscience.

graznar [graz·nár] *v.* to caw, croak, squawk, cackle, quack.

graznido [graz·ní·ḏo] *m.* caw, croak, squawk, cackle, quack.

greca [gré·ka] *f.* fret; ornamental design.

greda [gré·ḏa] *f.* clay, chalk; chalk cleaner.

gremial [gre·mjál] *adj.* pertaining to a labor union; *m.* member of a union.

gremio [gré·mjo] *m.* guild, society, brotherhood, trade union; fold (*referring to the Church*).

greña [gré·ña] *f.* shock of hair, tangled mop of hair (*usually* **greñas**); **greñudo** [gre·ñú·ḏo] *adj.* shaggy, with long, unkempt hair.

grey [grej] *f.* flock; congregation (*of a church*).

griego [grjé·ḡo] *adj.* Greek, Grecian; *m.* Greek.

grieta [grjé·ta] *f.* crevice; crack; fissure.

grifo [grí·fo] *m.* faucet; *Carib.* cheap tavern (*where* **chicha** *is sold*); *Peru* gas station; *Am.* colored person; *Col.* drug addict; *Am.* drunkard; *adj.* curly, kinky, woolly (*hair*); *Col.* vain, conceited; **letra grifa** script; **ponerse —** to bristle, stand on end (*said of hair*).

grillo [grí·yo] *m.* cricket; sprout, shoot; **-s** fetters; obstacle, hindrance.

grima [grí·ma] *f.* uneasiness; displeasure, disgust; *Riopl.*, *Carib.* sadness, compassion, pity; *Am.* bit, small particle; **dar —** to disgust; to make uneasy; *Am.* to make sad, inspire pity.

gringo [griŋ·go] *adj. Ch. Riopl.* (*Italian*) foreign (*not Spanish*); *m. Ch.*, *Riopl.* (*Italian*) foreigner (*not Spanish*); *Mex.*, *C.A.*, *Andes*, *Col.*, *Ven.* Yankee or English-speaking person.

gripe [grí·pe] *f.* grippe, flu, influenza.

gris [gris] *adj.* grey; **grisáceo** *adj.* greyish.

grita [grí·ta] *f.* shouting, hooting; clamor, uproar.

gritar [gri·tár] *v.* to shout, cry.

gritería [gri·te·rí·a] *f.* shouting, clamor, uproar.

grito [grí·to] *m.* shout, cry; **poner el — en el cielo** to complain loudly, "hit the ceiling".

grosella [gro·sé·ya] *f.* currant; **— blanca** gooseberry; **grosellero** [gro·se·yé·ro] *m.* currant bush.

grosería [gro·se·rí·a] *f.* rudeness; coarseness; crudeness; insult.

grosero [gro·sé·ro] *adj.* rough, coarse; rude, impolite.

grosor [gro·sór] *m.* thickness.

grotesco [gro·tés·ko] *adj.* grotesque, fantastic; absurd.

grúa [grú·a] *f.* crane, derrick.

gruesa [grwé·sa] *f.* gross, twelve dozen.

grueso [grwé·so] *adj.* (*voluminoso*) fat, stout; thick;

bulky, big, heavy; (*burdo*) dense; coarse; *m.* thickness; bulk; density; main part; **en —** in gross, in bulk, by wholesale.

grulla [grú·ya] *f.* crane (*bird*).

gruñido [gru·ñí·ḏo] *m.* growl, grumble; grunt.

gruñir[19] [gru·ñír] *v. irr.* to grunt; to growl; to snarl; to grumble.

gruñón [gru·ñón] *adj.* growling; grunting; grumbly; *m.* growler; grumbler.

grupa [grú·pa] *f.* rump; **volver -s** to turn around (*usually on horseback*).

grupo [grú·po] *m.* group; set.

gruta [grú·ta] *f.* grotto, cavern.

guacal [gwa·kál] *m. Col.*, *Mex.*, *C.A.* crate (*for transporting fruit, vegetables, etc., carried on the back*). Also **huacal**.

guacamayo [gwa·ka·má·yo] *m. Am.* macaw (*large parrot*); *Am.* flashily dressed person.

guacamole [gwa·ka·mó·le] *m. Mex.*, *C.A.*, *Cuba* avocado salad; also **guacamol**.

guacho [gwá·čo] *m.* birdling, chick; young animal; *Andes*, *Riopl.* orphan; *Andes*, *Riopl.* foundling, abandoned child; *adj. Am.* odd, not paired; *Andes*, *Riopl.* forlorn, alone, abandoned.

guadal [gwa·ḏál] *m. Am.* small dune, sand hill; *Ven.* quagmire, bog, swamp; *Am.* growth of bamboo grass.

guadaña [gwa·ḏá·ña] *f.* scythe.

guagua [gwá·ḡwa] *f. Carib.*, *Ven.* bus; trifle, insignificant thing; *m.* & *f. Andes*, *Ch.*, *Riopl.* baby; **de —** for nothing, gratis, free.

guaje [gwá·xe] *m. Am.* a species of gourd; *Am.* vessel or bowl made of a gourd; *Am.* simpleton, fool; *Am.* trifle, trinket, piece of junk; *adj. Am.* foolish; *Am.* **hacerse uno —** to play the fool; *Am.* **hacer a uno —** to fool, deceive someone.

guajiro [gwa·xi·ro] *m.* Indian of the Guajira peninsula (*in Venezuela and Colombia*); *Cuba* rustic, peasant.

guajolote [gwa·xo·ló·te] *m. Mex.* turkey; *Mex.* fool.

guanaco [gwa·ná·ko] *m. Andes*, *Ch.*, *Riopl.* guanaco (*a kind of llama*); *Am.* tall, lanky, gawky person; *Am.* fool, simpleton; nickname for Salvadoreans.

guanajo [gwa·ná·xo] *m. Am.* turkey; *Am.* fool, dunce.

guano [gwá·no] *m. Carib.* palm tree; *Carib.* palm leaves (*used for thatching*); *Am.* guano, bird dung, fertilizer.

guantada [gwan·tá·ḏa] *f.* wallop, blow, slap.

guante [gwán·te] *m.* glove; *Andes* whip, scourge; **echar el — a uno** to seize or grab a person; **guantelete** [gwan·te·lé·te] *m.* gauntlet.

guapo [gwá·po] *adj. Am.* handsome, good-looking; ostentatious, showy; daring, brave; *Ch.*, *Andes* harsh, severe; *Carib.*, *Mex.* angry; *m.* brawler, quarreler, bully.

guarache [gwa·rá·če] *m. Mex.* Mexican leather sandal; *Mex.* tire patch. Also **huarache** [wa·rá·če].

guaraní [gwa·ra·ní] *adj.* pertaining to the Guarani Indians of Paraguay; *m.* & *f.* Guarani Indian.

guarapo [gwa·rá·po] *m. Col.*, *C.A.*, *Andes* juice of the sugar cane; *Col.*, *C.A.*, *Andes* sugar-cane liquor; *Col.*, *C.A.*, *Andes* low-grade brandy.

guarda [gwár·ḏa] *m.* & *f.* guard; keeper; *Riopl.* ticket collector on a streetcar; *f.* custody, care, keeping; observance of a law; **-s** outside ribs of a fan; flyleaves.

guardabarros [gwar·ḏa·ḇa·rros] *m.*, **guardafango** [gwar·ḏa·fáŋ·go] *m.* fender.

guardabosques [gwar·ḏa·ḇós·kes] *m.* forest ranger,

forester, forest keeper.
guardabrisa [gwar·da·brí·sa] *f.* windshield.
guardacostas [gwar·da·kós·tas] *m.* coast guard.
guardafrenos [gwar·da·fré·nos] *m.* brakeman.
guardagujas [gwar·da·gú·xas] *m.* switchman.
guardamonte [gwar·da·món·te] *m.* trigger guard;
forest keeper.
guardapapeles [gwar·da·pa·pé·les] *m.* file, filing
cabinet or box.
guardapelo [gwar·da·pé·lo] *m.* locket.
guardar [gwar·dár] *v.* to guard, watch over; to
keep; to store; to observe (*laws, customs*); **-se de**
to guard against, keep from, avoid.
guardarropa [gwar·da·rró·pa] *m.* wardrobe;
cloakroom; keeper of a cloakroom.
guardia [gwár·/ja] *f.* guard, body of guards;
defense, protection; *m.* guard, guardsman.
guardiamarina [gwar·dja·ma·rí·na] *f.* midshipman.
guardián *m.* guardian, keeper; superior of a
Franciscan monastery.
guarecer[13] [gwa·re·sér] *v. irr.* to protect, shelter;
-se to take shelter.
guarida [gwa·rí·da] *f.* den, cave, lair.
guarismo [gwa·ríz·mo] *m.* number.
guarnecer[13] [gwar·ne·sér] *v. irr.* to garnish,
decorate; to adorn; to trim; to harness; to
garrison; to set (*jewels*).
guarnición [gwar·ni·sjón] *f.* adornment; trimming;
setting of a jewel; guard of a sword; garrison;
-es trappings, harness.
guaro [gwá·ro] *m. C.A.* rum.
guasa [gwá·sa] *f.* joking; foolishness.
guasca [gwás·ka] *f. Andes, Ch., Ríopl.* leather
thong; *Andes, Ch., Ríopl.* rope, cord; *Andes, Ch.*
whip; *Andes, Ch., Ríopl.* **dar —** to whip, beat,
thrash.
guaso [gwá·so] *m. Am.* stag, male deer; *Ch., Andes,
Ríopl.* peasant; *Cuba* half-breed; *Am.* lasso; *adj.*
rustic, peasant-like.
guasón [gwa·són] *adj.* funny, comical; *m.* joker,
jester.
guata [gwá·ta] *f. Am.* padding; *Ven.* fib; *Col.* a
species of potato; *Ch., Andes* paunch, belly; *Am.*
echar — to get fat.
guatemalteco [gwa·te·mal·té·ko] *m. & adj.*
Guatemalan.
guayaba [gwa·yá·ba] *f.* guava (*pear-shaped tropical
fruit*); **guayabo** *m.* guava tree; *Am.* lie, fraud, trick.
guayabera [gwa·ya·bé·ra] *f.* tropical pleated jacket.
gubernativo [gu·ber·na·tí·bo] *adj.* governmental,
administrative.
guedeja [ge·dé·xa] *f.* forelock; lock of hair; lion's
mane.
güero [gwé·ro] *adj. Mex.* blond; *m. Ven.* cassava
liquor. *See* **huero.**
guerra [gé·rra] *f.* war; **— a muerte** war to the
finish; **dar —** to bother, trouble.
guerrear [ge·rre·ár] *v.* to war; *Am.* to do mischief
or to bother (*said of children*).
guerrero [ge·rré·ro] *adj.* warlike, martial; *m.* warrior,
soldier.
guerrilla [ge·rrí·ya] *f.* small war; skirmish; body of
soldiers; band of fighters.
guerrillero [ge·rri·yé·ro] *m.* guerrilla fighter.
guía [gí·a] *m. & f.* guide, leader; *f.* guidebook,
directory; signpost; shoot, sprout; *Ríopl.* garland
of flowers.
guiar[17] [gjar] *v.* to guide; to drive (*a car*).
guija [gí·xa] *f.* pebble; **guijarro** [gi·xá·rro] *m.*
cobblestone.
guijo [gí·xo] *m.* gravel.

guinda [gín·da] *f.* sour cherry.
guindilla [gin·dí·ya] *f. Spain* small hot pepper.
guineo [gi·né·o] *m. C.A.* banana.
guiñada [gi·ñá·da] *f.* wink.
guiñapo [gi·ñá·po] *m.* tag, tatter, rag; ragamuffin,
ragged person.
guiñar [gi·ñár] *v.* to wink.
guiño [gí·ño] *m.* wink.
guión [gjón] *m.* hyphen; repeat sign (*in music*); cross
(*carried before a prelate in a procession*); guide,
leader (*among birds and animals*); leader in a
dance.
guirnalda [gir·nál·da] *f.* garland, wreath.
guisa [gí·sa] *f.* way, manner; **a — de** like, in the
manner of.
guisado [gi·sá·do] *m.* stew.
guisante [gi·sán·te] *m.* pea; **— de olor** sweet pea.
guisar [gi·sár] *v.* to cook; to prepare, arrange.
guiso [gí·so] *m.* dish, dish of food.
güisquil [gwis·kil] *m. C.A.* chayote (*a pear-shaped
fruit*).
guitarra [gi·tá·rra] *f.* guitar.
gula [gú·la] *f.* gluttony.
gusano [gu·sá·no] *m.* worm; caterpillar; **— de la
conciencia** remorse; **— de luz** glowworm; *Col.,
Mex.* **matar el —** to satisfy a need or desire
(*particularly hunger or thirst*).
gustar [gus·tár] *v.* (*agradar*) to please, be pleasing;
(*saborear*) to taste; to experience; **-le a uno una
cosa** to like something; **— de** to have a liking
for, be fond of.
gusto [gús·to] *m.* (*agrado*) pleasure; whim, fancy;
(*sabor*) taste; flavor; **dar —** to please; **estar a —**
to be comfortable, contented; **tener — en** to be
glad to; **tomar el — a una cosa** to become fond of
something.
gustoso [gus·tó·so] *adj.* (*con agrado*) glad; pleasant;
willing; merry; (*sabroso*) tasty; *adv.* willingly.

H:h

haba [á·ba] *f.* large bean; Lima bean.
habano [a·bá·no] *m.* Havana cigar.
haber[30] [a·bér] *v. irr.* to have (*auxiliary verb*);
habérselas con to have it out with; **ha de llegar
mañana** he is to arrive tomorrow; **ha de ser
verdad** it must be true; **hay (había, hubo,** *etc.*)
there is, there are (there was, there were, *etc.*);
hay que (+ *inf.*) it is necessary; **no hay de qué**
you are welcome? **¿qué hay?** what's the matter?
haber [a·bér] *m.* credit, credit side (*in book-keeping*);
-es property, goods, cash, assets.
habichuela [a·bi·čwé·la] *f.* bean; **— verde** string
bean.
hábil [á·bil] *adj.* skilful, capable, able.
habilidad [a·bi·li·dád] *f.* ability, skill.
habilitar [a·bi·li·tár] *v.* to enable; to equip; to
qualify.
habitación [a·bi·ta·sjón] *f.* apartment; room;
lodging.
habitante [a·bi·tán·te] *m.* inhabitant; resident.
habitar [a·bi·tár] *v.* to inhabit; to live, reside.
hábito [á·bi·to] *m.* habit; custom.
habitual [a·bi·twál] *adj.* habitual, customary.
habituar[18] [a·bi·twár] *v.* to accustom; **-se** to get
used, accustomed.
habla [á·bla] *f.* speech; language, dialect; **al —**
within speaking distance; in communication

(with).

hablador [a·ƀla·ḓór] *m.* talker; gossip; *adj.* talkative.
habladuría [a·ƀla·ḓu·rí·a] *f.* gossip, rumor; empty talk; impertinent remark.
hablar [a·ƀlár] *v.* to speak; to talk; — **alto** (*or* **en voz alta**) to speak loudly; — **bajo** (**quedo** *or* **en voz baja**) to speak softly; — **por los codos** to chatter constantly.
hablilla [a·ƀlí·ya] *f.* gossip, rumor, malicious tale.
hacedero [a·se·ḓé·ro] *adj.* feasible.
hacedor [a·se·ḓór] *m.* maker; **el Supremo Hacedor** the Maker.
hacendado [a·sen·dá·ḓo] *m.* landholder; *Ríopl., Ch., Ven.* owner of a farm, plantation, or ranch.
hacendoso [a·sen·dó·so] *adj.* industrious, diligent.
hacer[31] [a·sér] *v. irr.* (*crear*) to do; to make; (*formar*) to form; to accustom; (*causar*) to cause, order (*followed by inf.*); — **caso** to mind, pay attention; — **frío** (**calor**) to be cold (warm); — **la maleta** to pack one's suitcase; — **un papel** to play a part; *Am.* — **aprecio** to pay attention; *Ríopl., Mex.* — **caras** (*or* **caritas**) to flirt; **no le hace** it makes no difference; **-se** to become, grow, get to be; **-se a** to get used to; **-se de rogar** to want to be coaxed.
hacia [á·sja] *prep.* toward; about; — **adelante** forward; — **atrás** backward.
hacienda [a·sjén·da] *f.* estate; property; finance; large farm; *Ríopl.* cattle, livestock.
hacina [á·si·na] *f.* shock (*of grain*), stack, pile.
hacinar [a·si·nár] *v.* to shock (*grain*); to stack, pile up; to accumulate.
hacha [á·ča] *f.* ax; hatchet; torch.
hachero [a·čé·ro] *m.* axman, woodcutter.
hada [á·ḓa] *f.* fairy.
hado [á·ḓo] *m.* fate, fortune, destiny.
halagar[7] [a·la·ǥár] *v.* to coax; to flatter; to allure, attract.
halago [a·lá·ǥo] *m.* flattery; caress; allurement.
halagüeño [a·la·ǥwé·ño] *adj.* alluring, attractive; flattering; promising.
halar [a·lár] = **jalar.**
halcón [al·kón] *m.* falcon.
hálito [á·li·to] *m.* breath; vapor.
hallar [a·yár] *v.* to find; to discover, find out; **-se** to be; to fare, get along.
hallazgo [a·yáz·ǥo] *m.* find; discovery; reward (*for finding something*).
hamaca [a·má·ka] *f.* hammock.
hambre [ám·bre] *f.* hunger; famine; appetite; **tener** — to be hungry; **hambruna** [am·brú·na] *f. Am.* great hunger, starvation.
hambrear [am·bre·ár] *v.* to starve; to be hungry.
hambriento [am·brjén·to] *adj.* hungry; greedy; *C.A., Mex., Andes* stingy.
hampa [ám·pa] *f. Spain* underworld.
hangar [aŋ·gár] *m.* hangar.
haragán [a·ra·ǥán] *adj.* lazy, indolent; *m.* loafer, idler.
haraganear [a·ra·ǥa·ne·ár] *v.* to lounge, loaf, be lazy.
haraganería [a·ra·ǥa·ne·rí·a] *f.* laziness.
harapiento [a·ra·pjén·to] *adj.* tattered, ragged.
harapo [a·rá·po] *m.* rag, tatter; **andar hecho un** — to be in tatters.
haraposo [a·rá·pó·so] *adj.* tattered, ragged.
harina [a·rí·na] *f.* flour; **eso es — de otro costal** that is something entirely different; **harinoso** [a·ri·nó·so] *adj.* floury; flourlike.
harmonía [ar·mo·ní·a] *f.* harmony.
hartar [ar·tár] *v.* to fill up, gorge; to sate, satiate;

-se to have one's fill; to overeat, eat too much.
harto [ár·to] *adj.* full; sated, satiated; fed up; too much; *adv.* too much; *Mex., C.A., Col., Ven., Ríopl., Andes* much, very much.
hasta [ás·ta] *prep.* till, until; up to; — **luego** good-bye, see you later; *conj.* even; — **que** until.
hastiar[17] [as·tjár] *v.* to surfeit; to cloy; to disgust.
hastío [as·tí·o] *m.* surfeit, excess; boredom; loathing, disgust.
hato [á·to] *m.* herd; flock; sheepfold; shepherd's hut; gang, crowd; pile; *Col., Ven.* cattle ranch.
haya [á·ya] *f.* beech; **hayuco** *m.* beechnut.
haz [as] *f.* face; surface; *m.* fagot, bundle, bunch.
hazaña [a·sá·ña] *f.* deed, exploit, feat.
hazmerreír [az·me·rre·ír] *m.* laughing stock.
he [e] (*used with* **aquí** *or* **alli**) behold, here is, here you have; **heme aquí** here I am; **helo aquí** here it is.
hebilla [e·ƀí·ya] *f.* buckle.
hebra [é·ƀra] *f.* thread; fiber; fine string; *Am.* **de una** — all at once, at one stroke, *Am.* **ni** — absolutely nothing; **hebroso** *adj.* fibrous, stringy.
hecatombe [e·ka·tóm·be] *m.* massacre, great slaughter; hecatomb (*sacrifice of 100 oxen*).
hectárea [ek·tá·re·a] *m.* hectare.
hechicera [e·či·sé·ra] *f.* witch, enchantress; hag.
hechicería [e·či·se·rí·a] *f.* witchcraft; magic; charm; enchantment.
hechicero [e·či·sé·ro] *adj.* bewitching, charming; *m.* magician; charmer; sorcerer.
hechizar[5] [e·či·sár] *v.* to bewitch; to charm.
hechizo [e·čí·so] *m.* charm; enchantment.
hecho [é·čo] *m.* fact; act, deed; **de** — in fact; *p.p. of* **hacer** done, made.
hechura [e·čú·ra] *f.* make; shape, cut; workmanship.
heder[1] [e·ḓér] *v. irr.* to stink; to reek.
hediondez [e·djon·dés] *f.* stink, stench.
hediondo [e·djón·do] *adj.* foul-smelling, stinking; filthy; *m. Ríopl.* skunk.
hedor [e·ḓór] *m.* stink, stench.
helada [e·lá·ḓa] *f.* frost.
helado [e·lá·ḓo] *adj.* frozen; freezing; frosty; icy; *m.* ice cream; ice, sherbet; **heladería** [e·la·ḓe·rí·a] *f. Am.* ice-cream parlor.
heladora [e·la·ḓó·ra] *f.* freezer.
helar[1] [e·lár] *v. irr.* to freeze.
helecho [e·lé·čo] *m.* fern.
hélice [é·li·se] *f.* screw propeller; helix, spiral.
helicóptero [e·li·kóp·te·ro] *m.* helicopter.
helio [é·ljo] *m.* helium.
helipuerto [e·li·pwér·to] *m.* heliport.
hembra [ém·bra] *f.* female; staple; nut (*of a screw*); **macho y** — hook and eye.
hemisferio [e·mis·fé·rjo] *m.* hemisphere.
hemofilia [e·mo·fí·lja] *f.* hemophilia.
hemoglobina [e·mo·glo·ƀí·na] *f.* hemoglobin.
hemorragia [e·mo·rrá·xja] *f.* hemorrhage.
henchir[5] [en·čír] *v. irr.* to swell, stuff, fill.
hendedura [en·de·ḓú·ra], **hendidura** [en·di·ḓú·ra] *f.* crack, crevice, fissure.
hender[1] [en·dér] *v. irr.* to split, crack, cleave.
henequén [e·ne·kén] *m. Mex., Ven., C.A., Col.* sisal, sisal hemp.
heno [é·no] *m.* hay.
henil [e·níl] *m.* hayloft.
hepatitis [e·pa·tí·tis] *f.* hepatitis.
heráldico [e·rál·di·ko] *adj.* heraldic; **heráldica** heraldry.
heraldo [e·rál·do] *m.* herald.
herbazal [er·ƀa·sál] *m.* field of grass.

herboso [er·ƀó·so] *adj.* grassy; weedy.
heredad [e·re·ḍáḍ] *f.* parcel of land; rural property; estate.
heredar [e·re·ḍár] *v.* to inherit; to bequeath, leave in a will.
heredero [e·re·ḍé·ro] *m.* heir; successor; **heredera** [e·re·ḍé·ra] *f.* heiress.
hereditario [e·re·ḍi·tá·rjo] *adj.* hereditary.
hereje [e·ré·xe] *m.* heretic; **cara de —** hideous face.
herejía [e·re·xí·a] *f.* heresy; offensive remark.
herencia [e·ren·sja] *f.* inheritance; heritage; heredity.
herida [e·rí·ḍa] *f.* wound; injury.
herido [e·rí·ḍo] *adj.* wounded; *m.* wounded man; *Am.* small drainage channel.
herir[3] [e·rír] *v. irr.* to wound; to hurt; to strike; to offend.
hermana [er·má·na] *f.* sister.
hermanastro [er·ma·nás·tro] *m.* stepbrother, half brother; **hermanastra** [er·ma·nás·tra] *f.* stepsister, half sister.
hermandad [er·man·dáḍ] *f.* brotherhood, fraternity.
hermano [er·má·no] *m.* brother.
hermético [er·mé·ti·ko] *adj.* hermetic; airtight; tight-lipped; close-mouthed; **hermetismo** [er·me·tíz·mo] *m.* complete silence.
hermosear [er·mo·se·ár] *v.* to beautify, adorn.
hermoso [er·mó·so] *adj.* beautiful, handsome.
hermosura [er·mo·sú·ra] *f.* beauty.
hernia [ér·nja] *f.* hernia.
héroe [e·ro·é] *m.* hero; **heroína** [e·ro·í·na] *f.* heroine; heroin (*drug*).
heroico [e·rój·ko] *adj.* heroic.
heroísmo [e·ro·íz·mo] *adj.* heroism.
herradura [e·rra·ḍú·ra] *f.* horseshoe.
herraje [e·rrá·xe] *m.* ironwork; iron trimmings; horseshoes and nails; *Am.* silver saddle trimmings; *Am.* horseshoe.
herramienta [e·rra·mjén·ta] *f.* tool; *pl.* set of tools.
herrar[1] [e·rrár] *v. irr.* to shoe (*a horse*); to brand; to trim with iron.
herrería [e·rre·rí·a] *f.* blacksmith's shop or trade; forge; ironworks.
herrero [e·rré·ro] *m.* blacksmith.
herrete [e·rré·te] *m.* metal tip (*for a shoelace, for instance*); *Am.* branding iron.
herrumbre [e·rrúm·bre] *f.* rust; plant rot.
hervidero [er·ƀi·ḍé·ro] *m.* bubbling sound (*of boiling water*); bubbling spring; swarm, crowd; **un — de gente** a swarm of people.
hervir[3] [er·ƀír] *v. irr.* to boil; **— de gente** to swarm with people.
hervor [er·ƀór] *m.* boiling; boiling point; **soltar el —** to come to a boil.
heterodoxia [e·te·ro·ḍók·sja] *f.* heterodoxy.
heterogéneo [e·te·ro·xé·ne·o] *adj.* heterogeneous.
hez [es] *f.* scum; **la — del pueblo** the scum of society; **heces** [é·ses] dregs, sediment.
hiato [já·to] *m.* hiatus.
híbrido [í·ƀri·ḍo] *adj. & m.* hybrid.
hidalgo [i·ḍal·ǥo] *m.* hidalgo (*Spanish nobleman*); *adj.* noble, courteous.
hidalguía [i·ḍal·ǥí·a] *f.* nobility; generosity; courtesy.
hidrato [i·ḍrá·to] *m.* hydrate.
hidráulico [i·ḍráw·li·ko] *adj.* hydraulic; **fuerza hidráulica** water power; **ingeniero —** hydraulic engineer.
hidroavión [i·ḍro·a·ƀjón] *m.* hydroplane, seaplane.
hidroeléctrico [i·ḍro·e·lék·tri·ko] *adj.* hydroelectric.
hidrógeno [i·ḍró·xe·no] *m.* hydrogen.

hidropesía [i·ḍro·pe·sí·a] *f.* dropsy.
hidroplano [i·ḍro·plá·no] *m.* hydroplane.
hiedra [jé·ḍra] *f.* ivy.
hiel [jel] *f.* gall, bile; bitterness.
hielo [jé·lo] *m.* ice; frost.
hierba [jér·ƀa] *f.* grass; herb; weed; *Riopl., Andes* mate (*Paraguayan tea*); *Mex., Ven., Cuba* marihuana (*a narcotic*); *C.A.* **ciertas -s** so-and-so (*person not named*).
hierbabuena [jer·ƀa·ƀwé·na] *f.* mint. *Also* **yerbabuena** [ỿer·ƀa·ƀwé·na].
hierro [jé·rro] *m.* iron; brand; iron tool, instrument, or weapon; **-s** irons, chains, handcuffs.
hígado [í·ǥa·ḍo] *m.* (*órgano*) liver; (*valentía*) courage; valor; **malos -s** ill will.
higiene [i·xjé·ne] *f.* hygiene; **higiénico** [i·xjé·ni·ko] *adj.* hygienic, sanitary.
higo [í·ǥo] *m.* fig; **higuera** [i·ǥé·ra] *f.* fig tree; **higuerilla** [i·ǥe·rí·ya] *f. Am.* castor-oil plant.
hija [í·xa] *f.* daughter; native daughter.
hijo [í·xo] *m.* son; native son; offspring; fruit, result.
hilachas [i·lá·čas] *f. pl.* lint; **mostrar uno la hilacha** to show one's worst side or nature; **hilachos** [i·lá·čos] *m. pl. Am.* rags, tatters.
hilado [i·lá·ḍo] *m.* yarn; *p.p. of* **hilar.**
hilandera [i·lan·dé·ra] *f.* spinner.
hilandería [i·lan·de·rí·a] *f.* spinning mill; art of spinning; spinning.
hilandero [i·lan·dé·ro] *m.* spinner; spinning room.
hilar [i·lár] *v.* to spin, make into thread; **— muy delgado** to be very subtle.
hilas [í·las] *f. pl.* lint, fine ravelings (*for dressing wounds*).
hilaza [i·lá·sa] *f.* coarse thread; yarn.
hilera [i·lé·ra] *f.* file, row, line; **— de perlas** strand or string of pearls.
hilo [í·lo] *m.* (*hebra*) thread; fine yarn; string; (*alambre*) filament; thin wire; (*tela*) linen; **a —** without interruption; **al —** along the thread; *Am.* very well, all right; **de —** straight, without stopping; *Am.* **de un —** constantly, without stopping; **tener el alma en un —** to be frightened to death; to be in great anxiety or suspense.
hilván [il·ƀán] *m.* basting stitch; basting; *Am.* hem.
hilvanar [il·ƀa·nár] *v.* to baste; to put together, connect; to do hastily; *Am.* to hem.
himno [ím·no] *m.* hymn.
hincapié [iŋ·ka·pjé] : **hacer —** to emphasize, stress; to insist (upon).
hincar[6] [iŋ·kár] *v.* to drive, thrust (into); **-se** (*or* **-se de rodillas**) to kneel down.
hinchado [in·čá·ḍo] *adj. & p.p.* swollen; inflated; presumptuous.
hinchar [in·čár] *v.* to swell; **-se** to swell; to swell up, puff up.
hinchazón [in·ča·són] *f.* swelling; inflation; conceit; bombast, inflated style.
hinojos [i·nó·xos] : **de —** on one's knees.
hipérbole [i·pér·ƀo·le] *f.* hyperbole.
hiperbólico [i·per·ƀó·li·ko] *adj.* hyperbolic.
hipo [í·po] *m.* hiccough; sob; longing; grudge, ill will.
hipocresía [i·po·kre·sía] *f.* hypocrisy.
hipócrita [i·pó·kri·ta] *adj.* hypocritical, insincere; *m. & f.* hypocrite.
hipódromo [i·pó·ḍro·mo] *m.* race track.
hipoteca [i·po·té·ka] *f.* mortgage.
hipotecar[6] [i·po·te·kár] *v.* to mortgage.
hipótesis [i·pó·te·sis] *f.* hypothesis, theory.

hipotético [i·po·té·ti·ko] *adj.* hypothetic(al).
hirviente [ir·bjén·te] *adj.* boiling.
hispanidad [is·pa·ni·dád] *f.* Hispanic solidarity.
hispanista [is·pa·nís·ta] *m. & f.* Hispanist; one who is interested in Hispanic studies.
hispano [is·pá·no] *adj.* Hispanic, Spanish; *m.* Spanish-speaking person.
hispanoamericano [is·pa;no·a·me·ri·ká·no] *adj.* Spanish-American.
histamina [is·ta·mí·na] *f.* histamine.
histérico [is·té·ri·ko] *adj.* hysterical.
historia [is·tó·rja] *f.* history; story; tale, fable; **dejarse de -s** to stop fooling and come to the point; **historieta** [is·to·rjé·ta] *f.* story, anecdote.
historiador [is·to·rja·dór] *m.* historian.
historial [is·to·rjal] *m.* record, data (*concerning a person or firm*); *adj.* historic.
histórico [is·tó·ri·ko] *adj.* historic, historical.
hito [í·to] *adj.* firm, fixed; **de hito en hito** fixedly.
hocico [o·sí·ko] *m.* snout; **caer de -s** to fall on one's face; **meter el — en todo** to meddle, stick one's nose in everything.
hogaño [o·gá·ño] *adv.* nowadays.
hogar [o·gár] *m.* hearth, fireplace; home.
hogareño [o·ga·ré·ño] *adj.* home-loving, domestic; homelike.
hoguera [o·gé·ra] *f.* bonfire.
hoja [ó·xa] *f.* leaf; petal; sheet of paper or metal; blade; **— de lata** tin plate.
hojalata [o·xa·lá·ta] *f.* tin plate.
hojaldre [o·xál·dre] *m. & f.* puff pastry.
hojarasca [o·xa·rás·ka] *f.* fallen leaves; dry foliage; superfluous ornament; trash; useless words.
hojear [o·xe·ár] *v.* to leaf, turn the pages of; to browse.
hojuela [o·xwé·la] *f.* leaflet, small leaf; thin leaf (*of metal*); flake; thin pancake; **— de estaño** tin foil.
¡hola! [ó·la] *interj.* hello!; ho!; ah!
holandés [o·lan·dés] *adj.* Dutch; *m.* Dutchman; Dutch language.
holgado [ol·gá·do] *adj.* (*libre*) free, at leisure; comfortable; (*ancho*) wide, loose; roomy, spacious; *p.p. of* **holgar.**
holganza [ol·gán·sa] *f.* idleness.
holgar [ol·gár] *v. irr.* to rest; to loaf; **-se** to be glad; to relax, have a good time; **huelga decir** needless to say.
holgazán [ol·ga·sán] *m.* idler, loafer; *adj.* lazy, idle.
holgazanear [ol·ga·sa·ne·ár] *v.* to loiter, lounge, idle, bum around.
holgazanería [ol·ga·sa·ne·rí·a] *f.* idleness, laziness.
holgorio [ol·gó·rjo] *m.* spree.
holgura [ol·gú·ra] *f.* (*descanso*) ease; rest, comfort; (*lugar*) roominess, plenty of room.
holocausto [o·lo·káws·to] *m.* holocaust, burnt offering, sacrifice.
hollar [o·yár] *v.* to tread, trample upon.
hollejo [o·yé·xo] *m.* skin, peel; husk.
hollín [o·yín] *m.* soot.
hombrada [om·brá·da] *f.* manly act; show of bravery.
hombre [óm·bre] *m.* man; **hombría** [om·bri·a] *f.* manliness, manly strength; **— de bien** honesty.
hombro [óm·bro] *m.* shoulder; **arrimar** (*or* **meter**) **el —** to help.
hombruno [om·brú·no] *adj.* mannish, masculine.
homenaje [o·me·ná·xe] *m.* homage, honor.
homeópata [o·me·ó·pa·ta] *adj.* homeopathic.
homicida [o·mi·sí·da] *m.* murderer; *f.* murderess; *adj.* homicidal, murderous.
homicidio [o·mi·sí·djo] *m.* homicide, murder.

homófono [o·mó·fo·no] *adj.* homophonous.
homogeneidad [o·mo·xe·nej·dád] *f.* homogeneity.
homogéneo [o·mo·xé·ne·o] *adj.* homogeneous, of the same kind or nature.
honda [ón·da] *f.* sling, slingshot.
hondo [ón·do] *adj.* deep; low; *m.* bottom, depth.
hondonada [on·do·ná·da] *f.* hollow, dip, gully, ravine.
hondura [on·dú·ra] *f.* depth; **meterse en -s** to go beyond one's depth; to get into trouble.
honestidad [o·nes·ti·dád] *f.* chastity, modesty, decency; decorum, propriety.
honesto [o·nés·to] *adj.* chaste, modest, decent; just; honest.
hongo [óŋ·go] *m.* mushroom; fungus; derby hat.
honor [o·nór] *m.* honor; glory; dignity.
honorario [o·no·rá·rjo] *m.* fee (*for professional services*); *adj.* honorary.
honorífico [o·no·rí·fi·ko] *adj.* honorary; **mención honorífica** honorable mention.
honra [ón·rra] *f.* honor; reputation; **-s** obsequies, funeral rites.
honradez [on·rra·dés] *f.* honesty, honor, integrity.
honrado [on·rrá·do] *adj.* honest, honorable; honored.
honrar [on·rrár] *v.* to honor; **-se** to be honored; to consider it an honor.
honroso [on·rró·so] *adj.* honorable; honoring.
hora [ó·ra] *f.* hour; time; **-s** canonical hours, office (*required daily prayers for priests and nuns*); **es — de** it is time to; **no ver la — de** (+ *inf.*) to be anxious to; **¿qué — es?** what time is it?
horadar [o·ra·dár] *v.* to pierce, bore, perforate.
horario [o·rá·rjo] *m.* schedule, timetable; hour hand.
horca [ór·ka] *f.* (*cadalso*) gallows; (*horcón*) pitchfork; *P.R.* birthday present; **— de ajos** string of garlic.
horcajadas [or·ka·xá·das]: **a —** astride (*with one leg on each side*); **ponerse a —** to straddle.
horcón [or·kón] *m.* forked pole, forked prop; *Mex., Cuba, Ven.* post, roof support; *Am.* roof.
horda [ór·da] *f.* horde.
horizontal [o·ri·son·tál] *adj.* horizontal.
horizonte [o·ri·són·te] *m.* horizon.
horma [ór·ma] *f.* form, mold; block (*for shaping a hat*); shoe last; shoe tree.
hormiga [or·mí·ga] *f.* ant.
hormigón [or·mi·gón] *m.* concrete.
hormigonera [or·mi·go·né·ra] *f.* concrete mixer.
hormiguear [or·mi·ge·ár] *v.* to swarm; to be crawling with ants; **me hormiguea el cuerpo** I itch all over.
hormigueo [or·mi·ge·o] *m.* itching, creeping sensation; tingle, tingling sensation.
hormiguero [or·mi·gé·ro] *m.* ant hill; ant nest; swarm; **oso —** anteater.
hormona [or·mó·na] *f.* hormone.
hornada [or·ná·da] *f.* batch of bread, baking.
hornear [or·ne·ár] *v.* to bake (*in an oven*).
hornilla [or·ní·ya] *f.* burner; grate (*of a stove*).
hornillo [or·ní·yo] *m.* kitchen stove; hot plate.
horno [or·no] *m.* furnace; oven; kiln (*for baking bricks*); **alto —** blast furnace.
horquilla [or·kí·ya] *f.* hairpin; forked pole; small pitchfork.
horrendo [o·rrén·do] *adj.* horrible, hideous.
horrible [o·rri·ble] *adj.* horrible.
horripilante [o·rri·pi·lán·te] *adj.* horrifying.
horror [o·rrór] *m.* horror; atrocity; **dar —** to cause fright; to horrify; **tenerle — a uno** to feel a

strong dislike for one.
horrorizar[9] [o·rro·ri·sár] *v.* to horrify, shock, terrify.
horroroso [o·rro·ró·so] *adj.* horrid; frightful, hideous.
hortaliza [or·ta·li·sa] *f.* vegetables; vegatable garden.
hortelano [or·te·lá·no] *m.* gardener.
hosco [ós·ko] *adj.* sullen; frowning; dark.
hospedaje [os·pe·đá·xe] *m.* board and lodging; lodging.
hospedar [os·pe·đár] *v.* to lodge, give lodging; **-se** to take lodging; to room, to stop (*at a hotel*).
hospedero [os·pe·đé·ro] *m.* innkeeper.
hospicio [os·pí·sjo] *m.* asylum; orphanage, orphan asylum; poorhouse; **hospiciano** [os·pi·sjá·no] *m.* inmate of a poorhouse or asylum.
hospital [os·pi·tál] *m.* hospital; — **de primera sangre** first-aid station.
hospitalidad [os·pi·ta·li·đáđ] *f.* hospitality.
hostería [os·te·rí·a] *f.* hostelry, inn.
hostia [ós·tja] *f.* host (*consecrated wafer*).
hostigar[7] [os·ti·gár] *v.* to harass, vex; to beat, lash; *C.A., Col.* to cloy.
hostil [os·tíl] *adj.* hostile; **hostilidad** [os·ti·li·đáđ] *f.* hostility.
hotel [o·tél] *m.* hotel; villa; **hotelero** [o·te·lé·ro] *m.* hotel-keeper; *adj.* pertaining to hotels.
hoy [oj] *adv.* today; — **día** nowadays; **de** — **en adelante** from now on; — **por** — at present; **de** — **más** henceforth.
hoya [ó·ya] *f.* pit, hole; grave; valley; *Am.* river basin.
hoyo [ó·yo] *m.* hole; pit; grave; *Ríopl., Carib.* dimple.
hoyuelo [o·ywé·lo] *m.* dimple; tiny hole.
hoz [os] *f.* sickle; narrow ravine.
hozar[9] [o·sár] *v.* to root, turn up the earth with the snout (*as hogs*).
huacal [wa·kál] = **guacal.**
huarache [wa·rá·če] = **guarache.**
huaso [wá·so] = **guaso.**
hueco [wé·ko] *adj.* (*vacío*) hollow, empty; (*vano*) vain, affected; puffed up; high-sounding; *m.* gap, space, hole.
huelga [wél·ga] *f.* labor strike; rest; leisure; **declararse en** — to strike.
huelguista [wel·gís·ta] *m.* striker.
huella [wé·ya] *f.* trace; footprint.
huérfano [wér·fa·no] *adj. & m.* orphan.
huero [wé·ro] *adj.* empty; rotten, spoiled (*egg*). *See* **güero.**
huerta [wér·ta] *f.* orchard and vegetable garden; irrigated land.
huerto [wér·to] *m.* small orchard and vegetable garden; garden patch.
hueso [wé·so] *m.* bone; stone, pit; big seed; **la sin** — the tongue; **soltar la sin** — to talk too much; **no dejarle un** — **sano** to pick him to pieces.
huésped [wés·peđ] *m.* (*convidado*) guest; (*anfitrión*) host; **ser** — **en su casa** to be seldom at home.
hueste [wés·te] *f.* host, army, multitude.
huesudo [we·sú·đo] *adj.* bony.
huevo [wé·ɓo] *m.* egg; — **duro** hard-boiled egg; — **estrellado** fried egg; — **pasado por agua** soft-boiled egg; **-s revueltos** scrambled eggs; *Mex., C.A., Col., Ven.* **-s tibios** soft-boiled eggs; *Col., Mex.* **-s pericos** scrambled eggs; *Ven., Andes* **costar un** — to be very expensive.
huída [wí·đa] *f.* flight; escape.
huir[32] [wir] *v. irr.* to flee, escape; to avoid, shun.

huizache [wi·sá·ce] *m. Mex., C.A.* huisache (*a species of acacia*).
hule [ú·le] *m.* rubber; oilcloth; *Col., Ven.* rubber tree.
hulla [ú·ya] *f.* soft coal.
humanidad [u·ma·ni·đáđ] *f.* humanity, mankind; humaneness; **-es** humanities, letters.
humanitario [u·ma·ni·tá·rjo] *adj.* humanitarian, humane, kind, charitable.
humano [u·má·no] *adj.* human; humane; *m.* man, human being.
humareda [u·ma·ré·đa] *f.* cloud of smoke.
humeante [u·me·án·te] *adj.* smoking, smoky; steaming.
humear [u·me·ár] *v.* to smoke, give off smoke; to steam; *Am.* to fumigate.
humedad [u·me·đáđ] *f.* humidity, moisture, dampness.
humedecer[13] [u·me·đe·sér] *v. irr.* to moisten, wet, dampen.
húmedo [ú·me·đo] *adj.* humid, moist, wet, damp.
humildad [u·mil·dáđ] *f.* humility; humbleness; meekness.
humilde [u·míl·de] *adj.* humble, lowly, meek.
humillación [u·mi·ya·sjón] *f.* humiliation; submission.
humillar [u·mi·yár] *v.* to humiliate, humble, lower, crush; **-se** to humiliate oneself; to bow humbly.
humillos [u·mí·yos] *m. pl.* airs, conceit, vanity.
humo [ú·mo] *m.* smoke, fume, vapor; **-s** conceit, vanity.
humor [u·mór] *m.* substance; mood, disposition.
humorada [u·mo·rá·đa] *f.* pleasantry, witty remark; caprice, notion.
humorismo [u·mo·ríz·mo] *m.* humor, humorous style.
humorístico [u·mo·rís·ti·ko] *adj.* humorous.
humoso [u·mó·so] *adj.* smoky.
hundimiento [un·di·mjén·to] *m.* sinking, collapse, cave-in.
hundir [un·dír] *v.* (*sumir*) to sink, submerge; (*batir*) to crush, oppress; to destroy; **-se** to sink; to collapse, cave in.
huracán [u·ra·kán] *m.* hurricane.
huraño [u·rá·ño] *adj.* diffident, shy, bashful; unsociable.
¡hurra! [ú·rra] *interj.* hurrah!
hurtadillas [ur·ta·đí·yas]: **a** — on the sly, secretly, stealthily.
hurtar [ur·tár] *v.* to steal, rob; **-se** to withdraw, slip away; to hide; — **el cuerpo** to dodge; to flee.
hurto [úr·to] *m.* robbery, theft; stolen article; **a** — stealthily, on the sly.
husmear [uz·me·ár] *v.* to scent, smell, follow the track of; to nose, pry (into).
husmeo [uz·mé·o] *m.* sniff, sniffing, smelling; prying.
huso [ú·so] *m.* spindle.

I: i

I: i **ibérico** [i·ɓé·ri·ko], **ibero** [i·ɓé·ro] *adj.* Iberian; **iberoamericano** [i·ɓe·ro·a·mé·ri·ká·no] *adj.* Ibero-American (*Spanish or Portuguese American*).
iconoclasta [i·ko·no·klás·ta] *m. & f.* iconoclast.
ida [í·đa] *f.* departure; sally; **billete de** — **y vuelta** round-trip ticket; **-s y venidas** goings and comings.

idea [i·dé·a] *f.* idea; notion.
ideal [i·de·ál] *m.* & *adj.* ideal.
idealismo [i·de·a·líz·mo] *m.* idealism.
idealista [i·de·a·lís·ta] *adj.* idealistic; *m.* & *f.* idealist; dreamer.
idear [i·de·ár] *v.* to form an idea of; to devise, think out, plan.
idem [í·den] idem (*abbreviation*: id.), ditto, the same.
idéntico [i·dén·ti·ko] *adj.* identical.
identidad [i·den·ti·dád] *f.* identity.
identificar[6] [i·den·ti·fi·kár] *v.* to identify
idilio [i·dí·ljo] *m.* idyl.
idioma [i·dí·ljo] *m.* language, tongue.
idiosincrasia [i·djo·siŋ·krá·sja] *f.* idiosyncrasy.
idiota [i·djó·ta] *m.* & *f.* idiot; *adj.* idiotic, foolish.
idiotez [i·djo·tés] *f.* idiocy.
idiotismo [i·djo·tíz·mo] *m.* idiom; idiocy.
idolatrar [i·do·la·trár] *v.* to idolize, worship.
idolo [í·do·lo] *m.* idol.
idóneo [i·dó·ne·o] *adj.* fit, suitable; qualified.
iglesia [i·glé·sja] *f.* church.
ignición [ig·ni·sjón] *f.* ignition.
ignominia [ig·no·mí·nja] *f.* infamy, shame, disgrace.
ignominioso [ig·no·mi·njó·so] *adj.* ignominious; infamous, shameful, disgraceful.
ignorancia [ig·no·rán·sja] *f.* ignorance.
ignorante [ig·no·rán·te] *adj.* ignorant.
ignorar [ig·no·rár] *v.* to be ignorant of, not to know.
ignoto [ig·nó·to] *adj.* unknown, undiscovered.
igual [i·gwál] *adj.* (*semejante*) equal; (*liso*) even, smooth; uniform; (*siempre*) constant; **serle — a uno** to be all the same to one, make no difference to one; *m.* equal; **al — equally.**
igualar [i·gwa·lár] *v.* to equal; to equalize; to match; to level, smooth; to adjust; to be equal.
igualdad [i·gwal·dád] *f.* equality.
igualitario [i·gwa·li·tá·rjo] *adj.* equalitarian (*promoting the doctrine of equality*).
iguana [i·gwá·na] *f.* iguana.
ijada [i·xá·da] *f.* loin; flank (*of an animal*); pain in the side; **ijar** *m.* flank (*of an animal*).
ilegal [i·le·gál] *adj.* illegal, unlawful.
ilegítimo [i·le·xí·ti·mo] *adj.* illegitimate; illegal.
ileso [i·lé·so] *adj.* unharmed, uninjured, unhurt, safe and sound.
ilícito [i·lí·si·to] *adj.* illicit, unlawful.
ilimitado [i·li·mi·tá·do] *adj.* unlimited.
iluminación [i·lu·mi·na·sjón] *f.* illumination.
iluminar [i·lu·mi·nár] *v.* to illuminate; to light; to enlighten.
ilusión [i·lu·sjón] *f.* illusion.
ilusivo [i·lu·sí·bo] *adj.* illusive.
iluso [i·lú·so] *adj.* deluded; *m.* visionary, dreamer.
ilusorio [i·lu·só·rjo] *adj.* illusive; deceptive; worthless.
ilustración [i·lus·tra·sjón] *f.* illustration; elucidation, explanation.
ilustrado [i·lus·trá·do] *adj.* learned; enlightened.
ilustrador [i·lus·tra·dór] *m.* illustrator.
ilustrar [i·lus·trár] *v.* to illustrate.
ilustre [i·lús·tre] *adj.* illustrious, distinguished.
imagen [i·má·xen] *f.* image.
imaginable [i·ma·xi·ná·ble] *adj.* imaginable, conceivable.
imaginación [i·ma·xi·na·sjón] *f.* imagination.
imaginar [i·ma·xi·nár] *v.* to imagine.
imaginario [i·ma·xi·ná·rjo] *adj.* imaginary.
imaginativo [i·ma·xi·na·tí·bo] *adj.* imaginative; **imaginativa** [i·ma·xi·na·tí·ba] *f.* imagination.

imán [i·mán] *m.* magnet; attraction.
imantar [i·man·tár] *v.* to magnetize.
imbécil [im·bé·sil] *adj.* imbecile, stupid.
imborrable [im·bo·rrá·ble] *adj.* indelible, not erasable; unforgettable.
imbuir[32] [im·bwír] *v. irr.* to imbue; to instill, infuse, inspire (with).
imitación [i·mi·ta·sjón] *f.* imitation.
imitador [i·mi·ta·dor] *m.* imitator; follower; *adj.* imitative, imitating.
imitar [i·mi·tár] *v.* to imitate.
impaciencia [im·pa·sjén·sja] *f.* impatience.
impaciente [im·pa·sjén·te] *adj.* impatient.
impar [im·pár] *adj.* odd; **número — odd number.**
imparcial [im·par·sjál] *adj.* impartial; **imparcialidad** [im·par·sja·li·dád] *f.* impartiality, fairness, justice.
impasible [im·pa·sí·ble] *adj.* impassive, insensitive, insensible, unfeeling, unmoved.
impávido [im·pá·bi·do] *adj.* fearless; calm; *Am.* impudent, brazen.
impedimento [im·pe·di·mén·to] *m.* impediment, hindrance, obstacle.
impedir[5] [im·pe·dír] *v. irr.* to impede, prevent, hinder.
impeler [im·pe·lér] *v.* to impel, push; to incite, spur.
impenetrable [im·pe·ne·trá·ble] *adj.* impenetrable; impervious; incomprehensible.
impensado [im·pen·sá·do] *adj.* unforeseen, unexpected; offhand, done without thinking; **impensadamente** [im·pen·sa·da·mén·te] *adv.* offhand, without thinking; unexpectedly.
imperar [im·pe·rár] *v.* to rule, command, dominate.
imperativo [im·pe·ra·tí·bo] *adj.* imperative; urgent, compelling; *m.* imperative mood.
imperceptible [im·per·sep·tí·ble] *adj.* imperceptible.
imperdible [im·per·dí·ble] *m.* safety pin; *adj.* safe, that cannot be lost.
imperecedero [im·pe·re·se·dé·ro] *adj.* imperishable, enduring, everlasting.
imperfecto [im·per·fék·to] *adj.* imperfect; *m.* imperfect tense.
imperial [im·pe·rjál] *adj.* imperial; *f.* coach top; top seats on a coach or bus.
impericia [im·pe·rí·sja] *f.* inexperience.
imperio [im·pé·rjo] *m.* empire; command, rule; sway, influence.
imperioso [im·pe·rjó·so] *adj.* imperious, arrogant, domineering; urgent.
impermeable [im·per·me·á·ble] *adj.* waterproof, impervious, rainproof; *m.* raincoat.
impersonal [im·per·so·nál] *adj.* impersonal.
impertinencia [im·per·ti·nén·sja] *f.* impertinence; impudence; insolent remark or act; **decir -s** to talk nonsense; to make insolent remarks.
impertinente [im·per·ti·nén·te] *adj.* impertinent, impudent; meddlesome; irrelevant, not to the point; **-s** *m. pl.* lorgnette (*eyeglasses mounted on a handle*).
ímpetu [ím·pe·tu] *m.* impetus; violent force; impulse; *C.A., Ríopl.* vehement desire; **— de ira** fit of anger.
impetuoso [im·pe·twó·so] *adj.* impetuous, violent.
impío [im·pí·o] *adj.* impious, irreligious; profane.
implacable [im·pla·ká·ble] *adj.* implacable, relentless.
implantación [im·plan·ta·sjón] *f.* implantation, establishment, introduction (*of a system*).
implantar [im·plan·tár] *v.* to implant, establish, introduce.

implicar[6] [im·pli·kár] *v.* to imply; to implicate, involve.

implorar [im·plo·rár] *v.* to implore, entreat, beg.

imponente [im·po·nén·te] *adj.* imposing.

imponer[40] [im·po·nér] *v. irr.* to impose; to invest (*money*); — **miedo** to inspire fear; — **respeto** to inspire or command respect; **-se** to inspire fear or respect; to dominate; *Am.* **-se a** to get accustomed ur used to.

importancia [im·por·tán·sja] *f.* importance.

importante [im·por·tán·te] *adj.* important.

importar [im·por·tár] *v.* to be important; to matter; to amount to; to be necessary; to concern; to import.

importe [im·pór·te] *m.* amount, price, value.

importunar [im·por·tu·nár] *v.* to importune, nag, tease, pester.

importuno [im·por·tú·no] *adj.* annoying, persistent.

imposibilidad [im·po·si·ƀi·li· đáđ] *f.* impossibility.

imposibilitado [im·po·si·ƀi·li·tá·đo] *p.p. & adj.* disabled, unfit; helpless.

imposibilitar [im·po·si·ƀi·li·tár] *v.* to make impossible; to disable.

imposible [im·po·si·ƀle] *adj.* impossible; intolerable, unbearable; *Col., Ven.* disabled (*because of illness*); *Am.* slovenly, untidy.

imposición [im·po·si·sjón] *f.* imposition; burden; tax.

impostor [im·pos·tór] *m.* impostor, cheat; **impostura** [im·pos·tú·ra] *f.* imposture, fraud, deceit.

impotencia [im·po·ten·sja] *f.* impotence.

impotente [im·po·tén·te] *adj.* impotent, powerless.

impreciso [im·pre·sí·so] *adj.* vague, indefinite; inaccurate.

impregnar [im·preǥ·nár] *v.* to impregnate, saturate.

imprenta [im·prén·ta] *f.* press; printing shop; printing.

imprescindible [im·pre·sin·dí·ƀle] *adj.* essential, indispensable.

impresión [im·pre·sjón] *f.* impression; printing; mark; footprint.

impresionante [im·pre·sjo·nán·te] *adj.* impressive.

impresionar [im·pre·sjo·nár] *v.* to impress; to move, affect, stir; **-se** to be stirred, moved.

impreso [im·pré·so] *p.p. irr. of* **imprimir** printed; impressed, imprinted; *m.* printed matter.

impresor [im·pre·sór] *m.* printer.

imprevisión [im·pre·ƀi·sjón] *f.* carelessness, lack of foresight.

imprevisto [im·pre·ƀís·to] *adj.* unforeseen, unexpected.

imprimir [im·pri·mír] *v.* to print; to imprint, impress.

improbable [im·pro·ƀá·ƀle] *adj.* improbable, unlikely.

improperio [im·pro·pé·rjo] *m.* affront, insult.

impropio [im·pró·pjo] *adj.* improper; unsuitable.

improvisar [im·pro·ƀi·sár] *v.* to improvise.

improviso [im·pro·ƀí·so] *adj.* unforeseen; **de —** suddenly; *Col., Ven., Mex.* **en un —** in a moment, in the twinkling of an eye.

imprudencia [im·pru·đén·sja] *f.* imprudence, indiscretion, rash act.

imprudente [im·pru·đén·te] *adj.* imprudent; unwise; indiscreet.

impuesto [im·pwés·to] *p.p. of* **imponer** imposed; informed; *Am.* **estar — a** to be used or accustomed to; *m.* tax, duty.

impulsar [im·pul·sár] *v.* to impel, push, move; to force.

impulso [im·púl·so] *m.* impulse; push.

impureza [im·pu·ré·sa] *f.* impurity.

impuro [im·pú·ro] *adj.* impure.

imputar [im·pu·tár] *v.* to impute, attribute.

inacabable [i·na·ka·ƀá·ƀle] *adj.* unending, endless.

inacabado [i·na·ka·ƀá·đo] *adj.* unfinished.

inaccesible [i·nak·se·sí·ƀle] *adj.* inaccessible, unobtainable.

inacción [i·nak·sjón] *f.* inaction, inactivity, idleness.

inaceptable [i·na·sep·tá·ƀle] *adj.* unacceptable, unsatisfactory.

inactividad [i·nak·ti·ƀi·đáđ] *f.* inactivity.

inactivo [i·nak·tí·ƀo] *adj.* inactive.

inadecuado [i·na·đe·kwá·đo] *adj.* inadequate.

inadvertencia [i·nađ·ƀer·tén·sja] *f.* oversight; inattention, heedlessness.

inadvertido [i·nađ·ƀer·tí·đo] *adj.* careless, heedless; unnoticed.

inafectado [i·na·fek·tá·đo] *adj.* unaffected.

inagotable [i·na·ǥo·ta·ƀle] *adj.* inexhaustible.

inaguantable [i·na·ǥwan·tá·ƀle] *adj.* insufferable, unbearable.

inalámbrico [i·na·lám·bri·ko] *adj.* wireless.

inalterable [i·nal·te·rá·ƀle] *adj.* unalterable, unchangeable.

inalterado [i·nal·te·rá·đo] *adj.* unchanged.

inamovible [i·na·mo·ƀí·ƀle] *adj.* = **inmovible.**

inanición [i·na·ni·sjón] *f.* starvation.

inanimado [i·na·ni·má·đo] *adj.* inanimate, lifeless.

inapelable [i·na·pe·lá·ƀle] *adj.* unappealable; unavoidable.

inapetencia [i·na·pe·tén·sja] *f.* lack of appetite.

inaplicable [i·na·pli·ká·ƀle] *adj.* inapplicable, unsuitable; **— al caso** irrelevant.

inapreciable [i·na·pre·sjá·ƀle] *adj.* invaluable; inappreciable, too small to be perceived, very slight.

inasequible [i·na·se·ki·ƀle] *adj.* inaccessible, not obtainable; hard to attain or obtain.

inaudito [i·naw·đi·to] *adj.* unheard-of; unprecedented.

inauguración [i·naw·ǥu·ra·sjón] *f.* inauguration.

inaugurar [i·naw·ǥu·rár] *v.* to inaugurate, begin, open.

incaico [iŋ·káj·ko], **incásico** [in·ká·si·ko] *adj.* Incan (*of or pertaining to the Incas*).

incalculable [iŋ·kal·ku·lá·ƀle] *adj.* incalculable; innumerable, untold.

incandescente [iŋ·kan·de·sén·te] *adj.* incandescent.

incansable [iŋ·kan·sá·ƀle] *adj.* untiring, tireless.

incapacidad [iŋ·ka·pa·si·đáđ] *f.* incompetence, inability, unfitness.

incapacitar [iŋ·ka·pa·si·tár] *v.* to cripple, disable, handicap, unfit, make unfit.

incapaz [iŋ·ka·pás] *adj.* incapable, unable.

incauto [iŋ·káw·to] *adj.* unwary, heedless, reckless.

incendiar [iŋ·sen·djár] *v.* to set fire to; **-se** to catch fire.

incendio [iŋ·sén·djo] *m.* conflagration, fire.

incentivo [in·sén·ti·ƀo] *m.* incentive, inducement.

incertidumbre [in·ser·ti·đúm·bre] *f.* uncertainty, doubt.

incesante [in·se·sán·te] *adj.* incessant.

incidental [in·si·đen·tál] *adj.* incidental.

incidente [in·si·đen·te] *adj.* incidental; *m.* incident.

incienso [in·sjén·so] *m.* incense.

incierto [in·sjér·to] *adj.* uncertain, doubtful; unstable; unknown; untrue.

incisión [in·si·sjón] *f.* incision, cut, slit, gash.

incisivo [in·si·sí·ƀo] *adj.* incisive; *m.* incisor.

incitamiento [in·si·ta·mjén·to] *m.* incitement,

inducement, incentive.
incitar [in·si·tár] *v.* to incite, rouse, stir up.
incivil [in·si·ƀíl] *adj.* uncivil, rude, impolite.
inclemencia [in·kle·mén·sja] *f.* inclemency, severity, harshness; **inclemente** [in·kle·mén·te] *adj.* unmerciful, merciless.
inclinación [in·kli·na·sjón] *f.* inclination, affection; tendency, bent; bow; incline, slope.
inclinar [in·kli·nár] *v.* (*bajar*) to incline; (*persuadir*) to persuade; **-se** to bow; to stoop; to incline, slope, slant; to lean, bend.
incluir[32] [in·klwír] *v. irr.* to include; to inclose.
inclusive [in·klu·sí·ƀe] *adv.* inclusive, including; even; **inclusivo** [in·klu·sí·ƀo] *adj.* inclusive; comprehensive.
incluso [in·klú·so] *adj.* inclosed; included; including; even.
incógnito [in·kóg·ni·to] *adj.* unknown; **de —** incognito (*with one's name or rank unknown*); **incógnita** *f.* unknown quantity (*in mathematics*).
incoherente [in·ko·e·rén·te] *adj.* incoherent, disconnected, rambling.
incoloro [in·ko·ló·ro] *adj.* colorless.
incombustible [in·kom·bus·tí·ƀle] *adj.* incombustible; fireproof.
incomestible [in·ko·mes·ti·ƀle] *adj.* inedible.
incomodar [in·ko·mo·ɖár] *v.* to inconvenience, disturb, trouble, annoy.
incomodidad [in·ko·mo·ɖi·ɖáɖ] *f.* inconvenience, discomfort; bother, annoyance.
incómodo [in·kó·mo·ɖo] *adj.* inconvenient, bothersome: uncomfortable.
incomparable [in·kom·pa·ra·ƀle] *adj.* incomparable.
incompasivo [in·kom·pa·sí·ƀo] *adj.* merciless, pitiless.
incompatible [in·kom·pa·ti·ƀle] *adj.* incompatible; unsuitable, uncongenial.
incompetencia [in·kom·pe·tén·sja] *f.* incompetence, inability, unfitness; **incompetente** [in·kom·pe·tén·te] *adj.* incompetent, unfit.
incompleto [in·kom·plé·to] *adj.* incomplete.
incomprensible [in·kom·pren·sí·ƀle] *adj.* incomprehensible.
inconcebible [in·kon·se·ƀí·ƀle] *adj.* inconceivable.
inconcluso [in·kon·klú·so] *adj.* unfinished.
incondicional [in·kon·di·sjo·nál] *adj.* unconditional.
inconexo [in·ko·nék·so] *adj.* unconnected; incoherent, disconnected.
inconfundible [in·kon·fun·dí·ƀle] *adj.* unmistakable.
incongruente [in·koŋ·grwén·te] *adj.* unsuitable, not appropriate; not harmonious.
inconquistable [in·koŋ·kis·tá·ƀle] *adj.* unconquerable.
inconsciencia [in·kon·sjén·sja] *f.* unconsciousness; unawareness.
inconsciente [in·kon·sjén·te] *adj.* unconscious; unaware.
inconsecuente [in·kon·se·kwén·te] *adj.* inconsistent; illogical.
inconsiderado [in·kon·si·ɖe·rá·ɖo] *adj.* inconsiderate, thoughtless.
inconstancia [in·kons·tán·sja] *f.* inconstancy, changeableness, fickleness.
inconstante [in·kons·tán·te] *adj.* inconstant, fickle, changeable, variable.
incontable [in·kon·tá·ƀle] *adj.* countless, innumerable.
inconveniencia [in·kom·be·njén·sja] *f.* inconvenience; trouble.
inconveniente [in·kom·be·njén·te] *adj.* inconvenient; improper; *m.* obstacle; objection.

incorporar [in·kor·po·rár] *v.* to incorporate, unite; to embody; to include; **-se** to sit up; **-se a** to join.
incorrecto [in·ko·rrék·to] *adj.* incorrect.
incredulidad [in·kre·ɖu·li·ɖáɖ] *f.* incredulity, unbelief.
incrédulo [in·kré·ɖu·lo] *adj.* incredulous, unbelieving; *m.* unbeliever.
increíble [in·kre·í·ƀle] *adj.* incredible, unbelievable.
incremento [in·kre·mén·to] *m.* increment, increase.
incrustar [in·krus·tár] *v.* to inlay; to encrust (*cover with a crust or hard coating*); **-se en** to penetrate impress itself deeply into.
incubadora [in·ku·ƀa·ɖó·ra] *f.* incubator.
inculcar[6] [in·kul·kár] *v.* to inculcate, instill, impress.
inculto [in·kúl·to] *adj.* uncultured; uncultivated; unrefined.
incumbencia [in·kum·bén·sja] *f.* concern, duty, obligation; **no es de mi —** it does not concern me, it is not within my province.
incurable [in·ku·rá·ƀle] *adj.* incurable.
incurrir [in·ku·rrír] *v.* to incur, fall (into); **— en un error** to fall into or commit an error; **— en el odio de** to incur the hatred of.
incursión [in·kur·sjón] *f.* raid, invasion.
indagación [in·da·ga·sjón] *f.* investigation, inquiry.
indagador [in·da·gá·ɖór] *m.* investigator; inquirer; *adj.* investigating; inquiring.
indagar[7] [in·da·gár] *v.* to find out, investigate; to inquire.
indebido [in·de·ƀí·ɖo] *adj.* undue, improper; illegal; **indebidamente** [in·de·ƀi·ɖa·mén·te] *adv.* unduly; illegally.
indecencia [in·de·sén·sja] *f.* indecency, obscenity, indecent act or remark.
indecente [in·de·sén·te] *adj.* indecent, improper.
indecible [in·de·sí·ƀle] *adj.* inexpressible, untold.
indeciso [in·de·sí·so] *adj.* undecided; doubtful, uncertain.
indefectible [in·de·fek·tí·ƀle] *adj.* unfailing; **-mente** unfailingly.
indefenso [in·de·fén·so] *adj.* defenseless, unprotected.
indefinible [in·de·fi·ní·ƀle] *adj.* indefinable.
indefinido [in·de·fi·ní·ɖo] *adj.* indefinite.
indeleble [in·de·le·ƀle] *adj.* indelible.
indemnización [in·dem·ni·sa·sjón] *f.* indemnity, compensation.
indemnizar[9] [in·dem·ni·sár] *v.* to indemnify, compensate.
independencia [in·de·pen·dén·sja] *f.* independence.
independiente [in·de·pen·djén·te] *adj.* independent.
indescriptible [in·des·krip·tí·ƀle] *adj.* indescribable.
indeseable [in·de·se·á·ƀle] *adj.* undesirable, unwelcome.
indiada [in·djá·ɖa] *f.* Ríopl., C.A., Col. community, group, or crowd of Indians; Col., Ven., Carib., Andes an Indian-like remark or act; Am. an uncontrollable fit of anger.
indianista [in·dja·nís·ta] *m. & f.* student of Indian culture; *adj.* pertaining to Indian culture.
indiano [in·djá·no] *adj.* of or pertaining to the West or East Indies; *m.* Spaniard who goes back to settle in his country after having lived for some time in Spanish America.
indicación [in·di·ka·sjón] *f.* indication.
indicar[6] [in·di·kár] *v.* to indicate, show, point out.
indicativo [in·di·ka·tí·ƀo] *adj.* indicative; *m.* indicative, indicative mood.
índice [ín·di·se] *m.* index; catalogue; sign; pointer;

forefinger.
indicio [in·dí·sjo] *m.* indication, sign.
indiferencia [in·di·fe·rén·sja] *f.* indifference.
indiferente [in·di·fe·rén·te] *adj.* indifferent.
indígena [in·dí·xe·na] *adj.* indigenous, native; *m.* &
    f. native inhabitant; *Am.* Indian.
indigestión [in·di·xes·tjón] *f.* indigestion.
indignación [in·dig·na·sjón] *f.* indignation.
indignado [in·dig·ná·đo] *p.p.* & *adj.* indignant,
    irritated, angry.
indignar [in·dig·nár] *v.* to irritate, anger; **-se** to
    become indignant, angry.
indignidad [in·dig·ni·đáđ] *f.* indignity, affront,
    insult; unworthy or disgraceful act.
indigno [in·dig·no] *adj.* unworthy; low,
    contemptible.
indio [ín·djo] *adj.* & *m.* Indian; Hindu; indium
    (*element*).
indirecta [in·di·rék·ta] *f.* hint, indirect remark,
    innuendo, insinuation.
indirecto [in·di·rék·to] *adj.* indirect.
indisciplinado [in·di·si·pli·ná·đo] *adj.* undisciplined,
    untrained.
indiscreto [in·dis·kré·to] *adj.* indiscreet, imprudent,
    unwise, rash.
indiscutible [in·dis·ku·tí·ble] *adj.* indisputable,
    unquestionable.
indispensable [in·dis·pen·sá·ble] *adj.* indispensable.
indisponer[40] [in·dis·po·nér] *v. irr.* to indispose; to
    make ill; — **a uno con otro** to prejudice someone
    against another; **-se** to become ill; **-se con** to fall
    out with, quarrel with.
indisposición [in·dis·po·si·sjón] *f.* indisposition,
    upset, slight illness; reluctance, unwillingness.
indispuesto [in·dis·pwés·to] *p.p. of* **indisponer** & *adj.*
    indisposed, unwilling; ill.
indisputable [in·dis·pu·tá·ble] *adj.* unquestionable.
indistinto [in·dis·tín·to] *adj.* indistinct, dim, vague,
    not clear.
individual [in·di·bi·đwál] *adj.* individual.
individualidad [in·di·bi·đwa·li·đáđ] *f.* individuality.
individualismo [in·di·bi·đwa·líz·mo] *m.*
    individualism.
individuo [in·di·bí·đwo] *adj.* individual; indivisible;
    m. individual; person; member.
indócil [in·dó·sil] *adj.* unruly, disobedient,
    headstrong.
indocto [in·dók·to] *adj.* uneducated, ignorant.
índole [ín·do·le] *f.* disposition, temper; kind, class.
indolencia [in·do·lén·sja] *f.* indolence, laziness;
    insensitiveness, indifference.
indolente [in·do·lén·te] *adj.* indolent, lazy;
    insensitive, indifferent.
indomable [in·do·má·ble] *adj.* indomitable,
    unconquerable; unmanageable; untamable.
indómito [in·dó·mi·to] *adj.* untamed;
    uncontrollable, unruly.
inducir[25] [in·du·sír] *v. irr.* to induce; to persuade.
indudable [in·du·đá·ble] *adj.* unquestionable,
    certain.
indulgencia [in·dul·xén·sja] *f.* indulgence, tolerance,
    forgiveness; remission of sins.
indulgente [in·dul·xén·te] *adj.* indulgent, lenient.
indultar [in·dul·tár] *v.* to pardon, set free; to
    exempt.
indulto [in·dúl·to] *m.* pardon, forgiveness;
    exemption; privilege.
indumentaria [in·du·men·tá·rja] *f.* costume, dress;
    manner of dressing.
industria [in·dús·trja] *f.* industry; cleverness, skill;
    de — intentionally, on purpose.

industrial [in·dus·trjál] *adj.* industrial; *m.*
    industrialist; manufacturer.
industrioso [in·dus·trjó·so] *adj.* industrious.
inédito [i·né·đi·to] *adj.* unpublished.
inefable [i·ne·fá·ble] *adj.* ineffable, inexpressible.
ineficaz [i·ne·fi·kás] *adj.* ineffective; inefficient.
inepto [i·nép·to] *adj.* incompetent; unsuitable.
inequívoco [i·ne·kí·bo·ko] *adj.* unmistakable.
inercia [i·nér·sja] *f.* inertia, lifelessness; inactivity.
inerme [i·nér·me] *adj.* unarmed, defenseless.
inerte [i·nér·te] *adj.* inert; inactive, sluggish, slow.
inesperado [i·nes·pe·rá·đo] *adj.* unexpected.
inestable [i·nes·tá·ble] *adj.* unstable; unsettled;
    unsteady.
inestimable [i·nes·ti·má·ble] *adj.* inestimable,
    invaluable.
inevitable [i·ne·bi·tá·ble] *adj.* inevitable,
    unavoidable.
inexacto [i·nek·sák·to] *adj.* inexact, inaccurate.
inexorable [i·nek·so·rá·ble] *adj.* inexorable.
inexperiencia [i·nes·pe·rjén·n·sja] *f.* inexperience.
inexperto [i·nes·pér·to] *adj.* unskilful, unskilled,
    inexperienced.
inexplicable [i·nes·pli·ká·ble] *adj.* inexplicable.
inextinguible [i·nes·tiŋ·gí·ble] *adj.* inextinguishable,
    unquenchable.
infalible [in·fa·lí·ble] *adj.* infallible.
infame [in·fá·me] *adj.* infamous; *m.* scoundrel.
infamia [in·fá·mja] *f.* infamy, dishonor; wickedness.
infancia [in·fán·sja] *f.* infancy.
infante [in·fán·te] *m.* infant; infante (*royal prince of
    Spain, except the heir to the throne*); infantryman.
infantería [in·fan·te·rí·a] *f.* infantry.
infantil [in·fan·tíl] *adj.* infantile, childlike, childish.
infatigable [in·fa·ti·gá·ble] *adj.* tireless, untiring.
infausto [in·fáws·to] *adj.* unfortunate; unhappy.
infección [in·fek·sjón] *f.* infection; **infeccioso** *adj.*
    infectious.
infectar [in·fek·tár] *v.* to infect; to corrupt; **-se** to
    become infected.
infeliz [in·fe·lís] *adj.* unhappy, unfortunate; *m.* poor
    wretch.
inferior [in·fe·rjór] *adj.* inferior; lower; *m.* inferior.
inferioridad [in·fe·rjo·ri·đáđ] *f.* inferiority.
inferir[3] [in·fe·rír] *v. irr.* (*concluir*) to infer; to
    imply; (*causar*) to inflict.
infernal [in·fer·nál] *adj.* infernal.
infestar [in·fes·tár] *v.* to infest, invade, overrun,
    plague; to corrupt, infect.
inficionar [in·fi·sjo·nár] *v.* to infect; to contaminate.
infiel [in·fjél] *adj.* unfaithful, faithless; infidel;
    inaccurate.
infiernillo [in·fjer·ni·yo] *m.* chafing dish.
infierno [in·fjér·no] *m.* hell; **en el quinto** — very
    far away.
infiltrar [in·fil·trár] *v.* to filter through; **-se** to leak
    (into), filter (through), infiltrate.
infinidad [in·fi·ni·đáđ] *f.* infinity; **una** — **de** a large
    number of.
infinito [in·fi·ní·to] *adj.* infinite; *adv.* infinitely; *m.*
    infinity.
inflamación [in·fla·ma·sjón] *f.* inflammation.
inflamado [in·fla·má·đo] *p.p.* & *adj.* inflamed; sore.
inflamar [in·fla·már] *v.* to inflame, excite; to kindle,
    set on fire; **-se** to become inflamed.
inflar [in·flár] *v.* to inflate; to exaggerate; **-se** to
    become inflated; to swell up with pride.
inflexible [in·flek·sí·ble] *adj.* inflexible, stiff, rigid;
    unbending.
inflexión [in·flek·sjón] *f.* inflection.
infligir[11] [in·fli·xír] *v.* to inflict.

IN

influencia [in·flwén·sja] *f.* influence.
influenza [in·flwén·sa] *f.* influenza, grippe, flu.
influir³² [in·flwír] *v. irr.* to influence.
influjo [in·flú·xo] *m.* influence; influx, inward flow.
influyente [in·flu·yén·te] *adj.* influential.
información [in·for·ma·sjón] *f.* information.
informal [in·for·mál] *adj.* informal; unconventional; unreliable, not dependable, not punctual.
informar [in·for·már] *v.* to inform; to give form to; to give a report; to present a case; **-se** to find out.
informe [in·fór·me] *m.* report, account; information; brief; *adj.* formless, shapeless.
infortunio [in·for·tú·njo] *m.* misfortune, mishap; misery.
infracción [in·frak·sjón] *f.* infraction, breach, violation (*of a law, treaty, etc.*).
infractor [in·frak·tór] *m.* transgressor, lawbreaker, violator (*of a law*).
infrascrito [in·fras·krí·to] *m.* undersigned, subscriber, signer (*of a letter, document, etc.*); **el — secretario** the secretary whose signature appears below.
infringir¹¹ [in·friŋ·xír] *v.* to infringe, break, violate.
infructuoso [in·fruk·twó·so] *adj.* fruitless.
ínfulas [ín·fu·las] *f. pl.* airs, false importance; **darse — to** put on airs.
infundado [in·fun·dá·ḍo] *adj.* groundless, without foundation.
infundir [in·fun·dír] *v.* to infuse, inspire; to instill.
infusión [in·fu·sjón] *f.* infusion (*liquid extract obtained by steeping*); infusion, inspiration; **poner en —** to steep (*as tea leaves*).
ingeniería [iŋ·xe·nje·rí·a] *f.* engineering.
ingeniero [iŋ·xe·njé·ro] *m.* engineer.
ingenio [iŋ·xé·njo] *m.* genius; talent; ingenuity; mentality, mental power, mind; wit; **— de azúcar** sugar refinery; sugar plantation.
ingeniosidad [iŋ·xe·njo·si·ḍáḍ] *f.* ingenuity, cleverness.
ingenioso [iŋ·xe·njó·so] *adj.* ingenious, clever.
ingenuidad [iŋ·xe·nwi·ḍáḍ] *f.* candor, frankness; unaffected simplicity.
ingenuo [iŋ·xé·nwo] *adj.* frank, sincere; simple, unaffected; naive.
ingerir [iŋ·xe·rír] **= injerir.**
ingestión [iŋ·xes·tjón] *f.* ingestion.
ingle [íŋ·gle] *f.* groin.
inglés [iŋ·glés] *adj.* English; **a la inglesa** in the English fashion; *Am.* **ir a la inglesa** to go Dutch treat; *m.* Englishman; the English language.
ingobernable [iŋ·go·ḅer·ná·ḅle] *adj.* ungovernable, unruly, uncontrollable.
ingratitud [iŋ·gra·ti·túḍ] *f.* ingratitude.
ingrato [iŋ·grá·to] *adj.* ungrateful, thankless; harsh; cruel; disdainful.
ingrediente [iŋ·gre·ḍjén·te] *m.* ingredient.
ingresar [iŋ·gre·sár] *v.* to enter; **— en** to join (*a society, club, etc.*).
ingreso [iŋ·gré·so] *m.* entrance; entry; **-s** receipts, profits; revenue.
inhábil [i·ná·ḅil] *adj.* unskilled; unskilful; unfit.
inhabilidad [i·na·ḅi·li·ḍáḍ] *f.* inability; unfitness.
inhabilitar [i·na·ḅi·li·tár] *v.* to disqualify; to unfit, disable.
inherente [i·ne·rén·te] *adj.* inherent.
inhibir [i·ni·ḅír] *v.* to inhibit.
inhospitalario [i·nos·pi·ta·lá·rjo] *adj.* inhospitable.
inhumano [i·nu·má·no] *adj.* inhuman, cruel.
iniciador [i·ni·sja·ḍór] *m.* initiator; pioneer; *adj.* initiating.

inicial [i·ni·sjál] *adj. & f.* initial.
iniciar [i·ni·sjár] *v.* to initiate; to begin.
iniciativa [i·ni·sja·ti·ḅa] *f.* initiative.
inicuo [i·ní·kwo] *adj.* wicked.
iniquidad [i·ni·ki·ḍáḍ] *f.* iniquity, wickedness; sin.
injerir³ [iŋ·xe·rír] *v. irr.* to inject, insert; **-se** to interfere, meddle.
injertar [iŋ·xer·tár] *v.* to graft.
injerto [iŋ·xér·to] *m.* graft.
injuria [iŋ·xú·rja] *f.* affront, insult; harm, damage.
injuriar [iŋ·xu·rjár] *v.* to insult, offend; to harm, damage.
injurioso [iŋ·xu·rjó·so] *adj.* insulting, offensive; harmful.
injusticia [iŋ·xus·tí·sja] *f.* injustice.
injustificado [iŋ·xus·ti·fi·ká·ḍo] *adj.* unjustified; unjustifiable.
injusto [iŋ·xús·to] *adj.* unjust, unfair.
inmaculado [im·ma·ku·lá·ḍo] *adj.* immaculate, clean; pure.
inmediación [im·me·ḍja·sjón] *f.* vicinity; nearness; **-es** environs, outskirts.
inmediato [im·me·ḍjá·to] *adj.* near, close; *Am.* **de — immediately; suddenly; inmediatamente** *adv.* immediately, at once.
inmejorable [im·me·xo·rá·ḅle] *adj.* unsurpassable.
inmensidad [im·men·si·ḍáḍ] *f.* immensity, vastness; vast number.
inmenso [im·mén·so] *adj.* immense, vast, huge; boundless.
inmersión [im·mer·sjón] *f.* immersion, dip.
inmigración [im·mi·ɡra·sjón] *f.* immigration.
inmigrante [im·mi·ɡrán·te] *adj., m. & f.* immigrant.
inmigrar [im·mi·ɡrár] *v.* to immigrate.
inminente [im·mi·nén·te] *adj.* imminent.
inmiscuir³² [im·mis·kwír] *v. irr.* to mix; **-se** to meddle, interfere.
inmoble [im·mó·ḅle] *adj.* motionless; unshaken.
inmoral [im·mo·rál] *adj.* immoral; **inmoralidad** [im·mo·ra·li·ḍáḍ] *f.* immorality.
inmortal [im·mor·tál] *adj.* immortal; **inmortalidad** *f.* immortality.
inmovible [im·mo·ḅí·ḅle] *adj.* immovable, fixed; steadfast.
inmóvil [im·mó·ḅil] *adj.* motionless, still; immovable.
inmuebles [im·mwé·ḅles] *m. pl.* real estate.
inmundicia [im·mun·di·sja] *f.* filth, dirt; nastiness.
inmundo [im·mún·do] *adj.* filthy, dirty; impure; nasty.
inmune [im·mú·ne] *adj.* immune; exempt.
inmunidad [im·mu·ni·ḍáḍ] *f.* immunity.
inmutable [im·mu·tá·ḅle] *adj.* unchangeable, invariable.
inmutar [im·mu·tár] *v.* to alter, change; **-se** to show emotion (*either by turning pale or blushing*).
innato [in·ná·to] *adj.* innate, natural, inborn.
innecesario [in·ne·se·sá·rjo] *adj.* unnecessary.
innegable [in·ne·ɡá·ḅle] *adj.* undeniable, not to be denied.
innocuo [in·nó·kwo] *adj.* innocuous, harmless; **innocuidad** *f.* harmlessness.
innovación [in·no·ḅa·sjón] *f.* innovation; novelty.
innumerable [in·nu·me·rá·ḅle] *adj.* innumerable.
inobservancia [i·noḅ·ser·ḅán·sja] *f.* nonobservance, violation (*of a law*), lack of observance (*of a law, rule, or custom*).
inocencia [i·no·sén·sja] *f.* innocence.
inocente [i·no·sén·te] *adj.* innocent; *m.* innocent person; **inocentón** *adj.* quite foolish or simple; easily fooled; *m.* dupe, unsuspecting victim.

inocular [i·no·ku·lár] *v.* to inoculate.
inodoro [i·no·đó·ro] *adj.* odorless; *m. C.A., Ven., Col.* toilet, water closet.
inofensivo [i·no·fen·sí·ƀo] *adj.* inoffensive; harmless.
inolvidable [i·nol·ƀi·đá·ƀle] *adj.* unforgettable.
inopinado [i·no·pi·ná·đo] *adj.* unexpected.
inoportuno [i·no·por·tú·no] *adj.* inopportune, untimely, unsuitable.
inoxidable [i·nok·si·đá·ƀle] *adj.* rust proof.
inquietar [iŋ·kje·tár] *v.* to worry, disturb, make uneasy; **-se** to become disturbed, uneasy.
inquieto [iŋ·kjé·to] *adj.* restless; uneasy, anxious.
inquietud [iŋ·kje·túđ] *f.* restlessness; anxiety, uneasiness; fear.
inquilino [iŋ·ki·lí·no] *m.* tenant, renter; lodger.
inquina [iŋ·kí·na] *f.* aversion, grudge, dislike.
inquirir[35] [iŋ·ki·rír] *v. irr.* to inquire, investigate; to find out.
inquisición [iŋ·ki·si·sjón] *f.* inquisition; inquiry, investigation.
insaciable [in·sa·sjá·ƀle] *adj.* insatiable, never satisfied, greedy.
insalubre [in·sa·lu·ƀre] *adj.* unhealthy, unhealthful, unwholesome.
insano [in·sá·no] *adj.* insane, crazy; unhealthy.
inscribir[52] [ins·kri·ƀír] *v.* to inscribe; to register, enroll; to record; **-se** to register.
inscripción [ins·krip·sjón] *f.* inscription; registration.
inscripto [ins·kríp·to], **inscrito** [ins·krí·to] *p.p. of* inscribir.
insecto [in·sék·to] *m.* insect.
inseguro [in·se·ǥú·ro] *adj.* insecure; unsafe; doubtful, uncertain.
insensato [in·sen·sá·to] *adj.* senseless; foolish.
insensibilidad [in·sen·si·ƀi·li·đáđ] *f.* insensibility, unconsciousness; lack of feeling.
insensible [in·sen·sí·ƀle] *adj.* insensible; unfeeling; imperceptible.
inseparable [in·se·pa·rá·ƀle] *adj.* inseparable.
inserción [in·ser·sjón] *f.* insertion; insert.
insertar [in·ser·tár] *v.* to insert.
inserto *adj.* inserted.
inservible [in·ser·ƀi·ƀle] *adj.* useless.
insidioso [in·si·đjó·so] *adj.* insidious; sly, crafty.
insigne [in·siǥ·ne] *adj.* famous.
insignia [in·siǥ·nja] *f.* badge, medal, decoration; flag, pennant; **-s** insignia.
insignificante [in·siǥ·ni·fi·kán·te] *adj.* insignificant.
insinuación [in·si·nwa·sjón] *f.* insinuation; intimation, hint.
insinuar[18] [in·si·nwár] *v.* to insinuate, hint; **-se** to insinuate oneself (*into another's friendship*); to creep (into) gradually.
insipidez [in·si·pi·đés] *f.* flatness, tastelessness, dullness; **insípido** *adj.,* insipid; tasteless.
insistencia [in·sis·tén·sja] *f.* insistence, persistence, obstinacy; **insistente** [in·sis·tén·te] *adj.* insistent, persistent.
insistir [in·sis·tír] *v.* to insist; to persist.
insociable [in·so·sjá·ƀle] *adj.* unsociable.
insolación [in·so·la·sjón] *f.* sunstroke.
insolencia [in·so·lén·sja] *f.* insolence.
insolentarse [in·so·len·tár·se] *v.* to sauce, become insolent, act with insolence.
insolente [in·so·lén·te] *adj.* insolent.
insólito [in·só·li·to] *adj.* unusual; uncommon.
insolvente [in·sol·ƀén·te] *adj.* insolvent, bankrupt.
insomne [in·sóm·ne] *adj.* sleepless.
insondable [in·son·dá·ƀle] *adj.* fathomless, deep; impenetrable.

insoportable [in·so·por·tá·ƀle] *adj.* unbearable.
insospechado [in·sos·pe·čá·đo] *adj.* unsuspected.
inspección [ins·pek·sjón] *f.* inspection.
inspeccionar [ins·pek·sjo·nár] *v.* to inspect.
inspector [ins·pek·tór] *m.* inspector; overseer.
inspiración [ins·pi·ra·sjón] *f.* inspiration; inhalation, breathing in.
inspirar [ins·pi·rár] *v.* to inspire; to inhale.
instalación [ins·ta·la·sjón] *f.* installation.
instalar [ins·ta·lar] *v.* to install.
instancia [ins·tán·sja] *f.* instance, urgent request; petition; **a -s de** at the request of.
instantánea [ins·tan·tá·ne·a] *f.* snapshot.
instantáneo [ins·tan·tá·ne·o] *adj.* instantaneous; sudden.
instante [ins·tán·te] *m.* instant, moment; **al —** at once, immediately; **por -s** continually; from one moment to another; *adj.* instant, urgent.
instar [ins·tár] *v.* to urge, press; to be urgent.
instigar[7] [ins·ti·ǥár] *v.* to instigate, urge on, incite.
instintivo [ins·tin·tí·ƀo] *adj.* instinctive.
instinto [ins·tín·to] *m.* instinct.
institución [ins·ti·tu·sjón] *f.* institution; establishment, foundation; **-es** institutes, collection of precepts and principles.
instituir[32] [ins·ti·twír] *v. irr.* to institute; **— por heredero** to appoint as heir.
instituto [ins·ti·tú·to] *m.* institute; established principle, law, or custom; **— de segunda enseñanza** high school.
institutriz [ins·ti·tu·trís] *f.* governess.
instrucción [ins·truk·sjón] *f.* instruction; education.
instructivo [ins·truk·tí·ƀo] *adj.* instructive.
instruir[32] [ins·trwír] *v. irr.* to instruct, teach; to inform.
instrumento [ins·tru·mén·to] *m.* instrument.
insuficiencia [in·su·fi·sjén·sja] *f.* insufficiency, deficiency; incompetence; dearth, scarcity, lack.
insuficiente [in·su·fi·sjén·te] *adj.* insufficient.
insufrible [in·su·frí·ƀle] *adj.* insufferable, unbearable.
insula [ín·su·la] *f.* island.
insulina [in·su·lí·na] *f.* insulin.
insultante [in·sul·tán·te] *adj.* insulting, abusive.
insultar [in·sul·tár] *v.* to insult; **-se** to be seized with a fit.
insulto [in·súl·to] *m.* insult; sudden fit or attack.
insuperable [in·su·pe·rá·ƀle] *adj.* insuperable; insurmountable.
insurgente [in·sur·xén·te] *adj., m. & f.* insurgent.
insurrección [in·su·rrek·sjón] *f.* insurrection, uprising, revolt.
insurrecto [in·su·rrék·to] *m.* insurgent, rebel; *adj.* rebellious.
intacto [in·ták·to] *adj.* intact.
intachable [in·ta·čá·ƀle] *adj.* faultless, irreproachable.
integral [in·te·ǥrál] *adj.* integral; *f.* integral (*math*).
integrante [in·te·ǥrán·te] *adj.* integral; integrating.
integrar [in·te·ǥrár] *v.* to form; to integrate.
integridad [in·te·ǥri·đáđ] *f.* integrity; wholeness; honesty; purity.
íntegro [ín·te·ǥro] *adj.* whole, complete; honest, upright.
intelecto [in·te·lék·to] *m.* intellect.
intelectual [in·te·lek·twál] *adj.* intellectual.
inteligencia [in·te·li·xén·sja] *f.* intelligence.
inteligente [in·te·li·xén·te] *adj.* intelligent.
intemperancia [in·tem·pe·rán·sja] *f.* intemperance, excess.
intemperie [in·tem·pé·rje] *f.* open air; bad weather;

IN

a la — unsheltered, outdoors, in the open air; exposed to the weather.
intención [in·ten·sjón] *f.* intention; **intencional** [in·ten·sjo·nál] *adj.* intentional.
intendente [in·ten·dén·te] *m.* manager, superintendent, supervisor; *Ríopl.* governor of a province; *Am.* police commissioner.
intensidad [in·ten·si·dáḍ] *f.* intensity; stress.
intenso [in·tén·so] *adj.* intense; intensive; ardent, vehement.
intentar [in·ten·tár] *v.* to attempt, try; to intend.
intento [in·tén·to] *m.* intent, purpose, intention; **de** — on purpose.
intercalar [in·ter·ka·lár] *v.* to insert, place between.
intercambio [in·ter·kám·bjo] *m.* interchange; exchange.
interceder [in·ter·se·ḍér] *v.* to intercede.
interceptar [in·ter·sep·tár] *v.* to intercept.
intercesión [in·ter·se·sjón] *f.* intercession, mediation.
interdental [in·ter·ḍen·tál] *adj.* interdental.
interdicción [in·ter·ḍik·sjón] *f.* interdiction; prevention.
interés [in·te·rés] *m.* interest.
interesante [in·te·re·sán·te] *adj.* interesting.
interesar [in·te·re·sár] *v.* to interest; to give an interest or share; **-se** to be or become interested.
interferencia [in·ter·fe·rén·sja] *f.* interference.
interin [ín·te·rin] *m.* interim, meantime; **en al** — in the meantime.
interino [in·te·rí·no] *adj.* acting, temporary.
interior [in·te·rjór] *adj.* interior; inner; internal; *m.* interior, inside.
interjección [in·ter·xek·sjón] *f.* interjection, exclamation.
interlineal [in·ter·li·ne·ál] *adj.* interlinear.
interlocutor [in·ter·lo·ku·tór] *m.* participant in a dialogue.
intermedio [in·ter·me·ḍjo] *adj.* intermediate; intervening; *m.* intermission; interval; **por — de** by means of, through the intervention of.
interminable [in·ter·mi·ná·ḅle] *adj.* interminable, unending, endless.
intermisión [in·ter·mi·sjón] *f.* intermission, interruption, pause, interval.
intermitente [in·ter·mi·tén·te] *adj.* intermittent, occurring at intervals; **calentura** (*or* **fiebre**) — intermittent fever.
internacional [in·ter·na·sjo·nál] *adj.* international.
internado [in·ter·ná·ḍo] *m.* a boarding student.
internar [in·ter·nár] *v.* to intern, confine; **-se** to penetrate, go into the interior.
interno [in·tér·no] *adj.* internal; interior; *m.* boarding-school student.
interoceánico [in·te·ro·se·á·ni·ko] *adj.* interoceanic; transcontinental.
interpelar [in·ter·pe·lár] *v.* to interrogate, question, demand explanations; to ask the aid of.
interponer[40] [in·ter·po·nér] *v. irr.* to interpose, put between, insert; to place as a mediator; **-se** to intervene, mediate.
interpretación [in·ter·pre·ta·sjón] *f.* interpretation.
interpretar [in·ter·pre·tár] *v.* to interpret.
intérprete [in·tér·pre·te] *m. & f.* interpreter.
interpuesto [in·ter·pwés·to] *p.p. of* **interponer.**
interrogación [in·te·rro·ga·sjón] *f.* interrogation, question; **signo de** — question mark.
interrogador [in·te·rro·ga·ḍór] *m.* questioner; *adj.* questioning.
interrogar[7] [in·te·rro·gár] *v.* to interrogate, question.
interrogativo [in·te·rro·ga·tí·ḅo] *adj.* interrogative.

interrogatorio [in·te·rro·ga·tó·rjo] *m.* interrogation, questioning.
interrumpir [in·te·rrum·pír] *v.* to interrupt.
interrupción [in·te·rrup·sjón] *f.* interruption.
interruptor [in·te·rrup·tór] *m.* interrupter; electric switch.
intersección [in·ter·sek·sjón] *f.* intersection.
intersticio [in·ters·tí·sjo] *m.* interval.
intervalo [in·ter·ḅá·lo] *m.* interval.
intervención [in·ter·ḅen·sjón] *f.* intervention; mediation; participation; auditing of accounts.
intervenir[48] [in·ter·ḅe·nír] *v. irr.* to intervene; to mediate; to audit (*accounts*).
interventor [in·ter·ḅen·tór] *m.* inspector; controller, comptroller; auditor.
intestino [in·tes·tí·no] *m.* intestine; *adj.* intestine, internal.
intimación [in·ti·ma·sjón] *f.* intimation; hint, insinuation, suggestion.
intimar [in·ti·már] *v.* to announce, notify; to intimate, hint; to become intimate, become friendly.
intimidad [in·ti·mi·ḍáḍ] *f.* intimacy.
intimidar [in·ti·mi·ḍár] *v.* to intimidate.
íntimo [ín·ti·mo] *adj.* intimate.
intitular [in·ti·tu·lár] *v.* to entitle; to give a title to (*a person or a thing*); **-se** to be entitled, be called; to call oneself (*by a certain name*).
intolerable [in·to·le·rá·ḅle] *adj.* intolerable.
intolerancia [in·to·le·rán·sja] *f.* intolerance; **intolerante** [in·to·le·rán·te] *adj.* intolerant, narrow-minded.
intoxicante [in·tok·si·kán·te] *m.* poison.
intoxicar[6] [in·tok·si·kár] *v.* to poison.
intranquilo [in·traŋ·kí·lo] *adj.* disturbed, uneasy.
intranquilidad [in·traŋ·ki·li·ḍáḍ] *f.* uneasiness, restlessness.
intransigencia [in·tran·si·xén·sja] *f.* uncompromising act or attitude; intolerance.
intransigente [in·tran·si·xén·te] *adj.* uncompromising, unwilling to compromise or yield; intolerant.
intratable [in·tra·tá·ḅle] *adj.* unsociable; rude; unruly.
intravenoso [in·tra·ḅe·nó·so] *adj.* intravenous (*within a vein or the veins*; *into a vein*).
intrepidez [in·tre·pi·ḍés] *f.* fearlessness, courage.
intrépido [in·tré·pi·ḍo] *adj.* intrepid, fearless.
intriga [in·trí·ga] *f.* intrigue; scheme; plot.
intrigante [in·tri·gán·te] *m. & f.* intriguer, plotter; *adj.* intriguing.
intrigar[7] [in·tri·gár] *v.* to intrigue.
intrincado [in·triŋ·ká·ḍo] *adj.* intricate, complicated, entangled.
introducción [in·tro·ḍuk·sjón] *f.* introduction.
introducir[25] [in·tro·ḍu·sír] *v. irr.* to introduce; **-se** to introduce oneself; to get in; to penetrate.
intromisión [in·tro·mi·sjón] *f.* meddling; insertion.
introvertido [in·tro·ḅer·tí·ḍo] *m. & f.* introvert.
intruso [in·trú·so] *adj.* intrusive, intruding; *m.* intruder.
intuición [in·twi·sjón] *f.* intuition.
intuir[32] [in·twír] *v. irr.* to sense, feel by intuition.
inundación [i·nun·da·sjón] *f.* inundation, flood.
inundar [i·nun·dár] *v.* to inundate, flood.
inusitado [i·nu·si·tá·ḍo] *adj.* unusual, rare.
inútil [i·nú·til] *adj.* useless.
inutilidad [i·nu·ti·li·ḍáḍ] *f.* uselessness.
inutilizar[9] [i·nu·ti·li·sár] *v.* to make useless, put out of commission; to disable; to ruin, spoil.
invadir [im·ba·ḍír] *v.* to invade.

invalidar [im·ba·li·dár] v. to render invalid; to void, annul.
inválido [im·bá·li·d̦o] adj. invalid; void, null; sickly, weak; m. invalid.
invariable [im·ba·rjá·b̦le] adj. invariable.
invasión [im·ba·sjón] f. invasion.
invasor [im·ba·sór] m. invader; adj. invading; **ejército** — invading army.
invencible [im·ben·sí·b̦le] adj. invincible, unconquerable.
invención [im·ben·sjón] f. invention.
invendible [im·ben·dí·b̦le] adj. unsaleable.
inventar [im·ben·tár] v. to invent.
inventariar[17] [im·ben·ta·rjár] v. to inventory, take an inventory of.
inventario [im·ben·tá·rjo] m. inventory.
inventiva [im·ben·tí·b̦a] f. inventiveness, power of inventing, ingenuity.
inventivo [im·ben·tí·b̦o] adj. inventive.
invento [im·bén·to] m. invention.
inventor [im·ben·tór] m. inventor; storyteller, fibber.
invernáculo [im·ber·ná·ku·lo] m. greenhouse, hothouse.
invernada [im·ber·ná·d̦a] f. wintering; Am. pasturing.
invernadero [im·ber·na·d̦é·ro] m. winter quarters; winter resort; winter pasture; greenhouse, hothouse.
invernal [im·ber·nál] adj. wintry, winter.
invernar[1] [im·ber·nár] v. irr. to winter, spend the winter.
inverosímil [im·be·ro·sí·mil] **inverisímil** [im·be·ri·sí·mil] adj. unlikely, improbable.
inversión [im·bér·sjón] f. inversion; investment.
inverso [im·bér·so] adj. inverse, inverted; reverse; **a** (or **por**) **la inversa** on the contrary.
invertir[3] [im·ber·tír] v. irr. to invert; to reverse; to invest; to employ, spend (time).
investigación [im·bes·ti·ga·sjón] f. investigation.
investigador [im·bes·ti·ga·d̦ór] m. investigator; adj. investigating.
investigar[7] [im·bes·ti·gár] v. to investigate.
invicto [im·bík·to] adj. unconquered; always victorious.
invierno [im·bjér·no] m. winter; C.A., Col., Ven., Ec., Peru the rainy season.
invisible [im·bi·si·b̦le] adj. invisible.
invitación [im·bi·ta·sjón] f. invitation.
invitar [im·bi·tár] v. to invite.
invocación [im·bo·ka·sjón] f. invocation.
invocar[6] [im·bo·kár] v. to invoke.
involuntario [im·bo·lun·tá·rjo] adj. involuntary.
inyección [in·ẏek·sjón] f. injection.
inyectado [in·ẏek·tá·d̦o] p.p. injected; adj. bloodshot, inflamed.
inyectar [in·ẏek·tár] v. to inject.
ion [jon] m. ion.
ionizar[9] [jo·ni·sár] v. irr. to ionize.
ir[33] [ir] v. irr. to go; to walk; — **corriendo** to be running; — **entendiendo** to understand gradually; to begin to understand; — **a caballo** to ride horseback; — **a pie** to walk; — **en automóvil** to drive, ride in an automobile; **no irle ni venirle a uno** to make no difference to one; ¿**cómo le va?** how are you? **no me va nada en eso** that doesn't concern me; ¡**vamos!** let's go! come on! ¡**vaya!** well now!, ¡**vaya un hómbre!** what a man!; **-se** to go, go away; to escape; **-se abajo** to fall down, topple over; to collapse; **-se a pique** yo founder, sink.
ira [í·ra] f. ire, anger.

iracundo [i·ra·kún·do] adj. irritable; angry.
iridio [i·rí·d̦jo] m. iridium.
iris [í·ris] m. iris (of the eye); **arco** — rainbow.
irisado [i·ri·sá·d̦o] adj. iridescent, rainbow-hued.
ironía [i·ro·ní·a] f. irony.
irónico [i·ró·ni·ko] adj. ironic, ironical.
irracional [i·rra·sjo·nál] adj. irrational, unreasonable.
irradiar [i·rra·djár] v. to radiate.
irreal [i·rre·ál] adj. unreal.
irreflexión [i·rre·flek·sjón] f. thoughtlessness.
irreflexivo [i·rre·flek·sí·b̦o] adj. thoughtless.
irrefrenable [i·rre·fre·ná·b̦le] adj. uncontrollable.
irrefutable [i·rre·fu·tá·b̦le] adj. irrefutable.
irregular [i·rre·ġu·lár] adj. irregular.
irreligioso [i·rre·li·xjó·so] adj. irreligious.
irremediable [i·rre·me·d̦já·b̦le] adj. irremediable; hopeless, incurable.
irreprochable [i·rre·pro·čá·b̦le] adj. irreproachable, flawless.
irresistible [i·rre·sis·tí·b̦le] adj. irresistible.
irresoluto [i·rre·so·lú·to] adj. irresolute, undecided, hesitating.
irrespetuoso [i·rres·pe·twó·so] adj. disrespectful.
irreverencia [i·rre·b̦e·rén·sja] f. irreverence.
irreverente [i·rre·b̦e·rén·te] adj. irreverent.
irrigación [i·rre·ġa·sjón] f. irrigation.
irrigar[7] [i·rri·ġár] v. to irrigate.
irrisión [i·rri·sjón] f. mockery, ridicule, derision.
irritación [i·rri·ta·sjón] f. irritation.
irritante [i·rri·tán·te] adj. irritating.
irritar [i·rri·tár] v. to irritate.
irrumpir [i·rrum·pír] v. to enter violently; to invade.
irrupción [i·rrup·sjón] f. sudden attack, raid, invasion.
isla [iz·la] f. island.
islamismo [iz·la·míz·mo] m. islamism.
islandés [iz·lan·dés] adj. Icelandic.
isleño [iz·lé·ño] m. islander.
isobara [i·so·b̦á·ra] f. isobar.
islote [iz·ló·te] m. islet, small rocky island.
istmo [íz·mo] m. isthmus.
italiano [i·ta·ljá·no] adj. & m. Italian.
itinerario [i·ti·ne·rá·rjo] m. itinerary; timetable, schedule; railroad guide.
itrio [í·trjo] m. yttrium.
izar[9] [i·sár] v. to hoist; to heave.
izquierda [is·kjér·d̦a] f. left hand; left side; left wing (in politics); **a la** — to the left; **izquierdista** [is·kjer·dís·ta] m. & f. leftist, radical.
izquierdo [is·kjér·d̦o] adj. left; left-handed.

J: j

jabalí [xa·b̦a·lí] m. wild boar.
jabalina [xa·b̦a·lí·na] f. javelin; wild sow.
jabón [xa·b̦ón] m. soap; Riopl. fright, fear; **dar** — to soft-soap, flatter; **dar un** — to give a good scolding; to beat, thrash.
jabonadura [xa·b̦o·na·d̦ú·ra] f. washing, soaping; **-s** suds, lather; **dar a uno una** — to reprimand or scold someone.
jabonar [xa·b̦o·nár] v. (lavar) to lather, soap; (reprender) to scold; reprimand.
jabonera [xa·b̦o·né·ra] f. soap dish; woman soap vendor or maker.
jaca [xá·ka] f. pony, small horse; **jaco** [xa·ko] m. small nag; poor horse.
jacal [xa·kál] m. Mex. shack, adobe hut; **jacalucho** [xa·ka·lú·čo] m. Am. poor, ugly shack.

jacinto [xa·sín·to] *m.* hyacinth.
jactancia [xak·tán·sja] *f.* boast, brag; boasting.
jactancioso [xak·tan·sjó·so] *adj.* braggart, boastful.
jactarse [xak·tár·se] *v.* to brag, boast.
jaculatoria [xa·ku·la·tó·rja] *f.* short, fervent prayer.
jadeante [xa·ḍe·án·te] *adj.* breathless, panting, out of breath.
jadear [xa·ḍe·ár] *v.* to pant.
jadeo [xa·ḍé·o] *m.* pant, panting.
jaez [xa·és] *m.* harness; kind, sort; **jaeces** [xa·é·ses] trappings.
jaguar [xa·ǵwár] *m.* jaguar.
jagüey [xa·ǵwéj] *m.* puddle, pool.
jai alai [xaj·a·láj] *m.* Basque game played with basket and *pelota*.
jalar [xa·lár] *v.* to pull; to haul; to jerk; *C.A.* to court, make love; *Ven., Andes* to flunk (*a student*); *Mex.* **¡jala!** [xá·la] (*or* **¡jálale!** [xá·la·le]) get going! get a move on there!; **-se** *Am.* to get drunk; *Mex.* to go away, move away.
jalea [xa·lé·a] *f.* jelly.
jalear [xa·le·ár] *v.* to shout (*to hunting dogs*); to rouse, beat up (*game*); to shout and clap (*to encourage dancers*).
jaleo [xa·lé·o] *m.* shouting and clapping (*to encourage dancers*); an Andalusian dance; revelry, merrymaking; jesting; gracefulness.
jaletina [xa·le·tí·na] *f.* gelatin.
jalón [xa·lón] *m.* marker (*for boundaries*); *Am.* pull, jerk, tug; *Mex., C.A.* swallow of liquor; *Bol., C.A.* stretch, distance.
jalonear [xa·lo·ne·ár] *v. C.A., Mex.* to pull, jerk.
jamás [xa·más] *adv.* never.
jamón [xa·món] *m.* ham; *P.R.* fix, difficulty.
jamona [xa·mó·na] *f.* popular term for a fat middle-aged woman.
japonés [xa·po·nés] *adj. & m.* Japanese.
jaque [xá·ke] *m.* check (*in chess*); braggart, bully; **— mate** checkmate (*in chess*); **tener a uno en —** to hold someone under a threat.
jaqueca [xa·ké·ka] *f.* headache; sick headache.
jara [xá·ra] *f.* rockrose (*shrub*); *Ven., Col.* reed; **jaral** [xa·rál] *m.* bramble of rockroses; *Am.* reeds, clump of reeds.
jarabe [xa·rá·ḅe] *m.* syrup; sweet beverage; *Mex., C.A.* a kind of tap dance; *Mex.* song and musical accompaniment of the **jarabe.**
jarana [xa·rá·na] *f.* merrymaking, revelry; trick; fib; jest; *Col., Ec., Carib.* a dance; *Mex.* small guitar; **ir de —** to go on a spree.
jarcia [xár·sja] *f.* rigging (*ropes, chains, etc. for the masts, yards and sails of a ship*); fishing tackle; pile, heap; jumble of things.
jardín [xar·ḍín] *m.* flower garden.
jardinero [xar·ḍi·né·ro] *m.* gardener.
jarra [xá·rra] *f.* jar, vase, pitcher; **de** (*or* **en**) **-s** akimbo (*with hands on the hips*).
jarro [xá·rro] *m.* jar, jug, pitcher.
jarrón *m.* large vase or jar.
jaspe [xás·pe] *m.* jasper; veined marble; **jaspeado** *adj.* veined, streaked, mottled.
jaula [xáw·la] *f.* cage; cagelike cell or prison; *Am.* roofless cattle car or freight car.
jauría [xaw·rí·a] *f.* pack of hounds.
jazmín [xaz·mín] *m.* jasmine.
jefatura [xe·fa·tú·ra] *f.* position of chief; headquarters of a chief.
jefe [xé·fe] *m.* chief, leader, head.
jengibre [xeŋ·xí·ḅre] *m.* ginger.
jerez [xe·rés] *m.* sherry wine.
jerga [xér·ǵa] *f.* (*tela*) thick coarse cloth; straw

mattress; (*dialeeto*) jargon; slang; *Am.* saddle pad; *Col.* poncho made of coarse cloth.
jergón [xer·ǵón] *m.* (*material*) straw mattress; ill-fitting suit or dress; (*persona*) big clumsy fellow; *Ríopl., Mex., Ven.* cheap coarse rug.
jerigonza [xe·ri·ǵón·sa] *f.* jargon; slang.
jeringa [xe·ríŋ·ga] *f.* syringe; **jeringazo** [xe·riŋ·gá·so] *m.* injection; squirt.
jeringar[7] [xe·riŋ·gár] *v.* to inject; to squirt; to bother, molest, vex, annoy.
jeroglífico [xe·ro·ǵlí·fi·ko] *m.* hieroglyphic.
jesuita [xe·swi·ta] *m.* Jesuit.
jeta [xé·ta] *f.* snout; thick lips.
jiba [xí·ḅa] = **giba.**
jíbaro [xí·ḅa·ro] *adj. P.R.* rustic, rural, rude, uncultured; *m. P.R.* bumpkin, peasant.
jibia [xi·ḅja] *f.* cuttlefish.
jícara [xí·ka·ra] *f.* chocolate cup; *Am.* small bowl made out of a gourd; *Am.* any small bowl; *Am.* bald head.
jilguero [xil·ǵé·ro] *m.* linnet.
jinete [xi·né·te] *m.* horseman, rider.
jineteada [xi·ne·te·á·ḍa] *f. Ríopl., C.A.* roughriding, horse-breaking.
jinetear [xi·ne·te·ár] *v.* to ride horseback; to perform on horseback; *Am.* to break in (*a horse*); *Am.* to ride a bronco or bull.
jira [xí·ra] *f.* excursion, tour; outing, picnic; strip of cloth.
jirafa [xi·rá·fa] *f.* giraffe; boom mike (*broadcasting*).
jitomate [xi·to·má·te] *m. Mex.* tomato. *Also* **gitomate.**
jocoso [xo·kó·so] *adj.* jocular.
jofaina [xo·fáj·na] *f.* basin, washbowl.
jolgorio [xol·ǵó·rjo] = **holgorio.**
jornada [xor·ná·ḍa] *f.* day's journey; military expedition; working day; act (*of a Spanish play*).
jornal [xor·nál] *m.* day's wages; bookkeeping journal; **a —** by the day.
jornalero [xor·na·lé·ro] *m.* day laborer.
joroba [xo·ró·ḅa] *f.* hump; nuisance, annoyance.
jorobado [xo·ro·ḅá·ḍo] *adj.* hunchbacked; annoyed, bothered, in a bad fix; *m.* hunchback.
jorobar [xo·ro·ḅár] *v.* to bother, pester, annoy.
jorongo [xo·róŋ·go] *m. Mex.* Mexican poncho.
jota [xó·ta] *f.* name of the letter *j*; iota (*anything insignificant*); Aragonese and Valencian dance and music; *Am.* (= **ojota**) leather sandal; **no saber una —** not to know anything.
joven [xó·ḅen] *adj.* young; *m. & f.* youth; young man; young woman.
jovial [xo·ḅjál] *adj.* jovial, jolly, merry; **jovialidad** [xo·ḅja·li·ḍáḍ] *f.* gaiety, merriment, fun.
joya [xó·ya] *f.* jewel; piece of jewelry; **-s** jewels, trousseau.
joyería [xo·ye·rí·a] *f.* jeweler's shop.
joyero [xo·ro·yé·ro] *m.* jeweler; jewel box.
juanete [xwa·né·te] *m.* bunion.
jubilación [xu·ḅi·la·sjón] *f.* retirement (*from a position or office*); pension.
jubilar [xu·ḅi·lár] *v.* to pension; to retire; **-se** to be pensioned or retired; to rejoice; *Col.* to decline, fall into decline; *Ven., Guat.* to play hooky or truant.
jubileo [xu·ḅi·lé·o] *m.* jubilee; time of rejoicing; concession by the Pope of plenary (*complete*) indulgence.
júbilo [xú·ḅi·lo] *m.* joy, glee.
jubiloso [xu·ḅi·ló·so] *adj.* jubilant, joyful.
jubón [xu·ḅón] *m.* jacket; bodice.

judía [xu·dí·a] *f. Spain* bean; string bean; Jewess; **-s tiernas** (*or* **verdes**) string beans.

judicial [xu·ḍi·sjál] *adj.* judicial; **-mente** *adv.* judicially.

judío [xu·ḍí·o] *adj.* Jewish; *m.* Jew.

judo [xú·ḍo] *m.* judo.

juego [xwé·ḡo] *m.* game; play; sport; gambling; pack of cards; set; — **de palabras** pun, play on words; — **de te** tea set; **hacer** — to match; **poner en** — to coordinate; **to set in motion.**

juerga [xwér·ḡa] *f.* spree, revelry, wild festivity; **irse de** — to go out on a spree; **juerguista** *m. & f.* merrymaker.

jueves [xwé·ḅes] *m.* Thursday.

juez [xwes] *m.* judge; juror, member of a jury; — **arbitrador** (*or* **árbitro**) arbitrator, umpire.

jugada [xu·ḡá·ḍa] *f.* play, move; stroke; trick.

jugador [xu·ḡa·ḍór] *m.* player; gambler; — **de manos** juggler.

jugar[34] [xu·ḡár] *v. irr.* to play; to gamble; to toy; — **a la pelota** to play ball; *Am.* — **a dos cartas** to be double-faced.

jugarreta [xu·ḡa·rré·ta] *f.* bad play, wrong play; mean trick; tricky deal; *Am.* noisy game.

jugo [xú·ḡo] *m.* juice; sap.

jugosidad [xu·ḡo·si·ḍáḍ] *f.* juiciness; **jugoso** *adj.* juicy.

juguete [xu·ḡé·te] *m.* plaything, toy; jest, joke; — **cómico** skit; **por** (*or* **de**) — jokingly.

juguetear [xu·ḡe·te·ár] *v.* to play around, romp, frolic; to toy; to tamper (with), fool (with).

juguetón [xu·ḡe·tón] *adj.* playful.

juicio [xwí·sjo] *m.* judgment; sense, wisdom; opinion; trial; **perder el** — to lose one's mind, go crazy.

juicioso [xwi·sjó·so] *adj.* judicious, wise; sensible.

julio [xú·ljo] *m.* July.

jumento [xu·mén·to] *m.* ass, donkey.

juncal [xun·kál] *m.* growth of rushes.

junco [xúŋ·ko] *m.* rush, reed; junk (*Chinese sailboat*).

jungla [xúŋ·gla] *f. Am.* jungle.

junio [xú·njo] *m.* June.

junquillo [xuŋ·kí·yo] *m.* reed; jonquil (*yellow flower similar to the daffodil*), species of narcissus.

junta [xún·ta] *f.* (*reunión*) meeting, conference; (*funcionarios*) board, council.

juntar [xun·tár] *v.* to join, unite; to connect; to assemble; to collect; **-se** to assemble, gather; to be closely united; to associate (with).

junto [xún·to] *adj.* joined, united;**-s** together; *adv.* near; — **a** near to, close to; **en** — all together, in all; **por** — all together, in a lump; wholesale.

juntura [xun·tú·ra] *f.* juncture; junction; joint, seam.

jurado [xu·rá·ḍo] *m.* jury; juror, juryman; *adj. & p.p.* sworn.

juramentar [xu·ra·men·tár] *v.* to swear in; **-se** to take an oath, be sworn in.

juramento [xu·ra·mén·to] *m.* oath; vow; curse.

jurar [xu·rár] *v.* to swear, vow; to take oath; to curse.

jurisconsulto [xu·ris·kon·súl·to] *m.* jurist, expert in law; lawyer.

jurisdicción [xu·riz·ḍik·sjón] *f.* jurisdiction.

jurisprudencia [xu·ris·pru·ḍén·sja] *f.* jurisprudence, law.

juro: de — [xú·ro] *adv.* certainly, of course.

justa [xús·ta] *f.* joust, tournament, combat (*between horsemen with lances*); contest.

justicia [xus·tí·sja] *f.* justice; court of justice; judge; police.

justiciero [xus·ti·sjé·ro] *adj.* strictly just, austere (*in matters of justice*).

justificación [xus·ti·fi·ka·sjón] *f.* justification.

justificante [xus·ti·fi·kán·te] *adj.* justifying; *m.* voucher; written excuse; proof.

justificar[6] [xus·ti·fi·kár] *v.* to justify; to vindicate, clear of blame.

justo [xús·to] *adj.* just; pious; exact, correct; tight; *adv.* duly; exactly; tightly; *m.* just man; **los -s** the just.

juvenil [xu·ḅe·níl] *adj.* juvenile, young, youthful.

juventud [xu·ḅen·túḍ] *f.* youth; young people.

juzgado [xuz·ḡá·ḍo] *m.* court, tribunal.

juzgar[7] [xuz·ḡár] *v.* to judge.

K : k

kermesse [ker·mé·se] *f.* country fair; bazaar for charity.

keroseno [ke·ro·sé·no] *f.* kerosene, coal oil.

kilo [kí·lo] *m.* kilo, kilogram.

kilociclo [ki·lo·sí·klo] *m.* kilocycle.

kilogramo [ki·lo·ḡrá·mo] *m.* kilogram.

kilometraje [ki·lo·me·trá·xe] *m.* number of kilometers.

kilómetro [ki·ló·me·tro] *m.* kilometer.

kilovatio [ki·lo·ḅá·tjo] *m.* kilowatt.

L : l

la [la] *def. art. f.* the; — **de** the one with, that one with; *obj. pron.* her; it; — **que** *rel. pron.* she who, the one that; which.

la [la] *m.* sixth note on the musical scale.

laberinto [la·ḅe·rín·to] *m.* labyrinth, maze; labyrinth, internal ear.

labia [la·ḅja] *f.* fluency, talkativeness, gift of gab; **tener mucha** — to be a good talker.

labial [la·ḅjál] *adj.* labial.

labio [lá·ḅjo] *m.* lip.

labiodental [la·ḅjo·ḍen·tál] *adj.* labiodental.

labor [la·ḅór] *f.* (*trabajo*) labor, work; (*cosido*) embroidery; needlework; (*agrícola*) tillage; — **de punto** knitting; **laborable** [la·ḅo·rá·ḅle] *adj.* workable; tillable; **día laborable** work day; **laboral** [la·ḅo·rál] *adj.* pertaining to labor.

laboratorio [la·ḅo·ra·tó·rjo] *m.* laboratory.

laboriosidad [la·ḅo·rjo·si·ḍáḍ] *f.* laboriousness, industry.

laborioso [la·ḅo·rjó·so] *adj.* laborious; industrious.

laborista [la·ḅo·rís·ta] *m. & f.* laborite.

labrado [la·ḅrá·ḍo] *p.p. & adj.* (*agrícola*) tilled, cultivated; (*hecho*) wrought; manufactured; carved; *m.* carving; — **en madera** woodwork, carving; **-s** cultivate··· ·ands.

labrador [la·ḅra·ḍór]   ·mer; peasant.

labranza [la·ḅrán·sa]   ·ng, tillage, plowing; cultivated land, far··

labrar [la·ḅrár] *v.* (*la tier··a*) to till, cultivate, farm; to plow; (*crear*) to carve; to embroider; to work (*metals*); to build (*a monument*).

labriego [la·ḅrjé·ḡo] *m.* peasant.

laca [lá·ka] *f.* lacquer; shellac.

lacayo [la·ká·yo] *m.* lackey, footman, flunky.

lacio [lá·sjo] *adj.* withered; languid; limp; straight

(*hair*).

lacra [lá·kra] *f.* trace of an illness; blemish, defect; *Am.* sore, ulcer, scab, scar.

lacre [lá·kre] *m.* red sealing wax; *adj. Am.* red.

lacrimógeno [la·kri·mó·xe·no] *adj.* tear-producing.

lactar [lak·tár] *v.* to nurse, suckle; to feed with milk.

lácteo [lák·te·o] *adj.* milky; **fiebre láctea** milk fever; **régimen** — milk diet; **Vía láctea** milk Way.

ladear [la·de·ár] *v.* to tilt, tip; to go along the slope or side of; to turn aside (*from a way or course*); **-se** to tilt; to sway; to incline or lean (towards); to move to one side; *Am.* to fall in love.

ladeo [la·dé·o] *m.* inclination, tilt.

ladera [la·dé·ra] *f.* slope.

ladino [la·dí·no] *adj.* crafty, sly, shrewd; conversant with two or three languages; *m.* Sephardic Jew (*Spanish-speaking*); Romansch (*a Romance language of Switzerland*); *Guat.* Spanish-speaking person (*as opposed to one who speaks an Indian language*); *Am.* mestizo, half-breed; *Mex., Ven.* talker, talkative person.

lado [lá·do] *m.* side; **al** — near, at hand, at one's side; **de** — tilted, obliquely; sideways; — **a** — side by side; **¡a un** —**!** gangway! **hacerse a un** — to move over, step aside, move to one side; *Mex., Ven.* **echársela de** — to boast.

ladrar [la·drár] *v.* to bark.

ladrido [la·drí·do] *m.* bark, barking.

ladrillo [la·drí·yo] *m.* brick.

ladrón [la·drón] *m.* thief, robber; **ladronzuelo** [la·dron·swé·lo] *m.* petty thief.

lagartija [la·gar·tí·xa] *f.* small lizard.

lagarto [la·gár·to] *m.* lizard; rascal, sly fellow.

lago [lá·go] *m.* lake.

lágrima [lá·gri·ma] *f.* tear; **llorar a** — **viva** to weep abundantly.

lagrimear [la·gri·me·ár] *v.* to weep, shed tears.

laguna [la·gú·na] *f.* lagoon; gap, blank space.

laico [láj·ko] *adj.* lay; *m.* layman.

laísta [la·ís·ta] *m. & f.* one who uses *la* for indirect object.

laja [lá·xa] *f.* slab; flat stone.

lamedero [la·me·dé·ro] *m.* salt lick (*for cattle*).

lamentable [la·men·tá·ble] *adj.* lamentable, pitiful.

lamentación [la·men·ta·sjón] *f.* lamentation.

lamentar [la·men·tár] *v.* to lament, deplore; **-se** to moan, complain, wail.

lamento [la·mén·to] *m.* lament, moan, cry.

lamer [la·mér] *v.* to lick; to lap.

lamida [la·mí·da] *f. Mex., C.A.* lick; also **lambida**.

lámina [lá·mi·na] *f.* metal plate; sheet of metal; engraving; book illustration.

laminar [la·mi·nár] *v.* to laminate.

lámpara [lám·pa·ra] *f.* lamp.

lampiño [lam·pí·ño] *adj.* hairless; beardless.

lana [lá·na] *f.* wool; *Am.* tramp, vagabond.

lanar [la·nár] *adj.* wool-bearing; of wool.

lance [lán·se] *m.* occurrence, event; cast, throw, move, turn; accident; quarrel; predicament.

lancear [lan·se·ár] *v.* to lance, spear.

lancha [lán·ča] *f.* launch; boat; slab; **lanchón** [lan·čón] *m.* barge.

langosta [lan·gós·ta] *f.* lobster; locust.

languidecer[13] [lan·gi·de·sér] *v. irr.* to languish.

languidez [lan·gi·dés] *f.* languor, faintness, weakness.

lánguido [lán·gi·do] *adj.* languid.

lanilla [la·ní·ya] *f.* nap (*of cloth*).

lanudo [la·nú·do] *adj.* woolly; *Ven.* coarse, crude, ill-bred; *Am.* dull, slow, weak-willed; *Ch., C.A., Col.* wealthy.

lanza [lán·sa] *f.* lance, spear; *Col.* swindler, cheat; *m.* **lanzabombas** [lan·sa·bóm·bas] bomb launcher; *m.* **lanzacohetes** [lan·sa·ko·é·tes] rocket launcher; *m.* **lanzallamas** [lan·sa·yá·mas] flame thrower.

lanzada [lan·sá·da] *f.* thrust (*with a spear*).

lanzadera [lan·sa·dé·ra] *f.* shuttle.

lanzamiento [lan·sa·mjén·to] *m.* launching (*boat or rocket*).

lanzar[9] [lan·sár] *v.* to fling, throw; to eject; to launch; **-se** to rush, fling oneself; to dart out.

lanzazo [lan·sá·so] *m.* thrust with a lance.

lapicero [la·pi·sé·ro] *m.* pencil (*a mechanical pencil, one with an adjustable lead*).

lápida [lá·pi·da] *f.* slab, tombstone; stone tablet.

lapidar [la·pi·dár] *v.* to stone; *Col., Ch.* to cut precious stones.

lapidario [la·pi·dá·rjo] *m.* lapidary.

lápiz [lá·pis] *f.* pencil; crayon; — **para los labios** lipstick.

lapso [láp·so] *m.* lapse.

lardo [lár·do] *m.* lard.

lares [lá·res] *m. pl.* home.

largar[7] [lar·gár] *v.* to loosen; to let go; to set free; to unfold (*a flag or sails*); *Am.* to hurl, throw; *Col.* to strike (*a blow*); *Riopl.* to give, hand over; **-se** to go away, slip away; to leave.

largo [lár·go] *adj.* long; generous; *m.* length; largo (*music*); **a la larga** in the long run; slowly; **a lo** — along; lengthwise; **¡— de aquí!** get out of here!

largor [lar·gór] *m.* length.

largucho [lar·gú·čo] *adj.* lanky.

largueza [lar·ge·sa] *f.* generosity, liberality; length.

larguísimo [lar·gi·si·mo] *adj.* very long.

largura [lar·gú·ra] *f.* length.

laringe [la·rín·xe] *f.* larynx.

laríngeo [la·rín·xe·o] *adj.* laryngeal.

laringitis [la·rin·xí·tis] *f.* laryngitis.

larva [lár·ba] *f.* larva.

las [las] *def. art. f. pl.* the; *obj. pron.* them; — **que** *rel. pron.* those which; which.

lascivia [la·si·bja] *f.* lewdness.

lascivo [la·sí·bo] *adj.* lascivious, lewd.

lástima [lás·ti·ma] *f.* pity; compassion, grief.

lastimadura [las·ti·ma·dú·ra] *f.* sore, hurt.

lastimar [las·ti·már] *v.* to hurt; to offend; **-se** to get hurt; **-se de** to feel pity for.

lastimero [las·ti·mé·ro] *adj.* pitiful; mournful.

lastimoso [las·ti·mó·so] *adj.* pitiful.

lastre [lás·tre] *m.* ballast, weight.

lata [lá·ta] *f.* (*metal*) tin plate; tin can, can; (*madero*) small log; thin board; (*pesadez*) annoyance; embarrassment; boring speech; *Am.* gaucho saber; *Am.* prop.

latente [la·tén·te] *adj.* latent.

lateral [la·te·rál] *adj.* lateral, side; [1] (*phonetically*).

latido [la·tí·do] *m.* palpitation, throb, beat; bark, howl.

latifundio [la·ti·fún·djo] *m.* large landed estate.

latigazo [la·ti·gá·so] *m.* lash, stroke with a whip; crack of a whip; harsh reprimand; unexpected blow or offense.

látigo [lá·ti·go] *m.* whip; *Am.* whipping, beating; *Ch.* end or goal of a horse race.

latín [la·tín] *m.* Latin language.

latinismo [la·ti·níz·mo] *m.* Latinism; imitating

Latin.
latino [la·tí·no] *adj.* Latin; *m.* Latinist, Latin
scholar; Latin.
latir [la·tír] *v.* to throb, beat, palpitate; to bark.
latitud [la·ti·túḍ] *f.* latitude; extent, breadth.
latón [la·tón] *m.* brass.
latrocinio [la·tro·sí·njo] *m.* larceny, theft, robbery.
laúd [la·úḍ] *m.* lute; catboat (*long, narrow boat
with a lateen sail*).
laudable [law·ḍá·ḅle] *adj.* laudable, praiseworthy.
laurel [law·rél] *m.* laurel; laurel wreath.
lauro [láw·ro] *m.* laurel; glory, fame.
lava [lá·ḅa] *f.* lava; washing of minerals.
lavable [la·ḅá·ḅle] *adj.* washable.
lavabo [la·ḅá·ḅo] *m.* lavatory, washroom;
washstand; washbowl.
lavadero [la·ḅa·dé·ro] *m.* washing place.
lavado [la·ḅá·ḍo] *m.* wash, washing; laundry,
laundry work; — **de cerebro** brain washing.
lavador [la·ḅa·ḍór] *m.* washer; cleaner; *adj.*
washing; cleaning; **lavadora** [la·ḅa·ḍó·ra] *f.*
washer, washing machine.
lavadura [la·ḅa·ḍú·ra] *f.* washing; slops, dirty
water.
lavamanos [la·ḅa·má·nos] *m.* lavatory, washbowl,
washstand.
lavendera [la·ḅan·dé·ra] *f.* laundress,
washerwoman.
lavandería [la·ḅan·de·rí·a] *f.* laundry.
lavar [la·ḅár] *v.* to wash; to launder; to whitewash.
lavativa [la·ḅa·tí·ḅa] *f.* enema; syringe; bother,
nuisance.
lavatorio [la·ḅa·tó·rjo] *m.* washing (*act of washing*);
wash (*liquid or solution for washing*); lavatory
(*ceremonial act of washing*); washbowl,
washstand; *Am.* washroom.
lavazas [la·ḅá·sas] *f. pl.* slops, dirty water.
laxante [lak·sán·te] *m.* laxative.
lazada [la·sá·ḍa] *f.* bow, bowknot; *Am.* throwing
of the lasso, lassoing.
lazar [la·sár] *v.* to rope, lasso; to noose.
lazarillo [la·sa·rí·yo] *m.* blindman's guide.
lazo [lá·so] *m.* (*nudo*) bow, knot; slipknot; lasso,
lariat; (*vínculo*) tie, bond; (*trampa*) snare, trap;
trick.
le [le] *obj. pron.* him; you (*formal*); to him; to her;
to you (*formal*).
leal [le·ál] *adj.* loyal.
lealtad [le·al·táḍ] *f.* loyalty.
lebrel [le·ḅrél] *m.* greyhound.
lebrillo [le·ḅrí·yo] *m.* earthenware basin or tub.
lección [lek·sjón] *f.* lesson; reading; **dar la** — to
recite the lesson; **dar** — to teach; **tomarle a
uno la** — to have someone recite his lesson.
lector [lek·tór] *m.* reader; lecturer.
lectura [lek·tú·ra] *f.* reading; **libro de** — reader.
lechada [le·čá·ḍa] *f.* whitewash; *Am.* milking.
leche [lé·če] *f.* milk; *Col., Ven., C.A., Andes, Riopl.*
luck (*in games*).
lechería [le·če·rí·a] *f.* dairy, creamery; **lechero**
[le·čé·ro] *adj.* milk; milch, giving milk (*applied
to animals*); *Am.* lucky (*in games of chance*); *m.*
milkman; **lechera** [le·čé·ra] *f.* milkmaid; milk
can; milk pitcher.
lecho [lé·čo] *m.* bed; river bed.
lechón [le·čón] *m.* suckling pig; pig.
lechoso [le·čó·so] *adj.* milky; *m.* papaya tree;
lechosa [le·čó·sa] *f. P.R.* papaya (*tropical fruit*).
lechuga [le·čú·ga] *f.* lettuce.
lechuza [le·čú·sa] *f.* screech owl, barn owl.
leer[14] [le·ér] *v.* to read.

legación [le·ga·sjón] *f.* legation.
legado [le·gá·ḍo] *m.* (*donación*) legacy; legato;
(*representante*) representative, ambassador.
legajo [le·gá·xo] *m.* bundle of papers; dossier.
legal [le·gál] *adj.* legal, lawful; truthful; reliable;
Col., Ven., Andes excellent, best; *Am.* just,
honest.
legalizar[9] [le·ga·li·sár] *v.* to legalize.
legar[7] [le·gár] *v.* to will, bequeath; to send as a
delegate.
legendario [le·xen·dá·rjo] *adj.* legendary.
legión [le·xjón] *f.* legion.
legislación [le·xiz·la·sjón] *f.* legislation.
legislador [le·xiz·la·ḍór] *m.* legislator; *adj.*
legislating, legislative.
legislar [le·xiz·lár] *v.* to legislate.
legislativo [le·xiz·la·tí·ḅo] *adj.* legislative.
legislatura [le·xiz·la·tú·ra] *f.* legislature, legislative
assembly.
legítimo [le·xí·ti·mo] *adj.* legitimate; real, genuine.
lego [lé·go] *adj.* lay; ignorant; *m.* layman.
legua [lé·gwa] *f.* league (*about 3 miles*).
leguleyo [le·gu·lé·yo] *m.* shyster.
legumbre [le·gúm·bre] *f.* vegetable.
leída [le·í·ḍa] *f. Am.* reading. *See* **lectura**.
leísta [le·ís·ta] *m. & f.* one who uses the pronoun
le for masculine direct object (*le conozco*).
lejanía [le·xa·ní·a] *f.* distance; distant place.
lejano [le·xá·no] *adj.* distant; remote.
lejía [le·xi·a] *f.* lye; harsh reprimand.
lejos [lé·xos] *adv.* far, far away; **a lo** — in the
distance; *Am.* **a un** — in the distance; **de** (or
desde) — from afar; *m.* view, perspective;
background.
lelo [lé·lo] *adj.* silly, stupid, foolish.
lema [lé·ma] *m.* motto; theme; slogan.
lencería [len·se·rí·a] *f.* dry goods; dry-goods store;
linen room or closet.
lengua [léŋ·gwa] *f.* tongue; language; interpreter;
— **de tierra** point, neck of land.
lenguado [leŋ·gwá·ḍo] *m.* flounder, sole (*a fish*).
lenguaje [leŋ·gwá·xe] *m.* language (*manner of
expression*).
lenguaraz [leŋ·gwa·rás] *adj.* talkative,
loose-tongued.
lengüeta [leŋ·gwé·ta] *f.* small tongue; **lengüetada**
[leŋ·gwe·ta·ḍa] *f.* lick.
leninismo [le·ni·níz·mo] *m.* Leninism.
lente [lén·te] *m. & f.* lens; **-s** *m. pl.* eyeglasses.
lenteja [len·té·xa] *f.* lentil; lentil seed; **lentejuela**
[len·te·xwé·la] *f.* spangle.
lentitud [len·ti·túḍ] *f.* slowness.
lento [lén·to] *adj.* slow; dull.
leña [lé·ña] *f.* firewood; kindling; beating;
leñera [le·ñé·ra] *f.* woodshed; woodbox.
leñador [le·ña·ḍór] *m.* woodcutter; woodman.
leño [lé·ño] *m.* log; timber; piece of firewood.
león [le·ón] *m.* lion; **leona** [le·ó·na] *f.* lioness;
leonera [le·o·né·ra] *f.* lion's den or cage; dive,
gambling joint; disorderly room.
leontina [le·on·tí·na] *f. Mex., Carib., Col.* watch
chain.
leopardo [le·o·pár·ḍo] *m.* leopard.
leopoldina [le·o·pol·dí·na] *f. Mex., Ven.* watch
chain.
lerdo [lér·ḍo] *adj.* dull, heavy, stupid, slow.
les [les] *obj. pron.* to them; to you (*formal*).
lesión [le·sjón] *f.* wound, injury.
lesionar [le·sjo·nár] *v.* to injure; to wound; to
hurt; to damage.
lesna [léz·na] = **lezna**.

letargo [le·tár·ǵo] *m.* lethargy, stupor, drowsiness.
letra [lé·tra] *f.* letter (*of the alphabet*); printing type; hand; handwriting; letter (*exact wording or meaning*); words of a song; — **abierta** letter of credit; — **de cambio** draft, bill of exchange; — **mayúscula** capital letter; — **minúscula** small letter; **al pie de la** — literally; **-s** letters, learning.
letrado [le·trá·ḓo] *adj.* learned; *m.* lawyer.
letrero [le·tré·ro] *m.* notice, poster, sign; legend (*under an illustration*).
leva [lé·ḅa] *f.* levy, draft; weighing anchor, setting sail; **echar** — to draft, conscript; *Col.* **echar -s** to boast.
levadizo [le·ḅa·dí·so] *adj.* lift (*bridge*).
levadura [le·ḅa·ḓú·ra] *f.* leaven, yeast.
levantamiento [le·ḅan·ta·mjén·to] *m.* (*revuelta*) uprising, revolt, insurrection; (*altura*) elevation; lifting, raising; adjournment (*of a meeting*); — **de un plano** surveying.
levantar [le·ḅan·tár] *v.* to raise, lift; to set up; to erect; to rouse, stir up; to recruit; *Ch.* to break land, plow; — **el campo** to break camp; — **la mesa** to clear the table; — **la sesión** to adjourn the meeting; — **un plano** to survey, map out; — **falso testimonio** to bear false witness; **-se** to stand up, get up, rise; to rebel.
levante [le·ḅán·te] *m.* east; east wind.
levantisco [le·ḅan·tís·ko] *adj.* turbulent; rebellious.
levar [le·ḅár] *v.* to weigh (*anchor*); — **el ancla** to weigh anchor; **-se** to weigh anchor, set sail.
leve [lé·ḅe] *adj.* light; slight; unimportant.
levita [le·ḅí·ta] *f.* frock coat; *m.* Levite, member of the tribe of Levi.
léxico [lék·si·ko] *m.* lexicon, dictionary; vocabulary; glossary.
lexicografía [lek·si·ko·ǵra·fí·a] *f.* lexicography.
lexicología [lek·si·ko·lo·xí·a] *f.* lexicology.
ley [lej] *f.* law; rule; loyalty; standard quality; **de buena** — of good quality; **plata de** — sterling silver; **-es** jurisprudence, law; system of laws.
leyenda [le·yén·da] *f.* legend; reading; inscription.
lezna [léz·na] *f.* awl.
liar [ljar] *v.* to tie, bind; to roll up; to deceive; **-se** to bind oneself; to get tangled up.
libelo [li·ḅé·lo] *m.* libel.
libélula [li·ḅé·lu·la] *f.* dragon fly.
liberación [li·ḅe·ra·sjón] *f.* liberation; deliverance.
liberal [li·ḅe·rál] *adj.* liberal; generous; **liberalidad** [li·ḅe·ra·li·ḓáḓ] *f.* liberality; generosity.
liberalismo [li·ḅe·ra·líz·mo] *m.* liberalism.
libertad [li·ḅer·táḓ] *f.* liberty.
libertador [li·ḅer·ta·ḓór] *m.* liberator, deliverer.
libertar [li·ḅer·tár] *v.* to liberate, free, set free; **-se** to get free; to escape.
libertinaje [li·ḅer·ti·ná·xe] *m.* license, licentiousness, lack of moral restraint.
libertino [li·ḅer·tí·no] *m.* libertine (*person without moral restraint*).
libido [li·ḅí·ḓo] *m.* libido.
libra [lí·ḅra] *f.* pound; Libra (*sign of the Zodiac*).
librador [li·ḅra·ḓór] *m.* drawer (*of a bill, draft, etc.*); deliverer, liberator; measuring scoop.
libranza [li·ḅrán·sa] *f.* bill of exchange, draft.
librar [li·ḅrár] *v.* to free, set free; to issue; to draw (*a draft*); — **guerra** to wage war; **-se** to save oneself; to escape; **-se de** to get rid of, escape from.
libre [lí·ḅre] *adj.* free; unmarried; loose; vacant.
librea [li·ḅré·a] *f.* livery (*uniform*).
librería [li·ḅre·rí·a] *f.* bookstore.
librero [li·ḅré·ro] *m.* bookseller; *Am.* bookcase, bookshelves.

libreta [li·ḅré·ta] *f.* notebook, memorandum book,
libreto [li·ḅré·to] *m.* libretto.
libro [lí·ḅro] *m.* book; — **de caja** cashbook; — **mayor** ledger.
licencia [li·sén·sja] *f.* license; permission; furlough, leave; looseness; license to practice.
licenciado [li·sen·sjá·ḓo] *m.* licenciate (*person having a degree approximately equivalent to a master's degree*); *Ríopl., Mex., C.A.* lawyer.
licenciar [li·sen·sjár] *v.* to license; to give a license or permit; to dismiss, discharge (*from the army*); to confer the degree of **licenciado**; **-se** to get the degree of **licenciado**.
licenciatura [li·sen·sja·tú·ra] *f.* degree of **licenciado**.
licencioso [li·sen·sjó·so] *adj.* licentious, lewd.
liceo [li·sé·o] *m.* lyceum; high school; *Col.* primary school or high school.
lícito [lí·si·to] *adj.* lawful; permissible, allowable.
licor [li·kór] *m.* liquid; liquor.
lid [liḓ] *f.* fight; contest.
líder [lí·ḓer] *m. Am.* leader.
lidiar [li·ḓjár] *v.* to fight; to combat; to contend.
liebre [ljé·ḅre] *f.* hare; coward.
lienzo [ljén·so] *m.* cotton or linen cloth; canvas; painting.
liga [lí·ǵa] *f.* (*alianza*) league; alliance; (*cinta*) garter; alloy; birdlime.
ligadura [li·ǵa·ḓú·ra] *f.* binding; tie, bond.
ligar[7] [li·ǵár] *v.* to bind, tie, unite; to alloy (*combine metals*); **-se** to unite, combine, form an alliance.
ligereza [li·xe·ré·sa] *f.* lightness; swiftness; flippancy; frivolity.
ligero [li·xé·ro] *adj.* (*leve*) light; (*rápido*) swift; nimble; flippant; *adv. Am.* quickly; **a la ligera** quickly, superficially.
lija [lí·xa] *f.* sandpaper.
lijar [li·xár] *v.* to sandpaper.
lila [lí·la] *f.* lilac; pinkish-purple.
lima [lí·ma] *f.* file; lime (*fruit*); finishing, polishing.
limar [li·már] *v.* to file; to file down; to smooth, polish.
limeño [li·mé·ño] *adj.* of or from Lima, Peru.
limero [li·mé·ro] *m.* lime tree.
limitación [li·mi·ta·sjón] *f.* limitation; district.
limitar [li·mi·tár] *v.* to limit; to restrict; to bound.
límite [lí·mi·te] *m.* limit; boundary.
limítrofe [li·mí·tro·fe] *adj.* limiting; bordering.
limo [lí·mo] *m.* slime.
limón [li·món] *m.* lemon; lemon tree; **limonada** *f.* lemonade; **limonero** *m.* lemon tree lemon dealer or vendor.
limosna [li·móz·na] *f.* alms, charity.
limosnero [li·moz·né·ro] *m.* beggar.
limpiabotas [lim·pja·ḅó·tas] *m.* bootblack; *Ch.* bootlicker, flatterer.
limpiadientes [lim·pja·ḓjén·tes] *m.* toothpick.
limpiaparabrisas [lim·pja·pa·ra·ḅrí·sas] *m.* windshield wiper.
limpiar [lim·pjár] *v.* to clean; to wipe; to cleanse, purify; *Am.* to beat up, whip, lash.
límpido [lím·pi·ḓo] *adj.* limpid, clear.
limpieza [lim·pjé·sa] *f.* cleanliness, neatness; purity; honesty.
limpio [lím·pjo] *adj.* clean; neat; pure; **poner en** — to make a clean copy; *Am.* — **y soplado** absolutely broke, wiped out.
linaje [li·ná·xe] *m.* lineage, family, race.
linajudo [li·na·xú·ḓo] *adj.* highborn.
linaza [li·ná·sa] *f.* linseed.

lince [lín·se] *m.* lynx; sharp-sighted person.
linchar [lin·čár] *v.* to lynch.
lindar [lin·dár] *v.* to border, adjoin.
linde [lín·de] *m.* & *f.* limit, border, boundary; landmark.
lindero [lin·dé·ro] *adj.* bordering upon; *m. Carib., C.A.* landmark; boundary.
lindeza [lin·dé·sa] *f.* prettiness; exquisiteness; neatness; witty act or remark.
lindo [lín·do] *adj.* pretty; **de lo** — wonderfully; very much; to the utmost.
línea [lí·ne·a] *f.* line; limit.
lineal [li·ne·ál] *adj.* lineal, linear.
lingüista [liŋ·gwís·ta] *m.* & *f.* linguist.
lingüística [liŋ·gwís·ti·ka] *f.* linguistics.
lingüístico [liŋ·gwís·ti·ko] *adj.* linguistic.
lino [lí·no] *m.* linen; flax; **linón** *m.* lawn, thin linen or cotton.
linotipia [li·no·tí·pja] *f.* linotype.
linterna [lin·tér·na] *f.* lantern.
lío [lí·o] *m.* (*bulto*) bundle; (*enredo*) fib; mess, confusion; **armar un** — to raise a rumpus; to cause confusion; **hacerse un** — to be confused, get tangled up; **meterse en un** — to get oneself into a mess.
liquidación [li·ki·ḑa·sjón] *f.* liquidation; settlement (*of an account*).
liquidar [li·ki·ḑár] *v.* to liquidate; to settle (*an account*).
líquido [lí·ki·ḑo] *m.* liquid.
lira [lí·ra] *f.* lyre, small harp; a type of metrical composition; lira (*Italian coin*).
lírico [lí·ri·ko] *adj.* lyric, lyrical; *Am.* fantastic; *m. Ríopl.* visionary, dreamer.
lirio [lí·rjo] *m.* lily.
lirismo [li·ríz·mo] *m.* lyricism (*lyric quality*); *Am.* idle dream, fantasy.
lisiado [li·sjá·ḑo] *adj.* lame, hurt, injured.
liso [lí·so] *adj.* smooth, even; flat; evident, clear; *Am.* crafty, sly; *Col., Ven., C.A., Andes* fresh, impudent.
lisonja [li·sóŋ·xa] *f.* flattery.
lisonjear [li·soŋ·xe·ár] *v.* to flatter; to fawn on; to please.
lisonjero [li·soŋ·xé·ro] *adj.* flattering, pleasing; *m.* flatterer.
lista [lís·ta] *f.* list; strip; stripe; **pasar** — to call the roll; — **de correos** general delivery.
listado [lis·tá·ḑo] *adj.* striped.
listar [lis·tár] *v.* to register, enter in a list; *Ríopl., Mex., Ven.* to stripe, streak.
listo [lís·to] *adj.* ready, prompt; clever; *Ríopl., Ch.* mischievous.
listón [lis·tón] *m.* ribbon, tape; strip.
lisura [li·sú·ra] *f.* smoothness; sincerity, frankness; *Am.* freshness, impudence; *Andes* insulting or filthy remark.
litera [li·té·ra] *f.* berth (*on a boat or train*); litter (*for carrying a person*).
literario [li·te·rá·rjo] *adj.* literary.
literato [li·te·rá·to] *adj.* literary, learned; *m.* literary man, writer.
literatura [li·te·ra·tú·ra] *f.* literature.
litigio [li·tí·xjo] *m.* litigation, lawsuit.
litio [lí·tjo] *m.* lithium.
litoral [li·to·rál] *adj.* seaboard, coastal; *m.* coast, shore.
litro [lí·tro] *m.* liter (*about 1.05 quarts*).
liviandad [li·ƀja·ni·ḑáḑ] *f.* lightness; frivolity; lewdness.
liviano [li·ƀjá·no] *adj.* (*leve*) light; slight,

unimportant; (*lascivo*) frivolous, fickle; lewd; unchaste.
lívido [lí·ƀi·ḑo] *adj.* livid, having a dull-bluish color; pale.
lo [lo] *obj. pron.* him; you (*formal*); it; so; *dem. pron.* — **de** that of, that affair of, that matter of; — **bueno** the good, what is good; **sé** — **bueno que Vd. es** I know how good you are; — **que** that which, what.
loable [lo·á·ƀle] *adj.* laudable, worthy of praise.
loar [lo·ár] *v.* to praise.
lobanillo [lo·ƀa·ní·yo] *m.* growth, tumor.
lobo [ló·ƀo] *m.* wolf.
lóbrego [ló·ƀre·go] *adj.* dark, gloomy.
lobreguez [lo·ƀre·gés] *f.* darkness, gloominess.
lóbulo [ló·ƀu·lo] *m.* lobe.
lobuno [lo·ƀú·no] *adj.* related to the wolf.
local [lo·kál] *adj.* local; *m.* place, quarters; site; premises.
localidad [lo·ka·li·ḑáḑ] *f.* location; locality, town; place; seat (*in a theater*).
localización [lo·ka·li·sa·sjón] *f.* localization, localizing.
localizar [lo·ka·li·sár] *v.* to localize.
loco [ló·ko] *adj.* insane, mad, crazy; — **de remate** stark mad; *m.* lunatic, insane person.
locomotor [lo·ko·mo·tór] *adj.* locomotive.
locomotora [lo·ko·mo·tó·ra] *f.* locomotive; — **diesel** diesel locomotive.
locuaz [lo·kwás] *adj.* loquacious, talkative.
locución [lo·ku·sjón] *f.* phrase; diction.
locura [lo·kú·ra] *f.* madness, insanity.
locutor [lo·ku·tór] *m.* radio announcer.
lodazal [lo·ḑa·sál] *m.* muddy place; mire.
lodo [ló·ḑo] *m.* mud; **lodoso** [lo·ḑó·so] *adj.* muddy, miry.
logaritmo [lo·ga·rím·mo] *m.* logarithm.
logia [ló·xja] *f.* lodge (*secret society*).
lógica [ló·xi·ka] *f.* logic; reasoning.
lógico [ló·xi·ko] *adj.* logical.
lograr [lo·grár] *v.* to gain, obtain, accomplish; — (+ *inf.*) to succeed in; **-se** to succeed; to turn out well.
logrero [lo·gré·ro] *m.* usurer; profiteer.
logro [ló·gro] *m.* profit, gain; usury; attainment; realization.
loísta [lo·ís·ta] *m.* & *f.* one who uses the pronoun *lo* for the masculine direct object (*lo conozco*).
loma [ló·ma] *f.* small hill; **lomerío** [lo·me·rí·o] *m. Am.* group of hills.
lombriz [lom·brís] *f.* earthworm.
lomillo [lo·mí·yo] *m.* cross-stitch.
lomo [ló·mo] *m.* back (*of an animal, book, knife, etc.*); loin; ridge between two furrows; *Mex., Ven.* **hacer** — to bear with patience, resign oneself.
lona [ló·na] *f.* canvas.
lonche [lón·če] *m. Col., Ven., Mex.* lunch; **lonchería** [lon·če·rí·a] *f. Col., Ven., Mex.* lunchroom.
londinense [lon·di·nén·se] *m.* & *f.* of or from London.
longaniza [loŋ·ga·ní·sa] *f.* pork sausage.
longevidad [loŋ·xe·ƀi·ḑáḑ] *f.* longevity, long life; span of life, length of life.
longitud [loŋ·xi·túḑ] *f.* longitude; length.
longitudinal [loŋ·xi·tu·ḑi·nál] *adj.* longitudinal, lengthwise; **-mente** *adv.* longitudinally, lengthwise.
lonja [lón·xa] *f.* (*mercado*) exchange; market; (*carne*) slice of meat; (*correa*) leather strap; *Ríopl.* raw hide.

LE

lontananza [lon·ta·nán·sa] *f.* background; **en —** in the distance, in the background.

loro [ló·ro] *m.* parrot.

los [los] *def. art. m. pl.* the; *obj. pron.* them; **— que** *rel. pron.* those which; which.

losa [ló·sa] *f.* flagstone; slab; gravestone.

lote [ló·te] *m.* lot, share, part; *Am.* remnant lot; *Col.* swallow of liquor; *Am.* blockhead, dunce.

lotear [lo·te·ár] *v. Am.* to subdivide into lots; *Am.* to divide into portions.

lotería [lo·te·rí·a] *f.* lottery; raffle.

loza [ló·sa] *f.* fine earthenware; crockery; **— fina** chinaware.

lozanía [lo·sa·ní·a] *f.* luxuriance (*rich foliage or growth*); vigor.

lozano [lo·sá·no] *adj.* luxuriant; exuberant, vigorous, lusty.

lubricar[6] [lu·βri·kár] *v.* to lubricate, or grease.

lucero [lu·sé·ro] *m.* morning star; any bright star; star on the forehead of certain animals; splendor, brightness.

lúcido [lú·si·đo] *adj.* lucid, clear; shining, bright.

luciente [lu·sjén·te] *adj.* shining, bright.

luciérnaga [lu·sjér·na·ğa] *f.* firefly; glowworm.

lucimiento [lu·si·mjén·to] *m.* splendor; brilliance; success.

lucir[13] [lu·sír] *v. irr.* (*brillar*) to shine; to illuminate; to brighten; (*superar*) to excel; (*alardear*) to show off; **-se** to shine, be brilliant; show off; to be successful.

lucrativo [lu·kra·tí·βo] *adj.* lucrative, profitable.

lucro [lú·kro] *m.* profit, gain.

luctuoso [luk·twó·so] *adj.* sad, mournful, dismal.

lucha [lú·ča] *f.* fight, struggle; dispute; wrestling match.

luchador [lu·ča·đór] *m.* fighter; wrestler.

luchar [lu·čár] *v.* to fight; to wrestle; to struggle; to dispute.

luego [lwé·ğo] *adv.* soon, presently; afterwards, then, next; **desde —** immediately, at once; naturally; **— de** after; **— que** as soon as; **hasta — good-bye**, so long; **— —** right away.

luengo [lwén·go] *adj.* long; **-s años** many years.

lugar [lu·ğár] *m.* (*sitio*) place; site; town; space; (*empleo*) position, employment; (*ocasión*) time, occasion, opportunity; **dar — a** to give cause or occasion for; **hacer** (*or* **dar**) **—** to make room; **en — de** instead of.

lugareño [lu·ğa·ré·ño] *m.* villager.

lúgubre [lú·ğu·βre] *adj.* mournful, gloomy.

lujo [lú·xo] *m.* luxury, extravagance.

lujoso [lu·xó·so] *adj.* luxurious; elegant; showy.

lujuria [lu·xú·rja] *f.* lust, lewdness, sensuality.

lujurioso [lu·xu·rjó·so] *adj.* lustful, lewd, sensual.

lumbre [lúm·bre] *f.* fire; brightness.

luminoso [lu·mi·nó·so] *adj.* luminous, bright, shining.

luna [lú·na] *f.* moon; mirror, glass for mirrors.

lunar [lu·nár] *adj.* lunar; *m.* mole; blemish, spot.

lunático [lu·ná·ti·ko] *adj.* & *m.* lunatic.

lunes [lú·nes] *m.* Monday; *Ch.* **hacer San Lunes** to lay off on Monday.

lunfardo [lun·fár·đo] *m.* social dialect of the Buenos Aires underworld.

lustre [lús·tre] *m.* luster, shine; glory.

lustroso [lus·tró·so] *adj.* lustrous, glossy, shining.

luto [lú·to] *m.* mourning; sorrow, grief.

luz [lus] *f.* light; clarity; hint, guidance; **dar a —** to give birth; to publish; **entre dos luces** at twilight.

LL:11

llaga [yá·ğa] *f.* wound; ulcer, sore.

llama [yá·ma] *f.* flame; llama (*a South American beast of burden*).

llamada [ya·má·đa] *f.* call; beckon, sign; knock; reference mark (*as an asterisk*).

llamador [ya·ma·đór] *m.* knocker (*of a door*); caller.

llamamiento [ya·ma·mjén·to] *m.* call, calling; calling together; appeal.

llamar [ya·már] *v.* to call; to summon; to name; to invoke; **— a la puerta** to knock at the door; **-se** to be called, named; *Am.* to break one's word or promise.

llamarada [ya·ma·rá·đa] *f.* flash; sudden flame or blaze; sudden flush, blush.

llamativo [ya·ma·tí·βo] *adj.* showy, loud, gaudy, flashy; thirst-exciting.

llameante [ya·me·án·te] *adj.* flaming.

llana [yá·na] *f.* mason's trowel.

llanero [ya·né·ro] *m. Ven., Col.* plainsman.

llaneza [ya·né·sa] *f.* simplicity; frankness; sincerity; plainness.

llano [yá·no] *adj.* plain, simple; even, smooth, level; frank; *m.* plain, flat ground.

llanta [yán·ta] *f. Spain* rim of a wheel; *Am.* tire; tire casing; *Peru* large sunshade (*used in Peruvian markets*).

llanto [yán·to] *m.* crying, weeping; tears.

llanura [ya·nú·ra] *f.* extensive plain; prairie; evenness, flatness.

llapa [yá·pa] *f. Andes, Ríopl.* a small gift from the vendor to the purchaser; also **yapa, ñapa.**

llave [yá·βe] *f.* key; faucet; clef; **— de tuercas** wrench; **— inglesa** monkey wrench; **— maestra** master key.

llavera [ya·βé·ra] *f. Am.* housekeeper.

llavero [ya·βé·ro] *m.* key ring; key maker; keeper of the keys.

llavín [ya·βín] *m.* small key.

llegada [ye·ğá·đa] *f.* arrival.

llegar[7] [ye·ğár] *v.* to arrive; to reach; to amount; **— a ser** to get or come to be; **— a las manos** to come to blows; **-se** to approach, get near.

llenar [ye·nár] *v.* to fill; to stuff; **-se** to fill up; to overeat; **-se de** to get filled with; to get covered with, spattered with.

lleno [yé·no] *adj.* full; *m.* fullness, completeness; **de — totally**, completely; **un — completo** a full house (*said of a theater*).

llenura [ye·nú·ra] *f.* fullness; abundance.

llevadero [ye·βa·đé·ro] *adj.* bearable, tolerable.

llevar [ye·βár] *v.* (*transportar*) to carry; to bear; to transport; to wear; (*conducir*) to take; to lead; (*cobrar*) to charge; to ask a certain price; to keep (*accounts*); **— ventaja** to be ahead, have the advantage; **— un año a** to be one year older than; **— un mes aquí** to have been here one month; **— un castigo** to suffer punishment; **-se** to carry away; **-se bien con** to get along with.

llorar [yo·rár] *v.* to cry, weep.

lloriquear [yo·ri·ke·ár] *v.* to whimper, whine, weep.

lloriqueo [yo·ri·ké·o] *m.* whimper, whining.

lloro [yó·ro] *m.* weeping.

llorón [yo·rón] *adj.* weeping; **sauce —** weeping willow; *m.* weeper, crybaby, whiner.

llorona [yo·ró·na] *f.* weeping woman; **-s** *Am.* large spurs.

lloroso [yo·ró·so] *adj.* tearful; weeping.

llovedizo [yo·βe·đí·so] *adj.* rain (*used as adj.*); **agua llovediza** rain water.

llover[2] [ẏo·ḃér] *v. irr.* to rain, shower.
llovizna [ẏo·ḃíz·na] *f.* drizzle.
lloviznar [ẏo·ḃiz·nár] *v.* to drizzle, sprinkle.
lluvia [ẏu·ḃja] *f.* rain; shower.
lluvioso [ẏu·ḃjó·so] *adj.* rainy.

M:m

macana [ma·ká·na] *f. Am.* club, cudgel, stick; *Am.* lie, absurdity, nonsense. **macanudo** [ma·ka·nú·ḍo] *adj. Ríopl.* tremendous! great!

macarrón [ma·ka·rrón] *m.* macaroon; **-es** macaroni.

maceta [ma·sé·ta] *f.* (*tiesto*) flowerpot; (*martillo*) small mallet; stonecutter's hammer; handle of tools; *Am.* head; *adj. Am.* slow.

macilento [ma·si·lén·to] *adj.* thin, emaciated; pale.

macizo [ma·sí·so] *adj.* solid, firm; massive; *m.* massiveness; firmness; thicket; clump.

machacar[6] [ma·ča·kár] *v.* to pound, crush; to insist, harp on.

machacón [ma·ča·kón] *adj.* persistent; tenacious.

machete [ma·čé·te] *m.* machete, large heavy knife; **machetazo** *m.* large machete; blow with a machete.

machismo [ma·číz·mo] *m.* the quality of being a male; proven daring.

macho [má·čo] *m.* male; he-mule; hook (*of a hook and eye*); abutment; pillar; stupid fellow; sledgehammer; *C.R.* a blond; North American; *Am.* **pararle a uno el** — to halt or repress a person; *adj.* masculine, male; strong.

machucar[6] [ma·ču·kár] *v.* to pound, beat, bruise; *Am.* to crush; *Am.* to break (*a horse*).

machucón [ma·ču·kón] *m.* smash; bruise.

madeja [ma·ḍé·xa] *f.* skein; mass of hair; limp, listless person.

madera [ma·ḍé·ra] *f.* wood; timber; lumber; **maderero** *m.* lumberman, lumber dealer.

maderaje [ma·ḍe·rá·xe] *m.* timber, lumber; timber work; woodwork.

maderamen [ma·ḍe·rá·men] *m.* timber; timber work; woodwork.

madero [ma·ḍé·ro] *m.* beam; plank; timber, piece of lumber; blockhead, dunce.

madrastra [ma·ḍrás·tra] *f.* stepmother.

madre [má·ḍre] *f.* mother; womb; root, origin; river bed; **salirse de** — to overflow (*said of rivers*).

madrepeña [ma·ḍre·pé·ña] *f. Am.* moss.

madreperla [ma·ḍre·pér·la] *f.* mother-of-pearl.

madreselva [ma·ḍre·sél·ḃa] *f.* honeysuckle.

madriguera [ma·ḍri·ǵé·ra] *f.* burrow; den, lair.

madrileño [ma·ḍri·lé·ño] *adj.* Madrilenian, from or pertaining to Madrid; *m.* Madrilenian.

madrina [ma·ḍrí·na] *f.* (*patrocinadora*) godmother; bridesmaid; sponsor; (*correa*) strap for yoking two horses; (*ganado*) leading mare; prop; *Am.* small herd of tame cattle (*used for leading wild cattle*).

madrugada [ma·ḍru·ǵá·ḍa] *f.* dawn; early morning; **de** — at daybreak.

madrugador [ma·ḍru·ga·ḍór] *m.* early riser.

madrugar[7] [ma·ḍru·gár] *v.* to rise early; to be ahead of others; to "get the jump" on someone.

madurar [ma·ḍu·rár] *v.* to mature; to ripen.

madurez [ma·ḍu·rés] *f.* maturity; ripeness.

maduro [ma·ḍú·ro] *adj.* ripe; mature; prudent,
wise; *Am.* bruised, sore.

maestría [ma·es·trí·a] *f.* mastery; great skill; advanced teaching degree.

maestro [ma·és·tro] *m.* master, teacher; chief craftsman; *adj.* master; masterly, skillful; **llave maestra** master key; **obra maestra** masterpiece.

magia [má·xja] *f.* magic; charm.

mágico [má·xi·ko] *adj.* magic; *m.* magician.

magín [ma·xín] *m.* imagination, fancy.

magisterio [ma·xis·té·rjo] *m.* teaching profession.

magistrado [ma·xis·trá·ḍo] *m.* magistrate, judge.

magistral [ma·xis·trál] *adj.* masterly; masterful; authoritative.

magnánimo [maǵ·ná·ni·mo] *adj.* magnanimous, noble, generous.

magnesia [maǵ·né·sja] *f.* magnesia.

magnesio [maǵ·né·sjo] *m.* magnesium.

magnético [maǵ·né·ti·ko] *adj.* magnetic; attractive.

magnetofónico [maǵ·ne·to·fó·ni·ko] *adj.* recording (*tape or wire*).

magnetófono [maǵ·ne·tó·fo·no] *m.* tape recorder.

magnificencia [maǵ·ni·fi·sén·sja] *f.* magnificence, splendor.

magnífico [maǵ·ní·fi·ko] *adj.* magnificent, splendid.

magnitud [maǵ·ni·túḍ] *f.* magnitude, greatness.

magno [máǵ·no] *adj.* great.

magnolia [maǵ·nó·lja] *f.* magnolia.

mago [má·ǵo] *m.* magician, wizard; **los tres Reyes Magos** the Three Wise Men.

magra [máǵ·ra] *f.* slice of ham.

magro [máǵ·ro] *adj.* lean.

maguey [ma·ǵéj] *m.* maguey, century plant.

magullar [ma·ǵu·yár] *v.* to bruise; to maul; to mangle; *Ríopl., Ch., Col., Andes, P.R.* to crumple.

magullón [ma·ǵu·yón] *m.* a bruise.

mahometano [ma·o·me·tá·no] *adj. & m.* Mohammedan.

maicillo [maj·sí·yo] *m. Am.* gravel.

maíz [ma·ís] *m.* corn; **maizal** [maj·sál] *m.* cornfield.

majada [ma·xá·ḍa] *f.* sheepfold; dung, manure; *Ríopl., Ch.* flock of sheep or goats.

majadería [ma·xa·ḍe·rí·a] *f.* foolishness, nonsense.

majadero [ma·xa·ḍé·ro] *adj.* foolish; bothersome.

majar [ma·xár] *v.* to pound; to crush; to bruise; to crumple; to mash; to annoy, bother.

majestad [ma·xes·táḍ] *f.* majesty; dignity.

majestuoso [ma·xes·twó·so] *adj.* majestic, stately.

majo [má·xo] *adj.* gaudy, showy; gaily attired; pretty; *m.* dandy; **maja** [má·xa] *f.* belle.

mal [mal] *m.* evil; illness; harm; wrong. *See* **malo.**

malabarista [ma·la·ḃrís·ta] *m. & f.* juggler; *Ch.* sly thief.

malacate [ma·la·ká·te] *m.* hoist, hoisting machine; winch; *Am.* spindle (*for cotton*); *Am.* **parecer uno un** — to be constantly on the go, be in constant motion.

malagueña [ma·la·ǵé·ña] *adj.* song and dance of Málaga.

malandanza [ma·lan·dán·sa] *f.* misfortune.

malaquita [ma·la·kí·ta] *f.* malachite.

malaventura [ma·la·ḃen·tú·ra] *f.* misfortune, disaster.

malazo [ma·lá·so] *adj.* perverse, evil, wicked; vicious.

malbaratar [mal·ḃa·ra·tár] *v.* to undersell, sell at a loss; to squander.

malcontento [mal·kon·tén·to] *adj.* discontented; *m.* malcontent, troublemaker.

malcriado [mal·krjá·ḍo] *adj.* ill-bred, rude.

maldad [mal·dáḍ] *f.* badness, evil, wickedness.

LO

maldecir[27,52] [mal·de·sír] *v. irr.* to curse; to damn.
maldiciente [mal·di·sjén·te] *adj.* cursing.
maldición [mal·di·sjón] *f.* curse.
maldispuesto [mal·dis·pwés·to] *adj.* unwilling, not inclined.
maldito [mal·dí·to] *p.p. of* **maldecir** & *adj.* cursed; wicked; damned; *Am.* tricky; *Am.* bold, boastful.
maleable [ma·le·á·ble] *adj.* malleable; easily spoiled.
maleante [ma·le·án·te] *m.* crook, rogue, rascal, villain.
malecón [ma·le·kón] *m.* mole; dike.
maledicencia [ma·le·di·sén·sja] *f.* slander.
maleficio [ma·le·fí·sjo] *m.* spell, charm, witchery.
maléfico [ma·lé·fi·ko] *adj.* evil, harmful.
malestar [ma·les·tár] *m.* indisposition; slight illness; discomfort.
maleta [ma·lé·ta] *f.* travelling bag; suitcase; *Col.,* *Ven.,* C.A. bundle of clothes; *Col.* hump (*on the back*); *Am.* saddlebag; *C.A.* rogue, rascal; *Am.* lazy fellow.
maletín [ma·le·tín] *m.* small valise, satchel.
malevo [ma·lé·bo] *adj. Bol., Ríopl.* bad, wicked.
malévolo [ma·lé·bo·lo] *adj.* bad, evil, wicked.
maleza [ma·lé·sa] *f.* underbrush; thicket; weeds.
malgastar [mal·gas·tár] *v.* to squander, waste.
¡malhaya! [ma·lá·ya] *interj.* cursed; *Ríopl.* were it so!
malhechor [ma·le·čór] *m.* malefactor, evildoer, criminal.
malhora [ma·ló·ra] *f. Ríopl., C.A., Ven.* trouble, misfortune.
malhumorado [ma·lu·mo·rá·do] *adj.* ill-humored.
malicia [ma·lí·sja] *f.* malice; wickedness; shrewdness; suspicion; *Ch.* bit of brandy or cognac added to another drink.
maliciar [ma·li·sjár] *v.* to suspect.
malicioso [ma·li·sjó·so] *adj.* malicious; wicked; shrewd; suspicious.
maligno [ma·líg·no] *adj.* malign, malignant; pernicious, harmful.
malmandado [mal·man·dá·do] *adj.* disobedient; stubborn.
mal(o) [mál(o)] *adj.* bad, evil; wicked; ill; difficult; *Am.* **a la mála** treacherously; *Ríopl.* **de malas** by force; **estar de malas** to be out of luck; **por la mala** unwillingly, by force; **venir de malas** to come with evil intentions; **mal** *adv.* badly; poorly; wrongly.
malograr [ma·lo·grár] *v.* to waste, lose; **-se** to turn out badly; to fail.
malón [ma·lón] *m.* mean trick; *Ríopl.* surprise Indian raid; *Ven.* tin-pan serenade, boisterous surprise party.
malpagar[7] [mal·pa·gár] *v.* to underpay, pay poorly.
malparto [mal·pár·to] *m.* miscarriage, abortion.
malquerencia [mal·ke·rén·sja] *f.* aversion, dislike, ill will.
malsano [mal·sá·no] *adj.* unhealthy; sickly.
malta [mál·ta] *f.* malt.
maltratar [mal·tra·tár] *v.* to treat badly; to misuse, abuse.
maltrato [mal·trá·to] *m.* mistreatment, abuse.
maltrecho [mal·tré·čo] *adj.* battered, bruised, injured.
malvado [mal·bá·do] *adj.* wicked; malicious.
malversación [mal·ber·sa·sjón] *f.* graft, corruption, misuse of public funds.
malversar [mal·ber·sár] *v.* to misuse (*funds in one's trust*); to embezzle.
malla [má·ya] *f.* mesh; coat of mail; *Ch.* species of

potato; **hacer** — to knit.
mamá [ma·má] *f.* mamma.
mamada [ma·má·da] *f.* suck, sucking.
mamado [ma·má·do] *adj. Am.* drunk.
mamar [ma·már] *v.* to suckle; to suck; to gorge; **-se** *Ríopl., C.A.* to get drunk; *Col.* to go back on one's promise; *Am.* to fold up, crack up; **-se a uno** to get the best of someone, decieve someone; *Col., C.A.* to kill someone.
mamarracho [ma·ma·rrá·čo] *m.* a mess; a worthless guy.
mamífero [ma·mí·fe·ro] *m.* mammal; *adj.* mammalian, of mammals.
mamón [ma·món] *adj.* suckling; *m.* suckling (*very young animal or child*); shoot, sucker (*of a tree*); *Ríopl.* cherimoya (*tree and fruit*); *Am.* papaya (*tree and fruit*); *Mex.* a kind of cake; *C.A.* public employee.
mampara [mam·pá·ra] *f.* screen.
mampostería [mam·pos·te·rí·a] *f.* masonry, stone masonry.
manada [ma·ná·da] *f.* herd; drove; pack; flock.
manantial [ma·nan·tjál] *m.* spring; source, origin.
manar [ma·nár] *v.* to spring, flow (from); to abound.
manaza [ma·ná·sa] *f.* large hand.
manazo [ma·ná·so] *m. Ríopl.* slap. See **manotazo**.
mancarrón [maŋ·ka·rrón] *m.* one-armed or one-handed man; cripple; old nag; *Ríopl., Andes* crude, clumsy fellow; *Am.* disabled workman; *Am.* dike, small dam.
mancebo [man·sé·bo] *m.* youth, young man; bachelor.
mancera [man·sé·ra] *f.* handle of a plough.
mancilla [man·sí·ya] *f.* stain, spot; dishonor.
manco [máŋ·ko] *adj.* one-armed; one-handed; maimed; lame (*referring to an arm* or *the front leg of an animal*); faulty, defective; *m. Ch.* nag.
mancuerna [maŋ·kwér·na] *f.* pair of animals tied together; *Mex., C.A. f. pl.* cuff links.
mancha [mán·ča] *f.* spot, stain, blemish; *Am.* cloud, swarm; *Ven., Cuba, Col.* roving herd of cattle.
manchar [man·čár] *v.* to stain, soil, spot; to tarnish.
manchego [man·čé·go] *adj.* of or belonging to La Mancha (*region of Spain*); *m.* inhabitant of La Mancha.
manchón [man·čón] *m.* large stain; large patch.
mandadero [man·da·dé·ro] *m.* messenger, errand boy.
mandado [man·dá·do] *m.* (*orden*) command, order; (*recado*) errand; *p.p. of* **mandar; bien** — well-behaved; **mal** — ill-behaved.
mandamiento [man·da·mjén·to] *m.* command, order; writ; commandment.
mandar [man·dár] *v.* (*pedir*) to command, order; rule; (*enviar*) to send; to bequeath; will; *Col., Ven.* to throw, hurl; — **hacer** to have made, order; *Col., Ven., Mex., Carib., Andes* — **una bofetada** to give a slap; *Col., Ven., Mex., Carib., Andes* — **una pedrada** to throw a stone; **-se** *Am.* to be impudent; **-se mudar** *Ríopl., Carib.* to go away.
mandatario [man·da·tá·rjo] *m.* attorney, representative; *Am.* magistrate, chief.
mandato [man·dá·to] *m.* mandate; order, command; term of office.
mandíbula [man·dí·bu·la] *f.* jaw, jawbone.
mandioca [man·djó·ka] *f.* manioc.
mando [mán·do] *m.* command, authority, power.
mandolina [man·do·lí·na] *f.* mandolin.

mandón [man·dón] *adj.* bossy, domineering; *m.* bossy person; *Am.* boss or foreman of a mine; *Am.* race starter.

maneador [ma·ne·a·dór] *m. Ríopl., Ven., Col.* hobble, leather lasso (*for the legs of an animal*); *Am.* whip; *Ven., Andes* halter.

manear [ma·ne·ár] *v.* to hobble, lasso, tie the legs of (*an animal*); **-se** *Col., Ven.* to get tangled up.

manecilla [ma·ne·sí·ya] *f.* small hand; hand of a watch or clock.

manejable [ma·ne·xá·ƀle] *adj.* manageable.

manejar [ma·ne·xár] *v.* to manage, handle; to drive (*a car*); **-se** to move about, get around (*after an illness or accident*); *Carib., Ven.* to behave oneself.

manejo [ma·né·xo] *m.* handling; management; trick, intrigue.

manera [ma·né·ra] *f.* manner, way, mode; side opening in a shirt; front opening in breeches; **-s** customs; manners, behavior; **a — de** (*or* **a la — de**) like, in the style of; **de — que** so that; **sobre —** exceedingly; extremely.

manga [máŋ·ga] *f.* sleeve; bag; hose (*for watering*); body of troops; *Am.* multitude, herd, swarm; *Am.* cattle chute (*narrow passageway*); *Am.* corral; **— de agua** waterspout, whirlwind over the ocean; *Am.* **— de hule** raincape; **por angas o por -s** by hook or crook, in one way or another.

mangana [maŋ·gá·na] *f.* lariat, lasso.

manganeso [maŋ·ga·né·so] *m.* manganese.

mangle [máŋ·gle] *m.* mangrove.

mango [máŋ·go] *m.* handle; *Am.* mango (*tropical tree and its fruit*).

manguera [maŋ·gé·ra] *f.* hose (*for water*); waterspout; *Ríopl.* large corral (*for livestock*).

manguito [maŋ·gí·to] *m.* muff; knitted half-sleeve (*worn on the forearm*); oversleeve.

maní [ma·ní] *m. Carib., C.A., Ch., Andes, Ven., Col.* peanut; **manicero** [ma·ni·sé·ro] *m. Carib., C.A., Ch., Andes, Ven., Col.* peanut vendor.

manía [ma·ní·a] *f.* mania, frenzy; craze, whim.

maniatar [ma·nja·tár] *v.* to tie the hands; to handcuff; to hobble (*an animal*).

maniático [ma·njá·ti·ko] *m.* crank, queer fellow; *adj.* cranky, queer, odd.

manicomio [ma·ni·kó·mjo] *m.* insane asylum.

manicura [ma·ni·kú·ra] *f.* manicure; manicurist.

manicurar [ma·ni·ku·rár] *v.* to manicure.

manido [ma·ní·đo] *adj.* rotting; *Ríopl., Carib., Col., Andes* trite, commonplace.

manifestación [ma·ni·fes·ta·sjón] *f.* manifestation; demonstration.

manifestar[1] [ma·ni·fes·tár] *v. irr.* to manifest; to show.

manifiesto [ma·ni·fjés·to] *adj.* manifest, clear, plain; *m.* manifesto, public declaration; customhouse manifest.

manigua [ma·ni·ǵwa] *f. Col., Ríopl., Cuba, P.R.* Cuban jungle or thicket; *Carib.* **coger —** to get feverish; *Ríopl., Carib.* **irse a la —** to rise up in rebellion.

manija [ma·ni·xa] *f.* handle; crank; fetter.

manilla [ma·ni·ya] *f.* small hand; bracelet; **-s de hierro** handcuffs.

maniobra [ma·njó·ƀra] *f.* maneuver; operation.

maniobrar [ma·njo·ƀrár] *v.* to maneuver.

manipulación [ma·ni·pu·la·sjón] *f.* manipulation.

manipular [ma·ni·pu·lár] *v.* to manipulate, handle.

maniquí [ma·ni·kí] *m.* manikin, model, dummy, figure of a person; puppet.

manivela [ma·ni·ƀé·la] *f.* crank.

manjar [maŋ·xár] *m.* dish, food; choice bit of food.

mano [má·no] *f.* (*del cuerpo*) hand; forefoot; (*reloj*) clock hand; (*acabado*) coat of paint or varnish; quire (*25 sheets*) of paper; *Am.* adventure, mishap; *Am.* handful; **— de obra** workmanship; labor; **a —** at hand; by hand; *Am.* **estamos a —** we are even, we are quits; *Am.* **doblar las -s** to give up; **ser —** to be first (*in a game*); to lead (*in a game*); **venir a las -s** to come to blows.

manojo [ma·nó·xo] *m.* handful; bunch.

manopla [ma·nó·pla] *f.* gauntlet; heavy glove; huge hand.

manosear [ma·no·se·ár] *v.* to handle, touch, feel with the hands; *Am.* to fondle, pet, caress.

manotada [ma·no·tá·đa] *f.* slap, blow; sweep of the hand; *Col.* handful, fistful; **manotazo** [ma·no·tá·so] *m.* slap.

manotear [ma·no·te·ár] *v.* to gesticulate; to strike with the hands; *Ríopl.* to embezzle, steal; *Am.* to snatch away (*what is given*).

mansalva [man·sál·ƀa]: **a —** without danger or risk; treacherously; **matar a —** to kill without warning or without giving a person a chance to defend himself.

mansedumbre [man·se·đúm·bre] *f.* meekness; gentleness.

mansión [man·sjón] *f.* sojourn, stay; abode, dwelling.

manso [mán·so] *adj.* meek; mild, gentle; tame; *Ríopl., Ch.* cultivated (*plant*), civilized (*Indian*); *m.* leading sheep, goat, or ox.

manta [mán·ta] *f.* blanket; large shawl; tossing in a blanket; *Mex., C.A., Ven., Ríopl.* coarse cotton cloth; *Am.* poncho; *Am.* **— mojada** dull person, dunce; **darle a uno una —** to toss someone in a blanket.

mantear [man·te·ár] *v.* to toss (*someone*) in a blanket.

manteca [man·té·ka] *f.* fat; lard; butter; *Am.* **— de cacao** cocoa butter; *Am.* **— de coco** coconut oil; **mantequera** [man·te·ké·ra] *f.* churn; butter dish; woman who makes or sells butter.

mantecado [man·te·ká·đo] *m.* ice cream.

mantel [man·tél] *m.* tablecloth; altar cloth; *C.A., Mex.* **estar de -es largos** to dine in style.

mantener[4][5] [man·te·nér] *v. irr.* to maintain; to support; to sustain; to defend; **-se** to continue, remain; to support oneself; **-se firme** to remain firm; **-se quieto** to stay or keep quiet.

mantenimiento [man·te·ni·mjén·to] *m.* maintenance, support; sustenance; livelihood.

mantequilla [man·te·ki·ya] *f.* butter; **mantequillería** [man·te·ki·ye·rí·a] *f. Am.* creamery, dairy (*for making butter*).

mantilla [man·tí·ya] *f.* mantilla (*Spanish veil or scarf for the head*); saddlecloth.

manto [mán·to] *m.* mantle, cloak; cape; large mantilla; mantel, mantelpiece.

mantón [man·tón] *m.* large shawl; **— de Manila** embroidered silk shawl.

manuable [ma·nwá·ƀle] *adj.* handy, easy to handle.

manual [ma·nwál] *adj.* manual; handy; *m.* manual, handbook.

manubrio [ma·nú·ƀrjo] *m.* crank; handle.

manufacturar [ma·nu·fak·tu·rár] *v.* to manufacture.

manufacturero [ma·nu·fak·tu·ré·ro] *adj.* manufacturing; *m.* manufacturer.

manuscrito [ma·nus·krí·to] *adj.* written by hand; *m.* manuscript.

manutención [ma·nu·ten·sjón] *f.* maintenance; support; conservation.

MA

manzana [man·sá·na] *f.* apple; block of houses;
Ríopl., Ch., Col., Ven., C.A. Adam's apple;
manzano [man·sá·no] *m.* apple tree.

manzanar [man·sa·nár] *m.* apple orchard.

maña [má·ña] *f.* skill, knack; cunning; **malas -s**
bad tricks or habits.

mañana [ma·ñá·na] *f.* morning; *Ríopl.* **media —**
mid-morning snack; *adv.* tomorrow, in the near
future; **pasado —** day after tomorrow; **muy de
— very** early in the morning; *m.* morrow;
mañanitas [ma·ña·ní·tas] *f. pl. Mex., C.A.*
popular song sung early in the morning to
celebrate a birthday, saint's day, etc.

mañanero [ma·ña·né·ro] *m.* early riser; *adj.* early
rising; **mañanista** [ma·ña·nís·ta] *m. & f. Am.*
procrastinator, one who puts things off until
tomorrow.

mañero [ma·ñe·ro] *adj.* astute, artful, clever; *Am.*
tricky; *Ch.* shy *(animal); Ríopl.* indolent, lazy
(child).

mañoso [ma·ñó·so] *adj.* skillful; clever; sly; tricky;
deceitful; *Am.* slow, lazy; *Am.* greedy, gluttonous
(child).

mapa [má·pa] *m.* map, chart.

mapache [ma·pá·če] *m. Ch.* raccoon.

mapurite [ma·pu·rí·te], **mapurito** [ma·pu·rí·to] *m.
Col., Ven.* skunk. *See zorrino, zorrillo.*

máquina [má·ki·na] *f.* machine; engine; **— de coser**
sewing machine; **— de escribir** typewriter.

maquinación [ma·ki·na·sjón] *f.* machination,
scheming, plotting; plot, scheme.

maquinador [ma·ki·na·ḍór] *m.* schemer, plotter.

maquinal [ma·ki·nál] *adj.* mechanical, automatic;
-mente *adv.* mechanically, automatically, in a
mechanical manner.

maquinar [ma·ki·nár] *v.* to plot, scheme.

maquinaria [ma·ki·ná·rja] *f.* machinery;
mechanism; mechanics.

maquinista [ma·ki·nís·ta] *m.* engineer, locomotive
engineer; machinist; mechanic.

mar [mar] *m. & f.* sea; **— alta** rough sea; **—
llena** high tide *(see* **pleamar);** **— de fondo** swell;
a -es abundantly; **baja — low** tide; **en alta — on**
the high seas; **la — de cosas** a lot of things.

maraca [ma·rá·ka] *f. Carib., Col., Ven.* maraca
*(rhythm instrument made of a dried gourd filled
with seeds or pebbles).*

maraña [ma·rá·ña] *f.* tangle; snarl; thicket; maze;
plot, intrigue.

marañón [ma·ra·ñón] *m.* cashew.

maravedí [ma·ra·ḅe·ḍí] *m.* maravedi *(an old
Spanish coin).*

maravilla [ma·ra·ḅi·ya] *f.* wonder, marvel;
marigold; **a las mil -s** wonderfully, perfectly.

maravillar [ma·ra·ḅi·yár] *v.* to astonish, dazzle; **-se**
to wonder, marvel.

maravilloso [ma·ra·ḅi·yó·so] *adj.* marvellous,
wonderful.

marbete [mar·ḅé·te] *m.* label, stamp; baggage tag
or check.

marca [már·ka] *f.* mark, stamp; sign; brand, make;
gauge, rule; march, frontier province; **— de
fábrica** trademark; **de — of** excellent quality.

marcar[6] [mar·kár] *v.* to mark, stamp, brand; to
note, observe.

marcial [mar·sjál] *adj.* martial, warlike; frank,
abrupt.

marco [már·ko] *m.* frame; mark *(German coin);*
mark *(unit of weight, equal to 8 ounces).*

marcha [már·ča] *f.* march; course, progress; speed;
gait; running, functioning; movement of a

watch.

marchamo [mar·čá·mo] *m.* customhouse mark;
Am. tax on each slaughtered animal.

marchante [mar·čán·te] *m. (vendedor)* merchant,
dealer; *(cliente)* customer, regular client.

marchar [mar·čár] *v.* to march, mark step; to
walk; to parade; to run *(said of machinery);*
-se to go away.

marchitar [mar·či·tár] *v.* to wither; **-se** to wither;
to fade; to shrivel up.

marchito [mar·čí·to] *adj.* withered; faded; shriveled
up.

marea [ma·ré·a] *f.* tide; *Ríopl., Ch.* sea fog.

mareado [ma·re·á·ḍo] *adj.* seasick; dizzy.

marear [ma·re·ár] *v. (navegar)* to navigate, sail;
(fastidiar) to annoy, upset *(a person);* to make
dizzy, **-se** to get seasick, nauseated; dizzy.

mareo [ma·ré·o] *m.* seasickness; nausea; vexation,
annoyance.

marfil [mar·fíl] *m.* ivory; *Ven.* fine-toothed comb.

margarita [mar·ġa·rí·ta] *f.* marguerite, daisy; pearl.

margen [már·xen] *m. & f.* margin, border; river
bank; **dar — a** to give an occasion to.

mariachi [ma·rjá·či] *m. Mex.* band and music
typical of Guadalajara; *pl.* members of the band.

maricón [ma·ri·kón] *adj.* sissy, effeminate; *m.* sissy.

marido [ma·rí·ḍo] *m.* husband.

marimacho [ma·ri·má·čo] *m.* mannish woman.

marimba [ma·rím·ba] *f.* marimba.

marina [ma·rí·na] *f. (costa)* seacoast, shore; *(fuerza
naval)* fleet; navy; *(arte u oficio)* seascape;
seamanship; **— de guerra** navy; **— mercante**
merchant marine.

marinero [ma·ri·né·ro] *m.* mariner, seaman, sailor.

marino [ma·rí·no] *adj.* marine; *m.* mariner, seaman,
sailor.

mariposa [ma·ri·pó·sa] *f.* butterfly; moth; *Am.*
blindman's buff *(a game).*

mariquita [ma·ri·ki·ta] *f.* sissy; *(cap.)* Molly.

mariscal [ma·ris·kál] *m.* marshal; blacksmith; **—
de campo** field marshal.

marisco [ma·rís·ko] *m.* shellfish.

marítimo [ma·rí·ti·mo] *adj.* maritime, marine.

marmita [mar·mí·ta] *f.* kettle, boiler, teakettle.

mármol [már·mol] *m.* marble.

marmóreo [mar·mó·re·o] *adj.* marble, of marble,
like marble.

maroma [ma·ró·ma] *f.* rope; *Am.* somersault; *Am.*
acrobatic performance; *Col.* sudden change of
political views; **andar en la — to** walk the
tightrope; **maromero** [ma·ro·mé·ro] *m. Carib.*
acrobat.

marqués [mar·kés] *m.* marquis.

marquesa [mar·ké·sa] *f.* marquise; *Ch.* couch.

marrano [ma·rrá·no] *m.* pig, hog; filthy person.

marrazo [ma·rrá·so] *m. Am.* bayonet, dagger.

marrón [ma·rrón] *adj.* maroon.

marroquí [ma·rro·kí] *adj.* from Morocco; *pl.*
marroquíes [ma·rro·kí·es].

marrullero [ma·rru·yé·ro] *adj.* sly, wily.

martes [már·tes] *m.* Tuesday; **— de carnestolendas**
Shrove Tuesday *(Tuesday before Lent).*

martillar [mar·ti·yár] *v.* to hammer, pound.

martillo [mar·tí·yo] *m.* hammer.

martinete [mar·ti·ne·te] *m.* pile driver; drop hammer;
hammer of a piano.

mártir [már·tir] *m. & f.* martyr.

martirio [mar·tí·rjo] *m.* martyrdom; torture,
torment.

martirizar[9] [mar·ti·ri·sár] *v.* to martyr; to torture,
torment.

marxismo [mark·síz·mo] *m.* Marxism.
marzo [már·so] *m.* March.
mas [mas] *conj.* but.
más [mas] *adj.* more; most; *adv.* more; most; plus; — **bien** rather; — **de** more than, over; — **que** more than; **no . . .** — **que** only; **a** — **de** in addition to; **a lo** — at the most; **está de** — it is superfluous, unnecessary; *Am.* **no** — only; *Am.* **no quiero** — **nada** (*instead of* **no quiero nada** —) I don't want anything more.
masa [má·sa] *f.* (*volumen*) mass; volume; (*pueblo*) crowd, the masses; (*pasta*) dough, paste; mortar; — **coral** glee club, choral society; **agarrarle a uno con las manos en la** — to catch someone in the act; **masilla** *f.* putty.
masaje [ma·sá·xe] *m.* massage.
mascada [mas·ká·ða] *f.* chewing; *Am.* mouthful; *Ríopl.* chew or quid of tobacco; *Am.* reprimand, scolding; *Mex.* silk handkerchief, scarf.
mascar[6] [mas·kár] *v.* to chew.
máscara [más·ka·ra] *f.* mask; **-s** masquerade; *m. & f.* masquerader; **mascarada** [mas·ka·rá·ða] *f.* masquerade.
masculino [mas·ku·lí·no] *adj.* masculine.
mascullar [mas·ku·yár] *v.* to mumble; to munch.
masón [ma·són] *m.* mason, freemason; **masonería** [ma·so·ne·rí·a] *f.* masonry, freemasonry.
masticar[6] [mas·ti·kár] *v.* to chew.
mástil [más·til] *m.* mast; post.
mastín [mas·tín] *m.* mastiff.
mastuerzo [mas·twér·so] *m.* (*flor*) nasturtium; (*tonto*) simpleton, fool.
mata [má·ta] *f.* shrub, plant, bush; grove; clump of trees; *Ven., Col.* thicket, jungle; — **de pelo** head of hair.
matadero [ma·ta·ðé·ro] *m.* slaughterhouse; hard work.
matador [ma·ta·ðór] *m.* killer, murderer; bullfighter who kills the bull.
matamoros [ma·ta·mó·ros] *m.* bully; boastful person.
matamoscas [ma·ta·mós·kas] *m.* fly swatter.
matanza [ma·tán·sa] *f.* massacre, butchery; slaughter of livestock; *Mex.* slaughterhouse.
matar [ma·tár] *v.* to kill; to murder; **-se** to commit suicide; to overwork; **-se con alguien** to fight with somebody.
matasanos [ma·ta·sá·nos] *m.* quack, quack doctor.
matasellos [ma·ta·sé·yos] *m.* canceller (*of stamps*).
mate [má·te] *m.* checkmate (*winning move in chess*); *Ríopl., Ch.* Paraguayan tea (*used also in Argentina and Uruguay*); *Andes, Col.* teapot (*for* **mate**), any small pot; *Am.* bald head; *adj.* unpolished, dull (*surface*).
matear [ma·te·ár] *v.* to plant seeds or shoots; to hunt among the bushes; *Ríopl., Ch.* to drink **mate**; *Am.* to checkmate (*make the winning move in chess*).
matemática [ma·te·má·ti·ka] *f. pl.* mathematics.
matemático [ma·te·má·ti·ko] *adj.* mathematical; *m.* mathematician.
materia [ma·té·rja] *f.* matter; material; school subject; pus; — **prima** (*or* **primera** —) raw material.
material [ma·te·rjál] *adj.* material; rude, coarse; *m.* ingredient; material; equipment; *Ven.* **de** — made of adobe.
maternal [ma·ter·nál] *adj.* maternal.
maternidad [ma·ter·ni·ðáð] *f.* maternity, motherhood.
materno [ma·tér·no] *adj.* maternal.

matinal [ma·ti·nál] *adj.* morning, of the morning.
matiné [ma·ti·né] *m. Am.* matinée.
matiz [ma·tís] *m.* tint, shade, color, hue; shading.
matizar[9] [ma·ti·sár] *v.* to blend (*colors*); to tint; to shade, tone down.
matón [ma·tón] *m.* bully.
matorral [ma·to·rrál] *m.* thicket.
matoso [ma·tó·so] *adj.* bushy; weedy, full of weeds.
matrero [ma·tré·ro] *adj.* astute, shrewd; cunning, sly; *m. Col.* trickster, swindler; *Ríopl.* bandit, outlaw, cattle thief.
matrícula [ma·trí·ku·la] *f.* register, list; matriculation, registration; certificate of registration.
matricular [ma·tri·ku·lár] *v.* to matriculate, enroll, register.
matrimonio [ma·tri·mó·njo] *m.* matrimony, marriage; married couple.
matriz [ma·trís] *f.* matrix, mold, form; womb; screw nut; *adj.* main, principal, first; **casa** — main office (*of a company*).
matungo [ma·tún·go] *m. Ríopl.* nag, old worn-out horse.
matutino [ma·tu·tí·no] *adj.* morning, of the morning.
maula [máw·la] *m.* a good-for-nothing.
maullar [maw·yár] *v.* to mew.
maullido, **maúllo** [ma·ú·yo] *m.* mew.
máxima [mák·si·ma] *f.* maxim, rule; proverb.
máxime [mák·si·me] *adj.* principally, especially.
máximo [mák·si·mo] *adj. & m.* maximum.
maya [má·ya] *f.* daisy; May queen; *m. & f.* Maya, Mayan Indian; *m.* Mayan language.
mayo [má·yo] *m.* May; Maypole; *Am.* Mayo Indian (*from Sonora, Mexico*); *Am.* language of the Mayo Indian.
mayonesa [ma·yo·né·sa] *f.* mayonnaise; dish served with mayonnaise.
mayor [ma·yór] *adj.* greater; larger; older; greatest; largest; oldest; main; major; high (*altar, mass*); *m.* major; chief; **-es** elders; ancestors; — **de edad** of age; **por** — (*or* **al por** —) wholesale; *f.* major premise (*of a syllogism*).
mayoral [ma·yo·rál] *m.* head shepherd; stagecoach driver; foreman; overseer, boss.
mayorazgo [ma·yo·ráz·ġo] *m.* primogeniture (*right of inheritance by the first-born*); first-born son and heir; family estate left to the eldest son.
mayordomo [ma·yor·ðó·mo] *m.* majordomo, steward, butler; manager of an estate.
mayorear [ma·yo·re·ár] *v. Am.* to wholesale, sell at wholesale.
mayoreo [ma·yo·ré·o] *m. Am.* wholesale.
mayoría [ma·yo·rí·a] *f.* majority.
mayorista [ma·yo·rís·ta] *m. Am.* wholesale dealer.
maza [má·sa] *f.* mace (*weapon, staff*); — **química** chemical mace.
mazmorra [maz·mó·rra] *f.* dungeon.
mazo [má·so] *m.* mallet; sledgehammer; bunch, handful.
mazorca [ma·sór·ka] *f.* ear of corn; *Ríopl.* tyrannical government; *Am.* cruel torture (*imposed by tyrants*).
me [me] *obj. pron.* me; to me; for me; myself.
mear [me·ár] *v.* to urinate.
mecánico [me·ká·ni·ko] *adj.* mechanical; *m.* mechanic, machinist, repairman; driver, chauffeur.
mecanismo [me·ka·níz·mo] *m.* mechanism.
mecanografía [me·ka·no·ġra·fí·a] *f.* stenography, typewriting.

MA

mecanógrafo [me·ka·nó·ǥra·fo] *m.* stenographer, typist.

mecate [me·ká·te] *m. Mex., C.A., Col., Ven.* rope, cord.

mecedor [me·se·ɖór] *m.* swing; *adj.* swinging, rocking.

mecedora [me·se·ɖó·ra] *f.* rocking chair.

mecer[10] [me·sér] *v.* to swing, rock, sway; to shake.

mecha [mé·ča] *f.* wick; lock of hair; fuse; strip of salt pork or bacon (*for larding meat*); *Ven.* tip of a whip; *Am.* scare, fright; *Andes, Col.* fib; *Andes, Col.* jest, joke; *Col.* trifle, worthless thing.

mechar [me·čár] *v.* to lard (*meat or fowl*).

mechero [me·čé·ro] *m.* (*canutillo*) lamp burner; gas jet; candlestick socket; (*encendedor*) pocket lighter; large wick; *Col.* disheveled hair; *Am.* joker, jester.

mechón [me·čón] *m.* large wick; large lock of hair.

medalla [me·ɖa·ya] *f.* medal.

médano [mé·ɖa·no] *m.* dune, sand hill, sand bank; *Riopl., Carib.* sandy marshland.

media [mé·ɖja] *f.* stocking; *Col., Riopl., Ven.* — **corta** (*or* — —) sock.

mediación [me·ɖja·sjón] *f.* mediation.

mediador [me·ɖja·ɖór] *m.* mediator.

mediados: [me·ɖjá·ɖos] **a** — **de** about the middle of.

medianero [me·ɖja·né·ro] *m.* mediator; go-between; *adj.* mediating; intermediate; **pared medianera** partition wall.

medianía [me·ɖja·ní·a] *f.* mediocrity; average; middle ground; moderate circumstances; moderation; *Col.* partition wall.

mediano [me·ɖjá·no] *adj.* medium; moderate; middle-sized; average; mediocre.

medianoche [me·ɖja·nó·če] *f.* midnight.

mediante [me·ɖján·te] *adj.* intervening; **Dios** — God willing; *prep.* by means of, through, with the help of.

mediar [me·ɖjár] *v.* to mediate, intervene; to intercede; to arrive at, or be in, the middle.

medible [me·ɖi·ƀle] *adj.* measurable.

medicamento [me·ɖi·ka·mén·to] *m.* medicament, medicine.

medicastro [me·ɖi·kás·tro] *m.* quack, quack doctor.

medicina [me·ɖi·sí·na] *f.* medicine.

medicinar [me·ɖi·si·nár] *v.* to doctor, treat, prescribe medicine for; **-se** to take medicine.

medición [me·ɖi·sjón] *f.* measurement; measuring.

médico [mé·ɖi·ko] *m.* doctor, physician; *adj.* medical.

medida [me·ɖí·ɖa] *f.* measure; measurement; gauge, rule; — **para áridos** dry measure; **a** — **del deseo** according to one's desire; **a** — **que** as, in proportion as; at the same time as.

medidor [me·ɖi·ɖór] *m. Am.* meter, gauge.

medio [mé·ɖjo] *adj.* half; middle; intermediate; medium, average; **media noche** midnight; **hacer una cosa a medias** to do something halfway; **ir a medias** to go halves; *adv.* half, not completely; *m.* middle; means, way; medium; environment; **-s** means, resources; **meterse de por** — to intervene, meddle in a dispute.

mediocre [me·ɖjó·kre] *adj.* mediocre; **mediocridad** [me·ɖjo·kri·ɖáɖ] *f.* mediocrity.

mediodía [me·ɖjo·ɖí·a] *m.* midday, noon; south.

medioeval [me·ɖjo·e·ƀál], **medieval** [me·ɖje·ƀál] *adj.* medieval.

medir[5] [me·ɖír] *v. irr.* to measure; to scan (*verses*); *Col., Ven., Mex.* — **las calles** to walk the streets, be out of a job; **-se** to measure one's words or

actions; *Mex., C.A., Ven., Col., Ríopl.* **-se con otro** to try one's strength or ability against another; to fight with another.

meditación [me·ɖi·ta·sjón] *f.* meditation.

meditar [me·ɖi·tár] *v.* to meditate; to muse.

medrar [me·ɖrár] *v.* to flourish, thrive; to prosper.

medroso [me·ɖró·so] *adj.* timid, faint-hearted; fearful, dreadful.

médula [mé·ɖu·la] *f.* marrow; pith; — **oblongada** medulla ablongata (*the posterior part of the brain tapering off into the spinal cord*).

megáfono [me·ǥá·fo·no] *m.* megaphone.

megatón [me·ǥa·ton] *m.* megaton.

mejicano [me·xi·ká·no] *adj.* Mexican; *m.* Mexican; the Aztec language; inhabitant of Mexico City. *Also* **mexicano.**

mejilla [me·xí·ya] *f.* cheek.

mejor [me·xór] *adj.* better; **el** — the best; *adv.* better; **a lo** — suddenly, unexpectedly; **tanto** — so much the better.

mejora [me·xó·ra] *f.* betterment; improvement.

mejoramiento [me·xo·ra·mjén·to] *m.* improvement.

mejorar [me·xo·rár] *v.* to better, improve; to get better, recover; **-se** to get better, recover.

mejoría [me·xo·rí·a] *f.* betterment, improvement; superiority.

melado [me·lá·ɖo] *adj.* honey-colored; *m.* sugar-cane syrup; honey cake.

melancolía [me·laŋ·ko·lí·a] *f.* melancholy, gloom.

melancólico [me·laŋ·kó·li·ko] *adj.* melancholy, gloomy.

melaza [me·lá·sa] *f.* molasses.

melena [me·lé·na] *f.* mane.

melindre [me·lín·dre] *m.* (*acto*) affectation; affected act or gesture; whim; (*comestible*) fritter, marzipan (*sweetmeat made of almond paste*).

melindroso [me·lin·dró·so] *adj.* affected; too particular, finicky, fussy.

melocotón [me·lo·ko·tón] *m.* peach; **melocotonero** [me·lo·ko·to·ne·ro] *m.* peach tree.

melodía [me·lo·dí·a] *f.* melody; **melodioso** [me·lo·djó·so] *adj.* melodious.

melón [me·lón] *m.* melon; cantaloupe; musk-melon; melon vine.

melosidad [me·lo·si·ɖáɖ] *f.* sweetness; softness, gentleness.

meloso [me·ló·so] *adj.* honeyed; soft, sweet; *m. Am.* honey-voiced person; *Am.* over-affectionate person.

mella [mé·ya] *f.* nick; dent; **hacer** — to make a dent or impression; to cause pain, worry, or suffering.

mellar [me·yár] *v.* to notch; to nick; to dent; to impair, damage.

mellizo [me·yi·so] *adj. & m.* twin.

membrete [mem·bré·te] *m.* heading; letterhead; memorandum.

membrillo [mem·brí·yo] *m.* quince (*tree and its fruit*).

membrudo [mem·brú·ɖo] *adj.* sinewy, robust, strong, muscular.

memorable [me·mo·rá·ƀle] *adj.* memorable, notable.

memorándum [me·mo·rán·dun] *m.* memorandum, note; memorandum book, notebook.

memoria [me·mór·ja] *f.* memory; remembrance; reminiscence; memoir, note, account; memorandum; **de** — by heart; **hacer** — to remember, recollect; — **de gallo** poor memory; **-s** regards; memoirs.

memorial [me·mo·rjál] *m.* memorandum book;

memorial, brief, petition.
mención [men·sjón] *f.* mention.
mencionar [men·sjo·nár] *v.* to mention.
mendigar[7] [men·di·gár] *v.* to beg; to ask alms.
mendigo [men·dí·go] *m.* beggar.
mendrugo [men·drú·go] *m.* crumb of bread.
menear [me·ne·ár] *v.* to move, shake, stir; to wiggle; to wag; **-se** to hustle about; to wag; to wiggle.
meneo [me·né·o] *m.* shaking; swaying; wagging; wiggle; wiggling.
menester [me·nes·tér] *m.* need; job, occupation; **-es** bodily needs; implements, tools; tasks, chores; **ser — to** be necessary.
menesteroso [me·nes·te·ró·so] *adj.* needy, in want.
mengua [méŋ·gwa] *f.* diminution, decrease; waning; poverty, want; discredit.
menguante [meŋ·gwán·te] *adj.* waning, diminishing, declining.
menguar[8] [meŋ·gwár] *v.* to diminish, decrease; to wane.
menjurje [meŋ·xúr·xe] *m.* stuff, mixture.
menor [me·nór] *adj.* smaller, lesser, younger; smallest, least, youngest; minor; *m. & f.* **— de edad** minor; *m.* minor (*music*); Minorite, Franciscan; *f.* minor premise (*of a syllogism*); **por — (al por —)** at retail; in small quantities.
menoría [me·no·rí·a] = **minoría.**
menos [mé·nos] *adv.* less; least; except; *adj. & pron.* less, least; *m.* minus; **— de** (*or* **— que**) less than; **a lo — (al —,** *or* **por lo —)** at least; **a — que** unless; **echar de —** to miss, feel or notice the absence of ; **no puede — de hacerlo** he cannot help doing it; **venir a —** to decline; to become weak or poor.
menoscabar [me·nos·ka·βár] *v.* to diminish, lessen; to impair, damage; **— la honra de** to undermine the reputation of.
menoscabo [me·nos·ká·βo] *m.* impairment; damage; diminution, lessening.
menospreciar [me·nos·pre·sjár] *v.* to despise, scorn; to underestimate.
menosprecio [me·nos·pré·sjo] *m.* scorn, contempt; underestimation.
mensaje [men·sa·xe] *m.* message.
mensajero [men·sa·xé·ro] *m.* messenger.
menstruo [méns·trwo] *m.* menstruation.
mensual [men·swál] *adj.* monthly.
mensualidad [men·swa·li·ðáð] *f.* monthly allowance; monthly payment.
mensurable [men·su·rá·βle] *adj.* measurable.
menta [mén·ta] *f.* mint; peppermint; *Ríopl.* rumor, hearsay; *Ríopl., Andes* **por -s** by hearsay; *Ríopl.* **persona de —** famous person.
mentado [men·tá·ðo] *adj.* famous; *p.p.* mentioned.
mental [men·tál] *adj.* mental.
mentalidad [men·ta·li·ðáð] *f.* mentality.
mentar[1] [men·tár] *v. irr.* to mention; to call, name.
mente [mén·te] *f.* mind; intellect.
mentecato [men·te·ká·to] *adj.* foolish, simple; *m.* fool.
mentir[3] [men·tír] *v. irr.* to lie, tell lies.
mentira [men·tí·ra] *f.* lie, falsehood, fib; white spot on the fingernails.
mentiroso [men·ti·ró·so] *adj.* lying; deceptive, false; *m.* liar, fibber; **mentirosillo** *m.* little fibber.
mentís [men·tís]: **dar un —** to give the lie (to).
mentón [men·tón] *m.* chin.
menú [me·nú] *m.* menu.
menudear [me·nu·de·ár] *v.* to occur frequently; to repeat over and over; to fall incessantly (*as rain,*

stones, projectiles, etc.); to tell in detail; *Am.* to retail, sell at retail; *Am.* to meet together often.
menudeo [me·nu·dé·o] *m.* retail; **vender al —** to retail, sell at retail.
menudo [me·nú·ðo] *adj.* minute, small; insignificant; exact, detailed; **dinero —** change; **a — often; por —** in detail; retail; *m.* entrails, "innards"; change, small coins.
meñique [me·ñí·ke] *adj.* tiny, wee; **dedo —** little finger.
meollo [me·ó·yo] *m.* marrow; pith; kernel; substance; brain; brains.
meple [mé·ple] *m. Ríopl.* maple.
merca [mér·ka] *f.* purchase.
mercachifle [mer·ka·čí·fle] *m.* peddler, vendor; cheap merchant; cheap fellow.
mercader [mer·ka·ðér] *m.* trader, merchant.
mercadería [mer·ka·de·rí·a] *f.* merchandise; trade.
mercado [mer·ká·ðo] *m.* market; mart.
mercancía [mer·kan·sí·a] *f.* merchandise; goods.
mercantil [mer·kan·tíl] *adj.* mercantile, commercial.
mercar[6] [mer·kár] *v.* to purchase, buy.
merced [mer·séð] *f.* favor; present, gift; mercy; **Vuestra Merced** Your Honor; **a — de** at the mercy of; at the expense of.
mercería [mer·se·rí·a] *f.* notions (*pins, buttons, etc.*); notions store; *Ríopl., P.R.* drygoods store.
mercurio [mer·kú·rjo] *m.* mercury; quicksilver.
merecedor [me·re·se·ðór] *adj.* worthy, deserving.
merecer[13] [me·re·sér] *v. irr.* to deserve.
merecido [me·re·sí·ðo] *adj. & p.p.* deserved; *m.* deserved punishment.
merecimiento [me·re·si·mjén·to] *m.* merit.
merendar[1] [me·ren·dár] *v. irr.* to have an afternoon snack or refreshment; *Carib., Ven.* **-se uno a alguien** to fleece or skin someone (*in a game or business deal*); to kill someone.
merendero [me·ren·dé·ro] *m.* lunchroom.
meridiano [me·ri·djá·no] *adj. & m.* meridian.
meridional [me·ri·djo·nál] *adj.* southern; *m.* southerner.
merienda [me·rjén·da] *f.* light afternoon meal; afternoon refreshments.
mérito [mé·ri·to] *m.* merit; **de —** notable.
merito [me·rí·to] *dim. of* **mero.**
meritorio [me·ri·tó·rjo] *adj.* meritorious, worthy, deserving; *m.* employee without salary (*learning trade or profession*).
merluza [mer·lú·sa] *f.* hake (*species of codfish*); drunken state.
merma [mér·ma] *f.* reduction, decrease.
mermar [mer·már] *v.* to dwindle; to decrease, reduce.
mermelada [mer·me·lá·ða] *f.* marmalade.
mero [mé·ro] *adj.* mere, pure; *Mex., C.A.* exact, real; **la mera verdad** the real truth; *adv. Mex., C.A.* very, very same, exactly; *Mex., C.A.* soon; *Col.* only; *Mex., C.A.* **una mera de las tres** only one of the three; *Mex., C.A.* **ya — (or merito)** very soon; *Mex., C.A.* **allí — (or merito)** right there; *m.* species of perch; *Ch.* species of thrush.
merodear [me·ro·de·ár] *v.* to rove in search of plunder.
mes [mes] *m.* month.
mesa [mé·sa] *f.* table; executive board; staircase landing; mesa, plateau; **levantar la —** to clear the table; **poner la —** to set the table; *Col., Carib., C.A., Mex.* **quitar la —** to clear the table.
mesada [me·sá·ða] *f.* monthly salary or allowance.
mesarse [me·sár·se] *v.* to tear (*one's hair or beard*).
mesero [me·sé·ro] *m. Mex., C.A., Ven., Col.* waiter.

ME

meseta [me·sé·ta] *f.* plateau; staircase landing.
mesón [me·són] *m.* inn (*usually a large one-story shelter for men and pack animals*).
mesonero [me·so·né·ro] *m.* innkeeper.
mestizo [mes·tí·so] *adj.* half-breed; hybrid; **perro** — mongrel dog; *m.* mestizo, half-breed.
mesura [me·sú·ra] *f.* moderation; composure; dignity; politeness.
mesurado [me·su·rá·ḍo] *adj.* moderate, temperate; dignified.
meta [mé·ta] *f.* goal; objective.
metabolismo [me·ta·ḅo·líz·mo] *m.* metabolism.
metafísica [me·ta·fi·sí·ka] *f.* metaphysics.
metáfora [me·tá·fo·ra] *f.* metaphor.
metafórico [me·ta·fó·ri·ko] *adj.* metaphorical.
metal [me·tál] *m.* metal.
metálico [me·tá·li·ko] *adj.* metallic, metal; *m.* specie, coined money; cash in coin.
metalurgia [me·ta·lúr·xja] *f.* metallurgy.
metamorfosis [me·ta·mor·fó·sis] *f.* metamorphosis.
metate [me·tá·te] *m. Mex.* flat stone (*used for grinding corn, etc.*).
metátesis [me·tá·te·sis] *f.* metathesis.
meteorito [me·te·o·rí·to] *m.* meteorite.
meteoro [me·te·ó·ro] *m.* meteor.
meteorología [me·te·o·ro·lo·xí·a] *f.* meteorology; **meteorológico** [me·te·o·ro·ló·xi·ko] *adj.* meteorological; **oficina meteorológica** weather bureau.
meter [me·tér] *v.* to put (in); to get (in); to insert; to smuggle; to make (*noise, trouble, etc.*); to cause (*fear*); *Carib.* to strike (*a blow*); *Ríopl., Carib.* **-le** to hurry up; **-se** to meddle, interfere; to plunge (into); **-se monja** (*Am.* **-se de monja**) to become a nun; also **-se a monja; -se con** to pick a quarrel with.
metódico [me·tó·ḍi·ko] *adj.* methodical.
método [mé·to·ḍo] *m.* method.
metralleta [me·tra·yé·ta] *f.* hand machine gun.
metrico [mé·tri·ko] *adj.* metric.
metro [mé·tro] *m.* meter; subway.
metrópoli [me·tró·po·li] *f.* metropolis.
metropolitano [me·tro·po·li·tá·no] *adj.* metropolitan; *m.* archbishop.
mexicano [me·xi·ká·no] = **mejicano** (*pronounced identically*).
mezcal [mez·kál] *m. Mex.* mescal (*a species of maguey and an alcoholic beverage made from it*).
mezcla [més·kla] *f.* mixture; mortar; mixed cloth; **mezclilla** [mes·klí·ya] *f.* mixed cloth (*generally black and white*); tweed.
mezclar [mes·klár] *v.* to mix, blend; **-se** to mix, mingle; to meddle.
mezcolanza [mes·ko·lán·sa] *f.* jumble, mess, mixture.
mezquindad [mes·ki·ni·ḍáḍ] *f.* meanness; stinginess; dire poverty.
mezquino [mes·kí·no] *adj.* poor, needy; mean, stingy; meager; small, tiny; *m. Col., Mex.* wart (*usually on a finger*).
mezquita [mes·kí·ta] *f.* mosque.
mi [mi] *adj.* my.
mí [mi] *pers. pron.* (*used after prep.*) me, myself.
miaja [mjá·xa] = **migaja**.
miau [mjáw] *m.* mew.
mico [mí·ko] *m.* long-tailed monkey; *C.A.* jack (*for lifting heavy objects*).
microbio [mi·kró·ḅjo] *m.* microbe.
microbús [mi·kro·ḅús] *m.* microbus.
microfilm [mi·kro·fíln] *m.* microfilm.
micrófono [mi·kró·fo·no] *m.* microphone.

microscopio [mi·kros·kó·pjo] *m.* microscope; — **electrónico** electron microscope; **microscópico** [mi·kro·skó·pi·ko] *adj.* microscopic.
miedo [mjé·ḍo] *m.* fear; dread; **tener** — to be afraid.
miedoso [mje·ḍó·so] *adj.* afraid, fearful, timid.
miel [mjel] *m.* honey; molasses.
mielga [mjél·ḡa] *f.* plot of ground for planting.
miembro [mjém·bro] *m.* member; limb.
mientes [mjén·tes] *f. pl.* thought, mind; **parar** — **en** to consider, reflect on; **traer a las** — to recall; **venírsele a uno a las** — to occur to one, come to one's mind.
mientras [mjén·tras] *conj.* while; — **que** while; — **tanto** in the meantime, meanwhile; — **más . . .** — **menos . . .** the more . . . the less . . .
miércoles [mjér·ko·les] *m.* Wednesday.
mies [mjes] *f.* ripe grain; harvest; **-es** fields of grain.
miga [mí·ḡa] *f.* crumb; soft part of bread; substance; **-s** crumbs; fried crumbs of bread; **hacer buenas -s** (*or* **malas -s**) **con** to get along well (*or* badly) with.
migaja [mi·ḡá·xa] *f.* crumb; bit, fragment, small particle.
migración [mi·ḡra·sjón] *f.* migration.
milagro [mi·lá·ḡro] *m.* miracle; wonder.
milagroso [mi·la·ḡró·so] *adj.* miraculous.
milicia [mi·lí·sja] *f.* militia; military science; military profession.
miligramo [mi·li·ḡrá·mo] *m.* milligram.
milímetro [mi·lí·me·tro] *m.* millimeter.
militar [mi·li·tár] *adj.* military; *m.* soldier, military man; *v.* to serve in the army; to militate, fight (against).
milpa [míl·pa] *f. Mex., C.A.* cornfield.
milla [mí·ya] *f.* mile.
millar [mi·yár] *m.* thousand; **-es** thousands, a great number.
millón [mi·yón] *m.* million; **millonario**. [mi·yo·ná·rjo] *adj. & m.* millionaire; **millonésimo** [mi·yo·né·si·mo] *adj. & m.* millionth.
mimar [mi·már] *v.* to pamper, spoil, humor; to pet.
mimbre [mím·bre] *m.* wicker; **mimbrera** [mim·bré·ra] *f.* willow.
mímico [mí·mi·ko] *adj.* mimic.
mimo [mí·mo] *m.* pampering; caress; coaxing.
mimoso [mi·mó·so] *adj.* tender, sensitive; delicate; finicky, fussy.
mina [mí·na] *f.* mine; source; fortune.
minar [mi·nár] *v.* to mine; to undermine; to sow with explosive mines.
mineral [mi·ne·rál] *m.* mineral; mine; ore; wealth, fortune; *adj.* mineral.
minería [mi·ne·rí·a] *f.* mining; miners.
minero [mi·né·ro] *m.* miner; wealth, fortune; source; *adj.* mining; **compañía minera** mining company.
miniatura [mi·nja·tú·ra] *f.* miniature.
minifalda [mi·ni·fál·da] *f.* miniskirt.
minifundio [mi·ni·fún·djo] *m.* small farm (*privately owned*).
mínimo [mí·ni·mo] *adj.* least, smallest; *m.* minimum.
minino [mi·ní·no] *m.* kitten, kitty, pussy.
ministerio [mi·nis·té·rjo] *m.* ministry; administration, ministering; portfolio (*office of a cabinet member*); minister's office.
ministrar [mi·nis·trár] *v.* to minister; to give (*money, aid, etc.*).
ministro [mi·nís·tro] *m.* minister; cabinet member;

office of justice.

minoría [mi·no·rí·a] *f.* minority.

minoridad [mi·no·ri·ḍáḍ] *f.* minority (*in age*).

minucioso [mi·nu·sjó·so] *adj.* minute, detailed; scrupulous.

minúsculo [mi·nús·ku·lo] *adj.* small; **letra minúscula** small letter.

minuta [mi·nú·ta] *f.* minutes; memorandum; first draft (*of a contract, deed, etc.*); memorandum list; lawyer's bill; *Am.* **a la** — breaded and fried (*said of meat or fish*).

minuto [mi·nú·to] *m.* minute; **minutero** [mi·nu·té·ro] *m.* minute hand.

mío [mí·o] *poss. adj.* my, of mine; *poss. pron.* mine; *Riopl.,* *Ch.* **detrás** — behind me.

miope [mjó·pe] *adj.* shortsighted, nearsighted; *m. & f.* nearsighted person.

miopía [mjo·pi·a] *f.* near-sightedness.

mira [mí·ra] *f.* (*de puntería*) gun sight; guiding point; (*intención*) intention, design; outlook; **estar a la** — **de** to be on the lookout for; to be on the alert for; **poner la** — **en** to fix one's eyes on; to aim at.

mirada [mi·rá·ḍa] *f.* glance, gaze, look.

mirador [mi·ra·ḍór] *m.* mirador, enclosed balcony (*commanding an extensive view*); watchtower; lookout site; onlooker, spectator; *Riopl.* penthouse (*small house built on a roof for recreation*).

miramiento [mi·ra·mjén·to] *m.* consideration, respect, regard; reverence; circumspection, prudence.

mirar [mi·rár] *v.* to look; to glance; to behold; to see; — **por alguien** to take care of someone; **¡mira (tú)!** look!

miríada [mi·rjá·ḍa] *f.* myriad, multitude, great number.

miriñaque [mi·ri·ñá·ke] *m.* crinoline.

mirlo [mír·lo] *m.* blackbird.

mirón [mi·rón] *m.* bystander, onlooker, spectator; *adj.* curious.

mirra [mí·rra] *f.* myrrh.

mirto [mír·to] *m.* myrtle.

misa [mí·sa] *f.* mass; — **del gallo** midnight mass.

misántropo [mi·sán·tro·po] *m.* misanthrope.

misceláneo [mi·se·lá·ne·o] *adj.* miscellaneous.

miserable [mi·se·rá·ḅle] *adj.* miserable, unhappy; forlorn; miserly, stingy; mean.

miseria [mi·sé·rja] *f.* misery; poverty; stinginess; bit, trifle.

misericordia [mi·se·ri·kor·ḍja] *f.* mercy, compassion, pity.

misericordioso [mi·se·ri·kor·ḍjó·so] *adj.* merciful, compassionate.

mísero [mí·se·ro] *adj.* miserable, unhappy; forlorn; stingy.

misi [mi·si] *interj.* word used to call cats.

misión [mi·sjón] *f.* mission.

misionero [mi·sjo·né·ro] *m.* missionary.

mismo [míz·mo] *adj.* same; self, very; **ahora** — right away.

misterio [mis·té·rjo] *m.* mystery; secret.

misterioso [mis·te·rjó·so] *adj.* mysterious.

místico [mís·ti·ko] *adj.* mystical, mystic; *m.* mystic.

mitad [mi·táḍ] *f.* half; middle.

mitigar [mi·ti·gár] *v.* to mitigate, soften, soothe.

mitin [mí·tin] *m.* meeting.

mito [mí·to] *m.* myth; **mitología** [mi·to·lo·xí·a] *f.* mythology.

mitra [mí·tra] *f.* bishop's miter.

mixto [mís·to] *adj.* mixed; half-breed; *m.*

composite; match; explosive compound.

mobiliario [mo·ḅi·ljá·rjo] *m.* furniture.

moblaje [mo·ḅlá·xe] = **mueblaje.**

mocasín [mo·ka·sín] *m.* moccasin.

mocedad [mo·se·ḍáḍ] *f.* youth; youthfulness; youthful prank.

mocetón [mo·se·tón] *m.* tall, robust lad.

moción [mo·sjón] *f.* motion.

moco [mó·ko] *m.* mucus; snot.

mocoso [mo·kó·so] *adj.* sniffling; *m.* brat, scamp; sniffling boy.

mochar [mo·čár] *v. Am.* to cut off, chop off, cut, trim (*see* **desmochar**); *Am.* to snitch, pilfer; *Col.* to depose, dismiss, put out of a job.

mochila [mo·čí·la] *f.* knapsack; soldier's kit.

mocho [mó·čo] *adj.* cut off; cropped, shorn; *Am.* maimed, mutilated; *Mex.* reactionary, conservative; *m.* butt of a firearm; *Col., Ven.* nag; *Carib.* cigar butt.

moda [mó·ḍa] *f.* mode, custom, style, fashion; **de** — fashionable.

modelar [mo·ḍe·lár] *v.* to model.

modelo [mo·ḍé·lo] *m.* model, copy, pattern; *m. & f.* life model.

moderación [mo·ḍe·ra·sjón] *f.* moderation.

moderado [mo·ḍe·rá·ḍo] *adj.* moderate; conservative.

moderar [mo·ḍe·rár] *v.* to moderate, temper; to regulate; to restrain.

moderno [mo·ḍér·no] *adj.* modern.

modestia [mo·ḍés·tja] *f.* modesty.

modesto [mo·ḍés·to] *adj.* modest.

módico [mó·ḍi·ko] *adj.* moderate, reasonable (*price*).

modificación [mo·ḍi·fi·ka·sjón] *f.* modification.

modificar[6] [mo·ḍi·fi·kár] *v.* to modify.

modismo [mo·ḍíz·mo] *m.* idiom.

modista [mo·ḍís·ta] *f.* dressmaker; milliner.

modo [mó·ḍo] *m.* mode, manner, way; mood (*grammar*); **a** (*or* **al**) — **de** like, in the manner of; **de** — **que** so that; and so; **de todos -s** at any rate, anyway.

modorra [mo·ḍo·rra] *f.* drowsiness; gid (*a disease of sheep*).

modular [mo·ḍu·lár] *v.* to modulate, tone down.

mofa [mó·fa] *f.* scoff, jeer, taunt; mockery.

mofar [mo·fár] *v.* to mock, scoff, jeer; **-se de** to make fun of, scoff at.

moflete [mo·flé·te] *m.* fat cheek; **mofletudo** [mo·fle·tú·ḍo] *adj.* fat-cheeked.

mohín [mo·ín] *m.* grimace; wry face.

mohíno [mo·í·no] *adj.* moody, discontented, sad, melancholy; black (*referring to a horse, cow, or bull*).

moho [mó·o] *m.* rust; mold.

mohoso [mo·ó·so] *adj.* musty, moldy; rusty.

mojada [mo·xá·ḍa] *f.* drench, drenching, wetting.

mojado [mo·xá·ḍo] *adj.* wet, damp, moist; *p.p. of* **mojar.**

mojadura [mo·xa·ḍú·ra] *f.* wetting, dampening, drenching.

mojar [mo·xár] *v.* to dampen, wet, moisten; *Riopl., Ch.* to accompany (*a song*); *Am.* to bribe; *Riopl., Carib., Mex.* to celebrate by drinking; *Am.* **mojársele a uno los papeles** to get things mixed up.

mojicón [mo·xi·kón] *m.* punch, blow; muffin, bun.

mojigatería [mo·xi·ga·te·rí·a] *f.* prudery; false humility; affected piety.

mojigato [mo·xi·gá·to] *adj.* prudish; affectedly pious, overzealous (*in matters of religion*);

ME

hypocritical; *m.* prude; hypocrite.

mojón [mo·xón] *m.* landmark; milestone; heap, pile.

molde [mól·de] *m.* mold, cast; form; pattern, model; **venir de** — to come pat, be to the point; **letras de** — printed letters; print.

moldear [mol·de·ár] *v.* to mold; to cast; to decorate with moldings.

moldura [mol·dú·ra] *f.* molding.

mole [mó·le] *f.* mass, bulk; *adj.* soft, mild; *m. Mex.* — **de guajolote** a Mexican dish of turkey served with a chili gravy.

molécula [mo·lé·ku·la] *f.* molecule.

moler[2] [mo·lér] *v. irr.* to mill; to grind; to tire, fatigue; to wear out, destroy; to bother; — **a palos** to give a thorough beating.

molestar [mo·les·tár] *v.* to molest, disturb; to bother, annoy.

molestia [mo·lés·tja] *f.* bother, annoyance; discomfort.

molesto [mo·lés·to] *adj.* bothersome, annoying; uncomfortable.

molibdeno [mo·lib̶·đe·no] *m.* molybdenum.

molicie [mo·li·sje] *f.* softness; fondness for luxury.

molienda [mo·ljén·da] *f.* grind, grinding, milling; portion to be, or that has been, ground; grinding season (*for sugar cane or olives*); fatigue, weariness; bother.

molinero [mo·li·né·ro] *m.* miller.

molinete [mo·li·né·te] *m.* small mill; ventilating fan; pin wheel; twirl, whirl, flourish.

molinillo [mo·li·ní·yo] *m.* small mill or grinder; chocolate beater; restless person.

molino [mo·lí·no] *m.* mill; restless person; — **de viento** windmill.

molusco [mo·lús·ko] *m.* mollusk.

mollera [mo·yé·ra] *f.* crown of the head; judgment, good sense; **ser duro de** — to be stubborn; **no tener sal en la** — to be dull, stupid.

momentáneo [mo·men·tá·ne·o] *adj.* momentary; sudden, quick.

momento [mo·mén·to] *m.* moment; importance; momentum; **al** — immediately, without delay; **a cada** — continually; frequently.

mona [mó·na] *f.* female monkey; mimic; drunkenness; **dormir la** — to sleep it off; **pillar una** — to get drunk.

monada [mo·ná·đa] *f.* (*típico de mono*) monkeyshine; monkey face; (*cosa graciosa*) cute little thing; cute gesture; nonsense; flattery.

monarca [mo·nár·ka] *m.* monarch.

monarquía [mo·nar·kí·a] *f.* monarchy.

monasterio [mo·nas·té·rjo] *m.* monastery.

mondadientes [mon·da·đjen·tes] *m.* toothpick.

mondadura [mon·da·đú·ra] *f.* trimming; peeling.

mondar [mon·dár] *v.* to pare; to peel; to prune; to clean out; *Am.* to beat, thrash; *Am.* to beat, defeat; **-se los dientes** to pick one's teeth.

moneda [mo·né·đa] *f.* coin; money; — **corriente** currency; — **menuda** (*or* **suelta**) change, small coins; **casa de** — mint.

monería [mo·ne·rí·a] *f.* monkeyshine, antic; trifle, trinket; cute little thing.

monetario [mo·ne·tá·rjo] *adj.* monetary, pertaining to money; financial.

monigote [mo·ni·ǵó·te] *m.* puppet, ridiculous figure; dunce.

monitorear [mo·ni·to·re·ár] *v.* to monitor (*a radio or TV program*).

monja [món̶·xa] *f.* nun.

monje [món̶·xe] *m.* monk.

mono [mó·no] *m.* monkey; silly fool; mimic; coveralls; *Ch.* pile of fruit or vegetables (*in a market*); **-s** *Ch.* worthless household utensils and furniture; *Am.* **meterle a uno los -s en el cuerpo** to frighten, terrify someone; *adj.* pretty, neat, cute; *Am.* sorrel, reddish-brown; *Col.* blond.

monóculo [mo·nó·ku·lo] *m.* monocle.

monologar[7] [mo·no·lo·ǵár] *v.* to soliloquize, talk to oneself; to recite monologues; to monopolize the conversation.

monólogo [mo·nó·lo·ǵo] *m.* monologue.

monopolio [mo·no·pó·ljo] *m.* monopoly.

monopolizar[9] [mo·no·po·li·sar] *v.* to monopolize, to corner (*a market*).

monosílabo [mo·no·sí·la·b̶o] *adj.* monosyllabic, of one syllable; *m.* monosyllable.

monotonía [mo·no·to·ní·a] *f.* monotony; **monótono** [mo·nó·to·no] *adj.* monotonous.

monserga [mon·sér·ǵa] *f.* gabble.

monstruo [móns·trwo] *m.* monster.

monstruosidad [mons·trwo·si·đáđ] *f.* monstrosity; monster, freak.

monstruoso [mons·trwó·so] *adj.* monstrous.

monta [món·ta] *f.* amount, sum; value, importance; **de poca** — of little value or importance.

montaje [mon·tá·xe] *m.* assembly, assembling (*of machinery*); mount, support for a cannon.

montante [mon·tán·te] *m.* broadsword; transom; upright; post; *Carib., Ven.* sum, amount, cost; *f.* high tide.

montaña [mon·tá·ña] *f.* mountain; — **rusa** roller coaster.

montañés [mon·ta·nés] *adj.* mountain (*used as adj.*) of, from or pertaining to the mountains; *m.* mountaineer; native of the province of Santander, Spain.

montañismo [mon·ta·níz·mo] *m.* mountaineering.

montañoso [mon·ta·ñó·so] *adj.* mountainous.

montar [mon·tár] *v.* to mount; to ride horseback; to amount (to); to set (*jewels*); to cock (*a gun*); to assemble, set up (*machinery*); *Carib., C.A.* to organize, establish.

montaraz [mon·ta·rás] *adj.* wild, primitive, uncivilized; *m.* forester.

monte [món·te] *m.* mount, mountain; forest; thicket; monte (*a card game*); *C.A., Mex.* grass, pasture; *Am.* country, outskirts; **montecillo** [mon·te·sí·yo] *m.* mound, small hill; **montepío** [mon·te·pí·o] *m.* pawnshop.

montera [mon·té·ra] *f.* cap; *Andes* Bolivian cone-shaped hat (*worn by Indians*).

montés [mon·tés] *adj.* wild, mountain (*used as adj.*); **cabra** — mountain goat; **gato** — wildcat.

montículo [mon·tí·ku·lo] *m.* mound.

montón [mon·tón] *m.* pile, heap, mass, great number; **a -es** in abundance, in heaps, by heaps.

montonera [mon·to·né·ra] *f. Col., Ven., Ríopl.* band of mounted rebels or guerrilla fighters; *Col.* pile of wheat, hay, straw, etc.; *Am.* pile, heap (*of anything*).

montuoso [mon·twó·so] *adj.* hilly; mountainous.

montura [mon·tú·ra] *f.* mount, horse; saddle and trappings.

monumento [mo·nu·mén·to] *m.* monument; **monumental** [mo·nu·men·tál] *adj.* monumental.

moña [mo·ña] *f.* doll; hair ribbon.

moño [mó·ño] *m.* knot or roll of hair; bow of ribbon; crest, tuft of feathers; *Mex.* forelock (*lock of hair on the fore part of the head*); *Am.* crest, peak (*of anything*); *Col.* whim; *Am.* a

Colombian popular dance; -s frippery, gaudy ornaments; *Col.* estar con el — torcido to be in an ugly humor.

mora [mó·ra] *f.* blackberry; mulberry; brambleberry; *Ch.* blood pudding, sausage.

morada [mo·rá·ḍa] *f.* dwelling, residence; stay.

morado [mo·rá·ḍo] *adj.* purple.

morador [mo·ra·ḍór] *m.* dweller, resident.

moral [mo·rál] *adj.* moral; *f.* ethics, moral philosophy; morale; *m.* mulberry tree; blackberry bush.

moraleja [mo·ra·lé·xa] *f.* moral, lesson, maxim.

moralidad [mo·ra·li·ḍáḍ] *f.* morality.

moralista [mo·ra·lís·ta] *m. & f.* moralist.

morar [mo·rár] *v.* to live, dwell, reside.

morbidez [mor·ḅi·ḍés] *f.* softness; mellowness.

mórbido [mór·ḅi·ḍo] *adj.* morbid; soft.

morboso [mor·ḅó·so] *adj.* morbid, unhealthy, diseased.

morcilla [mor·sí·ya] *f.* blood pudding, blood sausage; gag (*an amusing remark by a comedian*).

mordacidad [mor·ḍa·si·ḍáḍ] *f.* sharpness (*of tongue*).

mordaz [mor·ḍás] *adj.* biting, cutting, sarcastic.

mordaza [mor·ḍá·sa] *f.* gag (*for the mouth*).

mordedor [mor·ḍe·ḍór] *adj.* biting; snappy; *m.* biter; slanderer.

mordedura [mor·ḍe·ḍú·ra] *f.* bite; sting.

mordelón [mor·ḍe·lón] *adj. Col., Ven.* biting, snappy; *m. Am.* biter; *Mex.* public official who accepts a bribe.

morder[2] [mor·ḍér] *v. irr.* to bite; to nip; to gnaw; to corrode; to backbite, slander; *Ven.* to swindle; *Mex., C.A.* to "shake down", exact a bribe.

mordida [mor·ḍí·ḍa] *f. Am.* bite; *Mex., C.A., Carib., Ven.* graft, money obtained by graft.

mordiscar[6] [mor·ḍis·kár], **mordisquear** [mor·ḍis·ke·ár] *v.* to nibble; to gnaw.

mordisco [mor·ḍis·ko] *m.* bite; nibble.

moreno [mo·ré·no] *adj.* brown; dark, brunette; *m. Riopl., Carib., Mex., Ven., Andes* colored person.

moretón [mo·re·tón] *m.* bruise, black-and-blue mark.

morfema [mor·fé·m'a] *m.* morpheme.

morfina [mor·fí·na] *f.* morphine; **morfinómano** [mor·fi·nó·ma·no] *m.* morphine addict, drug fiend.

morfología [mor·fo·lo·xí·a] *f.* morphology.

moribundo [mo·ri·ḅún·do] *adj.* dying.

morir[4,52] [mo·rír] *v. irr.* to die; -se to die; to die out, be extinguished.

morisco [mo·rís·ko] *adj.* Moorish; Moresque, in the Moorish style; *m.* Morisco (*Christianized Moor*); language of the Moriscos.

mormonismo [mor·mo·níz·mo] *m.* Mormonism.

moro [mó·ro] *adj.* Moorish; *Mex., Ven., Riopl., Cuba* dappled, spotted (*horse*); *Col., Ch., Andes* unbaptized; *m.* Moor; *Am.* frosted cookie.

morocho [mo·ró·čo] *adj. Am.* robust, strong; *Riopl.* of dark complexion; *Ch.* rough, tough; *Andes* of low social condition.

morral [mo·rrál] *m.* nose bag; knapsack; hunter's bag.

morrillo [mo·rrí·yo] *m.* fat of the neck (*especially the bull*).

morriña [mo·rrí·ña] *f.* melancholy, blues, sadness.

morro [mó·rro] *m.* knoll.

morsa [mór·sa] *f.* walrus.

mortaja [mor·tá·xa] *f.* shroud; *Am.* cigarette paper.

mortal [mor·tál] *adj.* mortal; fatal; deadly; *m.* mortal; **mortalidad** [mor·ta·li·ḍáḍ] *f.* mortality;

death rate.

mortandad [mo·tan·dáḍ] *f.* mortality, death rate; massacre, slaughter.

mortecino [mor·te·sí·no] *adj.* deathly pale; dying; **hacer la mortecina** to pretend to be dead.

morterete [mor·te·ré·te] *m.* small mortar, small canon.

mortero [mor·té·ro] *m.* mortar (*for grinding*).

mortífero [mor·tí·fe·ro] *adj.* deadly, fatal.

mortificar[6] [mor·ti·fi·kár] *v.* to mortify; to torment; to vex, annoy; -se to do penance; to be grieved; *Mex., C.A., Ven.* to be embarrassed.

mortuorio [mor·twó·rjo] *adj.* funeral; funereal, mournful; *m.* funeral, burial.

mosaico [mo·sáj·ko] *adj. & m.* mosaic.

mosca [mós·ka] *f.* fly; bore; bother; *Am.* sponger, parasite; *Mex., C.A., Ven.* bull's-eye, center of a target; **moscón** *m.* large fly; *Am.* ir de moscón to go along as a chaperone.

mosquear [mos·ke·ár] *v.* to brush off or drive away flies; to whip, beat; *Riopl.* to rage, be furious; -se to show pique or resentment; *Ch.* to go away.

mosquito [mos·kí·to] *m.* mosquito; gnat; *Am.* Mosquito Indian of Nicaragua; **mosquitero** *m.* mosquito net.

mostacho [mos·tá·čo] *m.* mustache.

mostaza [mos·tá·sa] *f.* mustard; mustard seed; bird shot.

mostrador [mos·tra·ḍór] *m.* demonstrator; store counter; clock dial.

mostrar[2] [mos·trár] *v. irr.* to show; to demonstrate; to exhibit.

mostrenco [mos·tréŋ·ko] *adj.* (*sin dueño*) ownerless; homeless; stray (*animal*); (*torpe*) slow, dull; fat, heavy; *m.* dunce; *C.A.* worthless animal.

mota [mó·ta] *f.* mote, speck; knot in cloth; slight defect; mound, knoll; *Col., Ven., Carib.* powder puff; *Am.* tuft.

mote [mó·te] *m.* motto; slogan; nickname; *Andes, Ch., Col.* stewed corn; *Andes* grammatical error (*made by illiterate people and children*); *Am.* — **pelado** hominy.

motear [mo·te·ár] *v.* to speck, speckle; to spot; *Am.* to mispronounce, enunciate badly.

motejar [mo·te·xár] *v.* to jeer at; to call bad names; to insult; to censure; — de to brand as.

motín [mo·tín] *m.* mutiny; riot.

motivar [mo·ti·ḅár] *v.* to cause; to give a cause for.

motivo [mo·tí·ḅo] *m.* motive, reason; motif, theme; *m.* con — de because of; on the occasion of; *adj.* motive.

motocicleta [mo·to·si·klé·ta] *f.* motorcycle; **motociclista** [mo·to·si·kle·tis·ta] *m. & f.* motorcyclist, motorcycle rider.

motociclismo [mo·to·si·klíz·mo] *m.* motorcycling.

motor [mo·tór] *m.* motor; — de reacción jet engine; *adj.* motor, causing motion.

motorista [mo·to·rís·ta] *m. & f.* motorist; motorman, motorwoman.

motorreactor [mo·to·rre·ak·tór] *m.* jet engine.

motriz [mo·tris] *adj.* motive, impelling, driving; **fuerza** — power, driving force.

movedizo [mo·ḅe·ḍi·so] *adj.* movable; shaky; shifting; **arena movediza** quicksand.

mover[2] [mo·ḅér] *v. irr.* (*físicamente*) to move; (*persuadir*) to persuade; to stir, excite; to touch, affect; -se to move.

movible [mo·ḅi·ḅle] *adj.* movable; mobile; fickle.

móvil [mó·ḅil] *m.* motive, inducement, incentive; *adj.* mobile, movable; unstable.

movilización [mo·þi·li·sa·sjón] f. mobilization.
mobilizar[9] [mo·þi·li·sár] v. to mobilize.
movimiento [mo·þi·mjén·to] m. movement;
motion; commotion, disturbance.
moza [mó·sa] f. maid; girl; last hand of a game;
Ch. last song or dance of a fiesta.
mozalbete [mo·sal·þé·te] m. youth, lad.
mozárabe [mo·sá·ra·þe] adj. Mozarabic (Christian
in Moslem Spain).
mozo [mó·so] adj. young; unmarried; m. youth;
manservant; waiter; porter; errand boy; buen —
handsome man.
mozuela [mo·swé·la] f. lass, young girl.
mozuelo [mo·swé·lo] m. lad, young boy.
mucama [mu·ká·ma] f. Andes, Ríopl. servant girl;
mucamo [mu·ká·mo] m. Andes, Ríopl. servant.
mucoso [mu·kó·so] adj. mucous; slimy; membrana
mucosa mucous membrane.
muchacha [mu·čá·ča] f. child; girl; servant, maid.
muchacho [mu·čá·čo] m. child; boy, lad.
muchedumbre [mu·če·dúm·bre] f. multitude; crowd.
mucho [mú·čo] adj. much, a lot of; long (referring
to time); -s many; adv. much; a great deal; ni
con — not by far, not by a long shot; ni —
menos not by any means, nor anything like it;
por — que no matter how much; no es — que
it is no wonder that.
muda [mú·da] f. change; change of clothes; molt
(act or time of shedding feathers); Ríopl. relay of
draft animals.
mudable [mu·dá·þle] adj. changeable; fickle.
mudanza [mu·dán·sa] f. change; removal;
inconstancy.
mudar [mu·dár] v. to change; to remove; to molt;
— de casa to move; — de traje to change one's
suit or costume; -se to change one's clothes; to
change one's habits; to move, change one's
abode.
mudez [mu·dés] f. muteness, dumbness.
mudo [mú·do] adj. mute, dumb; silent; m. dumb
person.
mueblaje [mwe·þlá·xe] m. furniture.
mueble [mwé·þle] m. piece of furniture; -s
furniture, household goods; adj. movable;
bienes -s chattels, movable possessions.
mueblería [mwe·þle·rí·a] f. furniture store.
mueca [mwé·ka] f. grimace; wry face.
muela [mwé·la] f. (diente) molar tooth; (piedra)
millstone; grindstone; — cordal (or — del juicio)
wisdom tooth.
muelle [mwé·ye] adj. soft; voluptuous; m. spring;
wharf; loading platform; — real main spring of
a watch.
muerte [mwér·te] f. death.
muerto [mwér·to] p.p. of morir & adj. dead;
withered; faded; naturaleza muerta still life; m.
corpse.
muesca [mwés·ka] f. notch; groove.
muestra [mwés·tra] f. sample; pattern, model; shop
sign; sign, indication; presence, bearing; face,
dial (of a clock or watch); muestrario
[mwes·trá·rjo] m. book or collection of samples.
mugido [mu·xi·do] m. moo; mooing, lowing of
cattle.
mugir[11] [mu·xír] v. to moo, low.
mugre [mú·gre] f. dirt, grime.
mugriento [mu·grjén·to] adj. grimy, dirty.
mujer [mu·xér] f. woman; wife.
mujeriego [mu·xe·rjé·go] adj. fond of women;
womanly.
mujeril [mu·xe·ríl] adj. womanly, feminine;

womanish, like a woman.
mula [mú·la] f. mule; Am. cushion for carrying
loads; Am. worthless merchandise; Ríopl. cruel,
treacherous person; Am. echar a uno la — to
give someone the dickens, scold someone.
muladar [mu·la·dár] m. rubbish pile or dump;
dunghill, pile of manure.
mulato [mu·lá·to] adj. & m. mulatto.
muleta [mu·lé·ta] f. crutch; red cloth draped over
a rod (used by bullfighters).
muletilla [mu·le·tí·ya] f. cane with a crutchlike
handle; red cloth draped over a rod (used by
bullfighters); cliché (hackneyed or trite phrase);
refrain; repetitious word or phrase; braid frog
(fastener for a coat).
mulo [mú·lo] m. mule.
multa [múl·ta] f. fine.
multicolor [mul·ti·ko·lór] adj. many-colored,
motley.
múltiple [múl·ti·ple] adj. multiple.
multiplicación [mul·ti·pli·ka·sjón] f. multiplication.
multiplicar[6] [mul·ti·pli·kár] v. to multiply.
multiplicidad [mul·ti·pli·si·dád] f. multiplicity,
manifold variety.
múltiplo [múl·ti·plo] m. multiple number.
multitud [mul·ti·túd] f. multitude; crowd.
mullido [mu·yí·do] adj. soft; fluffy; m. stuffing for
mattresses or pillows; soft cushion or mattress.
mullir[20] [mu·yír] v. to fluff; to soften.
mundanal [mun·da·nál] adj. worldly.
mundano [mun·dá·no] adj. mundane, worldly.
mundial [mun·djál] adj. universal; la guerra — the
World War.
mundo [mún·do] m. world; trunk; todo el —
everybody.
munición [mu·ni·sjón] f. ammunition; buckshot;
es de guerra war supplies.
municipal [mu·ni·si·pál] adj. municipal;
municipalidad [mu·ni·si·pa·li·dád] f.
municipality; town hall; city government.
municipio [mu·ni·sí·pjo] m. municipality.
muñeca [mu·ñé·ka] f. doll; wrist; manikin (figure
for displaying clothes); muñeco m. boy doll;
dummy, puppet.
muñón [mu·ñón] m. stump (of an arm or leg).
muralla [mu·rá·ya] f. surrounding wall; rampart.
murciano [mur·sjá·no] adj. of or from Murcia,
Spain; m. native of Murcia.
murciélago [mur·sjé·la·go] m. bat.
murga [múr·ga] f. brass band.
murmullo [mur·mú·yo] m. murmur, rumor;
whisper; muttering.
murmuración [mur·mu·ra·sjón] f. slander, gossip;
grumbling.
murmurar [mur·mu·rár] v. to murmur; to slander,
gossip; to whisper; to grumble.
muro [mú·ro] m. wall.
murria [mú·rrja] f. sulkiness, sullenness,
melancholy, blues; tener — to be sulky; to have
the blues.
musa [mú·sa] f. Muse; muse, poetic inspiration;
poetry; -s fine arts.
muscular [mus·ku·lár] adj. muscular.
musculatura [mus·ku·la·tú·ra] f. muscles; muscular
system.
músculo [mús·ku·lo] m. muscle.
musculoso [mus·ku·ló·so] adj. muscular; sinewy.
muselina [mu·se·lí·na] f. muslin.
museo [mu·sé·o] m. museum.
musgo [múz·go] m. moss.
musgoso [muz·gó·so] adj. mossy.

música [mú·si·ka] *f.* music.
musical [mu·si·kál] *adj.* musical.
músico [mú·si·ko] *adj.* musical; *m.* musician.
musitar [mu·si·tár] *v.* to mutter, mumble; to whisper.
muslo [múz·lo] *m.* thigh.
mustio [mús·tjo] *adj.* sad; withered; humble.
mutación [mu·ta·sjón] *f.* mutation; unsettled weather.
mutilar [mu·ti·lár] *v.* to mutilate; to butcher; to mar.
mutismo [mu·tíz·mo] *m.* muteness, silence.
mutuo [mú·two] *adj.* mutual; reciprocal.
muy [mwi(múj)] *adv.* very; greatly; most.

N:n

nabo [ná·ƀo] *m.* turnip.
nácar [ná·kar] *m.* mother-of-pearl; pearl color.
nacarado [na·ka·rá·đo] *adj.* pearly.
nacer[13] [na·sér] *v. irr.* (*salir del vientre*) to be born; (*brotar*) to spring, originate; to bud; to sprout, grow (*said of plants*); — **de pie** (*or* — **de pies**) to be born lucky.
naciente [na·sjén·te] *adj.* rising (*sun*); *m.* orient, east.
nacimiento [na·si·mjén·to] *m.* birth; origin; beginning; descent; source; crèche (*representation of the Nativity*).
nación [na·sjón] *f.* nation.
nacional [na·sjo·nál] *adj.* national; *m.* national, citizen.
nacionalidad [na·sjo·na·li·đáđ] *f.* nationality.
nada [ná·đa] *f.* nothingness; *indef. pron.* nothing, not ... anything; *adv.* not at all; **de** — you are welcome, don't mention it (*as a reply to* «**gracias**»); *Am.* **a cada** — constantly; **una nadita** [na·đí·ta] a trifle, just a little.
nadada [na·đá·đa] *f.* swim.
nadador [na·đa·đór] *m.* swimmer; *Ven.* fish-net float.
nadar [na·đár] *v.* to swim; to float.
nadería [na·đe·rí·a] *f.* a mere nothing, trifle, worthless thing.
nadie [ná·đje] *indef. pron.* nobody, no one, not ... anyone.
nafta [náf·ta] *f.* naphtha.
naguas [ná·ǥwas] = **enaguas.**
náhuatl [ná·watl] *adj.* the language of the Aztec Indians.
naipe [náj·pe] *m.* playing card.
nalgas [nál·ǥas] *f. pl.* buttocks; rump; **nalgada** [nal·ǥá·đa] *f.* spank; **-s** spanking.
nana [ná·na] *f.* grandma; lullaby; *Mex., Riopl., Ven.* child's nurse; *Spain* nice old lady.
naranja [na·ráŋ·xa] *f.* orange; — **tangerina** [taŋ·xe·rí·na] tangerine; **naranjada** [na·raŋ·xá·đa] *f.* orangeade; orange juice; orange marmalade; **naranjal** [na·raŋ·xál] *m.* orange grove; **naranjo** [na·ráŋ·xo] *m.* orange tree.
narciso [nar·sí·so] *m.* narcissus; daffodil; fop, dandy.
narcótico [nar·kó·ti·ko] *adj. & m.* narcotic.
narcotizar[5] [nar·ko·ti·sár] *v.* to dope, drug with narcotics.
nariz [na·rís] *f.* nose; nostril; **narices** [na·rí·ses] nostrils.
narración [na·rra·sjón] *f.* narration, account, story.

narrar [na·rrár] *v.* to narrate, tell, relate.
narrativo [na·rra·tí·ƀo] *adj.* narrative; **narrativa** [na·rra·tí·ƀa] *f.* narrative.
nata [ná·ta] *f.* cream; best part; scum; **-s** whipped cream with sugar; custard; **natoso** [na·tó·so] *adj.* creamy.
natación [na·ta·sjón] *f.* swimming.
natal [na·tál] *adj.* natal; native; **natalicio** [na·ta·lí·sjo] *m.* birthday; **natalidad** [na·ta·li·đáđ] *f.* birth rate.
natillas [na·tí·yas] *f. pl.* custard.
nativo [na·tí·ƀo] *adj.* native.
natural [na·tu·rál] *adj.* natural; native; simple, unaffected; *m. & f.* native; *m.* nature, disposition; **al** — without affectation; **del** — from nature, from life.
naturaleza [na·tu·ra·lé·sa] *f.* nature; disposition; nationality; naturalization; — **muerta** still life.
naturalidad [na·tu·ra·li·đáđ] *f.* naturalness; simplicity; birthright.
naturalista [na·tu·ra·lís·ta] *adj.* naturalistic; *m. & f.* naturalist.
naturalización [na·tu·ra·li·sa·sjón] *f.* naturalization.
naturalizar[9] [na·tu·ra·li·sár] *v.* to naturalize; to acclimatize, accustom to a new climate; **-se** to become naturalized.
naufragar[7] [naw·fra·ǥár] *v.* to be shipwrecked; to fail.
naufragio [naw·frá·xjo] *m.* shipwreck; failure, ruin.
náufrago [náw·fra·ǥo] *m.* shipwrecked person.
náusea [náw·se·a] *f.* nausea; **dar -s** to nauseate, sicken; to disgust; **tener -s** to be nauseated, be sick to one's stomach.
nauseabundo [naw·se·a·ƀún·do] *adj.* nauseating, sickening.
nauseado [naw·se·á·đo] *adj.* nauseated, sick to one's stomach.
náutica [náw·ti·ka] *f.* navigation (*science of navigation*).
navaja [na·ƀá·xa] *f.* jackknife, pocketknife; penknife; razor.
navajazo [na·ƀa·xá·so] *m.* stab with a jackknife or razor; stab wound.
naval [na·ƀál] *adj.* naval.
navarro [na·ƀá·rro] *adj.* Navarrese, of or pertaining to Navarre, Spain; *m.* Navarrese.
nave [ná·ƀe] *f.* ship, boat; nave; — **cósmica** spaceship; — **cósmica pilotada** manned space vehicle.
navegable [na·ƀe·ǥá·ƀle] *adj.* navigable.
navegación [na·ƀe·ǥa·sjón] *f.* navigation; sea voyage; — **aérea** aviation.
navegador [na·ƀe·ǥa·đór] **navegante** [na·ƀe·ǥán·te] *m.* navigator; *adj.* navigating.
navegar[7] [na·ƀe·ǥár] *v.* to navigate; to sail.
navidad [na·ƀi·đáđ] *f.* Nativity; Christmas; **-es** Christmas season.
navideño [na·ƀi·đé·ño] *adj.* pertaining to Christmas.
navío [na·ƀí·o] *m.* vessel, ship — **de guerra** warship.
neblina [ne·ƀlí·na] *f.* fog, mist.
nebulosidad [ne·ƀu·lo·si·đáđ] *f.* cloudiness; nebulousness.
necedad [ne·se·đáđ] *f.* foolishness, nonsense.
necesario [ne·se·sá·rjo] *adj.* necessary.
neceser [ne·se·sér] *m.* toilet case; sewing kit.
necesidad [ne·se·si·đáđ] *f.* necessity, need, want.
necesitado [ne·se·si·tá·đo] *adj.* needy; in need, destitute, poor; *p.p. of* **necesitar;** *m.* needy person.
necesitar [ne·se·si·tár] *v.* to need; to necessitate.
necio [né·sjo] *adj.* stupid, ignorant; foolish;

stubborn; *Col.* touchy.
necrología [ne·kro·lo·xí·a] *f.* necrology.
nefando [ne·fán·do] *adj.* abominable; wicked.
nefasto [ne·fás·to] *adj.* ominous; tragic.
nefritis [ne·frí·tis] *f.* nephritis.
negación [ne·ga·sjón] *f.* negation, denial; negative (*negative particle*).
negar [1. 7] [ne·gár] *v. irr.* to deny; to refuse; to prohibit; to disown; **-se** to refuse, decline.
negativa [ne·ga·tí·ba] *f.* negative; denial, refusal.
negativo [ne·ga·tí·bo] *adj.* negative.
negligencia [ne·gli·xén·sja] *f.* negligence, neglect, carelessness.
negligente [ne·gli·xén·te] *adj.* negligent, neglectful, careless.
negociación [ne·go·sja·sjón] *f.* negotiation; business; business house; management; transaction, deal.
negociante [ne·go·sján·te] *m.* merchant, trader, dealer; businessman; *adj.* negotiating.
negociar [ne·go·sjár] *v.* to negotiate; to trade; to transact.
negocio [ne·gó·sjo] *m.* business; business deal; negotiation, transaction; *Ríopl., Carib., C.A., Ven., Andes* store; **hombre de -s** businessman.
negrear [ne·gre·ár] *v.* to become black; to appear black, look black (*in the distance*).
negrero [ne·gré·ro] *m.* slave trader.
negro [né·gro] *adj.* black; dark; sad, gloomy; unfortunate; *m.* black color; negro; *Ríopl., C.A., Ven., Col.* dear, darling; **negra** [né·gra] *f.* negress; *Ríopl., C.A., Ven., Col.* dear, darling.
negrura [ne·grú·ra] *f.* blackness.
negruzco [ne·grús·ko] *adj.* blackish.
nena [né·na] *f.* baby girl; **nene** [né·ne] *m.* baby boy.
neón [ne·ón] *m.* neon.
neófito [ne·ó·fi·to] *m. & f.* neophyte.
neologismo [ne·o·lo·xíz·mo] *m.* neologism.
neoplasma [ne·o·pláz·ma] *m.* neoplasm.
nepotismo [ne·po·tíz·mo] *m.* nepotism.
nervio [nér·bjo] *m.* nerve.
nervioso [ner·bjó·so], **nervoso** [ner·bó·so] *adj.* nervous, sinewy, strong.
nerviosidad [ner·bjo·si·dád], **nervosidad** [ner·bo·si·dád] *f.* nervousness; flexibility; vigor.
nervudo [ner·bú·do] *adj.* sinewy, tough, powerful.
neto [né·to] *adj.* clear, pure; net (*profit, price, etc.*); **netamente** [ne·ta·mén·te] *adv.* clearly, distinctly.
neumático [new·má·ti·ko] *m.* tire; *adj.* pneumatic.
neuralgia [new·rál·xja] *f.* neuralgia.
neurastenia [new·ras·té·nja] *f.* neurasthenia.
neutralidad [new·tra·li·dád] *f.* neutrality.
neutralizar [9] [new·tra·li·sár] *v.* to neutralize, counteract.
neutro [néw·tro] *adj.* neutral; neuter; sexless.
neutrón [new·trón] *m.* neutron.
nevada [ne·bá·da] *f.* snowfall.
nevado [ne·bá·do] *adj.* snowy, white as snow; covered with snow.
nevar [1] [ne·bár] *v. irr.* to snow.
nevasca [ne·bás·ka] *f.* snowstorm.
nevera [ne·bé·ra] *f.* icebox; refrigerator; ice storehouse; ice or ice-cream vendor (*woman*).
nevería [ne·be·rí·a] *f.* ice cream parlor.
ni [ni] *conj. & adv.* not; not even; neither; — **siquiera** not even.
nicotina [ni·ko·tí·na] *f.* nicotine.
nicho [ní·čo] *m.* niche; recess, hollow in a wall.
nidada [ni·dá·da] *f.* nestful of eggs; brood of chicks; hatch, brood.
nido [ní·do] *m.* nest; abode; *Am.* **patearle el — a**

alguien to "upset the applecart", upset someone's plans.
niebla [njé·bla] *f.* fog, mist; confusion.
nieto [njé·to] *m.* grandson, grandchild; **nieta** [njé·ta] *f.* granddaughter.
nieve [njé·be] *f.* snow; *Mex., Riopl., Ven.* sherbet, ice cream; **tiempo de -s** snowy season.
nigua [ní·gwa] *f.* chigger, chigoe, "sand flea," "red bug."
nihilismo [ni·i·líz·mo] *m.* nihilism.
nimio [ní·mjo] *adj.* miserly, stingy; *Am.* very small, insignificant.
ninfa [nín·fa] *f.* nymph.
ningun(o) [nin·gún(o)] *indef. adj. & pron.* no one, none, not ... any; nobody.
niña [ní·ña] *f.* girl; baby girl; *Andes, Riopl., Mex., Carib.* lady, mistress (*title of respect and endearment given to adults*); — **del ojo** pupil of the eye.
niñada [ni·ña·da] *f.* childishness, childish act or remark.
niñera [ni·ñé·ra] *f.* child's nurse.
niñería [ni·ñé·rí·a] *f.* childish act; child's play; trifle; foolishness.
niñez [ni·ñés] *f.* infancy; childhood.
niño [ní·ño] *m.* child, boy; infant; *Am.* master (*title of respect given to a young man by his servants*); *adj.* childlike, childish; very young, immature.
níquel [ní·kel] *m.* nickel.
niquelado [ni·ke·lá·do] *adj.* nickel-plated; *m.* nickel plating; nickel plate.
níspero [nís·pe·ro] *m.* loquat; medlar tree.
nitidez [ni·ti·dés] *f.* clarity, clearness.
nítido [ní·ti·do] *adj.* clear.
nitrato [ni·trá·to] *m.* nitrate; saltpeter.
nítrico [ní·tri·ko] *adj.*
nitro [ní·tro] *m.* niter, saltpeter.
nitrógeno [ni·tró·xe·no] *m.* nitrogen.
nitroglicerina [ni·tro·gli·se·rí·na] *f.* nitroglycerine.
nivel [ni·bél] *m.* level.
nivelar [ni·be·lár] *v.* to level; to grade; to equalize.
no [no] *adv.* no; not; nay; — **bien** as soon as; **un — sé qué** something indefinable; **por sí o por —** just in case, anyway.
noble [nó·ble] *adj.* noble; *m.* nobleman.
nobleza [no·blé·sa] *f.* nobility; nobleness.
noción [no·sjón] *f.* notion, idea.
nocivo [no·sí·bo] *adj.* noxious, harmful, injurious.
nocturno [nok·túr·no] *adj.* nocturnal, night, nightly; *m.* nocturne (*musical or lyrical composition*).
noche [nó·če] *f.* night; darkness; **a la —** tonight; **de —** by (at) night; **por (en) la —** at night, in the evening; **dejar a uno a buenas -s** to leave a person in the lurch.
Nochebuena [no·če·bwé·na] *f.* Christmas Eve.
nocherniego [no·čer·njé·go] *m.* night owl (*person*).
nodriza [no·drí·sa] *f.* child's nurse; wet nurse.
nogal [no·gál] *m.* walnut (*tree and wood*).
nomás [no·más] *Am* = **no más** just; only.
nombradía [nom·bra·dí·a] *f.* renown, fame.
nombramiento [nom·bra·mjén·to] *m.* nomination; appointment; naming.
nombar [nom·brár] *v.* to nominate; to name; to appoint.
nombre [nóm·bre] *m.* name; fame; noun; watchword; — **de pila** (*or* — **de bautismo**) Christian name.
nomenclatura [no·men·kla·tú·ra] *f.* nomenclature.
nomeolvides [no·me·ol·bí·des] *f.* forget-me-not.
nómina [nó·mi·na] *f.* list (*of names*); pay roll.
nominación [no·mi·na·sjón] *f.* nomination;

appointment.

nominal [no·mi·nál] *adj*. nominal; **valor —** small, insignificant value.

nominar [no·mi·nár] *v*. to nominate.

non [non] *adj*. odd, uneven; *m*. odd number, uneven number; **estar** (*or* **quedar**) **de —** to be left alone, be left without a partner or companion.

nonada [no·ná·ḍa] *f*. trifle, mere nothing.

nopal [no·pál] *m*. nopal, prickly pear tree (*species of cactus*).

nordeste [nor·ḍés·te] *adj*. & *m*. northeast.

nórdico [nór·ḍi·ko] *adj*. Nordic.

noria [nó·rja] *f*. draw well; chain pump.

norma [nór·ma] *f*. norm, standard, model.

normal [nor·mál] *adj*. normal; standard; *f*. perpendicular line.

normalizar[9] [nor·ma·li·sár] *v*. to normalize, make normal; to standardize.

noroeste [nor·o·és·te] *adj*. & *m*. northwest.

nortada [nor·tá·ḍa] *f*. strong north wind.

nortazo [nor·tá·so] *m*. *Mex.*, *Ven.* sudden gust of wind, strong north wind.

norte [nór·te] *m*. north; north wind; guide; North Star; direction.

norteamericano [nor·te·a·me·ri·ká·no] *adj*. North American; American (*from or of the United States*).

nortear [nor·te·ár] *v*. to blow from the north; *Sal.* to blow from any direction.

norteño [nor·té·ño] *adj*. northern; *m*. northener.

noruego [no·rwé·ḡo] *adj*. & *m*. Norwegian.

nostalgia [nos·tál·xja] *f*. nostalgia, longing, homesickness.

nostálgico [nos·tál·xi·ko] *adj*. homesick; lonesome; longing.

nota [nó·ta] *f*. note; mark; fame.

notable [no·tá·ḅle] *adj*. notable; noticeable.

notar [no·tár] *v*. to note, observe; to mark; to write down.

notario [no·tá·rjo] *m*. notary.

noticia [no·tí·sja] *f*. notice, information; news; **recibir -s** to receive word, hear (from).

noticiario [no·ti·sjá·rjo] *m*. news sheet, news column, news bulletin or film; **noticiero** [no·ti·sjé·ro] *m.* = **noticiario;** *adj*. news (*used as adj*.); newsy, full of news.

noticioso [no·ti·sjó·so] *adj*. newsy, full of news; well-informed.

notificación [no·ti·fi·ka·sjón] *f*. notification, notifying; notice; summons.

notificar[6] [no·ti·fi·kár] *v*. to notify.

notorio [no·tó·rjo] *adj*. well-known; obvious, evident.

novato [no·ḅá·to] *m*. novice, beginner.

novedad [no·ḅe·ḍáḍ] *f*. novelty; latest news, event, or fashion; change; newness; **hacerle a uno —** to seem strange or new to one; to excite one's curiosity or interest; **sin —** as usual; well.

novel [no·ḅél] *adj*. new, inexperienced.

novela [no·ḅé·la] *f*. novel; fiction.

novelesco [no·ḅe·lés·ko] *adj*. novelistic, fictional; fantastic.

novelista [no·ḅe·lís·ta] *m*. & *f*. novelist.

novena [no·ḅé·na] *f*. novena of the Church.

novia [nó·ḅja] *f*. fiancée; sweetheart; bride.

noviazgo [no·ḅjáz·ḡo] *m*. betrothal, engagement; courtship.

novicio [no·ḅí·sjo] *m*. novice; beginner; apprentice; *adj*. inexperienced.

noviembre [no·ḅjém·bre] *m*. November.

novilla [no·ḅí·ya] *f*. heifer, young cow.

novillada [no·ḅi·yá·ḍa] *f*. herd of young bulls; bullfight (*using young bulls*).

novillero [no·ḅi·yé·ro] *m*. a novice bullfighter; a fighter of 3-year-old bulls.

novillo [no·ḅí·yo] *m*. young bull; steer; **-s** bullfight (*using young bulls*); **hacer -s** to play hooky, cut classes; to play truant.

novio [nó·ḅjo] *m*. fiancé; sweetheart; bridegroom.

nubarrón [nu·ḅa·rrón] *m*. large storm cloud.

nube [nú·ḅe] *f*. cloud; film on the eyeball; **poner por las -s** to praise to the skies.

nublado [nu·ḅlá·ḍo] *m*. storm cloud; imminent danger; *adj*. cloudy.

nublar [nu·ḅlar] *v*. to cloud; to darken, obscure; **-se** to grow cloudy.

nubloso [nu·ḅló·so] *adj*. cloudy; gloomy.

nuboso [nu·ḅó·so] *adj*. *Spain* cloudy.

nuca [nú·ka] *f*. nape.

nuclear [nu·kle·ár] *adj*. nuclear.

núcleo [nú·kle·o] *m*. nucleus; kernel.

nudillo [nu·ḍí·yo] *m*. small knot; knuckle; loop, knitted stitch.

nudo [nú·ḍo] *m*. (*vínculo*) knot; joint; union, bond, tie (*crisis*) crisis, turning point (*of a play*); knot, nautical mile; **— ciego** hard knot.

nudoso [nu·ḍó·so] *adj*. knotty, gnarled, knotted.

nuera [nwé·ra] *f*. daughter-in-law.

nueva [nwé·ḅa] *f*. news.

nuevecito [nwe·ḅe·sí·to] *adj*. nice and new, brandnew.

nuevo [nwé·ḅo] *adj*. new; newly arrived; **de —** again; **¿qué hay de —?** what's new? what's the news?

nuez [nwes] *f*. walnut; nut; **—** (*or* **— de Adán**) Adam's apple; **— moscada** (*or* **— de especia**) nutmeg.

nulidad [nu·li·ḍáḍ] *f*. nullity (*state or quality of being null*); incompetence; nonentity, a nobody.

nulo [nú·lo] *adj*. null, void; useless.

numeral [nu·me·rál] *adj*. & *m*. numeral.

numerar [nu·me·rár] *v*. to number; to calculate; to enumerate.

numérico [nu·mé·ri·ko] *adj*. numerical.

número [nú·me·ro] *m*. number; numeral.

numeroso [nu·me·ró·so] *adj*. numerous.

numismática [nu·miz·má·ti·ka] *f*. numismatics.

nunca [núṇ·ka] *adv*. never; **no ... —** not ... ever; **más que —** more than ever.

nuncio [núṇ·sjo] *m*. herald, messenger; nuncio, Papal envoy.

nupcial [nup·sjál] *adj*. nuptial, relating to marriage or weddings.

nupcias [núp·sjas] *f*. *pl*. nuptials, wedding.

nutria [nú·trja] *f*. otter.

nutrición [nu·tri·sjón] *f*. nutrition; nourishment.

nutrido [nu·trí·ḍo] *adj*. full, abundant; substantial; *p.p. of* **nutrir.**

nutrimento [nu·tri·mén·to], **nutrimiento** [nu·tri·mjén·to] *m*. nutrition; nourishment, food.

nutrir [nu·trír] *v*. nourish, feed.

nutritivo [nu·tri·tí·ḅo] *adj*. nutritious, nourishing.

nylon [náj·lon] *m*. nylon.

NE

Ñ:ñ

ñandú [ñan·dú] *m.* nandu; American ostrich.
ñapa [ñá·pa] *f. Andes, Riopl., Cuba, Ven., Col.* additional amount, something extra; *Am.* **de** — to boot, in addition, besides.
ñato [ñá·to] *adj. C.A., Col., Ven., Andes* flat-nosed, pug-nosed, snub-nosed; *Am.* ugly, deformed; *Am.* insignificant.
ñoñería [ño·ñe·rí·a] *f.* silly remark or action; *Am.* dotage.
ñoño [ñó·ño] *adj.* feeble-minded; silly; *Am.* old, decrepit, feeble; *Col., Ec.* old-fashioned, out of style.
ñu [ñu] *m.* gnu.

O:o

o [o] *conj.* or, either.
oasis [o·á·sis] *m.* oasis.
obedecer[13] [o·ƀe·de·sér] *v. irr.* to obey; — **a cierta causa** to arise from, be due to, a certain cause; **esto obedece a que** ... this is due to the fact that ...
obediencia [o·ƀe·djén·sja] *f.* obedience.
obediente [o·ƀe·djén·te] *adj.* obedient.
obelisco [o·ƀe·lís·ko] *m.* obelisk.
obertura [o·ƀer·tú·ra] *f.* musical overture.
obispado [o·ƀis·pá·ḓo] *m.* bishopric.
obispo [o·ƀís·po] *m.* bishop; *Cubp, Andes* **a cada muerte de** (*or* **por la muerte de un**) — once in a blue moon.
objeción [oƀ·xe·sjón] *f.* objection.
objetar [oƀ·xe·tár] *v.* to object.
objetivo [oƀ·xe·tí·ƀo] *adj.* objective; *m.* objective (*lens of any optical instrument*); objective.
objeto [oƀ·xé·to] *m.* object, purpose, aim; thing.
oblea [o·ƀlé·a] *f.* water.
oblicuo [o·ƀlí·kwo] *adj.* oblique, slanting, bias.
obligación [o·ƀli·ga·sjón] *f.* obligation; duty; bond, security; engagement.
obligar[7] [o·ƀli·gár] *v.* to oblige; to obligate, bind, compel, put under obligation; **-se** to bind oneself, obligate oneself.
obligatorio [o·ƀli·ga·tó·rjo] *adj.* obligatory; compulsory; binding.
oboe [o·ƀó·e] *m.* oboe.
óbolo [ó·ƀo·lo] *m.* mite, small contribution.
obra [ó·ƀra] *f.* (*resultado de acción*) work; act; labor, toil; (*creación artística*) book; building (*under construction*); masterpiece of art; repair; — **de** approximately; **por** — **de** through, by virtue of power of; **hacer mala** — to interfere, hinder; **poner por** — to undertake, begin; to put into practice.
obrar [o·ƀrár] *v.* to work; to act; to operate; to function; to perform; to make; to do; **obra en nuestro poder** we are in receipt of; **la carta que obra en su poder** the letter that is in his possession.
obrero [o·ƀré·ro] *m.* workman, laborer.
obscenidad [oƀ·se·ni·ḓáḓ] *f.* obscenity.
obsceno [oƀ·sé·no] *adj.* obscene.
obscurecer[13] [oƀs·ku·re·sèr] *v. irr.* to obscure. darken; to tarnish; to grow dark; **-se** to get dark or cloudy.
obscuridad [oƀs·ku·ri·ḓáḓ] *f.* obscurity; darkness; dimness.
obscuro [oƀs·kú·ro] *adj.* obscure; dark; dim; **a obscuras** (=**a oscuras**) in the dark; *m.* shade (*in painting*).

obsequiar [oƀ·se·kjár] *v.* to regale, entertain; to court; *Am.* to give, make a present of.
obsequio [oƀ·sé·kjo] *m.* attention, courtesy; gift; **en** — **de** for the sake of, in honor of.
obsequioso [oƀ·se·kjó·so] *adj.* attentive, courteous, obliging; obsequious, servile.
observación [oƀ·ser·ƀa·sjón] *f.* observation; remark.
observador [oƀ·ser·ƀa·ḓór] *m.* observer; *adj.* observing.
observancia [oƀ·ser·ƀán·sja] *f.* observance (*of a law, rule, custom, etc.*).
observante [oƀ·ser·ƀán·te] *adj.* observant (*of a law, custom, or rule*).
observar [oƀ·ser·ƀár] *v.* to observe; to watch; to remark.
observatorio [oƀ·ser·ƀa·tó·rjo] *m.* observatory.
obsesión [oƀ·se·sjón] *f.* obsession.
obsesionar [oƀ·se·sjo·nár] *v.* to obsess.
obstáculo [oƀs·tá·ku·lo] *m.* obstacle.
obstante: [oƀs·tán·te] **no** — notwithstanding; nevertheless.
obstar [oƀs·tár] *v.* to hinder, impede, obstruct.
obstétrica [oƀs·té·tri·ka] *f.* obstetrics.
obstinación [oƀs·ti·na·sjón] *f.* obstinacy. stubbornness.
obstinado [oƀs·ti·ná·ḓo] *adj.* obstinate, stubborn.
obstinarse [oƀs·ti·nár·se] *v.* to persist (in); to be obstinate, stubborn (about).
obstrucción [oƀs·truk·sjón] *f.* obstruction.
obstruir[32] [oƀs·trwir] *v. irr.* to obstruct, block.
obtener[45] [oƀ·te·nér] *v. irr.* to obtain, get; to attain.
obtenible [oƀ·te·ní·ƀle] *adj.* obtainable, available.
obturador [oƀ·tu·ra·ḓór] *m.* choke (*of an automobile*); throttle; plug, stopper; shutter (*of a camera*).
obviar [oƀ·ƀjár] *v.* to obviate, clear away, remove.
obvio [óƀ·ƀjo] *adj.* obvious.
ocasión [o·ka·sjón] *f.* occasion, opportunity; cause; danger, risk; **de** — reduced, bargain; **avisos de** — want "ads" (*advertisements*); *Am.* **esta** — this time.
ocasional [o·ka·sjo·nál] *adj.* occasional.
ocasionar [o·ka·sjo·nár] *v.* to occasion, cause.
ocaso [o·ká·so] *m.* sunset; setting (*of any star or planet*); west; decadence, decline, end.
occidental [ok·si·ḓen·tál] *adj.* occidental, western.
occidente [ok·si·ḓén·te] *m.* occident, west.
océano [o·sé·a·no] *m.* ocean.
oceanografía [o·se·a·no·gra·fí·a] *f.* oceanography.
ocelote [o·se·ló·te] *m.* ocelot.
ocio [ó·sjo] *m.* leisure, idleness; recreation, pastime.
ociosidad [o·sjo·si·ḓáḓ] *f.* idleness, leisure.
ocioso [o·sjó·so] *adj.* idle; useless.
ocre [ó·kre] *m.* ocher.
octava [ok·tá·ƀa] *f.* octave.
octubre [ok·tú·ƀre] *m.* October.
ocular [o·ku·lár] *adj.* ocular; **testigo** — eye witness; *m.* eyepiece, lens (*for the eye in a microscope or telescope*).
oculista [o·ku·lís·ta] *m. & f.* oculist; *Am.* flatterer.
ocultar [o·kul·tár] *v.* to hide, conceal.
oculto [o·kúl·to] *adj.* hidden, concealed; *m. Am.* species of mole (*small animal*).
ocupación [o·ku·pa·sjón] *f.* occupation; employment.
ocupante [o·ku·pán·te] *m. & f.* occupant.
ocupar [o·ku·pár] *v.* to occupy; to employ; **-se en**

(*Am.* **-se de**) to be engaged in; to pay attention to, be interested in.

ocurrencia [o·ku·rrén·sja] *f.* occurrence, event; witticism, joke; bright or funny idea.

ocurrente [o·ku·rrén·te] *adj.* witty, funny, humorous; occurring.

ocurrir [o·ku·rrír] *v.* to occur.

ocurso [o·kúr·so] *m. Ríopl.* petition, application.

ochavo [o·čá·ƀo] *m.* an ancient coin; **no tener —** not to have a red cent.

ochentón [o·čen·tón] *m.* octogenarian.

oda [ó·ɗa] *f.* ode.

odiar [o·ɗjár] *v.* to hate.

odio [ó·ɗjo] *m.* hatred.

odioso [o·ɗjó·so] *adj.* odious, hateful.

odontología [o·ɗon·to·lo·xi·a] *f.* odontology.

odre [ó·ɗre] *m.* wine bag; drunk.

oeste [o·és·te] *m.* west; west wind.

ofender [o·fen·dér] *v.* to offend; to displease; **-se** to get offended; to become angry, take offense.

ofensa [o·fén·sa] *f.* offense.

ofensivo [o·fen·sí·ƀo] *adj.* offensive; obnoxious; attacking; **ofensiva** [o·fen·sí·ƀa] *f.* offensive.

ofensor [o·fen·sór] *m.* offender; *adj.* offending.

oferta [o·fér·ta] *f.* offer; promise.

oficial [o·fi·sjál] *m.* official, officer, skilled workman; *adj.* official.

oficiar [o·fi·sjár] *v.* to officiate, serve, minister, perform the duties of a priest or minister; to communicate officially; **— de** to serve as, act as.

oficina [o·fi·sí·na] *f.* office; shop; **oficinesco** *adj.* clerical, pertaining to an office.

oficio [o·fi·sjo] *m.* trade; function; official communication; religious office (*prayers*).

oficioso [o·fi·sjó·so] *adj.* officious, meddlesome.

ofrecer[13] [o·fre·sér] *v. irr.* to offer; to promise; **-se** to offer, occur, present itself; to offer oneself, volunteer; **¿qué se le ofrece a Vd.?** what do you wish?

ofrecimiento [o·fre·si·mjén·to] *m.* offer; offering.

ofrenda [o·frén·da] *f.* offering, gift.

ofuscamiento [o·fus·ka·mjén·to] *m.* clouded vision, blindness; cloudiness of the mind, bewilderment, mental confusion.

ofuscar[6] [o·fus·kár] *v.* to darken, cast a shadow on; to blind; to cloud; to bewilder, confuse.

ogro [ó·gro] *m.* ogre.

oído [o·í·ɗo] *m.* hearing; ear; **al —** confidentially; **de** (*or* **al**) **—** by ear; **de -s** (*or* **de oídas**) by hearsay or rumor.

oidor [oj·ɗór] *m.* hearer, listener; judge.

oír[36] [o·ír] *v. irr.* to hear; to listen; to understand; **— misa** to attend mass; **— decir que** to hear that; **— hablar de** to hear about.

ojal [o·xál] *m.* buttonhole; hole.

¡ojalá! [o·xa·lá] *interj.* God grant!; I hope so!; **— que** would that. I hope that.

ojazo [o·xá·so] *m.* large eye.

ojeada [o·xe·á·ɗa] *f.* glimpse, quick glance.

ojear [o·xe·ár] *v.* to eye, stare; to bewitch; to beat up, rouse (*wild game*).

ojera [o·xé·ra] *f.* dark circle under the eye; eyecup.

ojeriza [o·xe·rí·sa] *f.* grudge, spite.

ojeroso [o·xe·ró·so] *adj.* with dark circles under the eyes.

ojete [o·xé·te] *m.* eyelet.

ojiva [o·xi·ƀa] *f.* pointed arch; **ojival** [o·xi·ƀál] *adj.* pointed (*arch*); **ventana ojival** window with a pointed arch.

ojo [ó·xo] *m.* (*órgano*) eye; (*agujero*) keyhole; hole; **¡—!** careful! look out!; **a —** by sight, by guess;

a -s vistas visibly, clearly; **— de agua** spring (*of water*); **— de buey** porthole; **mal** (*or* **mal de**) **—** evil eye; *Am.* **hacer —** to cast the evil eye; *Am.*

pelar el — to be alert, keep one's eye peeled; *Mex., Ven.* **poner a uno los -s verdes** to deceive someone; **tener entre -s a** to have ill will toward, have a grudge against.

ojoso [o·xó·so] *adj.* full of holes.

ojota [o·xó·ta] *f. Andes, Ch., Ríopl.* leather sandal.

ola [ó·la] *f.* wave.

¡ole! [ó·le] *interj.* bravo! good!

oleada [o·le·á·ɗa] *f.* big wave; swell; surge; abundant yield of oil.

oleaje [o·le·á·xe] **olaje** [o·lá·xe] *m.* swell, surge, succession of waves.

oleo [ó·le·o] *m.* oil, holy oil; **pintura al —** oil painting.

oleoducto [o·le·o·ɗúk·to] *m.* pipe line.

oleoso [o·lo·ó·so] *adj.* oily.

oler[37] [o·lér] *v. irr.* to smell; to scent; **— a** to smack of; to smell like; *Am.* **olérselas** to suspect it, "smell a rat".

olfatear [ol·fa·te·ár] *v.* to scent, sniff, smell.

olfateo [ol·fa·te·ó] *m.* sniff, sniffing.

olfato [ol·fá·to] *m.* sense of smell.

olfatorio [ol·fa·tó·rjo] *adj.* olfactory.

oligarquía [o·li·gar·ki·a] *f.* oligarchy.

olimpiada [o·lim·pjá·ɗa] *f.* Olympiad; Olympic games.

olímpico [o·lím·pi·ko] *adj.* Olympian.

oliva [o·li·ƀa] *f.* olive; olive tree; **olivar** *m.* olive grove; **olivo** *m.* olive tree.

olmo [ól·mo] *m.* elm.

olor [o·lór] *m.* (*en el olfato*) smell, odor, fragrance; (*fama*) smack, trace, suspicion; *Am.* spice; **olorcillo** [o·lor·sí·yo] *m.* faint odor.

oloroso [o·lo·ró·so] *adj.* fragrant.

olote [o·ló·te] *m. Mex., C.A.* cob, corncob.

olvidadizo [ol·ƀi·ɗa·ɗi·so] *adj.* forgetful.

olvidar [ol·ƀi·ɗár] *v.* to forget; to neglect; **-se de** to forget; **olvidársele a uno algo** to forget something.

olvido [ol·ƀi·ɗo] *m.* forgetfulness; oblivion; neglect; **echar al —** to cast into oblivion; to forget on purpose.

olla [ó·ya] *f.* pot, kettle; olla (*vegetable and meat stew*); **— podrida** Spanish stew of mixed vegetables and meat.

ombligo [om·blí·go] *m.* navel; middle center.

ombú [om·bú] *m.* umbra tree.

omisión [o·mi·sjón] *f.* omission; oversight, neglect.

omiso [o·mí·so] *adj.* careless, neglectful; *N. Arg.* guilty; **hacer caso —** to omit.

omitir [o·mi·tír] *v.* to omit; to overlook.

ómnibus [óm·ni·ƀus] *m.* omnibus, bus.

omnipotente [om·ni·po·tén·te] *adj.* omnipotent, almighty.

onda [ón·da] *f.* wave; ripple; sound wave; scallop.

ondear [on·de·ár] *v.* to wave; to waver; to ripple; to sway, swing.

ondulación [on·du·la·sjón] *f.* undulation, waving motion; wave; **— permanente** permanent wave.

ondulado [on·du·lá·ɗo] *p.p. & adj.* wavy; scalloped (*edge*); **— permanente** permanent wave.

ondulante [on·du·lán·te] *adj.* wavy, waving.

ondular [on·du·lár] *v.* to undulate, wave.

oneroso [o·ne·ró·so] *adj.* onerous.

onomástico [o·no·más·ti·ko] *adj.* onomastic; *m.* saint's day.

onomatopeya [o·no·ma·to·pé·ya] *f.* onomatopoeia.

ontología [on·to·lo·xi·a] *f.* ontology.

onza [ón·sa] *f.* ounce; ounce, wildcat; *Ríopl., Bol.* small tiger.

opacidad [o·pa·si·dád] *f.* opacity; sadness.

opaco [o·pá·ko] *adj.* opaque, dim, dull.

ópalo [ó·pa·lo] *m.* opal.

ópera [ó·pe·ra] *f.* opera.

operación [o·pe·ra·sjón] *f.* operation; business transaction.

operador [o·pe·ra·dór] *m.* operator, surgeon.

operante [o·pe·rán·te] *adj.* operant (*behavior*).

operar [o·pe·rár] *v.* to operate; to take effect, work; to speculate (*in business*); to manipulate, handle.

operario [o·pe·rá·rjo] *m.* operator, workman, worker.

opereta [o·pe·ré·ta] *f.* operetta.

opinar [o·pi·nár] *v.* to express an opinion; to think; to judge; to argue.

opinión [o·pi·njón] *f.* opinion; reputation.

opio [ó·pjo] *m.* opium.

oponer[40] [o·po·nér] *v. irr.* to oppose; **-se** to disapprove; **-se a** to oppose, be against.

oporto [o·pór·to] *m.* port wine.

oportunidad [o·por·tu·ni·dád] *f.* opportunity.

oportuno [o·por·tú·no] *adj.* opportune; convenient, timely.

oposición [o·po·si·sjón] *f.* opposition; competition; **-es** competitive examinations.

opositor [o·po·si·tór] *m.* opponent; competitor.

opresión [o·pre·sjón] *f.* oppression.

opresivo [o·pre·sí·bo] *adj.* oppressive.

opresor [o·pre·sór] *m.* oppressor.

oprimir [o·pri·mír] *v.* to oppress; to crush; to press down.

oprobio [o·pró·bjo] *m.* infamy; insult; shame; dishonor.

optar [op·tár] *v.* to choose, select; **— por** to decide upon; to choose.

óptica [óp·ti·ka] *f.* optics.

óptico [óp·ti·ko] *adj.* optical, optic; *m.* optician.

optimismo [op·ti·míz·mo] *m.* optimism; **optimista** *m. & f.* optimist; *adj.* optimistic.

óptimo [óp·ti·mo] *adj.* very good, very best.

opuesto [o·pwés·to] *p.p.* of **oponer** opposed; *adj.* opposite; contrary.

opulencia [o·pu·lén·sja] *f.* opulence, abundance, wealth.

opulento [o·pu·lén·to] *adj.* opulant, wealthy.

oquedad [o·ke·dád] *f.* cavity, hollow; chasm.

ora [ó·ra] *conj.* now, then; whether; either.

oración [o·ra·sjón] *f.* oration; prayer; sentence.

oráculo [o·rá·ku·lo] *m.* oracle.

orador [o·ra·dór] *m.* orator, speaker.

oral [o·rál] *adj.* oral.

orar [o·rár] *v.* to pray.

oratoria [o·ra·tó·rjo] *f.* oratory, eloquence.

oratorio [o·ra·tó·rjo] *m.* oratory, private chapel; oratorio (*a religious musical composition*); *adj.* oratorical, pertaining to oratory.

orbe [ór·be] *m.* orb, sphere, globe; the earth; world, universe.

órbita [ór·bi·ta] *f.* orbit; eye socket.

orden [ór·den] *m.* (*colocación*) order; succession, series; class, group; relation; proportion; *f.* (*mando*) order, command; (*sociedad*) honorary or religious order; *m. & f.* sacrament of ordination; **a sus órdenes** at your service.

ordenado [or·de·ná·do] *p.p. & adj.* ordered; ordained; orderly; neat.

ordenanza [or·de·nán·sa] *f.* ordinance, decree, law; command, order; *m.* orderly (*military*).

ordenar [or·de·nár] *v.* to arrange, put in order; to order, command; to ordain; **-se** to become ordained.

ordeño [or·dé·ña] *m.* milking.

ordeñar [or·de·ñár] *v.* to milk.

ordinariez [or·di·na·rjés] *f.* commonness, lack of manners.

ordinario [or·di·ná·rjo] *adj.* ordinary; usual; common, coarse; *m.* ordinary (*a bishop or judge*); ordinary mail; daily household expense; **de —** usually, ordinarily.

orear [o·re·ár] *v.* to air; **-se** to be exposed to the air; to dry in the air.

orégano [o·ré·ga·no] *m.* wild marjoram, oregano.

oreja [o·ré·xa] *f.* ear; hearing; loop; small flap; *Am.* handle (*shaped like an ear*); **orejano** [o·re·xá·no] *adj.* unbranded (*cattle*); *Ven., Col.* cautious; *m. Cuba* aloof, unsociable person; **orejera** [o·re·xé·ra] *f.* ear muff, ear flap; **orejón** [o·re·xón] *m.* pull by the ear; *Col.* rancher or inhabitant of the *sabana*; *adj. Col.* long-eared, long-horned; *Col.* unbranded (*cattle*); *Col.* coarse, crude, uncouth.

orfandad [or·fan·dád] *f.* orphanage (*state of being an orphan*).

orfanato [or·fa·ná·to] *m.* orphanage, orphan asylum.

orfanatorio [or·fa·na·tó·rjo] *Am.* = **orfanato**.

orfebre [or·fé·bre] *m.* goldsmith; silversmith.

orfebrería [or·fe·bre·rí·a] *f.* silver or gold work.

orfeón [or·fe·ón] *m.* glee club, choir.

orgánico [or·gá·ni·ko] *adj.* organic.

organillo [or·ga·ní·yo] *m.* hand organ, hurdy-gurdy.

organismo [or·ga·níz·mo] *m.* organism.

organización [or·ga·ni·sa·sjón] *f.* organization.

organizador [or·ga·ni·sa·dór] *m.* organizer.

organizer[9] [or·ga·ni·sár] *v.* to organize; to arrange.

órgano [ór·ga·no] *m.* organ; **organillo** [or·ga·ní·yo] *m.* hand organ.

orgía [or·xí·a] *f.* orgy, wild revel.

orgullo [or·gú·yo] *m.* pride; haughtiness, arrogance.

orgulloso [or·gu·yó·so] *adj.* proud; haughty, arrogant.

oriental [o·rjen·tál] *adj.* oriental, eastern.

orientar [o·rjen·tár] *v.* to orientate, orient; **-se** to orient oneself, find one's bearings.

oriente [o·rjén·te] *m.* orient, east; east wind; source, origin.

orificación [o·ri·fi·ka·sjón] *f.* gold filling.

orificio [o·ri·fi·sjo] *m.* orifice, small hole, aperture, outlet.

origen [o·rí·xen] *m.* origin; source.

original [o·ri·xi·nál] *adj.* original; strange, quaint; *m.* original; manuscript, copy; queer person; **originalidad** [o·ri·xi·na·li·dád] *f.* originality.

originar [o·ri·xi·nár] *v.* to originate, cause to be; **-se** originate, arise.

orilla [o·rí·ya] *f.* shore, bank; beach; edge, border; **-s** *Am.* outskirts, environs.

orillar [o·ri·yár] *v.* border, trim the edge of; to skirt, go along the edge of; to reach the edge or shore.

orín [o·rín] *m.* rust; **orines** *m. pl.* urine.

orina [o·rí·na] *f.* urine.

orinar [o·ri·nár] *v.* to urinate.

oriol [o·rjól] *m.* oriole.

oriundo [o·rjún·do] *adj.* native; **ser — de** to hail from, come from.

orla [ór·la] *f.* border; trimming, fringe.

orlar [or·lár] *v.* to border, edge, trim with a border or fringe.

orlón [or·lón] *m.* orlon.
ornado [or·ná·do] *adj.* ornate; *p.p.* adorned, ornamented.
ornamentar [or·na·men·tár] *v.* to ornament, adorn.
ornamento [or·na·mén·to] *m.* ornament; decoration; **-s** sacred vestments.
ornar [or·nár] *v.* to adorn.
oro [ó·ro] *m.* gold; gold ornament; **-s** "gold coins" (*Spanish card suit*).
orondo [o·rón·do] *adj.* self-satisfied, puffed up, vain; *Am.* serene, calm.
oropel [o·ro·pél] *m.* tinsel.
orquesta [or·kés·ta] *f.* orchestra.
orquestar [or·kes·tár] *v.* to orchestrate.
orquídea [or·kí·de·a] *f.* orchid.
ortiga [or·tí·ga] *f.* nettle.
ortodoxo [or·to·dók·so] *adj.* orthodox.
ortografía [or·to·gra·fí·a] *f.* orthography, spelling.
ortográfico [or·to·grá·fi·ko] *adj.* orthographic (*pertaining to orthography or spelling*).
oruga [o·rú·ga] *f.* caterpillar.
orzuelo [or·swé·lo] *m.* sty (*on the eyelid*).
osadía [o·sa·dí·a] *f.* boldness, daring.
osado [o·sá·do] *adj.* bold, daring.
osamenta [o·sa·mén·ta] *f.* bones; skeleton.
osar [o·sár] *v.* to dare, venture.
oscilación [o·si·la·sjón] *f.* oscillation, sway; fluctuation, wavering.
oscilar [o·si·lár] *v.* to oscillate, swing, sway; to waver.
oscilatorio [o·si·la·tó·rjo] *adj.* oscillatory.
oscurecer [os·ku·re·sér] = **obscurecer**.
oscuridad [os·ku·ri·dád] = **obscuridad**.
oscuro [os·kú·ro] = **obscuro**.
oso [ó·so] *m.* bear; — **blanco** polar bear; — **hormiguero** anteater; — **marino** seal.
ostentación [os·ten·ta·sjón] *f.* ostentation, show. display.
ostentar [os·ten·tár] *v.* to display, show; to show off; to boast.
ostentoso [os·ten·tó·so] *adj.* ostentatious, showy.
ostión [os·tjón] *m.* large oyster.
ostra [ós·tra] *f.* oyster.
otate [o·tá·te] *m. Mex.*, *C.A.* species of bamboo; *Mex.*, *C.A.* bamboo stick or cane.
otero [o·té·ro] *m.* hillock, small hill, knoll.
otoñal [o·to·ñál] *adj.* autumnal, of autumn.
otoño [o·tó·ño] *m.* autumn, fall.
otorgar [o·tor·gár] *v.* to grant; to promise; to consent to.
otro [ó·tro] *adj.* another; **otra vez** again; *Am.* **como dijo el** — as someone said.
otrora [o·tró·ra] *adv.* formerly, in other times.
ovación [o·ba·sjón] *f.* ovation, enthusiastic applause.
oval [o·bál], **ovalado** [o·ba·lá·do] *adj.* oval; **óvalo** [ó·ba·lo] *m.* oval.
oveja [o·bé·xa] *f.* sheep.
ovejero [o·be·xé·ro] *m.* shepherd; sheep dog.
ovejuno [o·be·xú·no] *adj.* sheep, pertaining or relating to sheep.
overo [o·bé·ro] *adj.* peach-colored (*applied to horses and cattle*); *Ríopl.* mottled, spotted; *Ríopl.* multicolored; *Ríopl.* **ponerle a uno** — to insult someone.
overol [o·be·ról], **overoles** [o·be·ró·les] *m. Ch.*, *Col.* overalls.
ovillar [o·bi·yár] *v.* to ball, wind or form into a ball; **-se** to curl up into a ball.
ovillo [o·bí·yo] *m.* ball of yarn or thread; tangle; **hacerse uno un** — to curl up into a ball; to

become entangled, confused.
oxidado [ok·si·dá·do] *p.p.* rusted; *adj.* rusty.
oxidar [ok·si·dár] *v.* to oxidize; to rust; **-se** to become oxidized; to rust.
óxido [ók·si·do] *m.* oxide.
oxígeno [ok·sí·xeno] *m.* oxygen.
oyente [o·yén·te] *m. & f.* listener, auditor, hearer; *adj.* listening.
ozono [o·só·no] *m.* ozone.

P·p

pabellón [pa·be·yón] *m.* pavilion; canopy; banner, flag; shelter, covering; external ear.
pabilo [pa·bí·lo] *m.* wick; snuff (*of a candle*).
pacer[13] [pa·sér] *v. irr.* to pasture; to graze.
paciencia [pa·sjén·sja] *f.* patience.
paciente [pa·sjén·te] *adj.* patient; *m. & f.* patient.
pacienzudo [pa·sjen·sú·do] *adj.* patient, long-suffering.
pacificar[6] [pa·si·fi·kár] *v.* to pacify; to appease.
pacífico [pa·sí·fi·ko] *adj.* pacific, peaceful, calm.
pacifismo [pa·si·fíz·mo] *m.* pacifism.
pacto [pák·to] *m.* pact, agreement.
padecer[13] [pa·de·sér] *v. irr.* to suffer.
padecimiento [pa·de·si·mjén·to] *m.* suffering.
padrastro [pa·drás·tro] *m.* stepfather; hangnail.
padre [pá·dre] *m.* father; **-s** parents; ancestors; *adj. Am.* very great, stupendous.
padrenuestro [pa·dre·nwés·tro] *m.* paternoster, the Lord's Prayer.
padrino [pa·drí·no] *m.* godfather; sponsor, patron; second in a duel; best man (*at a wedding*).
paella [pa·é·ya] *f.* a popular rice dish with chicken, vegetables, etc.
paga [pá·ga] *f.* payment; pay, salary.
pagadero [pa·ga·dé·ro] *adj.* payable.
pagado [pa·gá·do] *p.p. & adj.* paid; self-satisfied, conceited; — **de sí mismo** pleased with oneself.
pagador [pa·ga·dór] *m.* payer; paymaster; paying teller (*in a bank*).
paganismo [pa·ga·níz·mo] *m.* paganism, heathenism.
pagano [pa·gá·no] *adj.* pagan; *m.* pagan; payer; dupe, sucker.
pagar[7] [pa·gár] *v.* to pay; to pay for; to requite, return (*love*); **-se de** to be proud of; to boast of; to be pleased with; *Ríopl.* **-se de palabras** to let oneself be tricked; *Am.* — **a nueve** to pay in excess.
pagaré [pa·ga·ré] *m.* promissory note; I.O.U.
página [pá·xi·na] *f.* page.
paginar [pa·xi·nár] *v.* to page.
pago [pá·go] *m.* (*premio*) payment; prize, reward; (*distrito*) country district; *Ríopl.* one's native farm land or district; *adj.* paid; *Am.* **estar -s** to be quits.
paila [páj·la] *f.* large pan; *C.A.* saucer.
país [pa·ís] *m.* nation, country; region.
paisaje [paj·sá·xe] *m.* landscape.
paisanaje [paj·sa·ná·xe] *m.* peasantry, country people; civilians; *Andes* gang of farm laborers.
paisano [paj·sá·no] *m.* countryman; peasant; fellow countryman; civilian.
paja [pá·xa] *f.* straw; chaff; rubbish; *Andes* grass for pasture; **echar -s** to draw lots; **por quítame allá esas -s** for an insignificant reason or pretext; **en un quítame allá esas -s** in a jiffy, in a second; **a**

humo de -s thoughtlessly; lightly; **no lo hizo a humo de -s** he did not do it without a special reason or intention.

pajar [pa·xár] *m.* straw loft, barn.

pájaro [pá·xa·ro] *m.* bird; shrewd, cautious person; *Ch.* absent-minded person; *Ch., Riopl.* person of suspicious conduct; — **carpintero** woodpecker; — **mosca** humming bird.

paje [pá·xe] *m.* page, valet, attendant.

pajizo [pa·xí· so] *adj.* made of straw; covered with straw; straw colored.

pajonal [pa·xo·nál] *m.* plain or field of tall coarse grass.

pala [pá·la] *f.* shovel; trowel; scoop; paddle; blade of an oar; racket; upper (*of a shoe*); cunning, craftiness; **meter la** — to deceive with cunning; *Am.* **hacer la** — to deceive with cunning; to stall, pretend to work; to flatter; **palada** [pa·lá·ɖa] *f.* scoop, shovelful; stroke of an oar.

palabra [pa·lá·ꞵra] *f.* word; promise; **de** — by word of mouth; **cuatro -s** a few words; **empeñar la** — to promise, pledge; **tener la** — to have the floor; *Am.* **¡—!** I mean it, it is true!

palabrero [pa·la·ꞵré·ro] *adj.* wordy, talkative.

palabrita [pa·la·ꞵrí·ta] *f.* a little word, a few words; a word of advice.

palacio [pa·lá·sjo] *m.* palace; **palaciego** [pa·la·sjé·ɡo] *m.* courtier; *adj.* relating to a palace or court; court (*used as an adj.*).

paladar [pa·la·ɖár] *m.* palate; taste, relish.

paladear [pa·la·ɖe·ár] *v.* to relish, taste with relish.

paladín [pa·la·ɖín] *m.* knight; champion, defender.

paladio [pa·lá·ɖjo] *m.* palladium.

palanca [pa·láŋ·ka] *f.* lever; crowbar; bar used for carrying a load; influence, a "pipe line".

palangana [pa·laŋ·gá·na] *f.* washbowl, basin; *S.A.* platter; *Ch.* large wooden bowl; *m. Andes* bluffer, charlatan.

palatal [pa·la·tál] *adj.* palatal.

palco [pál·ko] *m.* theater box; — **escénico** stage.

palenque [pa·léŋ·ke] *m.* palisade, fence; enclosure; *Riopl.* hitching post or plank.

paleta [pa·lé·ta] *f.* small flat shovel; mason's trowel; shoulder blade; blade (*of a rudder, of a ventilating fan*); paddle (*of a paddle wheel*); painter's palette; *Am.* candy, sweetmeat or ice cream attached to a stick; *Am.* a wooden paddle to stir with, or for beating clothes; **en dos -s** in a jiffy, in a second; **paletilla** [pa·le·tí·ya] *f.* shoulder blade.

palidecer[13] [pa·li·ɖe·sér] *v. irr.* to turn pale.

palidez [pa·li·ɖés] *f.* pallor, paleness.

pálido [pá·li·ɖo] *adj.* pallid, pale.

palillo [pa·lí·yo] *m.* small stick; toothpick; **tocar todos los -s** (*Ch.* **menear uno los -s**) to try every possible means.

paliza [pa·lí·sa] *f.* beating (*with a stick*), thrashing.

palizada [pa·li·sá·ɖa] *f.* palisade; stockade.

palma [pál·ma] *f.* palm tree; palm leaf; palm of the hand; **batir -s** to clap, applaud; **llevarse la** — to triumph, win, carry off the honors; to be the best.

palmada [pal·má·ɖa] *f.* slap; clap.

palmario [pal·má·rjo] *adj.* clear, evident.

palmatoria [pal·ma·tó·rja] *f.* small candlestick with handle.

palmear [pal·me·ár] *v.* to clap, applaud; *Am.* to pat, clap on the back; *Riopl.* to flatter.

palmera [pal·mé·ra] *f.* palm tree.

palmo [pál·mo] *m.* span (*about 9 inches*); — **a** — slowly, foot by foot.

palmotear [pal·mo·te·ár] *v.* to clap, applaud.

palo [pá·lo] *m.* stick; pole; log; mast; wood; blow with a stick; suit (*in a deck of cards*); *Am.* tree; *Riopl.* reprimand, reproof; *P.R., Ven.* large swallow of liquor; — **del Brasil** Brazil wood; *Ven.* — **a pique** rail fence, barbed wire fence; *Mex., C.A.* **a medio** — half-done; half-drunk; *Am.* **a** — **entero** drunk.

paloma [pa·ló·ma] *f.* dove, pigeon; pleasant, mild person; **-s** whitecaps.

palomar [pa·lo·már] *m.* dovecot (*shelter for doves or pigeons*).

palomilla [pa·lo·mí·ya] *f.* little dove; moth; small butterfly; **-s** small whitecaps.

palomita [pa·lo·mí·ta] *f.* little dove; **-s** *Am.* popcorn.

palpable [pal·pá·ꞵle] *adj.* palpable (*that can be felt or touched*); clear, obvious, evident.

palpar [pal·pár] *v.* to feel; to touch; to grope.

palpitación [pal·pi·ta·sjón] *f.* palpitation; beat, throb.

palpitante [pal·pi·tán·te] *adj.* palpitating; throbbing, trembling; exciting; **la cuestión** — the burning question.

palpitar [pal·pi·tár] *v.* to palpitate; to throb, beat.

palta [pál·ta] *f. Col., Ven., Andes, Riopl., Ch.* avocado, alligator pear; **palto** [pál·to] *m. Col., Ven., Andes, Riopl., Ch.* avocado tree. See **aguacate.**

palúdico [pa·lú·ɖi·ko] *adj.* marshy; **fiebre palúdica** malarial, or marsh fever; malaria; **paludismo** *m.* malaria.

pampa [pám·pa] *f. Am.* (*vast treeless plain of South America*); *Am.* prairie; *Ch.* drill field (*military*); *m. & f.* pampa Indian of Argentina; *m. Am.* language of the pampa Indian; *adj. Am.* pertaining to the pampa Indian *Riopl.* **caballo** — horse with head and body of different colors; *Riopl.* **trato** — dubious or dishonest deal; *Am.* **estar a la** — to be in the open; *Riopl.* **tener todo a la** — to be ragged or to be indecently exposed; *Ch.* **quedar en** — to be left without clothes; to be left in the lurch.

pampeano [pam·pe·á·no] *adj. Riopl.* of, or pertaining to, the pampa.

pampero [pam·pé·ro] *adj. Riopl.* of, or pertaining to, the pampas; *m. Riopl.* inhabitant of the pampas; *Riopl.* violent wind of the pampa.

pan [pan] *m.* bread; loaf of bread; wheat; **-es** fields of grain; breadstuffs; *Am.* **echar -es** to brag, boast.

pana [pá·na] *f.* corduroy.

panadería [pa·na·ɖe·rí·a] *f.* bakery.

panadero [pa·na·ɖé·ro] *m.* baker; *Ch.* flatterer.

panal [pa·nál] *m.* honeycomb; sweetmeat (*made of sugar, egg white, and lemon*).

panamericano [pa·na·me·ri·ká·no] *adj.* Pan-American.

pandearse [pan·de·ár·se] *v.* to bulge, warp; to sag.

pandeo [pan·dé·o] *m.* sag; bulge.

pandilla [pan·dí·ya] *f.* gang, band.

panela [pa·né·la] *f. Col., C.A.* unrefined sugar.

panfleto [pan·flé·to] *m. Am.* pamphlet.

pánico [pá·ni·ko] *m.* panic; *adj.* panic, panicky.

panne [pán·ne] *f.* accident, car trouble.

panocha [pa·no·ča] *f.* ear of corn; *Mex.* Mexican raw sugar; *Col., C.R.* a kind of tamale.

panqué [paŋ·ké] *m. Col., C.A., Mex.* small cake, cup cake; *Am.* pancake.

pantalón [pan·ta·lón] *m.* trousers; pants; **un par de -es** a pair of trousers.

pantalla [pan·tá·ya] *f.* light shade; screen; fireplace screen; motion-picture screen; *C.R.* fan, palm leaf fan; *P.R.* earring.

pantano [pan·tá·no] *m.* swamp; dam; difficulty.

pantanoso [pan·ta·nó·so] *adj.* swampy, marshy; muddy.

panteón [pan·te·ón] *m.* cemetery.

pantera [pan·té·ra] *f.* panther.

pantorrilla [pan·to·rrí·ya] *f.* calf (*of the leg*).

pantufla [pan·tú·fla] *f.* bedrom slipper.

panza [pán·sa] *f.* paunch, belly.

panzón [pan·són], **panzudo** [pan·sú·ḍo] *adj.* big-bellied.

pañal [pa·ñál] *m.* diaper; **estar en -es** to be in one's infancy; to have little or no knowledge of a thing.

paño [pá·ño] *m.* cloth (*any cloth, especially woolen*); blotch or spot on the skin; film on the eyeball; *Mex., Cuba* parcel of tillable land; *Mex.* kerchief; shawl; **— de manos** towel; **— de mesa** tablecloth; **al —** off-stage; **-s** clothes, garments; **-s menores** underwear; **pañero** *m.* clothier.

pañolón [pa·ño·lón] *m.* scarf, large kerchief; shawl.

pañuelo [pa·ñwé·lo] *m.* handkerchief.

papa [pá·pa] *m.* Pope; *f.* potato; fib, lie; *Am.* snap, easy job; **-s** pap (*soft food for babies*); soup; *Ríopl., Ch.* **cosa —** something good to eat; excellent thing; **echar -s** to fib, lie; *Am.* **importarle a uno una —** not to matter to one a bit; *Am.* **no saber ni —** not to a know a thing; to be completely ignorant.

papá [pa·pá] *m.* papa; *Mex., C.A., Andes* **— grande** grandfather.

papagayo [pa·pa·gá·yo] *m.* parrot; talker, chatterer.

papal [pa·pál] *adj.* papal.

papalote [pa·pa·ló·te], **papelote** [pa·pe·ló·te] *m. Carib., Mex.* kite.

papamoscos [pa·pa·mós·kos] *m.* flycatcher (*a bird*); simpleton, half-wit, dunce.

papanatas [pa·pa·ná·tas] *m.* simpleton, fool, dunce.

paparrucha [pa·pa·rrú·ča] *f.* fib, lie; **paparruchero** [pa·pa·rru·čé·ro] *m.* fibber.

papaya [pa·pá·ya] *f.* papaya.

papel [pa·pél] *m.* (*hoja*) paper; sheet of paper; document; (*parte dramática*) role; **— de estraza** brown wrapping paper; **— de lija** sandpaper; **— de seda** tissue paper; **— moneda** paper money; **— secante** blotting paper; **hacer el — de** to play the role of; **hacer buen** (*or* **mal**) **—** to cut a good (*or* bad) figure.

papelera [pa·pe·lé·ra] *f.* folder, file, case or device for keeping papers; *Am.* wastepaper basket; **papelero** [pa·pe·lé·ro] *m.* paper manufacturer; *adj.* pertaining to paper; vain, ostentatious.

papelería [pa·pe·le·rí·a] *f.* stationery store; stationery; lot of papers.

papeleta [pa·pe·lé·ta] *f.* card, file card, slip of paper.

papelucho [pa·pe·lú·čo] *m.* worthless piece of paper.

papera [pa·pé·ra] *f.* goiter; **-s** mumps.

paquete [pa·ké·te] *m.* package; bundle; dandy; packet boat (*mail boat*); *adj. Am.* dolled up, dressed up; *Ríopl., Col.* important, pompous; *Ríopl., Col.* insincere.

par [par] *adj.* even; *m.* pair, couple; peer; **a la —** at par; jointly; at the same time; **al — de** on a par with; **bajo —** below par; **sin —** peerless, without an equal, having no equal; **sobre —** above par; **de — en —** wide-open.

para [pá·ra] *prep.* for; to; toward; in order to; **¿— qué?** what for; **— que** so that; **— siempre** forever; **— mis adentros** to myself; **sin qué ni — qué** without rhyme or reason; *m. Ríopl.* Paraguayan tobacco; *Ríopl.* Paraguayan (*used as nickname*).

parabién [pa·ra·ḅjén] *m.* congratulations; **dar el —** to congratulate.

parabrisas [pa·ra·ḅrí·sas] *m.* windshield.

paracaídas [pa·ra·ka·i·ḍas] *m.* parachute; **paracaidista** [pa·ra·kaj·ḍís·ta] *m. & f.* parachutist.

parachoques [pa·ra·čó·kes] *m.* bumper.

parada [pa·rá·ḍa] *f.* stop; stopping place; bet, stake; military review; *P.R.* parade; *Ríopl.* boastfulness; *Ríopl.* **tener mucha —** to dress very well.

paradero [pa·ra·ḍé·ro] *m.* stopping place; whereabouts; end.

parado [pa·rá·ḍo] *p.p. & adj.* stopped; unoccupied, unemployed; fixed, motionless; *Am.* standing, erect, straight up; *Ch., P.R.* stiff, proud; *Ríopl.* cold, unenthusiastic; *P.R., Ch., Andes* **caer uno —** to land on one's feet; to be lucky; *Am.* **estar bien —** to be well-fixed, well-established; to be lucky; *m. Am.* air, appearance.

paradoja [pa·ra·ḍó·xa] *f.* paradox.

paradójico [pa·ra·ḍó·xi·ko] *adj.* paradoxical.

parafina [pa·ra·fí·na] *f.* paraffin.

paráfrasis [pa·rá·fra·sis] *f.* paraphrase.

paraguas [pa·rá·ǵwas] *m.* umbrella; **paragüero** [pa·ra·ǵwé·ro] *m.* umbrella stand; umbrella maker or seller.

paraguayo [pa·ra·ǵwá·yo] *adj. & m.* Paraguayan.

paraíso [pa·ra·í·so] *m.* paradise, heaven; upper gallery (*in a theater*).

paraje [pa·rá·xe] *m.* place; spot; situation.

paralelo [pa·ra·lé·lo] *adj.* parallel; similar; *m.* parallel; similarity; **paralela** [pa·ra·lé·la] *f.* parallel line; **paralelismo** [pa·ra·le·líz·mo] *m.* parallelism.

parálisis [pa·rá·li·sis] *f.* paralysis.

paralítico [pa·ra·lí·ti·ko] *adj.* paralytic.

paralizar[9] [pa·ra·li·sár] *v.* to paralyze; to stop.

parámetro [pa·rá·me·tro] *m.* parameter.

páramo [pá·ra·mo] *m.* high, bleak plain; cold region; *Andes* blizzard or a cold drizzle.

parangón [pa·raŋ·gón] *m.* comparison.

parangonar [pa·raŋ·go·nár] *v.* to compare.

paraninfo [pa·ra·nín·fo] *m.* assembly hall, lecture hall, auditorium.

parapeto [pa·ra·pé·to] *m.* parapet.

parar [pa·rár] *v.* to stop; to end, end up, come to an end; to parry (*in fencing*); to set up (*type*); *Am.* to stand, place in upright position; **— atención** to notice; **— mientes en** to observe; notice; *Ríopl.* **— las orejas** to prick up one's ears; to pay close attention; **-se** to stop; *Am.* to stand up, get up.

pararrayos [pa·ra·rrá·yos] *m.* lightning rod.

parásito [pa·rá·si·to] *m.* parasite; *adj.* parasitic.

parasol [pa·ra·sól] *m.* parasol.

parcela [par·sé·la] *f.* parcel of land; particle, small piece.

parcial [par·sjál] *adj.* partial; *m.* follower, partisan; **parcialidad** [par·sja·li·ḍáḍ] *f.* partiality; faction, party.

parche [pár·če] *m.* mending patch; sticking plaster; medicated plaster; drum.

pardal [par·ḍál] *m.* sparrow; linnet; sly fellow.

pardear [par·ḍe·ár] *v.* to grow dusky; to appear brownish-grey.
pardo [pár·ḍo] *adj.* dark-grey; brown; dark; cloudy; *m.* leopard; *Carib., Ríopl.* mulatto; **pardusco** [par·ḍús·ko] *adj.* greyish; brownish.
parear [pa·re·ár] *v.* to pair, couple, match, mate.
parecer¹³ [pa·re·sér] *v. irr.* to seem; to appear, show up; **-se** to resemble each other, look alike; *m.* opinion; appearance, looks; **al — apparently, seemingly.
parecido [pa·re·sí·ḍo] *adj.* alike, similar; **bien —** good-looking; *p.p. of* **parecer**; *m.* similarity, likeness, resemblance.
pared [pa·réḍ] *f.* wall; **— maestra** main wall; **— medianera** partition wall.
paredón [pa·re·ḍón] *m.* execution wall; thick wall.
pareja [pa·ré·xa] *f.* pair; couple; match; partner; *Am.* team of two horses; *Ríopl.* horse race.
parejero [pa·re·xé·ro] *m. Ríopl.* race horse; *Ríopl.* over-familar person, backslapper, hail-fellow-well-met.
parejo [pa·ré·xo] *adj.* even; smooth; equal; *adv. Ríopl.* hard.
parentela [pa·en·té·la] *f.* relatives, kin.
parentesco [pa·ren·tés·ko] *m.* kinship, relationship.
paréntesis [pa·rén·te·sis] *m.* parenthesis; digression; **entre —** by the way.
pargo [pár·ġo] *m.* red snapper.
paria [pá·rja] *m. & f.* outcast.
paridad [pa·ri·ḍáḍ] *f.* par, equality.
pariente [pa·rjén·te] *m. & f.* relative, relation.
parir [pa·rír] *v.* to give birth; to bear (*children*).
parlamentar [par·la·men·tár] *v.* to converse; to parley, discuss terms with an enemy.
parlamentario [par·la·men·tá·rjo] *adj.* parliamentary; *m.* member of parliament; envoy to a parley.
parlamento [par·la·mén·to] *m.* speech (*of a character in a play*); parley; parliament; legislative assembly.
parlanchín [par·lan·čín] *adj.* talkative; *m.* talker, chatterer.
parlero [par·lé·ro] *adj.* talkative; gossipy; chattering, chirping.
parlotear [par·lo·te·ár] *v.* to prate, prattle, chatter, chat.
parloteo [par·lo·té·o] *m.* chatter, prattle, idle talk.
paro [pá·ro] *m.* work, stoppage; lockout; *Am.* throw (*in the game of dice*); *Am.* **— y pinta** game of dice.
parodia [pa·ró·ḍja] *f.* parody, take-off, humorous imitation.
parodiar [pa·ro·ḍjár] *v.* to parody, take off, imitate.
parótidas [pa·ró·ti·ḍas] *f. pl.* mumps.
parpadear [par·pa·ḍe·ár] *v.* to wink; to blink; to flutter the eyelids; to twinkle.
parpadeo [par·pa·ḍé·o] *m.* winking; blinking; fluttering of the eyelids; twinkling.
párpado [pár·pa·ḍo] *m.* eyelid.
parque [pár·ke] *m.* park; *Am.* ammunition.
parra [pá·rra] *f.* grapevine; earthenware jug.
parrafada [pa·rra·fá·ḍa] *f.* chat.
párrafo [pá·rra·fo] *m.* paragraph; **echar un — con** to have a chat with.
parral [pa·rrál] *m.* grape arbor.
parranda [pa·rrán·da] *f.* revel, orgy, spree; *Col.* gang, band; **andar** (*or* **ir**) **de —** to go on a spree.
parrandear [pa·rran·de·ár] *v.* to revel, make merry, go on a spree.
parrilla [pa·rri·ya] *f.* grill, gridiron, broiler; grate.
párroco [pá·rro·ko] *m.* parish priest.

parroquia [pa·rró·kja] *f.* parish; parish church; clientele, customers.
parroquiano [pa·rro·kjá·no] *m.* client, customer; parishioner; *adj.* parochial, of a parish.
parsimonia [par·si·mó·nja] *f.* thrift, economy; moderation; prudence.
parsimonioso [par·si·mo·njó·so] *adj.* thrifty; stingy; cautious; slow.
parte [pár·te] *f.* part; share; place; party (*legal term*); **-s** qualities; **parte** *m.* notice, announcement; *Am.* unnecessary excuses or explanations; **de algún tiempo a ésta —** for some time past; **de — de** on behalf of; in favor of; **de — a —** through, from one side to the other; **dar —** to inform; **echar a mala —** to take amiss; **en —** partly; **por todas -s** everywhere; *m.* telegram; message.
partera [par·té·ra] *f.* midwife.
partición [par·ti·sjón] *f.* partition, division.
participación [par·ti·si·pa·sjón] *f.* participation, share; notice.
participante [par·ti·si·pán·te] *m. & f.* participant; *adj.* participating, sharing.
participar [par·ti·si·pár] *v.* to participate, share; to inform, notify.
partícipe [par·tí·si·pe] *m. & f.* participant; *adj.* participating.
participio [par·ti·sí·pjo] *m.* participle.
partícula [par·tí·ku·la] *f.* particle.
particular [par·ti·ku·lár] *adj.* particular, special; peculiar; private; personal; odd, strange; **en —** specially; **lecciones -es** private lessons; *m.* private citizen; individual; point, detail; matter.
partida [par·tí·ḍa] *f.* (*salida*) departure, leave; (*entidad*) item, entry; record; band, group; squad; shipment; game; set (*in tennis*); *Am.* part in the hair; **— de bautismo** (**de matrimonio** *or* **de defunción**) birth (marriage, *or* death) certificate; **— de campo** picnic; **— de caza** hunting party; **— doble** double-entry bookkeeping; *Mex., Ríopl.* **confesar la —** to tell the truth, speak plainly; **jugar una mala —** to play a mean trick.
partidario [par·ti·ḍá·rjo] *m.* partisan, follower, supporter.
partido [par·tí·ḍo] *m.* party, faction, group; contest, game; profit; district; *Bol.* **a** (*or* **al**) **—** in equal shares; *Am.* **dar —** to give a handicap or advantage (*in certain games*); **darse a —** to yield, give up; **sacar — de** to derive advantage from, make the best of; **tomar un —** to decide, make a decision.
partir [par·tír] *v.* (*dividir*) to split, divide; to crack, break; (*salir*) to depart, leave; **a — de hoy** starting today; from this day on; *Am.* **a** (*or* **al**) **— in equal parts**; *Am.* **— a uno por el eje** to ruin someone.
partitura [par·ti·tú·ra] *f.* musical score.
parto [pár·to] *m.* childbirth, delivery; product, offspring; **estar de —** to be in labor.
parvada [par·ḅá·ḍa] *f.* pile of unthreshed grain; brood; *Andes* flock (*of birds or children*).
parvedad [par·ḅe·ḍáḍ] *f.* smallness; trifle; snack, bit of food.
párvulo [pár·ḅu·lo] *m.* child; *adj.* small; innocent.
pasa [pá·sa] *f.* raisin; woolly hair of negros.
pasada [pa·sá·ḍa] *f.* passing, passage; *Am.* stay; *Am.* embarrassment, shame; **una mala —** a mean trick; **de —** on the way; incidentally, by the way; **dar una — por** to pass by, walk by.
pasadizo [pa·sa·ḍí·so] *m.* aisle; narrow hall;

narrow passageway.

pasado [pa·sá·ḍo] *m.* past; *p.p.* past, gone; *adj.* overripe, spoiled; *Mex.* dried (*fruits*). *Col.* thin, bony (*animal*); — **mañana** day after tomorrow; **el año** — last year; **en días -s** in days gone by.

pasaje [pa·sá·xe] *m.* passage; fare, ticket; total number of passengers; *Carib., Mex., Col.* private alley; *Col., Ven.* anecdote.

pasajero [pa·sa·xé·ro] *adj.* passing, temporary, fleeting, transitory; *m.* passenger; guest (*of a hotel*).

pasamano [pa·sa·má·no] *m.* railing, hand rail; gangplank; gangway (*of a ship*).

pasaporte [pa·sa·pór·te] *m.* passport.

pasar [pa·sár] *v.* to pass; to cross; to surpass, exceed; to pierce; to go forward; to go over (in, by, to); to enter; to carry over, take across; to happen; to get along; to swallow; to overlook; to tolerate; to suffer; — **las de Caín** to have a hard time; — **por alto** to omit, overlook; — **por las armas** to execute; **-se** to transfer, change over; to get overripe, spoiled; to exceed, go beyond; **se me pasó decirte** I forgot to tell you; *Ch.* **pasársela a uno** to deceive someone, break someone's confidence; **un buen** — enough to live on.

pasarela [pa·sa·ré·la] *f.* gangplank.

pasatiempo [pa·sa·tjém·po] *m.* pastime; *Am.* cookie.

pascua [pás·kwa] *f.* Easter; Jewish Passover; — **florida** (*or* **de resurrección**) Easter Sunday; — **de Navidad** Christmas.

pase [pá·se] *m.* pass, permit; thrust (*in fencing*); pass (*with the cape in bullfighting*).

pasear [pa·se·ár] *v.* to walk; to take a walk; to ride; **-se** to take a walk; to parade; **-se en automóvil** to take an automobile ride; **-se a caballo** to go horseback riding.

paseo [pa·sé·o] *m.* walk, ride; parade; public park; boulevard; — **en automóvil** automobile ride; **dar un** — to take a walk.

pasillo [pa·sí·yo] *m.* aisle; hallway, corridor; short step; short skit; *Col., Ec.* a type of dance music; *Mex.* runner, hall carpet.

pasión [pa·sjón] *f.* passion; suffering.

pasivo [pa·sí·ḅo] *adj.* passive; inactive; *m.* liabilities, debts; debit, debit side (*in bookkeeping*).

pasmar [paz·már] *v.* to astound, stun; **-se** to be amazed, stunned; to marvel; to get a sudden chill; to get frostbitten; *P.R.* to become dried up, shriveled up; *P.R., Mex.* to get bruised by the saddle or pack (*said of horses and mules*).

pasmo [páz·mo] *m.* amazement, astonishment; wonder, awe.

pasmoso [paz·mó·so] *adj.* astonishing, astounding; marvellous.

paso [pá·so] *m.* pass; step; pace; gait; passage; passing; skit; incident; *P.R., Ch., Andes* ford; *Mex.* ferry, ferryboat wharf; *adv.* slowly; **de** — by the way, in passing; **al** — **que** while; **salir del** — to get out of a difficulty; *Am.* **marcar el** — to mark step, obey humbly; *adj.* dried (*figs, grapes, prunes, etc.*); **paso a nivel** grade crossing.

pasta [pás·ta] *f.* paste; dough; noodles; book cover, binding; *Am.* cookie, cracker; **de buena** — of good temper or disposition.

pastal [pas·tál] *m. Am.* range, grazing land, large pasture.

pastar [pas·tár] *v.* to pasture, graze.

pastear [pas·te·ár] *v. Mex., Riopl.* to graze, pasture.

pastel [pas·tél] *m.* pie; pastry roll; filled pastry;

trick, fraud; secret pact, plot; pastel crayon; **pintura al** — pastel painting.

pastelería [pas·te·le·rí·a] *f.* pastry shop, bakery; pastry.

pastelero [pas·te·lé·ro] *m.* pastry cook; *Cuba* turncoat (*person who changes easily from one political party to another*); *Riopl.* political intriguer.

pasterizar[9] [pas·te·ri·sár], **pasteurizar**[9] [pas·tew·ri·sár] *v.* to pasteurize.

pastilla [pas·tí·ya] *f.* tablet (*of medicine, candy, etc.*); bar (*of chocolate*); cake (*of soap*).

pastizal [pas·ti·sál] *m.* pasture, grassland.

pasto [pás·to] *m.* pasture; grassland; grazing; nourishment; *Am.* grass; **a todo** — without restraint.

pastor [pas·tór] *m.* shepherd; pastor.

pastoral [pas·to·rál] *adj.* pastoral; *f.* pastoral play; idyll; pastoral letter; **pastorela** [pas·to·ré·la] *f.* pastoral, pastoral play; **pastoril** [pas·tó·ríl] *adj.* pastoral.

pastoso [pas·tó·so] *adj.* pasty, soft; mellow (*said of the voice*); *Am.* grassy.

pastura [pas·tú·ra] *f.* pasture; fodder, feed.

pata [pá·ta] *f.* foot, leg (*of an animal, table, chair, etc.*); female duck; — **de gallo** crow's-foot (*wrinkle at the corner of the eye*); *Ch., Andes* — **de perro** wanderer; *Riopl.* **hacer** — **ancha** to stand firm, face a danger; **meter la** — to put one's foot in it, make an embarrassing blunder; **-s arriba** upside down, head over heels.

patacón [pa·ta·kón] *m. Riopl.* silver coin worth about one peso.

patada [pa·tá·ḍa] *f.* kick; stamp (*with the foot*); footprint; "kick," intoxicating effect; **a -s** with kicks; in great abundance; *Andes* **en dos -s** in a jiffy, in a second.

patalear [pa·ta·le·ár] *v.* to kick around; to stamp.

pataleo [pa·ta·lé·o] *m.* kicking; stamping.

pataleta [pa·ta·lé·ta] *f.* convulsion; fainting fit.

patán [pa·tán] *m.* boor, ill-mannered person; rustic; *adj.* rude, boorish, ill-mannered.

patata [pa·tá·ta] *f.* potato.

patear [pa·te·ár] *v.* to kick; to stamp the foot; to tramp about; to trample on; to humiliate; *Am.* to kick, spring back (*as a gun*); *Ch.* to have a kick or intoxicating effect.

patentar [pa·ten·tár] *v.* to patent.

patente [pa·tén·te] *adj.* patent, evident, clear; *f.* patent; grant; privilege; *Carib.* **de** — excellent, of best quality.

patentizar[9] [pa·ten·ti·sár] *v.* to evidence, reveal, show.

paternal [pa·ter·nál] *adj.* paternal; fatherly.

paternidad [pa·ter·ni·ḍáḍ] *f.* paternity, fatherhood; authorship.

paterno [pa·tér·no] *adj.* paternal, fatherly.

patético [pa·té·ti·ko] *adj.* pathetic.

patibulario [pa·ti·ḅu·lá·rjo] *adj.* harrowing, frightful, hair-raising; criminal.

patíbulo [pa·tí·ḅu·lo] *m.* scaffold, gallows.

patilla [pa·tí·ya] *f.* small foot or paw; *Col., Ven.* watermelon; *Riopl.* stone or brick bench (*near a wall*); *Riopl.* railing of a balcony; *Ch.* slip from a plant; **-s** side whiskers; **Patillas** [pa·tí·yas] the Devil.

patín [pa·tín] *m.* skate; a small patio; goosander (*a kind of duck*); — **de ruedas** roller skate; **patinadero** [pa·ti·na·ḍé·ro] *m.* skating rink.

patinar [pa·ti·nár] *v.* to skate; to skid.

patio [pá·tjo] *m.* patio, open court, courtyard;

PA

Am. railway switchyard; *Am.* **pasarse uno al —** to take undue liberties.

patitieso [pa·ti·tjé·so] *adj.* dumbfounded.

patituerto [pa·ti·twér·to] *adj.* crook-legged; knock-kneed; bow-legged.

patizambo [pa·ti·sám·bo] *adj.* knock-kneed.

pato [pá·to] *m.* duck; **pagar el —** to be the goat; to get the blame; *Ríopl.* **andar —** to be flat broke, penniless; *Am.* **hacerse —** to play the fool; *Mex., Ríopl.* **pasarse de — a ganso** to take undue liberties; *Am.* **ser el — de la boda** to be the life of the party; **patito** *m.* duckling.

patochada [pa·to·čá·ḍa] *f.* stupidity, blunder, nonsense.

patojo [pa·tó·xo] *adj.* crooked-legged; bowlegged; *m. & f. Guat.* child; young person.

patología [pa·to·lo·xí·a] *f.* pathology.

patológico [pa·to·ló·xi·ko] *adj.* pathological.

patraña [pa·trá·ña] *f.* fabulous tale; lie, falsehood.

patria [pá·trja] *f.* fatherland, native country.

patriarca [pa·trjár·ka] *m.* patriarch; **patriarcal** [pa·trjar·kál] *adj.* patriarchal.

patrimonio [pa·tri·mó·njo] *m.* patrimony; inheritance.

patrio [pá·trjo] *adj.* native, of one's native country; paternal, belonging to the father.

patriota [pa·trjó·ta] *m. & f.* patriot.

patriótico [pa·trjó·ti·ko] *adj.* patriotic.

patriotismo [pa·trjo·tíz·mo] *m.* patriotism.

patrocinar [pa·tro·si·nár] *v.* to patronize, favor, sponsor.

patrocinio [pa·tro·sí·njo] *m.* patronage, protection.

patrón [pa·trón] *m.* (*protector*) patron; patron saint; sponsor; (*amo*) master, boss; proprietor, landlord; host; skipper; (*dechado*) pattern, standard, model; **patrona** [pa·tró·na] *f.* landlady; patroness; hostess.

patronato [pa·tro·ná·to] *m.* board of trustees; foundation (*for educational, cultural, or charitable purposes*).

patrono [pa·tró·no] *m.* patron, protector; trustee; patron saint.

patrulla [pa·trú·ya] *f.* patrol; squad, gang.

patrullar [pa·tru·yár] *v.* to patrol.

pausa [páw·sa] *f.* pause, stop, rest.

pausar [paw·sár] *v.* to pause.

pauta [páw·ta] *f.* norm, rule, standard; guide lines (*for writing*).

pava [pá·ḅa] *f.* turkey hen; *Ríopl.* kettle, teapot, teakettle; *Andes, Ch.* jest, coarse joke; **pelar la —** to talk by night at the window (*said of lovers*).

pavear [pa·ḅe·ár] *v.* to talk nonsense.

pavesa [pa·ḅé·sa] *f.* cinder; small firebrand; burnt wick or snuff of a candle; **-s** cinders.

pavimentar [pa·ḅi·men·tár] *v.* to pave.

pavimento [pa·ḅi·mén·to] *m.* pavement.

pavo [pá·ḅo] *m.* turkey; *Ch.* sponger, parasite; **— real** peacock; **comer —** to be a wallflower at a dance; *adj.* silly, foolish; vain.

pavón [pa·ḅón] *m.* peacock.

pavonearse [pa·ḅo·ne·ár·se] *v.* to strut, swagger.

pavoneo [pa·ḅo·né·o] *m.* strut, swagger.

pavor [pa·ḅór] *m.* awe, dread, terror.

pavoroso [pa·ḅo·ró·so] *adj.* frightful, dreadful.

payador [pa·ya·ḍór] *m. Ríopl.* one who sings an improvised song accompanied on the guitar.

payasada [pa·ya·sá·ḍa] *f.* clownish act or remark.

payasear [pa·ya·se·ár] *v.* to clown, play the fool.

payaso [pa·yá·so] *m.* clown.

paz [pas] *f.* peace.

pazguato [paz·ǥwá·to] *adj.* simple, dumb, stupid;

m. simpleton.

peaje [pe·á·xe] *m.* toll (*for crossing a bridge or ferry*).

peal [pe·ál] = **pial.**

pealar [pe·a·lár] = **pialar.**

peatón [pe·a·tón] *m.* pedestrian.

peca [pé·ka] *f.* freckle.

pecado [pe·ká·ḍo] *m.* sin.

pecador [pe·ka·ḍór] *m.* sinner; *adj.* sinful.

pecaminoso [pe·ka·mi·nó·so] *adj.* sinful.

pecar[6] [pe·kár] *v.* to sin; **— de bueno** to be too good; **— de oscuro** to be exceedingly unclear, too complicated.

pecera [pe·sé·ra] *f.* fish bowl.

pécora [pé·ko·ra] *f.* head of sheep.

pecoso [pe·kó·so] *adj.* freckly, freckled.

peculado [pe·ku·lá·ḍo] *m.* embezzlement.

peculiar [pe·ku·ljár] *adj.* peculiar; **peculiaridad** [pe·ku·lja·ri·ḍáḍ] *f.* peculiarity.

pechada [pe·ča·ḍa] *f. Ríopl.* bump, push, shove with the chest; *Am.* bumping contest between two riders; *Ríopl., Ch.* overthrowing an animal (*by bumping it with the chest of a horse*).

pechar [pe·čár] *v. Ríopl., Ch., Bol.* to bump, push, shove with the chest; *Ríopl., Ch., Bol.* to drive one's horse against; *Ch., Ríopl.* to borrow, strike (*someone*) for a loan.

pechera [pe·čé·ra] *f.* shirtfront; chest protector; bib (*of an apron*).

pecho [pé·čo] *m.* chest; breast; bosom; heart; courage; **dar el —** to nurse; **tomar a -s** to take to heart; *P.R., Col.* **a todo —** shouting; *Am.* **en -s de camisa** in shirt sleeves.

pechuga [pe·čú·ǥa] *f.* breast, breast meat of a fowl; bosom; *C.A., Col., Ch., Andes* courage, nerve, audacity, impudence.

pedagogía [pe·ḍa·ǥo·xí·a] *f.* pedagogy, science of education.

pedagógico [pe·ḍa·ǥó·xi·ko] *adj.* pedagogic, relating to education or teaching.

pedagogo [pe·ḍa·ǥó·ǥo] *m.* pedagogue, teacher, educator.

pedal [pe·ḍál] *m.* pedal.

pedalear [pe·ḍa·le·ár] *v.* to pedal.

pedante [pe·ḍán·te] *adj.* pedantic, affected, vain, superficial; *m.* pedant; **pedantesco** [pe·ḍan·tés·ko] *adj.* pedantic.

pedazo [pe·ḍá·so] *m.* piece, portion, bit; **hacer -s** to tear or break into pieces; **caerse a -s** fall into pieces.

pedernal [pe·ḍer·nál] *m.* flint.

pedestal [pe·ḍes·tál] *m.* pedestal, base.

pedestre [pe·ḍés·tre] *adj.* pedestrian, walking, going on foot; commonplace, vulgar, low.

pedido [pe·ḍí·ḍo] *m.* commercial order; request, petition; *p.p. of* **pedir.**

pedigüeño [pe·ḍi·ǥwé·ño] *adj.* begging, demanding.

pedir[5] [pe·ḍír] *v. irr.* to ask, beg, petition; to ask for; to demand; to require; to order (*merchandise*); **a — de boca** exactly as desired.

pedo [pé·ḍo] *m.* wind, flatulence; *Mex.* **andar —** to be drunk.

pedrada [pe·ḍrá·ḍa] *f.* hit or blow with a stone; throw with a stone; mark or bruise made by a stone (*thrown*); **a -s** by stoning; with stones; **dar una —** to hit with a stone; **echar a alguien a -s** to stone someone out; **matar a -s** to stone to death.

pedregal [pe·ḍre·ǥál] *m.* rocky ground, ground strewn with rocks.

pedregoso [pe·ḍre·ǥó·so] *adj.* rocky, stony, pebbly.

pedrería [pe·ḍre·rí·a] *f.* precious stones; precious stone ornament; jewelry.

pedrusco [pe·ḍrús·ko] *m.* boulder.

pedúnculo [pe·ḍúŋ·ku·lo] *m.* stem (*of a leaf, flower or fruit*), stalk.

pegajoso [pe·ġa·xó·so] *adj.* sticky; contagious.

pegar[7] [pe·ġár] *v.* (*golpear*) to hit, strike, slap, beat; (*adherir*) to stick, paste, glue; to sew on (*a button*); to infect; to be becoming; to be fitting, opportune, to the point; *Am.* to tie, fasten; *Am.* to yoke; — **fuego** to set on fire; — **un chasco** to play a trick; to surprise; disappoint; — **un susto** to give a scare; — **un salto (una carrera)** to take a jump (a run); **-se** to stick, cling; **pegársela a uno** to fool somebody.

pegote [pe·ġó·te] *m.* sticky thing; sticking plaster; clumsy patch; sponger; thick, sticky concoction; clumsy addition or insertion (*in a literary or artistic work*).

peinado [pej·ná·ḍo] *m.* coiffure, hairdo; hairdressing; *p.p.* combed; groomed; *adj.* effeminate; **bien** — spruce, trim.

peinador [pej·na·ḍór] *m.* hairdresser; short wrapper or dressing gown; **peinadora** [pej·na·ḍó·ra] *f.* woman hairdresser.

peinar [pej·nár] *v.* to comb; *Ríopl.* to flatter.

peine [péj·ne] *m.* comb.

peineta [pej·né·ta] *f.* large ornamental comb.

peje [pé·xe] *m. C.A.* fish.

peladilla [pe·la·ḍí·ya] *f.* small pebble.

pelado [pe·lá·ḍo] *p.p. & adj.* peeled; plucked; skinned; hairless; featherless; barren, treeless, bare; penniless, broke; *m. Mex.* ragged fellow (*generally a peon*); *Mex.* ill-bred person; *Col.* child.

pelafustán [pe·la·fus·tán] *m.* tramp, vagabond.

pelagatos [pe·la·ġá·tos] *m.* ragged fellow, tramp.

pelaje [pe·lá·xe] *m.* animal's coat, fur; external appearance.

pelar [pe·lár] *v.* to cut the hair of; to pluck the feathers or hair from; to peel, shell, skin, husk; to fleece, rob; *Am.* to beat, thrash; *Am.* to slander; *C.R.* — **los dientes** to show one's teeth; to smile affectedly; *C.A., Mex., Carib., Col., Andes* — **los ojos** to keep one's eyes peeled; to open one's eyes wide; **-se** to peel off; to lose one's hair; *Col., Ven.* to be confused; *Col., Ven.* to be careless, unaware; *Col., Ven.* to slip away; *Col., Ven.* to die; **pelárselas por algo** to be dying for something, want something very much.

peldaño [pel·dá·ño] *m.* step (*of a staircase*).

pelea [pe·lé·a] *f.* fight, quarrel.

pelear [pe·le·ár] *v.* to fight; to quarrel.

peletería [pe·le·te·rí·a] *f.* fur store; fur trade; furs; *Am.* leather goods, leather shop; *Cuba* shoe store.

pelicano [pe·li·ká·no] *adj.* gray-haired.

pelícano [pe·lí·ka·no] *m.* pelican.

película [pe·lí·ku·la] *f.* thin skin; membrane; film; motion-picture film.

peligrar [pe·li·ġrár] *v.* to be in danger.

peligro [pe·lí·ġro] *m.* danger.

peligroso [pe·li·ġró·so] *adj.* dangerous.

pelillo [pe·lí·yo] *m.* short, fine hair; **-s** trouble, nuisance; **echar -s a la mar** to "bury the hatchet", become reconciled; **no pararse en -s** not to stop at small details, not to bother about trifles; **no tener -s en la lengua** to speak frankly.

pelirrojo [pe·li·rró·xo] *adj.* redheaded, red-haired.

pelo [pé·lo] *m.* (*cabello*) hair; (*haz*) nap (*of cloth*); (*fibra*) grain (*in wood*); **al** — perfectly; agreed; apropos, to the point; along the grain; **eso me viene al** — that suits me perfectly; **con todos sus -s y señales** with every possible detail; *Am.* **por** (*or* **en**) **un** — on the point of, almost, by a hair's breadth; **montar en** — to ride bareback; **tomar el** — **a** to kid, make fun of; *Ríopl., Carib., Mex., Andes* **no aflojar un** — not to yield an inch.

pelón [pe·lón] *adj.* bald.

pelota [pe·ló·ta] *f.* ball; ball game; *Am.* boat made of cowhide; **en** — (*or* **en -s**) naked; *Am.* **darle a la** — to hit upon by chance; **pelotilla** [pe·lo·tí·ya] *f.* pellet, little ball.

pelotari [pe·lo·tá·ri] *m.* pelota (*jai-alai*) player.

pelotera [pe·lo·té·ra] *f.* brawl, row, riot; *C.A., Ven.* crowd.

pelotón [pe·lo·tón] *m.* large ball; crowd, gang; heap, pile; platoon of soliders; firing squad.

peluca [pe·lú·ka] *f.* wig.

pelucón [pe·lu·kón] *adj.* wig-wearing; *Ch.* conservative.

peludo [pe·lú·ḍo] *adj.* hairy; shaggy; *m.* plush carpet with shaggy pile; *Am.* a species of armadillo; *Ríopl.* **agarrar un** — to get drunk.

peluquería [pe·lu·ke·rí·a] *f.* barbershop, hairdresser's shop.

peluquero [pe·lu·ké·ro] *m.* hairdresser, barber.

pelusa [pe·lú·sa] *f.* down; fuzz; nap (*of cloth*).

pellejo [pe·yé·xo] *m.* hide; skin; peel; **salvar el** — to save one's skin, escape punishment; *Am.* **jugarse el** — to gamble one's life.

pellizcar[6] [pe·yis·kár] *v.* to pinch, nip.

pellizco [pe·yis·ko] *m.* pinching, nipping; pinch, nip.

pena [pé·na] *f.* penalty; grief, worry; hardship; toil; *Mex., Carib., C.A., Col., Ven.* embarrassment; **a duras -s** with great difficulty; hardly; **me da** — it grieves me; *C.A., Ven., Col., Carib.* it embarrasses me; **valer la** — to be worthwhile; **tener** (*or* **estar con**) **mucha** — to be terribly sorry; *Am.* to be greatly embarrassed.

penacho [pe·ná·čo] *m.* tuft, crest; plume.

penado [pe·ná·ḍo] *adj.* afflicted.

penal [pe·nál] *adj.* penal; **código** — penal code.

penalidad [pe·na·li·ḍáḍ] *f.* hardship; trouble; penalty.

penar [pe·nár] *v.* to suffer; to worry, fret; to impose a penalty; — **por** to long for; to suffer because of.

penca [péŋ·ka] *f.* leaf of a cactus plant; *Am.* sweetheart; *Ven.* **coger una** — to get drunk.

penco [péŋ·ko] *m.* nag, horse; *Am.* boor.

pendencia [pen·dén·sja] *f.* quarrel; scuffle, fight.

pendenciero [pen·den·sjé·ro] *adj.* quarrelsome.

pender [pen·dér] *v.* to hang; to dangle; to depend.

pendiente [pen·djén·te] *f.* slope; *m.* earring; pendant; *Am.* watch chain; *adj.* hanging, dangling; pending.

pendón [pen·dón] *m.* banner.

péndulo [pén·du·lo] *m.* pendulum.

pene [pé·ne] *m.* penis.

penetración [pe·ne·tra·sjón] *f.* penetration; acuteness; keen judgment.

penetrante [pe·ne·trán·te] *adj.* penetrating; acute; keen.

penetrar [pe·ne·trár] *v.* to penetrate; to pierce; to fathom, comprehend.

penicilina [pe·ni·si·lí·na] *f.* penicillin.

península [pe·nín·su·la] *f.* peninsula.

peninsular [pe·nin·su·lár] *adj.* peninsular.

penitencia [pe·ni·tén·sja] *f.* penance.

penitenciaría [pe·ni·ten·sja·rí·a] *f.* penitentiary.
penitente [pe·ni·tén·te] *adj.* repentant, penitent; *m.* & *f.* penitent.
penoso [pe·nó·so] *adj.* painful; hard, difficult; embarrassing; fatiguing; *Mex., Carib., C.A., Ven., Col.* timid, shy.
pensador [pen·sa·đór] *m.* thinker; *adj.* thinking.
pensamiento [pen·sa·mjén·to] *m.* thought; mind; pansy.
pensar [pen·sár] *v. irr.* to think; to think over; to intend.
pensativo [pen·sa·tí·ƀo] *adj.* pensive.
pensión [pen·sjón] *f.* pension; board; scholarship for study; boardinghouse; *Col.* apprehension, anxiety; — **completa** room and board.
pensionado [pen·sjo·ná·đo] *m.* pensioner (*person receiving a pension*); *adj.* & *p.p.* pensioned.
pensionar [pen·sjo·nár] *v.* to pension.
pensionista [pen·sjo·nís·ta] *m.* & *f.* boarder; pensioner (*person receiving a pension*).
pentagrama [pen·ta·grá·ma] *m.* musical staff.
penúltimo [pe·núl·ti·mo] *adj.* next to the last.
penumbra [pe·núm·bra] *f.* partial shadow, dimness.
penumbroso [pe·num·bró·so] *adj.* dim.
peña [pé·ña] *f.* rock, large stone.
peñasco [pe·ñás·ko] *m.* large rock; crag.
peñascoso [pe·ñas·ko·so] *adj.* rocky.
peón [pe·ón] *m.* unskilled laborer; foot soldier; spinning top; pawn (*in chess*); *Ch., Riopl., C.A., Carib., Mex.* farm hand; *Am.* apprentice; *Mex.* — **de albañil** mason's helper.
peonada [peo·ná·đa] *f.* gang of laborers or peons.
peonaje [pe·o·ná·xe] *m.* gang of laborers.
peonza [pe·on·sa] *f.* top (*toy*).
peor [pe·ór] *adj.* & *adv.* worse; worst; — **que** worse than; — **que** — that is even worse; **tanto** — so much the worse.
pepa [pé·pa] *f. Andes, Col., Ven., Ch., Mex., Riopl.* seed (*of an apple, melon, etc.*); *Am.* marble (*to play with*); **Pepa** nickname for **Josefa.**
pepenar [pe·pe·nár] *v. Mex.* to pick up; *Am.* to seize, grab.
pepino [pe·pí·no] *m.* cucumber.
pepita [pe·pí·ta] *f.* seed (*of an apple, melon, etc.*); pip (*a disease of birds*); nugget (*lump of gold or other minerals*); *Am.* fruit stone, pit; **Pepita** = **Josefita** dim. of **Josefa.**
pequeñez [pe·ke·ñés] *f.* smallness; childhood; trifle; meanness.
pequeño [pe·ké·ño] *adj.* small, little; young; low, humble; *m.* child.
pera [pé·ra] *f.* pear; goatee; sinecure, easy job; *Am.* Peruvian alligator pear (*see* **aguacate**); *Am.* **hacerle a uno la** — to play a trick on someone; **peral** *m.* pear tree; pear orchard.
percal [per·kál] *m.* percale (*fine cotton cloth*).
percance [per·kán·se] *m.* misfortune, accident; occurrence.
percepción [per·sep·sjón] *f.* perception; idea.
perceptible [per·sep·tí·ƀle] *adj.* perceptible, noticeable.
percibir [per·si·ƀír] *v.* to perceive; to collect, receive.
percudido [per·ku·đí·đo] *adj.* dirty, grimy.
percudir [per·ku·đir] *v.* to soil, make dirty or grimy; **-se** to get grimy.
percusión [per·ku·sjón] *f.* percussion.
percusor [per·ku·sór] *m.* firing pin.
percha [pér·ča] *f.* clothes or hat rack; pole; perch, roost; perch (*a fish*); **perchero** [per·čé·ro] *m.* clothes or hat rack.

perder [per·đér] *v. irr.* to lose; to squander; to ruin, harm; to miss (*a train*); — **de vista** to lose sight of; **-se** to lose one's way; to get lost; to go astray; to get spoiled; to become ruined.
perdición [per·đi·sjón] *f.* perdition, damnation, hell, ruin.
pérdida [pér·đi·đa] *f.* loss; damage.
perdidamente [per·đi·đa·mén·te] *adv.* excessively.
perdido [per·đi·đo] *p.p.* & *adj.* lost; strayed; mislaid; ruined; **estar** — **por alguien** to be crazy about, or very fond of, someone; *m.* rake, dissolute fellow; bum, vagabond.
perdigón [per·đi·gón] *m.* young partridge; bird shot, buckshot; losing gambler.
perdiz [per·đís] *f.* partridge.
perdón [per·đón] *m.* pardon; forgiveness; remission.
perdonar [per·đo·nár] *v.* to pardon; to forgive.
perdulario [per·đu·lá·rjo] *m.* rake, dissolute person; reckless fellow; good-for-nothing; tramp.
perdurable [per·đu·rá·ƀle] *adj.* lasting, everlasting.
perdurar [per·đu·rár] *v.* to last, endure.
perecedero [pe·re·se·đé·ro] *adj.* perishable.
perecer[13] [pe·re·sér] *v. irr.* to perish; to die; **-se** to long (for), pine (for).
peregrinación [pe·re·gri·na·sjón] *f.* pilgrimage; long journey.
peregrinar [pe·re·gri·nár] *v.* to journey; to go through life.
peregrino [pe·re·grí·no] *m.* pilgrim; *adj.* foreign, strange; rare; beautiful, perfect; travelling, wandering; **ave peregrina** migratory bird, bird of passage.
perejil [pe·re·xíl] *m.* parsley; **-es** frippery, showy clothes or ornaments.
perenne [pe·rén·ne] *adj.* perennial, enduring, perpetual.
pereza [pe·ré·sa] *f.* laziness; idleness.
perezoso [pe·re·só·so] *adj.* lazy; *m. Am.* sloth (*an animal*); *Am.* safety pin; *Am.* bed cushion.
perfección [per·fek·sjón] *f.* perfection; **a la** — to perfection, perfectly.
perfeccionamiento [per·fek·sjo·na·mjén·to] *m.* perfecting, perfection; completion.
perfeccionar [per·fek·sjo·nár] *v.* to perfect, finish, complete.
perfecto [per·fék·to] *adj.* perfect.
perfidia [per·fí·đja] *f.* perfidy, treachery.
pérfido [pér·fi·đo] *adj.* perfidious, treacherous, faithless.
perfil [per·fíl] *m.* profile; outline; *Am.* pen or pen point.
perfilar [per·fi·lár] *v.* to silhouette; to outline; **-se** to show one's profile; to be silhouetted.
perforación [per·fo·ra·sjón] *f.* perforation, hole; puncture; perforating, boring, drilling.
perforar [per·fo·rár] *v.* to perforate, pierce; to drill, bore.
perfumar [per·fu·már] *v.* to perfume, scent.
perfume [per·fú·me] *m.* perfume; fragrance.
perfumería [per·fu·me·rí·a] *f.* perfumery; perfume shop.
pergamino [per·ga·mí·no] *m.* parchment.
pericia [pe·rí·sja] *f.* expertness, skill.
perico [pe·rí·ko] *m.* parakeet, small parrot; *Col.* **huevos -s** scrambled eggs.
perifollos [pe·ri·fó·yos] *m. pl.* frippery, finery, showy ornaments.
perifrasear [pe·ri·fra·se·ár] *v.* to paraphrase.
perifrasis [pe·rí·fra·sis] *f.* paraphrase.
perigeo [pe·ri·xé·o] *m.* perigee.

perilla [pe·rí·ya] *f.* small pear; pear-shaped ornament; knob; pommel of a saddle; goatee; **de** — apropos, to the point.

perímetro [pe·rí·me·tro] *m.* perimeter.

periódico [pe·rjó·đi·ko] *m.* newspaper; periodical; *adj.* periodic, periodical.

periodismo [pe·rjo·đíz·mo] *m.* journalism; **periodista** [pe·rjo·đís·ta] *m. & f.* journalist; newspaper editor or publisher; **periodístico** [pe·rjo·đís·ti·ko] *adj.* journalistic.

período [pe·rí·o·đo] [pe·rjó·đo] *m.* period; cycle; sentence.

peripecia [pe·ri·pé·sja] *f.* vicissitude, change in fortune; unforeseen incident.

peripuesto [pe·ri·pwés·to] *adj.* dressed up, dolled up, decked out.

perito [pe·rí·to] *adj.* learned; experienced; skillful; skilled; *m.* expert.

peritoneo [pe·ri·to·né·o] *m.* peritoneum.

peritonitis [pe·ri·to·ní·tis] *f.* peritonitis.

perjudicar[6] [per·xu·đi·kár] *v.* to damage, impair, harm.

perjudicial [per·xu·đi·sjál] *adj.* harmful, injurious.

perjuicio [per·xwí·sjo] *m.* damage, ruin, mischief; harm.

perjurar [per·xu·rár] *v.* to perjure oneself; to commit perjury; to curse, swear.

perjurio [per·xú·rjo] *m.* perjury.

perla [pér·la] *f.* pearl; **de -s** perfectly, just right, to the point.

perlino [per·lí·no] *adj.* pearly, pearl-colored.

permanecer[13] [per·ma·ne·sér] *v. irr.* to remain, stay.

permanencia [per·ma·nén·sja] *f.* permanence, duration; stability; stay, sojourn.

permanente [per·ma·nén·te] *adj.* permanent.

permiso [per·mí·so] *m.* permission; permit.

permitir [per·mi·tír] *v.* to permit, let; to grant.

permuta [per·mú·ta] *f.* exchange, barter.

permutar [per·mu·tár] *v.* to exchange; to barter; to change around.

pernetas [per·né·tas] **: en** — barelegged, with bare legs.

pernicioso [per·ni·sjó·so] *adj.* pernicious, harmful.

perno [pér·no] *m.* bolt; spike; **-s** *Am.* tricks, frauds.

pero [pé·ro] *conj.* but, except, yet; *m.* objection, exception; defect; a variety of apple tree; a variety of apple; **perón** [pe·rón] *m. Am.* a variety of apple.

perogrullada [pe·ro·ġru·yá·đa] *f.* platitude, trite or commonplace remark.

peroración [pe·ro·ra·sjón] *f.* peroration, speech, harangue.

perorar [pe·ro·rár] *v.* to make an impassioned speech; to declaim, harangue; to plea, make a plea.

perorata [pe·ro·rá·ta] *f.* harangue, speech.

peróxido [pe·rók·si·đo] *m.* peroxide.

perpendicular [per·pen·di·ku·lár] *adj., m. & f.* perpendicular.

perpetuar[18] [per·pe·twár] *v.* to perpetuate.

perpetuo [per·pé·two] *adj.* perpetual; **perpetua** [per·pé·twa] *f.* everlasting (*plant*).

perplejidad [per·ple·xi·đáđ] *f.* perplexity.

perplejo [per·plé·xo] *adj.* perplexed, bewildered.

perra [pé·rra] *f.* bitch, female dog; drunkenness; — **chica** five-centime copper coin; — **grande** (*or* **gorda**) ten-centime copper coin.

perrada [pe·rrá·đa] *f.* pack of dogs; **hacer una** — to play a mean trick.

perrera [pe·rré·ra] *f.* kennel; toil, hard work, hard

job; tantrum; *Carib., Mex., Ven.* brawl, dispute.

perrilla [pe·rrí·ya] *f. Am.* sty (*on the eyelid*). *See* **orzuelo.**

perro [pé·rro] *m.* dog; — **de busca** hunting dog; — **dogo** bulldog; — **de lanas** poodle; *adj.* dogged, tenacious; *Mex., C.A.* hard, selfish, mean, stingy; *Ven.*, vagabond.

perruno [pe·rrú·no] *adj.* canine, doglike.

persecución [per·se·ku·sjón] *f.* persecution; pursuit.

perseguidor [per·se·ġi·đór] *m.* pursuer; persecutor.

perseguimiento [per·se·ġi·mjén·to] *m.* pursuit; persecution.

perseguir[5, 12] [per·se·ġír] *v. irr.* to pursue; to persecute; to harass, annoy.

perseverancia [per·se·ƀe·rán·sja] *f.* perseverance.

perseverar [per·se·ƀe·rár] *v.* to persevere.

persiana [per·sjá·na] *f.* Venetian blind; window shade.

persistencia [per·sis·tén·sja] *f.* persistence; **persistente** [per·sis·tén·te] *adj.* persistent.

persistir [per·sis·tír] *v.* to persist.

persona [per·só·na] *f.* person; personage.

personaje [per·so·ná·xe] *m.* personage; character (*in a book or play*).

personal [per·so·nál] *adj.* personal; *m.* personnel.

personalidad [per·so·na·li·đáđ] *f.* personality; individuality; person, personage.

personalismo [per·so·na·líz·mo] *m.* personalism; individualism.

perspectiva [per·spek·tí·ƀa] *f.* perspective; view; appearance; outlook; prospect.

perspicacia [pers·pi·ká·sja] *f.* keenness of mind, penetration, keen insight.

perspicaz [pers·pi·kás] *adj.* keen, shrewd.

persuadir [per·swa·đír] *v.* to persuade.

persuasión [per·swa·sjón] *f.* persuasion.

persuasivo [per·swa·sí·ƀo] *adj.* persuasive.

pertenecer[13] [per·te·ne·sér] *v. irr.* to belong; to pertain; to concern.

perteneciente [per·te·ne·sjén·te] *adj.* pertaining, belonging, concerning.

pértiga [pér·ti·ġa] *f.* pole, bar, rod; **salto con** — pole vault.

pertinente [per·ti·nén·te] *adj.* pertinent, to the point, apt, fitting.

pertrechos [per·tré·čos] *m. pl.* military supplies; tools, implements.

perturbación [per·tur·ƀa·sjón] *f.* uneasiness, agitation, disturbance.

perturbar [per·tur·ƀár] *v.* to perturb, disturb.

perunano [pe·rwá·no] *adj. & m.* Peruvian.

perulero [pe·ru·lé·ro] *adj. m. & f.* Peruvian (*slang expression*).

perversidad [per·ƀer·si·đáđ] *f.* perversity, wickedness.

perverso [per·ƀér·so] *adj.* perverse, wicked; *m.* pervert.

pervertir[3] [per·ƀer·tír] *v. irr.* to pervert; to; corrupt; to distort; **-se** to become perverted; to go wrong.

pesa [pé·sa] *f.* weight (*for scales*); — **de reloj** clock weight; **-s y medidas** weights and measures.

pesadez [pe·sa·đés] *f.* heaviness; dullness, drowsiness; slowness; bother; stubbornness.

pesadilla [pe·sa·đí·ya] *f.* nightmare.

pesado [pe·sá·đo] *adj.* heavy; sound (*sleep*); tiresome, boring; annoying; slow; dull.

pesadumbre [pe·sa·đúm·bre] *f.* grief, sorrow; weight, heaviness.

pésame [pé·sa·me] *m.* condolence, expression of sympathy.

PE

pesantez [pe·san·tés] *f.* gravity; heaviness.
pesar [pe·sár] *v.* (*penar*) to cause grief, sorrow, or regret; (*tener gravedad*) to weigh; to consider, to have weight, value, or importance; *m.* grief, sorrow; **a — de** in spite of.
pesaroso [pe·sa·ró·so] *adj.* grieved, sad; repentant.
pesca [pés·ka] *f.* fishing; catch, fish caught.
pescadería [pes·ka·de·rí·a] *f.* fish market; **pescadero** [pes·ka·dé·ro] *m.* fishmonger, dealer in fish.
pescado [pes·ká·do] *m.* fish (*especially after being caught*); salted codfish.
pescador [pes·ka·dór] *m.* fisherman.
pescar[6] [pes·kár] *v.* to fish; to catch; to catch unaware, catch in the act.
pescozón [pes·ko·són] *m.* blow on the back of the head or neck.
pescuezo [pes·kwé·so] *m.* neck.
pesebre [pe·sé·bre] *m.* manger.
peseta [pe·sé·ta] *f.* peseta (*monetary unit of Spain*).
pesimismo [pe·si·míz·mo] *m.* pessimism; **pesimista** [pe·si·mís·ta] *m. & f.* pessimist; *adj.* pessimistic.
pésimo [pé·si·mo] *adj.* very bad.
peso [pé·so] *m.* weight; weighing; burden; importance; *Am.* peso (*monetary unit of several Spanish American countries*).
pesquera [pes·ké·ra] *f.* fishery (*place for catching fish*); **pesquería** [pes·ke·rí·a] *f.* fishery; fishing.
pesquero [pes·ké·ro] *adj.* fishing; **buque —** fishing boat; **industria pesquera** fishing industry.
pesquisa [pes·kí·sa] *f.* investigation, inquiry; *m. Am.* police investigator.
pestaña [pes·tá·ña] *f.* eyelash; edging, fringe; **quemarse las -s** to burn the midnight oil, study hard at night.
pestañear [pes·ta·ñe·ár] *v.* to blink; to wink; to flicker.
peste [pés·te] *f.* pest, pestilence, plague; epidemic; strench, stink, foul odor; overabundance. excess; *Am.* smallpox; *Col.* head cold; **echar -s** to utter insults.
pestillo [pes·tí·yo] *m.* bolt; latch; lock.
pesuña [pe·sú·ña] *f.* hoof (*cloven*).
pesuño [pe·sú·ño] *m.* half of the cloven hoof.
petaca [pe·tá·ka] *f.* tobacco pouch; cigar case; leather covered hamper (*used as a pack*); *Mex., adj. Andes* heavy, clumsy.
pétalo [pé·ta·lo] *m.* petal.
petate [pe·tá·te] *m.* bundle; impostor; *Mex., C.A., Ven., Col.* mat (*of straw or palm leaves*); *Am.* dunce; *Andes* coward; **liar el —** to pack up and go; *Mex.* to die; *Col., Ven.* **dejar a uno en un —** to ruin a person, leave him penniless.
petición [pe·ti·sjón] *f.* petition, request.
petirrojo [pe·ti·rró·xo] *m.* robin, robin redbreast.
petiso [pe·tí·so] *adj. Riopl., Ch., Andes* small, short, dwarfish; *m. Am.* small horse, pony.
pétreo [pé·tre·o] *adj.* stone, stony.
petróleo [pe·tró·le·o] *m.* petroleum.
petrolero [pe·tro·lé·ro] *m.* oil man; dealer in petroleum; **compañía petrolera** oil company.
petulancia [pe·tu·lán·sja] *f.* flippancy; insolence; **petulante** [pe·tu·lán·te] *adj.* impertinent, flippant.
petunia [pe·tú·nja] *f.* petunia.
pez [pes] *m.* fish; *f.* pitch, tar.
pezón [pe·són] *m.* nipple; stem, stalk (*of a fruit, leaf or flower*); small point of land.
pezuña [pe·sú·ña] *f.* hoof.
piadoso [pja·dó·so] *adj.* pious; kind, merciful.
pial [pjal] *m. Mex.* lasso, lariat (*thrown in order to trip an animal*); *Riopl.* snare, trap.
pialar [pja·lár] *v.* to lasso by tripping with a **pial**.

piano [pjá·no] *m.* piano; **— de cola** grand piano; **— vertical** upright piano.
piar[17] [pjar] *v.* to peep, chirp; to cry, whine.
pibe [pí·be] *m. Riopl.* urchin, boy.
pica [pí·ka] *f.* pike, spear; picador's goad or lance; stonecutter's hammer; *Col.* trail; *Col., Ch.* pique, resentment; *Am.* cockfight.
picada [pi·ká·da] *f.* prick; bite (*as of an insect or fish*); puncture; sharp pain; dive (*of a plane*); *Cuba, Riopl.* path, trail (*cut through a forest*); *Am.* narrow ford; *Col., Ven., Mex.* peck.
picadillo [pi·ka·dí·yo] *m.* meat and vegetable hash; minced meat, mincement.
picador [pi·ka·dór] *m.* picador (*mounted bullfighter armed with a goad*); horse-breaker; chopping block; *Ven.* tree tapper.
picadura [pi·ka·dú·ra] *f.* biting; pricking; bite; prick; sting; puncture; cut tobacco.
picante [pi·kán·te] *adj.* (*acerbo*) pricking, biting, stinging; (*con chile o ají*) spicy; highly seasoned; *m.* strong seasoning; *Am.* highly seasoned sauce (*usually containing chili pepper*).
picapleitos [pi·ka·pléj·tos] *m.* quarrelsome person (*one who likes to pick a fight*); shyster.
picaporte [pi·ka·pór·te] *m.* latch; latchkey; door knocker.
picar[6] [pi·kár] *v.* to prick; to pierce; to bite (*said of fish or insects*); to sting; to peck; to nibble; to mince, chop up; to goad; to stick, poke; to hew, chisel; to pique, vex; to itch, smart, burn; *Am.* to chop (*wood*); *Am.* to open a trail; *Am.* to tap (*a tree*); *Am.* to slaughter (*cattle*); **— muy alto** to aim very high; **— en** to border on, be somewhat of; *Mex., Ven.* **¡pícale!** [pi·ka·le] hurry! **-se** to be piqued, angry; to be motheaten; to begin to sour; to begin to rot; *C.A., Ven.* **-se** to get tipsy; **-se de** to boast of.
picardía [pi·kar·dí·a] *f.* roguishness; offensive act or remark; roguish trick; mischief.
picaresco [pi·ka·rés·ko] *adj.* picaresque, roguish.
pícaro [pí·ka·ro] *m.* rogue, rascal; *adj.* roguish; mischievous; crafty, sly; low, vile; **picarón** [pa·ka·rón] *m.* big rascal.
picazón [pi·ka·són] *f.* itch, itching.
pico [pí·ko] *m.* beak, bill; sharp point; peak; pickaxe, pick, spout; mouth; additional amount, a little over; *C.A., Carib., Riopl., Ven.* a small balance; *Mex.* a goodly sum; **tener el — de oro** to be very eloquent; **tener mucho —** to be very talkative.
picotada [pi·ko·tá·da] *f.*, **picotazo** [pi·ko·tá·so] *m.* peck.
picotear [pi·ko·te·ár] *v.* to peck; to chatter; *Am.* to mince, cut into small pieces.
pichel [pi·čél] *m.* pitcher; mug.
pichón [pi·čón] *m.* young pigeon; *C.A.* any male bird (*except a rooster*); *Am.* dupe, easy mark; *Am.* novice, inexperienced person, apprentice; *adj. Am.* timid, shy.
pie [pje] *m.* foot; leg; stand; stem; base; *Am.* down payment; *Mex.* strophe, stanza; *Am.* **— de amigo** wedge; prop; **— de banco** silly remark; **a — juntillas** steadfastly, firmly; **al — de la letra** to the letter, literally, exactly; **de —** (*or* **en —**) standing; **a cuatro -s** on all fours; **dar — a** to give an opportunity or occasion; *Am.* **estar a — en** to be ignorant of; **ir a —** to walk.
piececito [pje·se·sí·to], **piecito** [pje·si·to] *m.* little foot.
piedad [pje·dád] *f.* piety; pity; mercy; **monte de —**

pawnshop.
piedra [pjé·dra] *f.* stone; gravel; hailstone; *Ven.*
piece of a domino set; **— angular** (*or*
fundamental) cornerstone; **— caliza** limestone;
— pómez pumice, pumice stone; **a — y lodo**
shut tight; **ser — de escándalo** to be an object;
of scandal.
piel [pjel] *f.* skin; hide; leather; fur.
piélago [pjé·la·ǵo] *m.* high sea; sea; great
abundance, great plenty.
pienso [pjén·so] *m.* feed; thought; **ni por —** not
even in thought.
pierna [pjér·na] *f.* leg; **dormir a — suelta** to sleep
like a log, sleep soundly; *Am.* **ser una buena —**
to be a good fellow, be always in a good mood.
pieza [pjé·sa] *f.* (*pedazo*) piece; part; (*cuarto*)
room; (*comedia*) play; **de una —** solid, in one
piece; *Am.* **ser de una —** to be an honest,
upright man.
pifia [pí·fja] *f.* a miss, miscue.
pigmento [piǵ·men·to] *m.* pigment.
pijama [pi·yá·ma] [pi·xá·ma] *m.* pajamas.
pila [pí·la] *f.* (*pieza cóncava*) basin; baptismal font;
trough; (*cúmulo*) pile; heap; electric battery; **—
atómica** atomic pile; *Am.* fountain; *Andes*
hairless dog; *Am.* bald head; **nombre de —**
Christian name; *Andes* **andar —** to go naked;
Mex. **tener las -s** (*or* **tener por -s**) to have a lot,
have heaps.
pilar [pi·lár] *m.* pillar, column; basin of a fountain.
pilcha [píl·ča] *f. Riopl.* any article of clothing; *Am.*
mistress; **-s** *Riopl.* belongings.
píldora [píl·do·ra] *f.* pill.
pilmama [pil·má·ma] *f. Mex.* child's nurse, wet
nurse.
pilón [pi·lón] *m.* basin (*of a fountain*); watering
trough; sugar loaf; large wooden or metal
mortar (*for grinding grain*); counterpoise; *Mex.*
an additional amount, premium (*given to a
buyer*); *Mex.* **de —** to boot, in addition, besides;
piloncillo [pi·lon·sí·yo] *m. Am.* unrefined sugar
loaf.
pilotar [pi·lo·tár], **pilotear** [pi·lo·te·ár] *v.* to pilot.
pilote [pi·ló·te] *m.* pile (*for building*).
piloto [pi·ló·to] *m.* pilot; *Mex.* generous entertainer
or host.
pillaje [pi·yá·xe] *m.* pillage, plunder.
pillar [pi·yár] *v.* to pillage, plunder; to pilfer; to
seize, snatch, grasp; to catch; *Am.* to surprise,
catch in the act.
pillo [pí·yo] *adj.* roguish; sly, crafty; *m.* rogue,
rascal; *Am.* a species of heron; *Am.* long-legged
person; **pilluelo** [pi·ywé·lo] *m.* little rascal,
scamp.
pimentero [pi·men·té·ro] *m.* pepper plant;
pepperbox, pepper shaker.
pimentón [pi·men·tón] *m.* large pepper; cayenne,
red pepper; paprika.
pimienta [pi·mjén·ta] *f.* black pepper.
pimiento [pi·mjén·to] *m.* green pepper; red pepper.
pimpollo [pim·pó·yo] *m.* rosebud; bud; shoot,
sprout; attractive youth.
pináculo [pi·ná·ku·lo] *m.* pinnacle, top, summit.
pinar [pi·nár] *m.* pine grove.
pincel [pin·sél] *m.* artist's brush; **pincelada**
[pin·se·lá·da] *f.* stroke of the brush.
pinchar [pin·čár] *v.* to prick; to puncture.
pinchazo [pin·čá·so] *m.* prick; puncture; stab.
pingajo [piŋ·gá·xo] *m.* tag, tatter, rag.
pingo [piŋ·go] *m. Riopl., Andes* saddle horse; *Mex.*
devil.

pingüe [píŋ·gwe] *adj.* abundant, copious; fat, greasy.
pingüino [piŋ·gwí·no] *m.* penguin.
pino [pí·no] *m.* pine; *Am.* filling for a meat pie;
hacer -s (*or* **hacer pinitos**) to begin to walk (*said
of a baby*); to begin to do things (*said of a
novice*).
pinta [pín·ta] *f.* spot, mark; outward sign, aspect;
pint; *Mex.* **hacer —** to play hooky, cut class.
pintar [pin·tár] *v.* to paint; to describe, depict; to
feign; to begin to turn red, begin to ripen (*said
of fruit*); to fancy, imagine; *Mex.* to play hooky,
play truant; *Am.* to fawn, flatter; **no — nada** to
be worth nothing, count for nothing; **las cosas
no pintaban bien** things did not look well; *Mex.*
— venados to play hooky; **-se** to put on
make-up; *Am.* to excel (in); to praise oneself;
Ven. to go away.
pintarrajear [pin·ta·rra·xe·ár] *v.* to daub; to smear
with paint or rouge.
pinto [pín·to] *adj. Am.* spotted, speckled.
pintor [pin·tór] *m.* painter, artist; **— de brocha
gorda** house painter; poor artist; *adj. Am.*
boastful, conceited.
pintoresco [pin·to·rés·ko] *adj.* picturesque.
pintura [pin·tú·ra] *f.* painting; picture; paint, color;
description.
pinzas [pín·sas] *f. pl.* pincers; tweezers; claws (*of
lobsters, crabs, etc.*); *Riopl., Mex., Carib.* pliers,
tongs.
piña [pí·ña] pineapple; pine cone; piña cloth;
cluster; *Cuba* pool (*a billiard game*).
piñata [pi·ñá·ta] *f.* pot; hanging pot or other
container (*filled with candies, fruit, etc.*).
piñón [pi·ñón] *m.* pine nut; nut pine; pinion.
pío [pí·o] *adj.* pious, devout; kind; merciful;
dappled, spotted (*horse*); **obras pías** pious works,
charitable deeds.
piocha [pjó·ča] *adj. Mex.* great! excellent.
piojo [pjó·xo] *m.* louse.
piojoso [pjo·xó·so] *adj.* lousy; mean, stingy.
pionero [pjo·né·ro] *m.* pioneer; boy scout.
pipa [pí·pa] *f.* tobacco pipe; keg, barrel; reed pipe
(*musical instrument*); fruit seed (*of a lemon,
orange, melon*); *Col.* green coconut; *Am.* potato;
Ven. **estar —** to be drunk; *m. Am.* species of
green frog.
pipiar [pi·pjár] *v.* to peep, chirp.
pipiolo [pi·pjó·lo] *m.* novice, beginner; *Am.* child,
youngster.
pique [pi·ke] *m.* pique, resentment; chigger (*insect*);
flea; *Am.* small chili pepper; *Am.* trail; **a — de** in
danger of, on the point of; **echar a —** to sink (*a
ship*); to destroy; **irse a —** to capsize; to sink.
piquete [pi·ké·te] *m.* prick; bite, sting (*of insects*);
small hole; picket, stake; picket (*military*); *Am.*
small band of musicians; *Am.* small corral; *Am.*
cutting edge of scissors.
piragua [pi·rá·ǵwa] *f. Riopl., Carib., Ven., Col.,
Andes* Indian canoe; dugout.
pirámide [pi·rá·mi·de] *f.* pyramid.
pirata [pi·rá·ta] *m.* pirate.
piratear [pi·ra·te·ár] *v.* to pirate.
piropo [pi·ró·po] *m.* flattery, compliment; a variety
of garnet (*a semiprecious stone*); **echar un —** to
"throw a bouquet"; to compliment.
pirotecnia [pi·ro·ték·nja] *f.* pyrotechnics; fireworks.
pirueta [pi·rwé·ta] *f.* whirl; somersault; caper;
hacer -s to cut capers; to turn somersaults; to
do stunts.
pisada [pi·sá·da] *f.* footstep; footprint; **dar una —**
to step on, stamp on; **seguir las -s de** to follow

PE

in the footsteps of; to imitate.
pisapapeles [pi·sa·pa·pé·les] *m.* paperweight.
pisar [pi·sár] *v.* to step on, tread upon; to trample under foot; to pound; to cover (*said of a male bird*).
piscina [pi·sí·na] *f.* swimming pool, swimming tank; fish pond.
pisco [pis·ko] *m. Peru, Col.* a rum-based mixed drink.
pise [pí·se] *m. Ven.* rut; *Am.* tread (*of a wheel*). *See* **rodadura.**
piso [pí·so] *m.* floor; story; pavement; apartment, flat; tread; *Ríopl., Mex., Carib., Ven.* fee for pasturage rights; *Am.* table scarf; *Am.* stool, footstool; *Am.* small rug.
pisón [pi·són] *m.* heavy mallet (*for pounding, flattening, crushing*).
pisotear [pi·so·te·ár] *v.* to tramp, tramp on, trample; to tread.
pisotón [pi·so·tón] *m.* hard step, stamp (*of the foot*); **dar un —** to step hard, stamp (upon).
pista [pís·ta] *f.* track, trace, trail; clew; race track; **— de aterrizaje** landing field.
pistola [pis·tó·la] *f.* pistol; **pistolera** [pis·to·lé·ra] *f.* holster.
pistolero [pis·to·lé·ro] *m.* gangster; body guard.
pistón [pis·tón] *m.* piston; *Col.* cornet.
pita [pí·ta] *f. Am.* agave or century plant; *Am.* fiber, or thread made from the fiber, of the agave or maguey.
pitar [pi·tár] *v.* to toot; to whistle; *Ríopl., Andes* to smoke; *Ven.* to hiss; *Carib., Mex.* to slip away, escape; *Am.* **-se una cosa** to steal something; *Ch., Col., Ven., C.A.* (*pitado*) **salir pitando** to leave on the run.
pitazo [pi·tá·so] *m.* toot, whistle, blast.
pitillo [pi·tí·yo] *m. Spain* cigarette; **pitillera** [pi·ti·yé·ra] *f.* cigarette case.
pito [pí·to] *m.* whistle; cigarette; *Am.* tick (*an insect*); **no vale un —** it is not worth a straw; *Am.* **no saber ni — de una cosa** not to know anything about a subject.
pitón [pi·tón] *m.* lump; horn of an animal.
pizarra [pi·sá·rra] *f.* slate; blackboard; **pizarrín** [pi·sa·rrín] *m.* slate pencil; **pizarrón** [pi·sa·rrón] *m.* blackboard.
pizca [pís·ka] *f.* pinch, small bit; *Mex.* harvest.
placa [plá·ka] *f.* badge, insignia; plaque, tablet; metal plate; photographic plate; license plate; *Ven.* scab or skin blemish.
placentero [pla·sen·té·ro] *adj.* pleasant, agreeable.
placer[38] [pla·sér] *v. irr.* to please, content; *m.* pleasure; sand bank, shoal; placer (*place where gold is obtained by washing*); *Am.* pearl fishing.
placero [pla·sé·ro] *m.,* **placera** *f.* market vendor.
plácido [plá·si·do] *adj.* placid, calm.
plaga [plá·ga] *f.* plague; calamity.
plagar [pla·gár] *v.* to plague, infest; **-se de** to become plagued or infested with.
plagiar [pla·xjár] *v.* to plagiarize, steal and use as one's own (*the writings, ideas, etc. of another*); to kidnap, abduct.
plan [plan] *m.* plan; design; project; drawing; mine floor; *Am.* clearing; *Am.* building grounds of a ranch.
plana [plá·na] *f.* page (*of a newspaper*); plain, flat country; mason's trowel; tally sheet; **enmendar la — a uno** to correct a person's mistakes.
plancton [plánk·ton] *m.* plankton.
plancha [plán·ča] *f.* flatiron; metal plate; gangplank; blunder; *Cuba* railway flatcar; *Ven.,*

Col. dental plate; **— de blindaje** armor plate; **hacer una —** to make a ridiculous blunder; **tirarse una —** to place oneself in a ridiculous situation.
planchado [plan·čá·do] *m.* ironing; clothes ironed or to be ironed; *adj. Am.* smart, clever; *Am.* brave; *Ven.* dolled up, dressed up; *Am.* broke, penniless.
planchar [plan·čár] *v.* to iron; to smooth out; *Mex.* to leave (*someone*) waiting; *Am.* to strike with the flat of a blade; *Am.* to flatter; *Mex., Ven.* — **el asiento** to be a wallflower at a dance.
planeador [pla·ne·a·dór] *m.* glider airplane.
planear [pla·ne·ár] *v.* to plan; to glide (*said of an airplane or bird*).
planeo [pla·né·o] *m.* planning; glide, gliding (*of an airplane*).
planeta [pla·né·ta] *m.* planet.
planetario [pla·ne·tá·rjo] *m.* planetary.
plano [plá·no] *adj.* plane, flat, level; *m.* plane; plan; map; **de —** flatly, clearly, openly; **dar de —** to hit with the flat of anything.
planta [plán·ta] *f.* (*ser orgánico*) plant; plantation; (*proyecto*) plan; ground plan, ground floor; (*del pie*) sole of the foot; **— baja** ground floor; **buena —** good looks; **echar -s** to brag.
plantación [plan·ta·sjón] *f.* plantation; planting.
plantar [plan·tár] *v.* plant; to strike (*a blow*); **-se** to stand firm; to balk; *Am.* to doll up, dress up; **dejar a uno plantado** to "stand someone up", keep someone waiting indefinitely.
plantear [plan·te·ár] *v.* to plan; to establish; to carry out; to state, present (*a problem*); to try.
plantel [plan·tél] *m.* establishment; firm; plant; nursery.
plantío [plan·tí·o] *m.* planting; plantation; recently planted garden; tree nursery.
plañidero [pla·ñi·dé·ro] *m.* professional mourner.
plasma [pláz·ma] *m.* plasma.
plástico [plás·ti·ko] *adj.* plastic.
plata [plá·ta] *f.* silver; silver money; **hablar en —** to speak in plain language; *Carib., C.A., Ven., Col.* money.
plataforma [pla·ta·fór·ma] *f.* platform; **— de lanzamiento** launching pad.
platanal [pla·ta·nál], **platanar** [pla·ta·nár] *m.* grove of banana trees; banana plantation.
plátano [plá·ta·no] *m.* banana; banana tree; plane tree.
platea [pla·té·a] *f.* main floor of a theatre; a lower box seat.
plateado [pla·te·á·do] *adj.* silver-plated; silvery.
platear [pla·te·ár] *v.* to silver, plate, cover with silver.
platel [pla·tél] *m.* platter; tray.
platero [pla·té·ro] *m.* silversmith; jeweler.
plática [plá·ti·ka] *f.* conversation, talk, chat; informal lecture.
platicador [pla·ti·ka·dór] *m.* talker; *adj.* talkative.
platicar[6] [pla·ti·kár] *v.* to converse, talk, chat.
platillo [pla·tí·yo] *m.* saucer; pan (*of a pair of scales*); cymbal; stew.
platino [pla·tí·no] *m.* platinum.
plato [plá·to] *m.* plate; dish; dinner course; **— de tocadiscos** turntable.
platón [pla·tón] *m.* large plate; platter.
platudo [pla·tú·do] *adj. Am.* wealthy, rich.
playa [plá·ya] *f.* beach, shore; *Ven.* wide, open space in front of a ranch house; *Ríopl., Andes* **— de estacionamiento** parking lot.
plaza [plá·sa] *f.* (*pública*) plaza, public square;

public market; (*empleo*) job; employment; *Riopl.*, *Ch.*, *Cuba*, *Ven.* park, promenade; — **de armas** parade ground; public square; fortress; — **fuerte** fortress; — **de gallos** cockpit (*for cockfights*); — **de toros** bull ring; **sacar a** — to bring out into the open, make public; **sentar** — to enlist; **plazoleta** [pla·so·lé·ta], **plazuela** [pla·swé·la] *f.* small square, court.

plazo [plá·so] *m.* term, time; **a** — on credit; in installments.

pleamar [ple·a·már] *m.* flood tide, high tide.

plebe [plé·ƀe] *f.* rabble; masses.

plebeyo [ple·ƀé·yo] *adj.* plebeian.

plebiscito [ple·ƀi·sí·to] *m.* plebiscite, direct vote.

plegadizo [ple·ga·ɖí·so] *adj.* folding; pliable, easily bent.

plegar[1,7] [ple·gár] *v.* to fold; to pleat; to crease; **-se** to bend, yield, submit.

plegaria [ple·gá·rja] *f.* supplication, prayer; prayer hour.

pleito [pléj·to] *m.* litigation, lawsuit; dispute; debate; duel; — **de acreedores** bankruptcy proceedings; **pleitista** *m. & f.* quarrelsome person.

plenario [ple·ná·rjo] *adj.* plenary (*session*).

plenipotenciario [ple·ni·po·ten·sjá·rjo] *m.* plenipotentiary (*diplomatic agent having full power or authority*); *adj.* plenipotentiary, having full power.

plenitud [ple·ni·túɖ] *f.* plenitude, fullness, completeness; abundance.

pleno [plé·no] *adj.* full, complete; **sesión plena** joint session; **en** — **día** in broad daylight, openly; **en** — **rostro** (*or* **en plena cara**) right on the face; *m.* joint session (*of a legislative body*).

pleuresía [plew·re·sí·a] *f.* pleurisy.

pliego [pljé·go] *m.* sheet of paper; sealed letter or document.

pliegue [pljé·ge] *m.* fold, crease, pleat.

plomada [plo·má·ɖa] *f.* plumb, lead weight, plumb bob.

plomazo [plo·má·so] *m. Col.*, *Ven.*, *Mex.* shot, bullet.

plomería [plo·me·rí·a] *f.* plumbing; plumber's shop; lead roof.

plomero [plo·mé·ro] *m.* plumber.

plomizo [plo·mí·so] *adj.* leaden, lead-colored.

plomo [pló·mo] *m.* lead; plumb, lead weight; bullet; boring person; **a** — vertical; vertically; *adj. Carib.*, *Mex.* lead-colored.

pluma [plú·ma] *f.* (*de ave*) feather; plume; (*instrumento*) pen; quill; — **estilográfica** (*or* — **fuente**) fountain pen; **plumada** [plu·má·ɖa] *f.* dash, stroke of the pen, flourish; **plumaje** [plu·má·xe] *m.* plumage; plume, **plumero** [plu·mé·ro] *m.* feather duster; box for feathers; feather ornament (*on hats, helmets, etc.*); **plumón** [plu·món] *m.* down; feather mattress; **plumoso** [plu·mó·so] *adj.* downy, feathery.

plural [plu·rál] *adj.* plural.

plutonio [plu·tó·njo] *m.* plutonium.

pluralidad [plu·ra·li·ɖáɖ] *f.* plurality.

pluvial [plu·ƀjál] *adj.* rain (*used as adj.*); **capa** — cope (*long cape used by priests during certain religious ceremonies*).

pluviómetro [plu·ƀjó·me·tro] *m.* rain gauge.

población [po·ƀla·sjón] *f.* (*acto*) populating; settlement; (*número*) population; (*lugar*) town, city.

poblado [po·ƀlá·ɖo] *m.* inhabited place; village; *p.p.* populated; covered with growth.

poblador [po·ƀla·ɖór] *m.* settler (*of a colony*).

poblar[2] [po·ƀlár] *v. irr.* to populate, people; to colonize, settle; to stock (*a farm*); to breed; **-se** to become covered (*with leaves or buds*).

pobre [pó·ƀre] *adj.* poor; *m.* poor man; beggar; **pobrete** [po·ƀré·te] *m.* poor devil, poor wretch; **pobretón** [po·ƀre·tón] *m.* poor old fellow, poor wretch.

pobreza [po·ƀré·sa] *f.* poverty; need; lack, scarcity; barrenness.

pocilga [po·síl·ga] *f.* pigsty, pigpen.

pocillo [po·sí·yo] *m.* cup.

poco [pó·ko] *adj.* little, scanty; small; short (*time*); **-s** few, some; *m.* a little, a bit; *adv.* little; **a** — presently, after a short time; **a** — **rato** (*or* **al** — **rato**) after a short while; — **a** — slowly, little by little; **a los -s meses** after a few months; **por** — **me caigo** I almost fell; **tener en** — **a** to hold in low esteem.

podadera [po·ɖa·ɖé·ra] *f.* pruning hook or knife.

podar [po·ɖár] *v.* to prune, trim, cut off.

podenco [po·ɖén·ko] *m.* hound.

poder[39] [po·ɖér] *v. irr.* to be able; can; may; **él puede mucho** (*or* **poco**) he has much (*or* little) power; **puede que** it is possible that, it may be that, perhaps; **hasta más no** — to the utmost, to the limit; **no** — **más** not to be able to do more; to be exhausted; **no puede menos de hacerlo** he cannot help doing it; **no** — **con la carga** not to be equal to the burden, not to be able to lift the load; *Col.*, *Ven.* **-le a uno algo** to be worried or affected by something, *m.* power, authority.

poderío [po·ɖe·rí·o] *m.* power, dominion; might; wealth.

poderoso [po·ɖe·ró·so] *adj.* powerful; wealthy.

podre [pó·ɖre] *f.* pus; decayed matter; **podredumbre** [po·ɖre·ɖúm·bre] *f.* corruption, decay; pus; rotten matter.

podrido [po·ɖri·ɖo] *adj.* rotten; *p.p.* of **podrir**.

podrir[16] [po·ɖrír] = **pudrir**[16].

poema [po·é·ma] *m.* poem.

poesía [po·e·sí·a] *f.* poetry; poem.

poeta [po·é·ta] *m.* poet; **poetastro** [po·e·tás·tro] *m.* bad poet.

poético [po·é·ti·ko] *adj.* poetic; **poética** [po·é·ti·ka] *f.* poetics.

poetisa [po·e·tí·sa] *f.* poetess.

polaco [po·lá·ko] *adj.* Polish; *m.* Polish, Polish language; Pole.

polaina [po·láj·na] *f.* legging.

polar [po·lár] *adj.* polar.

polea [po·lé·a] *f.* pulley.

polémica [po·lé·mi·ka] *f.* controversy; polemics.

polen [po·len] *m.* pollen.

policía [po·li·sí·a] *f.* police; *m.* policeman.

policial [po·li·sjál] *m. Col.*, *Ven.* policeman.

policiaco [po·li·sjá·ko] [po·li·sí·a·ko] *adj.* police, detective (*story*).

poligamia [po·li·gá·mja] *f.* polygamy.

políglota [po·lí·glo·ta] *m. & f.* polyglot; one who speaks several languages.

polilla [po·lí·ya] *f.* moth; larva of the moth.

poliomielitis [po·ljo·mje·lí·tis] *f.* poliomyelitis, polio.

política [po·lí·ti·ka] *f.* politics; policy; *Am.* — **de campanario** politics of a clique.

politicastro [po·lí·ti·kás·tro] *m.* bad or incapable politician.

político [po·lí·ti·ko] *adj.* political; politic; polite; **madre política** mother-in-law; *m.* politician.

póliza [pó·li·sa] *f.* policy, written contract; draft;

Pl

customhouse certificate; — **de seguros** insurance policy.
polizonte [po·li·són·te] *m.* policeman.
polo [pó·lo] *m.* pole (*of a magnet or of an axis*); polo (*a game*); — **acuático** water polo.
polonio [po·ló·njo] *m.* polonium.
poltrón [pol·trón] *adj.* lazy, idle; **silla poltrona** easy chair.
polvareda [pol·ƀa·ré·ƌa] *f.* cloud of dust; **armar** (*or* **levantar**) **una** — to kick up the dust; to raise a rumpus.
polvera [pol·ƀé·ra] *f.* powder box; compact; powder puff.
polvo [pól·ƀo] *m.* dust; powder; pinch of snuff or powder; — **férrico** iron oxide filings (*coating for recording tape*); **-s** toilet powder; **-s para dientes** tooth powder; **limpio de** — **y paja** entirely free; net; *Am.* cleaned out, without a penny; *Am.* innocent, ignorant, unaware; *Mex., Col., Ven.* **tomar el** — to escape, "beat it".
pólvora [pól·ƀo·ra] *f.* gunpowder; fireworks.
polvorear [pol·ƀo·re·ár] *v.* to powder, sprinkle with powder.
polvoriento [pol·ƀo·rjén·to] *adj.* dusty.
polvorin [pol·ƀo·rín] *m.* powder magazine; priming powder; powder flask; *Am.* tick (*parasitic insect*); *Ríopl.* spitfire, quick-tempered person.
polla [pó·ya] *f.* pullet (*young hen*); young lass; pool (*in cards*).
pollada [po·yá·ƌa] *f.* hatch, brood; flock of chicks.
pollera [po·yé·ra] *f.* woman who raises and sells chickens; chicken coop; a bell-shaped basket for chickens; petticoat; *Riopl., Ch., Col., Andes* skirt.
pollino [po·yí·no] *m.* young donkey, ass.
pollo [pó·yo] *m.* young chicken ; nestling, young bird; *Spain* young man; **polluelo** [po·ywé·lo] *m.* chick.
pomelo [po·mé·lo] *m. Spain* grapefruit.
pómez [pó·mes] *m.* pumice.
pompa [póm·pa] *f.* pomp; pageant, procession; bubble; pump.
pomposo [pom·pó·so] *adj.* pompous.
pómulo [pó·mu·lo] *m.* cheek bone.
ponche [pón·če] *m.* punch (*a beverage*); **ponchera** [pon·čé·ra] *f.* punch bowl.
poncho [pón·čo] *m. Andes, Ch., Ríopl.* poncho; cape.
ponderación [pon·de·ra·sjón] *f.* pondering, careful consideration, weighing; exaggeration.
ponderar [pon·de·rár] *v.* (*pensar*) to ponder, consider, weigh; (*exagerar*) to exaggerate; to extol.
ponderativo [pon·de·ra·tí·ƀo] *adj.* exaggerating.
ponderoso [pon·de·ró·so] *adj.* ponderous, heavy.
poner[40] [po·nér] *v. irr.* to put; to place; to set; to lay; to suppose; — **como nuevo a alguien** to cover someone with insults; — **en claro** to clarify; — **en limpio** to recopy, make a clean copy; — **todo de su parte** to do one's best; **pongamos que . . .** let us suppose that . . .; **-se** to place oneself; to become; **-se a** to begin to; **-se al corriente** to become informed; **-se de pie** to stand up; *Carib., Mex., Ch., Andes* **-se bien con alguien** to ingratiate oneself with someone, get on his good side; *Am.* **ponérsela** to get drunk.
poniente [po·njén·te] *m.* west; west wind; **el sol** — the setting sun.
pontón [pon·tón] *m.* pontoon; scow, flat-bottomed boat; log bridge; pontoon bridge.
ponzoña [pon·só·ña] *f.* venom, poison.

ponzoñoso [pon·so·ñó·so] *adj.* venomous, poisonous.
popa [pó·pa] *f.* poop, stern; **viento en** — speedily; going well.
popote [po·pó·te] *m. Mex.* straw for brooms; *Mex.* drinking straw or tube.
populacho [po·pu·lá·čo] *m.* populace, rabble.
popular [po·pu·lár] *adj.* popular.
popularidad [po·pu·la·ri·ƌáƌ] *f.* popularity.
populoso [po·pu·ló·so] *adj.* populous, densely populated.
popurrí [po·pu·rrí] *m.* potpourri.
poquito [po·kí·to] *adj.* very little; *Cuba, Ven., Col.* timid, shy; *m.* a small bit; **a -s** in small quantities.
por [por] *prep.* by; for; for the sake of, on account of, on behalf of; because of; through; along; on exchange for; in the place of; during; about, around; to, with the idea of; — **ciento** percent; — **consiguiente** consequently; — **entre** among, between; — **escrito** in writing; — **poco se muere** he almost died; **está** — **hacer** it is yet to be done; **él está** — **hacerlo** he is in favor of doing it; **recibir** — **esposa** to receive as a wife; **tener** — to consider, think of as; ¿— **que?** *interr. adv.* why? for what reason?
porcelana [por·se·lá·na] *f.* porcelain, china; enamel.
porcentaje [por·sen·tá·xe] *m.* percentage.
porcino [por·sí·no] *adj.* porcine; related to the pig.
porción [por·sjón] *f.* portion; part, share; **una** — **de gente** a lot of people.
porche [pór·če] *m.* porch.
pordiosear [por·djo·se·ár] *v.* to beg.
pordiosero [por·djo·sé·ro] *m.* beggar.
porfia [por·fí·a] *f.* stubbornness, obstinacy; persistence, insistence; **a** — in competition; with great insistence.
porfiado[por·fjá·ƌo] *adj.* stubborn, obstinate, persistent.
porfiar[17] [por·fjár] *v.* to persist; to insist; to dispute obstinately; to argue.
pormenor [por·me·nór] *m.* detail.
pormenorizar[9] [por·me·no·ri·sár] *v.* to detail, tell in detail; to itemize.
pornografía [por·no·ǥra·fí·a] *f.* pornography.
pornográfico [por·no·ǥrá·fi·ko] *adj.* pornographic.
poro [pó·ro] *m.* pore.
poroso [po·ró·so] *adj.* porous.
poroto [po·ró·to] *m. Ch., Ríopl., Andes* bean; *Ch., Ríopl., Andes* runt; urchin.
porque [pór·ke] *conj.* because; so that.
porqué [por·ké] *m.* cause, reason, motive.
porquería [por·ke·rí·a] *f.* filth; filthy act or word; nasty piece of food; trifle, worthless object.
porra [pó·rra] *f.* club, stick; *Am.* **mandar a uno a la** — to send someone to the devil; **porrazo** *m.* blow; knock; bump; **porrón** *m.* wine vessel with long snout.
porta [pór·ta] *f.* porthole; cover for a porthole; goal (*in football*).
portaaviones [por·ta·a·ƀjó·nes] *m.* airplane carrier.
portada [por·tá·ƌa] *f.* façade, front (*of a building*); title page.
portador [por·ta·ƌór] *m.* carrier; bearer; tray.
portal [por·tál] *m.* portal; entrance, vestibule; portico, porch; *Am.* Christmas crèche; **-es** arcades, galleries; **portalón** [por·ta·lón] *m.* large portal; gangway (*of a ship*).
portamonedas [por·ta·mo·ne·ƌas] *m.* pocketbook, coin purse.

portapapeles [por·ta·pa·pé·les] *m.* briefcase.
portaplumas [por·ta·plú·mas] *m.* penholder.
portar [por·tár] *v. Am.* to carry; **-se** to behave.
portátil [por·tá·til] *adj.* portable.
portaviones [por·ta·ƀjo·nes] *m.* aircraft carrier; also **portaaviones.**
portavoz [por·ta·ƀos] *m.* megaphone; mouthpiece; spokesman.
portazgo [por·táz·ǥo] *m.* toll.
portazo [por·tá·so] *m.* bang or slam of a door; **dar un —** to bang or slam the door.
porte [pór·te] *m.* portage, cost of carriage; freight; postage; manner, bearing; size, capacity; *Am.* birthday present; *C.A.* size.
portear [por·te·ár] *v.* to carry on one's back; *Am.* to get out in a hurry.
portento [por·tén·to] *m.* portent; wonder, marvel.
portentoso [por·ten·tó·so] *adj.* marvelous, extraordinary, amazing, terrifying.
porteño [por·té·ño] *adj.* from a port; *Riopl.* from Buenos Aires.
portería [por·te·ría] *f.* porter's quarters; main door of a building.
portero [por·té·ro] *m.* doorkeeper, doorman; janitor.
pórtico [pór·ti·ko] *m.* portico, porch.
portilla [por·ti·ya] *f.* porthole; small gate or passageway.
portón *m.* gate.
portugués [por·tu·ǥés] *adj.* Portuguese; *m.* Portuguese; Portuguese language.
porvenir [por·ƀe·nír] *m.* future.
pos [pos]: **en — de** after; in pursuit of.
posada [po·sá· đa] *f.* lodging; inn; boardinghouse; dwelling, home; *Mex.* **las -s** a Christmas festivity lasting nine days; **posadero** [po·sa·đé·ro] *m.* innkeeper.
posaderas [po·sa·đé·ras] *f. pl.* posterior, buttocks, rump.
posar [po·sár] *v.* to lodge; to rest; to sit down; to pose (*as a model*); to perch (*said of birds*); **-se** to settle (*said of sediment*); to perch (*said of birds*).
posdata [poz·đá·ta] *f.* postscript.
poseedor [po·se·e·đór] *m.* possessor, owner.
poseer[14] [po·se·ér] *v.* to possess, own; to master, know well; **-se** to have control of oneself.
posesión [po·se·sjón] *f.* possession.
posesivo [po·se·si·ƀo] *adj. & m.* possessive.
posesor [po·se·sór] *m.* possessor, owner.
posibilidad [po·si·ƀi·li·đáđ] *f.* possibility.
posible [po·si·ƀle] *adj.* possible; **hacer lo —** to do one's best; **-s** *m. pl.* goods, property, means.
posición [po·si·sjón] *f.* position; posture; status, rank, standing; placing.
positivo [po·si·tí·ƀo] *adj.* positive; effective; true; practical.
posponer[40] [pos·po·nér] *v. irr.* to postpone, put off; to put after; to subordinate.
pospuesto [pos·pwés·to] *p.p. of* **posponer.**
posta [pós·ta] *f.* (*bala*) small bullet; (*apuesta*) bet, wager; (*relevo*) relay (*of post horses*); post station; **-s** buckshot; **por la —** posthaste; fast, speedily; *m.* postboy, courier, messenger.
postal [pos·tál] *adj.* postal; **tarjeta —** postcard.
postdata [poz·đá·ta] = **posdata.**
poste [pós·te] *m.* post, pillar.
postergar[7] [pos·ter·ǥár] *v.* to delay; to postpone; to disregard someone's right.
posteridad [pos·te·ri·đáđ] *f.* posterity.
posterior [pos·te·rjór] *adj.* posterior, back, rear; later.

postigo [pos·tí·ǥo] *m.* wicket, small door or gate; shutter; peep window.
postizo [pos·tí·so] *adj.* false, artificial; *m.* switch, false hair.
postración [pos·tra·sjón] *f.* prostration, collapse, exhaustion; dejection, lowness of spirits.
postrar [pos·trár] *v.* to prostrate; to humiliate; to throw down; to weaken, exhaust; **-se** to kneel to the ground; to be weakened, exhausted; to collapse.
postre [pós·tre] *m.* dessert; **a la —** at last.
postrer(o) [pos·tré·r(o)] *adj.* last; hindmost, nearest the rear.
postulante [pos·tu·lán·te] *m. & f.* petitioner; applicant, candidate.
póstumo [pós·tu·mo] *adj.* posthumous, after one's death.
postura [pos·tú·ra] *f.* posture, position; bid; wager; pact, agreement; egg-laying.
potable [po·tá·ƀle] *adj.* drinkable; **agua —** drinking water.
potaje [po·tá·xe] *m.* pottage, thick soup; porridge; mixed drink.
potasio [po·tá·sjo] *m.* potassium.
pote [pó·te] *m.* pot; jar; jug; *Carib., Ven., Mex., Riopl.* flask; *Am.* buzzard.
potencia [po·tén·sja] *f.* potency; power; faculty, ability; powerful nation.
potentado [po·ten·tá·đo] *m.* potentate.
potente [po·tén·te] *adj.* potent, powerful, strong.
potestad [po·tes·táđ] *f.* power; dominion, authority.
potranca [po·trán·ka] *f.* filly, young mare.
potrero [po·tré·ro] *m.* herdsman of colts; fenced-in pasture land; *Carib., Mex., C.A., Ven., Col., Ch.* cattle ranch, stock farm.
potro [pó·tro] *m.* colt; rack, torture; *Col., Ven., Mex., Ch., Riopl.* wild horse.
poyo [pó·yo] *m.* stone or brick bench (*usually built against a wall*).
pozo [pó·so] *m.* well; hole, pit; mine shaft; hold of a ship; *Am.* pool, puddle; *Riopl., Ch., Ven., Col., Mex.* spring, fountain.
pozole [po·só·le] *m. Mex.* stew made of hominy and pig's head.
práctica [prák·ti·ka] *f.* practice; exercise; custom, habit; method.
practicante [prak·ti·kán·te] *m. & f.* doctor's assistant; hospital intern.
practicar[6] [prak·ti·kár] *v.* to practice; to put into practice.
práctico [prák·ti·ko] *adj.* practical; experienced, skilful; *m.* **— de puerto** harbor pilot.
pradera [pra·đé·ra] *f.* prairie; meadow.
prado [prá·đo] *m.* meadow, field; lawn.
preámbulo [pre·ám·bu·lo] *m.* preamble, introduction, prologue.
precario [pre·ká·rjo] *adj.* precarious.
precaución [pre·kaw·sjón] *f.* precaution.
precaver [pre·ka·ƀér] *v.* to guard (against), keep (from); to warn, caution; **-se** to guard oneself (against); to take precautions.
precavido [pre·ka·ƀí·đo] *adj.* cautious, on guard.
precedencia [pre·se·đén·sja] *f.* precedence; priority.
precedente [pre·se·đén·te] *adj.* preceding; *m.* precedent.
preceder [pre·se·đér] *v.* to precede; to have precedence.
precepto [pre·sép·to] *m.* precept; rule; order.
preceptor [pre·sep·tór] *m.* teacher, tutor.
preciado [pre·sjá·đo] *adj.* prized, esteemed; precious, valuable.

PO

preciar [pre·sjár] *v.* to appraise; to value; **-se de** to boast of, be proud of.

precio [pré·sjo] *m.* price; value, worth; esteem.

precioso [pre·sjó·so] *adj.* precious, valuable; fine, exquisite; beautiful.

precipicio [pre·si·pí·sjo] *m.* precipice; ruin.

precipitación [pre·si·pi·ta·sjón] *f.* precipitation; rush, haste, hurry.

precipitado [pre·si·pi·tá·ɖo] *adj.* precipitate, hasty, rash; *m.* precipitate (*chemical term*).

precipitar [pre·si·pi·tár] *v.* to precipitate; to hasten, rush; to hurl, throw headlong; **-se** to throw oneself headlong; to rush (into).

precipitoso [pre·si·pi·tó·so] *adj.* precipitous, steep; rash.

precisar [pre·si·sár] *v.* to determine precisely; to force, compel, make necessary; *Riopl., Col., Ven., Mex., Andes*; to be necessary or urgent; *Am.* to need.

precisión [pre·si·sjón] *f.* precision, exactness; accuracy; compulsion, force, necessity; *Am.* haste.

preciso [pre·sí·so] *adj.* necessary; precise, exact; clear; *m. Am.* small travelling bag.

precoz [pre·kós] *adj.* precocious.

precursor [pre·kur·sór] *m.* precursor, forerunner.

predecir[27] [pre·ɖe·sír] *v. irr.* to predict, prophesy, forecast, foretell.

predestinar [pre·ɖes·ti·nár] *v.* to predestine.

predicación [pre·ɖi·ka·sjón] *f.* preaching.

predicado [pre·ɖi·ká·ɖo] *adj. & m.* predicate; *p.p. of* **predicar.**

predicador [pre·ɖi·ka·ɖór] *m.* preacher.

predicar[6] [pre·ɖi·kár] *v.* to preach.

predicción [pre·ɖik·sjón] *f.* prediction.

predilección [pre·ɖi·lek·sjón] *f.* predilection, preference, liking.

predilecto [pre·ɖi·lek·to] *adj.* favorite, preferred.

predisponer[40] [pre·ɖis·po·nér] *v. irr.* to predispose, bias, prejudice.

predispuesto [pre·ɖis·pwés·to] *p.p. of* **predisponer** & *adj.* predisposed, prejudiced, biased.

predominante [pre·ɖo·mi·nán·te] *adj.* predominant; prevailing, ruling.

predominar [pre·ɖo·mi·nár] *v.* to predominate, prevail.

predominio [pre·ɖo·mí·njo] *m.* predominance; sway, influence.

prefacio [pre·fa·sjo] *m.* preface.

prefecto [pre·fék·to] *m.* prefect (*military or civil chief; sometimes a mayor, sometimes governor of a province, as in Peru*).

preferencia [pre·fe·rén·sja] *f.* preference; **de — with** preference; preferably.

preferente [pre·fe·rén·te] *adj.* preferable; preferred; preferential; **acciones -s** preferred shares.

preferible [pre·fe·ri·ɓle] *adj.* preferable.

preferir[3] [pre·fe·rír] *v. irr.* to prefer.

prefijar [pre·fi·xár] *v.* to prefix; to set beforehand (*as a date*).

prefijo [pre·fi·xo] *m.* prefix.

pregonar [pre·ɡo·nár] *v.* to proclaim, cry out; to make known.

pregunta [pre·ɡún·ta] *f.* question; **hacer una — to** ask a question.

preguntar [pre·ɡun·tár] *v.* to ask, inquire.

preguntón [pre·ɡun·tón] *adj.* inquisitive.

prejuicio [pre·xwí·sjo] *m.* prejudice.

prejuzgar[7] [pre·xuz·ɡár] *v. irr.* to prejudge.

prelado [pre·lá·ɖo] *m.* prelate.

preliminar [pre·li·mi·nár] *adj. & m.* preliminary.

preludiar [pre·lu·ɖjár] *v.* to be the prelude or beginning of; to initiate, introduce; to try out (*a musical instrument*).

preludio [pre·lú·ɖjo] *m.* prelude; introduction.

prematuro [pre·ma·tú·ro] *adj.* premature, untimely.

premeditado [pre·me·ɖi·tá·ɖo] *adj.* premeditated, deliberate.

premiar [pre·mjár] *v.* to reward.

premio [pré·mjo] *m.* prize; reward; recompense; premium; **a — with** interest, at interest.

premisa [pre·mí·sa] *f.* premise (*either of the first two propositions of a syllogism*).

premura [pre·mú·ra] *f.* pressure, urgency, haste.

prenda [prén·da] *f.* (*fianza*) pawn, pledge, security; token; (*partes del vestido*) article of clothing; anything valuable; loved person; jewel; **-s good** qualities, gifts, talents; **— de vestir** garment; **juego de -s** game of forfeits; **en — de** as a proof of, as a pledge of.

prendar [pren·dár] *v.* to pawn, pledge; to charm, please; **-se de** to get attached to; to fall in love with.

prendedor [pren·de·ɖór] *m.* clasp; stickpin; tie pin; brooch; *Am.* light.

prender [pren·dér] *v.* (*asir*) to seize, catch, grab; to bite (*said of an insect*); to fasten, clasp; to arrest, imprison; (*empezar*) to take root; to begin to burn; catch fire; *Riopl., Carib., C.A., Mex.* to light (*a lamp*); *Am.* to start, begin, undertake; **— el fuego** to start the fire; *Col.* **-las** to take to one's heels; **-se** to dress up.

prendero [pren·dé·ro] *m.* pawnbroker; second-hand dealer.

prensa [prén·sa] *f.* press; printing press.

prensar [pren·sár] *v.* to press.

prensil [pren·síl] *adj.* prehensile.

preñado [pre·ñá·ɖo] *adj.* pregnant; full.

preñez [pre·ñés] *f.* pregnancy.

preocupación [pre·o·ku·pa·sjón] *f.* preoccupation; worry; bias, prejudice.

preocupar [pre·o·ku·pár] *v.* to preoccupy; to worry; to prejudice; **-se** to be preoccupied; to worry; to be prejudiced.

preparación [pre·pa·ra·sjón] *f.* preparation.

preparar [pre·pa·rár] *v.* to prepare; **-se** to get ready; to be prepared.

preparativo [pre·pa·ra·tí·ɓo] *adj.* preparatory; *m.* preparation.

preparatorio [pre·pa·ra·tó·rjo] *adj.* preparatory.

preponderancia [pre·pon·de·rán·sja] *f.* preponderance.

preposición [pre·po·si·sjón] *f.* preposition.

prerrogativa [pre·rro·ɡa·tí·ɓa] *f.* prerogative, right, privilege.

presa [pré·sa] *f.* prey; dam; fang, tusk; claw; **hacer — to** seize.

presagiar [pre·sa·xjár] *v.* to foretell.

presagio [pre·sá·xjo] *m.* presage, omen, sign.

presbítero [prez·ɓí·te·ro] *m.* priest.

prescindir [pre·sin·dír] *v.* to disregard, set aside, leave aside; to omit; to dispense (with).

prescribir[52] [pres·kri·bír] *v.* to prescribe.

prescrito [pres·kri·to] *p.p. of* **prescribir.**

presencia [pre·sén·sja] *f.* presence; figure, bearing; **— de animo** presence of mind, serenity.

presenciar [pre·sen·sjár] *v.* to see, witness; to be present at.

presentación [pre·sen·ta·sjón] *f.* presentation; personal introduction; *Ven.* petition.

presentar [pre·sen·tár] *v.* to present; to introduce; **-se** to appear, present oneself; to introduce oneself; to offer one's services; *Am.* to have recourse to justice, file suit.

presente [pre·sén·te] *adj.* present; *m.* present, gift; **al** — now, at the present time; **por el (la,** *or* **lo)** — for the present; **mejorando lo** — present company excepted; **tener** — to bear in mind.

presentimiento [pre·sen·ti·mjén·to] *m.* presentiment, foreboding.

presentir[3] [pre·sen·tír] *v. irr.* to have a presentiment, foreboding or hunch.

preservación [pre·ser·ba·sjón] *f.* preservation.

preservar [pre·ser·bár] *v.* to preserve, guard, protect, keep.

presidencia [pre·si·dén·sja] *f.* presidency; office of president; presidential term; chairmanship.

presidencial [pre·si·den·sjál] *adj.* presidential.

presidente [pre·si·dén·te] *m.* president; chairman; presiding judge.

presidiario [pre·si·djá·rjo] *m.* prisoner, convict.

presidio [pre·sí·djo] *m.* garrison; fortress; penitentiary, prison; **diez años de** — ten years at hard labor (*in a prison*).

presidir [pre·si·dír] *v.* to preside; to direct.

presilla [pre·si·ya] *f.* loop, fastener; clip.

presión [pre·sjón] *f.* pressure.

preso [pré·so] *m.* prisoner; *p.p. irr.* of **prender** imprisoned.

prestado [pres·tá·do] *adj.* & *p.p.* loaned, lent; **dar** — to lend; **pedir** — to borrow.

prestamista [pres·ta·mís·ta] *m.* & *f.* moneylender.

préstamo [prés·ta·mo] *m.* loan.

prestar [pres·tár] *v.* to loan, lend; *Col., Ven., C.A., Andes* to borrow; — **ayuda** to give help; — **atención** to pay attention; *Andes* **presta acá** give it here, give it to me; **-se** to lend oneself or itself.

presteza [pres·té·sa] *f.* promptness, speed.

prestidigitación [pres·ti·di·xi·ta·sjón] *f.* juggling, sleight of hand.

prestidigitador [pres·ti·di·xi·ta·dór] *m.* juggler.

prestigio [pres·tí·xjo] *m.* prestige; influence; authority; good reputation.

presto [prés·to] *adj.* quick; nimble; prompt; ready; *adv.* soon, at once; **de** — quickly, promptly.

presumido [pre·su·mí·do] *adj.* conceited, presumptuous; *p.p. of* **presumir.**

presumir [pre·su·mír] *v.* to presume; to boast; to show off; *Am.* to court, woo; — **de valiente** to boast of one's valor.

presunción [pre·sun·sjón] *f.* presumption, assumption; conceit, arrogance.

presunto [pre·sún·to] *adj.* presumed; supposed; prospective; **heredero** — heir apparent.

presuntuoso [pre·sun·twó·so] *adj.* presumptuous, conceited.

presuponer[40] [pre·su·po·nér] *v. irr.* to presuppose, take for granted, imply; to estimate.

presupuesto [pre·su·pwés·to] *p.p. of* **presuponer** presupposed; estimated; *m.* budget, estimate.

presuroso [pre·su·ró·so] *adj.* quick, prompt; hasty.

pretencioso [pre·ten·sjó·so] *adj.* presumptuous; conceited.

pretender [pre·ten·dér] *v.* to pretend; to solicit; seek; to claim; to try; to court.

pretendiente [pre·ten·djén·te] *m.* pretender, claimant; suitor; office seeker.

pretensión [pre·ten·sjón] *f.* pretension; claim; presumption; pretense.

pretérito [pre·té·ri·to] *adj.* preterite, past; *m.* preterite, the past tense.

pretexto [pre·tés·to] *m.* pretext, pretense, excuse.

pretil [pre·til] *m.* stone or brick railing; *Am.* ledge; *Mex., Ven.* stone or brick bench (*built against a wall*).

pretina [pre·tí·na] *f.* belt, girdle; waistband.

prevalecer[13] [pre·ba·le·sér] *v. irr.* to prevail.

prevaleciente [pre·ba·le·sjén·te] *adj.* prevalent, current.

prevención [pre·ben·sjón] *f.* prevention; foresight, preparedness; bias, prejudice; provision, supply; admonition, warning; police station; guardhouse.

prevenido [pre·be·ní·do] *adj.* & *p.p.* prepared, ready; forewarned; cautious; supplied.

prevenir[48] [pre·be·nír] *v. irr.* to prevent, avoid; to prepare beforehand; to foresee; to warn; to predispose; **-se** to get prepared, get ready.

prever[49] [pre·bér] *v. irr.* to foresee.

previo [pré·bjo] *adj.* previous; *m. Am.* preliminary examination.

previsión [pre·bi·sjón] *f.* foresight.

previsto [pre·bís·to] *p.p. of* **prever.**

prieto [prjé·to] *adj.* dark, black; tight; compact; *Riopl., Ven., Col., Mex., C.A., Andes* dark-complexioned, swarthy.

prima [prí·ma] *f.* female cousin; premium; prime (*first of the canonical hours*).

primacía [pri·má·sja] *f.* priority, precedence; superiority.

primario [pri·má·rjo] *adj.* primary, principal.

primavera [pri·ma·bé·ra] *f.* spring; primrose; print, flowered silk cloth.

primaveral [pri·ma·be·rál] *adj.* spring, pertaining to spring.

primer(o) [pri·mér(o)] *adj.* first; former; leading, principal; **primera enseñanza** primary education; **primera materia** raw material; **de buenas a primeras** all of a sudden, unexpectedly; **a primera luz** at dawn; *adv.* first; rather.

primicia [pri·mí·sja] *f.* first fruit; first profit; **-s** first fruits.

primitivo [pri·mi·tí·bo] *adj.* primitive; primary; original.

primo [prí·mo] *m.* cousin; simpleton, sucker, dupe; — **hermano** (*or* — **carnal**) first cousin; *Carib.* **coger a uno de** — to deceive someone easily; *adj.* first; **número** — prime number.

primogénito [pri·mo·xé·ni·to] *adj.* & *m.* first-born; **primogenitura** [pri·mo·xe·ni·tú·ra] *f.* birthright; rights of the first-born.

primor [pri·mór] *m.* beauty; excellence; exquisiteness; skill, ability.

primordial [pri·mor·djál] *adj.* primordial.

primoroso [pri·mo·ró·so] *adj.* excellent, fine, exquisite; skillful.

prímula [prí·mu·la] *f.* primrose.

princesa [prin·sé·sa] *f.* princess.

principal [prin·si·pál] *adj.* principal; renowned, famous; **piso** — main floor (*usually, the second floor*); *m.* principal, capital sum; chief, head.

príncipe [prín·si·pe] *m.* prince; *adj.* princeps, first (*edition*).

principiante [prin·si·pján·te] *m.* beginner.

principiar [prin·si·pjár] *v.* to begin.

principio [prin·si·pjo] *m.* principle; beginning; origin, source; entrée (*main dinner course*); **a -s de** towards the beginning of.

pringar[7] [prin·gár] *v. irr.* to dip (*in grease*).

pringoso [prin·gó·so] *adj.* greasy.

pringue [prin·ge] *m.* & *f.* grease drippings (*from bacon, ham, etc.*).

prioridad [prjó·ri·dád] *f.* priority; precedence.

PR

prisa [prí·sa] *f.* speed, haste; **de** (*or* **a**) — quickly, speedily; **a toda** — with the greatest speed; **eso corre** — that is urgent; **dar** — **a** to hurry; **darse** — to hurry; **tener** (*or* **estar de**) — to be in a hurry.

prisión [pri·sjón] *f.* prison; imprisonment; seizure; shackle; **-es** shackles, fetters, chains.

prisionero [pri·sjo·né·ro] *m.* prisoner.

prisma [príz·ma] *f.* prism.

pristino [pris·tí·no] *adj.* first, early, former, primitive.

privación [pri·βa·sjón] *f.* privation; want, lack; loss.

privado [pri·βá·ḍo] *adj.* private; personal; unconscious; *p.p.* deprived; *m.* favorite.

privar [pri·βár] *v.* (*destituir*) to deprive; to prohibit; (*tener aceptación*) to enjoy the favor of someone; to be in vogue; **-le a uno del sentido** to stun, daze; **ya no privan esas costumbres** those customs are no longer in vogue or in existence; **-se** to lose consciousness; **-se de** to deprive oneself of.

privativo [pri·βa·tí·βo] *adj.* exclusive; particular, distinctive.

privilegiado [pri·βi·le·xjá·ḍo] *adj.* privileged.

privilegiar [pri·βi·le·xjár] *v.* to favor; to give a privilege to.

privilegio [pri·βi·lé·xjo] *m.* privilege; exemption; patent; copyright; — **de invención** patent on an invention.

pro [pro] *m.* & *f.* profit, advantage; **en** — **de** on behalf of; **en** — **y en contra** pro and con, for and against; **hombre de** — man of worth.

proa [pró·a] *f.* prow.

probabilidad [pro·βa·βi·li·ḍáḍ] *f.* probability.

probable [pro·βá·ble] *adj.* probable.

probar[2] [pro·βár] *v. irr.* (*examinar*) to test; to taste; to prove; to try; to try on; (*gustar*) to suit, agree with; **no me prueba el clima** the climate does not agree with me.

probeta [pro·βé·ta] *f.* test tube; pressure gauge.

probidad [pro·βi·ḍáḍ] *f.* integrity, uprightness, honesty.

problema [pro·blé·ma] *m.* problem.

problemático [pro·ble·má·ti·ko] *adj.* problematic.

procedente [pro·se·ḍén·te] *adj.* proceeding (from), originating; according to law.

proceder [pro·se·ḍér] *v.* to proceed; to originate; to behave; to take action (against); *m.* behavior, conduct.

procedimiento [pro·se·ḍi·mjén·to] *m.* procedure; method; process; conduct.

prócer [pró·ser] *m.* distinguished person; hero; great statesman.

procesado [pro·se·sá·ḍo] *p.p.* & *adj.* relating to, or included in, a lawsuit; accused, prosecuted; *m.* defendant.

procesar [pro·se·sár] *v.* to prosecute; to accuse; to indict; to sue.

procesión [pro·se·sjón] *f.* procession; parade.

proceso [pro·sé·so] *m.* process; lawsuit, legal proceedings; lapse of time; — **verbal** minutes, record.

proclama [pro·klá·ma] *f.* proclamation, ban; marriage banns.

proclamación [pro·kla·ma·sjón] *f.* proclamation.

proclamar [pro·kla·már] *v.* to proclaim.

proclítico [pro·klí·ti·ko] *adj.* proclitic.

procurador [pro·ku·ra·ḍór] *m.* attorney.

procurar [pro·ku·rár] *v.* (*pretender*) to try, endeavor; (*obtener*) to procure, obtain, get.

prodigar[7] [pro·ḍi·gár] *v.* to lavish; to bestow upon; to squander, waste.

prodigio [pro·ḍí·xjo] *m.* prodigy, wonder, marvel; miracle.

prodigioso [pro·ḍi·xjóso] *adj.* prodigious, marvelous; fine, exquisite.

pródigo [pró·ḍi·go] *adj.* prodigal, wasteful; lavish; generous; *m.* spendthrift.

producción [pro·ḍuk·sjón] *f.* production; produce.

producir[25] [pro·ḍu·sír] *v. irr.* to produce; to bring about; to yield; **-se** to express oneself, explain oneself; *Col., Ven.* to occur, happen.

productivo [pro·ḍuk·tí·βo] *adj.* productive; fruitful; profitable.

producto [pro·ḍúk·to] *m.* product; yield; result.

productor [pro·ḍuk·tór] *m.* producer; *adj.* producing, productive.

proeza [pro·é·sa] *f.* prowess; *Col.* boast, exaggeration.

profanación [pro·fa·na·sjón] *f.* profanation.

profanar [pro·fa·nár] *v.* to profane; to defile.

profano [pro·fá·no] *adj.* profane, not sacred; irreverent; lay, uninformed (*about a branch of learning*).

profecía [pro·fe·sí·a] *f.* prophecy; prediction.

proferir[3] [pro·fe·rír] *v. irr.* to utter, express, speak.

profesar [pro·fe·sár] *v.* to profess; to avow, confess.

profesión [pro·fe·sjón] *f.* profession; avowal, declaration.

profesional [pro·fe·sjo·nál] *adj., m.* & *f.* professional.

profesionista [pro·fe·sjo·nís·ta] *m.* & *f. Am.* professional.

profesor [pro·fe·sór] *m.* professor, teacher; **profesorado** [pro·fe·so·rá·ḍo] *m.* faculty; body of teachers; teaching profession; professorship.

profeta [pro·fé·ta] *m.* prophet.

profético [pro·fé·ti·ko] *adj.* prophetic.

profetizar[9] [pro·fe·ti·sár] *v.* to prophesy.

proficiente [pro·fi·sjén·te] *adj.* proficient, skilled.

profilaxis [pro·fi·lák·sis] *f.* prophylaxis (*disease prevention*).

prófugo [pró·fu·go] *adj.* & *m.* fugitive.

profundidad [pro·fun·di·ḍáḍ] *f.* profundity, depth.

profundizar[9] [pro·fun·di·sár] *v.* to deepen; to go deep into.

profundo [pro·fún·do] *adj.* profound; deep; low.

profuso [pro·fú·so] *adj.* profuse; lavish.

progenitor [pro·xe·ni·tór] *m.* progenitor.

programa [pro·grá·ma] *m.* program; plan.

programar [pro·gra·már] *v.* to plan; to program.

progresar [pro·gre·sár] *v.* to progress.

progresista [pro·gre·sís·ta] *m., f.* & *adj.* progressive.

progresivo [pro·gre·sí·βo] *adj.* progressive.

progreso [pro·gré·so] *m.* progress.

prohibición [proj·bi·sjón] *f.* prohibition; ban.

prohibir [proj·bír] *v.* to prohibit, forbid.

prohijar [pro·i·xár] *v.* to adopt.

prójimo [pró·xi·mo] *m.* neighbor, fellow being; *Riopl., Carib., C.A.* **ese** — that fellow.

prole [pró·le] *f.* progeny, offspring.

proletariado [pro·le·ta·rjá·ḍo] *m.* proletariat, working class.

proletario [pro·le·tá·rjo] *adj.* proletarian, belonging to the working class; plebeian; *m.* proletarian.

prolijo [pro·lí·xo] *adj.* prolix, too long, drawn out; too detailed; boring, tedious.

prologar[7] [pro·lo·gár] *v.* to preface, write a preface for.

prólogo [pró·lo·go] *m.* prologue.

prolongación [pro·loŋ·ga·sjón] *f.* prolongation,

extension; lengthening.
prolongar[7] [pro·loŋ·gár] *v.* to prolong, lengthen, extend.
promediar [pro·me·djár] *v.* to average; to divide or distribute into two equal parts; to mediate; **antes de — el mes** before the middle of the month.
promedio [pro·mé·djo] *m.* middle; average.
promesa [pro·mé·sa] *f.* promise.
prometedor [pro·me·te·đór] *adj.* promising, hopeful.
prometer [pro·me·tér] *v.* to promise; to show promise; *Ríopl., C.A.* to affirm, assure; **-se** to become engaged, betrothed.
prometido [pro·me·ti·đo] *adj. & p.p.* betrothed; *m.* fiancé, betrothed; promise.
prominente [pro·mi·nén·te] *adj.* prominent.
promiscuo [pro·mís·kwo] *adj.* promiscuous.
promisorio [pro·mi·só·rjo] *adj.* promissory.
promoción [pro·mo·sjón] *f.* promotion, advancement.
promontorio [pro·mon·tó·rjo] *m.* promontory, headland, cape; anything bulky; bulge.
promotor [pro·mo·tór] *m.* promoter.
promovedor [pro·mo·ƀe·đór] *m.* promoter.
promover[2] [pro·mo·ƀér] *v. irr.* to promote; to advance.
promulgación [pro·mul·ga·sjón] *f.* promulgation, publication, proclamation (*of a law*).
promulgar[7] [pro·mul·gár] *v.* to promulgate, proclaim, announce publicly.
pronombre [pro·nóm·bre] *m.* pronoun.
pronominal [pro·no·mi·nál] *adj.* pronominal.
pronosticar[6] [pro·nos·ti·kár] *v.* to prophesy, predict.
pronóstico [pro·nós·ti·ko] *m.* forecast; prediction; omen.
prontitud [pron·ti·túđ] *f.* promptness; quickness.
pronto [prón·to] *adj.* quick, speedy; ready; prompt; *adv.* soon; quickly; **de —** suddenly; **al —** at first; **por de** (*or* **por lo**) — for the present; *m.* sudden impulse.
pronunciación [pro·nun·sja·sjón] *f.* pronunciation.
pronunciar [pro·nun·sjár] *v.* to pronounce; to utter; **-se** to rise up in rebellion.
propagación [pro·pa·ga·sjón] *f.* propagation, spread, spreading.
propaganda [pro·pa·gán·da] *f.* propaganda; advertising.
propagar[7] [pro·pa·gár] *v.* to propagate, reproduce; to spread.
propalar [pro·pa·lár] *v.* to spread (*news*).
propasarse [pro·pa·sár·se] *v.* to overstep one's bounds; to exceed one's authority, go too far.
propensión [pro·pen·sjón] *f.* tendency, inclination; bent, natural tendency or ability.
propenso [pro·pén·so] *adj.* prone, susceptible, inclined.
propiciar [pro·pi·sjár] *v.* to calm one's anger; *Am.* to propose.
propicio [pro·pí·sjo] *adj.* propitious, favorable.
propiedad [pro·pje·đáđ] *f.* property; ownership; attribute, quality; propriety, appropriateness.
propietario [pro·pje·tá·rjo] *m.* proprietor, owner.
propina [pro·pí·na] *f.* tip (*voluntary gift of money for service*).
propinar [pro·pi·nár] *v.* to give (*something to drink*); to give (*a beating, kick, slap*); *Am.* to tip, give a tip to; **— una paliza** to give a beating.
propio [pró·pjo] *adj.* proper; suitable; own; same; **amor —** vanity, pride, self-esteem; *m.* messenger.
proponer[40] [pro·po·nér] *v. irr.* to propose; to

resolve; to present; **-se** to resolve, make a resolution.
proporción [pro·por·sjón] *f.* proportion; dimension; ratio; opportunity, chance.
proporcionar [pro·por·sjo·nár] *v.* to proportion; to adapt, adjust; to furnish, supply; give.
proposición [pro·po·si·sjón] *f.* proposition; proposal; assertion.
propósito [pro·pó·si·to] *m.* purpose, aim, design; **a —** apropos, suitable, fitting; by the way; **de —** on purpose; **fuera de —** irrelevant, beside the point.
propuesta [pro·pwés·to] *f.* proposal, offer; proposition.
propuesto [pro·pwés·to] *p.p. of* **proponer**.
propulsar [pro·pul·sár] *v.* to propel.
propulsión [pro·pul·sjón] *f.* propulsion; **— a chorro** (*por reacción*) jet propulsion; **— a cohete** rocket propulsion.
propulsor [pro·pul·sór] *m.* propeller; *adj.* propelling; *m.* propelling force.
prorratear [pro·rra·te·ár] *v.* to prorate, distribute or assess proportionally; to average.
prorrateo [pro·rra·té·o] *m.* apportionment, proportional distribution.
prórroga [pró·rro·ga] *f.* renewal, extension of time.
prorrogar[7] [pro·rro·gár] *v.* to put off, postpone; to adjourn; to extend (*time limit*).
prorrumpir [pro·rrum·pír] *v.* to break forth; **— en llanto** to burst into tears; **— en una carcajada** to let out a big laugh.
prosa [pró·sa] *f.* prose.
prosaico [pro·sáj·ko] *adj.* prosaic; dull; tedious.
proscribir[52] [pros·kri·ƀír] *v.* to proscribe, banish; to outlaw.
proscripción [pros·krip·sjón] *f.* banishment.
proscripto [pros·kríp·to], **proscrito** [pros·krí·to] *p.p. of* **proscribir**; *m.* exile, outlaw.
proseguir[5, 12] [pro·se·gír] *v. irr.* to continue; to follow.
prosélito [pro·sé·li·to] *m.* proselyte.
prosódico [pro·só·đi·ko] *adj.* prosodic.
prosperar [pros·pe·rár] *v.* to prosper.
prosperidad [pros·pe·ri·đáđ] *f.* prosperity; success.
próspero [prós·pe·ro] *adj.* prosperous; successful.
próstata [prós·ta·ta] *f.* prostate.
prostituir[32] [pros·ti·twír] *v.* to prostitute, corrupt.
prostituta [pros·ti·tú·ta] *f.* prostitute.
protagonista [pro·ta·go·nís·ta] *m. & f.* protagonist (*main character or actor*).
protección [pro·tek·sjón] *f.* protection; support.
proteccionista [pro·tek·sjo·nís·ta] *adj.* protective; **tarifa —** protective tariff; *m. & f.* protectionist (*follower of the economic principles of protection*).
protector [pro·tek·tór] *m.* protector, guardian; *adj.* protecting, protective.
protectorado [pro·tek·to·rá·đo] *m.* protectorate.
proteger[11] [pro·te·xér] *v.* to protect; to shelter; to defend.
protegido [pro·te·xí·đo] *m.* protege.
proteína [pro·te·í·na] *f.* protein.
proteínico [pro·te·í·ni·ko] *adj.* related to the proteins.
protesta [pro·tés·ta] *f.* protest; protestation.
protestación [pro·tes·ta·sjón] *f.* protestation, solemn declaration; protest.
protestante [pro·tes·tán·te] *m.* Protestant; one who protests.
protestar [pro·tes·tár] *v.* (*confesar*) to assert, assure; to avow publicly; (*negar*) to protest;

— **una letra** to protest a draft.
protocolo [pro·to·kó·lo] *m.* protocol.
protón [pro·tón] *m.* proton.
protoplasma [pro·to·pláz·ma] *m.* protoplasm.
protuberancia [pro·tu·ƀe·rán·sja] *f.* protuberance, bulge.
protuberante [pro·tu·ƀe·rán·te] *adj.* protuberant, prominent, bulging.
provecho [pro·ƀé·čo] *m.* profit; benefit; utility; advantage; **hombre de** — worthy, useful man.
provechoso [pro·ƀe·čó·so] *adj.* profitable; useful; beneficial; advantageous.
proveedor [pro·ƀe·e·ðór] *m.* provisioner, provider; supply man.
proveer[14, 52] [pro·ƀe·ér] *v. irr.* to provide; to supply; to confer, bestow; to decide; **-se de** to supply oneself with.
provenir[48] [pro·ƀe·nír] *v. irr.* to originate, arise, come (from).
proverbio [pro·ƀer·ƀjo] *m.* proverb.
providencia [pro·ƀi·ðén·sja] *f.* providence; foresight; Providence, God; legal decision, sentence; provision, measure; **tomar una** — to take a step or measure.
providencial [pro·ƀi·ðen·sjál] *adj.* providential.
provincia [pro·ƀín·sja] *f.* province.
provincial [pro·ƀin·sjál] *adj.* provincial.
provinciano [pro·ƀin·sjá·no] *adj. & m.* provincial.
provisión [pro·ƀi·sjón] *f.* provision; supply, stock.
provisional [pro·ƀi·sjo·nál] *adj.* temporary; provisional.
provisorio [pro·ƀi·só·rjo] *adj.* provisional, temporary.
provisto [pro·ƀís·to] *p.p. of* **proveer.**
provocación [pro·ƀo·ka·sjón] *f.* provocation; dare, defiance.
provocador [pro·ƀo·ka·ðór] *adj.* provoking; — provoker.
provocar[6] [pro·ƀo·kár] *v.* to provoke; to excite, rouse; to stimulate.
provocativo [pro·ƀo·ka·tí·ƀo] *adj.* provocative.
proximidad [prok·si·mi·ðáð] *f.* proximity, nearness.
próximo [prók·si·mo] *adj.* next; neighboring; near; **del** — **pasado** of last month.
proyección [pro·yek·sjón] *f.* projection; jut.
proyectar [pro·yek·tár] *v.* to project; to plan; to throw; to cast; **-se** to be cast (*as a shadow*).
proyectil [pro·yek·tíl] *m.* projectile.
proyectista [pro·yek·tís·ta] *m. & f.* designer; schemer, planner.
proyecto [pro·yék·to] *m.* project; plan; — **de ley** bill (*in a legislature*).
prudencia [pru·ðén·sja] *f.* prudence, practical wisdom, discretion.
prudente [pru·ðén·te] *adj.* prudent, wise, discreet.
prueba [prwé·ƀa] *f.* proof; trial; test; fitting; sample; evidence; *Andes, Ríopl., Col., C.A.* acrobatic performance, stunt, trick, sleight of hand; **a** — **de incendio** fireproof.
prurito [pru·rí·to] *m.* itch; keen desire.
psicología [si·ko·lo·xí·a] *f. see* **sicología.**
psicosis [si·kó·sis] *f. see* **sicosis.**
psiqiatría [si·kja·trí·a] *f. see* **siqiatría.**
psitacosis [si·ta·kó·sis] *f. see* **sitacosis.**
ptomaína [toma·í·na] *f.* ptomaine.
púa [pú·a] *f.* prick; barb; prong; thorn; quill (*of a porcupine, etc.*); sharp, cunning person; *Ríopl.* cock's spur; **alambre de -s** barbed wire.
publicación [pu·ƀli·ka·sjón] *f.* publication.
publicar[6] [pu·ƀli·kár] *v.* to publish; to reveal; to announce.

publicidad [pu·ƀli·si·ðáð] *f.* publicity.
público [pú·ƀli·ko] *adj. & m.* public.
puchero [pu·čé·ro] *m.* pot, kettle; meat and vegetable stew; pout; **hacer -s** to pout.
pucho [pú·čo] *m.* cigar or cigarette butt; *C.A.* something of little value.
pudiente [pu·ðjén·te] *adj.* powerful; rich, wealthy; *m.* man of means.
pudín [pu·ðín] *m.* pudding.
pudor [pu·ðór] *m.* modesty; shyness.
pudrir[16] [pu·ðrír] *v.* to rot; to vex, annoy; **-se** to rot.
pueblero [pwe·ƀlé·ro] *m. Ríopl.* townsman (*as opposed to countryman*).
pueblo [pwé·ƀlo] *m.* town, village; people, race, nation; populace; common people.
puente [pwén·te] *m.* bridge; *Carib., Mex., Ríopl.* dental bridge; *Am.* knife and fork rest; — **colgante** suspension bridge; — **levadizo** drawbridge.
puerca [pwér·ka] *f.* sow.
puerco [pwér·ko] *m.* pig, hog; — **espín** porcupine; — **jabalí** wild boar; *adj.* filthy, dirty; coarse, ill-bred.
pueril [pwe·ríl] *adj.* puerile, childish.
puerro [pwé·rro] *m.* scallion.
puerta [pwér·ta] *f.* door; gate; entrance; — **accessoria (excusada,** *or* **falsa)** side door; — **de golpe** spring door; trap door; — **franca** open door; free entrance or entry; — **trasera** back door; **a** — **cerrada** secretly, behind closed doors; *Am.* **en** — in view, in sight, very near.
puerto [pwér·to] *m.* port; harbor; refuge; mountain pass; — **franco** free port.
puertorriqueño [pwer·to·rri·ké·ño] *adj. & m.* Puerto Rican.
pues [pwes] *conj.* since, because, for, inasmuch as; then; *adv.* then; well; — **bien** well then, well; — **que** since.
puesta [pwés·ta] *f.* set, setting (*of a star or planet*); stake at cards; — **de sol** sunset.
puestero [pwes·té·ro] *m. Carib., Mex., Ríopl.* vendor, seller (*at a stand or stall*); *Ríopl.* man in charge of livestock on Argentine ranches.
puesto [pwés·to] *p.p. of* **poner** placed, put, set; **mal** (*or* **bien**) — badly (*or* well) dressed; *m.* place; vendor's booth or stand; post, position, office; military post; *Andes, Ríopl.* station for watching and taking care of cattle on a ranch; — **de socorros** first-aid station; — **que** *conj.* since.
pugilato [pu·xi·lá·to] *m.* boxing.
pugilista [pu·xi·lís·ta] *m.* boxer, prize fighter.
pugna [púǥ·na] *f.* struggle; conflict; **estar en** — **con** to be in conflict with; to be opposed to.
pugnar [puǥ·nár] *v.* to fight; to struggle; to strive; to persist.
pujanza [pu·xán·sa] *f.* push, force, power.
pujar [pu·xár] *v.* to make a strenuous effort; to grope for words; to falter; to outbid (*offer a higher bid than*); *C.A.* to grunt; *Am.* to reject; *Ven.* to dismiss; *Am.* — **para adentro** to forbear, keep silent; *Am.* **andar pujado** to go around crestfallen; to be in disgrace.
pujido [pu·xí·ðo] *m. Am.* grunt (*due to strenuous effort*).
pulcritud [pul·kri·túð] *f.* neatness, trimness; excellence, perfection.
pulcro [púl·kro] *adj.* neat, trim; beautiful.
pulga [púl·ǥa] *f.* flea; *Ríopl.* small and insignificant person; **tener malas -s** to be illtempered; *Col.,*

Andes **ser de pocas -s** to be touchy, oversensitive; **pulgón** *m.* blight, plant louse.

pulgada [pul·gá·đa] *f.* inch.

pulgar [pul·gár] *m.* thumb.

pulguero [pul·gé·ro] *m.* jail (*slang*).

pulido [pu·lí·đo] *adj.* polished, refined; polite; neat; exquisite.

pulidor [pu·li·đór] *adj.* polishing; *m.* polisher.

pulimentar [pu·li·men·tár] *v.* to polish.

pulimento [pu·li·mén·to] *m.* polish; gloss.

pulir [pu·lír] *v.* to polish.

pulmón [pul·món] *m.* lung.

pulmonar [pul·mo·nár] *adj.* pulmonary, pertaining to the lungs.

pulmonía [pul·mo·ní·a] *f.* pneumonia.

pulpa [púl·pa] *f.* pulp; boneless meat.

pulpería [pul·pe·rí·a] *f. Ríopl., C.A., Ch., Ven., Andes* country general store; *Am.* tavern.

pulpero [pul·pé·ro] *m. Ríopl., C.A., Ch., Ven., Andes* owner of a country store or tavern.

púlpito [púl·pi·to] *m.* pulpit.

pulpo [púl·po] *m.* octopus.

pulque [púl·ke] *m. Mex.* pulque (*fermented juice of the maguey*).

pulquería [pul·ke·rí·a] *f. Mex.* pulque bar or cantina.

pulsación [pul·sa·sjón] *f.* pulsation, beat, throb; pulse, beating.

pulsar [pul·sár] *v.* to pulsate, throb, beat; to feel the pulse of; to sound out; examine; to play (*the harp*); *Mex., C.A.* to judge or try the weight of (*by lifting*).

pulsera [pul·sé·ra] *f.* bracelet; wrist bandage; **reloj de —** wrist watch.

pulso [púl·so] *m.* pulse; steadiness; tract; *Ríopl., Carib., Col.* bracelet, wrist watch; **un hombre de —** a prudent, steady man; *Cuba, Mex.* **beber a —** to drink straight down, gulp down; **levantar a —** to lift with the strength of the wrist or hand; **sacar a — un negocio** to carry out a deal by sheer perseverance.

pulsorreactor [pul·so·rre·ak·tór] *m.* jet engine of movable intake valves.

pulular [pu·lu·lár] *v.* to swarm; to multiply rapidly; to sprout, bud.

pulverizar[9] [pul·βe·ri·sár] *v.* to pulverize.

pulla [pú·ya] *f.* taunt; mean dig, quip, cutting remark; filthy word or remark.

puma [pú·ma] *f.* puma, mountain lion.

puna [pú·na] *f. Andes* cold, arid tableland of the Andes; *Ríopl.* desert; *Andes* sickness caused by high altitude.

pundonor [pun·do·nór] *m.* point of honor.

púnico [pú·ni·ko] *adj.* Punic.

punta [pún·ta] *f.* point, tip; bull's horn; cigar or cigarette butt; *Ven.*, gang, band, herd, a lot (*of things, people, etc.*); *Am.* small leaf of fine tobacco; *Am.* jeer, cutting remark; **-s** point lace; scallops; **de —** on end; **de -s** (*or* **de puntillas**) on tiptoe; *Am.* **a — de** by dint of, by means of; **estar de — con** to be on bad terms with; **sacar — a un lápiz** to sharpen a pencil; **tener sus -s de poeta** to be something of a poet.

puntada [pun·ta·đa] *f.* stitch; hint; *Andes* prick, pricking, sting, sharp pain; **no he dado — en este asunto** I have left this matter completely untouched.

puntal [pun·tál] *m.* prop; support, basis; bull's horn; *Col.* snack (*between meals*).

puntapié [pun·ta·pjé] *m.* kick (*with the toe of the shoe*).

puntazo [pun·tá·so] *m. Col., Ven., Mex., Cuba* stab, jab.

puntear [pun·te·ár] *v.* to pluck (*the strings of a guitar*); to play (*a guitar*); to make dots; to engrave, draw or paint by means of dots; to stitch; to tack (*said of a boat*).

puntería [pun·te·rí·a] *f.* aim.

puntero [pun·té·ro] *m.* pointer; chisel; blacksmith's punch; *C.A., Col., Ch.* clock or watch hand; *Am.* leader of a parade; *Cuba, Mex., Ven., Col.* leading ox (*or other animal*); *Am.* guide.

pentiagudo [pun·tja·gú·đo] *adj.* sharp, sharp-pointed.

puntilla [pun·tí·ya] *f.* small point; tip; small dagger; tracing point; point lace; *Ven.* penknife; *Am.* toe rubber; *Am.* ridge (*of a hill*); **de -s** on tiptoe; **puntillazo** *m.* stab (*with a dagger*).

punto [pún·to] *m.* (*parada*) period; stop; point; dot; (*puntada*) stitch; mesh; (*sitio*) place; moment; (*mira*) gun sight; **— de admiración** exclamation mark; **— de interrogación** question mark; **— y coma** semicolon; **dos -s** colon; **al —** at once, immediately; **a — de** on the point of; **de —** knitted, porous knit, stockinet or jersey weave; **en —** exactly, on the dot; **a — fijo** with certainty; **subir de —** to increase or get worse.

puntuación [pun·twa·sjón] *f.* punctuation.

puntual [pun·twál] *adj.* punctual, prompt; exact.

puntualidad [pun·twa·li·đáđ] *f.* punctuality, promptness; certainty.

puntuar[18] [pun·twár] *v.* to punctuate.

punzada [pun·sá·đa] *f.* puncture; prick; sharp pain.

punzante [pun·sán·te] *adj.* sharp; pricking; piercing, penetrating.

punzar[9] [pun·sár] *v.* to puncture; to sting; to prick; to punch, perforate.

punzón [pun·són] *m.* punch, puncher; pick; awl.

puñada [pu·ñá·đa] *f.* punch, box, blow with the fist.

puñado [pu·ñá·đo] *m.* fistful, handful; **a -s** abundantly; by handfuls.

puñal [pu·ñál] *m.* dagger.

puñalada [pu·ña·la·đa] *f.* stab; sharp pain; **coser a -s** to stab to death.

puñetazo [pu·ñe·tá·so] *m.* punch, blow with the fist.

puño [pú·ño] *m.* fist; fistful, handful; cuff; hilt, handle; *Ven., Col.* blow with the fist; **a — cerrado** firmly; **ser como un —** to be stingy; **tener -s** to be strong, courageous.

pupila [pu·pí·la] *f.* pupil (*of the eye*).

pupilo [pu·pí·lo] *m.* ward; boarding-school pupil; boarder.

pupitre [pu·pí·tre] *m.* desk, school desk.

puré [pu·ré] *m.* purée, thick soup.

pureza [pu·ré·sa] *f.* purity; chastity.

purga [púr·ga] *f.* purge, laxative, physic.

purgante [pur·gán·te] *adj.* purgative, laxative; *m.* purgative, physic, laxative.

purgar[7] [pur·gár] *v.* to purge; to purify; to atone for; **-se** to purge oneself; to take a laxative.

purgatorio [pur·ga·tó·rjo] *m.* purgatory.

purificar[6] [pu·ri·fi·kár] *v.* to purify.

purista [pu·rís·ta] *m. & f.* purist.

puro [pú·ro] *adj.* (*limpio*) pure; clean; chaste; (*sólo*) mere, only, sheer; **a pura fuerza** by sheer force; **a puros gritos** by just shouting; *m.* cigar.

púrpura [púr·pu·ra] *f.* purple; purple cloth.

purpúreo [pur·pú·re·o] *adj.* purple.

pus [pus] *m.* pus.

pusilánime [pu·si·lá·ni·me] *adj.* pusillanimous.

puta [pú·ta] *f.* whore, prostitute.

putativo [pu·ta·tí·βo] *adj.* reputed, supposed; **padre**

— foster father.

putrefacción [pu·tre·fak·sjón] *f.* putrefaction, decay, rotting.

putrefacto [pu·tre·fák·to] *adj.* putrid, rotten, decayed.

puya [pú·ya] *f.* goad; lance head.

Q:q

que [ke] *rel. pron.* that; which; who; whom; **el** — who; which; the one who; the one which; *conj.* that; for, because; **más (menos)** — more (less) than; **el mismo** — the same as; — (= *subj.*) let, may you, I hope that; **por mucho** no matter how much; **quieras — no** whether you wish or not.

qué [ke] *interr. adj. & pron.* what?; what a!; *interr. adv.* how; **¡**— **bonito!** how beautiful!; **¿a** —? what for?; **¿para** —? what for?; **¿por** —? why?; **¿**— **tal?** how?; hello!; **¡**— **más da!** what's the difference!; **¡a mí** —! so what! and what's that to me!

quebracho [ke·ḅrá·čo] *m.* quebracho, breakax wood.

quebrada [ke·ḅrá·ḍa] *f.* ravine; gorge; failure, bankruptcy; *Ríopl., Col., Ven., C.A., Mex.* brook.

quebradizo [ke·ḅra·ḍí·so] *adj.* breakable; brittle; fragile; delicate.

quebrado [ke·ḅrá·ḍo] *adj.* broken; weakened; ruptured; bankrupt; rough or rugged (*ground*); *m.* common fraction; *Ven.* navigable waters between reefs.

quebrantar [ke·ḅran·tár] *v.* to break; to break open; to pound, crush; to violate (*a law*); to weaken; to vex; *Mex., Col.* to tame, break in (*a colt*); — **el agua** to take the chill off the water.

quebranto [ke·ḅrán·to] *m.* breaking; grief, affliction; discouragement; damage, loss.

quebrar[1] [ke·ḅrár] *v. irr.* to break; to crush; to interrupt; to wither (*said of the complexion*); to become bankrupt; **-se** to break; to get broken; to be ruptured; **-se uno la cabeza** to rack one's brain.

quebrazón [ke·ḅra·són] *m. Ven., Col.* breakage, breaking.

quechua [ké·čwa] *adj. Am.* Quichuan; *m. & f.* Quichua, Quichuan Indian; *m.* Quichuan language.

quedar [ke·ḍár] to stay; to remain; to be left over; to be left (*in a state or condition*); — **en** to agree to; *Am.* — **de** to agree to; — **bien** to acquit oneself well; to come out well; *Am.* to suit, become (*said of a dress, hat, etc.*); *Am.* — **bien con alguien** to please someone; **-se** to remain; **-se con una cosa** to keep something; to take something (*buy it*); *Am.* **-se como si tal cosa** to act as if nothing had happened.

quedo [ké·ḍo] *adj.* quiet, still; gentle; *adv.* softly; in a low voice; **quedito** [ke·ḍí·to] *adj.* nice and quiet; *adv.* very softly.

quehacer [ke·a·sér] *m.* work, occupation; task, duty, chore.

queja [ké·xa] *f.* complaint; groan, moan; grudge.

quejarse [ke·xár·se] *v.* to complain; to grumble; to moan; to lament.

quejido [ke·xí·ḍo] *m.* moan; groan.

quejoso [ke·xó·so] *adj.* complaining, whining.

quejumbre [ke·xúm·bre] *f.* whine, moan; murmur,

complaint; **-s** *m. Cuba, Ven.* grumbler, whiner; **quejumbroso** [ke·xum·bró·so] *adj.* whining, complaining.

quemada [ke·má·ḍa] *f.* burned forest; *Am.* burn.

quemado [ke·má·ḍo] *m.* burned portion of a forest; *Col.* burned field; *Am.* hot alcoholic drink; *adj.* dark, tan; *Am.* peeved, piqued; *Col., Ven., Cuba, Mex.* ruined; *p.p. of* **quemar.**

quemadura [ke·ma·ḍú·ra] *f.* burn; scald; smut (*plant disease*).

quemar [ke·már] *v.* to burn; to scald; to scorch; to sell at a loss; to annoy; *Am.* to deceive, swindle; **-se** to burn; to be hot.

quemazón [ke·ma·són] *f.* (*calor*) burn, burning; great heat; fire, conflagration; (*desazón*) pique, anger; bargain sale; *Am.* mirage on the pampas.

quena [ké·na] *f. Andes* flute of the Quechua Indians.

querella [ke·ré·ya] *f.* quarrel; complaint; controversy.

querellarse [ke·re·yár·se] *v.* to complain.

querencia [ke·rén·sja] *f.* affection; longing; favorite spot; haunt; stable.

querer[41] [ke·rér] *v. irr.* to want, wish, desire; to will; to be willing; to love; — **decir** to mean; **sin** — unwillingly; **no quiso hacerlo** he refused to do it; **quiere llover** it is trying to rain, it is about to rain; **como quiera** in any way; **como quiera que** since; no matter how; **cuando quiera** whenever; **donde quiera** wherever; anywhere; **-se** to love each other; *Ríopl., Ven., Col.* to be on the point of, be about to; **se quiere caer esa pared** that wall is about to fall.

querido [ke·rí·ḍo] *p.p.* wanted, desired; *adj.* beloved, dear; *m.* lover; **querida** *f.* darling; mistress.

queroseno [ke·ro·sé·no] *m. variant of* **keroseno.**

querubín [ke·ru·bín] *m.* cherub.

quesería [ke·se·rí·a] *f.* dairy, creamery, cheese factory; **quesera** [ke·sé·ra] *f.* dairy, cheese factory; cheese dish; dairymaid, woman cheese vendor or cheesemaker; **quesero** [ke·sé·ro] *adj.* pertaining to cheese; *m.* cheesemaker.

queso [ké·so] *m.* cheese; *Ven.* — **de higos** fig paste.

quetzal [ket·sál] *m.* bird of paradise; quetzal (*monetary unit of Guatemala*).

quicio [kí·sjo] *m.* hinge of a door; **sacar a uno de** — to exasperate someone.

quichua [kí·čwa] = **quechua.**

quiebra [kjé·ḅra] *f.* (*rotura*) break; crack; fissure; fracture; (*pérdida*) loss, damage; bankruptcy.

quien [kjen] *rel. pron.* who, whom; he who, she who; **quién** *interr. pron.* who? whom?

quienquiera [kjen·kjé·ra] *pron.* whoever, whosoever, whomsoever.

quieto [kjé·to] *adj.* quiet, still; calm.

quietud [kje·túḍ] *f.* quiet, stillness, calmness.

quijada [ki·xá·ḍa] *f.* jaw; jawbone.

quijotada [ki·xo·tá·ḍa] *f.* quixotic deed.

quilate [ki·lá·te] *m.* carat (*twenty-fourth part in weight and value of gold*); unit of weight for precious stones and pearls; **-s** qualities; degree of perfection or purity.

quilla [kí·ya] *f.* keel.

quimera [ki·mé·ra] *f.* absurd idea, wild fancy.

química [kí·mi·ka] *f.* chemistry.

químico [kí·mi·ko] *adj.* chemical; *m.* chemist.

quina [kí·na], **quinina** [ki·ní·na] *f.* quinine.

quincalla [kin·ká·ya] *f.* hardware.

quincallería [kin·ka·ye·rí·a] *f.* hardware; hardware store; hardware trade.

quincena [kin·sé·na] *f.* fortnight; semimonthly pay.
quinqué [kin·ké] *m.* oil lamp.
quinta [kín·ta] *f.* (*casa*) villa, country house; (*militar*) draft, military conscription; (*cartas*) sequence of five cards.
quintaesencia [kin·ta·e·sén·sja] *f.* quintessence, pure essence, purest form.
quiosco [kjós·ko] *m.* kiosk, small pavilion.
quirúrgico [ki·rúr·xi·ko] *adj.* surgical.
quisquilloso [kis·ki·yó·so] *adj.* touchy, oversensitive.
quisto [kís·to]: **bien** — well-liked, well received, welcome; **mal** — disliked; unwelcome.
quitamanchas [ki·ta·mán·čas] *m.* cleaner, stain remover.
quitar [ki·tár] *v.* to remove; to take away (off, *or* from); to rob of; to deprive of; to subtract; to parry (*in fencing*); **-se** to take off (*clothing*); to remove oneself, withdraw; **-se de una cosa** to give up something, get rid of something; **-se a alguien de encima** to get rid of someone; **¡quita allá!** don't tell me that!; **¡quítese de aquí!** get out of here!
quitasol [ki·ta·sól] *m.* large sunshade, parasol.
quite [kí·te] *m.* parry (*in fencing*); revenge; dodge, dodging; *Ven., Col., Mex.* **andar a los -s** to be on the defensive; to take offense easily; to be afraid of one's own shadow; **eso no tiene —** that can't be helped.
quizá [ki·sá], **quizás** [ki·sás] *adv.* perhaps, maybe.

R:r

rabadilla [rra·ƀa·đí·ya] *f.* end of the spinal column; tail of a fowl; rump.
rábano [rrá·ƀa·no] *m.* radish; **tomar el — por las hojas** to take one thing for another; to misinterpret something.
rabia [rrá·ƀja] *f.* rabies; rage; **tener — a alguien** to hate someone; *Riopl., Carib., Mex.* **volarse de —** to get furious, angry.
rabiar [rra·ƀjár] *v.* to have rabies; to rage; to rave; to suffer a severe pain; **— por** to be dying to or for, be very eager to; **quema que rabia** it burns terribly.
rabieta [rra·ƀjé·ta] *f.* tantrum, fit of temper.
rabino [rra·ƀí·no] *m.* rabbi.
rabioso [rra·ƀjó·so] *adj.* rabid (*having rabies*), mad; furious, angry, violent.
rabo [rrá·ƀo] *m.* tail; **de cabo a —** from beginning to end; **mirar con el — del ojo** to look out of the corner of one's eye.
rabón [rra·ƀón] *m.* bobtail.
racimo [rra·sí·mo] *m.* bunch; cluster.
raciocinio [rra·sjo·sí·njo] *m.* reasoning.
ración [rra·sjón] *f.* ration; allowance; supply.
racional [rra·sjo·nál] *adj.* rational; reasonable.
racionamiento [rra·sjo·na·mjén·to] *m.* rationing.
racionar [rra·sjo·nár] *v.* to ration.
racismo [rra·síz·mo] *m.* racism.
racista [rra·sís·ta] *m. & f.* racist.
radar [rra·đár] *m.* radar.
radaroscopio [rra·đa·ros·kó·pjo] *m.* radarscope.
radiación [rra·đja·sjón] *f.* radiation; **— cósmica** cosmic radiation.
radiatividad [rra·đjak·ti·ƀi·đáđ] *f.* radioactivity.
radiactivo [rra·đjak·ti·ƀo] *adj.* radioactive.
radiador [rra·đja·đór] *m.* radiator.
radiante [rra·đján·te] *adj.* radiant; shining; beaming.

radiar [rra·đjár] *v.* to radiate; to radio; to broadcast.
radical [rra·đi·kál] *adj.* (*básico*) fundamental, basic; radical; (*extremista*) extreme; *m.* radical; root of a word.
radicalismo [rra·đi·ka·líz·mo] *m.* radicalism.
radicar[6] [rra·đi·kár] *v.* to take root; to be, be found (*in a certain place*); **-se** to take root; to locate, settle.
radio [rrá·đjo] *m.* radius; radium; *m. & f.* radio.
radiodifundir [rra·đjo·đi·fun·dír] *v.* to broadcast by radio. *See* **difundir**.
radiodifusión [rra·đjo·đi·fu·sjón] *f.* broadcasting. *See* **difusión**.
radiodifusora [rra·đjo·đi·fu·só·ra], **radioemisora** [rra·đjo·e·mi·só·ra] *f.* broadcasting station.
radioeléctrico [rra·đjo·e·lék·tri·ko] *adj.* radioelectric.
radioescucha [rra·đjo·es·kú·ča] *m. & f.* radio listener.
radiofónico [rra·đjo·fó·ni·ko] *adj.* radio (*used as adj.*); **estación radiofónica** radio station.
radiografía [rra·đjo·ǥra·fí·a] *f.* radiography, X-ray photography; X-ray picture.
radiografiar[17] [rra·đjo·ǥra·fjár] *v.* to take X-ray pictures.
radiolocutor [rra·đjo·lo·ku·tór] *m.* radio announcer. *See* **locutor**.
radiotelefonía [rra·đjo·te·le·fo·ní·a] *f.* radiotelephony, radio, wireless.
radiotelegrafía [rra·đjo·te·le·ǥra·fí·a] *f.* radiotelegraphy, radio, wireless telegraphy.
radiotransmisor [rra·đjo·trans·mi·sór] *m.* radio transmitter.
radon [rra·đon] *m.* radon.
radioyente [rra·đjo·yén·te] = **radioescucha**.
raer[24] [rra·ér] *v. irr.* to scrape off; to rub off; to scratch off; to fray; to erase.
ráfaga [rrá·fa·ǥa] *f.* gust of wind; flash of light.
raído [rra·í·đo] *p.p. & adj.* scraped off; rubbed off; frayed; worn, threadbare.
raigón [rraj·ǥón] *m.* large root; root of a tooth.
raíz [rra·ís] *f.* root; origin; foundation; **— cuadrada** square root; **a — de** close to, right after; **de —** by the roots, completely; **echar raíces** to take root, become firmly fixed.
raja [rrá·xa] *f.* slice; splinter; crack; split, crevice; **hacer -s** to slice; to tear into strips; to cut into splinters; **hacerse uno -s** to wear oneself out (*by dancing, jumping or any violent exercise*).
rajá [rra·xá] *m.* rajah.
rajadura [rra·xa·đú·ra] *f.* crack, crevice.
rajar [rra·xár] *v.* to split; to crack; to cleave; to slice; to chatter; to brag; *Col., Cuba, Mex., Andes* to defame, insult; *Col.* to flunk, fail (*a student*); **-se** to split open; to crack; *Mex.* to get afraid, back down.
rajatablas [rra·xa·tá·ƀlas] *m. Col.* reprimand, scolding; **a —** in great haste.
ralea [rra·lé·a] *f.* breed, race, stock; species, kind.
ralear [rra·le·ár] *v.* to thin out, make less dense; to become less dense.
ralo [rrá·lo] *adj.* sparse, thin, thinly scattered.
rallador [rra·ya·đór] *m.* grater.
rallar [rra·yár] *v.* to grate; to grate on, annoy; *Am.* to goad, spur.
rama [rrá·ma] *f.* branch, limb; **en —** crude, raw; **andarse por las -s** to beat about the bush, not to stick to the point.
ramada [rra·má·đa] *f.* branches, foliage; arbor;

Am. shed, tent.
ramaje [rra·má·xe] *m.* foliage; branches.
ramal [rra·mál] *m.* strand (*of a rope, etc.*); branch; branch railway line; halter.
rambla [rrám·bla] *f.* avenue (*especially in Barcelona*).
ramera [rra·mé·ra] *f.* harlot, prostitute.
ramificarse[6] [rra·mi·fi·kár·se] *v.* to branch off, divide into branches.
ramillete [rra·mi·yé·te] *m.* bouquet; flower cluster.
ramo [rrá·mo] *m.* bunch (*of flowers*), bouquet; line, branch (*of art, science, industry, etc.*); branch, bough; **domingo de –s** Palm Sunday.
ramonear [rra·mo·ne·ár] *v.* to cut off twigs or tips of branches; to nibble grass, twigs, or leaves; *Am.* to eat scraps or leftovers.
rampa [rrám·pa] *f.* ramp; apron (*airport*); **– de cohetes, – de lanzamiento** launching ramp.
ramplón [rram·plón] *adj.* coarse; crude, uncouth; slovenly.
ramplonería [rram·plo·ne·rí·a] *f.* coarse act or remark; crudeness, coarseness; slovenliness.
rana [rrá·na] *f.* frog.
rancio [rrán·sjo] *adj.* rancid, stale; old (*wine*); **linaje –** old, noble lineage.
ranchero [rran·čé·ro] *m. Mex.* rancher, farmer; **ranchería** [rran·če·rí·a] *f.* group of huts; *Col.* inn (*for* **arrieros**).
rancho [rrán·čo] *m.* camp; hamlet; mess (*meal for a group and the group itself*); *Carib., Ven., Col., Andes, Ríopl.* hut; *Carib., Ven., Col., Andes, Ríopl.* country house; *Mex.* ranch, small farm (*usually for cattle raising*).
rango [rraŋ·go] *m.* rank, position.
ranura [rra·nú·ra] *f.* groove; slot.
rapar [rra·pár] *v.* to shave off; to crop (*hair*); to strip bare, rob of everything.
rapaz [rra·pás] *adj.* rapacious, grasping, greedy; *m.* lad; **rapaza** *f.* lass, young girl.
rape [rrá·pe] *m.* quick or close haircut.
rapé [rra·pé] *m.* snuff (*pulverized tobacco*).
rapidez [rra·pi·dés] *f.* rapidity, speed.
rápido [rrá·pi·do] *adj.* rapid, swift; *m.* rapids.
rapiña [rra·pí·ña] *f.* plunder; **ave de –** bird of prey.
rapiñar [rra·pi·ñár] *v.* to plunder; to steal.
raposa [rra·pó·sa] *f.* fox.
raptar [rrap·tár] *v.* to kidnap, abduct.
rapto [rráp·to] *m.* (*delito*) abduction, kidnapping; (*sentimiento*) ecstasy, rapture; outburst.
raqueta [rra·ké·ta] *f.* racket (*used in games*); tennis.
raquítico [rra·kí·ti·ko] *adj.* rickety, feeble, weak, skinny, sickly.
rareza [rra·ré·sa] *f.* rarity; oddity; strangeness; freak; curiosity; queer act or remark; peculiarity; **por –** seldom.
raro [rrá·ro] *adj.* rare; thin, not dense; scarce; strange, odd; ridiculous; **rara vez** (*or* **raras veces**) rarely, seldom.
ras [rras] **a – de** flush with, even with; **al – con** flush with; **estar – con –** to be flush, perfectly even.
rascacielos [rras·ka·sjé·los] *m.* skyscraper.
rascar[6] [rras·kár] *v.* to scratch; to scrape; *Andes* to dig up potatoes; *Am.* **– uno para adentro** to seek one's own advantage, look out for oneself.
rasete [rra·sé·te] *m.* sateen.
rasgado [rraz·gá·do] *adj.* torn; open; *Col.* generous; *Am.* outspoken; **ojos –s** large, wideopen eyes.

rasgadura [rraz·ga·dú·ra] *f.* tear, rip, rent.
rasgar[7] [rraz·gár] *v.* to tear; to rip.
rasgo [rráz·go] *m.* (*propiedad*) trait, characteristic; (*rúbrica*) stroke of the pen, flourish; (*hazaña*) feat; *Am.* irrigation ditch; *Ven.* **un – de terreno** a parcel of land; **–s** features; traits.
rasgón [rraz·gón] *m.* large tear, rent, rip.
rasguñar [rraz·gu·ñár] *v.* to scratch; to claw.
rasguño [rraz·gú·ño] *m.* scratch.
raso [rrá·so] *adj.* (*llano*) plain; flat, smooth; (*despejado*) clear, cloudless; *Ríopl., Mex.* even, level (*when measuring wheat, corn, etc.*); *Am.* scarce, scanty; **soldado –** private; **al –** in the open air; *m.* satin.
raspadura [rras·pa·dú·ra] *f.* scrape; scraping; erasure; shaving (*of wood or metal*).
raspar [rras·pár] *v.* to scrape, scrape off; to steal; *Andes* to scold, upbraid; *Col.* to leave.
rastra [rrás·tra] *f.* drag; sled; large rake; harrow; **a –s** dragging; unwillingly.
rastreador [rras·tre·a·dór] *m.* trailer, tracker, tracer.
rastrear [rras·tre·ár] *v.* to trail, track, trace; to rake, harrow; to drag (*a dragnet*); to skim, scrape the ground.
rastrero [rras·tré·ro] *adj.* low, vile.
rastrillar [rras·tri·yár] *v.* to rake; to comb (*flax or hemp*); *Ven.* to scrape; *Am.* to shoot; *Am.* to barter, exchange; *Am.* to pilfer, steal (*in stores*).
rastrillo [rras·trí·yo] *m.* rake; *Am.* barter, exchange; *Am.* business deal.
rastro [rrás·tro] *m.* track, trail, scent; trace, sign; rake, harrow; slaughterhouse.
rastrojo [rras·tró·xo] *m.* stubble.
rasura [rra·sú·ra] *f.* shave, shaving.
rasurar [rra·su·rár] *v.* to shave.
rata [rrá·ta] *f.* rat; *m.* pickpocket.
ratear [rra·te·ár] *v.* to pilfer; to pick pockets; to creep, crawl.
ratería [rra·te·rí·a] *f.* petty larceny; meanness.
ratero [rra·té·ro] *m.* pickpocket; *adj.* contemptible, mean.
ratificar[6] [rra·ti·fi·kár] *v.* to ratify.
rato [rrá·to] *m.* short time, little while; **buen –** pleasant time; long time; **–s perdidos** leisure hours; **a –s** at intervals, from time to time; **pasar el –** to while away the time, kill time; *Am.* **¡hasta cada –!** so long!; see you later!
ratón [rra·tón] *m.* mouse; *Am.* **tener un –** to have a hangover; **ratonera** [rra·to·né·ra] *f.* mousetrap.
raudal [rraw·dál] *m.* torrent, downpour, flood; *Ríopl., Ch., Col., Ven., Andes* rapids.
raudo [rraw·do] *adj.* rapid swift.
raya [rrá·ya] *f.* line; dash; stripe; boundary line; part in the hair; *Mex.* pay, wage; *Mex.* **día de – payday; **tener a –** to keep within bounds; to hold in check; **pasar de la –** to overstep one's bounds, take undue liberties; *m.* sting ray (*a species of fish*).
rayador [rra·ya·dór] *m. Mex.* paymaster; *Am.* umpire in a game.
rayar [rra·yár] *v.* to line, make lines on; to streak; to scratch, mark; to cross out; *Mex.* to pay or collect wages; *Am.* to stop a horse all of a sudden; *Am.* to spur a horse to run at top speed; **– el alba** to dawn; **– en** to border on; *Am.* **-se uno** to help oneself; to get rich.
rayo [rrá·yo] *m.* ray, beam; lightning, thunderbolt; spoke; **-s X** X-rays; **-s infrarrojos** infrared rays.
rayón [rra·yón] *m.* rayon.
raza [rrá·sa] *f.* race; clan; breed; fissure, crevice; **caballo de –** thoroughbred horse.

razón [rra·són] *f.* (*facultad*) reason; (*justicia*) right, justice; (*cuenta*) ratio; account, information, word, message; — **social** firm, firm name; **a** — **de** at the rate of; **icon** —! no wonder!; **dar** — to inform; **dar la** — **a una persona** to admit that a person is right; **perder la** — to lose one's mind; **poner en** — to pacify; **tener** — to be right.

razonable [rra·so·ná·ḅle] *adj.* reasonable.

razonamiento [rra·so·na·mjén·to] *m.* reasoning.

razonar [rra·so·nár] *v.* to reason; to discourse, talk; to argue.

re [rre] *m.* second note of the musical scale (*solfeggio*).

reabierto [rre·a·ḅjér·to] *p.p. of* reabrir.

reabrir[52] [rre·a·ḅrír] *v.* to reopen.

reacción [rre·ak·sjón] *f.* reaction; — **nuclear** nuclear reaction; — **en cadena** chain reaction.

reaccionar [rre·ak·sjo·nár] *v.* to react.

reaccionario [rre·ak·sjo·ná·rjo] *adj. & m.* reactionary.

reacio [rre·á·sjo] *adj.* stubborn, obstinate.

reactor [rre·ak·tór] *m.* reactor; — **atómico** atomic reactor; — **nuclear** nuclear reactor.

reajustar [rre·a·xus·tár] *v.* to readjust.

reajuste [rre·a·xús·te] *m.* readjustment.

real [rre·ál] *adj.* real; royal; *m.* army camp; fairground; real (*Spanish coin worth one fourth of a peseta*); **-es** *Andes* money (*in general*); **levantar el** — (*or* **los -es**) to break camp.

realce [rre·ál·se] *m.* (*adorno*) embossment, raised work, relief; (*lustre*) prestige; lustre, splendor; **dar** — to enhance; to emphasize.

realeza [rre·a·lé·sa] *f.* royalty (*royal dignity*).

realidad [rre·a·li·ḍáḍ] *f.* reality; truth; fact; **en** — really, truly, in fact.

realismo [rre·a·líz·mo] *m.* realism; royalism.

realista [rre·a·lís·ta] *adj.* realistic; royalist; *m.* realist; royalist.

realización [rre·a·li·sa·sjón] *f.* realization, fulfillment; conversion into money, sale.

realizar[9] [rre·a·li·sár] *v.* to realize, fulfill, make real; to convert into money; to sell out.

realzar[9] [rre·al·sár] *v.* to emboss; to raise; to enhance; to make stand out; to emphasize.

reanimar [rre·a·ni·már] *v.* to revive; to comfort; to cheer; to encourage.

reanudación [rre·a·nu·ḍa·sjón] *f.* renewal.

reanudar [rre·a·nu·ḍár] *v.* to renew, resume, begin again.

reaparecer[13] [rre·a·pa·re·sér] *v. irr.* to reappear.

reasumir [rre·a·su·mír] *v.* to resume.

reata [rre·á·ta] *f.* lariat, rope, lasso.

reavivar [rre·a·ḅi·ḅár] *v.* to revive.

rebaja [rre·ḅá·xa] *f.* deduction; reduction; discount.

rebajar [rre·ḅa·xár] *v.* to diminish; to lower, reduce; to tone down (*a painting*); to humiliate; **-se** to lower or humble oneself.

rebanada [rre·ḅa·ná·ḍa] *f.* slice.

rebanar [rre·ḅa·nár] *v.* to slice.

rebaño [rre·ḅá·ño] *m.* flock; herd.

rebatir [rre·ḅa·tír] *v.* to beat over and over; to repel, resist; to refute; to rebut (*come back with an argument*); to argue; to parry (*in fencing*).

rebato [rre·ḅá·to] *m.* alarm, call to arms; surprise attack.

rebelarse [rre·ḅe·lár·se] *v.* to rebel.

rebelde [rre·ḅél·de] *adj.* rebellious; *m.* rebel; defaulter (*one who fails to appear in court*).

rebeldía [rre·ḅel·dí·a] *f.* rebelliousness; defiance; default, failure to appear in court; **en** — in revolt.

rebelión [rre·ḅe·ljón] *f.* rebellion, revolt.

rebencazo [rre·ḅeŋ·ká·so] *m. Ríopl., Ch., Andes* crack of a whip; *Am.* lash, stroke with a whip.

rebenque [rre·ḅéŋ·ke] *m.* rawhide whip.

reborde [rre·ḅór·ḍe] *m.* edge, border.

rebosante [rre·ḅo·sán·te] *adj.* brimming, overflowing.

rebosar [rre·ḅo·sár] *v.* to overflow, brim over; to abound.

rebotar [rre·ḅo·tár] *v.* to rebound, bounce back or again; to make rebound; to repel, reject; to annoy, vex; **-se** to become vexed, upset; *Col., Mex.* to become cloudy or muddy (*said of water*); *Am.* **rebotársele a uno la bilis** to get angry, become upset.

rebote [rre·ḅó·te] *m.* rebound, bounce; **de** — on the rebound; indirectly.

rebozar[9] [rre·ḅo·sár] *v.* to muffle up; **-se** to muffle oneself up; to wrap oneself up.

rebozo [rre·ḅó·so] *m.* shawl; **sin** — frankly, openly.

rebullir[20] [rre·ḅu·yír] *v. irr.* to stir, move; to boil up.

rebusca [rre·ḅús·ka] *f.* research; search; searching; gleaning; residue.

rebuscar[6] [rre·ḅus·kár] *v.* to search thoroughly; to pry into; to glean.

rebuznar [rre·ḅuz·nár] *v.* to bray.

rebuzno [rre·ḅúz·no] *m.* bray.

recabar [rre·ka·ḅár] *v.* to obtain, gain by entreaty.

recado [rre·ká·ḍo] *m.* message; errand; gift; daily food supply, daily marketing; precaution; equipment; *Ríopl., Andes* saddle and trappings; — **de escribir** writing materials; **-s a** regards to.

recaer[24] [rre·ka·ér] *v. irr.* to fall (upon); to fall again; to relapse; to have a relapse.

recaída [rre·ka·í·ḍa] *f.* relapse; falling again.

recalar [rre·ka·lár] *v.* to saturate, soak through; to reach port; to come within sight of land; to land, end up, stop at; *Am.* — **con alguien** to "land" on somebody, take it out on somebody.

recalcar[6] [rre·kal·kár] *v.* to emphasize; to harp on; to press down.

recalcitrante [rre·kal·si·trán·te] *adj.* obstinate, disobedient, stubborn.

recalentar[1] [rre·ka·len·tár] *v. irr.* to reheat, warm over; to overheat, heat too much.

recamar [rre·ka·már] *v.* to embroider (*usually with gold or silver*).

recámara [rre·ká·ma·ra] *f.* dressing room; *Mex., C.A., Col.* bedroom; *Ríopl., Col.* chamber for an explosive charge.

recapitular [rre·ka·pi·tu·lár] *v.* to recapitulate, sum up, tell briefly.

recargar[7] [rre·kar·gár] *v.* to overload; to emphasize.

recargo [rre·kár·go] *m.* overload; extra load; extra charge; increase (*of fever*); new charge, new accusation.

recatado [rre·ka·tá·ḍo] *adj.* cautious, prudent; modest; *p.p.* concealed.

recatar [rre·ka·tár] *v.* to cover, conceal; **-se** to show timidity; to be cautious; to hide (from), shun.

recato [rre·ká·to] *m.* caution, prudence; reserve, restraint, secrecy; modesty.

recaudación [rre·kaw·ḍa·sjón] *f.* collection, collecting; office of tax collector.

recaudador [rre·kaw·ḍa·ḍór] *m.* tax collector.

recaudar [rre·kaw·ḍár] *v.* to collect (*money, taxes, rents, etc.*).

recaudo [rre·kaw·d̦o] *m.* collection, collecting; precaution; bond, security; *Mex.* spices, seasonings; *Am.* daily supply of vegetables; **estar a buen** — to be safe; **poner a buen** — to place in safety.

recelar [rre·se·lár] *v.* to suspect, fear; **-se de** to be suspicious or afraid of.

recelo [rre·sé·lo] *m.* suspicion, fear.

receloso [rre·se·ló·so] *adj.* suspicious, distrustful, fearful.

recepción [rre·sep·sjón] *f.* reception; admission.

receptáculo [rre·sep·tá·ku·lo] *m.* receptacle.

receptivo [rre·sep·tí·d̦o] *adj.* receptive, capable of receiving, quick to receive.

receptor [rre·sep·tór] *m.* receiver; *adj.* receiving.

receta [rre·sé·ta] *f.* recipe; prescription.

recetar [rre·se·tár] *v.* to prescribe (*a medicine*).

recibidor [rre·si·d̦i·d̦ór] *m.* receiver; reception room.

recibimiento [rre·si·d̦i·mjén·to] *m.* reception; welcome; reception room; parlor.

recibir [rre·si·d̦ír] *v.* to receive; to admit, accept; to go out to meet; — **noticias de** to hear from; **-se de** to receive a title or degree of.

recibo [rre·si·d̦o] *m.* (*monetario*) receipt; (*acción*) reception; (*sala*) reception room; parlor; **sala de** — reception room; **estar de** — to be at home for receiving callers; **ser de** — to be acceptable, be fit for use.

reciedumbre [rre·sje·d̦úm·bre] *f.* strength, force, vigor.

recién [rre·sjén] *adv.* recently, lately, newly (*used before a past participle*); *Ríopl., Ch., Andes* just now; *Ríopl., Ch., Andes* a short time ago; *Ríopl., Ch., Andes* — **entonces** just then.

reciente [rre·sjén·te] *adj.* recent, new.

recinto [rre·sín·to] *m.* enclosure; precinct.

recio [rré·sjo] *adj.* strong, robust; harsh; hard, severe; fast; *adv.* strongly; harshly; rapidly; hard; loud.

recipiente [rre·si·pjén·te] *m.* receptable, container; recipient, receiver (*he who receives*).

recíproco [rre·sí·pro·ko] *adj.* reciprocal, mutual.

recitación [rre·si·ta·sjón] *f.* recitation, recital.

recital [rre·si·tál] *m.* musical recital.

recitar [rre·si·tár] *v.* to recite.

reclamación [rre·kla·ma·sjón] *f.* protest, complaint; claim, demand.

reclamador [rre·kla·ma·d̦ór] *m.* claimant; complainer.

reclamante [rre·kla·mán·te] *m. & f.* claimant; complainer; *adj.* complaining, claiming.

reclamar [rre·kla·már] *v.* (*protestar*) to complain, protest (*against*); (*exigir*) to claim, demand; to lure, call back (*a bird*).

reclamo [rre·klá·mo] *m.* (*protesta*) protest; claim; advertisement; (*llamada*) call; bird call; decoy bird; lure.

reclinar [rre·kli·nár] *v.* to recline, lean; **-se** to recline, lean back.

recluir³² [rre·klwír] *v. irr.* to seclude, shut up; **-se** to isolate oneself.

recluso [rre·klú·so] *m.* recluse, hermit; *adj.* shut in, shut up.

recluta [rre·klú·ta] *f.* recruiting; *Am.* roundup of cattle; *m.* recruit.

reclutamiento [rre·klu·ta·mjén·to] *m.* recruiting; levy, draft.

reclutar [rre·klu·tár] *v.* to recruit, enlist; *Am.* to round up (*cattle*).

recobrar [rre·ko·d̦rár] *v.* to recover, regain; **-se** to

recover; to recuperate.

recobro [rre·kó·d̦ro] *m.* recovery.

recodo [rre·kó·d̦o] *m.* bend, turn; elbow (*of a road*).

recoger¹¹ [rre·ko·xér] *v.* (*juntar*) to gather; to collect; to pick up; (*ceñir*) to take in, tighten; (*abrigar*) to shelter; **-se** to retire, go home; to withdraw; to seclude oneself; to take shelter.

recogida [rre·ko·xí·d̦a] *f.* harvest.

recogimiento [rre·ko·xi·mjén·to] *m.* seclusion; concentration of thought, composure; retreat; collecting, gathering.

recolección [rre·ko·lek·sjón] *f.* collecting, gathering; harvest, crop; summary.

recolectar [rre·ko·lek·tár] *v.* to harvest; to gather.

recomendable [rre·ko·men·dá·d̦le] *adj.* praiseworthy, laudable; advisable.

recomendación [rre·ko·men·da·sjón] *f.* recommendation; request.

recomendar¹ [rre·ko·men·dár] *v. irr.* to recommend; to commend, praise; to enjoin, urge; to advise.

recompensa [rre·kom·pén·sa] *f.* recompense; compensation.

recompensar [rre·kom·pen·sár] *v.* to recompense, reward; to compensate.

reconcentrar [rre·kon·sen·trár] *v.* to concentrate, bring together; to hide in the depth of one's heart; **-se** to concentrate, become absorbed in thought, collect one's thoughts.

reconciliación [rre·kon·si·lja·sjón] *f.* reconciliation.

reconciliar [rre·kon·si·ljár] *v.* to reconcile; **-se** to become reconciled.

recóndito [rre·kón·di·to] *adj.* hidden, concealed; profound.

reconocer¹³ [rre·ko·no·sér] *v. irr.* to recognize; to admit, acknowledge; to examine carefully; to reconnoiter, scout, explore.

reconocimiento [rre·ko·no·si·mjén·to] *m.* recognition; acknowledgment; gratitude; examination; scouting, exploring.

reconstruir³² [rre·kons·trwír] *v. irr.* to reconstruct, rebuild.

recontar² [rre·kon·tár] *v. irr.* to recount; to tell, relate.

recopilar [rre·ko·pi·lár] *v.* to compile; to digest, make a digest of.

récord [rré·kor] *m.* record.

recordación [rre·kor·d̦a·sjón] *f.* recollection; remembrance.

recordar² [rre·kor·d̦ár] *v. irr.* to remember; to recall; to remind; *Am.* to rouse, awaken; **-se** to remember; to wake up.

recordativo [rre·kor·d̦a·tí·d̦o] *m.* reminder; *adj.* reminding.

recordatorio [rre·kor·d̦a·tó·rjo] *m.* reminder.

recorrer [rre·ko·rrér] *v.* to go over; to travel over; to read over; to look over; to overhaul.

recorrido [rre·ko·rri·d̦o] *m.* trip, run; mileage, distance traveled.

recortar [rre·kor·tár] *v.* to trim, clip; to shorten; to cut out (*figures*); to pare off; **-se** to project itself (*as a shadow*); to outline itself.

recorte [rre·kór·te] *m.* clipping; cutting; outline; *Mex.* gossip, slander.

recostar² [rre·kos·tár] *v. irr.* to recline, lean; **-se** to recline, lean back.

recoveco [rre·ko·d̦é·ko] *m.* turn, bend; nook; sly or underhanded manner.

recreación [rre·kre·a·sjón] *f.* recreation.

recrear [rre·kre·ár] *v.* to entertain, amuse; to gratify, please; **-se** to amuse oneself; to take delight (in).

recreo [rre·kré·o] *m.* recreation, entertainment; place of amusement.

recrudecer[13] [rre·kru·ɖe·sér] *v.* to recur, break out again, flare up, become worse (*said of an illness or evil*).

rectángulo [rrek·táŋ·gu·lo] *m.* rectangle; *adj.* rectangular, right-angled.

rectificar[6] [rrek·ti·fi·kár] *v.* to rectify, correct, amend; to refine (*liquors*).

rectitud [rrek·ti·túɖ] *f.* rectitude, uprightness, righteousness; straightness; accuracy.

recto [rrék·to] *adj.* straight; right; just, honest; **ángulo** — right angle; *m.* rectum; *adv. C.A.* straight ahead.

rector [rrek·tór] *m.* college or university president; principal; rector, curate, priest.

recua [rré·kwa] *f.* drove of pack animals; drove, crowd.

recuento [rre·kwén·to] *m.* recount.

recuerdo [rre·kwér·ɖo] *m.* remembrance; recollection; souvenir, keepsake; memory; **-s** regards; *adj. Riopl., Col., Ven.* awake.

reculada [rre·ku·lá·ɖa] *f.* recoil.

recular [rre·ku·lár] *v.* to recoil, spring back; to fall back, go back, retreat; to yield, back down.

recuperación [rre·ku·pe·ra·sjón] *f.* recovery.

recuperar [rre·ku·pe·rár] *v.* to recuperate, recover, regain; **-se** to recuperate, recover one's health.

recurrir [rre·ku·rrír] *v.* to resort (to); to have recourse (to).

recurso [rre·kúr·so] *m.* recourse, resort; petition, appeal; **-s** means, resources; **sin** — without remedy; without appeal.

recusar [rre·ku·sár] *v.* to reject, decline.

rechazar[9] [rre·ča·sár] *v.* to reject; to repel, drive back; to rebuff.

rechifla [rre·čí·fla] *f.* hooting; hissing; ridicule.

rechiflar [rre·či·flár] *v.* to hoot; to hiss; to ridicule.

rechinamiento [rre·či·na·mjén·to] *m.* creak; squeak; squeaking; gnashing.

rechinar [rre·či·nár] *v.* to squeak; to creak; *Am.* to be furious, angry; *Am.* to grumble, growl; — **los dientes** to gnash one's teeth.

rechino [rre·čí·no] = **rechinamiento**.

rechoncho [rre·čon·čo] *adj.* plump; chubby; squat.

rechuparse [rre·ču·pár·se] *v.* to smack one's lips.

red [rreɖ] *f.* net; netting; network; snare; **redecilla** [rre·ɖe·si·ya] *f.* small net; mesh; hair net.

redacción [rre·ɖak·sjón] *f.* (*acto*) wording; editing; (*lugar*) newspaper offices; editorial department; (*cuerpo*) editorial staff.

redactar [rre·ɖak·tár] *v.* to word, compose; to edit.

redactor [rre·ɖak·tór] *m.* editor.

redada [rre·ɖá·ɖa] *f.* catch; haul (*of criminals*).

redarguir[32] [rre·ɖar·ǵwír] *v. irr.* to retort, answer back; to contradict, call in question; to reargue.

rededor [rre·ɖe·ɖór] *m.* surroundings; **al** (*or* **en**) — around, about.

redención [rre·ɖen·sjón] *f.* redemption.

redentor [rre·ɖen·tór] *m.* redeemer, savior; **el Redentor** the Savior.

redil [rre·ɖíl] *m.* sheepfold.

redimir [rre·ɖi·mír] *v.* to redeem; to ransom; to set free.

rédito [rré·ɖi·to] *m.* interest, revenue, yield.

redituar[18] [rre·ɖi·twár] *v.* to produce, yield (*interest*).

redoblar [rre·ɖo·ƀlár] *v.* to double; to clinch (*a nail*); to reiterate, repeat; to roll (*a drum*).

redoble [rre·ɖó·ƀle] *m.* roll (*of a drum*).

redoma [rre·ɖó·ma] *f.* flask, vial.

redomón [rre·ɖo·món] *m. Ríopl.* half-tame horse or bull; *adj. Ríopl.* half-civilized, rustic.

redonda [rre·ɖón·da] *f.* surrounding district, neighborhood; whole note (*music*); **a la** — all around, round-about.

redondear [rre·ɖon·de·ár] *v.* to round, make round; to round off; to round out.

redondel [rre·ɖon·dél] *m.* arena, bull ring; circle.

redondez [rre·ɖon·dés] *f.* roundness.

redondo [rre·ɖón·do] *adj.* round; whole, entire; clear, evident; *Andes* stupid; *Mex.* honest; **en** — all around.

redopelo [rre·ɖo·pé·lo]: **a** — against the grain.

redor [rre·ɖór] *m.* round mat; **en** — around.

reducción [rre·ɖuk·sjón] *f.* reduction; cut, discount; decrease.

reducido [rre·ɖu·sí·ɖo] *p.p. & adj.* reduced; compact, small.

reducir[25] [rre·ɖu·sír] *v. irr.* to reduce; to diminish; to convert (into); to reset (*a bone*); **-se** to adapt oneself, adjust oneself; to be constrained, forced.

redundante [rre·ɖun·dán·te] *adj.* redundant.

reedificar[6] [rre·e·ɖi·fi·kár] *v.* to rebuild, reconstruct.

reelección [rre·e·lek·sjón] *f.* re-election.

reelegir[11] [rre·e·le·xír] *v.* to re-elect.

reembolsar [rre·em·bol·sár] *v.* to reimburse, refund, repay, pay back.

reembolso [rre·em·ból·so] *m.* reimbursement, refund.

reemitir [rre·mi·tír] *v.* to emit again; to issue again; to rebroadcast; to relay (*a broadcast*).

reemplazable [rre·em·pla·sá·ƀle] *adj.* replaceable.

reemplazar[9] [rre·em·pla·sár] *v.* to replace; to substitute.

reemplazo [rre·em·plá·s̩o] *m.* replacement; substitute, substitution.

reexpedir[5] [rre·es·pe·ɖír] *v. irr.* to forward (*mail*).

refacción [rre·fak·sjón] *f.* (*alimento*) light lunch, refreshment; (*compostura*) repair, reparation; *Mex., Col.* spare part; *Carib.* help, aid, loan.

refajo [rre·fá·xo] *m.* underskirt; short skirt.

referencia [rre·fe·rén·sja] *f.* reference; narration, account.

referente [rre·fe·rén·te] *adj.* referring.

referir[3] [rre·fe·rír] *v. irr.* to refer; to narrate; to relate; **-se** to refer (to), relate (to).

refinamiento [rre·fi·na·mjén·to] *m.* refinement.

refinar [rre·fi·nár] *v.* to refine; to purify.

refinería [rre·fi·ne·ri·a] *f.* refinery.

reflector [rre·flek·tór] *m.* reflector; floodlight.

reflejar [rre·fle·xár] *v.* to reflect; to think over; **-se** to be reflected.

reflejo [rre·flé·xo] *m.* reflection, image, reflex; *adj.* reflected; reflex.

reflexión [rre·flek·sjón] *f.* reflection; meditation, consideration.

reflexionar [rre·flek·sjo·nár] *v.* to reflect, meditate, think over.

reflexivo [rre·flek·sí·ƀo] *adj.* reflexive; reflective, thoughtful.

reflujo [rre·flú·xo] *m.* ebb; ebb tide.

refocilar [rre·fo·si·lár] *v.* to cheer.

reforma [rre·fór·ma] *f.* reform; reformation; improvement.

reformador [rre·for·ma·ɖór] *m.* reformer.

reformar [rre·for·már] *v.* to reform; to correct, amend; to improve; **-se** to reform.

reformista [rre·for·mís·ta] *m. & f.* reformer.

reforzar[2, 9] [rre·for·sár] *v. irr.* to reinforce; to

RE

strengthen.
refracción [rre·frak·sjón] *f.* refraction.
refractario [rre·frak·tó·rjo] *adj.* refractory;
impervious; rebellious, unruly; stubborn.
refrán [rre·frán] *m.* popular proverb or saying.
refrenar [rre·fre·nár] *v.* to restrain, keep in check;
to curb; to rein.
refrendar [rre·fren·dár] *v.* to legalize by signing; to
countersign (*confirm by another signature*); —
un pasaporte to visé a passport.
refrescante [rre·fres·kán·te] *adj.* refreshing.
refrescar⁶ [rre·fres·kár] *v.* to refresh, renew; to
cool; to get cool (*said of the weather*); **-se** to
cool off; to take the fresh air; to take a cooling
drink or refreshment; *Cuba, C.A.* to take an
afternoon refreshment.
refresco [rre·frés·ko] *m.* refreshment.
refresquería [rre·fres·ke·rí·a] *f. Mex., C.A., Ven.*
refreshment shop, outdoor refreshment stand.
refriega [rre·frjé·ǥa] *f.* strife, fray, scuffle.
refrigeración [rre·fri·xe·ra·sjón] *f.* refrigeration;
light meal or refreshment.
refrigerador [rre·fri·xe·ra·ǫór] *m. Am.* refrigerator,
freezer; *adj.* refrigerating, freezing; refreshing.
refrigerar [rre·fri·xe·rár] *v.* to cool.
refrigerio [rre·fri·xé·rjo] *m.* refreshment; relief,
comfort; coolness.
refrito [rre·frí·to] *adj.* refried; frijoles refritos
(*Mexican fried beans*).
refuerzo [rre·fwér·so] *m.* reinforcement.
refugiado [rre·fu·xjá·ǫo] *m.* refugee; *p.p. of* **refugiar**.
refugiar [rre·fu·xjár] *v.* to shelter; **-se** to take
shelter or refuge.
refugio [rre·fú·xjo] *m.* refuge, shelter.
refulgente [rre·ful·xén·te] *adj.* refulgent, radiant,
shining.
refundir [rre·fun·dír] *v.* to remelt, refound, recast
(*metals*); to recast, rewrite, reconstruct.
refunfuñar [rre·fun·fu·ñár] *v.* to grumble, mumble,
growl, mutter.
refunfuño [rre·fun·fú·ño] *m.* grumble, growl;
refunfuñón [rre·fun·fu·ñón] *adj.* grouchy;
grumbly, grumbling.
refutar [rre·fu·tár] *v.* to refute.
regadera [rre·ga·ǫé·ra] *f.* sprinkler; *Mex.* shower
bath.
regadío [rre·ga·ǫí·o] *adj.* irrigable, that can be
irrigated; irrigated; *m.* irrigated land; **tierras de**
— irrigable lands.
regalar [rre·ga·lár] *v.* (*dar*) to give, present as a
gift; to regale; (*recrear*) to entertain; to delight,
please; **-se** to treat oneself well, live a life of
ease.
regalo [rre·ǥá·lo] *m.* present, gift; pleasure,
delight; dainty, delicacy; luxury, comfort.
regañadientes [rre·ga·ña·ǫjén·tes]: **a** — much
against one's wishes; unwillingly.
regañar [rre·ga·ñár] *v.* to growl; to grumble; to
quarrel; to scold.
regaño [rre·ǥá·ño] *m.* scolding, reprimand.
regañón [rre·ga·ñón] *adj.* grumbling; scolding;
quarrelsome; *m.* growler, grumbler, scolder.
regar¹·⁷ [rre·ǥár] *v. irr.* to irrigate; to water; to
sprinkle, scatter; *Col.* to spill, throw off (*said of*
a horse); **-se** *Am.* to scatter, disperse (*said of a*
group, herd, etc.).
regatear [rre·ga·te·ár] *v.* to haggle, bargain; to
dispute; to sell at retail; to race (*in a regatta or*
boat race).
regateo [rre·ga·té·o] *m.* bargaining.
regazo [rre·ǥá·so] *m.* lap.

regencia [rre·xén·sja] *f.* regency.
regentar [rre·xen·tár] *v.* to direct, conduct,
manage; — **una cátedra** to teach a course (*at*
a university).
regente [rre·xén·te] *m.* regent; manager; *adj.* ruling.
regidor [rre·xi·ǫór] *m.* councilman, alderman; *adj.*
governing, ruling.
régimen [rré·xi·men] *m.* regime; government, rule,
management; — **lácteo** milk diet.
regimiento [rre·xi·mjén·to] *m.* regiment;
(*administrativo*) administration; municipal
council; position of alderman.
regio [rré·xjo] *adj.* regal, royal; splendid,
magnificient.
región [rre·xjón] *f.* region.
regir⁵·¹¹ [rre·xír] *v. irr.* to rule, govern; to direct,
manage; to be in force (*said of a law*); to move
(*said of the bowels*).
registrador [rre·xis·tra·ǫór] *m.* registrar, recorder;
city clerk, official in charge of records; inspector
(*in a customhouse*); searcher; *adj.* registering;
caja registradora cash register.
registrar [rre·xis·trár] *v.* to examine, inspect,
scrutinize; to register, record; **-se** to register,
enroll.
registro [rre·xís·tro] *m.* search, inspection;
registration; census; registration office; register;
record; registration certificate; watch regulator;
bookmark; organ stop; *Ven.* wholesale textile
store.
regla [rré·ǥla] *f.* (*precepto*) rule; ruler; order;
precept, principle; (*medida*) measure,
moderation; menstruation; **en** — in order, in
due form; **por** — **general** as a general rule;
usually.
reglamento [rre·ǥla·mén·to] *m.* regulations, rules;
rule, bylaw.
regocijado [rre·ǥo·si·xá·ǫo] *adj.* joyful, merry, gay;
p.p. of **regocijar**.
regocijar [rre·ǥo·si·xár] *v.* to gladden, delight; **-se**
to be glad; to rejoice.
regocijo [rre·ǥo·sí·xo] *m.* joy; rejoicing.
regordete [rre·ǥor·ǫé·te] *adj.* plump.
regresar [rre·ǥre·sár] *v.* to return.
regreso [rre·ǥré·so] *m.* return; **estar de** — to be
back.
reguero [rre·ǥé·ro] *m.* stream, rivulet; trickle;
irrigation ditch.
regulación [rre·ǥu·la·sjón] *f.* regulation;
adjustment.
regulador [rre·ǥu·la·ǫór] *m.* regulator; controller;
governor (*of a machine*); *adj.* regulating.
regular [rre·ǥu·lár] *v.* to regulate; to adjust; *adj.*
regular; ordinary; moderate; fair, medium; **por**
lo — as a rule, usually; *adv.* fairly well.
regularidad [rre·ǥu·la·ri·ǫáǫ] *f.* regularity.
regularizar⁹ [rre·ǥu·la·ri·sár] *v.* to regulate, make
regular.
rehacer³¹ [rre·a·sér] *v. irr.* to remake; to make over;
to repair; **-se** to recover one's strength; to rally.
rehen [rre·én] *m.* hostage; **en rehenes** as a hostage.
rehuir³² [rre·wír] *v. irr.* to shun, avoid; to shrink
(from).
rehusar [rre·u·sár] *v.* to refuse; **-se a** to refuse to.
reina [réj·na] *f.* queen.
reinado [rrej·ná·ǫo] *m.* reign.
reimante [rrej·nán·te] *adj.* reigning; prevailing.
reinar [rrej·nár] *v.* to reign; to rule; to prevail.
reincidir [rrej·si·ǫír] *v.* to relapse, slide back (into).
reino [rréj·no] *m.* kingdom.
reintegro [rrejn·te·ǥro] *m.* reimbursement, refund.

reir[15] [rre·ír] *v. irr.* to laugh; **-se de** to laugh at;
Ríopl., Andes, Col., Ven., Carib. — **de dientes
para afuera** to laugh outwardly, laugh
hypocritically.

reiterar [rrej·te·rár] *v.* to reiterate, repeat.

reivindicación [rrej·ƀin·di·ka·sjón] *f.* recovery.

reja [rré·xa] *f.* grate, grating; plowshare (*blade of
the plow*); plowing; *Carib., C.A.* jail.

rejilla [rre·xí·ya] *f.* small grating, lattice; small
latticed window; fireplace grate; cane upholstery;
Ch. wire dish-cover.

rejo [rré·xo] *m.* point; plow share.

rejonear [rre·xo·ne·ár] *v.* to fight a bull from
horseback (*Portuguese style*).

rejuvenecer[13] [rre·xu·ƀe·ne·sér] *v. irr.* to rejuvenate,
make young; **-se** to become rejuvenated.

relación [rre·la·sjón] *f.* relation; story, account;
long speech in a play; *Ríopl.* verse recited
alternately by a couple in a folk dance; **-es**
personal relations, connections; acquaintances.

relacionar [rre·la·sjo·nár] *v.* to relate, connect; **-se**
to be related, connected; to become acquainted,
establish friendly connections.

relajación [rre·la·xa·sjón] *f.*, **relajamiento**
[rre·la·xa·mjén·to] *m.* relaxation; laxity;
slackening; hernia.

relajar [rre·la·xár] *v.* to relax; to slacken; to
release from a vow or oath; **-se** to get a hernia
or rupture; to become weakened; to become lax
(*said of laws, customs, etc.*).

relajo [rre·lá·xo] *m. Carib., Mex.* disorderly
conduct; lewdness; scandal.

relamerse [rre·la·mér·se] *v.* to lick one's lips; to
gloat; to boast; to slick oneself up.

relámpago [rre·lám·pa·ǥo] *m.* lightning; flash.

relampaguear [rre·lam·pa·ǥe·ár] *v.* to lighten; to
flash; to sparkle.

relampagueo [rre·lam·pa·ǥé·o] *m.* flashing; sheet
lightning.

relatar [rre·la·tár] *v.* to relate, narrate.

relativo [rre·la·tí·ƀo] *adj.* relative; — **a** relative to,
regarding.

relato [rre·lá·to] *m.* narration, account, story.

relé [rre·lé] *m.* relay; — **de televisión** television
relay system.

relegar[7] [rre·le·ǥár] *v.* to relegate, banish; to
postpone; to set aside, put away.

relente [rre·lén·te] *m.* night dampness; *Am.* fresh
night breeze.

relevar [rre·le·ƀár] *v.* to relieve; to release; to
absolve; to replace, substitute; to emboss; to
make stand out in relief.

relevo [rre·lé·ƀo] *m.* relief (*from a post or military
duty; person who relieves another from the
performance of a duty*).

relicario [rre·li·ká·rjo] *m.* reliquary (*small box or
casket for keeping relics*); *Col., Ven., Cuba, Mex.,
Andes* locket.

relieve [rre·ljé·ƀe] *m.* relief, embossment, raised
work; **-s** scraps, leftovers; **de** — in relief;
prominent, outstanding; **poner de** — to make
stand out; to emphasize.

religión [rre·li·xjón] *f.* religion.

religiosidad [rre·li·xjo·si·ðáð] *f.* religiousness, piety;
faithfulness.

religioso [rre·li·xjó·so] *adj.* religious; faithful;
punctual; *m.* friar, monk.

relinchar [rre·lin·čár] *v.* to neigh.

relincho [rre·lín·čo] *m.* neigh.

reliquia [rre·li·kja] *f.* relic; vestige; **-s** relics,
remains.

reloj [rre·ló] *m.* clock; watch; — **de pulsera**
wristwatch; — **de sol** (*or* — **solar**) sundial; —
despertador alarm clock.

relojería [rre·lo·xe·rí·a] *f.* watch shop; jewelry
store.

reluciente [rre·lu·sjén·te] *adj.* shining; sparkling.

relucir[13] [rre·lu·sír] *v. irr.* to glitter, sparkle; to
shine.

relumbrante [rre·lum·brán·te] *adj.* brilliant, flashing,
resplendent.

relumbrar [rre·lum·brár] *v.* to glare; to glitter.

relumbre [rre·lúm·bre] *m.* glare, glitter.

rellenar [rre·ye·nár] *v.* to refill; to fill up; to pad;
to stuff.

relleno [rre·yé·no] *adj.* stuffed; *m.* meat stuffing;
filling.

remachar [rre·ma·čár] *v.* to clinch; to hammer
down; to flatten; to rivet; to fix firmly; **-se** *Am.*
to be tight-lipped, stubbornly silent.

remache [rre·má·če] *m.* clinching; fastening,
securing; riveting; rivet.

remanente [rre·ma·nén·te] *m.* remainder, balance;
remnant; residue.

remar [rre·már] *v.* to row; to struggle.

rematado [rre·ma·tá·ðo] *adj. & p.p.* (*acabado*)
finished; (*vendido en subasta*) sold at auction;
loco — completely crazy.

rematar [rre·ma·tár] *v.* (*acabar*) to finish; to end;
to give the final or finishing stroke; (*vender*) to
auction; (*afianzar*) to fasten (*a stitch*); *Am.* to
stop (*a horse*) suddenly; *Am.* to buy or sell at
auction; **-se** to be finished, be completely
destroyed or ruined.

remate [rre·má·te] *m.* (*fin*) finish, end; (*postura*)
highest bid at an auction; sale at auction;
(*punta*) pinnacle, spire; *Am.* selvage, edge of a
fabric; **de** — absolutely, without remedy; **loco de**
— completely crazy, stark mad.

remedar [rre·me·ðár] *v.* to imitate; to mimic.

remediar [rre·me·ðjár] *v.* to remedy; to help; to
avoid.

remedio [rre·mé·ðjo] *m.* remedy; help;
amendment; recourse, resort; **sin** — without
help, unavoidable; **no tiene** — it can't be helped.

remedo [rre·mé·ðo] *m.* imitation; mockery.

remembranza [rre·mem·brán·sa] *f.* remembrance,
memory.

rememorar [rre·me·mo·rár] *v.* to remember, call to
mind.

remendar[1] [rre·men·dár] *v. irr.* to mend, patch; to
darn; to repair.

remendón [rre·men·dón] *m.* cobbler, shoe
repairman; mender, patcher.

remero [rre·mé·ro] *m.* rower.

remesa [rre·mé·sa] *f.* shipment; remittance,
payment.

remesar [rre·me·sár] *v.* to remit; to ship.

remiendo [rre·mjén·do] *m.* mend; mending; patch;
darn; repair; **a -s** piecemeal, piece by piece.

remilgado [rre·mil·ǥá·ðo] *adj.* prudish, prim,
affected.

remilgo [rre·míl·ǥo] *m.* prudery, primness, affection.

reminiscencia [rre·mi·ni·sén·sja] *f.* reminiscence.

remisión [rre·mi·sjón] *f.* (*disculpa*) remission;
forgiveness; (*remesa*) remittance, remitting;
(*diminución*) abatement, slackening; *Mex., Ven.*
anything shipped or sent.

remitente [rre·mi·tén·te] *m. & f.* sender; shipper.

remitir [rre·mi·tír] *v.* (*enviar*) to remit; to send;
(*diferir*) to defer; to pardon; to refer; to abate;
-se to defer, yield (*to another's judgment*).

RE

remo [rré·mo] *m.* oar; hard and long work; leg of a horse; **al —** at the oar; at hard labor.

remojar [rre·mo·xár] *v.* to soak; to steep; *Am.* to tip, bribe.

remojo [rre·mó·xo] *m.* soaking; steeping; *Am.* tip, bribe.

remolacha [rre·mo·lá·ča] *f.* beet.

remolcador [rre·mol·ka·đór] *m.* towboat, tug, tugboat; **lancha remolcadora** tugboat.

remolcar[6] [rre·mol·kár] *v.* to tow, tug; to take (*a person*) in tow.

remolino [rre·mo·lí·no] *m.* swirl, whirl; whirlwind; whirlpool; commotion; *Ríopl.* pin wheel; *Am.* ventilating wheel (*fan*); **— de gente** throng, crowd.

remolón [rre·mo·lón] *adj.* indolent, lazy.

remolque [rre·mól·ke] *m.* tow; towrope; **llevar a —** to tow; to take in tow.

remontar [rre·mon·tár] *v.* (*alzar*) to elevate, raise; (*reparar*) to repair, patch up; to resole; to revamp; *Am.* to go up; *Ríopl., Carib., C.A., Ven., Col.* to go upstream; **-se** to rise; to soar, fly upward; to date (from), go back (to); *Ríopl.* to take to the woods or hills.

rémora [rré·mo·ra] *f.* impediment, obstacle, hindrance.

remorder[4] [rre·mor·đér] *v. irr.* to sting.

remordimiento [rre·mor·di·mjén·to] *m.* remorse.

remoto [rre·mó·to] *adj.* remote, distant; improbable.

remover[2] [rre·mo·ɓér] *v. irr.* to remove; to dismiss; to stir.

rempujar [rrem·pu·xár] *v.* to jostle, push.

rempujón [rrem·pu·xón] *m.* jostle, push.

remuda [rre·mú·đa] *f.* change; substitution; replacement; change of clothes; spare tire; relay of horses; *Am.* spare horse, spare pack animal.

remudar [rre·mu·đár] *v.* to change; to replace.

remuneración [rre·mu·ne·ra·sjón] *f.* remuneration, compensation, pay, reward.

remunerar [rre·mu·ne·rár] *v.* to remunerate, compensate, pay, reward (*for services*).

renacer[13] [rre·na·sér] *v. irr.* to be reborn; to spring up, grow up again.

renacimiento [rre·na·si·mjén·to] *m.* renascence, renaissance; revival; rebirth.

rencilla [rren·sí·ya] *f.* quarrel.

renco [rréŋ·ko] *adj.* lame.

rencor [rreŋ·kór] *m.* rancor, resentment, hatred, grudge.

rencoroso [rreŋ·ko·ró·so] *adj.* resentful, spiteful.

rendición [rren·di·sjón] *f.* surrender; submission; yield, profit.

rendido [rren·dí·đo] *p.p. & adj.* tired out, fatigued; devoted; obsequious, servile.

rendija [rren·dí·xa] *f.* crack, crevice.

rendimiento [rren·di·mjén·to] *m.* yield, output, profit; surrender, submission; fatigue.

rendir[5] [rren·dír] *v. irr.* to subdue; to surrender, hand over; to yield, produce; to fatigue; to render, do (*homage*); *Cuba, Ven.* **— la jornada** to end or suspend the day's work; **-se** to surrender, give up; to become fatigued, worn out.

renegado [rre·ne·ǵá·đo] *m.* renegade, traitor; *adj.* renegade, disloyal; wicked.

renegar[1, 7] [rre·ne·ǵár] *v. irr.* to deny insistently; to detest; to blaspheme, curse; **— de** to deny, renounce (*one's faith*); *Am.* to hate, protest against.

renglón [rreŋ·glón] *m.* line (*written or printed*);

item; *Ríopl., Col., Ven., Mex., Carib., Andes* line of business, specialty.

renio [rré·njo] *m.* rhenium.

reno [rré·no] *m.* reindeer.

renombrado [rre·nom·brá·đo] *adj.* renowned, famous.

renombre [rre·nóm·bre] *m.* renown, fame.

renovación [rre·no·ɓa·sjón] *f.* renovation, restoration; renewal.

renovar[2] [rre·no·ɓár] *v. irr.* to renovate; to renew; to replace.

renquear [rreŋ·ke·ár] *v.* to limp.

renta [rrén·ta] *f.* rent, rental; income; revenue.

renuencia [rre·nwén·sja] *f.* reluctance, unwillingness.

renuente [rre·nwén·te] *adj.* reluctant, unwilling.

renuevo [rre·nwé·ɓo] *m.* (*vástago*) sprout, shoot; (*acto*) renovation, restoration.

renunciar [rre·nun·sjár] *v.* to renounce; to resign; to refuse; to renege (*fail to follow suit in cards*).

reñidor [rre·ñi·đór] *adj.* quarrelsome.

reñir[5, 19] [rre·ñír] *v. irr.* to quarrel; to fight; to scold.

reo [rré·o] *adj.* guilty; *m.* culprit, criminal; defendant.

reojo : [rre·ó·xo] **mirar de —** to look out of the corner of one's eye; to look scornfully.

repantigarse[7] [rre·pan·ti·ǵár·se] *v.* to lounge, stretch out (*in a chair*).

reparación [rre·pa·ra·sjón] *f.* reparation; repair; indemnity.

reparar [rre·pa·rár] *v.* (*renovar*) to repair; to regain; to recover; (*corregir*) to make amends for, atone for; to remedy; to ward off (*a blow*); *Am.* to rear, buck (*said of horses*); **— en** to observe, notice.

reparo [rre·pá·ro] *m.* (*arreglo*) repair; restoration; (*observación*) notice; observation; (*duda*) doubt, objection; (*abrigo*) shelter; parry (*fencing*); *Mex.* sudden bound or leap of a horse.

repartimiento [rre·par·ti·mjén·to] *m.* distribution, division; assessment.

repartir [rre·par·tír] *v.* to distribute; to allot.

reparto [rre·pár·to] *m.* distribution; mail delivery; cast of characters.

repasar [rre·pa·sár] *v.* to review, look over, go over again; to mend (*clothes*); to pass by again.

repaso [rre·pá·so] *m.* review; revision.

repelente [rre·pe·lén·te] *adj.* repellent, repulsive; repugnant.

repeler [rre·pe·lér] *v.* to repel; to reject.

repelón [rre·pe·lón] *m.* pull; kink.

repente [rre·pén·te] *m.* sudden movement; *Am.* attack, fit; **de —** suddenly.

repentino [rre·pen·tí·no] *adj.* sudden.

repercutir [rre·per·ku·tír] *v.* to resound, echo back; to rebound; to reflect back (*as light*).

repetición [rre·pe·ti·sjón] *f.* repetition.

repetido [rre·pe·tí·đo] *p.p.* repeated; **repetidas veces** repeatedly, often.

repetir[5] [rre·pe·tír] *v. irr.* to repeat; to belch.

repicar[6] [rre·pi·kar] *v.* (*tañer*) to chime, ring; (*hacer menudo*) to mince, chop fine; *Carib., Ven.* to drum, tap (*with the fingers or heels*); **-se** to boast; to be conceited.

repique [rre·pí·ke] *m.* (*tañido*) chime, ringing, peal; (*acción de picar*) mincing, chopping.

repiquetear [rre·pi·ke·te·ár] *v.* to chime, ring; to jingle; *Am.* to tap (*with fingers or heels*).

repiqueteo [rre·pi·ke·té·o] *m.* chiming, ringing; jingling, tinkling; *Ríopl., Carib., Ven.* clicking sound of heels.

repisa [rre·pí·sa] *f*. shelf, ledge; sill; wall bracket; — **de ventana** window sill.

replegar[1, 7] [rre·ple·gár] *v*. *irr*. to fold, pleat; **-se** to retreat, fall back.

réplica [rré·pli·ka] *f*. reply, answer, retort; replica, copy; *Am*. *m*. examiner.

replicar[6] [rre·pli·kár] *v*. to reply, answer back; to retort.

repliegue [rre·pljé·ǥe] *m*. fold, crease; retreat (*of troops*).

repollo [rre·pó·yo] *m*. cabbage.

reponer[40] [rre·po·nér] *v*. *irr*. (*devolver*) to replace, put back; to restore; (*contestar*) to reply, retort; **-se** to recover one's health or fortune; to collect oneself, become calm.

reportaje [rre·por·tá·xe] *m*. newspaper report; reporting.

reportar [rre·por·tár] *v*. to check, control, restrain; to attain, obtain; to bring; to carry; *Am*. to report; **-se** to control oneself.

reporte [rre·pór·te] *m*. report, news.

repórter [rre·pór·ter], **reportero** *m*. reporter.

reposado [rre·po·sá·ǫo] *p.p*. & *adj*. reposed; quiet, calm; restful.

reposar [rre·po·sár] *v*. to repose; to rest; to lie buried; **-se** to settle (*said of sediment*).

reposición [rre·po·si·sjón] *f*. replacement; recovery (*of one's health*).

reposo [rre·pó·so] *m*. repose, rest; calm.

repostada [rre·pos·tá·ǫa] *f*. sharp answer, back talk.

repostería [rre·pos·te·rí·a] *f*. pastry shop.

reprender [rre·pren·dér] *v*. to reprimand, scold.

reprensible [rre·pren·si·ɓle] *adj*. reprehensible, deserving reproof.

reprensión [rre·pren·sjón] *f*. reproof, rebuke.

represa [rre·pré·sa] *f*. dam; damming, stopping; *Col*., *Ven*. reservoir.

represalia [rre·pre·sá·lja] *f*. reprisal.

represar [rre·pre·sár] *v*. to bank, dam; to recapture (*a ship*) from the enemy; to repress, check.

representación [rre·pre·sen·ta·sjón] *f*. representation; play, performance; authority, dignity; petition, plea.

representante [rre·pre·sen·tán·te] *adj*. representing; *m*. & *f*. representative; actor.

representar [rre·pre·sen·tár] *v*. (*declarar*) to represent; to declare, state; to express, show; (*actuar*) to act, play, perform; **-se** to imagine, picture to oneself.

representativo [rre·pre·sen·ta·tí·ɓo] *adj*. representative.

represión [rre·pre·sjón] *f*. repression, control, restraint.

reprimenda [rre·pri·mén·da] *f*. reprimand, rebuke.

reprimir [rre·pri·mír] *v*. to repress, check, curb; **-se** to repress oneself; to refrain.

reprobar[2] [rre·pro·ɓár] *v*. *irr*. to reprove, blame; to condemn; to flunk, fail.

reprochar [rre·pro·čár] *v*. to reproach.

reproche [rre·pró·če] *m*. reproach.

reproducción [rre·pro·duk·sjón] *f*. reproduction.

reproducir[25] [rre·pro·ǫu·sír] *v*. *irr*. to reproduce.

reptil [rrep·til] *m*. reptile.

república [rre·pú·ɓi·ka] *f*. republic.

republicano [rre·pu·ɓi·ká·no] *adj*. & *m*. republican.

repudiar [rre·pu·ǫjár] *v*. to repudiate; to disown.

repuesto [rre·pwés·to] *m*. stock, supply, provisions; sideboard; **de** — spare, extra; *p.p. of* **reponer** & *adj*. recovered (*from an illness, loss, fright, etc.*);

replaced; restored.

repugnancia [rre·pug·nán·sja] *f*. repugnance, disgust; aversion; dislike, reluctance.

repugnante [rre·pug·nán·te] *adj*. repugnant, disgusting, loathsome.

repugnar [rre·pug·nár] *v*. to be repugnant; to disgust; to oppose, contradict.

repulido [rre·pu·li·ǫo] *adj*. polished up, slick; shiny; spruce.

repulsa [rre·púl·sa] *f*. repulse; rebuff; rebuke.

repulsar [rre·pil·sár] *v*. to repulse, repel, reject.

repulsivo [rre·pul·sí·ɓo] *adj*. repulsive, repugnant.

repuntar [rre·pun·tár] *v*. *Am*. to round up (*cattle*).

reputación [rre·pu·ta·sjón] *f*. reputation.

reputar [rre·pu·tár] *v*. to repute.

requebrar[1] [rre·ke·ɓrár] *v*. *irr*. to compliment; to flatter; to flirt with; to court, woo; to break again.

requemado [rre·ke·má·ǫo] *p.p*. & *adj*. burned; parched; tanned, sunburned.

requemar [rre·ke·már] *v*. to parch, dry up; to burn; to overcook; **-se** to become overheated; to burn inwardly; to get tanned, sunburned.

requerimiento [rre·ke·ri·mjén·to] *m*. requisition; requirement; summons; **-s** amorous advances, insinuations.

requerir[3] [rre·ke·rír] *v*. *irr*. (*exigir*) to require; to need; to summon; (*indagar*) to examine, investigate; (*avisar*) to notify; — **de amores** to court, woo.

requesón [rre·ke·són] *m*. cottage cheese.

requiebro [rre·kjé·ɓro] *m*. flattery; compliment.

requisito [rre·ki·sí·to] *m*. requirement, requisite; — **previo** prerequisite.

res [rres] *f*. head of cattle; any large animal.

resabio [rre·sa·ɓjo] *m*. disagreeable aftertaste; bad habit.

resaca [rre·sá·ka] *f*. undertow; surge, surf; redraft (*of a bill of exchange*); *Am*. beating, thrashing; *Mex*., *Ríopl*. mud and slime (*left by a flood*).

resaltar [rre·sal·tár] *v*. to stand out; to project, jut out; to rebound, bounce or spring back; to be evident, obvious.

resarcir[10] [rre·sar·sír] *v*. to indemnify, compensate, repay; to make amends for; **-se de** to make up for.

resbaladero [rrez·ɓa·la·ǫé·ro] *m*. slide, slippery place.

resbaladizo [rrez·ɓa·la·ǫí·so] *adj*. slippery.

resbalar [rrez·ɓa·lár] *v*. to slide; **-se** to slip; to slide; to skid; **resbalársele a uno una cosa** to let a thing slide off one's back, be impervious to a thing.

resbalón [rrez·ɓa·lón] *m*. sudden or violent slip; slide; error; **darse un** — to slip.

resbaloso [rrez·ɓa·ló·so] *adj*. slippery.

rescatar [rres·ka·tár] *v*. to ransom; to redeem; to barter, exchange, trade; *Am*. to resell.

rescate [rres·ká·te] *m*. ransom; redemption; barter, exchange.

rescoldo [rres·kól·do] *m*. embers, hot cinders, hot ashes; doubt, scruple.

resecar[6] [rre·se·kár] *v*. to dry up; to parch.

reseco [rre·sé·ko] *adj*. very dry; dried up, parched; thin, skinny.

resentimiento [rre·sen·ti·mjén·to] *m*. resentment; impairment, damage (*to one's health*).

resentirse[3] [rre·sen·tír·se] *v*. *irr* (*tener pesar*) to show resentment, hurt, or grief; to resent; (*empeorar*) to weaken; to become worse.

reseña [rre·sé·ña] *f*. military review; book review;

RE

brief account; sign, signal.

reseñar [rre·se·ñár] *v.* to review (*a book*); to review (*troops*); to outline briefly, give a short account of.

resero [rre·sé·ro] *m. Ríopl.* cowboy, herdsman; *Am.* dealer in livestock.

reserva [rre·ser·ƀa] *f.* reserve; reservation; exception; caution; **a — de** reserving the right to, intending to; **sin —** without reserve, frankly.

reservación [rre·ser·ƀa·sjón] *f.* reservation.

reservar [rre·ser·ƀár] *v.* to reserve; to put aside; to postpone; to exempt; to keep secret; **-se** to conserve one's strength, spare oneself (*for another time*).

resfriado [rres·frjá·ɖo] *m.* cold (*illness*); *p.p. of* **resfriar**; *adj. Ríopl.* indiscreet.

resfriar[17] [rres·frjár] *v.* to cool; to chill; **-se** to catch cold; to cool.

resfrío [rres·frí·o] *m.* chill; cold.

resguardar [rrez·ǥwar·ɖár] *v.* to guard, defend; to shield; **-se de** to guard oneself against; to seek shelter from.

resguardo [rrez·ǥwár·ɖo] *m.* defense; security; guarantee; guard.

residencia [rre·si·ɖén·sja] *f.* residence; office or post of a resident foreign minister; *Am.* luxurious dwelling.

residente [rre·si·ɖén·te] *adj.* resident, residing; *m. & f.* resident, dweller; resident foreign minister; *Col., C.A., Ríopl.* alien resident.

residir [rre·si·ɖír] *v.* to reside; to live, dwell; to be inherent, belong (to).

residuo [rre·sí·ɖwo] *m.* residue; remainder.

resignación [rre·siǥ·na·sjón] *f.* resignation.

resignar [rre·siǥ·nár] *v.* to resign; to hand over; **-se** to resign oneself.

resina [rre·sí·na] *f.* resin.

resistencia [rre·sis·tén·sja] *f.* resistance.

resistente [rre·sis·tén·te] *adj.* resistant; resisting.

resistir [rre·sis·tír] *v.* to resist; to tolerate, endure; **-se** to resist, struggle.

resolución [rre·so·lu·sjón] *f.* (*ánimo*) resolution; courage, determination; (*resultado*) solution; **en — in** brief.

resolver[2, 52] [rre·sol·ƀér] *v. irr.* to resolve, decide; to solve; to dissolve; **-se** to resolve, decide; to be reduced (to), dissolve (into).

resollar[2] [rre·so·yár] *v. irr.* to breathe hard; to pant.

resonar[2] [rre·so·nár] *v. irr.* to resound.

resoplar [rre·so·plár] *v.* to puff, breathe hard; to snort.

resoplido [rre·so·plí·ɖo] *m.* puff, pant; snort.

resorte [rre·sór·te] *m.* spring; elasticity; means (*to attain an object*); *Col.* elastic, rubber band; *Ven.* **no es de mi —** it doesn't concern me.

respaldar [rres·pal·dár] *v.* to endorse; to guarantee; *Am.* to back, support; **-se** to lean back; *Ch.* to protect one's rear.

respaldo [rres·pál·do] *m.* back (*of a chair or sheet of paper*); protecting wall; endorsement; *Am.* protection, security, guarantee.

respectivo [rres·pek·tí·ƀo] *adj.* respective.

respecto [rres·pék·to] *m.* respect, relation, reference; point, matter; **(con) — a** (*or* **— de**) with respect to, with regard to.

respetable [rres·pe·tá·ƀle] *adj.* respectable.

respetar [rres·pe·tár] *v.* to respect.

respeto [rres·pé·to] *m.* respect; reverence, regard; consideration.

respetuoso [rres·pe·twó·so] *adj.* respectful;

respectable.

respingar[7] [rres·piŋ·gár] *v.* to buck; to balk (*said of a horse*); to grumble; to curl up (*said of the edge of a garment*).

respingo [rres·píŋ·go] *m.* buck, balking; muttering, grumbling.

respiración [rres·pi·ra·sjón] *f.* respiration, breathing.

respirar [rres·pi·rár] *v.* to breathe.

respiro [rres·pi·ro] *m.* breathing; breath; respite, pause, moment of rest; extension of time (*for payment*).

resplandecer[13] [rres·plan·de·sér] *v. irr.* to shine; to glitter.

resplandeciente [rres·plan·de·sjén·te] *adj.* resplendent, shining.

resplandor [rres·plan·dór] *m.* splendor, brilliance, brightness; *Am.* sun's glare.

responder [rres·pon·dér] *v.* to respond; to answer; to correspond, harmonize; to answer (for), be responsible (for).

respondón [rres·pon·dón] *adj.* saucy, pert, insolent (*in answering*).

responsabilidad [rres·pon·sa·ƀi·li·ɖáɖ] *f.* responsibility.

responsable [rres·pon·sá·ƀle] *adj.* responsible.

respuesta [rres·pwés·ta] *f.* response; answer, reply.

resquebradura [rres·ke·ƀra·dú·ra], **resquebrajadura** [rres·ke·ƀra·xa·dú·ra] *f.* fissure, crevice, crack.

resquebrajar [rres·ke·ƀra·xár] = **resquebrar.**

resquebrar[1] [rres·ke·ƀrár] *v. irr.* to crack; to split.

resquicio [rres·kí·sjo] *m.* crack, slit, crevice; opening; *Col., Ven., Mex.* vestige, sign, trace.

resta [rrés·ta] *f.* subtraction (*as an arithmetical operation*); remainder.

restablecer[13] [rres·ta·ƀle·sér] *v. irr.* to re-establish; to restore; **-se** to recover.

restante [rres·tán·te] *adj.* remaining; *m.* residue, remainder.

restañar [rres·ta·ñár] *v.* to staunch (*a wound*); to check the flow of.

restar [rres·tár] *v.* to deduct; to subtract; to remain, be left over; to strike back (*a ball*).

restauración [rres·taw·ra·sjón] *f.* restoration.

restaurante [rres·taw·rán·te] *m.* restaurant.

restaurar [rres·taw·rár] *v.* to restore; to recover; to re-establish; to repair.

restitución [rres·ti·tu·sjón] *f.* restitution, restoration, return.

restituir[32] [rres·ti·twír] *v. irr.* to return, give back; to restore.

resto [rrés·to] *m.* rest, remainder; stakes at cards; return (*of a tennis ball*); player who returns the ball; **-s** remains.

restorán [rres·to·rán] *m. Am.* restaurant.

restregar[1, 7] [rres·tre·ǥár] *v. irr.* to rub hard; to scrub.

restricción [rres·trik·sjón] *f.* restriction; restraint; curb; limitation.

restringir[11] [rres·triŋ·xír] *v.* to restrict; to restrain; to limit.

resucitar [rre·su·si·tár] *v.* to resuscitate, bring to life; to come to life; to revive.

resuelto [rre·swél·to] *p.p. of* **resolver** resolved, determined; *adj.* resolute, bold; quick.

resuello [rre·swé·yo] *m.* breath; breathing, panting.

resulta [rre·súl·ta] *f.* result; effect, consequence; **de -s** as a result, in consequence.

resultado [rre·sul·tá·ɖo] *m.* result, effect, consequence.

resultante [rre·sul·tán·te] *adj.* resulting; *f.* resultant (*force*).

resultar [rre·sul·tár] *v.* to result; to spring, arise as a consequence; to turn out to be; **resulta que** it turns out that.

resumen [rre·sú·men] *m.* résumé, summary; **en —** summing up, in brief.

resumidero [rre·su·mi·dé·ro] *m. Am.* = **sumidero.**

resumir [rre·su·mír] *v.* to summarize, sum up; **-se** to be reduced or condensed.

resurgir[11] [rre·sur·xír] *v.* to arise again; to reappear.

retablo [rre·tá·blo] *m.* altarpiece; religious picture hung as a votive offering; series of pictures that tell a story.

retaguardia [rre·ta·gwár·dja] *f.* rear guard.

retal [rre·tál] *m.* remnant.

retar [rre·tár] *v.* to challenge, defy; to reprimand, scold; *Ch., Andes* to insult.

retardar [rre·tar·dár] *v.* to retard, delay.

retazo [rre·tá·so] *m.* remnant; piece; fragment.

retener[45] [rre·te·nér] *v. irr.* to retain; to keep; to withhold; to detain.

retintín [rre·tin·tín] *m.* jingle, tinkle; sarcastic tone of ring.

retirada [rre·ti·rá·da] *f.* retreat; withdrawal.

retirado [rre·ti·rá·do] *p.p. & adj.* retired; distant, remote; isolated; pensioned.

retirar [rre·ti·rár] *v.* to withdraw; to take away; **-se** to retire, withdraw; to retreat.

retiro [rre·tí·ro] *m.* retreat; retirement; withdrawal; place of refuge; pension of a retired officer.

reto [rré·to] *m.* challenge; defiance; *Ríopl.* scolding; *Andes* insult.

retobado [rre·to·bá·do] *adj. Col., Ríopl.* saucy; *Andes* stubborn, unruly; *Andes* peevish; *Am.* sly, astute.

retobar [rre·to·bár] *v. Col., Andes* to cover with leather; *Am.* to wrap with leather, oilcloth, or burlap; *Am.* to tan (*leather*); **-se** *Ríopl.* to revel, talk back, act saucy; *Andes, Col.* to become disagreeable and aloof.

retocar[6] [rre·to·kár] *v.* to retouch, touch up; to finish, perfect.

retoñar [rre·to·ñár] *v.* to sprout; to bud; to sprout again; to reappear.

retoño [rre·tó·ño] *m.* sprout, shoot; bud.

retoque [rre·tó·ke] *m.* retouching; finishing touch.

retorcer[2, 10] [rre·tor·sér] *v. irr.* to twist; to retort; to distort; **-se** to wriggle; to squirm.

retorcimiento [rre·tor·si·mjén·to] *m.* twisting; squirming.

retórica [rre·tó·ri·ka] *f.* rhetoric.

retornar [rre·tor·nár] *v.* to return; to give back.

retorno [rre·tór·no] *m.* return; repayment; barter.

retozar[9] [rre·to·sár] *v.* to gambol, frisk about, frolic, romp; to stir within (*said of passions*).

retozo [rre·tó·so] *m.* frolic; **retozón** [rre·to·són] *adj.* frisky, playful.

retractarse [rre·trak·tár·se] *v.* to retract, take back one's word.

retraer[46] [rre·tra·ér] *v. irr.* to withdraw, draw back, take back; **-se de** to withdraw from; to keep aloof or away from; to shun.

retraído [rre·tra·í·do] *adj.* shy, reserved.

retraimiento [rre·traj·mjén·to] *m.* retirement; reserve, aloofness, shyness.

retranca [rre·tráŋ·ka] *f. Cuba* brake; **retranquero** [rre·traŋ·ké·ro] *m. Am.* brakeman.

retrancar[6] [rre·traŋ·kár] *v. Cuba* to brake, put the brake on; *Cuba* **se ha retrancado el asunto** the

affair has come to a standstill.

retrasado [rre·tra·sá·do] *p.p. & adj.* behind, behind time; backward; postponed, delayed.

retrasar [rre·tra·sár] *v.* to delay, retard; to set back; to go backward; **-se** to fall behind; to be late, behind time.

retraso [rre·trá·so] *m.* delay.

retratar [rre·tra·tár] *v.* to portray; to photograph; to copy, imitate; **-se** to be portrayed; to be photographed; to be reflected.

retrato [rre·trá·to] *m.* portrait; photograph; copy, imitation; reflection.

retrete [rre·tré·te] *m.* toilet, water closet; place of retreat.

retroactivo [rre·tro·ak·tí·bo] *adj.* retroactive.

retroceder [rre·tro·se·dér] *v.* to turn back; to fall back, draw back; to recede.

retroceso [rre·tro·sé·so] *m.* retrogression, backward step; retreat; setback, relapse.

retrocohete [rre·tro·ko·é·te] *m.* retro-rocket.

retropropulsión [rre·tro·pro·pul·sjon] *f.* retropropulsion.

retruécano [rre·trwé·ka·no] *m.* pun.

retumbar [rre·tum·bár] *v.* to resound; to rumble.

retumbo [rre·túm·bo] *m.* loud echo or sound; rumble (*of thunder, cannon, etc.*).

reuma [rréw·ma] *m. & f.*, **reumatismo** [rrew·ma·tíz·mo] *m.* rheumatism.

reunión [rrew·njón] *f.* reunion; meeting.

reunir [rrew·nír] *v.* to reunite; to unite; to group; to gather; to assemble; to collect; **-se** to meet, assemble; to reunite.

revancha [rre·bán·ča] *f.* revenge; return game or match.

revelación [rre·be·la·sjón] *f.* revelation.

revelador [rre·be·la·dór] *adj.* revealing; *m.* developer (*in photography*).

revelar [rre·be·lár] *v.* reveal; to develop (*a film*).

revendedor [rre·ben·de·dór] *m.* retailer; reseller; ticket scalper.

reventa [rre·bén·ta] *f.* resale.

reventar[1] [rre·ben·tár] *v. irr.* (*estallar*) to burst; to burst forth; to explode; to smash; (*fatigar*) to fatigue, exhaust; to bother; **-se** to burst; to blow out, explode.

reventón [rre·ben·tón] *m.* burst, bursting; blowout; steep hill; hard work, toil; *adj.* bursting.

reverdecer[13] [rre·ber·de·sér] *v. irr.* to grow fresh and green again; to gain new strength and vigor.

reverencia [rre·be·rén·sja] *f.* reverence; bow.

reverenciar [rre·be·ren·sjár] *v.* to revere, venerate.

reverendo [rre·be·rén·do] *adj.* reverend; *Cuba, Ríopl., Mex., Andes* large, big (*ironically*).

reverente [rre·be·rén·te] *adj.* reverent.

reverso [rre·bér·so] *m.* reverse; back side.

revertir[3] [rre·ber·tir] *v. irr.* to revert.

revés [rre·bés] *m.* reverse; back, wrong side; black stroke or slap; backhanded thrust (*in fencing*); misfortune; **al —** backwards; wrong side out; in the opposite way; from left to right.

revestir[5] [rre·bes·tír] *v. irr.* to dress, clothe; to coat, cover with a coating; **-se** to dress, put on an outer garment or vestment; to be invested (*with power, authority, etc.*); **-se de paciencia** to arm oneself with patience.

revisar [rre·bi·sár] *v.* to revise; to review; to examine, inspect.

revisión [rre·bi·sjón] *m.* revision; review (*of a case*), new trial; inspection (*of baggage*).

revisor [rre·bi·sór] *m.* corrector; inspector,

RE

overseer.

revista [rre·ḅís·ta] *f.* (*inspección*) review; inspection; (*publicación*) magazine, journal; (*proceso*) second trial or hearing; **pasar** — to pass in review; to examine carefully; to review (*troops*).

revistar [rre·ḅis·tár] *v.* to review, inspect (*troops*).

revivir [rre·ḅi·ḅír] *v.* to revive.

revocación [rre·ḅo·ka·sjón] *f.* repeal, cancellation.

revocar[6] [rre·ḅo·kár] *v.* to revoke, repeal.

revolcar[6] [rre·ḅol·kár] *v.* (*derribar*) to knock down; to turn over and over; to floor, defeat; (*suspender*) to fail, flunk; **-se** to wallow; to roll over and over; to flounder.

revolotear [rre·ḅo·lo·te·ár] *v.* to fly about, flutter around; to hover; to circle around.

revoltijo [rre·ḅol·tí·xo], **revoltillo** [rre·ḅol·tí·yo] *m.* jumble, mixture, mess; tangle, muddle; **revoltillo de huevos** scrambled eggs.

revoltoso [rre·ḅol·tó·so] *adj.* turbulent, unruly, rebellious; mischievous; intricate; *m.* agitator, troublemaker; rebel.

revolución [rre·ḅo·lu·sjón] *f.* revolution.

revolucionario [rre·ḅo·lu·sjo·ná·rjo] *adj.* revolutionary; *m.* revolutionist, revolutionary.

revolver[2] [rre·ḅol·ḅér] *v. irr.* to revolve; to turn over; to stir up; to mix up; to turn around swiftly (*a horse*); **-se** to move back and forth; to roll over and over; to change (*said of the weather*).

revólver [rre·ḅól·ḅer] *m.* revolver, pistol.

revuelo [rre·ḅwé·lo] *m.* whirl; stir, commotion; flying around.

revuelta [rre·ḅwél·ta] *f.* revolt, revolution; second turn; turn, bend; quarrel, fight; *Am.* sudden turning of a horse.

revuelto [rre·ḅwél·to] *p.p. of* **revolver** & *adj.* confused; mixed up; intricate, complicated; choppy (*sea*); changeable (*weather*); **huevos -s** scrambled eggs.

rey [rrej] *m.* king.

reyerta [rre·yér·ta] *f.* quarrel, dispute.

rezagado [rre·sa·ḡá·ḏo] *adj.* back, behind; *m.* straggler, slowpoke, latecomer.

rezagar[7] [rre·sa·ḡár] *v.* to leave behind; to separate (*the weak cattle*) from the herd; *Am.* to reserve, set aside; **-se** to lag behind.

rezar[9] [rre·sár] *v.* to pray; to say or recite (*a prayer*); to mutter, grumble; **así lo reza el libro** so the book says; **eso no reza conmigo** that has nothing to do with me.

rezo [rré·so] *m.* prayer.

rezongar[7] [rre·son·gár] *v.* to grumble, growl, mutter.

rezongón [rre·son·gón] *adj.* growling, grumbling; *m.* grumbler, growler; scolder.

rezumar [rre·su·már] *v.* to ooze; to leak; **se rezuma** it oozes, it seeps through.

ria [rrí·a] *f.* mouth of a river, estuary.

riachuelo [rrja·čwé·lo] *m.* rivulet, brook.

ribazo [rri·ḅá·so] *m.* bank, ridge.

ribera [rri·ḅé·ra] *f.* shore, bank, beach.

ribereño [rri·ḅe·ré·ño] *adj.* of, pertaining to, or living on, a river bank.

ribete [rri·ḅé·te] *m.* trimming, border, edge, binding; addition; **tiene sus -s de poeta** he is something of a poet.

ribetear [rri·ḅe·te·ár] *v.* to bind, put a binding on; to border, trim the edge or border of.

ricacho [rri·ká·čo] *adj.* quite rich (*often said sarcastically*); **ricachón** [rri·ka·čón] *adj.* extremely rich, disgustingly rich.

rico [rrí·ko] *adj.* rich, wealthy; delicious; exquisite; **ricote** [rri·kó·te] = **ricacho.**

ridiculizar[9] [rri·ḏi·ku·li·sár] *v.* to ridicule, deride.

ridículo [rri·ḏí·ku·lo] *adj.* ridiculous; queer, strange; *m.* ridicule; ridiculous situation; **hacer el** — to be ridiculous; to act the fool.

riego [rrjé·ḡo] *m.* irrigation; watering.

riel [rrjel] *m.* rail; **-es** track, railroad track.

rienda [rrjén·da] *f.* rein, bridle; moderation, restraint; **a — suelta** with free rein, without restraint; violently, swiftly; **soltar la** — to let loose, act without restraint; **tirar las -s** to draw rein, tighten the reins; to restrain.

riente [rrjén·te] *adj.* laughing, smiling.

riesgo [rrjez·ḡo] *m.* risk.

rifa [rrí·fa] *f.* raffle; scuffle, quarrel.

rifar [rri·fár] *v.* to raffle; to scuffle, quarrel.

rifeño [rri·fé·ño] *m.* riff.

rifle [rrí·fle] *m.* rifle.

rigidez [rri·xi·ḏés] *f.* rigidity, stiffness; severity, strictness.

rígido [rrí·xi·ḏo] *adj.* rigid, stiff; severe, strict.

rigor [rri·ḡór] *m.* rigor; severity; harshness; rigidity, stiffness; **en** — in reality; strictly; **ser de** — to be absolutely indispensable, be required by custom.

rigoroso [rri·ḡo·ró·so], **riguroso** [rri·ḡu·ró·so] *adj.* rigorous; harsh; severe; strict.

rima [rrí·ma] *f.* rhyme; **-s** poems.

rimar [rri·már] *v.* to rhyme.

rimbombante [rrim·bom·bán·te] *adj.* high-sounding; resounding.

rimero [rri·mé·ro] *m.* pile, heap.

rincón [rriŋ·kón] *m.* corner; nook; *Am.* narrow valley.

rinconada [rriŋ·ko·ná·ḏa] *f.* corner; nook.

rinconera [rriŋ·ko·né·ra] *f.* corner cupboard, corner table, corner bracket.

ringlera [rriŋ·glé·ra] *f.* tier, row, line.

rinoceronte [rri·no·se·rón·te] *m.* rhinoceros.

riña [rri·ña] *f.* quarrel, dispute, fight.

riñón [rri·ñón] *m.* kidney; center, interior.

río [rrí·o] *m.* river.

ripio [rrí·pjo] *m.* rubble, stone or brick fragments; padding (*in a verse, speech, etc.*), useless word.

riqueza [rri·ké·sa] *f.* riches; wealth.

risa [rrí·sa] *f.* laugh; laughter; **reventar de** — to burst with laughter; **tomar a** — to take lightly; to laugh off.

risada [rri·sá·ḏa] *f.* gale of laughter, loud laugh.

risco [rrís·ko] *m.* rocky cliff, crag; honey fritter.

risible [rri·sí·ḅle] *adj.* laughable, ridiculous.

risotada [rri·so·tá·ḏa] *f.* guffaw, big laugh.

ristra [rrís·tra] *f.* string (*of onions, garlic, etc.*); series, row.

risueño [rri·swé·ño] *adj.* smiling; pleasant; delightful.

rítmico [rríḏ·mi·ko] *adj.* rhythmical.

ritmo [rríḏ·mo] *m.* rhythm.

rito [rrí·to] *m.* rite, ceremony.

rival [rri·ḅál] *m.* & *f.* rival, competitor; enemy.

rivalidad [rri·ḅa·li·ḏáḏ] *f.* rivalry, competition; enmity.

rivalizar[9] [rri·ḅa·li·sár] *v.* to rival, compete.

rizado [rri·sá·ḏo] *p.p.* curled; *adj.* wavy, curly; *m.* curling; curls.

rizar[9] [rri·sár] *v.* to curl; to ripple; to ruffle, gather into ruffles; **-se** to curl one's hair; to curl.

rizo [rrí·so] *m.* curl; *adj.* curly; **rizoso** [rri·só·so] *adj.* curly.

roano [rro·á·no] *adj.* roan (*red, bay, or chestnut-colored, mixed with white; applied to a horse*).

robalo [rro·ba·lo] *m.* bass.
robar [rro·bár] *v.* to rob, steal; to abduct, kidnap.
roble [rró·ble] *m.* oak tree; oak wood; **robledal** [rro·ble·dál], **robledo** [rro·blé·do] *m.* oak grove.
robo [rró·bo] *m.* robbery, theft; loot, plunder.
robusto [rró·bús·to] *adj.* robust, vigorous.
roca [rró·ka] *f.* rock, boulder; rocky cliff, crag.
rocalloso [rro·ka·yó·so] *adj.* rocky.
roce [rró·se] *m.* graze; friction; contact; **no tener — con** to have no contact with (*a person*).
rociada [rro·sjá·da] *f.* sprinkling; spray; dew; sprinkle, shower; volley of harsh words.
rociar[17] [rro·sjár] *v.* to sprinkle; to spray; to fall (*said of dew*).
rocín [rro·sín] *m.* nag, hack; draft horse; coarse, ill-bred man; *Ríopl., Mex., Andes* riding horse.
rocío [rro·sí·o] *m.* dew; sprinkle; shower; spray; *adj. Am.* reddish, roan (*horse*).
rocoso [rro·kó·so] *adj.* rocky.
rodada [rro·dá·da] *f.* rut, wheel track; *Ríopl.* tumble, fall.
rodado [rro·dád·do] *adj.* dapple (*horse*); *p.p. of* **rodar.**
rodadura [rro·da·dú·ra] *f.* rolling; rut; **— del neumático** tire tread.
rodaja [rro·dá·xa] *f.* disk; small wheel; round slice.
rodaje [rro·dá·xe] *m.* works (*of a watch*); **— de película** the filming of a movie.
rodar[2] [rro·dár] *v. irr.* to roll; to revolve; to roam, wander about; to fall down (*rolling*); *Am.* **— a patadas** to kick down.
rodear [rro·de·ár] *v.* to go around; to go by a roundabout way; to surround, encircle; *Ríopl., Cuba, Ven.* to round up (*cattle*).
rodela [rro·dé·la] *f.* round shield; *Mex.* padded ring for carrying loads on the head; *Am.* round slice; *Am.* kettle lid; *Am.* hoop; *Am.* game of rolling a hoop.
rodeo [rro·dé·o] *m.* detour, roundabout way; circumlocution, roundabout expression; dodge, evasion; corral, stockyard; rodeo, roundup.
rodilla [rro·dí·ya] *f.* knee; **de -s** on one's knees; **hincarse de -s** to kneel down.
rodillo [rro·dí·yo] *m.* roller; rolling pin; road roller.
rodio [rró·djo] *m.* rhodium.
rododendro [rro·do·dén·dro] *m.* rhododendron.
roedor [rro·e·dór] *m.* rodent.
roer[51] [rro·ér] *v. irr.* to gnaw; to corrode, eat away; to torment, harass.
rogar[2, 7] [rro·gár] *v. irr.* to pray, beg, beseech; **hacerse de —** to let oneself be coaxed.
rojez [rro·xés] *f.* redness.
rojizo [rro·xí·so] *adj.* reddish.
rojo [rró·xo] *adj.* red; red, radical.
rojura [rro·xú·ra] *f.* redness.
rollizo [rro·yí·so] *adj.* plump; *m.* log.
rollo [rró·yo] *m.* roll; bundle; rolling pin; log.
romadizo [rro·ma·dí·so] *m.* nasal catarrh, head cold.
romance [rro·mán·se] *adj.* Romance, Romanic (*language*); *m.* Romance language; Spanish language; romance, chivalric novel; ballad; eight-syllable meter with even verses rhyming in assonance; **en buen —** in plain language.
románico [rro·má·ni·ko] *adj.* Romanesque (*architecture*); Romance (*language*).
romano [rro·má·no] *adj. & m.* Roman.
romanticismo [rro·man·ti·síz·mo] *m.* romanticism.
romántico [rro·mán·ti·ko] *adj.* romantic; sentimental; *m.* romantic; sentimentalist.

rombo [rróm·bo] *m.* rhombus.
romería [rro·me·rí·a] *f.* pilgrimage.
romero [rro·mé·ro] *m.* pilgrim; rosemary (*shrub*).
romo [rró·mo] *adj.* blunt; snub-nosed.
rompe [rróm·pe]: **de — y rasga** resolute, bold; **al —** *Am.* suddenly.
rompecabezas [rrom·pe·ka·bé·sas] *m.* puzzle, riddle.
rompenueces [rrom·pe·nwé·ses] *m.* nutcracker.
rompeolas [rrom·pe·ó·las] *m.* breakwater, mole.
romper[52] [rrom·pér] *v.* to break; to shatter; to tear; to wear through; *Ven.* to leave suddenly or on the run; **— el alba** to dawn; **— a** to start to; **-se** to break.
rompiente [rrom·pjén·te] *m.* shoal, sand bank, reef; **-s** breakers, surf.
rompimiento [rrom·pi·mjén·to] *m.* rupture, break; crack; breach; quarrel.
rompopo [rrom·pó·po] *m.* eggnog.
ron [rron] *m.* rum.
roncar[6] [rron·kár] *v.* to snore; to roar; to brag.
ronco [rróŋ·ko] *adj.* hoarse; harsh-sounding.
roncha [rrón·ča] *f.* hive; welt.
ronda [rrón·da] *f.* patrol; night serenaders; round (*of a game, of drinks, etc.*); *Ríopl., C.A., Andes* ring-around-a-rosy (*a children's game*); **hacer la — a** to court; *Am.* to surround, trap (*an animal*).
rondar [rron·dár] *v.* to go around, hover around; to patrol; to make the rounds; to serenade.
ronquera [rron·ké·ra] *f.* hoarseness.
ronquido [rron·kí·do] *m.* snore; snort.
ronronear [rron·rro·ne·ár] *v.* to purr.
ronroneo [rron·rro·né·o] *m.* purr.
ronzal [rron·sál] *m.* halter.
roña [rró·ña] *f.* scab, mange; filth; infection; stinginess; trickery; *Ríopl., Col., Ven., Cuba* ill will, grudge; *Am.* **hacer —** to fake an illness.
roñoso [rro·ñó·so] *adj.* scabby, mangy; dirty; stingy; *Carib., Mex.* spiteful; *Am.* fainthearted, cowardly.
ropa [rró·pa] *f.* clothing, clothes; **— blanca** linen; **— vieja** old clothes; stew made from leftover meat; **a quema —** at close range (*when shooting*); suddenly, without warning.
ropaje [rro·pá·xe] *m.* clothes, clothing, apparel; robe.
ropería [rro·pe·rí·a] *f.* clothing store.
ropero [rro·pé·ro] *m.* clothier; wardrobe, clothespress; wardrobe keeper; *Am.* clothes rack.
roqueño [rro·ké·ño] *adj.* rocky; hard, like rock.
rorro [rró·rro] *m.* popular term for a baby.
rosa [rró·sa] *f.* rose; red spot on the skin; rose color; *Ch., Mex.* rosebush; **— de los vientos** (*or* **— náutica**) mariner's compass.
rosado [rro·sá·do] *adj.* rosy, rose-colored; frosted (*drink*); *Am.* roan, reddish-brown (*horse*).
rosal [rro·sál] *m.* rosebush.
rosario [rro·sá·rjo] *m.* rosary; **— de desdichas** chain of misfortunes.
rosbif [rroz·bíf] *m.* roast beef.
rosca [rrós·ka] *f.* screw and nut; screw thread; spiral, twist; ring-shaped roll; *Mex., Ven., Col.* ring-shaped cushion (*for carrying loads on the head*); *Am.* circle of card players.
roseta [rro·sé·ta] *f.* rosette; small rose; **-s** popcorn; **rosetón** [rro·se·tón] *m.* large rosette; rose window.
rosillo [rro·sí·yo] *adj.* light red; roan (*horse*).
rostro [rrós·tro] *m.* face; **hacer —** to face.
rota [rró·ta] *f.* rout, defeat; ship's course; Rota

(*ecclesiastical court*); rattan palm tree.
rotación [rro·ta·sjón] *f.* rotation.
rotario [rro·tá·rjo] *m.* member of the Rotary Club.
rotativo [rro·ta·tí·ƀo] *adj.* rotary; *f.* printing press.
rotatorio [rro·ta·tó·rjo] *adj.* rotary.
roto [rró·to] *p.p. irr.* of **romper** & *adj.* broken;
shattered; torn; worn out, ragged; *m. Ch.* person
of the poorer class.
rotular [rro·tu·lár] *v.* to label; to letter.
rótulo [rró·tu·lo] *m.* title, inscription; label.
rotundo [rro·tún·do] *adj.* round; sonorous; **una
negativa rotunda** a flat denial.
rotura [rro·tú·ra] *f.* breach, opening; break; tear,
rip; rupture; fracture.
roturar [rro·tu·rár] *v.* to break ground; to plow
(*new ground*).
rozadura [rro·sa·đú·ra] *f.* friction; chafe; chafing.
rozamiento [rro·sa·mjén·to] *m.* friction; rubbing.
rozar[9] [rro·sár] *v.* to graze; to scrape; to chafe;
to clear of underbush; **-se con alguien** to have
connections, contact, or dealings with someone.
rozón [rro·són] *m.* graze, sudden or violent scrape;
short, broad scythe.
ruana [rrwá·na] *f. Col., Ven.* a woolen poncho.
ruano [rrwá·no] = **roano**.
rubí [rru·ƀí] *m.* ruby.
rubicundo [rru·ƀi·kún·do] *adj.* reddish; ruddy,
healthy red; reddish-blond.
rubidio [rru·ƀí·djo] *m.* rubidium.
rubio [rrú·ƀjo] *adj.* blond, blonde.
rubor [rru·ƀór] *m.* blush; bashfulness, shyness.
ruborizarse[9] [rru·ƀo·ri·sar·se] *v.* to blush; to feel
ashamed.
rúbrica [rrú·ƀri·ka] *f.* scroll, flourish (*added to a
signature*); title, heading; **de** — according to
ritual, rule, or custom.
rucio [rrú·sjo] *adj.* grey (*horse or donkey*); —
rodado dapple-grey.
rudeza [rru·đé·sa] *f.* rudeness; coarseness;
roughness.
rudo [rrú·đo] *adj.* rude; coarse; rough; stupid.
rueca [rrwé·ka] *f.* distaff (*used for spinning*).
rueda [rrwé·đa] *f.* (*maquina*) wheel; circle; spread
of a peacock's tail; round object; (*grupo*) circle;
group; **en** — in turn; in a circle; **hacer la** — **a**
to court; to flatter.
ruedo [rrwé·đo] *m.* circuit, tour; border, rim;
circumference.
ruego [rrwé·ǥo] *m.* prayer, supplication, request.
rufián [rru·fján] *m.* ruffian; bully.
rugido [rru·xí·đo] *m.* roar; rumbling.
rugir[11] [rru·xír] *v.* to roar; to bellow.
rugoso [rru·ǥó·so] *adj.* wrinkled; furrowed.
ruibarbo [rrwi·ƀár·ƀo] *m.* rhubarb.
ruidazo [rrwi·đá·so] *m.* big noise.
ruido [rrwí·đo] *m.* noise; din; dispute; talk,
rumor; **hacer** (*or* **meter**) — to make a noise; to
create a sensation; to cause a disturbance.
ruidoso [rrwi·đó·so] *adj.* noisy; loud; sensational.
ruin [rrwin] *adj.* (*vicioso*) vile, base, mean; vicious
(*animal*); (*mezquino*) small; petty; puny; stingy.
ruina [rrwí·na] *f.* ruin; destruction; downfall.
ruindad [rrwin·dáđ] *f.* baseness; meanness;
stinginess; mean or vile act.
ruinoso [rrwi·nó·so] *adj.* ruinous; in a state of ruin
or decay.
ruiseñor [rrwi·se·ñór] *m.* nightingale.
rumba [rrúm·ba] *f. Ven., Col., Carib., Mex., Riopl.*
rumba (*dance and music*); *Carib., Ven., Andes*
spree; *Carib., Ven., Andes* **irse de** — to go on a
spree.

rumbear [rrum·be·ár] *v. Riopl., Andes* to head
(towards), take a certain direction; *Am.* to cut a
path through a forest; *Am.* to go on a spree.
rumbo [rrúm·bo] *m.* (*ruta*) direction, course; route;
(*pompa*) pomp; ostentation; *Am.* cut on the
head; *Am.* revel, noisy spree; **hacer** — **a** to head
or sail towards; *Am.* **ir al** — to be going in the
right direction, be on the right track.
rumboso [rrum·bó·so] *adj.* pompous, ostentatious;
generous.
rumiante [rru·mján·te] *m.* ruminant.
rumiar [rru·mjár] *v.* to ruminate; to chew the cud;
to ponder, meditate.
rumor [rru·mór] *m.* rumor, report; murmur;
rumble.
runfla [rrún·fla] *f.* series (*of things of the same
kind*); sequence (*in cards*).
runrún [rrun·rrún] *m.* rumor; murmur.
ruptura [rrup·tú·ra] *f.* rupture; break; fracture.
rural [rru·rál] *adj.* rural.
ruso [rrú·so] *adj.* Russian; *m.* Russian; Russian
language.
rústico [rrús·ti·ko] *adj.* rustic, rural; crude, coarse;
m. peasant; **en** (*or* **a la**) **rústica** unbound,
paper-bound.
ruta [rrú·ta] *f.* route, course, way.
rutenio [rru·té·njo] *m.* ruthenium.
rutina [rru·tí·na] *f.* routine.

S:s **sábado** [sá·ƀa·đo] *m.* Saturday.
sábalo [sá·ƀa·lo] *m.* shad; *Am.* tarpon.
sábana [sá·ƀa·na] *f.* bed sheet; altar
cloth.
sabana [sa·ƀá·na] *f. Col.* savanna, treeless plain;
Col. **ponerse en la** — to become suddenly rich.
sabandija [sa·ƀan·dí·xa] *f.* small reptile; small
lizard.
sabañón [sa·ƀa·ñón] *m.* chilblain.
sabedor [sa·ƀe·đór] *adj.* knowing; aware, informed.
saber[42] [sa·ƀér] *v. irr.* to know; to know how to,
be able to; to learn, find out; *Riopl., Ven.,
Col.* to be in the habit of; — **a** to taste of,
taste like; **sabe bien** it tastes good; **a** —
namely; that is; *Am.* **¿a** — **si venga!** who
knows whether he will come!; **un no sé qué** an
indefinable something; **¿sabe Vd. a la plaza?** do
you know the way to the square?; *m.*
knowledge, learning.
sabiduría [sa·ƀi·đu·rí·a] *f.* wisdom; knowledge.
sabiendas [sa·ƀjén·das] : **a** — consciously,
knowingly.
sabino [sa·ƀí·no] *adj.* roan.
sabio [sá·ƀjo] *adj.* wise; judicious; learned; *m.*
savant, scholar; sage, wise man.
sable [sá·ƀle] *m.* saber; **sablazo** [sa·ƀlá·so] *m.*
blow with a saber; saber wound; **dar un sablazo**
to strike for a loan.
sabor[sa·ƀór] *m.* savor, taste, flavor.
saborear [sa·ƀo·re·ár] *v.* to savor, flavor, season;
to relish, taste with pleasure; to enjoy; **-se** to eat
or drink with relish; to smack one's lips.
sabotaje [sa·ƀo·tá·xe] *m.* sabotage.
sabotear [sa·ƀo·te·ár] *v.* to sabotage.
sabroso [sa·ƀró·so] *adj.* savory, tasty; delicious;
delightful.
sabueso [sa·ƀwé·so] *m.* hound.
sacabocados [sa·ka·ƀo·ká·đos] *m.* punch (*tool*).
sacacorchos [sa·ka·cór·čos] *m.* corkscrew.

sacamuelas [sa·ka·mwé·las] *m. & f.* tooth puller; quack dentist.

sacar[6] [sa·kár] *v.* to draw, draw out, pull out, get out, or take out; to get, obtain; to infer; to make (*a copy*); to take (*a snapshot or picture*); to stick out (*one's tongue*); to serve (*a ball*); — **a bailar** to ask to dance, lead on to the dance floor; — **a luz** to publish; — **el cuerpo** to dodge; — **en claro** (*or* — **en limpio**) to deduce, conclude; *Am.* — **el sombrero** to take off one's hat; *Am.* ¡**sáquese de allí!** get out of there!

sacarina [sa·ka·rí·na] *f.* saccharine.

sacerdocio [sa·ser·ḍó·sjo] *m.* priesthood.

sacerdote [sa·ser·ḍó·te] *m.* priest.

saciar [sa·sjár] *v.* to satiate, satisfy; **-se** to be satiated, satisfied completely.

saco [sá·ko] *m.* sack, bag; sackful, bagful; loose-fitting coat; sack, plundering; *Am.* suit coat; — **de noche** overnight bag, satchel.

sacramento [sa·kra·mén·to] *m.* sacrament.

sacrificar[6] [sa·kri·fi·kár] *v.* to sacrifice.

sacrificio [sa·kri·fí·sjo] *m.* sacrifice.

sacrilegio [sa·kri·lé·xjo] *m.* sacrilege.

sacrílego [sa·kri·le·ḡo] *adj.* sacrilegious.

sacristán [sa·kris·tán] *m.* sacristan, sexton; *Am.* busybody, meddler.

sacro [sá·kro] *adj.* sacred.

sacrosanto [sa·kro·sán·to] *adj.* sacrosanct, holy and sacred.

sacudida [sa·ku·ḍí·ḍa] *f.* shake, jolt, jerk.

sacudimiento [sa·ku·ḍi·mjén·to] *m.* shaking; shake, jerk; shock, jolt.

sacudir [sa·ku·ḍír] *v.* to shake; to jerk; to beat; to beat the dust from; to shake off; **-se** to shake oneself; to brush oneself off; **-se de alguien** to shake someone off, get rid of someone.

sádico [sá·ḍi·ko] *adj.* sadistic, cruel.

sadismo [sa·ḍíz·mo] *m.* sadism.

saeta [sa·é·ta] *f.* arrow, dart.

sagacidad [sa·ḡa·si·ḍáḍ] *f.* sagacity.

sagaz [sa·ḡás] *adj.* sagacious, shrewd.

sagrado [sa·ḡrá·ḍo] *adj.* sacred; consecrated; *m.* asylum, refuge.

sahumar [sa·u·már] *v.* to perfume with incense; to fumigate.

sahumerio [sa·u·mé·rjo] *m.* vapor, fume; incense; burning of incense; fumigation.

sainete [sáj·né·te] *m.* one-act comedy or farce; delicacy, tasty tidbit; flavor, relish; sauce.

sajón [sa·xón] *adj. & m.* Saxon.

sal [sal] *f.* salt; wit, humor; grace; *Mex., Cuba, C.A., Col., Andes* misfortune, bad luck.

sala [sá·la] *f.* parlor; hall, large room; — **de justicia** courtroom.

salado [sa·lá·ḍo] *adj.* salty; salted; witty; charming; *Am.* costly; *Mex., Cuba, C.A., Col., Andes* **estar** — to be unlucky; *m. Am.* salt pit, salt mine.

salar [sa·lár] *v.* to salt; to cure or preserve with salt; *Mex., Cuba, C.A., Col., Andes* to bring bad luck (to); *Am.* to dishonor; *Am.* to ruin, spoil; *Am.* to bribe; *Am.* to feed salt to cattle; *m. Am.* salt pit.

salario [sa·lá·rjo] *m.* salary, wages.

salchicha [sal·čí·ča] *f.* sausage; **salchichón** [sal·či·čón] *m.* large sausage.

saldar [sal·dár] *v.* to balance, settle (*an account*).

saldo [sál·do] *m.* balance, settlement (*of an account*); bargain sale.

saledizo [sa·le·ḍí·so] = **salidizo**.

salero [sa·lé·ro] *m.* (*vaso*) saltcellar, saltshaker; place for storing salts; salt lick; (*gracia*) wit, grace, charm; *Am.* salt dealer.

saleroso [sa·le·ró·so] *adj.* charming; witty; attractive (*more common in feminine*).

salida [sa·lí·ḍa] *f.* departure; exit; sally; outlet; way out; loophole; outskirts; outcome; jut, projection; outlay, expenditure; witty remark; — **de pie de banco** silly remark, nonsense; — **del sol** sunrise; *Cuba* — **de teatro** evening wrap.

salidizo [sa·li·ḍí·so] *m.* jut, ledge, projection; *adj.* salient, jutting, projecting.

saliente [sa·ljén·te] *adj.* salient, standing out; projecting; *m.* salient, salient angle; jut, projection.

salina [sa·lí·na] *f.* salt mine or pit; salt works.

salir[43] [sa·lír] *v. irr.* (*partir*) to go out; to leave, depart; to get out (*of*); to come out; to sprout; to come (*from*); (*resultar*) to turn out to be; — **bien** to turn out well; to come out well; — **a su padre** to turn out to be or look like his father; *Am.* — **a mano** to come out even; **-se** to get out, slip out; to leak out; **-se con la suya** to get one's own way.

salitral [sa·li·trál] *m.* saltpeter bed or mine.

salitre [sa·lí·tre] *m.* saltpeter; **salitrera** [sa·li·tré·ra] *f.* saltpeter mine or bed; **salitroso** [sa·li·tró·so] *adj.* nitrous, abounding in saltpeter.

saliva [sa·lí·ḇa] *f.* saliva.

salmo [sál·mo] *m.* psalm.

salmodiar [sal·mo·ḍjár] *v.* to chant; to talk in a monotone or singsong.

salmón [sal·món] *m.* salmon.

salmuera [sal·mwé·ra] *f.* brine.

salobre [sa·ló·ḇre] *adj.* briny, salty.

salón [sa·lón] *m.* salon, hall, large room; salted meat or fish.

salpicadero [sal·pi·ka·ḍé·ro] *m.* dashboard.

salpicadura [sal·pi·ka·ḍú·ra] *f.* spatter, splash.

salpicar[6] [sal·pi·kár] *v.* to sprinkle, spray, spatter.

salpicón [sal·pi·kón] *m.* hash; hodgepodge; *Ec.* fruit drink.

salpimentar[1] [sal·pi·men·tár] *v. irr.* to salt and pepper.

salpimienta [sal·pi·mjén·ta] *f.* salt and pepper.

salpullido [sal·pu·yí·ḍo] *m.* rash, skin eruption.

salsa [sál·sa] *f.* sauce; gravy; *Am.* sound whipping or beating; **salsera** [sal·sé·ra] *f.* sauce dish.

saltamontes [sal·ta·món·tes] *m.* grasshopper.

saltar [sal·tár] *v.* (*brincar*) to jump; to jump over; to leap; to bounce; to skip; (*estallar*) to burst, break into pieces; to come off; — **a la vista** to be obvious, evident; — **a tierra** to disembark, land; *Mex.* — **las trancas** to lose one's patience; to lose one's head.

salteador [sal·te·a·ḍór] *m.* bandit, highway robber.

saltear [sal·te·ár] *v.* to assault, attack; to hold up, rob; to take by surprise; to jump or skip around.

salto [sál·to] *m.* jump; leap; precipice; gap; — **de agua** waterfall; **a -s** by jumps; **en un** (*or* **de un**) — in a jiffy; quickly; **dar un** — to jump, leap.

saltón [sal·tón] *adj.* jumping, skipping, hopping; jumpy; protruding; *Col.* half-cooked; **ojos -es** popeyes, bulging eyes; *m.* grasshopper.

salubre [sa·lú·ḇre] *adj.* healthy, healthful.

salubridad [sa·lu·ḇri·ḍáḍ] *f.* healthfulness, health; sanitation.

salud [sa·lúḍ] *f.* health; welfare; salvation; ¡—! greetings!; your health!

saludable [sa·lu·ḍá·ḇle] *adj.* wholesome, healthful beneficial.

saludador [sa·lu·ḍa·ḍór] *m.* greeter; healer, quack.
saludar [sa·lu·ḍár] *v.* to salute, greet; to fire a salute.
saludo [sa·lú·ḍo] *m.* salute, nod, greeting.
salutación [sa·lu·ta·sjón] *f.* salutation; greeting.
salva [sál·ḅa] *f.* salvo, salute with guns; greeting, welcome.
salvación [sal·ḅa·sjón] *f.* salvation.
salvado [sal·ḅá·ḍo] *m.* bran.
salvador [sal·ḅa·ḍór] *m.* savior, rescuer; Savior (Saviour); *adj.* saving.
salvaguardar [sal·ḅa·ǵwar·ḍár] *v.* to safeguard, defend, protect.
salvaguardia [sal·ḅa·ǵwár·ḍja] *m.* safeguard, protection; guard; *f.* safe-conduct paper, passport; password.
salvajada [sal·ḅa·xá·ḍa] *f.* savage act or remark.
salvaje [sal·ḅá·xe] *adj.* savage, wild; *m.* savage.
salvajez [sal·ḅa·xés] *f.* wildness, savagery.
salvajismo [sal·ḅa·xíz·mo] *m.* savagery; *Am.* savage act or remark. *See* **salvajada.**
salvamento [sal·ḅa·mén·to] *m.* salvation, rescue; place of safety; salvage (*rescue of property*); **bote de —** lifeboat.
salvar [sal·ḅár] *v.* (*librar*) to save; to except; to exclude; (*vencer*) to clear, jump over; **-se** to be saved; to save oneself, escape.
salvavidas [sal·ḅa·ḅí·ḍas] *m.* life preserver; **lancha —** lifeboat.
¡salve! [sál·ḅe] *interj.* hail!; **Salve** [sál·ḅe] *f.* Salve Regina, prayer to the Virgin Mary.
salvia [sal·ḅja] *f.* sage (*a plant*).
salvo [sál·ḅo] *adj.* saved; safe; *prep.* save, except but; **a —** safe, without injury; **en —** in safety; out of danger.
salvoconducto [sal·ḅo·kon·dúk·to] *m.* safe-conduct, pass.
san [san] *adj.* (*contr. of* **santo**) saint.
sánalotodo [sá·na·lo·tó·ḍo] *m.* cure-all.
sanar [sa·nár] *v.* to heal, cure; to recover, get well.
sanatorio [sa·na·tó·rjo] *m.* sanitarium.
sanción [san·sjón] *f.* sanction.
sancionar [san·sjo·nár] *v.* to sanction; to authorize, ratify.
sancocho [saŋ·kó·čo] *m.* parboiled meat.
sandalia [san·dá·lja] *f.* sandal.
sandez [san·dés] *f.* stupidity; folly; foolish remark.
sandía [san·dí·a] *f.* watermelon.
sandio [san·dí·o] *adj.* silly, foolish.
saneamiento [sa·ne·a·mjén·to] *m.* sanitation; drainage of land.
sanear [sa·ne·ár] *v.* to make sanitary (*land, property, etc.*); to drain, dry up (*land*).
sangrar [saŋ·gár] *v.* to bleed; to drain; to tap (*a tree*); to pilfer; to exploit (*someone*); to indent (*a line*).
sangre [sáŋ·gre] *f.* blood; **— fría** calmness, coolness of mind; **a — fría** in cold blood.
sangría [saŋ·grí·a] *f.* a refreshing Spanish drink made of red wine, fruit juice, and sugar.
sangriento [saŋ·grjén·to] *adj.* bleeding; bloody; bloodstained; bloodthirsty, cruel.
sanguijuela [saŋ·gi·xwé·la] *f.* leech.
sanguinario [saŋ·gi·ná·rjo] *adj.* bloody, cruel; bloodthirsty, murderous.
sanidad [sa·ni·ḍáḍ] *f.* health; soundness; healthfulness; sanitation; **— publica** health department.
sanitario [sa·ni·tá·rjo] *adj.* sanitary.
sano [sá·no] *adj.* (*de salud*) sound, healthy; healthful; sane, sensible; (*integro*) whole;

unbroken; undamaged; **— y salvo** safe and sound.
sanseacabó [san·se·a·ka·ḅó] that's all; that's the end.
santiamén [san·tja·mén]: **en un —** in a jiffy.
santidad [san·ti·ḍáḍ] *f.* sanctity, holiness, saintliness; **su Santidad** his Holiness.
santificar⁶ [san·ti·fi·kár] *v.* to sanctify; to consecrate.
santiguar⁸ [san·ti·ǵwár] *v.* to bless; to make the sign of the cross; to beat, hit, punish; **-se** to cross oneself; to show astonishment (*by crossing oneself*).
santísimo [san·tí·si·mo] *adj.* most holy; *m.* the Holy Sacrament.
santo [sán·to] *adj.* saintly, holy; sacred; **esperar todo el — día** to wait the whole blessed day; **— y bueno** well and good; *Ríopl., Col., Ven., Mex., Carib., Andes* **¡santa palabra!** that's my final and last word! *m.* saint; saint's day; *Mex., Ven.* **tener el — de espaldas** to have a streak of bad luck; **santurrón** *m.* religious hypocrite, affectedly pious person.
santuario [san·twá·rjo] *m.* sanctuary; *Col.* buried treasure; *Am.* Indian idol.
saña [sá·ña] *f.* fury, rage.
sañudo [sa·ñú·ḍo] *adj.* furious, enraged.
sapo [sá·po] *m.* toad; *Col.* despicable little man; *Col.* chubby person; *Am.* sly person; **echar -s y culebras** to swear, curse.
saque [sá·ke] *m.* serve, service (*in tennis*); server.
saquear [sa·ke·ár] *v.* to sack, plunder, pillage, loot.
saqueo [sa·ké·o] *m.* sacking, pillaging, plunder; loot, booty.
saquillo [sa·kí·yo] *m.* small bag, handbag, satchel.
sarampión [sa·ram·pjón] *m.* measles.
sarao [sa·rá·o] *m.* soirée, evening party.
sarape [sa·rá·pe] *m.* *Mex.* serape, blanket.
sarcasmo [sar·káz·mo] *m.* sarcasm.
sarcástico [sar·kás·ti·ko] *adj.* sarcastic.
sarcófago [sar·kó·fa·ǵo] *m.* sarcophagus.
sardina [sar·ḍí·na] *f.* sardine.
sardo [sár·ḍo] *adj.* Sardinian.
sargento [sar·xén·to] *m.* sergeant.
sarmentoso [sar·men·tó·so] *adj.* vinelike; full of vine shoots; gnarled, knotty.
sarmiento [sar·mjén·to] *m.* shoot or branch of a vine.
sarna [sár·na] *f.* itch; mange.
sarnoso [sar·nó·so] *adj.* itchy, scabby, mangy.
sarpullido [sar·pu·yí·ḍo] = **salpullido.**
sarro [sá·rro] *m.* tartar (*on teeth*); crust, sediment (*in utensils*).
sarta [sár·ta] *f.* string (*of beads*); series.
sartén [sar·tén] *f.* frying pan.
sastre [sás·tre] *m.* tailor.
sastrería [sas·tre·rí·a] *f.* tailor shop.
satánico [sa·tá·ni·ko] *adj.* satanic, devilish.
satélite [sa·té·li·te] *m.* satellite; suburban development; **— artificial** artificial satellite.
satén [sa·tén] *m.* sateen.
sátira [sá·ti·ra] *f.* satire.
satírico [sa·tí·ri·ko] *adj.* satirical.
satirizar⁹ [sa·ti·ri·sár] *v.* to satirize.
satisfacción [sa·tis·fak·sjón] *f.* satisfaction; apology, excuse; **tomar —** to vindicate oneself; to take revenge; **dar una —** to offer an apology; to apologize.
satisfacer³¹ [sa·tis·fa·sér] *v. irr.* to satisfy; to pay (*a debt*); **— una letra** to honor a draft; **-se** to be satisfied; to take satisfaction.

satisfactorio [sa·tis·fak·tó·rjo] *adj.* satisfactory.
satisfecho [sa·tis·fé·čo] *p.p. of* **satisfacer** satisfied, gratified; *adj.* content, contented.
saturar [sa·tu·rár] *v.* to saturate; to satiate.
sauce [sáw·se] *m.* willow.
savia [sá·bja] *f.* sap.
saxófono [sak·só·fo·no] *m.* saxophone; also **saxofón** [sak·so·fón], **sazón** [sa·són] *f.* (*época*) season, opportune time; (*sabor*) taste, flavor; ripeness; **a la** — then, at that time; **en** — in season; ripe; opportunely; *adj. Ríopl., Mex., Cuba* ripe.
sazonado [sa·so·ná·do] *adj. & p.p.* seasoned; mellow, ripe; expressive (*said of a phrase*).
sazonar [sa·so·nár] *v.* to season; to flavor; **-se** to become seasoned; to ripen, mature.
se [se] *obj. pron.* (*before* **le, la, lo, las,** *and* **los**) to him, to her; to you (*formal*); to them; *refl. pron.* himself, herself, yourself (*formal*), yourselves (*formal*) themselves; *reciprocal pron.* each other, one another.
sebo [sé·bo] *m.* tallow, fat.
seboso [se·bó·so] *adj.* fatty; tallowy.
secador [se·ka·dór] *m. Am.* dryer (*clothes, hair*).
secante [se·kán·te] *adj.* drying, blotting; **papel** — blotter; *f.* secant (*math.*).
secar[6] [se·kár] *v.* to dry; to wipe dry; **-se** to dry or wipe oneself; to dry up; to wither; to get thin.
sección [sek·sjón] *f.* section; division; cutting.
seccionar [sek·sjo·nár] *v.* to section.
seco [sé·ko] *adj.* (*sin humedad*) dry; dried; withered; (*áspero*) harsh; abrupt; plain, unadorned; **en** — on dry land, out of the water; **parar en** — to stop short, stop suddenly; **a secas** plain; alone, without anything else; *Mex., Carib., Ríopl., Andes* simply, straight to the point; **comer pan a secas** to eat just bread; *Mex., Ven.* **bailar a secas** to dance without musical accompaniment.
secreción [se·kre·sjón] *f.* secretion.
secretar [se·kre·tár] *v.* to secrete.
secretaría [se·kre·ta·rí·a] *f.* secretary's office; position of secretary.
secretariado [se·kre·ta·rjá·do] *m.* secretariat.
secretario [se·kre·tá·rjo] *m.* secretary; confidant; **secretaria** [se·kre·ta·rja] *f.* woman secretary; secretary's wife.
secretear [se·kre·te·ár] *v.* to whisper; **-se** to whisper to each other.
secreto [se·kré·to] *adj.* secret, hidden; secretive; *m.* secret; secrecy; secret place; — **a voces** open secret; **en** — secretly; **hablar en** — to whisper.
secta [sék·ta] *f.* sect.
secuaz [se·kwás] *m.* partisan, follower.
secuela [se·kwé·la] *f.* sequel, outcome, consequence.
secuencia [se·kwén·sja] *f.* sequence.
secuestrador [se·kwes·tra·dór] *m.* kidnapper; confiscator.
secuestrar [se·kwes·trár] *v.* to seize; to kidnap; to confiscate.
secuestro [se·kwés·tro] *m.* kidnapping; seizure.
secular [se·ku·lár] *adj.* secular; lay, worldly; centennial; *m.* secular, secular priest.
secundar [se·kun·dár] *v.* to second, favor, back up.
secundario [se·kun·dá·rjo] *adj.* secondary.
sed [sed] *f.* thirst; craving, desire; **tener** — to be thirsty.
seda [sé·da] *f.* silk; **como una** — soft as silk; sweet-tempered; smoothly, easily.
sedal [se·dál] *m.* fishing line.

sedán [se·dán] *m.* sedan.
sedativo [se·da·tí·bo] *adj. & m.* sedative.
sede [sé·de] *f.* seat, see; **Santa Sede** Holy See.
sedentario [se·den·tá·rjo] *adj.* sedentary.
sedeño [se·dé·ño] *adj.* silky, silken.
sedería [se·de·rí·a] *f.* silk goods; silk shop.
sedero [se·dé·ro] *m.* silk dealer or weaver; *adj.* silk, pertaining to silk; **industria sedera** silk industry.
sedición [se·di·sjón] *f.* sedition.
sedicioso [se·di·sjó·so] *adj.* seditious, turbulent.
sediento [se·djén·to] *adj.* thirsty; dry, parched; anxious, desirous.
sedimento [se·di·mén·to] *m.* sediment; dregs, grounds.
sedoso [se·dó·so] *adj.* silken, silky.
seducción [se·duk·sjón] *f.* seduction.
seducir[25] [se·du·sír] *v. irr.* to seduce; to entice; to charm.
seductivo [se·duk·tí·bo] *adj.* seductive, alluring; inviting, enticing.
seductor [se·duk·tór] *adj.* tempting, fascinating; *m.* seducer; tempter; charming person.
sefardí [se·far·dí] *adj.* Sephardic; *m.* Spanish-speaking Jew.
segador [se·ga·dór] *m.* harvester, reaper; **segadora** [se·ga·dó·ra] *f.* harvester, mowing machine; woman reaper.
segar[1,7] [se·gár] *v. irr.* to mow, reap; to cut off.
seglar [se·glár] *adj.* secular, lay; *m.* layman.
segmento [seg·mén·to] *m.* segment.
segregar[7] [se·gre·gár] *v. irr.* to segregate.
seguida [se·gí·da] *f.* succession; series, continuation; **de** — without interruption, continuously; **en** — at once, immediately.
seguido [se·gí·do] *p.p.* followed; continued; *adj.* continuous; straight, direct; *adv.* without interruption; *Am.* often; *Col., Ven.* **de** — at once, immediately.
seguidor [se·gi·dór] *m.* follower.
seguimiento [se·gi·mjén·to] *m.* pursuit.
seguir[5,12] [se·gír] *v. irr.* to follow; to continue; to pursue; **-se** to follow as a consequence.
según [se·gún] *prep.* according to; *conj.* as; according to; — **y conforme** (*or* — **y como**) exactly as, just as; that depends.
segundar [se·gun·dár] *v.* to repeat a second time; to second.
segundero [se·gun·dé·ro] *m.* second hand (*of a watch or clock*).
segundo [se·gún·do] *adj. & m.* second.
segundón [se·gun·dón] *m.* second child.
seguridad [se·gu·ri·dád] *f.* security; safety; certainty; **alfiler de** — safety pin.
seguro [se·gú·ro] *adj.* secure; sure, certain; safe; *Ríopl., Mex., Carib., Andes* honest, trustworthy; *m.* assurance; insurance; safety device; **a buen** — (**al** —, *or* **de** —) truly, certainly; **en** — in safety; **sobre** — without risk; without taking a chance; *Am.* **irse uno del** — to lose one's temper; *Ch., Mex., Cuba, Andes* **a la segura** without risk.
seibó [sej·bó] *m. Cuba, Ven.* sideboard, hutch.
selección [se·lek·sjón] *f.* selection choice.
seleccionar [se·lek·sjo·nár] *v.* to select, choose.
selecto [se·lék·to] *adj.* select, choice.
selenio [se·lé·njo] *m.* selenium.
selectivo [se·lek·tí·bo] *adj.* selective.
selva [sél·ba] *f.* forest; jungle.
sellar [se·yár] *v.* (*imprimir*) to stamp; to seal; (*cerrar*) to close tightly, seal; (*concluir*) to

SA

conclude.

sello [sé·yo] *m.* seal; stamp; *Am.* official stamped paper.

semáforo [se·má·fo·ro] *m.* traffic light.

semana [se·má·na] *f.* week; week's wages; **días de** — week days; **entre** — during the week.

semanal [se·ma·nál] *adj.* weekly; **-mente** *adv.* weekly, every week.

semanario [se·ma·ná·rjo] *m.* weekly publication; *adj.* weekly.

semblante [sem·blán·te] *m.* countenance; facial expression; appearance.

semblanza [sem·blán·sa] *f.* portrait, literary sketch.

sembrado [sem·brá·ɖo] *m.* sown ground; cultivated field.

sembradora [sem·bra·ɖó·ra] *f.* seeder, sowing machine.

sembrar[1] [sem·brár] *v. irr.* to sow; to scatter.

semejante [se·me·xán·te] *adj.* similar, like; such a; *m.* fellow man; **nuestros -s** our fellow men.

semejanza [se·me·xán·sa] *f.* resemblance, similarity; simile; **a — de** in the manner of.

semejar [se·me·xár] *v.* to resemble; **-se** to resemble.

semental [se·men·tál] *adj.* sowing (*crops*); breeding (*animals*); used as stud.

semestre [se·més·tre] *m.* semester.

semiconsonante [se·mi·kon·so·nán·te] *f.* semiconsonant.

semilla [se·mi·ya] *f.* seed.

semillero [se·mi·yé·ro] *m.* seed bed; plant nursery; **— de vicios** hotbed of vice.

seminario [se·mi·ná·rjo] *m.* seminary; plant nursery, seed plot.

semítico [se·mí·ti·ko] *adj.* Semitic.

semivocal [se·mi·ƀo·kál] *f.* semivowel.

sempiterno [sem·pi·tér·no] *adj.* everlasting; evergreen.

senado [se·ná·ɖo] *m.* senate.

senador [se·na·ɖór] *m.* senator.

sencillez [sen·si·yés] *f.* simplicity; plainness.

sencillo [sen·si·yo] *adj.* simple; easy; plain; unadorned; unaffected; *m.* loose change, small coins.

senda [sén·da] *f.* path; way, course.

sendero [sen·dé·ro] *m.* path.

sendos [sén·dos] *adj. pl.* one for each of two or more persons or things.

senectud [se·nek·túɖ] *f.* senility, old age.

senil [se·níl] *adj.* senile.

seno [sé·no] *m.* (*pecho*) breast, bosom; (*hueco*) cavity, hollow; womb; lap; cove, bay; innermost recess; sinus (*cavity in a bone*); sine (*math.*); *C.A.* armpit.

sensación [sen·sa·sjón] *f.* sensation.

sensacional [sen·sa·sjo·nál] *adj.* sensational.

sensatez [sen·sa·tés] *f.* prudence, common sense.

sensato [sen·sá·to] *adj.* sensible, wise, prudent.

sensibilidad [sen·si·ƀi·li·ɖáɖ] *f.* sensibility; sensitiveness.

sensible [sen·sí·ƀle] *adj.* sensitive; perceptible; regrettable.

sensitivo [sen·si·tí·ƀo] *adj.* sensitive.

sensual [sen·swál] *adj.* sensual; sensuous.

sensualidad [sen·swa·li·ɖáɖ] *f.* sensuality; lewdness.

sentada [sen·tá·ɖa] *f.* sitting; **de una —** at one sitting.

sentado [sen·tá·ɖo] *adj.* seated, sitting; **dar por —** to take for granted.

sentar[1] [sen·tár] *v. irr.* to seat; to set; to establish; to become, suit, fit; to agree with one (*as food or climate*); **-se** to sit down; to settle down; *Col.* **-se**

en la palabra to do all the talking, monopolize the conversation.

sentencia [sen·tén·sja] *f.* sentence; verdict; judgment, maxim, proverb; statement.

sentenciar [sen·ten·sjár] *v.* to sentence; to pass judgment on; to decide.

sentido [sen·tí·ɖo] *p.p.* felt; experienced; *adj.* heartfelt, filled with feeling; sensitive; touchy; **darse por —** to take offense; to have one's feelings hurt; **estar — con alguien** to be offended or peeved at someone; *m.* sense; meaning; judgment; **aguzar el —** to prick up one's ears; **perder el —** to faint.

sentimental [sen·ti·men·tál] *adj.* sentimental.

sentimentalismo [sen·ti·men·ta·líz·mo] *m.* sentimentalism, sentimentality.

sentimiento [sen·ti·mjén·to] *m.* sentiment; sensation, feeling; grief, regret.

sentir[3] [sen·tír] *v. irr.* to feel; to sense; to hear; to regret; **-se** to feel (*well, strong, sad, etc.*); to feel oneself, consider oneself; to feel resentment; to feel a pain; **sin —** without being realized or felt; inadvertently; unnoticed; *m.* feeling; judgment, opinion.

señá [sé·ña] *familiar contraction of* **señora.**

seña [sé·ña] *f.* sign, mark; signal; password; **-s** address (*name and place of residence*); **por mas -s** as an additional proof.

señal [se·ñál] *f.* (*marca*) sign, mark; signal; trace, vestige; scar; (*indicio*) reminder; indication; token, pledge; *Riopl., Andes* earmark, brand (*on the ear of livestock*); **en — de** in proof of, in token of.

señalar [se·ña·lár] *v.* to mark; to point out; to indicate; to determine, fix; to appoint; to signal; to assign; *Am.* to earmark, brand (*cattle*); **-se** to distinguish oneself.

señero [se·ñé·ro] *adj.* unique.

señor [se·ñór] *m.* mister; sir; owner; master, lord; gentleman; **el Señor** the Lord.

señora [se·ñó·ra] *f.* lady; madam; mistress; Mrs.

señorear [se·ño·re·ár] *v.* to lord it over, domineer; to dominate; to master, control.

señoría [se·ño·rí·a] *f.* lordship.

señoril [se·ño·ríl] *adj.* lordly.

señorío [se·ño·rí·o] *m.* dominion, rule; domain of a lord; lordship; dignity; mastery, control; body of noblemen.

señorita [se·ño·rí·ta] *f.* miss; young lady.

señorito [se·ño·rí·to] *m.* master, young gentleman.

señuelo [se·ñwé·lo] *m.* decoy; lure, bait; *Ven.* leading or guiding oxen.

separación [se·pa·ra·sjón] *f.* separation.

separado [se·pa·rá·ɖo] *p.p. & adj.* separate; separated; **por —** separately.

separar [se·pa·rár] *v.* to separate; to set aside; to remove (from); to dismiss (from); **-se** to separate; to retire, resign; to withdraw, leave.

separata [se·pa·rá·ta] *f.* reprint (*of an article*).

septentrional [sep·ten·trjo·nál] *adj.* northern.

septiembre [sep·tjém·bre] *m.* September.

sepulcral [se·pul·král] *adj.* sepulchral (*pertaining to sepulchers or tombs*); **lápida —** tombstone.

sepulcro [se·púl·kro] *m.* sepulcher, tomb, grave.

sepultar [se·pul·tár] *v.* to bury; to hide.

sepultura [se·pul·tú·ra] *f.* burial; grave; **dar —** to bury.

sepulturero [se·pul·tu·ré·ro] *m.* gravedigger.

sequedad [se·ke·ɖáɖ] *f.* dryness; gruffness.

sequía [se·kí·a] *f.* drought.

séquito [sé·ki·to] *m.* retinue, following.

ser⁴⁴ [ser] *v. irr.* to be; to exist; to happen, occur;
— **de** (*or* **para**) **ver** to be worth seeing; *m.* being;
essence, nature; existence; *Am.* **estar en un** — to
be always in the same condition.
serafín [se·ra·fín] *m.* seraph.
serenar [se·re·nár] *v.* to pacify; to calm down; *Col.*
to drizzle, rain gently; **-se** to become serene,
calm down; to clear up (*said of the weather*).
serenata [se·re·ná·ta] *f.* serenade.
serenidad [se·re·ni·dád] *f.* serenity, calm.
sereno [se·ré·no] *adj.* serene, calm; clear, cloudless;
m. night humidity, dew; night watchman; **al** —
in the night air.
serie [sé·rje] *f.* series.
seriedad [se·rje·dád] *f.* seriousness; gravity;
earnestness; dignity.
serio [sé·rjo] *adj.* serious; grave; earnest; dignified;
formal; **en** — seriously.
sermón [ser·món] *m.* sermon; reproof.
sermonear [ser·mo·ne·ár] *v.* to preach; to
admonish, reprimand.
serpentear [ser·pen·te·ár] *v.* to wind, twist, turn,
zigzag.
serpentino [ser·pen·tí·no] *adj.* serpentine.
serpiente [ser·pjén·te] *f.* serpent, snake.
serrado [se·rrá·do] *adj.* toothed, notched (*like a
saw*); jagged.
serrana [se·rrá·na] *f.* mountain girl; **serranilla**
[se·rra·ní·ya] *f.* lyric poem with a rustic theme.
serranía [se·rra·ní·a] *f.* mountainous region; chain
of mountains.
serrano [se·rrá·no] *m.* mountaineer; *adj.* of,
pertaining to, or from the mountains.
serrar [se·rrár] = **aserrar.**
serrín [se·rrín] *m.* sawdust.
serrucho [se·rrú·čo] *m.* handsaw.
servible [ser·bí·ble] *adj.* serviceable, useful.
servicial [ser·bi·sjál] *adj.* helpful, obliging.
servicio [ser·bí·sjo] *m.* service; table service; tea or
coffee set; chamber pot; *Am.* toilet, water closet.
servidor [ser·bi·dór] *m.* servant; waiter; — **de Vd.**
at your service; **su seguro** — yours truly.
servidumbre [ser·bi·dúm·bre] *f.* domestic help,
servants; servitude, slavery; service.
servil [ser·bíl] *adj.* servile; **servilón** [ser·bi·lón] *adj.*
very servile; *m.* bootlicker, great flatterer.
servilismo [ser·bi·líz·mo] *m.* servility, servile
behavior or attitude, servile submission.
servilleta [ser·bi·yé·ta] *f.* napkin.
servir⁵ [ser·bír] *v. irr.* to serve; to be of use; — **de**
to serve as, act as; to be used as; — **para** to be
good for; to be used for; **-se** to serve or help
oneself; to be pleased to; **-se de** to make use of;
sírvase Vd. hacerlo please do it.
seseo [se·sé·o] *m.* pronunciation of all sibilantsas
/s/.
sesgado [sez·gá·do] *adj.* slanting, oblique, bias.
sesgar⁷ [sez·gár] *v.* to slant; to cut on the bias; to
follow an oblique line.
sesgo [séz·go] *m.* bias; slant; diagonal cut; turn; **al**
— on the bias; diagonally, obliquely.
sesión [se·sjón] *f.* session; meeting, conference.
seso [sé·so] *m.* brain; wisdom, intelligence;
devanarse los -s to rack one's brain.
sestear [ses·te·ár] *v.* to snooze, take a nap.
sesudo [se·sú·do] *adj.* sensible, wise, prudent;
Mex., C.A. stubborn.
seta [sé·ta] *f.* mushroom.
setiembre [se·tjém·bre] *m. Spain* preferred form for
septiembre.
sétimo [sé·ti·mo] *adj. Spain* preferred form for

séptimo.
seto [sé·to] *m.* fence; hedge.
seudónimo [sew·dó·ni·mo] *m.* pseudonym, pen
name.
severidad [se·be·ri·dád] *f.* severity; strictness;
seriousness.
severo [se·bé·ro] *adj.* severe; strict; stern.
sevillano [se·bi·yá·no] *adj.* of, from, or pertaining
to Seville, Spain.
sexo [sék·so] *m.* sex.
sexual [sek·swál] *adj.* sexual.
si [si] *conj.* if; whether; **i— ya te lo dije!** but I
already told you!; — **bien** although; **por** —
acaso just in case.
sí [si] *adv.* yes; — **que** certainly, really; **un** — **es no**
es a trifle, somewhat; *m.* assent, consent; *refl.*
pron. (*used after a prep.*) himself, herself, yourself
(*formal*), themselves; **de por** — separately, by
itself; **estar sobre** — to be on the alert.
sibilante [si·bi·lán·te] *adj.* sibilant, whistling.
sicología [si·ko·lo·xi·a] *f.* psychology.
sicológico [si·ko·ló·xi·ko] *adj.* psychological.
sicólogo [si·kó·lo·go] *m.* psychologist.
sicosis [si·kó·sis] *f.* psychosis.
siderurgia [si·de·rúr·xja] *f.* iron and steel industry.
sidra [sí·dra] *f.* cider.
siega [sjé·ga] *f.* reaping, mowing; harvesting;
harvest, harvest season.
siembra [sjém·bra] *f.* sowing; seedtime, sowing
time; sown field.
siempre [sjém·pre] *adv.* always; *Mex., C.A., Col.,
Andes* in any case, anyway; **para** (*or* **por**) —
forever, for always; **por** — **jamás** forever and
ever; — **que** whenever; provided that; *Am.* — **si**
me voy I've decided to go anyway.
siempreviva [sjem·pre·bí·ba] *f.* evergreen;
everlasting.
sien [sjen] *f.* temple (*of the forehead*).
sierpe [sjér·pe] *f.* serpent, snake.
sierra [sjé·rra] *f.* saw; rocky mountain range.
siervo [sjér·bo] *m.* serf; slave; servant.
siesta [sjés·ta] *f.* siesta, afternoon nap; early
afternoon; **dormir la** — to take an afternoon
nap.
sifón [si·fón] *m.* siphon; siphon bottle; trap (*in
plumbing fixtures*).
sigilo [si·xi·lo] *m.* secret; secrecy.
sigla [sí·gla] *f.* initial abbreviation.
siglo [sí·glo] *m.* century; period, epoch; the world,
worldly matters.
significación [sig·ni·fi·ka·sjón] *f.* meaning;
significance.
significado [sig·ni·fi·ká·do] *m.* significance,
meaning.
significar⁶ [sig·ni·fi·kár] *v.* to signify; to mean; to
make known, show; to matter, have
importance.
significativo [sig·ni·fi·ka·tí·bo] *adj.* significant.
signo [sí·gno] *m.* sign; mark; symbol.
siguiente [si·gjén·te] *adj.* following.
sílaba [sí·la·ba] *f.* syllable.
silabario [si·la·bá·rjo] *m.* speller, spelling book.
silabear [si·la·be·ár] *v.* to syllabicate.
silbar [sil·bár] *v.* to whistle; to hiss.
silbato [sil·bá·to] *m.* whistle.
silbido [sil·bí·do] *m.* whistle; hiss.
silenciador [si·len·sja·dór] *m.* silencer; muffler (*of
an automobile*).
silencio [si·lén·sjo] *m.* silence; pause; *adj. Am.*
silent, quiet, motionless.
silencioso [si·len·sjó·so] *adj.* silent, quiet.

SE

silicio [si·lí·sjo] *m.* silicon.
silo [sí·lo] *m.* silo; cave.
silogismo [si·lo·xíz·mo] *m.* syllogism.
silueta [si·lwé·ta] *f.* silhouette.
silvestre [sil·βés·tre] *adj.* wild, uncultivated.
silvicultor [sil·βi·kul·tór] *m.* forester; **silvicultura**
[sil·βi·kul·tú·ra] *f.* forestry.
silla [sí·ya] *f.* chair; saddle; — **de montar** saddle;
Ven. — **de balanza** rocking chair. *See* **mecedora.**
sillón [si·yón] *m.* large chair; easy chair; *Am.* — **de**
hamaca rocking chair.
sima [sí·ma] *f.* chasm, abyss.
simbólico [sim·bó·li·ko] *adj.* symbolic.
simbolismo [sim·bo·líz·mo] *m.* symbolism.
símbolo [sím·bo·lo] *m.* symbol; — **de la fe** (*or de*
los Apóstoles) the Apostle's creed.
simetría [si·me·trí·a] *f.* symmetry.
simétrico [si·mé·tri·ko] *adj.* symmetrical.
simiente [si·mjén·te] *f.* seed.
símil [sí·mil] *m.* simile; similarity; *adj.* similar.
similar [si·mi·lár] *adj.* similar.
simpatía [sim·pa·tí·a] *f.* attraction, attractiveness;
accord, harmony; liking.
simpático [sim·pá·ti·ko] *adj.* sympathetic,
congenial; pleasant, agreeable, nice.
simpatizar[9] [sim·pa·ti·sár] *v.* to be attractive to; to
get on well with; to be congenial; **no me**
simpatiza I don't like him.
simple [sím·ple] *adj.* simple; mere; plain; pure,
unmixed; naïve, innocent; silly, foolish; *m.*
simpleton.
simpleza [sim·plé·sa] *f.* simplicity; simpleness,
stupidity, foolishness.
simplicidad [sim·pli·si·dád] *f.* simplicity; candor.
simplificar[6] [sim·pli·fi·kár] *v.* to simplify.
simplista [sim·plís·ta] *adj.* simplistic; *m.* & *f.* a
person who is inclined to oversimplify.
simplón [sim·plón] *m.* simpleton.
simposio [sim·pó·sjo] *m.* symposium.
simulacro [si·mu·lá·kro] *m.* mimic battle, sham or
mock battle; image, vision.
simular [si·mu·lár] *v.* to simulate, feign.
simultáneo [si·mul·tá·ne·o] *adj.* simultaneous.
sin [sin] *prep.* without; besides, not counting; —
que *conj.* without; — **embargo** nevertheless, still,
yet; — **qué ni para qué** without rhyme or reason.
sinagoga [si·na·ǵó·ǵa] *f.* synagogue.
sinapismo [si·na·píz·mo] *m.* mustard plaster;
irritating person, nuisance, pest, bore.
sincerar [sin·se·rár] *v.* to square, justify, excuse; **-se**
to square oneself (with), justify oneself (with).
sinceridad [sin·se·ri·dád] *f.* sincerity.
sincero [sin·sé·ro] *adj.* sincere.
síncopa [sín·ko·pa] *f.* syncopation; syncope.
sincronizar[9] [sin·kro·ni·sár] *v. irr.* to synchronize.
sindicar[6] [sin·di·kár] *v.* to syndicate; **-se** to
syndicate, form a syndicate.
sindicato [sin·di·ká·to] *m.* syndicate; labor union.
síndico [sín·di·ko] *m.* receiver (*person appointed to*
take charge of property under litigation or to
liquidate a bankrupt business); trustee.
sinecura [si·ne·kú·ra] *f.* sinecure (*easy and well paid*
position).
sinfonía [sin·fo·ní·a] *f.* symphony.
singular [sin·gu·lár] *adj.* singular; unique; striking;
odd, strange.
singularizar[9] [sin·gu·la·ri·sár] *v.* to single out,
choose; to distinguish; **-se** to distinguish oneself;
to be singled out.
siniestro [si·njés·tro] *adj.* sinister; left (*side*); *m.*
unforeseen loss, damage; **siniestra** [si·njés·tra] *f.*

left hand; left-hand side.
sinnúmero [sin·nú·me·ro] *m.* great number, endless
number.
sino [sí·no] *conj.* but; *prep.* except; **no hace** — **lo**
que le mandan he only does what he is told; —
que *conj.* but; *m.* fate, destiny.
sinónimo [si·nó·ni·mo] *m.* synonym; *adj.*
synonymous.
sinrazón [sin·rra·són] *f.* injustice, wrong.
sinsabor [sin·sa·βór] *m.* displeasure; trouble, grief,
distress.
sintaxis [sin·ták·sis] *f.* syntax.
síntesis [sín·te·sis] *f.* synthesis; summary.
sintético [sin·té·ti·ko] *adj.* synthetic.
sintetizar[9] [sin·te·ti·sár] *v.* to synthesize.
síntoma [sín·to·ma] *m.* symptom; indication, sign.
sintonizar[9] [sin·to·ni·sár] *v.* to tune in (on).
sinuoso [si·nwó·so] *adj.* sinuous, winding; wavy.
sinvergüenza [sim·ber·ǵwén·sa] *m.* & *f.* shameless
person; scoundrel.
siquiatra [si·kjá·tra] *m.* & *f.* psychiatrist, alienist.
siquiatría [si·kja·trí·a] *f.* psychiatry.
siquiera [si·kjé·ra] *adv.* at least; even; **ni** — not
even; *conj.* even though.
sirena [si·ré·na] *f.* siren; whistle, foghorn.
sirviente [sir·βjén·te] *m.* servant; waiter; **sirvienta**
[sir·βjén·ta] *f.* housemaid; waitress.
sisa [sí·sa] *f.* petty theft; dart (*made in a garment*).
sisal [si·sál] *m. Am.* sisal or sisal hemp (*fiber used*
in ropemaking).
sisar [si·sár] *v.* to take in (*a garment*); to pilfer; to
cheat out of, defraud.
sisear [si·se·ár] *v.* to hiss.
siseo [si·sé·o] *m.* hiss, hissing.
sistema [sis·té·ma] *m.* system.
sistemático [sis·te·má·ti·ko] *adj.* systematic.
sitial [si·tjál] *m.* chair of a presiding officer; place
of honor.
sitiar [si·tjál] *v.* to besiege; to surround.
sitio [sí·tjo] *m.* site, location; place, spot, space;
siege; *Am.* cattle ranch; *Mex.* taxicab station;
poner — **a** to lay siege to.
sito [sí·to] *adj.* situated, located.
situación [si·twa·sjón] *f.* situation; position;
location; state, condition; *Mex., Carib., Ven.,*
Col. **hombre de la** — man of the hour, man of
influence.
situado [si·twá·do] *p.p.* situated; placed.
situar[18] [si·twár] *v.* to locate; to place; **-se** to
station oneself, place oneself; to be located,
placed, situated.
snobismo [ez·no·βíz·mo] *m.* snobism (*in the*
European sense); the tendency to try to do
whatever seems to be in style.
so [so]: — **capa de** under the guise of; — **pena de**
under penalty of; — **pretexto de** under the
pretext of.
sobaco [so·βá·ko] *m.* armpit.
sobar [so·βár] *v.* (*ablandar*) to rub; to knead; to
massage; to touch, handle; to fondle, pet;
(*fastidiar*) to bother; to beat, slap; *Col., Ven.,*
Mex. to set bones; *Col.* to flay, skin; *Am.* to win
(*in a fight*); *Am.* to tire out (*a horse*).
soberanía [so·βe·ra·ní·a] *f.* sovereignty.
soberano [so·βe·rá·no] *adj.* & *m.* sovereign.
soberbia [so·βer·βja] *f.* pride, arrogance;
ostentation, pomp.
soberbio [so·βer·βjo] *adj.* proud, haughty,
arrogant; pompous; superb, magnificent;
spirited (*horse*).
sobornar [so·βor·nár] *v.* to bribe.

soborno [so·b̶ór·no] *m.* bribery; bribe; *Andes* overload (*on a pack animal*), extra load.

sobra [só·b̶ra] *f.* surplus, excess; **-s** leftovers, leavings; **de** — more than enough; superfluous, unnecessary.

sobrado [so·b̶rá·d̶o] *m.* attic; loft; *Am.* pantry shelf; **-s** *Col., Ven.* leftovers, leavings; *adj.* leftover; excessive; superfluous; forward, brazen; **sobradas veces** many times, repeatedly.

sobrante [so·b̶rán·te] *adj.* leftover, surplus, excess, spare; *m.* surplus, excess, remainder.

sobrar [so·b̶rár] *v.* to exceed; to remain, be left over; to be more than enough.

sobre [só·b̶re] *prep.* (*encima de*) over; above; on, upon; (*acerca de*) about; approximately; besides; — **manera** excessively; **estar** — **si** to be cautious, on the alert; — **que** besides, in addition to the fact that; *m.* envelope; address (*on an envelope*).

sobrecama [so·b̶re·ká·ma] *f.* bedspread.

sobrecarga [so·b̶re·kár·g̶a] *f.* overload; overburden.

sobrecargar[7] [so·b̶re·kar·g̶ár] *v.* to overload; to overburden.

sobrecargo [so·b̶re·kár·g̶o] *m.* purser (*on a ship*); *f.* airline hostess.

sobrecoger[11] [so·b̶re·ko·xér] *v.* to surprise, catch unaware; to startle; **-se** to be startled; **-se de miedo** to be seized with fear.

sobreexcitación [so·b̶re·ek·si·ta·sjón] *f.* overexcitement; thrill.

sobreexcitar [so·b̶re·ek·si·tár] *v.* to overexcite.

sobrehumano [so·b̶re·u·má·no] *adj.* superhuman.

sobrellevar [so·b̶re·ye·b̶ár] *v.* to endure, bear; to tolerate; to lighten (*another's burden*).

sobremesa [so·b̶re·mé·sa] *f.* table runner; after dinner conversation at the table; **de** — during the after dinner conversation.

sobrenadar [so·b̶re·na·d̶ár] *v.* to float.

sobrenatural [so·b̶re·na·tu·rál] *adj.* supernatural.

sobrenombre [so·b̶re·nóm·bre] *m.* surname; nickname.

sobrentender[1] [so·b̶ren·ten·dér] *v. irr.* to assume, understand; **-se** to be assumed, be obvious, be understood.

sobrepasar [sob̶·re·pa·sár] *v.* to exceed; to excel; **-se** to overstep, go too far.

sobreponer[40] [so·b̶re·po·nér] *v. irr.* to lay on top; **-se** to dominate oneself; **-se a** to overcome; to dominate.

sobrepuesto [so·b̶re·pwés·to] *p.p. of* **sobreponer**; *m.* appliqué (*trimming laid on a dress*); *C.A.* mend, patch.

sobrepujar [so·b̶re·pu·xár] *v.* to exceed, excel, surpass; to outweigh.

sobresaliente [so·b̶re·sa·ljén·te] *adj.* outstanding; projecting; excellent; *m. & f.* substitute (*a person*); understudy (*substitute actor*).

sobresalir[43] [so·b̶re·sa·lír] *v. irr.* to stand out; to project, jut out; to excel.

sobresaltar [so·b̶re·sal·tár] *v.* to startle, frighten; to assail; to stand out clearly **-se** to be startled, frightened.

sobresalto [so·b̶re·sál·to] *m.* start, scare, fright, shock; **de** — suddenly.

sobrescrito [so·b̶res·krí·to] *m.* address (*on an envelope*).

sobresdrújulo [so·b̶rez·drú·xu·lo] *adj.* accented on syllable before antepenult.

sobrestante [so·b̶res·tán·te] *m.* overseer; boss, foreman.

sobresueldo [so·b̶re·swél·do] *m.* overtime pay, extra pay or wages.

sobretodo [so·b̶re·tó·d̶o] *m.* overcoat.

sobrevenir[48] [so·b̶re·b̶e·nír] *v. irr.* to happen, occur, come unexpectedly; to follow, happen after.

sobreviviente [so·b̶re·b̶i·b̶jén·te] *m. & f.* survivor; *adj.* surviving.

sobrevivir [so·b̶re·b̶i·b̶ír] *v.* to survive.

sobriedad [so·brje·d̶ád̶] *f.* sobriety, soberness, temperance, moderation.

sobrina [so·brí·na] *f.* niece.

sobrino [so·brí·no] *m.* nephew.

sobrio [só·brjo] *adj.* sober, temperate, moderate.

socarrón [so·ka·rrón] *adj.* cunning, sly, crafty.

socarronería [so·ka·rro·ne·rí·a] *f.* craftiness, slyness, cunning.

socavar [so·ka·b̶ár] *v.* to dig under; to undermine.

socavón [so·ka·b̶ón] *m.* tunnel; cave, cavern; underground passageway.

social [so·sjál] *adj.* social; sociable, friendly.

socialismo [so·sja·líz·mo] *m.* socialism.

socialista [so·sja·lís·ta] *adj.* socialist, socialistic; *m. & f.* socialist.

sociedad [so·sje·d̶ád̶] *f.* society; partnership; company, firm, corporation; — **anónima** (*or* — **por acciones**) stock company.

socio [só·sjo] *m.* associate, partner; member.

sociología [so·sjo·lo·xí·a] *f.* sociology.

socorrer [so·ko·rrér] *v.* to help, aid, assist.

socorro [so·kó·rro] *m.* help, aid, assistance, relief; *Am.* partial advance payment on a workman's wages.

sodio [só·d̶jo] *m.* sodium.

sodomía [so·d̶o·mí·a] *f.* sodomy.

soez [so·és] *adj.* low, vile, vulgar; coarse, ill-mannered.

sofá [so·fá] *m.* sofa, davenport.

sofocante [so·fo·kán·te] *adj.* suffocating, stifling.

sofocar[6] [so·fo·kár] *v.* to suffocate, choke; to smother; to bother; to embarrass.

sofoco [so·fó·ko] *m.* suffocation, choking; upset, annoyance; embarrassment.

sofrenar [so·fre·nár] *v.* to check; to control; to reprimand.

sofrito [so·frí·to] *m.* a preparation of lightly fried ingredients.

soga [só·g̶a] *f.* rope; *Ven., Col., Andes, Ch.* leather lasso or rope.

sojuzgamiento [so·xuz·g̶a·mjén·to] *m.* subjugation, subjection.

sojuzgar[7] [so·xuz·g̶ár] *v.* to subjugate, subdue, subject.

sol [sol] *m.* sun; sunshine; sol (*fifth note of the scale*); *Am.* sol (*monetary unit of Peru*); **de** — **a** — from sunrise to sunset; **hace** — it is sunny; **tomar el** — to bask in the sun; to enjoy the sunshine.

solana [so·lá·na] *f.* sunny place; sunroom; sun porch; intense sunlight; **solanera** [so·la·né·ra] *f.* sunburn; sunny place.

solapa [so·lá·pa] *f.* lapel.

solapado [so·la·pá·d̶o] *adj.* sly, crafty, cunning, deceitful, underhanded.

solar [so·lár] *m.* lot, plot of ground; ancestral mansion, manor; *Carib., Mex.* tenement house; *Mex., Ven.* back yard; *Col.* town lot, field (*for growing alfalfa, corn, etc.*); *adj.* solar, of the sun.

solar[2] [so·lár] *v. irr.* to sole (*shoes*); to pave, floor.

solariego [so·la·rjé·g̶o] *adj.* manorial, pertaining to a manor; **casa solariega** ancestral manor or mansion.

solaz [so·lás] *m.* solace, comfort; relaxation,

recreation.

solazar[9] [so·la·sár] *v.* to console, cheer, comfort; **-se** to seek relaxation or pleasure; to enjoy oneself.

soldado [sol·dá·do] *m.* soldier; — **raso** private; — **de línea** regular soldier.

soldadura [sol·da·dú·ra] *f.* soldering; welding; solder.

soldar[2] [sol·dár] *v. irr.* to solder; to weld.

soleado [so·le·á·do] *adj.* sunny; *p.p.* sunned.

solear [so·le·ár] = **asolear.**

soledad [so·le·dád] *f.* solitude; loneliness; homesickness; lonely retreat.

solemne [so·lém·ne] *adj.* solemn; imposing; — **disparate** downright foolishness, huge blunder.

solemnidad [so·lem·ni·dád] *f.* solemnity; solemn ceremony.

soler[2,51] [so·lér] *v. irr.* to have the custom of, be in the habit of.

solfeo [sol·fé·o] *m.* sol-faing, solfeggio style.

solferino [sol·fe·rí·no] *adj.* reddish-purple.

solicitante [so·li·si·tán·te] *m. & f.* solicitor; applicant.

solicitar [so·li·si·tár] *v.* to solicit; to apply for; to beg, ask for; to court, woo.

solícito [so·lí·si·to] *adj.* solicitous, careful; anxious, concerned, diligent.

solicitud [so·li·si·túd] *f.* solicitude; care, concern, anxiety.

solidaridad [so·li·da·ri·dád] *f.* solidarity; union; bond, community of interests.

solidez [so·li·dés] *f.* solidity; compactness.

solidificar[6] [so·li·di·fi·kár] *v.* to solidify.

sólido [so·li·do] *adj.* solid; firm; strong; *m.* solid.

soliloquio [so·li·ló·kjo] *m.* soliloquy, monologue.

solista [so·lis·ta] *m. & f.* soloist.

solitaria [so·li·tá·rja] *f.* tapeworm.

solitario [so·li·tá·rjo] *adj.* solitary; lonely; *m.* recluse, hermit; solitaire (*card game*); solitaire (*gem set by itself*).

sólito [só·li·to] *adj.* customary.

solo [só·lo] *adj.* sole, only; single; alone; lonely **a solas** alone; *m.* solo; **sólo** [só·lo] *adv.* only.

solomillo [so·lo·mí·yo], **solomo** [so·ló·mo] *m.* sirloin; loin; loin of pork.

solsticio [sols·tí·sjo] *m.* solstice.

soltar[2] [sol·tár] *v. irr.* to loosen, untie, unfasten; to let loose; to set free; to let go; to let out; to utter; **-se** to set oneself free; to come loose; to lose restraint; to loosen up; **-se a** to begin to, start to.

soltero [sol·té·ro] *adj.* single, unmarried; *m.* bachelor; **soltera** [sol·té·ra] *f.* spinster; **solterón** [sol·te·rón] *m.* old bachelor; **solterona** [sol·te·ró·na] *f.* old maid.

soltura [sol·tú·ra] *f.* looseness; freedom; facility, ease; agility, nimbleness; release (*of a prisoner*).

solución [so·lu·sjón] *f.* solution; loosening, untying.

solucionar [so·lu·sjo·nár] *v.* to solve, to resolve.

solventar [sol·ben·tár] *v.* to pay (*a bill*), settle (*an account*); to solve (*a problem or difficulty*).

sollozar[9] [so·yo·sár] *v.* to sob.

sollozo [so·yó·so] *m.* sob.

sombra [sóm·bra] *f.* (*oscuridad*) shadow; shade; darkness; (*abrigo*) shelter, protection; (*imagen*) image, reflection (*in the water*); *Am.* guide lines (*under writing paper*); *Ven.* awning, sunshade; **hacer** — to shade; to cast a shadow (on).

sombreado [som·bre·á·do] *adj.* shady; shaded.

sombrear [som·bre·ár] *v.* to shade; **-se** *Mex., Ven.,*

Col. to seek the shade, stand in the shade.

sombrería [som·bre·re·rí·a] *f.* hat shop.

sombrero [som·bré·ro] *m.* hat; — **de copa** top hat, high hat; — **hongo** derby; — **de jipijapa** Panama hat; *C.A., Col., Ven.* — **de pelo** top hat.

sombrilla [som·brí·ya] *f.* parasol, sunshade.

sombrío [som·brí·o] *adj.* somber, gloomy; shady.

somero [so·mé·ro] *adj.* superficial, shallow; summary, concise.

someter [so·me·tér] *v.* to submit; to subject; **-se** to submit.

sometimiento [so·me·ti·mjén·to] *m.* submission; subjection.

somnolencia [som·no·lén·sja] *f.* drowsiness, sleepiness; **con** — sleepily.

son [son] *m.* sound; tune; rumor; **en** — **de guerra** in a warlike manner; **sin ton ni** — without rhyme or reason.

sonaja [so·ná·xa] *f.* jingles, tambourine (*to accompany certain dances*); rattle; **sonajero** [so·na·xé·ro] *m.* child's rattle.

sonámbulo [so·nám·bu·lo] *m.* sleepwalker.

sonante [so·nán·te] *adj.* sounding; ringing; sonorous; **en dinero** — **y contante** in hard cash.

sonar[2] [so·nár] *v. irr.* to sound; to ring; to sound familiar; — **a** to sound like; seem like; **-se** to blow one's nose; **se suena que** it is rumored that.

sonda [són·da] *f.* plumb, string with lead weight (*for sounding the depth of water*); sounding; surgeon's probe.

sondar [son·dár] = **sondear.**

sondear [son·de·ár] *v.* to sound, fathom; to sound out; to probe; to examine into.

sondeo [son·dé·o] *m.* sounding, fathoming.

soneto [so·né·to] *m.* sonnet.

sonido [so·ní·do] *m.* sound.

sonoro [so·nó·ro] *adj.* sonorous; **consonante sonora** voiced consonant.

sonreír[15] [son·rre·ír] *v. irr.* to smile; **-se** to smile.

sonriente [son·rrjén·te] *adj.* smiling, beaming, radiant.

sonrisa [son·rrí·sa] *f.* smile.

sonrojarse [son·rro·xár·se] *v.* to blush.

sonrojo [son·rró·xo] *m.* blush.

sonrosado [son·rro·sá·do] *adj.* rosy.

sonsacar[6] [son·sa·kár] *v.* to lure away; to draw (*someone*) out; to extract (*a secret*); to take on the sly.

sonsonete [son·so·né·te] *m.* singsong; rhythmical tapping sound.

soñador [so·ña·dór] *m.* dreamer.

soñar[2] [so·ñár] *v. irr.* to dream; — **con** (*or* — **en**) to dream of; — **despierto** to daydream.

soñoliento [so·ño·ljén·to] *adj.* sleepy, drowsy.

sopa [só·pa] *f.* soup; sop; **estar hecho una** — to be sopping wet; *Am.* **es un -s** he is a fool.

sopapo [so·pá·po] *m.* chuck, tap, pat (*under the chin*); slap.

sopera [so·pé·ra] *f.* soup tureen.

sopero [so·pé·ro] *m.* soup dish.

sopetón [so·pe·tón] *m.* box, slap; **de** — all of a sudden, unexpectedly.

soplar [sop·lár] *v.* (*despedir aire*) to blow; to blow away; to blow up, inflate; (*robar*) to swipe, steal; (*informar*) to prompt; to "squeal" on, inform against; *Col., Ven., Mex., Cuba, Andes* — **una bofetada** to strike a blow; **-se** to swell up, puff up; to eat up, gobble up; to gulp down; **se sopló el pastel** he gobbled up the pie; *Am.* **-se a uno** to deceive someone, get the best of someone.

soplete [so·plé·te] *m.* blow torch; blowpipe.

soplo [só·plo] *m.* (*de aire*) blowing; puff, gust of wind; breath; (*aviso*) whispered warning or advice; "squealing", informing; **en un** — in a jiffy, in a second.

soplón [so·plón] *m.* informer, "squealer" (*one who tells on someone*), tattletale.

sopor [so·pór] *m.* stupor; lethargy.

soportal [so·por·tál] *m.* arcade.

soportar [so·por·tár] *v.* to support, hold up, bear; to stand, endure, tolerate.

soporte [so·pór·te] *m.* support.

sorber [sor·bér] *v.* to sip; to suck; to swallow; to absorb; to snuff up one's nose.

sorbete [sor·b̞é·te] *m.* sherbet; fruit ice; *C.A., Mex., Ven.* cone, ice-cream cone; *Am.* silk top hat.

sorbo [sór·b̞o] *m.* sip, swallow, gulp; sniff.

sordera [sor·d̞é·ra], **sordez** [sor·d̞és] *f.* deafness.

sórdido [sór·d̞i·d̞o] *adj.* sordid.

sordina [sor·d̞í·na] *f.* mute (*of a musical instrument*).

sordo [sór·d̞o] *adj.* deaf; silent, noiseless; dull; muffled; **consonante sorda** voiceless consonant; *m.* deaf person; **hacerse el** — to pretend not to hear; to turn a deaf ear.

sordomudo [sor·d̞o·mú·d̞o] *adj.* deaf and dumb; *m.* deaf-mute.

sorna [sór·na] *f.* slyness, cunning; sneer.

soroche [so·ró·če] *m. Andes* shortness of breath, sickness caused by high altitude; *Am.* blush, flush.

sorprendente [sor·pren·dén·te] *adj.* surprising.

sorprender [sor·pren·dér] *v.* to surprise; **-se** to be surprised.

sorpresa [sor·pré·sa] *f.* surprise.

sortear [sor·te·ár] *v.* to draw lots; to raffle; to dodge; to shun; to fight (*bulls*) skillfully.

sorteo [sor·té·o] *m.* drawing or casting of lots; raffle.

sortija [sor·tí·xa] *f.* ring; finger ring; ringlet, curl.

sosa [só·sa] *f.* soda.

sosegado [so·se·g̞á·d̞o] *adj.* calm, quiet, peaceful.

sosegar[1,7] [so·se·g̞ár] *v.* to calm, quiet; to be quiet; **-se** to quiet down.

sosiego [so·sjé·g̞o] *m.* calm, peace, quiet.

soslayo [soz·lá·yo]: **al** — obliquely; slanting; on the bias; **de** — oblique, slanting; at a slant; sideways; **mirada de** — side glance; **pegar de** — to glance, hit at a slant.

soso [só·so] *adj.* flat, tasteless, insipid; dull, silly; awkward.

sospecha [sos·pé·ča] *f.* suspicion; mistrust.

sospechar [sos·pe·čár] *v.* to suspect; to mistrust.

sospechoso [sos·pe·čó·so] *adj.* suspicious; *m.* suspect.

sostén [sos·tén] *m.* support; prop; supporter; brassière.

sostener[4,5] [sos·te·nér] *v. irr.* to sustain; to hold; to support, maintain; to defend, uphold; to endure.

sostenido [sos·te·ni·d̞o] *p.p.* & *adj.* sustained; supported, held up; *m.* sharp (*in music*).

sota [só·ta] *f.* jack (*at cards*); *m. Am.* foreman, boss, overseer.

sotana [so·tá·na] *f.* cassock (*black outer robe of a priest*).

sótano [só·ta·no] *m.* cellar, basement.

soterrar [so·te·rrár] *v.* to bury.

soto [só·to] *m.* grove; thicket.

sotreta [so·tré·ta] *m. Andes, Ríopl.* nag, old horse.

soviet [so·b̞jét] *m.* soviet; **soviético** [so·b̞jé·ti·ko] *adj.* soviet, of, or pertaining to, soviets.

sténcil [es·tén·sil] *m.* stencil.

suave [swá·b̞e] *adj.* soft; smooth; mild; bland; gentle.

suavidad [swa·b̞i·d̞ád̞] *f.* softness; smoothness; mildness; gentleness.

suavizar[9] [swa·b̞i·sár] *v.* to smooth; to soften.

subalterno [su·b̞al·tér·no] *adj.* & *m.* subordinate.

subasta [su·b̞ás·ta] *f.* public auction.

subastar [su·b̞ás·tar] *v.* to sell at auction.

subconsciente [su·b̞·kon·sjén·te] *adj.* subconscious.

subdesarrollado [su·b̞·d̞e·sa·rro·yá·d̞o] *adj.* underdeveloped.

súbdito [sú·b̞·d̞i·to] *m.* subject.

subida [su·b̞í·d̞a] *f.* rise; ascent; carrying up; **de** — on the way up; **muchas -s y bajadas** many ups and downs; much going up and down.

subir [su·b̞ír] *v.* to ascend, go up, climb; to raise, lift; to carry up; to mount; — **al tren** to board the train, get on the train.

súbito [sú·b̞i·to] *adj.* sudden; **de** — suddenly.

sublevación [su·b̞le·b̞a·sjón] *f.* revolt, uprising, insurrection.

sublevar [su·b̞·le·b̞ár] *v.* to excite to rebellion; **-se** to revolt.

sublimado [su·b̞·li·má·d̞o] *adj.* sublimated.

sublime [su·b̞lí·me] *adj.* sublime.

submarino [su·b̞·ma·ri·no] *m.* & *adj.* submarine; *m.* — **atómico** atomic submarine.

subordinado [su·b̞or·d̞i·ná·d̞o] *adj.* & *m.* subordinate.

subordinar [su·b̞or·d̞i·nár] *v.* to subordinate; to subdue.

subrayar [su·b̞·rra·yár] *v.* to underline; to emphasize.

subsanar [su·b̞·sa·nár] *v.* to mend, remedy, repair (*a damage, error, defect, etc.*); to make up for (*an error, fault, etc.*); to excuse (*a fault or error*).

subscribir [su·b̞s·kri·b̞ír] = **suscribir.**

subscripción [su·b̞s·krip·sjón] = **suscripción.**

subscriptor [su·b̞s·krip·tór] = **suscritor.**

subsecretario [su·b̞·se·kre·tá·rjo] *m.* undersecretary.

subsecuente [su·b̞·se·kwén·te] *adj.* subsequent.

subsiguiente [su·b̞·si·g̞jén·te] *adj.* subsequent.

subsistencia [su·b̞·sis·tén·sja] *f.* living, livelihood; sustenance; permanence.

subsistir [su·b̞·sis·tír] *v.* to subsist; to exist; to last.

substancia [su·b̞s·tán·sja] = **sustancia.**

substancial [su·b̞s·tan·sjál] = **sustancial.**

substancioso [su·b̞s·tan·sjó·so] = **sustancioso.**

substituíble [su·b̞s·ti·twí·b̞le] = **sustituíble.**

substantivo [su·b̞s·tan·tí·b̞o] = **sustantivo.**

substitución [su·b̞s·ti·tu·sjón] = **sustitución.**

substituir [su·b̞s·ti·twír] = **sustituir.**

substituto [su·b̞s·ti·tú·to] = **sustituto.**

substracción [su·b̞s·trak·sjón] = **sustracción.**

substraer [su·b̞s·tra·ér] = **sustraer.**

subsuelo [su·b̞·swé·lo] *m.* subsoil.

subteniente [su·b̞·te·njén·te] *m.* second lieutenant.

subterfugio [su·b̞·ter·fú·xjo] *m.* subterfuge.

subterráneo [su·b̞·te·rrá·ne·o] *adj.* subterranean, underground; *m.* underground; cave, tunnel, vault.

suburbano [su·b̞ur·b̞á·no] *adj.* suburban; *m.* suburban resident.

suburbio [su·b̞ur·b̞jo] *m.* suburb.

subvención [su·b̞·b̞en·sjón] *f.* subsidy.

subvencionar [su·b̞·b̞en·sjo·nár] *v.* to subsidize.

subyugar [su·b̞·yu·g̞ár] *v.* to subdue.

succión [suk·sjón] *f.* suction.

suceder [su·se·d̞ér] *v.* to happen, occur; to succeed, follow.

sucesión [su·se·sjón] *f.* succession; heirs, offspring.

sucesivo [su·se·sí·b̞o] *adj.* successive; **en lo** —

SO

hereafter, in the future.

suceso [su·sé·so] *m.* event; outcome, result.

sucesor [su·se·sór] *m.* successor.

suciedad [su·sje·đáđ] *f.* dirt, filth; filthiness; filthy act or remark.

sucinto [su·sín·to] *adj.* compact, concise, brief.

sucio [sú·sjo] *adj.* dirty; foul, filthy.

suculento [su·ku·lén·to] *adj.* juicy.

sucumbir [su·kum·bír] *v.* to succumb; to yield.

sucursal [su·kur·sál] *f.* branch, branch office (*of a post office, bank, etc.*); *adj.* branch (*used as an adj.*).

suche [sú·če] *adj. Ven.* sour, unripe; *m. Andes* pimple; *Ch.* office boy, insignificant employee; *Andes* suche (*a tree*).

sud [suđ] *m.* south; south wind; **sudeste** [su·đés·te] *m. & adj.* southeast; **sudoeste** [su·đo·és·te] *m. & adj.* southwest.

sudamericano [su·đa·me·ri·ká·no] *adj. & m.* South American.

sudar [su·đár] *v.* to sweat, perspire; to ooze; to toil.

sudario [su·đá·rjo] *m.* shroud.

sudor [su·đór] *m.* sweat, perspiration; toil.

sudoroso [su·đo·ró·so] *adj.* sweaty, sweating, perspiring.

sueco [swé·ko] *adj.* Swedish; *m.* Swede; Swedish language; **hacerse el** — to pretend not to see or understand.

suegra [swé·ǥra] *f.* mother-in-law.

suegro [swé·ǥro] *m.* father-in-law.

suela [swé·la] *f.* sole of a shoe; shoe leather.

sueldo [swél·do] *m.* salary.

suelo [swé·lo] *m.* soil, ground; floor; pavement; bottom.

suelto [swél·to] *adj.* (*no atado*) loose; free, easy; (*ágil*) agile, nimble; blank (*verse*); *m.* small change; short newspaper article, news item.

sueño [swé·ño] *m.* sleep; dream; sleepiness, drowsiness; **en -s** in one's sleep; **conciliar el** — to get to sleep; **tener** — to be sleepy.

suero [swé·ro] *m.* serum.

suerte [swér·te] *f.* (*fortuna*) fate; fortune; chance; luck; (*clase*) sort, kind; way, manner; (*truco*) trick; **de — que** so that, in such a way that; and so; **echar -s** to cast lots; **tener** — to be lucky; **tocarle a uno la** — to fall to one's lot; to be lucky.

suéter [swé·ter] *m. Am.* sweater.

suficiente [su·fi·sjén·te] *adj.* sufficient; competent, able.

sufijo [su·fí·xo] *m.* suffix; *adj.* suffixed.

sufragar[7] [su·fra·ǥár] *v.* to defray, pay; to help, aid; *Am.* — **por** to vote for.

sufragio [su·frá·xjo] *m.* suffrage; vote; help, aid.

sufrido [su·frí·do] *adj.* suffering, long-suffering, patient; **mal** — impatient.

sufridor [su·fri·đór] *m.* sufferer; *adj.* suffering.

sufrimiento [su·fri·mjén·to] *m.* suffering; patience, endurance.

sufrir [su·frír] *v.* to suffer; to endure; to allow, permit; to sustain; to undergo; — **un examen** to take an examination.

sugerencia [su·xe·rén·sja] *f. Am.* suggestion, hint.

sugerir[3] [su·xe·rír] *v. irr.* to suggest; to hint.

sugestión [su·xes·tjón] *f.* suggestion; hint.

sugestivo [su·xes·tí·ƀo] *adj.* suggestive.

suicida [swi·sí·da] *m. & f.* suicide (*person who commits suicide*). ·

suicidarse [swi·si·đár·se] *v.* to commit suicide.

suicidio [swi·sí·djo] *m.* suicide (*act of suicide*).

suizo [swí·so] *adj. & m.* Swiss.

sujeción [su·xe·sjón] *f.* subjection; control; submission.

sujetapapeles [su·xe·ta·pa·pé·les] *m.* paper clip.

sujetar [su·xe·tár] *v.* to subject; to control; to subdue; to fasten; to grasp, hold; **-se** to subject oneself; to submit; to adhere (to).

sujeto [su·xé·to] *adj.* subject; liable; fastened; under control; *m.* subject matter; subject; fellow, individual.

sulfamida [sul·fa·mí·đa] *f.* common name for the sulfa drugs.

sulfato [sul·fá·to] *m.* sulphate.

sulfurarse [sul·fu·rár·se] *v.* to get angry.

sulfúrico [sul·fú·ri·ko] *adj.* sulphuric.

sulfuro [sul·fú·ro] *m.* sulphide.

sultán [sul·tán] *m.* sultan.

suma [sú·ma] *f.* sum; addition; substance; summary; **en** — in short.

sumador [su·ma·đór] *adj.* adding; **máquina sumadora** adding machine.

sumar [su·már] *v.* to add; to add up (to), amount (to); to sum up; **-se a** to join.

sumario [su·má·rjo] *m.* summary; indictment; *adj.* summary, brief, concise; swift (*punishment*).

sumergible [su·mer·xi·ƀle] *adj.* submergible; *m.* submarine.

sumergir[11] [su·mer·xír] *v.* to submerge, plunge, sink; to immerse; **-se** to submerge; to sink.

sumidero [su·mi·đé·ro] *m.* sink; sewer, drain.

suministrar [su·mi·nis·trár] *v.* to give, supply with, provide with.

sumir [su·mír] *v.* to sink; to submerge; to immerse; *Riopl., Mex., Carib.* to dent; **-se** to sink; *Andes* to shrink, shrivel; *Andes* to cower, crouch in fear; *Am.* **-se el sombrero hasta las cejas** to pull one's hat over one's eyes.

sumisión [su·mi·sjón] *f.* submission; obedience.

sumiso [su·mí·so] *adj.* submissive; obedient; meek.

sumo [sú·mo] *adj.* supreme, highest, high; greatest; — **pontífice** Sovereign Pontiff (*the Pope*); **a lo** — at the most.

suntuoso [sun·twó·so] *adj.* sumptuous, magnificent, luxurious.

superable [su·pe·rá·ƀle] *adj.* superable.

superabundancia [su·pe·ra·ƀun·dán·sja] *f.* superabundance, great abundance, overflow.

superar [su·pe·rár] *v.* to surpass; to exceed; to overcome.

superávit [su·pe·rá·ƀit] *m.* surplus.

superficial [su·per·fi·sjál] *adj.* superficial; shallow; frivolous; **superficialidad** [su·per·fi·sja·li·đáđ] *f.* superficiality, shallowness, frivolity.

superficie [su·per·fí·sje] *f.* surface; area.

superfluo [su·pér·flwo] *adj.* superfluous.

superintendente [su·pe·rin·ten·dén·te] *m.* superintendent; supervisor; overseer.

superior [su·pe·rjór] *adj.* superior; higher; better; upper; *m.* superior; father superior; **superiora** [su·pe·rjó·ra] *f.* superior, mother superior.

superioridad [su·pe·rjo·ri·đáđ] *f.* superiority; excellence.

superlativo [su·per·la·tí·ƀo] *adj. & m.* superlative.

supersónico [su·per·só·ni·ko] *adj.* supersonic.

superstición [su·pers·ti·sjón] *f.* superstition.

supersticioso [su·pers·ti·sjó·so] *adj.* superstitious.

supervivencia [su·per·ƀi·ƀén·sja] *f.* survival.

superviviente [su·per·ƀi·ƀjén·te] = **sobreviviente**.

suplantar [su·plan·tár] *v.* to supplant; to forge (*a document or check*).

suplementar [su·ple·men·tár] *v.* supplement.

suplementario [su·ple·men·tá·rjo] *adj.* supplementary, extra.

suplemento [su·ple·mén·to] *m.* supplement; supply, supplying.

suplente [su·plén·te] *adj., m. & f.* substitute.

súplica [sú·pli·ka] *f.* entreaty; request; petition; prayer.

suplicante [su·pli·kán·te] *adj.* suppliant, beseeching; *m. & f.* suppliant; petitioner.

suplicar[6] [su·pli·kár] *v.* to beg, entreat, implore; to pray humbly; to appeal, petition.

suplicio [su·plí·sjo] *m.* torture; torment; anguish; execution; instrument of torture; scaffold, gallows.

suplir [su·plír] *v.* to supply; to make up for; to substitute, take the place of (*temporarily*).

suponer[40] [su·po·nér] *v. irr.* to suppose; to assume; to be important.

suposición [su·po·si·sjón] *f.* supposition; assumption.

supremacía [su·pre·má·sía] *f.* supremacy.

supremo [su·pré·mo] *adj.* supreme; final, last.

supresión [su·pre·sjón] *f.* suppression; omission; elimination.

suprimir [su·pri·mír] *v.* to suppress; to abolish; to omit.

supuesto [su·pwés·to] *p.p. of* **suponer** supposed, assumed; — **que** supposing that; since; **por** — of course; naturally; *m.* supposition; assumption.

supuración [su·pu·ra·sjón] *f.* formation or discharge of pus.

supurar [su·pu·rár] *v.* to fester, form or discharge pus.

sur [sur] *m.* south; south wind; **sureste** [su·rés·te] *m.* southeast; **suroeste** [su·ro·és·te] *m.* southwest.

suramericano [su·ra·me·ri·ká·no] = **sudamericano.**

surcar[6] [sur·kár] *v.* to furrow; to plow; to plow through; to cut through.

surco [súr·ko] *m.* furrow; rut; groove; wrinkle.

sureño [su·ré·ño] *adj.* southern, from the south; *m.* a southerner.

surgir[11] [sur·xír] *v.* to surge, rise; to spurt; spout; to appear.

surrealismo [su·rre·a·líz·mo] *m.* surrealism.

surtido [sur·tí·ḍo] *m.* stock, supply, assortment; *adj.* assorted.

surtidor [sur·ti·ḍór] *m.* supplier; spout, jet.

surtir [sur·tír] *v.* to provide, supply, stock (with); to spout, spurt; — **efecto** to produce the desired result; — **un pedido** to fill an order.

susceptible [su·sep·tí·ḅle] *adj.* susceptible; sensitive; touchy.

suscitar [su·si·tár] *v.* to raise, stir up, provoke.

suscribir[52] [sus·kri·ḅír] *v.* to subscribe; to endorse; to agree (to); **-se** to subscribe.

suscripción [sus·krip·sjón] *f.* subscription.

suscrito [sus·kri·to] *p.p. of* **suscribir.**

suscritor [sus·kri·tór] *m.* subscriber.

susodicho [su·so·ḍi·čo] *adj.* aforesaid, above-mentioned.

suspender [sus·pen·dér] *v.* (*colgar*) to suspend; to hang; (*detener*) to stop; to defer; (*no aprobar*) to fail, flunk; to dismiss temporarily; to astonish.

suspensión [sus·pen·sjón] *f.* suspension; postponement, delay; uncertainty; cessation; a system of supporting devices (*automobile*).

suspenso [sus·pén·so] *adj.* suspended; hanging; pending; perplexed, astonished; **en** — in suspense; *m.* failure (*in an examination*).

suspicaz [sus·pi·kás] *adj.* suspicious.

suspirar [sus·pi·rár] *v.* to sigh; to sigh (for), long (for).

suspiro [sus·pí·ro] *m.* sight; brief pause (*in music*).

sustancia [sus·tán·sja] *f.* substance; essence; *Andes* broth.

sustancial [sus·tan·sjál] *adj.* substantial; nourishing.

sustancioso [sus·tan·sjó·so] *adj.* substantial; nourishing.

sustantivo [sus·tan·tí·ḅo] *m.* noun; *adj.* substantive; real; independent.

sustentar [sus·ten·tár] *v.* to sustain; to support; to feed, nourish; to maintain; uphold.

sustento [sus·tén·to] *m.* sustenance; food; support.

sustitución [sus·ti·tu·sjón] *f.* substitution.

sustituible [sus·ti·twí·ḅle] *adj.* replaceable.

sustituir[32] [sus·ti·twír] *v. irr.* to substitute.

sustituto [sus·ti·tú·to] *m.* substitute.

susto [sús·to] *m.* scare, fright.

sustracción [sus·trak·sjón] *f.* subtraction.

sustraer[46] [sus·tra·ér] *v. irr.* to subtract; to remove, withdraw; **-se a** to evade, avoid, slip away from.

susurrar [su·su·rrár] *v.* to whisper; to murmur; to rustle; **-se** to be whispered or rumored about.

susurro [su·sú·rro] *m.* whisper; murmur; rustle.

sutil [su·til] *adj.* subtle; keen; clever; crafty; thin, fine, delicate.

sutileza [su·ti·lé·sa], **sutilidad** [su·ti·li·ḍáḍ] *f.* subtlety; keenness, cleverness; cunning; thinness, fineness.

suyo [sú·yo] *adj.* his, of his; her, of hers; your, of yours (*formal*); their, of theirs; *pron.* his, hers, yours (*formal*), theirs; **de** — naturally, by nature; **salirse con la suya** to get one's own way; **hacer de las suyas** to be up to one's tricks; **los -s** his (hers, theirs); his (her, their) own people.

T:t **tabaco** [ta·ḅá·ko] *m.* tobacco; *Carib., Ven., Col.* cigar; snuff; *Col.* blow with the fist; **tabaquería** [ta·ḅa·ke·rí·a] *f.* tobacco store, cigar store.

tábano [tá·ḅa·no] *m.* horsefly, gadfly.

taberna [ta·ḅér·na] *f.* tavern, bar, liquor store.

tabernáculo [ta·ḅer·ná·ku·lo] *m.* tabernacle.

tabique [ta·ḅí·ke] *m.* partition, partition wall.

tabla [tá·ḅla] *f.* board, plank; plate of metal; slab; table, list; strip of ground; *Col.* chocolate tablet; **-s** draw, tie (*in games*); stage boards, the stage; **a raja** — cost what it may; *Am.* in great haste; **hacer** — **rasa de algo** to disregard, omit, or ignore something; *Am.* to clear away all obstacles in the way of something.

tablado [ta·ḅlá·ḍo] *m.* platform, stage; scaffold; floor boards.

tablero [ta·ḅlé·ro] *m.* board; panel; timber, piece of lumber; chessboard, checkerboard; store counter; large work table; gambling table; *Col., Ven., Mex.* blackboard; **poner al** — to risk, endanger; — **de mando** control panel.

tableta [ta·ḅlé·ta] *f.* tablet; small thin board; memorandum pad.

tabletear [ta·ḅle·te·ár] *v.* to rattle; to make a continuous rattling or tapping sound.

tableteo [ta·ḅle·té·o] *m.* rattling sound; tapping.

tablilla [ta·ḅlí·ya] *f.* tablet; slat, small thin board; splint; small bulletin board; **-s** wooden clappers.

tablón [ta·ḅlón] *m.* plank; large, thick board.

taburete [ta·bu·ré·te] *m.* stool; footstool; *Sal.* chair.
tacañería [ta·ka·ñe·rí·a] *f.* stinginess, tightness, miserliness.
tacaño [ta·ka·ño] *adj.* stingy, tight, miserly; sly.
tácito [tá·si·to] *adj.* tacit, implied; silent.
taciturno [ta·si·túr·no] *adj.* taciturn, silent, sullen; sad.
taco [tá·ko] *m.* wad; roll; plug, stopper; billiard cue; bite, snack; swear word; *Mex., C.A.* Mexican folded tortilla sandwich; *Am.* leather legging; *Ch., Andes* short, fat person; *Mex.* heel of a shoe; *Am.* pile, heap; **echar -s** to curse, swear; *Mex.* **darse uno —** to strut, put on airs.
tacón [ta·kón] *m.* heel of a shoe.
taconear [ta·ko·ne·ár] *v.* to click the heels, walk hard on one's heels.
taconeo [ta·ko·né·o] *m.* click, clicking (*of the heels*).
táctica [ták·ti·ka] *f.* tactics.
tacto [ták·to] *m.* tact; touch, sense of touch.
tacha [tá·ča] *f.* flaw, defect, blemish.
tachar [ta·čár] *v.* (*borrar*) to cross out; to scratch out; to blot out; (*culpar*) to blame; to find fault with; to censure.
tachón [ta·čón] *m.* stud; trimming, braid; blot.
tachonar [ta·čo·nár] *v.* to stud, ornament with studs; to adorn with trimming.
tachuela [ta·čwé·la] *f.* tack, small nail; *Am.* metal dipper; *Am.* runt, "shorty".
tafetán [ta·fe·tán] *m.* taffeta; **— inglés** court plaster; **— adhesivo** "Band-Aid".
tahur [ta·úr] *m.* gambler; cardsharp.
taimado [taj·má·ḍo] *adj.* sly, crafty; *Am.* sullen, gloomy, gruff.
taita [táj·ta] = **tatita.** *See* **tata.**
tajada [ta·xá·ḍa] *f.* slice; cut.
tajalápiz [ta·xa·lá·pis] *m.* pencil sharpener.
tajante [ta·xán·te] *adj.* cutting, sharp.
tajar [ta·xár] *v.* to slice; to cut; to sharpen (*a pencil*).
tajo [tá·xo] *m.* cut; gash; cutting edge; sheer cliff; chopping block.
tal [tal] *adj.* such; such a; **— cual** such as; so-so, fair; **— vez** perhaps; **el — Pedro** that fellow Peter; **un — García** a certain García; **— para cual** two of a kind; **un — por cual** a nobody; *adv.* just as, in such a way; **estaba — como le dejé** he was just as I left him; **con — (de) que** provided that; **¿qué —?** how are you?; hello!
talabarte [ta·la·bár·te] *m.* sword belt.
taladrar [ta·la·ḍrár] *v.* to bore, drill; to pierce; to penetrate.
taladro [ta·lá·ḍro] *m.* auger, drill; bore, drill hole; *Am.* mine tunnel.
tálamo [tá·la·mo] *m.* bridal bed or chamber.
talante [ta·lán·te] *m.* disposition; mood; appearance, manner.
talar [ta·lár] *v.* to cut down; *Am.* to prune.
talco [tál·ko] *m.* talc (*a soft mineral*); **— en polvo** talcum powder.
talega [ta·lé·ga] *f.* money bag, sack.
talento [ta·lén·to] *m.* talent; ability, natural gift.
talentoso [ta·len·tó·so] *adj.* talented, gifted.
talio [tá·ljo] *m.* thallium.
talismán [ta·liz·mán] *m.* talisman, charm.
talón [ta·lón] *m.* heel; stub, check, coupon.
talonario [ta·lo·ná·rjo] *m.* stub book; **libro —** stub book.
talonear [ta·lo·ne·ár] *v.* to tap with one's heel; to walk briskly.
taloneo [ta·lo·né·o] *m.* tapping with the heel; loud footsteps.

talla [tá·ya] *f.* (*altura*) stature, height; size; (*labrado*) carving; (*lance entero*) round of a card game; (*rescate*) ransom; *Am.* chat; *Am.* thrashing, beating.
tallar [ta·yár] *v.* to carve; to cut (*stone*); to appraise; to deal (*cards*); *Am.* to court, make love; *Andes, Col.* to bother, disturb.
tallarín [ta·ya·rín] *m.* noodle.
talle [tá·ye] *m.* figure, form; waist; fit (*of a dress*); looks, appearance; *Ven.* bodice.
taller [ta·yér] *m.* workshop; laboratory; studio; factory.
tallo [tá·yo] *m.* stalk; stem; shoot, sprout.
tamal [ta·mál] *m. Mex., C.A.* tamale; *Am.* vile trick, intrigue; *Am.* clumsy bundle.
tamaño [ta·má·ño] *m.* size; *adj.* such a; of the size of; **— disparate** such a (big) mistake; **— como un elefante** big as an elephant; **tamañito** [ta·ma·ñí·to] *adj.* very small; **tamañito así** about this little; **se quedó tamañito** he was (left) astonished, amazed.
tamarindo [ta·ma·rín·do] *m.* tamarind; *Mex.* traffic cop (*because of color of uniform*).
tambalearse [tam·ba·le·ár·se] *v.* to totter, stagger, sway, reel.
también [tam·bjén] *adv.* also, too; likewise.
tambor [tam·bór] *m.* drum; drum-like object; drummer; pair of embroidery hoops; *Mex.* bedspring, spring mattress; **— de freno** brake drum; **tambora** [tam·bó·ra] *f.* bass drum; **tamboril** [tam·bo·ríl] *m.* small drum; **tamborilero** [tam·bo·ri·lé·ro] *m.* drummer.
tamborilear [tam·bo·ri·le·ár] *v.* to drum; to extol.
tamiz [ta·mís] *m.* fine sieve.
tamizar [ta·mi·sár] *v.* to sift; to blend.
tampoco [tam·pó·ko] *conj.* either (*after a negative*); **no lo hizo —** he did not do it either; **ni yo —** nor I either.
tan [tan] *adv.* (*contr. of* **tanto**) so, as; such a.
tanda [tán·da] *f.* turn; round, bout; task; gang, group; shift, relay; *Col., Ven., Mex., Carib.* section of a theatrical performance.
tangente [tan·xén·te] *adj. & f.* tangent; **salirse por la —** to go off at a tangent; to avoid the issue.
tangible [tan·xi·ble] *adj.* tangible.
tango [tán·go] *m.* tango.
tanque [tán·ke] *m.* tank; reservoir; *Col., Ven.* pond; *Mex.* swimming pool.
tantán [tan·tán] *m.* clang; knock! knock!; sound of a bell, drum, etc.
tantear [tan·te·ár] *v.* to probe, test; to sound out, feel out; to estimate, calculate approximately; *Cuba, Ven., Riopl.* to grope, feel one's way; *Am.* to lie in wait; *Mex.* to fool, make a fool of; *Ven., Mex., C.A.* **¡tantee Vd.!** just imagine!
tanteo [tan·té·o] *m.* trial, test; calculation, estimate; score; **al —** by guess; hit or miss.
tanto [tán·to] *adj., pron. & adv.* so much, as much; so; **-s** so many, as many; *m.* certain amount; counter, chip (*to keep score*); **cuarenta y -s** forty odd; **el — por ciento** percentage, rate; **un —** (*or* **algún —**) somewhat; **— como** as well as; as much as; **— ... como** both ... and; **— en la ciudad como en el campo** both in the city and in the country; **entre** (*or* **mientras**) **—** meanwhile; **por lo —** therefore.
tañer [ta·ñér] *v.* to play (*an instrument*); to ring.
tañido [ta·ñí·ḍo] *m.* sound, tune; ring; twang (*of a guitar*).
tapa [tá·pa] *f.* cover; lid; book cover; heel lift.

tapacubos [ta·pa·kú·bos] *m.* hubcap.
tapadera [ta·pa·dé·ra] *f.* cover, lid; one who shields another.
tapar [ta·pár] *v.* to cover; to plug, stop up; to veil; to hide; *Am.* to fill (*a tooth*); *Am.* to crush, crumple; *Am.* to cover with insults; **-se** to cover up; to wrap oneself up.
taparrabo [ta·pa·rrá·bo] *m.* loincloth; trunks.
tapera [ta·pé·ra] *f. Am.* ruins; *Riopl., Andes* abandoned room or house.
tapete [ta·pé·te] *m.* rug; table scarf.
tapia [tá·pja] *f.* abode wall; wall fence.
tapiar [ta·pjár] *v.* to wall up; to block up (*a door or window*).
tapicería [ta·pi·se·rí·a] *f.* tapestry; upholstery; tapestry shop; tapestry making.
tapioca [ta·pjó·ka] *f.* tapioca.
tapiz [ta·pís] *m.* tapestry.
tapizar[9] [ta·pi·sár] *v. irr.* to carpet; to cover.
tapón [ta·pón] *m.* plug, stopper, cork; bottle cap.
taquigrafía [ta·ki·ɡra·fí·a] *f.* shorthand.
taquígrafo [ta·kí·ɡra·fo] *m.* stenographer.
taquilla [ta·kí·ya] *f.* ticket office; box office; file (*for letters, papers, etc.*); *Am.* tavern, liquor store.
tarántula [ta·rán·tu·la] *f.* tarantula.
tararear [ta·ra·re·ár] *v.* to hum.
tarareo [ta·ra·ré·o] *m.* hum, humming.
tarascada [ta·ras·ká·da] *f.* snap, bite; snappy or harsh answer.
tardanza [tar·dán·sa] *f.* delay; slowness.
tardar [tar·dár] *v.* to delay; to be late; to be long (in); to take long (in); **-se** to delay oneself; to be delayed; **a más** — at the very latest.
tarde [tár·de] *f.* afternoon; *adv.* late; **de — en —** from time to time, now and then.
tardío [tar·dí·o] *adj.* late; slow.
tardo [tár·do] *adj.* slow, lazy; tardy, late; stupid, dull; **tardón** [tar·dón] *adj.* very slow; *m.* slowpoke, slow person.
tarea [ta·ré·a] *f.* task, job; anxiety, care.
tarifa [ta·rí·fa] *f.* tariff; list of duties, taxes, or prices; fare.
tarima [ta·rí·ma] *f.* wooden platform; low bench.
tarjeta [tar·xé·ta] *f.* card; **— postal** postcard.
tarro [tá·rro] *m.* earthen jar; glass jar; *Mex.* horn (*of an animal*); *Ch., Cuba, Andes* can; *Andes* top hat.
tarta [tár·ta] *f.* tart.
tartamudear [tar·ta·mu·de·ár] *v.* to stutter, stammer.
tartamudeo [tat·ta·mu·dé·o] *m.* stammer, stammering.
tartamudo [tar·ta·mú·do] *m.* stutterer, stammerer; *adj.* stuttering, stammering.
tártaro [tár·ta·ro] *m.* tartar.
tartera [tar·té·ra] *f.* griddle; baking pan.
tarugo [tar·ú·ɡo] *m.* wooden block; wooden peg; blockhead, dunce; *adj. Andes* mischievous, devilish.
tasa [tá·sa] *f.* measure; standard; rate; appraisal; valuation.
tasación [ta·sa·sjón] *f.* assessment, valuation, appraisal.
tasajo [ta·sá·xo] *m.* piece of jerked beef.
tasar [ta·sár] *v.* to measure; to appraise; to rate.
tata [tá·ta] *f.* daddy, dad; *Mex., Andes* chief (*said by Indians to a superior*); **tatita** [ta·tí·ta] *m.* daddy; *Mex., Andes* dear chief or daddy (*said by Indians*).
tataranieto [ta·ta·ra·njé·to] *m.* great-great-grandson.
tatuar[18] [ta·twár] *v.* to tattoo.
taurino [taw·rí·no] *adj.* related to bullfighting.
tauromaquia [taw·ro·má·kja] *f.* bullfighting.
taxear [tak·se·ár] *v.* to taxi (*said of a plane*).
taxi [ták·si], **taxímetro** [tak·sí·me·tro] *m.* taxi, taxicab.
taxista [tak·sís·ta] *m. & f.* taxi driver.
taxonomía [tak·so·no·mí·a] *f.* taxonomy.
taza [tá·sa] *f.* cup; bowl; basin of a fountain.
tazón [ta·són] *m.* large cup; bowl; basin of a fountain.
té [te] *m.* tea; *f.* T-square, T-shaped ruler.
te [te] *obj. pron.* you (*fam. sing.*); to you; for you; yourself.
teatral [te·a·trál] *adj.* theatrical.
teatro [te·á·tro] *m.* theater; stage; scene, setting; **hacer —** to put on airs, show off.
tecla [té·kla] *f.* key (*of a piano, typewriter, etc.*); **dar uno en la —** to hit the nail on the head, find the right way to do something.
teclado [te·klá·do] *m.* keyboard.
teclear [te·kle·ár] *v.* to finger the keys; to play the piano; to type.
tecleo [te·klé·o] *m.* fingering; movement of the keys (*typewriter, piano*).
técnica [ték·ni·ka] *f.* technique.
técnico [ték·ni·ko] *adj.* technical; *m.* technical expert, technician.
tecnología [tek·no·lo·xí·a] *f.* technology.
tecolote [te·ko·ló·te] *m. Mex.* owl.
techado [te·čá·do] *m.* roof; shed; *p.p. of* **techar**.
techar [te·čár] *v.* to roof.
techo [té·čo] *m.* roof; ceiling.
techumbre [te·čúm·bre] *f.* roof; ceiling.
tedio [te·djo] *m.* tediousness; boredom; bother.
tedioso [te·djó·so] *adj.* tedious, boring, tiresome.
teja [té·xa] *f.* tile; linden tree; *Am.* rear part of a saddle; **de -s abajo** here below, in this world.
tejado [te·xá·do] *m.* roof; shed.
tejamanil [te·xa·ma·níl] *m.* shingle; small thin board.
tejar [te·xár] *m.* tile factory; *v.* to cover with tiles.
tejedor [te·xe·dór] *m.* weaver.
tejer [te·xér] *v.* to weave; to interlace; to braid; to knit.
tejido [te·xí·do] *m.* textile, fabric; texture; weave; weaving; tissue.
tejo [té·xo] *m.* disk; quoit; weight.
tejón [te·xón] *m.* badger; bar of gold.
tela [té·la] *f.* cloth; membrane; web; film (*on the surface of liquids*); **— adhesiva** adhesive tape; **— de cebolla** onion skin; flimsy fabric; *Am.* **— emplástica** court plaster; **— metálica** wire screen; **poner en — de juicio** to call in question.
telar [te·lár] *m.* loom.
telaraña [te·la·rá·ña] *f.* cobweb, spider's web.
teleférico [te·le·fé·ri·ko] *m.* telpher; car suspended on aerial cables.
telefonear [te·le·fo·ne·ár] *v.* to telephone.
telefónico [te·le·fó·ni·ko] *adj.* telephonic, telephone (*used as adj.*); **receptor —** telephone receiver.
teléfono [te·lé·fo·no] *m.* telephone; **telefonista** [te·le·fo·nísta] *m. & f.* telephone operator.
telegrafía [te·le·ɡra·fí·a] *f.* telegraphy.
telegrafiar[17] [te·le·ɡra·fjár] *v.* to telegraph.
telegráfico [te·le·ɡrá·fi·ko] *adj.* telegraphic.
telégrafo [te·lé·ɡra·fo] *m.* telegraph; **— sin hilos** (*or* **— inalámbrico**) wireless telegraph; **telegrafista** [te·le·ɡra·fís·ta] *m. & f.* telegraph operator.

telegrama [te·le·gra·ma] *m.* telegram.
telémetro [te·lé·me·tro] *m.* telemeter; range finder.
teleparía [te·le·pa·tí·a] *f.* telepathy.
telescopio [te·les·kó·pjo] *m.* telescope.
telesquí [te·les·kí] *m.* ski lift.
teletipo [te·le·tí·po] *m.* teletype.
televidente [te·le·bi·dén·te] *m. & f.* televiewer; one who watches television.
televisión [te·le·bi·sjón] *f.* television.
telón [te·lón] *m.* theater curtain; — **de boca** drop curtain; — **de foro** drop scene.
telurio [te·lú·rjo] *m.* tellurium.
tema [té·ma] *m.* theme; subject; *f.* fixed idea, mania.
temático [te·má·ti·ko] *adj.* thematic; persistent.
temblar[1] [tem·blár] *v. irr.* to tremble; to shake; to quiver.
temblón [tem·blón] *adj.* tremulous, trembling, shaking, quivering.
temblor [tem·blór] *m.* tremor, trembling; shiver; quake; — **de tierra** earthquake.
tembloroso [tem·blo·ró·so] *adj.* trembling, shaking.
temer [te·mér] *v.* to fear; to dread; to suspect.
temerario [te·me·rá·rjo] *adj.* rash, reckless.
temeridad [te·me·ri·dád] *f.* temerity, recklessness; folly.
temeroso [te·me·ró·so] *adj.* fearful; suspicious; timid.
temible [te·mí·ble] *adj.* terrible, dreadful.
temor [te·mór] *m.* fear; dread, suspicion.
témpano [tém·pa·no] *m.* thick slice or chunk (*of anything*); kettledrum; drumhead (*parchment stretched over the end of a drum*); — **de hielo** block of ice; iceberg.
temperamento [tem·pe·ra·mén·to] *m.* temperament; climate.
temperatura [tem·pe·ra·tú·ra] *f.* temperature.
tempestad [tem·pes·tád] *f.* tempest, storm.
tempestuoso [tem·pes·twó·so] *adj.* tempestuous, stormy.
templado [tem·plá·do] *p.p. & adj.* (*moderado*) tempered; tuned; moderate; temperate; lukewarm; (*valiente*) brave; *Andes* in love; *Am.* half-drunk; *Am.* hard, severe; **estar mal** — to be in a bad humor.
templanza [tem·plán·sa] *f.* temperance; moderation; mildness.
templar [tem·plár] *v.* to temper; to moderate; to calm; to soften; to tune; **-se** to be tempered, moderate; to control oneself; *Andes* to fall in love; *Col.* to take to one's heels; *Am.* to stuff oneself.
temple [tém·ple] *m.* temper; temperament; valor, courage; harmony (*of musical instruments*); *Am.* sweetheart; **de mal** — in a bad humor.
templo [tém·plo] *m.* temple; church.
temporada [tem·po·rá·da] *f.* period of time, season; — **de ópera** opera season.
temporal [tem·po·rál] *adj.* temporal; secular, worldly; temporary; *m.* weather; storm; spell of rainy weather.
tempranero [tem·pra·né·ro] *adj.* habitually early or ahead of time; **ser** — to be an early riser.
temprano [tem·prá·no] *adj.* early; premature; *adv.* early.
tenacidad [te·na·si·dád] *f.* tenacity; tenaciousness; perseverance.
tenacillas [te·na·sí·yas] *f. pl.* small tongs; pincers, tweezers; sugar tongs; curling iron.
tenaz [te·nás] *adj.* tenacious; firm; strong, resistant; stubborn.

tenazas [te·ná·sas] *f. pl.* pincers; pliers; tongs; forceps (*for pulling teeth*); **tenazuelas** [te·na·swé·las] *f. pl.* tweezers, small pincers.
tendedero [ten·de·dé·ro] *m.* place to hang or spread clothes; clothesline.
tendencia [ten·dén·sja] *f.* tendency, inclination.
tender[1] [ten·dér] *v. irr.* (*extender*) to spread out; to hang to dry; to stretch out; to lay out; (*propender*) to tend, have a tendency, move (*toward*); *Carib., Mex., C.A., Riopl., Andes* to make (*a bed*); **-se** to stretch oneself out; to lay all one's cards on the table; to run at full gallop.
ténder [tén·der] *m.* tender (*of a train*).
tendero [ten·dé·ro] *m.* storekeeper; tentmaker.
tendido [ten·dí·do] *m.* laying; a wash hung up to dry.
tendón [ten·dón] *m.* tendon, sinew.
tenducho [ten·dú·čo] *m.* wretched little shop.
tenebroso [te·ne·bró·so] *adj.* dark, shadowy; gloomy.
tenedor [te·ne·dór] *m.* table fork; holder, possessor, keeper; — **de libros** bookkeeper.
teneduría [te·ne·du·rí·a] *f.* office and position of bookkeeper; — **de libros** bookkeeping.
tener[4,5] [te·nér] *v. irr.* to have; to possess; to hold; — **en mucho** to esteem highly; — **por** to consider, judge; — **que** (+ *inf.*) to have to; — **gana** (*or* — **ganas**) **de** to desire, feel like; — **miedo** (**sueño, frío, hambre,** *etc.*) to be afraid (sleepy, cold, hungry, *etc.*); — **... años** to be ... years old; **-se** to stand firm; to hold on.
tenería [te·ne·rí·a] *f.* tannery.
tenia [té·nja] *f.* tapeworm.
teniente [te·njén·te] *m.* first lieutenant; substitute, deputy.
tenis [té·nis] *m.* tennis.
tenista [te·nís·ta] *m. & f.* tennis player.
tenor [te·nór] *m.* tenor; text, literal meaning; kind, sort, nature.
tensión [ten·sjón] *f.* tension; strain.
tenso [tén·so] *adj.* tense; tight, taut.
tentación [ten·ta·sjón] *f.* temptation.
tentáculo [ten·tá·ku·lo] *m.* tentacle, feeler.
tentador [ten·ta·dór] *adj.* tempting; *m.* tempter; the devil.
tentalear [ten·ta·le·ár] *v.* to grope, feel around; to finger, touch; to fumble (*for something*).
tentar[1] [ten·tár] *v. irr.* to tempt; to touch, feel with the fingers; to grope; to attempt, try; to test; to probe, examine with a probe.
tentativa [ten·ta·tí·ba] *f.* attempt, trial.
tentativo [ten·ta·tí·bo] *adj.* tentative.
tenue [té·nwe] *adj.* delicate, thin; flimsy; worthless.
teñir[5,19] [te·ñír] *v. irr.* to dye; to tinge; to darken (*the color of a painting*).
teologal [te·o·lo·gál], **teológico** *adj.* theological.
teología [te·o·lo·xí·a] *f.* theology.
teólogo [te·ó·lo·go] *m.* theologian.
teoría [te·o·rí·a] *f.* theory.
teórico [te·ó·ri·ko] *adj.* theoretical.
tequila [te·kí·la] *m. Mex.* tequila (*liquor made from the maguey plant*).
terapéutico [te·ra·péw·ti·ko] *adj.* therapeutic.
tercero [ter·sé·ro] *adj.* third; *m.* third person; mediator; go-between; tertiary (*member of the third order of St. Francis*).
terciar [ter·sjár] *v.* (*atravesar*) to sling across one's shoulders; (*dividir*) to divide into three parts; (*intervenir*) to intervene, mediate; to meddle, join (*in*); (*equilibrar*) to balance the load on a pack animal; *Mex., Col.* to load or carry on the

back; *Am.* to adulterate, add water to; *Am.* to mix.

tercio [tér·sjo] *adj.* third; *m.* one third; half of a mule load; military regiment or division; *Col., Carib., Mex.* bale, bundle; **hacer uno mal —** to hinder, interfere; **— de varas** the banderilla part of the bullfight.

terciopelo [ter·sjo·pé·lo] *m.* velvet.

terco [tér·ko] *adj.* obstinate, stubborn; hard; *Am.* harsh, severe.

tergiversar [ter·xi·ƀer·sár] *v.* to distort, twist.

terminación [ter·mi·na·sjón] *f.* termination, end; ending.

terminal [ter·mi·nál] *adj.* terminal, final.

terminante [ter·mi·nán·te] *adj.* closing, ending; decisive, final.

terminar [ter·mi·nár] *v.* to terminate, end; to finish; **-se** to end.

término [tér·mi·no] *m.* end; completion; goal, object; boundary, limit; terminal; term; word, phrase; **en otros -s** in other words; **por — medio** on an average; as a rule; **primer —** foreground.

termo [tér·mo] *m.* thermos bottle.

termómetro [ter·mó·me·tro] *m.* thermometer.

termonuclear [ter·mo·nu·kle·ár] *adj.* thermonuclear.

Termos [tér·mos] *f.* Thermos bottle (*trademark*).

termóstato [ter·mós·ta·to] *m.* thermostat.

ternera [ter·né·ra] *f.* calf; veal.

terneza [ter·né·sa] *f.* tenderness; softness; affection; affectionate word; caress.

terno [tér·no] *m.* group or combination of three; suit of clothes; *Carib., Mex.* set of jewels (*earrings, necklace, and brooch*); *Am.* cup and saucer; **echar** (*or* **soltar**) **un —** to utter a bad word; to curse, swear.

ternura [ter·nú·ra] *f.* tenderness.

terquedad [ter·ke·dád] *f.* obstinacy, stubbornness.

terrado [te·rrá·do] *m.* terrace; flat roof.

terramicina [te·rra·mi·sí·na] *f.* Terramycin.

terraplén [te·rra·plén] *m.* railroad embankment.

terrateniente [te·rra·te·njén·te] *m.* & *f.* landholder.

terraza [te·rrá·sa] *f.* terrace, veranda; flat roof.

terremoto [te·rre·mó·to] *m.* earthquake.

terrenal [te·rre·nál] *adj.* earthly, worldly.

terreno [te·rré·no] *m.* land; ground; field; *adj.* earthly, worldly.

terrestre [te·rrés·tre] *adj.* terrestrial; earthly.

terrible [te·rrí·ƀle] *adj.* terrible.

terrífico [te·rrí·fi·ko] *adj.* terrific.

territorial [te·rri·to·rjál] *adj.* territorial.

territorio [te·rri·tó·rjo] *m.* territory.

terrón [te·rrón] *m.* clod; lump (*of sugar*).

terror [te·rrór] *m.* terror.

terrorista [te·rro·rís·ta] *m.* & *f.* terrorist.

terruño [te·rrú·ño] *m.* native soil.

terso [tér·so] *adj.* polished, smooth.

tertulia [ter·tú·lja] *f.* evening party; social gathering; club; conversation; *Ríopl., Cuba, Ven.* theater gallery.

tertuliano [ter·tu·ljá·no], **tertulio** [ter·tú·ljo] *m.* member of a **tertulia**.

tesis [té·sis] *f.* thesis.

tesón [te·són] *m.* grit, endurance, pluck, persistence.

tesonero [te·so·né·ro] *adj. Mex., Cuba, Andes* tenacious, stubborn, persevering, persistent.

tesorería [te·so·re·rí·a] *f.* treasury; **tesorero** [te·so·ré·ro] *m.* treasurer.

tesoro [te·só·ro] *m.* treasure; treasury.

testa [tés·ta] *f.* head; crown of the head; front.

testamento [tes·ta·mén·to] *m.* testament; will.

testarudez [tes·ta·ru·dés] *f.* stubbornness, obstinacy.

testarudo [tes·ta·rú·do] *adj.* stubborn.

testigo [tes·tí·ɡo] *m.* & *f.* witness; *m.* testimony, proof, evidence; **— de cargo** witness for the prosecution; **— de vista** eyewitness.

testimoniar [tes·ti·mo·njár] *v.* to give testimony of; to serve as a witness.

testimonio [tes·ti·mó·njo] *m.* testimony; proof, evidence; **levantar falso —** to bear false witness.

testuz [tes·tús] *m.* nape; crown of the head (*of certain animals*).

teta [té·ta] *f.* teat, nipple; breast; udder.

tétano [té·ta·no] *m.* tetanus.

tetera [te·té·ra] *f.* teapot; teakettle; *Mex., Cuba, Col.* **tetero** [te·té·ro] nursing bottle.

tétrico [té·tri·ko] *adj.* sad, melancholy, gloomy.

teutónico [tew·tó·ni·ko] *adj.* teutonic.

textil [tes·tíl] *adj.* textile.

texto [tés·to] *m.* text; quotation; textbook.

tez [tes] *f.* complexion, skin.

ti [ti] *pers. pron.* (*used after prep.*) you; yourself (*fam. sing.*).

tía [tí·a] *f.* aunt; older woman; *Ven.* **— rica** pawnshop; **no hay tu —** there is no use or hope; there is no way out of it; **quedarse una para —** to remain an old maid.

tibio [tí·ƀjo] *adj.* tepid, lukewarm; indifferent; *Am.* annoyed, angry.

tiburón [ti·ƀu·rón] *m.* shark.

tico [tí·ko] *adj.* & *m. Am.* Costa Rican (*humorous nickname*).

tictac [tik·ták] *m.* tick-tock.

tiempo [tjém·po] *m.* time; weather; tense; **a —** in time, on time; **a su —** in due time, at the proper time; **a un —** at one and the same time; **andando el —** in time, as time goes on.

tienda [tjén·da] *f.* store; tent; **— de campaña** camping tent, army tent.

tienta [tjén·ta] *f.* probe (*surgical instrument*); **a -s** gropingly, feeling one's way; **andar a -s** to grope, feel one's way.

tiento [tjén·to] *m.* touch; tact; blind man's stick; steady hand; blow; tentacle, feeler (*of an insect*); *Andes, Ríopl.* saddle strap, leather strap, thong; *Am.* snack; *Am.* swallow of liquor; **dar un —** to make a trial or attempt; **hacer algo con mucho —** to do something with great care or caution; **perder el —** to lose one's skill; *Andes* **tener a uno a los -s** to keep someone within sight; *Ven.* **tener la vida en un —** to be in great danger.

tierno [tjér·no] *adj.* tender; soft; young; recent, new; sensitive; affectionate; *Am.* green, unripe.

tierra [tjé·rra] *f.* earth; land; ground; soil; native land; **— adentro** inland; **— firme** mainland; solid ground; **dar en — con alguien** to overthrow someone; **echar por —** to knock down; to demolish; **tomar —** to land.

tieso [tjé·so] *adj.* stiff, rigid; stuck-up; firm; stubborn.

tiesto [tjés·to] *m. Spain* flowerpot; broken piece of earthenware; *Ch.* pot.

tiesura [tje·sú·ra] *f.* stiffness.

tifo [tí·fo] *m.* typhus; **tifoidea** [ti·foj·dé·a] *f.* typhoid fever.

tifón [ti·fón] *m.* typhoon; waterspout.

tifus [tí·fus] *m.* typhus.

tigre [tí·ɡre] *m.* tiger.

tijera [ti·xé·ra] *f.* (*usually* **tijeras**) scissors; sawhorse; **silla de —** folding chair; **tener buena —** (*or* **tener buenas -s**) to have a sharp tongue;

TE

to be a gossip.

tijeretada [ti·xe·re·tá·d̬a] *f.*, **tijeretazo** [ti·xe·re·tá·so] *m.* snip, cut, clip (*with the scissors*).

tijeretear [ti·xe·re·te·ár] *v.* to snip, cut, clip (*with scissors*); to criticize others, gossip.

tila [tí·la] *f.* linden; linden blossom tea.

tildar [til·dár] *v.* to accent (*a word*); to put a tilde over the **n**; to stigmatize.

tilde [tíl·de] *f.* tilde (*mark over an* **n**); blemish; jot, bit, speck; *Col.* accent mark.

timbrar [tim·brár] *v.* to stamp, mark with a seal.

timbrazo [tim·brá·so] *m.* ring of an electric bell.

timbre [tím·bre] *m.* revenue stamp; seal; crest (*on a coat of arms*); call bell; timbre (*quality of tone, tone color*); merit, fame; glorious deed; *Am.* postage stamp.

timidez [ti·mi·d̬és] *f.* timidity; shyness.

tímido [tí·mi·d̬o] *adj.* timid; shy.

timón [ti·món] *m.* helm; rudder; beam of a plow; *Col.* steering wheel.

timonear [ti·mo·ne·ár] *v.* to steer (*a ship*).

timorato [ti·mo·rá·to] *adj.* timorous, timid.

tímpano [tím·pa·no] *m.* eardrum; kettledrum.

tina [tí·na] *f.* large earthen jar; vat, tank, tub; bathtub.

tinaco [ti·ná·ko] *m.* tank, vat, tub.

tinaja [ti·ná·xa] *f.* large earthen jar.

tinglado [tiŋ·glá·d̬o] *m.* shed.

tinieblas [ti·njé·b̬las] *f. pl.* darkness; obscurity; ignorance, confusion; Tenebrae (*Holy Week religious service*).

tino [tí·no] *m.* acumen, keen insight, good judgment; tact; accurate aim; good sense of touch; tank, vat.

tinta [tín·ta] *f.* ink; dye; tint, hue; **-s** paints; **— simpática** invisible ink; **saber de buena —** to know on good authority.

tinte [tín·te] *m.* tint, hue; tinge; color; dye; dyeing.

tinterillo [tin·te·rí·yo] *m.* shyster. *See* **picapleitos**.

tintero [tin·té·ro] *m.* inkwell, inkstand; ink roller (*printing*); *Am.* writing materials, desk set.

tintinear [tin·ti·ne·ár] *v.* to tinkle.

tintineo [tin·ti·né·o] *m.* tinkle, tinkling.

tinto [tín·to] *adj.* tinged; red (*wine*); *Col.* black coffee; *Am.* dark-red; *p.p. irr. of* **teñir**.

tintorería [tin·to·re·rí·a] *f.* cleaner's and dyer's shop.

tintorero [tin·to·ré·ro] *m.* dyer.

tintura [tin·tú·ra] *f.* tincture; tint; color; dye.

tinturar [tin·tu·rár] *v.* to tincture; to tinge; to dye.

tiñoso [ti·ñó·so] *adj.* scabby, mangy; stingy.

tío [tí·o] *m.* uncle; old man; good old man; fellow, guy; *Ríopl., Mex., Ven., Andes* **el cuento del —** deceitful story (*told to extract money*).

tiovivo [ti·o·b̬í·b̬o] *m.* merry-go-round.

típico [tí·pi·ko] *adj.* typical; *Am.* corrected (*edition*).

tiple [tí·ple] *m. & f.* high soprano singer; *m.* treble; soprano voice; treble guitar.

tipo [tí·po] *m.* type; class; model, standard; fellow, guy; *Am.* rate of interest; *Am.* **— de cambio** rate or exchange; **buen —** good-looking fellow.

tipografía [ti·po·ǥra·fí·a] *f.* typography, printing; press, printing shop.

tira [tí·ra] *f.* strip; stripe; *Mex.* **estar hecho -s** to be in rags; *Ven.* **sacar a uno las -s** to tan one's hide, beat one to pieces.

tirabuzón [ti·ra·b̬u·són] *m.* corkscrew.

tirada [ti·rá·d̬a] *f.* throw; issue, edition, printing; *Am.* tirade, long speech; *Am.* sly trick; *Am.* dash

(*on horseback*); **de una —** all at once, at one fell swoop.

tirador [ti·ra·d̬ór] *m.* shooter; thrower; slingshot; bell cord; handle; printer; *Am.* leather belt with pockets; **— de goma** slingshot.

tiranía [ti·ra·ní·a] *f.* tyranny.

tiránico [ti·rá·ni·ko] *adj.* tyrannical.

tirano [ti·rá·no] *adj.* tyrannical; *m.* tyrant.

tirante [ti·rán·te] *adj.* pulling; stretched, taut; strained; *m.* trace (*of a harness*); brace; **-s** suspenders; supporters (*for stockings*).

tirantez [ti·ran·tés] *f.* tension, tightness; strain; pull.

tirar [ti·rár] *v.* (*lanzar*) to throw; to throw away; to shoot, fire; (*imprimir*) to draw; to print; (*atraer*) to pull; to attract; *Am.* to cart; **— a** to tend toward; to resemble; to aim at; **— de** to pull, tug; **— bien a la espada** to handle a sword well; **ir tirando** to get along; **a todo** (or **a más**) **—** at the most; *Am.* **al —** haphazardly; **-se** to throw oneself; to lie down; *Mex., C.A., Col., Ven., Riopl., Andes* **tirársela de** to boast of.

tiritar [ti·ri·tár] *v.* to shiver.

tiro [tí·ro] *m.* (*disparo*) throw; shot; (*pieza*) piece of artillery; (*alcance*) range of a gun; shooting range; (*carga*) charge of a gun; team (*of horses*); chimney draft; mine shaft; *Am.* issue, printing; *Am.* cartage, transport; **-s** *Am.* suspenders; **— al blanco** target practice; *Ch., Andes* **al —** at once; *Ven.* **de a** (or **de al**) **—** all at once; completely; **caballo de —** draft horse; **ni a -s** absolutely not (*not even if you shoot me*).

tirón [ti·rón] *m.* jerk, sudden pull; **de un —** all at once, with one big pull.

tironear [ti·ro·ne·ár] *v. C.A., Mex., Riopl.* to pull, jerk; *Col.* to attract.

tirotear [ti·ro·te·ár] *v.* to shoot around; to shoot at random; **-se** to exchange shots.

tiroteo [ti·ro·té·o] *m.* shooting; exchange of shots; skirmish.

tirria [tí·rrja] *f.* aversion, grudge; **tenerle — a una persona** to have a strong dislike for someone; to hold a grudge against someone.

tísico [tí·si·ko] *adj.* tubercular, consumptive.

tisis [tí·sis] *f.* tuberculosis, consumption.

titanio [ti·tá·njo] *m.* titanium.

títere [tí·te·re] *m.* puppet; ridiculous little fellow; **-s** puppet show.

titilación [ti·ti·la·sjón] *f.* flicker; twinkle; **titileo** *m.* flickering; twinkling; glimmer.

titilar [ti·ti·lár] *v.* to flicker; to twinkle.

titubear [ti·tu·b̬e·ár] *v.* to hesitate; to totter, stagger; to grope; to stutter, stammer.

titubeo [ti·tu·b̬é·o] *m.* hesitation, wavering.

titular [ti·tu·lár] *v.* to entitle; to name; **-se** to be called or named; to call oneself; to receive a title; *adj.* titular, in name only; *m.* officer; holder of a title.

título [tí·tu·lo] *m.* (*letrero*) title; heading; sign; inscription; (*derecho*) claim, legal right; (*grado*) degree, diploma; credential; titled person; merit; bond, certificate; **a — de** under the pretext of; in the capacity of.

tiza [tí·sa] *f.* chalk.

tiznado [tiz·ná·d̬o] *adj.* sooty, covered with soot; smutty; dirty; *Ven.* drunk; *p.p. of* **tiznar**.

tiznar [tiz·nár] *v.* to smudge, smut; to smear with soot.

tizne [tíz·ne] *m.* soot; smut; **tiznón** [tiz·nón] *m.* smudge.

tizón [ti·són] *m.* firebrand (*piece of burning wood*);

rust, blight (*on plants*); stain (*on one's honor*).
toalla [to·á·ya] *f.* towel.
tobillo [to·bí·yo] *m.* ankle.
tocadiscos [to·ka·dís·kos] *m.* record player;
phonograph.
tocado [to·ká·do] *m.* headdress; hairdo, coiffure;
adj. "touched", half-crazy; *p.p. of* **tocar**.
tocador [to·ka·dór] *m.* dressing table; boudoir,
dressing room; dressing case; player (*of a
musical instrument*).
tocar[6] [to·kár] *v.* to touch; to play (*an instrument*);
to toll, ring; to knock, rap; — **en** to stop over
in; **-le a uno** to fall to one's lot; to be one's
share; to be one's turn; to concern one; **-se** to
fix one's hair; to become "touched", go slightly
crazy.
tocayo [to·ká·yo] *m.* namesake; one who has the
same name.
tocino [to·sí·no] *m.* bacon; salt pork; lard.
tocón [to·kón] *m.* stub, stump (*of a tree, arm or
leg*).
todavía [to·da·bí·a] *adv.* still; yet; even.
todo [tó·do] *adj.* all, whole; every, each; —
hombre every man; **-s los días** every day; **a** —
correr at full or top speed; *m.* whole; all;
everything; **-s** everybody; **ante** — first of all;
así y — in spite of that; **con** — in spite of that;
del — wholly.
todopoderoso [to·do·po·de·ró·so] *adj.* almighty.
toga [tó·ga] *f.* gown, robe (*worn by a judge,
professor, etc.*); Roman toga.
toldería [tol·de·rí·a] *f.* *Riopl.* Indian camp, Indian
village.
toldo [tól·do] *m.* awning; pomp, vanity; *Riopl.*
Indian hut.
tolerancia [to·le·rán·sja] *f.* tolerance, toleration;
tolerante [to·le·rán·te] *adj.* tolerant.
tolerar [to·le·rár] *v.* to tolerate; to allow; to
overlook, let pass.
tolete [to·lé·te] *m.* *Col., Mex., Cuba* stick, club,
cudgel; *Am.* raft.
toma [tó·ma] *f.* taking; seizure, capture; dose; tap
(*of a water main*); *Am.* irrigation ditch; — **de
corriente** plug, electric outlet.
tomar [to·már] *v.* (*asir*) to take; to grasp, catch;
to capture; (*beber*) to drink; — **a pechos** to take
to heart, take seriously; **-lo a mal** to take it
amiss; — **el pelo a** to make fun of, make a fool
of; — **por la derecha** to turn to the right;
-se con to quarrel with.
tomate [to·má·te] *m.* tomato.
tómbola [tóm·bo·la] *f.* raffle for charity.
tomillo [to·mí·yo] *m.* thyme.
tomo [tó·mo] *m.* tome, volume; *Am.* heavy person;
Am. dull, silent person; *Am.* **buen** — a heavy
drinker; **de** — **y lomo** bulky; important.
ton [ton]: **sin** — **ni son** without rhyme or reason.
tonada [to·ná·da] *f.* tune, song; *Andes* singsong;
Andes, Mex., Carib., Riopl. local accent;
tonadilla [to·na·dí·ya] *f.* little tune; short
popular song.
tonel [to·nél] *m.* keg, cask, barrel.
tonelada [to·ne·lá·da] *f.* ton.
tonelaje [to·ne·lá·xe] *m.* tonnage.
tónico [tó·ni·ko] *adj. & m.* tonic.
tono [tó·no] *m.* tone; tune; key, pitch; accent;
manner; vigor, strength; **de buen** — of good
taste, stylish; **subirse de** — to put on airs.
tonsura [ton·sú·ra] *f.* shearing.
tontera [ton·té·ra] = **tontería**.
tontería [ton·te·rí·a] *f.* foolishness; stupidity.

tonto [tón·to] *adj.* foolish; stupid; **a tontas y a
locas** recklessly, without thought; *m.* fool;
dunce; *Col., Ch.* a game of cards.
topar [to·pár] *v.* to collide with, run into, bump
into; to encounter; to find; to run across; to
butt; *Am.* to gamble; *Col.* to fight with the fists;
Carib., Mex., Riopl., Andes, Col. to meet, greet.
tope [tó·pe] *m.* butt, bump, collision; encounter;
bumper; dead-end; **hasta el** — up to the top;
estar hasta los -s to be filled up.
topetada [to·pe·tá·da] *f.*, **topetazo** [to·pe·tá·so] *m.*
butt; bump, bump on the head; **topetón**
[to·pe·tón] *m.* hard bump, collision; butt.
topetear [to·pe·te·ár] *v.* to butt; to bump.
tópico [tó·pi·ko] *m.* topic, subject.
topo [tó·po] *m.* mole (*small animal*); dunce;
awkward person.
topografía [to·po·gra·fí·a] *f.* topography.
toque [tó·ke] *m.* touch; ringing; beat (*of a drum*);
tap, sound (*of a trumpet, clarinet, etc.*); assay;
piedra de — touchstone; **¡allí está el** —**!** there
is the difficulty!; there is the real test!
toquilla [to·kí·ya] *f.* triangular handkerchief;
ribbon; hatband.
tórax [tó·raks] *m.* thorax.
torbellino [tor·be·yí·no] *m.* whirlwind; rush, bustle,
confusion.
torcedura [tor·se·dú·ra] *f.* twist; sprain, strain.
torcer[2, 10] [tor·sér] *v. irr.* to twist; to turn; to
bend; to sprain; to distort; **-se** to become
twisted, bent, or sprained; to get crooked; to go
astray; to turn sour (*said of wine*); *Am.* to get
offended, angry.
torcido [tor·sí·do] *p.p. & adj.* twisted, turned,
bent; crooked; angry, resentful; *Am.*
unfortunate, unlucky; **estar** — **con** to be on
unfriendly terms with; *m.* twisted roll of candied
fruit; coarse silk twist; *Mex., Carib.* gesture or
look of disdain; *Andes* lasso made of twisted
leather.
tordillo [tor·dí·yo] *adj.* greyish, dapple-grey.
tordo [tór·do] *adj.* dapple-grey; *m.* thrush;
dapple-grey horse.
torear [to·re·ár] *v.* to perform in a bullfight; to
incite, provoke (*a bull*); to tease.
torero [to·ré·ro] *m.* bullfighter; *adj.* relating to
bullfighting
tormenta [tor·mén·ta] *f.* storm, tempest;
misfortune.
tormento [tor·mén·to] *m.* torment; torture; rack
(*instrument of torture*); anguish; pain.
tornar [tor·nár] *v.* to return; to turn; to change,
alter; — **a hacerlo** to do it again.
tornasol [tor·na·sól] *m.* sunflower.
tornadizo [tor·na·dí·so] *adj.* changeable; fickle.
tornasolado [tor·na·so·lá·do] *adj.* iridescent,
rainbow-colored; changeable (*silk*).
tornear [tor·ne·ár] *v.* to turn in a lathe; to do lathe
work; to fight in a tournament.
torneo [tor·né·o] *m.* tournament.
tornillo [tor·ní·yo] *m.* screw; clamp, vise; **faltarle a
uno un** — to have little sense, "have a screw
loose".
torniquete [tor·ni·ké·te] *m.* turnbuckle; tourniquet.
torno [tór·no] *m.* turn; lathe; turnstile; revolving
server; winch or windlass (*machine for lifting or
pulling, turned by a crank*); — **de hilar** spinning
wheel; **en** — around.
toro [tó·ro] *m.* bull; *Mex. Col.* difficult question;
-s bullfight; *Am.* **estar en las astas del** — to be in
a predicament.

TI

toronja [to·rón·xa] *f*. grapefruit.
torpe [tór·pe] *adj*. stupid, dull; clumsy; slow; lewd.
torpedo [tor·pé·ḍo] *m*. torpedo; **torpedero** [tor·pe·ḍé·ro] *m*. torpedo boat.
torpeza [tor·pé·sa] *f*. stupidity, dullness; clumsiness; slowness; moral turpitude, lewdness.
torre [tó·rre] *f*. tower; turret; castle (*in chess*).
torrencial [to·rren·sjál] *adj*. torrential.
torrente [to·rrén·te] *m*. torrent; flood; — **de voz** powerful voice.
torreón [to·rre·ón] *m*. large tower (*of a fortress, castle, etc.*).
tórrido [tó·rri·ḍo] *adj*. torrid.
torsión [tor·sjón] *f*. twist; sprain.
torta [tór·ta] *f*. torte, round cake; round loaf.
tortilla [tor·tí·ya] *f*. omelet; *Mex., C.A.* tortilla (*flat, thin cornmeal cake*).
tórtola [tór·to·la] *f*. turtledove.
tortuga [tor·tú·ga] *f*. tortoise; turtle.
tortuoso [tor·twó·so] *adj*. tortuous, twisting, winding; sly.
tortura [tor·tú·ra] *f*. torture; grief, affliction.
torturar [tor·tu·rár] *v*. to torture.
torvo [tór·ḅo] *adj*. grim, stern, severe.
tos [tos] *f*. cough; — **ferina** whooping cough.
tosco [tós·ko] *adj*. coarse, harsh, rough.
toser [to·sér] *v*. to cough; *Am.* to brag, boast.
tosquedad [tos·ke·ḍáḍ] *f*. coarseness, crudeness, roughness; rudeness.
tostada [tos·tá·ḍa] *f*. toast, toasted bread; *Am.* boring visit or conversation; *Ven.* toasted **tortilla; dar** (*or* **pegar**) **una** — **a uno** to play a mean trick on someone; *Am.* to make someone very angry.
tostado [tos·tá·ḍo] *p.p.* & *adj*. toasted; roasted; tanned; *Am.* worn out, tired out; *m*. toasting; *Am.* roasted corn.
tostador [tos·ta·ḍór] *m*. toaster.
tostar[2] [tos·tár] *v. irr*. to toast; to tan; to overheat; to roast (*coffee*).
tostón [tos·tón] *m*. toast dipped in oil; small roasted pig; *Mex., C.A.* coin worth half a Mexican peso.
total [to·tál] *adj*. & *m*. total.
totalidad [to·ta·li·ḍáḍ] *f*. entirety, whole.
totalitario [to·ta·li·tá·rjo] *adj*. totalitarian.
totuma [to·tú·ma] *f*. calabash.
tóxico [tók·si·ko] *adj*. toxic.
toxina [tok·si·na] *f*. toxin (*poison produced within animals and plants*).
toza [tó·sa] *f*. wooden block; stump; log; piece of bark.
traba [trá·ḅa] *f*. bond, tie; binding or locking device; fastener, fetter, shackle; hindrance, obstacle
trabado [tra·ḅá·ḍo] *adj. Col., Ríopl., Mex.* tongue-tied; *p.p. of* **trabar.**
trabajador [tra·ḅa·xa·ḍor] *adj*. industrious; *m*. worker, laborer.
trabajar [tra·ḅa·xár] *v*. to work; to labor; to strive.
trabajo [tra·ḅá·xo] *m*. work; labor; difficulty, obstacle; trouble; hardship.
trabajoso [tra·ḅa·xó·so] *adj*. laborious, difficult; troublesome; *Am.* unobliging; *Am.* demanding.
trabalenguas [tra·ḅa·lén·gwas] *m*. tongue twister.
trabar [tra·ḅár] *v*. to join, fasten; to clasp; to shackle; to brace; to impede; — **amistad con alguien** to become friends with someone; — **batalla** to join in battle; — **conversación** to be engaged in conversation; to engage in conversation; **-se** *Ríopl., Mex., Ven.* to stammer;

-se de palabras to get into an argument.
tracción [trak·sjón] *f*. traction.
tractor [trak·tór] *m*. tractor.
tradición [tra·ḍi·sjón] *f*. tradition.
tradicional [tra·ḍi·sjo·nál] *adj*. traditional.
traducción [tra·ḍuk·sjón] *f*. translation.
traducir[25] [tra·ḍu·sír] *v. irr*. to translate; to interpret.
traductor [tra·ḍuk·tór] *m*. translator.
traer[46] [tra·ér] *v. irr*. to bring; to carry; to lead, conduct; to have; to bring about; to wear; — **a uno inquieto** to keep one disturbed; — **a uno a mal** — to mistreat someone; to bother someone; **-se bien** to dress well; to carry oneself well.
trafagar[7] [tra·fa·gár] *v*. to traffic, trade; to roam about; to bustle, hustle; to toil.
tráfago [trá·fa·go] *m*. trade, commerce; bustle, hustle; toil.
traficante [tra·fi·kán·te] *m*. trader; dealer; tradesman.
traficar[6] [tra·fi·kár] *v*. to traffic, trade; *Ven.* to pass or move back and forth (*as traffic*). *See* **transitar.**
tráfico [trá·fi·ko] *m*. traffic; trade, commerce.
tragaluz [tra·ga·lús] *f*. skylight.
tragar[7] [tra·gár] *v*. to swallow; to gulp; to engulf, swallow up.
tragedia [tra·xé·dja] *f*. tragedy.
trágico [trá·xi·ko] *adj*. tragic.
trago [trá·go] *m*. swallow, gulp; misfortune; *Am.* brandy, hard liquor; **a -s** slowly, by degrees; **echar un** — to take a drink; **tragón** *m*. glutton; *adj*. gluttonous.
traición [traj·sjón] *f*. treason; treachery; **a** — treacherously; deceitfully.
traicionar [traj·sjo·nár] *v*. to betray.
traicionero [traj·sjo·né·ro] *adj*. treacherous; deceitful; *m*. traitor.
traído [tra·í·ḍo] *adj*. used, old, worn out; **muy** — **y llevado** very worn out; *p.p. of* **traer.**
traidor [traj·ḍór] *adj*. treacherous; *m*. traitor; betrayer.
traje [trá·xe] *m*. dress; suit; gown; — **de etiqueta** (— **de ceremonia**, *or Am.* — **de parada**) formal gown; formal suit; dress uniform; — **de luces** bullfighter's costume; *Col., C.A., Mex., Ríopl.* — **sastre** woman's tailor-made suit.
trajeado [tra·xe·á·ḍo] *p.p.* & *adj*. dressed, clothed.
trajín [tra·xín] *m*. traffic, going and coming; hustle, bustle, commotion.
trajinar [tra·xi·nár] *v*. to carry, cart back and forth; to go back and forth; to bustle, hustle.
trama [trá·ma] *f*. plot; scheme; conspiracy; woof (*horizontal threads of a fabric*).
tramar [tra·már] *v*. to weave; to plot; to scheme.
tramitar [tra·mi·tár] *v*. to transact; to take legal steps; to negotiate.
trámite [trá·mi·te] *m*. transaction, procedure, step, formality.
tramo [trá·mo] *m*. stretch, lap, span; short distance; regular interval; flight of stairs.
tramoya [tra·mó·ya] *f*. stage devices and machinery.
trampa [trám·pa] *f*. trap; snare; hatch, trap door; hinged section of a counter; spring door; fraud; trick.
trampear [tram·pe·ár] *v*. to trick, cheat, swindle.
trampista [tram·pís·ta] *m*. & *f*. cheat, crook, swindler.
trampolín [tram·po·lín] *m*. springboard.
tramposo [tram·pó·so] *adj*. deceitful, tricky; *m*.

swindler, cheat.

tranca [tráŋ·ka] *f.* crossbar, bolt; pole, prop; club, stick; *Ven., Ríopl.* rustic gate; *Ríopl.* fence with gates; *Mex., Ven.* **saltar las -s** to jump over the fence; to lose one's patience, rebel, get angry; *Ch., Ríopl., Andes, Mex.* **tener una —** to be drunk.

trance [trán·se] *m.* critical moment; dangerous situation; **el último —** the last moment of life; **a todo —** at any cost, cost what it may.

tranco [tráŋ·ko] *m.* stride, long step; threshold; **a -s** hurriedly; **en dos -s** in a jiffy; *Ríopl.* **al —** striding, with long steps.

tranquear [traŋ·ke·ár] *v.* to stride along.

tranquera [traŋ·ké·ra] *f.* stockade, wooden fence; *Ríopl., Cuba, Ven.* large gate (*made with trancas*).

tranquilidad [traŋ·ki·li·ḍáḍ] *f.* tranquility, peacefulness.

tranquilizar[9] [traŋ·ki·li·sár] *v.* to quiet, calm down; to pacify; **-se** to become tranquil, calm down.

tranquilo [traŋ·kí·lo] *adj.* tranquil, peaceful.

transacción [tran·sak·sjón] *f.* transaction, negotiation; compromise.

transar [tran·sár] *v. Am.* to compromise, yield, give in.

transatlántico [tran·sa·tlán·ti·ko] *adj.* transatlantic; *m.* transatlantic steamer.

transbordar [trans·ḅor·ḍár] = **trasbordar.**

transbordo [trans·ḅór·ḍo] = **trasbordo.**

transcendencia [trans·sen·dén·sja] *f.* consequence, importance; penetration.

transcendental [tran·sen·den·tál] *adj.* consequential, important, far-reaching.

transcribir [trans·kri·ḅír] *v.* to transcribe.

transcurrir [trans·ku·rrír] *v.* to pass elapse.

transcurso [trans·kúr·so] *m.* passing, lapse (*of time*).

transeúnte [tran·se·ún·te] *m.* passer-by; pedestrian; transient; *adj.* transient.

transferencia [trans·fe·rén·sja] *f.* transference, transfer.

transferible [trans·fe·rí·ḅle] *f.* transference, transfer.

transferible [trans·fe·rí·ḅle] *adj.* transferable.

transferir[3] [trans·fe·rír] *v. irr.* to transfer.

transformación [trans·for·ma·sjón] *f.* transformation.

transformador [trans·for·ma·ḍór] *m.* transformer.

transformar [trans·for·már] *v.* to transform.

transfusión [trans·fu·sjón] *f.* transfusion.

transgredir[51] [trans·ǥre·ḍír] *v.* to transgress.

transgresión [trans·ǥre·sjón] *f.* transgression.

transgresor [trans·ǥre·sór] *m.* transgressor. offender.

transición [tran·si·sjón] *f.* transition.

transigente [tran·si·xén·te] *adj.* compromising, yielding, pliable.

transigir[11] [tran·si·xír] *v.* to compromise, yield, make concessions; to settle by compromise.

transistor [tran·sis·tór] *m.* transistor.

transitable [tran·si·tá·ḅle] *adj.* passable (*road*).

transitar [tran·si·tár] *v.* to pass or move back and forth (*as traffic*).

tránsito [trán·si·to] *m.* transit; traffic; passing; passage; transition; **de —** on the way, in transit, passing through.

transitorio [tran·si·tó·rjo] *adj.* transitory.

transmisión [trans·mi·sjón] *f.* transmission; **automática** automatic transmission.

transmisor [trans·mi·sór] *m.* transmitter; *adj.* transmitting.

transmitir [trans·mi·tír] *v.* to transmit.

transparencia [trans·pa·rén·sja] *f.* transparency.

transparente [trans·pa·rén·te] *adj.* transparent; lucid, clear; *m.* window shade; stained-glass window.

transpirar [trans·pi·rár] *v.* to transpire; to leak out.

transponer[40] [trans·po·nér] *v. irr.* to transpose; to transfer; to transplant; to go beyond, go over to the other side; **-se** to hide from view, go behind; to set, go below the horizon.

transportación [trans·por·ta·sjón] *f.* transportation, transport.

transportar [trans·por·tár] *v.* to transport; to transpose (*music*); **-se** to be transported, carried away by strong feeling; to be in ecstasy.

transporte [trans·pór·te] *m.* transport; transportation; transport vessel; ecstasy; **— de locura** fit of madness.

transpuesto [trans·pwés·to] *p.p. of* **transponer.**

transversal [trans·ḅer·sál] *adj.* transversal, transverse; **sección —** cross section.

transverso [trans·ḅér·so] *adj.* transverse, cross.

tranvía [tram·bí·a] *m.* streetcar; streetcar track.

trapacear [tra·pa·se·ár] *v.* to swindle, cheat; to racketeer.

trapacería [tra·pa·se·rí·a] *f.* racket, fraud, swindle.

trapacero [tra·pa·sé·ro] *m.* racketeer; cheat, swindler; *adj.* cheating, deceiving.

trapacista [tra·pa·sís·ta] *m. & f.* racketeer; swindler, cheat.

trapeador [tra·pe·a·ḍór] *m. Am.* mopper; *Andes, Ven., Col., C.A., Mex., Cuba* mop.

trapear [tra·pe·ár] *v. Am.* to mop; *Am.* to beat up, give (*someone*) a licking.

trapecio [tra·pé·sjo] *m.* trapeze.

trapiche [tra·pí·če] *m.* sugar mill; press (*for extracting juices*); *Andes* grinding machine (*for pulverizing minerals*).

trapisonda [tra·pi·són·da] *f.* escapade, prank; brawl; noisy spree.

trapo [trá·po] *m.* rag; *C.A., Ven., Ur.* cloth; **-s** clothes; **a todo —** at full sail; speedily; **poner a uno como un —** to make one feel like a rag; **sacarle a uno los -s al sol** to exhibit somebody's dirty linen; **soltar el —** to burst out laughing or crying.

traposo [tra·pó·so] *adj. Am.* ragged, tattered, in rags.

tráquea [trá·ke·a] *f.* trachea, windpipe.

traquetear [tra·ke·te·ár] *v.* to rattle; to shake; to jolt; to crack, crackle.

traqueteo [tra·ke·té·o] *m.* rattling; shaking; jolting; cracking, crackling; *Ríopl., Col., Ven., C.A., Mex. Carib., Andes* uproar, din; *Am.* noisy. disorderly traffic.

tras [tras] *prep.* after; in search of; behind, in back of; **— de** behind, after; besides, in addition to; *interj.* ¡ **—** ! bang!

trasbordar [traz·ḅor·ḍár] *v.* to transfer.

trasbordo [traz·ḅór·ḍo] *m.* transfer.

trascendencia [tra·sen·dén·sja] = **transcendencia.**

trascendental [tra·sen·den·tál] = **transcendental.**

trasegar[1, 7] [tra·se·ǥár] *v. irr.* to upset, overturn; to change from one place to another; to pour from one container to another.

trasero [tra·sé·ro] *adj.* rear, hind, back; *m.* rump.

trasladar [traz·la·ḍár] *v.* to move, remove; to transfer; to postpone; to translate; to transcribe, copy.

traslado [traz·lá·ḍo] *m.* transfer; transcript, written copy.

traslucirse[13] [traz·lu·sír·se] *v. irr.* to be translucent;

TO

to be transparent, clear, evident.

trasnochar [traz·no·čár] *v.* to sit up all night; to stay awake all night; to spend the night out.

traspalar [tras·pa·lár] *v.* to shovel.

traspapelar [tras·pa·pe·lár] *v.* to mislay, misplace (*a paper, letter, document, etc.*); **-se** to become mislaid among other papers.

traspasar [tras·pa·sár] *v.* to pass over, cross over; to go beyond; to pass through; to pierce; to transfer (*property*); to trespass.

traspaso [tras·pá·so] *m.* transfer; transgression, trespass.

traspié [tras·pjé] *m.* stumble, slip; **dar un** — to stumble or trip.

trasplantar [tras·plan·tár] *v.* to transplant.

trasponer[40] [tras·po·nér] = **transponer.**

trasquila [tras·kí·la], **trasquiladura** [tras·ki·la·ḍú·ra] *f.* shearing, clip, clipping; bad haircut.

trasquilar [tras·ki·lár] *v.* to shear; to clip; to crop; to cut badly (*hair*).

trastazo [tras·tá·so] *m.* thump, blow.

traste [trás·te] *m.* fret, stop (*of a guitar*); *C.A.* utensil, implement; **dar al** — **con** to destroy, ruin.

trasto [trás·to] *m.* household utensil; piece of junk; rubbish, trash; **-s** utensils; implements; **-s de pescar** fishing tackle.

trastornar [tras·tor·nár] *v.* to overturn; to upset; to disturb.

trastorno [tras·tór·no] *m.* upset; disorder; disturbance.

trastrocar[2, 6] [tras·tro·kár] *v. irr.* to invert, change; to upset.

trasudar [tra·su·ḍár] *v.* to perspire, sweat slightly.

trasudor [tra·su·ḍór] *m.* slight perspiration or sweat.

tratable [tra·tá·ḅle] *adj.* friendly, sociable; manageable.

tratado [tra·tá·ḍo] *m.* treaty; treatise.

tratamiento [tra·ta·mjén·to] *m.* treatment; title of courtesy; form of address.

tratante [tra·tán·te] *m. & f.* dealer, tradesman, trader.

tratar [tra·tár] *v.* to treat; to handle; to discuss; to have social relations with; — **con** to have dealings with; — **de** to try to; to treat of, deal with; **-le a uno de** to address someone as; to treat someone as; — **en** to deal in; **-se bien** to treat oneself well; to behave well; **-se de** to be a question of; **no se trata de eso** that isn't the question, that isn't the point.

trato [trá·to] *m.* (*acuerdo*) treatment; deal, pact; trade; (*manera*) manner, behavior; social relations; dealings; *Am.* — **pampa** unfair deal; **¡ — hecho!** it's a deal!; **tener buen** — to be affable, sociable.

traumático [traw·má·ti·ko] *adj.* traumatic.

través [tra·ḅés] *m.* crossbeam; reverse, misfortune; **a** (*or* **al**) — **de** through, across; **de** — across; **dar al** — **con** to ruin, destroy; to squander; **mirar de** — to squint in a sinister manner.

travesaño [tra·ḅe·sá·ño] *m.* crosspiece, crossbar; bolster, long bedpillow; *Ven., Andes* railway tie.

travesear [tra·ḅe·se·ár] *v.* to romp, frisk, frolic; to fool around; to misbehave.

travesía [tra·ḅe·sí·a] *f.* crossing; sea voyage; wind blowing towards a coast; *Am.* wasteland, desert land; *Am.* partition wall or fence.

travesura [tra·ḅe·sú·ra] *f.* mischief; prank; lively wit.

traviesa [tra·ḅjé·sa] *f.* railway tie; rafter, crossbeam;

Col. midyear crop.

travieso [tra·ḅjé·so] *adv.* mischievous; lively; restless; **a campo** · (*or* **a campo traviesa**) cross-country.

trayecto [tra·yék·to] *m.* run, stretch, lap, distance (*traveled over*).

trayectoria [tra·yek·tó·rja] *f.* path (*of a bullet, missile, etc.*).

traza [trá·sa] *f.* (*plan*) plan; design; plot; invention; (*apariencia*) appearance; semblance; aspect; indication, sign; **darse -s** to use one's wits or ingenuity; **tener -s de** to have the appearance or signs of; **tiene** (*or* **lleva**) **-s de no acabar nunca** it looks as if he would never end.

trazado [tra·sá·ḍo] *m.* draft, plan, sketch, outline; drawing; *p.p. & adj.* traced, sketched, outlined.

trazar[9] [tra·sár] *v.* to trace, sketch; to draw, mark out; to plan.

trébol [tré·ḅol] *m.* clover.

trecho [tré·čo] *m.* space, distance; lap (*in a race*); **a -s** by or at intervals; **de** — **en** — at certain points or intervals; from time to time.

tregua [tré·ǵwa] *f.* truce; rest, respite.

tremedal [tre·me·ḍál] *m.* quagmire, bog.

tremendo [tre·mén·do] *adj.* tremendous, huge; terrible.

trementina [tra·men·tí·na] *f.* turpentine.

tremolar [tre·mo·lár] *v.* to flutter, wave (*as a flag*).

trémolo [tré·mo·lo] *m.* tremolo (*of the voice*), quaver.

trémulo [tré·mu·lo] *adj.* tremulous, trembling, quivering; flickering.

tren [tren] *m.* train; *Am.* traffic; — **correo** mail train; — **de aterrizaje** landing gear; *Ven., Carib.* — **de lavado** laundry; *Cuba, Ven.* — **de mudadas** moving company; — **de recreo** excursion train; — **mixto** freight and passenger train.

trenza [trén·sa] *f.* tress; braid; *Mex., Cuba, Ven.* string (*of garlic, onions, etc.*); **trencilla** *f.* braid.

trenzar[9] [tren·sár] *v.* to braid; **-se** to braid one's hair; *Riopl., Andes, Col.* to fight hand to hand.

trepador [tre·pa·ḍór] *adj.* climbing.

trepar [tre·pár] *v.* to climb; to clamber; **-se** to climb; to clamber; to perch.

trepidación [tre·pi·ḍa·sjón] *f.* jar, vibration; trembling, shaking.

trepidar [tre·pi·ḍár] *v.* to shake, vibrate, tremble, jar.

treta [tré·ta] *f.* trick, wile; **malas -s** bad tricks, bad habits.

triangular [trjaŋ·gu·lár] *adj.* triangular.

triángulo [trján·gu·lo] *m.* triangle.

tribu [trí·ḅu] *f.* tribe.

tribulación [tri·ḅu·la·sjón] *f.* tribulation, trouble.

tribuna [tri·ḅú·na] *f.* rostrum (*speaker's platform*).

tribunal [tri·ḅu·nál] *m.* tribunal; court of justice; body of judges.

tributar [tri·ḅu·tár] *v.* to pay tribute, pay homage.

tributario [tri·ḅu·tá·rjo] *adj. & m.* tributary.

tributo [tri·ḅú·to] *m.* tribute; contribution, tax.

triciclo [tri·sí·klo] *m.* tricycle.

trifulca [tri·fúl·ka] *f.* fight, quarrel, wrangle, row.

trigo [trí·go] *m.* wheat.

trigueño [tri·ǵé·ño] *adj.* swarthy; brunet; dark.

trilogía [tri·lo·xi·a] *f.* trilogy.

trillado [tri·yá·ḍo] *p.p.* beaten; *adj.* trite, hackneyed, commonplace; **camino** — beaten path.

trilladora [tri·ya·ḍó·ra] *f.* threshing machine.

trillar [tri·yár] *v.* to thresh; to beat, mistreat; *Cuba* to cut a path.

trimestre [tri·més·tre] *m.* quarter, period of three months; quarterly payment, income, or salary; **trimestral** [tri·mes·trál] *adj.* quarterly.

trinar [tri·nár] *v.* to trill (*in singing*); to warble; to quaver (*siad of the voice*); to get furious.

trinchante [trin·čán·te] *m.* carving fork; carving knife; carver.

trinchar [trin·čár] *v.* to carve (*meat*).

trinche [trín·če] *m. Col., Ven., C.A., Mex.* fork; *Am.* carving table; *Am.* **plato** — carving platter.

trinchera [trin·čé·ra] *f.* trench; ditch; *C.A., Ven., Andes* stockade, fence; *Am.* curved knife.

trinchero [trin·čé·ro] *m.* carving table; **plato** — carving platter.

trineo [tri·né·a] *m.* sleigh; sled.

trino [trí·no] *m.* trill (*in singing*).

tripa [trí·pa] *f.* intestine, bowel; paunch, belly; **-s** entrails, insides.

triple [trí·ple] *adj. & m.* triple.

triplicar[6] [tri·pli·kár] *v.* to triplicate, triple, treble.

tripode [trí·po·de] *m.* tripod.

tripulación [tri·pu·la·sjón] *f.* crew, ship's company.

tripular [tri·pu·lár] *v.* to man (*a ship*).

trique [trí·ke] *m.* crack, snap; *Mex.* utensil, trinket; *Col.* clever trick in a game; *Am.* drink made from barley; **-s** *Mex.* poor household utensils, goods, etc.

triquinosis [tri·ki·nó·sis] *f.* trichinosis.

triscar[6] [tris·kár] *v.* to romp, frisk, frolic; to stamp or shuffle the feet; *Am.* to tease, make fun of.

triste [trís·te] *adj.* sad; sorrowful; *Mex.* bashful, backward; *m. Ríopl.* melancholy love song.

tristeza [tris·té·sa] *f.* sadness; sorrow; *Am.* tick fever.

tristón [tris·tón] *adj.* wistful, quite sad, melancholy.

triunfal [trjun·fál] *adj.* triumphal.

triunfante [trjun·fán·te] *adj.* triumphant.

triunfar [trjun·fár] *v.* to triumph; to trump (*at cards*).

triunfo [trjún·fo] *m.* triumph; trump card; trophy.

trivial [tri·bjál] *adj.* trivial, commonplace, trite.

triza [trí·sa] *f.* shred, fragment, small piece; cord, rope (*for sails*); **hacer -s** to tear into shreds; to tear to pieces.

trocar[2, 6] [tro·kár] *v. irr.* to change; to barter, exchange; to do one thing instead of another; **-se** to change; to be transformed; to exchange.

trocha [tró·ča] *f.* path, trail; *Ríopl.* gauge (*of a railway*); *Col.* trot; *Am.* slice or serving of meat.

trofeo [tro·fé·o] *m.* trophy; booty, spoils.

troj [tro], **troje** [tró·xe] *m.* barn, granary.

trole [tró·le] *m.* trolley.

trolebús [tro·le·βús] *m.* trolleybus.

tromba [tróm·ba] *f.* waterspout.

trombón [trom·bón] *m.* trombone.

trompa [tróm·pa] *f.* trumpet; trunk of an elephant; large spinning top; *Am.* snout; *Col.* cowcatcher (*of a locomotive*).

trompada [trom·pa·ḍa] *f.* blow with the fist; bump.

trompeta [trom·pé·ta] *f.* trumpet; *m.* trumpeter; useless individual; *Andes* drunk, drunkard; *Andes* bold, shameless fellow.

trompetear [trom·pe·te·ár] *v.* to trumpet, blow the trumpet.

trompo [tróm·po] *m.* spinning top; stupid fellow, dunce.

tronada [tro·na·ḍa] *f.* thunderstorm.

tronar[2] [tro·nár] *v. irr.* to thunder; to explode, burst; *Mex., C.A.* to execute by shooting; — **los dedos** to snap one's fingers; **por lo que pueda** —

just in case.

tronco [tróŋ·ko] *m.* tree trunk; log; stem; trunk (*of the human body*); team (*of horses*).

tronchar [tron·čár] *v.* to bend or break (*a stalk or trunk*); to chop off; to break off; **-se** to break off or get bent (*said of a stalk or trunk*); *Col.* to get twisted or bent.

tronera [tro·né·ra] *f.* opening; porthole (*through which to shoot*); small, narrow window; pocket of a billiard table; *m.* madcap, reckless fellow.

tronido [tro·ní·ḍo] *m.* thunder; detonation; sharp, sudden sound.

trono [tró·no] *m.* throne.

tropa [tró·pa] *f.* troop; crowd; *Ríopl.* herd of cattle, drove of horses (*often* **tropilla**).

tropel [tro·pél] *m.* throng; bustle, rush; jumble, confusion.

tropezar[1, 9] [tro·pe·sár] *v. irr.* to stumble; to blunder; — **con** to meet, come across, encounter.

tropezón [tro·pe·són] *m.* stumbling; stumble; slip; **a -es** falteringly, stumbling along clumsily; **darse un** — to stumble, trip.

tropical [tro·pi·kál] *adj.* tropical.

trópico [tró·pi·ko] *m.* tropic.

tropiezo [tro·pjé·so] *m.* stumble; stumbling block; slip, fault; dispute.

tropilla [tro·pí·ya] *f.* small troop; *Am.* drove of horses guided by the **madrina**; *Mex.* pack of dogs; *Am.* group of spare saddle horses.

tropillero [tro·pi·yé·ro] *m. Am.* horse wrangler, herdsman.

trotar [tro·tár] *v.* to trot; to hurry.

trote [tró·te] *m.* trot; **al** — quickly.

trovador [tro·βa·ḍór] *m.* troubadour, minstrel.

troza [tró·sa] *f.* log.

trozar[9] [tro·sár] *v.* to cut off, break off (*a piece*); to break or cut into pieces.

trozo [tro·so] *m.* piece, bit, fragment; passage, selection.

truco [trú·ko] *m.* clever trick; pocketing of a ball (*in the game of pool*); *Am.* blow with the fist; *Andes, Ríopl.* a card game; **-s** game of pool (*game similar to billiards*).

truculencia [tru·ku·lén·sja] *f.* cruelty, ferocity, ruthlessness.

truculento [tru·ku·lén·to] *adj.* cruel, fierce, ruthless.

trucha [trú·ča] *f.* trout; *Am.* vendor's portable stand.

trueno [trwé·no] *m.* thunder; explosion, report of a gun; wild youth, troublemaker; *Am.* firecracker, rocket.

trueque [trwé·ke], **trueco** [trwé·ko] *m.* exchange; barter; *Col., Ven., Andes* change, small money; **a** (*or* **en**) — **de** in exchange for.

truhán [tru·án] *m.* scoundrel; swindler; cheat; buffoon, jester.

truncar[6] [truŋ·kár] *v. irr.* to truncate.

tu [tu] *adj.* thy; your (*fam. sing.*).

tú [tu] *pers. pron.* thou; you (*fam. sing.*).

tualet [twa·lét] = **lavabo.**

tuba [tú·βa] *f.* tuba (*instrument*).

tuberculosis [tu·βer·ku·ló·sis] *f.* tuberculosis; **tuberculoso** [tu·βer·ku·ló·so] *adj.* tuberculous, tubercular.

tubería [tu·βe·rí·a] *f.* tubing, piping; pipe line.

tubo [tú·βo] *m.* tube; pipe; lamp chimney; — **de ensayo** test tube; — **de escape** tail pipe.

tuerca [twér·ka] *f.* nut (*of a screw*); **llave de -s** wrench.

tuerto [twér·to] *adj.* one-eyed; blind in one eye; *m.*

TR

wrong, injustice; **a — o a derecho** (*or* **a tuertas o a derechas**) rightly or wrongly; thoughtlessly.

tuétano [twé·ta·no] *m.* marrow; pith; innermost part; **mojado hasta los -s** soaked through and through.

tufo [tú·fo] *m.* vapor, fume; disagreeable odor; airs, conceit; **tufillo** [tu·fí·yo] *m.* whiff, pungent odor.

tul [tul] *m.* tulle (*a thin, fine net for veils*); **tul** [tul], **tule** [tú·le] *m. Mex.* a kind of reed or bulrush (*used in the manufacture of seats and backs of chairs*).

tulipán [tu·li·pán] *m.* tulip; *Mex.* hibiscus.

tullido [tu·yí·đo] *p.p.* crippled; paralyzed; numb.

tullirse[20] [tu·yír·se] *v. irr.* to become crippled; to become numb or paralyzed.

tumba [túm·ba] *f.* tomb; grave; *Col., Cuba, Mex.* felling of timber; *Ven.* forest clearing.

tumbar [tum·bár] *v.* to knock down; *Col., Mex., Cuba* to fell timber; **-se** to lie down.

tumbo [túm·bo] *m.* tumble; somersault; **dar -s** to jump, bump along.

tumor [tu·mór] *m.* tumor; **tumorcillo** [tu·mor·sí·yo] *m.* boil; small tumor.

tumulto [tu·múl·to] *m.* tumult, uproar; mob, throng.

tumultuoso [tu·mul·twó·so] *adj.* tumultuous.

tuna [tú·na] *f.* prickly pear; *Spain* singing group.

tunante [tu·nán·te] *m. & f.* rascal, rogue, scamp; loafer; *Andes, Ch., C.A.* libertine, licentious or lewd person.

tunco [tún·ko] *m. Sal.,* pig.

tunda [tún·da] *f.* whipping, thrashing; shearing (*the nap of cloth*).

tundir [tun·dír] *v.* to lash, beat, whip; to shear (*the nap of cloth*).

túnel [tú·nel] *m.* tunnel.

túnica [tú·ni·ka] *f.* tunic; gown, robe.

tungsteno [tuns·té·no] *m.* tungsten.

tupido [tu·pí·đo] *adj.* dense; compact, thick; blocked, obstructed.

tupir [tu·pír] *v.* to press, pack, squeeze together; to stop up, clog; **-se** to get stopped up; to stuff oneself; to become dense (*as a forest*); *Am.* to get astonished or confused.

turba [túr·ba] *f.* mob, throng.

turbación [tur·ba·sjón] *f.* disturbance, confusion; embarrassment.

turbamulta [tur·ba·múl·ta] *f.* throng, mob, crowd.

turbar [tur·bár] *v.* to perturb; to disturb; to trouble; **-se** to get disturbed, confused, embarrassed.

turbina [tur·bí·na] *f.* turbine.

turbio [túr·bjo] *adj.* muddy; muddled, confused.

turbión [tur·bjón] *m.* thunderstorm; heavy shower.

turbogenerador [tur·bo·xe·ne·ra·dór] *m.* turbogenerator.

turbopropulsor [tur·bo·pro·pul·sór] *m.* turboprop.

turborreactor [tur·bo·rre·ak·tór] *m.* turbojet.

turbulento [tur·bu·lén·to] *adj.* turbulent; restless; disorderly.

turco [túr·ko] *adj.* Turkish; *m.* Turk; Turkish, Turkish language; *Am.* peddler.

turismo [tu·ríz·mo] *m.* tourist travel; touring, sightseeing; **oficina de —** travel bureau; **turista** [tu·rís·ta] *m. & f.* tourist; **turístico** [tu·rís·ti·ko] *adj.* tourist; related to tourism.

tunar [tur·nár] *v.* to alternate; **-se** to alternate; to take turns.

turno [túr·no] *m.* turn, alternate order.

turquesa [tur·ké·sa] *f.* turquoise.

turrón [tu·rrón] *m.* nougat, nut confection; almond

cake; *Mex.* **romper el —** to decide to use the **tú** form of address (*as a mark of close friendship*).

tusa [tú·sa] *f. Am.* corn, corncob; *Cuba, Mex.* corn husk; *Am.* corn silk, tassel of an ear of corn.

tusar [tu·sár] *v. Cuba, Mex., Ríopl., Andes* to shear; *Ríopl.* to crop, cut badly (*hair*).

tutear [tu·te·ár] *v.* to address familiarly (*using the* **tú** *form*).

tutela [tu·té·la] *f.* guardianship; guidance, protection.

tutelar [tu·te·lár] *v.* to guide, coach, direct; *adj.* guiding, guardian (*used as adj.*).

tutor [tu·tór] *m.* tutor; guardian.

tuyo [tú·yo] *poss. adj.* your, of yours (*fam. sing.*); *poss. pron.* yours.

U : u

u [u] *conj.* (*before words beginning with* **o** *or* **ho**) or.

ubicar[6] [u·bi·kár] *v.* to be located; **-se** *Am.* to situate.

ubre [ú·bre] *f.* udder.

ufanarse [u·fa·nár·se] *v.* to glory (in); to be proud (of).

ufano [u·fá·no] *adj.* proud; gay; self-satisfied.

ujier [u·xjér] *m.* usher, doorman.

úlcera [úl·se·ra] *f.* ulcer; sore.

ulterior [ul·te·rjór] *adj.* ulterior; further; later.

ultimar [ul·ti·már] *v.* to put an end to; *Am.* to give the finishing blow, kill.

último [úl·ti·mo] *adj.* last, final; ultimate; latest; **estar en las últimas** to be on one's last legs; to be at the end of one's rope, be at the end of one's resources.

ultrajar [ul·tra·xár] *v.* to outrage, insult; to scorn.

ultraje [ul·trá·xe] *m.* outrage, insult.

ultramar [ul·tra·már] *m.* country or place across the sea; **de —** overseas, from across the sea; **en** (*or* **a**) **—** overseas.

ultramarinos [ul·tra·ma·rí·nos] *m. pl.* delicatessen; imported foods.

ultratumba [ul·tra·túm·ba] *adv.* beyond the grave.

ultravioleta [ul·tra·bjo·lé·ta] *adj.* ultraviolet.

ulular [u·lu·lár] *v.* to howl, shriek, hoot.

umbral [um·brál] *m.* threshold.

umbrío [um·brí·o] *adj.* shady.

un(o) [ú·no] *indef. art.* a, an; **-s** some, a few; **-s cuantos** a few; **uno** *pron. & num.* one.

unánime [u·ná·ni·me] *adj.* unanimous.

unanimidad [u·na·ni·mi·đáđ] *f.* unanimity, complete accord.

unción [un·sjón] *f.* unction (*anointing with oil*); religious fervor; spiritual grace; **Extremaunción** [es·tre·mawn·sjón] Extreme Unction (*the Last Sacrament of the Church*).

uncir[10] [un·sír] *v.* to yoke.

ungir[11] [un·xír] *v.* to anoint; to consecrate.

ungüento [un·gwén·to] *m.* ointment; salve.

único [ú·ni·ko] *adj.* only, sole; unique, singular, rare.

unicornio [u·ni·kór·njo] *m.* unicorn.

unidad [u·ni·đáđ] *f.* unity; unit.

unificar[6] [u·ni·fi·kár] *v.* to unify; to unite.

uniformar [u·ni·for·már] *v.* to standardize; to make uniform; to furnish with uniforms.

uniforme [u·ni·fór·me] *adj. & m.* uniform.

uniformidad [u·ni·for·mi·đáđ] *f.* uniformity.

unilateral [u·ni·la·te·rál] *adj.* unilateral, one-sided.

unión [u·njón] *f.* union.

unir [u·nír] *v.* to unite; to join; to bring together; -se to unite, join together; to wed.
unísono [u·ní·so·no] *adj.* unison.
universal [u·ni·ber·sál] *adj.* universal.
universidad [u·ni·ber·si·dád] *f.* university.
universitario [u·ni·ber·si·tá·rjo] *adj.* pertaining to the university; *m. Am.* a university student.
universo [u·ni·bér·so] *m.* universe.
untar [un·tár] *v.* to anoint; to smear; to oil, grease; to bribe; to corrupt; -se to smear oneself; to get smeared.
unto [ún·to] *m.* grease, fat; ointment.
untuosidad [un·two·si·dád] *f.* greasiness; **untuoso** *adj.* unctuous; oily, greasy.
uña [ú·ña] *f.* fingernail; toenail; claw; hoof; hook (*on a tool*); **a — de caballo** at full gallop, at full speed; **largo de -s** prone to stealing; *Mex., C.A., Ven., Col., Andes* **largas -s** a thief; **vivir de sus -s** to live by stealing; *Mex., C.A., Ven., Col., Andes* **echar la —** to steal; **ser — y carne** to be inseparable friends.
uranio [u·rá·njo] *m.* uranium.
urbanidad [ur·ba·ni·dád] *f.* courtesy, politeness; refinement.
urbanizar[9] [ur·ba·ni·sár] *v. irr.* to urbanize.
urbano [ur·bá·no] *adj.* urban; courteous, polite.
urbe [úr·be] *f.* metropolis, large city.
urdimbre [ur·dím·bre] *f.* warp (*of a fabric*); scheme.
urdir [ur·dír] *v.* to warp (*in weaving*); to plot, scheme; to invent (*a lie, story, etc.*).
uremia [u·ré·mja] *f.* uremia.
uretra [u·ré·tra] *f.* urethra.
urgencia [ur·xén·sja] *f.* urgency; pressing need.
urgente [ur·xén·te] *adj.* urgent, pressing.
urgir[11] [ur·xír] *v.* to urge; to be urgent.
úrico [ú·ri·ko] *adj.* uric.
urna [úr·na] *f.* urn; **— electoral** ballot box.
urraca [u·rrá·ka] *f.* magpie.
usado [u·sá·do] *p.p. & adj.* used; accustomed; worn; threadbare.
usanza [u·sán·sa] *f.* usage, custom, habit.
usar [u·sár] *v.* to use; to wear; to wear out; to be accustomed; -se to be in use, be in vogue.
uso [ú·so] *m.* (*empleo*) use; usage; wear; (*costumbre*) usage; practice; habit; custom; **al — de la época** according to the custom or usage of the period; **estar en buen —** to be in good condition (*said of a thing*).
usted [us·té(d)] *pers. pron.* (*abbreviated as* **Vd., V.,** *or* **Ud.**) you.
usual [u·swál] *adj.* usual; ordinary, customary.
usufructo [u·su·frúk·to] *m.* use, enjoyment; profit.
usufructuar[18] [u·su·fruk·twár] *v.* to enjoy the use of; to make use of.
usura [u·sú·ra] *f.* usury.
usurero [u·su·ré·ro] *m.* usurer, loan shark.
usurpar [u·sur·pár] *v.* to usurp.
utensilio [u·ten·si·ljo] *m.* utensil; implement, tool.
útero [ú·te·ro] *m.* uterus, womb.
útil [ú·til] *adj.* useful; profitable; -es *m. pl.* tools, instruments.
utilidad [u·ti·li·dád] *f.* utility; profit; usefulness.
utilitario [u·ti·li·tá·rjo] *adj.* utilitarian.
utilizar[9] [u·ti·li·zár] *v.* to utilize; to use.
utopía [u·to·pí·a] *f.* utopia.
uvula [u·bu·la] *f.* uvula.
uva [ú·ba] *f.* grape; **— espina** gooseberry; **— pasa** raisin; **estar hecho una —** to be tipsy, drunk.
uvula [u·bu·la] *f.* uvula.
uvular [u·bu·lár] *adj.* uvular.
¡uy! [uj] *interj.* ouch! oh!

V:v

vaca [bá·ka] *f.* cow; **carne de —** beef; **cuero de —** cowhide; *Am.* **hacer —** to play hooky, play truant, cut class; to join in a quick business deal.
vacación [ba·ka·sjón] *f.* vacation (*usually* **vacaciones**).
vacada [ba·ká·da] *f.* herd of cows.
vacancia [ba·kán·sja] *f.* vacancy.
vacante [ba·kán·te] *adj.* vacant, unfilled, unoccupied; *f.* vacancy.
vaciar[17] [ba·sjár] (*dejar vacío*) to empty; to drain; to flow; (*amoldar*) to cast into a mold; (*ahuecar*) to hollow out; -se to spill; to empty; to become empty; to flow (into).
vaciedad [ba·sje·dád] *f.* emptiness; nonsense, silliness.
vacilación [ba·si·la·sjón] *f.* hesitation; wavering; doubt.
vacilante [ba·si·lán·te] *adj.* vacillating, hesitating, wavering; unsteady.
vacilar [ba·si·lár] *v.* to vacillate, waver, hesitate; to sway.
vacío [ba·sí·o] *adj.* empty; vacant; unoccupied; hollow; *m.* void; hollow; vacuum; vacancy; gap, blank.
vacuna [ba·kú·na] *f.* vaccine; vaccination; cowpox (*eruptive disease of the cow*); **vacunación** [ba·ku·na·sjón] *f.* vaccination; **— antipoliomelítica** antipolio inoculation.
vacunar [ba·ku·nár] *v.* to vaccinate.
vadear [ba·de·ár] *v.* to ford; to wade; to avoid (*a difficulty*).
vado [bá·do] *m.* ford; **no hallar —** to find no way out.
vagabundear [ba·ga·bun·de·ár] *v.* to tramp around, wander, rove; to loiter.
vagabundo [ba·ga·bún·do] *adj.* vagabond, wandering; *m.* vagabond, tramp; vagrant; wanderer.
vagar[7] [ba·gár] *v.* to wander, roam; to loiter; to loaf; *m.* leisure; loitering.
vagina [ba·xi·na] *f.* vagina.
vago [bá·go] *adj.* vague; roaming; idle; vagrant; *m.* vagrant, tramp.
vagón [ba·gón] *m.* railway car or coach; **vagoneta** [ba·go·né·ta] *f.* small railway car or tram (*used in mines*); **vagonada** [ba·go·ná·da] *f.* carload.
vaguear [ba·ge·ár] *v.* = **vagar**.
vahído [ba·í·do] *m.* dizziness, dizzy spell.
vaho [bá·o] *m.* vapor, steam, fume, mist; odor.
vaina [báj·na] *f.* sheath, scabbard; case; pod, husk; *Ven., Col., C.A., Mex.* bother, nuisance; *Ven., Col.* luck.
vainilla [baj·ní·ya] *f.* vanilla.
vaivén [baj·bén] *m.* sway; fluctuation, wavering; traffic, coming and going; -es comings and goings; ups and downs; inconstancy.
vajilla [ba·xi·ya] *f.* tableware; set of dishes; **— de plata** silverware; **— de porcelana** chinaware.
vale [bá·le] *m.* bond, promissory note; voucher; adieu, farewell; *m. & f. Col., Ven., Mes.* comrade, pal, chum.
valedero [ba·le·de·ro] *adj.* valid, binding, effective.
valedor [ba·le·dór] *m.* defender, protector; *Am.* pal, comrade.
valenciano [ba·len·sjá·no] *adj.* Valencian, of or from Valencia, Spain; *m.* Valencian.
valentía [ba·len·tí·a] *f.* courage, valor; exploit; boast.
valentón [ba·len·tón] *adj.* blustering, boastful; *m.*

bully, braggart.

valer[47] [ba·lér] *v. irr.* to favor, protect; to cost; to be worth; to be worthy; to be equivalent to; to be valid; to prevail; to be useful; *Spain* ¡**vale!** O.K.; now you're talking; — **la pena** to be worth while; — **por** to be worth; **-se de** to avail oneself of, make use of; **más vale** it is better; ¡**válgame Dios!** heaven help me! good heavens!

valeroso [ba·le·ró·so] *adj.* valiant, brave; valuable.

valía [ba·lí·a] *f.* worth, value; influence.

validez [ba·li·dés] *f.* validity; stability, soundness.

válido [bá·li·do] *adj.* valid.

valiente [ba·ljén·te] *adj.* valiant, brave; powerful; *m.* brave man; bully.

valija [ba·lí·xa] *f.* valise, satchel; mailbag.

valimiento [ba·li·mjén·to] *m.* favor, protection; **gozar de** — to enjoy protection or favor.

valioso [ba·ljó·so] *adj.* valuable; worthy; wealthy.

valor [ba·lór] *m.* value; worth; price; significance; valor, courage; boldness; efficacy, power; **-es** stocks, bonds.

valoración [ba·lo·ra·sjón] *f.* valuation, appraisal.

valorar [ba·lo·rár] *v.* to evaluate, value, appraise.

valorizar[9] [ba·lo·ri·sár] *v. Cuba, Ven., Ríopl., Andes* to value, appraise; *Am.* to realize, convert into money.

vals [bals] *m.* waltz.

valsar [bal·sár] *v.* to waltz.

valuación [ba·lwa·sjón] *f.* valuation, appraisal.

valuar[18] [ba·lwár] *v.* to value, price, appraise; to rate.

válvula [bál·bu·la] *f.* valve.

valla [bá·ya] *f.* stockade, fence; barrier; obstacle; *Cuba, Col.* cockpit (*for cockfights*).

vallado [ba·yá·do] *m.* stockade, fenced-in place; fence.

valle [bá·ye] *m.* valley; vale.

vampiro [bam·pí·ro] *m.* vampire.

vanadio [ba·ná·djo] *m.* vanadium.

vanagloria [ba·na·gló·rja] *f.* vainglory, boastful vanity.

vanagloriarse[17] [ba·na·glo·rjár·se] *v.* to glory, take great pride (in), boast (of).

vanaglorioso [ba·na·glo·rjó·so] *adj.* vain, boastful, conceited.

vándalo [bán·da·lo] *m.* vandal.

vanguardia [ban·gwár·dja] *f.* vanguard.

vanidad [ba·ni·dád] *f.* vanity; conceit; emptiness.

vanidoso [ba·ni·dó·so] *adj.* vain, conceited.

vano [bá·no] *adj.* vain; empty; hollow; *m.* opening in a wall (*for a door or window*).

vapor [ba·pór] *m.* vapor, steam, mist; steamer; steamship.

vaporoso [ba·po·ró·so] *adj.* vaporous, steamy, misty; vaporlike.

vapulear [ba·pu·le·ár] *v.* to beat, whip, thrash.

vapuleo [ba·pu·lé·o] *m.* beating, whipping, thrashing.

vaquería [ba·ke·rí·a] *f.* herd of cows; stable for cows; dairy.

vaquerizo [ba·ke·rí·so] *m.* herdsman; *adj.* pertaining to cows; **vaqueriza** [ba·ke·rí·sa] *f.* stable for cows.

vaquero [ba·ké·ro] *m.* cowherd, herdsman; cowboy; *Cuba* milkman; *adj.* relating to cowherds, cowboys, or cattle.

vaqueta [ba·ké·ta] *f.* sole leather; cowhide; *Mex.* **zurrar a uno la** — to tan someone's hide, beat someone up.

vara [bá·ra] *f.* twig; stick; rod; wand; staff; yard, yardstick; thrust with a picador's lance.

varadero [ba·ra·de·ro] *m.* shipyard.

varar [ba·rár] *v.* to beach (*a boat*); to run aground; to stop, come to a standstill (*said of business*).

varear [ba·re·ár] *v.* to beat; to whip; to sell by the yard; to measure with a **vara**; *Am.* to exercise (*a horse before a race*).

variable [ba·rjá·ble] *adj.* variable, unstable, changeable; *f.* variable.

variación [ba·rja·sjón] *f.* variation.

variado [ba·rjá·do] *p.p. & adj.* varied; variegated.

variar[17] [ba·rjár] *v.* to vary; to change; to shift; to differ.

variedad [ba·rje·dád] *f.* variety; variation, change.

varilla [ba·rí·ya] *f.* small rod; wand; long, flexible twig; rib (*of an umbrella or fan*); corset stay; *Mex.* peddler's wares.

varillero [ba·ri·yé·ro] *m. Mex.* peddler.

vario [bá·rjo] *adj.* various; different; changeable; varied; **-s** various, several.

varón [ba·rón] *m.* male, man; *Am.* long beam, timber.

varonil [ba·ro·níl] *adj.* manly; strong; brave.

vasallo [ba·sá·yo] *adj. & m.* vassal, subject.

vasco [bás·ko], **vascongado** [bas·kon·gá·do] *adj. & m.* Basque.

vascuence [bas·kwén·se] *m.* the Basque language.

vaselina [ba·se·lí·na] *f.* vaseline.

vasija [ba·sí·xa] *f.* vessel, container, receptacle.

vaso [bá·so] *m.* drinking glass; glassful; vase; vessel; hull of a ship; horse's hoof; — **de elección** person chosen by God.

vástago [bás·ta·go] *m.* (*de planta*) shoot, sprout; stem; (*persona*) scion, offspring; *Mex., Col., Ven.* stem, trunk of a banana tree.

vasto [bás·to] *adj.* vast, extensive, large.

vate [bá·te] *m.* bard, poet.

vaticinar [ba·ti·si·nár] *v.* to prophesy, predict, foretell.

vaticinio [ba·ti·sí·njo] *m.* prophecy, prediction.

vecindad [be·sin·dád] *f.* vicinity; neighborhood; neighborliness; **casa de** — tenement.

vecindario [be·sin·dá·rjo] *m.* neighborhood; neighbors; vicinity.

vecino [be·sí·no] *m.* neighbor; resident; citizen; *adj.* neighboring; next, near.

vedar [be·dár] *v.* to prohibit; to impede.

vega [bé·ga] *f.* fertile lowland or plain; *Cuba, Ven.* tobacco plantation.

vegetación [be·xe·ta·sjón] *f.* vegetation.

vegetal [be·xe·tál] *adj.* vegetable; *m.* vegetable, plant.

vegetar [be·xe·tár] *v.* to vegetate.

vegetariano [be·xe·ta·rjá·no] *m.* vegetarian.

vehemente [be·e·mén·te] *adj.* vehement, passionate, impetuous; violent.

vehículo [be·í·ku·lo] *m.* vehicle.

veintena [bejn·té·na] *f.* score, twenty.

vejamen [be·xá·men] annoyance, vexation.

vejar [be·xár] *v.* to annoy; to criticize.

vejestorio [be·xes·tó·rjo] *m.* wrinkled old person.

vejete [be·xé·te] *m.* little old man.

vejez [be·xés] *f.* old age.

vejiga [be·xí·ga] *f.* bladder; blister; smallpox sore; — **de la bilis** (*or* — **de la hiel**) gall baldder.

vela [bé·la] *f.* vigil, watch; night watch; candle; sail; **a toda** — under full sail; at full speed; **en** — on watch, without sleep; **hacerse a la** — to set sail.

velada [be·lá·da] *f.* watch, vigil; evening party; evening function or meeting.

velador [be·la·dór] *m.* night watchman; keeper,

guard; lamp table; bedside table; candlestick;
Ríopl., *Mex.*, *Cuba*, *Col.* lamp shade.
velar [be·lár] *v.* to keep vigil; to stay up at night;
to be vigilant; to watch over; to veil; to cover
hide.
velatorio [be·la·tó·rjo] *m.* wake (*vigil over a
corpse*). See **velorio.**
veleidoso [be·lej·đó·so] *adj.* inconstant, fickle,
changeable.
velero [be·lé·ro] *m.* sailboat; sailmaker;
candlemaker; *adj.* swift-sailing; **buque —**
sailboat.
veleta [be·lé·ta] *f.* weathervane, weathercock; *m.*
& *f.* fickle person.
velis [be·lís] *m. Mex.* valise.
velo [bé·lo] *m.* veil; curtain, covering; **— del
paladar** velum, soft palate.
velocidad [be·lo·si·đáđ] *f.* velocity.
velocímetro [be·lo·sí·me·tro] *m.* speedometer.
velorio [be·ló·rjo] *m. Am.* wake (*vigil over a
corpse*); *Mex.*, *C.A.*, *Ven.*, *Col.*, *Ch.*, *Andes* dull
party.
veloz [be·lós] *adj.* swift, quick, fast.
vello [bé·yo] *m.* hair (*on the body*); down, fuzz;
nap (*of cloth*).
vellón [be·yón] *m.* fleece; tuft of wool; sheepskin
with fleece; silver and copper alloy; an ancient
copper coin.
velloso [be·yó·so] *adj.* hairy; downy, fuzzy.
velludo [be·yú·đo] *adj.* hairy; downy; fuzzy; *m.*
plush; velvet.
vena [bé·na] *f.* vein; lode, vein of metal ore;
mood, disposition; **estar en —** to be in the
mood; to be inspired.
venado [be·ná·đo] *m.* deer; venison, deer meat;
Mex. **pintar —** to play hooky.
vencedor [ben·se·đór] *adj.* conquering, winning,
victorious; *m.* conqueror, winner, victor.
vencer[10] [ben·sér] *v.* to conquer; vanquish; to
defeat; to overcome; to surpass; to win; **-se** to
control oneself; to mature, fall due; **se venció el
plazo** the time limit expired.
vencido [ben·sí·đo] *p.p.* & *adj.* conquered; defeated;
due, fallen due.
vencimiento [ben·si·mjén·to] *m.* conquering, defeat;
maturity (*of a debt*), falling due; expiration
(*of a period of time*).
venda [bén·da] *f.* bandage.
vendaje [ben·dá·xe] *m.* bandage.
vendar [ben·dár] *v.* to bandage; to blindfold.
vendaval [ben·da·bál] *m.* strong wind, gale.
vendedor [ben·de·đór] *m.* vendor, seller, peddler.
vender [ben·dér] *v.* to sell; to betray; **-se** to be
sold; to sell oneself; accept a bribe.
vendimia [ben·dí·mja] *f.* vintage; profit.
venduta [ben·dú·ta] *f. Col.* auction; *Cuba* small
fruit and vegetable store.
veneno [be·né·no] *m.* venom, poison.
venenoso [be·ne·nó·so] *adj.* poisonous.
venerable [be·ne·rá·ble] *adj.* venerable.
veneración [be·ne·ra·sjón] *f.* veneration, reverence.
venerando [be·ne·rán·do] *adj.* venerable, worthy of
respect.
venerar [be·ne·rár] *v.* to venerate, revere; to
worship.
venero [be·né·ro] *m.* water spring; source, origin;
lode, layer, seam (*of mineral*).
venezolano [be·ne·so·lá·no] *adj.* Venezuelan; *m.*
Venezuelan; *Ven.* Venezuelan silver coin.
vengador [beŋ·ga·đór] *adj.* avenging, revenging; *m.*
avenger.

venganza [beŋ·gán·sa] *f.* vengeance, revenge.
vengar[7] [beŋ·gár] to avenge, revenge; **-se de** to
take revenge on.
vengativo [beŋ·ga·tí·ƀo] *adj.* vindictive, revengeful.
venia [bé·nja] *f.* pardon; permission, leave; bow,
nod; *C.A.*, *Ven.*, *Ríopl.* military salute.
venida [be·ní·đa] *f.* arrival; return; river flood,
onrush of water; attack (*in fencing*).
venidero [be·ni·đé·ro] *adj.* coming, future; **en lo —**
in the future; **-s** *m. pl.* successors.
venir[48] [be·nír] *v. irr.* to come; to arrive; to fit;
-le a uno bien (*or* **mal**) to be becoming (*or
unbecoming*); **— a menos** to decline, decay;
— a pelo to come just at the right moment; to
suit perfectly; to be pat, opportune, to the point;
— en to agree to; **— sobre** to fall upon;
¿a qué viene eso? what is the point of that?
-se abajo to fall down; to collapse; to fail.
venoso [be·nó·so] *adj.* veined; venous (*of or
pertaining to the veins*; *with veins*).
venta [bén·ta] *f.* sale; roadside inn; *Ur.* store,
vendor's stand; **— pública** auction.
ventaja [ben·tá·xa] *f.* advantage; gain, profit;
bonus; odds.
ventajoso [ben·ta·xó·so] *adj.* advantageous,
beneficial, profitable; *Mex.* self-seeking,
profiteering.
ventana [ben·tá·na] *f.* window; window shutter;
Col. clearing (*in a forest*); **—** (*or* **ventanilla**
[ben·ta·ní·ya]) **de la nariz** nostril.
ventarrón [ben·ta·rrón] *m.* gale, strong wind.
ventear [ben·te·ár] *v.* (*oler*) to scent, sniff; (*soplar*)
to blow, be windy; (*poner al aire*) to air;
(*indagar*) to nose around; *Ven.* to toss in the
wind; *Am.* to flee; *Am.* to outrun; **-se** to expel
air, break wind; *Col.* to stay outdoors.
ventero [ben·té·ro] *m.* innkeeper.
ventilación [ben·ti·la·sjón] *f.* ventilation.
ventilador [ben·ti·la·đór] *m.* ventilator; fan (*for
ventilation*).
ventilar [ben·ti·lár] *v.* to ventilate; to air.
ventisca [ben·tís·ka] *f.* blizzard, snowstorm;
snowdrift.
ventiscar[6] [ben·tis·kár] *v.* to snow hard and blow
(*as in a blizzard*); to drift (*as snow in a blizzard*).
ventisquero [ben·tis·ké·ro] *m.* blizzard, snowstorm;
glacier; snowdrift; snow-capped mountain peak.
ventolera [ben·to·lé·ra] *f.* gust of wind; pride,
vanity; whim; pin wheel; **darle a uno la — de**
to take the notion to.
ventoso [ben·tó·so] *adj.* windy.
ventura [ben·tú·ra] *f.* happiness; fortune, chance;
risk, danger; **a la —** at random; **buena —**
fortune; **por —** perchance.
venturoso [ben·tu·ró·so] *adj.* fortunate, lucky;
happy.
ver[49] [ver] *v. irr.* to see; to look; to look at; to
look into, examine; **— de** to try to, see to it
that; **a más** (*or* **hasta más** **—** good-bye; **no — la
hora de** to be anxious to; **no tener nada que —
con** not to have anything to do with; **-se** to be
seen; to be; **-se obligado a** to be obliged to, be
forced, to; **a mi modo de —** in my opinion; **de
buen —** good-looking; **ser de —** to be worth
seeing.
vera [bé·ra] *f.* edge; **a la — del camino** at the
edge of the road.
veracidad [ve·ra·si·đáđ] *f.* truthfulness.
veraneante [be·ra·ne·án·te] *m.* & *f.* summer
resorter, vacationist, or tourist.
veranear [be·ra·ne·ár] *v.* to spend the summer.

veraneo [be·ra·né·o] *m.* summering, summer vacation.

veraniego [be·ra·njé·ǥo] *adj.* summer, of summer.

verano [be·rá·no] *m.* summer.

veras [bé·ras] *f. pl.* reality, truth; **de** — in truth; truly; in earnest.

veraz [be·rás] *adj.* truthful.

verbal [ber·ƀál] *adj.* verbal; oral.

verbena [ber·ƀé·na] *f.* verbena (*a plant*); festival or carnival (*on eve of a religious holiday*).

verbigracia [ber·ƀi·ǥra·sja] *adv.* for instance, for example.

verbo [bér·ƀo] *m.* verb; **el Verbo** the Word (*second person of the Trinity*).

verboso [ber·ƀó·so] *adj.* verbose, wordy.

verdad [ber·ɖáɖ] *f.* truth; ¿—? really?; is that so?; isn't that so?; — **de Perogrullo** truism, evident truth; **de** — (*or* **a la** —) in truth, in earnest; **en** — really, truly.

verdadero [ber·ɖa·ɖé·ro] *adj.* real; true; truthful; sincere.

verde [bér·ɖe] *adj.* green; unripe; young; offcolor, indecent; *m.* green; verdure; *Ur., Ven.* country, countryside.

verdear [ber·ɖe·ár] *v.* to grow green; to look green.

verdinegro [ber·ɖi·ne·ǥro] *adj.* dark-green.

verdor [ber·ɖór] *m.* verdure, greenness.

verdoso [ber·ɖó·so] *adj.* greenish.

verdugo [ber·ɖú·ǥo] *m.* executioner; cruel person; torment; rapier (*light sword*); lash, whip; welt; shoot of a tree; **verdugón** [ber·ɖu·ǥón] *m.* large welt.

verdulera [ber·ɖu·lé·ra] *f.* woman vendor of green vegetables; **verdulería** [ber·ɖu·le·rí·a] *f.* green vegetable store or stand.

verdura [ber·ɖú·ra] *f.* verdure; greenness; green vegetables.

vereda [be·ré·ɖa] *f.* path; *Ch., Riopl., Andes* sidewalk; *Col.* small village; *C.R.* bank of a stream.

veredicto [be·re·ɖík·to] *m.* verdict.

vergonzoso [ber·ǥon·só·so] *adj.* shameful. disgraceful; shy, bashful; *m.* species of armadillo.

vergüenza [ber·ǥwén·sa] *f.* shame; disgrace; shyness, bashfulness; **tener** — to have shame; to be ashamed.

vericueto [be·ri·kwé·to] *m.* rugged, wild place (*often rocky*).

verídico [be·rí·ɖi·ko] *adj.* truthful; true.

verificar[6] [be·ri·fi·kár] *v.* to verify; to confirm; to test, check; to carry out, fulfill; **-se** to be verified; to take place.

verijas [be·rí·xas] *f. pl. Riopl., Mex.* groin (*hollow between lower part of abdomen and thigh*); *Am.* flanks of a horse.

verja [bér·xa] *f.* grate, grating.

verónica [be·ró·ni·ka] *f.* veronica; a bullfighting pass executed with the cape held behind the body with both hands.

verruga [be·rrú·ǥa] *f.* wart; nuisance.

versado [ber·sá·ɖo] *adj.* versed, skilled, expert.

versar [ber·sár] *v.* to deal (with), treat (of); **-se en** to become versed in.

versátil [ber·sá·til] *adj.* versatile.

versificar[6] [ber·si·fi·kár] *v. irr.* to versify.

versión [ber·sjón] *f.* version; translation.

verso [bér·so] *m.* verse; meter; — **suelto** (*or* — **libre**) free or blank verse.

vertebrado [ber·te·ƀrá·ɖo] *adj. & m.* vertebrate.

verter[1] [ber·tér] *v. irr.* to pour; to empty; to spill;

to translate; to flow down.

vertical [ber·ti·kál] *adj.* vertical.

vértice [bér·ti·se] *m.* top, apex, summit.

vertiente [ber·tjén·te] *f.* slope; watershed; *adj.* flowing.

vertiginoso [ber·ti·xi·nó·so] *adj.* whirling, dizzy, giddy.

vértigo [bér·ti·ǥo] *m.* dizziness, giddiness; fit of madness.

vesícula [be·sí·ku·la] *f.* gall bladder.

vestíbulo [bes·tí·ƀu·lo] *m.* vestibule; lobby.

vestido [bes·tí·ɖo] *m.* clothing, apparel; dress; garment; suit.

vestidura [bes·ti·ɖú·ra] *f.* vestment; attire, apparel; raiment.

vestigio [bes·tí·xjo] *m.* vestige, sign, trace.

vestir[5] [bes·tír] *v. irr.* (*cubrir*) to dress; to clothe; to put on; to adorn; to cover; (*llevar*) to wear; **-se** to dress, get dressed; to be clothed; to be covered.

vestuario [bes·twá·rjo] *m.* wardrobe, apparel; theatrical costumes; cloakroom; dressing room; vestry (*room for church vestments*).

veta [bé·ta] *f.* vein, seam (*of mineral*); streak, grain (*in wood*); stripe; *Am.* rope.

veteado [be·te·á·ɖo] *adj.* veined; striped; streaked.

veterano [be·te·rá·no] *adj. & m.* veteran.

veterinario [be·te·ri·ná·rjo] *m.* veterinary.

veto [bé·to] *m.* veto.

vetusto [be·tús·to] *adj.* old, ancient.

vez [bes] *f.* time, occasion; turn; **a la** — at the same time; **cada** — **más** more and more; **cada** — **que** whenever; **de** — **en cuando** from time to time; **de una** — all at once; **en** — **de** instead of; **otra** — again; **una que otra** — rarely, once in a while; **tal** — perhaps; **a veces** sometimes; **raras veces** seldom; **hacer las veces de** to take the place of.

vía [bí·a] *f.* way; road; track; railroad track; conduit; **Vía Crucis** the Way of the Cross; **Vía Láctea** the Milky Way.

viaducto [bja·ɖúk·to] *m.* viaduct.

viajante [bja·xán·te] *m.* traveler; — **de comercio** traveling salesman.

viajar [bja·xár] *v.* tò travel.

viaje [bjá·xe] *m.* voyage; trip; travel; — **de ida y vuelta** (*or* — **redondo**) round trip.

viajero [bja·xé·ro] *m.* traveler; *adj.* traveling.

vianda [bján·da] *f.* viands, food; meal.

viandante [bjan·dán·te] *m. & f.* wayfarer, walker, pedestrian; passer-by; vagabond.

viático [bjá·ti·ko] *m.* provisions for a journey; viaticum (*communion given to dying persons*).

víbora [bí·ƀo·ra] *f.* viper.

vibración [bi·ƀra·sjón] *f.* vibration.

vibrante [bi·ƀrán·te] *adj.* vibrant, vibrating.

vibrar [bi·ƀrár] *v.* to vibrate.

vicecónsul [bi·se·kón·sul] *m.* vice consul.

vicepresidente [bi·se·pre·si·dén·te] *m.* vice-president.

viceversa [bi·se·ƀér·sa] *adv.* vice versa, conversely.

viciado [bi·sjá·ɖo] *adj.* contaminated, foul; corrupt; *p.p. of* **viciar.**

viciar [bi·sjár] *v.* to vitiate, corrupt; to adulterate; to falsify; **-se** to become corrupt.

vicio [bí·sjo] *m.* vice; bad habit; fault; craving; **de** — as a habit; **hablar de** — to talk too much; **-s** *Am.* articles and ingredients used for serving **mate.**

vicioso [bi·sjó·so] *adj.* vicious, evil, wicked; having bad habits; licentious; faulty, incorrect (*grammatical construction, reasoning, etc.*).

vicisitud [bi·si·si·túd] *f.* vicissitude; **-es** vicissitudes, ups and downs, changes of fortune or condition.

víctima [bík·ti·ma] *f.* victim.

victoria [bik·tó·rja] *f.* victory, triumph; victoria (*carriage*).

victorioso [bik·to·rjó·so] *adj.* victorious.

vicuña [bi·kú·ña] *f.* vicuña (*an Andean animal allied to the alpaca and llama*); vicuña wool; vicuña cloth.

vid [bid] *f.* vine, grapevine.

vida [bí·da] *f.* life; living; livelihood; — **mía** dearest; **hacer** — to live together; **pasar a mejor** — to die; **tener la** — **en un hilo** to be in great danger.

vidalita [bi·da·lí·ta] *f. Am.* melancholy song of Argentina and Chile.

vidente [bi·dén·te] *m.* seer, prophet; *adj.* seeing.

vidriado [bi·drjá·do] *m.* glaze; glazed earthenware; *p.p. & adj.* glazed.

vidriar[17] [bi·drjár] *v.* to glaze (*earthenware*).

vidriera [bi·drjé·ra] *f.* glass window; glass door; *Am.* show case, show window; — **de colores** stained-glass window.

vidriero [bi·drjé·ro] *m.* glazier (*one who installs windowpanes*); glass blower; glass maker; glass dealer.

vidrio [bi·drjo] *m.* glass; any glass article.

vidrioso [bi·drjó·so] *adj.* glassy; brittle; slippery, icy; touchy; irritable.

viejo [bjé·xo] *adj.* old; ancient; worn-out; *m.* old man; — **verde** old man who boasts of his youth and vigor; "dirty" old man; *Am.* **los -s** the old folks (*applied to one's parents*); **viejota** *f.* old hag.

viento [bjén·to] *m.* wind; scent; **hace** — it is windy; **a los cuatro -s** in all directions; **vientecito** *m.* gentle breeze.

vientre [bjén·tre] *m.* abdomen; belly; bowels; entrails; womb.

viernes [bjér·nes] *m.* Friday.

viga [bí·ga] *f.* beam; rafter.

vigencia [bi·xén·sja] *f.* operation (*of a law*); **entrar en** — to take effect (*said of a law*); **estar en** — to be in force (*said of a law*).

vigente [bi·xén·te] *adj.* effective, in force (*as a law*).

vigía [bi·xí·a] *f.* lookout, watchtower; watch (*act of watching*); reef; *m.* lookout, watchman.

vigilancia [bi·xi·lán·sja] *f.* vigilance.

vigilante [bi·xi·lán·te] *adj.* vigilant, watchful; *m.* watchman.

vigilar [bi·xi·lár] *v.* to keep guard; to watch over.

vigilia [bi·xi·lja] *f.* vigil, watch; wakefulness, sleeplessness; night hours (*spent in study*); eve before certain church festivals; vesper service; **día de** — day of abstinence; **comer de** — to abstain from meat.

vigor [bi·gór] *m.* vigor; **en** — in force (*said of a law*); **entrar en** — to become effective (*as a law, statute, etc.*).

vigorizar[6] [bi·go·ri·sár] *v.* to invigorate, tone up, give vigor to, strengthen.

vigoroso [bi·go·ró·so] *adj.* vigorous.

vihuela [bi·wé·la] *f.* guitar.

vil [bil] *adj.* vile, base, low, mean.

vileza [bi·lé·sa] *f.* villainy; baseness; vile act.

vilipendiar [bi·li·pen·djár] *v.* to revile.

vilo [bí·lo] : **en** — in the air; suspended; undecided; in suspense; **llevar en** — to waft.

villa [bí·ya] *f.* village; villa, country house.

villancico [bi·yan·sí·ko] *n.* carol; Christmas carol.

villanía [bi·ya·ní·a] *f.* villainy; lowliness.

villano [bi·yá·no] *adj.* rustic; uncouth; villainous;

mean, base; *m.* villain; rustic, peasant.

villorrio [bi·yó·rrjo] *m.* small village, hamlet.

vinagre [bi·ná·gre] *m.* vinegar; **vinagrera** [bi·na·gré·ra] *f.* vinegar cruet.

vincular [bin·ku·lár] *v.* to tie, bond, unite; to entail (*limit the inheritance of property*); to found, base (on).

vínculo [bíŋ·ku·lo] *m.* bond, tie, chain; entailed inheritance.

vindicar[6] [bin·di·kár] *v.* to vindicate; to avenge; to defend, assert (*one's rights*); **-se** to avenge oneself; to defend oneself.

vino [bí·no] *m.* wine; — **amontillado** good grade of pale sherry (*originally from Montilla*); — **tinto** dark-red wine; **vinería** [bi·ne·rí·a] *f. Ríopl., Andes* wineshop; **vinero** [bi·né·ro] *adj. Am.* pertaining to wine; **vinoso** [bi·nó·so] *adj.* winy.

viña [bí·ña] *f.* vineyard.

viñedo [bi·ñé·do] *m.* vineyard.

viola [bjó·la] *f.* viola.

violación [bjo·la·sjón] *f.* violation.

violado [bjo·lá·do] *adj.* violet; *m.* violet, violet color; *p.p.* violated.

violar [bjo·lár] *v.* to violate; to rape.

violencia [bjo·lén·sja] *f.* violence.

violentar [bjo·len·tár] *v.* to force; to break into (*a house*); **-se** to force oneself; to get angry.

violento [bjo·lén·to] *adj.* violent; impetuous; forced; strained; unnatural.

violeta [bjo·lé·ta] *f.* violet.

violín [bjo·lín] *m.* violin; *m. & f.* violinist; *Ven.* **estar hecho un** — to be very thin.

violinista [bjo·li·nís·ta] *m. & f.* violinist.

violonchelo [bjo·lon·čé·lo] *m.* violincello, cello.

virada [bi·rá·da] *f.* tack, change of direction, turn.

viraje [bi·rá·xe] *m.* change of direction; turn.

virar [bi·rár] *v.* to turn, turn around, change direction; to tack (*said of a ship*).

virgen [bír·xen] *adj. & f.* virgin.

virginal [bir·xi·nál] *adj.* virginal, virgin, pure.

viril [bi·ril] *adj.* virile, manly.

virilidad [bi·ri·li·dád] *f.* virility, manhood, manly strength, vigor.

virreinal [bi·rrej·nál] *adj.* viceregal.

virreinato [bi·rrej·ná·to] *m.* viceroyalty (*office or jurisdiction of a viceroy*).

virrey [bi·rréj] *m.* viceroy.

virtud [bir·túd] *f.* virtue.

virtuoso [bir·twó·so] *adj.* virtuous; *m.* virtuoso (*person skilled in an art*).

viruela [bir·wé·la] *f.* smallpox; pock (*mark left by smallpox*); **-s locas** (*or* **-s bastardas**) chicken pox.

virtua [bi·rú·ta] *f.* wood shaving.

visado [bi·sá·do] *m.* visa.

visaje [bi·sá·xe] *m.* grimace; wry face; **hacer -s** to make faces.

visar [bi·sár] *v.* to visé; to approve; to O.K.

viscoso [bis·kó·so] *adj.* slimy, sticky.

visera [bi·sé·ra] *f.* visor; eye shade; *Cuba, Mex.* blinder (*on a horse's bridle*).

visible [bi·sí·ble] *adj.* visible; evident; conspicuous, notable.

visigodo [bi·si·gó·do] *adj.* visigothic; *m.* visigoth.

visillo [bi·sí·yo] *m.* window curtain.

visión [bi·sjón] *f.* vision; sight; fantasy; apparition; sight (*ridiculous-looking person or thing*).

visionario [bi·sjo·ná·rjo] *adj. & m.* visionary.

visita [bi·sí·ta] *f.* visit, call; visitor; callers, company; — **de cumplimiento** (*or* — **de cumplido**) formal courtesy call, — **domiciliaria** police inspection of a house; home call (*of a*

VE

social worker, doctor, etc.).

visitación [bi·si·ta·sjón] f. visitation, visit.

visitador [bi·si·ta·đór] m. visitor, caller; inspector.

visitante [bi·si·tán·te] m. & f. caller, visitor; adj. visiting.

visitar [bi·si·tár] v. to visit; to inspect.

vislumbrar [biz·lum·brár] v. to catch a glimpse of; to guess, surmise; **-se** to be faintly visible.

vislumbre [biz·lúm·bre] f. glimmer; glimpse; vague idea; faint appearance.

viso [bí·so] m. appearance; semblance; pretense, pretext; luster, brilliance, glitter; glass curtain; **a dos -s** with a double view; with a double purpose.

visón [bi·són] m. mink.

víspera [bís·pe·ra] f. eve, evening or day before; time just before; **-s** vespers; **en -s de** on the eve of; about to.

vista [bís·ta] f. (panorama) view; landscape; sight; (sentido) sight; vision; (acción) look, glance; **a — de** in the presence of; in front of, within view of; **pagadero a la —** payable at sight or upon presentation; **¡hasta la —!** good-bye!; **bajar la —** to lower one's eyes; **conocer de —** to know by sight; **hacer la — gorda** to pretend not to see; **pasar la — por** to glance over; **perder de —** to lose sight of; **tener a la —** to have before one; to have received (a letter).

vistazo [bis·tá·so] m. glance; **dar un — a** to glance over.

visto [bís·to] p.p. of **ver** seen; adj. evident, clear **bien —** well thought of, proper; **mal —** looked down upon, improper; **— bueno** V⁰.B⁰.) approved (O.K.); **dar el — bueno** to approve, O.K.; **dar el — bueno** to approve, O.K.; **— que** whereas, considering that.

vistoso [bis·tó·so] adj. showy; colorful.

vital [bi·tál] adj. vital; important, necessary.

vitalicio [bi·ta·lí·sjo] adj. for life; m. life-insurance policy; lifetime pension.

vitalidad [bi·ta·li·đáđ] f. vitality.

vitamina [bi·ta·mí·na] f. vitamin.

vitaminado [bi·ta·mi·ná·đo] adj. containing vitamins.

vítor [bí·tor] m. cheer, applause; **¡—!** hurrah!

vitorear [bi·to·re·ár] v. to cheer, applaud.

vitrina [bi·trí·na] f. glass case; show case; show window.

vituallas [bi·twá·yas] f. pl. victuals, food, provisions.

vituperar [bi·tu·pe·rár] v. to revile, insult, call bad names.

vituperio [bi·tu·pé·rjo] m. affront, insult; reproach; censure.

viuda [bjú·đa] f. widow.

viudez [bju·đés] f. widowhood.

viudo [bjú·đo] m. widower.

¡viva! [bí·ba] interj. hurrah for; long live!

vivac [bi·bák], **vivaque** [bi·bá·ke] m. bivouac, military encampment; Am. police headquarters.

vivacidad [bi·ba·si·đáđ] f. vivacity; brightness; liveliness.

vivaracho [bi·ba·rá·čo] adj. lively; vivacious, gay.

vivaz [bi·bás] adj. vivacious, lively; bright, keen, witty.

víveres [bí·be·res] m. pl. food supplies, provisions.

vivero [bi·bé·ro] m. fish pond, fish hatchery, tree nursery.

viveza [bi·bé·sa] f. vivacity; animation, liveliness; quickness; brilliance, cleverness.

vívido [bí·bi·đo] adj. vivid; colorful.

vivienda [bi·bjén·da] f. dwelling; apartment.

viviente [bi·bjén·te] adj. living.

vivir [bi·bír] v. to live; to endure, last; **¡viva!** hurrah! long live!; **¿quién vive?** who goes there?; m. existence, living.

vivisección [bi·bi·sek·sjón] f. vivisection.

vivo [bí·bo] adj. (no muerto) alive; living; (ágil) lively; quick; (vistoso) vivid; bright; (listo) clever, wide-awake; **tío —** merry-go-round; **al —** vividly; **de viva voz** by word of mouth; **tocar en lo —** to hurt to the quick, touch the most sensitive spot.

vizcacha [bis·ká·ča] f. Andes, Ríopl. viscacha (South American rodent about the size of a hare).

vizcachera [bis·ka·čé·ra] f. Andes, Ríopl. viscacha burrow or hole; Am. room filled with junk; **vizcacheral** [bis·ka·če·rál] m. Andes, Ríopl. ground full of viscacha burrows.

vizcaíno [bis·ka·í·no] adj. Biscayan, of or from Biscay, Spain.

vocablo [bo·ká·blo] m. word, term.

vocabulario [bo·ka·bu·lá·rjo] m. vocabulary.

vocación [bo·ka·sjón] f. vocation; aptness, talent.

vocal [bo·kál] adj. vocal; oral; vowel; f. vowel; m. voter (in an assembly or council).

vocear [bo·se·ár] v. to shout; to cry out; to hail.

vocecita [bo·se·sí·ta] f. sweet little voice.

vocería [bo·se·rí·a] f. clamor, shouting.

vocerío [bo·se·rí·o] m. Am. clamor, shouting.

vocero m. spokesman.

vociferar [bo·si·fe·rár] v. to shout, clamor; to yell; to boast loudly of.

vodevil [bo·đe·bíl] m. vaudeville.

volado [bo·lá·đo] m. superior letter in printing; Col. angry person.

volante [bo·lán·te] adj. flying; floating; **papel** (or **hoja**) **—** handbill, circular; m. ruffle, frill; steering wheel; balance wheel; flywheel.

volar² [bo·lár] v. irr. to fly; to fly away; to explode; to irritate, pique; to rouse (bird game); **-se** Carib., Col. to fly off the handle, lose one's temper.

volátil [bo·lá·til] adj. volatile, fickle, changeable; flying.

volcán [bol·kán] m. volcano; Col. precipice; Am. swift torrent; C.A. **un — de** many; lots of; a pile of.

volcánico [bol·ká·ni·ko] adj. volcanic.

volcar²,⁶ [bol·kár] v. irr. to overturn; to capsize; to upset; to make dizzy; **-se** to upset, get upset.

volear [bo·le·ár] v. to volley, hit (a ball) in the air.

volición [bo·li·sjón] f. volition.

voltaje [bol·tá·xe] m. voltage.

voltear [bol·te·ár] v. to turn, turn around; to revolve; to turn inside out; to overturn; to tumble or roll over; to turn a somersault; Am. to go prying around; Col., Ven., C.A., Mex., Andes **— la espalda** to turn one's back; **-se** to turn over; to change sides.

voltereta [bol·te·ré·ta] f. somersault, tumble.

voltio [ból·tjo] m. volt. m. volt.

voluble [bo·lú·ble] adj. fickle; moody; changeable; twining (as a climbing vine).

volumen [bo·lú·men] m. volume.

voluminoso [bo·lu·mi·nó·so] adj. voluminous, bulky, very large.

voluntad [bo·lun·táđ] f. will; desire; determination; benevolence, good will; consent; **última —** last will, testament; **de** (or **de buena**) **—** willingly, with pleasure.

voluntario [bo·lun·tá·rjo] adj. voluntary; willful; m.

volunteer.
voluntarioso [bo·lun·ta·rjó·so] *adj.* willful.
voluptuoso [bo·lup·twó·so] *adj.* voluptuous; sensual.
voluta [bo·lú·ta] *f.* scroll, spiral-like ornament; **-s de humo** spirals of smoke.
volver[2,52] [bol·ƀér] *v. irr.* (*regresar*) to return; (*dar vuelta*) to turn; to turn up, over, or inside out; to restore; — **loco** to drive crazy; — **a** (+*inf.*) to do again; — **en sí** to come to, recover one's senses; — **por** to return for; to defend; **-se** to become; to turn; to turn around; to change one's ideas; **-se atrás** to go back; to back out, go back to one's word; **-se loco** to go crazy.
vomitar [bo·mi·tár] *v.* to vomit.
vómito [bó·mi·to] *m.* vomit; vomiting.
voracidad [bo·ra·si·ƌáƌ] *f.* voraciousness, greediness.
vorágine [bo·rá·xi·ne] *f.* vortex, whirlpool.
voraz [bo·rás] *adj.* voracious, ravenous, greedy.
vórtice [bór·ti·se] *m.* vortex, whirlpool; whirlwind, tornado; center of a cyclone.
votación [bo·ta·sjón] *f.* voting; vote, total number of votes.
votante [bo·tán·te] *m. & f.* voter.
votar [bo·tár] *v.* to vote; to vow; to curse; ¡**voto a tal!** by Jove!
voto [bó·to] *m.* vote; vow; prayer; votive offering; oath; wish; — **de confianza** vote of confidence.
voz [bos] *f.* (*capacidad*) voice; (*sonido*) shout, outcry; (*palabra*) word; rumor; — **común** common rumor or gossip; **a** — **en cuello** (*or* **a** — **en grito**) shouting; at the top of one's lungs; **en** — **alta** aloud; **a voces** shouting, with shouts; **secreto a voces** open secret; **dar voces** to shout, yell.
vozarrón [bo·sa·rrón] *m.* loud, strong voice.
vuelco [bwél·ko] *m.* upset; overturning; capsizing; tumble.
vuelo [bwé·lo] *m.* flight; width, fullness (*of a dress or cloak*); frill, ruffle; jut, projection (*of a building*); **al** (*or* **a**) — on the fly; quickly; **levantar** (*or* **alzar**) **el** — to fly away; to soar.
vuelta [bwél·ta] *f.* (*giro*) turn; return; repetition; (*parte opuesta*) reverse side; cuff, facing of a sleeve; cloak lining; (*cambio*) change (*money returned*); **a la** — around the corner; on returning; **a la** — **de los años** within a few years; *Am.* **otra** — again; **dar -s** to turn over and over; to wander about; **dar una** — to take a walk; **estar de** — to be back; **no tiene** — **de hoja** there are no two ways about it.
vuelto [bwél·to] *p.p. of* **volver**; *m. Am.* change (*money returned*).
vuestro [bwés·tro] *poss. adj.* your, of yours (*fam. pl.*); *poss. pron.* yours.
vulgar [bul·ǥár] *adj.* common, ordinary; in common use; low, vile, base.
vulgaridad [bul·ǥa·ri·ƌáƌ] *f.* vulgarity, coarseness, commonness.
vulgarismo [bul·ǥa·ríz·mo] *m.* slang, slang expression, vulgar or ungrammatical expression.
vulgo [búl·ǥo] *m.* populace, the common people; *adv.* commonly, popularly.
vulva [búl·ƀa] *f.* external female genitalia.

W:w

water [gwá·ter] *m. Spain* toilet.

X:x

xilófono [si·ló·fo·no] *m.* xylophone.

Y:y

y [i] *conj.* and.
ya [ya] *adv.* already; now; finally; soon, presently; in time; ¡—! now I see!; I understand; enough!; ¡— **lo creo!** I should say so!; yes, of course!; — **no** no longer; — **que** since; although; — **se ve** of course; it is clear; — **voy** I am coming.
yacer[50] [ya·sér] *v. irr.* to lie (*in the grave*); to be lying down; to lie, be situated.
yacimiento [ya·si·mjén·to] *m.* bed, layer (*of ore*); — **de petróleo** oil field.
yanqui [yáŋ·ki] *m. & f.* North American, native of the United States; Yankee.
yantar [yan·tár] *v.* to eat; *m.* food, meal.
yararÁ [ya·ra·rÁ] *f. Ríopl.* Argentine poisonous snake.
yarda [yár·ƌa] *f.* yard (*unit of measure*).
yate [yá·te] *m.* yacht.
yedra [yé·ƌra] = **hiedra.**
yegua [yé·ǥwa] *f.* mare; *Am.* cigar butt; *adj. Am.* big, large; **yeguada** [ye·ǥwá·ƌa] *f.* herd of mares.
yelmo [yél·mo] *m.* helmet.
yema [yé·ma] *f.* egg yolk; bud, shoot; candied egg yolk; — **del dedo** finger tip.
yerba [yér·ƀa] = **hierba.**
yerbabuena [yer·ƀa·ƀwé·na] *f.* mint; peppermint.
yerbero [yer·ƀé·ro] *m. Mex., Cuba, Ven., Col., Andes* herb vendor.
yermo [yér·mo] *m.* desert, wilderness; *adj.* desert uninhabited; uncultivated; sterile.
yerno [yér·no] *m.* son-in-law.
yerro [yé·rro] *m.* error, fault, mistake.
yerto [yér·to] *adj.* stiff, motionless, rigid.
yesca [yés·ka] *f.* tinder; anything highly inflammable; incentive (*to passion*); *Ríopl., Mex.* **estar hecho una** — to be in great anger.
yeso [yé·so] *m.* gypsum, chalk; plaster; chalk (*for blackboard*); — **blanco** whitewash; — **mate** plaster of Paris; **yesoso** [ye·só·so] *adj.* chalky.
yo [yo] *pers. pron.* I.
yod [yoƌ] *f.* yod (linguistic symbol).
yodo [yó·ƌo] *m.* iodine.
yoduro [yo·ƌú·ro] *m.* iodide.
yogi [yo·xi] *m* ≡ **yogi.**
yuca [yú·ka] *f.* yucca; cassava.
yugo [yú·ǥo] *m.* yoke; marriage tie; burden.
yogur [yo·ǥúr] *m.* yogurt.
yoyo [yó·yo] *m.* yo-yo.
yunga [yuŋ·ga] *f.* valley of Peru and Bolivia.
yunque [yuŋ·ke] *f.* anvil.
yunta [yun·ta] *f.* yoke of oxen; pair of draft animals.
yuyo [yú·yo] *m. Cuba, Mex., Ríopl., Andes* wild grass, weeds; *Am.* an herb sauce; *Am.* garden stuff; *Andes* **estar** — to be lifeless insipid; *Col.* **volverse uno** — to faint.

Z:z

zacate [sa·ká·te] *m. Mex., C.A.* grass, forage; hay.

zafado [sa·fá·ḍo] *adj.* impudent, brazen, shameless; *Ven.* smart, wide-awake, keen; *Col., Mex., Andes* "touched", half-crazy; *p.p.* of **zafar**.

zafar [sa·fár] *v.* to release, set free; to dislodge; *Am.* to exclude; **-se** to slip away; to dodge; to get rid (of); to get loose; *Col., Ven., Andes* to get dislocated (*said of a bone*); *Col., Mex., Andes* to go crazy; *Col.* to use foul language.

zafio [sá·fjo] *adj.* coarse, uncouth, rude.

zafir [sa·fír], **zafiro** [sa·fi·ro] *m.* sapphire.

zafra [sá·fra] *f.* sugar-making season; sugar making; sugar crop.

zaga [sá·ga] *f.* rear; **a la — (a** *or* **en —)** behind.

zagal [sa·gál] *m.* young shepherd; lad; **zagala** [sa·gá·la] *f.* young shepherdess; lass, maiden; **zagalejo** [sa·ga·lé·xo] *m.* young shepherd; short skirt; petticoat.

zaguán [sa·gwán] *m.* vestibule.

zaherir[3] [sa·e·rír] *v. irr.* to hurt (*feelings*); to censure, reprove; to reproach.

zaino [sáj·no] *adj.* treacherous; vicious; chestnut-colored (*horse*).

zalamero [sa·la·mé·ro] *m.* fawner, flatterer, servile person; **zalamería** [sa·la·me·rí·a] *f.* flattery, scraping and bowing.

zalea [sa·lé·a] *f.* pelt, undressed sheepskin.

zamacueca [sa·ma·kwé·ka] *f.* popular dance of Peru and Chile.

zambo [sám·bo] *adj.* knock-kneed; *m. Ríopl., Ven., Andes* Indian and negro half-breed; *Col.* a species of South American monkey.

zambra [sám·bra] *f. Spain* uproar; lively *fiesta.*

zambullida [sam·bu·yí·ḍa] *f.* dive, dip, plunge.

zambullir[20] [sam·bu·yír] *v.* to plunge, dip, duck; **-se** to dive; to plunge.

zambullón [sam·bu·yón] *m.* quick, sudden dip or dive.

zanahoria [sa·na·o·rja] *f.* carrot.

zanca [sáŋ·ka] *f.* long leg of any fowl; long leg; long prop; **zancada** [saŋ·ká·ḍa] *f.* stride, long step.

zanco [sáŋ·ko] *m.* stilt; **andar en -s** to walk on stilts.

zancón [saŋ·kón] *adj.* lanky, long-legged; *Col., Guat., Mex.* too short (*skirt or dress*).

zancudo [saŋ·kú·ḍo] *adj.* long-legged; *m. Mex., C.A., Ven., Col., Andes* mosquito.

zángano [sáŋ·ga·no] *m.* drone; loafer, sponger; *Am.* rogue, rascal.

zangolotear [saŋ·go·lo·te·ár] *v.* to shake, jiggle; **-se** to shake; to waddle; to sway from side to side.

zangoloteo [saŋ·go·lo·té·o] *m.* jiggle, jiggling; shaking; waddling.

zanguanga [saŋ·gwáŋ·ga] *f.* feigned illness; **hacer la —** to pretend to be ill; **zanguango** [saŋ·gwáŋ·go] *adj.* lazy; silly; *m.* fool.

zanja [sáŋ·xa] *f.* ditch; trench; *Am.* irrigation ditch.

zanjar [saŋ·xár] *v.* to excavate; to dig ditches in; to settle (*disputes*).

zapallo [sa·pá·yo] *m. Pan., Col., Ven., Andes* pumpkin; squash.

zapapico [sa·pa·pí·ko] *m.* pickaxe.

zapata [sa·pá·ta] *f.* half-boot; **— de freno** brake shoe.

zapateado [sa·pa·te·á·ḍo] *m.* a Spanish tap dance.

zapatear [sa·pa·te·ár] *v.* to tap with the feet; to tap-dance.

zapateo [sa·pa·té·o] *m.* tapping with the feet; *Am.*

a popular tap dance.

zapatería [sa·pa·te·rí·a] *f.* shoe store; shoemaker's shop.

zapatero [sa·pa·té·ro] *m.* shoemaker; shoe dealer.

zapatilla [sa·pa·tí·ya] *f.* slipper, pump.

zapato [sa·pá·to] *m.* shoe.

zapote [sa·pó·te] *m.* sapodilla.

zaragüeya [sa·ra·gwe·ya] *f.* opossum.

zarandajas [sa·ran·dá·xas] *f. pl.* trifles, trinkets, worthless things.

zarandear [sa·ran·de·ár] *v.* to winnow (*separate the chaff from grain*); to sift; to sift out; to move (*something*) quickly, wiggle, jiggle; *C.A., Ríopl.* to whip, lash, mistreat, abuse; **-se** to wiggle, jiggle; to bump along; to waddle; to strut, swagger.

zarandeo [sa·ran·dé·o] *m.* jiggle, jiggling; sifting; waddling; strutting.

zarcillo [sar·sí·yo] *m.* earring; tendril (*coil of a climbing vine*); *Andes, Mex.* earmark (*on the ear of an animal*).

zarco [sár·ko] *adj.* light-blue (*eyes*).

zarpa [sár·pa] *f.* paw, claw; weighing anchor; **echar la —** to grasp, seize; **zarpada** [sar·pá·ḍa] *f.* pounce; blow with a paw; **zarpazo** [sar·pá·so] *m.* blow with the paw; big blow, thud; hard fall.

zarpar [sar·pár] *v.* to weigh anchor; to set sail.

zarpazo [sar·pá·so] *m.* blow with a claw or paw.

zarza [sár·sa] *f.* bramble; blackberry bush.

zarzamora [sar·sa·mó·ra] *f.* blackberry.

zarzuela [sar·swé·la] *f.* Spanish musical comedy.

¡zas! *interj.* [sas] *interj.* bang!

zigzag [sig·sáǵ] *m.* zigzag.

zigzaguear [sig·sa·ǵe·ár] *v.* to zigzag.

zinc [siŋk] = **cinc.**

zócalo [só·ka·lo] *m.* base (*of a pedestal*); *Mex.* public square.

zodíaco [so·ḍí·a·ko] *m.* zodiac.

zona [só·na] *f.* zone; band, girdle; shingles (*a disease*).

zonzo [són·so] *adj.* dull, stupid, silly, foolish.

zoología [so·o·lo·xí·a] *f.* zoology.

zoológico [so·o·ló·xi·ko] *adj.* zoological; **jardín —** zoo.

zopenco [so·péŋ·ko] *adj.* studpid, dull, thick-headed *m.* blockhead, dunce.

zopilote [so·pi·ló·te] *m. Mex. C.A.* buzzard.

zoquete [so·ké·te] *m.* (*cosa*) block, chunk of wood; hunk of bread; (*persona*) blockhead, dunce, fool; ugly fat person; *Am.* grease, dirt, filth; *Am.* slap.

zorra [só·rra] *f.* fox; foxy person; drunkenness; prostitute; **pillar una —** to get drunk.

zorro [só·rro] *m.* fox; foxy person; **-s** fox skins; duster made of cloth or leather strips; **estar hecho un —** to be drowsy; **hacerse uno el —** to pretend to be stupid or not to hear; *adj.* foxy; **zorrillo** [so·rrí·yo], **zorrino** [so·rrí·no] *m. Ríopl.* skunk; **zorruno** [so·rrú·no] *adj.* foxy.

zorzal [sor·sál] *m.* thrush; crafty fellow; *Am.* fool, scapegoat, dupe.

zozobra [so·só·ƀra] *f.* foundering; sinking; anxiety, worry.

zozobrar [so·so·ƀrár] *v.* to founder; to capsize; to sink; to be in great danger; to fret, worry.

zumbar [sum·bár] *v.* to buzz; to hum; to ring (*said of the ears*); to scoff at; to strike, hit; *Ven., Col.* to throw out or away; *Andes* to punish; **una bofetada** to give a slap; **-se** *Am.* to slip away, disappear.

zumbido [sum·bí·ḍo] *m.* buzzing, humming; ringing (*in one's ears*); hit, blow, whack.

zumbón [sum·bón] *adj.* funny, playful; sarcastic;

m. jester.

zumo [sú·mo] *f. Spain* juice; profit; **zumoso** [su·mó·so] *adj.* juicy.

zurcido [sur·si·ḍo] *m.* darn; darning; *p.p. of* **zurcir.**

zurcir[10] [sur·sír] *v.* to darn; to invent, make up (*lies*).

zurdo [súr·ḍo] *adj.* left-handed; left; **a zurdas** with the left hand; clumsily.

zuro [sú·ro] *m.* cob, corncob.

zurra [sú·rra] *f.* beating, flogging; tanning (*of leather*).

zurrar [su·rrár] *v.* to flog, thrash; to tan (*leather*).

zurrón [su·rrón] *m.* pouch; bag; leather bag; *Ven., Col.* coward.

Zutano [su·tá·no] *m.* so-and-so; a certain person. (*Used often with* **Fulano** *and* **Mengano**).

ZA

A Spanish–English List of 1000 Common Idioms and Proverbs, with Dialectal Variants

The Spanish idioms, proverbs, and sayings are listed alphabetically, followed by American Spanish variants, then English equivalents, some of which are also idiomatic. American Spanish locutions that seem to be fairly common to most of Latin America are listed without regional designation, while local variations are indicated by country or region with the abbreviations employed in the text of the Dictionary. An English index follows the chart of idioms to facilitate the use of the compilation. It is to be noted that the basic element is the Spanish expression and also that the Spanish variants are intentionally more numerous than the English. This is because of the many political entities represented in the Spanish-speaking world, in contrast to American English idiomatic expression which tends to level to a general American form.

Mil Modismos, Refranes, y Dichos Españoles con Variantes Dialectales y Tradducción al Inglés

El cuadro de modismos, refranes, y dichos españoles tiene orden alfabético según la letra inicial de la primera palabra. Siguen variantes hispanoamericanas y luego equivalentes o semejantes del inglés, con ciertas variantes. Los modismos hispanoamericanos que son bastante generales no llevan indicación regional, y se señalan con abreviaturas del texto del Diccionario los que son típicos de ciertos países o regiones. Sigue al cuadro un índice inglés con los números de las locuciones castellanas correspondientes. Se nota que lo básico es la locución española y también que se dan más variantes dialectales en español, con motivo de las numerosas entidades políticas de América. El inglés, por lo visto, ha sufrido más nivelación en este siglo.

	Academy Spanish	American Spanish Variants	English Equivalents
1.	A aquél loar debemos cuyo pan comemos	No hay que darle patadas al pesebre	Don't bite the hand that feeds you
2.	¡A buenas horas!	¡Qué horitas! (*Mex.*)	Better late than never; It's about time!
3.	A buen hambre no hay pan duro	A buen hambre no hay gordas duras (*Mex.*)	Hunger is the best sauce
4.	A caballo regalado no hay que mirarle el diente	A caballo dado no se le mira el colmillo	Don't look a gift horse in the mouth
5.	A cambio de		In exchange for
6.	A carta cabal		Through and through
7.	A centenares	A cientos	By the hundreds
8.	A ciegas	A tientas	Blindly
9.	A conciencia		Conscientiously
10.	A continuación	Como sigue	Following; as follows
11.	A costa de		By dint of; at the expense of

241

Academy Spanish	American Spanish Variants	English Equivalents
12. ¿A cuántos estamos?	¿Cuál es la fecha?	What is the date?
13. A decir verdad	Francamente	Frankly
14. A duras penas	Con gran dificultad	With great difficulty
15. A empujones (empellones)	A codazos	By pushing; by shoving; by elbowing
16. A escondidas	Al aguaite (*Ven., Col.*)	Without the knowledge of
17. A ese efecto	Con ese motivo	To that end; for that purpose
18. A falta de		For lack of
19. A favor de	En favor de	In behalf of; in favor of; aided by
20. A fines de		Toward (around) the end of (month, week)
21. A fondo		Thoroughly
22. A fuerza de		By dint of; through; by
23. A grandes rasgos		Briefly; in outline form; in a sketchy way
24. Ahí vamos	Pasándola	(To be) getting along; (to say one) can't complain
25. A juzgar por	Juzgando por	Judging by
26. A la americana; a escote	Al aleluya, cada quien paga la suya; Americanamente (*Col.*)	Dutch treat; go Dutch
27. A la buena de Dios		Casually; as luck would have it
28. A la carrera	Fletado (*Ven., Col.*)	On the run
29. A la corta o a la larga	Tarde o temprano	Sooner or later
30. A la fuerza		By force
31. A la larga	Al fin	In the long run; when all is said and done
32. A la luz de		In light of
33. A la moda	En boga	In style; the "in" thing
34. A la postre	A las cansadas (*Riopl. Andes*); a la cansada (*Ec.*)	In the end
35. A la vez		At the same time
36. A lo grande	Como gringo (*Mex.*); al olor y flor (*Carib.*)	(To do something) in great style
37. A lo largo de		Along; bordering
38. A lo lejos	Allá lejos	In the distance; away off
39. A lo más	Cuando más	At (the) most
40. A lo mejor	Puede que; a la mejor (*Mex.*)	Like as not; it could be that
41. A lo vivo		Vividly described
42. A mano		By hand; at hand; tied (even)
43. A manos llenas	A Dios dar	By the handful
44. A más no poder	Hasta sacarse los zapatos (*Ch.*)	To the utmost
45. A más tardar	Cuando más tarde	At the latest
46. A mediados de		About (around) the middle of (month)
47. A medio camino		Halfway
48. A medio hacer		Half done
49. A menos que	A no ser que	Unless
50. A menudo		Often
51. A mi ver	En mi opinión	In my opinion; to my way of thinking
52. A modo de	Una especie de	A kind (sort) of
53. A palabras necias, oídos sordos	A boca de borracho, oídos de cantinero	For foolish talk, deaf ears
54. A pedir de boca		Exactly as desired; just as you want it
55. A pesar de		In spite of
56. A petición de		At the request of
57. A principios de		The early part of; around the first of (month)
58. A propósito		By the way; on purpose
59. A prueba de		Proof against (fire, etc.)
60. A punto fijo	Precisamente	Exactly
61. A que ...		I'll bet
62. A quemarropa	A boca de jarro	Point blank; at very close range

	Academy Spanish	*American Spanish Variants*	*English Equivalents*
63.	A quien corresponda		To whom it may concern
64.	¡A quién le importa!	¿Quién te mete, Juan Copete?	Mind your own business; what's it to you?
65.	A quien madruga, Dios le ayuda		The early bird catches the worm
66.	A ratos perdidos	En los ratos de ocio	In moments of leisure; in (one's) spare time
67.	A razón de		At the rate of
68.	A rienda suelta		Without restraint
69.	A saber	Es decir; o sea	Namely; that is
70.	A tal·efecto	Con tal motivo	To that end; for such purpose
71.	A tal punto	Hasta tal punto	To such an extent
72.	A toda costa	Cueste lo que cueste	At all hazards; whatever the cost
73.	A toda prisa	A toda orquesta; a toda vela	At full speed; all out; in high gear
74.	A todo correr	Como alma que lleva el diablo; Echando diablos (*Andes*); a todo ful (Andes)	At breakneck speed; like mad
75.	A todo trance		At any cost; at all costs
76.	A través de		Through, across
77.	A última hora		At the last moment; in the nick of time
78.	A un paso de aquí	Ahí tras lomita	Just a stone's throw; just a hop, skip, and jump
79.	A veces	De repente (pronto) (*Ríopl.*)	At times; now and then
80.	A ver si como repican doblan	A ver si como roncan duermen	His bark is worse than his bite; all talk and no cider
81.	Abandonar la partida	Arrojar la esponja (*Ch.*)	To give up; to say uncle
82.	Abierto de par en par		Wide open
83.	Abrir la marcha	Hacer la punta	To lead the (pack) parade
84.	Abrirse el pecho		To bare one's heart; to let off steam; to get a load off one's chest
85.	Abundar como la mala hierba	Ser ajonjolí de todos los moles (*Mex.*)	To be as common as dirt; to be a dime a dozen
86.	Abrirse paso (camino)		To make (force) one's way through
87.	Acabar de	Venir de (*Col.*); recién (*plus verb*) (*Ríopl., Ch.*)	To have just
88.	Acerca de	Sobre	Having to do with; about
89.	Acusar recibo de		To acknowledge receipt of
90.	Además de		In addition to; besides
91.	Advertirle algo a alguien		To inform one; to tell someone so
92.	Aguzar los oídos	Parar la oreja	To prick up one's ears
93.	Ahora bien	Pues; entonces	Now then; so
94.	Ahora mismo	Ahorita (*Mex., C.A.*)	Right now
95.	Al contrario		On the contrary; on the other hand
96.	Al fin	Por fin	At last
97.	Al fin y al cabo	Al fin y al fallo (*Ch.*)	In the very end; when all is said and done
98.	Al fin se canta la gloria	Nadie diga ¡zape! hasta que no escape; el que quiera huevos, que aguante los cacareos (*Ríopl.*)	Don't count your chickens before they're hatched
99.	Al gusto		As one wills; to the taste
100.	Al mejor cazador se le escapa la liebre	Al mejor mono se le cae el zapote (*C.A.*); A la mejor cocinera se le queman los frijoles	Everyone makes mistakes; it's a good horse that never stumbles
101.	Al menos	Cuando menos	At least
102.	Al minuto	Al golpe; Al tiro (*Ch., Ríopl.*)	Right away; directly (*South*)
103.	Al parecer	Por lo visto	Apparently
104.	Al pie de la letra		To the letter; thoroughly
105.	Al por mayor	Al mayoreo	Wholesale
106.	Al por menor		Retail; in detail

	Academy Spanish	American Spanish Variants	English Equivalents
107.	Al primer golpe de vista	A primera vista	At first glance
108.	Al principio	De primero	At first; at the outset
109.	Al revés		The opposite; inside out
110.	Alegrarse de	Darse por contento con	To be happy (glad) about
111.	Algo por el estilo		Something like that; something on that order
112.	Amigo del buen tiempo, múdase con el viento	Al nopal lo van a ver sólo cuando tiene tunas (Mex.)	Fair-weather friend
113.	Andar como loco	Andar como trompo chillador	To run around like a chicken with its head cut off
114.	Andar de fiesta en fiesta	Andar de parranda; andar de farras (Ríopl.); andar de jarana (Col., Ven., Carib.)	To lead a fast life; to be a swinger
115.	Andar de malas	Tener la de malas	To be out of luck (jinxed)
116.	Andar de prisa	Apurarse	To be in a hurry
117.	Andarse por las ramas	Andarse con medias tazas; emborrachar la perdiz (Ch.)	To beat around the bush
118.	Ante todo		Above all
119.	Antes doblar que quebrar	Más vale rodear que rodar	Better bend than break; if you can't lick 'em, join 'em
120.	Apretar el paso		To hasten; to hurry
121.	Aprovecha gaviota, que no hay otra	Atáscate ahora que hay lodo	Gather ye rosebuds while ye may; here's your chance
122.	Aprovechar la ocasión		To take advantage of the situation
123.	Aquí mismo	Aquí mero (Mex.)	Right here
124.	Armar un San Quintín	Armar una bronca; revolver el gallinero (Ch.)	To start a fight; to raise Cain
125.	¡Arriba los corazones!	¡No le afloje!	Courage! Cheer up! Chin up!
126.	Así es la vida	Así es la vida, tango	Such is life; that's the way the ball bounces; that's the way the cookie crumbles
127.	A sus órdenes	Para servirle	At your service
128.	Atender razones		To listen to reason
129.	Atrasado de noticias		Behind the times
130.	Aunque la mona se vista de seda, mona se queda		Clothes don't make the man
131.	Bajo cuerda	Por debajo del agua	In an underhanded manner; under the table
132.	Barrer para adentro	Rascarse para adentro es gran contento; antes mis dientes que mis parientes	To look after oneself first; to take care of number one
133.	Beber como una esponja	Beber hasta reventar	To drink like a fish
134.	Bien inclinado		Well-disposed; good-natured
135.	Bien mirado	Considerándolo bien	On second thought; come to think of it
136.	Boca abajo		Face down
137.	Boca arriba		Face (up) upward
138.	Borracho como una cuba	Borracho perdido	Dead drunk; plastered; tight
139.	Buen genio		Good-natured
140.	¡Buen provecho!	¡Que aproveche!	Good appetite!
141.	¡Bueno, bueno! ¡Conforme!	¡De acuerdo!	All right; agreed; O.K.
142.	Burlarse de	Reírse de; tener a uno para el fideo (Ch.)	To make fun of
143.	Buscarle tres pies al gato	Buscarle mangas al chaleco; buscarle cuatro pies al gato (Ec.)	To look for knots in a bulrush; to complicate things
144.	Buscar pelos en la sopa		To be given to fault finding; to look for an excuse to gripe
145.	Cada muerte de obispo	Como visita de obispo	In a month of Sundays; once in a blue moon
146.	Cada uno sabe dónde le aprieta el zapato	Cada quien sabe lo que carga su costal	Every man knows best where his own shoe pinches
147.	Caer atravesado	Caer gordo; caer mal; caer gacho (Col.)	To rub (one) the wrong way; to be a pain in the neck
148.	Caer como un balde de agua fría	Caer como un cubetazo de agua fría (Mex.)	To be like a dash of cold water; to be a wet blanket
149.	Caer de bruces	Dar el azotón; caer de ancho; echarse de boca (Andes)	To fall flat; to bite the dust

Academy Spanish	American Spanish Variants	English Equivalents
150. Caer en la cuenta		To realize; to take note of
151. Caer en la red	Caer en la ratonera; pisar el palito (*Ch.*); ensartarse (*Andes*)	To fall into the trap; to fall for it
152. Caerse de su propio peso		To be self-evident (obvious)
153. Calentarse los cascos		To rack one's brains
154. Callarse la boca	Cerrar el pico; no chillar (*Ven., C.A.*)	To keep still; to hold one's tongue
155. Cambiar de opinión		To change one's mind
156. Cambiar de tema	Cambiar el disco	To change the subject; to turn the record over
157. Caminar de arriba abajo	Andar vuelta y vuelta	To pace the floor; to pace up and down
158. Cara a cara		Right to one's face
159. Cara o cruz	Aguila o sol (*Mex.*); cara o sello	Heads or tails
160. Carne de gallina		Goose flesh; goose pimples; burr(brrr) bumps (South)
161. Cerca de		Near; about
162. Colgarle a uno el milagro	Colgarle a uno el muerto	To shift responsibility; to pass the buck
163. Como dijo el otro	Como dice el dicho	As the saying goes; as they say
164. Como Dios manda		As it should be; according to Cocker; according to Hoyle
165. Como dos y dos son cuatro		As sure as two and two are four; as sure as God made little green apples; as sure as shooting
166. Como el más pintado		As (with) the best of them
167. Como llovido del cielo		Like manna from heaven
168. Como perros y gatos	Como dos gatos en un costal	Like cats and dogs
169. Como quiera que sea	Sea lo que sea	However it be; in any case
170. ¿Cómo te (le) va?	¿Qué tal?	How are you? How's it going? What gives?
171. Como una fiera		Furiously
172. Compadecerse de alguien	Compadecerle a alguien	To pity; to sympathize with someone
173. Comprar a ciegas	Comprar potrillo en panza de yegua	To buy blindly; to buy a pig in a poke
174. Comunicarse con		To get in touch with
175. Con destino a		(To be) going to; (to be) bound for
176. Con el ojo y con la fe jamás me burlaré	Aunque te digan que sí, espérate a que lo veas	Seeing is believing; (to say one is) from Missouri
177. Con ese no se juega	A jugar con las muñecas	Don't trifle with that; don't mess with that
178. Con guante blanco	Con mucha mano izquierda	With kid gloves
179. Con intención	Adrede	Deliberately; on purpose
180. Con la condición de que		With the understanding that
181. Con la cuchara que elijas, con ésa comerás	Cada quien se pone la corona que se labra	As you make your bed, so you must lie in it
182. Con las bocas cosidas	¡Chitón!	To keep to oneself; mum's the word; button the lip
183. Con las manos en la masa		To be caught in the act; to be caught red-handed
184. Estar con los pelos de la dehesa	Estar con el pelo del potrero	To be a country bumkin; (hayseed, hick)
185. Con mucho gusto		Gladly
186. Con objeto de	Con el propósito de	With the object of
187. Con permiso		Excuse me; I beg your pardon
188. Con razón		No wonder! Small wonder!
189. Con respecto a		With regard to
190. Con tal que	A condición de que	Provided that; if
191. Con tiempo	Con anticipación; de antemano	In advance; ahead of time
192. Contigo pan y cebolla	Más vale atole con risas que chocolate con lágrimas	Whither thou goest ...; love in a cottage

Academy Spanish	American Spanish Variants	English Equivalents
193. Con todas las de ley	Como Dios manda	According to Cocker (Hoyle)
194. Confiar en	Fiarse de	To rely on; to trust
195. Conforme a	Según	In accordance with
196. Conocerle a uno el juego	Ponerse chango (Mex.)	To be wise to someone; to be onto someone's schemes
197. Constarle a uno		To be evident to one
198. Consultar con la almohada		To think something over; to sleep on something
199. Contar con		To count on; to depend on
200. Contentarse con		To be satisfied with
201. Contra viento y marea		Come what may; come hell or high water
202. Convenirle a uno		To be to one's advantage; to be advisable; to be to one's good
203. Correr la voz	Correr la bola (C.A.); dizque (Col. Andes)	To be rumored; to be noised about; they say; people say
204. Correr peligro		To run a risk; to take a chance
205. Correr riesgo		To run a risk; to take a chance
206. Cortar de raíz		To nip in the bud
207. Cortar el hilo	Cortar la hebra	To interrupt; to cut off
208. Corto de vista		Nearsighted
209. Cosa de		About; more or less; a matter of
210. Cosa de risa	Digno de risa	A laughing matter
211. Cosa de ver		Something worth seeing; something to see
212. Cosido a faldas de		To be tied to the apron strings of
213. Costar un ojo de la cara	Costar un huevo (Ven., Col., Andes)	To cost a mint; to cost plenty; to bring a stiff price
214. Cruzarse de brazos		To remain indifferent; to be not interested
215. Cuando quiera		Whenever; any time now
216. Cuanto antes	Tan pronto como posible	As soon as possible; the sooner the better
217. Cuanto más . . . más	Mientras más . . . más; entre más . . . más (C.A., Col., Andes)	The more . . . the more
218. Cuatro letras		A few lines (in a letter)
219. Cuesta abajo		Downhill; easy
220. Cuesta arriba		Uphill; difficult
221. ¡Cuidado!	¡Aguas! ¡Aguila! (Mex.); ¡Hay que pelar el ojo! (Col.)	Look out! Watch out!
222. Dar a entender		To insinuate; to pretend; to give to understand
223. Dar a luz		To give birth
224. Dar al borracho las llaves de la bodega	Poner la iglesia en manos de Lutero	To set the fox to keep the geese; to put the cat among the pigeons
225. Dar ánimo	Animar	To cheer up
226. Dar calabazas	Cortar; dar ayotes (C.A.); dar opio (Andes)	To break off relations; to give (one) the brush-off; to give (one) the mitten (N.E.)
227. Dar cuerda a		To wind (clock, etc.)
228. Dar de baja		To discharge; to drop (from a team, list, etc.)
229. Dar disgustos a		To cause grief to; to distress; to bug
230. Dar el pésame por		To present one's condolences for; to extend one's sympathy for
231. Dar en		To hit; take a notion to
232. Dar en el clavo		Hit the nail on the head
233. Dar forma a		To put in final shape
234. Dar gato por liebre	Hacerle guaje a uno (Mex.); pasársela a uno (Ch.)	To deceive; to cheat

Academy Spanish	American Spanish Variants	English Equivalents
235. Dar guerra		To make trouble
236. Dar (la) lata	Poner gorro (*Mex.*); poner pereque (*Col.*)	To bother; to annoy; to be a nuisance; to bug
237. Dar la razón a alguien		To acknowledge (a person) to be right; give credit for being right
238. Dar la vuelta a algo		To go around something; to rotate something
239. Dar las gracias		To thank; to be grateful
240. Dar lástima	Dar pena	To arouse pity
241. Dar mucha pena		To be very embarrassing
242. Dar muestras de	Dar señales de	To show signs of
243. Dar parte	Avisar	To inform; to report
244. Dar por cierto	Estar seguro	To be certain (sure)
245. Dar por descontado	Tomar por cierto	To take for granted
246. Dar por hecho	Suponer	To assume; to take for granted
247. Dar por seguro	Estar seguro	To be certain (sure)
248. Dar que hacer		To make work; to cause work
249. Dar rienda suelta a	Dar curso libre	To give free rein to; to let go
250. Dar salida a	Disponer de	To dispose of; to clear out; to get rid of
251. Dar señales de		To show signs of
252. Dar un paseo	Dar una vuelta	To take a walk (stroll)
253. Dar un paso en falso	Dar una metida de pata	To make a false move; to pull a boner
254. Dar una mano		To apply (a coat of paint, etc.)
255. Dar una vuelta		To take a turn (through a place); to turn over
256. Darle a uno coraje	Darle rabia a uno (*Carib.*);	To make one angry (mad)
257. Darle a uno en la matadura	Darle a uno en la mera matada (*Mex.*)	To touch to the quick; to strike home
258. Darle a uno la gana; apetecer	Provocarle a uno (*Col.*)	To feel like; to want to
259. Darle a uno lo mismo	Serle a uno igual	To be all the same to one; to make no difference to one
260. Darle a uno una carda	Echarle a uno la viga	To preach at; to give a good talking to; to bawl out; to tell off
261. Darle a uno vergüenza	Darle a uno mucha pena	To be ashamed; to be shy
262. Darle a uno una soberana paliza	Darle a uno hasta por debajo de la lengua; aplanchar a uno (*Col.*)	To give one a trouncing; to knock the spots off one
263. Darse aires; darse tono; ¡cuántos humos!	Darse mucho taco (*Mex.*); Botarse el pucho (*Ch.*); Darse corte; darse paquete (*Ec.*)	To put on airs; to put on the dog; to be stuck up
264. Darse cuenta de		To realize; to be aware of
265. Darse la gran vida	Darse vida de rey; darse vida de cachos para arriba (*Ch.*); darse vida de oro (*Col.*)	To live off the fat of the land; to live the life of Riley; to live it up
266. Darse prisa	Apurarse	To hurry; to move quickly
267. De acuerdo con		In accordance with
268. De ahora en adelante	De aquí en adelante	From now on; from here on
269. De bote en bote	Hasta el tope (*Mex.*)	Full to the brim; full up
270. De broma	De vacilada (*Mex.*)	As a joke; in jest
271. De buena gana		Willingly
272. De buenas a primeras	En un improviso (*Ven.*, *Col.*)	Without warning; suddenly
273. De cabo a rabo	De punta a punta	From beginning to end; from head to tail
274. De categoría	De número (*Riopl.*); de oro (*Col.*); de mentas (*Arg.*)	Of importance; of class
275. De cuando en cuando	De vez en cuando; de pronto (*C.A.*; *Riopl.*)	From time to time
276. De día en día	De día a día	From day to day
277. De dirección única	De un solo sentido	One-way

	Academy Spanish	*American Spanish Variants*	*English Equivalents*
278.	De enfrente		(The one) directly opposite; across the way
279.	De esta manera		In this way
280.	De etiqueta		Formal dress
281.	De golpe	En un improviso (*Ven., Col.*)	Suddenly; all of a sudden
282.	De gran subida, gran caída	De la subida más alta es la caída más lastimosa	The bigger they are, the harder they fall
283.	De hecho	El hecho es que; es que	As a matter of fact
284.	De hoy en adelante	De ahora en adelante	From now on
285.	De intento	Adrede; a propósito	On purpose
286.	De la noche a la mañana		Overnight; all at once
287.	De lado		Sideways
288.	De lleno		Fully; adequately
289.	De lo contrario		Otherwise
290.	De mal en peor	De Guatemala en guatepeor	From bad to worse
291.	De mala fe		In bad faith
292.	De mala gana		Unwillingly
293.	De mala muerte	Chafa (*Mex.*)	Worthless; crumby
294.	De manera que	Así es que	So that; as a result
295.	De memoria		By heart; from memory
296.	De modo que		So that; so
297.	De ningún modo	Ni modo (*Mex.*)	By no means; not on your life
298.	De ninguna manera	Ni loco; ¡qué esperanza!	By no means; no way!
299.	De nuevo	Otra vez	Again; anew; once more
300.	De paso		In passing; on the way
301.	De pronto	De repente	All of a sudden
302.	De pura casualidad		Purely by chance
303.	De repente	De golpe; en un improviso (*Ven., Col.*)	All of a sudden
304.	De tal palo, tal astilla	Cual el cuervo, tal su huevo; de tal jarro, tal tepalcate (*Mex.*)	Like father, like son; a chip off the old block
305.	Descubrir el pastel	Hacer aparecer el peine	To let the cat out of the bag; to spill the beans
306.	De todas maneras	De toda cuenta (*Col.*)	At any rate; anyway
307.	De trecho en trecho		At intervals (space and time)
308.	De un día para otro	De día a día	Day by day
309.	De un modo u otro		In one way or another
310.	De una vez y para siempre	De una vez	Once and for all
311.	De un solo sentido		One-way
312.	De vuelta a las andadas	Otra vez la burra en el trigo	Back to the old tricks
313.	Decidirse a		To make up one's mind to; to decide to
314.	Decir a todo amén		To be a yes man
315.	Decir agudezas	Tener buenas puntadas	To be witty; to be a wise guy
316.	Decir entre dientes		To mumble; to mutter
317.	Decir para sí	Decir para sus adentros	To say to oneself
318.	Dejar de		To cease; to stop
319.	Dejar a uno en la calle	Dejar a uno en la tendida Dejar a uno en un petate (*Col.; Ven.*)	To bleed (one) white; to take (one) to the cleaners
320.	Dejar en paz		To leave alone
321.	Dejar a uno plantado	Dejar a uno en la estacada; dejar a uno embarcado (*Mex.*)	To stand someone up
322.	Dejarse de cuentos	Dejarse de historias; dejarse de rodeos	To come to the point; to stop beating around the bush
323.	Del dicho al hecho hay gran trecho		Saying and doing are two different things; there's many a slip twixt the cup and the lip
324.	Delante de		In front of; in the presence of
325.	Dentro de	Entre (*C.A.*)	Inside; within
326.	Dentro de poco	En breve; at rato	Soon; shortly; right away; directly (South)
327.	Desde ahora		From now on
328.	Desde entonces		Since then

Academy Spanish	American Spanish Variants	English Equivalents
329. Desde fuera		From the outside
330. Desde lejos		From a distance
331. Desde luego		Of course; naturally
332. Desde un principio		Right from the start; from the very beginning
333. Despedirse a la francesa	Irse como burro sin mecate; Pintarse (*Ven.*); emplumárselas (*Col., Ven.*)	To take French leave
334. Después de		After; following
335. Detrás de	Detrás mío (tuyo, etc.) (*Ch., Ríopl.*)	Behind
336. Día hábil		Workday
337. Dicho y hecho		No sooner said than done
338. Digno de confianza		Reliable; trustworthy
339. Dijo la sartén a la caldera, quítate de allá, que me tiznas	El comal le dijo a la olla, qué tiznada estás (*Mex.*)	The pot called the kettle black
340. Dime con quien andas y te diré quién eres	Dime quien es tu junta y te diré si haces yunta	A man is known by the company he keeps; birds of a feather flock together
341. Dios mediante	Si Dios nos da vida; primero Dios (*C.A.*)	God willing; I hope so
342. Dirigir la palabra		To address; to speak to; to talk to
343. Disculparse por		To apologize for
344. Disponer de		To have at one's disposal; to spend; to get rid of
345. Disponerse a		To get ready to
346. Divertirse en grande	Pachanguear (*Mex.*); pasarla a todo dar	To have the time of one's life; to have a ball
347. Doblar la hoja	Cambiar el disco	To change the subject
348. Don de gentes		Winning manners; a way with people
349. Donde hubo fuego hay cenizas	Donde camotes quemaron, cenizas quedaron (*Andes*)	Where there's smoke, there's fire
350. Donde menos se piensa salta la liebre	De cualquier maya salta un ratón (*Ríopl.*)	The unexpected always happens; it happens when least expected
351. Echar a perder		To spoil; to go to waste
352. Echar al correo		To post, mail (letters, etc.)
353. Echar de menos	Extrañar; añorar; hacerle falts a uno (*Andes*)	To feel the absence of; to miss; to long for
354. Echar de ver	Catar de ver (*Col., Ven.*)	To notice; to observe
355. Echar flores	Decir piropos	To flatter; to sweet-talk
356. Echar indirectas		To make insinuations
357. Echar la casa por la ventana		To go all out; to kill the fatted calf; to blow the works
358. Echar la culpa a		To lay (put) the blame on
359. Echar la llave		To lock the door
360. Echar los bofes	¡A darle duro! (*Mex.*)	To work hard; to throw oneself into a job
361. Echar sapos y culebras	Echar tacos (*Mex.*) Echar ajos y cebollas; subir la prima (*Arg.*)	To swear a blue streak; to turn the air blue
362. Echar todo a rodar	Patearle el nido a alguien	To spoil things; to upset everything; to make a mess of everything
363. Echar un sueño (una siesta)	Tomar una siestita; tomar una pestañita (*Mex.*)	To take a nap; to catch a little shut-eye
364. Echar una mano		To lend a hand; to help out
365. Echar un párrafo	Echar guáguara (*Mex.*)	To pass the time of day; to chew the rag (fat)
366. Echarse a		To begin; to suddenly start
367. Echarse para atrás	Rajarse (*Mex.*)	To back out; to back down; to give in
368. Echarse un trago	Echarse un fogonazo (*Mex.*); empinar el codo; empinar el cacho (*Ch.*); pegarse un palo (*Carib., Col.*)	To take a drink (swig); to wet the whistle

Academy Spanish	American Spanish Variants	English Equivalents
369. El día menos pensado	Un día de éstos	One of these fine days
370. El gallito del lugar	El mero mero (*Mex.*)	The cock of the walk; the top banana; the top dog
371. El hombre propone y Dios dispone	El hombre propone, Dios dispone y la mujer descompone	Man proposes, God disposes
372. El mejer día		Some fine day
373. El que no se arriesga no pasa la mar	El que no arriesga no gana	Nothing ventured, nothing gained
374. Empeñarse en		To insist on; to be bent on
375. Empleo de cuello y levita	Empleo de camisa blanca y corbata	White-collar job
376. En aquel entonces		At that time; in those days
377. En breve plazo	Dentro de poco	Within a short time
378. En broma		As a joke; in jest
379. En calidad de		In the capacity of
380. En cambio		On the other hand; but
381. En cierta manera	Hasta cierto punto	In a way
382. En cuanto	Tan pronto como	As soon as
383. En cuanto a		Regarding; as for
384. En cueros	En traje de Adán; en pelota; pila (*Andes*)	Naked; in one's birthday suit; naked as a jay bird
385. En efectivo	En dinero contante y sonante; al chaz-chaz (*Mex.*)	In hard cash; in cold cash; cash on the barrel-head
386. En efecto	El hecho es que	In fact; as a matter of fact
387. En el extranjero		Abroad
388. En el peligro se conoce al amigo	En la cárcel se conocen los amigos	A friend in need is a friend indeed
389. En el fondo		At bottom; at heart; by nature
390. En favor de		On behalf of
391. En fila		In line
392. En fin	Así es que	In short; so
393. En firme	A la segura (*Ch., Andes*); a la fija (*Col.*)	Definite; binding
394. En grande		On a large scale; in a big way
395. En gustos no hay disputa	Sobre gustos se rompen géneros	Every man to his taste; some like it hot; some like it cold
396. En hora buena		Safely; luckily; o.k.
397. En la actualidad	Hoy; estos días	At the present time; nowadays
398. En lo alto de		On top of
399. En lo futuro	En el porvenir	Hereafter; in the future
400. En lugar de		Instead of
401. En mangas de camisa		In shirt sleeves
402. En mi perra vida	En mi cochina vida	Never in all my life; never in all my born days
403. En presencia de		Before; in the presence of; in front of
404. En primer lugar		In the first place
405. En principio		In principle; basically
406. En punto		Exactly (time); on the dot
407. En regla		In order
408. En rueda	Entre pura raza (*Mex.*)	A friendly gathering; among friends
409. En su apogeo		At the height of one's glory; at one's peak
410. En suma	Total	In short; briefly
411. En tal caso		In such a case
412. En todo caso		In any event; anyway
413. En total	Total	In short; to sum up
414. En un abrir y cerrar de ojos		In the twinkling of an eye
415. En un descuido	En un improviso (*Ven., Col.*)	When least expected
416. En un dos por tres	En menos que canta un gallo	When least expected; quick as a wink; in the shake of a lamb's tail
417. En vano	Al ñudo (*Ríopl.*)	In vain
418. En vez de		Instead of
419. En voz alta		Out loud

Academy Spanish	*American Spanish Variants*	*English Equivalents*
420. En voz baja	Despacio	In a soft (low) voice
421. Encargarse de		To take charge of
422. Encogerse de hombros		To shrug one's shoulders
423. Enfrente de		Opposite; across the way from
424. Enterarse de	Informarse	To find out about; to learn
425. Entrado en años	Ya vetarro	Well along in years; to be no spring chicken
426. Entrar en materia	Llegar al caso	To come to the point; get down to business
427. Entre azul y buenas noches	Entre dos aguas; ni un sí ni un no	To be undecided; to be on the fence
428. Entre bastidores		To be behind the scenes
429. Entre la espada y la pared	Entre dos fuegos	To be between the devil and the deep blue sea
430. Equivocarse de	Salirle a uno gabacho	To be mistaken about
431. Es decir	O sea	That is to say; in other words
432. Es fama que	Dizque (*Col.*); corre la bola que (*C.A.*)	It is rumored that; they say that
433. Es harina de otro costal	Es otro cantar; no viene al cuento	That's a horse of a different color
434. Es más bravo que un león	Es un perro; es una fiera	He is a tiger (wildcat)
435. ¡Esto es Jauja!	¡Esta es la tierra de Dios y María Santísima!	This is Seventh Heaven! This is Never-Never Land!
436. Escapársele a uno		To escape one's attention; to get by one
437. Escurrir el bulto	Emplumárselas (*Col., Ven.*); pelarse	To sneak away; to slip away
438. Esforzarse en (por)	Luchar por	To strive to; to struggle to
439. Está bien (bueno)		All right; o.k.
440. Está hasta en la sopa	Le dicen el diosito	There's no getting away from him; I'm sick of the sight of him
441. Está que pela	Está como para desplumar pollos	It's piping hot; It's as hot as blue blazes
442. Estar a cargo		To be in charge
443. Estar a disgusto		To be ill at ease; to feel awkward
444. Estar a gusto		To be contented; to be comfortable
445. Estar a la expectativa	Catiar la laucha (*Ch.*)	To be on the lookout for
446. Estar a la merced de		To be at the mercy of
447. Estar a punto de	Estar por	To be about to
448. Estar en su elemento	Estar en su cancha (*Ríopl.; Andes*); Estar en su mole (*Mex.*)	To be in one's element
449. Estar con ánimo de		To have a notion to
450. Estar chiflado	Le patina el embrague a uno; tener los alambres pelados (*Ch.*)	To have a screw loose; not to have all one's marbles
451. Estar de acuerdo		To agree
452. Estar de buen humor		To be in a good humor; to be in a good frame of mind
453. Estar de luto	Estar de duelo	To be in mourning
454. Estar de malas	Tener la de malas; tener el santo a espaldas (*Ven., Mex.*); estar salado (*Col., Andes*)	To be out of luck
455. Estar de moda	Estar en boga	To be fashionable; to be popular; to be the "in" thing
456. Estar de sobra		To be superfluous; to be too much
457. Estar de turno		To be on duty; to be on one's shift
458. Estar de viaje		To be traveling; to be on the road
459. Estar en buen uso	Estar en buenas condiciones	To be in good condition; to be in good shape

Academy Spanish	American Spanish Variants	English Equivalents
460. Estar en el pellejo de otro		To be in somebody else's shoes
461. Estar en la luna		To be up in the clouds
462. Estar en las nubes		To daydream; to be high (prices)
463. Estar en lo cierto		To be right; to be correct
464. Estar en lo firme		To be in the right
465. Estar en los huesos	Estar hecho un violín (*Ven.*); no quedarle a uno más que hueso y cuero	To be nothing but skin and bone
466. Estar en plan de		To be in the mood for; to be out for
467. Estar en un error	Estar equivocado	To be mistaken; to be wrong
468. Estar en vigor		To be in effect; to be in force
469. Estar en vísperas de		To be on the eve of; to be about to
470. Estar hecho una furia	Estar como agua para chocolate; estar hecho un chivo; estar hecho un quique (*Ch.*)	To be beside oneself; to be hot under the collar
471. Estar muy metido en		To be deeply involved in
472. Estar para	Estar por	To be about to
473. Estar por	Estar a favor de	To be in favor of; to be for
474. Estar prevenido		To be prepared; to be forewarned
475. Estar quebrado	Estar arrancado; estar bruja (*Mex.*); estar pato (*Ch.*)	To be broke (flat broke)
476. Estar rendido	Estar reventado	To be exhausted; to be all tired out; to be pooped
477. Estar sentido	Estar resentido	To be offended; to be hurt
478. Estar todo patas arriba	Ser todo un verdadero relajo	To be topsy-turvy; to be helter-skelter
479. Estrechar la mano	Chocarla	To shake hands
480. Extrañarle a uno		To seem strange (funny) to one
481. Faltar a		To absent oneself from; to miss
482. Fiarse en (de)		To trust; to rely on
483. Figurarse que	Se me hace que	Imagine that
484. Fijarse en		To pay attention to; to notice
485. Formar parte de		To be a member of; to be a part of
486. Frente a		Facing; opposite; in front of
487. Fuerte como un roble	Bien trabado	As strong as an ox; as strong as a bull moose
488. Fuera de sí		Unconscious; beside oneself
489. Función corrida	Permanencia voluntaria	All-day program; come-and-go function
490. Fulano	Ciertas hierbas (*Col., C.A.*)	Mr. So-and-so; what's-his-name
491. Ganar a uno la mano	Coger a uno la delantera; madrugarle a uno	To get up too early for one; to beat one to it
492. Ganarse la vida	Ganarse el pan de cada día; pegarse para ganar la gorda (*Mex.*)	To work for a living
493. Genio y figura hasta la sepultura	Al que nace barrigón, es al ñudo que lo fajen (*Ríopl.*)	You can't make a silk purse out of a sow's ear; the leopard doesn't change its spots
494. Gente menuda	La chiquillería	Small fry
495. Gracias a		Thanks to
496. Gritar como si le mataran	Gritar como marrano atorado en un caño	To scream bloody murder; to scream like a stuck pig
497. Guardarse de		To guard against; to avoid
498. Guiñar un ojo	Hacer ojos (*Col.*); hacer ojitos (*Mex.*); hacer caras (*Ríopl.*)	To make eyes at; to flirt; to give the glad eye to
499. Haber de		To be expected to; to be scheduled to

Academy Spanish	*American Spanish Variants*	*English Equivalents*
500. Haber de todo como en botica		There's a little of everything
501. Haber noros en la costa		The coast is not clear; something's up
502. Habituarse a	Acostumbrarse a; amañarse (*Col..*)	To accustom oneself to; to get used to
503. Hablar como una cotorra	No pararle la boca a uno (*Mex.*)	To be a chatterbox; to be a windbag
504. Hablar en voz baja	Hablar despacio; hablar quedito	To speak softly; to speak in a low voice
505. Hablar entre dientes		To mumble; to mutter
506. Hablar hasta por los codos	Ser lengualarga	To chatter; to talk idly; to talk too much
507. Hablar sin rodeos	Cantar claro; Pelar el cobre; Ser claridoso (*Ven., C.A.*); Hablar a calzón quitado (*Col., Ch.*)	Not to mince any words; to speak straight from the shoulder; tell it like it is
508. Hacer alarde	Echársela; echar flotas (*Col., Ven.*); levantarse el tarro (*Ch.*)	To boast; to brag
509. Hacer algo a medias		To do a halfway job; to do a poor job
510. Hacer arrancar	Dar un empujón	To set the ball rolling; to get the show on the road
511. Hacer buen papel	Jugar buen papel	To make a good showing
512. Hacer buenas migas		To get along well together
513. Hacer caso a uno	Dar boleto a uno	To pay attention to one
514. Hacer cola		To queue up; to stand in line; to line up
515. Hacer comedia	Hacer tango	To put on a show; to make a scene
516. Hacer la vista gorda		To pretend not to see; to wink at
517. Hacer escala		To make a scheduled stop; to stopover
518. Hacer falta		To be necessary; to have need of
519. Hacer frente a		To confront; to face up to
520. Hacer gestos		To make faces (gestures)
521. Hacer gracia	Parecer chistoso	To strike one as funny
522. Hacer hincapié	Poner énfasis; porfiar	To emphasize; to insist upon
523. Hacer juego		To match; to go well with
524. Hacer mal papel	Jugar mal papel	To make a poor showing; to play a poor role
525. Hacer novillos	Pintar venado (*Mex.*)	To cut classes; to play hooky
526. Hacer presente		To notify; to remind
527. Hacer puente		To take the intervening day off
528. Hacer su agosto		To feather one's nest; to make a killing
529. Hacer un mandado	Hacer un recado	To run an errand
530. Hacerle a uno un flaco servicio	Hacerle a uno la pera; jugar sucio (*Ch.*)	To do someone a bad turn; to play a dirty trick on someone
531. Hacerle daño a uno		To hurt or harm someone
532. Hacerse de noche		To get dark
533. Hacerse el sordo	Hacerse el cucho (*Ch.*)	To turn a deaf ear; to refuse to consider
534. Hacerse el tonto	Hacerse el loco; hacerse el menso (*Mex.*)	To play (act) the fool; to play dumb
535. Hacerse ilusiones		To build castles in Spain; to blow bubbles in the air
536. Hacerse tarde		To become (get) late
537. Hallarse en el pellejo de otro		To be in somebody else's shoes
538. Harto da quien da lo que tiene	El que da lo suyo, harto hace	You can't get blood from a turnip (stone)
539. Hasta aquí		So far; up to now
540. Hasta cierto punto		To a certain point (extent)

Academy Spanish	American Spanish Variants	English Equivalents
541. Hasta el tuétano	Hasta las cachas (*Mex.*)	To the core; to the very center
542. Hasta la fecha		To date; up to now
543. Hasta luego	Ahí nos vemos; hasta lueguito (*Mex.*)	So long; see you later; hurry back
544. Hay que	Es necesario	It is necessary; you have to
545. Hecho a la medida		Custom-made; made to order
546. Hecho y derecho		Mature; grown-up
547. Hincarse de rodillas	Arrodillarse	To kneel down
548. Historias de cuartel	Cuentos colorados; chistes verdes (*Mex.*)	Off-color jokes; pool-room talk
549. Hoy en día	Hoy día; hoy	These days; nowadays
550. Hoy por hoy	Actualmente	Under the present circumstances; for the time being
551. Ida y vuelta		Round-trip
552. Idas y venidas		Comings and goings
553. Impedir el paso		To block the way
554. Imponerse a	Apretar el breque (*Col.*)	To dominate; to command respect
555. Importarle a uno		To be of importance to one; to concern one
556. Incorporarse a		To join (a society or unit)
557. Inocente como una paloma	Como una blanca paloma (*Mex.*)	As harmless as a fly; as innocent as a new-born baby
558. Informarse de		To find out about
559. Ir a medias	Ir mitad mitad	To go fifty-fifty
560. Ir al grano	Ir a lo que truje	To get down to brass tacks; to get to the point
561. Ir de compras	Ir de tiendas	To go shopping
562. Ir del brazo		To walk arm in arm
563. Irle a uno bien (mal)		To be becoming (unbecoming); to be well
564. Irse de juerga	Irse de parranda; irse de tuna (*Col.*); irse de farras (*Riopl.*); irse de jarana (*Ven.*); irse de rumba (*Carib.*)	To go on a spree; to paint the town red
565. Irsele a uno el santo al cielo	Irsele a uno la onda	One's mind goes blank; one clean forgets; to be spacy
566. Jugar con dos barajas	Mamar a dos tetas	To double-cross; to play both ends against the middle
567. Jugarle una mala pasada a uno	Hacerle a uno la cama (*Ch.*)	To play foul with one; to play a dirty trick on one
568. Juntarse con		To associate with; to join
569. La alta sociedad	La gente copetuda	High society; the upper crust; the jet set
570. La esperanz es lo último que se pierde	Como el tiempo dure, lugar tiene la esperanza	Hope springs eternal; while there's life there's hope
571. La mar de	Cantidad de; un montón de; un volcán de (*C.A.*); patadas (*Ec.*); a ponchadas (*Andes*)	Lots of; loads of; oodles of; right smart of
572. La madeja se enreda	Se enreda la pita	The plot thickens
573. La letra con sangre entra		There's no royal road to learning
574. La mayor parte de	Los más de	The majority of; most of
575. La niña de mis (tus, etc.) ojos		The apple of one's eye
576. La necesidad hace maestro		Necessity is the mother of invention
577. La piedra quieta cría malva	Piedra que rueda no cría moho	A rolling stone gathers no moss
578. La vida no es senda de rosas	No todo es vida y dulzura	Life is not a bed of roses; Life is not all beer and skittles
579. Las verdades amargan	La verdad no peca pero incomoda	Truth begets hatred; the truth hurts

Academy Spanish	*American Spanish Variants*	*English Equivalents*
580. Leer entre renglones		To read between the lines
581. Lejos de		Far from
582. Levantar la mesa	Quitar la mesa	To clear the table
583. Levantarse del pie izquierdo	Levantarse de malas	To get up on the wrong side of the bed
584. Librarse de		To get rid of; to escape from
585. Lo de menos		The least of it
586. Lo indicado		What has been stated; that which is stated
587. Lo que el agua trae el agua lleva	Lo del agua, al agua	Easy come, easy go
588. Los estadistas de café		Arm-chair strategists; sidewalk superintendents
589. Los niños y los locos dicen las verdades	Los niños y los borrachos siempre dicen la verdad	Out of the mouths of babes and sucklings
590. Llamar la atención		To attract attention; to reprimand
591. Llegar a las manos	Irse a los moquetes; irse al moño (entre mujeres) (*Ch.*)	To come to blows; to get into a fight
592. Llegar a ser		To become; to get to be
593. Llevar a cabo		To accomplish; to carry out
594. Llevar la contra		To oppose; to contradict
595. Llevar la delantera		To be ahead
596. Llevar puesto		To be wearing
597. Llevar uno su merecido		To get what's coming (to one)
598. Llevar ventaja		To be ahead; to have a lead
599. Llevarse bien con		To get along well with
600. Llevarse un chasco	Pegarse palo	To be disappointed; to have a setback
601. Llorar a lágrima viva	Llorar como becerro en llano; soltar puchero (*Ch.*)	To cry like a baby
602. Llover a cántaros	Llover con rabia (*Carib.*); caer burros aparejados (*Carib.*)	To rain bucketsful; to pour; to rain cats and dogs
603. Llovido del cielo		Out of a clear blue sky
604. Mal genio	De maleta (*Andes*)	Bad temper
605. Mal que le pese a uno		Whether one likes it or not
606. Mandar a uno al diablo	Mandar a uno a la porra	(Tell someone to) Go to the devil; (Tell someone to) go jump in the lake
607. Mandar a uno a paseo	Mandar a uno a ver si ya puso la marrana	(Tell someone to) Go fly a kite
608. Más adelante		Farther on; later on
609. ¡Manos a la obra!		Let's get to work
610. Más allá (de)		Farther on; beyond
611. Más bien		Rather
612. Más falso que Judas		As false as a counterfeit penny; worthless as a plugged nickel
613. Más vale pájaro en mano que buitre volando	Más vale pájaro en mano que cien(to) volando; más vale guajito tengo que acocote tendré (*Mex.*)	A bird in the hand is worth two in the bush
614. Más vale prevenir que lamentar	Un gramo de previsión vale más que una tonelada de curación	An ounce of prevention is worth a pound of cure
615. Más vale tarde que nunca	Nunca es tarde cuando la dicha es buena	Better late than never
616. Matar dos pájaros de un tiro	Matar dos pájaros de una pedrada	To kill two birds with one stone
617. Media naranja		Better half; spouse
618. Mejor dicho		Or rather; better yet
619. Mejor que mejor	Tanto mejor	All the better; so much the better
620. Menos de		Fewer than; less than
621. Menos mal	Date de santos que no fue peor	So much the better; it could have been worse

Academy Spanish	American Spanish Variants	English Equivalents
622. Merecer la pena		To be worthwhile; to be worth the trouble
623. Meter en un puño a uno	Tener a uno agarrado de las greñas	To have someone by the neck; to have someone over a barrel
624. Meter la nariz en todas partes	Meter uno su cuchara en todo	To put one's oar in everywhere; to stick one's nose in others' business
625. Meterlo en el bolsillo	Echarse a uno a la bolsa	To wrap someone around one's little finger
626. Meterse a		To become; to decide to become
627. Meterse con		To pick a fight with
628. Meterse de hoz y coz	Meterse a la brava	To elbow one's way into
629. Mientras más ... más	Entre más ... más (*C.A.*, *Col.*)	The more ... the more
630. Mientras menos ... menos	Entre menos ... menos (*C.A.*, *Col.*)	The less ... the less
631. Mirar alrededor		To look around
632. Mirar de hito en hito	Mirar fijamente	To stare at; to eye up and down
633. Mirar de lado		To look askance at; to look at with a side glance
634. Mirar por		To take care of; to look after
635. Molestarse con		To bother about; to take the trouble to
636. Morderse la lengua		To hold one's tongue; to keep quiet
637. ¡Mucho ojo!	Un ojo al gato y otro al garabato	Look out! Watch your step!
638. Mucho ruido, pocas nueces	Tanto cacarear para no poner hueva; más la bulla que la cabuya (*Ven.*); es más la bulla que las mazorcas (*Col.*)	Much ado about nothing; his bark is worse than his bite
639. Muchos recuerdos a		Kindest regards to; the best to
640. Muy campante	Como si nada; de muchas correas	Cool as a cucumber
641. Muy de noche		Very late at night
642. Nacer con estrella	Nacer de pie	To be born lucky; to be born with a silver spoon in one's mouth
643. Nada de particular		Nothing unusual; nothing special
644. Nadar en la abundancia	Estar muy pesudo; estar bien parado	To be rolling in money (dough)
645. Negarse a		To refuse to
646. Negocio redondo		Good sound bargain
647. Negro como el carbón	Prieto retinto	As black as ink; as black as the ace of spades
648. ¡Ni a tiros!	¡En absoluto! ¡ni de vainas! (*Col.*); ¡ni bamba! (*Col.*)	Not for anything; not for love or money
649. ¡Ni en sueños!	¡Qué esperanza! (*Ríopl.*; *Andes*); ¡cuando! (*Ec.*); ¡frijoles! (*Carib.*)	By no means! Not on your life!
650. ¡Ni mucho menos!		Far from it! Not by a long shot!
651. Ni siquiera		Not even; not a single
652. ¡Ni soñar!	¡Ni por pienso!	Not even in your dreams! Not by a long shot!
653. Ninguna parte	Ningún lado	Nowhere; no place
654. No andarse por las ramas	No andarse con medias tazas	Not to beat around the bush
655. No cabe duda		There is no doubt; beyond a shadow of a doubt; have (has) got to be (*Jones has got to be the best pitcher*)
656. No caber en sí de gozo	No caber en el pellejo de gozo	To be beside oneself with joy; to be overcome with joy

	Academy Spanish	*American Spanish Variants*	*English Equivalents*
657.	No caer en la cuenta	No encontrarle el chiste	Not to see the point; not to get it
658.	No dar el brazo a torcer	No aflojar un pelo (*Ríopl.*) *Andes*); hacer pata ancha (*Ríopl.*)	To be stubborn; to be not easily deceived; to be unyielding; to stick to one's guns
659.	No dar ni un vaso de agua	Ser muy codo; no darle un grano de arroz al gallo de la Pasión	To be a real Scrooge; to be very stingy
660.	No darse por entendido		To pretend not to understand
661.	No dejar piedra por mover		To leave no stone unturned
662.	No dejarle a uno ni a sol ni a sombra	Seguirlo hasta que se eche	To breathe down someone's neck; to dog someone's footsteps; to bug someone
663.	No despegar los labios	No chillar	To keep silent; to keep one's mouth shut
664.	No estar para bromas	No estar de humor	To be in no mood for joking; not to be in a laughing mood
665.	No hay de qué	De nada; por nada (*Mex.*)	Don't mention it; you're welcome
666.	No hay excusa que valga	No hay pero que valga; o la bebes o la derramas	Excuse or no excuse; no buts about it
667.	No hay mal que por bien no venga -	Una afortunada desgracia	It's an ill wind that blows no good; it's a blessing in disguise
668.	¡No hay que achicarse!	¡No hay que rajarse! (*Mex.*)	Keep your chin up! Keep a stiff upper lip! Don't give in!
669.	No hay que darle vueltas		There's no getting around it
670.	No importa	No le hace	It doesn't matter; Never mind!
671.	No me importa un comino	No me importa un pito; no me importa un cacahuate (*Mex.*); no me importa un cacao (*C.A.*)	I don't care a bit
672.	No le suena a uno		It doesn't mean a thing; It doesn't ring a bell
673.	No morderse la lengua	Cantar claro; ser claridoso (*Ven., C.A.*)	Not to mince words; to speak straight from the shoulder
674.	No poder con	No ser un hueso fácil de roer	Not to be able to stand something (someone); to be too much for one
675.	No poder ver a alguien	No poder aguantar a uno; no tragar a uno ni con bombilla de plata (*Ríopl.*)	Not to be able to tolerate (stand) someone
676.	No saber dónde meterse	Estar del pin al pon (*Carib.*)	Not to know which way to turn
677.	No saber ni jota	No saber ni papa	Not to know a blessed thing; not to know enough to come in out of the rain
678.	No se ganó Zamora en una hora	No se ganó Toledo en un credo	Rome wasn't built in a day
679.	No ser ni la sombra de uno		Not to be the shadow of one's former self
680.	No tener ni en qué caerse muerto	No tener ni segunda camisa; estar arrancado; andar pato (*Ch., Ríopl.*)	Not to have a penny to call one's own; not to have a red cent
681.	No tener pelos en la lengua	Ser claridoso (*Ven., C.A.*); hablar a calzón quitado (*Ch., Col.*)	To be outspoken; to speak one's mind
682.	No tener pies ni cabeza		Not to make sense
683.	No tener precio		To be much esteemed; to be priceless
684.	No tener remedio		To be beyond repair (help, recourse); (to say something) can't be helped

Academy Spanish	*American Spanish Variants*	*English Equivalents*
685. No todo el monte es orégano	No todo ha de ser chayotes ni vainicas (*C.A.*)	Things aren't always as we should like them
686. No valer un comino	No valer un cacahuate (*Mex.*); no valer un cacao; (*C.A.*); no valer un palo de tabaco (*Col.*); no valer un taco (*Col.*); estar para el gato (*Ch.*)	Not to be worth a brass farthing (cent)
687. Obras son amores, que no buenas razones	Acciones son amores, no besos ni apachurrones	Actions speak louder than words
688. Obstinarse en	Ponerle pino a algo (*Ch.*); hacer lomo en (*Ven.*)	To persist in; to insist on
689. Ocurrírsele a uno		To occur to one; to cross one's mind
690. Oír hablar de	Oír mentar	To hear about
691. Ojos que no ven, corazón que no siente	Ojos que no ven tienen menos que sentir	Ignorance is bliss; out of sight, out of mind
692. Oponer resistencia	Pararle el carro a uno; pararle el macho a uno	To offer resistance
693. Otra vez		Again; once more
694. Padre mercader, hijo caballero, nieto limosnero	Padre pulpero, hijo caballero, nieto limosnero (*Perú*)	Three generations from shirt sleeve to shirt sleeve
695. Pagar a plazos		To pay in installments
696. Pagar en la misma moneda		To get even; tit for tat
697. Pagar los gastos		To pay the expenses; to foot the bill
698. ¡Palabra!	¡Palabra de honor! ¡En serio!	Word of honor! On the level! No fooling! Sure enough!
699. ¡Pamplinas!	¡Pura guasa! ¡Frijoles! (*Carib.*)	Nonsense! Horsefeathers! Baloney!
700. Para colmo de males	¡No faltaba más!	That's the last straw! That does it! That's the straw that broke the camel's back
701. Parar (la) oreja		To prick up one's ears; to sit up and take notice
702. Pararle los pies a uno	Pararle el carro a uno; pararle el macho a uno	To put an end to something; to put one's foot down
703. Parece mentira		It hardly seems possible; it seems impossible
704. Parecido a		Similar to; like
705. Pares y nones		Odds and evens
706. Participar de		To share in
707. Pasado de moda		Out of style; out of date
708. Pasar de la raya		To go too far
709. Pasar de largo	Pasar de hilo	To pass by (without stopping)
710. Pasar el rato		To pass the time away; to spend the time
711. Pasar estrecheces	Pasar hambres; andar torcido	To feel the pinch
712. Pasar la mano por el lomo	Darle la suave a uno; ser barbero (*Mex.*)	To butter someone up; to soft-soap someone; to polish the apple; to brown-nose
713. Pasarse sin		To get along without
714. Pasársele a uno		To get over; to forget
715. Pasársele a uno la mano		To overdo; to go too far
716. Paso a paso		Step by step; little by little
717. Pedir prestado	Prestar (*C.A., Col.*)	To ask (someone) to lend (one something); to borrow
718. Pedirle peras al olmo	Andar buscando guayabas en los magueyes	To try to get blood from a turnip (stone)
719. Pensar de		To have an opinion about; to think of
720. Pensar en		To think about
721. Perder de vista		To lose sight of
722. Perder el hilo de	Perder la hebra de	To lose the thread of
723. Perder la cabeza		To lose one's head (cool)
724. Perder la vista		To go blind

Academy Spanish	*American Spanish Variants*	*English Equivalents*
725. Perder los estribos		To lose one's mind; to flip one's lid
726. Perderse de vista		To vanish; to disappear
727. Perro ladrador nunca buen mordedor	Perro que ladra no muerde	Barking dogs seldom bite
728. Pesarle a uno		To be sorry for
729. Plan de estudios		Curriculum; course of study
730. Poco a poco		Little by little; gradually
731. Poco después (de)		A little later; soon after
732. Poco más o menos		More or less; about
733. Poner a uno al corriente	Ponerle al tanto a uno	To inform one; to bring one up to date
734. Poner el grito en el cielo		To make a great fuss; to hit the ceiling
735. Poner en claro		To clear up; to unravel
736. Poner en marcha		To start; to put in motion
737. Poner en ridículo		To humiliate; to make a fool of
738. Poner la mesa		To set the table
739. Poner mucho ojo		To pay close attention
740. Poner pies en polvorosa	Tomar el polvo (*Mex.*, *Col.*); Emplumárselas (*Col.*); salir fletado (*Ven.*)	To run away; to beat it; to take a powder; to hightail it
741. Poner pleito		To sue; to bring charges against
742. Poner reparo(s)		To raise objections
743. Ponerse a	Echarse a	To set about; to begin to
744. Ponerse a la obra		To get to work
745. Ponerse colorado		To blush
746. Ponerse de acuerdo		To come to an agreement
747. Ponerse de pie	Pararse	To get up; to stand
748. Ponerse disgustado	Ponerse bravo; picarse (*Col.*)	To get angry
749. Ponerse en camino		To start out; to hit the road
750. Ponerse en contra		To oppose
751. Ponérsele a uno carne de gallina		To get gooseflesh; to get goose pimples; to get burr (brrr) bumps
752. Por adelantado	Con anticipación	In advance; beforehand
753. Por ahora	Por el momento	For the present; for right now
754. Por aquí cerca		Around here; close by
755. Por casualidad		By chance; by the way
756. Por consiguiente	Por lo tanto	Therefore; so
757. Por dentro		Inside; within
758. Por detrás		From behind; in back
759. ¿Por dónde?		Which way? Where?
760. Por encima(de)		Above; superficially
761. Por entre		Among; between; through
762. Por extenso		At length; in detail
763. Por fin	A las cansadas (*Riopl.*, *Andes*); a la cansada (*Ec.*)	At last; at long last; Finally!
764. Por fórmula		As a matter of form
765. Por fortuna	Por suerte	Fortunately
766. Por fuera		On the outside
767. Por hoy	Por ahora	For the present
768. Por intermedio de		By means of; through
769. Por el hilo se saca el olvillo	Por la hebra se saca el olvillo; En el modo de cortar el queso se conoce al tendero	By their fruits shall ye know them; a fool is known by his laughing
770. Por la mitad		In the middle; in half
771. Por las buenas o por las malas	De mangas o de faldas (*Ec.*)	Whether one likes it or not; by hook or by crook
772. Por las nubes		Sky-high; up in the clouds
773. Por lo cual	Por cuyo motivo	For which reason; and so
774. Por lo demás		As for the rest; moreover
775. Por fuerza	De juro (*Riopl.*, *Andes*); juramente (*Andes*)	Of necessity; necessarily
776. Por lo general	Por regla general; por lo regular	Usually; in general

Academy Spanish	American Spanish Variants	English Equivalents
777. Por lo menos	Cuando menos; al menos	At least
778. Por lo pronto	Por el momento	For the time being
779. Por lo que toca a...		As far as ... is concerned
780. Por lo regular		Ordinarily; as a rule
781. Por lo visto		Apparently; evidently
782. Por más que		However much
783. Por ningún lado		Nowhere; no place
784. Por ningún motivo		Under no circumstances; no way!
785. Por ninguna parte		Nowhere; no place
786. Por otra parte		On the other hand
787. Por poco	Por un pelito de rana; casi, casi	Almost; like(d) to
788. Por primera vez		For the first time
789. Por regla general		Usually; as a rule
790. Por sabido se calla	¡Clarinete!	It goes without saying
791. Por si acaso		Just in case; if by chance
792. Por supuesto	Claro que sí; ¿cómo no?	Of course; certainly
793. Por sus puños		On one's own
794. Por término medio		On the average
795. Por última vez		For the last time
796. Por un lado ... por otro		On one hand ... on the other hand
797. Preguntar por		To inquire about; to ask for (a person)
798. Preguntarse si, cuándo, cómo, etc.		To wonder (if, when, how, etc.)
799. Prender fuego a	Prender candela (Col., Andes)	To set fire to; to set on fire
800. Preocuparse por		To worry about
801. Presentación en sociedad	Fiesta quinceañera	Debutantes' ball; coming-out party
802. Prestar atención		To pay attention; to be alert
803. Prestarse a		To lend itself to; to be used for
804. Presumir de		To consider oneself to be
805. Pretender decir		To mean; to imply
806. Pringar en todas	Ser sjonjolí de todos los moles (Mex.)	To have a finger in every pie
807. Proceder en contra		To take action against
808. Prometer el oro y el moro	Prometer las perlas de la Virgen	To promise wonders (the moon)
809. Pues bien	Pues entonces	All right then; so
810. Puesto que	Ya que	Because of the fact that; since
811. Punto de vista		Point of view; standpoint
812. Punto por punto		Step by step; in detail
813. Puro jarabe de pico	Pura guasa; pura parada (Mex.)	Just talk; lip service; eyewash
814. Que Dios le tenga en la gloria	Que en paz descanse	God rest his soul; may he rest in peace
815. ¿Qué más da?		What's the difference? So what?
816. ¿Qué mosca te picó?		What's the matter with you? What's bugging you?
817. ¿Qué hay de nuevo?	¿Quiubo? (qué hubo) (Mex., Col.)	What's up? What's the good word? How goes it?
818. Quedar bien con		To get along well with; to make a hit with
819. Quedar como postes	Quedarse hecho un idiota	To sit like a bump on a log; to stand there like an idiot
820. Quedar en		To agree (on)
821. Quedar en (de)		To promise to
822. Quedar en los huesos	No quedar más que hueso y cuero	To be a mere skeleton; to be nothing but skin and bones
823. Quedar en paz	Quedar a mano	To be even; to be square
824. Quedar entendido que		To be understood that
825. Quedar mal con		Not to be on good terms with; not to make a hit with

Academy Spanish	*American Spanish Variants*	*English Equivalents*
826. Quedarse a la luna de Valencia	Dejarle a uno de a pie; quedarse a la luna de Paita (*Andes*)	To be left holding the bag
827. Quedarse con		To agree to buy (take)
828. Quedarse confundido		To be confused
829. Quedarse para vestir santos	Quedarse para vender estampas y milagros	To be left on the shelf
830. Quemarse las cejas	Quemarse las pestañas; ponerse barbero (*Col.*); machetear (*Mex.*)	To burn the midnight oil; to cram for an exam
831. Querer decir		To mean
832. Quien bien te quiere, te hará llorar	Porque te quiero, te aporreo	Spare the rod and spoil the child
833. Quien fue a Sevilla perdió su silla	El que se fue para la villa perdió su silla	Finders keepers, losers weepers
834. Quien porfía mata venado	Quien mucho porfía logra algún día; hay que hacer collera (*Ch.*)	If at first you don't succeed, try, try again; never say die
835. Quitarse de en medio	Hacerse a un lado; borrarse	To get out of the way
836. Recaer sobre		To devolve upon; to revert to
837. Reducirse a		To amount to; to find oneself forced to
838. Referirse a		To refer to; to have reference to
839. Reflejarse en		To reflect on; to bring credit or discredit to
840. Reflexionar sobre		To reflect on; to think over
841. Rendir cuentas a		To render an accounting to; to present the facts to
842. Reparar en		To notice; to consider
843. Repetir como un perico	El perico dice lo que sabe pero no sabe lo que dice	To parrot (verb); to say by rote
844. Resistirse a		To be unwilling to; to refuse to
845. Responder por		To vouch for; to be responsible for
846. Rezar con	Tener que ver con	To have to do with
847. Risa de conejo	Reír de dientes afuera (*Col., Mex.*); reír a diente pelado (*Ven.*)	Half-hearted laugh
848. Rodearse de		To surround oneself with
849. Romper a		To begin; to suddenly start to; to burst out
850. Ropa blanca	Ropa interior; ropa íntima (feminine)	Underclothes; underwear
851. Saber a		Taste like
852. Saber a (la) gloria		To be delicious
853. Saber al dedillo		To know perfectly; to know in detail
854. Saber de sobra		To be fully aware; to know only too well
855. Saber llevar el compás		To be able to beat time
856. Sacar en limpio		To deduce; to understand
857. Sacar jugo de		To get a lot out of
858. Sacar partido de		To profit (gain) by
859. Sacar ventaja de		To profit by
860. Salir a pedir de boca	Salir al pelo	To be all one could wish for; to suit to a T
861. Salir al encuentro de		To go out to meet
862. Salir de Málaga y entrar en Malagón	Salir de Guatemala y entrar en Guatepeor	Out of the frying pan and into the fire
863. Salir del paso		To manage; to get by
864. Salir ganando		To come out ahead
865. Salirse con la suya		To get one's way; to get away with it
866. Saltar a la vista		To be obvious; not to be able to miss

Academy Spanish	American Spanish Variants	English Equivalents
867. Saludos a todos	Saludes a todos (*Col., Ec.*)	Greetings to all; say hello to everyone; say hey
868. ¡Sea bueno!	¡Tenga corazón! ¡No sea gacho!	Be a sport! Have a heart!
869. Seguir el rastro		To trace; to track down
870. Según el caso		According to the situation; it all depends
871. Según mi entender		As I understand (it)
872. Según parece	Por lo visto	Apparently
873. Sentir en el alma		To be terribly sorry
874. Sentir crecer la hierba	Tener oídos de tísico	To have ears like a fox; to have a sharp ear
875. Sentirse molesto	Embromarse	To be annoyed; to be bothered
876. Sentirse uno así no más	Andar bajo de forma	To feel below par; to be under the weather
877. Ser aficionado a		To be fond of; to be a fan of
878. Ser cabeza de turco		To be the scapegoat; to be the whipping boy; to be a patsy
879. Ser correcto		To be well-mannered
880. Ser de fiar		To be trustworthy; to be dependable
881. Ser de muchas vueltas	Ser muy mañoso	To know a trick (thing) or two
882. Ser de provecho		To be good for
883. Ser de rigor		To be proper; to be indispensable
884. Ser mala pieza	Ser una mala ficha (*Col.*)	To be a misfit (bad penny)
885. Ser mano	Llevar la punta	To lead; to be first
886. Ser menester		To be necessary
887. Ser muy ducho	Ser una trucha	To know the ropes
888. Ser preciso	Ser necesario	To be necessary
889. Ser presentada en sociedad	Cumplir los quince años; celebrar la fiesta quinceañera	To make (one's) social debut; to have a coming-out party
890. Ser una perla		To be a treasure (jewel)
891. Ser un burro; ser un zonzo	Ser un menso (*Mex.*); ser un pendejo (vulgar)	To be an ignoramus (dumbbell, moron)
892. Ser un éxito de taquilla		To be a box-office success (hit)
893. Ser un zángano	Ser un vampiro	To be a parasite (freeloader)
894. Serle a uno igual		To be all the same to one
895. Serle a uno indiferente		To be immaterial to one
896. Servir para	Prestarse a (*C.A.*)	To be used for
897. Sin embargo		Nevertheless
898. Sin falta		Without fail
899. Sin faltar una jota		In minutest detail
900. Sin fin de		Numberless; endless amount
901. Sin novedad		As usual; nothing new
902. Sin parar	De hilo	Endlessly; without a break
903. Sin perjuicio de	Dejando a salvo	Without affecting adversely; setting aside
904. Sin querer		Unintentionally
905. Sin remedio		Beyond solution; hopeless
906. Sin ton ni son		Without rhyme or reason
907. Sobre todo		Especially
908. Sudar la gota gorda	Sudar petróleo	To have a hard time; to sweat blood; to be in a sweat
909. Tal vez	A saber (*C.A.*); ¡quién quita! (*Col.*)	Perhaps; maybe
910. Tan pronto como		As soon as
911. Tanto como		As much as
912. Tanto mejor		So much the better
913. Tanto peor		So much the worse
914. Tarde o temprano		Sooner or later
915. Tener al corriente		To keep someone posted; to keep someone up to date
916. Tener antipatía		To dislike

Academy Spanish	*American Spanish Variants*	*English Equivalents*
917. Tener buenas aldabas	Tener buenas agarraderas; tener planca; tener enchufe (*Spain*)	To know the right people; to know influential people; to have a pipeline; to have pull
918. Tener cancha libre	Tener campo y tabla	To have a clear field; to have elbowroom
919. Tener cuidado	Pelar ojo	To be careful; to be watchful
920. Tener deseos de	Provocarle a uno (*Col.*); apetecer (*Spain*)	To be eager to; to want to
921. Tener el riñón bien cubierto	Estar bien parado; tener la canasta baja y el riñón bien cubierto (*Mex.*)	To be well-off; to be well-heeled
922. Tener en cuenta		To consider; to keep in mind
923. Tener en la punta de la lengua		To have on the tip of one's tongue
924. Tener en (la) mente		To have in mind
925. Tener en poco		To hold in low esteem; not to think much of
926. Tener fama de		To have the reputation of
927. Tener fe en		To have faith in
928. Tener ganas de	Apetecer (*Spain*); provocarle a uno (*Col.*)	To feel like; to desire
929. Tener gracia	Ser chistoso	To be funny
930. Tener la culpa		To be to blame
931. Tener la intención de		To mean to; to aim to (*South*)
932. Tener la palabra		To have permission to speak; to have the floor
933. Tener lugar		To take place; to be held
934. Tener mercado con		To trade with
935. Tener mucho mundo		To be sophisticated
936. Tener pesar por	Darle a uno pena	To be sorry about
937. Tener presente		To realize; to bear in mind
938. Tener prisa		To be in a hurry
939. Tener razón		To be right
940. Tener relación con		To have relation (connection) with
941. Tener retraso	Traer retraso; llegar placé (*Ch.*)	To be late
942. Tener sin cuidado		Not to be concerned; to care less
943. Tener trazas		To show signs
944. Tener vara alta	Tener mucha vara	To have far-reaching influence; to carry a big stick
945. Tocante a		Concerning; about; having to do with
946. Tocar de oído		To play by ear
947. Tocar en lo vivo		To hurt deeply; to cut to the quick
948. Tocarle a uno		To concern one; to be one's turn
949. Todas las veces que	Cada que	Whenever; every time that
950. Todavía no	Siempre no	Not yet
951. Todo bicho viviente		Every living soul
952. Todo lo contrario		Just the opposite
953. Todo lo demás		All the rest; everything else
954. Todo lo posible		Everything possible
955. Toma y daca	Dando y dando, pajarito volando	Cash and carry; put your money where your mouth is
956. Tomar a broma		To take as a joke
957. Tomar a pecho		To take to heart
958. Tomar cuerpo		To take shape
959. Tomar el gusto		To begin to like; to take a liking to
960. Tomar el rábano por las hojas		To put the cart before the horse
961. Tomar medidas		To take measures (measurements)

Academy Spanish	American Spanish Variants	English Equivalents
962. Tomar nota de		To take note of; jot down
963. Tomarla con		To pick on; to have a grudge against
964. Tomarle el pelo a uno	Hacerle guaje a uno (Mex.)	To pull someone's leg; to kid someone
965. Tomarle la palabra a uno		To take one at his word
966. Tomarse el trabajo de	Tomarse la molestia de	To take the trouble to
967. Tomarse la libertad de		To take the liberty to
968. Trabajar como una fiera	Trabajar como burro; trabajar como negro	To work like a dog
969. Trabar amistad		To strike up a friendship
970. Traer de cabeza a uno		To drive one crazy
971. Traer retraso		To be behind schedule; to be late
972. ¡Trato hecho!	¡Chóquela! ¡Echeme esos cinco!	It's a deal! Shake on it! Put 'er there!
973. ¡Tres hurras por fulano!	¡Una porra!	Three cheers for
974. Tropezar con	Trompezar con	To encounter; to run into
975. Un bribón de siete suelas	Uno capaz de empeñar la sábana sagrada	An errant rogue; a dirty rat
976. Un no sé qué		A certain something
977. Una comilona	Un banquetazo	A feast fit for a king; quite a spread
978. Una golondrina no hace verano		One swallow does not make a summer
979. Uno que otro		An occasional one; some; a few
980. Unos cuantos		Some; a few
981. Valer la pena		To be worthwhile; to be worth the trouble
982. Valerse de		To avail oneself of; to make use of
983. Variar de opinión		To hold a different opinion; to change one's mind
984. Velar por		To protect; to watch over; to take care of
985. Venir a parar		To turn out; to end up
986. Venirse a tierra		To collapse; to fail
987. Ver visiones		To have false notions; (to be) seeing things
988. ¡Vete a freír espárragos!	¡Vete a freír chongos! (Mex.); ¡vete a freír monos! (Col.); ¡vete a freír mocos! (Andes)	Go peddle your papers! Get lost!
989. Vísteme despacio que tengo prisa	Más vale paso que dure y no que apresure	Haste makes waste; easy does it
990. Volver el estómago	Huacarear (Mex.); echar las migas; dársele vuelta la vianda a uno (Ch.)	To vomit; to have the heaves; to upchuck; to toss one's cookies
991. Voy y vengo	No me tardo un minuto; oritita vengo (Mex.)	I'll be right back; it won't be a minute
992. Y así sucesivamente		And so on
993. Y pico		And some odd; and something
994. Y sanseacabó	Ahí muere	That's final; It's all over with
995. ¡Ya basta!	¡Ya párele! ¡Ya está suave!	That's enough! Hold it!
996. Ya cayó el chivo en el lazo	Este arroz ya se coció	It's in the bag
997. Ya le pasará		He'll get over it
998. Ya lo creo	A la fija (Ríopl.) ¿Cómo no?	Of course; certainly
999. Ya ni llorar es bueno	Nada logras con llorar delante del bien perdido	Don't cry over spilt milk
1000. Zapatero a tus zapatos		Mind your own business

English Index to Spanish Idioms and Proverbs

Parte Segundo Inglés-Español

Al Lector

El auge que desde el principio de la Segunda Guerra Mundial viene cobrando en la América española el aprendizaje del inglés, nos ha movido a recopilar en este breve Diccionario las voces y locuciones más indispensables de esta lengua tal como se habla y escribe en los Estados Unidos de América.

Al igual que en la Sección española-inglesa hemos antepuesto la abreviatura *Am.* y otras de señalados países o regiones a aquellos vocablos o modismos que son de uso exclusivo en alguna región de la América española, o bien de uso frecuentísimo en ésta, aunque ya hayan caído en desuso en la Península. Todo lo cual no excluye la posibilidad de que alguna acepción así designada se oiga en labios de español o sea de uso esporádico en España.

Lo que sí hemos procurado con gran ahinco y anhelamos lograr, presentando al estudioso este caudal indispensable de palabras, es el acercamiento lingüístico de las Américas, como base para nuestra mutua comprensión y como instrumento poderosísimo para nuestra solidaridad.

Los Editores

Lista de Abreviaturas

adj.	adjectivo	*irr.*	irregular
adv.	adverbio	*p.p.*	participio pasado o pasivo
art.	artículo	*pers.*	personal
art. indef.	artículo indefinido	*pl.*	plural
aux.	auxiliar	*pos.*	posesivo
comp.	comparativo	*prep.*	preposición
conj.	conjunción	*pron.*	pronombre
contr.	contracción	*pron. pers.*	pronombre personal
defect.	defectivo	*pron. pos.*	pronombre posesivo
etc.	etcétera	*s.*	sustantivo
ger.	gerundio	*sing.*	singular
gram.	gramatical, gramática	*subj.*	subjuntivo
imperf.	imperfecto	*v.*	verbo
indic.	indicativo	*v. defect.*	verbo defectivo
interj.	interjección	*v. irr.*	verbo irregular
interr.	interrogativo		

Abreviaturas Especiales de Indicación Regional

Am.[1]	Americanismo
Andalucía	
Andes	(Ecuador, Perú, Bolivia)
Arg.	Argentina
Bol.	Bolivia
Carib.	(Cuba, Puerto Rico, República Dominicana)
C.A.	Centroamérica (Guatemala, El Salvador, Honduras, Nicaragua, Costa Rica)

---

[1] Esta abreviatura se emplea para indicar uso general hispanoamericano; se implica a la vez carácter arcaizante en cuanto a España. Se usa también para señalar los vocablos ya poco usados que puedan encontrarse en obras literarias del siglo pasado.

Ch.	Chile
Col.	Colombia
C.R.	Costa Rica
Cuba	
Ec.	El Ecuador
Esp.	España
Guat.	Guatemala
Hond.	Honduras
Méx.	México
N. Esp.	Norte de España
Nic.	Nicaragua
Pan.	Panamá
Par.	Paraguay
Perú	
P.R.	Puerto Rico
Ríopl.	Río de la Plata (La Argentina oriental, el Uruguay)
S.A.	Sudamérica
Sal.	El Salvador
Ur.	El Uruguay
Ven.	Venezuela

Pronunciación Inglesa[2]

I. Vocales

Símbolo fonético	Ortografía inglesa	Ortografía fonética	Explicación de los sonidos
i	see pea	si pi	Equivale a la *i* in *hilo*.
ɪ	bit	bɪt	El sonido más aproximado es la *i* en *virtud*, pero la [ɪ] inglesa es una *i* más abierta tirando a *e* cerrada.
e	late they	lét ðe	Equivale aproximadamente a *ei*; la *i* de este diptongo es muy relajada y más abierta que en español.
ɛ	bet	bɛt	El sonido más aproximado en español es la *e* abierta de *perro*.
æ	sat	sæt	Es una vocal intermedia entre la *a* y la *e*.
ɑ	car	kɑr	Equivale aproximadamente a la *a* en *cargo*.
ɔ	forge	fɔrdʒ	Equivale aproximadamente a la *o* en *corto*, *corre*.
o	mode	mod	Equivale aproximadamente a *ou*; la *u* de este diptongo es muy relajada y más abierta que en español.
ʊ	pull	pʊl	El sonido más aproximado en español es la *u* en *turrón*, pero la [ʊ] inglesa es todavía más abierta.
u	June moon	dʒun mun	Equivale aproximadamente a la *u* en *uno*.
ə	cudgel apply	kʌdʒəl əplái	Es una *e* muy relajada. No tiene equivalente en español.
ɚ	teacher	títʃɚ	Es una *e* muy relajada, articulada simultáneamente con la *r*. No tiene equivalente en español.

[2] El estudioso puede consultar el importante diccionario de pronunciación norteamericana: Kenyon and Knott, *A Pronouncing Dictionary of American English* (Springfield, Massachusetts: G & C. Merriam Company, Publishers, 1944).

Símbolo fonético	Ortografía inglesa	Ortografía fonética	Explicación de los sonidos
ɜ	earth fur	ɜθ fɜ	Es un sonido intermedio entre la *e* y la *o* articulado simultáneamente con la *r*. Se acerca más a la *e* que a la *o*. No tiene equivalente en español.
ʌ	duck	dʌk	Es una vocal intermedia entre la *e* muy abierta y la *o*. Se acerca más a la *o* que a la *e*. No tiene equivalente en español.

II. Diptongos

aɪ	aisle nice	aɪl naɪs	Equivale aproximadamente a *ai* en *aire*.
aʊ	now	naʊ	Equivale aproximadamente a *au* en *causa*.
ɔɪ	coy	kɔɪ	Equivale aproximadamente a *oy* en *hoy*. El segundo elemento del diptongo es más abierto y débil, tirando a *e*.
ju	used	juzd	Equivale aproximadamente a *iu* en *ciudad*.
jʊ	cure	kjʊr	Equivale aproximadamente al diptongo *iu*, pero la *u* es más abierta.

III. Consonantes

p	paper	pépɚ	Equivale aproximadamente a la *p* española, pero es aspirada.
b	bat	bæt	La *b* inglesa es semejante a la *b* inicial española, pero se pronuncia más explosivamente.
t	tea	ti	Es bastante diferente de la *t* española. Se articula colocando flojamente la lengua arriba de los dientes incisivos superiores y es aspirada.
d	day	de	Equivale a la *d* inicial española pronunciada con mayor énfasis.
k	cat kill	kæt kɪl	Equivale aproximadamente a la *c* española delante de *a,o,u* pronunciada con aspiracion.
g	go gum ago	go gʌm əgó	Equivale aproximadamente, a la *g* inicial delante de *a,o,u*: *goma, guerra, gana*; sólo que la *g* inglesa se pronuncia con mayor explosión.
f	fun affair	fʌn əfɛr	Equivale aproximadamente a la *f* española.
v	very	vérɪ	No tiene equivalente en español. Es una labiodental que se articula con el labio inferior y los dientes incisivos superiores.
θ	thin	θɪn	Equivale aproximadamente a la *z* en el castellano *cazar*.
ð	then other	ðɛn ʌðɚ	Equivale aproximadamente a la *d* española en *pardo*.
s	send case cent	sɛnd kes sɛnt	Equivale aproximadamente a la *s* inicial española de Hispanoamérica; *santo*.
z	rose these zero	roz ðiz zíro	Equivale aproximadamente a la *s* sonora en *mismo*, pero se pronuncia con más sonoridad en inglés.
ʃ	sheet machine nation	ʃit maʃín néʃən	Es una *s* palatal que no tiene equivalente en español. Suena como la *ch* francesa; *chapeau*.
ʒ	vision	vɪʒən	No tiene equivalente en español. Es una palatal fricativa sonora, semejante a la *y* argentina y uruguaya.
tʃ	chase	tʃes	Equivale aproximadamente a la *ch* en *charla*.
dʒ	judge gentle	dʒʌdʒ dʒéntl̩	No tiene equivalente exacto en español. Se parece a la *y* de *inyectar* en la pronunciación de uruguayos y argentinos.
m	much	mʌtʃ	Equivale aproximadamente a la *m* española.
n	none any	nʌn énɪ	Equivale aproximadamente a la *n* española en *nada*.

Símbolo fonético	Ortografía inglesa	Ortografía fonética	Explicación de los sonidos
ŋ	eaten button lesson	ítŋ bʌ́tŋ lésŋ	No tiene equivalente en español. Representa la *n* sin la articulación de la vocal anterior.
ŋ	ankle angle ring	ǽŋkl̦ ǽŋgl̦ rɪŋ	Equivale a la *n* española en *mango, banco*.
l	late altar fall folly	let ɔ́ltɚ fɔl fálɪ	La *l* inicial equivale aproximadamente a la *l* española en *lado*. La *l* final de sílaba es más débil que la inicial y semejante a la portuguesa.
l̦	able ankle	ébl̦ ǽŋkl̦	No tiene equivalente en español. Se pronuncia como la *l* final de sílaba, omitiendo la vocal precedente.
w	weed well wall	wid wɛl wɔl	Equivale a la *u* de los diptongos; *ui, ue, ua, uo*.
h	hat whole	hæt hol	No tiene equivalente exacto en español. Equivale aproximadamente a una *j* suave que se reduce a una simple aspiración.
hw	where	hwɛr	Equivale a una *j* suave seguida de una *w* arriba explicada.
j	year yawn yet	jɪr jɔn jɛt	Equivale a la *i* española en los diptongos *ie, ia, io, iu: hiena*.
r	rose bear	roz bɛr	No tiene equivalente en español. La punta de la lengua se arrolla hacia atrás sin tocar el paladar. A veces se pierde al grado de vocalizarse.

Pronunciación de la *S* del Plural [3]

I. La **-s** del plural es sorda cuando la palabra termina en las consonantes sordas representadas por los símbolos fonéticos [p], [t], [k], [f], [θ]. Pronúnciase como la *s* de *santo*: **caps** [kæps], **gates** [gets], **cats** [kæts], **books** [bʊks], **cliffs** [klɪfs], **lengths** [lɛŋkθs].
Las excepciones más comunes son: **oath** [oθ], **oaths** [oðz]; **leaf** [lif], **leaves** [livz], **wife** [waɪf], **wives** [waɪvz]; **knife** [naɪf], **knives** [naɪvz]; **calf** [kæf], **calves** [kævz]; **half** [hæf], **halves** [hævz].

II. La **-s** del plural es sonora cuando la palabra termina en vocal (incluyendo la **-y** que se cambia en **-ies**), o en las consonantes sonoras representadas por los símbolos fonéticos [b], [d], [g], [v], [ð], [m], [n], [ŋ], [l]: **cries** [kraɪz], **robes** [robz], **beds** [bɛdz], **logs** [lɔgz], **stoves** [stovz], **lathes** [leðz], **farms** [fɑrmz], **bins** [bɪnz], **kings** [kɪŋz], falls [fɔlz], **furs** [fɝz], **papers** [pépɚz], **plows** [plaʊz].

III. Cuando la palabra termina **-en** las consonantes representadas por los símbolos [s], [ʃ], [tʃ], [z], [ʒ], [dʒ], se añade **-es** [ɪz], o **s** [ɪz], si la palabra termina en **-ce, -se, -dge, -ge**: **face** [fes], **faces** [fésɪz]; **kiss** [kɪs], **kisses** [kísɪz]; **ash** [æʃ], **ashes** [æʃɪz]; **lunch** [lʌntʃ], **lunches** [lʌntʃɪz]; **rose** [roz], **roses** [rózɪz]; **judge** [dʒʌdʒ], **judges** [dʒʌdʒɪz].

[3] Las mismas reglas se aplican a la pronunciación del genitivo y de la tercera persona del presente de indicativo, singular: **keeps** [kips]; **Kate's** [kets]; **saves** [sevz]; **John's** [dʒɑnz]; **judges** [dʒʌdʒɪz]; **Alice's** [ǽlɪsɪz].

El Sustantivo

I. Género

Son masculinos los nombres de varón o animal macho, y son femeninos los nombres de mujer o animal hembra. Los demás son neutros. El artículo definido **the** se aplica a todos los sustantivos, singular y plural: **the man** el hombre; **the men** los hombres; **the book** el libro; **the books** los libros; **the woman** la mujer; **the women** las mujeres.

En ciertos sustantivos se distingue el género femenino por medio del sufijo **-ess: poet** poeta; **poetess** poetisa. A veces es indispensable indicar el género por medio de las palabras **male** o **female, boy** o **girl, man** o **woman, she** o **he: baby boy** niño; **baby girl** niña; **woman writer** escritora; **she-bear** osa. En otros casos hay una palabra distinta para cada género; **uncle** tío; **aunt** tía.

II. Plural de los Sustantivos[4]

1. Generalmente se forma el plural añadiendo **-s** al singular: **paper, papers** papel, papeles; **book, books** libro, libros; **chief, chiefs** jefe, jefes.

2. Los sustantivos que terminan en **-ch** (pronunciada como la **ch** española), **-ss, -x, -sh, -z,** y **-o** añaden **-es** para formar el plural: **arch, arches** arco, arcos; **kiss, kisses** beso, besos; **box, boxes** caja, cajas; **dish, dishes** plato, platos; **buzz, buzzes** zumbido, zumbidos; **hero, heroes** héroe, héroes. Nótese que los sustantivos terminados en **-ch** (pronunciada [k]) forman el plural añadiendo **-s: monarch, monarchs** monarca, monarcas.

3. Los sustantivos que terminan en **-fe,** y ciertos sustantivos que terminan en **-f,** cambian estas letras en **v** y añaden **-es: leaf, leaves** hoja, hojas; **life, lives** vida, vidas; **wife, wives** esposa, esposas; **knife, knives** cuchillo, cuchillos.

4. Para formar el plural de los sustantivos terminados en **-y** precedida de consonante cámbiase la **-y** en **-ies: fly, flies** mosca, moscas; **cry, cries** grito, gritos; **family, families** familia, familias; **quantity, quantities** cantidad, cantidades. Nótese que los sustantivos terminados en **-y** precedida de vocal forman el plural añadiendo **-s** al singular: **day, days** día, días.

5. Ciertos sustantivos forman el plural de una manera irregular: **man, men** hombre, hombres; **woman, women** mujer, mujeres; **mouse, mice** ratón, ratones; **louse, lice** piojo, piojos; **goose, geese** ganso, gansos; **tooth, teeth** diente, dientes; **foot, feet** pie, pies; **ox, oxen** buey, bueyes.

6. Ciertos sustantivos que terminan en **-is** forman el plural cambiando la **i** de la terminación en **e: axis, axes** eje, ejes; **the crisis, the crises** la crisis, las crisis.

El Adjetivo

El adjetivo inglés es invariable en cuanto a género y número. Normalmente se coloca delante del sustantivo: **an interesting book** un libro interesante; **a large table** una mesa grande; **beautiful women** mujeres hermosas.

---

[4] Véase las reglas para la pronunciación del plural.

Los comparativos y superlativos. Aunque no hay una regla general, por lo común los adjetivos monosílabos, los adjetivos acentuados en la última sílaba y algunos bisílabos fácilmente pronunciados forman *el comparativo de aumento y el superlativo* añadiendo -er y -est. Los demás adjetivos van precedidos de **more** y **most**. Nótese que (1) sólo se añaden -r y -st a los que terminan en -e muda; (2) los adjetivos terminados en -y cambian esta letra en i; (3) los adjetivos terminados en consonante precedida de vocal doblan la consonante:

Positivo	*Comparativo*	*Superlativo*
tall alto	**taller** más alto	**the tallest** el más alto
wise sabio	**wiser** más sabio	**the wisest** el más sabio
polite cortés	**politer** más cortés	**the politest** el más cortés
happy feliz	**happier** más feliz	**the happiest** el más feliz
fat gordo	**fatter** más gordo	**the fattest** el más gordo
careful cuidadoso	**more careful** más cuidadoso	**the most careful** el más cuidadoso

El superlativo absoluto se forma anteponiendo **very** y a veces **most: very intelligent** muy inteligente; **she is a most beautiful woman** es una mujer hermosísima.

El comparativo y el superlativo de inferioridad se forman con los adverbios **less** y **least: less wise** menos sabio; **the least wise** el menos sabio.

El comparativo de igualdad se forma con el adverbio **as: as poor as** tan pobre como; **as much as** tanto como; **as much money as** tanto dinero como.

Los adjetivos siguientes forman el comparativo y el superlativo de una manera irregular:

good, well	**better**	**best**
bad, ill	**worse**	**worst**
little	**less, lesser**	**least**
far	**farther, further**	**farthest, furthest**
much, many	**more**	**most**
old	**older, elder**	**oldest, eldest**

El Adverbio

Fórmanse muchos adverbios, añadiendo -ly al adjetivo: **courteous** cortés, **courteously** cortésmente; **bold** atrevido, **boldly** atrevidamente. Existen las irregularidades siguientes en la formación de los adverbios que terminan en -ly: (1) los adjetivos terminados en -ble cambian la -e en -y: **possible, possibly**; (2) los terminados en ic añaden -ally: **poetic, poetically**; (3) los terminados en -ll añaden sólo la -y: **full, fully**; (4) los terminados en -ue pierden la -e final: **true, truly**; (5) los terminados en -y cambian la -y en i: **happy, happily**.

Como los adjetivos, la mayor parte de los adverbios forman el *comparativo* y el *superlativo* con los adverbios **more** (más), **most** (más), y **very** (muy). Asimismo los adverbios monosílabos añaden -er y -est:

Positivo	*Comparativo*	*Superlativo*	*Superlativo Absoluto*
boldly	**more boldly**	**most boldly**	**very boldly**
generously	**more generously**	**most generously**	**very generously**

soon	sooner	soonest	very soon
early	earlier	earliest	very early
late	later	latest	very late
near	nearer	nearest	very near
fast	faster	fastest	very fast

Los adverbios siguientes forman el comparativo y el superlativo de una manera irregular:

well	better	best	very well
badly, ill	worse	worst	very badly
little	less	least	very little
much	more	most	very much
far	farther, further	farthest, furthest	very far

Sufijos Comunes en Inglés

-dom   denota dominio, jurisdicción, estado, condición, etc.: **kingdom** reino; **martyrdom** martirio; **boredom** aburrimiento; **freedom** libertad.

-ed, -d   es la terminación del pretérito y del participio pasivo o pasado de los verbos regulares: **I called** llamé; **called** llamado.

-ee   indica la persona que recibe la acción: **addressee** destinatario; **employee** empleado.

-eer   denota oficio u ocupación: **engineer** ingeniero; **auctioneer** subastador.

-en   a) terminación del participio de muchos verbos irregulares: **fallen, broken, shaken;**
b) sufijo que significa *hecho de*: **golden** dorado, de oro; **wooden** de madera; **leaden** de plomo;
c) terminación verbal equivalente a *hacer*: **whiten** hacer blanco, emblanquecer; **darken** hacer obscuro, obscurecer.

-er   a) indica la persona que hace o el agente de la acción del verbo: **player** jugador; **talker** hablador;
b) indica el residente de un lugar: **New Yorker** habitante o residente de Nueva York; **islander** isleño;
c) denota ocupación: **carpenter** carpintero; **baker** panadero.
d) es la terminación del comparativo de adjetivos y adverbios; **taller** más alto; **faster** más aprisa.

-ess   úsase para formar el género femenino de ciertos sustantivos: **patroness** patrona; **poetess** poetisa; **countess** condesa.

-est   terminación del superlativo: **tallest** el más alto.

-fold   sufijo que significa *veces*: **twofold** dos veces; **hundredfold** cien veces.

-ful   a) equivale a *lleno*, y tratándose de adjetivos es igual a *-oso*: **hopeful** lleno de esperanzas; **careful** cuidadoso; **wilful** voluntarioso; **merciful** misericordioso; **glassful** un vaso (*lleno*);
b) indica a veces hábito o inclinación: **forgetful** olvidadizo;
c) es a veces equivalente a los sufijos españoles *-ado, -ada*: **handful** puñado; *spoonful* cucharada.

-hood	indica estado, condición, carácter, grupo; a menudo equivale a *-dad*: **motherhood** maternidad; **brotherhood** fraternidad; **childhood** niñez; **falsehood** falsedad.
-ician	denota especialidad en cierto ramo: **musician** músico; **technician** técnico; **electrician** electricista.
-ie	sufijo diminutivo: **birdie** pajarito; **Annie** Anita.
-ing	*a*) sufijo del gerundio: **speaking** hablando; *b*) sufijo del participio activo: **threatening** amenazante; **surprising** sorprendente; *c*) úsase a menudo para formar adjetivos: **running water** agua corriente; **drinking water** agua potable; **waiting room** sala de espera; **washing machine** máquina lavadora; *d*) úsase para formar sustantivos: **understanding** entendimiento; **supplying** abastecimiento; **clothing** ropa; **covering** cobertura; equivale al infinitivo castellano: **swimming is good exercise** el nadar es buen ejercicio.
-ish	*a*) úsase para formar ciertos adjetivos de nacionalidad: **Spanish** español; **English** inglés; **Turkish** turco; *b*) indica semejanza: **boyish** como niño, aniñado; **womanish** como mujer, mujeril, afeminado; **whitish** blancuzco, medio blanco, que tira a blanco.
-less	equivale a *sin, falto de*: **childless** sin hijos; **penniless** sin dinero; en ciertos casos el sufijo inglés se traduce por medio de un prefijo: **countless** innumerable, sin número; **endless** interminable, sin fin.
-like	significa *semejanza*, y equivale a *como, a manera de*: **lifelike** que parece vivo; **childlike** como niño, infantil; **tigerlike** como tigre.
-ly	*a*) sufijo adverbial: **slowly** lentamente; **happily** felizmente; **possibly** posiblemente; *b*) añadido a ciertos sustantivos equivale a *como, a la manera de*: **motherly** como madre, materno; **gentlemanly** como caballero, caballeroso; **friendly** amigable; **manly** varonil; *c*) equivale a *cada* en estos ejemplos: **daily** cada día; diario; **weekly** cada semana, semanal; **monthly** cada mes, mensual; **yearly** cada año, anual.
-ness	úsase para formar sustantivos abstractos: **goodness** bondad; **darkness** obscuridad; **foolishness** tontería; **shamelessness** desvergüenza.
-ship	*a*) úsase para formar sustantivos abstractos: **friendship** amistad; **relationship** relación, parentesco; *b*) denota arte o destreza: **horsemanship** equitación; *c*) expresa dignidad, oficio, cargo, o título: **professorship** profesorado o cátedra; **chairmanship** presidencia (*de un comité, asamblea, etc.*); **lordship** señoría; *d*) a veces expresa tan sólo un estado y su duración: **courtship** galanteo, cortejo, noviazgo.

-some	expresa en alto grado la cualidad representada por el vocablo al cual se añade: **tiresome** que cansa, cansado; **quarrelsome** dado a riñas, pendenciero; **loathsome** que repugna, asqueroso; **burdensome** gravoso.
-th	úsase para formar números ordinales: **fifth** quinto; **tenth** décimo.
-ty	*a*) terminación de los múltiples de diez: **twenty** veinte; **thirty** treinta; **forty** cuarenta; *b*) terminación de muchos sustantivos abstractos; equivale frecuentemente al sufijo español *-tad* o *-dad*: **beauty** beldad; **paternity** paternidad; **falsity** falsedad.
-ward, -wards	denotan *hacia*: **homeward** hacia casa; **downward** hacia abajo.
-ways, -wise	expresan manera, dirección, posición, etc.: **edgewise** de lado; **sideways** de lado; **lengthwise** a lo largo.
-y	*a*) terminación equivalente a los sufijos españoles *-ia, -ía*: **victory** victoria; **glory** gloria; **courtesy** cortesía; **biology** biología; **astronomy** astronomía; *b*) sufijo diminutivo: **doggy** perrito; **Johnny** Juanito; *c*) denota abundancia, y es a menudo equivalente a *-udo, -oso, -ado*: **rocky** lleno de rocas, rocoso, pedregoso; **rainy** lluvioso; **hairy** lleno de pelo, peludo; **bulky** abultado; **wavy** ondulado; **angry** enojado; *d*) expresa semejanza: **rosy** rosado, como una rosa, color de rosa.

Números

Consúltese la tabla de la página 35 de la Sección Española-Inglesa para el aprendizaje de los números cardinales y ordinales desde uno hasta un millón.

Verbos Irregulares de la Lengua Inglesa

Se denominan verbos irregulares los que no forman el pretérito o el participio pasivo con la adición de **-d** o **-ed** al presente. Obsérvese que en ciertos verbos coexiste la forma regular al lado de la irregular. En otros coexisten dos formas irregulares juntamente con la regular.

Presente	*Pretérito*	*Participio pasivo o pasado*
abide	abode	abode
am, is, are	was, were	been
arise	arose	arisen
awake	awoke, awaked	awaked, awoke
bear	bore	born, borne
beat	beat	beat, beaten
become	became	become
befall	befell	befallen
beget	begat	begotten
begin	began	begun
behold	beheld	beheld
bend	bent	bent
bereave	bereft, bereaved	bereft, bereaved
beseech	besought, beseeched	besought, beseeched
beset	beset	beset
bet	bet	bet

Presente	*Pretérito*	*Participio pasivo o pasado*
bid	bid, bade	bidden, bid
bind	bound	bound
bite	bit	bitten, bit
bleed	bled	bled
blow	blew	blown
break	broke	broken
breed	bred	bred
bring	brought	brought
build	built	built
burn	burnt, burned	burnt, burned
burst	burst	burst
buy	bought	bought
can (*verbo defectivo*)	could	—
cast	cast	cast
catch	caught	caught
chide	chided, chid	chided, chidden
choose	chose	chosen
cleave	cleft, clove, cleaved	cleft, cleaved, cloven
cling	clung	clung
clothe	clad, clothed	clad, clothed
come	came	come
cost	cost	cost
creep	crept	crept
crow	crew, crowed	crowed
cut	cut	cut
deal	dealt	dealt
dig	dug, digged	dug, digged
do	did	done
draw	drew	drawn
dream	dreamt, dreamed	dreamt, dreamed
drink	drank	drunk
drive	drove	driven
dwell	dwelt, dwelled	dwelt, dwelled
eat	ate	eaten
fall	fell	fallen
feed	fed	fed
feel	felt	felt
fight	fought	fought
find	found	found
flee	fled	fled
fling	flung	flung
fly	flew	flown
forbear	forbore	forborne
forbid	forbade	forbidden
foresee	foresaw	foreseen
foretell	foretold	foretold
forget	forgot	forgotten, forgot
forgive	forgave	forgiven
forsake	forsook	forsaken
freeze	froze	frozen
get	got	got, gotten
gild	gilt, gilded	gilt, gilded
gird	girt, girded	girt, girded
give	gave	given
go	went	gone
grind	ground	ground
grow	grew	grown
hang[5]	hung	hung
have, has	had	had
hear	heard	heard
heave	hove, heaved	hove, heaved
hew	hewed	hewn, hewed
hide	hid	hidden, hid
hit	hit	hit
hold	held	held
hurt	hurt	hurt
inlay	inlaid	inlaid

[5] Es regular cuando significa «ahorcar.»

Presente	*Pretérito*	*Participio pasivo o pasado*
keep	kept	kept
kneel	knelt	knelt
knit	knit, knitted	knit, knitted
know	knew	known
lay	laid	laid
lead	led	led
lean	leaned, leant	leaned, leant
leap	leapt, leaped	leapt, leaped
learn	learned, learnt	learned, learnt
leave	left	left
lend	lent	lent
let	let	let
lie[6] (**yacer; echarse**)	lay	lain
light	lit, lighted	lit, lighted
load	loaded	loaded, laden
lose	lost	lost
make	made	made
may (*verbo defectivo*)	might	—
mean	meant	meant
meet	met	met
melt	melted	melted, molten
mistake	mistook	mistaken
mow	mowed	mown, mowed
must (*verbo defectivo*)	—	—
ought (*verbo defectivo*)	ought	—
pay	paid	paid
put	put	put
quit	quit, quitted	quit, quitted
read [rid]	read [rɛd]	read [rɛd]
rend	rent	rent
rid	rid, ridded	rid, ridded
ride	rode	ridden
ring	rang, rung	rung
rise	rose	risen
run	ran	run
saw	sawed	sawn, sawed
say	said	said
see	saw	seen
seek	sought	sought
sell	sold	sold
send	sent	sent
set	set	set
sew	sewed	sewn, sewed
shake	shook	shaken
shall	should	—
shave	shaved	shaved, shaven
shear	sheared	shorn, sheared
shed	shed	shed
shine[7]	shone	shone
shoe	shod	shod
shoot	shot	shot
show	showed	shown, showed
shred	shred, shredded	shred, shredded
shrink	shrank, shrunk	shrunk, shrunken
shut	shut	shut
sing	sang, sung	sung
sink	sank	sunk
sit	sat	sat
slay	slew	slain
sleep	slept	slept
slide	slid	slid, slidden
sling	slung	slung
slink	slunk	slunk
slit	slit	slit
smell	smelt, smelled	smelt, smelled
smite	smote	smitten

[6] Es regular cuando significa «mentir.»
[7] Es por lo común regular cuando significa «pulir, dar brillo.»

Presente	*Pretérito*	*Participio pasivo o pasado*
sow	sowed	sown, sowed
speak	spoke	spoken
speed	sped, speeded	sped, speeded
spell	spelled, spelt	spelled, spelt
spend	spent	spent
spill	spilled, spilt	spilled, spilt
spin	spun	spun
spit	spit, spat	spit, spat
split	split	split
spread	spread	spread
spring	sprang, sprung	sprung
stand	stood	stood
stave	staved, stove	staved, stove
steal	stole	stolen
stick	stuck	stuck
sting	stung	stung
stink	stank, stunk	stunk
strew	strewed	strewn, strewed
stride	strode	stridden
strike	struck	struck, striken
string	strung	strung
strive	strove, strived	striven, strived
swear	swore	sworn
sweep	swept	swept
swell	swelled	swollen, swelled
swim	swam	swum
swing	swung	swung
take	took	taken
teach	taught	taught
tear	tore	torn
tell	told	told
think	thought	thought
thrive	throve, thrived	thriven, thrived
throw	threw	thrown
thrust	thrust	thrust
tread	trod	trod, trodden
understand	understood	understood
undertake	undertook	undertaken
undo	undid	undone
uphold	upheld	upheld
upset	upset	upset
wake	woke, waked	waked
wear	wore	worn
weave	wove	woven
wed	wedded	wedded, wed
weep	wept	wept
wet	wet, wetted	wet, wetted
will (*verbo auxiliar*)	would	—
win	won	won
wind	wound	wound
withdraw	withdrew	withdrawn
withhold	withheld	withheld
withstand	withstood	withstood
work	worked, wrought	worked, wrought
wring	wrung	wrung
write	wrote	written

A:a

a [ə, e] *art. indef.* un, una; **what — ...!** ¡qué ...!; **such —** tal; tan.

a·ban·don [əbǽndən] *v.* abandonar; dejar; *s.* abandono, desahogo, desenvoltura; entrega.

a·ban·doned [əbǽndənd] *adj.* abandondo; dejado; perverso; inmoral.

a·ban·don·ment [əbǽndənmənt] *s.* abandono, abandonamiento; desamparo; desenvoltura, desembarazo.

a·bashed [əbǽʃt] *adj.* humillado, avergonzado.

a·bate [əbét] *v.* bajar, rebajar; disminuir; acabar con; mitigar(se); calmarse.

a·bate·ment [əbétmənt] *s.* diminución, merma; rebaja, descuento; mitigación.

ab·bess [ǽbəs] *s.* abadesa.

ab·bey [ǽbɪ] *s.* abadía, monasterio.

ab·bot [ǽbət] *s.* abad.

ab·bre·vi·ate [əbrívɪet] *v.* abreviar, acortar, reducir.

ab·bre·vi·a·tion [əbrivɪéʃən] *s.* abreviación, abreviatura; **initial —** sigla.

ab·di·cate [ǽbdəket] *v.* abdicar, renunciar.

ab·do·men [ǽbdəmən] *s.* abdomen; vientre.

ab·duct [æbdʌ́kt] *v.* secuestrar, raptar, *Am.* plagiar (*a alguien*).

ab·duc·tion [æbdʌ́kʃən] *s.* rapto, robo, secuestro (*de una persona*).

ab·er·ra·tion [æbəréʃən] *s.* aberración, extravío (*de la mente*).

a·bet [əbét] *v.* incitar; fomentar.

a·bey·ance [əbéəns] *s.* suspensión; **in —** pendiente.

ab·hor [əbhɔ́r] *v.* aborrecer, odiar, abominar.

ab·hor·rence [əbhɔ́rəns] *s.* aborrecimiento, aversión.

a·bide [əbáɪd] *v.* quedar, permanecer; morar, habitar; aguardar; soportar, tolerar; **to — by** conformarse a; atenerse a.

a·bil·i·ty [əbílətɪ] *s.* habilidad, capacidad.

ab·ject [æbdʒékt] *adj.* abatido; vil.

ab·jure [æbdʒúr] *v.* abjurar.

ab·la·tive [ǽblətɪv] *adj.* ablativo.

a·ble [ébl] *adj.* hábil, capaz; competente; **a·ble-bod·ied** de cuerpo sano; **to be — to** poder; saber.

a·bly [éblɪ] *adv.* hábilmente.

ab·nor·mal [æbnɔ́rml] *adj.* anormal.

a·board [əbɔ́rd] *adv.* a bordo; en el tren; **to go —** embarcarse; **all —!** ¡viajeros al tren!; *Méx., C.A.* ¡vámonos!

a·bode [əbód] *s.* morada, domicilio, casa; *pret. & p.p. de* **to abide.**

a·bol·ish [əbálɪʃ] *v.* abolir; anular.

ab·o·li·tion [æbəlíʃən] *s.* abolición.

a·bom·i·na·ble [əbámnəbl] *adj.* abominable, aborrecible.

a·bort [əbɔ́rt] *v.* abortar.

a·bor·tion [əbɔ́rʃən] *s.* aborto.

a·bound [əbáʊnd] *v.* abundar; **to — with** abundar en.

a·bout [əbáʊt] *prep.* (*concerning*) acerca de, tocante a, respecto de; (*near, surrounding*) alrededor de, por; *adv.* (*almost*) casi, poco más o menos; **at — ten o'clock** a eso de las diez; **to be — one's business** atender a su negocio; **to be — to** estar para, estar a punto de; **to face —** dar media vuelta; **to have no money — one's person** no llevar dinero consigo.

a·bove [əbʌ́v] *prep.* por encima de; sobre; *adv.* arriba; **— all** sobre todo; **a·bove-men·tioned** susodicho, ya mencionado; **from —** de arriba;

del cielo, de Dios.

ab·ra·sive [əbrésɪv] *adj.* abrasivo; tosco.

a·breast [əbrést] *adj., adv.* al lado; **to keep abreast** ponerse al corriente.

a·bridge [əbrídʒ] *v.* abreviar; compendiar, condensar; privar (*a uno de sus derechos*).

a·broad [əbrɔ́d] *adv.* en el extranjero; fuera de casa; **to go —** ir al extranjero; **to spread —** divulgar o publicar por todas partes.

a·brupt [əbrʌ́pt] *adj.* repentino; precipitado; áspero, brusco; escarpado; **-ly** *adv.* de repente; bruscamente.

ab·scess [ǽbsɛs] *s.* absceso.

ab·sence [ǽbsns] *s.* ausencia; falta; **— of mind** abstracción; **leave of —** licencia (*para ausentarse*).

ab·sent [ǽbsnt] *adj.* ausente; abstraído, distraído; **ab·sent-mind·ed** absorto, abstraído; [ǽbsént] *v.* **to — oneself** ausentarse.

ab·sinthe [ǽbsɪnθ] *s.* ajenjo.

ab·so·lute [ǽbsəlut] *adj.* absoluto; **the —** lo absoluto; **-ly** *adv.* absolutamente; en absoluto.

ab·so·lu·tion [æbsəlúʃən] *s.* absolución.

ab·solve [æbsálv] *v.* absolver, remitir; perdonar, alzar la pena o el castigo.

ab·sorb [əbsɔ́rb] *v.* absorber.

ab·sorb·ent [əbsɔ́rbənt] *adj. & s.* absorbente.

ab·sorp·tion [əbsɔ́rpʃən] *s.* absorción; abstracción, embebecimiento.

ab·stain [əbstén] *v.* abstenerse, privarse.

ab·sti·nence [ǽstənəns] *s.* abstinencia.

ab·stract [ǽbstrækt] *adj.* abstracto; *s.* sumario; extracto; **in the —** en abstracto; [æbstrǽkt] *v.* abstraer; considerar aisladamente; separar, retirar; resumir, compendiar.

ab·strac·tion [æbstrǽkʃən] *s.* abstracción; idea abstracta.

ab·surd [əbsǽd] *adj.* absurdo; insensato; ridículo, disparatado.

ab·sur·di·ty [əbsǽdətɪ] *s.* absurdo, disparate.

a·bun·dance [əbʌ́ndəns] *s.* abundancia, copia.

a·bun·dant [əbʌ́ndənt] *adj.* abundante, copioso.

a·buse [əbjús] *s.* abuso; maltrato; ultraje; [əbjúz] *v.* abusar de; maltratar; injuriar; ultrajar.

a·bu·sive [əbjúsɪv] *adj.* abusivo; insultante, injurioso.

a·byss [əbís] *s.* abismo; sima.

ac·a·dem·ic [əkædémɪk] *adj.* académico; escolar.

a·cad·e·my [əkǽdəmɪ] *s.* academia; colegio; instituto; escuela preparatoria.

ac·cede [æksíd] *v.* acceder, consentir.

ac·cel·er·ate [ækséləret] *v.* acelerar(se).

ac·cel·er·a·tion [ækseləréʃən] *s.* aceleración.

ac·cel·er·a·tor [ækséləretə] *s.* acelerador.

ac·cent [ǽksnt] *s.* acento; [æksént] *v.* acentuar; recalcar.

ac·cen·tu·ate [ækséntʃʊet] *v.* acentuar; recalcar; realzar.

ac·cept [əksépt] *v.* aceptar; admitir; acoger; aprobar.

ac·cept·a·ble [əkséptəbl] *adj.* aceptable; grato; acepto.

ac·cep·tance [əkséptəns] *s.* aceptación; aprobación; buena acogida, recibimiento.

ac·cess [ǽksɛs] *s.* acceso; ataque (*de una enfermedad*); arrebato (*de furia*).

ac·ces·si·ble [æksésəbl] *adj.* accesible; asequible, obtenible.

ac·ces·so·ry [æksésərɪ] *adj.* accesorio; adjunto; *s.* accesorio; cómplice; **ac·ces·so·ries** cosas accesorias, adornos, adminículos.

ac·ci·dent [æksədənt] s. accidente; percance, contratiempo; **by —** por casualidad.

ac·ci·den·tal [æksədéntl] adj. accidental; casual; **-ly** adv. accidentalmente; por casualidad.

ac·claim [əklém] v. aclamar, aplaudir; s. aclamación, aplauso.

ac·cla·ma·tion [ækləméʃən] s. aclamación, aplauso.

ac·cli·mate [əkláɪmət], [ækləmet] v. aclimatar(se); acostumbrar(se).

ac·cli·ma·tize [əkláɪmətaɪz] v. aclimatar(se).

ac·com·mo·date [əkɑmədét] v. (adjust) acomodar, ajustar, ayudar, hacer un favor; (lodge) hospedar, alojar, tener cabida para; **to — oneself** conformarse, adaptarse.

ac·com·mo·da·tion [əkɑmədéʃən] s. favor, ayuda; conveniencia; alojamiento (en un hotel, casa, ect.); cabida; adaptación; ajuste.

ac·com·pa·ni·ment [əkʌmpənɪmənt] s. acompañamiento.

ac·com·pa·nist [əkʌmpənɪst] s. acompañador, acompañante.

ac·com·pa·ny [əkʌmpənɪ] v. acompañar.

ac·com·plice [əkɑmplɪs] s. cómplice.

ac·com·plish [əkɑmplɪʃ] v. cumplir; completar; lograr, conseguir; realizar, efectuar.

ac·com·plished [əkɑmplɪʃt] adj. cumplido; realizado; consumado; establecido; diestro; perfecto.

ac·com·plish·ment [əkɑmpɪʃmənt] s. cumplimiento; logro, realización; habilidad; perfección; mérito, proeza.

ac·cord [əkɔrd] s. acuerdo, convenio; armonía, concierto; **of one's own —** voluntariamente; espontáneamente; **in — with** de acuerdo con; **with one —** unánimemente; v. otorgar, conceder, dar; concordar.

ac·cord·ance [əkɔrdns] s. conformidad, acuerdo; **in — with** de acuerdo con, de conformidad con.

ac·cord·ing [əkɔrdɪŋ]: **— to** según; conforme a; de acuerdo con; **— as** según (que), a medida que.

ac·cord·ing·ly [əkɔrdɪŋlɪ] adv. en conformidad; así; como tal; por lo tanto; por consiguiente.

ac·cor·di·on [əkɔrdɪən] s. acordeón.

ac·cost [əkɔst] v. abordar (a alguien) en la calle, acosar; molestar, perseguir.

ac·count [əkáunt] s. (bill) cuenta, computación; (story) relato; **on — of** a causa de; con motivo de; por; **on my —** por mí; **on my own —** por mi propia cuenta; **on no —** de ninguna manera; **of no —** de ningún valor o importancia; **to turn to — aprovechar**, hacer útil o provechoso; v. dar cuenta (a); considerar, tener por; **to — for** dar cuenta o razón de; explicar; **how do you — for that?** ¿cómo se explica eso?

ac·count·a·ble [əkáuntəbl] adj. responsable; explicable.

ac·count·ant [əkáuntənt] s. contador, tenedor de libros.

ac·cout·ing [əkáuntɪŋ] s. contabilidad, contaduría.

ac·cred·it [əkrédɪt] v. acreditar.

ac·crue [əkrú] v. acumular(se).

ac·cul·tur·ate [əkʌltʃæet] v. aculturar(se).

ac·cu·mu·late [əkjúmjəlet] v. acumular(se), juntar(se), amontonar(se).

ac·cu·mu·la·tion [əkjumjəléʃən] s. acumulación, amontonamiento.

ac·cu·ra·cy [ækjərəsɪ] s. precisión, exactitud, esmero.

ac·cu·rate [ækjərɪt] adj. preciso, exacto; correcto; esmerado; cierto; certero; acertado; **-ly** adv. con

exctitud; correctamente; con esmero.

ac·cursed [əkɜst] adj. maldito; infame.

ac·cu·sa·tion [ækjəzéʃən] s. acusación.

ac·cu·sa·tive [əkjúzətɪv] adj. acusativo.

ac·cuse [əkjúz] v. acusar; denunciar.

ac·cus·er [əkjúzæ] s. acusador; delator, denunciador.

ac·cus·tom [əkʌstəm] v. acostumbrar; **to — oneself** acostumbrarse; **to be -ed to** tener la costumbre de, acostumbrar, soler; estar acostumbrado a, estar hecho a.

ace [es] s. as; as, el mejor de su clase (como un aviador excelente); **within an — of** a punto de; muy cerca de.

ac·e·tate [æsətet] s. acetato.

a·cet·y·lene [əsétəlin] s. acetileno.

ache [ek] s. dolor; **tooth —** dolor de muelas; v. doler.

a·chieve [ətʃív] v. acabar, llevar a cabo; realizar; conseguir, lograr; alcanzar.

a·chieve·ment [ətʃívmənt] s. logro, realización; proeza, hazaña.

ac·id [æsɪd] adj. ácido; agrio; s. ácido.

ac·id·i·ty [əsídətɪ] s. acidez.

ac·knowl·edge [əknálɪdʒ] v. reconocer, admitir; confesar; **to — receipt** acusar recibo.

ac·knowl·edg·ment [əknálɪdʒmənt] s. reconocimiento, expresión de gratitud; confesión, admisión; **— of receipt** acuse de recibo.

a·corn [ékɔrn] s. bellota.

a·cous·tics [əkústɪks] s. acústica.

ac·quaint [əkwént] v. enterar, informar; dar a conocer; familiarizar; **to — oneself with** ponerse al corriente de; enterarse de; **to be -ed with** conocer a (una persona); estar enterado de (algo); conocer (una ciudad, un país, etc.).

ac·quain·tance [əkwéntəns] s. conocimiento; conocido; **-s** amistades.

ac·qui·esce [ækwiés] v. asentir; consentir, quedar conforme.

ac·qui·es·cence [ækwiésns] s. asentimiento, consentimiento; conformidad.

ac·quire [əkwáɪr] v. adquirir; obtener, conseguir; contraer (costumbres, vicios).

ac·qui·si·tion [ækwəzíʃən] s. adquisición.

ac·quit [əkwít] v. absolver, exonerar; pagar, redimir, librar de (una obligación); **to — oneself well** quedar bien; portarse bien.

ac·quit·tal [əkwítl] s. absolución.

a·cre [ékæ] s. acre (medida de superficie).

ac·ro·bat [ækrəbæt] s. acróbata.

ac·ro·nym [ækrənɪm] s. acrónimo.

a·cross [əkrɔs] prep. a través de; al otro lado de; por; por en medio de; adv. a través, de través; **to go —** atravesar; **to come —, run —** encontrarse con; tropezar con.

a·cryl·ic [əkrílɪk] adj. acrílico.

act [ækt] s. acto; acción, hecho; v. hacer, desempeñar (un papel); representar (en el teatro); obrar; actuar; portarse; funcionar; **to — as** servir de, estar de.

act·ing [æktɪŋ] s. representación, desempeño (de un papel dramático); acción, actuación; adj. interino, suplente.

ac·tion [ækʃən] s. acción; acto; actuación; funcionamiento.

ac·ti·vate [æktɪvet] v. activar.

ac·tive [æktɪv] adj. activo.

ac·tiv·ism [æktəvɪzm] s. activismo.

ac·tiv·ist [æktəvɪst] s. activista.

ac·tiv·i·ty [ætkívətɪ] s. actividad.

ac·tor [ǽktɚ] *s.* actor.
ac·tress [ǽktrɪs] *s.* actriz.
ac·tu·al [ǽktʃʊəl] *adj.* (*legitimate*) verdadero, real; (*current*) actual, existente; **-ly** *adv.* realmente, en realidad; de hecho, efectivamente.
a·cu·men [əkjúmɪn] *s.* caletre, tino, perspicacia.
a·cute [əkjút] *adj.* agudo; perspicaz; penetrante.
ad·a·mant [ǽdəmænt] *adj.* duro; firme, inflexible.
a·dapt [ədǽpt] *v.* adaptar; **to — oneself** adaptarse, acomodarse.
ad·ap·ta·tion [ædəptéʃən] *s.* adaptación.
add [æd] *v.* sumar; añadir, agregar.
ad·dict [ǽdɪkt] *s.* adicto (*persona adicta al uso de narcóticos*); **drug —** morfinómano.
ad·dic·ted [ədíktɪd] *adj.* adicto, dado, entregado, habituado.
ad·di·tion [ədíʃən] *s.* adición; suma; añadidura, aditamento; **in — to** además de.
ad·di·tion·al [ədíʃənl] *adj.* adicional.
ad·di·tive [ǽdətɪv] *s.* & *adj.* aditivo.
ad·dress [ədrɛ́] *s.* (*street*) dirección, domicilio, señas; sobrescrito; (*speech*) discurso, arenga, conferencia; **form of —** tratamiento; *v.* dirigir, poner la dirección, señas o sobrescrito a; hablar, dirigir la palabra a; dirigirse a; **to — oneself to a task** aplicarse a una tarea.
ad·dress·ee [ədrɛsí] *s.* destinatario.
ad·duce [ədús] *v.* aducir.
a·dept [ədǽpt] *adj.* hábil; perito.
ad·e·quate [ǽdəkwɪt] *adj.* adecuado; proporcionado; suficiente.
ad·here [ədhír] *v.* adherirse; pegarse.
ad·her·ence [ədhírəns] *s.* adherencia.
ad·he·sion [ədhíʒən] *s.* adhesión.
ad·he·sive [ədhísɪv] *adj.* adhesivo; pegajoso; **— tape** tela adhesiva, esparadrapo.
ad·ja·cent [ədʒésṇt] *adj.* adyacente, contiguo.
ad·jec·tive [ǽdʒɪktɪv] *s.* adjetivo.
ad·join [ədʒɔ́ɪn] *v.* estar contiguo o adyacente a, lindar con.
ad·journ [ədʒə́n] *v.* aplazar, diferir; **to — the meeting** suspender o levantar la sesión; **meeting -ed** se levanta la sesión.
ad·journ·ment [ədʒə́nmənt] *s.* aplazamiento, levantamiento (*de una sesión*).
ad·junct [ǽdʒʌŋkt] *s.* adjunto, aditamento, añadidura; asociado, acompañante; *adj.* adjunto, unido, subordinado.
ad·just [ədʒʌ́st] *v.* ajustar; acomodar; arreglar; graduar; **to — oneself** adaptarse, conformarse.
ad·just·ment [ədʒʌ́stmənt] *s.* ajuste; ajustamiento; arreglo; regulación.
ad-lib [ǽdlíb] *v.* improvisar; expresarse espontáneamente.
ad·min·is·ter [ədmínəstɚ] *v.* administrar; dirigir, regir, gobernar; aplicar (*remedio, castigo, etc.*); **to — an oath** tomar juramento.
ad·min·is·tra·tion [ədmɪnəstréʃən] *s.* administración; dirección, gobierno; gerencia; manejo.
ad·min·is·tra·tive [ədmínəstretɪv] *adj.* administrativo; ejecutivo; gubernativo.
ad·min·is·tra·tor [ədmínəstretɚ] *s.* administrador.
ad·mi·ra·ble [ǽdmərəbl] *adj.* admirable.
ad·mi·ra·bly [*adv.* admirablemente.
ad·mi·ral [ǽdmərəl] *s.* almirante.
ad·mi·ra·tion [ædməréʃən] *s.* admiración.
ad·mire [ədmáɪr] *v.* admirar; estimar.
ad·mir·er [ədmáɪrɚ] *s.* admirador; pretendiente.
ad·mis·si·ble [ədmísəbl] *adj.* admisible.
ad·mis·sion [ədmíʃən] *s.* (*entrance*) entrada, precio

de entrada o de ingreso; (*confession*) confesión, admisión.
ad·mit [ədmít] *v.* admitir; aceptar; confesar, reconocer; conceder; dar entrada.
ad·mit·tance [ədmítṇs] *s.* entrada; derecho de entrar; admisión.
ad·mon·ish [ədmánɪʃ] *v.* amonestar.
ad·mo·ni·tion [ædmənɪʃən] *s.* amonestación, consejo.
a·do [ədú] *s.* actividad; bulla; disturbio.
a·do·be [ədóbɪ] *s.* adobe; casa de adobe.
ad·o·les·cence [ædlɛ́sṇs] *s.* adolescencia.
ad·o·les·cent [ædlɛ́sṇt] *adj.* & *s.* adolescente.
a·dopt [ədápt] *v.* adoptar; ahijar, prophijar.
a·dop·tion [ədápʃən] *s.* adopción.
a·dor·a·ble [ədórəbl] *adj.* adorable; encantador.
ad·o·ra·tion [ædəréʃən] *s.* adoración.
a·dore [ədór] *v.* adorar.
a·dorn [ədórn] *v.* adornar; ornar; embellecer.
a·dorn·ment [ədórnmənt] *s.* adorno.
ad·re·nal [ədrínl] *adj.* suprarrenal.
ad·ren·a·lin [ædrénəlɪn] *s.* adrenalina.
a·drift [ədríft] *adj.* & *adv.* a la deriva, flotando, flotante.
a·droit [ədrɔ́ɪt] *adj.* hábil, diestro.
a·dult [ədʌ́lt] *adj.* & *s.* adulto.
a·dul·ter·ate [ədʌ́ltəret] *v.* adulterar.
a·dul·ter·er [ədʌ́ltərɚ] *s.* adúltero.
a·dul·ter·y [ədʌ́ltərɪ] *s.* adulterio.
ad·vance [ədvǽns] *v.* (*progress*) avanzar, adelantar; progresar; acelerar; (*promote*) promover; proponer; (*pay beforehand*) pagar por adelantado (anticipado); *s.* avance; progreso; adelanto, anticipo; alza aumento de precio; **-s** requerimientos, pretensiones, insinuaciones; **in — por** adelantado, con anticipación.
ad·vanced [ədvǽnst] *adj.* avanzado; adelantado; **— in years** entrado en años, viejo, anciano.
ad·vance·ment [ədvǽnsmənt] *s.* adelantamiento, mejora, progreso; promoción.
ad·van·tage [ədvǽntɪdʒ] *s.* ventaja; beneficio; provecho; **to have the — over** llevar ventaja a; **to take — of** aprovecharse de; **to take — of a person** abusar de la confianza o paciencia de alguien.
ad·van·ta·geous [ædvəntédʒəs] *adj.* ventajoso; provechoso.
ad·vent [ædvent] *s.* advenimiento; venida.'
ad·ven·ture [ədvéntʃɚ] *s.* aventura; riesgo.
ad·ven·tur·er [ədvéntʃərɚ] *s.* aventurero.
ad·ven·tur·ous [ədvéntʃərəs] *adj.* aventurero; atrevido; aventurado; arriesgado.
ad·verb [ǽdvɚb] *m.* adverbio.
ad·ver·sar·y [ǽdvɚsɛrɪ] *s.* adversario, antagonista, contrario.
ad·verse [ədvə́s] *adj.* adverso; opuesto, contrario; hostil; desfavorable.
ad·ver·si·ty [ədvə́sətɪ] *s.* adversidad; infortunio.
ad·ver·tise [ǽdvətaɪz] *v.* anunciar; avisar, dar viso.
ad·ver·tise·ment [ædvətáɪzmənt] *s.* anuncio, aviso.
ad·ver·tis·er [ǽdvətaɪzɚ] *s.* anunciador, anunciante.
ad·ver·tis·ing [ǽdvətaɪzɪŋ] *s.* anuncios; arte o negocio de anunciar.
ad·vice [ədváɪs] *s.* aviso, advertencia; consejo; noticia.
ad·vis·a·ble [ədváɪzəbl] *adj.* conveniente; prudente; recomendable.
ad·vise [ədváɪz] *v.* (*counsel*) aconsejar; (*inform*) avisar, informar, advertir; **to — with** consultar con; aconsejarse con.

ad·vis·er, ad·vi·sor [ədváɪzɚ] s. consejero, aconsejador.

ad·vo·cate [ǽdvəkɪt] s. abogado; defensor, intercesor; partidario; [ǽdvəket] v. abogar por; defender.

aer·i·al [ɛ́rɪəl] adj. aéreo; s. antena.

aer·o·dy·nam·ic [ɛrodaɪnǽmɪk] adj. aerodinámico; aerodynamics; s. aerodinámica.

aer·o·plane [ɛ́rəplen] = **airplane**.

aer·o·sol [ɛ́rosol] s. aerosol.

aes·thet·ic [ɛsθɛ́tɪk] adj. estético; -s s. estética.

a·far [əfɑ́r] adv. lejos; **from** — desde lejos.

af·fa·ble [ǽfəbl] adj. afable, amable.

af·fair [əfɛ́r] s. (social) función, tertulia, fiesta, convite; (venture) asunto; negocio; lance; cosa; **love** — amorío.

af·fect [əfɛ́kt] v. afectar; conmover;.fingir; hacer ostentación de.

af·fec·ta·tion [æfɪktéʃən] s. afectación.

af·fect·ed [əfɛ́ktɪd] adj. (emotion) afectado, conmovido, enternecido; (feigned) fingido, artificioso.

af·fec·tion [əfɛ́kʃən] s. afecto, cariño; inclinación; afección, dolencia.

af·fec·tion·ate [əfɛ́kʃənɪt] adj. afectuoso, cariñoso.

af·fi·da·vit [æfədévɪt] s. declaración jurada.

af·fil·i·ate [əfíliet] v. afiliar; afiliarse, unirse, asociarse.

af·fin·i·ty [əfínətɪ] s. afinidad.

af·firm [əfɝm] v. afirmar, asegurar, aseverar.

af·firm·a·tive [əfɝmətɪv] adj. afirmativo; s. afirmativa.

af·fix [əfíks] v. fijar, pegar; **to** — **one's signature** poner su firma, firmar.

af·flict [əflíkt] v. afligir; **to be -ed with** padecer de sufrir de, adolecer de.

af·flic·tion [əflíkʃən] s. aflicción; pena, dolor; achaque; angustia; infortunio.

af·flu·ent [ǽfluənt] adj. acaudalado; abundante.

af·ford [əfórd] v. proveer, proporcionar; **I cannot** — **that expense** no puedo hacer ese gasto; **he cannot** — **to waste time** no le conviene perder el tiempo; no tiene tiempo que perder; **I cannot** — **that risk** no puedo (o no quiero) exponerme a ese riesgo.

af·fri·cate [ǽfrɪkət] adj. & s. africado.

af·front [əfrʌ́nt] s. afrenta, agravio, ultraje; v. afrentar, agraviar, ultrajar.

a·fire [əfáɪr] adj. ardiendo, quemándose.

a·float [əflót] adj. & adv. flotante; flotando; a flote; a flor de agua; a bordo; inundado; a la deriva, sin rumbo; **the rumor is** — corre la voz.

a·foot [əfút] adv. a pie; en marcha, en movimiento.

a·fore·said [əfórsɛd] adj. susodicho, ya dicho.

a·fraid [əfréd] adj. miedoso, medroso; atemorizado, amedrentado; **to be** — temer, tener miedo.

a·fresh [əfrɛ́ʃ] adv. de nuevo, desde el principio.

Af·ri·can [ǽfrɪkən] adj. & s. africano; negro.

af·ter [ǽftɚ] prep. (temporal) después de, tras, tras de; (position) detrás de; (following) en busca de; adv. después; detrás; conj. después (de) que; adj. subsiguiente; siguiente; — **all** después de todo; de todos modos; **day** — **tomorrow** pasado mañana; **after-dinner** de sobremesa; **—effect** consecuencia, resultado; **—math** consecuencias, resultados (usualmente desastrosos); **—thought** idea tardía.

af·ter·noon [æftɚnún] s. tarde.

af·ter·taste [ǽftɚtest] s. dejo, dejillo (sabor que queda en la boca).

af·ter·wards [ǽftɚwɚdz] adv. después.

a·gain [əgɛ́n] adv. otra vez, de nuevo; además; por otra parte; — **and** — repetidas veces; **never** — nunca jamás; **to come** — volver; **to do it** — volver a hacerlo.

a·gainst [əgɛ́nst] prep. contra; frente a; en contraste con; — **the grain** a contrapelo, a redopelo; — **a rainy day** para cuando llueva.

age [edʒ] s. edad; época; siglo; generación; **of** — mayor de edad; **old** — vejez, ancianidad; **to become of** — llegar a mayor edad; **under** — menor de edad; v. envejecer(se).

a·ged [édʒɪd, édʒd] adj. viejo, anciano; añejo; envejecido; — **forty years** de cuarenta años; — **in wood** añejado en toneles o barriles (dícese del vino).

a·gen·cy [édʒənsɪ] s. agencia; medio, intermedio.

a·gen·da [ədʒɛ́ndə] s. temario; asuntos que han de tratarse en una reunión.

a·gent [édʒənt] s. agente; intermediario, representante; apoderado.

ag·glu·ti·na·tive [əglútɪnətɪv] adj. aglutinante.

ag·gran·dize [ǽgrəndaɪz] v. engrandecer; agrandar.

ag·gra·vate [ǽgrəvet] v. agravar, empeorar; irritar, exasperar.

ag·gre·gate [ǽgrɪgɪt] s. agregado, conjunto, colección; adj. agregado, unido; **in the** — en conjunto.

ag·gres·sion [əgrɛ́ʃən] s. agresión.

ag·gres·sive [əgrɛ́sɪv] adj. agresivo; emprendedor.

ag·gres·sor [əgrɛ́sɚ] s. agresor.

a·ghast [əgǽst] adj. espantado, pasmado.

ag·ile [ǽdʒəl] adj. ágil.

a·gil·i·ty [ədʒílətɪ] s. agilidad.

ag·i·tate [ǽdʒətet] v. agitar; turbar, perturbar; alborotar; discutir acaloradamente; maquinar, tramar.

ag·i·ta·tion [ædʒətéʃən] s. agitación; alboroto.

ag·i·ta·tor [ǽdʒəteta] s. agitador, alborotador, revoltoso.

ag·nos·tic [ægnǽstɪk] adj. s. agnóstico.

a·go [əgó] adj. & adv. pasado; en el pasado; **many years** — hace muchos años; muchos años ha, mucho tiempo ha; **long** — hace mucho tiempo; ha mucho.

ag·o·nize [ǽgənaɪz] v. agonizar; sufrir angustiosamente; retorcerse de dolor; luchar.

ag·o·ny [ǽgənɪ] s. agonía; angustia, tormento; dolor; lucha.

a·gree [əgrí] v. (accede) acordar, concordar, consentir, estar de acuerdo, ponerse de acuerdo; (suit) sentarle bien a uno (dícese del clima, del alimento, etc.).

a·gree·a·ble [əgríəbl] adj. agradable, afable; complaciente; conveniente; satisfactorio.

a·gree·ment [əgrímənt] s. (concord) acuerdo, convenio, conformidad; (grammatical) concordancia; **to be in** — estar de acuerdo; **to come to an** — ponerse de acuerdo.

ag·ri·cul·tur·al [ægrɪkʌ́ltʃərəl] adj. agrícola.

ag·ri·cul·ture [ǽgrɪkʌltʃɚ] s. agricultura.

ag·ri·cul·tur·ist [ægrɪkʌ́ltʃərɪst] s. agricultor.

a·ground [əgráʊnd] adj. & adv. encallado.

a·head [əhɛ́d] adv. delante, al frente; adelante; — **of time** adelantado; antes de tiempo; **to go** — ir adelante; **to get** — adelantar(se).

aid [ed] s. ayuda, auxilio, socorro; ayudante, auxiliar; v. ayudar, auxiliar, socorrer.

aide-de-camp [édəkæmp] s. edecán.

ail [el] v. adolecer, padecer; **what -s you?** ¿qué tienes? ¿qué te aflige?

ai·le·ron [élərən] *s.* alerón.

ail·ment [élmənt] *s.* achaque, dolencia.

aim [em] *s. (pointing)* puntería; tino; *(objective)* fin, objeto; proposición; *v.* apuntar *(un arma);* dirigir, asestar; dirigir la puntería; aspirar (a); **to — to please** proponerse *(o* tratar de agradar.

aim·less [émlıs] *adj.* sin propósito, sin objeto.

air [ɛr] *s. (atmosphere)* aire, brisa; *(music)* tonada; **in the —** en el aire; indeciso; incierto; **in the open —** al raso, al aire libre; **to be on the —** emitir, radiodifundir; **to put on -s** darse tono; *adj.* de aire; aéreo; **— brake** freno neumático; **—line** línea aérea; ruta aérea; **— pocket** bache aéreo; bolsa de aire; **by —mail** por correo aéreo, por avión; **air-conditioned** de aire acondicionado; *v.* airear; orear; ventilar; publicar, pregonar; ostentar.

air·borne [ɛrborn] aéreo; aerotransportado.

air·craft [ɛrkræft] *s.* avión, aeroplano; aeronave; aviones; **— carrier** portaaviones.

air·foil [ɛrfɔıl] *s.* superficie de control en los aviones.

air·line [ɛrlaın] *s.* aerovía: línea aérea; compañía de transporte aéreo.

air·plane [ɛrplen] *s.* aeroplano, avión; **— carrier** portaaviones.

air·port [ɛrport] *s.* aeropuerto, aeródromo.

air·ship [ɛrʃıp] *s.* aeronave.

air·tight [ɛrtáıt] *adj.* hermético.

air·y [ɛrı] *adj.* airoso; aireado, ventilado; ligero; tenue.

aisle [aıl] *s.* pasillo, pasadizo; nave *(de una iglesia).*

a·jar [ədʒár] *adj.* entreabierto, entornado.

al·a·bas·ter [ǽləbæstɚ] *s.* alabastro.

a·larm [əlárm] *s.* alarma; rebato; inquietud; **— clock** despertador; *v.* alarmar; inquietar.

al·bi·no [æbáıno] *s.* albino.

al·bum [ǽlbəm] *álbum.*

al·che·my [ǽlkəmı] *s.* alquimia.

al·co·hol [ǽlkəhɔl] *s.* alcohol.

al·co·hōl·ic [ælkəhɔ́lık] *adj.* alcohólico.

al·cove [ǽlkov] *s.* alcoba.

al·der·man [ɔ́ldɚmən] *s.* concejal, regidor.

ale [el] *s.* cerveza de tipo espeso y amargo.

a·lert [əlɚ́t] *adj.* alerto, vigilante; despierto; vivo; listo; *s.* alarma, rebato; **to be on the —** estar alerta.

al·fal·fa [ælfǽlfə] *s.* alfalfa.

algae [ǽldʒı] *s. pl.* algas.

al·ge·bra [ǽldʒəbrə] *s.* álgebra.

al·i·bi [ǽləbaı] *s.* coartada; excusa.

a·li·en [éljən] *s.* extranjero; residente extranjero; *adj.* extraño, ajeno.

al·ien·ate [éljənet] *v.* enajenar; apartar, alejar *(a una persona de otra).*

al·ien·ist [éljənıst] *s.* alienista, psiquiatra.

a·light [əláıt] *v.* apearse, desmontarse, bajar(de); posarse *(dícese de pájaros, mariposas, etc.).*

a·lign [əláın] *v.* alinear(se).

a·like [əláık] *adj.* semejante; parecido; **to be —** parecerse, asemejarse; ser iguales; *adv.* del mismo modo.

al·i·mo·ny [ǽləmonı] *s.* asistencia de divorcio; alimento.

a·live [əláıv] *adj.* vivo; con vida; viviente; activo; **— with** lleno de.

al·ka·li [ǽlkəlaı] *s.* álcali.

all [ɔl] *adj.* todo (el); todos (los); *s.* todo; todo el mundo, todos; *adv.* enteramente; **— at once** de una vez; de un tirón; de repente; **— right** bueno; bien; **— the worse** tanto peor; **not at —**

de ninguna manera; no hay de qué; **nothing at — nada** en absoluto; **— told** *(o* **in —)** en conjunto; **once (and) for —** por última vez; una vez por todas; **to be — in** estar agotado, estar rendido de fatiga; **it is — over** se acabó, ha terminado todo.

al·lay [əlé] *v.* aliviar; calmar.

al·le·ga·tion [æləgéʃən] *s.* alegación, alegato; aseveración.

al·lege [əlédʒ] *v.* alegar; declarar; sostener, asegurar.

al·le·giance [əlídʒəns] *s.* lealtad, fidelidad; homenaje.

al·le·go·ry [ǽləgorı] *s.* alegoría.

al·ler·gy [ǽlɚdʒı] *s.* alergia *(sensibilidad anormal a ciertos alimentos o sustancias).*

al·le·vi·ate [əlívıet] *v.* aliviar.

al·ley [ǽlı] *s.* callejón; callejuela; **blind —** callejón sin salida; **bowling —** boliche, *Am.* bolera.

al·li·ance [əláıəns] *s.* alianza.

al·lied [əláıd] *adj.* aliado; relacionado.

al·li·ga·tor [ǽləgetɚ] *s.* lagarto; caimán; **— pear** aguacate.

al·lot [əlát] *v.* asignar; repartir.

al·low [əláú] *v.* permitir, dejar; conceder; admitir; asignar; abonar; **to — for certain errors** tener en cuenta ciertos errores.

al·low·a·ble [əláúəbl] *adj.* permisible, admisible, lícito.

al·low·ance [əláúəns] *s.* asignación; abono, pensión; ración; rebaja, descuento; permiso; concesión; **monthly —** mesada, mensualidad; **to make — for** tener en cuenta.

al·loy [ǽlɔı] *s.* aleación, liga, mezcla *(de dos o más metales);* [əlɔ́ı] *v.* alear, ligar, mezclar *(metales).*

al·lude [əlúd] *v.* aludir.

al·lure [əlúr] *v.* seducir, cautivar; atraer, halagar.

al·lure·ment [əlúrmənt] *s.* seducción, tentación; atractivo, halago.

al·lur·ing [əlúrıŋ] *adj.* seductivo, halagüeño, encantador.

al·lu·sion [əlúʒən] *s.* alusión; indirecta, insinuación.

al·lu·vi·um [əlúvıəm] *s.* aluvión.

al·ly [əláı] *v.* unir; aliarse; **to — oneself (itself) with** aliarse con, unirse con; [ǽlaı] *s.* aliado.

al·ma·nac [ɔ́lmənæk] *s.* almanaque, calendario.

al·might·y [ɔlmáıtı] *adj.* todopoderoso, omnipotente.

al·mond [ámənd] *s.* almendra; **— tree** almendro.

al·most [ɔ́lmost] *adv.* casi; **I — fell down** por poco me caigo.

alms [amz] *s.* limosna; **— box** cepo o cepillo, alcancía *(para limosnas).*

a·lone [əlón] *adj.* solo; solitario; único; *adv.* sólo, solamente; **all — a** solas; completamente solo; solito; **to let —** no tocar; no molestar; dejar en paz; no hacer caso de.

a·long [əlɔ́ŋ] *prep.* a lo largo de; por; al lado de; **— with** junto con; en compañía de; **all —** todo el tiempo; de un extremo a otro; **all — the coast** por toda la costa; **to carry — with** one llevar consigo; **to go — with** acompañar; **to get —** ir bien; **to get — with** llevarse bien con; **get —!** ¡vete! ¡váyase! ¡largo de aquí!

a·long·side [əlɔ́ŋsáıd] *prep. & adv.* al lado (de); al costado (de); lado a lado.

a·loof [əlúf] *adj.* aislado, apartado, retirado; huraño; reservado; *adv.* aparte; lejos.

a·loof·ness [əlúfnıs] *s.* alejamiento, desapego, aislamiento.

a·loud [ǝláʊd] *adv.* alto, recio, fuerte, en voz alta.
al·pha·bet [ǽlfǝbɛt] *s.* alfabeto.
al·read·y [ɔlrέdɪ] *adv.* ya.
al·so [ɔ́lso] *adv.* también, además, igualmente.
al·tar [ɔ́ltǝ] *s.* altar; **high** — altar mayor; —**piece** retablo.
al·ter [ɔ́ltǝ] *v.* alterar; cambiar; variar.
al·ter·a·tion [ɔltǝréʃǝn] *s.* alteración, cambio; mudanza; modificación.
al·ter·nate [ɔ́ltǝ·nɪt] *adj.* alternativo; alterno; alternado; *s.* suplente; **-ly** *adv.* alternativamente, por turno; [ɔ́ltǝnet] *v.* alternar; variar; turnar.
al·ter·na·tive [ɔltɝ́nǝtiv] *adj.* alternativo; *s.* alternativa.
al·ter·na·tor [ɔltɝ́nétǝ] *s.* alternador.
al·though [ɔlðó] *conj.* aunque, si bien, bien que.
al·tim·e·ter [ǽltímǝtǝ] *s.* altímetro.
al·ti·tude [ǽltǝtjud] *s.* altitud, altura, elevación; — **sickness** *Am.* soroche.
al·to [ǽlto] *s.* & *adj.* contralto.
al·to·geth·er [ɔltǝɡέðǝ] *adv.* del todo, completamente; en conjunto.
a·lu·mi·num [ǝlúmɪnǝm] *s.* aluminio.
a·lum·nus [ǝlʌ́mnǝs] *s.* graduado, exalumno.
al·ways [ɔ́lwɪz] *adv.* siempre.
am [æm] *1ª persona del presente de indic. del verbo* **to be**: soy, estoy.
a·mal·ga·mate [ǝmǽlgǝmet] *v.* amalgamar; combinar; unir.
a·mass [ǝmǽs] *v.* amontonar, acumular, apilar, *Am.* amasar.
am·a·teur [ǽmǝtʃʊr] *s.* aficionado; novicio, principiante.
a·maze [ǝméz] *v.* pasmar, maravillar, asombrar.
a·maze·ment [ǝmézmǝnt] *s.* pasmo, admiración, asombro.
a·maz·ing [ǝmézɪŋ] *adj.* pasmoso, asombroso, maravilloso.
am·bas·sa·dor [æmbǽsǝdǝ] *s.* embajador.
am·ber [ǽmbǝ] *s.* ámbar; color de ámbar; *adj.* ambarino; de ámbar.
am·bi·ance [ǽmbiǝns] *s.* ambiente.
am·bi·gu·i·ty [æmbɪgjúǝtɪ] *s.* ambigüedad.
am·big·u·ous [æmbíɡjʊǝs] *adj.* ambiguo.
am·bi·tion [æmbíʃǝn] *s.* ambición, aspiración.
am·bi·tious [æmbíʃǝs] *adj.* ambicioso.
am·biv·a·lent [æmbívǝlǝnt] *adj.* ambivalente.
am·ble [ǽmbl] *v.* andar, vagar.
am·bu·lance [ǽmbjǝlǝns] *s.* ambulancia.
am·bush [ǽmbʊʃ] *s.* emboscada; celada; acecho; **to lie in** — estar emboscado, estar al acecho; *v.* emboscar; poner celada a.
a·me·na·ble [ǝmínǝbl] *adj.* dócil; tratable.
a·mend [ǝménd] *v.* enmendar; rectificar; **-s** *s. pl.* satisfacción, compensación; **to make — for** resarcir, dar satisfacción por, compensar por.
a·mend·ment [ǝméndmǝnt] *s.* enmienda.
A·mer·i·can [ǝmérǝkǝn] *adj.* & *s.* (*continental*) americano; (*U.S.A.*) norteamericano.
A·mer·i·can·ism [ǝmérɪkǝnɪzǝm] *s.* americanismo.
am·e·thyst [ǽmǝθɪst] *s.* amatista.
a·mi·a·ble [émiǝbl] *adj.* amable, afable, amistoso.
am·i·ca·ble [ǽmɪkǝbl] *adj.* amigable, amistoso.
a·mid [ǝmíd] *prep.* en medio de; entre; **amidst** [ǝmídst] = **amid**.
a·miss [ǝmís] *adj.* errado, equivocado; impropio; *adv.* mal; fuera de lugar, impropiamente; **to take** — llevar a mal.
am·mo·nia [ǝmónjǝ] *s.* amoníaco.
am·mu·ni·tion [æmjǝníʃǝn] *s.* munición.
am·ne·sia [æmnízjǝ] *s.* amnesia.

am·nes·ty [ǽmnɛstɪ] *s.* amnestía.
a·mong [ǝmʌ́ŋ] *prep.* entre, en medio de; **amongst** [ǝmʌ́ŋst] = **among**.
am·o·rous [ǽmǝrǝs] *adj.* amoroso.
a·mor·phous [ǝmɔ́rfǝs] *adj.* amorfo.
am·or·tize [ǽmɔ́taɪz] *v.* amortizar.
a·mount [ǝmáʊnt] *s.* suma; cantidad; total; importe; valor; *v.* montar, subir, importar, ascender (a); valer; **that -s to stealing** eso equivale a robar.
am·pere [ǽmpɪr] *s.* amperio.
am·phib·i·ous [æmfíbɪǝs] *adj.* anfibio.
am·phi·the·a·ter [ǽmfǝθiǝtǝ] *s.* anfiteatro.
am·ple [ǽmpl] *adj.* amplio; abundante; bastante, suficiente.
am·pli·fy [ǽmplǝfaɪ] *v.* ampliar; amplificar.
am·pu·tate [ǽmpjǝtet] *v.* amputar.
a·muck [ǝmʌ́k] *adv.* con frenesí; **to run** — atacar a ciegas.
a·muse [ǝmjúz] *v.* divertir, entretener, distraer; **to — oneself** divertirse.
a·muse·ment [ǝmjúzmǝnt] *s.* diversión, entretenimiento, pasatiempo, recreo, distracción.
a·mus·ing [ǝmjúzɪŋ] *adj.* divertido, entretenido; gracioso, chistoso.
an [ǝn, æn] *art. indef.* un, una.
a·nach·ro·nism [ǝnǽkrǝnɪzm] *s.* anacronismo.
an·al·ge·sic [ænǝldʒízɪk] *s.* analgésico.
a·nal·o·gous [ǝnǽlǝgǝs] *adj.* análogo.
a·nal·o·gy [ǝnǽlǝdʒɪ] *s.* analogía, semejanza.
a·nal·y·sis [ǝnǽlǝsɪs] *s.* análisis.
an·a·lyt·ic [ænǝlítɪk] *adj.* analítico.
an·a·lyze [ǽnǝlaɪz] *v.* analizar.
an·ar·chist [ǽnǝkɪst] *s.* anarquista.
an·ar·chy [ǽnǝkɪ] *s.* anarquía.
a·nath·e·ma [ǝnǽθǝmǝ] *s.* anatema.
an·a·tom·i·cal [ænǝtámɪkl] *adj.* anatómico.
a·nat·o·my [ǝnǽtǝmɪ] *s.* anatomía.
an·ces·tor [ǽnsɛstǝ] *s.* antepasado; **-s** abuelos, antepasados.
an·ces·tral [ænséstrǝl] *adj.* solariego, de los antepasados; hereditario.
an·ces·try [ǽnsɛstrɪ] *s.* linaje, abolengo, ascendencia.
an·chor [ǽŋkǝ] *s.* ancla; **to drop** — anclar, echar anclas, dar fondo, fondear; **to weigh** — levar el ancla; *v.* anclar; echar anclas; fijar, asegurar.
an·cho·vy [ǽntʃovɪ] *s.* anchoa, anchova.
an·cient [énʃǝnt] *adj.* antiguo; vetusto; **the -s** los antiguos, la antigüedad.
and [ǝnd, ænd] *conj.* y; e (*delante de i o hi*); **— so forth** etcétera; y así sucesivamente; **let us try — do it** tratemos de hacerlo; **let us go — see** him vamos a verle.
An·da·lu·sian [ændǝlúʒǝn] *adj.* andaluz.
an·ec·dote [ǽnɪkdot] *s.* anécdota.
a·ne·mi·a [ǝnímiǝ] *s.* anemia.
an·es·the·sia [ænɪsθíʒǝ] *s.* anestesia.
an·es·thet·ic [ænǝsθétɪk] *adj.* & *s.* anestésico.
a·new [ǝnjú] *adv.* otra vez, de nuevo; nuevamente.
an·gel [éndʒǝl] *s.* ángel.
an·gel·ic [ændʒélɪk] *adj.* angélico.
an·ger [ǽŋgǝ] *s.* enojo, enfado, ira, cólera; *v.* enojar, enfadar, encolerizar.
an·gi·na [ændʒáɪnǝ] *s.* angina; — **pectoris** angina de pecho.
an·gle [ǽŋgl] *s.* ángulo; (*interior*) rincón; (*exterior*) esquina; punto de vista, aspecto; *v.* pescar.
An·glo-Sax·on [ǽŋglosǽksn] *adj.* & *s.* anglosajón.
an·gry [ǽŋgrɪ] *adj.* enojado; colérico; airado.
an·guish [ǽŋgwɪʃ] *s.* angustia, ansia, pena, dolor.

an·gu·lar [ǽŋgjʊlɚ] adj. angular; anguloso.

an·i·mal [ǽnəml] s. & adj. animal.

an·i·mate [ǽnəmɪt] adj. animado, viviente; **animated cartoon** dibujo animado; [ǽnəmet] v. animar; alentar.

an·i·ma·tion [ænəméʃən] s. animación; viveza.

an·i·mos·i·ty [ænəmásətɪ] s. animosidad, ojeriza, inquina, rencor.

an·ise [ǽnɪs] s. anís.

an·kle [ǽŋkl] s. tobillo.

an·nals [ǽnlz] s. pl. anales.

an·nex [ǽnɛks] s. (building) pabellón, ala; (dependent addition) anexo; añadidura; [ənéks] v. anexar.

an·nex·a·tion [ænɛkséʃən] s. anexión.

an·ni·hi·late [ənáɪələt] v. aniquilar; anonadar.

an·ni·ver·sa·ry [ænəvɝsərɪ] s. & adj. aniversario.

an·no·tate [ǽnotet] v. anotar.

an·no·ta·tion [ænotéʃən] s. anotación, acotación, nota.

an·nounce [ənáʊns] v. anunciar; proclamar.

an·nounce·ment [ənáʊnsmənt] s. anuncio; aviso; noticia.

an·nounc·er [ənáʊnsɚ] s. anunciador; **radio —** locutor.

an·noy [ənɔ́ɪ] v. molestar; fastidiar; incomodar; enfadar.

an·noy·ance [ənɔ́ɪəns] s. molestia; fastidio; enfado; vejamen.

an·nu·al [ǽnjʊəl] adj. anual; s. anuario; planta anual; **-ly** adv. anualmente, cada año, todos los años.

an·nu·i·ty [ənúətɪ] s. anualidad, renta anual.

an·nul [ənʌ́l] v. anular; abolir.

an·nul·ment [ənʌ́lmənt] s. revocación; anulación.

a·noint [ənɔ́ɪnt] v. ungir; untar; administrar la Extremaunción.

a·non [ənán] adv. pronto, luego; otra vez.

a·non·y·mous [ənánəməs] adj. anónimo.

an·oth·er [ənʌ́ðɚ] adj. & pron. otro; **one —** uno a otro, unos a otros.

an·swer [ǽnsɚ] s. respuesta, contestación; réplica; solución; v. responder; contestar; replicar; **to — for** ser responsable de (o por); responder de; ser (salir) fiador de; **to — the purpose** ser adecuado, servir para el objeto.

ant [ænt] s. hormiga; **—eater** oso hormiguero; **— hill** hormiguero.

ant·ac·id [æntǽsɪd] s. & adj. antiácido.

an·tag·o·nism [æntǽgənɪzəm] s. antagonismo, oposición, antipatía.

an·tag·o·nist [æntǽgənɪst] s. antagonista, adversario.

an·tag·o·nize [æntǽgənaɪz] v. contrariar, oponerse a, hostilizar.

an·te·ce·dent [æntəsídn̩t] adj. & s. antecedente.

an·te·lope [ǽntlop] s. antílope.

an·ten·na [ænténə] (pl. **antennae** [ænténi]) s. antena.

an·te·ri·or [æntírɪɚ] adj. anterior; delantero.

an·te·room [ǽntɪrum] s. antecámara; sala de espera.

an·them [ǽnθəm] s. himno.

an·thol·o·gy [ænθálədʒɪ] s. antología.

an·thra·cite [ǽnθrəsaɪt] s. antracita.

an·thro·pol·o·gist [ænθrəpálədʒɪst] s. antropólogo.

an·thro·pol·o·gy [ænθrəpálədʒɪ] s. antropología.

an·ti·air·craft [æntiérkræft] adj. antiaéreo.

an·ti·bi·ot·ic [æntɪbaɪátɪk] s. & adj. antibiótico.

an·ti·bod·y [ǽntɪbadɪ] s. anticuerpo.

an·tic·i·pate [æntísəpet] v. anticipar(se); prever;

esperar.

an·tic·i·pa·tion [æntɪsəpéʃən] s. anticipación; expectación; previsión.

an·tics [ǽntɪks] s. pl. travesuras, cabriolas.

an·ti·dote [ǽntɪdot] s. antídoto.

an·ti·freeze [ǽntɪfriz] s. anticongelante.

an·ti·mo·ny [ǽntəmónɪ] s. antimonio.

an·tip·a·thy [æntɪpəθɪ] s. antipatía, repugnancia.

an·ti·quat·ed [ǽntəkwetɪd] adj. anticuado; desusado.

an·tique [æntík] adj. antiguo; anticuado; s. antigualla.

an·tiq·ui·ty [æntíkwətɪ] s. antigüedad; vejez, ancianidad.

an·ti·sep·tic [æntəséptɪk] adj. & s. antiséptico.

an·ti·so·cial [æntɪsóʃel] adj. antisocial; s. Am. criminal.

an·tith·e·sis [æntíθəsɪs] s. antítesis.

ant·ler [ǽntlɚ] s. asta, cuerno (del venado, ciervo, etc.).

an·vil [ǽnvɪl] s. yunque.

anx·i·e·ty [æŋzáɪətɪ] s. ansiedad, zozobra; ansia, anhelo, afán.

anx·ious [ǽŋkʃəs] adj. ansioso; inquieto, preocupado; anheloso, deseoso; **-ly** adv. con ansiedad, con ansia, ansiosamente.

an·y [ɛ́nɪ] adj. & pron. cualquier(a), cualesquier (a); alguno, algunos; **in — case** de todos modos, en todo caso; **I have not — bread** no tengo pan; **she does not sing — more** ya no canta; **he does not want to work — more** no quiere trabajar más.

an·y·bod·y [ɛ́nɪbadɪ] pron. alguien, alguno; cualquiera; **not . . . —** no . . . nadie, no . . . ninguno; **he does not know —** no conoce a nadie.

an·y·how [ɛ́nɪhaʊ] adv. de todos modos; de cualquier modo.

an·y·one [ɛ́nɪwʌn] pron. = **anybody**.

an·y·thing [ɛ́nɪθɪŋ] pron. alguna cosa; cualquier cosa; algo; **not . . . —** no . . . nada; **not to know —** no saber nada; **— you wish** todo lo que quiera Vd.

an·y·way [ɛ́nɪwe] adv. de todos modos; en cualquier caso.

an·y·where [ɛ́nɪhwɛr] adv. dondequiera; en cualquier parte o lugar; en todas partes; **not . . . —** no . . . en (o a) ninguna parte; **not to go —** no ir a ninguna parte.

a·part [əpárt] adj. aparte; separadamente; a un lado; adj. aislado, separado; **to take —** desarmar, desmontar; **to tear —** despedazar, hacer pedazos.

a·part·ment [əpártmənt] s. departamento, piso, apartamento; vivienda, habitación.

ap·a·thet·ic [æpəθétɪk] adj. apático.

ap·a·thy [ǽpəθɪ] s. apatía, indiferencia, indolencia.

ape [ep] s. mono; v. remedar, imitar.

ap·er·ture [ǽpɚtʃɚ] s. abertura.

a·pex [épɛks] s. ápice, cumbre.

a·pha·sia [əfézɪə] s. afasia.

a·piece [əpís] adv. cada uno, a cada uno, por persona.

a·poc·o·pe [əpákəpɪ] s. apócope.

ap·o·gee [ǽpədʒɪ] s. apogeo.

a·pol·o·get·ic [əpalədʒétɪk] adj. que se excusa o disculpa.

a·pol·o·gize [əpálədʒaɪz] v. disculparse, excusarse.

a·pol·o·gy [əpálədʒɪ] s. apología; excusa, disculpa, justificación, satisfacción.

ap·o·plex·y [ǽpəplɛksɪ] s. apoplejía.

a·pos·tle [əpásl] *s*. apóstol.
ap·os·tol·ic [æpəstálɪk] *adj*. apostólico.
a·pos·tro·phe [əpástrəfɪ] *s*. apóstrofe; (*punctuation*) apóstrofo.
ap·pall [əpɔ́l] *v*. aterrorizar, aterrar; asombrar, espantar.
ap·pall·ing [əpɔ́lɪŋ] *adj*. aterrador; espantoso, asombroso.
ap·pa·ra·tus [æpərétəs] *s*. aparato; aparejo.
ap·par·el [əpǽrəl] *s*. ropa; ropaje; vestidos; indumentaria.
ap·par·ent [əpǽrənt] *adj*. aparente; visible; claro, evidente; patente; **heir** — heredero presunto; **-ly** *adv*. aparentemente, al parecer, por lo visto.
ap·pa·ri·tion [æpəríʃən] *s*. aparición; aparecido, espectro, fantasma.
ap·peal [əpil] *s*. (*legal*) apelación, recurso; (*request*) súplica; (*attraction*) atracción, atractivo, llamamiento; *v*. apelar; recurrir, acudir; atraer, despertar interés o simpatía; llamar la atención.
ap·pear [əpír] *v*. aparecer(se); parecer; comparecer.
ap·pear·ance [əpírəns] *s*. apariencia, semblante; porte, facha; aparición; cariz.
ap·pease [əpíz] *v*. apaciguar, aplacar; pacificar; conciliar; sosegar.
ap·pease·ment [əpízmənt] *s*. apaciguamiento; conciliación.
ap·pen·dix [əpéndɪks] *s*. apéndice.
ap·per·tain [æpə·tén] *v*. pertenecer.
ap·pe·tite [ǽpətaɪt] *s*. apetito; gana, deseo.
ap·pe·tiz·er [ǽpətaɪzɚ] *s*. aperitivo.
ap·pe·tiz·ing [ǽpətaɪzɪŋ] *adj*. apetecible; apetitoso.
ap·plaud [əplɔ́d] *v*. aplaudir.
ap·plause [əplɔ́z] *s*. aplauso.
ap·ple [ǽpl] *s*. manzana; — **tree** manzano; — **grove** manzanar; **Adam's** — nuez (*de la garganta*); *Ven., C.A., Col.* manzana; — **of my eye** niña de mis ojos.
ap·ple·sauce [ǽplsɔs] *s*. compota de manzana.
ap·pli·ance [əpláɪəns] *s*. utensilio, instrumento; herramienta.
ap·pli·ca·ble [ǽplɪkəbl] *adj*. aplicable.
ap·pli·cant [ǽpləkənt] *s*. solicitante, aspirante, candidato.
ap·pli·ca·tion [æpləkéʃən] *s*. (*dedication*) aplicación; (*petition*) solicitud, petición; *Méx., Carib., Ven.* aplicación.
ap·plied [əpláɪd] *adj.* & *p.p.* aplicado; — **for** pedido, solicitado.
ap·ply [əpláɪ] *v*. aplicar(se); **to** — **to** dirigirse a, acudir a, recurrir a; **to** — **for** solicitar, pedir; **to** — **oneself** aplicarse, dedicarse; **to** — **on account** acreditar en cuenta.
ap·point [əpɔ́ɪnt] *v*. (*designate*) nombrar, designar, señalar; (*furnish*) amueblar, equipar; **a well -ed house** una casa bien amueblada.
ap·point·ee [əpɔɪntí] *s*. electo.
ap·point·ment [əpɔ́ɪntmənt] *s*. (*designation*) nombramiento, designación; (*engagement*) cita, compromiso; **-s** mobiliario, mueblaje; accesorios.
ap·por·tion [əpɔ́rʃən] *v*. repartir proporcionadamente, prorratear.
ap·por·tion·ment [əpɔ́rʃənmənt] *s*. prorrateo, distribución, repartimiento.
ap·prais·al [əprézl] *s*. tasa, valuación.
ap·praise [əpréz] *v*. avaluar, valuar, tasar.
ap·pre·cia·ble [əpríʃɪəbl] *adj*. (*prized*) apreciable; (*perceived*) perceptible; (*quantity*) bastante.
ap·pre·ci·ate [əpríʃɪet] *v*. apreciar; estimar; agradecer; **to** — **in value** subir de valor.

ap·pre·ci·a·tion [əpriʃiéʃən] *s*. apreciación; aprecio; valuación; agradecimiento; aumento, alza, subida (*de precio*).
ap·pre·hend [æprɪhénd] *v*. aprehender, asir; prender; comprender; percibir.
ap·pre·hen·sion [æprɪhénʃən] *s*. aprehensión, aprensión, recelo, desconfianza, presentimiento; captura.
ap·pre·hen·sive [æprɪhénsɪv] *adj*. aprensivo.
ap·pren·tice [əpréntɪs] *s*. aprendiz; novicio, principiante; *v*. poner de aprendiz.
ap·pren·tice·ship [əpréntɪsʃɪp] *s*. aprendizaje.
ap·prise [əpráɪz] *v*. enterar, informar; apreciar.
ap·proach [əprótʃ] *s*. acercamiento; aproximación; acceso, entrada; **method of** — técnica o modo de plantear (*un problema*); *v*. acercarse, aproximarse; abordar (*a alguien*).
ap·pro·ba·tion [æprəbéʃən] *s*. aprobación.
ap·pro·pri·ate [əprópriɪt] *adj*. apropiado, propio, apto, conveniente, a propósito; [əprópriet] *v*. apropiarse, apoderarse de; asignar (*una suma de dinero*).
ap·pro·pri·a·tion [əpropriéʃən] *s*. apropiación; asignación, suma asignada.
ap·prov·al [əprúvl] *s*. aprobación, asentimiento.
ap·prove [əprúv] *v*. aprobar; asentir a.
ap·prox·i·mate [əprákəmɪt] *adj*. aproximado; aproximativo; **-ly** *adv*. aproximadamente, casi, poco más o menos; [əpráksəmet] *v*. aproximar; aproximarse, acercarse.
a·pri·cot [éprɪkat] *s*. albaricoque; *Am.* chabacano.
A·pril [éprəl] *s*. abril.
a·pron [éprən] *s*. delantal.
ap·ro·pos [æprəpó] *adv*. a propósito; *adj*. oportuno; pertinente; — **of** a propósito de.
apt [æpt] *adj*. apto, capaz; pertinente, a propósito; — **to** propenso a.
ap·ti·tude [ǽptətjud] *s*. aptitud, capacidad; habilidad.
aq·ua·ma·rine [akwəmərín] *s*. aguamarina.
a·quar·i·um [əkwériəm] *s*. acuario; pecera.
a·quat·ic [əkwǽtɪk] *adj*. acuático.
aq·ue·duct [ǽkwidʌkt] *s*. acueducto.
Ar·ab [ǽrəb] *adj*. & *s*. árabe.
Ar·a·go·nese [ærəgəníz] *adj*. & *s*. aragonés.
ar·bi·ter [árbɪtɚ] *s*. árbitro, arbitrador, juez árbitro.
ar·bi·trar·y [árbɪtrɛrɪ] *adj*. arbitrario; despótico.
ar·bi·trate [árbətret] *v*. arbitrar; decidir; someter al arbitraje.
ar·bi·tra·tion [arbətréʃən] *s*. arbitraje, arbitración.
ar·bi·tra·tor [árbətretɚ] *s*. arbitrador, árbitro, mediano.
ar·bor [árbɚ] *s*. emparrado, enramada, glorieta.
arc [ɑrk] *s*. arco; — **lamp** lámpara de arco.
ar·cade [ɑrkéd] *s*. arcada; galería; soportal.
arch [ɑrtʃ] *s*. arco; bóveda; **semicircular** — arco de medio punto; — **enemy** enemigo acérrimo; *v*. arquear(se); enarcar(se).
ar·chae·ol·o·gy [ɑrkɪáləd ʒɪ] *s*. arqueología.
ar·cha·ic [ɑrkéɪk] *adj*. arcaico, desusado, anticuado.
arch·bish·op [ɑrtʃbíʃəp] *s*. arzobispo.
arch·bish·op·ric [ɑrtʃbíʃəprɪk] *s*. arzobispado.
arch·er·y [ɑrtʃərɪ] *s*. tiro de flechas.
ar·chi·pel·a·go [ɑrkəpéləgo] *s*. archipiélago.
ar·chi·tect [árkətɛkt] *s*. arquitecto.
ar·chi·tec·tur·al [arkətɛktʃərəl] *adj*. arquitectónico.
ar·chi·tec·ture [árkətɛktʃɚ] *s*. arquitectura.
ar·chives [árkaɪvz] *s*. archivo.
arch·way [ɑrtʃwe] *s*. pasadizo (*bajo un arco*);

arcada, galería abovedada.
arc·tic [árktık] *adj.* ártico.
ar·dent [árdṇt] *adj.* ardiente apasionado.
ar·dor [árdə·] *s.* ardor; enardecimiento; fervor.
ar·du·ous (árdʒʊəs] *adj.* arduo, trabajoso.
are [ɑr] 2ᵃ *persona y pl. del presente de indic. del verbo* **to be:** eres, estás; somos, estamos; sois, estáis; son, están.
ar·e·a [ɛrıə] *s.* área, superficie; espacio; región.
a·re·na [ərínə] *s.* arena, redondel, plaza.
Ar·gen·ti·ne [árdʒəntin] *adj. & s.* argentino.
ar·gon [árgɑn] argón.
ar·gue [árgjʊ] *v.* argüir; debatir; altercar; **to —** **into** persuadir a.
ar·gu·ment [árgjəmənt] *s.* disputa; polémica; razonamiento; sumario, resumen.
ar·id [ǽrıd] *adj.* árido.
a·rise [əráız] *v.* levantarse; elevarse; surgir; provenir.
a·ris·en [ərízṇ] *p.p. de* **to arise.**
ar·is·toc·ra·cy [ærəstákrəsı] *s.* aristocracia.
a·ris·to·crat [ərístəkræt] *s.* aristócrata.
a·ris·to·crat·ic [ərıstəkrǽtık] *adj.* aristocrático.
a·rith·me·tic [əríθmətık] *s.* aritmética.
ark [ɑrk] *s.* arca; **— of the covenant** arca del testamento; **Noah's —** arca de Noé.
arm [ɑrm] *s.* (*anatomy*) brazo; (*weapon*) arma; **—** **in —** de bracete, de bracero; *Am.* de brazo, de brazos; **at -'s length** a una brazada; **with open -s** con los brazos abiertos; *v.* armar(se).
ar·ma·da [ɑrmádə] *s.* armada, flota.
ar·ma·ment [árməmənt] *s.* armamento.
ar·ma·ture [ármətʃə·] *s.* armaduar.
arm·chair [ármtʃɛr] *s.* silla de brazos, sillón, butaca.
armed for·ces [ármd fórsəz] *s.* fuerzas armadas.
arm·ful [ármfʊl] *s.* brazada.
ar·mi·stice [árməstıs] *s.* armisticio.
ar·mor [ármə·] *s.* armadura; blindaje, coraza; arnés; *v.* blindar, acorazar.
ar·mored [ármə·d] *p.p.* blindado, acorazado.
ar·mor·y [ármərı] *s.* armería; arsenal.
arm·pit [ármpıt] *s.* sobaco.
ar·my [ármı] *s.* ejército; muchedumbre; **— doctor** médico militar; **regular —** tropa de línea.
a·ro·ma [ərómə] *s.* aroma; fragancia.
ar·o·mat·ic [ærəmǽtık] *adj.* aromático.
a·rose [əróz] *pret. de* **to arise.**
a·round [əráʊnd] *adv.* alrededor; en redor; a la redonda, en torno; en derredor; cerca; **all —** por todos lados; *prep.* alrededor de; cerca de; **—** **here** por aquí; **to go — in circles** dar vueltas; **to** **go — the world** dar la vuelta al mundo.
a·rouse [əráʊz] *v.* despertar, *Riopl., C.A., Ven.* recordar (*al dormido*); excitar; promover.
ar·raign [ərén] *v.* acusar; procesar (*a un criminal*).
ar·range [əréndʒ] *v.* arreglar; disponer, colocar; acomodar; hacer arreglos (para), hacer planes (para).
ar·range·ment [əréndʒmənt] *s.* arreglo; disposición; colocación, orden; convenio.
ar·ray [əré] *s.* arreglo, formación, orden; orden (*de batalla*); pompa; gala, atavío; *v.* formar (*tropas*); poner en orden; ataviar, adornar.
ar·rears [ərírz] *s. pl.* atrasos, pagos o rentas vencidos y no cobrados; **in —** atrasado (*en el pago de una cuenta*).
ar·rest [ərɛst] *s.* arresto, captura, aprensión, detención; *v.* aprehender o prender, arrestar; detener; llamar, atraer (*la atención*).
ar·ri·val [əráıvl] *s.* llegada; arribo; venida; **the new**

-s los recién llegados.
ar·rive [əráıv] *v.* llegar; arribar; **to — at a result** lograr (*o conseguir*) un resultado.
ar·ro·gance [ǽrəgəns] *s.* arrogancia.
ar·ro·gant [ǽrəgənt] *adj.* arrogante.
ar·row [ǽro] *s.* saeta, flecha.
ar·se·nal [ársṇəl] *s.* arsenal.
ar·se·nic [ársṇık] *s.* arsénico.
ar·son [ársən] *s.* delito de incendio.
art [ɑrt] *s.* arte; destreza; astucia; **fine -s** bellas artes; **master of -s** licenciado en letras, maestro en artes.
ar·ter·y [ártərı] *s.* arteria.
art·ful [ártfəl] *adj.* artero, mañero, ladino.
ar·ti·choke [ártıtʃok] *s.* alcachofa.
ar·ti·cle [ártıkḷ] *s.* artículo; **— of clothing** prenda de vestir; **— of merchandise** mercancía, mercadería.
ar·tic·u·late [artíkjəlıt] *adj.* articulado; claro, inteligible; capaz de hablar; [artíkjəlet] *v.* articular; enunciar; enlazar.
ar·tic·u·la·tion [artıkjəléʃən] *s.* articulación; coyuntura.
ar·ti·fact [ártəfækt] *s.* artefacto.
ar·ti·fice [ártəfıs] *s.* artificio; ardid.
ar·ti·fi·cial [artəfíʃəl] *adj.* artificial; postizo; afectado, artificioso.
ar·til·ler·y [artílərı] *s.* artillería; **— man** artillero.
ar·ti·san [ártəzṇ] *s.* artesano; artífice.
art·ist [ártıst] *s.* artista.
ar·tis·tic [artístık] *adj.* artístico; **-ally** *adv.* artísticamente.
as [æz] *adv., conj., prep.* como; mientras; a medida que, según; en el momento en que; **— far —** hasta, hasta donde; **— for (— to)** en cuanto a; **— if** como si; **— it were** por decirlo así; **— large —** tan grande como; **— much —** tanto como; **— well** tan bien; también; **— yet** hasta ahora, todavía; **— long — you wish** todo el tiempo que Vd. quiera; **stong — he is** aunque es tan fuerte; **the same —** lo mismo que.
as·bes·tos [æsbéstəs] *s.* asbesto.
as·cend [əsɛnd] *v.* ascender; subir, elevarse.
as·cen·sion [əsɛnʃən] *s.* ascensión; subida.
as·cent [əsɛnt] *s.* ascenso; subida; ascensión.
as·cer·tain [æsə·tén] *v.* averiguar, indagar.
as·cet·ic [əsɛtık] *adj.* ascético; *s.* asceta.
as·cribe [əskráıb] *v.* atribuir, imputar, achacar.
ash [æʃ] *s.* ceniza; **— tray** cenicero; **— tree** fresno; **Ash Wednesday** miércoles de ceniza; **ash-colored** *adj.* ceniciento, cenizo.
a·shamed [əʃémd] *adj.* avergonzado, corrido; **to be —** tener vergüenza; avergonzarse.
a·shore [əʃór] *adv.* a tierra; en tierra; **to go —** desembarcar.
A·si·at·ic [əʒıǽtık] *adj. & s.* asiático.
a·side [əsáıd] *adv.* aparte; a un lado; al lado; *s.* aparte (*en un drama*).
ask [æsk] *v.* (*request*) pedir, rogar, solicitar; (*inquire*) preguntar; (*invite*) invitar; **to — for** pedir; **to — for (about, after)** preguntar por; **to — a question** hacer una pregunta.
a·skance [əskǽns] *adv.* de soslayo; con recelo; recelosamente; **to look —** mirar con recelo; no aprobar.
a·sleep [əslíp] *adj.* dormido; **to fall —** dormirse; **my arm is —** se me ha dormido (entumecido *o* entumido) el brazo.
as·par·a·gus [əspǽrəgəs] *s.* espárrago.
as·pect [æspɛkt] *s.* aspecto; cariz.
as·phalt [ǽsfɔlt] *s.* asfalto; chapapote.

as·pi·ra·tion [æspəréʃən] *s.* aspiración; anhelo.
as·pire [əspáɪr] *v.* aspirar; anhelar, ambicionar.
as·pi·rin [æspɜɪn] *s.* aspirina.
ass [æs] *s.* asno, burro; pollino.
as·sail [əsél] *v.* asaltar, acometer, agredir.
as·sail·ant [əsélənt] *s.* asaltador, agresor.
as·sas·sin [əsǽsɪn] *s.* asesino.
as·sas·si·nate [əsǽsŋet] *v.* asesinar.
as·sas·si·na·tion [əsæsŋéʃən] *s.* asesinato.
as·sault [əsɔ́lt] *s.* asalto, acometida; conato;
 ataque; *v.* asaltar, acometer, atacar; violar.
as·say [əsé] *v.* ensayar (*metales*); analizar,
 examinar; contrastar (*pesas, moneda*); *s.* ensaye
 (*de metales*); contraste (*de pesas, moneda*).
as·sem·ble [əsémbl] *v.* reunir(se), congregar(se),
 juntar(se); convocar; armar, montar
 (*maquinaria*).
as·sem·bly [əsémblɪ] *s.* asamblea; reunión;
 montaje (*de maquinaria*); — **hall** salón de
 sesiones; paraninfo.
as·sent [əsént] *s.* asentimiento; consentimiento; *v.*
 asentir; consentir.
as·sert [əsɜ́t] *v.* aseverar, asegurar, afirmar; **to —
 oneself** hacerse valer; obrar con firmeza;
 vindicarse.
as·ser·tion [əsɜ́ʃən] *s.* aserción, aserto, afirmación.
as·sess [əsés] *v.* avaluar; tasar; asignar, imponer
 (*impuestos, multas, contribuciones, etc.*).
as·sess·ment [əsésmənt] *s.* avaluación, tasación;
 imposición (*de contribuciones, multas, etc.*);
 contribución, impuesto.
as·set [æset] *s.* cualidad, ventaja; **-s** capital, fondos,
 caudal; haber, activo; **personal -s** bienes
 muebles.
as·sid·u·ous [əsidʒ∪əs] *adj.* asiduo, diligente.
as·sign [əsáɪn] *v.* asignar; señalar, designar;
 traspasar, ceder a favor de.
as·sign·ment [əsáɪnmənt] *s.* asignación;
 designación; cesión (*de bienes*); tarea (*asignada*);
 lección (*señalada*).
as·sim·i·late [əsimlet] *v.* asimilar(se), absorber(se).
as·sist [əsíst] *v.* asistir, ayudar.
as·sis·tance [əsístəns] *s.* asistencia, ayuda.
as·sis·tant [əsístənt] *s.* asistente; ayudante;
 auxiliar; *adj.* subordinado, auxiliar.
as·so·ci·ate [əsóʃɪt] *adj.* asociado; *s.* asociado;
 socio; compañero; colega; [əsóʃɪet] *v.*
 asociar(se); relacionar.
as·so·ci·a·tion [əsosɪéʃən] *s.* asociación; sociedad;
 conexión, relación.
as·sort [əsɔ́rt] *v.* ordenar, clasificar.
as·sort·ed [əsɔ́rtɪd] *adj.* surtido, mezclado, variado,
 de todas clases.
as·sort·ment [əsɔ́rtmənt] *s.* variedad; clasificación;
 surtido; colección, grupo.
as·sume [əsúm] *v.* asumir; tomar; dar por sentado,
 dar por supuesto; arrogarse, apropiarse.
as·sump·tion [əsʌ́mpʃən] *d.* suposición; toma,
 apropiación; presunción; asunción (*de la
 Virgen*).
as·sur·ance [əʃúrəns] *s.* seguridad, certeza;
 convicción; confianza; **life —** seguro de vida.
 Véase **insurance.**
as·sure [əʃúr] *v.* asegurar; afirmar; infundir
 confianza.
as·sur·ed·ly [əʃúrɪdlɪ] *adv.* seguramente; sin duda,
 con seguridad.
as·ta·tine [æstətin] *s.* astato.
as·ter·isk [æstərɪsk] *s.* asterisco.
a·stig·ma·tism [əstígmətɪzəm] *s.* astigmatismo.
as·ton·ish [əstánɪʃ] *v.* asombrar, pasmar, espantar.

as·ton·ish·ing [əstánɪʃɪŋ] *adj.* asombroso, pasmoso,
 maravilloso.
as·ton·ish·ment [əstánɪʃmənt] *s.* asombro, pasmo,
 sorpresa.
as·tound [əstá∪nd] *v.* pasmar; aterrar, aturdir.
a·stray [əstré] *adv.* fuera de camino; *adj.* desviado,
 extraviado, descaminado; **to go —** perderse;
 errar el camino; extraviarse; **to lead —** desviar,
 extraviar; llevar por mal camino; seducir.
a·stride [əstráɪd] *adv.* a horcajadas.
as·trin·gent [æstríndʒənt] *adj.*, *s.* astringente.
as·tro·dome [æstrədom] *s.* astródomo.
as·trol·o·gy [əstrálədʒɪ] *s.* astrología.
as·tro·naut [æstrənɔt] *s.* astronauta.
as·tron·o·mer [əstránəmə] *s.* astrónomo.
as·tron·o·my [estránəmɪ] *s.* astronomía.
as·tro·phys·ics [æstrofízɪks] *s.* astrofísica.
As·tu·ri·an [æstjúrɪən] *adj.* & *s.* asturiano.
as·tute [əstjút] *adj.* astuto, sagaz.
a·sun·der [əsʌ́ndə] *adj.* separado; **to cut —**
 separar, apartar; dividir en dos.
a·sy·lum [əsáɪləm] *s.* asilo; hospicio; **orphan —**
 orfanato, casa de huérfanos, *Méx., C.A., Andes*
 orfanatorio.
at [æt] *prep.* a; en; en (la) casa de; **— last** por fin,
 al fin; **— once** al punto; **to be — work** estar
 trabajando; **to enter — that door** entrar por
 aquella puerta.
at·a·vism [ǽtəvɪzəm] *s.* atavismo.
ate [et] *pret. de* **to eat.**
a·the·ist [éθɪɪst] *s.* ateo.
ath·lete [æθlit] *s.* atleta.
ath·let·ic [æθlétɪk] *adj.* atlético.
ath·let·ics [æθlétɪks] *s.* gimnasia; atletismo;
 deportes.
At·lan·tic [ətǽntɪk] *adj.* atlántico; *s.* el Atlántico.
at·las [ǽtləs] *s.* atlas.
at·mos·phere [ǽtməsfɪr] *s.* atmósfera; ambiente.
at·mos·pher·ic [ætməsférɪk] *adj.* atmosférico.
at·om [ǽtəm] *s.* átomo; **— bomb** bomba atómica.
a·tom·ic [ətámɪk] *adj.* atómico; **— age** edad
 atómica; **— energy** fuerza atómica; **— pile** pila
 atómica; **— weight** peso atómico.
a·tone [ətón] *v.* expiar, purgar; reparar.
a·tone·ment [ətónmənt] *s.* expiación; reparación.
a·tro·cious [ətróʃəs] *adj.* atroz.
a·troc·i·ty [ətrásətɪ] *s.* atrocidad; maldad.
at·ro·phy [ǽtrəfɪ] *s.* atrofia.
at·tach [ətǽtʃ] *v.* unir, juntar; sujetar, pegar,
 adherir; poner (*sello o firma*); embargar (*bienes*);
 asignar; atribuir.
at·ta·ché [ǽtəʃe] *s.* agregado.
at·tach·ment [ətǽtʃmənt] *s.* adhesión; apego;
 afición, cariño; embargo (*de bienes*); accesorio.
at·tack [ətǽk] *s.* ataque, asalto; acceso; *v.* atacar;
 acometer, embestir.
at·tain [ətén] *v.* lograr, conseguir, alcanzar; llegar
 a.
at·tain·ment [əténmənt] *s.* logro, consecución;
 adquisición; dote habilidad.
at·tempt [ətémpt] *s.* tentativa; prueba, ensayo;
 esfuerzo; atentado; *v.* tentar, intentar; procurar,
 tratar (de), probar; **to — the life of** atentar
 contra la vida de.
at·tend [əténd] *v.* atender, cuidar, mirar por; asistir
 a; acompañar.
at·ten·dance [əténdəns] *s.* asistencia; presencia;
 concurrencia.
at·ten·dant [əténdənt] *s.* acompañante; sirviente,
 servidor; asistente; *adj.* acompañante.
at·ten·tion [əténʃən] *s.* (*care*) cuidado; (*courtesy*)

fineza, urbanidad, atención; **to pay** — hacer caso; prestar atención.

at·ten·tive [ətέntɪv] *adj.* atento; cortés.

at·test [ətέst] *v.* atestiguar, atestar; certificar; dar fe.

at·tic [ǽtɪk] *s.* desván.

at·tire [ətáɪr] *s.* atavío; vestidura; vestido, traje; *v.* ataviar, adornar.

at·ti·tude [ǽtətjud] *s.* actitud; postura.

at·tor·ney [ətə́nɪ] *s.* abogado; procurador; apoderado; — **general** fiscal (*de una nación o estado*); **district** — fiscal de distrito; **power of** — procuración, poder.

at·tract [ətrǽkt] *v.* atraer; cautivar; **to** — **attention** llamar la atención.

at·trac·tion [ətrǽkʃən] *s.* atracción; atractivo; **-s** diversiones; lugares o sitios de interés.

at·trac·tive [ətrǽktɪv] *adj.* atractivo; seductor; simpático.

at·trac·tive·ness [ətrǽktɪvnɪs] *s.* atracción; atractivo.

at·trib·ute [ǽtrəbjut] *s.* atributo; propiedad; [ətríbjʊt] *v.* atribuir, achacar.

at·tri·tion [ətríʃən] *s.* agotamiento; atrición.

auc·tion [ɔ́kʃən] *s.* subasta, almoneda, remate, *Am.* venduta; *v.* subastar; rematar.

au·da·cious [ɔdéʃəs] *adj.* audaz, atrevido, osado.

au·dac·i·ty [ɔdǽsətɪ] *s.* audacia, osadía; descaro.

au·di·ble [ɔ́dəbl] *adj.* audible.

au·di·ence [ɔ́dɪəns] *s.* auditorio, concurrencia, público; audiencia.

au·di·o fre·quen·cy [ɔ́dɪofríkwɛnsɪ] *s.* audiofrecuencia.

au·di·o·vis·u·al [ɔ́dɪovíʒuəl] *adj.* audiovisual.

au·dit [ɔ́dɪt] *v.* intervenir [*cuentas*]; asistir a (*una clase*) de oyente; *s.* intervención, comprobación de cuentas.

au·di·tion [ɔdíʃən] *s.* audición.

au·di·tor [ɔ́dɪtə] *s.* interventor (*de cuentas*); oyente.

au·di·to·ri·um [ɔdətórɪəm] *s.* salón de conferencias o conciertos; paraninfo.

au·di·to·ry [ɔ́dətorɪ] *adj.* auditivo.

au·ger [ɔ́gə] *s.* taladro, barrena.

aught [ɔt] *s.* algo.

aug·ment [ɔgmɛ́nt] *v.* aumentar.

au·gur [ɔ́gə] *s.* agorero; *v.* augurar, pronosticar; **to** — **well** (*o* **ill**) ser de buen (*o* mal) agüero.

Au·gust [ɔ́gəst] *s.* agosto.

aunt [ænt] *s.* tía.

aus·pic·es [ɔ́spɪsɪz] *s. pl.* auspicios; protección.

aus·pi·cious [ɔspíʃəs] *adj.* propicio; favorable.

aus·tere [ɔstír] *adj.* austero, adustro, severo.

aus·ter·i·ty [ɔstέrətɪ] *s.* austeridad, severidad.

Aus·tri·an [ɔ́strɪən] *adj.* & *s.* austríaco.

au·then·tic [ɔθέntɪk] *adj.* auténtico.

au·thor [ɔ́θə] *s.* autor; escritor.

au·thor·i·ta·tive [əθɔ́rətetɪv] *adj.* autorizado, que tiene autoridad; autoritario.

au·thor·i·ty [əθɔ́rətɪ] *s.* autoridad; facultad; **to have on good** — saber de buena tinta.

au·thor·ize [ɔ́θəraɪz] *v.* autorizar.

au·to [ɔ́to] *s.* auto, automóvil.

au·to·crat [ɔ́təkræt] *s.* autócrata.

au·to·graph [ɔ́təgræf] *s.* autógrafo.

au·to·mat·ic [ɔtəmǽtɪk] *adj.* automático; **-ally** *adv.* automáticamente.

au·to·mo·bile [ɔ́təməbil] *s.* automóvil.

au·ton·o·my [ɔtɑ́nəmɪ] *s* — autonomía.

au·top·sy [ɔ́tɑpsɪ] *s.* autopsia.

au·tumn [ɔ́təm] *s.* otoño.

au·tum·nal [ɔtʌ́mnl] *adj.* otoñal.

aux·il·ia·ry [ɔgzíljərɪ] *adj.* & *s.* auxiliar.

a·vail [əvél] *v.* aprovechar; beneficiar; **to** — **oneself of** aprovecharse de; *s.* provecho; ventaja; **of no** — de ninguna utilidad o ventaja.

a·vail·a·ble [əvéləbl] *adj.* disponible; aprovechable; obtenible.

av·a·lanche [ǽvlæntʃ] *s.* alud; torrente.

av·a·rice [ǽvərɪs] *s.* avaricia.

av·a·ri·cious [ævəríʃəs] *adj.* avaro, avariento.

a·venge [əvɛ́ndʒ] *v.* vengar; vindicar.

a·veng·er [əvɛ́ndʒə] *s.* vengador.

av·e·nue [ǽvənu] *s.* avenida.

a·ver [əvɚ́] *v.* afirmar, asegurar.

av·er·age [ǽvrɪdʒ] *s.* promedio, término medio; **on an** — por término medio; *adj.* medio, mediano; ordinario; *v.* promediar, calcular o sacar el promedio; **to** — **a loss** prorratear una pérdida; **he -s 20 miles an hour** avanza o recorre un promedio de 20 millas por hora.

a·verse [əvɚ́s] *adj.* adverso, renuente.

a·ver·sion [əvɚ́ʒən] *s.* aversión; malquerencia, inquina.

a·vert [əvɚ́t] *v.* apartar, desviar; evitar; impedir.

a·vi·a·tion [evíéʃən] *s.* aviación.

a·vi·a·tor [évietə] *s.* aviador.

av·o·ca·do [ɑvəkádo] *s.* aguacate, *Andes* palta.

av·o·ca·tion [ævəkéʃən] *s.* distracción; ocupación de distracción o diversión.

a·void [əvɔ́ɪd] *v.* evitar; eludir.

a·vow [əváu] *v.* confesar, reconocer, admitir.

a·vow·al [əváuəl] *s.* confesión, admisión.

a·wait [əwét] *v.* esperar, aguardar.

a·wake [əwék] *adj.* despierto; alerto; **wide-awake** muy despierto; avispado; *v.* despertar(se).

a·wak·en [əwékən] *v.* despertar(se).

a·ward [əwɔ́rd] *s.* premio; decisión, sentencia; *v.* asignar; otorgar; conferir; adjudicar (*un premio, medalla, etc.*).

a·ware [əwɛ́r] *adj.* consciente; enterado, sabedor; cauto; sobre aviso.

a·way [əwé] *adv.* lejos; fuera; *adj.* ausente; **right** — ahora mismo, ahorita; **ten miles** — a diez millas de aquí; **to give** — regalar; **to go** — irse; **to take** — quitar.

awe [ɔ] *s.* pavor; pasmo; **to stand in** — quedarse, o estar, pasmado; pasmarse; *v.* atemoriżar; infundir avor; maravillar.

aw·ful [ɔ́fʊl] *adj.* terrible; horroroso; tremendo; impresionante; **-ly** *adv.* terriblemente; horrorosamente; muy.

a·while [əhwáɪl] *adv.* (or) un rato; (por) algún tiempo.

awk·ward [ɔ́kwəd] *adj.* torpe, desmañado; molesto, embarazoso; incómodo; inconveniente.

awl [ɔl] *s.* lezna, punzón.

aw·ning [ɔ́nɪŋ] *s.* toldo.

a·woke [əwók] *pret.* & *p.p.* de **to awake.**

ax, axe [æks] *s.* hacha.

ax·is [ǽksɪs] *pl.* **ax·es** (ǽksiz) *s.* eje.

ax·le [ǽksl] *s.* eje (*de una rueda*); **front** — eje delantero; **rear** — eje trasero.

aye [aɪ] *adv.* si; *s.* voto afirmativo.

Az·tec [ǽztɛk] *adj.* & *s.* azteca.

az·ure [ǽʒə] *adj.* azul; *s.* azur, azul celeste.

B:b

bab·ble [bǽbl] s. balbuceo; parloteo, charla; v. balbucear; parlotear, charlar.
babe [beb] = baby.
ba·boon [bæbún] s. mandril (especie de mono).
ba·by [bébɪ] s. nene, bebé, criatura; Andes, Ch. guagua; C.A. tierno; adj. infantil; de niño; — **girl** nena; — **sitter** [bébɪsɪtə] s. cuidaniños, niñera por horas; v. mimar.
bach·e·lor [bǽtʃələ] s. bachiller; soltero.
ba·cil·lus [bəsíləs] s. bacilo.
back [bæk] s. (anatomy) espalda; lomo (de animal); (opposite side) revés; respaldo (de silla), espaldar; **behind one's** — a espaldas de uno, a espaldas vueltas; **in** — **of** detrás de, tras; **to fall on one's** — caer de espaldas, caer boca arriba; **to turn one's** — volver las espaldas; adj. posterior; trasero; retrasado, atrasado, rezagado; — **pay** sueldo atrasado; — **yard** patio interior; corral; adv. atrás, detrás; — **and forth** de aquí para allá; **to come** — volver, regresar; **to give** — devolver; v. respaldar, endosar; sostener, apoyar, retroceder; hacer retroceder; **to** — **down** hacerse (para) atrás; retractarse.
back·bone [bǽkbón] s. espinazo, espina dorsal; firmeza; apoyo, sostén.
back·er [bǽkə] s. fiador; sostenedor, defensor.
back·fire [bǽkfaɪr] s. petardeo.
back·ground [bǽkɡraʊnd] s. fondo; educación; experiencia; **to keep in the** — dejar en último término; quedarse en último término; mantenerse retirado.
back·hand [bǽkhænd] s. revés; escritura inclinada a la izquierda; **-ed stroke** revés; **a -ed remark** una ironía; una indirecta.
back·ing [bǽkɪŋ] s. apoyo, garantía; endose, endoso; respaldo.
back·lash [bǽklæʃ] s. contragolpe; culateo.
back·log [bǽklɔɡ] s. reserva pendiente.
back·stage [bǽkstédʒ] adv. detrás del telón.
back-up [bǽkəp] adj. de reserva.
back·ward [bǽkwəd] adj. atrasado; retrasado; retrógrado; lerdo, tardo; huraño, tímido, esquivo; adv. = **backwards**.
back·ward·ness [bǽkwədnɪs] s. torpeza; atraso; timidez.
back·wards [bǽkwədz] adv. hacia (o para) atrás; de espaldas; **to go** — retroceder, andar hacia (o para) atrás.
ba·con [békən] s. tocino.
bac·te·ri·a [bæktíriə] s. pl. bacterias.
bac·te·ri·ol·o·gy [bæktɪriúlədʒɪ] s. bacteriología.
bad [bæd] adj. malo; perverso; dañoso; podrido; **to go from** — **to worse** ir de mal en peor; **to look** — tener mal cariz, tener mala cara o mal aspecto; **-ly** adv. mal, malamente.
bade [bæd] pret. de **to bid**.
badge [bædʒ] s. insignia, divisa; distintivo; Mex. chapa.
bad·ger [bǽdʒə] s. tejón; v. atormentar, acosar, molestar.
bad·ness [bǽdnɪs] s. maldad.
baf·fle [bǽfl] v. desconcertar, confundir; frustrar, impedir.
bag [bæɡ] s. (sack) saco, bolsa, talega; costal; (baggage) maleta; zurrón, morral; v. ensacar; cazar; agarrar; adueñarse de; inflarse; abolsarse.
bag·gage [bǽɡɪdʒ] s. equipaje; bagaje; — **car** furgón, vagón de equipajes; — **check** talón,

contraseña de equipajes; — **tag** marbete, etiqueta.
bag·pipe [bǽɡpaɪp] s. gaita.
bail [bel] s. fianza, caución; **to let out on** — poner en libertad bajo fianza; v. dar fianza; salir fiador; achicar (agua), vaciar; **to** — **out of a plane** tirarse (con paracaídas) de un aeroplano.
bait [bet] s. cebo; atractivo, aliciente; v. tentar, atraer; cebar; acosar, perseguir.
bake [bek] v. hornear, cocer al horno; calcinar.
bak·er [békə] s. panadero, pastelero, hornero.
bak·er·y [békərɪ] s. panadería, pastelería, tahona.
bak·ing [békɪŋ] s. hornada; cocimiento; — **powder** levadura.
bal·ance [bǽləns] s. (instrument) balanza; (equilibrium) contrapeso, equilibrio, balance; (debit, credit) saldo; — **of payments** balanza de pagos; — **wheel** volante del reloj; — **of trade** balanza comercial; — **of power** equilibrio político; **to lose one's** — perder el equilibrio; v. contrapesar; pesar; balancear(se); equilibrar; saldar (una cuenta).
bal·co·ny [bǽlkənɪ] s. balcón; galería (de teatro).
bald [bɔld] adj. calvo; pelado; pelón; sin vegetación; escueto, sin adornos; — **spot** calva.
bale [bel] s. bala, fardo (de mercancías); v. embalar, enfardar, empacar.
balk [bɔk] v. oponerse, rebelarse, resistirse; pararse de repente; negarse a seguir; encabritarse; **to** — **someone's plans** frustrar los planes de alguien.
ball [bɔl] s. (plaything) pelota, bola; (string, thread) ovillo; (weapon) bala; (dance) baile; — **bearing** cojinete de bolas; — **game** juego de pelota; beisbol; v. ovillar; **to** — **up** enredar, confundir.
bal·lad [bǽləd] s. romance; copla, canción; balada.
bal·last [bǽləst] s. lastre; grava (usada en terraplenes, caminos, etc.); v. lastrar, poner el lastre a (una embarcación).
bal·let [bǽlé] s. ballet.
bal·lis·tics [bəlístɪks] s. balística.
bal·loon [bəlún] s. globo (aerostático).
bal·lot [bǽlət] s. balota, Am. boleta, cédula para votar; voto; — **box** urna electoral; v. balotar, votar.
ball point [bɔ́lpɔɪnt] s. bolígrafo.
balm [bam] s. bálsamo.
bal·my [bámɪ] adj. balsámico; fragante; refrescante, suave; algo loco, chiflado.
bal·sam [bɔ́lsəm] s. bálsamo; especie de abeto.
bam·boo [bæmbú] s. bambú.
ban [bæn] s. bando, proclama; excomunión; prohibición; **marriage -s** (o **banns**) amonestaciones; v. proscribir, prohibir; condenar.
ba·nan·a [bənǽnə] s. plátano; banana; C.A. guineo. — **tree** banano; plátano.
band [bænd] s. (group) banda, partida, pandilla, cuadrilla; (musicians) banda; (strip) faja, lista, cinta, tira; partida, pandilla, cuadrilla; **rubber** — liga de goma; v. unit, juntar; atar, ligar; **to** — **together** confederarse, juntarse.
band·age [bǽndɪdʒ] s. venda, vendaje; v. vendar.
bandanna [bændǽnə] s. pañuelo de hierbas.
ban·dit [bǽndɪt] s. bandido, bandolero.
bang [bæŋ] s. golpe, golpazo; estallido; fleco (de pelo); **with a** — de golpe, de golpazo; de repente; con estrépito, —! ¡pum!; v. golpear; hacer estrépito; cortar (el pelo) en fleco; **to** — **the door** dar un portazo.

ban·ish [bǽnɪʃ] v. proscribir, desterrar; **to — fear**
desechar el temor.
ban·ish·ment [bǽnɪʃmənt] s. proscripción;
destierro.
ban·is·ter [bǽnɪstɚ] s. balaustre; barandilla,
barandal, pasamano.
ban·jo [bǽndʒo] s. banjo.
bank [bæŋk] s. (*institution*) banco; (*in card game*)
banca; (*of a river*) orilla, ribera, banda; escarpa;
(*pile*) montón; **savings — caja de ahorros**; *adj.*
bancario; de banco; v. depositar en un banco;
amontonar (*tierra o arena*); cubrir con cenizas,
tapar (*el fuego*); ladear (*un aeroplano*); **to —
upon** (*o* on) contar con.
bank·book [bǽŋkbʊk] s. libreta de banco.
bank·er [bǽŋkɚ] s. banquero.
bank·ing [bǽŋkɪŋ] s. transacciones bancarias
banca; *adj.* bancario, de banca; **— house** banca,
casa de banca.
bank·note [bǽŋknot] s. billete de banco.
bank·rupt [bǽŋkrʌpt] *adj.* en quiebra, arruinado,
insolvente; v. quebrar; arruinar.
bank·rupt·cy [bǽŋkrʌptsɪ] s. bancarrota, quiebra;
to go into — decalarse insolvente; quebrar,
hacer bancarrota.
ban·ner [bǽnɚ] s. bandera, estandarte, pendón;
adj. primero, principal, sobresaliente.
ban·quet [bǽŋkwɪt] s. banquete; v. banquetear.
bap·tism [bǽptɪzəm] s. bautismo; bautizo.
Bap·tist [bǽptɪst] s. bautista.
bap·tize [bæptáɪz] v. bautizar.
bar [bɑr] s. (*of iron*) barra; barrote; tranca;
(*obstacle*) barrera, obstáculo; (*of justice*)
tribunal; foro; (*saloon*) cantina, taberna;
(*counter*) mostrador; (*piece*) barra (*de jabón*);
pastilla (*de chocolate*); **sand — banco de arena;
-s reja; to be admitted to the — recibirse de
abogado**; v. atrancar (*la puerta*); estorbar;
prohibir; excluir.
barb [bɑrb] s. púa.
bar·bar·i·an [barbérɪən] s. & *adj.* bárbaro; salvaje.
bar·ba·rous [bárbərəs] *adj.* bárbaro; salvaje;
inculto.
bar·be·cue [bárbɪkju] s. *Méx.*, *C.A.*, *Col.* barbacoa;
Ríopl. churrasco; v. hacer barbacoa; *Ríopl.*
churrasquear.
barbed [barbd] *adj.* con púas; **— wire** alambre de
púas.
bar·ber [bárbɚ] s. barbero; peluquero.
bar·ber·shop [bárbɚʃap] s. barbería; peluquería.
bard [bɑrd] s. bardo, vate, poeta.
bare [ber] *adj.* (*naked*) desnudo; descubierto;
pelado; (*evident*) manifiesto, patente;
(*unfurnished*) desamueblado, vacío; **— majority**
mayoría escasa; **to lay — poner de manifiesto,
hacer patente, revelar; to ride —back montar en
pelo.**
bare·foot [bérfʊt] *adj.* descalzo, con los pies
desnudos; **-ed** [bérfʊtɪd] = **barefoot.**
bare·head·ed [bérhédɪd] *adj.* descubierto, sin
sombrero.
bare·leg·ged [bérlégɪd] *adj.* con las piernas
desnudas; sin medias.
bare·ly [bérlɪ] *adv.* apenas; escasamente; **— three
pounds** tres libras escasas.
bare·ness [bérnɪs] s. desnudez.
bar·gain [bárgɪn] s. (*agreement*) convenio, pacto;
negocio, trato; (*cheap*) ganga; **— sale** ganga,
Méx., *C.A.*, *Ven.*, *Andes* barata; **into the — por
añadidura; de ganancia; to make a — cerrar
un convenio; v. regatear; negociar; to — for**

regatear; contar con, esperar.
barge [bardʒ] s. lanchón; barca.
bar·i·tone [bǽrəton] s. & *adj.* barítono.
bar·i·um [bǽrɪəm] s. bario.
bark [bɑrk] s. ladrido; corteza (*de árbol*); barco
velero; v. ladrar; descortezar, quitar la corteza.
bar·ley [bárlɪ] s. cebada.
barn [bɑrn] s. establo, cuadra; granero, troje;
pajar; **streetcar — cobertizo para tranvías.**
bar·na·cle [bárnəkəl] s. cirrópodo.
barn·yard [bárnjard] s. corral; **— fowl** aves de
corral.
ba·rom·e·ter [bərámətɚ] s. barómetro.
bar·on [bǽrən] s. barón.
ba·roque [bərók] *adj.* & s. barroco.
bar·rage [bəráʒ] s. fuego de barrera; presa.
bar·rel [bǽrəl] s. barril, barrica, tonel, cuba; cañón
(*de fusil, pistola, etc.*); v. embarrilar (*meter en
barril*).
bar·ren [bǽrən] *adj.* árido; estéril.
bar·ren·ness [bǽrənnɪs] s. aridez; esterilidad.
bar·rette [bərét] s. broche, prendedor (*para sujetar
el pelo*).
bar·ri·cade [bærəkéd] s. barricada, barrera; v.
poner barricadas; obstruir el paso con
barricadas.
bar·ri·er [bǽrɪɚ] s. barrera, valla; obstáculo.
bar·room [bárum] s. cantina; bar.
bar·ter [bártɚ] v. permutar, trocar, cambiar; s.
permuta, trueque, cambio.
base [bes] s. base; basa; fundamento; *adj.* bajo, vil,
ruin; inferior; v. basar, fundar; establecer.
base·ball [bésból] s. baseball o beisbol.
base·ment [bésmənt] s. sótano.
base·ness [bésnɪs] s. bajeza, ruindad, vileza.
bash·ful [bǽʃfəl] *adj.* tímido, encogido, vergonzoso.
bash·ful·ness [bǽʃfəlnɪs] s. timidez, vergüenza,
cortedad, apocamiento.
ba·sic [bésɪk] *adj.* básico; fundamental.
ba·sin [bésṇ] s. palangana, jofaina; lebrillo; tazón
(*de fuente*); estanque, depósito de agua; **river —
cuenca de río.**
ba·sis [bésɪs] (*pl.* **bases** [bésiz]) s. base, fundamento.
bask [bæsk] v. calentarse (*al sol*); asolearse, tomar
el sol.
bas·ket [bǽskɪt] s. cesta, cesto, canasta.
bas·ket·ball [bǽskɪtbɔl] s. basquetbol.
Basque [bæsk] *adj.* & s. (*person*) vasco; (*language*)
vascuence, vasco; (*territory*) vascongado, vasco.
bass [bes] s. bajo (*en música*); *adj.* bajo, grave;
— drum tambora, bombo; **— horn** tuba.
bas·tard [bǽstəd] s. & *adj.* bastardo.
baste [best] v. hilvanar; pringar (*empapar la carne
con grasa*); apalear.
bat [bæt] s. palo, *Méx.*, *Carib.*, *Ven.*, *C.A.* bate
(*de beisbol*); garrote; golpe, garrotazo;
murciélago; v. apalear; dar palos; *Méx.*, *Carib.*,
Ven., *C.A.* batear; **not to — an eye** no
pestañear.
batch [bætʃ] s. hornada; colección, grupo,
conjunto.
bath [bæθ] s. baño.
bathe [beð] v. bañar(se).
bath·er [béðɚ] s. bañista.
bath·house [bǽθhaʊs] s. casa de baños; bañadero.
bath·robe [bǽθrob] s. bata de baño.
bath·room [bǽθrum] s. baño, cuarto de baño.
bath·tub [bǽθtʌb] s. bañera, tina.
bath·y·sphere [bǽθɪsfɪr] s. batisfera.
bat·tal·ion [bətǽljən] s. batallón.
bat·ter [bǽtɚ] s. batido, masa; *Am.* bateador (*de*

beisbol); *v.* golpear; **to — down** demoler.

bat·ter·y [bǽtərɪ] *s.* batería; acumulador; asalto.

bat·tle [bǽtl̩] *s.* batalla, lucha, combate; *v.* batallar, luchar, combatir.

bat·tle·field [bǽtl̩fild] *s.* campo de batalla.

bat·tle·ship [bǽtl̩ʃɪp] *s.* buque de guerra, acorazado.

bawl [bɔl] *s.* aullido; grito; *v.* aullar; gritar; pregonar; **to — out** regañar, reprender.

bay [be] *s.* bahía; ladrido, balido, aullido; **— rum** ron de laurel; **— tree** laurel; **— window** ventana saliente, mirador; **to hold at —** tener a raya; *adj.* bayo; *v.* dar aullidos, ladridos o balidos.

bay·o·net [béənɪt] *s.* bayoneta; *v.* traspasar; herir con bayoneta.

ba·zaar [bəzár] *s.* bazar; feria.

ba·zoo·ka [bəzúka] *s.* bazuca.

be [bi] *v.* (*innately*) ser; (*state or condition*) estar, verse, hallarse, encontrarse; **— that as it may** sea como sea; **to — cold (warm, hungry, right,** *etc.*) tener frío (calor, hambre, razón, *etc.*); **to — in a hurry** tener prisa; **he is to —** ha de ser; va a ser; **it is cold (hot, windy,** *etc.*) hace frío (calor, viento, *etc.*).

beach [bitʃ] *s.* playa, ribera; *v.* varar, poner en seco (*una embarcación*), encallar.

beach·head [bitʃhed] *s.* cabeza de playa.

bea·con [bíkən] *s.* faro, fanal; boya luminosa; señal; **aviation —** radiofaro.

bead [bid] *s.* cuenta (*de rosario, collar, etc.*); abalorio; glóbulo; gota (*de sudor*); **-s** rosario; collar de cuentas; *v.* adornar con abalorios o cuentecitas.

beak [bik] *s.* pico (*de ave*); espolón (*de nave*).

beak·er [bíkə] *s.* tazon.

beam [bim] *s.* rayo (*de luz o de calor*); sonrisa; viga; vigueta; brazo (*de balanza*); **radio —** línea de radiación, radiofaro; *v.* emitir (*luz, rayos*); brillar; sonreír, estar radiante de alegría; radiar, transmitir por radio.

beam·ing [bímɪŋ] *adj.* radiante, resplandeciente; sonriente.

bean [bin] *s.* judía, habichuela; *Méx., C.A., Ven., Col.* frijol; *Ch., Ríopl.* poroto; **coffee —** grano de café; **Lima —** haba; **string —** judía o habichuela verde; *Méx., C.A.* ejote; *Ch., Ríopl.* poroto.

bear [bɛr] *s.* oso, osa; bajista (*el que hace bajar los valores en la Bolsa*); *v.* (*stand*) soportar; llevar; sobrellevar; tolerar, aguantar; (*give birth*) parir, dar a luz; producir; **to — down** deprimir; apretar; **to — a grudge** guardar rencor; **to — in mind** tener en cuenta; **to — on a subject** tener relación con un asunto; **to — oneself with dignity** portarse con dignidad; **to — out** confirmar; **to — testimony** dar testimonio.

beard [bɪrd] *s.* barba, barbas; aristas (*de trigo o maíz*); **-ed** *adj.* barbado, barbudo.

bearer [bérə] *s.* portador; mensajero. **bearing** [bérɪŋ] *s.* (*posture*) porte, presencia; (*relation*) relación, conexión; (*direction*) rumbo, orientación; (*mechanical*) cojinete; **ball — —** cojinete de bolas; **beyond —** inaguantable, insufrible; **to lose one's -s** perder el rumbo, desorientarse; **fruit-bearing** *adj.* fructífero.

beast [bist] *s.* bestia, animal.

beat [bit] *s.* golpe; toque (*de tambor*); latido; palpitación; compás; ronda (*que hace el policía*); *v.* batir; golpear; azotar; vencer, ganar; marcar (*el compás*); pulsar, latir; sonar (*tambores*); **to —**

around the bush andarse por las ramas; valerse de rodeos; *pret. & p.p. de* **to beat.**

beat·en [bítn̩] *p.p. de* **to beat** & *adj.* batido; vencido; fatigado; **— path** camino trillado.

beat·er [bítə] *s.* batidor; molinillo; golpeador; **egg —** batidor de huevos.

be·a·tif·ic [buətífɪk] *adj.* beatífico.

beat·ing [bítɪŋ] *s.* paliza, tunda, zurra; latido; pulsación.

be·at·i·tude [bɪǽtətjud] *s.* beatitud, bienaventuranza; **the Beatitudes** las bienaventuranzas.

beau [bo] *s.* galán, pretendiente.

beau·te·ous [bjútɪəs] *adj.* bello, hermoso.

beau·ti·ful [bjútəfəl] *adj.* bello, hermoso.

beau·ti·fy [bjútəfaɪ] *v.* hermosear, embellecer.

beau·ty [bjútɪ] *s.* belleza, hermosura; beldad; **— parlor** salón de belleza.

bea·ver [bívə] *s.* castor; **— board** cartón para tabiques.

be·came [bɪkém] *pret. de* **to become.**

be·cause [bɪkɔz] *conj.* porque; **— of** *prep.* por, a causa de.

beck·on [békən] *s.* seña, llamada; *v.* llamar a señas.

be·come [bɪkʌm] *v.* (*suit*) sentar bien a, quedar bien a; convenir a; (*turn out to be*) hacerse; ponerse; llegar a ser; convertirse en; **to — crazy** volverse loco; enloquecer; **to — angry** enojarse; **to — frightened** asustarse; **to — old** envejecer(se); **what has — of him?** ¿qué ha sido de él?; ¿qué se ha hecho él?; *p.p. de* **to become.**

be·com·ing [bɪkámɪŋ] *adj.* propio, conveniente; decente, decoroso; **that dress is — to you** le sienta bien ese traje.

bed [bɛd] *s.* cama, lecho; cauce (*de un río*); fondo (*de lago o mar*); cuadro (*de jardín*); yacimiento (*mineral*); **to go to —** acostarse; **to put to —** acostar.

bed·bug [bédʌg] *s.* chinche.

bed·clothes [bédkloz] *s. pl.* ropa de cama.

bed·ding [bédɪŋ] **= bedclothes.**

bed·pan [bédpæn] *s.* silleta; cómodo.

bed·rid·den [bédrɪdən] *adj.* en cama; postrado.

bed·rock [bédrák] *s.* roca sólida; lecho de roca.

bed·room [bédrum] *s.* cuarto de dormir, alcoba, *Méx., C.A.* recámara.

bed·side [bédsaɪd] **: at the —** al lado de la cama; **— table** velador, mesilla de noche.

bed·spread [bédspred] *s.* colcha, sobrecama.

bed·time [bédtaɪm] *s.* hora de acostarse, hora de dormir.

bee [bi] *s.* abeja; reunión (*para trabajar o competir*); **to have a — in one's bonnet** tener una idea metida en la cabeza.

beech [bitʃ] *s.* haya; **— nut** nuez de haya, hayuco.

beef [bif] *s.* carne de vaca o toro; vaca, toro (*engordados para matar*); **roast —** rosbif.

beef·steak [bífstek] *s.* bistec, biftec o bisté.

bee·hive [bíhaɪv] *s.* colmena; abejera.

been [bɪn, bɛn] *p.p. de* **to be.**

beer [bɪr] *s.* cerveza; **— tavern** cervecería.

beet [bit] *s.* remolacha, *Am.* betabel.

bee·tle [bítl̩] *s.* escarabajo.

be·fall [bɪfɔl] *v.* sobrevenir, acaecer, suceder.

be·fall·en [bɪfɔlən] *p.p. de* **befall.**

be·fell [bɪfɛl] *pret. de* **befall.**

be·fit [bɪfít] *v.* convenir.

be·fore [bɪfór] *adv.* (*temporal*) antes; (*spatial*) delante; al frente; *prep.* antes de; delante de; enfrente de; ante; *conj.* antes (de) que.

be·fore·hand [bɪfórhænd] *adv.* de antemano, por

adelantado, con antelación, con anticipación.
be·friend [bɪfrɛ́nd] v. ofrecer o brindar amistad a;
favorecer; amparar.
beg [bɛg] v. rogar, suplicar, pedir; mendigar,
pordiosear; **to — the question** dar por sentado
lo mismo que se arguye.
be·gan [bɪgǽn] pret. de **to begin.**
be·get [bɪgɛ́t] v. engendrar; causar, producir.
beg·gar [bégɚ] s. mendigo, pordiosero; pobre;
infeliz, miserable.
be·gin [bɪgín] v. comenzar, empezar, principiar.
be·gin·ner [bɪgínɚ] s. principiante; novicio.
be·gin·ning [bɪgínɪŋ] s. principio; comienzo,
empiezo; origen; **— with** comenzando con (o
por); a partir de; **at the —** al principio.
be·got [bɪgát] pret. & p.p. de **to beget.**
be·got·ten [bɪgátn̩] p.p. de **to beget.**
be·grudge [bɪgrʌ́dʒ] v. envidiar; ceder de mala
gana.
be·guile [bɪgáɪl] v. enganar; defraudar; seducir.
be·gun [bɪgʌ́n] p.p. de **to begin.**
be·half [bɪhǽf]: **in (on) — of** por; en nombre de; a
favor de; en defensa de; **in my —** en mi nombre;
a mi favor; por mi.
be·have [bɪhév] v. portarse, conducirse, obrar,
proceder (bien o mal); **— yourself!** ¡pórtate bien!
be·hav·ior [bɪhévjɚ] s. comportamiento, proceder,
conducta; funcionamiento; reacción.
be·head [bɪhéd] v. decapitar, degollar, descabezar.
be·held [bɪhéld] pret. & p.p. de **to behold.**
be·hind [bɪháɪnd] adv. detrás; atrás; a la zaga, en
zaga; prep. detrás de, tras; **— one's back** a
espaldas de uno; **— time** atrasado, retrasado
from — por detrás; **to arrive ten minutes — time**
llegar con diez minutos de retraso; **to fall —**
atrasarse; retrasarse.
be·hold [bɪhóld] v. contemplar, mirar; **—!** ¡the
aqui!
be·hoove [bɪhúv] v. serle necesario a uno;
corresponderle a uno; atañerle a uno.
be·ing [bíɪŋ] s. ser; ente; esencia; existencia; ger. de
to be siendo; **for the time —** por ahora; por el
momento.
be·lat·ed [bɪlétɪd] adj. tardío; atrasado.
belch [bɛltʃ] v. eructar; **to — forth** echar, arrojar,
vomitar; s. eructo.
bel·fry [bélfrɪ] s. campanario.
Bel·gian [béldʒɪən] adj. & s. belga.
be·lief [bɪlíf] s. creencia; fe; convicción; opinión.
be·liev·a·ble [bəlívəbl̩] adj. creíble.
be·lieve [bəlív] v. creer; pensar; **to — in** creer en
tener fe en; confiar en.
be·liev·er [bəlívɚ] s. creyente, fiel.
be·lit·tle [bɪlít̩l] v. menospreciar, apocar,
empequeñecer; dar poca importancia a.
bell [bɛl] s. campana; campanilla; **cow —** cencerro,
esquila; **call —** timbre; **jingle —** cascabel; **—
flower** campanilla, campánula; **— jar** campana
de cristal.
bell·boy [bélbɔɪ] s. mozo de hotel, botones.
belle [bɛl] s. beldad, mujer bella.
bel·lig·er·ent [bəlídʒərənt] adj. & s. beligerante.
bel·low [bélo] s. bramido, rugido; v. rugir, bramar,
berrear; gritar.
bel·lows [béloz] s. (sing. & pl.) fuelle.
bel·ly [bélɪ] s. barriga; panza, vientre; estómago.
bel·ly·ache [bélɪek] s. dolor de barriga (estómago).
be·long [bəlɔ́ŋ] v. pertenecer, corresponder; **it does
not — here** está fuera de su sitio; está mal
colocado.
be·long·ings [bəlɔ́ŋɪŋz] s. pl. posesiones, bienes,

efectos, cosas.
be·lov·ed [bɪlʌ́vɪd] adj. querido, amado.
be·low [bəló] adv. abajo; bajo; debajo; **here —**
aquí abajo; en este mundo, de tejas abajo; prep.
bajo, debajo de.
belt [bɛlt] s. cinturón, cinto; correa; zona; **sword
—** talabarte; v. ceñir, fajar.
belt line [béltlaɪn] s. vía de circunvalación.
be·moan [bɪmón] v. lamentarse de, quejarse de.
bench [bɛntʃ] s. banco, banca; tribunal.
bend [bɛnd] s. curva; vuelta, recodo; v. encorvar(se),
doblar(se), Am. enchuecar(se); inclinar(se);
someter(se), ceder; **to — one's efforts** esforzarse
(por), dirigir sus esfuerzos.
be·neath (bɪníθ] prep. debajo de, bajo; indigno de;
inferior a.
ben·e·dic·tion [bɛnədíkʃən] s. bendición.
ben·e·fac·tor [bénəfæktɚ] s. benefactor, bienhechor;
patrón.
be·nef·i·cent [bənéfəsn̩t] adj. benéfico.
ben·e·fi·cial [bɛnəfíʃəl] adj. benéfico; ventajoso,
provechoso.
ben·e·fi·ci·ar·y [bɛnɪfíʃɪɛrɪ] s. beneficiario.
ben·e·fit [bénəfɪt] s. beneficio; provecho, ventaja;
— performance función de beneficio; v.
beneficiar; hacer bien; **to — by the advice**
aprovecharse del consejo; **he -ed by the medicine**
le hizo bien la medicina.
be·nev·o·lence [bənévələns] s. benevolencia.
be·nev·o·lent [bənévələnt] adj. benévolo.
be·nign [bɪnáɪn] adj. benigno; afable.
bent [bɛnt] s. inclinación; tendencia; propensión;
pret. & p.p. de **to bend**; adj. encorvado; inclinado,
doblado; corvo; gacho; **to be — on** estar
resuelto a.
ben·zene [bénzin] s. benceno.
be·queath [bɪkwíð] v. heredar, legar, dejar en
testamento.
be·quest [bɪkwɛ́st] s. legado, donación.
be·rate [bɪrét] v. regañar, reñir, reprender.
be·ret [bəré] s. boina.
ber·ry [bérɪ] s. baya (como mora, fresa, etc.); grano
(de café).
berth [bɝθ] s. litera (de un camarote); **to give a
wide —** de sacarle el cuerpo a, hacerse a un lado
para dejar pasar.
be·ryl·li·um [bəríliəm] s. berilio.
be·seech [bɪsít] v. suplicar, rogar.
be·set [bɪsɛ́t] v. atacar; rodear; acosar; pret. &
p.p. de **to beset.**
be·side [bɪsáɪd] prep. (spatial) al lado de; cerca de;
(in addition) además de; fuera de; **to be — oneself**
estar fuera de sí, estar loco; **that is — the
question** eso no hace al caso; no se trata de eso;
adv. además.
be·sides [bɪsáɪdz] adv. además; prep. además de.
be·siege [bɪsídʒ] v. sitiar, cercar; acosar,
importunar.
be·sought [bɪsɔ́t] pret. & p.p. de **to beseech.**
best [bɛst] adj. mejor; adv. mejor; más; **the —** el
mejor; lo mejor; **— girl** novia, querida; **— man**
padrino de boda; **— seller** éxito de venta; de
mayor venta; **at —** a lo más, cuando más; **to do
one's —** hacer todo lo posible; **to get the — of
a person** vencer o ganarle a una persona; **to
make the — of** sacar el major partido de
be·stow [bɪstó] v. otorgar, conferir; **to — gifts
upon** hacer regalos (o dádivas) a; **time well -ed**
tiempo bien empleado.
bet [bɛt] s. apuesta; v. apostar; pret. & p.p. de **to
bet.**

be·take [bɪték] v. to — oneself encaminarse, dirigirse.

be·tak·en [bɪtékən] p.p. de to betake.

be·took [bɪtúk] pret. de to betake.

be·tray [bɪtré] v. traicionar, vender, hacer tración; revelar, no guardar (un secreto); **to one's ignorance** hacer patente su ignorancia.

be·tray·er [bɪtréɚ] s. traidor, traicionera.

be·troth·al [bɪtróθəl] s. esponsales, compromiso, mutua promesa de matrimonio.

be·trothed [bɪtróθt] s. prometido, desposado; novio, novia.

bet·ter [bétɚ] adj. mejor; adv. mejor; más; — **half** cara mitad; **so much the** — tanto mejor; **to be** — **off** estar mejor así; estar en mejores condiciones; **to change for the** — mejorar(se); **to get** — (mejorar(se), restablecerse, aliviarse; v. mejorar; **to** — oneself mejorarse, mejorar de situación.

bet·ter·ment [bétɚmənt] s. mejoramiento, mejora, mejoría.

be·tween [bətwín] prep. entre, en medio de; adv. en medio.

bev·el [bévəl] s. bisel; adj. biselado; v. biselar.

bev·er·age [bévrɪdʒ] s. bebida.

be·wail [bɪwél] v. lamentar; quejarse de.

be·ware [btwér] v. guardarse (de), cuidarse (de); — ! ¡cuidado! ¡guárdese!

be·wil·der [bɪwíldɚ] v. confundir, turbar, perturbar, dejar perplejo; **to be -ed** estar turbado o perplejo; estar desorientado.

be·wil·der·ment [bɪwíldɚmənt] s. perplejidad, aturdimiento.

be·witch [bɪwítʃ] v. hechizar; aojar; encantar, cautivar.

be·yond [bɪjánd] adv. más allá, más lejos; prep. allende; más allá de; fuera de; — **my reach** fuera de mi alcance; — **the grave** ultratumba.

bi·as [báɪəs] s. (tendency) prejuicio; inclinación, tendencia; (diagonal) sesgo, oblicuidad; **on the** — sesgado, al sesgo, de lado; adj. sesgado, oblicuo; v. predisponer, inclinar, influir en.

bib [bɪb] s. babero; pechera (de delantal).

Bi·ble [báɪb] s. Biblia.

bib·li·cal [bíblɪk] adj. bíblico.

bib·li·og·ra·pher [bɪblɪágrəfɚ] s. bibliógrafo.

bib·li·og·ra·phy [bɪblɪágrəfɪ] s. bibliografía.

bi·car·bon·ate [baɪkárbənet] s. bicarbonato.

bick·er [bíkɚ] v. disputar, reñir.

bi·cy·cle [báɪsɪk] s. bicicleta; v. andar en bicicleta.

bid [bɪd] s. postura, oferta; envite (en naipes); turno (para envidar); invitación; v. ofrecer (precio); mandar; invitar, convidar; rogar; envidar (en naipes); **to** — **fair** parecer muy probable; **to** — **good-bye** decir adiós; despedirse; **to** — **up** alzar, pujar (la oferta en una subasta); pret. & p.p. de **to bid.**

bid·den [bídn] p.p. de to bid & to bide.

bide [baɪd] v. aguardar; **to** — **one's time** esperar una buena oportunidad.

bi·en·ni·um [baɪénɪəm] s. bienio.

bier [bɪr] s. féretro.

big [bɪg] adj. grande; importante; imponente; — **Dipper** Osa Mayor; — **game** caza mayor; — **sister** hermana mayor; — **with child** encinta; **to talk** — darse bombo, Am. darse corte; **big-bellied** panzudo, panzón, barrigón; **big-hearted** magnánimo.

big·a·my [bígəmɪ] s. bigamia.

big·ot [bígət] s. fanático.

big·ot·ry [bígətrɪ] s. fanatismo; intolerancia.

bi·ki·ni [bɪkíni] s. traje bikini.

bi·la·bi·al [baɪlébɪəl] adj. bilabial.

bile [baɪ] s. bills, hiel, cólera, mal humor.

bi·lin·gual [baɪlíŋgwəl] adj. & s. bilingüe.

bill [bɪl] s. (statement) cuenta; factura; (poster) cartel, anuncio; (bank note) billete de banco; programa de teatro; (bird) pico; (legislative) proyecto de ley; — **of exchange** libranza, letra de cambio; — **of fare** lista de platos; — **of lading** conocimiento de embarque; — **of rights** declaración de derechos; — **of sale** escritura o acta de venta; v. cargar en cuenta; enviar una cuenta a; **to** — **and coo** acariciarse y arrullar (como las palomas).

bill·board [bílbord] s. cartelera.

bill·fold [bílfold] s. cartera.

bil·liards [bíljɚdz] s. billar.

bill·ing [bílɪŋ] s. imortancia relativa de los anuncios de artistas de teatro.

bil·lion [bíljən] s. billón, millón de millones; mil millones (en los Estados Unidos y Francia).

bil·low [bílo] s. oleada; ola grande; v. alzarse en olas.

bin [bɪn] s. arcón, depósito; **coal** — carbonera; **grain** — granero.

bind [baɪnd] v. (unite) unir, juntar; (tie) ligar; amarrar; vendar; ceñir; (compel) restringir; obligar, compeler; (enclose) encuadernar, empastar; rivetear.

bind·ing [báɪndɪŋ] s. encuadernación; ribete, cinta; **cloth** — encuadernación en tela; **paper** — encuadernación en rústica; adj. obligatorio.

binge [bɪndʒ] s. jarana; parranda; borrachera.

bi·og·ra·phy [baɪágrəfɪ] s. biografía.

bi·ol·o·gy [baɪálədʒɪ] s. biologia.

bi·par·ti·san [baɪpártəzən] adj. de dos partidos; bipartito.

birch [bɚtʃ] s. abedul.

bird [bɚd] s. ave; pájaro; persona extraña o mal vista; — **of prey** ave de rapiña; — **seed** alpiste; — **shot** perdigones.

birth [bɚθ] s. nacimiento; parto; linaje; origen, principio; — **certificate** certificado (o fe) de nacimiento; — **control** control de la natalidad; anticoncepcionismo; limitación de partos; — **rate** natalidad; **to give** — dar a luz, parir.

birth·day [bɚθde] s. cumpleaños, natalicio.

birth·place [bɚθples] s. lugar de nacimiento, suelo natal.

birth·right [bɚθraɪt] s. derechos naturales o de nacimiento; naturalidad; primogenitura.

bis·cuit [bískɪt] s. bizcocho; galleta; panecillo.

bish·op [bíʃəp] s. obispo; alfil (en ajedrez).

bish·op·ric [bíʃəprɪk] s. obispado.

bis·muth [bízməθ] s. bismuto.

bi·son [báɪsn] s. bisonte, búfalo.

bit [bɪt] s. pedacito, trocito; pizca, miaja, migaja; poquito; bocado (del freno); taladro; **I don't care a** — no me importa un ardite; pret. & p.p. de **to bite.**

bitch [bɪtʃ] s. perra; ramera, prostituta.

bite [baɪt] s. mordedura, mordisco; bocado, bocadito; picadura (de insecto); v. morder; mordiscar; picar.

bit·ten [bítn] p.p. de to bite.

bit·ter [bítɚ] adj. amargo; agrio, acre; áspero; mordaz; **to fight to the** — **end** luchar hasta morir; **-s** s. pl. amargo; **-ly** adv. amargamente; con amargura.

bit·ter·ness [bítɚnɪs] s. amargura, amargor; rencor; aspereza.

black [blæk] adj. negro; obscuro; sombrío; **black-**

and-blue amoratado, lleno de moretones; —
mark mancha, estigma, marca de deshonra; s.
negro; luto; —**out** obscurecimiento; **to put
down in** — **and white** poner por escrito v. teñir
de negro; embetunar, dar bola o betún a (los
zapatos).

black·ber·ry [blǽkbɛri] s. zarzamora; mora.

black·bird [blǽkbɜd] s. mirlo.

black·board [blǽkbòrd] s. encerado; pizarrón;
pizarra.

black·en [blǽkən] v. ennegrecer; obscurecer; teñir
de negro; denigrar.

black·head [blǽkhɛd] s. espinilla.

black·ish [blǽkɪʃ] adj. negruzco.

black·jack [blǽkdʒæk] s. (weapon) cachiporra
flexible; (card game) veintiuna.

black·mail [blǽkmel] s. chantaje, extorsión; v.
ejercer el chantaje, extorsionar.

black·ness [blǽknɪs] s. negrura; obscuridad.

black·smith [blǽksmɪθ] s. herrero; -**'s shop** herrería.

black·top [blǽktap] s. camino de superficie
bituminosa.

blad·der [blǽdɚ] s. vejiga.

blade [bled] s. hoja (de navaja, cuchillo, etc.); hoja
(de hierba); espada; pala (de remo); aspa (de
hélice); **shoulder** — espaldilla o paletilla.

blame [blem] s. culpa; v. culpar, echar la culpa a;
to be to — tener la culpa.

blame·less [blémlɪs] adj. inculpable.

blanch [blæntʃ] v. blanquear; palidecer; escaldar
(almendras).

bland [blænd] adj. blando, suave.

blank [blæŋk] adj. (no writing) en blanco; (void)
vacío; (confused) aturdido; — **cartridge** cartucho
vacío; — **face** cara sin expresión; — **form**
blanco, forma en blanco, Méx., C.A., Ven.
esqueleto; — **verse** verso suelto o libre; s.
blanco; vacío; hueco, intermedio; papel en
blanco; forma en blanco; **application** — forma
(o blanco) para memorial o solicitud.

blan·ket [blǽŋkɪt] s. manta; frazada; cobertor;
Riopl., C.A., Méx., Ven., Col. cobija; Méx.
sarape, poncho; adj. general, inclusivo, que
abarca un grupo o clase.

blare [blɛr] s. fragor; son de trompetas; clarinada;
v. trompetear, proclamar; sonar (las trompetas);
hacer estruendo.

blas·pheme [blæsfím] v. blasfemar.

blas·phe·my [blǽsfɪmɪ] s. blasfemia.

blast [blæst] s. (wind) ráfaga de viento, golpe de
viento; soplo repentino; (trumpet) trompetazo;
(whistle) silbido; (explosion) explosión; estallido;
carga de dinamita; — **furnace** alto horno; v.
volar (con dinamita, etc.); destruir.

blaze [blez] s. llama, llamarada, incendio;
resplandor; — **of anger** arranque de ira; v.
arder; resplandecer; **to** — **a trail** abrir (o marcar)
una senda.

bleach [blitʃ] s. blanqueador; blanqueo; v.
blasquear(se); desteñir(se).

bleach·ers [blítʃɚz] s. pl. graderías.

bleak [blik] adj. yermo, desierto; helado.

blear [blɪr] v. nublar (los ojos).

blear·y [blírɪ] adj. nublado, inflamado, lagrimoso,
lagañoso.

bleat [blit] s. balido; v. balar.

bled [blɛd] pret. & p.p. de **to bleed.**

bleed [blid] v. sangrar; desangrar; extorsionar.

blem·ish [blémɪʃ] s. mancha, tacha, defecto; v.
manchar; empañar.

blend [blɛnd] s. mezcla, entremezcla; gradación (de

colores, sonidos, etc.); v. mezclar, entremezclar;
graduar (colores o sonidos); entremezclarse,
fundirse; armonizar.

bless [blɛs] v. bendecir; **God** — **you!** ¡que Dios te
bendiga!

bless·ed [blésɪd] adj. bendito; santo, beato;
bienaventurado; **the whole** — **day** todo el santo
día; [blɛst] pret. & p.p. de **to bless.**

bless·ing [blésɪŋ] s. bendición; gracia, don,
beneficio.

blest [blɛst] adj. = **blessed.**

blew [blu] pret. de **to blow.**

blight [blaɪt] s. pulgón (parásito); tizón (honguillo
parásito); quemadura (enfermedad de las plantas);
roña (de las plantas); malogro; ruina; v. destruir,
arruinar; frustrar (esperanzas).

blimp [blɪmp] s. dirigible pequeño.

blind [blaɪnd] adj. ciego; tapado, oculto; hecho a
ciegas; — **alley** callejón sin salida; — **choice**
selección hecha a ciegas; — **flying** vuelo ciego,
vuelo a ciegas; — **man** ciego; — **man's buff**
juego de la gallina ciega; — **date** [blaɪnddet] s.
cita a ciegas; persiana, cortinilla; biombo; venda
(para los ojos); anteojera (para resguardar los
ojos del caballo); **to be a** — **for someone** ser
tapadera de alguien; v. cegar; ofuscar; encubrir,
tapar.

blind·er [blaɪndɚ] s. anteojera, Am. visera (para
caballos de tiro).

blind·fold [blaɪndfold] v. vendar (los ojos); adj.
vendado (de ojos); s. venda (para los ojos).

blind·ly [blaɪndlɪ] adv. ciegamente; a ciegas.

blind·ness [blaɪndnɪs] s. ceguera, ceguedad.

blink [blɪŋk] s. pestañeo; parpadeo; guiño;
guiñada; v. pestañear; parpadear; guiñar.

blip [blɪp] s. bache de radar.

bliss [blɪs] s. beatitud, bienaventuranza, gloria;
felicidad.

blis·ter [blɪstɚ] s. ampolla, vejiga (en la piel o en
cualquipr superficie); v. ampollar, levantar
ampollas; ampollarse.

blitz [blɪts] s. ataque relámpago.

bliz·zard [blízɚd] s. ventisca; v. ventiscar.

bloat [blot] v. inflar(se); abotagarse.

blob [blab] s. burbuja.

block [blak] s. (piece) bloque, trozo de piedra;
zoquete; (city section) manzana (de casas); Am.
cuadra; (obstacle) estorbo, obstáculo; (group)
grupo, sección (hat) horma; — **pulley** polea;
chopping — tajo; v. estorbar; tapar; bloquear;
planchar (sobre horma); parar (una pelota, una
jugada); **to** — **out** esbozar, bosquejar; **to** — **the
door** impedir el paso; **to** — **up a door** tapiar una
puerta.

block·ade [blakéd] s. bloqueo; obstrucción v.
bloquear.

block·head [blákhɛd] s. zoquete, tonto, zopenco.

blond(e) [bland] adj. & s. rubio, blondo; Mex.
huero, güero; Guat. canche; Sal., Hond., chele;
C.R. macho; Col. mono; Ven. catire.

blood [blʌd] s. sangre; — **count** análisis
cuantitativo de la sangre; — **pudding** (o —
sausage) morcilla; — **relative** pariente
consanguíneo; — **vessel** vena; arteria; **in cold** —
en sangre fría; — **bank** banco de sangre; —
poisoning septicemia.

blood·shed [blʌdʃɛd] s. matanza; derrame,
derramamiento o efusión de sangre.

blood·shot [blʌdʃat] adj. inyectado de sangre.

blood·thirst·y [blʌdθɚstɪ] adj. sanguinario.

blood·y [blʌdɪ] adj. sangriento; ensangrentado;

sanguinario, feroz.

bloom [blum] *s.* flor; florecimiento floración; lozanía; color rosado (*en las mejillas*) *v.* florecer, *Am.* florear.

bloom·ing [blúmɪŋ] *adj.* floreciente; fresco, lozano, vigoroso.

blos·som [blásəm] *s.* flor; floración, florecimiento; *v.* florecer.

blot [blɑt] *s.* mancha, borrón; tacha; *v.* manchar; borrar; secar (*con papel secante*); emborronar, echar manchas o borrones; **to — out** borrar, tachar; destruir; **this pen -s** esta pluma echa borrones; **blotting paper** papel secante.

blotch [blɑtʃ] *v.* emborronar o borronear, manchar, cubrir con manchas; *s.* mancha, borrón.

blot·ter [blátɚ] *s.* palel secante; libro borrador.

blouse [blaʊs] *s.* blusa.

blow [blo] *s.* (*stroke*) golpe; porrazo; (*shock*) choque, sorpresa, desastre; (*wind*) soplo, soplido; **to come to -s** venir a las manos; *v.* soplar; ventear; *C.A.* nortear; resoplar; sonar (*una trompeta*); fanfarronear; **to — a fuse** quemar un fusible; **to — one's nose** sonarse; **to — one's brains out** levantarse la tapa de los sesos; **to — open** abrirse; **to — out** apagar(se); estallar, reventar(se) (*un neumático*); **to — over** pasar; disiparse; **to — up** inflar, hinchar; volar (*con dinamita*); estallar, reventar.

blow·er [blóɚ] *s.* soplador; fuelle; ventilador, aventador.

blown [blon] *p.p. de* **to blow** & *adj.* soplado; inflado; **full-blown rose** rosa abierta.

blow·out [blóaʊt] *s.* reventón (*de neumático*); escape violento de gas, aire, etc.

blow·pipe [blópaɪp] *s.* soplete.

blow·torch [blótɔrtʃ] *s.* soplete.

blue [blu] *adj.* azul; triste, melancólico; *s.* azul; **light —** (*ojos*) zarco; **the -s** melancolía, morriña, murria; *v.* azular, teñir de azul.

blue·bell [blúbɛl] *s.* campanilla azul (*flor*).

blue·bird [blúbɝd] *s.* pájaro azul, *Am.* azulejo.

blue·jay [blúdʒe] *s.* gayo, especie de azulejo (*pájaro*).

bluff [blʌf] *s.* acantilado, escarpa, risco; fanfarronada; fanfarrón, farsante; *v.* fanfarronear; alardear, hacer alarde; echar bravatas; embaucar.

bluff·er [blʌfɚ] *s.* farsante, fanfarrón.

blu·ing [blúɪŋ] *s.* añil (*para ropa blanca*).

blu·ish [blúɪʃ] *adj.* azulado, azulejo.

blun·der [blʌndɚ] *s.* disparate, desatino; despropósito; *v.* disparatar, desatinar; equivocarse.

blunt [blʌnt] *adj.* despuntado, embotado; brusco, grosero, *Méx.* claridoso; *v.* despuntar, embotar.

blur [blɝ] *s.* mancha; tacha; nube, cosa obscura o confusa; *v.* empañar, borronear, manchar; nublar, ofuscar; empañarse, nublarse.

blush [blʌʃ] *s.* sonrojo; rubor; *v.* sonrojarse, ruborizarse, ponerse colorado.

blus·ter [blʌstɚ] *v.* ventear o soplar recio (*el viento*); fanfarronear; *s.* ventolera, ventarrón, fuerte golpe de viento; jactancia, fanfarronada.

blus·ter·ing [blʌstərɪŋ] *adj.* fanfarrón, hactancioso; **— wind** ventarrón.

boar [bor] *s.* jabalí.

board [bord] *s.* (*wood*) tabla, tablero; mesa; (*meals*) comidas; (*directors*) junta, consejo; (*pasteboard*) en pasta; cartón; **the -s** las tablas, el teatro;

room and — cuarto y comida, pensión completa; asistencia; **— of directors** junta directiva; **bulletin —** tabilla para anuncios; **free on — (f.o.b.)** franco a bordo; **on —** a bordo; en el tren; **to go by the —** caer en el mar; perderse; ser descartado; *v.* ir a bordo; subir (*al tren*); entablar, cubrir con tablas; tomar a pupilaje, dar asistencia, pensión o pupilaje; residir o comer (*en casa de huéspedes*).

board·er [bórdɚ] *s.* huésped, pupilo, pensionista.

board·ing·house [bórdɪŋhaʊs] *s.* casa de huéspedes, pensión.

boast [bost] *s.* jactancia; alarde; bravata; gloria, orgullo; *v.* jactarse, alardear; hacer alarde de; ostentar.

boast·ful [bóstfəl] *adj.* jactancioso.

boast·ful·ness [bóstfəlnɪs] *s.* jactancia; ostentación.

boat [bot] *s.* bote; barco, buque; lancha, chalupa.

boat·house [bóthaʊs] *s.* casilla o cobertizo para botes.

boat·ing [bótɪŋ] *s.* paseo en lancha o bote; **to go —** pasear en bote.

boat·man [bótmən] (*pl.* **boatmen** [bótmɛn]) *s.* barquero.

bob [bɑb] *s.* meneo, sacudida; pesa (*de metal*); **to wear a —** llevar el pelo corto (*o* en melena); *v.* menearse; **to — one's hair** cortarse el pelo en melena; **to — up** aparecer de repente; **to — up and down** saltar, brincar; cabecear (*dícese de una embarcación*).

bob·bin [bábɪn] *s.* carrete; bobina.

bob·tail [bábtel] *s.* rabón.

bob·white [bábhwaɪt] *s.* cordorniz.

bode [bod] *pret.* & *p.p. de* **to bide**.

bod·ice [bádɪs] *s.* corpiño, jubón.

bod·i·ly [bádlɪ] *adj.* corpóreo; corporal; *adv.* todos juntos, colectivamente; **they rose —** se levantaron todos a una, se levantaron·todos juntos.

bod·y [bádɪ] *s.* cuerpo; agregado, conjunto; gremio; carrocería (*de automóvil*); fuselaje (*de aeroplano*); **— of water** extensión de agua; **— politic** grupo político; estado.

bod·y·guard [bádɪgard] *s.* guardaespaldas; *Am.* pistolero.

bog [bag] *s.* pantano; tremedal; *v.* hundir(se); atascarse.

Bo·he·mi·an [bohímɪən] *adj.* & *s.* bohemio.

boil [bɔɪl] *s.* hervor; tumorcillo; **to come to a —** soltar el hervor, hervir; *v.* hervir; cocer; bullir; **to — down** hervir hasta evaporar; abreviar.

boil·er [bɔɪlɚ] *s.* caldera, marmita; caldera de vapor; calorífero central.

boil·ing point [bɔɪlɪŋpɔɪnt] *s.* punto de ebullición.

bois·ter·ous [bɔɪstərəs] *adj.* bullicioso; esterpitoso, ruidoso; tumultuoso.

bold [bold] *adj.* atrevido, osado; arriesgado; audaz; insolente; claro, bien delineado; **— cliff** risco escarpado; **bold-faced** descarado; **bold-faced type** negritas.

bold·ness [bóldnɪs] *s.* atrevimiento; osadía; audacia; descaro, insolencia.

bo·lo·gna [bəlóní] *s.* especie de embutido.

Bol·she·vik [bólʃəvik] *adj.* & *s.* bolchevique.

bol·ster [bólstɚ] *s.* travesaño, almohada larga (*para la cabecera de la cama*); refuerzo, sostén; soporte; *v.* sostener, apoyar; apuntalar; **to — someone's courage** infundirle ámino a alguien.

bolt [bolt] *s.* (*door lock*) pestillo, cerrojo; (*pin*) perno, tornillo grande; (*movement*) salida de repente; (*cloth*) rollo; **thunder —** rayo; *v.* cerrar con cerrojo; tragar, engullir; romper con (*un partido político*); echarse a correr, lanzarse de repente; caer como rayo; **to — out** salir de golpe.

bomb [bɑm] *s.* bomba; *v.* bombardear; **— shelter** [bámʃɛltɚ] *s.* refugio antiaéreo.

bom·bard [bɑmbárd] *v.* bombardear, cañonear.

bom·bar·dier [bɑmbɚdír] *s.* bombardero.

bom·bard·ment [bɑmbárdmənt] *s.* bombardeo, cañoneo.

bom·bas·tic [bɑmbǽstɪk] *adj.* ampuloso, altisonante.

bom·ber [bámɚ] *s.* bombardero, avión de bombardeo.

bo·na fide [bónəfaɪd] *adj.* de buena fe.

bon·bon [bánbɑn] *s.* bombón, confite.

bond [bɑnd] *s.* (*tie*) lazo, vínculo; ligadura; (*obligation*) fianza, vale; obligación, bono.

bond·age [bándɪdʒ] *s.* servidumbre, esclavitud.

bonds·man [bándzmən] *s.* fiador.

bone [bon] *s.* hueso; espina (*de pez*); **-s** restos; osamenta; **— of contention** materia de discordia; **to make no -s about it** no pararse en pelillos; obrar francamente; *v.* deshuesar, quitar los huesos o espinas.

bon·fire [bánfaɪr] *s.* hoguera, fogata.

bon·net [bánɪt] *s.* gorra; sombrero (*de mujer*).

bo·nus [bónəs] *s.* prima, premio, gratificación.

bon·y [bóni] *adj.* huesudo.

boo [bu] *v.* mofarse, burlarse (*a gritos*); **— !** *interj.* ¡bu!; **-s** *s. pl.* rechifla, gritos de mofa.

boo·by [búbɪ] *s.* bobo, bobalicón.

book [bʊk] *s.* libro; **The book** la Biblia; **cash —** libro de caja; **memorandum —** libreta; **on the -s** cargado en cuenta; **to keep -s** llevar los libros o la contabilidad *v.* inscribir, asentar (*en un libro*); **to — passage** reservar pasaje.

book·case [búkkes] *s.* estante, estantería, armario para libros.

book·end [búkɛnd] *s.* apoyalibros, sujetalibros.

book·keep·er [búkkipɚ] *s.* tenedor de libros, contador.

book·keep·ing [búkkipɪŋ] *s.* teneduría de libros, contabilidad; **double entry —** partida doble.

book·let [búklɛt] *s.* librillo, librito, cuaderno, folleto.

book·sel·ler [búksɛlɚ] *s.* librero.

book·shelf [búkʃɛlf] *s.* estante, repisa para libros.

book·shop [búkʃɑp] *s.* librería.

book·store [búkstor] *s.* librería.

boom [bum] *s.* (*noise*) estampido; (*increase*) alza, auge (*en el mercado o bolsa*); bonanza, prosperidad momentánea; *v.* rugir, resonar, hacer estampido; prosperar, medrar, florecer, estar en bonanza; fomentar.

boon [bun] *s.* don; bendición, gracia, favor; *adj.* jovial, congenial.

boor [bʊr] *s.* patán, hombre zafio o grosero.

boor·ish [búrɪʃ] *adj.* grosero, zafio.

boost [bust] *s.* empuje, empujón (*de abajo arriba*); **— in prices** alza o auge de precios; *v.* empujar, alzar, levantar; hacer subir.

boost·er [bústɚ] *s.* aumentador; (*rocket*) cohete de lanzamiento; (*electronics*) amplificador.

boot [but] *s.* bota, calzado; **to —** por añadidura, de ganancia, *Méx.* de pilón, *Ven.* de ñapa; *Riopl., Andes* de yapa (*llapa*); *v.* dar un puntapié; **to — out** echar a puntapiés; echar a patadas.

boot·black [bútblæk] *s.* limpiabotas.

booth [buθ] *s.* casilla, puesto.

boot·leg·ger [bútlɛgɚ] *s.* contrabandista (*de licores*).

boot·lick·er [bútlɪkɚ] *s.* servilón, zalamero.

boo·ty [bútɪ] *s.* botín, saqueo.

bo·rax [bóræks] *s.* bórax.

bor·der [bórdɚ] *s.* borde, margen, orilla; orla, franja; ribete; frontera; *v.* ribetear, guarnecer (*el borde*); orlar; **to — on** (*o upon*) lindar con, confinar con; rayar en; **it -s on madness** raya en locura.

bor·der·ing [bórdɚɪŋ] *adj.* limítrofe.

bor·der·line [bórdɚlaɪn] *adj.* fronterizo; indefinido.

bore [bor] *s.* taladro, barreno; agujero (*hecho con taladro*); calibre (*de un cañón, cilindro, etc.*); persona o cosa aburrida; *v.* taladrar, horadar, barrenar; aburrir, fastidiar; *pret. de* to bear.

bored [bord] *adj.* cansado, aburrido; *p.p. de* to bore.

bore·dom [bórdəm] *s.* aburrimiento, tedio, hastío, fastidio.

bo·ric ac·id [bórɪk ǽsəd] *a.* ácido bórico.

bor·ing [bórɪŋ] *adj.* aburrido, fastidioso, tedioso.

born [bɔrn] *p.p. de* to bear & *adj.* nacido; innato; **to be — nacer.**

borne [bɔrn] *p.p.* to bear.

bo·ron [bóran] *s.* borón.

bor·ough [bɝo] *s.* villa; distrito de municipio.

bor·row [bɝo] *v.* pedir prestado; tomar prestado; tomar fiado.

bor·row·er [bórəwɚ] *s.* el que pide prestado.

bos·om [búzəm] *s.* seno, pecho, corazón; pechera (*de camisa*); **in the — of the family** en el seno de la familia; *adj.* querido; **— friend** amigo íntimo.

boss [bɔs] *s.* jefe; patrón; mayoral, capataz; *Am.* gamonal; **political —** cacique político; *v.* mandar, dominar, dirigir.

boss·y [bɔ́sɪ] *adj.* mandón, autoritario.

bo·tan·i·cal [bətǽnɪkl] *adj.* botánico.

bot·a·ny [bátn̩ɪ] *s.* botánica.

botch [batʃ] *s.* chapucería.

both [boθ] *adj. & pron.* ambos, entrambos, los dos; **— this and that** tanto esto como aquello; **— of them** ambos, ellos dos, los dos; **— (of) his friends** sus dos amigos, ambos amigos.

both·er [báðɚ] *s.* molestia; fastidio; incomodidad; enfado; *v.* molestar(se); fastidiar, enfadar; incomodar; estorbar.

both·er·some [báðɚsəm] *adj.* molesto.

bot·tle [bátl̩] *s.* botella; *v.* embotellar.

bot·tle·neck [bátl̩nɛk] *s.* embotellamiento, gollete.

bot·tom [bátəm] *s.* fondo; base; fundamento; asiento (*de silla*); **to be at the — of the class** ser el último de la clase; **what is at the — of all this?** ¿qué hay en el fondo de todo esto?

bou·doir [budwár] *s.* tocador.

bough [baʊ] *s.* rama.

bought [bɔt] *pret. & p.p. de* to buy.

bouil·lon [búljan] *s.* caldo.

boul·der [bóldɚ] *s.* peña, roca, guijarro grande, pedrusco.

boul·e·vard [búləvard] *s.* bulevar.

bounce [baʊns] *s.* bote, rebote (*de una pelota*); salto, brinco; *v.* hacer saltar; saltar, brincar; botar; echar, arrojar (*a alguien*); echar, despedir de un empleo.

bounc·er [baʊnsɚ] *s.* apagabroncas.

bound [baʊnd] *s.* (*jump*) salto, brinco; (*bounce*) bote, rebote; (*limit*) límite, confín; *adj.* ligado; confinado; obligado; ceñido; encuadernado; **to**

be — **for** ir para, ir con rumbo a; **to be** — **up in one's work** estar absorto en su trabajo; **it is** — **to happen** es seguro que sucederá; **I am** — **to do it** estoy resuelto a hacerlo; *v.* botar, resaltar; saltar, brincar; limitar; ceñir, cercar; *pret. & p.p. de* **to bind.**

bound·a·ry [báʊndərɪ] *s.* límite, linde; confín; frontera.

bound·less [báʊndlɪs] *adj.* ilimitado, sin límite, sin término.

boun·ti·ful [báʊntəfəl] *adj.* generoso, liberal; abundante.

boun·ty [báʊntɪ] *s.* largueza, generosidad; don, favor, gracia; premio, recompensa.

bou·quet [buké] *s.* ramillete, ramo de flores; aroma, fragancia.

bour·geois [bʊrʒwá] *adj. & s.* burgués.

bout [baʊt] *s.* combate, lucha, contienda, asalto; **a** — **of pneumonia** un ataque de pulmonía.

bow [baʊ] *s.* (*inclination*) reverencia; inclinación, saludo; (*of a ship*) proa; *v.* hacer una reverencia, inclinarse (*para saludar*); someterse; **to** — **one's head** inclinar la cabeza *-ed down* agobiado.

bow [bo] *s.* arco (*para tirar flechas*); arco (*de violín*); curva; lazo, moño (*de cintas*); **bow-legged** *adj.* patizambo, patituerto; *v.* arquear; tocar (*un instrumento*) con arco.

bow·els [báʊəlz] *s. pl.* intestinos; entrañas; tripas.

bow·er [báʊæ] *s.* enramada, ramada, glorieta.

bowl [bol] *s.* cuenco; tazón; jícara; boliche, bola; **wash** — palangana, lavamanos; *-s* juego de bolos; *v.* bolear, jugar a los bolos, jugar al boliche.

box [baks] *s.* caja; estuche; palco de teatro; casilla; compartimiento; bofetada; —**car** furgón; — **office** taquilla; — **seat** asiento de palco; *v.* encajonar; meter en una caja; abofetear; boxear.

box·er [báksæ] *s.* boxeador, pugilista.

box·ing [báksɪŋ] *s.* boxeo, pugilato.

boy [bɔɪ] *s.* niño; muchacho; mozo.

boy·cott [bɔ́ɪkat] *v.* boicotear; *s.* boicoteo.

boy·hood [bɔ́ɪhʊd] *s.* niñez; mocedad, juventud.

boy·ish [bɔ́ɪʃ] *adj.* pueril; juvenil; aniñado.

brace [bres] *s.* traba; tirante; apoyo, refuerzo; corchete ({}); **carpenter's** — berbiquí; *v.* trabar; apoyar, reforzar; asegurar; estimular, fortalecer; **to** — **up** animarse, cobrar ánimo.

brace·let [bréslɪt] *s.* brazalete, pulsera.

brack·et [brǽkɪt] *s.* ménsula, soporte, sostén; repisa; *-s* paréntesis cuadrados; *v.* colocar entre paréntesis; unir; agrupar.

brag [bræg] *s.* jactancia; *v.* jactarse (de); hacer alarde de.

brag·gart [brǽgæt] *adj. & s.* jactancioso, fanfarrón; matamoros, matamoscas.

braid [bred] *s.* trenza; galón, trencilla; *v.* trenzar; galonear, guarnecer con galones.

brain [bren] *s.* cerebro; seso; **to rack one's** *-s* devanarse los sesos, romperse la cabeza; *v.* saltar la tapa de los sesos; — **trust** [bréntrʌst] *s.* grupo de consejeros; — **washing** [brénwɔʃɪŋ] *s.* lavado cerebral.

brake [brek] *s.* freno; *Ven., Col.* retranca; *Méx., Riopl., C.A., Carib.* garrote; — **lining** forro de freno; — **shoe** zapata de freno; — **drum** tambor de freno; — **fluid** fluído de freno; **to apply the** *-s* frenar; *v.* frenar, enfrenar; *Ven., Col.* retrancar; *Méx., Riopl., C.A., Carib.* dar garrote.

brake·man [brékmən] *s.* guardafrenos, *Ven., Col.* retranquero, *Méx., Riopl., C.A., Carib.* garrotero.

bram·ble [brǽmbl] *s.* zarza, breña.

bran [bræn] *s.* salvado.

branch [bræntʃ] *s.* rama (*de árbol*); gajo; ramo (*de la ciencia*); sucursal; bifurcación; sección; tributario (*de un río*); ramificación; — **railway** ramal; *v.* ramificarse; bifurcarse.

brand [brænd] *s.* (*make*) marca; marca de fábrica; hechura; (*cattle mark*) hierro; *Riopl., Méx.* fierro (*de marcar*);estigma; **brand-new** nuevecito, flamante, acabado de hacer o comprar; *v.* marcar! herrar, marcar (*con hierro candente*); difamar; **to** — **as** motejar de.

bran·dish [brǽndɪʃ] *v.* blandir; *s.* floreo, molinete.

bran·dy [brǽndɪ] *s.* aguardiente; coñac.

brash [bræʃ] *adj.* insolente; impetuoso; temerario.

brass [bræs] *s.* (*metal*) latón, bronce; (*actitud*) desfachatez, descaro; **-es** utensilios de latón; instrumentos músicos de metal; — **band** banda murga.

bras·siere [brəzír] *s.* corpiño, sostén (*para ceñir los pechos*).

brat [bræt] *s.* mocoso.

bra·va·do [brəvádo] *s.* bravata; jactancia.

brave [brev] *adj.* bravo, valiente, valeroso; *v.* arrostrar; desafiar, hacer frente a.

brav·ery [brévərɪ] *s.* valor, valentía.

brawl [brɔl] *v.* reyerta, pendencia, riña; alboroto; *v.* armar una pendencia, alborotar, reñir.

bray [bre] *s.* rebuzno; *v.* rebuznar.

bra·zen [brézn] *adj.* bronceado; de bronce; de latón; descarado, desvergonzado.

bra·zier [brezjæ] *s.* brasero.

breach [britʃ] *s.* (*opening*) brecha, abertura; (*infraction*) infracción; rompimiento; — **of faith** abuso de confianza; — **of promise** violación de un compromiso; *v.* abrir brecha.

bread [brɛd] *s.* pan; —**box** caja para pan; — **line** cola del pan; *v. Méx., C.A.* empanizar; *Riopl., Ch.* empanar.

breadth [brɛdθ] *s.* anchura, ancho; extensión; amplitud.

break [brek] *s.* rompimiento; rotura; interrupción; pausa; bajón (*en la bolsa o mercado*); **to have a bad (good)** — tener mala (buena) suerte; **to make a bad** — cometer un disparate; *v.* romper(se), quebrantar(se), quebrar(se); amansar, domar; arruinar; **to** — **away** fugarse, escaparse; **to** — **into** forzar la entrada en, allanar (*una morada*); **to** — **loose** escaparse, desprenderse, soltarse; **to** — **out** estallar (*una guerra*); **to** — **out of prison** escaparse de la cárcel; **to** — **a promise** faltar a la palabra; **to** — **up** desmenuzar, despedazar; disolver; perturbar.

break·a·ble [brékəbl] *adj.* quebradizo.

break·down [brékdaʊn] *s.* parada imprevista; análisis. (*automobile*) avería, pane.

break·er [brékæ] *s.* rompiente (*ola*); **law** — infractor.

break·fast [brékfəst] *s.* desayuno; **to eat** — tomar el desayuno; *v.* desayunarse.

break·through [brékθru] *s.* adelanto repentino; brecha.

break·wa·ter [brékwɔtæ] *s.* rompeolas, malecón.

breast [brɛst] *s.* pecho; seno; teta; pechuga (*de ave*); **to make a clean** — **of it** confesarlo todo.

breath [brɛθ] *s.* aliento; resuello; respiro; soplo, hálito; **in the same** — al mismo instante, con el mismo aliento; **out of** — sin aliento, jadeando; **under one's** — en voz baja, entre dientes.

breathe [brið] *v.* respirar; resollar; tomar aliento; exhalar; **to** — **into** infundir; **he** *-ed* **his last** exhaló el último suspiro; **he did not** — **a word**

no dijo palabra.
breath·less [beέθlɪs] *adj.* jadeante; sin aliento.
breath·tak·ing [bréθtekɪŋ] *adj.* conmovedor;
emocionante.
bred [brɛd] *pret.* & *p.p. de* **to breed.**
breech·es [brítʃɪz] *s. pl.* bragas, calzones; **riding —**
pantalones de montar.
breed [brid] *s.* casta, raza; ralea, especie; *v.* criar;
procrear, engendrar; educar; producirse;
multiplicarse.
breed·er [brídɚ] *s.* criador; animal de cría.
breed·ing [brídɪŋ] *s.* cría, crianza; educación,
modales.
breeze [briz] *s.* brisa, vientecillo.
breez·y [brízɪ] *adj.* airoso, ventilado; refrescado
(*por la brisa*); animado, vivaz; **it is —** hace
brisa.
breth·ren [brέðrɪn] *s. pl.* hermanos (*los fieles de
una iglesia o los miembros de una sociedad*).
brev·i·ty [brέvətɪ] *s.* brevedad.
brew [bru] *s.* cerveza; mezcla; *v.* fermentar, hacer
(*licores*); preparar (*té*); fomentar, tramar;
fabricar cerveza; amenazar (*una tormenta,
calamidad etc.*).
brew·er·y [brúərɪ] *s.* cervecería, fábrica de cerveza.
bri·ar, bri·er [bráɪɚ] *s.* zarza; rosal silvestre.
bribe [braɪb] *s.* soborno, cohecho; *v.* sobornar,
cohechar.
brib·er·y [bráɪbərɪ] *s.* soborno, choecho.
brick [brɪk] *s.* ladrillo; ladrillos; *v.* enladrillar.
brick·bat [bríkbæt] *s.* pedazo de ladrillo; insulto.
bri·dal [bráɪdl] *adj.* nupcial; de bodas; de novia;
— dress vestido de novia.
bride [braɪd] *s.* novia, desposada.
bride·groom [bráɪdgrum] *s.* novio, desposado.
brides·maid [bráɪdzmed] *s.* madrina de boda.
bridge [brɪdʒ] *a.* puente; caballete de la nariz;
draw — puente levadizo; **suspension —** puente
colgante; *v.* tender un puente; **to — a gap** llenar
un vacío.
bri·dle [bráɪdl] *s.* brida, freno de caballo; freno,
restricción; **— path** camino de harradura; *v.*
embridar, enfrenar; reprimir, subyugar; erguirse,
erguir la cabeza.
brief [brif] *adj.* breve, corto, conciso; *s.* sumario,
resumen; informe, memorial; breve apostólico;
to hold a — for abogar por; **-ly** *adv.*
brevemente; en resumen, en breve.
brief·case [brífkes] *s.* portapapeles, cartera grande.
brief·ing [brifɪŋ] *s.* reunión preparatoria.
bri·gade [brɪgéd] *s.* brigada.
bright [braɪt] *adj.* (*light*) brillante, claro, luciente;
radiante; (*smart*) inteligente; (*cheerful*) alegre;
listo, vivo; **— color** color subido.
bright·en [bráɪtn] *v.* abrillantar, pulir, dar lustre;
avivar(se); alegrar(se); animar(se); aclararse,
despejarse (*el cielo*).
bright·ness [bráɪtnɪs] *s.* brillo, lustre, esplendor;
claridad; viveza, agudeza, inteligencia.
bril·liance [bríljəns] *s.* brillantez, brillo; lustre;
resplandor.
bril·liant [bríljənt] *adj.* brillante; resplandeciente;
espléndido; talentoso; *s.* brillante; diamante.
brim [brɪm] *s.* borde, margen, orilla; ala (*de
sombrero*); **to fill to the —** llenar o arrasar hasta
el borde; **to be filled to the —** estar hasta los
topes; estar de bote en bote; *v.* **to — over**
rebosar.
brine [braɪn] *s.* salmuera.
bring [brɪŋ] *v.* traer; llevar; ocasionar, causar;
to — about producir, efectuar, ocasionar; **to —**

down bajar; **to — forth** dar a luz; producir;
to — to resucitar; **to — up** criar, educar; **to —
up a subject** traer a discusión un asunto.
brink [brɪŋk] *s.* borde, orilla, margen; **on the — of**
al borde de.
brisk [brɪsk] *adj.* vivo, animado; fuerte; rápido;
-ly *adv.* aprisa; fuerte.
bris·tle [brɪsl] *s.* creda; *v.* erizar(se); **to — with**
estar erizado (*o lleno*) de.
bris·tly [brɪslɪ] *adj.* serdoso; erizado.
Brit·ish [brítɪʃ] *adj.* británico; **the —** los ingleses.
brit·tle [brítl] *adj.* quebradizo; frágil.
broach [brotʃ] *v.* tracer a colación, comenzar a
hablar de (*un asunto*).
broad [brɔd] *adj.* ancho; amplio, vasto, extenso;
tolerante; **— hint** insinuación clara; **in —
daylight** en pleno día; **broad-minded** tolerante;
de amplias miras.
broad·cast [brɔ́dkæst] *s.* radiodifusión, difusión,
emisión; transmisión; *v.* difundir; radiodifundir,
radiar, emitir.
broad·cloth [brɔ́dklɔθ] *s.* paño fino de algodón o
de lana.
broad jump [brɔ́ddʒəmp] *s.* salto de longitud.
broad·side [brɔ́dsaɪd] *s.* (*guns*) andanada;
(*announcement*) hoja suelta de propaganda.
bro·cade [brokéd] *s.* brocado.
broil [brɔil] *v.* asar(se).
broke [brok] *pret. de* **to break;** *adj.* quebrado,
arruinado; pelado, sin dinero; **to go —** quebrar,
arruinarse.
bro·ken [brókən] *p.p. de* **to break** & *adj.* roto;
rompido; quebrado; quebrantado; arruinado;
abatido; **— English** inglés champurrado o
champurreado; inglés mal pronunciado.
bro·ker [brókɚ] *s.* corredor, agente; bolsista;
money — cambista, corredor de cambio.
bro·mide [brómaɪd] *s.* bromuro.
bro·mine [brómin] *s.* bromo.
bron·chi·tis [brankáɪtɪs] *s.* bronquitis.
bron·co, bron·cho [bráŋko] *s.* potro o caballo
bronco, *Ríopl.* redomón; **— buster** domador.
bronze [branz] *s.* bronce; color de bronce; *v.*
broncear.
brooch [brutʃ] *s.* broche (*alfiler de pecho*).
brood [brud] *s.* pollada; nidada; cría; casta; *v.*
empollar; encobar; **to — over** cavilar.
brook [brʊk] *s.* arroyuelo, riachuelo, *C.A., Col.,
Ven.* quebrada; *Méx., Ríopl.* arroyo, cañada; *v.*
tolerar, aguantar.
broom [brum] *s.* escoba; retama (*arbusto*); **—stick**
palo o mango de escoba.
broth [brɔθ] *s.* caldo.
broth·er [brʌ́ðɚ]s. hermano; cofrade.
broth·er·hood [brʌ́ðɚhʊd] *s.* hermandad;
fraternidad; cofradía.
broth·er-in-law [brʌ́ðərɪnlɔ] *s.* cuñado.
broth·er·ly [brʌ́ðɚlɪ] *adj.* fraternal.
brought [brɔt] *pret. & p.p. de* **to bring.**
brow [braʊ] *s.* ceja; frente.
brown [braʊn] *adj.* moreno; café; castaño; pardo
oscuro; tostado; *v.* tostar(se).
browse [braʊz] *v.* hojear; ramonear, pacer, pastar
(*el ganado*).
bruise [bruz] *s.* magulladura, cardenal, magullón,
contusión; *v.* magullar(se); estropear(se).
bru·net, bru·nette [brunét] *adj.* moreno, atrigueño.
brunt [brʌnt] *s.* fuerza (*de un golpe o ataque*); **the
— of the battle** lo más reñido del combate.
brush [brʌʃ] *s.* (*tooth, clothes*) cepillo; (*paint,
shaving*) brocha; (*artist's*) pincel; (*vegetation*)

matorral; (*contact*) roce; encuentro; *v.* cepillar,
acepillar; rozar; **to — aside** desechar, echar a un
lado; **to — up** cepillarse; repasar (*una materia,
una técnica, etc.*).
brush·wood [brʌʃwʊd] *s.* broza; maleza, matorral,
zarzal.
brusque [brʌsk] *adj.* brusco.
bru·tal [brútl] *adj.* brutal, bruto.
bru·tal·i·ty [brutǽlɪtɪ] *s.* brutalidad.
brute [brut] *s.* bruto, bestia; *adj.* bruto, brutal;
bestial.
bub·ble [bʌbl] *s.* burbuja; borbollón; ampolla; *v.*
borbotar; hacer espuma; bullir; **to — over with
joy** rebosar de gozo.
bub·ble gum [bʌbl gʌm] *s.* chicle hinchable; chicle
de globo.
buck [bʌk] *s.* macho cabrío, cabrón; gamo; macho
(*del ciervo, antílope, etc.*); corveta, respingo (*de
un caballo*); embestida; **— private** soldado raso;
to pass the — Ríopl., Andes pasar el fardo; *v.*
cabriolear, respingar; embestir; encabritarse;
bregar con (*el viento*); **to — up** cobrar ánimo;
the horse -ed the rider el caballo tiró al jinete.
buck·et [bʌkɪt] *s.* cubo, cubeta, balde.
buck·le [bʌkl] *s.* hebilla; *v.* abrochar con hebilla;
doblarse; abollarse; **to — down to** aplicarse con
empeño a; **to — with** luchar con.
buck·shot [bʌkʃat] *s.* posta, perdigón.
buck·skin [bʌkskɪn] *s.* badana; ante.
buck·wheat [bʌkhwit] *s.* trigo sarraceno.
bud [bʌd] *s.* botón, yema; capullo, pimpollo;
retoño; *v.* echar botones o retoños; florecer.
bud·dy [bʌdɪ] *s.* camarada, compañero.
budge [bʌdʒ] *v.* mover(se), menear(se), bullir.
bud·get [bʌdʒɪt] *s.* presupuesto.
buff [bʌf] *s.* piel de ante o búfalo; color de ante;
pulidor; **blindman's —** juego de la gallina ciega;
v. pulir, pulimentar.
buf·fa·lo [bʌflo] *s.* búfalo.
buf·fet [bʌfé] *s.* aparador; repostería; mostrador
para refrescos; fonda de estación.
buf·fet·ing [bʌfǝtɪŋ] *s.* golpeteo, bataneo.
buf·foon [bʌfún] *s.* bufón; payaso.
bug [bʌg] *s.* insecto; bicho; microbio.
bug·gy [bʌgɪ] *s.* cochecillo.
bu·gle [bjúgl] *s.* clarín; corneta; trompeta.
build [bɪld] *s.* estructura; talle, forma, hechura; *v.*
edificar, construir; fabricar; **to — up one's health**
reconstituir su salud.
build·er [bɪldɚ] *s.* constructor.
build·ing [bɪldɪŋ] *s.* edificio; construcción.
build-up [bɪldʌp] *s.* refuerzo paulatino.
built [bɪlt] *pret. & p.p. de* **to build.**
bulb [bʌlb] *s.* bulbo (*de la cebolla y otras
plantas*); planta bulbosa; **electric light —**
bombilla, bujía eléctrica, ampolla, *Méx., C.A.,
Andes* foco; *Ríopl.* bombita.
bulge [bʌldʒ] *s.* bulto; protuberancia; panza; *v.*
abultar; combarse.
bulg·y [bʌldʒɪ] *adj.* abultado.
bulk [bʌlk] *s.* bulto, volumen; masa; **the — of the
army** el grueso del ejército.
bulk·y [bʌlkɪ] *adj.* abultado, voluminoso, grueso.
bull [bʊl] *s.* toro; alcista (*el que hace subir los
valores en la bolsa*); disparate, error; **Papal —**
bula; **—fight** corrida de toros; *adj.* taurino;
—fighter torero; **bull's-eye** centro del blanco;
tiro perfecto.
bull·dog [bʊldɔg] *s.* perro dogo, perro de presa.
bull·doz·er [bʊldozɚ] *s.* topadora; buldózer.
bul·let [bʊlɪt] *s.* bala.

bul·le·tin [bʊlǝtn] *s.* boletín; **— board** tablilla para
fijar anuncios o avisos.
bull·frog [bʊlfrag] *s.* rana grande.
bull·head·ed [bʊlhédɪd] *adj.* terco, obstinado.
bul·lion [bʊljǝn] *s.* oro (*o plata*) en barras;
metálico; lingotes de oro o plata.
bul·ly [bʊlɪ] *s.* pendenciero, valentón, fanfarrón,
matón; *adj.* excelente, magnífico; *v.* intimidar;
echar bravatas.
bul·wark [bʊlwɚk] *s.* baluarte; defensa.
bum [bʌm] *s.* holgazán, vagabundo; gorrón;
borracho; **to go on a —** irse de juerga; *adj.*
malo, mal hecho, de ínfima calidad; inútil,
inservible; **to feel —** estar indispuesto; *v.*
holgazanear; vivir de gorra.
bum·ble·bee [bʌmblbi] *s.* abejorro, abejón.
bump [bʌmp] *s.* (*blow*) tope, choque; golpe; (*lump*)
chichón; abolladura; hinchazón; joroba,
protuberancia; *v.* topar, topetear; chocar;
abollar; **to — along** zarandearse, ir
zarandeándose; **to — off** derribar; matar.
bump·er [bʌmpɚ] *s.* parachoques, defensa; tope;
adj. grande, excelente; **— crop** cosecha
abundante.
bun [bʌn] *s.* bollo (*de pan*).
bunch [bʌntʃ] *s.* manojo, puñado; racimo (*de uvas,
plátanos, etc.*); grupo; **— of flowers** ramillete de
flores; *v.* juntar(se), agrupar(se).
bun·dle [bʌndl] *s.* lío, bulto, fardo, hato; haz;
paquete; *v.* liar, atar; envolver; **to — up**
abrigarse, taparse bien.
bun·ga·low [bʌŋgǝlo] *s.* casita de un piso.
bun·gle [bʌŋgl] *v.* chapucear; estropear; echar a
perder.
bun·ion [bʌnjǝn] *s.* juanete.
bunk [bʌŋk] *s.* litera, camilla (*fija en la pared*);
embuste, tontería, paparrucha, papa.
bun·ny [bʌnɪ] *s.* conejito.
buoy [bɔɪ] *s.* boya; *v.* boyar, mantener a flote;
to — up sostener, apoyar.
buoy·ant [bɔɪǝnt] *adj.* boyante, flotante; vivaz,
animado, alegre.
bur·den [bɝdn] *s.* carga, peso; cuidado; gravamen;
v. cargar; agobiar.
bur·den·some [bɝdnsǝm] *adj.* gravoso; pesado.
bu·reau [bjúro] *s.* oficina; despacho; división,
ramo; cómoda; **travel —** oficina de turismo;
weather — oficina de meteorología, observatorio
meteorológico.
bu·reauc·ra·cy [bjurákrǝsɪ] *s.* burocracia.
bu·reau·crat [bjúrǝkræt] *s.* burócrata.
bur·glar [bɝglɚ] *s.* ladrón (*que se mete en casa
ajena*).
bur·gla·ry [bɝglǝrɪ] *s.* robo.
bur·i·al [bérɪǝl] *s.* entierro; **— place** cementerio.
bur·lap [bɝlæp] *s.* arpillera, tela burda de cáñamo.
bur·ly [bɝlɪ] *adj.* corpulento, voluminoso, grandote.
burn [bɝn] *s.* quemadura; *v.* quemar(se); incendiar;
arder; abrasar(se).
burn·er [bɝnɚ] *s.* quemador; mechero; hornilla.
bur·nish [bɝnɪʃ] *v.* bruñir; pulir; *s.* bruñido,
pulimento.
burnt [bɝnt] *pret. & p.p. de* **to burn.**
bur·row [bɝo] *s.* madriguera, conejera; *v.* hacer
madrigueras en; escarbar; socavar, minar;
esconderse.
burst [bɝst] *s.* reventón, explosión; estallido; **— of
laughter** carcajada; *v.* reventar(se); abrirse;
estallar; **to — into** entrar de repente; **to — into
tears** prorrumpir en lágrimas; **to — with
laughter** estallar o reventar de risa; *pret. & p.p.*

de **to burst.**

bur·y [bérɪ] *v.* enterrar; sepultar; soterrar; **to be buried in thought** estar absorto, meditabundo o pensativo.

bus [bʌs] *s.* autobús, ómnibus, *Méx.* camión; *C.A.* camioneta; *Ríopl.* colectivo; *Ch.* micro; *Carib.* guagua.

bus·boy [básbɔɪ] *s.* ayudante de camarero.

bush [buʃ] *s.* arbusto; mata; matorral, breñal; **rose** — rosal; **to beat around the** — andarse por las ramas.

bush·el [búʃəl] *s.* fanega *(medida de áridos).*

bush·ing [búʃɪŋ] *s.* buje.

bush·y [búʃɪ] *adj.* matoso, espeso; lleno de arbustos.

bus·i·ly [bízlɪ] *adv.* diligentemente.

busi·ness [bíznɪs] *s.* negocio; ocupación; comercio; asunto; — **house** casa de comercio, establecimiento mercantil; — **transaction** negocio, transacción comercial; **to do — with** negociar con, comerciar con; **he has no — doing it** no tiene derecho a hacerlo; **not to be one's** — no concernirle a uno, no importarle a uno; **to make a — deal** hacer un trato.

busi·ness·like [bíznɪslaɪk] *adj.* eficaz, eficiente, práctico; formal.

busi·ness·man [bíznɪsmæn] *s.* hombre de negocios, comerciante.

bust [bʌst] *s.* busto; pecho *(de mujer)*; **to go out on a** — salir o ir de parranda; *v.* reventar; quebrar; domar *(un potro).*

bus·tle [bʌsl] *s.* bulla, bullicio, trajín, alboroto; polisón *(para abultar las caderas)*; *v.* bullir(se); menearse; trajinar.

bus·y [bízɪ] *adj.* ocupado; activo; —**body** entremetido; — **street** calle de mucho tráfico; *v.* **to — oneself** ocuparse.

but [bʌt] *conj., prep. & adv.* pero, mas; sino; menos, excepto; sólo, no ... más que; — **for you** a no ser por Vd.; **not only ... — also** no sólo ... sino (que) también; **I cannot help** — no puedo menos de; **she is — a child** no es más que una niña.

bu·tane [bjutén] *s.* butano.

butch·er [bútʃɚ] *s.* carnicero; -**'s shop** carnicería; *v.* matar *(reses)*; hacer una matanza o carnicería; destrozar.

butch·er·y [bútʃɚɪ] *s.* carnicería, matanza.

but·ler [bátlɚ] *s.* despensero, mayordomo; -**'s pantry** despensa.

butt [bʌt] *s.* culata *(de rifle)*; colilla *(de cigarro)*; tope; topetazo; cabezada; **the — of ridicule** el blanco de las burlas; *v.* topetear, embestir; **to — in** entremeterse; **to — into a conversation** meter baza, *Am.* meter su cuchara.

but·ter [bátɚ] *s.* manteca, mantequilla; *v.* enmantecar, untar con manteca o mantequilla.

but·ter·cup [bátɚkʌp] *s.* botón de oro *(flor).*

but·ter·fly [bátɚflaɪ] *s.* mariposa; — **stroke** brazada mariposa.

but·ter·milk [bátɚmɪlk] *s.* suero de mantequilla.

but·ter·scotch [bátɚskátʃ] *s.* confite o jarabe de azúcar y mantequilla.

but·tocks [bátəks] *s. pl.* nalgas, asentaderas.

but·ton [bátn] *s.* botón; — **hook** abotonador; *v.* abotonar(se).

but·ton·hole [bátnhol] *s.* ojal; *v.* hacer ojales; **to — someone** detener, demorar a uno *(charlando).*

but·tress [bátrɪs] *s.* contrafuerte; refuerzo, sostén; *v.* sostener, reforzar, poner contrafuerte.

buy [baɪ] *v.* comprar; **to — off** sobornar; **to — up**

acaparar.

buy·er [báɪɚ] *s.* comprador.

buzz [bʌz] *s.* zumbido; murmullo; *v.* zumbar; murmurar; **to — the bell** tocar el timbre.

buz·zard [bázɚd] *s.* buitre, *Am.* aura, *Méx., C.A.* zopilote, *Ríopl.* carancho; *Col., Andes* gallinazo.

by [baɪ] *prep.* por; cerca de; al lado de; junto a; según; — **and** — luego, pronto; — **dint of a** fuerza de; — **far** con mucho; — **night** de noche; — **the way** de paso; a propósito; entre paréntesis; — **this time** ya; a la hora de ésta; — **two o'clock** para las dos; **days gone** — días pasados.

by·gone [báɪgɔn] *adj.* pasado; **let -s be -s** lo pasado pasado, lo pasado pisado.

by·law [báɪlɔ] *s.* estatuto; reglamento.

by·pass [báɪpæs] *s.* desviación.

by·path [báɪpæθ] *s.* atajo, vereda.

by·prod·uct [báɪprɑdəkt] *s.* producto secundario o accessorio.

by·stand·ers [báɪstændɚz] *s.* circunstantes, presentes; mirones.

C:c **cab** [kæb] *s.* coche de alquiler; taxímetro, taxi; casilla *(de una locomotora)*; — **driver** cochero; chófer.

cab·bage [kǽbɪdʒ] *s.* col, repollo, berza.

cab·in [kǽbɪn] *s.* cabaña, choza; bohío, *Mex.* jacal; *Carib.* barraca; camarote *(de buque)*; **airplane** — cabina de aeroplano.

cab·i·net [kǽbənɪt] *s.* gabinete; armario; escaparate, vitrina; *(dept. heads)* gabinete.

cab·i·net·ma·ker [kǽbənɪtmékɚ] *s.* ebanista.

ca·ble [kébl] *s.* cable, amarra; cablegrama; — **address** dirección cablegráfica; *v.* cablegrafiar.

ca·ble·gram [kébl|græm] *s.* cablegrama.

cab·man [kǽbmən] *s.* cochero; chófer.

cack·le [kǽkl] *s.* cacareo; charla; risotada; *v.* cacarear; parlotear, charlar.

cac·tus [kǽktəs] *(pl.* **cacti** [kǽktaɪ]*) s.* cacto.

cad [kæd] *s.* canalla *(m.)*; malcriado.

cad·die [kǽdɪ] *s.* muchacho que lleva los palos de golf; caddy.

ca·dence [kédn̩s] *s.* cadencia.

ca·det [kədét] *s.* cadete.

cad·mi·um [kǽdmɪəm] *s.* cadmio.

ca·fé [kǽfé] *s.* café, restaurante.

caf·e·te·ri·a [kæfətírɪə] *s.* restaurante *(en donde uno sirve uno mismo).*

caf·fein [kǽfiɪn] *·s.* cafeína.

cage [kedʒ] *s.* jaula; *v.* enjaular.

ca·jole [kədʒól] *v.* halagar para conseguir algo.

cake [kek] *s.* pastel; bizcocho; bollo; torta; *Ven., Col.* panqué; pastilla *(de jabón)*; — **of ice** témpano de hielo; *v.* apelmazarse, formar masa compacta.

cal·a·bash [kǽləbæʃ] *s.* totuma.

ca·lam·i·ty [kəlǽmətɪ] *s.* calamidad.

cal·ci·um [kǽlsɪəm] *s.* calcio.

cal·cu·late [kǽlkjəlet] *v.* calcular; **to — on** contar con.

cal·cu·la·tion [kælkjəléʃən] *s.* cálculo; cómputo, cuenta.

cal·cu·lus [kǽlkjələs] *s.* cálculo.

cal·en·dar [kǽləndɚ] *s.* calendario, almanaque; — **year** año corriente.

calf [kæf] *(pl.* **calves** [kævz]*) s.* ternero, ternera,

becerro, becerra; pantorrilla (*de la pierna*); —
skin piel de becerro o becerrillo.
cal·i·ber [kǽləbɚ] *s.* calibre.
cal·i·co [kǽləko] *s.* calicó (*tela de algodón*).
call [kɔl] *s.* (*summons*) llamada; llamamiento; (*visit*)
visita; (*demand*) demanda, pedido; **within** — al
alcance de la voz; *v.* llamar; gritar; hacer una
visita; pasar (*lista*); **to** — **at a port** hacer escala
en un puerto; **to** — **for** ir por; demandar,
pedir; **to** — **on** visitar a; acudir a (*en busca de
auxilio*); **to** — **to order a meeting** abrir la sesión;
to — **together** convocar; **to** — **up on the phone**
llamar por teléfono.
cal·ler [kɔ́lɚ] *s.* visita, visitante; llamador (*el que
llama*).
cal·lous [kǽləs] *adj.* calloso; duro.
cal·lus [kǽləs] *s.* callo.
calm [kɑm] *s.* calma; sosiego; *adj.* calmo,
tranquilo, quieto, sosegado; *v.* calmar,
tranquilizar, sosegar; desenfadar; **to** — **down**
calmarse; **-ly** *adv.* tranquilamente, con calma.
calm·ness [kámnɪs] *s.* calma, sosiego, tranquilidad.
cal·o·rie [kǽlərɪ] *s.* caloría.
cal·um·ny [kǽləmnɪ] *s.* calumnia.
cam [kæm] *s.* leva.
came [kem] *pret. de* **to come.**
cam·el [kǽml] *s.* camello.
cam·e·o [kǽmɪo] *s.* camafeo.
cam·er·a [kǽmərə] *s.* cámara fotográfica.
cam·ou·flage [kǽməflaʒ] *s.* camuflaje; disfraz; *v.*
encubrir, disfrazar.
camp [kæmp] *s.* campo, campamento; — **chair**
silla de tijera; **political** — partido político; *v.*
acampar.
cam·paign [kæmpén] *s.* campaña; *v.* hacer
campaña; hacer propaganda.
cam·phor [kǽmfɚ] *s.* alcanfor.
cam·pus [kǽmpəs] *s.* campo (*de una universidad*).
can [kæn] *s.* lata, bote, envase; — **opener** abrelatas;
v. envasar, enlatar; *v. defect. y aux.* (*usado sólo
en las formas* **can** *y* **could**) poder, saber.
Ca·na·di·an [kənédiən] *adj. & s.* canadiense.
ca·nal [kənǽl] *s.* canal; **irrigation** — acequia.
ca·nar·y [kənɛ́rɪ] *s.* canario.
can·cel [kǽnsl] *v.* cancelar; anular; revocar; techar.
can·cel·er [kǽnsələ] *s.* matasellos.
can·cel·la·tion [kænslé∫ən] *s.* cancelación;
anulación; revocación.
can·cer [kǽnsɚ] *s.* cáncer.
can·de·la·brum [kændəlǽbrəm] *s.* candelabro.
can·did [kǽndɪd] *adj.* cándido, franco, sincero.
can·di·da·cy [kǽndədəsɪ] *s.* candidatura.
can·di·date [kǽndədet] *s.* candidato; aspirante.
can·dle [kǽndl] *s.* candela, vela; bujía; cirio; —
power potencia lumínica (*en bujías*).
can·dle·stick [kǽndlstɪk] *s.* candelero; palmatoria.
can·dor [kǽndɚ] *s.* candor, sinceridad.
can·dy [kǽndɪ] *s.* dulce, confite, bombón; — **shop**
confitería, dulcería; *v.* confitar, azucarar;
almibarar, garapiñar; cristalizarse (*el almíbar*);
candied almonds almendras garapiñadas.
cane [ken] *s.* caña; — **plantation** (*o* —**field**)
cañaveral; *C.A.* cañal; — **chair** silla de bejuco;
sugar — caña de azúcar; **walking** — bastón;
chuzo (*de sereno*); **to beat with a** — bastonear,
apalear.
ca·nine [kénaɪn] *adj.* canino, perruno.
can·ker [kǽnkɚ] *s.* úlcera, llaga (*de la boca*).
canned [kǽnd] *adj.* enlatado, envasado, conservado
(*en lata o en vidrio*); — **goods** conservas
alimenticias.

can·ner·y [kǽnərɪ] *s.* fábrica de conservas
alimenticias.
can·ni·bal [kǽnəbl] *s.* caníbal.
can·non [kǽnən] *s.* cañón.
can·non·ade [kænənéd] *s.* cañoneo; *v.* cañonear.
can·not [kǽnɑt] = **can not** no puedo, no puede, no
podemos, etc.
can·ny [kǽnɪ] *adj.* sagaz; astuto.
ca·noe [kənú] *s.* canoa, *Riopl.* piragua, *Méx.*
chalupa.
can·on [kǽnən] *s.* canon; ley, regla; criterio,
norma; canónigo.
can·o·py [kǽnəpɪ] *s.* dosel, pabellón; (*airplane*)
capota, cúpula.
can·ta·loupe [kǽntlop] *s.* melón.
can·teen [kæntín] *s.* cantina; cantimplora.
can·ton [kǽntən] *s.* cantón, región, distrito.
can·vas [kǽnvəs] *s.* lona; lienzo; toldo; cañamazo.
can·vass [kǽnvəs] *s.* inspección; escrutinio;
indagación, encuesta, pesquisa; solicitación (*de
votos*); *v.* examinar, escudriñar; recorrer (*un
distrito solicitando algo*); hacer una encuesta;
solicitar votos o pedidos comerciales.
can·yon [kǽnjən] *s.* cañón, garganta.
cap [kæp] *s.* (*head covering*) gorro, gorra, boina;
Méx. cachucha; (*academic*) birrete; (*bottle*,
wheel) tapa, tapón; (*mountain*) cima, cumbre;
percussion — cápsula fulminante; *v.* tapar,
poner tapón a; **that -s the climax** eso es el
colmo.
ca·pa·bil·i·ty [kepəbíləti] *s.* capacidad, aptitud.
ca·pa·ble [képəbl] *adj.* capaz; hábil; competente.
ca·pa·cious [kəpé∫əs] *adj.* capaz, amplio, espacioso.
ca·pac·i·ty [kəpǽsətɪ] *s.* capacidad; cabida;
habilidad; aptitud; **in the** — **of a teacher** en
calidad de maestro.
cape [kep] *s.* capa; capote; cabo, promontorio.
ca·per [képɚ] *s.* cabriola; voltereta, brinco; **to cut
-s** cabriolar, retozar, hacer travesuras; *v.*
cabriolar, retozar, juguetear, brincar.
cap·il·lar·y [kǽpɪlɛrɪ] *s. & adj.* capilar.
cap·i·tal [kǽpətl] *s.* capital (*f.*), ciudad principal;
capital (*m.*), caudal; chapitel (*de una columna*);
letra mayúscula; **to make** — **of** sacar partido
de, aprovecharse de; *adj.* capital; principal;
excelente; —**punishment** pena capital, pena de
muerte.
cap·i·tal·ism [kǽpətlɪzəm] *s.* capitalismo.
cap·i·tal·ist [kǽpətlɪst] *s.* capitalista; **-ic** *adj.*
capitalista.
cap·i·tal·i·za·tion [kæpətləzéfən] *s.* capitalización.
cap·i·tal·ize [kǽpətlaɪz] *v.* capitalizar; sacar
provecho (de); escribir con mayúscula.
cap·i·tol [kǽpətl] *s.* capitolio.
ca·pit·u·late [kəpít∫əlet] *v.* capitular.
ca·price [kəprís] *s.* capricho.
ca·pri·cious [kəprí∫əs] *adj.* caprichoso.
cap·size [kǽpsaɪz] *v.* zozobrar, volcar(se).
cap·sule [kǽpsl] *s.* cápsula.
cap·tain [kǽptɪn] *s.* capitán; *v.* capitanear, mandar;
servir de capitán.
cap·ti·vate [kǽptəvet] *v.* cautivar.
cap·tive [kǽptɪv] *s. & adj.* cautivo, prisionero.
cap·tiv·i·ty [kæptívətɪ] *s.* cautiverio, prisión.
cap·tor [kǽptɚ] *s.* aprehensor o aprensor.
cap·ture [kǽpt∫ɚ] *s.* captura; aprensión; presa;
toma; *v.* capturar; prender; tomar (*una ciudad*).
car [kɑr] *s.* coche, automóvil, auto, *Am.* carro;
(*de ferrocarril*); camarín (*de ascensor*), ascensor,
Am. elevador; **dining** — coche comedor; **freight**
— furgón, vagón de carga.

car·a·mel [kǽrəml] *s.* caramelo.
car·at [kǽrət] *s.* quilate.
car·a·van [kǽrəvæn] *s.* caravana.
car·bol·ic [karbálık] *adj.* carbólico.
car·bon [kárbən] *s.* carbono; — **copy** copia en papel carbón; — **paper** papel carbón; — **monoxide** monóxido de carbono; — **dioxide** dióxido de carbono.
car·bu·re·tor [kárbəretəʳ] *s.* carburador.
car·cass [kárkəs] *s.* esqueleto; cuerpo descarnado, despojo; res (*muerta*); casco (*de un buque*).
card [kard] *s.* (*missive*) tarjeta; (*playing*) naipe, carta; carda (*para cardar lana*); — **index** índice de fichas; fichero; —**sharp** fullero; **file** — ficha, papeleta; **post**— tarjeta postal; **pack of -s** baraja, naipes; **to play -s** jugar a la baraja, jugar a los naipes; *v.* cardar (*lana*).
card·board [kárdbord] *s.* cartón; **fine** — cartulina.
car·di·ac [kárdıæk] *adj.* cardiaco, cardíaco.
car·di·nal [kárdɳəl] *adj.* cardinal; principal, fundamental; rojo, bermellón; — **number** número cardinal; *s.* cardenal (*dignatario eclesiástico*); — **bird** cardenal.
care [kɛr] *s.* (*worry*) cuidado; aflección; ansiedad; (*caution*) cuidado, cautela, esmero; (*responsibility*) cargo, custodia; **to take** — **of** cuidar de; *v.* tener interés (por); **to** — **about** tener interés en (*o* por); preocuparse de; importarle a uno; **to** — **for** cuidar de; estimar, tenerle cariño a; gustarle a uno; simpatizarle a uno (*una persona*); **to** — **to** querer, desear, tener ganas de; **what does he** —? ¿a él qué le importa?
ca·reen [kərín] *v.* moverse con rapidez y sin control; volcar (*un buque*).
ca·reer [kərír] *s.* carrera, profesión.
care·free [kɛ́rfri] *adj.* libre de cuidado, sin cuidados, despreocupado.
care·ful [kɛ́rfəl] *adj.* cuidadoso; esmerado; cauteloso; **to be** — tener cuidado; **-ly** *adv.* cuidadosamente, con cuidado; con esmero.
care·ful·ness [kɛ́rfəlnɪs] *s.* cuidado; esmero; cautela.
care·less [kɛ́rlɪs] *adj.* descuidado; negligente; indiferente; **-ly** *adv.* sin cuidado; sin esmero; descuidadamente.
care·less·ness [kɛ́rlɪsnɪs] *s.* descuido; falta de esmero; desaliño; negligencia.
ca·ress [kərɛ́s] *s.* caricia; *v.* acariciar.
care·tak·er [kɛ́rtekəʳ] *s.* cuidador, guardián, vigilante, celador.
car·fare [kárfɛr] *s.* pasaje de tranvía.
car·go [kárgo] *s.* carga, cargamento; flete.
car·i·ca·ture [kǽrɪkətʃəʳ] *s.* caricatura; *v.* caricaturar o caricaturizar.
car·load [kárlod] *s.* furgonada, vagonada, carga de un furgón o vagón.
car·nal [kárn̩] *adj.* carnal.
car·na·tion [karnéʃən] *s.* clavel; color encarnado o rosado.
car·ni·val [kárnəvl̩] *s.* carnaval; fiesta, holgorio; feria, verbena.
car·niv·o·rous [karnívərəs] *adj.* carnívoro, carnicero.
car·ol [kǽrəl] *s.* villancico; **Christmas** — villancico de Navidad; *v.* cantar villancicos; celebrar con villancicos.
car·om [kǽrəm] *s.* carambola; rebote.
ca·rouse [kəráʊz] *v.* andar de parranda, *Ríopl.*, *Ch.* andar de farra; embriagarse.
car·pen·ter [kárpəntəʳ] *s.* carpintero.

car·pen·try [kárpəntrɪ] *s.* carpintería.
car·pet [kárpɪt] *s.* alfombra; **small** — tapete; *v.* tapizar.
car·riage [kǽrɪdʒ] *s.* carruaje, coche; acarreo, transporte; porte; — **paid** porte pagado; **good** — buen porte, garbo, manera airosa.
car·ri·er [kǽrɪəʳ] *s.* portador; mensajero; carretero, trajinante; transportador; *Am.* cargador; **airplane** — portaaviones; **disease** — transmisor de gérmenes contagiosos; **mail** — cartero.
car·rot [kǽrət] *s.* zanahoria.
car·ry [kǽrɪ] *v.* llevar; acarrear, transportar; *Am.* cargar; sostener (*una carga*); traer consigo; ganar, lograr (*una elección, un premio, etc.*); **to** — **away** llevarse; cargar con; entusiasmar, encantar; **to** — **on** continuar; no parar; **to** — **oneself well** andar derecho, airoso, garboso; **to** — **out** llevar a cabo, realizar; sacar.
cart [kart] *s.* carro, carreta, vagoncillo; *v.* acarrear.
cart·age [kártɪdʒ] *s.* carretaje, acarreo.
cart·er [kártəʳ] *s.* carretero; àcarreador.
car·ton [kártn̩] *s.* caja de cartón.
car·toon [kartún] *s.* caricatura.
car·toon·ist [kartúnɪst] *s.* caricaturista.
car·tridge [kártrɪdʒ] *s.* cartucho; — **belt** cartuchera canana; — **box** cartuchera; — **shell** cápsula.
carve [karv] *v.* tallar; labrar; cincelar; esculpir; trinchar, tajar (*carne*).
carv·er [kárvəʳ] *s.* trinchador; trinchante (*cuchillo*); entallador, escultor.
carv·ing [kárvɪŋ] *s.* talla, obra de escultura, entalladura; — **knife** trinchante.
cas·cade [kæskéd] *s.* cascada, salto de agua.
case [kes] *s.* (*instance*) caso; (*box*) caja; (*pillow*) funda, cubierta; (*scabbard*) vaina; **window** — marco de ventana; **in** — **that** caso que, en caso de que; **in any** — en todo caso; **just in** — por si acaso; — **work** trabajo con casos.
case·ment [késmənt] *s.* puerta ventana.
cash [kæʃ] *s.* dinero contante; — **box** cofre; — **payment** pago al contado; — **on delivery (c.o.d.)** contra reembolso, cóbrese al entregar; — **register** caja registradora (*de dinero*); **to pay** — pagar al contado; *v.* cambiar, cobrar (*un cheque*).
ca·shew [kǽʃju] *s.* anacardo; marañón.
cash·ier [kæʃír] *s.* cajero.
cask [kæsk] *s.* tonel, barril, cuba.
cas·ket [kǽskɪt] *s.* ataúd; **jewel** — joyero, cofrecillo.
cas·se·role [kǽsərol] *s.* cacerola.
cas·sette [kəsét] *s.* carrete pequeña de cinta magnetofónica; pequeña grabadora.
cas·sock [kǽsək] *s.* sotana.
cast [kæst] *s.* tirada (*al pescar*); molde; matiz; apariencia; defecto (*del ojo*); reparto (*de papeles dramáticos*); actores; — **iron** hierro fundido o colado; *v.* echar; tirar; arrojar; lanzar; moldear; repartir (*papeles dramáticos*); escoger (*para un papel dramático*); **to** — **a ballot** votar; **to** — **a statue in bronze** vaciar una estatua en bronce; **to** — **about** buscar; hacer planes; **to** — **aside** desechar; **to** — **lots** echar suertes; **to be** — **down** estar abatido; *pret. & p.p. de* **to cast.**
cas·ta·nets [kǽstənɛts] *s. pl.* castañuelas.
caste [kæst] *s.* casta; **to lose** — perder el prestigio social.
Cas·til·ian [kæstíljən] *s. & adj.* castellano.
cas·tle [kǽsl̩] *s.* castillo; alcázar; fortaleza; torre, roque (*en ajedrez*).

cas·tor oil [kǽstə ɔıl] *s.* aceite de ricino.
cas·trate [kǽstret] *v.* capar, castrar.
cas·u·al [kǽʒʊəl] *adj.* casual; accidental.
cas·u·al·ty [kǽʒʊəltı] *s.* baja o pérdida (*en el ejército*); accidente.
cat [kæt] *s.* gato; gata.
cat·a·log [kǽtlɔg] *s.* catálogo; *v.* catalogar.
cat·a·lyst [kǽtəlıst] *s.* catalizador.
cat·a·ract [kǽtərækt] *s.* catarata.
ca·tarrh [kətár] *s.* catarro.
ca·tas·tro·phe [kətǽstrəfı] *s.* catástrofe.
catch [kætʃ] *s.* presa; botín; presa; pestillo (*de la puerta*); trampa; cogida (*de la pelota*); — **phrase** frase llamativa; — **question** pregunta tramposa; **he is a good** — es un buen partido; **to play** — jugar a la pelota; *v.* coger; prender; asir; alcanzar; enganchar; comprender; ser contagioso, pegarse; **to — a glimpse of** vislumbrar; **to — cold** coger un resfriado, resfriarse; **to — on** comprender, caer en la cuenta; **to — one's eye** llamarle a uno la atención; **to — sight of** avistar; **to — unaware** sorprender, coger desprevenido; **to — up with** alcanzar a, emparejarse con.
catch·er [kǽtʃə] *s.* cogedor, agarrador; parador, cácher o receptor (*en béisbol*).
catch·ing [kǽtʃıŋ] *adj.* pegajoso, contagioso; atractivo.
cat·e·chism [kǽtəkızəm] *s.* catecismo.
cat·e·go·ry [kǽtəgorı] *s.* categoría.
ca·ter [kétə] *v.*— surtir, abastecer, proveer los alimentos (*para banquetes, fiestas, etc.*) to — **to** proveer a las necesidades o al gusto de; **to — to the taste of** halagar el gusto de.
cat·er·pil·lar [kǽtəpılə] *s.* oruga; — **tractor** tractor.
ca·the·dral [kəθídrəl] *s.* catedral.
cath·ode [kǽθod] *s.* cátodo; — **rays** rayos catódicos.
Cath·o·lic [kǽθəlık] *s.* & *adj.* católico.
Ca·thol·i·cism [kəθɑ́ləsızəm] *s.* catolicismo.
cat·sup [kǽtsəp] *s.* salsa de tomate.
cat·tle [kǽtl] *s.* ganado, ganado vacuno; — **raiser** ganadero, *Ríopl.* estanciero; — **raising** ganadería; — **ranch** hacienda de ganado, *Méx., C.A.* rancho, *Ríopl.* estancia; *Ven., Col.* hato.
caught [kɔt] *pret.* & *p.p. de* **to catch.**
cau·li·flow·er [kɔ́ləflauə] *s.* coliflor.
cause [kɔz] *s.* causa; *v.* causar; originar; **to — to** hacer; inducir a.
caus·tic [kɔ́stık] *adj.* cáustico.
cau·ter·ize [kɔ́tʒraız] *v.* cauterizar.
cau·tion [kɔ́ʃən] *s.* precaución, cautela; aviso, advertencia; —! ¡cuidado! ¡atención!; *v.* prevenir, avisar, advertir.
cau·tious [kɔ́ʃəs] *adj.* cauto; cauteloso, cuidadoso; precavido.
cav·a·lier [kævəlír] *s.* caballero; galán; *adj.* orgulloso, altivo, desdeñoso.
cav·al·ry [kǽvlrı] *s.* caballería.
cave [kev] *s.* cueva; caverna; *v.* **to — in** hundirse; desplomarse.
cav·ern [kǽvən] *s.* caverna.
cav·i·ty [kǽvətı] *s.* cavidad, hueco; (*tooth*) carie.
ca·vort [kəvɔ́rt] *v.* cabriolar.
caw [kɔ] *s.* graznido; *v.* graznar.
cease [sis] *v.* cesar; parar, desistir; dejar de.
cease·less [síslıs] *adj.* incesante.
ce·dar [sídə] *s.* cedro.
cede [sid] *v.* ceder.
ce·dil·la [sıdılə] *s.* cedilla.

ceil·ing [sílıŋ] *s.* techo (*interior*); cielo máximo (*en aviación*); altura máxima (*en aviación*); — **price** precio máximo.
cel·e·brate [sɛ́ləbret] *v.* celebrar.
cel·e·brat·ed [sɛ́ləbretıd] *adj.* célebre, renombrado.
cel·e·bra·tion [sɛləbréʃən] *s.* celebración; fiesta.
ce·leb·ri·ty [səlébrətı] *s.* celebridad; renombre.
cel·er·y [sɛ́lərı] *s.* apio.
ce·les·tial [səléstʃəl] *adj.* celestial, celeste.
cell [sɛl] *s.* (*enclosure*) celda; (*structural*) célula; (*battery*) pila eléctrica.
cel·lar [sɛ́lə] *s.* bodega, sótano.
cel·lu·loid [séljəlɔıd] *s.* celuloide.
ce·ment [səmɛ́nt] *s.* cemento; hormigón; **reinforced** — cemento armado; — **mixer** hormigonera; *v.* unir, cementar, pegar con cemento; cubrir con cemento.
cem·e·ter·y [sɛ́mətɛrı] *s.* cementerio.
cen·sor [sɛ́nsə] *s.* censor; censurador, crítico; *v.* censurar (*cartas, periódicos, etc.*).
cen·sor·ship [sɛ́nsəʃıp] *s.* censura.
cen·sure [sɛ́nʃə] *s.* censura, crítica, reprobación; *v.* censurar, criticar, reprobar.
cen·sus [sɛ́nsəs] *s.* censo.
cent [sɛnt] *s.* centavo (*de peso o dólar*); **per** — por ciento.
cen·ten·ni·al [sɛntɛ́nıəl] *adj.* & *s.* centenario.
cen·ter [sɛ́ntə] *s.* centro; *v.* centrar; colocar en el centro; concentrar(se).
cen·ti·grade [sɛ́ntəgred] *adj.* centígrado.
cen·ti·pede [sɛ́ntəpid] *s.* ciempiés, cientopiés.
cen·tral [sɛ́ntrəl] *adj.* central; céntrico; *s.* (la) central de teléfonos.
cen·tral·ize [sɛ́ntrəlaız] *v.* centralizar.
cen·trif·u·gal [sɛntrífjʊgl] *adj.* centrífugo.
cen·trip·e·tal [sɛntrípətl] *adj.* centrípeto.
cen·tu·ry [sɛ́ntʃərı] *s.* siglo.
ce·ram·ic [sərǽmık] *adj.* cerámico; **ceramics** *s.* cerámica.
ce·re·al [sírıəl] *adj.* cereal; *s.* cereal; grano.
cer·e·mo·ni·al [sɛrəmónıəl] *adj.* ceremonial; *s.* ceremonial; rito.
cer·e·mo·ni·ous [sɛrəmónıəs] *adj.* ceremonioso.
cer·e·mo·ny [sɛ́rəmonı] *s.* ceremonia; ceremonial.
cer·tain [sɝ́tn] *adj.* cierto, seguro; **-ly** *adv.* ciertamente; por cierto; de cierto; seguramente; de seguro.
cer·tain·ty [sɝ́tntı] *s.* certeza; certidumbre; seguridad.
cer·tif·i·cate [sɝtífəkıt] *s.* certificado; documento; testimonio; — **of stock** bono, obligación; **birth** — partida de nacimiento; **death** — partida (*o* certificado) de defunción.
cer·ti·fi·ca·tion [sɝtıfıkéʃən] *s.* certificación.
cer·ti·fy [sɝ́təfaı] *v.* certificar; dar fe, atestiguar.
cer·vix [sɝ́vıks] *s.* cerviz.
ces·sa·tion [sɛséʃən] *s.* suspensión, paro.
cess·pool [sɛ́spul] *s.* cloaca, rezumadero.
chafe [tʃef] *s.* rozadura; irritación, molestia; *v.* rozar(se); frotar; irritar(se).
chaff [tʃæf] *s.* hollejo, cáscara; *v.* embromar, bromear.
cha·grin [ʃəgrín] *s.* mortificación, desazón, pesar; **-ed** *p.p.* mortificado, afligido.
chain [tʃen] *s.* cadena; — **of mountains** cordillera; — **store** tienda sucursal (*una entre muchas de una misma empresa*); — **reaction** reacción en cadena; reacción eslabonada; — **saw** aserradora de cadena; — **smoker** el que fuma cigarro tras cigarro; *v.* encadenar.
chair [tʃɛr] *s.* silla; cátedra; presidencia; **arm** —

sillón (de brazos); **easy** — butaca, poltrona;
folding — silla de tijera; **rocking** — mecedora.
chair·man [tʃɛ́rmən] s. presidente, director (de una
junta o de departamento).
chair·man·ship [tʃɛ́rmənʃɪp] s. presidencia (de una
junta).
chal·ice [tʃǽlɪs] s. cáliz (vaso sagrado).
chalk [tʃɔk] s. tiza, yeso; greda; v. enyesar; marcar
con tiza o yeso; **to — down** apuntar con tiza o
yeso (en el pizarrón); **to — out** bosquejar,
esbozar con tiza.
chalk·y [tʃɔ́kɪ] adj. yesoso; blanco.
chal·lenge [tʃǽlɪndʒ] s. desafío; reto; demanda; v.
desafiar, retar; disputar, poner a prueba; dar el
quienvive.
cham·ber [tʃémbɚ] s. cámara; aposento; — **of**
commerce cámara de comercio.
cham·ber·maid [tʃémbɚmed] s. camarera, sirvienta.
cham·ois [ʃǽmɪ] s. gamuza.
cham·pi·on [tʃǽmpɪən] s. campeón; defensor; v.
defender.
cham·pi·on·ship [tʃǽmpɪənʃɪp] s. campeonato.
chance [tʃæns] s. (opportunity) oportunidad,
ocasión; (possibility) posibilidad, probabilidad;
(fortune) suerte, fortuna; casualidad, azar; (risk)
riesgo; billete de rifa o lotería; **by** — por
casualidad; **game of** — juego de azar; **to run**
a — correr riesgo; adj. casual, accidental; v.
arriesgar; **to — to** acertar a, hacer (algo) por
casualidad.
chan·cel·lor [tʃǽnsəlɚ] s. canciller; primer
ministro; magistrado; rector de universidad.
chan·de·lier [ʃændlɪr] s. araña de luces, Am. candil.
change [tʃendʒ] s. (money) cambio; vuelta, Am.
vuelto; suelto; Méx. feria; (fresh clothes) muda
de ropa; (switch) mudanza; **the — of life** la
menopausia; v. cambiar; mudar; alterar; **to —**
clothes mudar de ropa; **to — trains**
transbordar(se), cambiar de tren.
change·a·ble [tʃéndʒəbl̩] adj. mudable, variable;
inconstante; tornadizo; — **silk** seda tornasolada.
chan·nel [tʃǽnl̩] s. canal; cauce; canal (de
televisión).
chant [tʃænt] s. canto llano o gregoriano;
sonsonete; v. cantar (psalmos, himnos, etc.).
cha·os [kéas] s. caos; desorden.
cha·ot·ic [keátɪk] adj. caótico.
chap [tʃæp] s. grieta, raja, rajadura (en la piel);
chico; **what a fine — he is!** ¡qué buen tipo (o
sujeto) es!; v. agrietarse, rajarse (la piel).
chap·el [tʃǽpl̩] s. capilla.
chap·er·on(e) [ʃǽpəron] s. acompañante, persona
de respeto; **to go along as a** — Am. ir de
moscón; v. acompañar, servir de acompañante.
chap·lain [tʃǽplɪn] s. capellán; **army** — capellán
castrense.
chap·ter [tʃǽptɚ] s. capítulo; cabildo (de una
catedral).
char [tʃar] v. requemar, carbonizar.
char·ac·ter [kǽrɪktɚ] s. carácter; personaje.
char·ac·ter·is·tic [kærɪktərístɪk] adj. característico;
típico; s. característica, rasgo característico;
distintivo; peculiaridad.
char·ac·ter·ize [kǽrɪktəraɪz] v. caracterizar.
cha·rade [ʃəréd] s. charada.
char·coal [tʃárkol] s. carbón; carboncillo (para
dibujar); — **drawing** dibujo al carbón.
charge [tʃardʒ] s. (custody) cargo; custodia;
cuidado; (order) mandato, encargo; (accusation)
cargo, acusación; (load) carga; peso; (cost)
precio, coste; (attack) embestida, asalto, ataque;

chargé d'affaires agregado; — **account** cuenta
abierta; — **prepaid** porte pagado; **under my** —a
mi cargo; **to be in** — **of** estar encargado de;
v. cargar; cargar en cuenta; cobrar (precio);
mandar; exhortar; atacar, embestir, asaltar; **to**
— **with murder** acusar de homicidio.

charg·er [tʃárdʒɚ] s. cargador (de batería); caballo
de guerra, corcel.
char·i·ot [tʃǽrɪət] s. carroza; carruaje.
cha·ris·ma [kərízmə] s. carisma.
char·i·ta·ble [tʃǽrətəbl̩] adj. caritativo.
char·i·ty [tʃǽrətɪ] s. caridad; limosna; beneficencia.
char·la·tan [ʃárlətn̩] s. charlatán; farsante.
charm [tʃarm] s. encanto; atractivo; hechizo;
talismán; **watch** — dije; v. encantar; cautivar;
hechizar.
charm·ing [tʃármɪŋ] adj. encantador, atractivo.
chart [tʃart] s. carta (hidrográfica o de navegar);
mapa; gráfica, representación gráfica; v.
cartografiar, delinear mapas o cartas; **to — a**
course trazar o planear una ruta o derrotero.
char·ter [tʃártɚ] s. carta constitucional,
constitución, código; título; carta de privilegio;
— **member** socio fundador; v. fletar (un barco);
alquilar (un ómnibus).
chase [tʃes] s. caza; persecución; v. cazar;
perseguir; **to — away** ahuyentar.
chasm [kǽzəm] s. abismo; vacío.
chaste [tʃest] adj. casto; honesto; puro.
chas·tise [tʃæstáɪz] v. castigar.
chas·tise·ment [tʃæstáɪzmənt] s. castigo,
escarmiento.
chas·ti·ty [tʃǽstətɪ] s. castidad; honestidad; pureza.
chat [tʃæt] s. charla, Mex. plática; v. charlar,
Mex. platicar.
chat·tels [tʃǽtl̩z] s. pl. enseres, bienes muebles.
chat·ter [tʃǽtɚ] s. charla, parloteo; castañeteo (de
los dientes); chirrido (de aves); v. charlar,
parlotear, cotorrear; castañetear (los dientes).
chauf·feur [ʃófɚ] s. chófer, cochero de automóvil.
cheap [tʃip] adj. barato; cursi, de mal gusto; **to feel**
— sentir vergüenza; **-ly** adv. barato, a poco
precio.
cheap·en [tʃípən] v. abaratar.
cheap·ness [tʃípnɪs] s. baratura; cursilería.
cheat [tʃit] s. fraude, engaño; trampa; trampista,
tramposo; estafador; embaucador; v. engañar;
trampear; embaucar; estafar.
check [tʃɛk] s. cheque (de banco); talón, marbete,
contraseña (de equipajes, etc.); marca, señal;
cuenta (de restaurante); restricción, represión;
cuadro (de un tejido o tela); comprobación;
jaque (en ajedrez); —**room** vestuario;
guardarropa; consigna (equipajes); — **point**
punto de inspección; — **list** lista comprobante.
v. refrenar, reprimir, restringir; facturar,
depositar (equipajes); inspeccionar; confrontar,
comprobar; marcar (con una señal); dar jaque
(en ajedrez); **to — out of a hotel** desocupar el
cuarto o alojamiento de un hotel.
check·book [tʃékbʊk] s. libreta de cheques; libro
talonario.
check·er [tʃékɚ] s. cuadro; casilla (de un tablero de
ajedrez, etc.); pieza (del juego de damas);
comprobador; inspector; -s juego de damas;
—**board** tablero; v. cuadricular, marcar con
cuadritos; **-ed career** vida azarosa, vida llena de
variedad; **-ed cloth** paño o tela a cuadros.
check·mate [tʃékmet] s. jaque mate.
cheek [tʃik] s. mejilla, carrillo; cachete; descaro,
desfachatez; **fat** — mejilla gorda, moflete; —

bone pómulo; **red —** chapetón.

cheer [tʃɪr] s. alegría; buen ánimo, jovialidad; consuelo; **-s** aplausos, vivas; v. alegrar, alentar, animar; refocilar; aplaudir, vitorear; **to — up** alentar, dar ánimo; cobrar ánimo, animarse.

cheer·ful [tʃɪrfəl] adj. animado, alegre, jovial; **-ly** adv. alegremente, con alegría, con júbilo; de buena gana, de buen grado.

cheer·ful·ness [tʃɪrfəlnɪs] s. jovialidad, alegría; buen humor.

cheer·i·ly [tʃɪrəlɪ] = **cheerfully**.

cheer·less [tʃɪrlɪs] adj. abatido, desalentado, desanimado; triste, sombrío.

cheer·y [tʃɪrɪ] = **cheerful**.

cheese [tʃiz] s. queso; **cottage —** requesón.

chef [ʃɛf] s. cocinero.

chem·i·cal [kɛmɪkl] adj. químico; s. producto químico.

chem·ist [kɛmɪst] s. químico.

chem·is·try [kɛmɪstrɪ] s. química.

cher·ish [tʃɛrɪʃ] v. acariciar, abrigar (una esperanza, un ideal, etc.); apreciar.

cher·ry [tʃɛrɪ] s. cereza; **— tree** cerezo.

cher·ub [tʃɛrəb] s. querubín.

chess [tʃɛs] s. ajedrez; **—board** tablero de ajedrez.

chest [tʃɛst] s. cofre, arca; caja; pecho; **— of drawers** cómoda.

chest·nut [tʃɛsnət] s. castaña; **— tree** castaño; adj. castaño; **— horse** caballo zaino.

chev·ron [ʃɛvrən] s. galón.

chew [tʃu] s. mascada, mordisco, bocado; v. mascar, masticar.

chew·ing gum [tʃúɪŋ gʌm] s. goma de mascar; Am. chicle.

chick [tʃɪk] s. polluelo, pollito; pajarito; **chick-pea** garbanzo.

chick·en [tʃɪkɪn] s. pollo; polluelo; **— pox** viruelas locas; **chicken-hearted** cobarde, gallina.

chic·o·ry [tʃɪkərɪ] s. achicoria.

chide [tʃaɪd] v. regañar, reprender, reprobar.

chief [tʃif] s. jefe, caudillo; cacique (de una tribu); **commander in —** comandante en jefe; adj. principal; **— clerk** oficial mayor; **— justice** presidente de la corte suprema; **-ly** adv. principalmente, mayormente; sobre todo.

chif·fon [ʃɪfán] s. gasa.

chig·ger [tʃɪgɚ] s. nigua.

chil·blain [tʃɪlblen] s. sabañón.

child [tʃaɪld] s. niño, niña; hijo, hija; **-'s play** cosa de niños; **to be with —** estar encinta.

child·birth [tʃáɪldbɜθ] s. parto, alumbramiento.

child·hood [tʃáɪldhʊd] s. niñez, infancia.

child·ish [tʃáɪdɪʃ] adj. pueril; infantil; **— action** niñería, niñada.

child·less [tʃáɪdlɪs] adj. sin hijos.

child·like [tʃáɪldlaɪk] adj. como niño, aniñado, pueril.

chil·dren [tʃɪldrən] pl. de **child**.

Chil·e·an [tʃɪlɪən] adj. & s. chileno.

chil·i [tʃɪlɪ] s. Méx., C.A. chile, Carib., S.A. ají.

chill [tʃɪl] s. frío, resfrío; enfriamiento; escalofrío; calofrío; **-s and fever** escalofríos; adj. frío; v. resfriar(se); enfriar(se); **to become -ed** resfriarse, escalofriarse.

chill·y [tʃɪlɪ] adj. frío; friolento.

chime [tʃaɪm] s. repique, campaneo; **-s** órgano de campanas, juego de campanas; v. repicar, campanear; tocar, sonar, tañer (las campanas); **to — with** estar en armonía con.

chim·ney [tʃɪmnɪ] s. chimenea; **lamp —** tubo de lámpara, Am. bombilla.

chin [tʃɪn] s. barba.

chi·na [tʃaɪnə] s. loza de china, porcelana, loza fina; vajilla de porcelana; **— closet** chinero.

chi·na·ware [tʃáɪnəwɛr] = **china**.

Chi·nese [tʃaɪníz] adj. chino; s. chino; idioma chino.

chink [tʃɪŋk] s. grieta, hendidura.

chip [tʃɪp] s. astilla, brizna; fragmento; desconchadura; desportilladura; ficha (de pócar); v. astillar; desconchar(se); descascarar(se); desportillar(se); picar, tajar (con cincel o hacha); **to — in** contribuir con su cuota.

chip·munk [tʃɪpmʌŋk] s. especie de ardilla.

chi·ro·prac·tic [kaɪrəpræktɪk] adj. quiropráctico.

chirp [tʃɝp] s. chirrido; pío; gorjeo; v. chirriar; piar; pipiar; gorjear.

chis·el [tʃɪzl] s. cincel; v. cincelar; sisar, estafar.

chiv·al·rous [ʃɪvlrəs] adj. caballeresco, caballeroso, galante, cortés.

chiv·al·ry [ʃɪvlrɪ] s. caballería; caballerosidad.

chlo·ride [klóraɪd] s. cloruro.

chlo·rine [klórin] s. cloro.

chlo·ro·form [klórəfɔrm] s. cloroformo.

chlo·ro·phyll [klórəfɪl] s. clorofila.

choc·o·late [tʃɔklɪt] s. chocolate; **— pot** chocolatera.

choice [tʃɔɪs] s. selección; preferencia; escogimiento; cosa elegida; favorito, preferido; alternativa; **to have no other —** no tener otra alternativa; adj. selecto; bien escogido; excelente.

choir [kwaɪr] s. coro.

choke [tʃok] s. sofoco, ahogo; tos ahogada; estrangulación; estrangulador, obturador (de automóvil); v. sofocar(se), ahogar(se); estrangular(se); obstruir, tapar; regularizar (el motor).

chol·er·a [kálərə] s. cólera (m.).

cho·les·ter·ol [kəléstərol] s. colesterol.

choose [tʃuz] v. escoger; elegir; seleccionar; **to — to** optar por; preferir; **I do not — to do it** no se me antoja (o no es mi gusto) hacerlo.

chop [tʃɑp] s. chuleta, costilla, tajada (de carne); **-s** quijadas (usualmente de animal); v. tajar, cortar; picar, desmenuzar (carne).

chop·py [tʃɑpɪ] adj. picado, agitado.

cho·ral [kórəl] adj. coral.

chord [kɔrd] s. cuerda; acorde.

chore [tʃor] s. tarea; quehacer.

cho·re·og·ra·phy [korɪágrəfɪ] s. coreografía.

cho·rus [kórəs] s. coro; v. cantar o hablar en coro; contestar a una voz.

chose [tʃoz] pret. de **to choose**.

cho·sen [tʃózn] p.p. de **to choose**.

chris·ten [krɪsn] v. bautizar.

chris·ten·ing [krɪnɪŋ] s. bautizo, bautismo.

Chris·tian [krɪstʃən] s. & adj. cristiano; **— name** nombre de pila o bautismo.

Chris·ti·an·i·ty [krɪstʃíænətɪ] s. cristiandad; cristianismo.

Christ·mas [krɪsməs] s. Navidad, Pascua de Navidad; adj. navideño; **— Eve** Nochebuena; **— gift** regalo de Navidad; aguinaldo; **Merry —!** ¡Felices Navidades! ¡Felices Pascuas!

chrome [krom] s. cromo; adj. cromado.

chro·mi·um [krómɪəm] s. cromo.

chro·mo·some [króməsom] s. cromosomo.

chron·ic [kránɪk] adj. crónico.

chron·i·cle [kránɪkl] s. crónica; v. relatar; escribir la crónica de.

chron·i·cler [kránɪklə·] s. cronista.
chron·o·log·i·cal [krɑnəládʒɪkl] adj. cronológico.
chro·nom·e·ter [krɑnámətə·] s. cronómetro.
chry·san·the·mum [krɪsǽnθəməm] s. crisantema, crisantemo.
chub·by [tʃʌ́bɪ] adj. rechoncho; gordiflón.
chuck [tʃʌk] s. mamola, golpecito, caricia (debajo de la barba); v. echar, tirar (lo que no sirve); to — under the chin hacer la mamola.
chuck·le [tʃʌ́kl] s. risita; v. reír entre dientes.
chum [tʃʌm] s. compañero, camarada, compinche.
chunk [tʃʌŋk] s. trozo; zoquete.
church [tʃɝt] s. iglesia.
church·man [tʃɝ́tʃmən] s. clérigo, eclesiástico, sacerdote; (parishoner) feligrés.
church·yard [tʃɝ́tʃjɑrd] s. patio de iglesia; camposanto, cementerio.
churn [tʃɝn] s. mantequera (para hacer manteca); v. batir (en una mantequera); agitar, revolver.
ci·der [sáɪdə·] s. sidra.
ci·gar [sɪgár] s. puro; Carib., Col., Ven. tabaco; — store tabaquería, estanquillo.
cig·a·rette [sɪgərɛ́t] s. cigarrillo, pitillo, Méx., C.A., Ven., Col. cigarro; — case cigarrera, pitillera; — holder boquilla; — lighter encendedor.
cinch [sɪntʃ] s. cincha; ganga, cosa fácil; v. cinchar; apretar.
cin·der [síndə·] s. ceniza; carbón, brasa, ascua; cisco; -s cenizas; rescoldo.
cin·na·mon [sínəmən] s. canela; — tree canelo.
ci·pher [sáɪfə·] s. cifra; número; cero.
cir·cle [sɝ́kl] s. círculo; cerco, rueda; v. cercar, circundar; circular, dar vueltas.
cir·cuit [sɝ́kɪt] s. circuito; rode o, vuelta.
cir·cu·lar [sɝ́kjələ·] adj. circular; redondo; s. circular; hoja volante.
cir·cu·late [sɝ́kjəlet] v. circular; poner en circulación.
cir·cu·la·tion [sɝkjəléʃən] s. circulación.
cir·cum·fer·ence [sə·kʌ́mfərəns] s. circunferencia.
cir·cum·flex [sɝ́kəmflɛks] adj. circunflejo.
cir·cum·lo·cu·tion [sɝkəmlokjúʃən] s. circunlocución, rodeo.
cir·cum·scribe [sɝ́kəmskráɪb] v. circunscribir, limitar.
cir·cum·spect [sɝ́kəmspɛkt] adj. circunspecto; prudente.
cir·cum·spec·tion [sɝkəmspékʃən] s. circunspección, miramiento, prudencia.
cir·cum·stance [sɝ́kəmstæns] s. circunstancia; incidente; ceremonia, pompa.
cir·cum·vent [sɝkəmvɛ́nt] v. evitar; embaucar.
cir·cus [sɝ́kəs] s. circo.
cir·rho·sis [sɪrósɪs] s. cirrosis.
cis·tern [sístə·n] s. cisterna.
cit·a·del [sítədl] s. ciudadela.
ci·ta·tion [saɪtéʃən] s. citación; cita; mención.
cite [saɪt] v. citar; citar a juicio; mencionar.
cit·i·zen [sítəzn] s. ciudadano, paisano.
cit·i·zen·ship [sítəznʃɪp] s. ciudadanía.
cit·ron [sítrən] s. acitrón.
cit·rus [sítrəs] s. cidro.
cit·y [sítɪ] s. ciudad, población; municipio; adj. municipal; urbano; — council ayuntamiento; — hall ayuntamiento, casa municipal.
civ·ic [sívɪk] adj. cívico.
civ·ics [sívɪks] s. derecho político.
civ·il [sívl] adj. civil; cortés; — engineer ingeniero civil; — rights derechos civiles; — disobedience desobediencia civil.
ci·vil·ian [səvíljən] s. civil; paisano (persona no militar).
ci·vil·i·ty [səvíləti] s. civilidad, cortesía, urbanidad.
civ·i·li·za·tion [sɪvləzéʃən] s. civilización.
civ·i·lize [sívlaɪz] v. civilizar.
civ·i·lized [sívlaɪzd] adj. civilizado.
clad [klæd] pret. & p.p. de to clothe.
claim [klem] s. demanda; reclamación, reclamo; derecho, título; pretensión; miner's — denuncia; v. reclamar; demandar; pedir, exigir; afirmar, sostener; to — a mine denunciar una mina; to — to be pretender ser.
claim·ant [klémənt] s. reclamante o reclamador; pretendiente (a un trono).
clair·voy·ant [klɛrvɔ́ɪənt] adj. clarividente.
clam [klæm] s. almeja.
clam·ber [klǽmbə·] v. trepar, encaramarse, subir a gatas, subir gateando.
clam·my [klǽmɪ] adj. frío y húmedo.
clam·or [klǽmə·] s. clamor; clamoreo; gritería, vocería; v. clamar; vociferar, gritar.
clam·or·ous [klǽmərəs] adj. clamoroso.
clamp [klæmp] s. grapa; tornillo de banco; v. afianzar, sujetar; pisar recio.
clan [klæn] s. clan; tribu.
clan·des·tine [klændɛ́stɪn] adj. clandestino.
clang [klæŋ] s. tantán, retintín; campanada, campanillazo; —! —! ¡tan! ¡tan!; v. sonar, repicar (una campana o timbre); hacer sonar, tocar fuerte.
clap [klæp] s. palmada; golpe seco; — of thunder trueno; v. palmear, palmotear, aplaudir, dar palmadas; cerrar de golpe (un libro); dar una palmada, Am. palmear (sobre la espalda); to — in jail meter (o encajar) en la cárcel.
clap·per [klǽpə·] s. badajo.
clar·i·fy [klǽrəfaɪ] v. aclarar.
clar·i·net [klǽrənɛt] s. clarinete.
clar·i·ty [klǽrətɪ] s. claridad, luz.
clash [klæʃ] s. choque, encontrón, colisión; riña, conflicto; estruendo; v. chocar; darse un encontrón; hacer crujir; oponerse, estar en conflicto.
clasp [klæsp] s. (fastener) broche; hebilla; cierre; traba; (grip) apretón, apretón de manos; v. abrochar; asir; agarrar; sujetar, asegurar; abrazar; apretar (la mano).
class [klæs] s. clase; v. clasificar.
clas·sic [klǽsɪk] adj. & s. clásico; — scholar humanista, erudito clásico.
clas·si·cal [klǽsɪkl] adj. clásico.
clas·si·cism [klǽsɪsɪzm] s. clasicismo.
clas·si·fi·ca·tion [klæsəfəkéʃən] s. clasificación.
clas·si·fy [klǽsəfaɪ] v. clasificar.
class·mate [klǽsmet] s. compañero de clase, condiscípulo.
class·room [klǽsrum] s. clase, aula.
clat·ter [klǽtə·] s. estrépito, boruca; traqueteo; bullicio; alboroto; v. hacer estrépito o boruca; traquetear; meter bulla o alboroto.
clause [klɔz] s. cláusula.
claw [klɔ] s. garra; zarpa; uña; pinza (de langosta, cangrejo, etc.); orejas (de un martillo); arañazo; v. desgarrar; arañar; rasgar.
claw·ing [klɔ́ɪŋ] s. zarpazo.
clay [kle] s. barro; arcilla, greda.
clean [klin] adj. limpio; puro; adv. limpiamente; clean-cut bien tallado, de buen talle, de buen parecer; v. limpiar; asear; desempañar; to — up limpiar(se), asear(se).
clean·er [klínə·] s. limpiador; quitamanchas.
clean·li·ness [klénlɪnɪs] s. limpieza; aseo.

CH

clean·ly [klénlɪ] *adj.* limpio; aseado; [klínlɪ] *adv.* limpiamente.

clean·ness [klínnɪs] *s.* limpieza; aseo.

cleanse [klɛnz] *v.* limpiar; asear; purificar, depurar.

cleans·er [klénzɚ] *s.* limpiador.

clear [klɪr] *adj.* (*evident*) claro; patente, manifiesto; (*clean*) límpido; despejado; libre (*de culpa, estorbos, deudas, etc.*); — **profit** ganancia neta; **clear-cut** *adj.* bien delineado; clarividente; **to pass** — **through** atravesar, traspasar de lado a lado; **to be in the** — estar sin deudas; estar libre de culpa; *v.* aclarar(se); despejar(se); escampar; clarificar; quitar (*estorbos*); desmontar (*un terreno*); salvar, saltar por encima de; librar (*de culpa, deudas, etc.*); sacar (*una ganancia neta*); pasar (*un cheque*) por un banco de liquidación; liquidar (*una cuenta*); **to — the table** levantar la mesa; **to — up** aclarar(se).

clear·ance [klírəns] *s.* espacio (*libre entre dos objetos*); despacho de aduana; — **sale** saldo, venta (*de liquidación*), *Am.* barata.

clear·ing [klírɪŋ] *s.* aclaramiento; claro, terreno desmontado o desarbolado; liquidación de balances; — **house** banco de liquidación.

clear·ness [klírnɪs] *s.* claridad.

cleav·age [klívɪdʒ] *s.* hendedura.

cleave [kliv] *v.* hender(se); tajar; rajar, partir.

cleav·er [klívɚ] *s.* cuchilla o hacha (*de carnicero*).

clef [klɛf] *s.* clave (*en música*).

cleft [klɛft] *s.* grieta, hendedura; *adj.* hendido, partido, rajado; *pret.* & *p.p. de* **to cleave.**

clem·en·cy [klémənsɪ] *s.* clemencia.

clem·ent [klémənt] *adj.* clemente.

clench [klɛntʃ] *s.* agarro, agarrada, agarrón; apretón; *v.* agarrar, asir; apretar (*los dientes, el puño*).

cler·gy [klɝdʒɪ] *s.* clero.

cler·gy·man [klɝdʒɪmən] *s.* clérigo, eclesiástico, pastor, sacerdote.

cler·i·cal [klérɪkl] *adj.* clerical, eclesiástico; oficinesco, de oficina; de dependientes.

clerk [klɝk] *s.* dependiente; empleado (*de oficina*); escribiente; archivero (*de municipio*); **law —** escribano; *v.* estar de dependiente.

clev·er [klévɚ] *adj.* diestro, hábil; listo; talentoso; mañoso; **-ly** *adv.* hábilmente; con destreza; con maña.

clev·er·ness [klévɚnɪs] *s.* destreza, habilidad, maña; talento.

clew [klu] *s.* indicio (*que indica el camino para resolver un misterio o problema*).

cli·ché [klɪʃé] *s.* (*plate*) clisé; *Am.* cliché; (*phrase*) cliché.

click [klɪk] *s.* golpecito; chasquido (*de la lengua*); gatillazo (*sonido del gatillo de una pistola*); tacóneo (*sonido de tacones*); *v.* sonar (*un pestillo, un broche, un gatillo, etc.*); chasquear (*la lengua*); **to — the heels** cuadrarse (*militarmente*); taconear.

cli·ent [kláɪənt] *s.* cliente.

cli·en·tele [klaɪəntél] *s.* clientela.

cliff [klɪf] *s.* risco, precipicio, peñasco, escarpa.

cli·mate [kláɪmɪt] *s.* clima.

cli·max [kláɪmæks] *s.* clímax, culminación; *v.* culminar; llegar al clímax.

climb [klaɪm] *s.* subida, ascenso; *v.* subir; trepar; encaramarse; **to — down** bajar a gatas; desprenderse (*de un árbol*).

climb·er [kláɪmɚ] *s.* trepador; enredadera, planta trepadora.

clime [klaɪm] *s.* clima.

clinch [klɪntʃ] *v.* remachar, redoblar (*un clavo*); afianzar, sujetar, asegurar bien; cerrar (*un trato*); abrazarse fuertemente; *s.* remache; abrazo; agarrón; **to be in a —** estar agarrados o abrazados.

cling [klɪŋ] *v.* pegarse, adherirse.

clin·ic [klínɪk] *s.* clínica.

clink [klɪŋk] *s.* tintín.

clip [klɪp] *s.* (*fastener*) broche, presilla; (*cutting*) tijeretada (*corte con tijeras*); trasquila, trasquiladura; **paper —** sujetapapeles; **to go at a good —** ir a paso rápido; andar de prisa; *v.* recortar; cortar; trasquilar (*el pelo o lana de los animales*); **to — together** sujetar.

clip·per [klípɚ] *s.* clíper (*velero o avión de gran velocidad*); trasquilador; recortador; **-s** tijeras; maquinilla (*para recortar el pelo*).

clip·ping [klípɪŋ] *s.* recorte.

cloak [klok] *s.* capa; manto; *v.* tapar, embozar, encubrir.

cloak·room [klókrum] *s.* guardarropa, vestuario.

clock [klɑk] *s.* reloj; **alarm —** despertador; *v.* marcar; cronometrar.

clock·wise [klákwaɪz] *adv.* en el sentido de las manecillas de reloj.

clock·work [klákwɝk] *s.* maquinaria de reloj; **like —** con precisión, puntualmente; sin dificultad.

clod [klɑd] *s.* terrón; tonto, necio.

clog [klɑg] *s.* estorbo, obstáculo; zueco (*zapato de suela gruesa o de madera*); — **dance** zapateado; *v.* estorbar, embarazar; obstruir, atorar, tapar; obstruirse, atascarse, azolvarse (*Am.* enzolvarse), atorarse (*un caño, acequia, etc.*).

clois·ter [klóɪstɚ] *s.* claustro; monasterio; convento; *v.* enclaustrar.

close [kloz] *s.* fin, terminación, conclusión; *v.* cerrar(se); concluir; **to — an account** saldar una cuenta; **to — in upon** cercar, rodear; **to — out** liquidar, vender en liquidación.

close [klos] *adj.* (*near*) cercano, próximo; aproximado; íntimo; (*tight*) estrecho, ajustado; (*stingy*) cerrado; tacaño, mezquino; (*suffocating*) opresivo; sofocante; — **attention** suma atención; — **questioning** interrogatorio detallado o minucioso; — **translation** traducción fiel; **at — range** de cerca; *adv.* cerca; **-ly** *adv.* aproximadamente; estrechamente; apretadamente; con sumo cuidado a atención.

closed cir·cuit [klozd sɝkət] *s.* & *adj.* circuito cerrado.

close·ness [klósnɪs] *s.* cercanía, proximidad; aproximación; estrechez; intimidad; tacañería, avaricia; mala ventilación, falta de aire; fidelidad (*de una traducción*).

clos·et [klázɪt] *s.* ropero; alacena, armario; gabinete, retrete, excusado; *v.* encerrar en un cuarto (*para una entrevista secreta*); **to — oneself** (**themselves**) encerrarse.

clot [klɑt] *v.* coagular(se), cuajar(se); *s.* coágulo, cuajarón.

cloth [klɔθ] *s.* tela, paño, género; trapo; *adj.* de paño; — **binding** encuadernación en tela.

clothe [kloð] *v.* vestir; cubrir; revestir; investir.

clothes [kloz] *s. pl.* ropa; ropaje, vestidos; **suit of —** terno, traje, *Carib.*, *Ven.* flux; **—line** tendedero; **—pin** pinzas, gancho (*para tender la ropa*).

cloth·ier [klóðjɚ] *s.* comerciante en ropa o paño; ropero, pañero.

cloth·ing [klóðɪŋ] *s.* ropa; ropaje, vestidos.

cloud [klaʊd] *s.* nube; **storm** — nubarrón; *v.*
nublar(se), anublar(se); obscurecer; manchar.

cloud·burst [kláʊdbɚst] *s.* chaparrón, aguacero.

cloud·less [kláʊdlɪs] *adj.* claro, despejado; sin
nubes.

cloud·y [kláʊdɪ] *adj.* nublado; *Esp.* nuboso;
sombrío.

clove [klov] *s.* clavo (*especia*); — **of garlic** diente
de ajo.

clo·ven [klóvən] *adj.* hendido; *s.* & *adj.* — **hoof**
patihendido, pie hendido.

clo·ver [klóvɚ] *s.* trébol; **to be in** — estar o vivir
en la abundancia; sentirse próspero.

clo·ver·leaf [klóvɚlif] *s.* (*highway*) cruce en trébol.

clown [klaʊn] *s.* payaso, bufón; *v.* payasear,
bufonear, hacer el payaso.

cloy [klɔɪ] *v.* empalagar; hastiar.

club [klʌb] *s.* club, círculo; casino; garrote, porra;
palo; basto (*de la baraja*); *v.* golpear, aporrear,
apalear; **to** — **together** formar club; escotar,
pagar la cuota que le toca a cada uno, *Am.*
cotizar.

club·house [klʌ́bhaʊs] *s.* club, casino.

cluck [klʌk] *s.* cloqueo; *v.* cloquear.

clue = **clew.**

clump [klʌmp] *s.* terrón; pisada fuerte; — **of
bushes** matorral; — **of trees** grupo de árboles,
arboleda; *v.* apiñar, amontonar; **to** — **along**
andar pesadamente.

clum·sy [klʌ́mzɪ] *adj.* torpe, desmañado;
incómodo; difícil de manejar; mal hecho.

clung [klʌŋ] *pret.* & *p.p. de* **to cling.**

clus·ter [klʌ́stɚ] *s.* racimo; grupo; *v.* agrupar(se);
arracimarse (*formar racimo*).

clutch [klʌtʃ] *s.* apretón fuerte; agarro, agarrón;
embrague (*de automóvil*); **-es** garras; uñas; —
pedal palanca del embrague; **to step on the** —
pisar el embrague; desembragar, soltar el
embrague; **to throw in the** — embragar; *v.*
agarrar, asir; apretar.

clut·ter [klʌ́tɚ] *v.* obstruir; atestar (*de cosas*);
poner en desorden; *s.* desorden, confusión.

coach [kotʃ] *s.* coche; entrenador (*en deportes*);
maestro particular; *v.* aleccionar; guiar,
adiestrar, *Am.* entrenar; **to** — **with** ser instruido
o entrenado por.

coach·man [kótʃmən] *s.* cochero.

co·ag·u·late [koǽgjəlet] *v.* coagular(se), cuajar(se).

coal [kol] *s.* carbón; ascua, brasa; **hard** — carbón
de piedra, antracita; **soft** — hulla; — **bin**
carbonera; — **dealer** carbonero; — **oil** kerosina;
— **tar** alquitrán de carbón; *v.* cargar de carbón,
echar carbón; proveer(se) de carbón.

co·a·li·tion [koəlíʃən] *s.* coalición.

coarse [kors] *adj.* (*crude*) burdo, basto; tosco;
áspero; (*rude*) rudo, grosero; vulgar; tosco;
— **sand** arena gruesa.

coarse·ness [kórsnɪs] *s.* tosquedad; vulgaridad,
grosería, rudeza.

coast [kost] *s.* costa, litoral; — **guard**
guardacostas, guarda de costas; *v.* costear,
navegar por la costa; deslizar(se), resbalar(se)
cuesta abajo.

coast·al [kóstl] *adj.* cóstero, costanero, de la costa;
— **traffic** cabotaje.

coast·line [kóstlaɪn] *s.* costa, litoral.

coat [kot] *s.* chaqueta, americana; *Am.* saco;
pelo (*de un animal*); **lady's** — abrigo de señora;
— **hanger** colgador; — **of arms** escudo de
armas; — **of paint** capa de pintura; *v.* cubrir;
revestir, dar una mano (*de pintura*); **to** — **with**

sugar azucarar, bañar en azúcar.

coat·ing [kótɪŋ] *s.* capa.

coat·tail [kóttel] *s.* faldón.

coax [koks] *v.* rogar o persuadir con halagos,
halagar, tentar.

cob [kɑb] *s.* carozo, zuro (*de la mazorca del maíz*),
Ven., Col., Carib. tusa, *Méx., C.A.* olote.

co·balt [kóbɔlt] *s.* cobalto.

cob·bler [kɑ́blɚ] *s.* remendón (*zapatero*); pudín
de bizcocho y fruta.

cob·ble·stone [kɑ́blston] *s.* guijarro; *adj.*
empedrado.

cob·web [kɑ́bwɛb] *s.* telaraña.

co·caine [kokén] *s.* cocaína.

cock [kak] *s.* gallo; macho de ave; espita, grifo;
martillo (*de armas de fuego*); **—sure** muy seguro
de sí mismo; *v.* amartillar (*un arma de fuego*);
ladear (*la cabeza*), ladearse (*el sombrero*).

cock·fight [kɑ́kfaɪt] *s.* pelea de gallos, riña de
gallos.

cock·pit [kɑ́kpɪt] *s.* gallera; (*airplane*) cabina.

cock·roach [kɑ́krotʃ] *s.* cucaracha.

cock·tail [kɑ́ktel] *s.* coctel; aperitivo (*de ostras*),
almejas, frutas, etc.).

cock·y [kɑ́kɪ] *adj.* arrogante, *Am.* retobado.

co·coa [kóko] *s.* cacao; bebida de cacao,
chocolate.

co·co·nut [kókənət] *s.* coco (*fruta*).

co·coon [kəkún] *s.* capullo (*del gusano de seda,
etc.*).

cod [kɑd] *s. N.Esp.* abadejo; *Andalucia, Am.*
bacalao; **cod-liver oil** aceite de hígado de
bacalao.

cod·dle [kɑ́dl] *v.* mimar, consentir.

code [kod] *s.* código; clave; — **message**
comunicación en clave; **signal** — código de
señales.

co·dex [kódɛks] *s.* codice.

cod·fish [kɑ́dfɪʃ] *s.* bacalao.

co·erce [koɚ́s] *v.* forzar, obligar.

co·er·cion [koɚ́ʃən] *s.* coacción.

co·ex·is·tence [koɛgzístəns] *s.* coexistencia.

cof·fee [kɔ́fi] *s.* café; — **shop** café; — **tree** cafeto;
black — café solo; *Col.* tinto.

cof·fee·pot [kɔ́fipɑt] *s.* cafetera.

cof·fer [kɔ́fɚ] *s.* cofre, arca.

cof·fin [kɔ́fin] *s.* ataúd, féretro.

cog [kag] *s.* diente; — **wheel** rueda dentada.

cog·nate [kɑ́gnet] *s.* cognato.

co·her·ent [kohírənt] *adj.* coherente; conexo.

co·he·sion [kohíʒən] *s.* cohesión.

coif·fure [kwafʊ́r] *s.* tocado, peinado.

coil [kɔɪl] *s.* rollo; rosca; espiral de alambre;
electric — bobina; *v.* arrollar(se), enrollar(se);
enroscar(se).

coin [kɔɪn] *s.* moneda; *v.* acuñar; inventar, forjar
(*una frase o palabra*).

coin·age [kɔ́ɪnɪdʒ] *s.* acuñación; sistema
monetario; moneda, monedas; invención (*de
una palabra o frase*).

co·in·cide [koɪnsáɪd] *v.* coincidir.

co·in·ci·dence [koínsədəns] *s.* coincidencia;
casualidad.

coke [kok] *s.* cok, coque (*combustible*).

cold [kold] *adj.* frío; — **cream** crema cosmética;
— **meat** fiambre; — **wave** ola de frío; — **war**
guerra fría; **to be** — tener frío; **it is** — **today**
hace frío hoy; *s.* frío; catarro, resfriado; **to catch
a** — resfriarse, acatarrarse.

cold·ness [kóldnɪs] *s.* frialdad; indiferencia,
despego.

col·ic [kálık] *s.* cólico.

col·lab·o·rate [kəlǽbəret] *v.* colaborar.

col·lab·o·ra·tion [kəlæbəréʃən] *s.* colaboración.

col·lapse [kəlǽps] *s.* desplome, derrumbe, derrumbamiento; hundimiento; postración; *v.* doblar(se), plegar(se); contraer (*el volumen*); hundirse, derrumbarse, desplomarse; sufrir una postración.

col·lar [kálɚ] *s.* collar; cuello (*de vestido, camisa, etc.*); collera (*para mulas o caballos de tiro*); *v.* acollarar, poner collar a; coger o agarrar por el cuello; prender.

col·late [kəlét, kólet] *v.* cotejar; colacionar.

col·lat·er·al [kəlǽtərəl] *adj.* colateral; auxiliar, subsidiario, accesorio; *s.* garantía (*para un préstamo bancario*).

col·league [kálig] *s.* colega.

col·lect [kəlékt] *v.* recoger; coleccionar; cobrar; recaudar (*impuestos*); reunir(se); congregarse; **to — oneself** calmarse; sosegarse, reportarse.

col·lec·tion [kəlékʃən] *s.* colección; agrupación (*de gente*); recolección, cobranza, cobro, recaudación, colecta.

col·lec·tive [kəléktɪv] *adj.* colectivo.

col·lec·tiv·ism [kəléktəvɪzm] *s.* colectivismo.

col·lec·tor [kəléktɚ] *s.* colector; coleccionista (*de sellos, objetos artísticos, etc.*); cobrador (*de billetes, deudas, etc.*); recaudador (*de impuestos*).

col·lege [kálɪdʒ] *s.* universidad; **— of engineering** facultad de ingeniería; **— of medicine** escuela (*facultad*) de medicina.

col·lide [kəláɪd] *v.* chocar; estar en conflicto, oponerse.

col·lie [kálɪ] *s.* perro de pastor.

col·li·sion [kəlíʒən] *s.* choque, colisión; oposición; pugna (*de intereses, ideas, etc.*).

col·lo·qui·al [kəlókwɪəl] *adj.* familiar; **— expression** locución o frase familiar.

col·lu·sion [kəlúʒɪən] *s.* confabulación.

co·lon [kólən] *s.* colon (*del intestino*); dos puntos (*signo de puntuación*).

colo·nel [kɝnl] *s.* coronel.

co·lo·ni·al [kəlónɪəl] *adj.* colonial.

col·o·nist [kálənɪst] *s.* colono, colonizador.

col·o·ni·za·tion [kalənəzéʃən] *s.* colonización.

col·o·nize [kálənaɪz] *v.* colonizar; establecerse en colonia.

col·o·ny [kálənɪ] *s.* colonia.

col·or [kʌlɚ] *s.* color; colorido; **the -s** la bandera; *v.* colorar; colorear; dar colorido; pintar; teñir; iluminar (*una fotografía, grabado, etc.*); ruborizarse.

col·ored [kʌlɚd] *adj.* colorado, teñido, colorido, pintado; de color; coloreado; **— person** persona de color.

col·or·ful [kʌlɚfəl] *adj.* lleno de color; colorido; vistoso; vívido; pintoresco.

col·or·ing [kʌlɚɪŋ] *s.* colorido; coloración; colorante.

col·or·less [kʌlɚlɪs] *adj.* incoloro; descolorido.

co·los·sal [kəlásl] *adj.* colosal.

colt [kolt] *s.* potro.

Co·lum·bi·an [kəlʌmbɪən] *adj.* colombiano, de Colombia; colombino, referente a Cristóbal Colón.

col·umn [káləm] *s.* columna.

co·ma [kómə] *s.* coma.

comb [kom] *s.* peine; peineta (*de mujer*); cresta (*de gallo*); rastrillo, carda (*para lana*); almohaza (*para caballos*); panal (*de miel*); *v.* peinar; rastrillar, cardar (*lana*); escudriñar; **to — one's**

hair peinarse.

com·bat [kámbæt] *s.* combate, pelea; *v.* combatir.

com·bat·ant [kámbətənt] *adj.* & *s.* combatiente.

com·bi·na·tion [kambənéʃən] *s.* combinación.

com·bine [kəmbáɪn] *v.* combinar(se), unir(se).

com·bo [kámbo] *s.* batería de jazz.

com·bus·ti·ble [kəmbʌ́stəbl] *adj.* & *s.* combustible.

com·bus·tion [kəmbʌ́stʃən] *s.* combustión.

come [kʌm] *v.* venir; llegar; provenir; **to — about** suceder; **to — again** volver, volver a venir; **to — back** volver, regresar; **to — downstairs** bajar; **to — in** entrar; **to — out** salir; **to — of age** llegar a mayor edad; **to — off** soltarse, zafarse; **to — to** volver en sí; **to — to terms** ponerse de acuerdo, ajustarse; **to — up** subir; surgir (*una cuestión*); *p.p. de* **to come.**

co·me·di·an [kəmídɪən] *s.* cómico, comediante.

com·e·dy [kámədɪ] *s.* comedia.

come·ly [kʌ́mlɪ] *adj.* agradable a la vista, gentil, bien parecido.

com·et [kámɪt] *s.* cometa.

com·fort [kʌ́mfɚt] *s.* comodidad; bienestar; alivio, consuelo; *v.* consolar, confortar, aliviar.

com·fort·a·ble [kʌ́mfɚtəbl] *adj.* cómodo; confortable; **— life** vida holgada; **— income** un buen pasar, renta suficiente; **comfortably** *adv.* cómodamente; con comodidad; holgadamente.

com·fort·er [kʌ́mfɚtɚ] *s.* consolador; edredón, cobertor acolchado.

com·fort·less [kʌ́mfɚtlɪs] *adj.* incómodo; desconsolado.

com·ic [kámɪk] *adj.* cómico; chistoso, gracioso; **-s** *s. pl.* caricaturas, historietas cómicas.

com·i·cal [kámɪkl] *adj.* cómico, gracioso.

com·ing [kámɪŋ] *adj.* que viene, que llega; próximo; venidero; *s.* venida, llegada; **— of Christ** advenimiento de Cristo.

com·ma [kámə] *s.* coma.

com·mand [kəmǽnd] *s.* (*order*) mando; mandato, orden; mandamiento; (*post*) comandancia; (*dominance*) dominio; **at your —** a la orden de Vd., a la disposición de Vd.; **he has a good — of English** domina bien el inglés; *v.* mandar; ordenar; dominar; comandar; **to — respect** inspirar respeto, imponerse.

com·mand·er [kəmǽndɚ] *s.* jefe; comandante; teniente de navío; comendador (*de ciertas órdenes*); **— in chief** comandante en jefe; general en jefe.

com·mand·ment [kəmǽndmənt] *s.* mandamiento; mandato, orden.

com·man·do [kəmǽndo] *s.* comando.

com·mem·o·rate [kəméməret] *v.* conmemorar.

com·mence [kəméns] *v.* comenzar.

com·mence·ment [kəménsmənt] *s.* comienzo, principio; acto de distribución de diplomas.

com·mend [kəménd] *v.* alabar, elogiar; encomendar, encargar; recomendar.

com·men·da·tion [kamən/déʃən] *s.* encomio, alabanza.

com·ment [kámɛnt] *s.* comentario, observación, nota; *v.* comentar; hacer observaciones; hacer comentarios.

com·men·tar·y [káməntɛrɪ] ʃ. comentario.

com·men·ta·tor [káməntetɚ] *s.* comentador; comentarista; **radio —** comentarista radial.

com·merce [kámɚs] *s.* comercio.

com·mer·cial [kəmɝ́ʃəl] *adj.* comercial.

com·mis·er·a·tion [kəmɪzəréʃən] *s.* compasión.

com·mis·sar [kámɪsar] *s.* comisario.

com·mis·sar·y [káməsɛrɪ] *s.* comisario.

com·mis·sion [kəmíʃən] *s.* comisión; encargo; junta; nombramiento; **to put out of —** inutilizar; descomponer, quebrar; retirar del servicio (*un navío*); *v.* comisionar; encargar; nombrar; poner en servicio (*un navío*); **-ed officer** oficial comisionado (*alférez u oficial superior a éste*).

com·mis·sion·er [kəmíʃənə⋅] *s.* comisionado; comisario; **police —** comisario de policía.

com·mit [kəmít] *v.* (*perpetrate*) cometer; (*entrust*) encargar; **to — to memory** aprender de memoria **to — to prison** encarcelar; **to — oneself** dar o expresar su opinión, expresarse abiertamente, comprometerse.

com·mit·tee [kəmítɪ] *s.* comité; comisión, junta; **— of one** comisionado o delegado único.

com·mod·i·ty [kəmádətɪ] *s.* mercancía; género, mercadería, artículo de comercio, producto.

com·mon [kámən] *adj.* común; general; corriente; vulgar, ordinario; público; **— law** derecho consuetudinario; **— sense** sentido común; **— soldier** soldado raso; **— market** mercado común; **-s** *s. pl.* refectorio (*de un colegio o universidad*); ejido, campo común; **-ly** *adv.* comúnmente, por lo común.

com·mon·ness [kámənnɪs] *s.* vulgaridad, ordinariez; frecuencia.

com·mon·place [kámənples] *adj.* común, trivial; *s.* lugar común.

com·mon·wealth [kámənwɛlθ] *s.* estado; república; pueblo, colectividad.

com·mo·tion [kəmóʃən] *s.* conmoción; tumulto; bullicio; levantamiento.

com·mune [kəmjún] *v.* comunicarse (con); comulgar.

com·mu·ni·cate [kəmjúnəket] *v.* comunicar(se); transmitir.

com·mu·ni·ca·tion [kəmjunəkéʃən] *s.* comunicación.

com·mu·ni·ca·tive [kəmjúnəketɪv] *adj.* comunicativo.

com·mun·ion [kəmjúnjən] *s.* comunión.

com·mu·nism [kámjʊnɪzəm] *s.* comunismo.

com·mu·nist [kámjʊnɪst] *s.* & *adj.* comunista.

com·mu·ni·ty [kəmjúnətɪ] *s.* comunidad; sociedad; vecindario, barrio; **— chest** caja de beneficencia, fondos de beneficencia.

com·mute [kəmjút] *v.* conmutar; viajar diario de una población a otra.

com·pact [kəmpǽkt] *adj.* compacto; denso; apretado; conciso; sucinto; [kámpækt] *s.* pacto, trato, convenio; polvera.

com·pact·ness [kəmpǽktnɪs] *s.* solidez; densidad; concisión.

com·pan·ion [kəmpǽnjən] *s.* compañero; acompañante.

com·pan·ion·ship [kəmpǽnjənʃɪp] *s.* compañerismo, camaradería; compañía.

com·pany [kʌmpənɪ] *s.* compañía; sociedad; visita; **ship's —** tripulación; **to keep — with** acompañar a; cortejar a; tener relaciones con, frecuentar la compañía de.

com·pa·ra·ble [kámpərəbl] *adj.* comparable.

com·par·a·tive [kəmpǽrətɪv] *adj.* comparativo.

com·pare [kəmpér] *v.* comparar; cotejar; confrontar; contrastar; **beyond —** incomparable, sin par, sin igual, sin comparación.

com·par·i·son [kəmpǽrəsn] *s.* comparación; símil; **beyond —** incomparable, sin comparación; **in — with** comparado con.

com·part·ment [kəmpártmənt] *s.* compartimiento, sección, división; departamento.

com·pass [kʌmpəs] *s.* compás (*para dibujar*); brújula; área, ámbito; alcance.

com·pas·sion [kəmpǽʃən] *s.* compasión, lástima.

com·pas·sion·ate [kəmpǽʃənɪt] *adj.* compasivo, misericordioso.

com·pat·i·ble [kəmpǽtəbl] *adj.* compatible.

com·pa·tri·ot [kəmpétrɪət] *s.* compatriota.

com·pel [kəmpél] *v.* compeler, obligar; exigir.

com·pen·sate [kámpənset] *v.* compensar; recompensar; remunerar.

com·pen·sa·tion [kampənséʃən] *s.* compensación; recompensa; remuneración.

com·pete [kəmpít] *v.* competir.

com·pe·tence [kámpətəns] *s.* competencia, aptitud, capacidad.

com·pe·tent [kámpətənt] *adj.* competente; calificado; capaz.

com·pe·ti·tion [kampətíʃən] *s.* competencia; concurso, certamen; contienda.

com·pet·i·tive [kəmpétətɪv] *adj.* en competencia; **— examination** oposición, concurso.

com·pet·i·tor [kəmpétətə⋅] *s.* competidor; rival; opositor.

com·pile [kəmpáɪl] *v.* compilar, recopilar.

com·pla·cen·cy [kəmplésṇsɪ] *s.* complacencia, contentamiento.

com·pla·cent [kəmplésṇt] *adj.* complaciente, satisfecho.

com·plain [kəmplén] *v.* quejarse; querellarse.

com·plaint [kəmplént] *s.* queja; quejido, lamento; dolencia, enfermedad; **to lodge a —** hacer una reclamación.

com·ple·ment [kámpləmənt] *s.* complemento; [kámpləmɛnt] *v.* complementar, completar.

com·plete [kəmplít] *adj.* completo; *v.* completar; terminar; **-ly** *adv.* completamente, por completo.

com·plete·ness [kəmplítnɪs] *s.* perfección; minuciosidad; lo completo; lo cabal; lo acabado.

com·ple·tion [kəmplíʃən] *s.* completamiento; terminación, conclusión; cumplimiento.

com·plex [kámplɛks] *s.* complejo; [kəmplɛ́ks] *adj.* complejo; compuesto; complicado.

com·plex·ion [kəmplɛ́kʃən] *s.* cutis, tez; aspecto.

com·plex·i·ty [kámplɛksətɪ] *s.* complejidad.

com·pli·ance [kəmpláɪəns] *s.* complacencia; condescendencia; conformidad; cumplimiento; **in — with** en conformidad con; de acuerdo con, conforme a.

com·pli·cate [kámpləket] *v.* complicar.

com·pli·cat·ed [kámpləketɪd] *adj.* complicado.

com·pli·ca·tion [kampləkéʃən] *s.* complicación.

com·plic·i·ty [kəmplísətɪ] *s.* complicidad.

com·pli·ment [kámpləmənt] *s.* cumplido, cumplimiento; requiebro, lisonja, galantería; **to send one's -s** enviar saludos; [kámpləmɛnt] *v.* cumplimentar; requebrar; lisonjear; alabar.

com·ply [kəmpláɪ] *v.* consentir, conformarse (con), obrar de acuerdo (con); cumplir (con).

com·po·nent [kəmpónənt] *adj.* & *s.* componente.

com·pose [kəmpóz] *v.* componer; **to — oneself** sosegarse, serenarse, calmarse.

com·posed [kəmpózd] *adj.* compuesto; tranquilo, sereno, sosegado; **to be — of** estar compuesto de, componerse de, constar de.

com·pos·er [kəmpózə⋅] *s.* compositor; autor.

com·pos·ite [kəmpázɪt] *adj.* compuesto; *s.* compuesto; mezcla.

com·po·si·tion [kampəzíʃən] *s.* composición; arreglo; compuesto.

com·po·sure [kəmpóʒə⋅] *s.* compostura, calma,

CO

serenidad.

com·pound [kámpaυnd] *adj. & s.* compuesto; [kɑmpáυnd] *v.* componer; mezclar, combinar; **to — interest** calcular el interés compuesto.

com·pre·hend [kɑmprɪhénd] *v.* comprender; abarcar, abrazar, incluir.

com·pre·hen·si·ble [kɑmprɪhénsəbl] *adj.* comprensible, inteligible.

com·pre·hen·sion [kɑmprɪhénʃən] *s.* comprensión.

com·pre·hen·sive [kɑmprɪhénsɪv] *adj.* comprensivo; inclusivo.

com·press [kámprɛs] *s.* compresa; [kəmprés] *v.* comprimir, apretar, condensar.

com·pres·sion [kəmpréʃən] *s.* compresión.

com·prise [kəmpráɪz] *v.* comprender, abarcar, incluir, abrazar; constar de.

com·pro·mise [kámprəmaɪz] *s.* compromiso; arreglo; avenencia; término medio; *v.* comprometer; avenirse, transigir; *Am.* transar.

comp·trol·ler [kəntrólɚ] *s.* interventor, *Am.* contralor.

com·pul·sion [kəmpʌlʃən] *s.* compulsión, coacción.

com·pul·so·ry [kəmpʌlsərɪ] *adj.* obligatorio.

com·pu·ta·tion [kɑmpjətéʃən] *s.* cómputo, cálculo.

com·pute [kəmpjút] *v.* computar.

com·put·er [kəmpjútɚ] *s. Esp.* calculadora electrónica; *Arg.* computadora; programadora.

com·put·er·ize [kəmpjútɚaɪz] *v.* someter datos a la calculadora electrónica; suplir con sistema computadora.

com·rade [kámræd] *s.* camarada, compañero.

con·cave [kankév] *adj.* cóncavo.

con·ceal [kansíl] *v.* encubrir, ocultar, esconder.

con·ceal·ment [kansílmənt] *s.* encubrimiento.

con·cede [kansíd] *v.* conceder; otorgar: admitir, reconocer.

con·ceit [kansít] *s.* presunción, amor propio, vanagloria; concepto, agudeza.

con·ceit·ed [kansítɪd] *adj.* presuntuoso, presumido, vanidoso, engreído.

con·ceiv·a·ble [kansívəbl] *adj.* concebible, imaginable, comprensible.

con·ceive [kansív] *v.* concebir; imaginar.

con·cen·trate [kánsn̩tret] *v.* concentrar(se), reconcentrar(se).

con·cen·tra·tion [kansn̩tréʃən] *s.* concentración; reconcentración; **— camp** reconcentración de presos.

con·cept [kánsɛpt] *s.* concepto, idea; opinión.

con·cep·tion [kansépʃən] *s.* concepción; concepto, idea.

con·cern [kansɝn] *s. (business)* compañía, negociación; negocio; establecimiento mercantil; *(interest)* cuidado; interés; preocupación; **to be of no —** no ser de consecuencia; *v.* concernir, importar, interesar; preocupar; **in all that -s him** en cuanto la atañe, en cuanto le concierne; **to whom it may —** a quien corresponda.

con·cerned [kansɝnd] *adj.* interesado; preocupado, intranquilo, inquieto, ansioso; **to be — about** interesarse por, preocuparse por; **as far as I am —** por lo que me concierne, por lo que me toca, en cuanto a mí me atañe.

con·cern·ing [kansɝnɪŋ] *prep.* tocante a, respecto a, acerca de.

con·cert [kánsɝt] *s.* concierto; [kansɝt] *v.* concertar, arreglar *(un plan).*

con·ces·sion [kansέʃən] *s.* concesión.

con·cil·i·ate [kansílɪet] *v.* conciliar, poner en armonía; ganar la voluntad de.

con·cise [kansáɪs] *adj.* conciso, sucinto.

con·cise·ness [kansáɪsnɪs] *s.* concisión, brevedad.

con·clude [kanklúd] *v.* concluir; acabar, terminar; deducir; decidir.

con·clu·sion [kanklúʒən] *s.* conclusión.

con·clu·sive [kanklúsɪv] *adj.* conclusivo, concluyente.

con·coct [kankákt] *v.* confeccionar; preparar *(combinando diversos ingredientes);* inventar, urdir.

con·coc·tion [kankákʃən] *s.* cocimiento, menjurje; mezcla.

con·cord [kánkɔrd] *s.* concordia, conformidad, acuerdo; convenio, pacto.

con·crete [kankrít] *adj.* concreto; de hormigón, de cemento; *s.* hormigón, cemento, *Am.* concreto.

con·cu·bine [káŋkjubaɪn] *s.* concubina.

con·cur [kankɝ] *v.* estar de acuerdo, ser del mismo parecer; unirse.

con·cus·sion [kankʌʃən] *s.* concusión.

con·demn [kandém] *v.* condenar; **to — a building** condenar un edificio.

con·dem·na·tion [kandɛmnéʃən] *s.* condenación.

con·den·sa·tion [kandɛnséʃən] *s.* condensación; resumen, compendio.

con·dense [kandέns] *v.* condensar(se).

con·de·scend [kandɪsέnd] *v.* condescender.

con·de·scen·sion [kandɪsέnʃən] *s.* condescendencia.

con·di·ment [kándəmənt] *s.* condimento.

con·di·tion [kandíʃən] *s.* condición; estado; nota o calificación provisional; **on — that** a condición de que, con tal que; *v.* acondicionar; poner en buena condición; estipular; reprobar provisionalmente *(a un estudiante).*

con·di·tion·al [kandíʃən̩l] *adj.* condicional.

con·dole [kandól] *v.* condolerse; **to — with** dar el pésame a; consolar a.

con·do·lence [kandólɛns] *s.* pésame.

con·do·min·i·um [kandəmínɪəm] *s.* condominio.

con·done [kandón] *v.* dispensar; perdonar; condonar.

con·duce [kandjús] *v.* conducir.

con·du·cive [kandjúsɪv] *adj.* conducente.

con·duct [kándʌkt] *s. (behavior)* conducta; comportamiento, proceder; *(handling)* dirección, manejo; [kandʌkt] *v.* conducir; dirigir; manejar; **to — oneself well** portarse bien.

con·duc·tor [kandʌktɚ] *s.* conductor; guía; **orchestra —** director de orquesta; **train —** revisor; cobrador, *Am.* conductor.

con·duit [kándυɪt] *s.* conducto; caño; cañería, tubería.

cone [kon] *s.* cono; **paper —** cucurucho; **pine —** piña.

con·fec·tion [kanfékʃən] *s.* confección; confitura; confite, dulce.

con·fec·tion·er·y [kanfékʃənɛrɪ] *s.* confitería; dulcería; confites, dulces.

con·fed·er·a·cy [kanfédərəsɪ] *s.* confederación.

con·fed·er·ate [kanfédərɪt] *adj. & s.* confederado; [kanfédəret] *v.* confederar(se).

con·fed·er·a·tion [kanfédəréʃən] *s.* confederación.

con·fer [kanfɝ] *v.* conferir; conceder; conferenciar, consultar.

con·fer·ence [kánfərəns] *s.* conferencia; congreso; consulta, junta, sesión.

con·fess [kanfés] *v.* confesar(se); reconocer, admitir.

con·fes·sion [kanféʃən] *s.* confesión.

con·fes·sion·al [kanféʃən̩l] *s.* confesionario.

con·fes·sor [kanfésɚ] *s.* confesor.

con·fi·dant [kanfədǽnt] *s.* confidente.

con·fide [kanfáɪd] *v.* confiar; fiar.

con·fi·dence [kánfədəns] s. confianza; confidencia; — **game** estafa; — **man** estafador.

con·fi·dent [kánfədənt] adj. confiado; seguro, cierto; **-ly** adv. confiadamente, con toda seguridad.

con·fi·den·tial [kɑnfədɛ́nʃəl] adj. confidencial; íntimo; secreto; **-ly** adv. en confianza.

con·fine [kánfaɪn] s. confín; [kɑnfáɪn] v. confinar; encerrar; **to — oneself to** limitarse a; **to be -ed in bed** estar encamado, guardar cama.

con·fine·ment [kənfáɪnmənt] s. encerramiento; encierro; prisión, encarcelación.

con·firm [kənfɝm] v. confirmar.

con·fir·ma·tion [kɑnfəméʃən] s. confirmación.

con·fis·cate [kánfɪskeɪ] v. confiscar.

con·fla·gra·tion [kɑnfləgréʃən] s. conflagración, incendio.

con·flict [kánflɪkt] s. conflicto, oposición, choque; lucha, combate; [kənflíkt] v. chocar, oponerse, estar en conflicto.

con·form [kənfɔ́rm] v. conformar(se).

con·form·i·ty [kənfɔ́rmətɪ] s. conformidad.

con·found [kɑnfáʊnd] v. confundir, perturbar, desconcertar, aturdir; — **it!** ¡caramba!

con·front [kənfrʌ́nt] v. confrontar; carear, poner cara a cara (a dos reos); encararse con, afrontar, hacer frente a, arrostrar.

con·fuse [kənfjúz] v. confundir; trastornar; embrollar; desconcertar.

con·fused [kənfjúzd] adj. confuso; revuelto; desconcertado, perplejo; **to become —** confundirse; desconcertarse.

con·fus·ing [kənfjúzɪŋ] adj. confuso, revuelto; desconcertante.

con·fu·sion [kənfjúʒən] s. confusión; desorden; tumulto; perplejidad.

con·geal [kəndʒíl] v. congelar(se), helar(se), cuajar(se).

con·gen·ial [kəndʒínjəl] adj. congenial; simpático; **to be — with** congeniar con, simpatizar con.

con·ges·tion [kəndʒɛ́stʃən] s. congestión; aglomeración.

con·glom·er·a·tion [kənglɑməréʃən] s. aglomeración.

con·grat·u·late [kəngrǽtʃəlet] v. congratular, felicitar, dar el parabién.

con·grat·u·la·tion [kəngrætʃəléʃən] s. congratulación, felicitación, parabién, enhorabuena.

con·gre·gate [káŋgrɪget] v. congregar(se), juntar(se), reunir(se).

con·gre·ga·tion [kaŋgrɪgéʃən] s. congregación; asamblea, reunión; colección, agregado; fieles, feligreses (de una iglesia).

con·gress [káŋgrəs] s. congreso; asamblea.

con·gres·sion·al [kəŋgréʃənl] adj. perteneciente al congreso.

con·gress·man [káŋgrəsmən] s. congresista, diputado, representante.

con·ic [kánɪk] adj. cónico.

con·jec·ture [kəndʒɛ́ktʃɚ] s. conjetura, suposición; v. conjeturar, suponer.

con·ju·gate [kándʒəget] v. conjugar.

con·ju·ga·tion [kandʒəgéʃən] s. conjugación.

con·junc·tion [kəndʒʌ́ŋkʃən] s. conjunción.

con·jure [kándʒɚ] v. conjurar; **to — up** evocar; [kəndʒúr] rogar, implorar.

con·nect [kənɛ́kt] v. conectar; unir(se), juntar(se); enlazar(se); relacionar(se); acoplar.

con·nect·ing rod [kənɛ́ktɪŋ rad] s. biela.

con·nec·tion [kənɛ́kʃən] s. conexión; enlace;

vínculo; unión; relación; **-s** parientes; amigos, amistades.

con·nip·tion [kənípʃən] s. pataleta; **to have a —** darle a uno una pataleta.

con·nive [kənáɪv] v. conspirar; disimular; hacerse cómplice.

con·nois·seur [kanəsɝ́] s. conocedor, perito.

con·quer [káŋkɚ] v. conquistar; vencer.

con·quer·or [káŋkərɚ] s. conquistador; vencedor.

con·quest [káŋkwɛst] s. conquista.

con·science [kánʃəns] s. conciencia.

con·sci·en·tious [kanʃiɛ́nʃəs] adj. concienzudo.

con·scious [kánʃəs] adj. consciente; sabedor; **-ly** adv. conscientemente; a sabiendas.

con·scious·ness [kánʃəsnɪs] s. consciencia, estado consciente; **to lose —** perder el sentido o conocimiento.

con·script [kənskrípt] v. reclutar; [kánskrɪpt] s. recluta.

con·se·crate [kánsɪkret] v. consagrar; dedicar.

con·se·cra·tion [kansɪkréʃən] s. consagración; dedicación.

con·sec·u·tive [kənsɛ́kjətɪv] adj. consecutivo.

con·sen·sus [kənsɛ́nsəs] s. consenso.

con·sent [kənsɛ́nt] s. consentimiento; permiso, asentimiento; v. consentir; permitir, asentir.

con·se·quence [kánsəkwɛns] s. consecuencia.

con·se·quent [kánsəkwɛnt] adj. consecuente; consiguiente; s. consecuente, consiguiente, consecuencia; **-ly** adv. por consiguiente, por consecuencia.

con·se·quen·tial [kansəkwɛ́ntʃl] adj. de consecuencia.

con·ser·va·tion [kansəvéʃən] s. conservación; preservación.

con·ser·va·tive [kənsɝ́vətɪv] adj. conservador; conservativo; s. conservador.

con·ser·va·to·ry [kənsɝ́vətorɪ] s. conservatorio; invernadero.

con·serve [kánsɝv] s. conserva, dulce; v. [kənsɝ́v] conservar; preservar.

con·sid·er [kənsídɚ] v. considerar.

con·sid·er·a·ble [kənsídərəbl] adj. considerable; cuantioso; **considerably** adv. considerablemente; **considerably older** bastante más viejo.

con·sid·er·ate [kənsídərɪt] adj. considerado.

con·sid·er·a·tion [kənsɪdəréʃən] s. (respect) respeto; consideración; importancia; (pay) remuneración; **in — of** en atención a, teniendo en cuenta, en razón de, en vista de.

con·sid·er·ing [kənsídərɪŋ] prep. en razón de, en vista de; en atención a, en consideración de.

con·sign [kənsáɪn] v. consignar; enviar; entregar.

con·sign·ee [kansaɪní] s. consignatario.

con·sign·ment [kənsáɪnmənt] s. consignación.

con·sist [kənsíst] v. consistir (en); constar (de).

con·sis·ten·cy [kənsístənsɪ] s. consecuencia; consistencia, firmeza, solidez.

con·sis·tent [kənsístənt] adj. consecuente, lógico; compatible; consistente, coherente.

con·so·la·tion [kansəléʃən] s. consolación; consuelo.

con·sole [kənsól] v. consolar.

con·sol·i·date [kənsáladet] v. consolidar(se); unir(se), combinar(se).

con·so·nant [kánsənənt] adj. consonante; conforme; s. consonante.

con·sort [kánsɔrt] s. consorte; [kənsɔ́rt] v. **to — with** asociarse con.

con·spic·u·ous [kənspíkjuəs] adj. conspicuo, notorio; manifiesto, sobresaliente.

CO

con·spir·a·cy [kənspírəsɪ] *s.* conspiración, conjuración.

con·spir·a·tor [kənspírətə] *s.* conspirador, conjurado.

con·spire [kənspáɪr] *v.* conspirar; tramar, maquinar.

con·sta·ble [kánstəbl] *s.* alguacil, policía; condestable (*titulo*).

con·stan·cy [kánstənsɪ] *s.* constancia.

con·stant [kánstənt] *adj.* constante; *s.* constante, cantidad constante; **-ly** *adv.* constantemente, continuamente, siempre; a menudo.

con·stel·la·tion [kanstəleʃən] *s.* constelación.

con·ster·na·tion [kanstənéʃən] *s.* consternación.

con·sti·pate [kánstəpet] *v.* estreñir.

con·sti·pa·tion [kanstəpéʃən] *s.* estreñimiento.

con·stit·u·ent [kənstítʃuənt] *adj.* constituyente; constitutivo; componente; *s.* componente, elemento; elector, votante.

con·sti·tute [kánstətjut] *v.* constituir; componer; establecer.

con·sti·tu·tion [kanstətjúʃən] *s.* constitución.

con·sti·tu·tion·al [kanstətjúʃənl] *adj.* constitucional; *s.* paseo a pie, caminata (*para hacer ejercicio*).

con·strain [kənstrén] *v.* constreñir; obligar, forzar; apretar, comprimir.

con·strict [kənstríkt] *v.* apretar; estrechar.

con·struct [kənstrʌ́kt] *v.* construir, fabricar.

con·struc·tion [kənstrʌ́kʃən] *s.* construcción; estructura; interpretación.

con·struc·tive [kənstrʌ́ktɪv] *adj.* constructivo; de utilidad positiva; provechoso.

con·strue [kənstrú] *v.* interpretar, explicar.

con·sul [kánsl] *s.* cónsul.

con·su·late [kánslɪt] *s.* consulado.

con·sult [kənsʌ́lt] *v.* consultar.

con·sult·ant [kənsʌ́ltənt] *s.* consultante.

con·sul·ta·tion [kansltéʃən] *s.* consulta.

con·sume [kənsúm] *v.* consumir; gastar; perder (*el tiempo*).

con·sum·er [kənsúmə] *s.* consumidor.

con·sum·mate [kánsəmet] *v.* consumar, completar; [kənsʌ́mɪt] *adj.* consumado, perfecto, completo.

con·sump·tion [kənsʌ́mpʃən] *s.* consumo, gasto; consunción; tisis, tuberculosis.

con·sump·tive [kənsʌ́mptɪv] *adj.* tísico.

con·tact [kántækt] *s.* contacto; *v.* tocar; poner(se) en contacto con; estar en contacto con.

con·ta·gion [kəntédʒən] *s.* contagio.

con·ta·gious [kəntédʒəs] *adj.* contagioso.

con·tain [kəntén] *v.* contener; encerrar; tener cabida para; reprimir, refrenar; **to — oneself** contenerse, refrenarse.

con·tain·er [kənténə] *s.* envase, caja, recipiente.

con·tam·i·nate [kəntǽmənet] *v.* contaminar, viciar, inficionar.

con·tam·i·na·tion [kəntæmənéʃən] *s.* contaminación; cruce.

con·tem·plate [kántəmplet] *v.* contemplar; meditar; tener la intención de; proyectar.

con·tem·pla·tion [kantəmpléʃən] *s.* contemplación; meditación; intención, propósito.

con·tem·po·rar·y [kəntémpərɛrɪ] *adj.* contemporáneo; coetáneo.

con·tempt [kəntémpt] *s.* desdén, menosprecio; desprecio; **— of court** contumacia.

con·tempt·i·ble [kəntémptəbl] *adj.* despreciable, vil.

con·temp·tu·ous [kəntémptʃuəs] *adj.* desdeñoso.

con·tend [kənténd] *v.* contender; competir; argüir; altercar; sostener, afirmar.

con·tent [kántɛnt] *s.* contenido; sustancia; capacidad, volumen; **-s** contenido; **table of -s** tabla de materias, índice general.

con·tent [kəntént] *adj.* contento; satisfecho; *s.* contento; satisfacción; **to one's heart's** — a pedir de boca; hasta saciarse; a su entera satisfacción; *v.* contentar; satisfacer.

con·tent·ed [kənténtɪd] *adj.* contento, satisfecho.

con·ten·tion [kənténʃən] *s.* contención, contienda, disputa, controversia; tema, argumento; aseveración.

con·tent·ment [kənténtmənt] *s.* contentamiento, contento.

con·test [kántɛst] *s.* concurso, certamen; debate; contienda; torneo; [kəntést] *v.* contender; disputar; luchar por; **to — with** competir con.

con·text [kántɛkst] *s.* contexto.

con·tig·u·ous [kəntígjuəs] *adj.* contiguo; adyacente.

con·ti·nent [kántənənt] *s.* continente; *adj.* continente, casto, moderado.

con·ti·nen·tal [kantənéntl] *adj. & s.* continental.

con·tin·gen·cy [kəntíndʒənsɪ] *s.* contingencia, eventualidad.

con·tin·gent [kəntíndʒənt] *adj. & s.* contingente.

con·tin·u·al [kəntínjuəl] *adj.* continuo; frecuente; **-ly** *adv.* de continuo, continuamente, frecuentemente.

con·tin·u·ance [kəntínjuəns] *s.* continuación; aplazamiento.

con·tin·u·a·tion [kəntɪnjuéʃən] *s.* continuación.

con·tin·ue [kəntínju] *v.* continuar.

con·ti·nu·i·ty [kantənúətɪ] *s.* continuidad.

con·tin·u·ous [kəntínjuəs] *adj.* continuo, sin parar, sin cesar.

con·tor·tion [kəntórʃən] *s.* contorsión.

con·tour [kántʊr] *s.* contorno; perímetro.

con·tra·band [kántrəbænd] *s.* contrabando.

con·tract [kántrækt] *s.* contrato, pacto, convenio; contrata; **marriage —** esponsales; [kəntrǽkt] *v.* contratar; contraer(se), encoger(se); **to — an illness** contraer una enfermedad; **to — the brows** fruncir las cejas.

con·trac·tion [kəntrǽkʃən] *s.* contracción.

con·trac·tor [kəntrǽktə] *s.* contratista.

con·tra·dict [kantrədíkt] *v.* contradecir; contrariar.

con·tra·dic·tion [kantrədíkʃən] *s.* contradicción; contrariedad.

con·tra·dic·to·ry [kantrədíktərɪ] *adj.* contradictorio; opuesto, contrario.

con·tra·ry [kántrɛrɪ] *adj.* contrario; opuesto; testarudo, obstinado; *s.* contrario; **on the —** al contrario.

con·trast [kántræst] *s.* contraste; [kəntrǽst] *v.* contrastar.

con·tra·vene [kantrəvín] *v.* contravenir a; oponerse a.

con·trib·ute [kəntríbjut] *v.* contribuir.

con·tri·bu·tion [kantrəbjúʃən] *s.* contribución; aportación; cuota; dádiva.

con·trib·u·tor [kəntríbjətə] *s.* contribuidor; colaborador.

con·trib·u·to·ry [kəntríbjutorɪ] *adj.* contribuidor.

con·trite [kántraɪt] *adj.* contrito.

con·tri·vance [kəntráɪvəns] *s.* traza, maquinación; artificio, invención; designio; artefacto, aparato, máquina.

con·trive [kəntráɪv] *v.* tramar, maquinar; inventar, idear; proyectar; **to — to** buscar el medio de, tratar de, procurar.

con·trol [kəntról] *s.* (*authority*) mando, manejo; dirección; (*instrument*) freno, regulador;

restricción; *Am.* control; **-s** mandos, controles; — **stick** palanca (*de un aeroplano*); — **tower** torre de mando; — **experiment** experimento controlado; **to lose** — **of one's temper** perder la paciencia; *v.* gobernar, manejar, *Am.* controlar; regular, regularizar; restringir; contener, reprimir; tener a raya; **to** — **oneself** contenerse dominarse.

con·trol·ler [kəntrólə] *s.* interventor, registrador, *Riopl., C.A., Andes, Ven., Col.* contralor, *Ch., Méx.* contralador; regulador; aparato de manejo y control.

con·tro·ver·sy [kántrəvɜsɪ] *s.* controversia, debate, disputa; polémica.

co·nun·drum [kənʌndrəm] *s.* adivinanza, acertijo.

con·va·lesce [kɑnvəlés] *v.* convalescer.

con·vene [kənvín] *v.* juntar, convocar; reunirse.

con·ven·ience [kənvínjəns] *s.* conveniencia, comodidad; **at one's** — cuando le convenga a uno, cuando tenga oportunidad, cuando buenamente pueda.

con·ven·ient [kənvínjənt] *adj.* conveniente; oportuno; cómodo; a propósito; **-ly** *adv.* convenientemente, cómodamente.

con·vent [kánvɛnt] *s.* convento.

con·ven·tion [kənvɛnʃən] *s.* convención; congreso, asamblea; convenio; costumbre, regla.

con·ven·tion·al [kənvɛnʃənl] *adj.* convencional; tradicional.

con·ven·tion·eer [kənvɛnʃənír] *s.* congresista.

con·verge [kənvɜdʒ] *v.* converger o convergir.

con·ver·sant [kánvɜsṇt] *adj.:* — **with** versado en.

con·ver·sa·tion [kɑnvəséʃən] *s.* conversación.

con·verse [kənvɜs] *v.* conversar, hablar, platicar.

con·ver·sion [kənvɜʒən] *s.* conversión.

con·vert [kánvɜt] *s.* converso, persona convertida; catecúmeno (*converso reciente*); [kənvɜt] *v.* convertir(se).

con·vex [kɑnvɛks] *adj.* convexo.

con·vey [kənvé] *v.* llevar; transportar; transferir; traspasar; transmitir; comunicar; **to** — **thanks** expresar agradecimiento, dar las gracias.

con·vey·ance [kənvéəns] *s.* vehículo; transporte; transmisión; entrega; comunicación; traspaso; escritura de propiedad o traspaso.

con·vey·er [kənvéə] *s.* correa de transmisión.

con·vict [kánvɪkt] *s.* presidiario; reo; [kənvíkt] *v.* convencer (*de un delito*), declarar culpable; probar la culpabilidad de.

con·vic·tion [kənvíkʃən] *s.* convicción; convencimiento; prueba de culpabilidad.

con·vince [kənvíns] *v.* convencer.

con·vinc·ing [kənvínsɪŋ] *adj.* convincente.

con·vo·ca·tion [kɑnvəkéʃən] *s.* convocación; asamblea.

con·voke [kənvók] *v.* convocar.

con·voy [kánvɔɪ] *s.* convoy, escolta, guardia; [kənvɔ́ɪ] *v.* convoyar.

con·vulse [kənvʌls] *v.* crispar; agitar; convulsionar.

con·vul·sion [kənvʌlʃən] *s.* convulsión, agitación.

coo [ku] *s.* arrullo; *v.* arrullar.

cook [kʊk] *s.* cocinero, cocinera; *v.* cocinar, guisar; cocer; **to** — **up a plan** urdir un plan.

cook·er·y [kʊ́kərɪ] *s.* cocina, arte de cocinar.

cook·ie, cook·y [kʊ́kɪ] *s.* bizcochito, bollito.

cook·ing [kʊ́kɪŋ] *s.* cocina, arte culinaria; — **stove** cocina de gas, cocina eléctrica, estufa; — **utensils** batería de cocina, trastos de cocina.

cool [kul] *adj.* fresco; frío, indiferente; calmo, sereno; *s.* fresco, frescura; *v.* refrescar; enfriar; templar, calmar; **to** — **off** enfriarse; calmarse.

cool·ant [kúlənt] *s.* líquido refrigerador.

cool·ness [kúlnɪs] *s.* fresco, frescura; frialdad, indiferencia.

coon [kun] *s.* coatí (*cuadrúpedo carnívoro*); negro; **a -'s age** una eternidad, mucho tiempo.

coop [kup] *s.* jaula; **chicken** — gallinero; *v.* enjaular; **to** — **up** encerrar.

co·op·er·ate [koápəret] *v.* cooperar.

co·op·er·a·tion [koɑpəréʃən] *s.* cooperación.

co·op·er·a·tive [koápəretɪv] *adj.* cooperativo; *s.* cooperativa, sociedad cooperativa.

co·or·di·nate [koórdṇet] *v.* coordinar; [koórdṇɪt] *adj.* coordinado.

co·or·di·na·tion [koordṇéʃən] *s.* coordinación.

cop [kɑp] *s.* polizonte, policía.

cope [kop] *v.* **to** — **with** tener suficiente fuerza para; **I cannot** — **with this** no puedo con esto, no puedo dar abasto a esto.

co·pi·ous [kópɪəs] *adj.* copioso, abundante.

cop·per [kápə] *s.* cobre; polizonte, policía; — **coin** moneda de cobre, centavo; — **kettle** marmita o caldera de cobre; *adj.* cobrizo.

cop·y [kápɪ] *s.* copia; ejemplar (*de un libro*); manuscrito (*para el impresor*); *v.* copiar; imitar; remedar.

cop·y·right [kápɪraɪt] *s.* derecho de propiedad literaria; *v.* registrar, obtener patente de propiedad literaria.

co·quette [kokét] *s.* coqueta.

cor·al [kórəl] *s.* coral; *adj.* coralino, de coral; — **reef** arrecife de coral.

cord [kord] *s.* cuerda; cordón, cordel; cuerda (*medida de leña*); tendón; **-s** pantalones de pana; **spinal** — espinazo, espina dorsal.

cor·dial [kórdʒəl] *adj.* & *s.* cordial.

cor·du·roy [kórdərɔɪ] *s.* pana; **-s** pantalones de pana; — **road** camino de troncos o maderos.

core [kor] *s.* corazón, centro; núcleo; esencia; *v.* cortar el centro o corazón de; despepitar (*una manzana*).

cork [kork] *s.* corcho; tapón; — **tree** alcornoque; *v.* tapar con corcho.

cork·screw [kórkskru] *s.* tirabuzón, sacacorchos; *adj.* espiral, de forma espiral.

corn [korn] *s.* maíz; grano, cereal; callo (*de los pies o manos*); — **bread** pan de maíz; — **meal** harina de maíz; — **cob** *Esp.* zuro; *Am.* tusa; *v.* salar, curar, acecinar.

corned beef [kórnd bif] *s.* carne de vaca curada (*en salmuera y salitre*).

cor·ner [kórnə] *s.* (*interior*) rincón; rinconada; ángulo; (*exterior*) esquina; ángulo; (*monopoly*) monopolio; — **stone** piedra angular; — **table** (— **shelf,** — **bracket**) rinconera; *v.* arrinconar; acorralar; acaparar, monopolizar.

cor·net [kornét] *s.* corneta.

corn·field [kórnfild] *s.* maizal, *Am.* milpa.

cor·nice [kórnɪs] *s.* cornisa.

cor·ol·lar·y [kórəlɛrɪ] *s.* corolario; consecuencia natural.

cor·o·na·tion [kɔrənéʃən] *s.* coronación.

cor·o·ner [kórənə] *s.* juez de guardia.

cor·o·net [kórənɪt] *s.* coronilla, guirnalda.

cor·po·ral [kórpərəl] *adj.* corporal; corpóreo; *s.* cabo (*militar*).

cor·po·ra·tion [kɔrpəréʃən] *s.* corporación; sociedad mercantil.

corps [kor] *s.* cuerpo (*grupo organizado*); **air** — cuerpo de aviación; **army** — cuerpo de ejército.

corpse [kɔrps] *s.* cadáver.

cor·pu·lent [kórpjələnt] *adj.* corpulento.

cor·pus·cle [kɔ́rpəsl] s. corpúsculo; glóbulo.
cor·ral [kərǽl] s. corral; v. acorralar.
cor·rect [kərɛ́kt] v. corregir; adj. correcto; **it is —** está bien; **-ly** adv. correctamente; **-ly done** bien hecho.
cor·rec·tion [kərɛ́kʃən] s. corrección.
cor·rect·ness [kərɛ́ktnɪs] s. corrección.
cor·rec·tor [kərɛ́ktɚ] s. corregidor, corrector.
cor·re·late [kɔ́rəlet] v. correlacionar.
cor·re·spond [kɔrəspánd] v. corresponder; corresponderse, cartearse, escribirse.
cor·re·spon·dence [kɔrəspándəns] s. correspondencia.
cor·re·spon·dent [kɔrəspándənt] adj. correspondiente; s. correspondiente; corresponsal.
cor·re·spond·ing [kɔrəspándɪŋ] adj. correspondiente; conforme.
cor·ri·dor [kɔ́rədɚ] s. corredor, pasillo, pasadizo.
cor·rob·o·rate [kərábəret] v. corroborar.
cor·rode [kəród] v. corroer(se).
cor·ru·gat·ed i·ron [kɔ́rəgetəd aiɚn] s. hierro acanalado.
cor·rupt [kərʌ́pt] adj. corrompido; perverso, depravado; **to become —** corromperse; v. corromper; pervertir; sobornar.
cor·rup·tion [kərʌ́pʃən] s. corrupción; soborno; descomposición.
cor·set [kɔ́rsɪt] s. corsé.
cor·ti·sone [kɔ́rtəzon] s. cortisono.
cos·met·ic [kɑzmɛ́tɪk] adj. & s. cosmético.
cos·mic [kázmɪk] adj. cósmico.
cos·mo·naut [kázmənɔt] s. cosmonauta.
cos·mo·pol·i·tan [kɑzməpálətn] adj. cosmopolita.
cost [kɔst] s. coste, costa o costo; **at all -s** a toda costa; **to sell at —** vender al costo; v. costar; pret. & p.p. de **to cost.**
cost·ly [kɔ́stlɪ] adj. costoso.
cos·tume [kástjum] s. vestuario, traje, vestido; atavío; indumentaria.
cot [kat] s. catre; **folding —** catre de tijera.
cot·tage [kátɪdʒ] s. casita, caseta; casa de campo; **— cheese** requesón.
cot·ter pin [kátɚ pɪn] s. chaveta.
cot·ton [katn] s. algodón; **—seed** semilla de algodón; **— wool** algodón en rama; **— yarn** hilaza.
couch [kautʃ] s. canapé, diván; v. expresar; estar escondido o en acecho; **-ed in difficult language** expresado en lenguaje difícil.
cough [kɔf] s. tos; **— drop** pastilla para la tos; **whooping —** tos ferina; v. toser; **to — up** expectorar.
could [kud] pret. del. v. defect. **can.**
coun·cil [káunsl] s. concilio; consejo; **city —** consejo muncipal.
coun·cil·man [káunslmən] s. concejal.
coun·cil·or [káunslɚ] s. concejal.
coun·sel [káunsl] s. (advice) consejo; parecer, dictamen; (lawyer) abogado consultor; v. aconsejar; recomendar.
coun·sel·or [káunslɚ] s. consejero; abogado consultor.
count [kaunt] s. (reckoning) cuenta, cálculo; cómputo; (charge) cargo, acusación; (noble) conde; v. contar; valer, tener importancia; **to — on** contar con, confiar en.
count·down [káuntdaun] s. recuento descendente hasta cero.
coun·te·nance [káuntənəns] s. semblante, aspecto; **to give — to** favorecer, apoyar; aprobar; v.

aprobar; favorecer, apoyar; tolerar.
count·er [káuntɚ] s. contador; mostrador; tablero; ficha; adj. contrario, opuesto; adv. al contrario; **to run — to** ser contrario a, oponerse a; v. oponerse; contradecir; **to — a blow** devolver un golpe.
coun·ter·act [kauntɚǽkt] v. contrarrestar, neutralizar.
coun·ter·bal·ance [kauntɚbǽləns] v. contrapesar; equilibrar; [káuntɚbæləns] s. contrapeso.
coun·ter·feit [káuntɚfɪt] s. falsificación; adj. falso; falsificado, falseado; contrahecho; **— money** moneda falsa; v. contrahacer, falsificar, falsear.
coun·ter·mand [káuntɚmænd] s. contraorden, contramando, revocación, canceleción; [kauntɚmǽnd] v. contramandar, revocar, cancelar.
coun·ter·part [káuntɚpart] s. contraparte.
coun·ter·poise [káuntɚpɔɪz] s. contrapeso; v. contrapesar.
coun·ter·rev·o·lu·tion [kauntɚrɛvəlúʃən] s. contrarrevolución.
coun·ter·sign [káuntɚsain] s. contraseña.
count·ess [káuntɪs] s. condesa.
count·less [káuntlɪs] adj. incontable, innumerable.
coun·try [kántrɪ] s. país; tierra; patria; campo; adj. campestre; rural; rústico; campesino.
coun·try·man [kántrɪmən] s. compatriota, paisano; (rural type) campesino, Méx., C.A. ranchero, P.R. jíbaro; Cuba guajiro; Ch. huaso; Arg. gaucho; Ec., Col. paisa.
coun·try·side [kántrisaid] s. campiña, campo.
coun·ty [káuntɪ] s. condado (división de un estado).
coup d'é·tat [ku detá] s. golpe de estado; cuartelazo.
cou·pé [kupé, kup] s. cupé.
coup·le [kʌ́pl] s. par; pareja; v. parear; unir; acoplar.
coup·let [kʌ́plɪt] s. copla, versos pareados.
coup·ling [kʌ́plɪŋ] s. unión, conexión; acoplamiento; enganche.
cou·pon [kúpan] s. cupón; talón.
cour·age [kɝ́ɪdʒ] s. coraje, ánimo, valor.
cou·ra·geous [kərédʒəs] adj. valeroso, valiente, animoso.
cou·ri·er [kúrɪɚ] s. mensajero.
course [kors] s. (way) curso; rumbo, trayecto; (advance) marcha, progreso; (mode) método; (study) asignatura; (dish) plato (de una comida); **— of conduct** conducta, proceder; **golf —** campo o cancha de golf; **race —** hipódromo, pista; **in the — of a year** en el transcurso de un año; **of —** claro, por supuesto; **to follow a straight —** seguir una línea recta.
court [kort] s. patio; plazuela, plazoleta; juzgado, tribunal de justicia; corte; **tennis —** cancha para tenis; **— plaster** tela adhesiva, tafetán inglés, esparadrapo; **to pay — to** hacer la corte a, cortejar, galantear; v. cortejar; galantear; buscar; **to — danger** exponerse al peligro.
cour·te·ous [kɝ́tɪəs] adj. cortés.
cour·te·sy [kɝ́təsɪ] s. cortesía; fineza, atención; reverencia.
court·i·er [kórtɪɚ] s. cortesano, palaciego.
court·mar·tial [kórtmarʃəl] s. consejo de guerra; v. someter a consejo de guerra.
court·ship [kórtʃɪp] s. cortejo, galanteo.
court·yard [kórtjard] s. patio.
cous·in [kázn] s. primo; prima; **first —** primo hermano, primo carnal.
cove [kov] s. cala, ensenada.

cov·e·nant [kʌvənənt] *s.* convenio, pacto; contrato.
cov·er [kʌvəˈ] *s. (lid)* cubierta, tapa, tapadera; *(blanket)* cobija; cobertor; *(binding)* encuadernación; envoltura; *(pillow)* funda; *(shelter)* albergue, abrido; **table** — tapete; — **charge** precio fijo que se agrega a la cuenta por servicios; **to send under separate** — enviar por separado; *v.* cubrir; tapar; encubrir; abrigar, proteger; abarcar; **to** — **a distance** recorrer una distancia.
cov·er·age [kʌvərɪdʒ] *s.* alcance; *(journalism)* reportaje.
cov·er·ing [kʌvrɪŋ] *s.* cubierta; cobertura; envoltura; cobija, abrigo.
cov·et [kʌvɪt] *v.* codiciar; ambicionar.
cov·et·ous [kʌvɪtəs] *adj.* codicioso.
cow [kaʊ] *s.* vaca; hembra *(de elefante y otros cuadrúpedos)*; *v.* atemorizar, acobardar.
cow·ard [káʊəd] *adj. & s.* cobarde.
cow·ard·ice [káʊədɪs] *s.* cobardía.
cow·ard·li·ness [káʊədlɪnɪs] *s.* cobardía.
cow·ard·ly [káʊədlɪ] *adj.* cobarde; *adv.* cobardemente.
cow·boy [káʊbɔɪ] *s.* vaquero, *Ríopl.* resero, gaucho; *Ven., Col.* llanero.
cow·er [káʊəˈ] *v.* agacharse *(de miedo o vergüenza)*, achicarse, encogerse *(de miedo)*, acobardarse.
cow·hide [káʊhaɪd] *s.* cuero de vaca, vaqueta.
cowl [kaʊl] *s.* capucha.
cox·swain [káksən] *s.* timonel.
coy [kɔɪ] *adj.* recatado, esquivo, modesto; tímido; gazmoño.
coy·o·te [káɪot, kaɪótɪ] *s.* coyote.
co·zy [kózɪ] *adj.* cómodo y abrigado; cómodo y agradable.
crab [kræb] *s.* cangrejo; cascarrabias *(persona de mal genio)*; — **apple** manzana silvestre.
crack [kræk] *s. (space)* raja, grieta, rendija; *(sound)* crujido; estallido; trueno, estampido; *(blow)* golpe; *(joke)* pulla, chanza; **at the** — **of dawn** al romper el alba; *adj.* excelente; *v.* rajar(se), hender(se), agrietarse; crujir; estallar; **to** — **a joke** soltar un chiste; **to** — **nuts** cascar nueces.
crack·down [krǽkdaʊn] *s.* represión severa.
cracked [krækt] *adj.* agrietado, rajado; quebrado; chiflado, loco.
crack·er [krǽkəˈ] *s.* galleta.
crack·le [krǽkl] *s.* crujido; crepitación; chasquido; *v.* crujir, crepitar.
crack·pot [krǽkpat] *s.* excéntrico.
cra·dle [krédl] *s.* cuna.
craft [kræft] *s. (skill)* maña, destreza; astucia, artificio, cautela; *(occupation)* arte, oficio; *(boat)* embarcación; embarcaciones.
crafts·man [krǽftsmən] *s.* artesano, artífice.
craft·y [krǽftɪ] *adj.* mañoso, astuto, cauteloso, taimado.
crag [kræg] *s.* risco, peñasco.
cram [kræm] *v.* rellenar; atestar; atracar(se), hartar(se); engullir.
cramp [kræmp] *s.* calambre; grapa; *v.* comprimir, apretar, estrechar; afianzar, sujetar *(con grapa)*.
cran·ber·ry [krǽnbɛrɪ] *s.* arándano.
crane [kren] *s.* grulla *(ave)*; grúa *(máquina para levantar pesos)*; *v.* **to** — **one's neck** estirar el cuello.
cra·ni·um [krénɪəm] *s.* cráneo.
crank [kræŋk] *s.* cigüeña, manubrio, manija, manivela; **he is a** — es un maniático; *v.* voltear el manubrio o la cigüeña.
crank·case [krǽŋkes] *s.* cárter del motor.

crank·shaft [krǽŋkʃæft] *s.* cigüeñal.
crank·y [krǽŋkɪ] *adj.* cascarrabias; maniático; enojadizo.
cran·ny [krǽnɪ] *s.* grieta, rendija.
crape [krep] *s.* crespón; crespón negro.
crash [kræʃ] *s. (noise)* estallido, golpazo, estruendo; *(collision)* choque; *(failure)* fracaso; quiebra; bancarrota; — **landing** aterrizaje violento; aterrizaje de barriga; *v.* estrellar(se); estallar; chocar; **to** — **an airplane** aterrizar de golpe un aeroplano; **to** — **into** chocar con, estrellarse contra.
crate [kret] *s.* canasto, cesta, jaula *(para el transporte de mercancías, etc.)*; *Am.* huacal; *v.* embalar en jaula.
cra·ter [krétəˈ] *s.* cráter.
cra·vat [krəvǽt] *s.* corbata.
crave [krev] *v.* ansiar, anhelar, apetecer; **to** — **mercy (pardon)** pedir misericordia (perdón).
crawl [krɔl] *s.* marcha lenta; natación a la marinera; *v.* arrastrarse; gatear, andar a gatas; marchar lentamente; **to be -ing with ants** hormiguear, estar lleno de hormigas.
cray·on [kréən] *s.* lápiz de color, *Am.* creyón; pastel; tiza, yeso.
craze [krez] *s.* manía, locura; moda; antojo; *v.* enloquecer.
cra·zy [krézɪ] *adj.* loco; trastornado; **to go** — volverse loco, perder el juicio.
creak [krik] *s.* crujido, rechino, rechinamiento; *v.* crujir, rechinar.
cream [krim] *s.* crema; nata; — **of tomato soup** puré de tomate; **cold** — crema cosmética; **ice** — helado; *v.* desnatar; batir, mezclar *(azúcar y mantequilla)*; preparar *(legumbres)* con salsa de crema.
cream·er·y [krímərɪ] *s.* lechería, quesería, *Am.* mantequillería.
cream·y [krímɪ] *adj.* natoso; lleno de crema o nata.
crease [kris] *s.* pliegue, arruga; *v.* plegar, hacer pliegues; arrugar.
cre·ate [krɪét] *v.* crear.
cre·a·tion [krɪéʃən] *s.* creación; obra.
cre·a·tive [krɪétɪv] *adj.* creativo, creador.
cre·a·tor [krɪétəˈ] *s.* creador.
crea·ture [krítʃəˈ] *s.* criatura; ser viviente; animalejo.
cre·dence [krídn̩s] *s.* creencia, crédito.
cre·den·tials [krɪdénʃəlz] *s. pl.* credenciales.
cred·i·ble [krédəbl] *adj.* creíble.
cred·it [krédɪt] *s.* crédito; buena fama; — **and debit** haber y deber; activo y pasivo; — **card** tarjeta de crédito; **on** — a crédito, al fiado, a plazo; **to give** — dar crédito, creer; acreditar, abonar; **that does him** — eso le acredita; *v.* acreditar; abonar en cuenta; creer, dar crédito; atribuir.
cred·it·a·ble [krédɪtəbl] *adj.* loable.
cred·i·tor [krédɪtəˈ] *s.* acreedor.
cred·u·lous [krédʒələs] *adj.* crédulo.
creed [krid] *s.* credo; creencia.
creek [krik, krɪk] *s.* riachuelo, arroyo.
creep [krip] *v.* arrastrarse; gatear, andar a gatas; trepar *(las plantas)*; andar lentamente; deslizarse; sentir hormigueo *(en le cuerpo)*; *s. pl.* hormigueo; aprensión, horror.
creep·er [krípəˈ] *s.* enredadera, planta trepadora.
cre·mate [krímet] *v.* incinerar.
Cre·ole [kríol] *s.* criollo; descendiente de los franceses de Luisiana; persona de sangre mestiza.

cre·o·sote [kriəsot] *s.* creosota.
crepe [krɛp] = **crape.**
crept [krɛpt] *pret. & p.p. de* **to creep.**
cres·cent [krɛsn̩t] *adj.* creciente; *s.* luna creciente; media luna (*emblema de turcos y mahometanos*).
crest [krɛst] *s.* cresta; penacho; copete; cima, cumbre; timbre (*de un escudo de armas*).
crest·fall·en [krɛstfɔlən] *adj.* cabizbajo, alicaído, abatido.
cre·tonne [krɪtán] *s.* cretona.
crev·ice [krɛvɪs] *s.* grieta, hendedura.
crew [kru] *s.* tripulación; cuadrilla (*de obreros*); *pret. de* **to crow.**
crib [krɪb] *s.* camita de niño; pesebre; granero, arcón; armazón (*usado en la construcción de edificios*); *v.* enjaular; usar traducción o clave fraudulenta (*en un examen*).
crick·et [krɪkɪt] *s.* grillo; vilorta (*juego*).
crime [kraɪm] *s.* crimen.
crim·i·nal [krímənl] *adj. & s.* criminal.
crimp [krɪmp] *v.* rizar; *s.* rizo.
crim·son [krɪmzn̩] *adj. & s.* carmesí.
cringe [krɪndʒ] *v.* encogerse; arrastrarse.
crip·ple [krípl̩] *s.* cojo, manco; tullido, baldado, inválido; *v.* estropear; mutilar, derrengar; baldar; incapacitar.
cri·sis [kráɪsɪs] *s.* crisis.
crisp [krɪsp] *adj.* (*brittle*) quebradizo; tieso; bien tostado; (*curly*) crespo, encrespado; — **answer** contestación aguda; — **wind** brisa refrescante; *v.* encrespar.
cri·te·ri·on [kraɪtírɪən] *s.* criterio.
crit·ic [krítɪk] *s.* crítico; criticón.
crit·i·cal [krítɪkl] *adj.* crítico; criticador, criticón.
crit·i·cism [krítəsɪzəm] *s.* crítica; criticismo.
crit·i·cize [krítəsaɪz] *v.* criticar; censurar.
croak [krok] *v.* croar; graznar; *s.* canto de ranas; graznido.
cro·chet [kroʃé] *s.* labor de gancho; — **hook** aguja de gancho; *v.* hacer labor de gancho.
crock [krak] *s.* vasija de loza, jarra.
crock·er·y [krákərɪ] *s.* loza.
croc·o·dile [krákədaɪl] *s.* cocodrilo, *Am.* caimán.
cro·ny [króni] *s.* compadre, compinche, camarada, compañero.
crook [kruk] *s.* (*thief*) falsario; estafador, maleante, pícaro; (*curve*) curva, vuelta; recodo; gancho; **shepherd's** — cayado; *v.* torcer(se); **to** — **one's arm** doblar el brazo o codo.
crook·ed [krúkɪd] *adj.* torcido; curvo, encorvado, *Am.* chueco; *Ríopl.* chingado; falso, fraudulento.
croon [krun] *v.* cantar «tristes» (*con exagerado patetismo y exagerando los sonidos nasales*).
crop [krap] *s.* cosecha; buche (*de ave*); látigo, *Am.* cuarta; — **of hair** cabellera; *v.* segar; recortar; rapar; **tò** — **out** aparecer, asomar; **to** — **up** brotar, manifestarse inesperadamente.
cross [krɔs] *s.* cruz; cruce; cruzamiento (*de razas*); mezcla; *v.* cruzar(se); atravesar(se); santiguar(se); encontrarse; contrariar; *adj.* en cruz, cruzado, transversal; malhumorado; **cross-country** a campo traviesa; **cross-examine** *v.* interrogar, repreguntar; **cross-eyed** bizco; —**word puzzle** crucigrama; — **walk** cruce para transeúntes.
cross·bar [krósbɑr] *s.* travesaño.
cross·ing [krósɪŋ] *s.* cruce; cruzamiento; encrucijada, crucero; travesía; **railroad** — cruce; **river** — vado.
cross·road [krósrod] *s.* vía transversal, encrucijada,

crucero.
cross sec·tion [krɛs sɛkʃən] *s.* corte transversal; sección transversal.
crouch [krautʃ] *v.* agacharse, agazaparse.
crow [kro] *s.* cuervo; canto del gallo; **crow's-foot** pata de gallo (*arrugas en el rabo del ojo*); *v.* cantar (*el gallo*); cacarear; jactarse, hacer alarde.
crow·bar [króbɑr] *s.* barra, palanca de hierro.
crowd [kraud] *s.* muchedumbre; gentío, gente; cuadrilla, pandilla; grupo; *v.* agolparse, apiñar(se); estrujar, empujar.
crowd·ed [kráudɪd] *adj.* atestado, lleno, apiñado.
crown [kraun] *s.* corona; copa (*de sombrero*); cima; *v.* coronar.
cru·ci·ble [krúsəbl] *s.* crisol.
cru·ci·fix [krúsəfɪks] *s.* crucifijo.
cru·ci·fy [krúsəfaɪ] *v.* crucificar.
crude [krud] *adj.* basto, tosco, rudo; inculto; — **oil** petróleo crudo; — **sugar** azúcar bruto, azúcar crudo.
cru·el [krúəl] *adj.* cruel.
cru·el·ty [krúəltɪ] *s.* crueldad.
cru·et [krúɪt] *s.* ampolla (*pequeña vasija de cristal*); vinajera (*para servir vino en la misa*); **oil** — aceitera; **vinegar** — vinagrera.
cruise [kruz] *s.* travesía, viaje por mar; excursión; *v.* navegar.
cruis·er [krúzɚ] *s.* crucero (*buque*).
crumb [krʌm] *s.* migaja; miga; mendrugo; *v.* desmenuzar, desmigajar.
crum·ble [krʌmbl̩] *v.* desmenuzar(se); desmoronarse.
crum·ple [krʌmpl̩] *v.* arrugar(se); ajar, apabullar.
crunch [krʌntʃ] *v.* crujir; mascullar.
cru·sade [krused] *s.* cruzada; *v.* hacer una campaña; hacer una cruzada.
cru·sad·er [kruséda-] *s.* cruzado.
crush [krʌʃ] *s.* compresión, presión; estrujamiento, apiñamiento de gente; *v.* estrujar; aplastar; majar; subyugar; **to** — **stone** moler piedra.
crust [krʌst] *s.* corteza (*de pan, queso, etc.*); costra; mendrugo; *v.* encostrarse, cubrir(se) de costra.
crust·y [krʌstɪ] *adj.* costroso.
crutch [krʌtʃ] *s.* muleta.
cry [kraɪ] *v.* grito; lloro, lamento; **a far** — **from** muy distante de, muy lejos de; *v.* gritar; llorar; clamar; exclamar; vocear; **to** — **for help** pedir socorro.
crys·tal [krístl] *s.* cristal; — **clear** cristalino.
crys·tal·line [krístlɪn] *adj.* cristalino.
crys·tal·lize [krístlaɪz] *v.* cristalizar(se).
cub [kʌb] *s.* cachorro (*de oso, tigre, lobo, león*); — **reporter** reportero novato.
Cu·ban [kjúbən] *adj. & s.* cubano.
cub·by·hole [kʌ́bɪhol] *s.* chiribitil.
cube [kjúb] *s.* cubo; — **root** raíz cúbica.
cu·bic [kjúbɪk] *adj.* cúbico.
cu·bism [kjúbɪzm] *s.* cubismo.
cuck·old [kʌkold] *s.* cornudo.
cuck·oo [kúku] *s.* cuco, cuclillo; *adj.* tocado, chiflado, medio loco.
cu·cum·ber [kjúkʌmbɚ] *s.* pepino.
cud [kʌd] *s.* rumia; **to chew the** — rumiar.
cud·dle [kʌdl̩] *v.* abrazar, tener en brazos; estar abrazados.
cudg·el [kʌ́dʒəl] *s.* garrote; porra; *v.* aporrear, apalear.
cue [kju] *s.* señal, indicación; pie (*últimas palabras de un parlamento que sirven de señal en el teatro*); **billiard** — taco de billar.
cuff [kʌf] *s.* puño (*de camisa o de vestido*); doblez

(*del pantalón*); bofetada; *v.* bofetear, dar de
bofetadas.
cull [kʌl] *v.* entresacar; extraer.
cul·mi·nate [kʌ́lmənet] *v.* culminar.
cul·prit [kʌ́lprɪt] *s.* reo, delincuente, culpable.
cult [kʌlt] *s.* culto; secta religiosa.
cul·ti·vate [kʌ́ltəvet] *v.* cultivar; labrar, barbechar.
cul·ti·vat·ed [kʌ́ltəvetɪd] *adj.* cultivado; culto.
cul·ti·va·tion [kʌltəvéʃən] *s.* cultivación, cultivo;
cultura.
cul·ti·va·tor [kʌ́ltəvetɚ] *s.* cultivador; máquina
cultivadora.
cul·ture [kʌ́ltʃɚ] *s.* (*societal*) cultura; (*tillage*)
cultivo.
cul·tured [kʌ́ltʃɚd] *adj.* culto; cultivado.
cum·ber·some [kʌ́mbɚsəm] *adj.* engorroso,
embarazoso, incómodo.
cu·mu·la·tive [kjúmjələtɪv] *adj.* acumulativo.
cun·ning [kʌ́nɪŋ] *adj.* astuto, socarrón, sagaz,
taimado; diestro; cuco, mono, gracioso; *s.*
astucia, maña, sagacidad.
cup [kʌp] *s.* taza, pocillo; copa (*trofeo*).
cup·board [kʌ́bɚd] *s.* armario, aparador; alacena.
cur [kɝ] *s.* perro mestizo, *Am.* perro chusco;
villano, vil, cobarde.
cu·rate [kjúrɪt] *s.* cura.
cu·ra·tor [kjúretɚ] *s.* conservador.
curb [kɝb] *s.* reborde, encintado (*de la acera*);
Riopl. cordón de la acera; freno, restricción;
barbada (*del freno de un caballo*); brocal de
pozo; *v.* refrenar, reprimir.
curd [kɝd] *s.* cuajada; *v.* cuajar(se), coagular(se).
cur·dle [kɝdl] *v.* cuajar(se), coagular(se).
cure [kjʊr] *s.* cura, curación; remedio; *v.* curar(se);
sanar.
cur·few [kɝfju] *s.* queda.
cu·ri·o [kjúrɪo] *s.* curiosidad, objeto raro y curioso.
cu·ri·os·i·ty [kjʊrɪásətɪ] *s.* curiosidad; rareza.
cu·ri·ous [kjúrɪəs] *adj.* curioso; extraño, raro.
curl [kɝl] *s.* rizo, bucle; espiral (*de humo*); *v.*
rizar(se); ensortijar(se); enroscar(se); retorcerse,
alzarse en espirales (*el humo*).
curl·y [kɝlɪ] *adj.* rizo, rizoso, rizado, crespo, *Am.*
chino.
cur·rant [kɝ́ənt] *s.* grosella; — **bush** grosellero.
cur·ren·cy [kɝ́ənsɪ] *s.* moneda corriente;
circulación; **paper** — papel moneda.
cur·rent [kɝ́ənt] *adj.* corriente; común,
prevaleciente, en boga; *s.* corriente.
cur·ric·u·lum [kərɪ́kjələm] *s.* programa de estudios.
curse [kɝs] *s.* maldición; calamidad; *v.* maldecir.
cursed [kɝst] *adj.* maldito.
curs·ing [kɝ́sɪŋ] *adj.* maldiciente.
cur·sive [kɝ́sɪv] *adj.* cursivo.
curt [kɝt] *adj.* corto; brusco.
cur·tail [kɝtél] *v.* cercenar; acortar; restringir,
reducir.
cur·tain [kɝ́tṇ] *s.* cortina; telón (*de teatro*); *v.*
poner cortinas.
cur·va·ture [kɝ́vətʃɚ] *s.* curvatura.
curve [kɝv] *s.* curva; *v.* encorvar(se); torcer(se);
doblar(se).
curved [kɝvd] *adj.* encorvado; torcido; curvo,
corvo, *Méx.*, *C.A.* chueco.
cush·ion [kúʃən] *s.* cojín; almohadilla; almohadón;
amortiguador (*para amortiguar un sonido o
golpe*) ; *v.* acojinar; amortiguar (*un choque*).
cus·tard [kʌ́stɚd] *s.* flan, natillas.
cus·to·dy [kʌ́stədɪ] *s.* custodia, cargo, cuidado; **to
hold in —** custodiar.
cus·tom [kʌ́stəm] *s.* costumbre, hábito, uso, usanza;

-s derechos de aduana; — **made** hecho a la
medida; — **tailor** maestro sastre; — **built**
construido según pedido.
cus·tom·ar·y [kʌ́stəmɛrɪ] *adj.* acostumbrado,
habitual, usual, de costumbre.
cus·tom·er [kʌ́stəmɚ] *s.* parroquiano, cliente,
marchante.
cus·tom·house [kʌ́stəmhaʊs] *s.* aduana; — **official**
aduanero; — **mark** marchamo.
cut [kʌt] *s.* corte (*m.*); cortadura, *Am.* cortada;
rebanada, tajada; rebaja, reducción (*de precios,
sueldos*); hechura (*de un traje*); ausencia (*de la
clase*); grabado; **short** — atajo, camino corto; *v.*
cortar; tajar; truncar; talar (*árboles*) labrar,
tallar; segar; rebajar, reducir (*precios, sueldos*);
negar el saludo a; alzar (*los naipes*); **to — across**
cruzar, atravesar; **to — capers** hacer cabriolas,
cabriolar; **to — class** faltar a la clase; **to — out**
recortar; excluir; **to be — out for** estar hecho
para, tener vocación para; *pret. & p.p. de* **to cut.**
cut-and-dried [kʌ́tænddráɪd] *adj.* ya determinado;
ordinario.
cut·back [kʌ́tbæk] *s.* reducción.
cute [kjut] *adj.* mono, cuco; astuto.
cu·ti·cle [kjútɪkl] *s.* cutícula.
cut·ler·y [kʌ́tlərɪ] *s.* cuchillería, cuchillos.
cut·let [kʌ́tlɪt] *s.* chuleta.
cut·off [kʌ́tɔf] *s.* límite ya indicado.
cut·ter [kʌ́tɚ] *s.* cortador; máquina para cortar;
trineo; **wood** — leñador; **coast guard** — barco
guardacostas.
cut·ting [kʌ́tɪŋ] *adj.* cortante; penetrante;
mordaz, sarcástico.
cy·ber·net·ics [saɪbɚnétɪks] *s.* cibernética.
cy·cle [sáɪkl] *s.* ciclo.
cy·clone [sáɪklon] *s.* ciclón; huracán.
cy·clo·tron [sáɪklətran] *s.* ciclotrón.
cyl·in·der [sɪ́lɪndɚ] *s.* cilindro; — **head** émbolo.
cy·lin·dri·cal [sɪlɪ́ndrɪkl] *adj.* cilíndrico.
cym·bal [sɪ́mbl] *s.* címbalo, platillo; **to play the -s**
tocar los platillos.
cyn·ic [sɪ́nɪk] *s.* cínico.
cyn·i·cal [sɪ́nɪkl] *adj.* cínico.
cyn·i·cism [sɪ́nəsɪzəm] *s.* cinismo.
cy·press [sáɪprəs] *s.* ciprés.
cyst [sɪst] *s.* quiste.

D:d

dab·ble [dǽbl] *v.* chapotear;
trabajar superficialmente.
dad [dæd] *s.* papá, tata; **daddy** *s.*
papaíto o papacito, tata, tatita,
Am. taita.
daf·fo·dil [dǽfədɪl] *s.* narciso.
dag·ger [dǽgɚ] *s.* daga; puñal; **to look -s at**
traspasar con la mirada.
dahl·ia [dǽljə] *s.* dalia.
dai·ly [délɪ] *adj.* diario; *adv.* diariamente; *s.* diario,
periódico.
dain·ty [déntɪ] *adj.* delicado, fino, primoroso,
exquisito; *s.* golosina, manjar exquisito.
dair·y [dérɪ] *s.* lechería, vaquería; quesería, quesera.
dai·sy [dézɪ] *s.* margarita, maya.
dale [del] *s.* cañada.
dal·ly [dǽlɪ] *v.* juguetear; holgazanear; entretenerse,
tardar; malgastar el tiempo.
dam [dæm] *s.* presa, represa; *v.* represar, estancar.
dam·age [dǽmɪdʒ] *s.* daño; perjuicio; avería; **to
pay for -s** indemnizar, pagar los daños y

perjuicios; *v.* dañar(se); averiar(se).
Dam·a·scene [dǽməsin] *adj. s.* damasquinado.
dame [dem] *s.* dama, señora; **old** — vieja.
damn [dæm] *v.* maldecir; condenar; blasfemar; —
it ¡maldito sea!
dam·na·tion [dæmnéʃən] *s.* condenación, perdición.
damp [dæmp] *adj.* húmedo; mojado; *s.* humedad;
v. humedecer, mojar.
damp·en [dǽmpən] *v.* mojar, humedecer;
desalentar; amortiguar.
damp·ness [dǽmpnɪs] *s.* humedad.
dam·sel [dǽmzl] *s.* damisela.
dance [dæns] *s.* baile; danza; — **music** música de
baile; *v.* bailar; danzar.
danc·er [dǽnsə·] *s.* bailador; bailarín, bailarina;
danzante.
dan·de·li·on [dǽndļaɪən] *s.* diente de león.
dan·druff [dǽndrəf] *s.* caspa.
dan·dy [dǽndɪ] *s.* currutaco, majo, afectado; chulo;
adj. elegante, excelente.
dan·ger [déndʒə·] *s.* peligro, riesgo.
dan·ger·ous [déndʒərəs] *adj.* peligroso;
arriesgado; **-ly** *adv.* peligrosamente; **-ly ill**
gravemente enfermo.
dan·gle [dǽŋgl] *v.* pender, colgar, bambolear(se)
(*en el aire*).
dap·ple(d) [dǽpl(d)] *adj.* rodado, con manchas
(*dícese de los caballos*); **dapple-grey** rucio rodado,
tordo, tordillo.
dare [dɛr] *s.* desafío, reto, provocación; **—devil**
atrevido, osado; *v.* atreverse, osar; desafiar.
dar·ing [dérɪŋ] *s.* atrevimiento, osadía; *adj.* osado,
atrevido, arrojado.
dark [dɑrk] *adj.* obscuro; sombrío; — **horse** caballo
desconocido (*que gana inesperadamente la
carrera*); candidato nombrado inesperadamente;
— **secret** secreto profundo; enigma;
darkskinned moreno, trigueño; *s.* obscuridad;
sombra.
dark·en [dɑ́rkən] *v.* obscurecer(se); nublarse.
dark·ness [dɑ́rknɪs] *s.* obscuridad; tinieblas;
sombra.
dark·y [dɑ́rkɪ] *s.* negro (*persona*).
dar·ling [dɑ́rlɪŋ] *adj. & s.* amado, querido; **my** —
vida mía (*o* mi vida), amor mío.
darn [dɑrn] *s.* zurcido; **it is not worth a** — no vale
un comino, no vale un pito; *v.* zurcir; **—!**
¡caramba! ¡canastos!; **-ing needle** aguja de zurcir.
dart [dɑrt] *s.* dardo, flecha; sisa (*en un vestido*);
movimiento rápido; *v.* lanzar(se); flechar; **to** —
out salir como una flecha; **to** — **in and out**
entrar y salir precipitadamente.
dash [dæʃ] *s.* (*line*) raya; (*run*) carrera corta; (*vigor*)
ímpetu; (*grace*) garbo; pizca (*de sal, azúcar, etc.*);
rociada (*de agua*); **—board** tablero de
instrumentos; **with a** — **of the pen** de una
plumada; *v.* lanzar(se); echar(se); estrellar(se);
salpicar; frustrar (*esperanzas*); **to** — **by** pasar
corriendo; **to** — **out** salir a la carrera; **to** — **off**
a letter escribir de prisa una carta.
da·ta [détə] *s. pl.* datos.
date [det] *s.* (*time*) fecha; (*statement*) data;
(*appointment*) cita, compromiso; (*fruit*) dátil; **out
of** — anticuado, desusado; fuera de moda; **up to
of** — al día, moderno; **up to this** — hasta ahora,
hasta la fecha; *v.* fechar; **to** — **from** datar de;
remontarse a.
daub [dɔb] *v.* embarrar, untar; pintarrajear.
daugh·ter [dɔ́tə·] *s.* hija; **daughter-in-law** nuera.
daunt [dɔnt] *v.* intimidar, asustar, espantar;
desanimar.

daunt·less [dɔ́ntlɪs] *adj.* denodado, intrépido.
dav·en·port [dǽvənport] *s.* sofá.
dawn [dɔn] *s.* alba; amanecer, madrugada; *v.*
amanecer; alborear, rayar (*el día*); **it just -ed
upon me** acabo de darme cuenta.
day [de] *s.* día; — **after tomorrow** pasado
mañana; — **before yesterday** anteayer o antier;
— **laborer** jornalero; **by** — de día; **by the** — por
día; **eight-hour** — jornada de ocho horas; **to win
the** — ganar la jornada, triunfar; *adj.* diurno.
day·break [débrek] *s.* amanecer, alba; **at** — al
amanecer, al romper el día, al rayar el día.
day·light [délaɪt] *s.* luz del día.
day·time [détaɪm] *s.* día (*tiempo de luz natural*); **in
the** — durante el día; de día.
daze [dez] *s.* aturdimiento; deslumbramiento; **to be
in a** — estar aturdido; *v.* aturdir; ofuscar;
deslumbrar.
daz·zle [dǽzl] *s.* brillantez; *v.* deslumbrar; ofuscar.
dea·con [díkən] *s.* diácono.
dead [dɛd] *adj.* muerto; — **air** aire viciado o
estancado; — **letter** carta no reclamada; — **loss**
pérdida absoluta; *adv.* completamente,
absolutamente; sumamente, muy; — **sure**
completamente seguro; — **tired** muerto de
cansancio; *s.* **the** — los muertos; **in the** — **of the
night** en el sigilo de la noche; **in the** — **of winter**
en lo más crudo del invierno.
dead·en [dɛ́dn̩] *v.* amortiguar.
dead·head [dɛ́dhɛd] *s.* persona que no paga la
entrada; colado.
dead·ly [dɛ́dlɪ] *adj.* mortal; fatal; como la muerte;
cadavérico; *adv.* mortalmente; — **dull** sumamente
aburrido.
deaf [dɛf] *adj.* sordo; **deaf-mute** *s. & adj.*
sordomudo.
deaf·en [dɛ́fən] *v.* ensordecer; amortiguar, apagar
(*un sonido*).
deaf·en·ing [dɛ́fənɪŋ] *adj.* ensordecedor,
estruendoso.
deaf·ness [dɛ́fnɪs] *s.* sordera.
deal [dil] *s.* trato, negocio; mano (*en el juego de
naipes*); distribución, reparto (*de los naipes*); **a
great** — of una gran cantidad de, mucho; **to
give a square** — tratar con equidad; *v.* tallar (*en
juegos de naipes*); distribuir, repartir; dar (*un
golpe*); **to** — **in** comerciar en; **to** — **with** tratar
de (*un asunto*); tratar con; negociar con.
deal·er [dilə·] *s.* negociante, comerciante, tratante;
tallador (*en el juego de naipes*).
deal·ings [dilɪŋz] *s. pl.* relaciones (*comerciales o
amistosas*); comercio, tratos, negocios.
dealt [dɛlt] *pret. & p.p. de* **to deal.**
dean [din] *s.* deán (*dignidad eclesiástica*); decano
(*de universidad*).
dear [dɪr] *adj.* (*beloved*) querido, amado; (*expensive*)
caro; costoso; *adv.* caro; **—me!** ¡Dios mío!; **oh
—!** ¡ay!; **my** — querido mío; **Dear Sir** Muy
señor mío; **-ly** *adv.* cariñosamente; a precio alto;
my -ly beloved muy amado mío; muy amados
míos.
dearth [dɝθ] *s.* escasez, carestía, insuficiencia.
death [dɛθ] *s.* muerte; mortandad; — **rate**
mortalidad.
death·bed [dɛ́θbɛd] *s.* lecho de muerte.
de·base [dɪbés] *v.* rebajar el valor de; degradar,
humillar, envilecer.
de·bat·a·ble [dɪbétəbl] *adj.* discutible, disputable.
de·bate [dɪbét] *s.* debate, discusión; *v.* debatir,
discutir; considerar; deliberar.
de·bil·i·tate [dəbílətet] *v.* debilitar.

deb·it [débɪt] s. débito, adeudo, cargo; debe (de una cuenta); pasivo (en contabilidad); v. adeudar, cargar en cuenta.

de·brief·ing [dibrífɪŋ] s. informe de vuelo bajo interrogación; informe.

de·bris [dəbrí] s. escombros; ruinas.

debt [dɛt] s. deuda; adeudo; débito; **bad** — cuenta incobrable; **to run into** — adeudarse, entramparse, cargarse de deudas.

bedt·or [détə·] s. deudor.

de·bunk [dibʌŋk] s. desbaratar; desenmascarar.

de·but [dibjú] s. estreno; **to make a** — debutar, estrenarse.

de·cade [déked] s. década, decenio.

de·ca·dence [dikédns] s. decadencia.

de·cant·er [dikǽntə·] s. garrafa; **large** — garrafón.

de·cay [diké] s. decaimiento; decadencia, ruina; podredumbre; caries (de la dentadura); v. decaer; venir a menos; pudrir(se) o podrir(se).

de·cease [disís] s. muerte, fallecimiento; v. morir, fallecer.

de·ceased [disíst] adj. & s. muerto, difunto.

de·ceit [disít] s. engaño; fraude; trampa.

de·ceit·ful [disítfəl] adj. engañador; tramposo; engañoso.

de·ceive [disív] v. engañar.

De·cem·ber [disɛmbə·] s. diciembre.

de·cen·cy [dísnsɪ] s. decencia.

de·cent [dísnt] adj. decente; decoroso.

de·ci·bel [dɛ̀sɪbɛl] s. decibelio; decibel.

de·cide [disáɪd] v. decidir, resolver, determinar; **to** — **to** resolverse a, decidirse a.

de·cid·ed [disáɪdɪd] adj. decidido, resuelto.

dec·i·mal [désəml] adj. decimal; s. decimal, fracción decimal.

dec·i·mate [désɪmet] v. diezmar.

de·ci·pher [disáɪfə·] v. decifrar.

de·ci·sion [disíʒən] s. decisión, resolución.

de·ci·sive [disáɪsɪv] adj. decisivo; terminante.

deck [dɛk] s. cubierta (de un buque); baraja; v. cubrir; ataviar; **to** — **oneself out** emperifollarse.

dec·la·ra·tion [dɛkləréʃən] s. declaración.

de·clare [dɪklǽr] v. declarar; afirmar.

de·cline [dɪkláɪn] s. declinación; decadencia; mengua; baja (de precios); v. declinar; decaer; rehusar; **to** — **to do something** negarse a hacer algo.

de·cliv·i·ty [dɪklívətɪ] s. declive.

de·col·le·te [dekɑlté] adj. escotado.

de·com·pose [dikəmpóz] v. descomponer(se); corromper(se), pudrir(se).

dec·o·rate [dékəret] v. decorar, adornar; condecorar.

dec·o·ra·tion [dɛkəréʃən] s. decoración; adorno; insignia, condecoración.

dec·o·ra·tive [dékəretɪv] adj. decorativo; ornamental.

de·co·rum [dikórəm] s. decoro; circunspección.

de·coy [dikɔ́ɪ] s. reclamo, señuelo, figura de ave (que sirve para atraer aves); cebo (artificio para atraer con engaño); trampa, lazo; v. atraer con señuelo o engaño.

de·crease [dikris] s. disminución o diminución; merma; mengua; [dɪkrís] v. disminuir(se); mermar; menguar.

de·cree [dɪkrí] s. decreto; v. decretar; mandar.

de·crep·it [dɪkrépɪt] adj. decrépito.

ded·i·cate [dédəket] v. dedicar.

ded·i·ca·tion [dɛdəkéʃən] s. dedicación; dedicatoria.

de·duce [dɪdjús] v. deducir, inferir.

de·duct [dɪdʌ́kt] v. deducir, descontar, rebajar.

de·duc·tion [dɪdʌ́kʃən] s. deducción; rebaja, descuento.

deed [did] s. hecho, acción, acto; hazaña; escritura (de venta o compra).

deem [dim] v. juzgar, creer, considerar.

deep [dip] adj. (down) hondo; profundo; (obscure) oscuro; (tone) grave, bajo; — **in debt** cargado de deudas; — **in thought** absorto; — **mourning** luto riguroso; **to go off the** — **end** echarse a pique; caer en el abismo; — **into the night** en las tinieblas de la noche; s. **the** — el mar; **-ly** adv. profundamente, hondamente; intensamente.

deep·en [dípən] v. ahondar, profundizar.

deer [dɪr] s. ciervo, venado; —**skin** piel o cuero de venado.

de·face [dɪfés] v. desfigurar, estropear, mutilar.

de·fame [dɪfém] v. difamar, calumniar, denigrar.

de·fault [dɪfɔ́lt] s. falta, falta, negligencia (de un deber, pago, obligación); deficiencia; v. fallar, faltar (en el cumplimiento de un deber, pago, obligación); no comparecer a la cita de un tribunal.

de·feat [dɪfit] s. derrota, vencimiento; frustración (de un plan); v. vencer, derrotar; frustrar.

def·e·cate [défəket] v. defecar.

de·fect [dɪfɛ́kt] s. defecto.

de·fec·tive [dɪfɛ́ktɪv] adj. defectuoso; incompleto; subnormal, falto de inteligencia; — **verb** verbo defectivo.

de·fend [dɪfénd] v. defender.

de·fen·dant [dɪféndənt] s. acusado, demandado, procesado.

de·fend·er [dɪféndə·] s. defensor; abogado defensor.

de·fense [dɪféns] s. defensa.

de·fense·less [dɪfénslɪs] adj. indefenso, inerme.

de·fen·sive [dɪfénsɪv] adj. defensivo; s. defensiva.

de·fer [dɪfɝ] v. diferir, posponer, aplazar; **to** — **to another's opinion** remitirse o ceder al dictamen de otro.

de·fi·ance [dɪfáɪəns] s. reto, desafío, provocación; oposición; **in** — **of** en abierta oposición con, a despecho de.

de·fi·cien·cy [dɪfíʃənsɪ] s. deficiencia; defecto; déficit.

de·fi·cient [dɪfíʃənt] adj. deficiente; defectuoso.

def·i·cit [défəsɪt] s. déficit.

de·file [dɪfáɪl] v. viciar, corromper; profanar; manchar, ensuciar.

de·fine [dɪfáɪn] v. definir.

def·i·nite [défənɪt] adj. definido; claro, preciso; fijo; —**article** artículo determinado o definido; **ly** adv. definidamente; claramente; **-ly not** terminantemente no.

def·i·ni·tion [dɛfəníʃən] s. definición.

de·fin·i·tive [dɪfínətɪv] adj. definitivo.

de·flate [dɪflét] v. desinflar.

de·flect [dɪflɛ́kt] v. desviar(se).

de·form [dɪfɔ́rm] v. deformar; desfigurar, afear.

de·formed [dɪfɔ́rmd] adj. deforme, disforme; deformado; desfigurado.

de·form·i·ty [dɪfɔ́rmətɪ] s. deformidad; deformación.

de·fraud [dɪfrɔ́d] v. defraudar.

de·fray [dɪfré] v. sufragar, costear, pagar (gastos).

deft [dɛft] adj. diestro, ágil.

de·funct [dɪfʌ́ŋkt] adj. difunto.

de·fy [dɪfáɪ] v. desafiar; retar; oponerse a, resistirse a.

de·gen·er·ate [dɪdʒɛ́nərɪt] adj. & s. degenerado; [dɪdʒɛ́nəret] v. degenerar.

deg·ra·da·tion [dɛgrədéʃən] s. degradación; envilecimiento.

DA

de·grade [dɪgréd] v. degradar; envilecer, rebajar.
de·gree [dɪgrí] s. grado; rango; **by -s** gradualmente; **to get a**—graduarse.
de·hu·man·ize [dihjúmənaɪz] v. deshumanizar.
de·hy·drate [dɪháɪdret] v. deshidratar(se).
deign [den] v. dignarse, condescender.
de·i·ty [díətɪ] s. deidad.
de·ject·ed [dɪdʒéktɪd] adj. abatido.
de·jec·tion [dɪdʒékʃən] s. abatimiento, melancolía, depresión.
de·lay [dɪlé] s. demora, tardanza, dilación, retraso; v. demorar; retardar, dilatar; diferir; tardarse.
de·layed ac·tion [dɪléd ǽkʃən] adj. atrasado; retardado.
del·e·gate [déləget] s. delegado, representante; v. delegar, diputar.
del·e·ga·tion [déləgéʃən] s. delegación diputación.
de·le·tion [dɪlíʃən] s. suspensión.
de·lib·er·ate [dɪlíbərɪt] adj. deliberado. premeditado; cauto, prudente; lento; **-ly** adv. deliberadamente; con premeditación; [dɪlíbəret] v. deliberar.
de·lib·er·a·tion [dɪlɪbəréʃən] s. deliberación.
del·i·ca·cy [déləkəsɪ] s. delicadeza; sensibilidad; finura; golosina.
del·i·cate [déləkət] adj. delicado; frágil; exquisito.
del·i·ca·tes·sen [déləkətésn] s. tienda de fiambres. queso, ensaladas, ultramarinos, etc.
de·li·cious [dɪlíʃəs] adj. delicioso.
de·light [dɪláɪt] s. deleite; delicia; v. deleitar(se); encantar; agradar; **to — in** gozarse en, deleitarse en.
de·light·ed [dɪláɪtɪd] adj. encantado; **to be — to** alegrarse de, tener mucho gusto en (o de).
de·light·ful [dɪláɪtfəl] adj. deleitoso; delicioso; ameno, agradable.
de·lin·e·ate [dɪlíniet] v. delinear, trazar.
de·lin·quent [dɪlíŋkwənt] adj. & s. delincuente.
de·lir·i·ous [dɪlírɪəs] adj. delirante; **to be —** delirar, desvariar.
de·lir·i·um [dɪlírɪəm] s. delirio, desvarío.
de·liv·er [dɪlívə·] v. entregar; librar, libertar; pronunciar (un discurso); dar (un golpe).
de·liv·er·ance [dɪlívərəns] s. liberación, rescate.
de·liv·er·er [dɪlívərə·] s. libertador; portador, mansejero.
de·liv·er·y [dɪlívərɪ] s. (giving) entrega; (saving) liberación; (birth) parto; (speaking) elocuencia, manera de hacer una conferencia; **— service** servicio de entrega; **— truck** camión (o camioneta) de reparto; **mail —** reparto de carreo.
dell [dɛl] s. cañada, hondonada.
del·ta wing [déltə wɪŋ] s. ala en delta.
de·lude [dɪlúd] v. engañar.
del·uge [déljudʒ] s. diluvio; v. inundar; abrumar.
de·lu·sion [dɪlúʒən] s. ilusión; engaño, error.
de·mand [dɪmǽnd] s. demanda; exigencia; solicitud; **on — a** solicitud; v. demandar, reclamar; exigir.
de·mand·ing [dɪmǽndɪŋ] adj. exigente.
de·mean·or [dɪmínə·] s. conducta, comportamiento, proceder.
de·ment·ed [dɪméntɪd] adj. demente.
dem·i·john [démidʒan] s. damajuana.
de·mise [dɪmáɪz] s. fallecimiento.
de·mo·bil·ize [dimóblaɪz] v. demovilizar.
de·moc·ra·cy [dəmákrəsɪ] s. democarcia.
dem·o·crat [déməkræt] s. demócrata.
dem·o·crat·ic [deməkrǽtɪk] adj. democrático.
de·mol·ish [dɪmálɪʃ] v. demoler.

de·mon [dímən] s. demonio.
dem·on·strate [démənstret] v. demostrar.
dem·on·stra·tion [dɛmənstréʃən] s. demostración; prueba; (protest) manifestación.
de·mon·stra·tive [dɪmánstrətɪv] adj. demostrativo; efusivo.
den [dɛn] s. guarida; escondrijo; cueva, lugar de retiro.
de·ni·al [dɪnáɪəl] s. negación; negativa; **self-denial** abnegación.
den·i·grate [dénɪgret] v. calumniar; ennegrecer.
de·nom·i·na·tion [dɪnɑmənéʃən] s. (name) denominación; nombre; título, designación; (sect) secta religiosa.
de·note [dɪnót] v. denotar.
de·nounce [dɪnáʊns] v. denunciar; delatar, acusar.
dense [dɛns] adj. denso; espeso, apretado; estúpido.
den·si·ty [dénsətɪ] s. densidad; estupidez.
dent [dɛnt] s. abolladura; mella; v. abollar; mellar.
den·tal [déntl] adj. dental; s. dental, consonante dental.
den·ti·frice [déntɪfrɪs] s. pasta dentífrica; dentífrico.
den·tist [déntɪst] s. dentista.
de·nun·ci·a·tion [dɪnʌnsiéʃən] s. denuncia, acusación.
de·ny [dɪnáɪ] v. negar; rehusar; **to — oneself** sacrificarse, abnegarse; **to — oneself to callers** negarse a recibir visitas.
de·o·dor·ant [diódərənt] s. desodorante.
de·ox·i·dize [diáksədaɪz] v. desoxidar.
de·part [dɪpárt] v. partir, salir, irse; desviarse, apartarse.
de·part·ed [dɪpártɪd] adj. ido; ausente; difunto.
de·part·ment [dɪpártmənt] s. departamento; distrito; ramo, división; **— store** almacén.
de·par·ture [dɪpártʃə·] s. salida, partida; desviación.
de·pend [dɪpénd] v. depender; **to — on** depender de; contar con, confiar en.
de·pend·a·ble [dɪpéndəbl] adj. seguro, fidedigno, digno de confianza.
de·pen·dence [dɪpéndəns] s. dependencia; confianza.
de·pen·den·cy [dɪpéndənsɪ] s. dependencia; sucursal.
de·pen·dent [dɪpéndənt] adj. dependiente; subordinado; s. dependiente, familiar.
de·pict [dɪpíkt] v. pintar, describir; representar.
dep·i·late [dépəlet] v. depilar.
de·pil·a·to·ry [dɪpílətorɪ] s. depilatorio.
de·plete [dɪplit] v. agotar; vaciar.
de·plor·a·ble [dɪplórəbl] adj. deplorable, lamentable.
de·plore [dɪplór] v. deplorar.
de·port [dɪpórt] v. deportar; **to — oneself well** portarse bien.
de·port·ment [dɪpórtmənt] s. comportamiento, conducta.
de·pose [dɪpóz] v. deponer; declarar, atestiguar.
de·pos·it [dɪpázɪt] s. depósito; v. depositar.
dep·o·si·tion [dɛpəzíʃən] s. deposición; declaración.
de·pos·i·tor [dɪpázɪtə·] s. depositador.
de·pot [dípo] s. depósito; almacén; estación de ferrocarril.
dep·re·cate [déprɪket] v. desaprobar.
de·pre·ci·ate [dɪpríʃiet] v. depreciar; bajar de precio; abaratar(se); menospreciar.
de·press [dɪprés] v. deprimir; abatir; desanimar; depreciar, rebajar el valor de.

de·pressed [dɪprést] *adj.* abatido, decaído.
de·press·ing [dɪprésɪŋ] *adj.* deprimente.
de·pres·sion [dɪpréʃən] *s.* depresión; decaimiento, abatimiento; rebaja (*de precios*).
de·prive [dɪpráɪv] *v.* privar.
depth [dɛpθ] *s.* profundidad; hondura; fondo; longitud (*de un solar*); gravedad (*de los sonidos*); viveza (*de los colores*); **in the — of the night** en las tinieblas de la noche; **in the — of winter** en lo más crudo del invierno.
dep·u·ta·tion [dɛpjətéʃən] *s.* diputación, delagación; comisión.
de·pute [dɪpjút] *v.* diputar, delegar.
dep·u·ty [dépjətɪ] *s.* diputado; agente; delegado.
de·range [dɪréndʒ] *v.* trastornar, desordenar.
der·by [dɝbɪ] *s.* sombrero hongo, *Méx., Ven., Col.* sombrero de bola.
der·e·lict [dérɪlɪkt] *adj.* abandonado; negligente.
de·ride [dɪráɪd] *v.* escarnecer, ridiculizar, mofarse de, burlarse de.
de·ri·sion [dɪríʒən] *s.* mofa, escarnio.
de·rive [dəráɪv] *v.* derivar(se); provenir; sacar (*provecho*); recibir (*placer*).
der·ma·tol·o·gy [dɝmətáledʒɪ] *s.* dermatología.
der·rick [dérɪk] *s.* grúa; armazón (*para la explotación del petróleo*).
de·scend [dɪsénd] *v.* descender; bajar; **to — upon** caer sobre, acometer.
de·scen·dant [dɪséndənt] *adj. & s.* descendiente.
de·scent [dɪsént] *s.* descenso; bajada; descendencia, linaje; descendimiento; declive.
de·scribe [dɪskráɪb] *v.* describir; trazar.
de·scrip·tion [dɪskrípʃən] *s.* descripción; **of all -s** de todas clases.
de·scrip·tive [dɪskríptɪv] *adj.* descriptivo; — **linguistics** lingüística descriptiva.
des·ert [dézɝt] *adj.* desierto, despoblado; estéril; *s.* desierto, yermo; páramo; [dɪzɝt] *v.* abandonar, desamparar; desertar.
de·sert·er [dɪzɝtɚ] *s.* desertor.
de·ser·tion [dɪzɝʃən] *s.* deserción, abandono, desamparo.
de·serve [dɪzɝv] *v.* merecer.
de·serv·ing [dɪzɝvɪŋ] *adj.* meritorio; merecedor.
de·sign [dɪzáɪn] *s.* (*sketch*) dibujo, diseño; (*plan*) designio, propósito, intención; plan, proyecto; *v.* diseñar, trazar; proyectar; idear.
des·ig·nate [dézɪgnet] *v.* designar; señalar, indicar, nombrar.
de·sign·er [dɪzáɪnɚ] *s.* diseñador; dibujante; proyectista; intrigante.
de·sir·a·bil·i·ty [dɪzaɪrəbílətɪ] *s.* conveniencia, utilidad.
de·sir·a·ble [dɪzáɪrəbl] *adj.* deseable; agradable; conveniente.
de·sire [dɪzáɪr] *s.* deseo; anhelo, ansia; *v.* desear; anhelar, ansiar.
de·sir·ous [dɪzáɪrəs] *adj.* deseoso.
de·sist [dɪzíst] *v.* desistir.
desk [dɛsk] *s.* escritorio, bufete, pupitre, mesa de escribir.
des·o·late [déslɪt] *adj.* desolado; despoblado; desierto; solitario; [déslet] *v.* desolar; asolar; arrasar; despoblar.
des·o·la·tion [désléʃən] *s.* desolación; soledad.
de·spair [dɪspér] *s.* desesperación; desesperanza; *v.* desesperarse, perder la esperanza.
de·spair·ing [dɪspérɪŋ] *adj.* desesperado, sin esperanza.
des·patch [dɪspǽtʃ] = **dispatch**.
des·per·ate [désprɪt] *adj.* desesperado; arriesgado,

temerario; — **illness** enfermedad gravísima; **-ly** *adv.* desesperadamente; **-ly ill** gravísimamente enfermo.
des·per·a·tion [dɛspəréʃən] *s.* desesperación; temeridad.
des·pi·ca·ble [déspɪkəbl] *adj.* despreciable; desdeñable.
de·spise [dɪspáɪz] *v.* despreciar; desdeñar; menospreciar.
de·spite [dɪspáɪt] *s.* despecho; *prep.* a despecho de, a pesar de.
de·spoil [dɪspɔ́ɪl] *v.* despojar.
de·spon·den·cy [dɪspándənsɪ] *s.* abatimiento desaliento, descaecimiento o decaimiento del ánimo.
de·spon·dent [dɪspándənt] *adj.* abatido, descaecido o decaído de ánimo, desalentado; desesperanzado.
des·pot [déspət] *s.* déspota.
des·pot·ic [dɪspátɪk] *adj.* despótico.
des·pot·ism [déspətɪzəm] *s.* despotismo.
des·sert [dɪzɝt] *s.* postre.
des·ti·na·tion [dɛstənéʃən] *s.* destinación, destino; paradero.
des·tine [déstɪn] *v.* destinar; **-ed for** con rumbo a, con destinación a; destinado a.
des·ti·ny [déstənɪ] *s.* destino, sino, hado.
des·ti·tute [déstətjut] *adj.* destituido, necesitado; falto, desprovisto.
de·stroy [dɪstrɔ́ɪ] *v.* destruir.
de·stroy·er [dɪstrɔ́ɪɚ] *s.* destruidor; destructor, cazatorpedero, destroyer.
de·struc·ti·ble [dɪstrʌ́ktəbl] *adj.* destructible.
de·struc·tion [dɪstrʌ́kʃən] *s.* destrucción; ruina.
de·struc·tive [dɪstrʌ́ktɪv] *adj.* destructivo.
de·tach [dɪtǽtʃ] *v.* separar, despegar, desprender; destacar (*una porción de tropa*).
de·tach·ment [dɪtǽtʃmənt] *s.* separación; desprendimiento; desapego, despego, alejamiento; destacamento (*militar*).
de·tail [dítel] *s.* detalle; pormenor; destacamento (*militar*); **to go into** — detallar, pormenorizar; [dɪtél] *v.* detallar; pormenorizar; destacar, asignar.
de·tain [dɪtén] *v.* detener; entretener, demorar, retardar.
de·tect [dɪtékt] *v.* descubrir.
de·tec·tive [dɪtéktɪv] *s.* detective, detectivo; policía secreto.
de·ten·tion [dɪténʃən] *s.* detención.
de·ter·gent [dɪtɝdʒənt] *s.* detergente.
de·te·ri·o·rate [dɪtíriəret] *v.* deteriorar(se).
de·te·ri·o·ra·tion [dɪtɪriəréʃən] *s.* deterioro.
de·ter·mi·na·tion [dɪtɝmənéʃən] *s.* determinación; decisión; resolución, firmeza.
de·ter·mine [dɪtɝmɪn] *v.* determinar; decidir; **to —** **to** determinarse a, decidirse a, resolverse a.
de·ter·mined [dɪtɝmɪnd] *adj.* determinado, decidido, resuelto.
de·test [dɪtést] *v.* detestar, aborrecer.
de·tour [dítʊr] *s.* rodeo, desvío, desviación, vuelta; *v.* dar o hacer un rodeo.
dev·as·tate [dévəstet] *v.* devastar, arruinar, asolar.
de·vel·op [dɪvéləp] *v.* desarrollar(se); desenvolver(se); revelar (*una película o placa fotográfica*); explotar (*una mina*).
de·vel·op·ment [dɪvéləpmənt] *s.* (*evolution*) desarrollo; desenvolvimiento; evolución; crecimiento; (*generation*) fomento; explotación; (*photo*) revelado.
de·vi·ate [dívɪet] *v.* desviar(se).

de·vi·a·tion [divıéʃən] s. desviación; desvío, extravío.

de·vice [dıváıs] s. artificio; mecanismo, aparato; ardid, recurso; divisa; **left to one's own -s** abandonado a sus propios recursos.

dev·il [dévl] s. diablo; demonio.

dev·il·ish [dévlıʃ] adj. diabólico; endiablado; travieso.

dev·il·try [dévltrı] s. diablura.

de·vi·ous [dívıəs] adj. desviado; tortuoso; indirecto.

de·vise [dıváız] v. idear, trazar, urdir.

de·void [dıvɔ́ıd] adj. exento, libre, falto, privado, desprovisto.

de·vote [dıvót] v. dedicar; consagrar; **to — oneself to** dedicarse a, consagrarse a, aplicarse a.

de·vot·ed [dıvótıd] adj. dedicado, consagrado; apegado; **— friend** amigo fiel o leal.

de·vo·tion [dıvóʃən] s. devoción; piedad; afecto; lealtad.

de·vour [dıváur] v. devorar.

de·vout [dıváut] adj. devoto, piadoso; sincero.

dew [dju] s. rocío, sereno; v. rociar; caer (el rocío).

dew·drop [djúdrap] s. gota de rocío.

dew·y [djúı] adj. rociado, húmedo de rocío.

dex·ter·i·ty [dɛkstérətı] s. destreza.

dex·ter·ous [dékstrəs] adj. diestro.

dex·trose [dékstros] s. dextrosa.

di·a·dem [dáıədɛm] s. diadema.

di·ag·nose [daıəgnós] v. diagnosticar.

di·ag·o·nal [daıǽgən̩l] adj. diagonal, oblicuo; s. diagonal.

di·a·gram [dáıəgræm] s. diagrama.

di·al [dáıəl] s. esfera; muestra (del reloj), Méx., C.A. carátula; **— telephone** teléfono automático; v. sintonizar o captar (una estación radiotelefónica).

di·a·lect [dáıəlɛkt] s. dialecto.

di·a·lec·tol·o·gy [daıəlɛktálədʒı] dialectología.

di·a·logue [dáıəlɔg] s. diálogo; v. dialogar.

di·am·e·ter [daıǽmətəˑ] s. diámetro.

dia·mond [dáımənd] s. diamante; rombo (figura geométrica).

di·a·per [dáıəpəˑ] s. pañal.

di·ar·rhe·a [daıəríə] s. diarrea.

di·a·ry [dáıərı] s. diario.

dice [daıs] s. pl. de **die** dados; v. cuadricular, cortar en cuarterones o cubos.

di·chot·o·my [daıkátəmı] s. dicotomía.

dic·tate [díktet] s. dictado, precepto; v. dictar.

dic·ta·tion [dıktéʃən] s. dictado; mando absoluto; **to take —** escribir al dictado.

dic·ta·tor [díktetəˑ] s. dictador.

dic·ta·tor·ship [dıktétəˑʃıp] s. dictadura.

dic·tion [díkʃən] s. dicción.

dic·tion·ar·y [díkʃənɛrı] s. diccionario.

did [dıd] pret. de **to do**.

die [daı] s. (pl. **dice**) dado (para jugar); (pl. **dies**) matriz, molde; cuño (sello para acuñar moneda).

die [daı] v. morir(se); marchitarse; secarse (las flores, plantas, etc.); **to — out** morirse, extinguirse, apagarse.

di·er·e·sis [daıérəsıs] s. diéresis.

di·et [dáıət] s. dieta; régimen; **to be on a —** estar a dieta; **to put on a —** adietar, poner a dieta; v. ponerse a dieta; estar a dieta.

dif·fer [dífəˑ] v. diferir, diferenciarse, distinguirse; disentir; **to — with** no convenir con, no estar de acuerdo con.

dif·fer·ence [dífrəns] s. diferencia; distinción; discordia, controversia; **it makes no —** no

importa, es igual, da lo mismo.

dif·fer·ent [dífrənt] adj. diferente; distinto.

dif·fer·en·tial [dıfˑrénʃəl] s. diferencial.

dif·fer·en·ti·ate [dıfərénʃıet] v. diferenciar(se); distinguir(se).

dif·fi·cult [dífəkʌlt] adj. difícil; dificultoso, trabajoso, penoso.

dif·fi·cul·ty [dífəkʌltı] s. dificultad: apuro, aprieto.

dif·fi·dence [dífədəns] s. timidez; desconfianza de sí propio.

dif·fi·dent [dífədənt] adj. huraño; tímido.

dif·fuse [dıfjús] adk. difuso; prolijo; [dıfjúz] v. difundir.

dif·fu·sion [dıfjúʒən] s. difusión; diseminación.

dig [dıg] v. cavar; excavar; ahondar; escarbar; trabajar duro; **to — under** socavar; **to — up** desenterrar; s. piquete; pulla, sarcasmo.

di·gest [dáıdʒɛst] s. sumario, compendio; recopilación; código; [dədʒɛ́st] v. digerir; recopilar.

di·gest·i·ble [dədʒéstəbl] adj. digestible, digerible.

di·ges·tion [dədʒéstʃən] s. digestión.

di·ges·tive [dədʒéstıv] adj. digestivo.

dig·ni·fied [dígnəfaıd] adj. digno, mesurado; serio, grave.

dig·ni·tar·y [dígnətɛrı] s. dignatario.

dig·ni·ty [dígnətı] s. dignidad.

di·graph [dáıgræf] s. dígrafo.

di·gress [dəgrés] v. divagar.

di·gres·sion [dəgréʃən] s. digresión, divagación.

dike [daık] s. dique, represa; zanja.

di·late [daılét] v. dilatar(se), extender(se), ensanchar(se).

dil·i·gence [dílədʒəns] s. diligencia; aplicación, esmero.

dil·i·gent [dílədʒənt] adj. diligente, activo, aplicado.

di·lute [dılút] v. diluir, desleír; aguar; adj. diluido.

dim [dım] adj. penumbroso, obscuro; nublado; confuso; indistinto; deslustrado, sin brillo; v. obscurecer; anublar, ofuscar; atenuar.

dime [daım] s. moneda de diez centavos.

di·men·sion [dəménʃən] s. dimensión.

di·min·ish [dəmínıʃ] v. disminuir; rebajar.

dim·i·nu·tion [dımənjúʃən] s. diminución, mengua.

di·min·u·tive [dəmínjətıv] adj. diminutivo; diminuto; s. diminutivo.

dim·ness [dímnıs] s. semi-obscuridad, penumbra; ofuscamiento.

dim·ple [dímpl] s. hoyuelo.

din [dın] s. estruendo, fragor, estrépito.

dine [daın] v. comer; festejar u obsequiar con una comida.

din·er [dáınəˑ] s. coche-comedor; comensal (persona que come a la mesa).

din·gy [díndʒı] adj. negruzco; manchado, sucio.

din·ing [dáınıŋ] ger. de **to dine**; **— car** coche-comedor; **— room** comedor.

din·ner [dínəˑ] s. comida; **— coat** smoking o esmoquin.

dint [dınt] s. **by — of** a fuerza de.

di·o·ram·a [daıərǽmə] s. diorama.

dip [dıp] s. zambullida; inmersión; bajada; declive; depresión; v. meter(se); zambullirse; mojar (la pluma en el tintero); teñir; agachar (la cabeza); saludar (con la bandera); inclinarse (un camino); dar un bajón (un avión); hundirse (el sol en el horizonte); **to — out** vaciar (con cucharón o cazo).

diph·the·ri·a [dıfθírıə] s. difteria.

diph·thong [dífθɔŋ] s. diptongo.

di·plo·ma [dıplómə] s. diploma.

di·plo·ma·cy [dɪplómǝsɪ] *s.* diplomacia.
dip·lo·mat [dípləmæt] *s.* diplomático.
dip·lo·mat·ic [dɪpləmǽtɪk] *adj.* diplomático.
dip·per [dípə·] *s.* cucharón, cazo; **the Big Dipper** la Osa Mayor.
dire [daɪr] *adj.* extremo; horrendo; fatal, de mal agüero.
di·rect [dərɛkt] *adj.* (*straight*) directo; derecho, en línea recta; *C.A.* recto; (*immediate*) inmediato; — **current** corriente continua; — **object** acusativo; *adv.* directamente; **-ly** *adv.* directamente; inmediatamente; en seguida; *v.* dirigir; guiar; encaminar; dar direcciones u órdenes.
di·rec·tion [dərɛkʃən] *s.* dirección; administración; gerencia; rumbo.
di·rec·tion·al an·ten·na [dərɛkʃən| æntɛnə] *s.* antena direccional.
di·rec·tion·al sig·nal [dərɛkʃən| sígnl] *s.* señal direccional.
di·rec·tive [dərɛktɪv] *adj.* directivo; *s.* orden, mandato.
di·rect·ness [dərɛktnɪs] *s.* derechura; franqueza; lo directo; **with** — sin rodeos.
di·rec·tor [dərɛktə·] *s.* director; gerente.
di·rec·to·ry [dərɛktərɪ] *s.* directorio; junta directiva; **telephone** — guía telefónica.
dir·i·gi·ble [dírədʒəbl] *adj. & s.* dirigible.
dirt [dɜrt] *s.* suciedad; mugre; tierra, polvo, lodo.
dirt·y [dɜrtɪ] *adj.* sucio; mugriento; cochino; enlodado; manchado; *v.* ensuciar; manchar; enlodar.
dis·a·ble [dɪsébl] *v.* incapacitar.
dis·ad·van·tage [dɪsədvǽntɪdʒ] *s.* desventaja; **to be at a** — estar en una situación desventajosa.
dis·a·gree [dɪsəgrí] *v.* (*dissent*) diferir, disentir; no convenir, no estar de acuerdo; (*bad effect*) no sentarle bien a uno (*el clima, la comida, etc.*).
dis·a·gree·a·ble [dɪsəgríəbl] *adj.* desagradable; áspero, de mal genio.
dis·a·gree·ment [dɪsəgrímənt] *s.* desavenencia, desacuerdo; disensión; discordia; discordancia.
dis·al·low [dɪsəlaʊ] *v.* desaprobar; rechazar.
dis·ap·pear [dɪsəpír] *v.* desaparecer.
dis·ap·pear·ance [dɪsəpírəns] *s.* desaparición.
dis·ap·point [dɪsəpóɪnt] *v.* chasquear; contrariar; decepcionar; faltar a lo prometido; desilusionar; **to be -ed** estar desilusionado o decepcionado; estar desengañado; quedar contrariado.
dis·ap·point·ing [dɪsəpóɪntɪŋ] *adj.* desilusionante, desengañador, decepcionante.
dis·ap·point·ment [dɪsəpóɪntmənt] *s.* desilusión, desengaño, decepción; chasco; contrariedad.
dis·ap·prov·al [dɪsəprúvl] *s.* desaprobación.
dis·ap·prove [dɪsəprúv] *v.* desaprobar.
dis·arm [dɪsárm] *v.* desarmar(se).
dis·ar·ma·ment [dɪsármǝmǝnt] *s.* desarme.
dis·ar·ray [dɪsəré] *s.* desarreglo, confusión, desorden; *v.* desarreglar, desordenar.
dis·as·ter [dizǽstə·] *s.* desastre.
dis·as·trous [dizǽstrəs] *adj.* desastroso.
dis·band [dɪsbǽnd] *v.* dispersar; licenciar (*las tropas*); desbandarse.
dis·be·lieve [dɪsbəlív] *v.* descreer, no creer.
dis·burse [dɪsbɜ́s] *v.* desembolsar.
dis·burse·ment [dɪsbɜ́smənt] *s.* desembolso; gasto.
disc [dɪsk] = **disk**.
dis·card [dískɑrd] *s.* descarte; desecho, cosa desechada; [dɪskárd] *v.* descartar; desechar.
dis·cern [dɪsɜ́n] *v.* discernir, distinguir; percibir.
dis·cern·ment [dɪsɜ́nmənt] *s.* discernimiento.

dis·charge [dɪstʃárdʒ] *s.* descarga (*de artillería*); descargo (*de una obligación*); desempeño (*de un deber*); exoneración; despedida; licencia (*militar*); pago (*de una deuda*); derrame, desagüe; supuración; *v.* descargar; exonerar; poner en libertad; despedir; echar, deponer; dar de baja (*a un soldado*); pagar (*una deuda*); arrojar, supurar; desaguar.
dis·ci·ple [dɪsáɪpl] *s.* discípulo.
dis·ci·pline [dísəplɪn] *s.* disciplina; *v.* disciplinar.
dis·close [dɪsklóz] *v.* descubrir; revelar.
dis·col·or [dɪskʌ́lə·] *v.* descolorar(se), desteñir(se).
dis·com·fort [dɪskʌ́mfə·t] *s.* incomodidad; malestar.
dis·con·cert [dɪskənsɜ́t] *v.* desconcertar.
dis·con·nect [dɪskənɛkt] *v.* desconectar; desacoplar; desunir, separar.
dis·con·nect·ed [dɪskənɛktɪd] *p.p. & adj.* desconectado; desunido; inconexo, incoherente.
dis·con·so·late [dɪskánslɪt] *adj.* desconsolado.
dis·con·tent [dɪskəntɛnt] *s.* descontento; *v.* descontentar.
dis·con·tent·ed [dɪskəntɛntɪd] *adj.* descontento; descontentadizo.
dis·con·tin·ue [dɪskəntínju] *v.* descontinuar; parar; suspender, interrumpir; abandonar.
dis·cord [dískɔrd] *s.* discordia; disonancia, discordancia; desavenencia.
dis·count [dískaʊnt] *s.* descuento; rebaja; — **rate** tipo de descuento; *v.* descontar; rebajar.
dis·cour·age [dɪskɜ́ɪdʒ] *v.* desanimar, desalentar, abatir; **to** — **from** disuadir de.
dis·cour·age·ment [dɪskɜ́ɪdʒmənt] *s.* desaliento, abatimiento.
dis·course [dískors] *s.* discurso; conversación; [dɪskórs] *v.* disertar, discurrir, hablar.
dis·cour·te·ous [dɪskɜ́tɪəs] *adj.* descortés, desatento.
dis·cour·te·sy [dɪskɜ́təsɪ] *s.* descortesía, desatención.
dis·cov·er [dɪskʌ́və·] *v.* descubrir.
dis·cov·er·er [dɪskʌ́vərə·] *s.* descubridor.
dis·cov·er·y [dɪskʌ́vrɪ] *s.* descubrimiento.
dis·cred·it [dɪskrɛ́dɪt] *s.* descrédito; deshonra; *v.* desacreditar; deshonrar; no creer.
dis·creet [dɪskrít] *adj.* discreto, prudente.
dis·crep·an·cy [dɪskrɛ́pənsɪ] *s.* discrepancia, diferencia; variación.
dis·cre·tion [dɪskrɛ́ʃən] *s.* discreción; prudencia; **at one's own** — a discreción.
dis·crim·i·nate [dɪskrímənət] *v.* discernir; distinguir; hacer distinciones, hacer favoritismos; dar trato de inferioridad con motivos de prejuicio; **to** — **against** hacer favoritismos en perjuicio de.
dis·cuss [dɪskʌ́s] *v.* discutir.
dis·cus·sion [dɪskʌ́ʃən] *s.* discusión.
dis·dain [dɪsdén] *s.* desdén, menosprecio; *v.* desdeñar, menospreciar; desdeñarse de.
dis·dain·ful [dɪsdénfəl] *adj.* desdeñoso.
dis·ease [dɪzíz] *s.* enfermedad.
dis·eased [dɪzízd] *adj.* enfermo.
dis·em·bark [dɪsɪmbárk] *v.* desembarcar.
dis·en·tan·gle [dɪsɪntǽŋgl] *v.* desenredar, desenmarañar, deshacer (*una maraña o enredo*).
dis·fig·ure [dɪsfígjə·] *v.* desfigurar; afear; desencajar.
dis·fran·chise [dɪsfrǽntʃaɪz] *v.* privar de derecho de voto o de ciudadanía.
dis·grace [dɪsgrés] *s.* ignominia, deshonra; vergüenza; **to be in** — estar desacreditado, haber perdido la gracia o el favor; *v.* deshonrar; degradar; desacreditar; avergonzar.

dis·grace·ful [dɪsgrésfəl] *adj.* vergonzoso.
dis·guise [dɪsgáɪz] *s.* disfraz; *v.* disfrazar.
dis·gust [dɪsgʌ́st] *s.* asco; repugnancia; disgusto; *v.* disgustar, dar asco; repugnar.
dis·gust·ed [dɪsgʌ́stɪd] *adj.* disgustado; descontento; asqueado.
dis·gust·ing [dɪsgʌ́stɪŋ] *adj.* asqueroso, repugnante.
dish [dɪʃ] *s.* plato; manjar, vianda; -es vajilla; *v.* servir.
dis·heart·en [dɪshártn̩] *v.* desalentar, desanimar, descorazonar.
di·shev·el [dɪʃévl̩] *v.* desgreñar.
di·shev·eled [dɪʃévl̩d] *adj.* desgreñado; desaliñado, desaseado; revuelto.
dis·hon·est [dɪsánɪst] *adj.* engañoso, falso, tramposo, falto de honradez, fraudulento.
dis·hon·es·ty [dɪsánɪstɪ] *s.* fraude, falta de honradez.
dis·hon·or [dɪsánɚ] *s.* deshonra; afrenta; *v.* deshonrar; recusar (*un giro o cheque*).
dis·hon·or·a·ble [dɪsánərəbl̩] *adj.* deshonroso; infame.
dish·wash·er [dɪʃwɔ́ʃɚ] *s.* (*person*) lavaplatos; (*machine*) máquina de lavar platos.
dis·il·lu·sion [dɪsɪlúʒən] *s.* desilusión, decepción, desengaño; *v.* desilusionar, decepcionar, desengañar.
dis·in·fect [dɪsɪnfékt] *v.* desinfectar.
dis·in·fec·tant [dɪsɪnféktənt] *s.* desinfectante.
dis·in·ter·est·ed [dɪsíntərəstɪd] *adj.* desinteresado.
disk [dɪsk] *s.* disco; — **brake** freno de disco.
dis·like [dɪsláɪk] *s.* antipatía, aversión; *v.* sentir o tener aversión por; **I** — **it** me repugna, no me gusta, me desagrada.
dis·lo·cate [dɪsloket] *v.* dislocar, descoyuntar; desencajar.
dis·lodge [dɪsládʒ] *v.* desalojar.
dis·loy·al [dɪslóɪəl] *adj.* desleal.
dis·mal [dɪzml̩] *adj.* lúgubre, sombrío, tétrico.
dis·man·tle [dɪsmǽntl̩] *v.* desmantelar; desmontar, desarmar.
dis·may [dɪsmé] *s.* desmayo, desaliento, pavor; *v.* desalentar, desanimar; atemorizar.
dis·miss [dɪsmís] *v.* (*discharge*) despedir, expulsar, destituir; (*dispel*) desechar; (*allow to leave*) licenciar, dar de baja; (*close*) dar por terminado (*un pleito o caso jurídico*); **to** — **the meeting** disolver la junta, levantar la sesión.
dis·miss·al [dɪsmísl̩] *s.* despedida, expulsión, destitución (*de un cargo*).
dis·mount [dɪsmáʊnt] *v.* desmontar; apear(se); desarmar (*un cañón, una máquina*); desengastar (*joyas*).
dis·o·be·di·ence [dɪsəbídɪəns] *s.* desobediencia.
dis·o·be·di·ent [dɪsəbídɪənt] *adj.* desobediente.
dis·o·bey [dɪsəbé] *v.* desobedecer.
dis·or·der [dɪsɔ́rdɚ] *s.* (*confusion*) desorden; trastorno; confusión; (*illness*) enfermedad; *v.* desordenar; trastornar; desarreglar.
dis·or·der·ly [dɪsɔ́rdɚlɪ] *adj.* desordenado; desarreglado; revoltoso; escandaloso; *adv.* desordenadamente.
dis·own [dɪsón] *v.* repudiar; desconocer, negar.
dis·par·age [dɪspǽrɪdʒ] *v.* desacreditar; desdorar.
dis·pas·sion·ate [dɪspǽʃənɪt] *adj.* desapasionado.
dis·patch [dɪspǽtʃ] *s.* despacho; envío; parte (*m.*), comunicación, mensaje; prontitud, expedición; *v.* despachar; enviar, expedir; matar.
dis·pel [dɪspél] *v.* disipar; dispersar.
dis·pen·sa·ry [dɪspénsərɪ] *s.* dispensario.
dis·pen·sa·tion [dɪspənséʃən] *s.* dispensa, exención;

dispensación; distribución.
dis·pense [dɪspéns] *v.* (*give*) dispensar, dar; repartir, distribuir; administrar (*la justicia*); despachar (*recetas, medicamentos*); **to** — **from** eximir de dispensar de; **to** — **with** omitir; pasarse sin, prescindir de.
dis·per·sal [dɪspɚ́sl̩] *s.* dispersión; desbandada.
dis·perse [dɪspɚ́s] *v.* dispersar(se), disipar(se), esparcir(se).
dis·place [dɪsplés] *v.* desalojar; desplazar; poner fuera de su lugar; suplantar.
dis·placed per·son [dɪsplést pɚ́sən] *s.* persona desplazada.
dis·play [dɪsplé] *s.* manifestación, exhibición; ostentación; *v.* exhibir; mostrar, manifestar; desplegar.
dis·please [dɪsplíz] *v.* desagradar; disgustar, fastidiar.
dis·pleas·ure [dɪsplɛ́ʒɚ] *s.* desagrado, disgusto, descontento.
dis·pos·al [dɪspózl̩] *s.* disposición; arreglo; venta (*de bienes*).
dis·pose [dɪspóz] *v.* disponer; arreglar; influir; **to** — **of** deshacerse de.
dis·po·si·tion [dɪspəzíʃən] *s.* disposición; arreglo; aptitud, inclinación; venta; **good (bad)** — buen (mal) genio.
dis·pos·ses [dɪspozés] *v.* desposeer; despojar.
dis·prove [dɪsprúv] *v.* refutar.
dis·pute [dɪspjút] *s.* disputa; *v.* disputar.
dis·qual·i·fy [dɪskwaləfaɪ] *v.* inhabilitar, incapacitar, descalificar.
dis·re·gard [dɪsrɪgárd] *s.* desatención, falta de atención, negligencia, descuido; falta de respeto o consideración; *v.* desatender, no hacer caso de, desentenderse de.
dis·re·spect [dɪsrɪspékt] *s.* desacato, falta de respeto.
dis·re·spect·ful [dɪsrɪspéktfəl] *adj.* irrespetuoso.
dis·rupt [dɪsrápt] *v.* desbaratar; romper.
dis·sat·is·fied [dɪssǽtɪsfaɪd] *adj.* descontento, malcontento, mal satisfecho.
dis·sat·is·fy [dɪssǽtɪsfaɪ] *v.* descontentar, no satisfacer.
dis·sect [dɪsékt] *v.* disecar, hacer una disección; analizar.
dis·sem·ble [dɪsémbl̩] *v.* disimular, fingir.
dis·sen·sion [dɪsénʃən] *s.* disensión, discordia.
dis·sent [dɪsént] *v.* disentir; *s.* desacuerdo; disensión, desavenencia.
dis·ser·ta·tion [dɪsɚtéʃən] *s.* disertacion; tratado; tesis.
dis·sim·u·la·tion [dɪsɪmjəléʃən] *s.* disimulo.
dis·si·pate [dɪsəpet] *v.* disipar; disipar(se).
dis·si·pa·tion [dɪsəpéʃən] *s.* disipación.
dis·so·lute [dɪsəlut] *adj.* disoluto.
dis·so·lu·tion [dɪsəlúʃən] *s.* disolución.
dis·solve [dɪzálv] *v.* disolver(se); anular.
dis·suade [dɪswéd] *v.* disuadir.
dis·taff [dɪstæf] *s.* rueca.
dis·tance [dɪstəns] *s.* distancia; lejanía; alejamiento; **in the** — a lo lejos, en lontananza.
dis·tant [dɪstənt] *adj.* (*far*) distante; apartado; lejano, remoto; (*aloof*) esquivo; **to be** — **from** distar de; **-ly** *adv.* de lejos; remotamente; a distancia; en lontananza.
dis·taste [dɪstést] *s.* disgusto, aversión, repugnancia.
dis·taste·ful [dɪstéstfəl] *adj.* desagradable, repugnante.
dis·tem·per [dɪstémpɚ] *s.* moquillo; pepita (*de las*

gallinas).

dis·tend [dɪsténd] *v.* dilatar, ensanchar.
dis·til [dɪstíl] *v.* destilar.
dis·til·la·tion [dɪstǀéʃən] *s.* destilación.
dis·till·er·y [dɪstílərɪ] *s.* destilería.
dis·tinct [dɪstíŋkt] *adj.* distinto, claro; diferente; **-ly** *adv.* distintamente, claramente, con claridad.
dis·tinc·tion [dɪstíŋkʃən] *s.* distinctión.
dis·tinc·tive [dɪstíŋktɪv] *adj.* distintivo.
dis·tin·guish [dɪstíŋgwɪʃ] *v.* distinguir; discernir.
dis·tin·guished [dɪstíŋgwɪʃt] *adj.* distinguido.
dis·tin·guish·ing [dɪstíŋgwɪʃɪŋ] *adj.* distintivo, característico.
dis·tort [dɪstɔ́ry] *v.* desfigurar, deformar, torcer, falsear; tergiversar.
dis·tract [dɪstrǽkt] *v.* distraer; perturbar.
dis·trac·tion [dɪstrǽkʃən] *s.* distracción, diversión; perturbación; **to drive to** — volver loco.
dis·tress [dɪstrés] *s.* angustia, aflicción, congoja; dolor; **to be in** — tener una aflicción; estar apurado; estar en zozobra (*un navío*); *v.* angustiar, acongojar, afligir; **to be -ed** estar afligido o apurado.
dis·trib·ute [dɪstríbjʊt] *v.* distribuir, repartir.
dis·tri·bu·tion [dɪstrəbjúʃən] *s.* distribución; repartimiento.
dis·trib·u·tor [dɪstríbjətɚ] *s.* distribuidor.
dis·trict [dístrɪkt] *s.* distrito; — **attorney** fiscal de distrito.
dis·trust [dɪstrást] *s.* deconfianza; recelo; *v.* desconfiar; recelar.
dis·trust·ful [dɪstrástfəl] *adj.* desconfiado, sospechoso, receloso.
dis·turb [dɪstɝ́b] *v.* turbar, perturbar, inquietar; desarreglar; incomodar, molestar; **don't** — **yourself!** ¡no se moleste Vd.!
dis·tur·bance [dɪstɝ́bəns] *s.* disturbio; perturbación; desorden; alboroto; molestia.
dis·use [dɪsjús] *s.* desuso; **to fall into** — caer en desuso; caducar.
ditch [dɪtʃ] *s.* zanja; foso; **irrigation** — acequia; *v.* zanjar, abrir zanjas; meter en la zanja; **to** — **someone** deshacerse de alguien.
dit·to [díto] *s.* ídem, lo mismo.
di·u·ret·ic [daɪjʊrétɪk] *adj. & s.* diurético.
di·van [dáɪvæn] *s.* diván.
dive [daɪv] *s.* zambullida (*echándose de cabeza*), buceada, chapuz; picada (*descenso rápido de un avión*); *Méx.* clavado; garito, leonera; *v.* echarse de cabeza; zambullirse (*de cabeza*); bucear; sumergirse (*un submarino*); **to** — **into someone** abalanzarse sobre alguien.
div·er [dáɪvɚ] *s.* buzo; zambullidor.
di·verge [dəvɝ́dʒ] *v.* divergir, irse apartando, separarse; diferir.
di·ver·gence [dəvɝ́dʒəns] *s.* divergencia; diferencia (*de opiniones*).
di·vers [dáɪvɚz] *adj.* diversos, varios.
di·verse [dəvɝ́s] *adj.* diverso; diferente.
di·ver·sion [dəvɝ́ʒən] *s.* diversión, recreo; desviación.
di·ver·si·ty [dəvɝ́sətɪ] *s.* diversidad, diferencia, variedad.
di·vert [dəvɝ́t] *v.* divertir, entretener; distraer; desviar, apartar.
di·vide [dəváɪd] *v.* dividir(se); partir.
div·i·dend [dívədɛnd] *s.* dividendo.
di·vid·ing [dɪváɪdɪŋ] *adj.* divisorio.
di·vine [dəváɪn] *adj.* divino; *v.* adivinar.
di·vin·i·ty [dəvínətɪ] *s.* divinidad; deidad; teología.
di·vi·sion [dəvíʒən] *s.* división.

di·vorce [dəvórs] *s.* divorcio; *v.* divorciar(se).
di·vulge [dəváldʒ] *v.* divulgar.
diz·zi·ness [dízɪnɪs] *s.* vahido o vaguido, desvanecimiento, mareo, vértigo.
diz·zy [dízɪ] *adj.* desvanecido, mareado; confuso; aturdido; — **speed** velocidad vertiginosa.
do [du] *v.* hacer; **to** — **away with** deshacerse de; prescindir de ; **to** — **a lesson** estudiar una lección; **to** — **one's hair** peinarse, arreglarse el pelo; **to** — **the dishes** lavar los platos; **to** — **up** envolver; limpiar, arreglar; lavar o planchar; **to** — **well in business** prosperar en los negocios; **to** — **without** pasarse sin; **to have nothing to** — **with** no tener nada que ver con; **that will** — basta, bastará; **that won't** — eso no sirve; eso no resultará bien; **this will have to** — habrá que conformarse con esto; **how** — **you** —? ¿cómo está Vd.?; — **you hear me?** ¿me oye Vd.?; **yes, I** — si, le oigo; **I** — **say it** sí lo digo.
doc·ile [dásǀ] *adj.* dócil.
dock [dɑk] *s.* muelle, desembarcadero; dársena; **dry** — carenero, dique de carena; *v.* entrar en el muelle; atracar, meter (*una embarcación*) en el muelle o dique; **to** — **the wages** rebajar la paga.
doc·tor [dáktɚ] *s.* doctor; médico, facultativo; *v.* medicinar, curar; **to** — **oneself** medicinarse, tomar medicinas.
doc·trine [dáktrɪn] *s.* doctrina.
doc·u·ment [dákjəmənt] *s.* documento; [dákjəment] *v.* documentar.
dod·der [dádɚ] *v.* tambalear; temblar.
dodge [dadʒ] *s.* evasión, evasiva; *v.* evadir(se); escabullirse; hurtar el cuerpo; **to** — **around a corner** dar un esquinazo.
doe [do] *s.* cierva; hembra (*del antílope, del gamo, de la liebre*).
dog [dɔg] *s.* perro, perra; can; **hot** — salchicha caliente, *Ch., C.A.* perro caliente; *Ríopl.* pancho; **to put on a lot of** — emperifollarse; darse mucho tono, *Ríopl.* darse mucho corte; *v.* seguir la pista de, perseguir, acosar; *adv.* sumamente, completamente; **dog-tired** cansadísimo.
dog·ma [dɔ́gmə] *s.* dogma.
dog·mat·ic [dɔgmǽtɪk] *adj.* dogmático.
doi·ly [dɔ́ɪlɪ] *s.* mantelito (*para platos, vasos, lámparas, etc.*).
do·ings [dúɪnz] *s. pl.* hechos, acciones, acontecimientos; **great** — mucha actividad, fiesta, función.
do-it-your·self [duɪtjʊrsélf] *adj.* proyectado para que uno pueda hacer sus propios trabajos manuales en casa; autodidáctico.
dole [dol] *s.* reparto gratuito (*de dinero o alimento*); ración, limosna; *v.* repartir gratuitamente.
dole·ful [dólfəl] *adj.* lúgubre, triste, lastimoso.
doll [dal] *s.* muñeca, muñeco; *v.* **to** — **up** emperifollarse, ataviarse; **dolly** *s.* muñequita.
dol·lar [dálɚ] *s.* dólar.
dol·phin [dólfɪn] *s.* delfín.
do·main [domén] *s.* dominio; heredad.
dome [dom] *s.* cúpula; media naranja (*de iglesia*).
do·mes·tic [dəméstɪk] *adj.* doméstico; hogareño; nacional, del país, *Am.* criollo; *s.* criado, sirviente.
do·mi·cile [dáməsaɪl] *s.* domicilio.
dom·i·nant [dámənənt] *adj.* dominante.
dom·i·nate [dámənet] *v.* dominar.
dom·i·na·tion [daménéʃən] *s.* dominación, dominio.
dom·i·neer [damənír] *v.* dominar, señorear.
dom·i·neer·ing [damənírɪŋ] *adj.* dominador,

mandón, imperioso, tiránico.

do·min·ion [dəmínjən] *s.* dominio.

dom·i·no [dáməno] *s.* dominó, traje de máscara; disfraz; ficha (*de dominó*); **dominoes** dominó (*juego*).

don [dɑn] *s.* don (*título*); caballero; *v.* ponerse, vestirse.

do·nate [dónet] *v.* donar, regalar, hacer donación.

do·na·tion [donéʃən] *s.* donación; regalo, dádiva.

done [dʌn] *p.p. de* to do hecho; terminado, acabado; **to be — in** estar rendido de cansancio; **the meat is well —** está bien asada la carne.

don·key [dáŋkɪ] *s.* burro, asno.

doo·dad [dúdæd] *s.* chuchería, chisme.

doom [dum] *s.* hado, sino, destino; mala suerte, perdición, ruina; **the day of —** el día del juicio final; *v.* condenar, sentenciar; predestinar; **to be -ed to failure** estar predestinado al fracaso.

door [dor] *s.* puerta; entrada.

door·bell [dórbɛl] *s.* campanilla o timbre (*de llamada*).

door·knob [dórnɑb] *s.* tirador de puerta, perilla, manija.

door·man [dórmæn] *s.* portero.

door·step [dórstɛp] *s.* escalón de la puerta; umbral.

door·way [dórwe] *s.* puerta, entrada, vano (*de la puerta*).

dope [dop] *s.* (*narcotic*) narcótico; opio; droga; menjurje, medicamento; (*information*) información; **— fiend** morfinómano; **he is a —** es un zoquete; *v.* narcotizar; **to — out** adivinar, conjeturar; **to — oneself up** medicinarse demasiado.

dor·mi·to·ry [dórmətorɪ] *s.* dormitorio.

dose [dos] *s.* dosis; *v.* medicinar; **to — oneself** medicinarse.

dos·si·er [dásie] *s.* expediente; legajo.

dot [dɑt] *s.* punto; **on the — en** punto; *v.* marcar con puntos; poner el punto (*sobre la* i).

do·tage [dótɪdʒ] *s.* chochez; **to be in one's —** chochear.

dote [dot] *v.* chochear; **to — on** estar loco por.

dou·ble [dʌbl] *adj.* doble; doblado; **— boiler** baño de María; **— deal** trato doble; **— entry** partida doble; **— standard** norma de conducta sexual mas restringida para la mujer; *s.* doble; **-s** juego de dobles (*en tenis*); *adv.* doblemente; **double-breasted** cruzado; **double-faced** de dos caras; *v.* doblar(se); duplicar(se); **to — up** doblarse; **doubly** *adv.* doblemente; por duplicado.

doubt [daʊt] *s.* duda; *v.* dudar.

doubt·ful [dáʊtfəl] *adj.* dudoso; dudable.

doubt·less [dáʊtlɪs] *adj.* indudable, cierto, seguro; *adv.* sin duda; indudablemente; probablemente.

douche [duʃ] *s.* ducha vaginal.

dough [do] *s.* pasta, masa; dinero.

dough·nut [dónət] *s.* bollito o buñuelo en rosca.

dove [dʌv] *s.* paloma.

dove [dov] *pret. de* to dive.

down [daʊn] *adv.* abajo, hacia abajo; **— to** hasta; **— East** en el este; **— the street** calle abajo; **to cut — prices** reducir o rebajar precios; **to get — to work** aplicarse; **to go (o come) — bajar; **to pay —** pagar al contado; **to put —** poner; anotar, apuntar, poner por escrito; *adj.* abatido, descorazonado; **— grade** declive, pendiente; **prices are —** han bajado los precios; **to be — on someone** tenerle ojeriza a alguien; *s.* plumón; vello; pelusa; *v.* echar por tierra, derribar; rebajar (*precios*).

down·cast [dáʊnkæst] *adj.* cabizbajo, abatido; **with — eyes** con los ojos bajos.

down·fall [dáʊnfɔl] *s.* caída; ruina.

down·pour [dáʊnpor] *s.* aguacero, chaparrón.

down·right [dáʊnraɪt] *adj.* claro, positivo, categórico, absoluto; **— foolishness** solemne disparate; *adv.* enteramente; absolutamente.

down·stairs [dáʊnstɛrz] *adv.* abajo; en el piso bajo; *adj.* del piso bajo; *s.* piso bajo, piso inferior.

down·stream [dáʊnstrim] *adv.* río abajo, aguas abajo; con la corriente.

down-to-earth [daʊntəˈθ] *adj.* sensato; practico.

down·town [dáʊntáʊn] *adv.* al centro, en el centro (*de una población*); *adj.* del centro; *s,* centro.

down·ward [dáʊnwəd] *adj.* descendente; inclinado; *adv.* (= **downwards**) hacia abajo.

dow·ny [dáʊnɪ] *adj.* suave, blando; velloso; plumoso.

dow·ry [dáʊrɪ] *s.* dote.

doze [doz] *s.* siestecita, sueño ligero; *v.* dormitar.

doz·en [dʌzn] *s.* docena.

drab [dræb] *adj.* pardo, pardusco; monótono.

draft [dræft] *s.* corriente de aire; trago; libranza, letra de cambio, giro bancario; trazado; plan; leva (*militar*), conscripción; tiro (*de estufa, hogar, etc.*); calado (*de un barco*); **— beer** cerveza de barril; **— horse** caballo de tiro; **rough —** croquis, borrador; *v.* trazar, dibujar, delinear, reclutar, echar leva; redactar (*un documento*).

drafts·man [dræftsmən] *s.* dibujante.

drag [dræg] *s.* rastra; traba, obstáculo; **to have a — with someone** tener buenas aldabas con alguien; *v.* arrastrar(se); rastrear; moverse despacio; **to — on and on** prolongarse demasiado, prolongarse hasta el fastidio.

drag·on [drægən] *s.* dragón.

drain [dren] *s.* (*channel*) desagüe; desaguadero, conducto; (*exhaust*) agotamiento; consumo; *v.* desaguar(se); apurar (*un vaso*); agotar, consumir; escurrir(se), secar(se); desecar (*un terreno*), *Am.* drenar.

drain·age [drénɪdʒ] *s.* desagüe, *Am.* drenaje; desaguadero; sistema de desaguaderos; desecamiento, desecación (*de un terreno, laguna, etc.*).

drake [drek] *s.* pato.

dra·ma [drámə] *s.* drama.

dra·mat·ic [drəmætɪk] *adj.* dramático.

dra·ma·tist [drámətɪst] *s.* dramaturgo, dramático.

dra·ma·tize [dræmətaɪz] *v.* dramatizar.

drank [dræŋk] *pret. de* to drink.

drape [drep] *s.* colgadura, cortina, tapiz; *v.* colgar, entapizar, adornar con tapices; cubrir, revestir.

drap·er·y [drépərɪ] *s.* tapicería, colgaduras, cortinas; pañería, paños, géneros.

dras·tic [dræstɪk] *adj.* extremo, fuerte, violento; **to take — steps** tomar medidas enérgicas.

draught [dræft] *véase* **draft**.

draw [drɔ] *v.* (*pull*) tirar; estirar; jalar (*halar*); (*attract*) atraer; sacar; (*design*) dibujar, trazar; (*withdraw*) girar, librar (*una libranza*); hacer (*una comparación*); correr (*la cortina*); **to — aside** apartar(se); **to — a breath** aspirar, tomar aliento; **to — lots** echar suertes, sortear; **to — near** acercarse; **to — out** sacar; sonsacar (*a una persona*); alargar, prolongar; **to — up** acercar(se); redactar (*un documento*); *s.* empate (*en deportes o juegos*); número sacado (*en una rifa*); atración; **—bridge** puente levadizo.

draw·back [drɔbæk] *s.* desventaja; obstáculi,

inconveniente.
drawer [drɔr] *s.* cajón, gaveta; **-s** calzoncillos.
draw·er [drɔ́ɚ] *s.* librador, girador; dibujante.
draw·ing [drɔ́ɪŋ] *s.* (*design*) dibujo; delineación,
trazado; (*raffle*) sorteo; — **paper** papel de dibujo;
— **room** sala de recibo, recibidor, recibimiento.
drawn [drɔn] *p.p. de* **to draw.**
dread [drɛd] *s.* pavor, temor, aprensión; *adj.*
terrible; temido; *v.* temer; sentir aprensión de.
dread·ful [drɛ́dfəl] *adj.* horrendo; espantoso.
dream [drim] *s.* sueño; ensueño; *v.* soñar; **to** — **of**
soñar con, soñar en.
dream·er [drímɚ] *s.* soñador.
dream·land [drímlænd] *s.* tierra del ensueño;
región de los sueños.
dreamt [drɛmpt] = **dreamed.**
drea·my [drími] *adj.* soñoliento; soñador;
melancólico; como un sueño; **a** — **recollection**
un vago recuerdo.
drea·ry [dríri] *adj.* sombrío; melancólico.
dredge [drɛdʒ] *s.* draga; *v.* dragar.
dregs [drɛgz] *s. pl.* heces, sedimento.
drench [drɛntʃ] *s.* mojada, mojadura, empapada; *v.*
empapar; mojar; remojar.
dress [drɛs] *s.* vestido, traje; vestidura, ropaje,
atavío; — **rehearsal** ensayo general y último
(*antes de una función*); — **suit** traje de etiqueta;
v. vestir(se); arreglarse, componerse; aderezar;
adobar (*carne o pieles*); curar (*heridas*); alinear,
formar (*las tropas*); **to** — **down** reprender,
regañar; **to** — **up** emperifollarse, acicalarse,
ataviarse.
dress·er [drɛ́sɚ] *s.* tocador, cómoda (*con espejo*);
she is a good — viste con elegancia o buen gusto.
dress·ing [drɛ́sɪŋ] *s.* aderezo; salsa (*para ensaladas*);
relleno (*para carne, pollo, etc.*); medicamento,
vendajes (*para heridas*); **a** — **down** regaño; —
gown bata; — **room** tocador; — **table** tocador.
dress·mak·er [drɛ́smekɚ] *s.* modista.
drew [dru] *pret. de* **to draw.**
drib·ble [dríbl] *v.* gotear; dejar caer en gotas;
babear; *s.* goteo; chorrito.
drib·let [dríblɪt] *s.* gota, gotita; **in -s** gota a gota;
en pequeñas cantidades.
dried [draɪd] *pret. & p.p. de* **to dry;** *adj.* seco; paso;
— **fig** higo paso.
drift [drɪft] *s.* (*direction*) rumbo, dirección,
tendencia, deriva; (*pile*) montón,
amontonamiento (*de arena, nieve, etc.*); (*off
course*) desvío (*de un barco o avión*); **to get the**
— **of a conversation** enterarse a medias de una
conversación; *v.* flotar; ir(se) a la deriva; dejarse
llevar por la corriente; amontonarse (*la nieve, la
arena*); esparcirse (*la arena, la nieve, las nubes*).
drift·wood [dríftwʊd] *s.* madera o leña flotante;
madera de playa.
drill [drɪl] *s.* (*tool*) taladro; barrena; (*training*)
ejercicio; adiestramiento; *Am.* entrenamiento;
dril (*tela*); *v.* taladrar, barrenar, perforar; hacer
ejercicio; aleccionar; disciplinar (*un ejército*);
adiestrar(se), *Am.* entrenar(se).
dri·ly [dráɪlɪ] *adv.* secamente.
drink [drɪŋk] *s.* bebida; trago; *v.* beber; **to** — **a
toast to** beber a la salud de, brindar por; — **it
down!** ¡bébaselo! ¡trágueselo!
drink·a·ble [dríŋkəbl] *adj.* potable.
drip [drɪp] *s.* goteo; *v.* gotear, caer gota a gota;
dejar caer gota a gota.
drive [draɪv] *s.* (*ride*) paseo en coche; (*road*) calzada,
carretera, paseo; (*campaign*) campaña; (*impulse*)
empuje; tiro, tirada (*de una pelota*); *v.* impulsar,

impeler, empujar; arrear (*animales*); conducir,
guiar o manejar (*un auto*); forzar; encajar, clavar
(*una estaca, cuña, o clavo*); tirar, lanzar (*una
pelota*); dar un paseo en auto; llevar (*a alguien*)
en auto; cavar (*un pozo, túnel, etc.*); **to** — **away**
ahuyentar; **to** — **a good bargain** hacer un buen
trato; **to** — **mad** volver loco; **what are you
driving at?** ¿qué quieres decir con eso?
drive-in [dráɪvɪn] *s. adj.* establecimiento como
tienda, banco, teatro que tiene pista
automovilística que permite al cliente
permanecer en su coche; automovilístico.
driv·el [drívl] *s.* baba; ñoñería, tontería; *v.* babear;
chochear, decir ñoñerías.
driv·el·ing [drívlɪŋ] *adj.* baboso.
driv·en [drívən] *p.p. de* **to drive.**
driv·er [dráɪvɚ] *s.* cochero, chófer, mecánico,
conductor (*de automóvil*); arriero (*de animales*);
uno de los palos de golf; **pile** — martinete (*para
clavar pilotes*); **slave** — mandón, tirano; **truck** —
carretero, camionero.
drive·way [dráɪvwe] *s.* calzada de entrada,
carretera de entrada.
driz·zle [drízl] *v.* lloviznar; *s.* llovizna.
drone [dron] *s.* zángano; holgazán; zumbido; *v.*
zumbar; hablar con monotonía; holgazanear,
perder el tiempo.
droop [drup] *v.* doblarse, andar o estar alicaído,
estar abatido; languidecer; marchitarse; bajar
(*los hombros, los párpados*); **his shoulders** — tiene
los hombros caídos; **-ing eyelids** párpados
caídos.
drop [drɑp] *s.* (*liquid*) gota; (*descent*) baja; caída;
(*incline*) declive; **cough** — pastilla para la tos;
letter — buzón; — **curtain** telón (*de teatro*); —
hammer martinete; — **out** dimitente; *v.* dejar
caer, soltar; gotear; caer; dejar (*un asunto, una
amistad*); **to** — **a line** poner unos renglones; **to**
— **asleep** quedarse dormido, dormirse; **to** —
behind dejar atrás; quedarse atrás; **to** — **in** hacer
una visita inesperada, *Am.* descolgarse; **to** — **in
a mailbox** echar al buzón; **to** — **out** retirarse;
desaparecer; **to** — **the curtain** bajar el telón.
drought [draʊt] *s.* sequía.
drove [drov] *s.* manada, recua, rebaño; tropel; *pret.
de* **drive.**
drown [draʊn] *v.* ahogar(se), anegar(se); apagar,
ahogar (*un sonido*).
drowse [draʊz] *v.* dormitar; estar amodorrado.
drows·i·ness [dráʊzɪnɪs] *s.* modorra, somnolencia.
drow·sy [dráʊzɪ] *adj.* soñoliento; adormilado,
amodorrado; **to become** — amodorrarse.
drudge [drʌdʒ] *v.* afanarse, atarearse; *s.* trabajador,
esclavo del trabajo.
drug [drʌg] *s.* droga; narcótico; **to be a** — **on the
market** ser invendible (*una mercancía*); *v.* jaropar
(*administrar drogas en demasía*); narcotizar.
drug·gist [drʌ́gɪst] *s.* boticario, droguista, droguero,
farmacéutico.
drug·store [drʌ́gstor] *s.* botica, droguería,
farmacia.
drum [drʌm] *s.* tambor; tímpano (*del oído*); barril,
tonel; **bass** — tambora, bombo; —**stick** bolillo
de tambor; — **major** tambor mayor; *v.* tocar el
tambor; tamborilear; **to** — **a lesson into someone**
meterle a uno la lección en la cabeza; **to** — **up
trade** solicitar o fomentar ventas.
drum·mer [drʌ́mɚ] *s.* tambor, tamborilevo;
viajante de comercio, agente.
drunk [drʌŋk] *p.p. de* **to drink;** *adj.* borracho, ebrio,
emborrachado, bebido; *Riopl.* mamado; *C.A.*

bolo; *Ch.* cufifo; **to get** — emborracharse, embriagarse.

drunk·ard [drʌ́ŋkəd] *s.* borracho, borrachón, beodo, bebedor.

drunk·en [drʌ́njən] *adj.* borracho, ebrio.

drunk·en·ness [drʌ́ŋkənnɪs] *s.* borrachera, embriaguez.

dry [draɪ] *adj.* seco; árido; **a — book** un libro aburrido; **— cleaner** quitamanchas; tintorero; **— cleaning** lavado o limpieza al seco; **— goods** lencería, géneros, tejidos, telas; **— measure** medida para áridos; **— run** ejercicio de ensayo; ensayo. **— wash** ropa lavada pero no planchada. *v.* secar(se); enjugar; **to — up** secarse, resecarse.

dry·ness [draɪnɪs] *s.* sequedad; aridez.

dub [dʌb] *v.* doblar (*una película*).

du·bi·ous [djúbɪəs] *adj.* dudoso.

duch·ess [dʌ́tʃɪs] *s.* duquesa.

duck [dʌk] *s.* pato, pata; ánade; dril (*género*); zambullida, chapuz; agachada rápida (*para evitar un golpe*); *v.* zambullir(se), chapuzar(se); agachar(se); agachar (*la cabeza*).

duck·ling [dʌ́klɪŋ] *s.* patito, añadeja.

duc·tile [dʌ́ktɪl] *adj.* dúctil.

dud [dʌd] *s.* bomba que no estalla.

dude [dud] *s.* caballerete; novato.

due [dju] *adj.* debido; vencido, pagadero; **in — time** a su debido tiempo; **the bill is** — se ha vencido la cuenta; **the train is—at two o'clock** el tren debe llegar a las dos; *adv.* directamente; **— east** hacia el este, rumbo al oriente; *s.* derecho, privilegio; **-s** cuota.

du·el [djúəl] *s.* duelo, desafío, combate; *v.* batirse en duelo.

du·et [djuét] *s.* duo, dueto.

dug [dʌg] *pret. & p.p. de* **to dig.**

dug·out [dʌ́gaʊt] *s.* piragua.

duke [djuk] *s.* duque.

duke·dom [djúkdəm] *s.* ducado.

dull [dʌl] *adj.* (*dim*) opaco, empañado, mate; sin brillo; (*boring*) aburrido; (*blunt*) embotado, sin punta, sin filo; (*stupid*) torpe; tardo; **— pain** dolor sordo; **— sound** sonido sordo o apagado; *v.* embotar(se); empañar(se); ofuscar; amortiguar (*un dolor o sonido*).

dull·ness [dʌ́lnɪs] *s.* (*dimness*) falta de brillo; (*sluggishness*) estupidez, torpeza; (*bluntness*) falta de punta o filo; (*monotony*) aburrimiento; (*heaviness*) pesadez.

du·ly [djúlɪ] *adv.* debidamente.

dumb [dʌm] *adj.* (*silent*) mudo; silencioso, callado; (*dull*) estúpido, torpe; **—creature** animal.

dumb·found·ed [dʌmfáʊndəd] *adj.* patitieso.

dumb·ness [dʌ́mnɪs] *s.* mudez; mutismo; estupidez.

dum·my [dʌ́mɪ] *s.* (*figure*) maniquí, figurón, muñeco; (*fool*) zoquete, tonto; *adj.* falso, fingido.

dump [dʌmp] *s.* montón (*de tierra, carbón, etc.*); terrero, vaciadero, escorial; **garbage—**muladar; basurero; **to be in the -s** estar abatido; *v.* echar, vaciar, descargar; echar a la basura.

dunce [dʌns] *s.* zopenco, zoquete, tonto.

dune [djun] *s.* duna o médano.

dung [dʌŋ] *s.* boñiga, estiércol.

dun·geon [dʌ́ndʒən] *s.* mazmorra, calabozo.

dung·hill [dʌ́ŋhɪl] *s.* muladar, estercolero.

dupe [djup] *s.* inocentón, incauto, víctima (*de un engaño*); *v.* embaucar.

du·pli·cate [djúpləkɪt] *adj. & s.* doble, duplicado; [djúpləket] *v.* duplicar, copiar.

du·plic·i·ty [djuplísətɪ] *s.* duplicidad, doblez.

du·ra·ble [djúrəbl] *adj.* durable, duradero.

du·ra·tion [djʊréʃən] *s.* duración.

dur·ing [dúrɪŋ] *prep.* durante.

dusk [dʌsk] *s.* crepúsculo (*vespertino*), anochecida; caída de la tarde; sombra, oscuridad; **at —**al atardecer.

dusk·y [dʌ́skɪ] *adj.* obscuro, negruzco; sombrío.

dust [dʌst] *s.* polvo; tierra; **cloud of—**polvareda; *v.* sacudir el polvo, desempolvar, quitar el polvo; empolvar, llenar de polvo; espolvorear.

dust·er [dʌ́stə] *s.* limpiador; quitapolvo; **feather —** plumero.

dust·y [dʌ́stɪ] *adj.* polvoriento; empolvado, lleno de polvo.

Dutch [dʌtʃ] *adj. & s.* holandés; **— treat** convite a escote.

Dutch·man [dʌ́tʃmən] *s.* holandés.

du·ty [djútɪ] *s.* deber, obligación; derechos aduanales; impuesto; **—free** libre de derechos aduanales.

dwarf [dwɔrf] *s. & adj.* enano; *v.* achicar, empequeñecer; impedir el desarrollo o crecimiento de.

dwell [dwel] *v.* residir, morar, habitar vivir; **to — on a subject** espaciarse o dilatarse en un asunto.

dwell·er [dwélə] *s.* habitante, morador.

dwell·ing [dwélɪŋ] *s.* morada, habitación, domicilio.

dwelt [dwelt] *pret. & p.p. de* **to dwell.**

dwin·dle [dwíndl] *v.* menguar, mermar; disminuir(se); gastarse.

dye [daɪ] *s.* tinte, tintura; *v.* teñir, tinturar.

dy·er [dáɪə] *s.* tintorero; **-'s shop** tintorería.

dy·ing [dáɪŋ] *adj.* moribundo; agonizante.

dy·nam·ic [daɪnǽmɪk] *adj.* dinámico; enérgico; **-s** *s.* dinámica.

dy·na·mite [dáɪnəmaɪt] *s.* dinamita; *v.* dinamitar, volar con dinamita.

dy·na·mo [dáɪnəmo] *s.* dínamo.

dy·nas·ty [dáɪnəstɪ] *s.* dinastía.

dys·en·ter·y [dísṇterɪ] *s.* disentería.

E:e

each [itʃ] *adj.* cada; *pron.* cada uno; **— other** el uno al otro, uno(s) a otro(s).

ea·ger [ígə] *adj.* anhelante, ansioso, deseoso; **-ly** *adv.* con anhelo; con ahinco; ansiosamente.

ea·ger·ness [ígənɪs] *s.* anhelo, ansia, deseo vehemente; ahinco; ardor.

ea·gle [ígl] *s.* águila.

ear [ɪr] *s.* (*outer*) oreja; (*hearing*) oído; **—drum** tímpano; **— muff** orejera; **— of corn** mazorca; **— of wheat** espiga; **by —** de oído; **within —shot** al alcance del oído.

earl [ɜl] *s.* conde.

ear·ly [ɜ́lɪ] *adv.* temprano; *adj.* temprano; primitivo, remoto; **— riser** madrugador, tempranero, mañanero; **at an — date** en fecha a próxima.

earn [ɜn] *v.* ganar; merecer.

ear·nest [ɜ́nɪst] *adj.* serio, formal; ardiente; **in —** en serio, con toda formalidad; de buena fe; **-ly** *adv.* seriamente; con ahinco; encarecidamente; ansiosamente.

ear·nest·ness [ɜ́nɪstnɪs] *s.* seriedad; celo; solicitud; sinceridad; **in all —** con todo ahinco; con toda formalidad; con toda sinceridad.

earn·ings [ɜ́nɪŋz] *s.* ganancias; sueldo, salario,

paga.
ear·ring [írrɪŋ] s. arete, zarcillo, pendiente, arracada; *C.A.* arito; *P.R.* pantalla.
earth [ɟθ] s. tierra; suelo.
earth·en [ɟθən] adj. de tierra; de barro.
earth·en·ware [ɟθənwɛr] s. loza de barro; trastos, cacharros.
earth·ly [ɟθlɪ] adj. terrenal, terrestre, mundano; terreno; **to be of no — use** no servir para nada.
earth·quake [ɟθkwek] s. terremoto, temblor de tierra.
earth·shak·ing [ɟθʃekɪŋ] adj. desmedido.
earth·worm [ɟθwɜm] s. lombriz.
ease [iz] s. (*facility*) facilidad; naturalidad; soltura; (*comfort*) comodidad; tranquilidad; **at —** tranquilo; cómodo; v. facilitar; aliviar; mitigar; tranquilizar; aligerar (*el peso*); aflojar.
ea·sel [ízl] s. caballete (*de pintor*).
eas·i·ly [ízəlɪ] adv. fácilmente; sin dificultad; cómodamente.
east [ist] s. este; oriente, levante; adj. del este, oriental; adv. al este, hacia el este; en el este.
East·er [ístɚ] s. Pascuas, Pascua Florida; **— Sunday** Domingo de Resurrección o de Pascuas.
east·ern [ístɚn] adj. oriental; del este.
east·ward [ístwɚd] adv. & adj. hacia el este u oriente.
eas·y [ízɪ] adj. (*simple*) fácil; (*comfortable*) cómodo; tranquilo; **— chair** silla cómoda, poltrona, butaca; **easy-going man** hombre cachazudo o calmo; **at an — pace** a paso moderado; **within — reach** al alcance; a la mano.
eat [it] v. comer; **to — away** corroer, destruir; **to — breakfast** desayunarse, tomar el desayuno; **to — dinner** tomar la comida, comer; **to — supper** tomar la cena, cenar; **to — one's heart out** sufrir en silencio; **to — one's words** retractarse.
eat·en [ítn] p.p. de **to eat**.
eaves [ivz] s. pl. alero (*de un tejado*).
ebb [ɛb] s. reflujo; decadencia; **— tide** marea menguante; **to be at a low —** estar decaído; v. menguar, decaer.
eb·on·y [ébənɪ] s. ébano.
ec·cen·tric [ɪksɛ́ntrɪk] adj. & s. excéntrico.
ec·cle·si·as·tic [ɪklɪziǽstɪk] adj. & s. eclesiástico.
ech·e·lon [ɛ́ʃəlɑn] s. escalón.
ech·o [ɛ́ko] s. eco; v. hacer eco, repetir; resonar, repercutir.
ec·lec·tic [ɪklɛ́ktɪk] adj. ecléctico.
e·clipse [ɪklíps] s. eclipse; v. eclipsar.
ec·o·nom·ic [ɪkənámɪk] adj. económico.
ec·o·nom·i·cal [ɪkənámɪk] adj. económico.
ec·o·nom·ics [ɪkənámɪks] s. economía política.
e·con·o·mist [ɪkánəmɪst] s. economista.
e·con·o·mize [ɪkánəmaɪz] v. economizar.
e·con·o·my [ɪkánəmɪ] s. economía; parsimonia.
e·con·o·my class [ɪkánəmɪ klæs] s. segunda clase en las líneas aéreas.
ec·sta·sy [ɛ́kstəsɪ] s. éxtasis.
ec·u·men·i·cal [ɛkjumɛ́nəkl] adj. ecuménico.
ed·dy [ɛ́dɪ] s. remolino; v. arremolinarse.
E·den [ídn] s. Edén; paraíso.
edge [ɛdʒ] s. orilla, borde; filo; **to be on —** estar nervioso.
edge·wise [ɛ́dʒwaɪz] adv. de lado; de filo.
ed·i·ble [ɛ́dəbl] adj. & s. comestible.
ed·i·fice [ɛ́dəfɪs] s. edificio.
ed·i·fy [ɛ́dəfaɪ] v. edificar (*moral, espiritualmente*).
ed·it [ɛ́dɪt] v. redactar; preparar o corregir (*un manuscrito*) para la imprenta; cuidar (*una edición*).

e·di·tion [ɪdíʃən] s. edición.
ed·i·tor [ɛ́dɪtɚ] s. redactor; director de un periódico; revisor (*de manuscritos*).
ed·i·to·ri·al [ɛdətórɪəl] adj. editorial; s. editorial (*m.*), artículo de fondo.
ed·i·to·ri·al·ize [ɛdɪtórɪəlaɪz] v. expresar opiniones como en artículo de fondo; editorializar.
ed·u·cate [ɛ́dʒəket] v. educar; instruir.
ed·u·ca·tion [ɛdʒəkéʃən] s. educación; crianza; instrucción, enseñanza; pedagogía.
ed·u·ca·tion·al [ɛdʒəkéʃənl] adj. educativo, docente; pedagógico.
ed·u·ca·tor [ɛ́dʒəketɚ] s. educador.
eel [il] s. anguila.
ef·fect [əfɛ́kt] s. efecto; **-s** bienes, efectos; **to go into —** hacerse vigente, ponerse en operación (*una ley*); v. efectuar; ejecutar; realizar.
ef·fec·tive [əfɛ́ktɪv] adj. efectivo, eficaz; vigente (*una ley*); **-ly** adv. eficazmente.
ef·fec·tu·al [əfɛ́ktʃʊəl] adj. eficaz.
ef·fem·i·nate [əfɛ́mənɪt] adj. afeminado.
ef·fete [ɪfít] adj. gastado; estéril; decadente.
ef·fi·ca·cy [ɛ́fəkəsɪ] s. eficacia.
ef·fi·cien·cy [əfíʃəsɪ] s. eficiencia; eficacia.
ef·fi·cient [əfíʃənt] adj. eficiente; eficaz.
ef·fi·gy [ɛ́fɪdʒɪ] s. efigie; **to burn in —** quemar en efigie.
ef·fort [ɛ́fɚt] s. esfuerzo; empeño; conato.
ef·front·er·y [əfrʌ́ntərɪ] s. descaro, desvergüenza, desfachatez.
ef·fu·sive [ɛfúsɪv] adj. efusivo, demostrativo, expansivo.
egg [ɛg] s. huevo; **fried —** huevo frito o estrellado; **hard-boiled —** huevo cocido, huevo duro; **scrambled -s** huevos revueltos; **soft-boiled —** huevo pasado por agua; *Mex.* huevo tibio; v. **to — on** incitar.
egg·nog [ɛ́gnag] s. rompopo.
egg·plant [ɛ́gplænt] s. berenjena.
e·go·cen·tric [igosɛ́ntrɪk] adj. egocéntrico.
e·go·tism [ígotɪzəm] s. egotismo; egoísmo.
E·gyp·tian [ɪdʒípʃən] adj. & s. egipcio.
ei·ther [íðɚ] adj. & pron. uno u otro; **— of the two** cualquiera de los dos; **in — case** en ambos casos; adv. tampoco; **nor I —** ni yo tampoco; conj. o.
ejac·u·late [ɪdʒǽkjulet] v. eyacular.
e·ject [ɪdʒɛ́kt] v. echar, arrojar, expulsar.
e·jec·tion [ɪdʒɛ́kʃən] s. expulsión; **— seat** asiento lanzable.
e·lab·o·rate [ɪlǽbərɪt] adj. elaborado, primoroso; esmerado; [ɪlǽbəret] v. elaborar.
e·lapse [ɪlǽps] v. transcurrir, pasar.
e·las·tic [ɪlǽstɪk] adj. elástico; s. elástico; goma elástica; cordón elástico; liga elástica.
e·las·tic·i·ty [ɪlæstísətɪ] s. elasticidad.
e·lat·ed [ɪlétɪd] adj. exaltado, gozoso, alborozado.
el·bow [ɛ́lbo] s. codo; recodo, ángulo; **to be within — reach** estar a la mano; v. codear, dar codazos; **to — one's way through** abrirse paso a codazos.
eld·er [ɛ́ldɚ] adj. mayor, más grande, más viejo, de más edad; s. mayor; anciano; dignatario (*en ciertas iglesias*); **our -s** nuestros mayores; nuestros antepasados.
el·der·ly [ɛ́ldɚlɪ] adj. viejo, anciano.
el·dest [ɛ́ldɪst] adj. mayor.
e·lect [ɪlɛ́kt] adj. & s. electo; elegido; v. elegir.
e·lec·tion [ɪlɛ́kʃən] s. elección.
e·lec·tor [ɪlɛ́ktɚ] s. elector.
e·lec·tor·al [ɪlɛ́ktərəl] adj. electoral.
e·lec·tric [ɪlɛ́ktrɪk] adj. eléctrico; **— meter**

electrómetro, contador eléctrico; — **storm** tronada, tempestad; — **eye** ojo eléctrico; *s.* tranvía o ferrocarril eléctrico.

e·lec·tri·cal [ɪlɛ́ktrɪkl] *adj.* eléctrico; — **engineering** electrotecnia, ingeniería eléctrica; — **engineer** ingeniero electricista; electrotécnico.

e·lec·tri·cian [ɪlɛktríʃən] *s.* electricista.

e·lec·tric·i·ty [ɪlɛktrísətɪ] *s.* electricidad.

e·lec·tri·fy [ɪlɛ́ktrəfaɪ] *v.* electrizar; electrificar.

e·lec·tro·car·di·o·graph [ɪlɛktrokárdɪəgræf] *s.* electrocardiógrafo.

e·lec·tro·cute [ɪlɛ́ktrəkjut] *v.* electrocutar.

e·lec·trol·y·sis [ɪlɛktrálɪsɪs] *s.* electrolisis.

e·lec·tro·mag·net [ɪlɛktromǽgnət] *s.* electroimán.

e·lec·tron [ɪlɛ́ktrɑn] *s.* electrón; — **microscope** microscopio electrónico.

e·lec·tron·ics [ɪlɛktrániks] *s.* electrónica.

el·e·gance [ɛ́ləgəns] *s.* elegancia.

el·e·gant [ɛ́ləgənt] *adj.* elegante.

el·e·ment [ɛ́ləmənt] *s.* elemento.

el·e·men·tal [ɛləméntl] *adj.* elemental.

el·e·men·ta·ry [ɛləméntərɪ] *adj.* elemental.

el·e·phant [ɛ́ləfənt] *s.* elefante.

el·e·vate [ɛ́ləvet] *v.* elevar; alzar, levantar.

el·e·va·tion [ɛləvéʃən] *s.* elevación; altura; exaltación.

el·e·va·tor [ɛ́ləvetɚ] *s.* ascensor, *Am.* elevador; **grain** — almacén de granos.

e·lic·it[ɪlísɪt] *v.* extraer, sonsacar; **to** — **admiration** despertar admiración; **to** — **applause** suscitar el aplauso o los aplausos.

el·i·gi·ble [ɛ́lɪdʒəbl] *adj.* elegible.

e·lim·i·nate [ɪlímənet] *v.* eliminar.

e·lim·i·na·tion [ɪlɪmənéʃən] *s.* eliminación.

e·lite [ɛlít] *s.* lo selecto; los selectos; los escogidos.

elk [ɛlk] *s.* ante.

el·lip·tic [ɪlíptɪk] *adj.* elíptico.

elm [ɛlm] *s.* olmo.

e·lope [ɪlóp] *v.* fugarse (*con su novio*).

el·o·quence [ɛ́ləkwəns] *s.* elocuencia.

el·o·quent [ɛ́ləkwənt] *adj.* elocuente.

else [ɛls] *adj. & adv.* otro (*úsase sólo en ciertas combinaciones*); más, además; **or** — de otro modo; si no; **nobody** — ningún otro; **nothing** — nada más; **somebody** — algún otro, otra persona; **what** —? ¿ qué más?

else·where [ɛ́lshwɛr] *adv.* en otra parte, a otra parte.

e·lu·ci·date [ɪlúsədet] *v.* elucidar, esclarecer, aclarar, clarificar.

e·lu·ci·da·tion [ɪlusədéʃən] *s.* elucidación, esclarecimiento, explicación.

e·lude [ɪlúd] *v.* eludir, evadir.

e·lu·sive [ɪlúsɪv] *adj.* evasivo; que elude.

e·ma·ci·at·ed [ɪméʃɪetɪd] *adj.* demacrado, escuálido, macilento.

em·a·nate [ɛ́mənet] *v.* emanar, brotar.

em·a·na·tion [ɛmənéʃən] *s.* emanación; efluvio.

e·man·ci·pate [ɪmǽnsəpet] *v.* emancipar.

e·man·ci·pa·tion [ɪmænsəpéʃən] *s.* emancipación.

em·balm [ɪmbám] *v.* embalsamar.

em·bank·ment [ɪmbǽŋkmənt] *s.* terraplén; dique.

em·bar·go [ɪmbɑrgo] *s.* embargo; prohibición; **to put an** — **on** embargar.

em·bark [ɪmbárk] *v.* embarcar(se).

em·bar·rass [ɪmbǽrəs] *v.* turbar, desconcertar; apenar; avergonzar; embarazar; **to be financially -ed** encontrarse escaso de fondos.

em·bar·rass·ing [ɪmbǽrəsɪŋ] *adj.* embarazoso, penoso; desconcertante; angustioso.

em·bar·rass·ment [ɪmbǽrəsmənt] *s.* turbación,

vergüenza, desconcierto; aprieto, apuro, dificultad; estorbo, embarazo.

em·bas·sy [ɛ́mbəsɪ] *s.* embajada.

em·bel·lish [ɪmbɛ́lɪʃ] *v.* embellecer, hermosear.

em·ber [ɛ́mbɚ] *s.* ascua; **-s** ascuas, rescoldo.

em·bez·zle [ɪmbɛ́zl] *v.* desfalcar.

em·bez·zle·ment [ɪmbɛ́z|mənt] *s.* desfalco, peculado.

em·bit·ter [ɪmbítɚ] *v.* amargar.

em·blem [ɛ́mbləm] *s.* emblema.

em·bod·y [ɪmbádɪ] *v.* encarnar, dar cuerpo a; incorporar, abarcar.

em·boss [ɪmbɔ́s] *v.* realzar, grabar en relieve.

em·brace [ɪmbrés] *s.* abrazo; *v.* abrazar(se); abarcar.

em·broi·der [ɪmbrɔ́ɪdɚ] *v.* bordar; recamar; ornar, embellecer.

em·broi·der·y [ɪmbrɔ́ɪdərɪ] *s.* bordado; bordadura; recamo.

em·bry·o [ɛ́mbrɪo] *s.* embrión.

em·er·ald [ɛ́mərəld] *s.* esmeralda.

e·merge [ɪmɝ́dʒ] *v.* emerger; surtir.

e·mer·gen·cy [ɪmɝ́dʒənsɪ] *s.* caso fortuito; aprieto; urgencia; emergencia.

em·i·grant [ɛ́məgrənt] *adj. & s.* emigrante.

em·i·grate [ɛ́məgret] *v.* emigrar.

em·i·gra·tion [ɛməgréʃən] *s.* emigración.

em·i·nence [ɛ́mənəns] *s.* eminencia.

em·i·nent [ɛ́mənənt] *adj.* eminente.

e·mit [ɪmít] *v.* emitir; exhalar, arrojar; despedir (*olor, humo, etc.*).

e·mo·tion [ɪmóʃən] *s.* emoción.

e·mo·tion·al [ɪmóʃənl] *adj.* emocional; emotivo; sentimental; sensible.

em·pa·thy [ɛ́mpəθɪ] *s.* empatía.

em·per·or [ɛ́mpərɚ] *s.* emperador.

em·pha·sis [ɛ́mfəsɪs] *s.* énfasis.

em·pha·size [ɛ́mfəsaɪz] *v.* dar énfasis; hacer hincapié en; subrayar, recalcar; acentuar.

em·phat·ic [ɪmfǽtɪk] *adj.* enfático; recalcado; **-ally** *adv.* enfáticamente.

em·phy·se·ma [ɛmfəsímə] *s.* enfisema.

em·pire [ɛ́mpaɪr] *s.* imperio.

em·pir·i·cal [ɛmpírəkl] *adj.* empírico.

em·ploy [ɪmplɔ́ɪ] *v.* emplear; dar empleo a; ocupar; **to be in his** — ser su empleado; trabajar a sus órdenes.

em·ploy·ee [ɪmplɔ́íí] *s.* empleado.

em·ploy·er [ɪmplɔ́ɪɚ] *s.* patrón, amo, principal.

em·ploy·ment [ɪmplɔ́ɪmənt] *s.* empleo; ocupación.

em·pow·er [ɪmpáʊɚ] *v.* autorizar; apoderar (*dar poder a un abogado*).

em·press [ɛ́mprɪs] *s.* emperatriz.

emp·ti·ness [ɛ́mptɪnɪs] *s.* vaciedad; futilidad, vanidad.

emp·ty [ɛ́mptɪ] *adj.* vacío; vacante, desocupado; vano; *v.* vaciar; desaguar, desembocar.

emp·ty-hand·ed [ɛmptɪhǽndɪd] *adj.* sin posesión.

em·u·late [ɛ́mjʊlet] *v.* emular.

en·a·ble [ɪnébl] *v.* capacitar, hacer capaz; habilitar; dar poder; facilitar; hacer posible.

en·act [ɪnǽkt] *v.* decretar, promulgar; hacer el papel de.

en·am·el [ɪnǽml] *s.* esmalte; *v.* esmaltar.

en·am·or [ɪnǽmɚ] *v.* enamorar, mover a amar; encantar; **to be -ed of** estar enamorado de.

en·camp [ɪnkǽmp] *v.* acampar.

en·chant [ɪntʃǽnt] *v.* encantar; embelesar; hechizar.

en·chant·er [ɪntʃǽntɚ] *s.* encantador; hechicero, mago, brujo.

en·chant·ment [ɪntʃǽntmənt] *s.* encanto;

encantamiento; hechicería.

en·chant·ress [ɪntʃǽntrɪs] s. encantadora; hechicera, bruja.

en·cir·cle [ɪnsɚ́kl] v. cercar, rodear, ceñir.

en·clit·ic [ɛnklítɪk] adj. enclítico.

en·close [ɪnklóz] v. encerrar; cercar, rodear, circundar; incluir.

en·clo·sure [ɪnklóʒɚ] s. recinto, cercado, vallado; remesa, lo remitido (dentro de una carta), lo adjunto; encerramiento.

en·com·pass [ɪnkʌ́mpəs] v. abarcar; encuadrar; rodear, ceñir, circundar.

en·coun·ter [ɪnkáʊntɚ] s. encuentro; combate; v. encontrar(se); encontrarse con; tropezar con.

en·cour·age [ɪnkɚ́ɪdʒ] v. alentar, animar; fomentar.

en·cour·age·ment [ɪnkɚ́ɪdʒmənt] s. aliento, ánimo; estímulo; fomento.

en·croach [ɪnkrótʃ] v. to — upon usurpar, invadir, meterse en; quitar (el tiempo).

en·cum·ber [ɛnkʌ́mbɚ] v. impedir; estorbar.

en·cy·clo·pe·di·a [ɪnsaɪkləpídɪə] s. enciclopedia.

end [ɛnd] s. (temporal) fin; cabo; término; (spatial) término; extremo; **no — of things** un sin fin de cosas; **odds and -s** retazos; **on —** de punta; **to put an — to** acabar con, poner fin a; v. acabar; terminar; concluir, dar fin.

en·dan·ger [ɪndéndʒɚ] v. poner en peligro, arriesgar.

en·dear [ɪndír] v. hacer amar, hacer querer; **to — oneself** hacerse querer.

en·deav·or [ɪndévɚ] s. esfuerzo, empeño; tentativa; tarea; v. procurar, tratar de, intentar; esforzarse por o en.

en·dem·ic [ɛndɛ́mɪk] adj. endémico.

end·ing [ɛ́ndɪŋ] s. final; terminación; conclusión.

end·less [ɛ́ndlɪs] adj. sin fin, interminable, inacabable; eterno.

en·dorse [ɛndórs] v. endosar; repaldar; apoyar, garanitzar.

en·dorse·ment [ɛndórsmənt] s. (signature) endose, endoso; (backing) respaldo; garantía, apoyo.

en·dors·er [ɛndórsɚ] s. endosante.

en·dow [ɪndáʊ] v. dotar.

en·dow·ment [ɪndáʊmənt] s. dotación; dote, don.

en·dur·ance [ɪndjúrəns] s. resistencia, aguante; paciencia; duración.

en·dure [ɪndjúr] v. aguantar, soportar, sufrir; durar, perdurar.

en·e·ma [ɛ́nəmə] s. lavativa.

en·e·my [ɛ́nəmɪ] s. enemigo.

en·er·get·ic [ɛnɚdʒɛ́tɪk] adj. enérgico.

en·er·gy [ɛ́nɚdʒɪ] s. energía.

en·er·vate [ɛ́nɚvet] v. enervar, debilitar.

en·fold = **infold**.

en·force [ɪnfórs] v. dar fuerza a; hacer cumplir (una ley); **to — obedience** hacer obedecer, imponer obediencia.

en·force·ment [ɪnfórsmənt] s. coacción; cumplimiento forzoso (de una ley).

en·gage [ɪngédʒ] v. (employ) ocupar; emplear, contratar; (reserve) alquilar; (attract) atraer; (mesh) engranar, acoplar; **to — in battle** trabar batalla; **to — (oneself) to do it** comprometerse a hacerlo; **to be -ed in something** estar ocupado en algo; **to be -ed to be married** estar comprometido para casarse.

en·gage·ment [ɪngédʒmənt] s. compromiso; cita; noviazgo; convenio, contrato; pelea; traba, engrane, acoplamiento (de maquinaria).

en·gen·der [ɪndʒɛ́ndɚ] v. engendrar, producir.

en·gine [ɛ́ndʒən] s. máquina; motor; locomotora.

en·gi·neer [ɛndʒənír] s. ingeniero; maquinista (de locomotora); v. dirigir, planear.

en·gi·neer·ing [ɛndʒənírɪŋ] s. ingeniería; manejo, planeo.

Eng·lish [íŋglɪʃ] adj. inglés; s. inglés, idioma inglés; **the —** los ingleses.

Eng·lish·man [íŋglɪʃmən] s. inglés.

en·grave [ɪngrév] v. grabar, esculpir.

en·grav·ing [ɪngrévɪŋ] s. grabado; estampa, lámina; **wood —** grabado en madera.

en·gross [ɛngrós] v. absorber; redactar en limpio.

en·grossed [ɪngróst] adj. absorto, ensimismado.

en·gulf [ɪngʌ́lf] v. engolfar, absorber, tragar.

en·hance [ɪnhǽns] v. realzar; engrandecer.

e·nig·ma [ɪnígmə] s. enigma.

en·join [ɪndʒɔ́ɪn] v. mandar, ordenar; **to — from** prohibir, vedar.

en·joy [ɪndʒɔ́ɪ] v. gozar de; disfrutar de; **to — oneself** divertirse, gozar, deleitarse; **to — the use of** usufructuar.

en·joy·a·ble [ɪndʒɔ́ɪəbl] adj. agradable, deleitable.

en·joy·ment [ɪndʒɔ́ɪmənt] s. placer, goce; disfrute; usufructo.

en·large [ɪnlárdʒ] v. agrandar(se); ensanchar; ampliar; **to — upon** explayarse en, extenderse en; comentar.

en·large·ment [ɪnlárdʒmənt] s. (photo) ampliación; ensachamiento.

en·light·en [ɪnláɪtn̩] v. alumbrar; iluminar; ilustrar, instruir.

en·list [ɪnlíst] v. alistar(se); sentar plaza (de soldado); reclutar.

en·list·ment [ɪnlístmənt] s. reclutamiento; alistamiento.

en·li·ven [ɪnláɪvən] v. avivar, animar, alegrar.

en·mi·ty [ɛ́nmətɪ] s. enemistad.

en·no·ble [ɪnóbl̩] v. ennoblecer.

e·nor·mous [ɪnórməs] adj. enorme.

e·nough [ənʌ́f] adj. & adv. bastante; s. lo bastante, lo suficiente; **that is —** eso basta, con eso basta; **—!** ¡basta!

en·quire = **inquire**.

en·rage [ɪnrédʒ] v. enrabiar, hacer rabiar; enfurecer.

en·rap·ture [ɪnrǽptʃɚ] v. extasiar, embelesar, enajenar.

en·rich [ɪnrítʃ] v. enriquecer.

en·roll [ɪnról] v. alistar(se); matricular(se); inscribir(se); hacerse miembro.

en·roll·ment [ɪnrólmənt] s. alistamiento; registro, matrícula.

en·sem·ble [ɑnsámbl̩] s. (music) conjunto musical; (dress) traje armonioso.

en·sign [ɛ́nsn̩] s. alférez (de la marina); [ɛ́nsaɪn] bandera; insignia.

en·slave [ɪnslév] v. esclavizar.

en·snare [ɛnsnér] v. enredar, entrampar, embaucar.

en·sue [ɛnsú] v. sobrevenir, seguir(se), resultar.

en·tail [ɪntél] v. envolver, ocasionar; vincular (una herencia).

en·tan·gle [ɪntǽŋgl̩] v. enredar, enmarañar, embrollar.

en·ter [ɛ́ntɚ] v. entrar en; ingresar en; asentar (una partida, cantidad, etc.); registrar; salir (al escenario).

en·ter·prise [ɛ́ntɚpraɪz] s. empresa.

en·ter·pris·ing [ɛ́ntɚpraɪzɪŋ] adj. emprendedor.

en·ter·tain [ɛntɚtén] v. divertir; agasajar; obsequiar; banquetear; acariciar (una idea); abrigar (una esperanza, un rencor); **she -s a great deal** es muy fiestera u obsequiosa.

en·ter·tain·ing [ɛntɚténɪŋ] adj. entretenido,

EL

divertido, chistoso.

en·ter·tain·ment [ɛntəténmənt] *s.* entretenimiento; pasatiempo; diversión; fiesta; convite.

en·thu·si·asm [ɪnθjúzɪæzəm] *s.* entusiasmo.

en·thu·si·ast [ɪnθjúzɪæst] *s.* entusiasta.

en·thu·si·as·tic [ɪnθjuzɪǽstɪk] *adj.* entusiasta, entusiástico; **to be** — estar entusiasmado.

en·tice [ɪntáɪs] *v.* atraer, tentar, seducir, halagar.

en·tire [ɪntáɪr] *adj.* entero, cabal; **the** — **world** todo el mundo; **-ly** *adv.* enteramente, por entero.

en·tire·ty [ɪntáɪrtɪ] *s.* totalidad, entereza; conjunto; todo.

en·ti·tle [ɪntáɪtl] *v.* titular, intitular; autorizar, dar derecho.

en·ti·ty [ɛntətɪ] *s.* entidad; ente, ser.

en·trails [ɛntrəlz] *s. pl.* entrañas; tripas.

en·trance [ɛntrəns] *s.* entrada; ingreso.

en·treat [ɪntrít] *v.* suplicar, rogar; instar.

en·treat·y [ɪntrítɪ] *s.* súplica, ruego; instancia.

en·trench = **intrench.**

en·trust [ɪntrʌst] *v.* confiar; depositar, entregar.

en·try [ɛntrɪ] *s.* entrada; ingreso; partida, registro, anotación; **double** — partida doble (*en teneduría*).

e·nu·mer·ate [ɪnjúməret] *v.* enumerar.

e·nun·ci·ate [ɪnʌnsɪet] *v.* articular; enunciar, declarar.

en·vel·op [ɪnvɛ́ləp] *v.* envolver.

en·ve·lope [ɛnvəlop] *s.* sobre, cubierta (*de una carta*).

en·vi·a·ble [ɛnvɪəbl] *adj.* envidiable.

en·vi·ous [ɛnvɪəs] *adj.* envidioso.

en·vi·ron·ment [ɪnváɪrənmənt] *s.* ambiente, medio ambiente.

en·vi·rons [ɪnváɪrənz] *s. pl.* cercanías, contornos, alrededores.

en·vis·age [ɛnvízɪdʒ] *v.* prever; encararse con.

en·voy [ɛnvɔɪ] *s.* enviado.

en·vy [ɛnvɪ] *s.* envidia; *v.* envidiar.

e·phem·er·al [ɪfɛ́mərl] *adj.* efímero.

ep·ic [ɛpɪk] *s.* epopeya, poema, épico; *adj.* épico.

ep·i·dem·ic [ɛpədɛ́mɪk] *s.* epidemia; peste; *adj.* epidémico.

ep·i·logue [ɛpəlɔg] *s.* epílogo.

E·piph·a·ny [ɪpífənɪ] *s.*— Epifanía.

ep·i·sode [ɛpəsod] *s.* episodio.

e·pis·tle [ɪpísl] *s.* epístola, carta.

ep·i·taph [ɛpətæf] *s.* epitafio.

e·pit·o·me [ɪpítəmɪ] *s.* epítome.

ep·och [ɛpək] *s.* época.

e·qual [íkwəl] *adj.* igual; **to be** — **to a task** ser competente (*o* tener suficientes fuerzas) para una tarea; *s.* igual; cantidad igual; *v.* igualar; ser igual a; **-ly** *adv.* igualmente; por igual.

e·qual·i·ty [ikwɑ́lətɪ] *s.* igualdad.

e·qual·ize [íkwəlaɪz] *v.* igualar; emparejar; equilibrar; nivelar.

e·qua·tion [ikwéʒən] *s.* ecuación.

e·qua·tor [ikwétə] *s.* ecuador.

e·qui·lib·ri·um [ikwəlíbrɪəm] *s.* equilibrio.

e·quip [ɪkwíp] *v.* equipar; proveer; habilitar.

e·quip·ment [ɪkwípmənt] *s.* equipo; aparatos; avíos; habilitación.

eq·ui·ta·ble [ɛ́kwɪtəbl] *adj.* equitativo.

eq·ui·ty [ɛ́kwətɪ] *s.* equidad; justicia.

e·quiv·a·lent [ɪkwívələnt] *adj. & s.* equivalente.

e·quiv·o·cal [ɪkwívəkl] *adj.* equívoco, ambiguo.

e·ra [írə] *s.* era, época.

e·rad·i·cate [ɪrǽdɪket] *v.* desarraigar, extirpar.

e·rase [ɪrés] *v.* borrar; tachar.

e·ras·er [ɪrésə] *s.* goma, *Am.* borrador; **blackboard** — cepillo.

e·ra·sure [ɪréʃə] *s.* borradura, raspadura.

ere [ɛr] *prep.* antes de; *conj.* antes (de) que.

e·rect [ɪrɛ́kt] *adj.* erguido; derecho; levantado; *Am.* parado; *v.* erigir; levantar, alzar.

er·mine [ɝmɪn] *s.* armiño.

e·rode [ɪród] *v.* erosionar.

e·ro·sion [ɪróʒən] *s.* erosión; desgaste.

e·rot·ic [ɪrɑ́tɪk] *adj.* erótico.

err [ɝ] *v.* errar; equivocarse; descarriarse.

er·rand [ɛrənd] *s.* mandado, recado, encargo; — **boy** mandadero.

er·rant [ɛrənt] *adj.* errante; **knight-errant** caballero andante.

er·rat·ic [ɛrǽtɪk] *adj.* inconstante errático; vagabundo.

er·ro·ne·ous [ərónɪəs] *adj.* erróneo, errado.

er·ror [ɛrə] *s.* error.

er·u·di·tion [ɛrudíʃən] *s.* erudición.

e·rupt [ɪrʌ́pt] *v.* arrojar.

e·rup·tion [ɪrʌ́pʃən] *s.* erupción.

es·ca·late [ɛ́skəlet] *v.* aumentar; intensificar.

es·ca·pade [ɛ́skəped] *s.* trapisonda, travesura.

es·cape [əskép] *s.* escape; fuga, huída; escapada; escapatoria; *v.* escapar(se); fugarse; huir(se); eludir, evadir; **it -s me** se me escapa.

es·cort [ɛ́skɔrt] *s.* escolta; acompañante; convoy; [ɪskɔ́rt] *v.* escoltar; convoyar; acompañar.

es·cutch·eon [ɪskʌ́tʃən] *s.* escudo de armas, blasón.

Es·ki·mo [ɛ́skəmo] *s.* esquimal.

es·pe·cial [əspɛ́ʃəl] *adj.* especial; **-ly** *adv.* especialmente.

es·pi·o·nage [ɛ́spɪənɪdʒ] *s.* espionaje.

es·pouse [ɛspáʊs] *v.* patrocinar; casarse.

es·say [ɛ́se] *s.* ensayo; [ɛsé] *v.* ensayar.

es·sence [ɛ́sn̩s] *s.* esencia.

es·sen·tial [əsɛ́nʃəl] *adj.* esencial.

es·tab·lish [əstǽblɪʃ] *v.* establecer.

es·tab·lish·ment [əstǽblɪʃmənt] *s.* establecimiento. ·

es·tate [əstét] *s.* hacienda, heredad; bienes, propiedades; estado, condición; **country** — finca rural.

es·teem [əstím] *s.* estima, estimación, aprecio; *v.* estimar, apreciar; considerar, juzgar.

es·ti·ma·ble [ɛ́stəməbl] *adj.* estimable.

es·ti·mate [ɛ́stəmɪt] *s.* (*calculation*) tasa, cálculo aproximado; presupuesto; (*judgment*) opinión; [ɛ́stəmet] *v.* estimar, tasar, calcular aproximadamente; hacer un presupuesto; juzgar, opinar.

es·ti·ma·tion [ɛstəméʃən] *s.* juicio, opinión; estima; estimación.

es·trange [əstréndʒ] *v.* enajenar; apartar.

es·tu·ar·y [ɛ́stʃʊɛrɪ] *s.* estuario o estero, desembocadura de un rio.

etch [ɛtʃ] *v.* grabar al agua fuerte.

etch·ing [ɛ́tʃɪŋ] *s.* agua fuerte, grabado al agua fuerte.

e·ter·nal [ɪtɝ́nl] *adj.* eterno.

e·ter·ni·ty [ɪtɝ́nətɪ] *s.* eternidad.

e·ther [íθə] *s.* éter.

e·the·re·al [iθírɪəl] *adj.* etéreo.

eth·i·cal [ɛ́θɪkl] *adj.* ético, moral.

eth·ics [ɛ́θɪks] *s.* ética, moral.

eth·nic [ɛ́θnɪk] *adj.* étnico.

eth·nol·o·gy [ɛθnálədʒɪ] *s.* etnología.

et·i·quette [ɛ́tɪkɛt] *s.* etiqueta (*regla de conducta social*).

et·y·mol·o·gy [ɛtəmálədʒɪ] *s.* etimología.

eu·ca·lyp·tus [jukəlíptəs] *s.* eucalipto.

Eu·cha·rist [júkərɪst] *s.* Eucaristía.

eu·phe·mism [júfəmɪzm] *s.* eufemismo.

eu·pho·ri·a [jufórɪə] s. euforia.

Eu·ro·pe·an [jʊrəpíən] adj. & s. europeo.

e·vac·u·ate [ɪvǽkjʊet] v. evacuar; desocupar.

e·vade [ɪvéd] v. evadir.

e·val·u·ate [ɪvǽljʊet] v. valorar, avaluar.

e·vap·o·rate [ɪvǽpəret] v. evaporar(se).

e·vap·o·ra·tion [ɪvæpəréʃən] s. evaporación.

e·va·sion [ɪvéʒən] s. evasión, evasiva.

e·va·sive [ɪvésɪv] adj. evasivo.

eve [iv] s. víspera, vigilia; **Christmas Eve** Nochebuena; **New Year's Eve** víspera del Año Nuevo; **on the — of** en vísperas de.

e·ven [ívən] adj. (level) liso, plano, llano, a nivel; (same) parejo; uniforme; igual; **— dozen** docena cabal; **— number** número par; **— temper** genio apacible; **to be — with someone** estar mano a mano (o estar a mano) con alguien; **to get — with someone** desquitarse de alguien; adv. aun, hasta; **— if** (o **— though**) aun cuando; **— so** aun así; **not —** ni siquiera, ni aun; v. allanar; nivelar(se); igualar(se); emparejar; **-ly** adv. igualmente; de un modo igual; con uniformidad; con suavidad.

eve·ning [ívnɪŋ] s. tarde; atardecer; noche (las primeras horas); **— gown** vestido de etiqueta; **— star** estrella vespertina, lucero de la tarde.

e·ven·ness [ívənnɪs] s. lisura; igualdad; **— of temper** apacibilidad o suavidad de genio.

e·vent [ɪvént] s. suceso, acontecimiento; incidente, evento; resultado, coneecuencia; **in any — en** todo caso; **in the — of** en caso de.

e·vent·ful [ɪvéntfəl] adj. lleno de sucesos; importante, memorable.

e·ven·tu·al [ɪvéntʃʊəl] adj. eventual; último, final, terminal; **-ly** adv. finalmente, por fin, con el tiempo; eventualmente.

ev·er [ɛvɚ] adv. siempre; jamás; alguna vez; **— so much** muchísimo; **for — and —** por (o para) siempre jamás; **hardly —** casi nunca, apenas; **if — si** alguna vez; **more than —** más que nunca; **the best friend I — had** el mejor amigo que en mi vida he tenido.

ev·er·green [ɛvɚgrin] s. siempreviva, sempiterna; adj. siempre verde.

ev·er·last·ing [ɛvəlǽstɪŋ] adj. sempiterno, eterno, perpetuo; duradero; s. eternidad; sempiterna (planta); siempreviva; perpetua, flor perpetua.

ev·er·more [ɛvəmór] adv. para siempre; **for —** para siempre jamás.

eve·ry [ɛvrɪ] adj. cada; todo; todos los, todas las; **— bit of it** todo, todito; **— day** todos los días; **— once in a while** de vez en cuando; **— one of them** todos ellos; **— other day** cada dos días, un día sí y otro no.

eve·ry·bod·y [ɛvrɪbadɪ] pron. todos, todo el mundo.

eve·ry·day [ɛvrɪdé] adj. diario, cuotidiano, de todos los días; ordinario.

eve·ry·one [ɛvrɪwʌn] pron. todos; todo el mundo; cada uno.

eve·ry·thing [ɛvrɪθɪŋ] pron. todo.

eve·ry·where [ɛvrɪhwɛr] adv. por (o en) todas partes; a todas partes.

e·vict [ɪvíkt] v. desalojar; expulsar.

ev·i·dence [ɛvədəns] s. evidencia; prueba; demostración, señal; testimonio; **to be in —** mostrarse; v. hacer evidente, evidenciar; patentizar, revelar, mostrar.

ev·i·dent [ɛvədənt] adj. evidente, patente.

e·vil [ívl] adj. malo, malvado, maligno; aciago, de mal agüero; **to cast the — eye** aojar; **the Evil**

One el Diablo; s. mal; maldad; adv. mal.

e·vil·do·er [ívldúə] s. malhechor.

e·voke [ɪvók] v. evocar; **to — laughter** provocar a risa.

ev·o·lu·tion [ɛvəlúʃən] s. evolución.

e·volve [ɪválv] v. desarrollar(se), desenvolver(se); urdir; evolucionar.

ewe [ju] s. oveja.

ex·act [ɪgzǽkt] adj. exacto; v. exigir; **-ly** adv. exactamente; en punto.

ex·act·ing [ɪgzǽktɪŋ] adj. exigente.

ex·ag·ger·ate [ɪgzǽdʒəret] v. exagerar.

ex·alt [ɪgzólt] v. exaltar, ensalzar.

ex·al·ta·tion [ɛgzɔltéʃən] s. exaltación.

ex·am·i·na·tion [ɪgzæmənéʃən] s. examen; reconocimiento (médico).

ex·am·ine [ɪgzǽmɪn] v. examinar; reconocer (dícese del médico).

ex·am·ple [ɪgzǽmpl] s. ejemplo.

ex·as·per·ate [ɪgzǽspəret] v. exasperar, irritar.

ex·ca·vate [ɛkskəvet] v. excavar.

ex·ca·va·tor [ɛkskəvetə] s. excavadora.

ex·ceed [ɪksíd] v. exceder; sobrepasar; propasarse.

ex·ceed·ing·ly [ɪksídɪŋlɪ] adv. sumamente, extremamente; **— well** extremamente bien.

ex·cel [ɪksél] v. sobresalir (en o entre); sobrepujar (a).

ex·cel·lence [ɛksləns] s. excelencia.

ex·cel·len·cy [ɛkslənsɪ] s. excelencia.

ex·cel·lent [ɛkslənt] adj. excelente.

ex·cept [ɪksépt] prep. excepto, menos; v. exceptuar.

ex·cept·ing [ɪkséptɪŋ] prep. excepto, salvo, menos, exceptuando.

ex·cep·tion [ɪksépʃən] s. (exclusion) excepción; (opposition) objeción; **with the — of** a excepción de, con excepción de; **to take —** objetar; ofenderse.

ex·cep·tion·al [ɪksépʃənl] adj. exceptional.

ex·cess [ɪksés] s. exceso; sobrante; **— baggage (weight)** exceso de equipaje (de peso); **to drink to —** beber en exceso.

ex·ces·sive [ɪksésɪv] adj. excesivo; desmedido; **-ly** adv. excesivamente, en exceso, demasiado.

ex·change [ɪkstʃéndʒ] s. (money) cambio; (interchange) trueque; intercambio, canje (de publicaciones, prisioneros); (stock) lonja, bolsa; **rate of —** cambio, Am. tipo de cambio; **telephone —** central de teléfonos; **foreign —** divisa. v. cambiar; trocar; canjear (publicaciones, prisioneros); **to — greetings** saludarse; mandarse felicitaciones.

ex·cite [ɪksáɪt] v. excitar; acalorar; agitar.

ex·cit·ed [ɪksáɪtɪd] adj. excitado, acalorado; animado; **to get —** entusiasmarse; sobreexcitarse; acalorarse; **-ly** adv. acaloradamente, agitadamente.

ex·cite·ment [ɪksáɪtmənt] s. excitación; acaloramiento; agitación, alboroto; animación.

ex·cit·ing [ɪksáɪtɪŋ] adj. excitante, excitador; estimulante.

ex·claim [ɪksklém] v. exclamar.

ex·cla·ma·tion [ɛkskləméʃən] s. exclamación; **— point** punto de admiración.

ex·clude [ɪksklúd] v. excluir.

ex·clu·sion [ɪksklúʒən] s. exclusión.

ex·clu·sive [ɪksklúsɪv] adj. exclusivo; privativo; **— of** sin contar.

ex·com·mu·ni·cate [ɛkskəmjúnəket] v. excomunicar.

ex·com·mu·ni·ca·tion [ɛkskəmjunəkéʃən] s. excomunión.

ex·cre·ment [ɛ́kskrɪmənt] s. excremento; caca.
ex·cur·sion [ɪkskə́ʒən] s. excursión; correría; expedición.
ex·cus·a·ble [ɪkskjúzəbl] adj. excusable, disculpable.
ex·cuse [ɪkskjús] s. excusa; disculpa; [ɪkskjúz] v. excusar; disculpar; perdonar, dispensar; eximir; — me! ¡dispense Vd.! ¡perdone Vd.!
ex·e·cute [ɛ́ksɪkjut] v. ejecutar; fusilar; adjusticiar; llevar a cabo.
ex·e·cu·tion [ɛksɪkjúʃən] s. ejecución; desempeño; — wall paredón.
ex·e·cu·tion·er [ɛksɪkjúʃənə] s. verdugo.
ex·ec·u·tive [ɪgzɛ́kjʊtɪv] adj. ejecutivo; s. ejecutivo, poder ejecutivo; gerente, administrador.
ex·ec·u·tor [ɪgzɛ́kjətə] s. albacea, ejecutor testamentario; [ɛ́ksɪkjutə] ejecutor.
ex·em·pla·ry [ɪgzɛ́mplərɪ] adj. ejemplar.
ex·empt [ɪgzɛ́mpt] adj. exento, libre; v. eximir, exentar.
ex·emp·tion [ɪgzɛ́mpʃən] s. exención.
ex·er·cise [ɛ́ksəsaɪz] s. ejercicio; v. ejercitar(se); ejercer (poder o autoridad); hacer ejercicio, hacer gimnasia; to be -d about something estar preocupado o sobreexcitado por algo.
ex·ert [ɪgzə́t] v. ejercer; to — oneself esforzarse, hacer esfuerzos, empeñarse.
ex·er·tion [ɪgzə́ʃən] s. ejercicio; esfuerzo, empeño.
ex·hale [ɛkshél] v. exhalar, emitir; espirar, soplar.
ex·haust [ɪgzɔ́st] s. escape (de gas o vapor); v. agotar; consumir; debilitar, fatigar; I am -ed no puedo más; estoy agotado.
ex·haus·tion [ɪgzɔ́stʃən] s. agotamiento; fatiga, postración.
ex·haus·tive [ɛgzɔ́stɪv] adj. comprensivo; detallado.
ex·hib·it [ɪgzíbɪt] v. exhibir; mostrar, exponer.
ex·hi·bi·tion [ɛksəbíʃən] s. exhibición; exposición, manifestación.
ex·hil·a·rate [ɪgzíləret] v. alborozar, excitar, animar, entusiasmar; refocilar.
ex·hort [ɪgzɔ́rt] v. exhortar.
ex·ile [ɛ́gzaɪl] s. destierro, exilio; desterrado; v. desterrar; expatriar.
ex·ist [ɪgzíst] v. existir.
ex·is·tence [ɪgzístəns] s. existencia.
ex·is·tent [ɪgzístənt] adj. existente.
ex·it [ɛ́gzɪt] s. salida; salida (del foro); v. vase o vanse (un personaje o personajes al fin de una escena).
ex·o·dus [ɛ́ksədəs] s. éxodo.
ex·on·er·ate [ɪgzánəret] v. exonerar.
ex·or·bi·tant [ɪgzɔ́rbətənt] adj. exorbitante.
ex·or·cism [ɛ́ksɔrsɪzəm] s. exorcismo; conjuro.
ex·ot·ic [ɪgzútɪk] adj. exótico; raro, extraño.
ex·pand [ɪkspǽnd] v. ensanchar(se); dilatar(se); extender(se) agrandar(se); desarrollar (una ecuación).
ex·panse [ɪkspǽns] s. espacio, extensión.
ex·pan·sion [ɪkspǽnʃən] s. expansión; ensanche; desarrollo (de una ecuación).
ex·pan·sive [ɪkspǽnsɪv] adj. expansivo; efusivo.
ex·pect [ɪkspɛ́kt] v. esperar; contar con; I — so supongo que sí.
ex·pec·ta·tion [ɛkspɛktéʃən] s. expectación; expectativa; esperanza.
ex·pec·to·rate [ɪkspɛ́ktəret] v. expectorar, desgarrar.
ex·pe·di·ent [ɪkspídɪənt] adj. conveniente, oportuno; ventajoso; prudente; s. expediente, medio.
ex·pe·dite [ɛ́kspədaɪt] v. facilitar; despachar.
ex·pe·di·tion [ɛkspɪdíʃən] s. expedición.

ex·pe·di·tion·ar·y [ɛkspɪdíʃənɛrɪ] adj. expedicionario.
ex·pel [ɪkspɛ́l] v. expeler; expulsar.
ex·pend [ɪkspɛ́nd] v. gastar; consumir.
ex·pen·di·ture [ɪkspɛ́ndɪtʃə] s. gasto; desembolso.
ex·pense [ɪkspɛ́ns] s. gasto; coste, costa o costo.
ex·pen·sive [ɪkspɛ́nsɪv] adj. costoso.
ex·pen·sive·ness [ɪkspɛ́nsɪvnɪs] s. precio subido, coste elevado.
ex·pe·ri·ence [ɪkspírɪəns] s. experiencia; aventura, lance; v. experimentar; pasar (penas, sufrimientos); sentir.
ex·pe·ri·enced [ɪkspírɪənst] adj. experimentado; ducho, perito, experto.
ex·per·i·ment [ɪkspɛ́rəmənt] s. experimento, prueba; v. experimentar, hacer un experimento.
ex·per·i·men·tal [ɪkspɛrəmɛ́ntl] adj. experimental.
ex·pert [ɛ́kspət] s. experto, perito; [ɪkspə́t] adj. experto, perito, experimentado.
ex·pi·ra·tion [ɛkspəréʃən] s. terminación; vencimiento (de un plazo); espiración (del aire).
ex·pire [ɪkspáɪr] v. expirar, morir; acabar; vencerse (un plazo); expeler (el aire aspirado).
ex·plain [ɪksplén] v. explicar.
ex·plain·a·ble [ɪksplénəbl] adj. explicable.
ex·pla·na·tion [ɛksplənéʃən] s. explicación.
ex·plan·a·to·ry [ɪksplǽnətorɪ] adj. explicativo.
ex·plic·it [ɛksplísɪt] adj. explícito.
ex·plode [ɪksplód] v. estallar, hacer explosión, Am. explotar; reventar; volar (con dinamita); desacreditar (una teoría).
ex·ploit [ɛ́ksplɔɪt] s. hazaña, proeza; [ɪksplɔ́ɪt] v. explotar; sacar partido de, abusar de.
ex·ploi·ta·tion [ɛksplɔɪtéʃən] s. explotación.
ex·plo·ra·tion [ɛkspləréʃən] s. exploración.
ex·plore [ɪksplór] v. explorar.
ex·plor·er [ɪksplórə] s. explorador.
ex·plo·sion [ɪksplóʒən] s. explosión, estallido.
ex·plo·sive [ɪksplósɪv] adj. & s. explosivo.
ex·port [ɛ́ksport] s. exportación; artículo exportado, mercancía exportada; [ɪksprót] v. exportar.
ex·por·ta·tion [ɛksportéʃən] s. exportación.
ex·pose [ɪkspóz] v. exponer; exhibir, mostrar, poner a la vista; revelar; desenmascarar.
ex·po·si·tion [ɛkspəzíʃn] s. exposición; exhibición.
ex·po·sure [ɪkspóʒə] s. exposición; revelación; to die of — morir a efecto de la intemperie.
ex·pound [ɪkspáʊnd] v. exponer, explicar.
ex·press [ɪksprɛ́s] adj. (rapid) expreso; (explicit) explícito, claro; — company compañía de expreso; expreso, Am. exprés; — train tren expreso; adv. por expreso, por exprés; s. expreso; tren expreso, Am. exprés; v. expresar; enviar por expreso (o por exprés).
ex·pres·sion [ɪksprɛ́ʃən] s. expresión.
ex·pres·sive [ɪksprɛ́sɪv] adj. expresivo.
ex·pul·sion [ɪkspʌ́lʃən] s. expulsión.
ex·qui·site [ɛkskwízɪt] adj. exquisito.
ex·qui·site·ness [ɪkskwízɪtnɪs] s. exquisitez; primor.
ex·stant [ɪkstǽnt] adj. existente.
ex·tem·po·ra·ne·ous [ɛkstɛmpərénɪəs] adj. improvisado.
ex·tend [ɪkstɛ́nd] v. extender(se); tender; prolongar(se); alargar(se); agrandar; dilatar; prorrogar (un plazo); dar (el pésame, el parabién, ayuda, etc.).
ex·tend·ed [ɪkstɛ́ndɪd] adj. extenso; prolongado; extendido.
ex·ten·sion [ɪkstɛ́nʃən] s. extensión; prolongación;

prórroga (*de un plazo*); añadidura, anexo.
ex·ten·sive [ɪksténsɪv] *adj.* extenso, ancho,
dilatado; extensivo; **-ly** *adv.* extensamente, por
extenso; extensivamente; **-ly used** de uso general
o común.
ex·tent [ɪkstént] *s.* extensión; grado; **to a great —**
en gran parte, generalmente; **to such an — that**
a tal grado que; **to the — one's ability** en
proporción a su habilidad; **up to a certain —**
hasta cierto punto.
ex·ten·u·ate [ɪksténjuet] *v.* atenuar, mitigar.
ex·te·ri·or [ɪkstíriɚ] *adj.* exterior; externo; *s.*
exterioridad; exterior, porte, aspecto.
ex·ter·mi·nate [ɪkstɝmənet] *v.* exterminar, destruir
por completo, extirpar.
ex·ter·mi·na·tion [ɪkstɝmənéʃən] *s.* exterminio.
ex·ter·nal [ɪkstɝnl] *adj.* externo; exterior; *s.*
exterioridad; lo externo.
ex·tinct [ɪkstíŋkt] *adj.* extinto; extinguido,
apagado.
ex·tin·guish [ɪkstíŋgwɪʃ] *v.* extinguir; apagar.
ex·tol [ɪkstól] *v.* enaltecer; ensalzar.
ex·tort [ɪkstórt] *v.* obtener por fuerza o amenaza,
exigir (*dinero, promesa, etc.*), *Am.* extorsionar.
ex·tor·tion [ɪkstórʃən] *s.* extorsión.
ex·tra [ɛ́kstrə] *adj.* extraordinario; de sobra, de
más, adicional; suplementario; **— tire** neumático
de repuesto o de recambio; **— workman** obrero
supernumerario; *adv.* extraordinariamente; *s.*
extra; extraordinario (*de un periódico*);
suplemento; gasto extraordinario; recargo
(*cargo adicional*); actor suplente o
supernumerario.
ex·tract [ékstrækt] *s.* extracto; cita, trozo
(*entresacado de un libro*); resumen; [ɪkstrǽkt] *v.*
extraer; seleccionar; citar.
ex·traor·di·nar·y [ɪkstrórdnɛrɪ] *adj.* extraordinario;
extraordinarily *adv.* extraordinariamente; de
manera extraordinaria.
ex·trav·a·gance [ɪkstrǽvəgəns] *s.* despilfarro,
derroche, gasto excesivo; lujo excesivo;
extravagancia, capricho.
ex·trav·a·gant [ɪkstrǽvəgənt] *adj.* gastador,
despilfarrado; extravagante, disparatado; **—
praise** elogios excesivos; **— prices** precios
exorbitantes.
ex·treme [ɪkstrím] *adj.* (*last*) último; extremo;
más remoto; (*excessive*) excesivo; riguroso;
radical; **— opinions** opiniones extremadas; *s.*
extremo; cabo; **to go to -s** extremar, exagerar;
hacer extremos; tomar las medidas más
extremas; **-ly** *adv.* extremamente, en extremo.
ex·trem·i·ty [ɪkstrémətɪ] *s.* extremidad, extremo;
medida extrema; **in —** en gran peligro; en un
apuro.
ex·u·ber·ant [ɪgzjúbərənt] *adj.* exuberante.
ex·ult [ɪgzʌ́lt] *v.* alborozarse, regocijarse.
eye [aɪ] *s.* ojo; **— shade** visera; **in a twinkling of
an —** en un abrir y cerrar de ojos; **hook and —**
macho y hembra; **to catch one's —** llamar la
atención; **to have good -s** tener buena vista; **to
have before one's -s** tener a (*o* tener ante) la
vista; **to keep an — on** cuidar, vigilar; **to see —
to —** estar completamente de acuerdo; *v.* mirar,
observar.
eye·ball [áɪbɔl] *s.* globo del ojo.
eye·brow [áɪbraʊ] *s.* ceja.
eye·glass [áɪglæs] *s.* lente, cristal (*de anteojo*);
ocular (*de microscopio o telescopio*); **-es** lentes,
anteojos.
eye·lash [áɪlæʃ] *s.* pestaña.

eye·lid [áɪlɪd] *s.* párpado.
eye·sight [áɪsaɪt] *s.* vista; **poor —** mala vista.

F·f

fa·ble [fébl] *s.* fábula.
fab·ric [fǽbrɪk] *s.* género, tela; tejido;
textura; estructura.
fab·u·lous [fǽbjələs] *adj.* fabuloso.
fa·çade [fəsád] *s.* fachada.
face [fes] *s.* (*human*) cara, rostro; (*building*) fachada,
frente; (*surface*) haz, superficie; (*watch*) muestra;
Riopl. esfera; *Méx., C.A., Ven., Col.* carátula; **—
value** valor nominal; **in the—of** en presencia de,
ante, frente a; **to lose —** perder prestigio; **to
make -s** hacer muecas o gestos; **to save one's —**
salvar el amor propio; *v.* encararse con;
enfrentarse con; hacer frente a; mirar hacia;
forrar; **to — about** volverse, *Méx., C.A., Ven.,
Col., Andes* voltearse; **to — danger** afrontar o
arrostrar el peligro; **to — with marble** revestir
de mármol; **it -s the street** da a la calle.

EX

fac·et [fǽsɪt] *s.* faceta.
fa·cil·i·tate [fəsílətet] *v.* facilitar.
fa·cil·i·ty [fəsílətɪ] *s.* facilidad.
fact [fækt] *s.* hecho; dato; verdad, realidad; **in —**
de hecho; en realidad.
fac·tion [fǽkʃən] *s.* facción, bando, partido,
pandilla.
fac·tor [fǽktɚ] *s.* factor; elemento; agente; *v.*
decomponer en factores.
fac·to·ry [fǽktrɪ] *s.* fábrica.
fac·ul·ty [fǽkltɪ] *s.* facultad; (*college*) profesorado;
cuerpo docente.
fad [fæd] *s.* novedad; manía; moda.
fade [fed] *v.* descolorar(se), desteñir(se);
marchitar(se); apagarse (*un sonido*);
desvanecerse.
fagged [fægd] *adj.* agotado, rendido de cansancio.
fail [fel] *v.* (*not effect*) faltar; fallar; fracasar; no
tener éxito; (*wane*) decaer; debilitarse; (*go broke*)
quebrar, hacer bancarrota; **to — in an
examination** fallar en un examen, salir mal en un
examen; **to — a student** reprobar o suspender a
un estudiante; **don't — to do it** dejar de hacerlo, no
hacerlo; **don't — to come** no deje Vd. de venir;
without — sin falta.
fail·ure [féljɚ] *s.* fracaso; malogro; falta; descuido;
negligencia; quiebra, bancarrota; debilitamiento.
faint [fent] *adj.* (*weak*) débil, lánguido; (*indistinct*)
imperceptible, tenue, vago, indistinto; **to feel —**
sentirse desvanecido; **—hearted** tímido, cobarde;
s. desmayo; *v.* desmayarse; languidecer; **-ly** *adv.*
débilmente; lánguidamente; indistintamente,
vagamente, tenuemente; apenas.
faint·ness [féntnɪs] *s.* languidez, debilidad,
desfallecimiento; falta de claridad; vaguedad.
fair [fɛr] *adj.* (*just*) justo, recto, honrado; imparcial;
equitativo; (*mediocre*) regular, mediano;
(*complexion*) rubio, blondo; *Méx.* huero; *Guat.*
canche; *C.R.* macho; *Pan.* fulo; *Col.* mono;
Ven. catire; (*Sal.*) chele; (*weather*) claro,
despejado; **— chance of success** buena
probabilidad de éxito; **— complexion** tez blanca;
— hair pelo rubio; **— name** reputación sin
mancilla; **— play** juego limpio; **— sex** sexo
bello; **— weather** buen tiempo, tiempo
bonancible; **to act —** obrar con imparcialidad (*o*
con equidad); **to play —** jugar limpio; *s.* feria;
mercado; exposición; (*Valencia*) falla; **-ly** *adv.*

justamente; imparcialmente; medianamente; **-ly**
difficult medianamente difícil; **-ly well** regular,
bastante bien.
fair·ness [férnɪs] *s.* justicia, equidad, imparcialidad;
blancura (*de la tez*); belleza.
fair·y [férɪ] *s.* hada; — **godmother** hada madrina;
— **tale** cuento de hadas.
fair·y·land [férɪlænd] *s.* tierra de las hadas.
faith [feθ] *s.* fe; fidelidad; **in good** — de buena fe;
to have — **in** tener fe o confianza en; **to keep** —
cumplir con la palabra.
faith·ful [féθfəl] *adj.* fiel; leal; **-ly** *adv.* fielmente;
con fidelidad; puntualmente; **-ly yours** suyo
afectísimo; siempre suyo.
faith·ful·ness [féθfəlnɪs] *s.* fidelidad; lealtad;
exactitud.
faith·less [féθlɪs] *adj.* infiel; sin fe; desleal; falso.
fake [fek] *s.* fraude, trampa; falsedad; embustero;
adj. falso, fingido; *v.* falsear; fingir; simular.
fal·con [fólkən] *n.* halcón.
fall [fɔl] *s.* (*drop*) caída; bajada; (*collapse*) ruina;
baja (*de precios*); (*season*) otoño; **-s** cascada,
catarata, salto de agua; *v.* caer(se); decaer;
bajar; **to** — **asleep** dormirse, quedarse dormido;
to — **back** retroceder; **to** — **behind** atrasarse,
rezagarse, quedarse atrás; **to** — **in love**
enamorarse; **to** — **out with** reñir con, enemistarse
con; **to** — **to one** tocarle a uno, corresponderle a
uno; **his plans fell through** fracasaron (*o se*
malograron*) sus planes.
fal·la·cy [fǽləsɪ] *s.* falsedad; error.
fall·en [fólən] *p.p. de* **to fall.**
fall·out [fólauʊt] *s.* precipitación radiactiva.
fal·low [fǽlo] *adj.* baldío; *s.* barbecho; *v.* barbechar.
false [fɔls] *adj.* falso; postizo (*dientes, barba, etc.*);
fingido, simulado.
false·hood [fólshʊd] *s.* falsedad, mentira.
false·ness [fólsnɪs] *s.* falsedad.
fal·si·fy [fólsəfaɪ] *v.* falsificar, falsear; mentir.
fal·si·ty [fólsətɪ] *s.* falsedad; mentira.
fal·ter [fóltəʳ] *v.* vacilar; titubear; tambalearse;
bambolearse; **to** — **an excuse** balbucear una
excusa; *s.* temblor, vacilación.
fame [fem] *s.* fama.
famed [femd] *adj.* afamado, famoso, renombrado.
fa·mil·iar [fəmíljəʳ] *adj.* familiar, íntimo;
confianzudo; **to be** — **with a subject** conocer bien,
estar versado en o ser conocedor de una materia;
s. familiar.
fa·mil·i·ar·i·ty [fəmɪlɪǽrətɪ] *s.* familiaridad;
confianza, franqueza.
fam·i·ly [fǽmlɪ] *s.* familia; — **name** apellido; — **tree**
árbol genealógico; **to be in the** — **way** estar
encinta.
fam·ine [fǽmɪn] *s.* hambre; escasez, carestía.
fam·ished [fǽmɪʃt] *adj.* hambriento, muerto de
hambre; **to be** — morirse de hambre.
fa·mous [féməs] *adj.* famoso.
fan [fæn] *s.* abanico; aventador; ventilador;
aficionado (*a deportes*); admirador; *v.* abanicar;
ventilar.
fa·nat·ic [fənǽtɪk] *adj. & s.* fanático.
fa·nat·i·cism [fənǽtəsɪzm] *s.* fanatismo.
fan·ci·ful [fǽnsɪfəl] *adj.* fantástico; caprichoso;
imaginario.
fan·cy [fǽnsɪ] *s.* fantasía, antojo, capricho;
imaginación; afición, gusto; **to have a** — **for** tener
afición a; **to strike one's** — antojársele a uno; **to**
take a — **to a person** caerle a uno bien (*o*
simpatizarle a uno) una persona; *adj.* fantástico,
de fantasía; de adorno; elegante; — **ball** baile de

fantasía o disfraces; — **free** libre de cuidados;
—**work** labor; bordado fino; *v.* imaginar(se);
fantasear; forjar, concebir (*una idea*); **to** —
oneself imaginarse; **just** — **the idea!** ¡figúrate qué
idea! **I don't** — **the idea of** no me gusta la idea
de.
fang [fæŋ] *s.* colmillo (*de ciertos animales*).
fan·tas·tic [fæntǽstɪk] *adj.* fantástico; extravagante.
fan·ta·sy [fǽntəsɪ] *s.* fantasía.
far [fɑr] *adv.* lejos; — **away** muy lejos; — **and wide**
por todas partes; — **better** mucho mejor; — **off**
muy lejos; a lo lejos; **by** — con mucho; **as** — **as**
hasta; en cuanto a; **as** — **as I know** según
parece; a lo que parece; que yo sepa; **so** —
hasta ahora; hasta aquí; hasta entonces; **how**
—**?** ¿hasta dónde?; *adj.* lejano, distante, remoto;
— **journey** largo viaje; **it is a** — **cry from** dista
mucho de.
far·a·way [fárəwé] *adj.* muy lejano, distante,
remoto; abstraído.
farce [fɑrs] *s.* farsa.
fare [fɛr] *s.* pasaje, tarifa de pasajes; pasajero;
comida, alimento; *v.* pasarla (*bien o mal*); irle a
uno (*bien o mal*); **to** — **forth** salir.
fare·well [fɛrwél] *s.* despedida, adiós; **to bid** — **to**
despedirse de; —**! ** ¡adiós!
far·fetched [fárfɛtʃt] *adj.* traído de muy lejos;
forzado; traído por los cabellos; que no hace al
caso; improbable, poco creíble.
far·flung [fárflʌŋ] *adj.* extenso, de gran alcance.
farm [fɑrm] *s.* hacienda, granja, *Riopl.* estancia,
Méx. rancho; — **hand** peón; — **produce**
productos agrícolas; *v.* cultivar, labrar (*la tierra*);
to — **out** dar en arriendo; repartir.
farm·er [fárməʳ] *s.* labrador; granjero; agricultor;
Méx. ranchero, *Riopl.* estanciero, *Am.*
hacendano.
farm·house [fármhaʊs] *s.* alquería, finca.
farm·ing [fármɪŋ] *s.* labranza, agricultura, cultivo
de los campos; *adj.* agrícola.
farm·yard [fármjɑrd] *s.* corral (*de una alquería*).
far·off [fárɔf] *adj.* distance, remoto.
far·sighted [fársáɪtəd] *adj.* (*sight*) présbite;
(*foresighted*) precavido.
far·ther [fárðəʳ] *adv.* más lejos; más; — **on** más
adelante; *adj.* más remoto, más lejano.
far·thest [fárðɪst] *adj.* más lejano; más remoto;
adv. más lejos.
fas·ci·nate [fǽsnet] *v.* fascinar.
fas·ci·na·tion [fæsnéʃən] *s.* fascinación.
fas·cism [fǽʃɪzm] *s.* fascismo.
fas·cist [fǽʃɪst] *s.* fascista.
fash·ion [fǽʃən] *s.* (*style*) moda, boga, estilo; (*way*)
manera, modo; — **plate** figurín; **the latest** — la
última moda (*o* novedad); **after a** —
medianamente, no muy bien; **to be in** — estar de
moda; estilarse; *v.* forjar, hacer, formar; idear.
fash·ion·a·ble [fǽʃnəbl] *adj.* de moda; de buen
tono; elegante.
fast [fæst] *adj.* rápido, veloz; adelantado (*dícese del
reloj*); firme (*amigo*); fijo; disipado,
disoluto; *adv.* aprisa, de prisa; firmemente,
fijamente; — **asleep** profundamente dormido; *s.*
ayuno; *v.* ayunar.
fas·ten [fǽsn] *v.* fijar(se); sujetar(se), asegurar(se);
atar, unir; abrochar(se).
fas·ten·er [fǽsnəʳ] *s.* broche, abrochador.
fas·tid·i·ous [fæstídɪəs] *adj.* melindroso.
fat [fæt] *adj.* gordo; grasiento; mantecoso; —
profits ganancias pingües; *s.* grasa, manteca;
gordura; **the** — **of the land** lo mejor y más rico

de la tierra.

fa·tal [fétḷ] *adj.* fatal.

fa·tal·i·ty [fətǽlətɪ] *s.* fatalidad; muerte.

fate [fet] *s.* hado, sino, destino; fortuna, suerte.

fa·ther [fáðɚ] *s.* padre.

fa·ther·hood [fáðɚhʊd] *s.* paternidad.

fa·ther-in-law [fáðɚrɪnlɔ] *s.* suegro.

fa·ther·land [fáðɚlænd] *s.* patria.

fa·ther·ly [fáðɚlɪ] *adv.* paternal.

fath·om [fǽðəm] *v.* sondar, sondear; penetrar; *s.* braza (*medida de profundidad*).

fath·om·less [fǽðəmlɪs] *adj.* insondable.

fa·tigue [fətíg] *s.* fatiga, cansancio; *v.* fatigar(se), cansar(se).

fat·ness [fǽtnɪs] *s.* gordura.

fat·ten [fǽtṇ] *v.* engordar.

fat·ty [fǽtɪ] *adj.* grasiento; seboso.

fau·cet [fɔ́sɪt] *s.* grifo, llave, espita, canilla, *Am.* bitoque.

fault [fɔlt] *s.* (*defect*) falta; defecto, tacha; (*blame*) culpa; (*geological*) falla; **to a** — excesivamente; **to be at** — ser, culpable; **to find** — **with** criticar a.

fault·find·er [fɔ́ltfaɪndɚ] *s.* criticón, criticador.

fault·less [fɔ́ltlɪs] *adj.* intachable, sin tacha, perfecto.

fault·y [fɔ́ltɪ] *adj.* defectuoso, imperfecto.

fa·vor [févɚ] *s.* favor; **your** — **of the ...** su grata (carta) del ...; *v.* favorecer.

fa·vor·a·ble [févrəbḷ] *adj.* favorable; **favorably** *adv.* favorablemente.

fa·vor·ite [févrɪt] *adj.* & *s.* favorito.

fa·vor·it·ism [févrɪtɪzəm] *s.* favoritismo.

fawn [fɔn] *s.* cervato; color de cervato; *v.* adular; halagar.

fear [fɪr] *s.* temor, miedo; pavor; *v.* temer.

fear·ful [fírfəl] *adj.* terrible, espantoso; temible, temeroso; miedoso.

fear·less [fírlɪs] *adj.* sin temor, intrépido, atrevido, arrojado.

fear·less·ness [fílɪsnɪs] *s.* intrepidez, arrojo, osadía, atrevimiento.

fea·si·ble [fízəbḷ] *adj.* factible, hacedero, dable.

feast [fist] *s.* fiesta; festín, banquete; *v.* festejar, obsequiar; banquetear; **to** — **one's eyes on** deleitar la vista en.

feat [fit] *s.* proeza, hazaña; acto de destreza; suerte (*en el circo*).

feath·er [féðɚ] *s.* pluma; **-s** plumaje; **a** — **in one's cap** un triunfo para uno; — **weight** de peso mínimo; *v.* emplumar.

feath·er·y [féðərɪ] *adj.* plumoso; ligero, como una pluma.

fea·ture [fítʃɚ] *s.* facción, rasgo distintivo; película principal (*en el cine*); **-s** facciones (*de la cara*); — **article** artículo sobresaliente o principal; *v.* destacar, hacer sobresalir; dar realce a; mostrar, exhibir (*como cosa principal*), hacer resaltar.

Feb·ru·ar·y [fébrʊɛrɪ] *s.* febrero.

fed [fed] *pret.* & *p.p. de* **to feed**; **to be** — **up** estar harto; estar hasta la coronilla, estar hasta el copete.

fed·er·al [fédərəl] *adj.* federal.

fed·er·a·tion [fedəréʃən] *s.* federación, confederación, liga.

fee [fi] *s.* honorario (honorarios); derechos; cuota; **admission** — derechos de entrada; precio de entrada.

fee·ble [fíbḷ] *adj.* débil, endeble; **feebly** *adv.* débilmente.

feed [fid] *s.* forraje, pasto, pienso (*para los caballos*); comida; *v.* alimentar(se); dar de comer; pacer, pastar; **to** — **coal** echar carbón.

feed·back [fídbæk] *s.* regeneración.

feel [fil] *v.* sentir; tocar, tentar; palpar; **to** — **better (sad, happy,** *etc.***)** sentirse mejor (triste, feliz, *etc*); **to** — **one's way** tantear el camino; **to** — **for someone** compadecer a alguien; **it -s soft** está suave; **it -s hot in here** se siente calor aquí; *s.* tacto, sentido del tacto; **this cloth has a nice** — esta tela es suave al tacto.

feel·er [fílɚ] *s.* tentáculo, antena (*de los insectos*); tiento; propuesta (*para averiguar la inclinación o pensamiento de alguien*).

feel·ing [fílɪŋ] *s.* (*touch*) tacto; sensación (*emotion*) sentimiento; emoción; pasión; (*pity*) compasión; ternura; **to hurt someone's -s** ofender la sensibildad de alguien; *adj.* sensible, compasivo.

feet [fit] *pl. de* **foot**.

feign [fen] *v.* fingir.

fell [fɛl] *v.* derribar, echar abajo; talar (*un árbol*); *pret. de* **to fall**.

fel·low [félo] *s.* socio, miembro (*de una sociedad, colegio, etc.*); becario (*estudiante que disfruta una beca*); camarada; compañero; individuo, tipo, sujeto, hombre; — **citizen** conciudadano; — **man** prójimo; — **member** consocio; colega; — **student** condiscípulo.

fel·low·ship [féloʃɪp] *s.* compañerismo; unión; confraternidad; sociedad; beca; **to get a** — obtener una beca.

fel·o·ny [félənɪ] *s.* crimen.

felt [fɛlt] *s.* fieltro; *adj.* de fieltro; *pret.* & *p.p. de* **to feel**.

fe·male [fímel] *s.* hembra; *adj.* hembra; femenino, mujeril, de la mujer; — **cat (dog,** *etc.***)** gata (perra, *etc.*); — **screw** tuerca, hembra de tornillo.

fem·i·nine [fémənɪn] *adj.* femenino, femenil.

fem·i·nin·i·ty [femɪnínɪtɪ] *s.* feminidad.

fe·mur [fímɚ] *s.* fémur.

fence [fɛns] *s.* cerca, valla, vallado; receptor de cosas robadas; **to be on the** — estar indeciso; *v.* esgrimir; **to** — **in** cercar, rodear con cerca.

fenc·ing [fénsɪŋ] *s.* esgrima; cercado.

fend·er [féndɚ] *s.* guardabarros, guardafango; *Am.* trompa (*de locomotora*); *Riopl.* parrilla.

fer·ment [fɚmɛnt] *s.* fermento; fermentación; [fɚmɛ́nt] *v.* fermentar; hacer fermentar.

fer·men·ta·tion [fɚməntéʃən] *s.* fermentación.

fern [fɚn] *s.* helecho.

fe·ro·cious [fəróʃəs] *adj.* feroz, fiero.

fe·roc·i·ty [fərásətɪ] *s.* ferocidad, fiereza.

fer·ret [férɪt] *v.* **to** — **out** buscar, cazar; escudriñar, indagar.

fer·ry [férɪ] *s.* barca de pasaje (*a través de un río o bahía*); embarcadero; *v.* transportar de una orilla a otra; atravesar (*un río*) en barca de pasaje.

fer·tile [fɚtḷ] *adj.* fértil; fecundo.

fer·til·i·ty [fɚtílətɪ] *s.* fertilidad.

fer·til·ize [fɚtḷaɪz] *v.* fertilizar; abonar; fecundar.

fer·til·iz·er [fɚtḷaɪzɚ] *s.* abono (*para la tierra*).

fer·vent [fɚvənt] *adj.* ferviente, fervoroso.

fer·vor [fɚvɚ] *s.* fervor; ardor.

fes·ter [féstɚ] *v.* supurar; enconarse (*una llaga*); *s.* llaga, úlcera.

fes·ti·val [féstəvḷ] *s.* fiesta.

fes·tive [féstɪv] *adj.* festivo; alegre.

fes·tiv·i·ty [festívətɪ] *s.* júbilo, regocijo; festividad.

fetch [fɛtʃ] *v.* ir a buscar; coger; traer.

fete [fet] *s.* fiesta; *v.* festejar; agasajar.

fet·ish [fétɪʃ] *s.* fetiche.

FA

fet·ter [fétəʳ] v. engrillar, meter en grillos encadenar; **-s'** s. pl. grillos, cadenas, trabas.

fe·tus [fítəs] s. feto.

feud [fjud] s. riña, pelea, contienda; **old —** enemistad antigua (entre dos personas o familias).

feu·dal [fjúdl] adj. feudal.

fe·ver [fívəʳ] s. fiebre, calentura.

fe·ver·ish [fívərɪʃ] adj. calenturiento, febril.

fe·ver·ish·ness [fívərɪʃnɪs] s. calentura; agitación febril.

few [fju] adj. & pron. pocos; **a —** unos pocos, unos cuantos.

fi·an·cé [fiɑnsé] s. novio; **fiancée** f. novia.

fi·as·co [fiǽsko] s. fiasco.

fib [fɪb] s. bola, mentirilla, paparrucha, papa; v. echar papas, decir o contar paparruchas.

fib·ber [fíbəʳ] s. paparruchero, cuentero, mentirosillo.

fi·ber [fáɪbəʳ] s. fibra.

fi·brous [fáɪbrəs] adj. fibroso.

fick·le [fíkl] adj. inconstante, voluble, veleidoso, mudable; tornadizo.

fic·tion [fíkʃən] s. ficción.

fic·tion·al [fíkʃənl] adj. novelesco; ficticio.

fic·ti·tious [fɪktíʃəs] adj. ficticio.

fid·dle [fídl] s. violín; v. tocar el violín; **to — around** malgastar el tiempo; juguetear.

fi·del·i·ty [faɪdélətɪ] s. fidelidad.

fid·get [fídʒɪt] v. estar inquieto; agitarse, menearse nerviosamente.

field [fild] s. campo; campo o cancha (de deportes); **— artillery** artillería de campaña; **— glasses** anteojos de larga vista; **— work** trabajo de investigación en el campo.

fiend [find] s. demonio, diablo; **dope —** morfinómano.

fiend·ish [fíndɪʃ] adj. diabólico.

fierce [fɪrs] adj. feroz, fiero; furioso, espantoso.

fierce·ness [fírsnɪs] s. ferocidad; fiereza; vehemencia.

fier·y [fáɪrɪ] adj. fogoso; ardiente; vehemente.

fife [faɪf] s. pífano.

fig [fɪg] s. higo; **— tree** higuera.

fight [faɪt] s. lucha; pelea; riña, pleito; **he has a lot of — left** le sobra fuerza para luchar; v. luchar (con) pelear; combatir; reñir; batirse; **to — it out** decidirlo a golpes o con argumentos; **to — one's way through** abrirse camino a la fuerza.

fight·er [fáɪtəʳ] s. luchador; combatiente, guerrero; **— airplane** avión de caza.

fight·ing [fáɪtɪŋ] s. lucha, combate pelea; adj. combatiente; luchador.

fig·ure [fígjəʳ] s. (form) figura; forma; talle (de una persona); (numerical) cifra, número; valor; precio; **-s** cuentas, cálculos; **— of speech** figura de dicción; **to be good at -s** sabe hacer bien las cuentas; ser listo en aritmética; **to cut a poor —** tener mala facha, hacer el ridículo; v. figurar; imaginarse, figurarse; adornar con dibujos; calcular; **to — on** contar con, confiar en; tener la intención de, proponerse; tomar en cuenta; **to — out** descifrar, resolver.

fil·a·ment [fíləmənt] s. filamento.

file [faɪl] s. (records) fichero; archivo; registro, lista; legajo; (cabinet) guardapapeles; (line) fila; (tool) lima; **— card** ficha, papeleta; v. archivar; guardar en el fichero; registrar, asentar en el registro; limar; desfilar, marchar en fila.

fil·i·al [fílɪəl] adj. filial.

fil·i·gree [fílɪgri] s. filigrana.

fill [fɪl] v. llenar(se); ocupar (un puesto); empastar

(un diente); servir, atender, despachar (un pedido); inflar (un neumático); tapar (un agujero); **to — out a blank** llenar un formulario (forma o esqueleto); **her eyes -ed with tears** se le arrasaron los ojos de lágrimas.

fil·let [fílé] s. filete; [fílɪt] cinta, lista de adorno.

fill·ing [fílɪŋ] s. relleno; empaste (dental); **gold —** orificación.

fil·ly [fílɪ] s. potranca.

film [fɪlm] s. película; membrana; tela (formada sobre la superficie de un líquido); nube (en el ojo); v. filmar (cinematografiar).

fil·ter [fíltəʳ] s. filtro; v. filtrar(se).

filth [fɪlθ] s. suciedad; porquería; mugre.

filth·i·ness [fílθɪnɪs] s. suciedad, porquería.

filth·y [fílθɪ] adj. sucio; puerco, cochino; mugriento.

fin [fɪn] s. aleta (de pez).

fi·nal [fáɪnl] adj. final; terminante; definitivo; **-ly** adv. finalmente; en fin, por fin.

fi·nance [fənǽns] s. teoría bancaria, Am. finanza; **-s** fondos, recursos monetarios; negocios bancarios, Am. finanzas; v. hacer operaciones bancarias; fomentar (un negocio o empresa), Am. financiar.

fi·nan·cial [fənǽnʃəl] adj. financiero; monetario.

fin·an·cier [finənsír] s. financiero, Am. financista.

fi·nanc·ing [fənǽnsɪŋ] s. Am. financiamiento.

find [faɪnd] v. hallar; encontrar; declarar; **to — fault with** criticar a, censurar a; **to — guilty** declarar o encontrar culpable; **to — out** descubrir; averiguar; s. hallazgo.

find·ing [fáɪndɪŋ] s. descubrimiento; hallazgo; fallo, decisión; **-s** resultados, datos (de una investigación).

fine [faɪn] adj. fino; perfecto, excelente; superior; primoroso; **— arts** bellas artes; **— sand** arena fina o menuda; **—weather** tiempo claro o despejado; **to feel —** sentirse muy bien de salud; **to have a — time** pasar un rato muy divertido; **fine-looking** bien parecido, guapo; s. multa; **in —** finalmente, en fin, en resumen; v. multar; **-ly** adv. finamente; con primor; excelentemente; muy bien, perfectamente.

fine·ness [fáɪnnɪs] s. finura; fineza; primor; excelencia, perfección.

fin·er·y [fáɪnərɪ] s. galas; atavíos, adornos.

fi·nesse [fɪnés] s. sutileza; artificio; soltura.

fin·ger [fíŋgəʳ] s. dedo (de la mano); **—print** impresión digital; **the little —** el dedo meñique; **middle —** dedo del corazón, dedo de enmedio; **ring —** dedo anular; v. tocar; manosear.

fin·ger·nail [fíŋgəʳnel] s. uña.

fin·ick·y [fíniki] adj. melindroso.

fin·ish [fíniʃ] s. fin, término, conclusión; (varnish) acabado; pulimiento; **to have a rough —** estar sin pulir, sin pulimento o al natural; v. acabar, acabar con, terminar, finalizar; pulir, pulimentar.

fin·ished [fíniʃt] adj. acabado; pulido, pulimentado; excelente.

fir [fɝ] s. abeto.

fire [faɪr] s. (flame) fuego; lumbre; (destructive) quemazón; incendio; **— alarm** alarma de incendios; **— department** cuerpo o servicio de bomberos; servicio de incendios; **— engine** bomba (para incendios); **— escape** escalera de salvamento; **— insurance** seguro contra incendios; **to be on —** estar ardiendo, estar quemándose; **to catch —** incendiarse, quemarse; **to set on —** pegar fuego, incendiar; **to be under enemy —** estar expuesto al fuego del enemigo; v. incendiar; pegar fuego; inflamar; disparar; **to — an employee** despedir (o expulsar) a un

empleado.
fire·arm [fáɪrɑrm] *s.* arma de fuego.
fire·brand [fáɪrbrænd] *s.* tizón; pavesa.
fire·crack·er [fáɪrkrækɚ] *s.* triquitraque.
fire·fly [fáɪrflaɪ] *s.* luciérnaga.
fire·man [fáɪrmən] *s.* bombero; fogonero.
fire·place [fáɪrples] *s.* chimenea, hogar.
fire·proof [fáɪrpruf] *adj.* incombustible; a prueba de
  incendio; *v.* hacer incombustible.
fire·side [fáɪrsaɪd] *s.* hogar.
fire·wood [fáɪrwʊd] *s.* leña.
fire·works [fáɪrwɝks] *s.* fuegos artificiales;
  pirotecnia.
fir·ing pin [fáɪrɪŋ pɪn] *s.* percusor.
firm [fɝm] *adj.* firme; fijo; estable; *s.* firma, razón
  social (*nombre de una casa comercial*); compañía
  (*comercial o industrial*); **-ly** *adv.* firmemente, con
  firmeza.
fir·ma·ment [fɝməmənt] *s.* firmamento.
firm·ness [fɝmnɪs] *s.* firmeza; estabilidad.
first [fɝst] *adj.* primero; *adv.* primero, en primer
  lugar, al principio, **from the** — desde el
  principio; **first-born** primogénito; **first-class** de
  primera clase; **first-cousin** primo hermano;
  first-rate de primera clase; muy bien; **—hand** de
  primera mano.
first aid [fɚst éd] *s.* primeros auxilios.
fish [fɪʃ] *s.* pez; *C.A.* peje; pescado; — **market**
  pescadería; — **story** patraña, cuento
  extravagante o increíble; **neither** — **nor fowl**
  ni chicha ni limonada; *v.* pescar.
fish·er [fíʃɚ] *s.* pescador.
fish·er·man [fíʃɚmən] *s.* pescador.
fish·er·y [fíʃɚrɪ] *s.* pesquera; pesquería, pesca.
fish·hook [fíʃhʊk] *s.* anzuelo.
fish·ing [fíʃɪŋ] *s.* pesca, pesquería; — **rod** caña de
  pescar; — **tackle** avíos o enseres de pescar; **to
  go** — ir de pesca.
fis·sure [fíʃɚ] *s.* grieta, hendedura, *Am.* rajadura.
fist [fɪst] *s.* puño; **to shake one's** — **at** amenazar
  con el puño.
fit [fɪt] *adj.* (*proper*) apto; a propósito, propio,
  conveniente; (*healthy*) sano, de buena salud, en
  buen estado; capaz; — **to be tied** frenético;
  not to see — **to do it** no tener a bien hacerlo;
  s. talle (*de un traje*); ajuste; encaje (*de una pieza
  en otra*); ataque, convulsión; — **of anger** acceso,
  arrebato o arranque de cólera; **by -s and starts**
  espasmódicamente; **that suit is a good** — ese
  traje le entalla (o le viene) bien; *v.* ajustar(se);
  adaptar; encajar(se), caber (en); acomodar;
  entallar (*un vestido*); venir bien (*un vestido,
  zapatos, sombrero, etc.*); ser a propósito para,
  ser propio para; capacitar, preparar; **to** — **in
  with** armonizar con; llevarse bien con; **to** — **out**
  equipar, proveer; **it does not** — **the facts** no está
  de acuerdo con los hechos; no hace al caso.
fit·ness [fítnɪs] *s.* aptitud; capacidad; conveniencia;
  propiedad (*de una idea, de una palabra, etc.*);
  physical — buena salud.
fit·ting [fítɪŋ] *adj.* propio, apropiado; a propósito,
  conveniente; *s.* ajuste; **dress** — prueba de un
  traje o vestido; **-s** avíos, guarniciones,
  accesorios.
fix [fɪks] *v.* (*repair*) remendar; componer; reparar;
  ajustar; arreglar; (*prearrange*) fijar; asegurar;
  to — **up** arreglar(se); componer(se); *s.* apuro,
  aprieto.
fixed [fíkst] *adj.* fijo, firme.
fix·ed·ly [fíksɪdlɪ] *adv.* de hito en hito; fijamente.
fix·ture [fíksʃɚ] *s.* (*thing*) accesorio fijo; (*person*)

persona firmemente establecida (*en un sitio o
  empleo*); **electric light -s** instalaciones eléctricas
  (*como brazos de lámparas, arañas*).
flab·by [flæbɪ] *adj.* blanducho.
flag [flæg] *s.* bandera; banderola; — **lily** flor de lis;
  v. hacer señas con banderola; adornar con
  banderas; decaer, debilitarse, menguar, flaquear.
fla·grant [flǽgrənt] *adv.* flagrante, notorio,
  escandaloso.
flag·staff [flǽgstæf] *s.* asta de bandera.
flag·stone [flǽgston] *s.* losa.
flair [flɛr] *s.* instinto, penetración, cacumen;
  disposición o aptitud natural.
flak [flæk] *s.* fuego antiaéreo; crítica abusiva.
flake [flek] *s.* copo (*de nieve*); escama; hojuela;
  corn -s hojuelas de maíz; *v.* descostrarse,
  descascararse.
flam·boy·ant [flæmbɔ́jənt] *adj.* rimbombante;
  flameante.
flame [flem] *s.* llama; flama; — **thrower**
  lanzallamas; *v.* llamear, flamear, echar llamas;
  inflamar(se); enardecer(se).
flam·ing [flémɪŋ] *adj.* llameante; flameante;
  encendido; ardiente, apasionado; — **red** rojo
  encendido.
flank [flæŋk] *s.* flanco; costado; lado; ijar (*de un
  animal*); *v.* flanquear; rodear.
flan·nel [flǽnl] *s.* franela.
flap [flæp] *s.* (*thing*) aleta; cubierta (*del bolsillo*);
  (*action*) golpeteo; aleteo; *v.* golpetear; aletear,
  batir (*las alas*); hojear con violencia (*las
  páginas*).
flare [flɛr] *s.* llamarada; llama; arranque (*de ira*);
  vuelo (*de una falda*); *v.* llamear, echar
  llamaradas; tener vuelo (*una falda*); **to** — **up**
  enfurecerse; encenderse; **the illness -ed up**
  recudeció la enfermedad.
flash [flæʃ] *s.* rayo; destello, llamarada; fogonazo;
  — **of hope** rayo de esperanza; — **of lightning**
  relámpago; — **of wit** agudeza; **—bulb** bombilla
  de destello; bombilla flash; **in a** — en un
  instante; **news** — última noticia (*enviada por
  radio o telégrafo*); *v.* relampaguear; destellar;
  brillar; centellear; radiar o telegrafiar (*noticias*).
  to — **by** pasar como un relámpago.
flash·ing [flǽʃɪŋ] *s.* relampagueo, centello; *adj.*
  relumbrante; flameante.
flash·light [flǽʃlaɪt] *s.* linterna eléctrica.
fiash·y [flǽʃɪ] *adj.* relumbrante; llamativo, de
  relumbrón, ostentoso; chillante, chillón (*dícese
  de los colores*).
flask [flæsk] *s.* frasco.
flat [flæt] *adj.* (*no curves*) plano, llano, chato;
  aplastado; (*tasteless*) insípido; monótono;
  (*without air*) desinflado; — **denial** negativa
  terminante; — **note** nota desentonada; — **rate**
  precio o número redondo; **D** — re bemol
  (*nota musical*); — **car** vagón de plataforma;
  to be — **broke** estar completamente pelado, estar
  sin dinero; **to fall** — caer de plano; caer mal (*un
  discurso, chiste, etc.*); **to sing** — desentonar,
  cantar desentonadamente; **to refuse -ly** negarse
  absolutamente; *s.* plano; palma (*de la mano*);
  apartamento, departamento, piso; bemol (*en
  música*).
flat·iron [flǽtaɪɚn] *s.* plancha.
flat·ness [flǽtnɪs] *s.* llanura; lisura; insipidez;
  desafinamiento (*en música*).
flat·ten [flǽtn] *v.* aplastar(se); aplanar(se);
  allanar(se).
flat·ter [flǽtɚ] *v.* lisonjear; adular.

FE

flat·ter·er [flǽtərɚ] s. lisonjero, adulador.
flat·ter·ing [flǽtərɪŋ] adj. lisonjero, halagüeño, adulador.
flat·ter·y [flǽtərɪ] s. lisonja, halago; adulación.
flat·u·lence [flǽtjʊləns] s. hinchazón, flatulencia.
flaunt [flɔnt] v. ostentar; hacer gala de.
fla·vor [flévɚ] s. sabor; gusto; condimento; v. sazonar; dar sabor a; condimentar.
fla·vor·less [flévɚlɪs] adj. insípido, sin sabor.
flaw [flɔ] s. defecto; falta; tacha; imperfección.
flaw·less [flɔ́lɪs] adj. sin tacha; intachable, irreprochable; perfecto.
flax [flæks] s. lino.
flay [fle] s. desollar.
flea [fli] s. pulga.
fled [flɛd] pret. & p.p. de to **flee**.
flee [fli] v. huir; huir de.
fleece [flis] s. vellón, lana; v. trasquilar, esquilar; despojar, estafar, defraudar.
fleet [flit] s. flota; armada; adj. veloz.
fleet·ing [flitɪŋ] adj. fugaz, transitorio, pasajero, efímero.
Flem·ish [flémɪʃ] adj. flamenco; s. flamenco, idioma flamenco; **the —** los flamencos.
flesh [flɛʃ] s. carne; **— and blood** carne y hueso; **— color** color encarnado; **in the —** en persona.
flesh·y [flɛ́ʃɪ] adj. carnoso; gordo, gordiflón.
flew [flu] pret. de to **fly**.
flex·i·bil·i·ty [flɛksəbílətɪ] s. flexibilidad.
flex·i·ble [flɛ́ksəbl] adj. flexible.
flick·er [flíkɚ] s. titilación, parpadeo, luz trémula; temblor momentáneo (de emoción); aleteo; especie de pájaro carpintero; v. titilar; temblar; parpadear; vacilar; aletear; **to — one's eyelash** pestañear.
fli·er [fláɚ] s. volador; aviador; tren rápido.
flight [flaɪt] s. vuelo; bandada (de pájaros); escuadrilla (de aviones); fuga, huída; **— of stairs** tramo de escalera; **to put to —** poner en fuga.
flim·sy [flímzɪ] adj. endeble, débil; tenue; quebradizo; frágil; baladí; **a — excuse** una excusa baladí.
fling [flɪŋ] v. arrojar(se), lanzar(se); tirar; echar; **to — open (shut)** abrir (cerrar) de golpe; s. tiro; tirada, lanzamiento; tentativa; **to go out on a —** irse a echar una cana al aire.
flint [flɪnt] s. pedernal.
flip [flɪp] v. arrojar, lanzar al aire; sacudir; dar un dedazo.
flip·pan·cy [flípənsɪ] s. ligereza; frivolidad; impertinencia; petulancia.
flip·pant [flípənt] adj. ligero (en sus acciones y modales), ligero de cascos; frívolo; inpertinente; petulante.
flirt [flɝt] s. coqueta; coquetón, coquetona; v. coquetear.
flir·ta·tion [flɝtéʃən] s. coquetería; **to carry on a —** coquetear.
flit [flɪt] v. pasar velozmente; volar; revolotear.
float [flot] s. boya; cosa flotante, flotador; corcho (de una caña de pescar); balsa; carro o carroza (de procesiones, fiestas, etc.); v. flotar; sobrenadar; boyar; poner a flote; lanzar al mercado (una nueva emisión de valores, bonos, etc.).
flock [flɑk] s. bandada (de pájaros, niños, etc.); rebaño, grey; manada (de animales); grupo; **— of people** gentío, muchedumbre; v. agruparse; congregarse; **to — to** acudir juntos (o en bandadas) a; **to — together** andar juntos, volar en bandadas, ir en grupo.

flog [flɑg] v. azotar.
flood [flʌd] s. inundación; diluvio; avenida (de agua), crecida; creciente; torrente; **—gate** compuerta (de una presa); esclusa (de un canal); **— light** reflector; proyector de luz; **— tide** flujo (o marea ascendiente); v. inundar.
floor [flor] s. (surface) suelo; piso; (story) piso; (bottom) fondo; **to have the —** tener la palabra; v. solar; entarimar, enladrillar, enlosar; echar al suelo, derribar; asombrar.
flop [flɑp] v. (flap) caer o colgar flojamente; aletear; menearse; (throw) lanzar; dejar caer; (fail) fracasar; fallar; **to — down** dejarse caer; desplomarse, tumbarse; **to — over** voltear(se); dar vueltas; s. fracaso.
flo·rist [flórɪst] s. florero, florera; **-'s shop** florería.
floss [flɔs] s. seda floja; pelusa; fibra sedosa; **dental —** seda dentál.
flound·er [fláʊndɚ] v. patalear (en el lodo, nieve, etc.); forcejear (por salir del lodo, nieve, o cualquier aprieto); revolcarse; tropezar, cometer errores; s. lenguado (pez).
flour [flaʊr] s. harina.
flour·ish [flɝ́ɪʃ] v. (prosper) florecer, prosperar, medrar; (blandish) blandir; agitar en el aire; s. floreo; adorno o rasgo caprichoso; ostentación; (with the signature) rúbrica.
flour·y [fláʊrɪ] adj. harinoso.
flow [flo] s. flujo; corriente; **— of words** torrente de palabras; v. fluir; correr; flotar, ondear; **to — into** desembocar en; **to be -ing with riches** nadar en la abundancia.
flow·er [fláʊɚ] s. flor; **— bed** cuadro de jardín; **— vase** florero; v. florecer, Am. florear.
flow·er·pot [fláʊrpɑt] s. N. Spain tiesto, And. Am. maceta.
flow·er·y [fláʊrɪ] adj. florido.
flow·ing [flóɪŋ] adj. fluído, corriente, fluente; suelto, ondeante.
flown [flon] p.p. de to **fly**.
flu [flu] s. influenza, gripe.
fluc·tu·ate [flʌ́ktʃʊet] s. fluctuar.
fluc·tu·a·tion [flʌktʃʊéʃən] s. fluctuación.
flue [flu] s. cañón (de chimenea); tubo de escape.
flu·en·cy [flúənsɪ] s. fluidez; labia.
flu·ent [flúənt] adj. fluente, flúido; **to speak -ly** hablar con facilidad.
fluff [flʌf] s. mullir; esponjar.
fluff·y [flʌ́fɪ] adj. mullido, suave, blando; cubierto de vello o plumón; **— hair** pelo esponjado o esponjoso.
flu·id [flúɪd] adj. & s. flúido.
flung [flʌŋ] pret. & p.p. de to **fling**.
flunk [flʌŋk] s. reprobación (en un examen o asignatura); v. reprobar, suspender (en un examen); salir mal, fracasar o fallar (en un examen).
flun·ky [flʌ́ŋkɪ] s. lacayo; ayudante servil; zalamero, persona servil.
flu·o·rine [flúərɪn] s. fluor.
flur·ry [flɝ́ɪ] s. (weather) ráfaga; nevisca; (action) agitación.
flush [flʌʃ] s. sonrojo, rubor; bochorno; flujo rápido; flux (de naipes); adj. lleno; rico; parejo, al mismo nivel; **— with** a flor de, a ras de; v. sonrojar(se), ruborizar(se), poner(se) colorado; hacer rebosar (de agua); **to — out** vaciar (un depósito), enjuagar.
flute [flut] s. flauta; estría (de una columna); v. acanalar, estriar (una columna).
flut·ter [flʌ́tɚ] s. aleteo; agitación; alboroto; vuelco

(*del corazón*); *v.* aletear; revolotear; agitar(se);
palpitar; menear(se); tremolar (*una bandera*).
flux [flʌks] *s.* flujo.
fly [flaɪ] *s.* mosca; pliegue (*para cubrir botones*);
bragueta (*abertura de los pantalones*); **on the —**
al vuelo; **to hit a —** pegar una planchita o
elevar una palomita (*en béisbol*); **— swatter**
matamoscas; *v.* volar; pasar velozmente; huir;
ondear; enarbolar (*una bandera*); **to — at**
lanzarse sobre; **to — away** volar, irse, escaparse;
to — off the handle perder los estribos (*o* la
paciencia); **to — open (shut)** abrirse (cerrarse) de
repente; **to — up in anger** montar en cólera.
fly·er = **flier.**
fly·leaf [fláɪlif] *s.* guarda (*hoja en blanco al
principio y al fin de un libro*).
foam [fom] *s.* espuma; *v.* espumar, hacer espuma.
fo·cus [fókəs] *s.* foco; distancia focal; *v.*
enfocar(se).
fod·der [fádɚ] *s.* forraje.
foe [fo] *s.* enemigo.
fog [fɑg] *s.* niebla, neblina, bruma; velo, nube (*en
una película o fotografía*); **—horn** sirena; *v.*
anublar, ofuscar, obscurecer; ponerse brumoso;
velar(se) (*una película*).
fog·gy [fágɪ] *adj.* brumoso, nublado; obscuro,
confuso.
foil [fɔɪl] *s.* oropel, hojuela, laminita de metal;
florete (*de esgrima*); realce, contraste; **tin —**
hojuela de estaño; *v.* frustrar.
fold [fold] *s.* (*double over*) pliegue, doblez;
(*enclosure*) redil; grey; **three —** tres veces;
hundred — cien veces; *v.* doblar(se); plegar(se);
envolver; **to — one's arms** cruzarse de brazos.
fold·er [fóldɚ] *s.* (*pamphlet*) folleto, circular;
(*holder*) papelera; plegadera (*máquina para
plegar*).
fold·ing [fóldɪŋ] *adj.* plegadizo; **— chair** silla
plegadiza, silla de tijera; **— machine** plegadora,
máquina plegadora; **— screen** biombo.
fo·li·age [fólɪdʒ] *s.* follaje, fronda.
fo·li·o [fólɪo] *s.* folio; infolio, libro en folio;
pliego; **— edition** edición en folio.
folk [fok] *s.* gente; pueblo; **-s** parientes, allegados;
familia; personas; amigos (*vocativo familiar*); *adj.*
popular, del pueblo; **— dance** danza o baile
tradicional; **—lore** folklore; cuentos, leyendas y
tradiciones populares; **— song** canción popular,
canción típica o tradicional; **— music** música
del pueblo; música tradicional.
fol·low [fálo] *v.* seguir; ejercer (*un oficio o
profesión*); seguir el hilo de (*un argumento*);
seguirse (*como consecuencia*); **to — suit** jugar el
mismo palo (*en naipes*); seguir el ejemplo,
imitar.
fol·low·er [fáləwɚ] *s.* seguidor; imitador;
partidario.
fol·low·ing [fáləwɪŋ] *s.* séquito, comitiva,
partidarios; *adj.* siguiente; subsiguiente.
fol·ly [fálɪ] *s.* locura; necedad, tontería; desatino.
fo·ment [fomént] *v.* fomentar.
fond [fɑnd] *adj.* aficionado (a); amigo (de); amante
(de), encariñado (con); cariñoso, afectuoso;
tierno; **to be — of** querer a (*una persona*); estar
encariñado con, ser aficionado a; gustar de
(*algo*); **-ly** *adv.* cariñosamente, afectuosamente.
fon·dle [fándl] *v.* acariciar.
fond·ness [fándnɪs] *s.* cariño, afecto; afición.
font [fɑnt] *s.* pila bautismal; fuente.
food [fud] *s.* alimento, sustento; comida.
food·stuff [fúdstʌf] *s.* alimento; producto

alimenticio; comestibles.
fool [ful] *s.* tonto, necio, zonzo; payaso; **to play the
—** payasear, hacer el payaso; *v.* chasquear,
chancear(se); bromear, embromar; engañar; **to
— away the time** malgastar el tiempo.
fool·ish [fúlɪʃ] *adj.* tonto; necio, bobo, zonzo.
fool·ish·ness [fúlɪʃnɪs] *s.* tontería, necedad,
bobería.
foot [fut] *s.* pie; pata (*de animal*); **on — a** pie;
— soldier soldado de infantería; **to put one's
— in it** meter la pata; *v.* andar a pie; **to — it**
andar a pie; **to — the bill** pagar la cuenta;
sufragar los gastos.
foot·ball [fútbɔl] *s.* fútbol, football.
foot·hold [fúthold] *s.* arraigo; puesto establecido.
foot·ing [fútɪŋ] *s.* base; posición firme; **to be on a
friendly — with** tener relaciones amistosas con;
to lose one's — perder pie.
foot·lights [fútlaɪts] *s. pl.* candilejas (*dei teatro*);
tablas, teatro.
foot·man [fútmən] *s.* lacayo.
foot·note [fútnot] *s.* nota al pie de una página.
foot·path [fútpæθ] *s.* vereda, senda, trocha (*para
gente a pie*).
foot·print [fútprɪnt] *s.* huella, pisada.
foot·step [fútstɛp] *s.* (*action*) pisada, paso; (*trace*)
huella; **to follow in the -s of** seguir las pisadas
o huellas de.
foot·stool [fútstul] *s.* banquillo, taburete, escabel.
fop [fɑp] *s.* currutaco.
for [fɔr] *prep.* por; para; **— all of her intelligence**
a pesar de su inteligencia; **— feat that** por
miedo (de) que; **— the present** por el presente,
por ahora; **as — him** en cuanto a él; **to know
— a fact** saber de cierto, saber de hecho; **to pay
him — it** pagárselo; **to thank him — it**
agradecérselo; *conj.* porque, pues.
for·age [fɔrɪdʒ] *s.* forraje; *v.* forrajear; dar forraje
a.
for·ay [fɔre] *s.* correría, incursión; saqueo; *v.* pillar,
saquear.
for·bade [fɚbæd] *pret. de* **to forbid.**
for·bear [fɔrbɛr] *s.* antepasado; [fɔrbér] *v.*
abstenerse de; tener paciencia.
for·bid [fɚbíd] *v.* prohibir; vedar.
for·bid·den [fɚbídn] *adj.* prohibido; vedado; *p.p. de*
to forbid.
for·bid·ding [fɚbídɪŋ] *adj.* austero, reservado;
pavoroso; impenetrable.
for·bore [fɔrbór] *pret. de* **to forbear.**
for·borne [fɔrbórn] *p.p. de* **to forbear.**
force [fɔrs] *s.* fuerza; cuerpo (*de policía, de
empleados, etc.*); **in — en** vigor, vigente; **armed -s**
fuerzas armadas; *v.* forzar, obligar; **to — one's
way** abrirse paso por fuerza; **to — out** echar por
fuerza, echar a la fuerza.
forced [fɔrst] *adj.* forzado.
force·ful [fɔrsfəl] *adj.* vigoroso; enérgico.
for·ceps [fɔrsəps] *s.* gatillo (*tenazas para sacar
muelas*); pinzas.
for·ci·ble [fɔrsəbl] *adj.* (*strong*) fuerte, enérgico;
potente; eficaz; (*by force*) violento; hecho a la
fuerza; **forcibly** *adv.* fuertemente; con energía;
forzosamente; por fuerza.
ford [fɔrd] *s.* vado; *v.* vadear.
fore [for] *adj.* anterior, delantero; de proa; *s.*
frente; puesto delantero; *adv.* delante, hacia
adelante; *interj.* ¡cuidado! (*dícese en el campo de
golf*).
fore·arm [fórɑrm] *s.* antebrazo.
fore·bode [forbód] *v.* presagiar; presentir.

fore·bod·ing [forbódɪŋ] *s.* presentimiento; presagio.
fore·cast [fórkæst] *s.* pronóstico; [forkǽst] *v.* pronosticar; predecir; *pret. & p.p. de* to forecast.
fore·fa·ther [fórfɑðə·] *s.* antepasado.
fore·fin·ger [fórfɪŋgə·] *s.* (dedo) índice.
fore·foot [fórfʊt] *s.* pata delantera, mano (*de cuadrúpedo*).
fore·go [forgó] *v.* abstenerse de.
fore·gone [forgón] *p.p. de* to forego; a — conclusion una conclusión inevitable.
fore·ground [fórgraʊnd] *s.* frente, primer plano, primer término.
fore·head [fórɪd] *s.* frente (*f.*).
for·eign [fɔ́rɪn] *adj.* extranjero; foráneo; extraño; — to his nature ajeno a su índole; — office ministerio de relaciones exteriores; departamento de negocios extranjeros; — trade comercio exterior; foreign-born extranjero de nacimiento.
for·eign·er [fɔ́rɪnə·] *s.* extranjero; forastero.
fore·lock [fórlɑk] *s.* guedeja.
fore·man [fórmən] *s.* capataz; presidente (*de un jurado*); *Méx., C.A., Ven., Col.* caporal (*de un rancho o hacienda*); *Ríopl.* capataz.
fore·most [fórmost] *adj.* (*first*) primero; delantero; (*most important*) principal, más notable, más distinguido.
fore·noon [fornún] *s.* (la) mañana.
fore·run·ner [forrΛnə·] *s.* precursor; presagio.
fore·saw [forsó] *pret. de* to foresee.
fore·see [forsí] *s.* prever.
fore·seen [forsín] *p.p. de* to foresee previsto.
fore·sight [fórsaɪt] *s.* previsión.
for·est [fɔ́rɪst] *s.* bosque, selva; — ranger guardabosques; *v.* arbolar, plantar de árboles.
fore·stall [forstól] *v.* prevenir; madrugar.
for·est·er [fɔ́rɪstə·] *s.* guardabosques; silvicultor; habitante de un bosque.
for·est·ry [fɔ́rɪstrɪ] *s.* silvicultura.
fore·tell [fortél] *v.* precedir, pronosticar, presagiar.
fore·told [fortóld] *pret. & p.p. de* to foretell.
for·ev·er [fəévə·] *adv.* por (*o* para) siempre.
for·feit [fórfɪt] *s.* multa; pena; prenda perdida; game of -s juego de prendas; *v.* perder, perder el derecho a.
for·gave [fəgév] *pret. de* to forgive.
forge [fordʒ] *s.* fragua; forja; *v.* fraguar; forjar; falsear, falsificar; to — ahead abrirse paso; avanzar.
for·ger·y [fórdʒərɪ] *s.* falsificación.
for·get [fəgét] *v.* olvidar; olvidarse de; to — oneself cometer un desmán impensadamente; perder el tino o la paciencia.
for·get·ful [fəgétfəl] *adj.* olvidadizo; negligente.
for·get·ful·ness [fəgétfəlnɪs] *s.* olvido; negligencia.
for·get-me-not [fəgétmɪnɑt] *s.* nomeolvides.
for·give [fəgív] *v.* perdonar.
for·giv·en [fəgívən] *p.p. de* to forgive.
for·give·ness [fəgívnɪs] *s.* perdón.
for·giv·ing [fəgívɪŋ] *adj.* perdonador, misericordioso, de buen corazón.
for·got [fəgát] *pret. & p.p. de* to forget.
for·got·ten [fəgátn̩] *p.p. de* to forget.
fork [fɔrk] *s.* tenedor, *Méx., Col., Ven., Andes* trinche; horquilla (*para heno*); horcón; bifurcación; *v.* bifurcarse; levantar o arrojar (*heno*) con horquilla.
for·lorn [fəlórn] *adj.* desamparado, desdichado.
form [fɔrm] *s.* forma; condición, estado; blank — blanco, forma en blanco, *Méx., Ven.* esqueleto; *v.* formar(se).

for·mal [fórml] *adj.* formal, perteneciente a la forma; convencional, ceremonioso; — party reunión de etiqueta; -ly *adv.* formalmente, con ceremonia, solemnemente.
for·mal·i·ty [fɔrmǽlətɪ] *s.* formalidad, ceremonia; formalismo.
for·ma·tion [fɔrméʃən] *s.* formación.
for·ma·tive [fɔ́rmətɪv] *adj.* formativo.
for·mer [fɔ́rmə·] *adj.* primero, precedente, anterior; antiguo; in — times en otro tiempo, en días de antaño, antiguamente, anteriormente; the — aquél (aquèlla, aquéllos, aquéllas); -ly *adv.* anteriormente; antes, en tiempos pasados.
for·mi·da·ble [fɔ́rmɪdəbl] *adj.* formidable.
for·mu·la [fɔ́rmjələ] *s.* fórmula.
for·mu·late [fɔ́rmjəlet] *v.* formular.
for·sake [fəsék] *v.* desamparar; abandonar.
for·sak·en [fəsékən] *p.p. de* to forsake & *adj.* desamparado, abandonado.
for·sook [fəsúk] *pret. de* to forsake.
for·swear [fɔrswér] *v.* abjurar.
fort [fort] *s.* fuerte, fortín, fortaleza.
forth [forθ] *adv.* adelante; hacia adelante; to go — salir; and so — etcétera, y así succesivamente.
forth·com·ing [fórθkΛmɪŋ] *adj.* venidero, próximo; funds will not be — until no habrá fondos disponibles hasta.
forth·with [forθwíθ] *adv.* en seguida, pronto, al punto.
for·ti·fi·ca·tion [fɔrtəfəkéʃən] *s.* fortificación.
for·ti·fy [fɔ́rtəfaɪ] *v.* fortificar; fortalecer.
for·ti·tude [fɔ́rtətjud] *s.* fortaleza.
fort·night [fɔ́rtnaɪt] *s.* quincena, quince días, dos semanas.
for·tress [fɔ́rtrɪs] *s.* fortaleza, fuerte.
for·tu·i·tous [fɔrtjúətəs] *adj.* fortuito; inopinado, inesperado.
for·tu·nate [fɔ́rtʃənɪt] *adj.* afortunado; -ly *adv.* afortunadamente, por fortuna.
for·tune [fɔ́rtʃən] *s.* fortuna; —teller agorero, adivino.
fo·rum [fórəm] *s.* foro; tribunal; ateneo.
for·ward [fɔ́rwəd] *adj.* (*leading*) delantero; (*progressive*) precoz; progresista; (*daring*) atrevido; descarado; *adv.* adelante, hacia adelante; *v.* transmitir; despachar; reenviar; reexpedir, to — a plan fomentar un plan.
fos·sil [fásl] *adj.* fósil; anticuado; *s.* fósil.
fos·ter [fásta·] *v.* criar, nutrir; fomentar; promover; *adj.* putativo; adoptivo.
fought [fɔt] *pret. & p.p. de* to fight.
foul [faʊl] *adj.* sucio; asqueroso; puerco, cochino; fétido; vil; injusto; — air aire viciado; — ball pelota foul (*en béisbol*); —mouthed mal hablado, obsceno; — play juego sucio; fraude; violencia; — weather mal tiempo; *s.* mala jugada (*contraria a las reglas del juego*), trampa, *Am.* chapuza, foul; *v.* ensuciar; violar (*las reglas de un juego*); *Am.* pegar un foul (*en béisbol*).
found [faʊnd] *v.* fundar, establecer; *pret. & p.p. de* to find.
foun·da·tion [faʊndéʃən] *s.* fundación; base; fundamento; principio.
foun·der [fáʊndə·] *s.* fundador; fundidor (*de metales*); *v.* zozobrar, irse a pique; fracasar; tropezar; hacer zozobrar.
foun·dry [fáʊndrɪ] *s.* fundición.
foun·tain [fáʊntɪ] *s.* fuente; manatial; — pen pluma (de) fuente, pluma estilográfica.
four·score [fórskór] *adj.* cuatro veintenas, ochenta.
fourth [forθ] *adj.* cuarto; *s.* cuarto, cuarta parte;

the — of July el cuarto de julio.
fowl [faʊl] s. ave; gallo, gallina; pollo.
fox [faks] s. zorra; zorro; persona astuta.
fox·y [fáksɪ] adj. zorro, zorruno, astuto.
frac·tion [frǽkʃən] s. fracción; quebrado.
frac·ture [frǽktʃəˠ] s. fractura; quiebra; rotura; v. fracturar; quebrar, romper.
frag·ile [frǽdʒəl] adj. frágil.
frag·ment [frǽgmənt] s. fragmento.
fra·grance [frégrəns] s. fragancia.
fra·grant [frégrənt] adj. fragante, oloroso.
frail [frel] adj. frágil; endeble, débil.
frail·ty [fréltɪ] s. debilidad, flaqueza.
frame [frem] s. armazón, armadura, esqueleto; estructura; marco (de un cuadro, ventana, puerta, etc.); disposición (de ánimo); **embroidery —** bastidor para bordar; **— house** casa con armazón de madera; v. formar, forjar; fabricar; enmarcar (poner en marco); inventar; **to — someone** conspirar contra una persona; **to — up a charge** forjar un cargo o acusación.
frame·work [frémwəˠk] s. armazón, esqueleto; estructura.
franc [fræŋk] s. franco (moneda francesa).
fran·chise [frǽntʃaɪz] s. (privilege) franquicia; derecho o privilegio político; (vote) sufragio, voto.
fran·ci·um [frǽnsɪəm] s. francio.
frank [fræŋk] adj. franco, sincero; **very —** francote; s. sello de franqueo; franquicia de correos; v. franquear, despachar, enviar (carta) exenta de franqueo.
frank·furt·er [frǽŋkfəˠtəˠ] s. salchicha.
frank·ness [frǽŋknɪs] s. franqueza, sinceridad.
fran·tic [frǽntɪk] adj. frenético; **-ally** adv. frenéticamente.
fra·ter·nal [frətɜˠnl] adj. fraternal.
fra·ter·ni·ty [frətɜˠnətɪ] s. fraternidad; confraternidad.
frat·er·nize [frǽtəˠnaɪz] v. fraternizar.
fraud [frɔd] s. fraude, engaño; trampa, Am. chapuza; trampista, tramposo.
fraud·u·lent [frɔ́dʒələnt] adj. fraudulento.
fray [fre] s. reyerta, riña, pelea, alboroto; raedura; v. raer(se); deshilacharse.
frayed [fred] adj. raído, deshilachado.
freak [frik] s. capricho; rareza, hombre o cosa rara; monstruosidad, fenómeno.
freck·le [frékl] s. peca; v. ponerse pecoso.
freck·led [frékld] adj. pecoso.
freck·ly [frékl] adj. pecoso.
free [fri] adj. (not bound) libre; suelto; (gratis) gratuito; exento; (generous) liberal, generoso; **— of charge** gratis; **— on board (f.o.b.)** libre a bordo; **— port** puerto franco; **postage —** franco de porte; **to give someone a — hand** dar rienda suelta o libertad de acción a una persona; **— hand drawing** dibujo a pulso, dibujo a mano; **— thinker** libre pensador; adv. libremente; gratis, de balde; v. librar; libertar; soltar; eximir; **-ly** adv. libremente; con soltura.
free·dom [fridəm] s. libertad; libre uso; exención.
freeze [friz] v. helar(se); congelar(se).
freez·ing [frizɪŋ] adj. helado, glacial; **— point** punto de congelación.
freight [fret] s. flete; carga; **— train** tren de carga, tren de mercancías; **by —** por carga; v. fletar, cargar; enviar por carga.
French [frɛntʃ] adj. francés; **to take — leave** marcharse a la francesa, irse sin despedirse; s. francés, idioma francés; **the —** los franceses.

French·man [frɛ́ntʃmən] s. francés.
fren·zy [frɛ́nzɪ] s. frenesí.
fre·quen·cy [fríkwənsɪ] s. frecuencia.
fre·quent [fríkwənt] adj. frecuente; v. frecuentar; **-ly** adv. frecuentemente, a menudo.
fresh [frɛʃ] adj. (not stale) fresco; (new) reciente; nuevo; (bold) impertinente, entremetido; **— water** agua dulce; **-ly** adv. frescamente; con frescura; nuevamente, recientemente; **-ly painted** recién pintado, acabado de pintar.
fresh·en [frɛ́ʃən] v. refrescar(se).
fresh·man [frɛ́ʃmən] s. novato, novicio, estudiante del primer año.
fresh·ness [frɛ́ʃnɪs] s. frescura; frescor, fresco; descaro.
fret [frɛt] v. irritar(se); apurarse; estar nervioso; agitarse; s. agitación, apuro, preocupación; traste (de guitarra, mandolina, etc.); **—work** calado.
fret·ful [frɛ́tfəl] adj. descontentadizo; malhumorado, enojadizo; nervioso.
fri·ar [fráɪəˠ] s. fraile ≡
fric·tion [fríkʃən] s. fricción; rozamiento; frotación; desavenencia.
Fri·day [fráɪdɪ] s. viernes.
fried [fraɪd] adj. frito; freído; p.p. de **to fry**.
friend [frɛnd] s. amigo, amiga.
friend·less [frɛ́ndlɪs] adj. sin amigos, solo.
friend·li·ness [frɛ́ndlɪnɪs] s. afabilidad; amistad.
friend·ly [frɛ́ndlɪ] adj. amistoso, afable, amigable; propicio, favorable; adv. amistosamente.
friend·ship [frɛ́nʃɪp] s. amistad.
frig·ate [frígət] s. fragata.
fright [fraɪt] s. espanto, susto; terror; espantajo; **she is a —** es un adefesio.
fright·en [fráɪtn] v. espantar, asustar, atemorizar; **to — away** espantar, ahuyentar; **to get -ed** espantarse, asustarse.
fright·ened [fráɪtnd] adj. espantado, asustado.
fright·ful [fráɪtfəl] adj. espantoso, terrible, horroroso.
frig·id [frídʒɪd] adj. frígido, frío.
fringe [frɪndʒ] s. fleco; flequillo; orla; v. adornar con fleco; orlar.
frip·per·y [frípərɪ] s. perifollos, moños, perejiles; cursilería.
frisk [frɪsk] v. retozar, cabriolar, saltar, brincar; registrar (los bolsillos), Ven., Méx. exculcar.
frisk·y [frískɪ] adj. retozón, juguetón.
frit·ter [frítəˠ] s. fritura, fruta de sartén; v. **to — away** malgastar, desperdiciar poco a poco.
fri·vol·i·ty [frɪválətɪ] s. frivolidad.
friv·o·lous [frívələs] adj. frívolo.
fro [fro]: **to and —** de una parte a otra; de aquí para allá.
frock [frak] s. vestido (de mujer); **— coat** levita.
frog [frag] s. rana; broche (de cordoncillos o galones); **— in the throat** gallo en la garganta.
frol·ic [frálɪk] s. retozo, juego; holgorio, diversión; v. retozar, travesear, juguetear.
from [frɑm, frʌm] prep. de; desde; **to take something away — a person** quitarle algo a una persona.
front [frʌnt] s. frente (m.); fachada; frontispicio; **in — of** enfrente de; delante de; **— shirt** pechera; adj. delantero; frontal; frontero; v. hacer frente a; **to — towards** mirar hacia; dar a, caer a.
fron·tier [frʌntír] s. frontera; adj. fronterizo.
frost [frɔst] s. escarcha; helada; v. escarchar; helar; cubrir de escarcha.

FO

frost·ing [frɔ́stɪŋ] *s.* escarcha, confitura (*para cubrir un pastel*).
frost·y [frɔ́stɪ] *adj.* escarchado, cubierto de escarcha; helado.
froth [frɔθ] *s.* espuma; *v.* espumar, hacer espuma; echar espuma o espumarajos; **to — at the mouth** echar espumarajos por la boca; enfurecerse.
frown [fraun] *s.* ceño; entrecejo; *v.* fruncir el ceño o las cejas; **to — at** mirar con ceño; desaprobar (*algo*).
froze [froz] *pret. de* **to freeze.**
fro·zen [frózn] *p.p. de* **to freeze.**
fru·gal [frúgl] *adj.* frugal.
fruit [frut] *s.* fruto (*en general*); fruta (*comestible*); **to eat** — comer fruta; — **tree** árbol frutal; *v.* fructificar, producir frutas.
fruit·ful [frútfəl] *adj.* fructuoso; productivo; provechoso.
fruit·less [frútlɪs] *adj.* infructuoso, improductivo, estéril.
frus·trate [frʌ́stret] *v.* frustrar.
frus·tra·tion [frʌstréʃən] *s.* frustración.
fry [fraɪ] *v.* freír(se); *s.* fritada; **small** — pececillos; gente menuda; **French fries** patatas fritas a la francesa; **-ing pan** sartén.
fudge [fʌdʒ] *s.* dulce (*usualmente de chocolate y nueces*).
fu·el [fjúəl] *s.* combustible; incentivo.
fu·gi·tive [fjúdʒətɪv] *adj.* fugitivo; transitorio; *s.* fugitivo, prófugo.
ful·fill [fulfíl] *v.* cumplir; cumplir con; realizar; llevar a cabo; llenar (*un requisito*).
ful·fill·ment [fulfílmənt] *s.* cumplimiento.
full [ful] *adj.* lleno; completo; harto; pleno; — **dress** traje de etiqueta; — **moon** plenilunio, luna llena; — **skirt** falda de vuelo entero; — **of fun** muy divertido, muy chistoso; **at** — **speed** a toda velocidad; **in** — completamente; por completo; **to the** — por completo, por entero, totalmente; *adv.* completamente, enteramente; **to know** — **well** saber perfectamente, saber a ciencia cierta; **full-blooded** de raza pura; **full-fledged** hecho y derecho; maduro; completo; **-y** *adv.* completamente, enteramente, por completo.
full·ness [fúlnɪs] *s.* plenitud; llenura.
fum·ble [fʌ́mbl] *v.* tentalear, buscar a tientas; chapucear, no coger la pelota o soltarla al correr.
fume [fjum] *v.* exhalar vapor o gas; rabiar; **-s** *s. pl.* vapores, emanaciones, gases.
fu·mi·gate [fjúməget] *v.* fumigar, sahumar, *Riopl.* humear.
fun [fʌn] *s.* diversión; burla, broma, chanza, *Carib., Méx., C.A.* choteo; **for** — en (*o de*) broma; de chanza; de chiste; **full of** — muy divertido; **to have** — divertirse; **to make** — **of** burlarse de, chancearse con, *Carib., Méx., C.A.* chotear, chotearse con; *Riopl.* jorobar.
func·tion [fʌ́ŋkʃən] *s.* función; *v.* funcionar.
fund [fʌnd] *s.* fondo, caudal; **-s** fondos, recursos; *v.* consolidar (*una deuda*); prorrogar el plazo de (*una deuda*).
fun·da·men·tal [fʌndəméntl] *adj.* fundamental; *s.* fundamento, principio.
fu·ner·al [fjúnərəl] *adj.* funeral, fúnebre; *s.* funeral, exequias, funerales.
fun·gus [fʌ́ŋgəs] *s.* hongo; fungosidad.
fun·nel [fʌ́nl] *s.* embudo; humero (*cañón de chimenea*).
fun·ny [fʌ́nɪ] *adj.* (*comical*) chistoso, cómico, gracioso, divertido; (*odd*) extraño, raro; **the**

funnies la sección cómica (*de un periódico*).
fur [fɝ] *s.* piel (*de animales peludos o lanudos*); sarro (*en la lengua*); — **coat** abrigo de pieles; *v.* forrar, cubrir o adornar con pieles.
fur·bish [fɝ́bɪʃ] *v.* acicalar, pulir.
fu·ri·ous [fjúrɪəs] *adj.* furioso.
furl [fɝl] *v.* arrollar, enrollar; plegar.
fur·lough [fɝ́lo] *s.* licencia militar; *s.* dar licencia militar.
fur·nace [fɝ́nɪs] *s.* calorífero; **blast** — alto horno.
fur·nish [fɝ́nɪʃ] *v.* (*equip*) equipar; amueblar; (*provide*) proveer, suministrar, surtir; **to** — **a room** amueblar un cuarto.
fur·ni·ture [fɝ́nɪtʃɚ] *s.* muebles, mobiliario, moblaje, mueblaje.
fur·row [fɝ́o] *s.* surco; arruga; *v.* surcar; arar.
fur·ther [fɝ́ðɚ] *adj.* adicional; más lejano, más remoto; *adv.* además; más; más lejos; *v.* promover, fomentar, adelantar.
fur·ther·more [fɝ́ðɚmor] *adv.* además.
fur·thest [fɝ́ðɪst] *adj.* (el) más lejano, (el) más remoto; *adv.* más lejos.
fur·tive [fɝ́tɪv] *adj.* furtivo.
fu·ry [fjúrɪ] *s.* furia; frenesí.
fuse [fjuz] *s.* fusible; mecha; *v.* fundir(se).
fu·se·lage [fjúzlɪdʒ] *s.* fuselaje.
fu·sion [fjúʒən] *s.* fusión; **nuclear** —fusión nuclear.
fuss [fʌs] *s.* melindre, preocupación inútil; bulla innecesaria; **to make a** — **over someone** darle a alguien demasiada importancia, desvivirse por alguien; *v.* hacer melindres, inquietarse (*por bagatelas*).
fuss·y [fʌ́sɪ] *adj.* melindroso; minucioso (*en demasía*); inquieto, nervioso; — **dress** vestido con demasiados adornos.
fu·tile [fjútl] *adj.* fútil; vano.
fu·ture [fjútʃɚ] *adj.* futuro; *s.* futuro; porvenir.
fuzz [fʌz] *s.* vello; pelusa.
fuzz·y [fʌ́zɪ] *adj.* velloso; cubierto de plumón fino; cubierto de pelusa.

G:g

gab [gæb] *v.* charlar, parlotear; *s.* charla; **gift of** — labia, facundia.
gab·ar·dine [gǽbɚdin] *s.* gabardina (*paño*).
gab·ble [gǽbl] *s.* charla, cotorreo; *v.* charlar, cotorrear.
ga·ble [gébl] *s.* gablete (*de un tejado*); — **roof** tejado de caballete o de dos aguas; — **window** ventana con gablete.
gad [gæd] *v.* vagar, callejear; andar de aquí para allá.
gadg·et [gǽdʒɪt] *s.* adminículo, artefacto, chisme.
gag [gæg] *s.* (*obstacle*) mordaza; (*joke*) broma, burla; morcilla, chiste (*improvisado por un actor*); *v.* amordazar; dar náuseas, hacer vomitar, basquear; interpolar chistes (*en la escena*).
gage *véase* **gauge.**
gai·e·ty [géətɪ] *s.* alegría, viveza, alborozo.
gai·ly [gélɪ] *adv.* alegremente; vistosamente.
gain [gen] *s.* ganancia, provecho; *v.* ganar.
gain·ful [génfl] *adj.* ganancioso.
gait [get] *s.* paso, andadura, marcha.
gale [gel] *s.* ventarrón; — **of laughter** risotada, carcajada, risada.
gall [gɔl] *s.* (*bile*) bilis, hiel; (*bitterness*) amargura; odio; descaro; — **bladder** vesícula; *v.* irritar.

gal·lant [gǽlənt] *adj.* valiente; noble; vistoso; [gəlǽnt] *adj.* galante, atento, cortés; galanteador; *s.* galán.
gal·lant·ry [gǽləntrɪ] *s.* galantería; gallardía, valor.
gal·ler·y [gǽlərɪ] *s.* galería; paraíso, gallinero *del* (*teatro*).
gal·ley [gǽlɪ] *s.* galera; cocina (*de un buque*); — **proof** galerada; — **slave** galeote.
gal·lium [gǽlɪəm] *s.* galio.
gal·lon [gǽlən] *s.* galón (*aproximadamente cuatro litros*).
gal·lop [gǽləp] *s.* galope; *v.* galopar, galopear; ir a galope.
gal·lows [gǽloz] *s.* horca.
gal·losh·es [gəláʃɪz] *s. pl.* chanclos, zapatos fuertes, zapatones.
gal·va·nom·e·ter [gǽlvənámətɚ] *s.* galvanómetro.
gam·ble [gǽmbl] *v.* jugar, apostar, aventurar (*algo*) en el juego; **to — away** perder en el juego; **to — everything** jugar el todo por el todo; — arriesgarlo todo; *s.* jugada (*en juegos de azar*), apuesta; riesgo.
gam·bol [gǽmbəl] *v.* retozar; cabriolar; juguetear; *s.* retozo, cabriola.
game [gem] *s.* juego; deporte; caza (*animales de caza y su carne*); **to make — of** mofarse de, burlarse de; *adj.* valiente, atrevido; resuelto; — **bird** ave de caza.
gam·ut [gǽmət] *s.* gama.
gan·der [gǽndɚ] *s.* ánsar, ganso.
gang [gǽŋ] *s.* cuadrilla; pandilla; juego (*de herramientas o máquinas*); *v.* agrupar(se); **to — up against** conspirar contra.
gang·plank [gǽŋplæŋk] *s.* plancha, pasamano (*de un buque*), pasarela.
gan·grene [gǽŋgrin] *s.* gangrena; *v.* gangrenar(se).
gang·ster [gǽŋstɚ] *s.* bandolero, bandido, maleante, atracador.
gang·way [gǽŋwe] *s.* paso, pasadizo; plancha, pasamano; portalón (*de un barco*); —! ¡a un lado! ¡ábranse!
gant·let = **gauntlet**.
gap [gæp] *s.* brecha, abertura; boquete; hueco; intervalo.
gape [gep] *s.* (*breach*) brecha, abertura; (*open jaws*) bostezo; boqueada; *v.* boquear, abrir la boca; estar boquiabierto (*mirando*); estar embobado; bostezar.
ga·rage [gəráʒ] *s.* garaje.
garb [garb] *s.* vestido; vestidura; aspecto, apariencia; *v.* vestir, ataviar.
gar·bage [gárbɪdʒ] *s.* desperdicios, basura.
gar·den [gárdn̩] *s.* jardín; huerta; huerto; *v.* cultivar un jardín.
gar·den·er [gárdnɚ] *s.* jardinero, hortelano; horticultor.
gar·gle [gárgl] *s.* gargarismo, *Am.* gárgaras; *v.* gargarizar, hacer gárgaras, *Am.* gargarear.
gar·land [gárlənd] *s.* guirnalda.
gar·lic [gárlɪk] *s.* ajo.
gar·ment [gármənt] *s.* prenda (*de vestir*).
gar·net [gárnɪt] *s.* granate.
gar·nish [gárnɪʃ] *s.* aderezo; adorno; *v.* aderezar; adornar; guarnecer.
gar·ret [gǽrɪt] *s.* desván, buhardilla.
gar·ri·son [gǽrəsn̩] *s.* guarnición; *v.* guarnecer o guarnicionar (*una fortaleza*).
gar·ter [gártɚ] *s.* liga (*para sujetar las medias*); *v.* sujetar con liga.
gas [gæs] *s.* (*gaseous*) gas; (*petroleum*) gasolina; — **burner** mechero; — **stove** estufa o cocina de

gas; **tear —** gas lacrimante o lacrimógeno; *v.* asfixiar con gas; envenenar con gas.
gas·e·ous [gǽsɪəs] *adj.* gaseoso.
gash [gæʃ] *s.* cuchillada, herida, incisión; *v.* dar una cuchillada, acuchillar.
gas·o·line [gǽslɪn] *s.* gasolina.
gasp [gæsp] *s.* boqueada; grito sofocado; *v.* boquear; jadear; sofocarse; abrir la boca (*de asombro*).
gas·tric [gǽstrɪk] *adj.* gástrico.
gas·tro·in·tes·ti·nal [gǽstroɪntéstɪnl̩] *adj.* gastrointestinal.
gate [get] *s.* portón, entrada; puerta; *Ven., Col.* tranquera (*puerta de trancas*).
gate·way [gétwe] *s.* paso, entrada.
gath·er [gǽðɚ] *v.* recoger; coger; reunir(se), juntar(se); deducir, colegir; fruncir (*en pliegues*); cobrar (fuerzas); **to — dust** llenarse de polvo, empolvarse; *s.* pliegue.
gath·er·ing [gǽðərɪŋ] *s.* asamblea, reunión; muchedumbre; pliegue.
gaud·y [gɔ́dɪ] *adj.* vistoso, llamativo, chillón, chillante.
gauge [gedʒ] *s.* calibrador; indicador; medidor; instrumento para medir; medida; calibre (*de un cañón, pistola, etc.*); ancho (*del ferrocarril*), *Ven.* trocha; *v.* medir; calibrar; estimar, calcular.
gaunt [gɔnt] *adj.* macilento, demacrado, flaco.
gaunt·let [gɔ́ntlɪt] *s.* guantelete; manopla; **to throw down the —** retar, desafiar.
gauze [gɔz] *s.* gasa; cendal.
gave [gev] *pret. de* **to give**.
gav·el [gǽvl] *s.* mazo del que preside.
gawk [gɔk] *v.* bobear, mirar embobado; *s.* simplón, bobo.
gawk·y [gɔ́kɪ] *adj.* torpe, desmañado; bobo.
gay [ge] *adj.* alegre; vivo; vistoso; festivo.
gay·e·ty *véase* **gaiety**.
gaze [gez] *s.* mirada (fija); *v.* contemplar, mirar con fijeza, clavar la mirada.
ga·zette [gəzɛ́t] *s.* gaceta.
gear [gɪr] *s.* (*equipment*) aperos; herramientas; aparejo; equipo; (*wheel*) rueda dentada; (*assembly*) engranaje (*de ruedas dentadas*); **foot—** calzado; **low —** primera velocidad; **steering —** mecanismo de dirección; **to be in —** estar engranado; **to shift —** cambiar de engrane o velocidad; **to throw in —** engranar; **to throw out of —** desengranar; **—shift lever** palanca de engrane, palanca de cambios; *v.* engranar.
geese [gis] *pl. de* **goose**.
Gei·ger count·er [gáɪgɚkáʊntɚ] *s.* contador (de) Geiger.
gel·a·tin [dʒélətn̩] *s.* gelatina, jaletina.
gem [dʒɛm] *s.* gema, piedra preciosa; joya, alhaja, panecillo, bollo.
gem·i·nate [dʒɛ́mənet] *v.* geminar(se).
gen·der [dʒɛ́ndɚ] *s.* género.
gene [dʒin] *s.* gen.
ge·ne·al·o·gy [dʒiniǽlədʒɪ] *s.* genealogía.
gen·er·al [dʒɛ́nərəl] *adj. & s.* general; **in —** en general, por lo común, por lo general; — **delivery** lista de correo.
gen·er·al·i·ty [dʒɛnərǽlətɪ] *s.* generalidad.
gen·er·al·ize [dʒɛ́nərəlaɪz] *v.* generalizar.
gen·er·ate [dʒɛ́nəret] *v.* engendrar; producir; originar.
gen·er·a·tion [dʒɛnəréʃən] *s.* generación; producción.
gen·er·a·tor [dʒɛ́nəetɚ] *s.* generador.
ge·ner·ic [dʒənérɪk] *adj.* genérico.

gen·er·os·i·ty [dʒɛnərásətɪ] s. generosidad.
gen·er·ous [dʒɛnərəs] adj. generoso; magnánimo, liberal; amplio; abundante.
ge·net·ics [dʒənétɪks] s. genética.
gen·ial [dʒínjəl] adj. genial, afable.
gen·i·tive [dʒénətɪv] adj. & s. genitivo.
gen·ius [dʒínjəs] s. genio; ingenio, talento.
gen·teel [dʒɛntíl] adj. gentil, cortés; elegante; gallardo.
gen·tile [dʒéntaɪ] adj. & s. gentil.
gen·tle [dʒéntl] adj. suave; afable; apacible; manso; gentil.
gen·tle·man [dʒéntl|mən] s. caballero; **gentlemen** pl. caballeros; señores.
gen·tle·man·ly [dʒént|mənlɪ] adj. caballeroso, caballero, cortés.
gen·tle·ness [dʒéntlnɪs] s. suavidad, dulzura, apacibilidad; mansedumbre.
gen·tly [dʒéntlɪ] adv. suavemente; despacio; dulcemente; con ternura; mansamente.
gen·u·ine [dʒénjʊɪn] adj. genuino; sincero.
ge·o·graph·i·cal [dʒiəgrǽfɪkl] adj. geográfico.
ge·og·ra·phy [dʒiágrəfɪ] s. geografía.
ge·o·log·i·cal [dʒiəládʒɪkl] adj. geológico.
ge·ol·o·gy [dʒiálədʒɪ] s. geología.
ge·o·met·ric [dʒiəmétrɪk] adj. geométrico.
ge·om·e·try [dʒiámətrɪ] s. geometría.
ge·o·phys·ics [dʒiofízɪks] s. geofísica.
ge·ra·ni·um [dʒərénɪəm] s. geranio.
germ [dʒɝm] s. germen; microbio.
Ger·man [dʒɝmən] adj. & s. alemán.
ger·mane [dʒɝmén] adj. pertinente, relacionado.
ger·ma·ni·um [dʒɝménɪəm] s. germanio.
ger·mi·nate [dʒɝmənət] v. germinar.
ger·und [dʒɛrənd] s. gerundio.
ges·ta·tion [dʒɛstéʃən] s. gestación.
ges·tic·u·late [dʒɛstíkjəlet] v. gesticular, hacer gestos o ademanes, accionar, manotear.
ges·ture [dʒéstʃɚ] s. gesto; ademán; **a mere —** una pura formalidad; v. gesticular, hacer gestos.
get [gɛt] v. (obtain) obtener, adquirir, lograr, conseguir; (earn) recibir, ganar; (reach) llegar (a); traer; (catch) coger, atrapar; preparar (la lección, la comida, etc.); **to — along** llevarse bien (con alguien); ir pasándolo (o ir pasándola); **to — angry** ponerse enojado, enojarse; **to — away** escaparse; irse; **to — down** bajar; **to — ill** ponerse enfermo, enfermar(se); **to — in** entrar; meter(se); llegar; **to — married** casarse; **to — off the train** bajar del tren; apearse del tren; **to — old** envejecer(se); **to — on** subir a; montar; **to — out** salir; irse; sacar; divulgarse (un secreto); **to — over** pasar por encima de; recuperarse de (una enfermedad); olvidar (una ofensa); pasársele a uno (el susto); **to — ready** preparar(se); alistar(se); **to — rich** enriquecerse, hacerse rico; **to — rid of** deshacerse de, desprenderse de; **to — through** pasar; terminar; **to — together** juntar(se), reunir(se); ponerse de acuerdo; **to — up** levantarse; **I got him to do it** le persuadí a que lo hiciese; **I (have) got to do it** tengo que hacerlo; **I don't — it** no lo comprendo; **that's what -s me** (or -s my goat) eso es lo que me irrita.
ghast·ly [gǽstlɪ] adj. horrible; pálido, lívido, cadavérico.
ghost [gost] s. espectro, fantasma; **the Holy Ghost** el Espíritu Santo; **not to have the — of a notion of** no tener la más remota idea de; **— writer** colaborador anónimo.
ghost·ly [góstlɪ] adj. como un espectro; de

espectros, de aparecidos.
gi·ant [dʒáɪənt] s. gigante; adj. gigantesco; enorme.
gid·dy [gídɪ] adj. ligero de cascos, frívolo; voluble, inconstante; desvanecido; **— speed** velocidad vertiginosa.
gift [gɪft] s. regalo; dádiva; don; dote, talento, prenda; donación.
gift·ed [gíftɪd] adj. talentoso, de talento.
gi·gan·tic [dʒaɪgǽntɪk] adj. gigantesco.
gig·gle [gígl] s. risita, risilla; risa falsa; v. reírse falsamente; reírse sofocando la voz; reír con una risilla afectada.
gild [gɪld] v. dorar.
gill [gɪl] s. agalla (de pez).
gilt [gɪlt] adj. & s. dorado; pret. & p.p. de **to gild**.
gim·mick [gímɪk] s. adminículo.
gin [dʒɪn] s. ginebra (licor).
gin·ger [dʒíndʒɚ] s. jengibre; **— ale** cerveza de jengibre.
gin·ger·bread [dʒíndʒɚbrɛd] s. pan de jengibre; ornato de mal gusto.
ging·ham [gíŋəm] s. guinga (tela de algodón).
gip·sy véase **gypsy**.
gi·raffe [dʒərǽf] s. jirafa.
gird [gɝd] v. ceñir; rodear; **to — oneself for** prepararse para.
gir·dle [gɝdl] s. ceñidor; cinto; faja; v. ceñir; fajar; cercar.
girl [gɝl] s. niña; muchacha; joven; chica, moza; criada.
girl·hood [gɝlhʊd] s. niñez; mocedad, juventud.
girl·ish [gɝlɪʃ] adj. pueril; de niña, de muchacha; juvenil.
girt [gɝt] pret. & p.p. de **to gird**; v. véase **gird**.
girth [gɝθ] s. circunferencia; cincha (para caballos); faja; v. cinchar; ceñir.
gist [dʒɪst] s. substancia, esencia.
give [gɪv] v. dar; regalar; ceder; dar de sí; **to — away** regalar; entregar; revelar (un secreto); **to — back** devolver; **to — birth** dar a luz, parir; **to — in** ceder; darse por vencido; **to — off** emitir; **to — out** divulgar; repartir; agotarse; **to — up** abandonar; desistir; renunciar a; perder la esperanza; rendir(se); ceder, darse por vencido; s. elasticidad.
giv·en [gívən] p.p. de **to give**; adj. (presented) (dado); regalado; (inclined) adicto, entregado; dispuesto, inclinado; **— name** nombre de pila, nombre de bautismo; **— time** hora determinada; **— that** dada que, suspuesto que.
giv·er [gívɚ] s. dador, donador.
gla·cial [gléʃəl] adj. glacial.
gla·cier [gléʃɚ] s. glaciar, helero.
glad [glæd] adj. contento; alegre; **to be — to** alegrarse de, tener mucho gusto en (o de); **-ly** adv. alegremente; con mucho gusto; de buena gana.
glad·den [glǽdn] v. regocijar, alegrar.
glade [gled] s. claro herboso (en un bosque).
glad·ness [glǽdnɪs] s. alegría, gozo.
glam·our [glǽmɚ] s. encanto, hechizo; fascinación, embrujo; **— girl** niña hechicera.
glam·or·ous [glǽmərəs] adj. fascinador, hechicero.
glance [glæns] s. mirada, vistazo, ojeada; vislumbre; v. echar (o dar) un vistazo; vislumbrar; pegar de soslayo; **to — off** rebotar de soslayo (o de lado).
gland [glænd] s. glándula.
glare [glɛr] s. (light) resplandor, relumbre; (stare) mirada furiosa; v. resplandecer, relumbrar; **to — at** mirar enfurecido a.

glass [glæs] *s.* (*substance*) vidrio; cristal;
(*receptacle*) vaso; copa (*de cristal*); (*eye*) lente;
looking — espejo; **-es** anteojos, lentes, gafas;
adj. de vidrio; — **blower** vidriero, soplador de
vidrio; — **case** escaparate.

glass·ware [glǽswɛr] *s.* vajilla de cristal, cristalería;
— **shop** cristalería.

glass·y [glǽsɪ] *adj.* vidrioso.

glau·co·ma [glɔkómə] *s.* glaucoma.

glaze [glez] *s.* vidriado; lustre; superficie lustrosa
o glaseada; *v.* vidriar; glasear; lustrar; poner
vidrios a.

gla·zier [gléʒɚ] *s.* vidriero.

gleam [glim] *s.* destello, rayo, fulgor, viso; *v.*
destellar, fulgurar, centellear.

glean [glin] *v.* recoger; espigar.

glee [gli] *s.* regocijo; júbilo; — **club** orfeón, masa
coral.

glib [glɪb] *adj.* locuaz; de mucha labia; — **excuse**
excusa fácil.

glide [glaɪd] *s.* deslizamiento; ligadura (*en música*);
planeo (*de un aeroplano*); *v.* deslizarse;
resbalarse; planear (*un aeroplano*).

glid·er [gláɪdɚ] *s.* deslizador, planeador
(*aeroplano*).

glim·mer [glímɚ] *s.* vislumbre; viso; titileo; — **of**
hope rayo de esperanza; *v.* titilar, centellear.

glimpse [glɪmps] *s.* vislumbre; vistazo, ojeada; **to**
catch a — **of** vislumbrar; *v.* vislumbrar.

glint [glɪnt] *s.* fulgor, rayo, destello.

glis·ten [glísn̩] *v.* relucir, brillar.

glit·ter [glítɚ] *s.* lustre, brillo, resplandor; *v.*
relumbrar, relucir, brillar.

gloat [glot] *v.* gozarse (en), deleitarse (en);
relamerse (*de gusto*).

globe [glob] *s.* globo; esfera.

glob·ule [glábjul] *s.* glóbulo.

gloom [glum] *s.* lobreguez, sombra; abatimiento,
tristeza, melancolía.

gloom·y [glúmɪ] *adj.* lóbrego, sombrío; triste,
melancólico; abatido.

glo·ri·fy [glórəfaɪ] *v.* glorificar.

glo·ri·ous [glórɪəs] *adj.* glorioso; espléndido.

glo·ry [glórɪ] *s.* gloria; *v.* gloriarse; vanagloriarse.

gloss [glɔs] *s.* (*shine*) lustre, brillo; pulimento;
(*note*) glosa, comentario; *v.* lustrar, dar brillo a;
pulir; glosar, comentar; **to** — **over** encubrir, dar
colorido de bueno (*a algo que no lo es*).

glos·sa·ry [glásərɪ] *s.* glosario.

gloss·y [glɔ́sɪ] *adj.* lustroso; pulido.

glove [glʌv] *s.* guante; *v.* enguantar, poner guantes.

glow [glo] *s.* incandescencia; brillo (*de un ascua*);
calor vivo; fosforescencia; *v.* lucir, brillar (*como*
un ascua); fosforecer; estar encendido o
enardecido.

glow·ing [glóɪŋ] *adj.* encendido, ardiente.

glow·worm [glówȝm] *s.* luciérnaga.

glue [glu] *s.* cola (*para pegar*); *v.* encolar, pegar
(*con cola*).

glum [glʌm] *adj.* hosco.

glut·ton [glʌ́tn̩] *s.* glotón.

glut·ton·ous [glʌ́tn̩əs] *adj.* glotón; goloso.

glut·ton·y [glʌ́tn̩ɪ] *s.* gula, glotonería.

glyc·er·in [glísəɪn] *s.* glicerina.

gnarled [nɑrld] *adj.* nudoso, torcido.

gnash [næʃ] *v.* crujir, rechinar (*los dientes*).

gnat [næt] *s.* jején (*insecto*).

gnaw [nɔ] *v.* roer.

gnu [ñu] *s.* nu.

go [go] *v.* (*move*) ir(se); andar; (*function*) marchar,
funcionar, servir; **to** — **around** andar alrededor

de; dar vueltas; **to** — **away** irse; **to** — **back on**
one's word faltar a la palabra; **to** — **by** pasar
por; guiarse por (*una regla*); **to** — **down** bajar;
to — **insane** volverse loco; **to** — **into** entrar en;
investigar; caber en; **to** — **off** hacer explosión;
dispararse; irse, salir disparado; **to** — **on**
proseguir, continuar; **to** — **out** salir; apagarse;
to — **over** pasar por encima de; examinar con
cuidado; releer; repasar; recorrer; **to** — **to sleep**
dormirse; **to** — **under** ir o pasar por debajo de;
hundirse; **to** — **up** subir; **to let** — soltar; **there**
is not enough to — **around** no hay (bastante)
para todos; *s.* empuje, energía; **it is a** — trato
hecho; **to be on the** — estar en continuo
movimiento.

goad [god] *s.* aguijón; puya; *v.* aguijonear; aguijar,
incitar.

goal [gol] *s.* meta; fin, objetivo.

goat [got] *s.* cabra; **male** — macho cabrío; **to be**
the — ser la víctima, pagar el pato.

goat·ee [goti] *s.* perilla.

goat·herd [góthɚd] *s.* cabrero.

gob·ble [gábl̩] *v.* tragar, engullir; **to** — **up**
engullirse.

gob·bler [gáblɚ] *s.* pavo.

go-be·tween [góbətwin] *s.* medianero.

gob·let [gáblɪt] *s.* copa grande.

gob·lin [gáblɪn] *s.* duende.

god [gɑd] *s.* dios; **God** Dios.

god·child [gádtʃaɪld] *s.* ahijado, ahijada.

god·dess [gádɪs] *s.* diosa.

god·fa·ther [gádfɑðɚ] *s.* padrino.

god·less [gádlɪs] *adj.* impío, ateo.

god·like [gádlaɪk] *adj.* como Dios; divino.

god·ly [gádlɪ] *adj.* pío, devoto; divino.

god·moth·er [gádmʌðɚ] *s.* madrina.

gog·gles [gáglz] *s. pl.* antiparras, gafas.

go·ing [góɪŋ] *ger.* & *adj.* que anda, marcha o
funciona bien; **to be** — **in**, irse; *s.* ida, partida;
comings and -s idas y venidas.

goi·ter [gɔ́ɪtɚ] *s.* papera; bocio; *Ríopl.*, *Méx.*,
C.A. buche; *C.A.* güecho.

gold [gold] *s.* oro; — **standard** patrón de oro.

gold·en [góldn̩] *adj.* de oro; áureo; dorado.

gold·finch [góldfɪntʃ] *s.* jilguero amarillo.

gold·fish [góldfɪʃ] *s.* carpa dorada.

gold·smith [góldsmɪθ] *s.* orfebre; — **shop**
orfebrería.

golf [gɑlf] *s.* golf.

gon·do·la [gándələ] *s.* góndola; cabina (*de una*
aeronave); — **car** vagón de mercancías (*sin*
techo), *Am.* jaula.

gone [gɔn] *p.p.* de **to go** & *adj.* ido; perdido; **he is**
— se fué; **it is all** — se acabó; ya no hay más.

gong [gɔŋ] *s.* gong, batintín.

good [gʊd] *adj.* bueno; válido; valedero; —
afternoon buenas tardes; — **day** buenos días;
adiós; — **evening** buenas noches; — **morning**
buenos días; — **night** buenas noches; **Good**
Friday Viernes Santo; **for** — para siempre,
permanentemente; **to have a** — **time** pasar un
buen rato; divertirse; **to make** — pagar,
compensar; cumplir (*una promesa*); salir bien,
tener buen éxito; *s.* bien; beneficio, provecho,
ventaja; **-s** bienes, efectos; mercancías.

good-bye [gʊdbáɪ] *s.* & *interj.* adiós.

good-look·ing [gúdlúkɪŋ] *adj.* bien parecido, guapo.

good·ly [gúdlɪ] *adj.* grande, considerable; de buena
apariencia.

good-na·tured [gúdnétʃɚd] *adj.* de buen genio,
bonachón, afable.

GE

good·ness [gúdnɪs] s. bondad; —! ¡Dios mío! ¡cielos!

good·y [gúdɪ] s. golosina, bonbón, dulce; interj. ¡qué gusto!; **goody-goody** beatuco (el que afecta virtud), papanatas.

goof [guf] v. chapucear.

goose [gus] s. ganso; bobo, tonto; — **flesh** carne de gallina.

goose·ber·ry [gúsbɛrɪ] s. grosella; grosellero (arbusto).

go·pher [gófɚ] s. roedor semejante a la ardilla.

gore [gor] s. (blood) cuajarón de sangre; sangre; (cloth) cuchillo (Am. cuchilla), sesga (tira de lienzo en figura de cuchilla); v. acornear, herir con los cuernos; hacer una sesga en (un traje).

gorge [gɔrdʒ] s. cañada, barranco, barranca; v. engullir(se), atracarse.

gor·geous [gɔ́rdʒəs] adj. primoroso, vistoso, hermosísimo.

go·ril·la [gərílə] s. gorila.

go·ry [gɔ́rɪ] adj. sangriento, ensangrentado.

gos·pel [gáspl] s. evangelio; **it is the — truth** es la pura verdad.

gos·sip [gásɪp] s. (rumors) chisme, chismería; murmuración, hablilla; (person) murmurador, chismero, chismoso; v. chismear, murmurar.

gos·sip·y [gásəpɪ] adj. chismero, chismoso.

got [gɑt] pret. & p.p. de **to get**.

Goth·ic [gáθɪk] adj. gótico; s. gótico (idioma de los godos); estilo gótico.

got·ten [gátn̩] p.p. de **to get**.

gouge [gaʊdʒ] s. gubia (especie de formón o escoplo curvo); v. excavar con gubia, formón o escoplo; **to — someone's eyes out** sacarle los ojos a alguien.

gourd [gord] s. calabaza.

gour·met [gʊrmé] s. gastrónomo.

gout [gaʊt] s. gota (enfermedad).

gov·ern [gávɚn] v. gobernar; regir.

gov·ern·ess [gávɚnɪs] s. institutriz.

gov·ern·ment [gávɚmənt] s. gobierno.

gov·ern·ment·al [gʌvɚméntl̩] adj. gubernativo.

gov·er·nor [gávɚnɚ] s. gobernador; regulador (de una máquina).

gown [gaʊn] s. vestido (de mujer); toga (de un juez, profesor, etc.); **dressing — bata**.

grab [græb] v. agarrar asir; arrebatar; s. arrebatiña; agarro, agarrón; presa.

grace [gres] s. gracia; favor; donaire, garbo; **to say — bendecir** la mesa, dar gracias; **to be in the good -s of someone** gozar del favor de uno; v. agraciar, adornar.

grace·ful [grésfəl] adj. gracioso, agraciado, garboso; **-ly** adv. graciosamente, con gracia, con garbo.

grace·ful·ness [grésfəlnɪs] s. gracia, donaire, gallardía, garbo.

gra·cious [gréʃəs] adj. afable; cortés; —! ¡válgame Dios!

gra·da·tion [gredéʃən] s. graduación; gradación; grado.

grade [gred] s. (degree) grado; (mark) nota, calificación; (slope) cuesta, declive, pendiente; Am. gradiente; — **crossing** cruce a nivel (de un ferrocarril con una carretera); **the -s** la escuela primaria; v. graduar, clasificar; calificar, dar una calificación; nivelar (un camino).

grad·u·al [grǽdʒʊəl] adj. gradual; **-ly** adv. gradualmente, poco a poco.

grad·u·ate [grǽdʒʊɪt] adj. graduado, que ha recibido un grado académico; **to do — work**

cursar asignaturas superiores (al bachillerato); s. estudiante graduado (que estudia para licenciado o doctor); [grǽdʒʊet] v. graduar(se).

grad·u·a·tion [grædʒʊéʃən] s. graduación.

graft [græft] s. (insertion) injerto; tejido injertado; (extortion) sisa, malversación (de caudales públicos); ganancia ilegal, Am. mordida; v. injertar; malversar fondos ajenos; sisar, exigir pago ilegal, Am. morder.

graft·er [grǽftɚ] s. malversador (de fondos públicos), estafador, C.A. coyote, Méx. mordelón.

grain [gren] s. (cereal) grano; (markings) fibra (de la madera), veta (del mármol o madera); **against the — a** (o al) redopelo, a contrapelo.

gram [græm] s. gramo.

gram·mar [grǽmɚ] s. gramática; — **school** escuela primaria.

gram·mat·i·cal [grəmǽtɪkl̩] adj. gramatical, gramático.

gran·a·ry [grǽnərɪ] s. granero.

grand [grænd] adj. grande; grandioso, admirable; magnífico.

grand·child [grǽntʃaɪld] s. nieto.

grand·chil·dren [grǽntʃɪldrən] s. pl. nietos.

grand·daugh·ter [grǽndɔtɚ] s. nieta.

gran·deur [grǽndʒɚ] s. grandeza, grandiosidad; majestad.

grand·fa·ther [grǽnfaðɚ] s. abuelo.

gran·di·ose [grǽndɪos] adj. grandioso, magnífico.

grand·ma [grǽnma] s. abuela, abuelita, Am. mamá grande.

grand·moth·er [grǽnmʌðɚ] s. abuela.

grand·ness [grǽndnɪs] s. grandeza; grandiosidad; magnificencia.

grand·pa [grǽnpa] s. abuelo, abuelito, Am. papá grande.

grand·par·ent [grǽnpɛrənt] s. abuelo, abuela; **-s** abuelos.

grand·son [grǽnsʌn] s. nieto.

grand·stand [grǽnstænd] s. andanada, gradería cubierta.

grange [grendʒ] s. granja; asociación de agricultores.

gran·ite [grǽnɪt] s. granito (roca).

gran·ny [grǽnɪ] s. abuelita; viejecita, viejita.

grant [grænt] s. concesión; subvención; donación; transferencia de propiedad (mediante escritura); v. conceder; otorgar; ceder, transferir (derechos, propiedad, etc.); **to take for -ed** dar por supuesto, dar por sentado.

gran·u·late [grǽnjələt] v. granular(se).

grape [grep] s. uva.

grape·fruit [grépfrut] s. toronja; Esp. pomelo.

grape·vine [grépvaɪn] s. vid; parra.

graph [græf] s. diagrama, gráfica; v. hacer una gráfica o diagrama.

graph·ic [grǽfɪk] adj. gráfico.

graph·ite [grǽfaɪt] s. grafito.

grap·ple [grǽpl̩] v. luchar, pelear cuerpo a cuerpo; aferrar, agarrar.

grasp [græsp] v. (seize) agarrar; asir; apretar; (understand) comprender; abarcar; s. agarro, asimiento; apretón de manos; **to be within one's — estar** al alcance de uno; **to have a good — of a subject** estar fuerte en una materia, saber a fondo una materia.

grass [græs] s. hierba; césped; pasto; Méx. zacate; Méx., Ven., Col. grama.

grass·hop·per [grǽshapɚ] s. saltamontes, saltón, Méx., C.A. chapulín.

grass·roots [grǽsruts] *adj.* del pueblo; de la gente.
grass·y [grǽsɪ] *adj.* herboso, *Am.* pastoso.
grate [gret] *s.* (*window*) reja, verja, enrejado; (*grill*) parrilla, brasero; *v.* enrejar, poner enrejado; crujir, rechinar (*los dientes*); rallar (*queso*); **to —** **on** molestar, irritar.
grate·ful [grétfəl] *adj.* agradecido; grato, agradable.
grat·er [grétɚ] *s.* rallador.
grat·i·fy [grǽtəfaɪ] *v.* complacer, dar gusto, agradar; satisfacer.
grat·ing [grétɪŋ] *s.* reja, enrejado, verja; *adj.* rechinante; molesto, áspero.
gra·tis [grétɪs] *adv.* gratis, de balde.
grat·i·tude [grǽtətjud] *s.* gratitud.
gra·tu·i·tous [grətjúətəs] *adj.* gratuito; sin fundamento; **— statement** afirmación arbitraria.
grave [grev] *adj.* grave; serio; *s.* tumba sepulcro, sepultura; acento grave; **—stone** losa o lápida sepulcral.
grave·dig·ger [grévdɪgɚ] *s.* sepulturero.
grav·el [grǽvl] *s.* grava, guijo, cascajo, *Am.* maicillo; cálculos (*en los riñones, la vejiga, etc.*); mal de piedra; *v.* cubrir con grava.
grave·yard [grévjɑrd] *s.* cementerio.
grav·i·ta·tion [grævɪtéʃən] *s.* atracción; gravitación.
grav·i·ty [grǽvətɪ] *s.* gravedad; seriedad.
gra·vy [grévɪ] *s.* salsa; jugo (*de carne*).
gray [gre] *adj.* gris; cano; pelicano; entrecano (*que empieza a encanecer*); **— horse** rucio, tordo, tordillo; **— matter** seso; **gray-headed** canoso; *s.* gris, color gris; *v.* encanecer; poner(se) gris.
gray·ish [gréɪʃ] *adj.* grisáceo, pardusco; **— hair** pelo entrecano.
gray·ness [grénɪs] *s.* grisura, gris, calidad de gris; encanecimiento.
graze [grez] *v.* (*feed*) pacer; apacentar, *Am.* pastear, pastar; (*brush*) rozar; raspar; *s.* roce, rozón, raspadura.
grease [gris] *s.* grasa; *v.* engrasar; untar; lubricar; **to — the palm** untar la mano, sobornar.
greas·y [grísɪ] *adj.* grasiento, grasoso; pringoso.
great [gret] *adj.* gran(de); eminente; magnífico, excelente; **a — deal** una gran cantidad; muchos; mucho; **a — many** muchos; **a — while** un largo rato o tiempo; **-ly** *adv.* grandemente; mucho; muy; en gran parte; sobremanera.
great-grand·child [grétgrǽntʃaɪld] *s.* biznieto.
great-grand·fa·ther [grétgrǽnfɑðɚ] *s.* bisabuelo.
great-grand·moth·er [grétgrǽnmʌðɚ] *s.* bisabuela.
great·ness [grétnɪs] *s.* grandeza.
Gre·cian [gríʃən] *adj. & s.* griego.
greed [grid] *s.* codicia; avaricia; gula.
greed·i·ly [grídlɪ] *adv.* vorazmente; con avaricia; con gula.
greed·i·ness [grídɪnɪs] *s.* codicia; avaricia; gula; voracidad.
greed·y [grídɪ] *adj.* codicioso; avaro; goloso; voraz.
Greek [grik] *adj. & s.* griego.
green [grin] *adj.* (*color*) verde; (*novice*) novato, inexperto; **to grow —** verdear; **the fields look —** verdean los campos; *s.* verde, verdor; césped; prado; campo de golf; **-s** verduras, hortalizas.
green·horn [grínhɔrn] *s.* novato, pipiolo.
green·house [grínhaʊs] *s.* invernáculo, invernadero.
green·ish [grínɪʃ] *adj.* verdoso.
green·ness [grínnɪs] *s.* (*color*) verdor, verdura; (*experience*) inmadurez; impericia.
greet [grit] *v.* saludar; **to — each other** saludarse.
greet·ing [grítɪŋ] *s.* saludo; salutación; **-s!** ¡salud! ¡saludos!
gre·nade [grɪnéd] *s.* granada, bomba pequeña.

grew [gru] *pret. de* **to grow.**
grey = **gray.**
grey·ish = **gray.**
grey·ness = **grayness.**
grey·hound [gréhaʊnd] *s.* lebrel, galgo.
grid·dle [grídl] *s.* tartera; plancha (*para tapar el hornillo*).
grief [grif] *s.* dolor, pesar; **to come to —** sobrevenirle a uno una desgracia; fracasar.
griev·ance [grívəns] *s.* queja; resentimiento; motivo de queja, injusticia, ofensa.
grieve [griv] *v.* afligir(se); lamentar(se), acongojar(se).
grieved [grivd] *adj.* penado.
griev·ous [grívəs] *adj.* doloroso, penoso; grave, altroz.
grill [grɪl] *s.* parrilla; **men's —** restaurante para hombres; *v.* asar en parrillas; interrogar (*a un sospechoso*).
grim [grɪm] *adj.* austero, áspero; fiero; torvo, siniestro.
gri·mace [grɪmés] *s.* mueca, gesto; *v.* hacer muecas o gestos.
grime [graɪm] *s.* mugre; *v.* ensuciar.
grim·y [gráɪmɪ] *adj.* mugriento.
grin [grɪn] *s.* sonrisa abierta; sonrisa maliciosa; sonrisa canina; *v.* sonreír (*mostrando mucho los dientes*).
grind [graɪnd] *v.* (*crush*) moler; machacar; (*sharpen*) afilar, amolar; (*study hard*) afanarse demasiado; estudiar con empeño; **to — a hand organ** tocar el organillo; **to — one's teeth** rechinar los dientes; *s.* molienda; faena, trabajo penoso; estudiante tesonero; **the daily —** la rutina diaria.
grind·er [gráɪndɚ] *s.* moledor; molinillo (*para moler café*); amolador, afilador; muela (*piedra para afilar*); muela (*diente molar*).
grind·stone [gráɪndston] *s.* piedra de amolar.
grip [grɪp] *v.* (*seize*) agarrar; asir; apretar; empuñar; (*impress*) impresionar; conmover; *s.* agarro; asimiento; apretón; asidero, asa; (*suitcase*) valija, maletín; *Méx.*, velís; **to have a — on someone** tener agarrado a alguien.
grippe [grɪp] *s.* gripe, influenza.
grit [grɪt] *s.* (*gravel*) arenilla, arena; piedra arenisca; (*pluck*) firmeza, tesón; **-s** maíz, avena, o trigo a medio moler; *v.* rechinar, crujir.
grit·ty [grítɪ] *adj.* arenoso; valeroso, firme.
griz·zly [grízlɪ] *adj.* grisáceo, pardusco; **— bear** oso pardo.
groan [gron] *s.* gemido, quejido; *v.* gemir; quejarse; crujir (*por exceso de peso*).
gro·cer [grósɚ] *s.* abacero, *Méx.* abarrotero, *Carib.*, *C.A.* bodeguero; *Ríopl.* almacenero.
gro·cer·y [grósɚɪ] *s.* abacería, tienda de comestibles, *Méx.* abarrotería, *Méx.* tienda de abarrotes; *Carib.*, *C.A.* bodega; **groceries** comestibles, *Méx.* abarrotes.
groom [grum] *s.* (*bridegroom*) novio; (*stable groom*) caballerizo, mozo de caballeriza; establero; *v.* almohazar, limpiar con la almohaza (*a los caballos*), cuidar (*a los caballos*); **to — oneself** asearse, peinarse, componerse; **well-groomed** bien vestido, aseado, limpio.
groove [gruv] *s.* estría, ranura, acanaladura; surco (*en un camino*); muesca, encaje; *v.* acanalar, estriar.
grope [grop] *v.* tentalear, tentar, andar a tientas; **to — for** buscar tentando, buscar a tientas.
gross [gros] *adj.* grueso; burdo; tosco; grosero;

— earnings ganancias totales; **— ignorance** ignorancia crasa; **— weight** peso bruto; *s.* grueso, totalidad; gruesa (*doce docenas*).

gro·tesque [grotésk] *adj.* & *s.* grotesco.

grot·to [gráto] *s.* gruta.

grouch [graᴜtʃ] *s.* mal humor; gruñón, refunfuñón, cascarrabias; **to have a — against someone** tenerle ojeriza (*o* mala voluntad) a una persona; guardarle rencor a alguien; *v.* grunñir, refunfuñar; estar de mal humor.

grouch·y [gráᴜtʃɪ] *adj.* gruñón, refunfuñón, malhumorado, cascarrabias.

ground [graᴜnd] *s.* (*earth*) suelo, tierra; terreno; (*motive*) motivo, rezón; base, fundamento; **— crew** personal de tierra; **-s** heces, desperdicios, sedimento; **— floor** piso bajo, planta baja, **to break** — roturar, arar; cavar; **to give —** retroceder, ceder; **to hold one's —** mantenerse firme; *v.* conectar (*un alambre*) con la tierra; encallar (*una embarcación*); aterrizar (*un aeroplano*); **to be well -ed** poseer las bases o principios fundamentales; *pret.* & *p.p. de* **to grind.**

ground·less [gráᴜndlɪs] *adj.* infundado.

group [grup] *s.* grupo; **— insurance** seguros sociales; *v.* agrupar.

grove [grov] *s.* arboleda, bosquecillo.

grow [gro] *v.* crecer; brotar; cultivar; criar; producir; **to — angry** ponerse enojado o enfadado, enfadarse, enojarse; **to — better** ponerse mejor, mejorar; **to — difficult** dificultarse, hacerse difícil; **to — late** hacerse tarde; **to — old** ponerse viejo, envejecer; **to — out of a habit** perder la costumbre; **to — pale** ponerse pálido, palidecer; **to — tired** cansarse.

growl [graᴜl] *s.* gruñido; *v.* gruñir.

growl·er [gráᴜlə·] *s.* gruñón; regañón.

grown [gron] *p.p. de* **to grow** & *adj.* crecido; desarrollado; **— man** hombre maduro, hombre hecho; **— with trees** poblado de árboles.

grown-up [grónʌp] *adj.* crecido, adulto; *s.* adulto.

growth [groθ] *s.* (*increase*) crecimiento, acrecentamiento; aumento; (*development*) desarrollo; (*vegetation*) vegetación; (*tissue*) tumor, lobanillo, excrecencia.

grub·by [grábɪ] *adj.* roñoso; sucio.

grudge [grʌdʒ] *s.* inquina, rencor, resentimiento, mala voluntad; *v.* tener inquina, evidia o mala voluntad; dar de mala gana.

gruff [grʌf] *adj.* áspero, rudo; grosero.

grum·ble [grámbl] *s.* refunfuño, gruñido, queja; *v.* refunfuñar, gruñir, quejarse.

grum·bler [grámblə·] *s.* gruñón; regañón.

grump·y [grámpɪ] *adj.* malhumorado; gruñón.

grunt [grʌnt] *s.* gruñido, *Méx., C.A., Col., Ven.* pujido; *v.* gruñir, *Riopl., Méx., C.A., Ven., Andes* pujar.

guar·an·tee [gærəntí] *s.* garantía; fianza; fiador; *v.* garantizar; dar fianza; salir fiador de.

guar·an·tor [gærəntə·] *s.* fiador.

guar·an·ty [gærəntɪ] *s.* garantía; fianza; fiador; *v. véase* **guarantee.**

guard [gɑrd] *s.* guarda; guardia; resguardo; **to be on —** estar alerta; estar en guardia; **to keep —** vigilar; *v.* guardar; resguardar; vigilar; **to — (oneself) against** guardarse de.

guard·i·an [gárdɪən] *s.* guardián, custodio; tutor; **— angel** ángel custodio, ángel de la guarda.

guard·i·an·ship [gárdɪənʃɪp] *s.* tutela; guarda, custodia.

guard·rail [gárdrel] *s.* baranda.

Gua·te·ma·lan [gwɑtəmálən] *adj.* & *s.* guatemalteco.

guess [gɛs] *s.* conjetura, suposición; adivinación; *v.* adivinar; suponer, creer.

guest [gɛst] *s.* convidado; visita; huésped, pensionista, inquilino.

guf·faw [gʌfɔ́] *s.* risotada, carcajada.

gui·dance [gáɪdn̩s] *s.* guía, dirección.

guide [gaɪd] *s.* guía.

guide·book [gáɪdbᴜk] *s.* guía del viajero; **railway —** guía de ferrocarriles.

guide·line [gáɪdlaɪn] *s.* norma; precepto.

guild [gɪld] *s.* gremio; cofradía; asociación.

guile [gaɪl] *s.* engaño, astucia.

guilt [gɪlt] *s.* culpa, delito; culpabilidad.

guilt·less [gɪltlɪs] *adj.* libre de culpa; inocente.

guilt·y [gɪltɪ] *adj.* culpable; reo, delincuente.

guise [gaɪz] *s.* aspecto, apariencia; modo; **under the — of** so capa de; disfrazado de.

gui·tar [gɪtár] *s.* guitarra.

gulf [gʌlf] *s.* golfo; abismo.

gull [gʌl] *s.* gaviota.

gul·let [gʌlɪt] *s.* gaznate.

gul·ly [gʌlɪ] *s.* barranco, barranca; hondonada.

gulp [gʌlp] *s.* trago; *v.* tragar; engullir; **to — it down** tragárselo.

gum [gʌm] *s.* (*product*) goma; (*of mouth*) encía; **chewing —** goma de mascar, *Am.* chicle; **— tree** arbol gomífero, *Col.* gomero; *v.* engomar, pegar con goma.

gun [gʌn] *s.* (*cannon*) cañón; (*rifle*) fusil, rifle; (*shotgun*) escopeta; pistola, revólver; **a 21 — salute** una salva de 21 cañonazos.

gun·boat [gánbot] *s.* cañonero, lancha cañonera.

gun·ner [gánə·] *s.* artillero, cañonero; ametrallador.

gun·pow·der [gánpaᴜdə·] *s.* pólvora.

gur·gle [gə́gl] *v.* borbotar, hacer borbollones; *s.* borbollón, borbotón.

gush [gʌʃ] *s.* chorro; borbollón, borbotón; efusión (*de cariño o entusiasmo*); *v.* chorrear, borbotar, borbollar, borbollonear; brotar; ser demasiado efusivo.

gust [gʌst] *s.* ráfaga, ventolera.

gut [gʌt] *s.* tripa, intestino; cuerda de tripa; **to have -s** tener agallas (*ánimo*).

gut·ter [gátə·] *s.* arroyo (*de la calle o de un camino*); gotera (*del techo*); zanja.

guy [gaɪ] *s.* (*person*) sujeto, tipo, individuo; (*wire*) tirante, alambre, cadena (*para sostener algo*); *v.* sostener (*algo*) con tirantes; burlarse de, mofarse de.

gym·na·si·um [dʒɪmnézɪəm] *s.* gimnasio.

gym·nas·tics [dʒɪmnǽstɪks] *s. pl.* gimnasia.

gy·ne·col·o·gy [gaɪnəkálədʒɪ] *s.* ginecología.

gyp·sy [dʒɪpsɪ] *s.* & *adj.* gitano.

gy·rate [dʒáɪret] *v.* girar.

gy·ro·scope [dʒáɪrəskop] *s.* giroscopio.

H:h

hab·it [hǽbɪt] *s.* hábito; costumbre; **drinking —** vicio de la bebida; **riding —** traje de montar.

ha·bit·u·al [həbɪtʃᴜəl] *adj.* habitual; acostumbrado.

hack [hæk] *s.* (*cut*) tajo; (*cough*) tos seca; (*horse*) caballo de alquiler; rocín; (*writer*) escritor mercenario; *v.* tajar, picar; toser con tos seca.

hack·neyed [hǽknɪd] *adj.* trillado, muy común.

had [hæd] *pret.* & *p.p. de* **to have; you — better**

do it es bueno que Vd. lo haga; sería bueno que
Vd. lo hiciese; **I — rather go than stay**
preferiría irme a quedarme.
haf·ni·um [hǽfniəm] s. hafnio.
hag [hæg] s. hechicera, bruja; viejota.
hag·gard [hǽgəd] adj. macilento, flaco.
hag·gle [hǽgl] v. regatear.
hail [hel] s. (storm) granizo; (greeting) saludo;
llamada, grito; **Hail Mary** Ave María; interj.
¡salud!; ¡salve!; v. granizar; saludar; llamar;
aclamar; **to — from** proceder de, ser oriundo de.
hail·storm [hélstɔrm] s. granizada.
hair [hɛr] s. pelo; cabello; vello; filamento (de las
plantas); **— net** red para el cabello.
hair·brush [hɛrbrʌʃ] s. cepillo para el cabello.
hair·cut [hɛrkʌt] s. corte de pelo; **close — rape**;
to have a — hacerse cortar el pelo.
hair·do [hɛrdu] s. peinado.
hair·dress·er [hɛrdrɛsə] s. peluquero; peinadora.
hair·less [hɛrlɪs] adj. sin pelo, pelado; lampiño.
hair·pin [hɛrpɪn] s. horquilla, Am. gancho (para el
pelo).
hair·y [hɛrɪ] adj. peludo, cabelludo; hirsuto,
velloso, velludo.
hale [hel] adj. sano, fuerte, robusto; v. llevar (a
una persona) por fuerza.
half [hæf] s. mitad; **— an apple** media manzana;
adj. medio; **— brother** hermanastro; **— cooked**
a medio cocer, medio cocido; **half-past one** la
una y media; **half-baked** a medio cocer; a medio
planear.
half-breed [hǽfbrid] adj. & s. mestizo.
half-hour [hǽfáʊr] s. media hora; adj. de media
hora.
half-mast [hǽfmǽst] s. media asta; v. poner a
media asta (la bandera).
half-o·pen [hǽfópən] adj. entreabierto; medio
abierto, entornado.
half·way [hǽfwe] adj. & adv. a medio camino;
parcial, incompleto; **— between** equidistante de;
— finished a medio acabar; **to do something —**
hacer algo a medias.
half-wit·ted [hǽfwɪtɪd] adj. imbécil, zonzo.
hal·i·but [hǽləbət] s. mero, hipogloso (pez).
hall [hɔl] s. salón (para asambleas, funciones, etc.);
edificio (de un colegio o universidad); vestíbulo;
corredor, pasillo; **town —** ayuntamiento.
hall·mark [hólmɑrk] s. distintivo.
hal·lo = **hello**.
hal·low [hǽlo] v. santificar; consagrar.
Hal·low·een [hǽloín] s. víspera de Todos los
Santos.
hall·way [hólwe] s. corredor, pasillo; zaguán.
ha·lo [hélo] s. halo; aureola.
halt [hɔlt] s. alto, parada; v. parar(se), detener(se);
hacer alto; vacilar.
hal·ter [hóltə] s. ronzal, cabestro.
halt·ing [hóltɪŋ] adj. vacilante; **-ly** adv. con
vacilación.
halve [hæv] v. partir por la mitad; partir en dos.
halves [hævz] pl. de **half**; **to go —** ir a medias.
ham [hæm] s. jamón.
ham·burg·er [hǽmbɝgə] s. carne picada de vaca;
bocadillo o emparedado de carne picada, Am.
hamburguesa.
ham·let [hǽmlɪt] s. caserío, aldehuela.
ham·mer [hǽmə] s. martillo; martinete (de piano);
sledge — macho; v. martillar; machacar; clavar.
ham·mock [hǽmək] s. hamaca, Ven., Col.
chinchorro; Ríopl. mangangá; coy.
ham·per [hǽmpə] s. canasto, cesto grande,

cuévano; v. estorbar, impedir, embarazar.
hand [hænd] s. mano; manecilla; aguja (de reloj);
obrero; letra (modo de escribir); **— and glove**
uña y carne; **— in —** (cogidos) de la mano;
at — a la mano, cerca; **made by —** hecho a
mano; **on —** disponible; en existencia; listo; a la
mano, presente; **on the other —** en cambio, por
otra parte; **to have one's -s full** estar
ocupadísimo; v. entregar, dar; **to — down** bajar
(una cosa para dársela a alguien); transmitir
(de una a otra generación); pronunciar (un fallo);
to — in entregar; **to — over** entregar.
hand·bag [hǽndbæg] s. bolsa o bolso; saco de
noche, maletín.
hand·ball [hǽndbɔl] s. pelota; juego de pelota.
hand·bill [hǽndbɪl] s. hoja volante (anuncio).
hand·cuff [hǽndkʌf] v. maniatar; **-s** s. pl. esposas,
manillas de hierro.
hand·ful [hǽndfəl] s. manojo, puñado.
hand·i·cap [hǽndɪkæp] s. desventaja, estorbo,
impedimento, obstáculo; ventaja o desventaja
(impuesta en ciertas contiendas); **— race** carrera
de handicap; v. estorbar, poner trabas a.
hand·i·work [hǽndɪwɝk] s. labor, trabajo hecho a
mano; artefacto.
hand·ker·chief [hǽŋkətʃɪf] s. pañuelo.
han·dle [hǽndl] s. mango, asa; tirador (de puerta o
cajón); puño (de espada); manubrio (de
bicicleta, organillo, etc.); v. manejar; manipular;
manosear, tocar; comerciar en; **-s easily** se
maneja con facilidad, es muy manuable.
hand·made [hǽndméd] adj. hecho a mano.
hand·saw [hǽndsɔ] s. serrucho.
hand·shake [hǽndʃek] s. apretón de manos.
hand·some [hǽnsəm] adj. (good-looking) hermoso,
guapo, bien parecido; (generous) generoso; **a —
sum** una suma considerable.
hand·writ·ing [hǽndraɪtɪŋ] s. letra (modo de
escribir), escritura.
hand·y [hǽndɪ] adj. a la mano, próximo; hábil,
diestro; manuable, fácil de manejar.
hang [hæŋ] v. colgar; suspender; ahorcar;
inclinar (la cabeza); **sentenced to —** condenado
a la horca; **to — around** andar holgazaneando
por un sitio; rondar; esperar sin hacer nada;
to — on colgarse de; depender de; estar
pendiente de; persistir; **to — paper on a wall**
empapelar una pared; **to — with tapestries**
entapizar; s. modo de caerle la ropa a una
persona; modo de manejar (un mecanismo);
modo de resolver (un problema); significado (de
un argumento); **I don't care a —** no me importa
un ardite.
han·gar [hǽŋə] s. hangar, cobertizo.
hang·er [hǽŋə] s. colgadero; percha, clavijero;
paper — empapelador.
hang·ing [hǽŋɪŋ] s. muerte en la horca; **-s**
colgaduras; adj. colgante; colgado.
hang·man [hǽŋmən] s. verdugo.
hang·nail [hǽŋnel] s. padrastro (pedacito de pellejo
que se levanta junto a las uñas).
hang·o·ver [hǽŋovə] s. sobrante, remanente, resto;
to have a — Ven., Col., Andes tener un ratón o
estar enratonado (tras una borrachera), Méx.
estar crudo o tener una cruda; Ch. la mona;
C.A. de goma; Ríopl. resaca.
hap·haz·ard [hǽphǽzəd] adv. al azar, al acaso, a la
ventura, a la buena de Dios; adj. casual;
impensado.
hap·haz·ard·ly [hǽphǽzədlɪ] adv. = **haphazard**.
hap·less [hǽplɪs] adj. desventurado, desgraciado.

GR

hap·pen [hǽpən] *v.* suceder, pasar, acontecer, sobrevenir, acaecer; **to — to hear (do, be,** *etc.***)** oír (hacer, estar, *etc.*) por casualidad; **to — to pass by** acertar a pasar; **to — on (upon)** encontrarse con, tropezar con.
hap·pen·ing [hǽpənɪŋ] *s.* acontecimiento, suceso.
hap·pi·ly [hǽplɪ] *adv.* felizmente; afortunadamente.
hap·pi·ness [hǽpɪnɪs] *s.* felicidad, dicha, contento.
hap·py [hǽpɪ] *adj.* feliz; dichoso, alegre; afortunado; **to be — to** alegrarse de.
ha·rangue [hərǽŋ] *s.* arenga, perorata; *v.* arengar, perorar.
har·ass [hǽrəs] *v.* acosar, hostigar, molestar.
har·bor [hárbɚ] *s.* puerto; asilo, refugio, abrigo; *v.* abrigar; hospedar; albergar.
hard [hard] *adj.* (*firm*) duro; (*stiff*) tieso; (*difficult*) arduo, difícil; **— cash** dinero contante y sonante, metálico; **— coal** antracita; **— liquor** licor espirituoso (*aguardiente, ron, etc.*); **— luck** mala suerte; **— of hearing** medio sordo; **— water** agua cruda; *adv.* fuerte, recio, con fuerza; con empeño, con ahínco; **— by** muy cerca; **— core** núcleo resistente (*de un grupo*); **—hearted** de corazón duro; **hard-working** muy trabajador, industrioso, aplicado.
hard·en [hárdn̩] *v.* endurecer(se).
hard·en·ing [hárdnɪŋ] *s.* endurecimiento.
hard·ly [hárdlɪ] *adv.* apenas; a duras penas; difícilmente; duramente, con aspereza; probablemente no.
hard·ness [hárdnɪs] *s.* dureza; aspereza; dificultad.
hard·ship [hárdʃɪp] *s.* apuro, aflicción; trabajo, penalidad.
hard·ware [hárdwɛr] *s.* quincalla, quincallería; **— shop** quincallería, ferretería.
har·dy [hárdɪ] *adj.* robusto, fuerte, recio, atrevido.
hare [hɛr] *s.* liebre.
hare·brained [hérbrénd] *adj.* atolondrado, ligero de cascos.
hare·lip [hérlɪp] *s.* labio leporino.
har·em [hérəm] *s.* harén.
har·lot [hárlət] *s.* ramera, prostituta.
harm [harm] *s.* daño, mal; perjuicio; *v.* dañar; hacer mal, hacer daño; perjudicar.
harm·ful [hármfəl] *adj.* dañoso; dañino, nocivo, perjudicial.
harm·less [hármlɪs] *adj.* innocuo; inofensivo; no dañoso, inocente.
harm·less·ness [hármlɪsnɪs] *s.* innocuidad; inocencia, falta de malicia.
har·mon·ic [harmánɪk] *adj.* armónico.
har·mo·ni·ous [harmónɪəs] *adj.* armonioso.
har·mo·nize [hármənaɪz] *v.* armonizar; concordar; congeniar.
har·mo·ny [hármənɪ] *s.* armonía.
har·ness [hárnɪs] *s.* guarniciones (*de caballerías*); jaez, aparejo; **to get back in** — volver al servicio activo, volver a trabajar; volver a la rutina; *v.* enjaezar, poner guarniciones a (*un caballo, mula, etc.*).
harp [harp] *s.* arpa; *v.* tocar el arpa; **to — on** repetir constantemente (*una nota, palabra, tema, etc.*); porfiar en.
har·poon [harpún] *s.* arpón; *v.* arponear, pescar con arpón.
har·row [hǽro] *s.* rastro, rastrillo, grada; *v.* rastrear, rastrillar; atormentar; horrorizar.
har·row·ing [hǽrəwɪŋ] *adj.* horrendo, horripilante, que pone los cabellos de punta; espeluznante.
har·ry [hǽrɪ] *v.* acosar, molestar; asolar.
harsh [harʃ] *adj.* tosco, áspero; severo, austero.

harsh·ness [hárʃnɪs] *s.* aspereza; tosquedad; severidad.
har·vest [hárvɪst] *s.* cosecha; siega, agosto; recolección; recogida; *v.* cosechar; segar.
hash [hæʃ] *s.* picadillo.
haste [hest] *s.* prisa; apresuramiento; **in — de** prisa; **to make** — darse prisa, apresurarse; *Am.* apurarse.
has·ten [hésn̩] *v.* apresurar(se), precipitar(se); darse prisa.
hast·i·ly [héstlɪ] *adv.* aprisa, de prisa, apresuradamente, precipitadamente.
hast·y [héstɪ] *adj.* apresurado; precipitado.
hat [hæt] *s.* sombrero.
hatch [hætʃ] *v.* empollar; criar pollos; idear, maquinar; *s.* cría, nidada, pollada; escotillón, trampa (*puerta en el suelo*); **—way** escotilla.
hatch·et [hǽtʃɪt] *s.* hacha; **to bury the** — echar pelillos a la mar, olvidar rencores o enemistades.
hate [het] *s.* odio; aborrecimiento; *v.* odiar; aborrecer; detestar.
hate·ful [hétfəl] *adj.* odioso, aborrecible.
ha·tred [hétrɪd] *s.* odio, aversión.
haugh·ti·ly [hótlɪ] *adv.* con altivez, altaneramente, arrogantemente.
haugh·ti·ness [hótnɪs] *s.* altanería, altivez.
haugh·ty [hótɪ] *adj.* altivo, altanero, arrogante.
haul [hɔl] *v.* (*transport*) acarrear, transportar; (*pull*) jalar (*halar*); tirar de; (*drag*) arrastrar; **to — down the flag** arriar (*o* bajar) la bandera; *s.* acarreo; transporte; tirón, estirón; buena pesca; ganancia, botín; (*round-up*) redada.
haunch [hɔntʃ] *s.* anca.
haunt [hɔnt] *v.* frecuentar a menudo; andar por, vagar por (*como fantasma o espectro*); **that idea -s me** me persigue esa idea; **-ed house** casa de espantos, fantasmas o aparecidos; *s.* guarida.
have [hæv] *v.* tener; poseer; haber (*v. aux.*); **to — a suit made** mandar hacer un traje; **to — a look at** dar un vistazo a, echar una mirada a; **to — to** tener que; deber; **I'll not — it** so no lo toleraré, no lo permitiré; **what did she — on?** ¿qué vestido llevaba (puesto)?
ha·ven [hévən] *s.* asilo, abrigo, refugio; puerto.
hav·oc [hǽvək] *s.* estrago, estropicio, ruina; **to cause** — hacer estragos.
hawk [hɔk] *s.* halcón; *v.* pregonar (*mercancías*).
haw·thorn [hóθɔrn] *s.* espino.
hay [he] *s.* heno, paja, hierba seca; **— fever** catarro asmático.
hay·loft [hélɔft] *s.* henil, pajar.
hay·stack [héstæk] *s.* montón de heno o paja.
haz·ard [hǽzɚd] *s.* azar; riesgo, peligro; estorbo, obstáculo (*en el campo de golf*); *v.* arriesgar, aventurar.
haz·ard·ous [hǽzɚdəs] *adj.* peligroso.
haze [hez] *s.* bruma, neblina, niebla; *v.* atormentar, hostigar (*con bromas estudiantiles*).
ha·zel [hézl̩] *s.* avellano; **—nut** avellana; *adj.* de avellano; avellanado, color de avellana.
haz·y [hézɪ] *adj.* (*weather*) nublado, brumoso; (*mind*) confuso.
he [hi] *pron. pers.* él; **— who** el que, quien; **he-goat** macho cabrío.
head [hɛd] *s.* cabeza; cabecera (*de cama*); jefe; **— of hair** cabellera; **game of -s or tails** juego de cara y cruz, juego de las chapas, *Ven., Col., Andes, Ch.* juego de cara y sello; *Méx.* juego de águila y sol; **to be out of one's** — delirar, estar delirante; **to come to a** — madurar; supurar (*un absceso*); **to keep one's** — conservar la calma, no

perder la cabeza; **it goes to his** — le desvanece; se le sube a la cabeza; *adj.* principal, primero; de proa, de frente; **head-on** de frente; *v.* encabezar; ir a la cabeza de; acaudillar; mandar, dirigir; **to** — **off** atajar; detener, refrenar; **to** — **towards** dirigirse a, encaminarse a.

head·ache [hédek] *s.* dolor de cabeza.

head·dress [héddrɛs] *s.* tocado, adorno para la cabeza.

head·gear [hédgɪr] *s.* sombrero, gorro, gorra; tocado, toca (*de mujer*); cabezada (*de guarnición para caballo*).

head·ing [hédɪŋ] *s.* encabezamiento, título.

head·land [hédlənd] *s.* cabo, promontorio.

head·light [hédlaɪt] *s.* linterna delantera, faro delantero.

head·line [hédlaɪn] *s.* título, encabezado.

head·long [hédlɔŋ] *adv.* de cabeza; precipitadamente.

head·quar·ters [hédkwɔrtəz] *s.* cuartel general; jefatura; oficina principal.

head·set [hédsɛt] *s.* receptor de cabeza.

head·strong [hédstrɔŋ] *adj.* testarudo, porfiado, obstinado.

head·way [hédwe] *s.* progreso, avance; **to make** — avanzar, adelantar, progresar.

heal [hil] *v.* curar; sanar; cicatrizar.

health [hɛlθ] *s.* salud; sanidad; salubridad.

health·ful [hɛlθfəl] *adj.* sano; salubre; saludable.

health·ful·ness [hɛlθfəlnɪs] *s.* salubridad; sanidad.

health·y [hɛlθɪ] *adj.* sano; saludable.

heap [hip] *s.* montón; pila; *v.* amontonar; apilar.

hear [hɪr] *v.* (*listen*) oír; escuchar; (*get news*) tener noticias; **to** — **about someone** oír hablar de alguien; **to** — **from someone** tener noticias de alguien; **to** — **of** saber de, tener noticias de, oír hablar de; **I -d that ...** oí decir que ...

heard [hɜd] *pret. & p.p. de* **to hear.**

hear·er [hírə] *s.* oyente.

hear·ing [híríŋ] *s.* (*sense*) oído; (*trial*) audiencia; examen de testigos; **hard of** — medio sordo, algo sordo; **within** — al alcance del oído; — **aid** aparato auditivo.

hear·say [hírse] *s.* habilla, rumor; **by** — de oídas.

hearse [hɜs] *s.* carroza fúnebre.

heart [hart] *s.* (*organ*) corazón; (*spirit*) ánimo; **at** — en realidad, en el fondo; **from the bottom of one's** — de corazón, con toda el alma; con toda sinceridad; **to learn by** — aprender de memoria; **to take** — cobrar ánimo; **to take to** — tomar en serio; tomar a pechos; — **attack** ataque cardíaco; — **of lettuce, cabbage** cogollo.

heart·ache [hártek] *s.* dolor del corazón; angustia, pesar, congoja.

heart·bro·ken [hártbrokən] *adj.* traspasado de dolor, acongojado, angustiado; desengañado.

heart·en [hártṇ] *v.* animar.

heart·felt [hártfɛlt] *adj.* sentido, cordial, sincero; **my** — **sympathy** mi más sentido pésame.

hearth [harθ] *s.* hogar; fogón.

heart·i·ly [hártḷɪ] *adv.* de corazón; cordialmente; de buena gana; **to eat** — comer con apetito; comer bien (*o* mucho).

heart·less [hártlɪs] *adj.* de mal corazón; cruel; insensible.

heart·rend·ing [hártrɛndɪŋ] *adj.* angustioso; agudo.

heart·y [hártɪ] *adj.* sincero, cordial; sano, fuerte; — **food** alimento nutritivo; **a** — **laugh** una buena carcajada; — **meal** comida abundante.

heat [hit] *s.* (*hot*) calor; ardor; (*emotion*) vehemencia; celo (*ardor sexual de la hembra*);

calefacción (*para las habitaciones*); corrida, carrera (*de prueba*); *v.* calentar(se); acalorar(se).

heat·er [hitə] *s.* calentador; calorífero.

hea·then [híðən] *s.* pagano, gentil, idólatra; paganos; *adj.* pagano; irreligioso.

heat·ing [hitɪŋ] *s.* calefacción.

heave [hiv] *v.* levantar, alzar (*con esfuerzo*); arrojar, lanzar; exhalar (*un suspiro*); jalar (*un cable*); jadear; basquear, hacer esfuerzos por vomitar.

heav·en [hévən] *s.* cielo.

heav·en·ly [hévənlɪ] *adj.* celeste; celestial; divino.

heav·i·ly [hévḷɪ] *adv.* pesadamente, lentamente; copiosamente, excesivamente.

heav·i·ness [hévɪnɪs] *s.* pesadez, pesantez; opresión; abatimiento.

heav·y [hévɪ] *adj.* (*weight*) pesado; (*thick*) grueso; (*coarse*) burdo; (*oppressive*) opresivo; — **rain** aguacero recio o fuerte; **with a** — **heart** abatido, acongojado.

heav·y·weight [hévɪwet] *s. & adj.* peso pesado (*fuerte*).

hectare [héktɛr] *s.* hectárea.

hec·tic [héktɪk] *adj.* febril; inquieto.

hedge [hɛdʒ] *s.* seto; vallado, barrera; *v.* cercar; poner valla o seto a; evitar o evadir contestaciones.

hedge·hog [hédʒhɑg] *s.* erizo.

he·don·ism [hídənɪzm] *s.* hedonismo.

heed [hid] *v.* atender; hacer caso; prestar atención; *s.* atención, cuidado; **to pay** — **to** prestar atención a; hacer caso de.

heed·less [hídlɪs] *adj.* descuidado; desatento.

heel [hil] *s.* talón (*del pie o de una media*); tacón (*del zapato*); **head over -s** patas arriba; *v.* poner tacón a; poner talón a.

he·gem·o·ny [hɪdʒémənɪ] *s.* hegemonía.

heif·er [héfə] *s.* novilla, vaquilla.

height [haɪt] *s.* altura; elevación; — **of folly** colmo de la locura.

height·en [háɪtṇ] *v.* avivar; aumentar(se); realzar.

hei·nous [hénəs] *adj.* aborrecible, odioso; malvado.

heir [ɛr] *s.* heredero.

heir·ess [érɪs] *s.* heredera.

held [hɛld] *pret. & p.p. de* **to hold.**

hel·i·cop·ter [héləkaptə] *s.* helicóptero.

he·li·um [hílɪəm] *s.* helio.

hell [hɛl] *s.* infierno.

hel·lo [hɛló] *interj.* ¡hola!; ¡halo!

helm [hɛlm] *s.* timón.

hel·met [hélmɪt] *s.* yelmo.

help [hɛlp] *s.* (*aid*) ayuda; auxilio; remedio; alivio; (*employee*) criado o criados, empleado o empleados; *v.* ayudar, asistir; auxiliar; remediar; servir (*algo de comer*); **to** — **down** equivale a bajar; — **yourself** sírvase Vd. (*de comer o beber*); tómelo Vd., está a la disposición de Vd.; **he cannot** — **it** no puede evitarlo; **he cannot** — **doing it** no puede menos de hacerlo; **he cannot** — **but come** no puede menos de venir.

help·er [hélpə] *s.* ayudante, asistente.

help·ful [hélpfəl] *adj.* útil, servicial; provechoso.

help·ing [hélpɪŋ] *s.* ayuda; porción (*que se sirve en la mesa*).

help·less [hélplɪs] *adj.* (*defenseless*) desamparado; (*handicapped*) desvalido; imposibilitado; incapaz; (*confused*) perplejo, indeciso (*sin saber qué hacer*); **a** — **situation** una situación irremediable.

help·less·ness [hélplɪsnɪs] *s.* incapacidad; incompetencia; impotencia, debilidad; abandono, desamparo.

hem [hɛm] *s.* dobladillo, bastilla; *v.* dobladillar, bastillar, hacer dobladillos en (*la ropa*); **to — in** rodear, cercar; **to — and haw** toser y retoser (*fingidamente*); tartamudear, vacilar.

hem·i·sphere [hémǝsfɪr] *s.* hemisferio.

hem·lock [hémlɑk] *s.* cicuta (*hierba venenosa*); abeto americano.

he·mo·glo·bin [hímoglobɪn] *s.* hemoglobina.

hem·or·rhage [hémǝrɪdʒ] *s.* hemorragia.

hemp [hɛmp] *s.* cáñamo, *Am.* sisal.

hem·stitch [hémstɪtʃ] *s.* dobladillo de ojo; *v.* hacer (*o* echar) dobladillo de ojo.

hen [hɛn] *s.* gallina; ave hembra.

hence [hɛns] *adv.* de (*o* desde) aquí; desde ahora; por lo tanto, por consiguiente; **a week —** de hoy en ocho días; de aquí a una semana.

hence·forth [hɛnsfórθ] *adv.* de aquí en adelante; de hoy en adelante; desde ahora.

hep·a·ti·tis [hɛpǝtáɪtɪs] *s.* hepatitis.

her [hɜ] *pron.* la; le, a ella; ella (*con preposición*); *adj.* su (sus), de ella.

her·ald [hérǝld] *s.* heraldo; anunciador, proclamador; precursor; *v.* anunciar, proclamar, publicar.

her·ald·ry [hérǝldrɪ] *s.* heráldica.

herb [ɝb] *s.* hierba (yerba).

herd [hɝd] *s.* (*animals*) hato; rebaño; manada; tropel; tropilla; (*cattle*) ganado; (*people*) muchedumbre; **the common —** el populacho, la chusma; *v.* reunir, juntar (*el ganado*); ir en manadas, ir juntos.

herds·man [hɝdzmǝn] *s.* vaquero, vaquerizo; pastor.

here [hɪr] *adv.* aquí; acá; **— it is** aquí está, helo aquí, aquí lo tiene Vd., **— is to you!** ¡a la salud de Vd.!; **that is neither — nor there** eso no viene al caso; (*to call a dog*) ¡cuz! ¡toma! (*a cat*) ¡misi! ¡mis!

here·af·ter [hɪrǽftǝ] *adv.* de aquí (*o* de hoy) en adelante; desde ahora en adelante; en lo futuro; *s.* **the —** la otra vida.

here·by [hɪrbáɪ] *adv.* por este medio; mediante la presente, por la presente; con estas palabras.

he·red·i·tar·y [hǝrédǝtɛrɪ] *adj.* hereditario.

he·red·i·ty [hǝrédǝtɪ] *s.* herencia.

here·in [hɪrín] *adv.* aquí dentro; en esto.

her·e·sy [hérǝsɪ] *s.* herejía.

her·e·tic [hérǝtɪk] *s.* hereje.

here·to·fore [hɪrtǝfór] *adv.* hasta ahora, hasta el presente.

here·with [hɪrwíθ] *adv.* aquí dentro, con esto, adjunto, incluso.

her·i·tage [hérǝtɪdʒ] *s.* herencia.

her·met·ic [hǝmétɪk] *adj.* hermético.

her·mit [hɝmɪt] *s.* ermitaño.

her·ni·a [hɝnɪǝ] *s.* hernia, ruptura, relajamiento.

he·ro [híro] *s.* héroe; protagonista.

he·ro·ic [hɪróɪk] *adj.* heroico.

her·o·in [héroɪn] *s.* heroína.

her·o·ine [héroɪn] *s.* heroína.

her·o·ism [héroɪzǝm] *s.* heroísmo.

he·ron [hérǝn] *s.* garza.

her·ring [hérɪŋ] *s.* arenque.

hers [hɝz] *pron. pos.* suyo (suya, suyos, suyas), de ella; el suyo (la suya, los suyos, las suyas); el (la, los, las) de ella; **a friend of —** un amigo suyo.

her·self [hǝsélf] *pron.* ella misma; se (*como reflexivo*); **by —** sola; por sí (sola); **she — did it** ella misma lo hizo; **she talks to —** ella habla para sí, habla consigo misma, habla para sus adentros, habla sola.

hes·i·tant [hézǝtǝnt] = **hesitating**.

hes·i·tate [hézǝtet] *v.* vacilar; titubear; dudar.

hes·i·tat·ing [hésǝtetɪŋ] *adj.* vacilante; indeciso; irresoluto, **-ly** *adv.* con vacilación.

hes·i·ta·tion [hezǝtéʃǝn] *s.* vacilación; titubeo, duda.

het·er·o·ge·ne·ous [hɛtǝǝdʒínɪǝs] *adj.* heterogeneo.

hew [hju] *v.* tajar, cortar; picar (*piedra*); labrar (*madera, piedra*).

hewn [hjun] *p.p. de* **to hew**.

hey [he] *interj.* ¡he!; ¡oiga!; ¡oye!

hi·a·tus [haɪétǝs] *s.* hiato.

hi·ber·nate [háɪbǝnet] *v.* invernar.

hic·cup, hic·cough [híkʌp] *s.* hipo; *v.* hipar, tener hipo.

hick·o·ry [híkǝrɪ] *s.* nogal americano; **— nut** nuez (*del nogal americano*).

hid [hɪd] *pret. & p.p. de* **to hide**.

hid·den [hídn] *p.p. de* **to hide**; *adj.* oculto, escondido.

hide [haɪd] *v.* ocultar(se); esconder(se); **to — from** esconderse de, recatarse de; *s.* cuero, piel; **to play — and seek** jugar al escondite.

hid·e·ous [hídɪǝs] *adj.* horrendo, horripilante, feote.

hi·er·ar·chy [háɪǝrɑrkɪ] *s.* jerarquía.

hi·er·o·glyph·ic [haɪǝroglífɪk] *adj. & s.* jeroglífico.

high [haɪ] *adj.* alto; **— altar** altar mayor; **— and dry** enjuto; en seco; solo, abandonado; **— antiquity** antigüedad remota; **— explosive** explosivo de gran potencia; **— tide** pleamar; **— wind** ventarrón, viento fuerte; **in — gear** en directa, en tercera velocidad; **two feet —** dos pies de alto; **it is — time that** ya es hora de que; **to be in — spirits** estar muy animado; *adv.* alto; a precio subido; en alto; **to look — and low** buscar por todas partes; **high-grade** de calidad superior; **high-handed** arbitrario, despótico; **high-minded** magnánimo; orgulloso; **high-sounding** altisonante, rimbombante; **high-strung** muy tenso.

high·land [háɪlǝnd] *s.* tierra montañosa; **the Highlands** las montañas de Escocia.

high·light [háɪlaɪt] *s.* lo más notable.

high·ly [háɪlɪ] *adv.* altamente; sumamente; muy; **— paid** muy bien pagado.

high·ness [háɪnɪs] *s.* altura; elevación; Alteza (*título*).

high·way [háɪwe] *s.* camino real; carretera, calzada.

high·way·man [háɪwemǝn] *s.* forajido, salteador de caminos, bandido.

hike [haɪk] *s.* caminata, paseo largo, *Am.* andada; *v.* dar (*o* echar) una caminata.

hill [hɪl] *s.* colina, collado, cerro; montoncillo de tierra; *Andes, Am.* loma; **— ant** hormiguero; **— down** cuesta abajo; **— up** cuesta arriba.

hill·ock [hílǝk] *s.* collado, otero, montecillo.

hill·side [hílsaɪd] *s.* ladera.

hill·top [híltǝp] *s.* cumbre, cima (*de una colina*).

hill·y [hílɪ] *adj.* montuoso; accidentado.

hilt [hɪlt] *s.* empuñadura, puño (*de una espada o daga*).

him [hɪm] *pron.* le; lo; él (*con preposición*).

him·self [hɪmsélf] *pron.* él mismo; se (*como reflexivo*); a sí mismo; *véase* **herself**.

hind [haɪnd] *adj.* trasero; posterior; *s.* cierva; **—most** *adj.* último, postrero.

hin·der [híndǝ] *v.* estorbar, impedir, obstruir.

hin·drance [híndrǝns] *s.* estorbo, obstáculo, impedimento.

hinge [hɪndʒ] *s.* gozne; bisagra; *v.* engoznar, poner goznes; **to — on** girar sobre; depender de.

hint [hɪnt] s. indirecta, insinuación; sugestión; **not to take the —** no darse por entendido; v. insinuar, intimar, sugerir indirectamente.

hip [hɪp] s. cadera.

hip·po·pot·a·mus [hɪpəpátəməs] s. hipopótamo.

hire [haɪr] s. (rent) alquiler; (pay) paga, sueldo; v. alquilar; emplear, dar empleo, C.A., Ven., Col. enganchar, Am. conchabar; **to — out** alquilarse, ponerse a servir a otro.

his [hɪz] pron. pos. suyo (suya, suyos, suyas), de él; el suyo (la suya, los suyos, las suyas); el (la, los, las) de él; **a friend of —** un amigo suyo; adj. su (sus), de él.

hiss [hɪs] s. silbido, chiflido; siseo; v. sisear, silbar, chiflar.

his·ta·mine [hístəmin] s. histamina.

his·to·ri·an [hɪstɔ́rɪən] s. historiador.

his·tor·ic [hɪstɔ́rɪk] adj. histórico.

his·tor·i·cal [hɪstɔ́rɪkḷ] adj. histórico.

his·to·ry [hístrɪ] s. historia.

his·tri·on·ics [hɪstrɪánɪks] s. histrionismo.

hit [hɪt] v. pegar, golpear; dar (un golpe); dar en (o con); chocar; **they — it off well** se llevan bien, congenian; **to — the mark** acertar, atinar, dar en el blanco; **to — upon** dar con; encontrarse con, encontrar por casualidad; pret. & p.p. de **to hit**; s. golpe; choque; golpe de fortuna; pulla, dicharacho; **to be a great —** ser un gran éxito; **to make a — with someone** caerle en gracia a una persona; **hit-and-run** adj. que abandona a su víctima atropellada.

hitch [hɪtʃ] v. atar, amarrar; enganchar; uncir (bueyes); dar un tirón; **to — one's chair nearer to** acercar su silla a; s. tirón; obstáculo, impedimento, tropiezo; enganche, enganchamiento.

hitch·hike [hítʃhaɪk] v. viajar de gorra (en automóvil), Méx. irse o viajar de mosca; Ch., Ríopl. hacer dedo, ir a dedo; Esp. viajar por auto-stop.

hith·er [hɪðɚ] adv. acá; **— and thither** acá y allá.

hith·er·to [hɪðɚtú] adv. hasta aquí, hasta ahora, hasta hoy.

hive [haɪv] s. colmena; enjambre; **-s** ronchas (de la piel).

hoard [hord] s. tesoro escondido; acumulamiento secreto de provisiones; v. atesorar, guardar (con avaricia); acumular secretamente.

hoarse [hors] adj. bronco, áspero, ronco.

hoarse·ness [hórsnɪs] s. ronquera; carraspera.

hoar·y [hórɪ] adj. cano, encanecido, canoso.

hob·ble [hábḷ] v. (limp) cojear, renquear; (tie) maniatar o manear (un animal); (impede) impedir, estorbar; s. cojera; traba, maniota o manea (cuerda con que se atan las manos de una bestia).

hob·by [hábɪ] s. afición; trabajo hecho por afición (no por obligación).

ho·bo [hóbo] s. vagabundo.

hodge·podge [hádʒpadʒ] s. mezcolanza, baturrillo.

hoe [ho] s. azada, azadón; v. cavar, escardar, limpiar con azadón.

hog [hɑg] s. puerco, cerdo, cochino; chancho; adj. porcino; v. apropiárselo todo.

hoist [hɔɪst] v. alzar, levantar; izar (la bandera, las velas); s. elevador, Am. malacate.

hold [hold] v. tener(se); retener; detener; tener cabida para; sostener; mantener(se); opinar; celebrar (una reunión, etc.); ocupar (un puesto); ser válido (un argumento o regla); **to — back someone** detener (o refrenar) a alguien; **to —**

forth perorar, hablar largamente; **to — in place** sujetar; **to — off** mantener(se) a distancia; mantenerse alejado; **to — on** agarrar(se); asir(se); persistir; **— on!** ¡agárrese bien!; ¡deténgase! ¡pare!; **to — someone responsible** hacerle a uno responsable; **to — someone to his word** obligar a uno a cumplir su palabra; **to — oneself erect** tenerse o andar derecho; **to — one's own** mantenerse firme; **to — one's tongue** callarse; **to — out** continuar, durar; mantenerse firme; **to — over** aplazar; durar; continuar en un cargo; **to — still** estarse quieto o callado; **to — tight** apretar; **to — to one's promise** cumplir con la promesa; **to — up** levantar, alzar; detener; asaltar, atracar (para robar); **how much does it —?** ¿cuánto le cabe? s. agarro; dominio; influencia; autoridad; bodega (de un barco); cabina de carga (de un aeroplano); **to get — of** asir, agarrar; atrapar; **to take — of** coger, agarrar, asir.

hold·er [hóldɚ] s. (person) tenedor, posesor; (device) receptáculo; cojinillo (para coger un trasto caliente); **cigarette —** boquilla; **pen—** portaplumas.

hold·up [hóldʌp] s. asalto, atraco.

hole [hol] s. agujero; abertura; hoyo, hueco, cavidad; bache (de un camino); **swimming —** charco, remanso; **to be in a —** hallarse en un apuro o aprieto.

hol·i·day [háləde] s. día de fiesta, día festivo, festividad; **-s** días de fiesta; vacaciones.

ho·li·ness [hólɪnɪs] s. santidad.

hol·low [hálo] adj. (empty) hueco; vacío; (concave) cóncavo; hundido; (insincere) falso; s. hueco; hoyo; cavidad; concavidad; depresión; cañada, hondonada; v. ahuecar; excavar; ahondar.

hol·ly [hálɪ] s. agrifolio, acebo.

hol·ster [hólstɚ] s. pistolera, funda (de pistola).

ho·ly [hólɪ] adj. santo; sagrado, sacro; **— water** agua bendita.

hom·age [hámɪdʒ] s. homenaje; reverencia; acatamiento; **to do —** acatar, rendir homenaje, honrar.

home [hom] s. casa, hogar; habitación, domicilio; **at —** en casa; adj. doméstico; casero; **— office** oficina matriz o central; **— rule** autonomía; **— run** Méx., C.A., Ven., Col. jonrón (en béisbol); **— stretch** último trecho (de una carrera); adv. a casa; en casa; **to strike —** herir en lo vivo; dar en el clavo o en el blanco.

home·land [hómlænd] s. tierra natal, suelo patrio.

home·less [hómlɪs] adj. sin casa; destituido.

home·like [hómlaɪk] adj. hogareño, cómodo.

home·ly [hómlɪ] adj. feo; llano; sencillo; casero, doméstico.

home·made [hómméd] adj. hecho en casa; doméstico, nacional, del país.

home·sick [hómsɪk] adj. nostálgico.

home·sick·ness [hómsɪknɪs] s. nostalgia.

home·stead [hómstɛd] s. heredad; casa y terrenos adyacentes.

home·ward [hómwɚd] adv. a casa; hacia la patria; **— voyage** retorno, viaje de vuelta.

home·work [hómwɝk] s. trabajo de casa; trabajo hecho en casa.

hom·i·cide [háməsaɪd] s. homicidio; homicida, asesino.

ho·mo·ge·ne·ous [homədʒínɪəs] adj. homogéneo.

ho·mog·e·nize [homádʒənaɪz] v. homogenizar.

ho·mo·sex·u·al [homəsɛ́kʃjʊl] adj. & s homosexual.

HE

hone [hon] *v.* amolar, asentar, afilar; *s.* piedra de afilar.
hon·est [ánɪst] *adj.* honrado, recto; genuino; — **goods** mercancías genuinas; **-ly** *adv.* honradamente; de veras.
hon·es·ty [ánɪstɪ] *s.* honradez, rectitud.
hon·ey [hʌ́nɪ] *s.* miel; dulzura; querido, querida.
hon·ey·comb [hʌ́nɪkom] *s.* panal.
hon·eyed [hʌ́nɪd] *adj.* meloso; dulce; melifluo.
hon·ey·moon [hʌ́nɪmun] *s.* luna de miel; viaje de novios, viaje de bodas; *v.* pasar la luna de miel.
hon·ey·suck·le [hʌ́nɪsʌkl] *s.* madreselva.
honk [hoŋk] *s.* pitazo (*de automóvil*); graznido (*voz del ganso*); *v.* donar la bocina; graznar.
hon·or [ánɚ] *s.* honor; honra; señoría (*título*); **upon my** — sobre mi palabra; *v.* honrar; dar honra.
hon·or·a·ble [ánɚəbl] *adj.* honorable; honroso; honrado.
hon·or·ar·y [ánɚɛrɪ] *adj.* honorario, honorífico.
hood [hʊd] *s.* capucha, caperuza; capirote, cubierta (*del motor*); *v.* encapuchar, encapirotar.
hood·lum [húdləm] *s.* maleante; antisocial.
hoof [hʊf] *s.* casco, pezuña; pata (*de caballo, toro, etc.*); (*half of cloven hoof*) pesuño.
hook [hʊk] *s.* gancho, garfio; anzuelo (*para pescar*); — **and eye** corchete; macho y hembra, **by** — **or crook** por la buena o por la mala, por angas o por mangas; **on his own** — por su propia cuenta; *v.* enganchar(se); abrochar(se); pescar, coger con anzuelo; robar, hurtar.
hook·y [hʊ́kɪ]: **to play** — hacer novillos, *Carib.* capear la escuela, *Méx.* pintar venado, *C.A., Ven., Col.* jubilarse; *Ríopl.* hacerse la rata (*la rabona*).
hoop [hup] *s.* aro; argolla; *v.* poner aro a; ceñir, cercar.
hoot [hut] *v.* ulular (*dícese del buho, lechuza, etc.*); rechiflar, ridiculizar; *s.* alarido, chillido.
hoot·ing [hútɪŋ] *s.* grita, rechifla.
hop [hap] *s.* salto, brinco; baile; *v.* saltar; brincar.
hope [hop] *s.* esperanza; *v.* esperar; **to** — **for** esperar; **to** — **against** — esperar desesperando; esperar lo que no puede ser, esperar lo imposible.
hope·ful [hópfəl] *adj.* esperanzado, lleno de esperanza; **a young** — un joven prometedor; **-ly** *adv.* con esperanza; con ansia; lleno de esperanza.
hope·less [hóplɪs] *adj.* sin esperanza, falto de esperanza, desesperanzado; desesperado; irremediable; — **cause** causa perdida; — **illness** enfermedad incurable; **it is** — no tiene remedio; **-ly** *adv.* sin esperanza, sin remedio.
hope·less·ness [hóplɪsnɪs] *s.* falta de esperanza; falta de remedio; desesperanza, desaliento.
horde [hord] *s.* horda; muchedumbre, gentío; enjambre.
ho·ri·zon [həráɪzn] *s.* horizonte.
hor·i·zon·tal [hɔrəzántl] *adj.* horizontal.
hor·mone [hɔ́rmon] *s.* hormona.
horn [hɔrn] *s.* (*animal*) cuerno; asta; cacho; (*automobile*) bocina, klaxon, trompa; (*musical*) corneta; trompeta; — **of plenty** cuerno de la abundancia; *v.* acornear, dar cornadas; **to** — **in** entremeterse; — **tip** pitón.
hor·net [hɔ́rnɪt] *s.* avispón; **-'s nest** avispero.
hor·o·scope [hɔ́rəskop] *s.* horóscopo.
hor·ri·ble [hɔ́rəbl] *adj.* horrible; **horribly** *adv.* horriblemente.
hor·rid [hɔ́rɪd] *adj.* horrendo, horrible.

hor·ri·fy [hɔ́rəfaɪ] *v.* horrorizar, aterrorizar, espantar.
hor·ror [hɔ́rɚ] *s.* horror.
hors d'oeuvre [ɔrdɚ́vrə] *s.* entremés; bocadillos.
horse [hɔrs] *s.* caballo; caballete (*de madera*), borriquete (*de carpinteros*); **saddle** — caballo de silla; — **dealer** chalán; — **race** carrera de caballos; — **sense** sentido común.
horse·back [hɔ́rsbæk] *s.* lomo de caballo; **to ride** — montar a caballo, cabalgar, jinetear.
horse·fly [hɔ́rsflaɪ] *s.* tábano, mosca de caballo.
horse·laugh [hɔ́rslæf] *s.* carcajada, risotada.
horse·man [hɔ́rsmən] *s.* jinete.
horse·man·ship [hɔ́rsmənʃɪp] *s.* equitación.
horse·pow·er [hɔ́rspaʊɚ] *s.* caballo de fuerza.
horse·rad·ish [hɔ́rsrædɪʃ] *s.* rábano picante.
horse·shoe [hɔ́rsʃu] *s.* herradura.
hose [hoz] *s.* medias; manga o manguera (*para regar*); **men's** — calcetines.
ho·sier·y [hóʒrɪ] *s.* medias; calcetines; calcetería (*negocio*); — **shop** calcetería.
hos·pi·ta·ble [háspɪtəbl] *adj.* hospitalario.
hos·pi·tal [háspɪtl] *s.* hospital.
hos·pi·tal·i·ty [háspɪtǽlətɪ] *s.* hospitalidad.
host [host] *s.* huésped (*el que hospeda*), anfitrión (*el que convida*); hospedero, mesonero; hueste; ejército, multitud; hostia; **sacred** — hostia consagrada.
hos·tage [hástɪdʒ] *s.* rehén (*persona que queda como prenda en poder del enemigo*).
hos·tel·ry [hástəlrɪ] *s.* hostería.
host·ess [hóstɪs] *s.* huéspeda (*la que hospeda o convida*).
hos·tile [hástl] *adj.* hostil.
hos·til·i·ty [hastílətɪ] *s.* hostilidad.
hot [hat] *adj.* caliente; caluroso; cálido; picante (*como el pimentón, chile, ají, etc.*); furioso; fresco, reciente; — **bed** semillero; **hot-headed** enojadizo, impetuoso; exaltado; — **house** invernáculo, invernadero; **it is** — **today** hace calor hoy.
ho·tel [hotél] *s.* hotel.
ho·tel-keep·er [hotélkipɚ] *s.* hotelero.
hot·ly [hátlɪ] *adv.* calurosamente, con vehemencia.
hound [haʊnd] *s.* perro de busca, lebrel, galgo, sabueso, podenco; *v.* acosar, perseguir; azuzar, incitar.
hour [aʊr] *s.* hora; — **hand** horario.
hour·ly [áʊrlɪ] *adv.* por horas; a cada hora; a menudo; *adj.* frecuente; por horas.
house [haʊs] *s.* (*residence*) casa; domicilio; (*legislature*) cámara, asamblea legislativa; **country** — casa de campo; **a full** — un lleno completo (*en al teatro*); [haʊz] *v.* alojar; hospedar.
house·hold [háʊshold] *s.* casa, familia; *adj.* casero; doméstico.
house·keep·er [háʊskipɚ] *s.* casera; ama de llaves; **to be a good** — ser una mujer hacendosa.
house·keep·ing [háʊskipɪŋ] *s.* gobierno de casa; quehaceres domésticos.
house·top [háʊstap] *s.* techumbre, tejado.
house·wife [háʊswaɪf] *s.* mujer de su casa; madre de familia; ama de casa.
house·work [háʊswɝk] *s.* trabajo de casa; quehaceres domésticos.
hous·ing [háʊzɪŋ] *s.* viviendas; programa de construcción de viviendas.
hove [hov] *pret.* & *p.p. de* **to heave.**
hov·el [hʌ́vl] *s.* choza, cabaña, *Carib., Ven.* bohío, *Méx.* jacal; cobertizo; *Ríopl.* tapera.
hov·er [hʌ́vɚ] *v.* cernerse (*como un pájaro*); vacilar;

to — **around** revolotear; rondar.
how [haʊ] *adv.* cómo; — **beautiful!** ¡qué hermoso!;
— **early (late, soon)?** ¿cuándo? ¿a qué hora?; —
far is it? ¡a qué distancia está? ¿cuánto dista de
aquí?; — **long?** ¿cuánto tiempo?; — **many?**
¿cuántos?; — **much is it?** ¿cuánto es? ¿a cómo
se vende? ¿cuál es el precio?; — **old are you?**
¿cuántos años tiene Vd.?; **no matter** — **much** por
mucho que; **he knows** — **difficult it is** él sabe lo
difícil que es; él sabe cuán difícil es.
how·ev·er [haʊévə] *adv.* & *conj.* sin embargo, no
obstante, con todo, empero; — **difficult it may
be** por muy difícil que sea; — **much** por mucho
que.
howl [haʊl] *s.* aullido, alarido, chillido, grito; *v.*
aullar; chillar, dar alaridos; gritar.
hub [hʌb] *s.* cubo (*de una rueda*); eje, centro de
actividad.
hub·bub [hʌbʌb] *s.* ajetreo; barullo.
huck·ster [hʌkstə] *s.* vendedor ambulante.
hud·dle [hʌdl] *s.* montón, confusión, tropel; **to be
in a** — estar agrupados (*en futbol para planear
una jugada*); **to get in a** — agruparse (*para
aconsejarse o planear algo*); *v.* amontonar(se);
acurrucarse.
hue [hju] *s.* tinte, matiz.
huff [hʌf] *s.* enojo, rabieta; **to get into a** — enojarse.
hug [hʌg] *v.* abrazar, estrechar; **to** — **the coast**
costear; *s.* abrazo fuerte.
huge [hjudʒ] *adj.* enorme; descomunal.
hull [hʌl] *s.* casco (*de una nave*); armazón (*de una
aeronave*); vaina, hollejo (*de ciertas legumbres*); *v.*
mondar, pelar desvainar, deshollejar.
hum [hʌm] *v.* canturrear (*o* canturriar), tararear;
zumbar (*dícese de insectos, maquinaria, etc.*); **to**
— **to sleep** arrullar; *s.* canturreo, tarareo;
zumbido; *interj.* ¡hum!; ¡ejém!
hu·man [hjúmən] *adj.* humano; *s.* ser humano.
hu·mane [hjumén] *adj.* humano; humanitario.
hu·man·ism [hjúmənɪzm] *s.* humanismo.
hu·man·i·tar·i·an [hjumænətérɪən] *adj.*
humanitario; *s.* filántropo.
hu·man·i·ty [hjumǽnətɪ] *s.* humanidad; **-ies**
humanidades.
hum·ble [hʌmbl] *adj.* humilde; *v.* humillar;
humbly *adv.* humildemente, con humildad.
hum·ble·ness [hʌmblnɪs] *s.* humildad.
hu·mid [hjúmɪd] *adj.* húmedo.
hu·mid·i·fy [hjumídəfaɪ] *v.* humedecer.
hu·mid·i·ty [hjumídətɪ] *d.* humedad.
hu·mil·i·ate [hjumíliet] *v.* humillar.
hu·mil·i·a·tion [hjumɪliéʃən] *s.* humillación.
hu·mil·i·ty [hjumílotɪ] *s.* humildad.
hum·ming·bird [hʌmɪŋbɜd] *s.* colibrí, pájaro mosca,
Méx. chuparrosa, *Am.* chupaflor, *Am.* guainumbí;
Riopl., Ch. picaflor.
hu·mor [hjúmə] *s.* humor, humorismo, gracia;
capricho; **out of** — de mal humor,
malhumorado, disgustado; *v.* seguir el humor (*a
una persona*), complacer; mimar.
hu·mor·ous [hjúmərəs] *adj.* humorístico, gracioso,
cómico, chistoso.
hump [hʌmp] *s.* joroba, corcova, giba; *v.*
encorvarse.
hump·back [hʌmpbæk] = **hunchback.**
hunch [hʌntʃ] *s.* joroba, corcova, giba;
presentimiento, corazonada; *v.* encorvar (*la
espalda*).
hunch·back [hʌntʃbæk] *s.* joroba; jorobado.
hun·dred [hʌndrəd] *adj.* cien(to); *s.* ciento; **-s**
centenares, cientos.

hun·dredth [hʌndrədθ] *adj.* centésimo.
hung [hʌŋ] *pret.* & *p.p. de* **to hang.**
hun·ger [hʌŋgə] *s.* hambre; *v.* tener hambre, estar
hambriento; **to** — **for** ansiar, anhelar.
hun·gri·ly [hʌŋgrɪlɪ] *adv.* con hambre,
hambrientamente.
hun·gry [hʌŋgrɪ] *adj.* hambriento; **to be** — tener
hambre.
hunk [hʌŋk] *s.* pedazo grande; mendrugo (*de pan*).
hunt [hʌnt] *v.* cazar; perseguir; buscar; escudriñar;
to — **down** dar caza a; seguir la pista de; **to** —
for buscar; *s.* caza, cacería; busca, búsqueda;
perseguimiento.
hunt·er [hʌntə] *s.* cazador; buscador; perro de
caza, perro de busca.
hunts·man [hʌntsmən] *s.* cazador.
hurl [hɜl] *v.* arrojar, lanzar.
hur·rah [hɜró] *interj.* ¡hurra! ¡viva!; ¡ole!; *v.*
vitorear.
hur·ri·cane [hɜɪken] *s.* huracán.
hur·ried [hɜɪd] *adj.* apresurado; **-ly** *adv.* de prisa,
apresuradamente, a escape.
hur·ry [hɜɪ] *v.* apresurar(se); precipitar(se); dar(se)
prisa; apurarse; correr; **to** — **in (out)** entrar
(salir) de prisa; **to** — **up** apresurar(se); dar(se)
prisa; *s.* prisa; precipitación; **to be in a** — tener
prisa, ir de prisa, estar de prisa.
hurt [hɜt] *v.* hacer daño; dañar; perjudicar; herir;
lastimar; doler; **to** — **one's feelings** darle a uno
que sentir; lastimar a uno; **my tooth -s** me duele
la muela; *pret.* & *p.p. de* **to hurt**; *s.* daño;
herida; lesión; dolor.
hus·band [hʌzbənd] *s.* marido, esposo.
hush [hʌʃ] *v.* acallar, aquietar; callar(se); **—!**
¡chitón! ¡silencio! ¡cállese! ¡quieto!; **to** — **up a
scandal** encubrir un escándalo; *s.* silencio,
quietud.
husk [hʌsk] *s.* cáscara, hollejo, vaina; *v.* mondar,
pelar, deshollejar.
husk·y [hʌskɪ] *adj.* ronco; forzudo, fuerte;
cascarudo.
hus·tle [hʌsl] *v.* apresurar(se); apurarse; menear(se);
atropellar; *s.* prisa, apresuramiento, meneo;
actividad; — **and bustle** vaivén.
hut [hʌt] *s.* choza, cabaña, *Carib.* bohío.
hy·a·cinth [háɪəsɪnθ] *s.* jacinto.
hy·brid [háɪbrɪd] *adj.* híbrido.
hy·drate [háɪdret] *s.* hidrato.
hy·drau·lic [haɪdrɔ́lɪk] *adj.* hidráulico.
hy·dro·e·lec·tric [haɪdroiléktrɪk] *adj.* hidroeléctrico.
hy·dro·gen [háɪdrədʒən] *s.* hidrógeno.
hy·dro·pho·bi·a [haɪdrofóbɪə] *s.* hidrofobia.
hy·dro·plane [háɪdrəplen] *s.* hidroplano, hidroavión.
hy·giene [háɪdʒin] *s.* higiene.
hymn [hɪm] *s.* himno.
hy·phen [háɪfən] *s.* guión.
hyp·no·sis [hɪpnósɪs] *s.* hipnosis.
hy·poc·ri·sy [hɪpákrəsɪ] *s.* hipocresía.
hyp·o·crite [hípəkrɪt] *s.* hipócrita.
hyp·o·crit·i·cal [hɪpəkrítɪkl] *adj.* hipócrita.
hy·poth·e·sis [haɪpáθəsɪs] *s.* hipótesis.
hys·ter·i·cal [hɪstérɪkl] *adj.* histérico.

HO

I·i I [aɪ] *pron. pers.* yo.

I·be·ri·an [aɪbírɪən] *adj.* ibérico, ibero.

ice [aɪs] *s.* (*solid*) hielo; (*food*) helado; mantecado; sorbete; — **cream** helado; **icecream parlor** *Am.* heladería; nevería; — **skates** patines de cuchilla; — **water** agua helada; *v.* helar; escarchar, alfeñicar, cubrir con escarcha (*un pastel*).

ice·berg [áɪsbɜg] *s.* montaña de hielo, témpano.

ice·box [áɪsbaks] *s.* nevera, *Am.* refrigerador.

ice·man [áɪsmæn] *s.* vendedor de hielo.

i·ci·cle [áɪsɪkḷ] *s.* carámbano.

i·con·o·clasm [aɪkánəklæzəm] *s.* iconoclasmo.

i·con·o·clast [aɪkánəklæst] *s.* iconoclasta.

i·cy [áɪsɪ] *adj.* helado, frío; congelado; cubierto de hielo.

i·de·a [aɪdíə] *s.* idea.

i·de·al [aɪdíəl] *adj.* & *s.* ideal.

i·de·al·ism [aɪdíəlɪzəm] *s.* idealismo.

i·de·al·ist [aɪdíəlɪst] *s.* idealista.

i·de·al·is·tic [aɪdiəlístɪk] *adj.* idealista.

i·den·ti·cal [aɪdɛ́ntɪkḷ] *adj.* idéntico.

i·den·ti·fi·ca·tion [aɪdɛntəfɪkéʃən] *s.* identificación; **I.D. card** carnet.

i·den·ti·fy [aɪdɛ́ntəfaɪ] *v.* identificar.

i·den·ti·ty [aɪdɛ́ntətɪ] *s.* identidad.

i·de·ol·o·gy [aɪdɪólədʒɪ] *s.* ideología.

id·i·o·cy [Ídɪəsɪ] *s.* idiotez.

id·i·om [ídɪəm] *s.* modismo, idiotismo.

id·i·o·syn·cra·sy [ɪdɪosínkrəsɪ] *s.* idiosincrasia.

id·i·ot [ídɪət] *s.* idiota.

id·i·ot·ic [ɪdɪátɪk] *adj.* idiota.

i·dle [áɪdḷ] *adj.* ocioso; perezoso, holgazán; vano; desocupado; *v.* holgazanear; perder el tiempo; funcionar (*el motor solo, sin engranar*); **idly** *adv.* ociosamente; inútilmente; perezosamente.

i·dle·ness [áɪdḷnɪs] *s.* ociosidad; ocio, desocupación; pereza, holgazanería.

i·dler [áɪdlə] *s.* holgazán, haragán.

i·dol [áɪdḷ] *s.* ídolo.

i·dol·a·try [aɪdálətrɪ] *s.* idolatría.

i·dol·ize [áɪdḷaɪz] *v.* idolatrar.

i·dyl [áɪdḷ] *s.* idilio.

if [ɪf] *conj.* si.

ig·nite [ɪgnáɪt] *v.* encender(se), inflamar(se); prender, pegar fuego a.

ig·ni·tion [ɪgníʃən] *s.* ignición, encendido (*de un motor*); — **switch** interruptor de encendido, *Méx., C.A., Ven., Carib.* switch de ignición.

ig·no·ble [ɪgnóbḷ] *adj.* innoble; bajo, vil.

ig·no·rance [ígnərəns] *s.* ignorancia.

ig·no·rant [ígnərənt] *adj.* ignorante.

ig·nore [ɪgnór] *v.* no hacer caso de, desatender; desairar.

ill [ɪl] *adj.* enfermo; malo; — **nature** mal genio, mala índole; — **will** mala voluntad, ojeriza, inquina; *s.* mal; enfermedad; calamidad; infortunio; *adv.* mal, malamente; — **at ease** inquieto, intranquilo; **ill-bred** mal criado; **ill-clad** mal vestido; **ill-humored** malhumorado; **ill-mannered** descortés, grosero; **ill-natured** de mala índole, *Ven., Col., Méx.* mal genioso; **ill-advised** mal aconsejado.

il·le·gal [ɪlígl] *adj.* ilegal; ilícito.

il·le·git·i·mate [ɪlɪdʒítəmɪt] *adj.* ilegítimo; bastardo.

il·lic·it [ɪlísɪt] *adj.* ilícito.

il·lit·er·a·cy [ɪlítərəsɪ] *s.* analfabetismo.

il·lit·er·ate [ɪlítərɪt] *adj.* & *s.* analfabeto.

ill·ness [ílnɪs] *s.* mal, enfermedad.

il·lu·mi·nate [ɪlúmənet] *v.* iluminar; alumbrar;

esclarecer.

il·lu·mi·na·tion [ɪlumənéʃən] *s.* iluminación; alumbrado.

il·lu·sion [ɪlúʒən] *s.* ilusión.

il·lu·sive [ɪlúsɪv] *adj.* ilusorio, ilusivo, falaz.

il·lu·so·ry [ɪlúsərɪ] *adj.* ilusorio, ilusivo, engañoso.

il·lus·trate [ɪləstrét] *v.* ilustrar; esclarecer.

il·lus·tra·tion [ɪləstréʃən] *s.* ilustración; grabado, estampa; aclaración, esclarecimiento.

il·lus·tra·tor [íləstretə] *s.* ilustrador.

il·lus·tri·ous [ɪlʌ́strɪəs] *adj.* ilustre.

im·age [ímɪdʒ] *s.* imagen.

im·age·ry [ímɪdʒrɪ] *s.* conjunto de imágenes, figuras; fantasía.

im·ag·i·nar·y [ɪmǽdʒənɛrɪ] *adj.* imaginario.

im·ag·i·na·tion [ɪmædʒənéʃən] *s.* imaginación; imaginativa.

im·ag·i·na·tive [ɪmǽdʒənetɪv] *adj.* imaginativo.

im·ag·ine [ɪmǽdʒɪn] *v.* imaginar(se); figurarse.

im·be·cile [ímbəsɪl] *adj.* & *s.* imbécil.

im·bibe [ɪmbáɪb] *v.* embeber, absorber; beber.

im·bue [ɪmbjú] *v.* imbuir, infundir; impregnar, empapar.

im·i·tate [ímətet] *v.* imitar; remedar.

im·i·ta·tion [ɪmətéʃən] *s.* imitación; remedo; *adj.* imitado, de imitación.

im·i·ta·tor [ímətetə] *s.* imitador; remedador.

im·mac·u·late [ɪmǽkjəlɪt] *adj.* inmaculado, sin mancha.

im·ma·te·ri·al [ɪmətírɪəl] *adj.* inmaterial, espiritual; **it is** — **to me** me es indiferente.

im·me·di·ate [ímídɪt] *adj.* inmediato; próximo; **-ly** *adv.* inmediatamente; en seguida; al punto, en el acto, al instante.

im·mense [ɪméns] *adj.* inmenso.

im·men·si·ty [ɪménsətɪ] *s.* inmensidad.

im·merse [ɪmɝ́s] *v.* sumergir, sumir.

im·mi·grant [íməgrənt] *adj.* & *s.* inmigrante.

im·mi·grate [íməgret] *v.* inmigrar.

im·mi·gra·tion [ɪməgréʃən] *s.* inmigración.

im·mi·nent [ímənənt] *adj.* inminente.

im·mo·bile [ɪmóbɪl] *adj.* inmóbil.

im·mod·est [ɪmádɪst] *adj.* deshonesto, impúdico, indecente.

im·mor·al [ɪmɔ́rəl] *adj.* inmoral; licencioso.

im·mor·al·i·ty [ɪmərǽlətɪ] *s.* inmoralidad.

im·mor·tal [ɪmɔ́rtl] *adj.* & *s.* inmortal.

im·mor·tal·i·ty [ɪmɔrtǽlətɪ] *s.* inmortalidad.

im·mov·a·ble [ɪmúvəbl] *adj.* inmovible (*o* inamovible); inmóvil; inmutable.

im·mune [ɪmjún] *adj.* inmune.

im·mu·ni·ty [ɪmjúnətɪ] *s.* inmunidad.

im·mu·ta·ble [ɪmjútəbl] *adj.* inmutable.

imp [ɪmp] *s.* diablillo.

im·pair [ɪmpér] *v.* dañar, perjudicar, menoscabar, desvirtuar, debilitar.

im·pair·ment [ɪmpérmənt] *s.* menoscabo; perjuicio; deterioro.

im·part [ɪmpárt] *v.* impartir, dar, comunicar.

im·par·tial [ɪmpárʃəl] *adj.* imparcial.

im·par·ti·al·i·ty [ɪmparʃǽlətɪ] *s.* imparcialidad.

im·pas·si·ble [ɪmpǽsəbl] *adj.* impasible.

im·pas·sioned [ɪmpǽʃənd] *adj.* apasionado, vehemente, ardiente.

im·pas·sive [ɪmpǽsɪv] *adj.* impasible.

im·pa·tience [ɪmpéʃəns] *s.* impaciencia.

im·pa·tient [ɪmpéʃənt] *adj.* impaciente.

im·peach [ɪmpitʃ] *v.* demandar o acusar formalmente (*a un alto funcionario de gobierno*); **to** — **a person's honor** poner en tela de juicio el honor de uno.

im·pede [ɪmpíd] *v.* impedir, estorbar, obstruir.
im·ped·i·ment [ɪmpédəmənt] *s.* impedimento, obstáculo, estorbo; traba.
im·pel [ɪmpél] *v.* impeler, impulsar.
im·pend·ing [ɪmpéndɪŋ] *adj.* inminente, amenazador.
im·per·a·tive [ɪmpérətɪv] *adj.* imperativo; imperioso, urgente; *s.* imperativo.
im·per·cep·ti·ble [ɪmpɚséptəbl] *adj.* imperceptible.
im·per·fect [ɪmpɚ́fɪkt] *adj.* imperfecto; defectuoso; *s.* imperfecto (*tiempo del verbo*).
im·pe·ri·al [ɪmpírɪəl] *adj.* imperial.
im·pe·ri·al·ism [ɪmpírɪəlɪzm] *s.* imperialismo.
im·per·il [ɪmpérəl] *v.* poner en peligro, arriesgar.
im·pe·ri·ous [ɪmpírɪəs] *adj.* imperioso; urgente.
im·per·son·al [ɪmpɚ́sɪl] *adj.* impersonal.
im·per·son·ate [ɪmpɚ́snet] *v.* representar (*un personaje*); remedar, imitar; fingirse otro, pretender ser otro.
im·per·ti·nence [ɪmpɚ́tnəns] *s.* impertinencia; insolencia, descaro.
im·per·ti·nent [ɪmpɚ́tnənt] *adj.* impertinente; insolente, descarado.
im·per·vi·ous [ɪmpɚ́vɪəs] *adj.* impermeable; impenetrable; — **to reason** refractario, testarudo.
im·pet·u·ous [ɪmpétʃʊəs] *adj.* impetuoso.
im·pe·tus [ɪmpətəs] *s.* ímpetu.
im·pi·ous [ɪmpɪəs] *adj.* impío.
im·pla·ca·ble [ɪmplékəbl] *adj.* implacable.
im·plant [ɪmplǽnt] *v.* implantar, plantar; inculcar, infundir.
im·ple·ment [ɪmpləmənt] *s.* herramienta, instrumento; -s utensilios, aperos, enseres.
im·pli·cate [ɪmplɪket] *v.* implicar, envolver, enredar.
im·plic·it [ɪmplísɪt] *adj.* implícito.
im·plore [ɪmplór] *v.* implorar, rogar; suplicar.
im·ply [ɪmplái] *v.* implicar; querer decir; insinuar.
im·po·lite [ɪmpəláɪt] *adj.* descortés.
im·port [ɪmpórt] *s.* significado, significación, sentido; importancia; importación; -s artículos importados; [ɪmpórt] *v.* importar; significar, querer decir.
im·por·tance [ɪmpórtns] *s.* importancia.
im·por·tant [ɪmpórtnt] *adj.* importante.
im·pose [ɪmpóz] *v.* imponer; **to — upon** abusar de (la amistad, hospitalidad, confianza de alguien); engañar.
im·pos·ing [ɪmpózɪŋ] *adj.* imponente; impresionante.
im·po·si·tion [ɪmpəzíʃən] *s.* imposición; carga, impuesto; abuso (de confianza).
im·pos·si·bil·i·ty [ɪmpasəbílətɪ] *s.* imposibilidad.
im·pos·si·ble [ɪmpásəbl] *adj.* imposible.
im·pos·tor [ɪmpástɚ] *s.* impostor, embaucador.
im·pos·ture [ɪmpástʃɚ] *s.* impostura, fraude, engaño.
im·po·tence [ɪmpətəns] *s.* impotencia.
im·po·tent [ɪmpətənt] *adj.* impotente.
im·pov·er·ish [ɪmpávərɪʃ] *v.* empobrecer.
im·preg·nate [ɪmprégnet] *v.* impregnar; empapar; empreñar.
im·press [ɪmprɛs] *s.* impresión, marca, señal, huella; [ɪmprés] *v.* imprimir, estampar, marcar, grabar; impresionar.
im·pres·sion [ɪmpréʃən] *s.* impresión; marca.
im·pres·sive [ɪmprésɪv] *adj.* impresionante; imponente.
im·print [ɪmprɪnt] *s.* impresión; pie de imprenta; [ɪmprínt] *v.* imprimir; estampar.

im·pris·on [ɪmprísn̩] *v.* aprisionar, encarcelar.
im·pris·on·ment [ɪmprízn̩mənt] *s.* prisión, encarcelación o encarcelamiento.
im·prob·a·ble [ɪmprábəbl] *adj.* improbable.
im·promp·tu [ɪmprámptu] *adv.* de improviso.
im·prop·er [ɪmprápɚ] *adj.* impropio.
im·prove [ɪmprúv] *v.* mejorar(se); **to — upon** mejorar; **to — one's time** aprovechar el tiempo.
im·prove·ment [ɪmprúvmənt] *s.* mejoramiento; mejora; progreso, adelanto; mejoría (de una enfermedad).
im·pro·vise [ɪmprəvaɪz] *v.* improvisar.
im·pru·dent [ɪmprúdn̩t] *adj.* imprudente.
im·pu·dence [ɪmpjədəns] *s.* impudencia, descaro, insolencia.
im·pu·dent [ɪmpjədənt] *adj.* impudente, descarado, insolente.
im·pulse [ɪmpʌls] *s.* impulso; ímpetu; inclinación; **to act on** — obrar impulsivamente.
im·pul·sive [ɪmpʌ́lsɪv] *adj.* impulsivo.
im·pu·ni·ty [ɪmpjúnətɪ] *s.* impunidad, falta o exención de castigo.
im·pure [ɪmpjúr] *adj.* impuro; sucio; adulterado.
im·pu·ri·ty [ɪmpjúrətɪ] *s.* impureza.
im·pute [ɪmpjút] *v.* imputar, achacar, atribuir.
in [ɪn] *prep.* en; dentro de; de (después de un superlativo); — **haste** de prisa; — **the morning** por (o en) la mañana; — **writing** por escrito; **at two** — **the morning** a las dos de la mañana; **dressed** — **white** vestido de blanco; **the tallest** — **his class** el más alto de su clase; **to come** — **a week** venir de hoy en ocho días, venir dentro de ocho días; *adv.* dentro; adentro; en casa; **to be** — **and out** estar entrando y saliendo; **to be all** — no poder más, estar rendido de cansancio; **to be** — **with someone** estar asociado con alguien; disfrutar el aprecio de una persona; **to come** — entrar; **to have it** — **for someone** tenerle ojeriza a una persona; **to put** — meter; **is the train** —? ¿ha llegado el tren?
in·a·bil·i·ty [ɪnəbílətɪ] *s.* inhabilidad, incapacidad.
in·ac·ces·si·ble [ɪnəksésəbl] *adj.* inaccesible; inasequible.
in·ac·cu·rate [ɪnǽkjərɪt] *adj.* inexacto, impreciso, incorrecto.
in·ac·tive [ɪnǽktɪv] *adj.* inactivo; inerte.
in·ac·tiv·i·ty [ɪnæktívətɪ] *s.* inactividad, inacción, inercia.
in·ad·e·quate [ɪnǽdəkwɪt] *adj.* inadecuado; insuficiente.
in·ad·ver·tent [ɪnədvɚ́tn̩t] *adj.* inadvertido; descuidado; -ly *adv.* inadvertidamente; descuidadamente.
in·ad·vis·a·ble [ɪnədváɪzəbl] *adj.* imprudente.
in·an·i·mate [ɪnǽnəmɪt] *adj.* inanimado.
in·as·much [ɪnəzmʌ́tʃ]: — **as** visto que, puesto que; en cuanto.
in·at·ten·tive [ɪnətɛ́ntɪv] *adj.* desatento.
in·au·gu·rate [ɪnɔ́gjoret] *v.* inaugurar, iniciar; investir de una dignidad o cargo.
in·au·gu·ra·tion [ɪnɔgjəréʃən] *s.* inauguración.
in·board [ínbord] *adj.* interior.
in·born [ínbɔrn] *adj.* innato, connatural.
in·can·des·cent [ɪnkəndésn̩t] *adj.* incandescente, candente.
in·can·ta·tion [ɪnkæntéʃən] *s.* conjuro.
in·ca·pa·ble [ɪnképəbl] *adj.* incapaz.
in·ca·pac·i·tate [ɪnkəpǽsɪtet] *v.* incapacitar.
in·cen·di·ar·y [ɪnsɛ́ndɪɛrɪ] *adj.* incendiario; — **bomb** bomba incendiaria.
in·cense [ínsɛns] *s.* incienso; [ɪnséns] *v.* inflamar,

exasperar.

in·cen·tive [ɪnséntɪv] *s.* incentivo, estimulo.

in·ces·sant [ɪnsésn̩t] *adj.* incesante, continuo.

inch [ɪntʃ] *s.* pulgada (*2.54 centímetros*); **by -es** poco a poco, gradualmente; **every — a man** nada menos que todo un hombre; **to be within an — of** estar a dos pulgadas de, estar muy cerca de; *v.* avanzar muy despacio (*por pulgadas*).

in·ci·dence [ɪ́nsɪdəns] *s.* incidencia.

in·ci·dent [ɪ́nsədənt] *s.* incidente, suceso, acontecimiento.

in·ci·den·tal [ɪnsədéntl̩] *adj.* incidental; accidental; contingente; **-s** *s. pl.* gastos imprevistos; **-ly** *adv.* incidentalmente; de paso.

in·cip·i·ent [ɪnsípɪənt] *adj.* incipiente.

in·ci·sion [ɪnsíʒən] *s.* incisión.

in·ci·sive [ɪnsáɪsɪv] *adj.* incisivo.

in·cite [ɪnsáɪt] *v.* incitar.

in·clem·ent [ɪnklɛ́mənt] *adj.* inclemente.

in·cli·na·tion [ɪnklənéʃən] *s.* inclinación.

in·cline [ɪ́nklaɪn] *s.* declive, pendiente, cuesta; [ɪnkláɪn] *v.* inclinar(se).

in·close = **enclose**.

in·clo·sure = **enclosure**.

in·clude [ɪnklúd] *v.* incluir, encerrar; abarcar.

in·clu·sive [ɪnklúsɪv] *adj.* inconcluso; **from Monday to Friday — del** lunes al viernes inclusive.

in·co·her·ent [ɪnkohírənt] *adj.* incoherente, inconexo.

in·come [ɪ́nkʌm] *s.* renta, rédito, ingreso, entrada; **— tax** impuesto sobre rentas.

in·com·pa·ra·ble [ɪnkámpərəbl̩] *adj.* incomparable, sin par, sin igual.

in·com·pat·i·ble [ɪnkəmpǽtəbl̩] *adj.* incompatible.

in·com·pe·tent [ɪnkámpətənt] *adj.* incompetente.

in·com·plete [ɪnkəmplít] *adj.* incompleto.

in·com·pre·hen·si·ble [ɪnkəmprɪhénsəbl̩] *adj.* incomprensible.

in·con·ceiv·a·ble [ɪnkənsívəbl̩] *adj.* inconcebible.

in·con·clu·sive [ɪnkənklúsɪv] *adj.* inconcluso.

in·con·sid·er·ate [ɪnkənsídərɪt] *adj.* inconsiderado, falto de miramiento.

in·con·sis·ten·cy [ɪnkənsístənsɪ] *s.* inconsecuencia; falta de uniformidad (*en la aplicación de una regla o principio*).

in·con·sis·tent [ɪnkənsístənt] *adj.* inconsecuente; falto de uniformidad.

in·con·spic·u·ous [ɪnkənspíkjuəs] *adj.* poco llamativo.

in·con·stan·cy [ɪnkánstənsɪ] *s.* inconstancia, mudanza.

in·con·stant [ɪnkánstənt] *adj.* inconstante, mudable, voluble.

in·con·test·a·ble [ɪnkəntéstəbl̩] *adj.* incontestable.

in·con·ven·ience [ɪnkənvínjəns] *s.* inconveniencia; molestia; *v.* incomodar; molestar.

in·con·ven·ient [ɪnkənvínjənt] *adj.* inconveniente, inoportuno.

in·cor·po·rate [ɪnkɔ́rpərɪt] *adj.* incorporado; asociado; [ɪnkɔ́rpəret] *v.* incorporar; incorporarse, asociarse (*para formar un cuerpo*).

in·cor·rect [ɪnkərɛ́kt] *adj.* incorrecto.

in·cor·ri·gi·ble [ɪnkɔ́rɪdʒəbl̩] *adj.* incorregible.

in·crease [ɪ́nkris] *s.* aumento; acrecentamiento; crecimiento; incremento; [ɪnkrís] *v.* aumentar(se); acrecentar(se), crecer; recargar.

in·creas·ing·ly [ɪnkrísɪŋlɪ] *adv.* más y más; cada vez más.

in·cred·i·ble [ɪnkrɛ́dəbl̩] *adj.* increíble.

in·cre·du·li·ty [ɪnkrədúlətɪ] *s.* incredulidad.

in·cred·u·lous [ɪnkrɛ́dʒələs] *adj.* incrédulo, descreído.

in·cre·ment [ɪ́nkrəmənt] *s.* incremento.

in·crim·i·nate [ɪnkrímənet] *v.* acriminar.

in·cu·ba·tor [ɪ́nkjubetəˑ] *s.* incubadora.

in·cul·cate [ɪnkʌ́lket] *v.* inculcar, infundir.

in·cur [ɪnkɝ́] *v.* incurrir en.

in·cur·a·ble [ɪnkjúrəbl̩] *adj.* incurable, irremediable; *s.* incurable.

in·debt·ed [ɪndɛ́tɪd] *adj.* adeudado, endeudado; obligado, agradecido.

in·debt·ed·ness [ɪndɛ́tɪdnɪs] *s.* deuda; obligación.

in·de·cen·cy [ɪndísn̩sɪ] *s.* indecencia.

in·de·cent [ɪndísn̩t] *adj.* indecente.

in·de·ci·sion [ɪndəsíʒən] *s.* indecisión.

in·deed [ɪndid] *adv.* en verdad, a la verdad; de veras; realmente.

in·de·fen·si·ble [ɪndɪfénsəbl̩] *adj.* indefendible.

in·def·i·nite [ɪndɛ́fənɪt] *adj.* indefinido.

in·del·i·ble [ɪndɛ́ləbl̩] *adj.* indeleble.

in·del·i·cate [ɪndɛ́ləkət] *adj.* indelicado, indecoroso.

in·dem·ni·fy [ɪndɛ́mnəfaɪ] *v.* indemnizar.

in·dem·ni·ty [ɪndɛ́mnətɪ] *s.* indemnización.

in·dent [ɪndɛ́nt] *v.* dentar, endentar; sangrar (*comenzar un renglón más adentro que los otros*).

in·de·pend·ence [ɪndɪpéndəns] *s.* independencia.

in·de·pend·ent [ɪndɪpéndənt] *adj.* independiente.

in·de·scrib·a·ble [ɪndɪskráɪbəbl̩] *adj.* indescriptible.

in·dex [ɪ́ndɛks] *s.* índice; *v.* alfabetizar, ordenar alfabéticamente; poner en un índice; **— finger** índice.

In·di·an [ɪ́ndɪən] *adj.* & *s.* indio; **— Ocean** Océano Indico.

in·di·cate [ɪ́ndəket] *v.* indicar.

in·di·ca·tion [ɪndəkéʃən] *s.* indicación.

in·dic·a·tive [ɪndíkətɪv] *adj.* & *s.* indicativo.

in·dict [ɪndáɪt] *v.* procesar, demandar (*ante un juez*); enjuiciar, formar causa a.

in·dict·ment [ɪndáɪtmənt] *s.* acusación (*hecha por el Gran Jurado*), denuncia, proceso judicial.

in·dif·fer·ence [ɪndífrəns] *s.* indiferencia; apatía.

in·dif·fer·ent [ɪndífrənt] *adj.* indiferente; apático.

in·dig·e·nous [ɪndídʒənəs] *adj.* indígena, autóctono, nativo.

in·di·gent [ɪ́ndədʒənt] *adj.* & *s.* indigente.

in·di·ges·tion [ɪndədʒéstʃən] *s.* indigestión.

in·dig·nant [ɪndígnənt] *adj.* indignado; **-ly** *adv.* con indignación.

in·dig·na·tion [ɪndɪgnéʃən] *s.* indignación.

in·dig·ni·ty [ɪndígnɪtɪ] *s.* indignidad, afrenta.

in·di·go [ɪ́ndɪgo] *s.* indigo, añil; **— blue** azul de añil.

in·di·rect [ɪndərɛ́kt] *adj.* indirecto.

in·dis·creet [ɪndɪskrít] *adj.* indiscreto.

in·dis·cre·tion [ɪndɪskréʃən] *s.* indiscreción.

in·dis·pen·sa·ble [ɪndɪspénsəbl̩] *adj.* indispensable.

in·dis·pose [ɪndɪspóz] *v.* indisponer.

in·dis·posed [ɪndɪspózd] *adj.* indispuesto.

in·dis·po·si·tion [ɪndɪspəzíʃən] *s.* indisposición; malestar.

in·dis·tinct [ɪndɪstíŋkt] *adj.* indistinto.

in·di·um [ɪ́ndɪəm] *s.* indio.

in·di·vid·u·al [ɪndəvídʒʊəl] *adj.* individual; *s.* individuo, sujeto, persona.

in·di·vid·u·al·ism [ɪndəvídʒʊəlɪzm̩] *s.* individualismo.

in·di·vid·u·al·ist [ɪndəvídʒuəlɪst] *s.* individualista.

in·di·vid·u·al·i·ty [ɪndəvɪdʒuǽlətɪ] *s.* individualidad, individuo, persona.

in·di·vis·i·ble [ɪndəvízəbl̩] *adj.* indivisible.

in·doc·tri·nate [ɪndáktrɪnet] *v.* adoctrinar.

in·do·lence [ɪ́ndələns] *s.* indolencia, desidia, apatía.

in·do·lent [ɪ́ndələnt] *adj.* indolente, desidioso,

apático.
in·dom·i·ta·ble [ɪndámətəbl] *adj.* indomable.
in·door [índor] *adj.* interior, de casa.
in·doors [índórz] *adv.* dentro, en casa; adentro; **to go** — entrar; ir adentro.
in·dorse = endorse.
in·dorse·ment = endorsement.
in·dors·er = endorser.
in·duce [ɪndjús] *v.* inducir.
in·duce·ment [ɪndjúsmənt] *s.* aliciente, incentivo.
in·duct [ɪndʌ́kt] *v.* introducir; iniciar; instalar (*en un cargo*).
in·duc·tion [ɪndʌ́kʃən] *s.* inducción; instalación (*en un cargo*).
in·dulge [ɪndʌ́ldʒ] *v.* gratificar, complacer; seguir el humor a (*una persona*); mimar, consentir (*a un niño*); **to** — **in** darse a, entregarse a (*un placer*); darse el lujo de, permitirse el placer de.
in·dul·gence [ɪndʌ́ldʒəns] *s.* indulgencia; complacencia (*en el vicio o placer*).
in·dul·gent [ɪndʌ́ldʒənt] *adj.* indulgente.
in·dus·tri·al [ɪndʌ́strɪəl] *adj.* industrial.
in·dus·tri·al·ist [ɪndʌ́strɪəlɪst] *s.* industrial; fabricante.
in·dus·tri·ous [ɪndʌ́strɪəs] *adj.* industrioso, aplicado, diligente.
in·dus·try [índəstrɪ] *s.* industria; aplicación, diligencia.
in·ed·i·ble [ɪnédəbl] *adj.* incomestible.
in·ef·fa·ble [ɪnéfəbl] *adj.* inefable.
in·ef·fec·tive [ɪnəféktɪv] *adj.* inefectivo, ineficaz.
in·ef·fi·cient [ɪnifíʃənt] *adj.* ineficaz.
in·el·i·gi·ble [ɪnélədʒəbl] *adj.* inelegible.
in·e·qual·i·ty [ɪnɪkwálətɪ] *s.* desigualdad; disparidad.
in·ert [ɪnə́t] *adj.* inerte.
in·er·tia [ɪnə́ʃə] *s.* inercia.
in·es·cap·a·ble [ɪnəsképəbl] *adj.* forzoso, inevitable.
in·es·ti·ma·ble [ɪnéstəməbl] *adj.* inestimable.
in·ev·i·ta·ble [ɪnévətəbl] *adj.* inevitable.
in·ex·haust·i·ble [ɪnɪgzóstəbl] *adj.* inagotable.
in·ex·o·ra·ble [ɪnéksərəbl] *adj.* inexorable; severo.
in·ex·pe·di·ent [ɪnɛkspídjənt] *adj.* inoportuno; imprudente.
in·ex·pen·sive [ɪnɪkspénsɪv] *adj.* económico, barato.
in·ex·pe·ri·ence [ɪnɪkspírɪəns] *s.* inexperiencia, falta de experiencia.
in·ex·pe·ri·enced [ɪnɪkspírɪənst] *adj.* inexperto, falto de experiencia.
in·ex·pli·ca·ble [ɪnéksplɪkəbl] *adj.* inexplicable.
in·ex·press·i·ble [ɪnɪksprésəbl] *adj.* inexpresable, indecible, inefable.
in·fal·li·ble [ɪnfǽləbl] *adj.* infalible.
in·fa·mous [ínfəməs] *adj.* infame, ignominioso.
in·fa·my [ínfəmɪ] *s.* infamia.
in·fan·cy [ínfənsɪ] *s.* infancia.
in·fant [ínfənt] *s.* infante, bebé, criatura, nene.
in·fan·tile [ínfəntaɪl] *adj.* infantil.
in·fan·try [ínfəntrɪ] *s.* infantería.
in·fect [ɪnfékt] *v.* infectar, inficionar; contagiar; contaminar.
in·fec·tion [ɪnfékʃən] *s.* infección; contagio.
in·fec·tious [ɪnfékʃəs] *adj.* infeccioso; contagioso.
in·fer [ɪnfə́] *v.* inferir, deducir, colegir.
in·fer·ence [ínfərəns] *s.* inferencia, deducción.
in·fe·ri·or [ɪnfírɪə] *adj. & s.* inferior.
in·fe·ri·or·i·ty [ɪnfɪríórətɪ] *s.* inferioridad; — **complex** complejo de inferioridad.
in·fer·nal [ɪnfə́nl] *adj.* infernal.
in·fer·no [ɪnfə́no] *s.* infierno.
in·fest [ɪnfést] *v.* infestar, plagar.

in·fi·del [ínfədl] *adj. & s.* infiel.
in·fil·trate [ɪnfíltret] *v.* infiltrar(se).
in·fi·nite [ínfənɪt] *adj. & s.* infinito.
in·fin·i·tive [ɪnfínətɪv] *adj. & s.* infinitivo.
in·fin·i·ty [ɪnfínətɪ] *s.* infinidad; infinito.
in·firm [ɪnfə́m] *adj.* enfermizo, achacoso, débil.
in·fir·ma·ry [ɪnfə́mərɪ] *s.* enfermería.
in·fir·mi·ty [ɪnfə́mətɪ] *s.* enfermedad, achaque; flaqueza.
in·flame [ɪnflém] *v.* inflamar(se); enardecer(se).
in·flam·ma·tion [ɪnfləméʃən] *s.* inflamación.
in·flate [ɪnflét] *v.* inflar; hinchar.
in·fla·tion [ɪnfléʃən] *s.* inflación; hinchazón.
in·flec·tion [ɪnflékʃən] *s.* inflexión.
in·flict [ɪnflíkt] *v.* infligir, imponer.
in·flu·ence [ínfluəns] *s.* influencia, influjo; *v.* influir en; ejercer influencia o influjo sobre.
in·flu·en·tial [ɪnfluénʃəl] *adj.* influyente.
in·flu·en·za [ɪnfluénzə] *s.* influenza, gripe.
in·flux [ínflʌks] *s.* entrada, afluencia (*de gente*).
in·fold [ɪnfóld] *v.* envolver; abrazar; abarcar.
in·form [ɪnfórm] *v.* informar; enterar; avisar; **to** — **against** delatar a, denunciar a.
in·for·mal [ɪnfórml] *adj.* informal, sin ceremonia; — **visit** visita de confianza; **-ly** *adv.* informalmente, sin ceremonia, de confianza.
in·form·ant [ɪnfórmənt] *s.* informante.
in·for·ma·tion [ɪnfəméʃən] *s.* (*service*) información; (*details*) informes; (*news*) noticias; (*knowledge*) conocimientos, saber.
in·frac·tion [ɪnfrǽkʃən] *s.* infracción.
in·fringe [ɪnfríndʒ] *v.* infringir, violar; **to** — **upon** violar.
in·fu·ri·ate [ɪnfjúrɪet] *v.* enfurecer.
in·fuse [ɪnfjúz] *v.* infundir; inculcar.
in·gen·ious [ɪndʒínjəs] *adj.* ingenioso.
in·ge·nu·i·ty [ɪndʒənúətɪ] *s.* ingeniosidad.
in·grat·i·tude [ɪngrǽtətjud] *s.* ingratitud.
in·gre·di·ent [ɪngrídɪənt] *s.* ingrediente.
in·hab·it [ɪnhǽbɪt] *v.* habitar, vivir en, residir en.
in·hab·i·tant [ɪnhǽbətənt] *s.* habitante.
in·hale [ɪnhél] *v.* inhalar, aspirar, inspirar.
in·her·ent [ɪnhírənt] *adj.* inherente.
in·her·it [ɪnhérɪt] *v.* heredar.
in·her·i·tance [ɪnhérətəns] *s.* herencia.
in·hib·it [ɪnhíbɪt] *v.* inhibir, cohibir, refrenar, reprimir; impedir.
in·hi·bi·tion [ɪnɪbíʃən] *s.* inhibición, cohibición; prohibición, restricción.
in·hos·pi·ta·ble [ɪnháspɪtəbl] *adj.* inhospitalario.
in·hu·man [ɪnhjúmən] *adj.* inhumano.
in·im·i·ta·ble [ɪnímətəbl] *adj.* inimitable.
in·iq·ui·ty [ɪníkwətɪ] *s.* iniquidad, maldad.
in·i·tial [ɪníʃəl] *adj. & s.* inicial; — **abbreviation** sigla; *v.* marcar o firmar con iniciales.
in·i·ti·ate [ɪníʃɪet] *v.* iniciar.
in·i·ti·a·tive [ɪníʃɪetɪv] *s.* iniciativa.
in·ject [ɪndʒékt] *v.* inyectar; injerir, introducir.
in·jec·tion [ɪndʒékʃən] *s.* inyección.
in·junc·tion [ɪndʒʌ́ŋkʃən] *s.* mandato, orden; entredicho.
in·jure [índʒə] *v.* dañar; herir, lesionar; lastimar.
in·ju·ri·ous [ɪndʒúrɪəs] *adj.* dañoso, dañino, perjudicial.
in·ju·ry [índʒərɪ] *s.* daño; herida, lesión; perjuicio.
in·jus·tice [ɪndʒʌ́stɪs] *s.* injusticia.
ink [ɪŋk] *s.* tinta; *v.* entintar; teñir o manchar con tinta.
ink·ling [íŋklɪŋ] *s.* indicación, indicio, idea, sospecha, noción vaga.
ink·stand [íŋkstænd] *s.* tintero.

IN

ink·well [íŋkwɛl] *s.* tintero.

in·laid [ɪnléd] *adj.* incrustado, embutido; **— work** embutido, incrustación; *pret.* & *p.p. de* **to inlay.**

in·land [ínlənd] *s.* interior (*de un país*); *adj.* interior, del interior de un país; *adv.* tierra adentro.

in·lay [ɪnlé] *v.* incrustar, embutir; [ínle] *s.* embutido.

in·mate [ínmet] *s.* residente, asilado (*de un hospicio, asilo, casa de corrección, etc.*); presidiario; hospiciano.

in·most [ínmost] *adj.* más interior, más íntimo, más secreto o recóndito; más profundo.

inn [ɪn] *s.* posada, mesón, fonda.

in·nate [ínét] *adj.* innato, connatural.

in·ner [ínɚ] *adj.* interior; íntimo, recóndito; **—most = inmost.**

in·ning [ínɪŋ] *s.* entrada, cuadro (*en béisbol*); turno (*del bateador en béisbol y otros juegos*).

inn·keep·er [ínkipɚ] *s.* ventero, mesonero, posadero.

in·no·cence [ínəsns] *s.* inocencia.

in·no·cent [ínəsnt] *adj.* & *s.* inocente.

in·noc·u·ous [ɪnákjuəs] *adj.* innocuo, inofensivo.

in·no·va·tion [ɪnəvéʃən] *s.* innovación.

in·nu·en·do [ɪnjuéndo] *s.* insinuación, indirecta.

in·nu·mer·a·ble [ɪnjúmərəbl] *adj.* innumerable.

in·oc·u·late [ɪnákjəlet] *v.* inocular; contaminar.

in·of·fen·sive [ɪnəfénsɪv] *adj.* inofensivo.

in·op·por·tune [ɪnɑpɚtjún] *adj.* inoportuno.

in·put [ínput] *s.* potencia consumida; (*electric*) entrada.

in·quire [ɪnkwáɪr] *v.* inquirir, indagar; preguntar; **to — about** preguntar por; **to — into** indagar, investigar.

in·qui·ry [ɪnkwáɪrɪ] *s.* indagación, investigación; pregunta; interrogatorio.

in·qui·si·tion [ɪnkwəzíʃən] *s.* inquisición; indagación.

in·quis·i·tive [ɪnkwízətɪv] *adj.* inquisitivo, investigador; preguntón; curioso.

in·road [ínrod] *s.* incursión, invasión, ataque; **to make -s upon** atacar; mermar.

in·sane [ɪnsén] *adj.* insano, loco; **— asylum** manicomio, casa de locos.

in·san·i·ty [ɪnsǽnətɪ] *s.* locura.

in·sa·tia·ble [ɪnséʃɪəbl] *adj.* insaciable.

in·scribe [ɪnskráɪb] *v.* inscribir.

in·scrip·tion [ɪnskrípʃən] *s.* inscripción; letrero.

in·sect [ínsɛkt] *s.* insecto.

in·se·cure [ɪnsɪkjúr] *adj.* inseguro.

in·sen·si·ble [ɪnsénsəbl] *adj.* insensible.

in·sen·si·tive [ɪnsénsətɪv] *adj.* insensible.

in·sep·a·ra·ble [ɪnsépərəbl] *adj.* inseparable.

in·sert [ɪnsɝt] *s.* inserción; intercalación; hoja (*insertada en un libro*); circular, folleto (*insertado en un periódico*); [ɪnsɝt] *v.* insertar; intercalar; encajar; meter.

in·ser·tion [ɪnsɝʃən] *s.* inserción; introducción.

in·side [ínsáɪd] *s.* interior; **-s** entrañas; *adj.* interior, interno; secreto; *adv.* dentro; adentro; **to turn — out** volver(se) al revés; *prep.* dentro de.

in·sight [ínsaɪt] *s.* penetración, discernimiento; intuición; perspicacia; comprensión.

in·sig·ni·a [ɪnsígnɪə] *s. pl.* insignias.

in·sig·nif·i·cant [ɪnsɪgnífəkənt] *adj.* insignificante.

in·sin·u·ate [ɪnsínjuet] *v.* insinuar.

in·sin·u·a·tion [ɪnsɪnjuéʃən] *s.* insinuación; indirecta.

in·sip·id [ɪnsípɪd] *adj.* insípido.

in·sist [ɪnsíst] *v.* insistir en; empeñarse(en); porfiar,

persistir.

in·sis·tence [ɪnsístəns] *s.* insistencia, empeño, porfía.

in·sis·tent [ɪnsístənt] *adj.* insistente; porfiado, persistente.

in·so·lence [ínsələns] *s.* insolencia.

in·so·lent [ínsələnt] *adj.* insolente.

in·sol·u·ble [ɪnsáljəbl] *adj.* insoluble.

in·spect [ɪnspékt] *v.* inspeccionar; examinar, registrar.

in·spec·tion [ɪnspékʃən] *s.* inspección; registro.

in·spec·tor [ɪnspéktɚ] *s.* inspector.

in·spi·ra·tion [ɪnspəréʃən] *s.* inspiración.

in·spire [ɪnspáɪr] *v.* inspirar.

in·stall [ɪnstɔ́l] *v.* instalar.

in·stal·la·tion [ɪnstəléʃən] *s.* instalación.

in·stall·ment, in·stal·ment [ɪnstɔ́lmənt] *s.* instalación; abono (*pago*); entrega o continuación (*semanal o mensual de una novela*); **to pay in -s** pagar por plazos; pagar en abonos.

in·stance [ínstəns] *s.* ejemplo, caso; vez, ocasión; instancia; **for —** por ejemplo.

in·stant [ínstənt] *s.* instante; *adj.* inmediato; urgente; **the 10th —** el 10 del (mes) corriente; **-ly** *adv.* al instante, inmediatamente.

in·stan·ta·ne·ous [ɪnstənténɪəs] *adj.* instantáneo.

in·stead [ɪnstéd] *adv.* en lugar de ello (eso, él, ella, *etc.*); **— of** en lugar de, en vez de.

in·step [ínstɛp] *s.* empeine (*del pie, del zapato*).

in·sti·gate [ínstəget] *v.* instigar.

in·still [ɪnstíl] *v.* inculcar, infundir.

in·stinct [ínstɪŋkt] *s.* instinto.

in·stinc·tive [ɪnstíŋktɪv] *adj.* instintivo.

in·sti·tute [ínstətjut] *s.* instituto; *v.* instituir.

in·sti·tu·tion [ɪnstətjúʃən] *s.* institución.

in·struct [ɪnstrʌ́kt] *v.* instruir; dar instrucciones.

in·struc·tion [ɪnstrʌ́kʃən] *s.* instrucción; enseñanza; **lack of —** falta de saber o conocimientos; **-s** órdenes, instrucciones.

in·struc·tive [ɪnstrʌ́ktɪv] *adj.* instructivo.

in·struc·tor [ɪnstrʌ́ktɚ] *s.* instructor.

in·stru·ment [ínstrəmənt] *s.* instrumento; **— panel** salpicadero.

in·stru·men·tal [ɪnstrəméntl] *adj.* instrumental; **to be —** in ayudar a, servir de instrumento para.

in·sub·or·di·nate [ɪnsəbɔ́rdɪnət] *adj.* insubordinado.

in·suf·fer·a·ble [ɪnsʌ́frəbl] *adj.* insufrible, inaguantable.

in·suf·fi·cien·cy [ɪnsəfíʃənsɪ] *s.* insuficiencia; incompetencia; falta, escasez.

in·suf·fi·cient [ɪnsəfíʃənt] *adj.* insuficiente; inadecuado.

in·su·late [ínsəlet] *v.* aislar.

in·su·la·tion [ɪnsəléʃən] *s.* aislamiento; aislación.

in·su·la·tor [ínsəletɚ] *s.* aislador.

in·su·lin [ínsələn] *s.* insulina.

in·sult [ínsʌlt] *s.* insulto; [ɪnsʌ́lt] *v.* insultar.

in·sur·ance [ɪnʃúrəns] *s.* aseguramiento; seguro; prima, premio (*de una póliza de seguro*); **— agent** agente de seguros; **· company** cómpañia de seguros; **— policy** póliza de seguro; **accident —** seguro contra accidentes; **fire —** seguro contra incendios; **life —** seguro sobre la vida.

in·sure [ɪnʃúr] *v.* asegurar; asegurarse de.

in·sur·gent [ɪnsɝ́dʒənt] *adj.* & *s.* insurgente, insurrecto.

in·sur·mount·a·ble [ɪnsɚmáʊntəbl] *adj.* insuperable.

in·sur·rec·tion [ɪnsərékʃən] *s.* insurrección, rebelión, alzamiento.

in·tact [ɪntǽkt] *adj.* intacto.

in·te·gral [íntəgrəl] *adj.* integral; integrante; *s.* integral.

in·te·grate [íntəgret] *v.* integrar.

in·teg·ri·ty [ɪntégrətɪ] *s.* integridad, entereza.

in·tel·lect [íntlɛkt] *s.* intelecto; entendimiento.

in·tel·lec·tu·al [ɪntléktʃʊəl] *adj.* & *s.* intelectual.

in·tel·li·gence [ɪntélədʒəns] *s.* inteligencia; información, noticias; policía secreta.

in·tel·li·gent [ɪntélədʒənt] *adj.* inteligente.

in·tel·li·gi·ble [ɪntélədʒəbl] *adj.* inteligible.

in·tem·per·ance [ɪntémpərəns] *s.* intemperancia.

in·tend [ɪnténd] *v.* intentar, pensar, tener la intención de; proponerse; destinar; **to — to do it** pensar hacerlo.

in·tense [ɪnténs] *adj.* intenso.

in·ten·si·fy [ɪnténsɪfaɪ] *v.* intensificar.

in·ten·si·ty [ɪnténsətɪ] *s.* intensidad.

in·ten·sive [ɪnténsɪv] *adj.* intenso; intensivo.

in·tent [ɪntént] *s.* intento, intención, propósito; significado; **to all -s and purposes** en todo caso, en todos sentidos; en realidad; *adj.* atento; **— on** absorto en, reconcentrado en; resuelto a, decidido a.

in·ten·tion [ɪnténʃən] *s.* intención.

in·ten·tion·al [ɪnténʃən.l] *adj.* intencional; **-ly** *adv.* intencionalmente, adrede, a propósito.

in·ter [ɪntɝ] *v.* enterrar, sepultar.

in·ter·cede [ɪntəsíd] *v.* interceder.

in·ter·cept [ɪntəsépt] *v.* interceptar; atajar.

in·ter·cep·tion [ɪntəsépʃən] *s.* interceptación.

in·ter·ces·sion [ɪntəséʃən] *s.* intercesión.

in·ter·change [ɪntɚtʃendʒ] *s.* intercambio; cambio, trueque; [ɪntɚtʃéndʒ] *v.* cambiar, trocar; permutar; alternar.

in·ter·course [íntɚkors] *s.* comunicación; comercio, trato; intercambio (*de ideas, sentimientos, etc.*).

in·ter·den·tal [ɪntɚdéntl] *adj.* interdental.

in·ter·est [íntərɪst] *s.* interés; rédito; participación (*en un negocio*); *v.* interesar.

in·ter·est·ed [íntərɪstɪd] *adj.* interesado; **to be** (*o* **become**) **—** **in** interesarse en (*o* por).

in·ter·est·ing [íntərɪstɪŋ] *adj.* interesante.

in·ter·fere [ɪntɚfír] *v.* intervenir; interponerse, entremeterse; estorbar; **to — with** estorbar, frustrar; dificultar.

in·ter·fer·ence [ɪntɚfírəns] *s.* intervención; obstáculo; interferencia (*en la radio*).

in·te·ri·or [ɪntírɪɚ] *adj.* interior; interno; *s.* interior.

in·ter·jec·tion [ɪntɚdʒékʃən] *s.* interjección, exclamación; intercalación.

in·ter·lace [ɪntɚlés] *v.* entrelazar, enlazar, entretejer.

in·ter·lin·e·ar [ɪntɚlínɪɚ] *adj.* interlineal.

in·ter·lock [ɪntɚlák] *v.* entrelazar(se); trabar(se).

in·ter·lude [íntɚlud] *s.* intervalo.

in·ter·me·di·ate [ɪntɚmídɪɪt] *adj.* intermedio.

in·ter·mi·na·ble [ɪntɝmɪnəbl] *adj.* interminable, inacabable.

in·ter·min·gle [ɪntɚmíŋgl] *v.* entremezclar(se), entreverar(se); mezclar(se).

in·ter·mis·sion [ɪntɚmíʃən] *s.* intermisión; intermedio, entreacto.

in·ter·mit·tent [ɪntɚmítŋt] *adj.* intermitente.

in·tern [ɪntɝn] *v.* internar, confinar, encerrar; [ɪntɝn] *s.* practicante (*de medicina en un hospital*).

in·ter·nal [ɪntɝnl] *adj.* interno; interior.

in·ter·na·tion·al [ɪntɚnǽʃənl] *adj.* internacional.

in·ter·o·ce·an·ic [ɪntɚoʃɪǽnɪk] *adj.* interoceánico.

in·ter·pose [ɪntɚpóz] *v.* interponer(se).

in·ter·pret [ɪntɝprɪt] *v.* interpretar.

in·ter·pre·ta·tion [ɪntɝprɪtéʃən] *s.* interpretación.

in·ter·pret·er [ɪntɝprɪtɚ] *s.* intérprete.

in·ter·ro·gate [ɪntérəget] *v.* interrogar.

in·ter·ro·ga·tion [ɪntɛrəgéʃən] *s.* interrogación.

in·ter·ro·ga·tive [ɪntɚrágətɪv] *adj.* interrogativo; *s.* pronombre o palabra interrogativa.

in·ter·rupt [ɪntɚɹʌ́pt] *v.* interrumpir.

in·ter·rup·tion [ɪntɚɹʌ́pʃən] *s.* interrupción.

in·ter·sect [ɪntɚsékt] *v.* cortar(se); cruzar(se).

in·ter·sec·tion [ɪntɚsékʃən] *s.* intersección; **street —** bocacalle.

in·ter·sperse [ɪntɚspɝs] *v.* entremezclar, esparcir.

in·ter·stice [ɪntɝstɪs] *s.* intersticio.

in·ter·twine [ɪntɚtwáɪn] *v.* entrelazar, entretejer, trenzar.

in·ter·val [íntɚvl] *s.* intervalo.

in·ter·vene [ɪntɚvín] *v.* intervenir; interponerse; mediar.

in·ter·ven·tion [ɪntɚvénʃən] *s.* intervención.

in·ter·view [íntɚvju] *s.* entrevista; *v.* entrevistar, entrevistarse con.

in·tes·tine [ɪntéstɪn] *s.* intestino; *adj.* intestino, interno.

in·ti·ma·cy [íntəməsɪ] *s.* intimidad.

in·ti·mate [íntəmɪt] *adj.* íntimo; *s.* amigo íntimo; [íntəmet] *v.* intimar, insinuar; indicar, dar a entender.

in·ti·ma·tion [ɪntəméʃən] *s.* intimación, insinuación.

in·tim·i·date [ɪntímədet] *v.* intimidar, acobardar, infundir miedo.

in·to [íntu, íntə] *prep.* en; dentro de; hacia el interior.

in·tol·er·a·ble [ɪntálərəbl] *adj.* intolerable, inaguantable.

in·tol·er·ance [ɪntálərəns] *s.* intolerancia.

in·tol·er·ant [ɪntálərənt] *adj.* intolerante.

in·to·na·tion [ɪntonéʃən] *s.* entonación.

in·tox·i·cate [ɪntáksəket] *v.* embriagar; emborrachar.

in·tox·i·ca·tion [ɪntaksəkéʃən] *s.* embriaguez; envenenamiento, intoxicación (*estado tóxico o envenenamiento parcial*).

in·tran·si·gent [ɪntrǽnsədʒənt] *adj.* intransigente.

in·tra·ve·nous [ɪntrəvínəs] *adj.* intravenoso.

in·trench [ɪntréntʃ] *v.* atrincherar; **to — oneself** atrincherarse; **to — upon another's rights** infringir los derechos ajenos; **to be -ed** estar atrincherado; estar firmemente establecido.

in·trep·id [ɪntrépɪd] *adj.* intrépido.

in·tri·cate [íntrəkɪt] *adj.* intrincado, enredado.

in·trigue [ɪntríg] *s.* intriga; enredo; trama; lío, embrollo; *v.* intrigar; tramar, maquinar.

in·tri·guer [ɪntrígɚ] *s.* intrigante.

in·tro·duce [ɪntrədjús] *v.* introducir; presentar.

in·tro·duc·tion [ɪntrədʌ́kʃən] *s.* introducción; presentación.

in·tro·spec·tion [ɪntrospékʃən] *s.* introspección.

in·tro·vert [íntrovɚt] *adj.* introvertido.

in·trude [ɪntrúd] *v.* entremeterse (*o* entrometerse); introducir, meter.

in·trud·er [ɪntrúdɚ] *s.* intruso, entremetido.

in·tru·sion [ɪntrúʒən] *s.* intrusión, entremetimiento.

in·tru·sive [ɪntrúsɪv] *adj.* intruso.

in·trust = entrust.

in·tu·i·tion [ɪntuíʃən] *s.* intuición.

in·un·date [ínəndet] *v.* inundar.

in·ure [ɪnjúr] *v.* habituar, acostumbrar.

in·vade [ɪnvéd] *v.* invadir.

in·vad·er [ɪnvédɚ] *s.* invasor.

in·va·lid [ɪnvǽlɪd] *adj.* inválido (*que no vale*), nulo, de ningún valor.

in·va·lid [ínvəlɪd] *adj.* inválido, enfermizo,

IN

achacoso; — **diet** dieta para inválidos; *s.*
inválido.
in·val·u·a·ble [ɪnvǽljebl̩] *adj.* de gran precio o
valor, inapreciable, inestimable.
in·var·i·a·ble [ɪnvɛ́rɪəbl̩] *adj.* invariable; **invariably**
adv. invariablemente; sin falta, sin excepción.
in·va·sion [ɪnvéʒən] *s.* invasión.
in·vent [ɪnvént] *v.* inventar.
in·ven·tion [ɪnvénʃən] *s.* invención; invento;
inventiva, facultad para inventar.
in·ven·tive [ɪnvéntɪv] *adj.* inventivo.
in·ven·tive·ness [ɪnvéntɪvnɪs] *s.* inventiva.
in·ven·tor [ɪnvéntɚ] *s.* inventor.
in·ven·to·ry [ɪnvəntorɪ] *s.* inventario; *v.* inventariar.
in·verse [ɪnvɝ́s] *adj.* inverso.
in·vert [ɪnvɝ́t] *v.* invertir; trastrocar; volver al
revés.
in·vest [ɪnvést] *v.* invertir, colocar (*fondos*); investir
(*de una dignidad o cargo*); revestir (*de autoridad*);
sitiar.
in·ves·ti·gate [ɪnvéstəget] *v.* investigar, indagar.
in·ves·ti·ga·tion [ɪnvɛstəgéʃən] *s.* investigación;
indagación.
in·ves·ti·ga·tor [ɪnvéstəgetɚ] *s.* investigador;
indagador.
in·vest·ment [ɪnvéstmənt] *s.* inversión (*de fondos*).
in·ves·tor [ɪnvéstɚ] *s.* el que invierte fondos.
in·vig·o·rate [ɪnvígəret] *v.* vigorizar, fortalecer.
in·vin·ci·ble [ɪnvínsəbl̩] *adj.* invencible.
in·vis·i·ble [ɪnvízəbl̩] *adj.* invisible.
in·vi·ta·tion [ɪnvətéʃən] *s.* invitación.
in·vite [ɪnváɪt] *v.* invitar; convidar.
in·vit·ing [ɪnváɪtɪŋ] *adj.* atractivo; seductivo,
tentador.
in·vo·ca·tion [ɪnvəkéʃən] *s.* invocación.
in·voice [ɪnvɔɪs] *s.* factura; envío, mercancías
enviadas; *v.* facturar.
in·voke [ɪnvók] *v.* invocar.
in·vol·un·tar·y [ɪnvɑ́lənterɪ] *adj.* involuntario.
in·volve [ɪnvɑ́lv] *v.* complicar, enredar; envolver;
implicar; comprometer; **to get -d in difficulties**
embrollarse, meterse en embrollos.
in·ward [ɪ́nwɚd] *adj.* interior; interno; secreto; *adv.*
hacia el interior; hacia dentro, adentro, para
dentro; **-s** *adv.* = **inward.**
i·o·dide [áɪədaɪd] *s.* yoduro.
i·o·dine [áɪədaɪn] *s.* yodo.
i·on [áɪən] *s.* ion.
i·on·ize [áɪənaɪz] *v.* ionizar.
ire [aɪr] *s.* ira.
ir·i·des·cent [ɪrədɛ́sn̩t] *adj.* iridiscente, tornasolado,
irisado.
i·rid·i·um [ɪrídɪəm] *s.* iridio.
i·ris [áɪrɪs] *s.* iris; arco iris; flor de lis.
I·rish [áɪrɪʃ] *adj.* irlandés; *s.* irlandés, idioma
irlandés; **the** — los irlandeses.
irk·some [ɝ́ksəm] *adj.* fastidioso, engorroso,
molesto, tedioso.
i·ron [áɪɚn] *s.* hierro; plancha (*de planchar ropa*);
adj. férro, de hierro; **—work** herraje, trabajo en
hierro; **—works** herrería; fábrica de hierro; *v.*
planchar; **to** — **out a difficulty** allanar una
dificultad.
i·ron·ic·al [aɪránɪk] *adj.* irónico.
i·ron·ing [áɪɚnɪŋ] *s.* planchado.
i·ro·ny [áɪrənɪ] *s.* ironía.
ir·ra·di·ate [ɪrédɪet] *v.* irradiar.
ir·ra·tion·al [ɪrǽʃənl̩] *adj.* irracional.
ir·re·fut·a·ble [ɪrɛfjútəbl̩] *adj.* irrefutable.
ir·reg·u·lar [ɪrégjələ] *adj.* irregular.
ir·rel·e·vant [ɪrɛ́ləvənt] *adj.* fuera de propósito,

inaplicable al caso, inoportuno, que no viene
(*o no hace*) al caso.
ir·re·li·gious [ɪrɪlídʒəs] *adj.* irreligioso, impío.
ir·re·me·di·a·ble [ɪrɪmídɪəbl̩] *adj.* irremediable;
incurable.
ir·re·proach·a·ble [ɪrɪprótʃəbl̩] *adj.* irreprochable,
intachable.
ir·re·sis·ti·ble [ɪrɪzístəbl̩] *adj.* irresistible.
ir·res·o·lute [ɪrɛ́zəlut] *adj.* irresoluto, indeciso.
ir·re·triev·a·ble [ɪrɪtrívəbl̩] *adj.* inapelable.
ir·rev·er·ence [ɪrɛ́vərəns] *s.* irreverencia, desacato.
ir·rev·er·ent [ɪrɛ́vərənt] *adj.* irreverente.
ir·ri·gate [ɪ́rəget] *v.* regar; irrigar, bañar.
ir·ri·ga·tion [ɪrəgéʃən] *s.* riego; irrigación; — **canal**
acequia, canal de irrigación.
ir·ri·ta·ble [ɪ́rətəbl̩] *adj.* irritable; colérico.
ir·ri·tate [ɪ́rətet] *v.* irritar.
ir·ri·tat·ing [ɪ́rətetɪŋ] *adj.* irritante.
ir·ri·ta·tion [ɪrətéʃən] *s.* irritación.
ir·rupt [ɪrʌ́pt] *v.* irrumpir.
is·land [áɪlənd] *s.* isla.
is·land·er [áɪləndɚ] *s.* isleño.
isle [aɪl] *s.* isla, ínsula.
i·so·bar [áɪsəbar] *s.* isobara.
i·so·late [áɪslet] *v.* aislar.
i·so·la·tion [aɪsléʃən] *s.* aislamiento.
i·so·la·tion·ism [aɪsəléʃənɪzəm] *s.* aislamiento.
i·so·met·ric [aɪsəmétrɪk] *adj.* isométrico.
Is·ra·el [ízrɪəl] *s.* Israel.
is·sue [íʃU] *s.* (*printing*) tirada, impresión; (*stock,
bonds*) emisión (*de valores*); (*problem*) problema,
tema; (*result*) resultado, consecuencia; **without**
— sin prole, sin sucesión; **to take** — **with**
disentir o diferir de; *v.* publicar, dar a luz; dar,
promulgar (*un decreto*); emitir (*valores, acciones,
etc.*); emanar; fluir; salir; brotar; provenir.
isth·mus [ísməs] *s.* istmo.
it [ɪt] *pron. neutro* lo, la (*acusativo*); ello, él, ella
(*después de una preposición*); *por lo general no
se traduce cuando es sujeto del verbo*; — **is there**
está allí; — **is I** soy yo; — **is raining** llueve,
está lloviendo; **what time is** —? ¿qué hora es?;
— **is two o'clock** son las dos; **how goes** —?
¿qué tal?
I·tal·ian [ɪtǽljən] *adj. & s.* italiano.
i·tal·ic [ɪtǽlɪk] *adj.* itálico; **-s** *s.* letra bastardilla.
i·tal·i·cize [ɪtǽlɪsaɪz] *v.* poner en letra bastardilla.
itch [ɪtʃ] *s.* comezón; picazón; sarna (*enfermedad
de la piel*); *v.* picar, darle a uno comezón; sentir
comezón; **to be -ing to** tener ansias de.
itch·y [ítʃɪ] *adj.* sarnoso, *Méx., Ven.* sarniento;
to feel — sentir comezón.
i·tem [áɪtəm] *s.* artículo; detalle; noticia, suelto
(*de un periódico*); partida (*de una lista*).
i·tem·ize [áɪtəmaɪz] *v.* pormenorizar detallar; hacer
una lista de.
i·tin·er·ant [aɪtínərənt] *adj.* ambulante.
i·tin·er·ar·y [aɪtínərɛrɪ] *s.* itinerario; ruta; guía de
viajeros.
its [ɪts] *pos. neutro* su (sus), de él, de ella, de ello.
it·self [ɪtsélf] *pron. neutro* mismo, misma; **by** —
por sí, de por sí, por sí solo; solo, aislado;
in — en sí.
i·vo·ry [áɪvrɪ] *s.* marfil; **—tower** torre de marfil.
i·vy [áɪvɪ] *s.* hiedra (yedra).

J:j

jab [dʒæb] v. picar; pinchar; s. piquete, pinchazo.

jack [dʒæk] s. gato (para alzar cosas pesadas); sota (en naipes); macho (del burro y otros animales); bandera de proa; — of all trades aprendiz de todo y oficial de nada; — pot premio gordo, premio mayor; — rabbit liebre americana; v. to — up solevantar, alzar con gato (un objeto pesado).

jack·ass [dʒǽkæs] s. asno, burro.

jack·et [dʒǽkɪt] s. chaqueta; envoltura; forro (de un libro); hollejo (de la patata).

jack·knife [dʒǽknaɪf] s. navaja.

jag·ged [dʒǽgɪd] adj. serrado, dentado.

jag·uar [dʒǽgwar] s. jaguar.

jail [dʒel] s. cárcel; v. encarcelar.

jail·er [dʒélɚ] s. carcelero.

ja·lop·y [dʒalápɪ] s. fotingo.

jam [dʒæm] v. estrujar, apachurrar; atorar(se); obstruir(se), atascar(se); apiñar(se); agolpar(se); to — on the brakes frenar de golpe; to — one's fingers machucarse los dedos; to — through forzar por, meter a la fuerza; s. conserva, compota; apretura; atascamiento; traffic — aglomeración de transeúntes o automóviles, Am. bola; to be in a — estar en un aprieto.

jan·i·tor [dʒǽnətɚ] s. conserje; portero; casero (encargado de un edificio).

Jan·u·ar·y [dʒǽnjʊɛrɪ] s. enero.

Jap·a·nese [dʒæpəníz] adj. & s. japonés.

jar [dʒar] s. jarra, jarro; tarro; choque; sacudida; trepidación, vibración; large earthen — tinaja; v. trepidar; hacer vibrar; hacer temblar; menear; to — one's nerves ponerle a uno los nervios de punta.

jar·gon [dʒárgən] s. jerga, jerigonza.

jas·mine [dʒǽzmɪn] s. jazmín.

jas·per [dʒǽspɚ] s. jaspe.

jaunt [dʒɔnt] s. caminata, excursión; v. dar un paseíto, hacer una corta caminata.

jaw [dʒɔ] s. quijada, mandíbula, Am. carretilla; -s grapa (de herramienta).

jaw·bone [dʒɔbón] s. mandíbula, quijada.

jay [dʒe] s. grajo; rústico, bobo; blue — azulejo; —walker el que cruza las bocacalles descuidadamente.

jazz [dʒæz] s. jazz (cierta clase de música sincopada); v. tocar el jazz; bailar el jazz; to — up sincopar; animar, alegrar.

jeal·ous [dʒéləs] adj. celoso; envidioso; to be — of someone tener celos de una persona, tenerle celos a una persona.

jeal·ou·sy [dʒéləsɪ] s. celos; envidia.

jeer [dʒɪr] s. mofa, befa, escarnio, Carib. choteo; v. mofar, befar, Carib. chotear; to — at mofarse de.

jel·ly [dʒélɪ] s. jalea; v. convertir(se) en jalea, hacer(se) gelatinoso.

jeop·ar·dy [dʒépɚdɪ] s. riesgo.

jerk [dʒɚk] s. tirón; sacudida, Méx., C.A., Ven., Col. jalón; espasmo muscular; v. sacudir(se); dar un tirón; atasajar (la carne); to — out sacar de un tirón; -ed beef tasajo, Am. charqui.

jerk·wa·ter [dʒɚkwɔtɚ] adj. de mala muerte.

jer·sey [dʒɝzɪ] s. tejido de punto, tejido elástico, Am. jersey; chaqueta, blusa, camisa (de punto), Am. jersey.

jest [dʒɛst] s. broma; chanza; chiste; v. bromear; chancear.

jest·er [dʒéstɚ] s. chancero, burlón; bufón.

Jes·u·it [dʒéʒʊɪt] s. jesuita.

jet [dʒɛt] s. chorro; surtidor (de fuente); — airplane avión de reacción; — engine motor de reacción; motorreactor; gas — mechero de gas; adj. de azabache; jet-black negro como el azabache; v. chorrear, salir en chorro.

Jew [dʒu] s. judío.

jew·el [dʒúəl] s. joya, alhaja; gema; — box estuche, joyero.

jew·el·er [dʒúələ] s. joyero; -'s shop joyería.

jew·el·ry [dʒúəlrɪ] s. joyas, alhajas, pedrería; — store joyería.

Jew·ish [dʒúɪʃ] adj. judío.

jif·fy [dʒífɪ] s. instante; in a — en un instante, en dos paletas; en un decir Jesús, en un santiamén.

jig [dʒɪg] s. jiga (música y baile); — saw sierra mecánica (para recortar figuras); —saw puzzle rompecabezas (de recortes); v. tocar una jiga; bailar una jiga; bailotear; menear(se).

jig·gle [dʒígl] v. zangolotear(se), zarandear(se), menear(se); s. zarandeo, meneo, zangoloteo.

jilt [dʒɪlt] v. desairar, dar calabazas, dejar plantado.

jin·gle [dʒíŋgl] s. retintín; verso o rima infantil; — bell cascabel; v. hacer retintín.

job [dʒab] s. tarea, faena; trabajo; empleo, ocupación; to be out of a — estar sin trabajo; estar desocupado.

jock·ey [dʒákɪ] s. jockey; v. maniobrar (para sacar ventaja o ganar un puesto).

join [dʒɔɪn] v. juntar(se); enlazar(se); acoplar; unirse a, asociarse a.

joint [dʒɔɪnt] s. (point) juntura, coyuntura; (function) articulación; conexión; bisagra; (public place) garito (casa de juego); fonducho, restaurante de mala muerte; out of — descoyuntado; desunido; adj. unido, asociado; copartícipe; colectivo; — account cuenta en común; — action acción colectiva; — committee comisión mixta; — creditor acreedor copartícipe; — heir coheredero; — session sesión plena; -ly adv. juntamente, juntos, unidamente, colectivamente.

joke [dʒok] s. broma, chiste, chanza; v. bromear; chancear(se), Carib. chotear; Ríopl. farrear; jorobar.

jok·er [dʒókɚ] s. bromista, chancero, guasón, Carib. choteador; (card) comodín.

jok·ing·ly [dʒókɪŋlɪ] adv. en (o de) chanza, en (o de) broma; de chiste.

jol·ly [dʒálɪ] adj. jovial; alegre; festivo; v. bromear, chancearse.

jolt [dʒolt] s. sacudida; sacudimiento; choque; v. sacudir.

jos·tle [dʒásl] v. rempujar o empujar, dar empellones; codear; s. rempujón, empujón, empellón.

jot [dʒat] v. to — down apuntar, tomar apuntes; s. jota, pizca.

jour·nal [dʒɝnl] s. diario; periódico; revista; acta (de una junta o concilio).

jour·nal·ism [dʒɝnlɪzm] s. periodismo.

jour·nal·ist [dʒɝnlɪst] s. periodista.

jour·nal·is·tic [dʒɝnlístɪk] adj. periodístico.

jour·ney [dʒɝnɪ] s. viaje; jornada; v. viajar; peregrinar.

joy [dʒɔɪ] s. júbilo, regocijo; alegría, gusto, deleite; felicidad.

joy·ful [dʒɔɪfəl] adj. regocijado, jubiloso; alegre; -ly adv. con regocijo, regocijadamente, con júbilo, alegremente.

IN

joy·ous [dʒɔ́ɪəs] *adj.* jubiloso, alegre, gozoso.
ju·bi·lant [dʒúb|ənt] *adj.* jubiloso, alegre.
ju·bi·lee [dʒúblɪ] *s.* jubileo; júbilo.
judge [dʒʌdʒ] *s.* juez; — **advocate** auditor de un consejo militar; *v.* juzgar.
judg·ment [dʒʌ́dʒmənt] *s.* juicio; sentencia, fallo; opinión; discernimiento; — **day** día del juicio final.
ju·di·cial [dʒudíʃəl] *adj.* judicial.
ju·di·cious [dʒudíʃəs] *adj.* juicioso, cuerdo.
jug [dʒʌg] *s.* cántaro; jarro, jarra; botija; chirona (*cárcel*) *Am.* chirola.
jug·gle [dʒʌ́gl] *v.* hacer juegos de manos; hacer suertes; **to — the accounts** barajar (*o* manipular) las cuentes; *s.* juego de manos, suerte; trampa.
jug·gler [dʒʌ́glə-] *s.* prestidigitador, malabarista.
juice [dʒus] *s.* jugo; zumo.
juic·i·ness [dʒúsɪnɪs] *s.* jugosidad.
juic·y [dʒúsɪ] *adj.* jugoso, zumoso; suculento; **a — story** un cuento picante.
juke box [dʒúkbɑks] *s.* tragamonedas; tragaquintos.
Ju·ly [dʒulái] *s.* julio.
jum·ble [dʒʌ́mbl] *s.* revolver(se), barajar; mezclar(se); -**s** mezcolanza, revoltijo; confusión.
jump [dʒʌmp] *v.* saltar; brincar; salvar (*de un salto*); hacer saltar; comerse una pieza (*en el juego de damas*); **to — at the chance** asir o aprovechar la oportunidad; **to — bail** perder la fianza por evasión; **to — over** saltar por encima de, salvar de un salto; **to — the track** descarrilarse; **to — to conclusions** hacer deducciones precipitadas; *s.* salto; brinco; subida repentina (*del precio*); **to be always on the — andar** siempre de aquí para allá; trajinar, trafagar, ser muy activo.
jump·er [dʒʌ́mpə-] *s.* saltador; chaquetón holgado (*de obrero*); vestido sin mangas (*puesto sobre la blusa de mujer*); -**s** traje de juego (*para miños*).
jump·y [dʒʌ́mpɪ] *adj.* saltón; asustadizo, nervioso.
junc·tion [dʒʌ́ŋkʃən] *s.* unión, juntura; confluencia (*de dos ríos*); empalme (*de ferrocarriles*).
junc·ture [dʒʌ́ŋktʃə-] *s.* juntura; coyuntura; **at this — a** esta sazón, en esta coyuntura.
June [dʒun] *s.* junio.
jun·gle [dʒʌ́ŋgl] *s.* selva; matorral; *Am.* jungla; *Carib.* manigua.
ju·nior [dʒúnjə-] *adj.* menor, más joven; — **college** colegio para los dos primeros años del bachillerato; **John Smith, Junior (Jr.)** John Smith, hijo; *s.* estudiante del tercer año (*en escuela superior, colegio o universidad*).
ju·ni·per [dʒúnɪpə-] *s.* junípero; enebro.
junk [dʒʌŋk] *s.* basura, desperdicios; trastos viejos; cosa inservible; **Chinese** — junco chino (*embarcación pequeña*); *v.* desechar, echar a la basura.
ju·ris·dic·tion [dʒurɪsdíkʃən] *s.* jurisdicción.
ju·ris·pru·dence [dʒurɪsprúdn̩s] *s.* jurisprudencia, derecho.
ju·ror [dʒúrə-] *s.* jurado, miembro de un jurado.
ju·ry [dʒúrɪ] *s.* jurado; **grand** — jurado de acusación.
just [dʒʌst] *adj.* justo; recto; exacto; *adv.* ni más ni menos, exactamente, justamente; precisamente; sólo, no más, nada más; apenas; — **now** ahora mismo; **he — left** acaba de salir, *Ríopl.* salió recién; **she is — a little girl** no es más que una niña, es una niña no más; **to have — acabar** de.
jus·tice [dʒʌ́stɪs] *s.* justicia; juez; magistrado.
jus·ti·fi·ca·tion [dʒʌstəfəkéʃən] *s.* justificación.

jus·ti·fy [dʒʌ́stəfaɪ] *v.* justificar.
just·ly [dʒʌ́stlɪ] *adv.* justamente; con razón.
jut [dʒʌt] *v.* sobresalir, proyectarse, extenderse; *s.* salidizo, proyección.
ju·ve·nile [dʒúvənl̩] *adj.* juvenil.

K : k

kan·ga·roo [kæŋgərú] *s.* canguro.
keel [kil] *s.* quilla; *v.* dar de quilla (*voltear un barco*); **to — over** volcar(se); zozobrar; caerse patas arriba, desplomarse.
keen [kin] *adj.* agudo; afilado; perspicaz; ansioso.
keen·ness [kínnɪs] *s.* agudeza; perspicacia; anhelo, ansia.
keep [kip] *v.* guardar; tener guardado; tener; retener; conservar(se); preservar(se); mantener(se); **to — accounts** llevar las cuentas; **to — at it** persistir, seguir dale que dale; **to — away** mantener(se) alejado; **to — back** tener a raya; detener; reprimir, restringir; **to — from** impedir; guardar(se) de; abstenerse de; **to — going** seguir andando, seguir adelante; seguir viviendo; **to — off** no arrimarse, no acercarse; no entrar; mantener(se) a distancia; **to — one's hands off** no tocar; **to — one's temper** contenerse, refrenarse, reprimirse; **to — quiet** estarse quieto o callado; **to — something up** seguir o continuar haciendo algo; **to — to the right** seguir a la derecha; mantenerse a la derecha; **to — track of** llevar la cuenta de; no perder de vista; *s.* manutención, subsistencia; **for -s** para siempre; para guardar; dado, no prestado.
keep·er [kípə-] *s.* guardián, custodio; **jail** — carcelero.
keep·ing [kípɪŋ] *s.* custodia; mantenimiento; preservación, conservación; **in — with** en armonía con.
keep·sake [kípsek] *s.* prenda, recuerdo, regalo.
keg [kɛg] *s.* tonel, barril.
ken·nel [kɛ́nl] *s.* perrera.
kept [kɛpt] *pret. & p.p. de* **to keep.**
ker·chief [kɝ́tʃɪf] *s.* pañuelo, pañolón.
ker·nel [kɝ́nl] *s.* simiente; grano (*de trigo o maíz*); meollo (*de ciertas frutas como la nuez*); núcleo.
ker·o·sene [kɛ́rəsin] *s.* kerosina, petróleo para lámparas.
ket·tle [kɛ́tl] *s.* caldera; —**drum** tímpano; **tea**—marmita, tetera, *Am.* pava (*para el mate*).
key [ki] *s.* (*lock*) llave; (*music*) clave; (*instrument*) tecla; (*land*) cayo; isleta; — **ring** llavero; **to be in** — estar a tono, estar templado; estar en armonía; *v.* poner a tono, afinar, templar (*con llave*); armonizar; **to — up** elevar el tono de; **to be -ed up** estar sobreexcitado, estar en tensión nerviosa.
key·board [kíbord] *s.* teclado.
key·hole [kíhol] *s.* ojo de la cerradura.
key·note [kínot] *s.* nota tónica; idea o principio fundamental.
key·stone [kíston] *s.* clave (*de un arco*); base, fundamento principal.
kha·ki [kɑ́kɪ] *s.* kaki, caqui; *adj.* de kaki.
kick [kik] *s.* (*foot*) *Esp.* coz; puntapié; patada; (*complaint*) queja; protesta; fuerza (*de una bebida*); estímulo; **to have a — Am.** patear (*dícese del licor*); *v.* cocear; dar coces o patadas;

dar puntapiés; patear; quejarse, protestar; **to —
out** echar a patadas; echar, expulsar; **to — the
bucket** estirar la pata, morir, *Am.* patear el
balde; **to — up a lot of dust** levantar una
polvareda.
kid [kɪd] *s.* cabrito; cabritilla (*piel curtida de
cabrito*); niño, niña; **— gloves** guantes de
cabritilla; *v.* bromear, embromar; chancearse
con, *Carib., Méx.* chotear.
kid·nap [kídnæp] *v.* secuestrar, raptar.
kid·nap·per [kídnæpə·] *s.* secuestrador; robachicos,
ladrón de niños.
kid·nap·ping [kídnæpɪŋ] *s.* rapto, secuestro.
kid·ney [kídnɪ] *s.* riñon; **— bean** judía, frijol; **—
stones** cálculos.
kill [kɪl] *v.* matar; destruir; amortiguar; parar (*el
motor*); *s.* animal o animales matados (*en la
caza*).
kill·er [kílə·] *s.* matador; asesino.
kiln [kɪln], [kɪl] *s.* horno.
ki·lo [kílo], **ki·lo·gram** [kíləgræm] *s.* kilo,
kilogramo.
ki·lo·cy·cle [kíləsaɪkḷ] *s.* kilociclo.
kil·o·me·ter [kíləmitə·] *s.* kilómetro.
kil·o·watt [kíləwat] *s.* kilovatio.
ki·mo·no [kəmónə] *s.* quimono; bata.
kin [kɪn] *s.* parentela, parientes, familia; **to notify
the nearest of —** avisar al pariente o deudo
más cercano.
kind [kaɪnd] *adj.* bondadoso; benévolo; amable;
to send one's — regards to enviar afectuosos
saludos a; **kindhearted** de buen corazón; **— of
tired** algo cansado; *s.* clase, especie, género;
to pay in — pagar en especie; pagar en la
misma moneda.
kin·der·gar·ten [kíndə·gartṇ] *s.* escuela de
párvulos.
kin·dle [kíndḷ] *v.* encender(se); inflamar(se);
incitar; prender (*el fuego*).
kin·dling [kíndlɪŋ] *s.* encendimiento; leña ligera,
astillas, *Andes* charamuscas.
kind·ly [káɪndlɪ] *adj.* bondadoso; benigno;
benévolo; amable, apacible; *adv.*
bondadosamente, ambablemente; con
benevolencia; por favor; **not to take — to
criticism** no aceptar de buen grado las
correcciones.
kind·ness [káɪndnɪs] *s.* bondad, amabilidad;
gentileza; benevolencia; favor.
kin·dred [kíndrɪd] *adj.* emparentado; allegado;
semejante; **— facts** hechos relacionados; **—
spirits** espíritus afines.
ki·nes·ics [kaɪnízɪks] *s.* kinésica, quinésica.
king [kɪŋ] *s.* rey; rey (*en ajedrez*); dama (*en el
juego de damas*).
king·dom [kíŋdəm] *s.* reino.
king·ly [kíŋlɪ] *adj.* regio; real; majestuoso; *adv.*
regiamente; majestuosamente.
kink [kɪŋk] *s.* (*bend*) enroscadura; (*pain*) tortícolis.
kink·y [kíŋkɪ] *adj.* crespo, ensortijado, *Am.* grifo.
kin·ship [kínʃɪp] *s.* parentesco; afinidad;
semejanza.
kins·man [kínzmən] *s.* pariente, deudo.
kiss [kɪs] *s.* beso; *v.* besar.
kit [kɪt] *s.* estuche, caja de herramientas; saco,
evoltura (*para guardar instrumentos,
herramientas, etc.*); gatito; **medicine —** botiquín;
soldier's — mochila.
kitch·en [kítʃɪn] *s.* cocina; **—ware** trastos de
cocina.
kite [kaɪt] *s.* cometa (*f.*), *Méx.* papalote; *Ch.*

volantín; *Arg.* barrilete; milano (*pájaro*).
kit·ten [kítṇ] *s.* gatito.
kit·ty [kítɪ] *s.* gatito, minino.
knack [næk] *s.* destreza, maña, habilidad.
knap·sack [næpsæk] *s.* mochila, morral, alforja.
knave [nev] *s.* bribón, bellaco, pícaro; sota (*de
naipes*).
knead [nid] *v.* amasar, sobar.
knee [ni] *s.* rodilla; **knee-deep** hasta la rodilla;
metido hasta las rodillas.
kneel [nil] *v.* arrodillarse; hincarse.
knell [nɛl] *s.* doble (*toque de campanas por los
difuntos*); *v.* doblar, tocar a muerto.
knelt [nɛlt] *pret. & p.p.* de **to kneel.**
knew [nju] *pret.* de **to know.**
knick·knack [níknæk] *s.* chuchería, baratija,
chisme.
knife [naɪf] *s.* cuchillo; cuchilla; **carving —**
trinchante; **pocket —** cortaplumas; navaja; *v.*
acuchillar.
knight [naɪt] *s.* caballero; campeón; caballo (*en
ajedrez*); **— errant** caballero andante; *v.* armar
caballero.
knight·hood [náɪthʊd] *s.* caballería, orden de la
caballería.
knit [nɪt] *v.* tejer (*a punto de aguja*); hacer calceta
o malla; enlazar; soldarse (*un hueso*) **to — one's
brow** fruncir las cejas, arrugar la frente; *pret.
& p.p.* de **to knit.**
knit·ting [nítɪŋ] *s.* labor de punto; **— needle** aguja
de media.
knives [naɪvz] *pl.* de **knife.**
knob [nab] *s.* perilla, botón, tirador (*de puerta,
cajón, etc.*); protuberancia.
knock [nak] *v.* (*pound*) golpear, golpetear; llamar
o tocar a la puerta; (*criticize*) criticar, censurar
o hablar mal de; **to — down** derribar;
desmontar (*una máquina o aparato*); **to — off**
suspender (*el trabajo*); rebajar (*del precio*);
derribar, echar abajo; **to — out** aplastar de un
golpe, poner fuera de combate; dejar sin
sentido; *s.* golpe; golpeteo; toque, llamada,
aldabonazo; crítica, censura; **knock-kneed**
zambo, patizambo.
knock·er [nákə·] *s.* llamador, aldaba, aldabón;
criticón, murmurador.
knoll [nol] *s.* colina, loma; eminencia.
knot [nat] *s.* nudo; lazo; *v.* anudar(se).
knot·ty [nátɪ] *adj.* nudoso; dificultoso, enredado.
know [no] *v.* (*to be acquainted with*) conocer; (*to
have knowledge of; to know how to*) saber; (*to
recognize*) reconocer; distinguir; **to — how to
swim** saber nadar; **to — of** saber de; tener
conocimiento de; tener noticias de; estar
enterado de.
know·ing·ly [nóɪŋlɪ] *adv.* a sabiendas; adrede.
knowl·edge [nálɪdʒ] *s.* conocimiento; saber,
sabiduría; pericia; **not to my —** no que yo sepa.
known [non] *p.p.* de **to know.**
knuck·le [nʌkḷ] *s.* nudillo; coyuntura, articulación;
artejo; *v.* someterse; **to — down** someterse;
aplicarse con empeño al trabajo.
kryp·ton [kríptan] *s.* criptón.

JO

L:1

la·bel [lébl] *s.* marbete, etiqueta, rótulo; *v.* marcar, rotular; apodar, llamar.

la·bor [lébɚ] *s.* trabajo; labor; obra; mano de obra; la clase obrera; — **union** sindicato; — **gang** peonaje; — **party** Partido Laborista; **to be in** — estar de parto; *v.* trabajar; afanarse; estar de parto; elaborar (*un punto*).

lab·o·ra·to·ry [lǽbrətɔrɪ] *s.* laboratorio.

la·bor·er [lébərɚ] *s.* trabajador, obrero; jornalero, peón.

la·bo·ri·ous [ləbóriəs] *adj.* laborioso, trabajoso, penoso; industrioso.

lab·y·rinth [lǽbərɪnθ] *s.* laberinto.

lace [les] *s.* (*cloth*) encaje; (*cord*) cordón, cordoncillo, cinta (*de corsé, etc.*); **gold** — galón de oro (*para guarnecer uniformes*); *v.* atar con cinta o cordón; guarnecer con encⁿies; enlazar, entrelazar.

lack [læk] *s.* falta; escasez, carencia; deficiencia; *v.* carecer de, faltarle a uno; necesitar; **he -s courage** le falta ánimo.

lack·ey [lǽkɪ] *s.* lacayo.

lack·ing [lǽkɪŋ] *adj.* falto, carente.

lac·quer [lǽkɚ] *s.* laca; *v.* barnizar con laca.

lad [læd] *s.* rapaz, chico.

lad·der [lǽdɚ] *s.* escalera de mano.

lad·en [lédn̩] *adj.* cargado; agobiado, abrumado; *v.* cargar; agobiar.

la·dies [lédɪz] *pl. de* **lady.**

laid [led] *pret. & p.p. de* **to lay; to be** — **up** estar incapacitado o estropeado.

lain [len] *p.p. de* **to lie.**

lair [lɛr] *s.* guarida; cueva de fieras.

lake [lek] *s.* lago.

lamb [læm] *s.* cordero; —**kin** corderito.

lame [lem] *adj.* cojo; lisiado; estropeado; — **excuse** disculpa falsa; *v.* hacer cojo; estropear, incapacitar.

la·ment [ləmént] *s.* lamento; *v.* lamentar(se).

lam·ent·a·ble [lǽməntəbl] *adj.* lamentable; doloroso.

lam·en·ta·tion [læməntéʃən] *s.* lamentación, lamento.

lam·i·nate [lǽmənet] *v.* laminar.

lamp [læmp] *s.* lámpara; linterna; farol; —**post** poste (de farol); —**shade** pantalla de lámpara.

lance [læns] *s.* lanza; *v.* alancear, lancear, herir con lanza; picar con bisturí.

land [lænd] *s.* tierra; terreno; suelo; *v.* desembarcar; aterrizar (*un avión*); llegar; coger (*un pez*); **to** — **a job** conseguir una colocacion, lograr un empleo.

land-grant [lǽndgrænt] *adj.* mediante donación federal de tierras.

land·hold·er [lǽndholdɚ] *s.* terrateniente, propietario, hacendado.

land·ing [lǽndɪŋ] *s.* (*act*) desembarco, desembarque; aterrizaje (*de un avión*); (*place*) desembarcadero; descanso (*de escalera*); — **field** campo de aterrizaje; aeropuerto; — **strip** pista de aterrizaje.

land·la·dy [lǽndledɪ] *s.* patrona, casera, dueña (*de la casa*).

land·lord [lǽndlɔrd] *s.* amo, patrón, propietario, dueño; casero.

land·mark [lǽndmɑrk] *s.* mojón, señal (*para fijar los confines*); marca; suceso culminante.

land·own·er [lǽndonɚ] *s.* terrateniente, propietario, hacendado.

land·scape [lǽndskep] *s.* paisaje.

land·slide [lǽndslaɪd] *s.* derrumbe, derrumbamiento, desplome; gran mayoría de votos.

lane [len] *s.* senda, vereda; callejuela; ruta, derrotero (*de vapores o aviones*).

lan·guage [lǽŋgwɪdʒ] *s.* lengua; idioma; lenguaje.

lan·guid [lǽŋgwɪd] *adj.* lánguido.

lan·guish [lǽŋgwɪʃ] *v.* languidecer.

lan·guor [lǽŋgɚ] *d.* languidez.

lank [læŋk] *adj.* alto y delgado, largucho.

lank·y [lǽŋkɪ] *adj.* largucho, zancón, zancudo.

lan·tern [lǽntɚn] *s.* linterna; farol.

lan·tha·nides [lǽnθənaɪdz] *s.* lantánidos.

lap [læp] *s.* falda, regazo; aleta; etapa, trecho (*de una carrera*); *v.* lamer; **to** — **over** cruzar(se) sobre, entrecruzar(se).

la·pel [ləpél] *s.* solapa.

lap·i·da·ry [lǽpɪdɛrɪ] *s. & adj.* lapidario.

lapse [læps] *s.* lapso; transcurso; desliz; error; *v.* deslizarse; pasar, transcurrir; caer en un desliz; decaer (*el entusiasmo, el interés, etc.*); caducar (*un plazo, un contrato, etc.*).

lar·board [lúrbɚd] *s.* babor; *adj.* de babor; — **side** banda de babor.

lar·ce·ny [lúrsn̩ɪ] *s.* latrocinio, hurto; ratería.

lard [lɑrd] *s.* lardo, manteca de puerco; *v.* mechar.

large [lɑrdʒ] *adj.* grande; **at** — suelto, libre; sin trabas; en general; **-ly** *adv.* grandemente, en gran parte.

large-scale [lúrdʒskél] *adj.* en grande escala.

lar·i·at [lǽrɪət] *s.* reata.

lark [lɑrk] *s.* (*bird*) alondra; (*fun*) diversión, holgorio, jarana; **to go on a** — ir o andar de jarana.

lar·va [lúrvə] *s.* larva.

lar·ynx [lǽrɪŋks] *s.* laringe.

las·civ·i·ous [ləsívɪəs] *adj.* lascivo.

lash [læʃ] *s.* látigo; azote, latigazo; pestaña; *v.* fustigar; azotar; censurar, reprender; amarrar.

lass [læs] *s.* moza, muchacha, doncella.

las·si·tude [lǽsətjud] *s.* dejadez, flojedad, decaimiento de fuerzas.

las·so [lǽso] *s.* lazo, reata, mangana; *v.* lazar, *Am.* enlazar.

last [læst] *adj.* (*in a series*) último; final; (*just passed*) pasado; — **night** anoche; — **year** el año pasado; **at** — por fin, finalmente, al fin; **next to the** — penúltimo; **to arrive** — llegar el último; *s.* fin, término; horma (*de zapato*); *v.* durar; perdurar; **-ly** *adv.* finalmente, en conclusión.

last·ing [lǽstɪŋ] *adj.* duradero; perdurable.

latch [lætʃ] *s.* pestillo, picaporte, aldaba, cerrojo; *v.* cerrar con aldaba.

late [let] *adj.* (*tardy*) tardío; tardo; (*recent*) reciente; último; —**comer** recién llegado; rezagado; **a** — **hour** una hora avanzada; **the** — **Mr. X** el finado (*o* difunto) Sr. X; **to have a** — **supper** cenar tarde; *adv.* tarde; — **afternoon** atardecer; — **in the night** a una hora avanzada de la noche; — **into the night** a deshoras de la noche; — **in the week** a fines de la semana; **of** — últimamente, recientemente; hace poco; **to**

be — ser tarde; llegar tarde; estar atrasado, venir o llegar con retraso (*el tren*); **the train was ten minutes** — el tren llegó con diez minutos de retraso; **-ly** últimamente, recientemente; hace poco, poco ha.

la·tent [létṇt] *adj.* latente.

lat·er [létɚ] *adv.* & *adj.* (*comp. de* late) más tarde; después, luego; más reciente; posterior.

lat·er·al [lǽtərəl] *adj.* lateral.

lat·est [létɪst] *adv.* & *adj.* (*superl. de* late) más tarde; más reciente, más nuevo; último; **the** — **fashion** la última moda, las últimas novedades; **the** — **news** las últimas novedades, las noticias más recientes; **at the** — a más tardar.

lathe [leθ] *s.* torno (*de carpintero o mecánico*).

lath·er [lǽðɚ] *s.* jabonadura, espuma de jabón; *v.* jabonar, enjabonar; espumar, hacer espuma.

Lat·in [lǽtṇ] *adj.* latino; *s.* latín.

lat·i·tude [lǽtətjud] *s.* latitud; libertad; amplitud.

lat·ter [lǽtɚ] *adj.* último; **towards the** — **part of the week** a (*o* hacia) fines de la semana; **the** — éste (ésta, esto, etc.).

lat·tice [lǽtɪs] *s.* celosía; enrejado, rejilla.

laud [lɔd] *v.* loar, encomiar, alabar.

laud·a·ble [lɔ́dəbl] *adj.* laudable, loable.

laugh [læf] *v.* reír(se); **to** — **at** reirse de; **to** — **loudly** reírse a carcajadas; **to** — **in one's sleeve** reírse para sus adentros; **she -ed in his face** se rió en sus barbas; *s.* risa; **loud** — risotada, carcajada, risada.

laugh·a·ble [lǽfəbl] *adj.* risible; ridículo.

laugh·ing·stock [lǽfɪŋstak] *s.* hazmerreír.

laugh·ter [lǽftɚ] *s.* risa.

launch [lɔntʃ] *v.* (*put into water*) botar o echar (*un barco*) al agua; (*a rocket*) lanzar; (*begin*) empezar, poner en operación; **to** — **forth** lanzarse; **to** — **forth on a journey** emprender un viaje; *s.* lancha.

laun·der [lɔ́ndɚ] *v.* lavar y planchar (*la ropa*).

laun·dress [lɔ́ndrɪs] *s.* lavandera.

laun·dry [lɔ́ndrɪ] *s.* lavandería; lavado; ropa (lavada).

lau·rel [lɔ́rəl] *s.* laurel; gloria, honor.

la·va [lávə] *s.* lava.

lav·a·to·ry [lǽvətorɪ] *s.* lavabo; lavamanos; lavatorio.

lav·en·der [lǽvəndɚ] *s.* espliego, lavándula; *adj.* lila, morado claro.

lav·ish [lǽvɪʃ] *adj.* gastador, pródigo, dadivoso; abundante, copioso; profuso; lujoso; *v.* prodigar; malgastar, despilfarrar; **to** — **praise upon** colmar de alabanzas a; **-ly** pródigamente, copiosamente; lujosamente.

law [lɔ] *s.* ley; derecho, jurisprudencia; regla; — **student** estudiante de leyes, estudiante de derecho; **law-abiding** observante de la ley.

law·break·er [lɔ́brekɚ] *s.* infactor, transgresor.

law·ful [lɔ́fəl] *adj.* legal; lícito; válido; permitido.

law·less [lɔ́lɪs] *adj.* sin ley; ilegal; desenfrenado; revoltoso; licencioso.

law·mak·er [lɔ́mekɚ] *s.* legislador.

lawn [lɔn] *s.* césped, prado; *Am.* pasto, grama; linón (*tela de hilo o algodón*); — **mower** cortadora de césped.

law·suit [lɔ́sut] *s.* pleito, litigio.

law·yer [lɔ́jɚ] *s.* abogado, jurisconsulto.

lax [læks] *adj.* flojo; suelto; relajado.

lax·a·tive [lǽksətɪv] *adj.* & *s.* laxante, purgante.

lax·i·ty [lǽksətɪ] *s.* flojedad, flojera; relajamiento (*de une regla, ley, etc.*).

lay [le] *pret. de* **to lie.**

lay [le] *v.* colocar; poner; tender, extender; poner (*huevos*); echar (*la culpa*); atribuir (*la responsabilidad*); presentar, exponer; asentar (*el polvo*); **to** — **a wager** apostar; **to** — **aside** poner a un lado; ahorrar; **to** — **away** (*o* **by**) guardar; **to** — **bare** revelar; exponer; **to** — **down** poner, colocar; rendir (*las armas*); **to** — **down the law** mandar, dictar; **to** — **hold of** asir, agarrar; **to** — **off a workman** suspender a un obrero; **to** — **open** exponer a la vista; **to** — **out a plan** trazar un plan; **to** — **up** almacenar; guardar, ahorrar; **to be laid up** estar incapacitado o estropeado; **to** — **waste** asolar; *s.* lay, balada, canción; situación, orientación (*del terreno*); *adj.* lego, laico; profano (*no iniciado en una ciencia*).

lay·er [léɚ] *s.* capa; estrato; gallina ponedora.

lay·man [lémən] *s.* lego, seglar, laico.

la·zi·ly [lézɪlɪ] *adv.* perezosamente.

la·zi·ness [lézɪnɪs] *s.* pereza.

la·zy [lézɪ] *adj.* perezoso, holgazán.

lead [lɛd] *s.* plomo; plomada, pesa de plomo.

lead [lid] *v.* (*guide*) guiar, dirigir; llevar; conducir; mandar (*un ejército*); (*precede*) ir a la cabeza de; sobresalir entre; ser mano (*en el juego de naipes*); **to** — **an orchestra** dirigir una orquesta, llevar la batuta; **to** — **astray** llevar por mal camino, extraviar, descarriar; **to** — **the way** ir por delante, mostrar el camino; *s.* delantera, primer lugar; mando, dirección; indicio; papel principal; primer actor.

lead·en [lédṇ] *adj.* plomizo; aplomado, color de plomo; pesado.

lead·er [lídɚ] *s.* jefe, caudillo, *Am.* líder; director; guía; caballo delantero; **-s** puntos suspensivos.

lead·er·ship [lídɚʃɪp] *s.* dirección, mando; iniciativa.

lead·ing [lídɪŋ] *adj.* principal; delantero; — **man** primer actor.

lead·off [lídɔf] *adj.* delantero; puntero.

leaf [lif] *s.* hoja; *v.* echar hojas (*un árbol*), cubrirse de hojas; **to** — **through a book** hojear un libro.

leaf·less [líflɪs] *adj.* sin hojas, deshojado.

leaf·let [líflɪt] *s.* hojilla; folleto, hoja volante, papel volante, circular.

leaf·y [lífɪ] *adj.* frondoso.

league [lig] *s.* (*alliance*) liga, confederación; sociedad; (*distance*) legua; *v.* asociar(se); ligarse, coligarse.

leak [lik] *s.* gotera (*en un techo*); agujero, grieta (*por donde se escapa el agua o el gas*); escape (*de gas, vapor, electricidad, etc.*); *v.* gotear(se); rezumar(se); hacer agua (*dícese de un barco*); salirse, escaparse (*el gas, el vapor, etc.*).

lean [lin] *v.* (*incline*) inclinar(se); recostar(se), reclinar(se); (*support*) apoyar(se); *adj.* magro; flaco; — **year** año estéril, año improductivo.

leant [lɛnt] = **leaned.**

leap [lip] *v.* saltar; brincar; *s.* salto, brinco; — **year** año bisiesto.

leapt [lɛpt] *pret.* & *p.p. de* **to leap.**

learn [lɝn] *v.* aprender; saber, averiguar, enterarse de.

learn·ed [lɝnɪd] *adj.* erudito; docto.

learn·er [lɝnɚ] *s.* aprendedor; estudiante, estudioso.

learn·ing [lɝnɪŋ] *s.* erudición, saber; aprendizaje.

learnt [lɝnt] *pret.* & *p.p. de* **learn.**

lease [lis] *v.* arrendar, dar o tomar en arriendo; *s.* arriendo, contrato de arrendamiento.

leash [liʃ] *s.* traílla; cuerda.

least [list] *adj.* (el) mínimo, (el) más pequeño; *adv.*

LA

menos; **at** — al menos, a lo menos, por lo
menos; **the** — lo (el, la) menos.
leath·er [léðə˞] *s.* cuero, piel; *adj.* de cuero, de piel;
— **strap** correa.
leave [liv] *v.* dejar; abandonar; salir (de); partir;
irse; **to** — **out** dejar fuera; omitir; *s.* permiso,
licencia; — **of absence** licencia; **to take** — **of**
despedirse de.
leav·en [lévən] *s.* levadura, fermento; *v.* fermentar
(*la masa*).
leaves [livz] *pl. de* **leaf**.
leav·ings [lívɪŋz] *s.* sobras, desperdicios.
lec·ture [lɛ́ktʃə˞] *s.* conferencia, discurso;
reprensión; *v.* dar una conferencia; explicar;
reprender.
lec·tur·er [lɛ́ktʃərə˞] *s.* conferenciante; lector (*de
universidad*).
led [lɛd] *pret. & p.p. de* **to lead**.
ledge [lɛdʒ] *s.* borde; salidizo.
ledg·er [lédʒə˞] *s.* libro mayor (*en contabilidad*).
leech [litʃ] *s.* sanguijuela.
leer [lɪr] *s.* mirada de soslayo, mirada lujuriosa;
v. mirar de soslayo; mirar con lujuria.
lee·ward [líwə˞d] *s. & adv.* sotavento.
left [lɛft] *pret. & p.p. de* **to leave**; **I have two
books** — me quedan dos libros; *adj.* izquierdo;
s. izquierda; mano izquierda; **at (on, to) the** —
a la izquierda.
left-hand·ed [lɛ́fthǽndɪd] *adj.* zurdo; a la
izquierda; torpe; malicioso, insincero; —
compliment alabanza irónica.
left·ist [lɛ́ftɪst] *s.* izquierdista.
left·o·ver [lɛ́ftovə˞] *adj.* sobrante; **-s** *s. pl.* sobras.
left-wing [lɛ́ftwɪŋ] *adj.* izquierdista.
leg [lɛg] *s.* pierna; pata (*de animal, mesa, etc.*);
pie o pata (*de banquillo, silla, etc.*); etapa,
trecho (*de una carrera o viaje*); **to be on one's
last -s** estar en las últimas.
leg·a·cy [légəsɪ] *s.* legado, herencia.
le·gal [lígl] *adj.* legal; lícito.
le·gal·ize [líglaɪz] *v.* legalizar; sancionar,
autorizar.
leg·ate [légɪt] *s.* legado; delegado.
le·ga·tion [lɪgéʃən] *s.* legación; embajada.
leg·end [lédʒənd] *s.* leyenda; letrero, inscripción.
leg·en·dar·y [lédʒəndɛrɪ] *adj.* legendario.
leg·gings [légɪŋz] *s. pl.* polainas.
leg·i·ble [lédʒəbl] *adj.* legible.
le·gion [lídʒən] *s.* legión.
leg·is·late [lédʒɪslet] *v.* legislar.
leg·is·la·tion [lɛdʒɪsléʃən] *s.* legislación.
leg·is·la·tive [lédʒɪsletɪv] *adj.* legislativo.
leg·is·la·tor [lédʒɪsletə˞] *s.* legislador.
leg·is·la·ture [lédʒɪsletʃə˞] *s.* legislatura, asamblea
legislativa.
le·git·i·mate [lɪdʒítəmɪt] *adj.* legítimo.
lei·sure [líʒə˞] *s.* ocio; — **hours** horas de ocio;
to be at — estar ocioso; estar libre o
desocupado; **do it at your** — hágalo Vd. cuando
pueda o le convenga; hágalo Vd. en sus ratos de
ocio.
lei·sure·ly [líʒə˞lɪ] *adj.* lento, deliberado, pausado;
adv. sin prisa, despacio, a sus (mis, tus, *etc.*)
anchas.
lem·on [lɛ́mən] *s.* limón; — **tree** limonero; *adj.* de
limón; — **color** cetrino.
lem·on·ade [lɛmənéd] *s.* limonada.
lend [lɛnd] *v.* prestar.
lend·er [léndə˞] *s.* prestador; **money** — prestamista.
length [lɛŋkθ] *s.* largo, largor, largura, longitud;
duración; cantidad (*de una sílaba*); **at** —

largamente, detenidamente; al fin; **to go to any**
— hacer cuanto esté de su parte.
length·en [lɛ́ŋkθən] *v.* alargar(se); prolongar(se).
length·wise [lɛ́ŋkθwaɪz] *adv.* a lo largo;
longitudinalmente; *adj.* longitudinal.
length·y [lɛ́ŋkθɪ] *adj.* largo, prolongado.
le·ni·ent [líniənt] *adj.* indulgente, clemente, poco
severo.
lens [lɛnz] *s.* lente; cristalino (*del ojo*).
lent [lɛnt] *pret. & p.p. de* **to lend**.
Lent [lɛnt] *s.* cuaresma.
leop·ard [lɛ́pə˞d] *s.* leopardo.
lep·ro·sy [lɛ́prəsɪ] *s.* lepra.
less [lɛs] *adj.* menor; *adv. & prep.* menos; — **and**
— cada vez menos.
less·en [lɛ́sn̩] *v.* aminorar(se), disminuir(se),
reducir(se); mermar.
less·er [lɛ́sə˞] *adj.* menor, más pequeño.
les·son [lɛ́sn̩] *s.* lección.
lest [lɛst] *conj.* no sea que, por miedo de que.
let [lɛt] *v.* (*permit*) dejar, permitir; (*rent*) alquilar,
arrendar; — **us** (*o* **let's**) **do it** vamos a hacerlo,
hagámoslo; — **him come** que venga; **to** — **be** no
molestar, dejar en paz; no tocar; **to** — **down**
nar; **to** — **go** soltar; **to** — **in**
dejar entrar, admitir; **to** — **know** avisar, enterar,
hacer saber; **to** — **off** soltar; dejar libre; **to** —
through dejar pasar; **to** — **up** disminuir; *pret. &
p.p. de* **to let**.
let·down [lɛ́tdaʊn] *s.* aflojamiento; desilusión.
le·thal [líθəl] *adj.* letal.
leth·ar·gy [lɛ́θə˞dʒɪ] *s.* letargo; **to fall into a** —
aletargarse.
let·ter [lɛ́tə˞] *s.* (*alphabet*) letra; (*missive*) carta; —
box buzón; — **carrier** cartero; —**head**
membrete; *v.* rotular, hacer a mano letras de
molde.
let·tuce [lɛ́tɪs] *s.* lechuga.
lev·el [lɛ́vl̩] *adj.* llano, plano; a nivel; igual;
parejo; **level-headed** bien equilibrado, sensato;
adv. a nivel; a ras; *s.* nivel; **to be on the** —
obrar rectamente, obrar sin engaño; ser o decir
la pura verdad; *v.* nivelar; igualar; allanar;
apuntar, asestar (*un arma*); **to** — **to the ground**
arrasar, echar por tierra.
le·ver [lɛ́və˞] *s.* palanca; **control** — palanca de
mando.
lev·i·ty [lɛ́vɪtɪ] *s.* frivolidad; levedad.
lev·y [lɛ́vɪ] *s.* imposición, recaudación (*de tributos,
impuestos, etc.*); leva, enganche, reclutamiento;
embargo (*de propiedad*); *v.* imponer, exigir,
recaudar (*tributos o multas*); reclutar; **to** — **on
someone's property** embargar la propiedad de
alguien.
lewd [lud] *adj.* lujurioso, lascivo, deshonesto.
lewd·ness [lúdnɪs] *s.* lascivia, lujuria.
lex·i·cal [lɛ́ksɪkl̩] *adj.* léxico.
lex·i·cog·ra·phy [lɛksɪkágrəfɪ] *s.* lexicografía.
lex·i·con [lɛ́ksɪkən] *s.* léxico.
li·a·bil·i·ty [laɪəbílətɪ] *s.* responsabilidad,
obligación; desventaja; **li·a·bil·i·ties**
obligaciones, deudas; pasivo.
li·a·ble [láɪəbl̩] *adj.* responsable, obligado; sujeto,
expuesto; propenso; probable.
li·ai·son [liezán] *s.* enlace; unión.
li·ar [láɪə˞] *s.* mentiroso, embustero.
li·bel [láɪbl̩] *s.* libelo; difamación; *v.* difamar.
lib·er·al [líbərəl] *adj. & s.* liberal.
lib·er·al·ism [líbərəlɪzm̩] *s.* liberalismo.
lib·er·al·i·ty [lɪbərǽlətɪ] *s.* liberalidad; largueza,
generosidad.

lib·er·al·ize [líbəˌlaɪz] v. liberalizar(se).
lib·er·ate [líbəret] v. libertar, librar; soltar.
lib·er·a·tion [lɪbəréʃən] s. liberación.
lib·er·a·tor [líbəretə] s. libertador.
lib·er·tine [líbətɪn] adj. & s. libertino.
lib·er·ty [líbətɪ] s. libertad; **at** — libre.
li·bi·do [lɪbído] s. libido.
li·brar·i·an [laɪbrérɪən] s. bibliotecario.
li·brar·y [láɪbrɛrɪ] s. biblioteca.
li·bret·to [lɪbréto] s. libreto.
lice [laɪs] pl. de **louse**.
li·cense, licence [láɪsns] s. licencia; permiso; título; **driver's** — licencia (pase, certificado o patente) de chófer; título de conductor; licencia para manejar; — **plate** placa (o chapa) de numeración, chapa de circulación, chapa de matrícula; v. licenciar, dar licencia a; permitir, autorizar.
li·cen·tious [laɪsénʃəs] adj. licencioso, disoluto.
lick [lɪk] v. (tongue) lamer; (thrash) dar una tunda o zurra; vencer; **to** — **someone's boots** adular a uno con servilismo; **to** — **the dust** morder el polvo; adular; s. lamedura, Am. lamida; lengüetada; C.A. lambida; **salt** — lamedero (lugar salino donde lame el ganado); **not to do a** — **of work** no hacer absolutamente nada.
lick·ing [líkɪŋ] s. zurra, tunda.
lid [lɪd] s. tapadera, tapa; **eye**— párpado.
lie [laɪ] s. mentira; embuste; **to give the** — **to** desmentir, dar un mentís; v. mentir (pret. & p.p. **lied**); tenderse, acostarse; yacer; estar; estar situado; consistir (en); **to** — **back** recostarse, echarse hacia atrás; **to** — **down** acostarse, echarse, tenderse; **to** — **in wait** acechar, espiar.
lieu·ten·ant [luténənt] s. teniente; **second** — subteniente.
life [laɪf] s. vida; **from** — del natural; **still** — naturaleza muerta; —**boat** bote de salvamento, lancha salvavidas; — **imprisonment** prisión perpetua; — **insurance** seguro sobre la vida; — **pension** pensión vitalicia; — **preserver** salvavidas, cinto o chaqueta de salvamento.
life·less [láɪflɪs] adj. sin vida; muerto; exánime; inanimado; desanimado.
life·less·ness [láɪflɪsnɪs] s. falta de vida; inercia; falta de animación.
life·like [láɪflaɪk] adj. como la vida; natural, que parece vivo.
life·long [láɪflɔ́ŋ] adj. perpetuo, de toda la vida.
life·time [láɪftaɪm] s. vida, transcurso de la vida.
lift [lɪft] v. levantar; alzar; elevar; disiparse (las nubes, la niebla, las tinieblas); **to** — **one's hat** quitarse el sombrero (para saludar); s. elevación; exaltación de ánimo; alzamiento, levantamiento; carga; ayuda (para levantar una carga); alza (de un zapato); ascensor, Am. elevador; **to give someone a** — **in a car** llevar a alguien en el auto.
lig·a·ture [lígətʃur] s. ligadura.
light [laɪt] s. luz; lumbre; **tail** — Am. farito trasero, Am. farol de cola, Méx. calavera; adj. claro; con luz; de tez blanca; ligero; leve; frívolo; — **drink** bebida suave; —**headed** frívolo, ligero de cascos; —**hearted** alegre; — **opera** opereta; **to make** — **of** dar poca importancia a; v. encender(se); iluminar, alumbrar; **to** — **upon** caer sobre; posarse en (dícese de los pájaros, mariposas, etc.).
light·en [láɪtn] v. aligerar; iluminar; aclarar; relampaguear; alegrar.
light·er [láɪtə] s. encendedor.
light·house [láɪthaʊs] s. faro.

light·ing [láɪtɪŋ] s. iluminación; alumbrado.
light·ly [láɪtlɪ] adv. ligeramente; levemente; frívolamente; sin seriedad.
light·ness [láɪtnɪs] s. ligereza; frivolidad; claridad.
light·ning [láɪtnɪŋ] s. relampagueo; relámpago; — **rod** pararrayos.
light·weight [láɪtwet] s. peso liviano; peso ligero.
lik·a·ble [láɪkəbl] adj. agradable, simpático, placentero.
like [laɪk] adv. & prep. como; del mismo modo que; semejante a; adj. semejante, parecido; **in** — **manner** de manera semejante, del mismo modo; **to feel** — **going** tener ganas de ir; **to look** — **someone** parecerse a alguien; **it looks** — **rain** parece que va a llover, quiere llover; s. semejante, igual; -**s** gustos; preferencias; v. gustarle a uno; **he** -**s books** le gustan los libros; **do whatever you** — haz lo que gustes.
like·ly [láɪklɪ] adj. probable, creíble; prometedor; — **place** lugar a propósito; **it is** — **to happen** es probable que suceda; adv. probablemente.
lik·en [láɪkən] v. asemejar, comparar.
like·ness [láɪknɪs] s. semejanza; parecido; retrato.
like·wise [láɪkwaɪz] adv. igualmente, asimismo; del mismo modo; también.
lik·ing [láɪkɪŋ] s. simpatía; afición; preferencia, gusto.
li·lac [láɪlək] s. lila; adj. lila, morado claro.
lil·y [lílɪ] s. lirio; azucena.
lil·y-white [líliwáɪt] adj. blanquísimo; puro; racialmente segregado.
limb [lɪm] s. rama (de árbol); miembro (del cuerpo), pierna, brazo.
lim·ber [límbə] adj. flexible; ágil; v. hacer flexible; **to** — **up** agilitar(se), hacer(se) flexible.
lime [laɪm] s. cal; lima (fruta); Am. limón; — **tree** limonero; liga (para cazar pájaros).
lime·light [láɪmlaɪt] s. luz de calcio; proscenio; **to be in the** — estar a la vista del público.
lime·stone [láɪmston] s. piedra caliza.
lim·it [límɪt] s. límite; confín; v. limitar.
lim·i·ta·tion [lɪmɪtéʃən] s. limitación; restricción.
lim·it·ed [límɪtɪd] adj. limitado; restringido.
lim·it·ing [límɪtɪŋ] adj. limítrofe.
lim·it·less [límɪtlɪs] adj. ilimitado, sin límites; desmedido.
limp [lɪmp] s. cojera; v. cojear; renquear; adj. flojo; flexible.
lim·pid [límpɪd] adj. límpido; claro, transparente.
line [laɪn] s. (mark) línea; renglón; raya; (cord) cuerda; (business) ramo; giro (de negocios); especialidad; — **of goods** surtido, línea (Am. renglón) de mercancías; **branch railway** — ramal; **pipe** — cañería, tubería; **to bring into** — alinear; obligar a proceder de acuerdo con un plan; poner de acuerdo; **to get in** — meterse en fila, hacer (o formar) cola; v. linear, rayar; alinear; forrar; **to** — **up** alinear(se); formarse, formar fila.
lin·e·age [línɪɪdʒ] s. linaje.
lin·e·ar [línɪə] adj. lineal.
lined [laɪnd] adj. rayado; forrado.
lin·en [línɪn] s. lino; ropa blanca.
lin·er [láɪnə] s. vapor, buque; **air** — avión, transporte aéreo.
line·up [láɪnəp] s. formación.
lin·ger [líŋgə] v. tardar(se), demorarse, dilatarse; andar ocioso, vagar; perdurar; prolongarse.
lin·ge·rie [lænʒərɪ] s. ropa interior de mujer.
lin·guist [líŋgwɪst] s. lingüista.
lin·guis·tics [lɪŋgwístɪks] s. lingüística.

LE

lin·ing [láɪnɪŋ] *s.* forro.
link [lɪŋk] *s.* eslabón; enlace; **cuff -s** gemelos; *v.* eslabonar(se); enlazar(se).
lin·net [línɪt] *s.* jilguero.
li·no·le·um [lɪnólɪəm] *s.* linóleo (*tela impermeable para cubrir el suelo*).
lin·seed [línsid] *s.* linaza; — **oil** aceite de linaza.
lint [lɪnt] *s.* hilas; hilachas.
li·on [láɪən] *s.* león.
li·on·ess [láɪənɪs] *s.* leona.
lip [lɪp] *s.* labio.
lip·stick [lípstɪk] *s.* lápiz para los labios.
liq·uid [líkwɪd] *adj.* líquido; — **assets** valores líquidos (*o realizables*); — **measure** medida para líquidos; *s.* líquido.
liq·ui·date [líkwɪdet] *v.* liquidar, saldar (*cuentas*); poner término a.
liq·ui·da·tion [lɪkwɪdéʃən] *s.* liquidación; saldo de cuentas.
liq·uor [líkɚ] *s.* licor; bebida espiritosa (*como aguardiente, ron, etc.*).
lisp [lɪsp] *s.* ceceo; *v.* cecear; balbucir.
list [lɪst] *s.* lista; registro; escora (*inclinación de un barco*); *v.* alistar, registrar poner o apuntar en una lista; hacer una lista de; escorar, inclinarse a la banda.
lis·ten [lísn] *v.* escuchar; atender, dar oídos, prestar atención; —! ¡oye! ¡escucha!; ¡oiga! ¡escuche!; **to — in** escuchar por radio; escuchar a hurtadillas (*una conversación*).
lis·ten·er [lísnɚ] *s.* escuchador, oyente; **radio** — radioescucha, radioyente.
list·less [lístlɪs] *adj.* abstraído; indiferente; indolente; desatento.
list·less·ness [lístlɪsnɪs] *s.* indiferencia, inatención, abstracción.
lit [lɪt] *pret. & p.p. de* **light**; *adj.* alumbrado; algo borracho.
lit·er·al [lítərəl] *adj.* literal; **-ly** *adv.* al pie de la letra, literalmente.
lit·er·ar·y [lítərɛrɪ] *adj.* literario.
lit·er·a·ture [lítərətʃʊr] *s.* literatura; impresos, folletos, circulares.
lith·i·um [líθɪəm] *s.* litio.
lit·i·ga·tion [lɪtəgéʃən] *s.* litigio, pleito.
lit·ter [lítɚ] *s.* (*young animals*) camada, cría; (*stretcher*) litera; camilla; cama de paja para animales; (*disorder*) cosas esparcidas; desorden; revoltillo; *v.* desarreglar, revolver, esparcir cosas.
lit·tle [lítl] *adj.* pequeño; poco; — **Bear** Osa Menor; **a — coffee** un poco de café; **a — while** un ratito (*o ratico*), un poco; *adv. & s.* poco; — **by** — poco a poco.
live [lɪv] *v.* vivir; **to — down** hacer olvidar, borrar (*el pasado*); **to — up to** vivir en conformidad con, vivir de acuerdo con.
live [laɪv] *adj.* (*not dead*) vivo; (*lively*) enérgico; vivo, activo; — **coal** ascua encendida; — **oak** encina; — **question** cuestión palpitante, cuestión de actualidad; — **wire** alambre cargado; persona muy activa.
live·li·hood [láɪvlɪhʊd] *s.* vida, alimento, subsistencia, manutención.
live·li·ness [láɪvlɪnɪs] *s.* viveza, animación; agilidad.
live·long [lívlɔŋ] *adj.* todo; absolutamente todo.
live·ly [láɪvlɪ] *adj.* vivo; vivaz; animado, alegre; airoso; — **horse** caballo brioso; *adv.* vivamente; de prisa.
liv·er [lívɚ] *s.* hígado; vividor.
liv·er·y [lívərɪ] *s.* librea; caballeriza (*para caballos de alquiler*); **auto** — garage para autos de alquiler.

lives [laɪvz] *pl. de* **life**.
live·stock [láɪvstɑk] *s.* ganado.
live wire [láɪvwáɪr] *s.* persona alerta y vivaz.
liv·id [lívɪd] *adj.* lívido; amoratado.
liv·ing [lívɪŋ] *s.* (*state*) vida; (*means*) manutención, subsistencia; *adj.* vivo; viviente; — **room** sala; — **wage** sueldo suficiente para vivir; **the** — los vivos.
liz·ard [lízɚd] *s.* lagarto; **small** — lagartija.
load [lod] *s.* carga; **ship** — cargamento; **-s of** gran cantidad de; montones de; *v.* cargar; agobiar; colmar.
loaf [lof] *s.* hogaza de pan; **sugar** — azúcar de pilón; *v.* holgazanear, haraganear.
loaf·er [lófɚ] *s.* holgazán, haragán, zángano.
loan [lon] *s.* préstamo; empréstito; — **shark** usurero; — **word** préstamo semántico; *v.* prestar (*dinero*).
loath [loθ] *adj.* maldispuesto, renuente; **to be — to** repugnarle a uno.
loathe [loð] *v.* repugnarle a uno; abominar.
loath·some [lóðsəm] *adj.* repugnante, asqueroso; aborrecible.
loaves [lovz] *pl. de* **loaf**.
lob [lab] *v.* volear.
lob·by [lábɪ] *s.* (*place*) vestíbulo; antecámara; salón de entrada; hall; (*influence*) camarilla (*que busca ventajas ante un cuerpo legislativo*); **hotel** — vestíbulo o patio del hotel, hall; *v.* cabildear (*procurar ventajas o partidarios en una asamblea*).
lobe [lob] *s.* lóbulo.
lob·ster [lábstɚ] *s.* langosta de mar.
lo·cal [lókl] *adj.* local; — **train** tren ordinario.
lo·cal·i·ty [lokælətɪ] *s.* localidad; comarca.
lo·cal·ize [lóklaɪz] *v.* localizar.
lo·cate [lóket] *v.* situar, establecer; localizar, averiguar la posición de; avecindarse, radicarse, establecerse.
lo·ca·tion [lokéʃən] *s.* situación; sitio, localidad.
lock [lak] *s.* (*door*) cerradura; (*canal*) esclusa (*de un canal*); llave (*de un arma de fuego*); guedeja (*de pelo*); bucle, rizo; *v.* cerrar con llave; trabar(se), juntar(se); entrelazar(se); **to — in** encerrar; **to — out** cerrar la puerta (*a alguien*), dejar afuera; **to — up** encerrar; encarcelar.
lock·er [lákɚ] *s.* alacena; armario.
lock·et [ákɪt] *s.* guardapelo.
lock·out [lákaʊt] *s.* paro (*suspensión del trabajo por parte de los empresarios*); cierre de fábrica.
lock·smith [láksmɪθ] *s.* cerrajero.
lo·co·mo·tive [lokəmótɪv] *s.* locomotora; — **engineer** maquinista.
lo·cust [lókəst] *s.* langosta, saltamontes; cigarra; — **tree** algarrobo; acacia falsa.
lodge [ladʒ] *s.* logia; casita accesoria; casa de campo; *v.* alojar(se); hospedar(se); colocar; **to — a complaint** presentar una queja.
lodg·er [ládʒɚ] *s.* huésped, inquilino.
lodg·ing [ládʒɪŋ] *s.* alojamiento, hospedaje; vivienda.
loft [lɔft] *s.* desván; galería, balcón interior (*de un templo*); **choir** — coro; **hay** — pajar.
loft·y [lɔ́ftɪ] *adj.* elevado; sublime; altivo.
log [lɔg] *s.* leño, troza, tronco aserrado; corredera (*aparato para medir las millas que anda la nave*); diario de navegación; — **cabin** cabaña de troncos; *v.* cortar (*árboles*); cortar leños y transportarlos; registrar (*en el diario de navegación*).
log·ic [ládʒɪk] *s.* lógica.

log·i·cal [ládʒɪkl] *adj.* lógico.
log·roll [lɔ́grol] *v.* lograr aprobación de leyes mediante favores.
loin [lɔɪn] *s.* ijada, ijar, lomo.
loi·ter [lɔ́ɪtɚ] *v.* holgazanear, vagar, malgastar el tiempo; **to — behind** rezagarse.
loll [lɑl] *v.* arrellanarse o repantigarse, recostarse con toda comodidad.
lone [lon] *adj.* solo, solitario.
lone·li·ness [lónlɪnɪs] *s.* soledad.
lone·ly [lónlɪ] *adj.* solo, solitario; triste, desamparado.
lone·some [lónsəm] *adj.* solo, solitario; triste, nostálgico.
long [lɔŋ] *adj.* largo; **the whole day —** todo el santo día; **three feet —** tres pies de largo; **to be — in coming** tardar en venir; *adv.* mucho, mucho tiempo; **— ago** hace mucho tiempo; **— live!** ¡viva! **as** (*o* **so**) **— as** en tanto que mientras que; **how — is it since … ?** ¿cuánto tiempo hace que … ?; **so —!** ¡hasta luego! ¡adiós!; **long-suffering** sufrido, paciente; **long-winded** prolijo, largo (*en hablar*); **long-distance** de larga distancia; *v.* anhelar; ansiar; **to — for** anhelar; suspirar por.
long·er [lɔ́ŋgɚ] *adj.* más largo; *adv.* más, más tiempo; **no — ya** no; **not … any —** ya no; no … más.
lon·gev·i·ty [lɑndʒévətɪ] *s.* longevidad.
long·ing [lɔ́ŋɪŋ] *s.* anhelo, añoranza, nostalgia; *adj.* anhelante, anheloso, nostálgico; **-ly** *adv.* con anhelo, anhelosamente, con ansia.
lon·gi·tude [lɑ́ndʒətjud] *s.* longitud.
long·shore·man [lɔ́ŋʃormən] *s.* estibador (*de barco o muelle*), cargador.
long-term [lɔ́ŋtɚm] *adj.* a largo plazo.
look [lʊk] *v.* (*see*) mirar; (*seem*) parecer; **it -s well on you** le cae (*o* le sienta) bien; **to — after** atender, cuidar; **to — alike** parecerse; asemejarse; **to — down on a person** mirar con desprecio (*o* menospreciar) a alguien; **to — for** buscar; esperar; **to — forward to** anticipar con placer; **to — into** examinar, investigar; **— out!** ¡cuidado!; ¡tenga cuidado!; **to — out of** asomarse a; **to — over** examinar; dar un vistazo a; **to — up** levantar la vista; buscar; **to — up to** admirar, mirar con respeto; *s.* mirada, vistazo; **-s** apariencia, aspecto; **to have good -s** ser bien parecido.
look·ing glass [lʊ́kɪŋglæs] *s.* espejo.
look·out [lʊ́kaʊt] *s.* vigía; atalaya; mirador; vista, perspectiva; **that is your —** ¡eso a usted!; **to be on the —** estar alerta.
loom [lum] *s.* telar; *v.* destacarse, descollar; asomar(se), aparecer.
loop [lup] *s.* (*closed*) lazo, gaza, presilla; (*road*) vuelta, curva; (*electric*) circuito; *v.* hacer una gaza (con *o* en); atar con gaza o presilla; hacer un circuito.
loop·hole [lúphol] *s.* agujero, abertura; salida; escapatoria.
loose [lus] *adj.* (*slack*) suelto; flojo; (*unfettered*) desatado; (*licentious*) disoluto; **— change** suelto, moneda suelta; **— jointed** de articulaciones flojas; **to let — soltar**; *v.* soltar, desatar; aflojar; **-ly** *adv.* sueltamente; flojamente; con poca exactitud, sin fundamento.
loos·en [lúsn] *v.* soltar(se); aflojar(se); desatar(se); **to — one's hold** desasirse, soltarse.
loose·ness [lúsnɪs] *s.* (*limberness*) soltura; flojedad; (*laxness*) flojera; holgura; relajación; (*of bowel*)

flujo.
loot [lut] *s.* botín, pillaje, saqueo; *v.* saquear, pillar, robar.
lop [lɑp] *v.* tronchar, desmochar (*Am.* mochar).
lo·qua·cious [lokwéʃəs] *adj.* locuaz, hablador, lenguaraz.
lo·quat [lókwat] *s.* níspero.
lord [lɔrd] *s.* señor; dueño, amo; lord; **Lord's Pray·er** Padre Nuestro; **Our Lord** Nuestro Señor; *v.* señorear, mandar; **to — it over** señorear, dominar.
lord·ly [lɔ́rdlɪ] *adj.* señoril; noble; altivo; despótico; *adv.* altivamente, imperiosamente.
lord·ship [lɔ́rdʃɪp] *s.* señoría (*título*); señorío, dominio.
lose [luz] *v.* perder; **to — sight of** perder de vista.
loss [lɔs] *s.* pérdida; **to be at a —** estar perplejo; no saber qué hacer; **to sell at a —** vender con pérdida.
lost [lɔst] *pret. & p.p. de* **to lose**; *adj.* perdido; extraviado; **— in thought** absorto, abstraído; **to get —** perderse extraviarse.
lot [lɑt] *s.* (*land*) lote; (*section*) parte, porción; (*luck*) suerte; solar, porción de terreno; **a — of** (*o* **-s of**) una gran cantidad de; mucho; muchos; **to draw -s** echar suertes; **to fall to one's —** tocarle a uno, caerle en suerte; *adv.* mucho; **a — better** mucho mejor.
lo·tion [lóʃən] *s.* loción.
lot·ter·y [lɑ́tɚɪ] *s.* lotería.
loud [laʊd] *adj.* ruidoso; recio, fuerte; chillón · (*dícese también de los colores*); *adv.* ruidosamente, fuerte, recio; alto, en voz alta.
loud-speak·er [láʊdspíkɚ] *s.* altavoz, altoparlante.
lounge [laʊndʒ] *s.* sala de descanso; sofá, diván, canapé; *v.* arrellanarse, repantigarse, recostarse cómodamente; sestear; holgazanear.
louse [laʊs] *s.* piojo.
lous·y [láʊzɪ] *adj.* piojoso; asqueroso.
lov·a·ble [lʌ́vəbl] *adj.* amable.
love [lʌv] *s.* (*affection*) amor; cariño; (*fondness*) afición; **— affair** amorío; **to be in —** estar enamorado; **to fall in — with** enamorarse de; **to make — to** enamorar a; *v.* amar, querer; gustar mucho de, gustarle a uno mucho; encantarle a uno algo.
love·li·ness [lʌ́vlɪnɪs] *s.* belleza, hermosura; amabilidad.
love·ly [lʌ́vlɪ] *adj.* amable; lindo, bello; exquisito; encantador; ameno.
lov·er [lʌ́vɚ] *s.* amante; **music —** aficionado a (*o* amante de) la música.
lov·ing [lʌ́vɪŋ] *adj.* amante, amoroso, cariñoso, afectuoso; **-ly** *adv.* cariñosamente, afectuosamente.
low [lo] *adj.* (*not high*) bajo; (*base*) vil; (*humble*) humilde; (*downcast*) abatido; débil; (*lacking*) deficiente; (*sick*) gravemente enfermo; **— comedy** farsa, sainete; **— gear** primera velocidad; **— Mass** misa rezada; **— key** de intensidad mínima; **dress with a — neck** vestido escotado (*o* con escote); **to be — on something** estar escaso de algo; **to be in — spirits** estar abatido o desanimado; *adv.* bajo; en voz baja, quedo, quedito; con bajeza, a precio bajo vilmente; *s.* mugido; *v.* mugir.
low·er [lóɚ] *adj.* más bajo; inferior; **— case letter** letra minúscula; **— classman** estudiante de los dos primeros años; **— house** cámara de diputados; *v.* bajar; disminuir; rebajar; abatir; humillar.

LI

low·land [lólænd] *s.* tierra baja.
low·li·ness [lólɪnɪs] *s.* bajeza; humildad.
low·ly [lólɪ] *adj.* bajo, humilde; inferior; *adv.* humildemente.
low·ness [lónɪs] *s.* bajeza; humildad; abatimiento; gravedad (*de tono*); debilidad (*de un sonido*); baratura.
loy·al [lɔ́ɪəl] *adj.* leal, fiel.
loy·al·ty [lɔ́ɪəltɪ] *s.* lealtad, fidelidad.
lu·bri·cant [lúbrɪkənt] *adj.* & *s.* lubricante.
lu·bri·cate [lúbrɪket] *v.* lubricar.
lu·cid [lúsɪd] *adj.* lúcido; claro; luciente.
luck [lʌk] *s.* suerte; fortuna; **in** — de buena suerte; **in bad** — de mala suerte.
luck·i·ly [lʌ́kɪlɪ] *adv.* afortunadamente, por fortuna.
luck·y [lʌ́kɪ] *adj.* afortunado, feliz; **to be** — tener suerte, tocarle a uno la suerte.
lu·cra·tive [lúkrətɪv] *adj.* lucrativo.
lu·di·crous [lúdɪkrəs] *adj.* ridículo.
lug [lʌg] *v.* llevar, traer, *Am.* carger; **to** — **away** cargar con, llevarse (*una cosa pesada*).
lug·gage [lʌ́gɪdʒ] *s.* equipaje.
luke·warm [lúkwórm] *adj.* tibio, templado; indiferente.
lull [lʌl] *v.* arrullar; sosegar; calmar(se); *s.* calma, momento de calma.
lul·la·by [lʌ́ləbaɪ] *s.* arrullo, canción de cuna.
lum·ber [lʌ́mbɚ] *s.* madera, maderaje; **—man** maderero, negociante en madera; **—yard** depósito de maderas; — **jack** leñador; *v.* cortar y aserrar madera; explotar los bosques; moverse pesadamente.
lu·mi·nous [lúmənəs] *adj.* luminoso.
lump [lʌmp] *s.* (*mass*) terrón; bulto; (*swelling*) hinchazón, chichón, protuberancia; — **of sugar** terrón de azúcar; *v.* amontonar; consolidar (*gastos*); apelotonarse, aterronarse, formar terrones.
lump·y [lʌ́mpɪ] *adj.* aterronado.
lu·na·tic [lúnətɪk] *adj.* & *s.* lunático, loco.
lunch [lʌntʃ] *s.* almuerzo; merienda; **—room** merendero, *Méx., Ven., Carib.* lonchería; *Ríopl.* confitería; *Spain* cafetería; *v.* almorzar; merendar; *Am.* tomar el lonche.
lun·cheon [lʌ́ntʃən] *s.* almuerzo; merienda.
lung [lʌŋ] *s.* pulmón.
lurch [lɝtʃ] *s.* sacudida; tambaleo repentino; **to give a** — tambalearse; **to leave someone in the** — dejar a uno plantado, dejar a uno a buenas noches; *v.* tambalearse; dar un tambaleo repentino.
lure [lʊr] *s.* aliciente, atractivo; tentación; cebo o reclamo (*para atraer*); *v.* atraer; seducir; atraer (*con cebo o reclamo*).
lurk [lɝk] *v.* estar oculto; estar en acecho; moverse furtivamente.
lus·cious [lʌ́ʃəs] *adj.* exquisito, delicioso, sabroso.
lust [lʌst] *s.* lujuria; deseo vehemente; codicia; *v.* **to** — **after** codiciar.
lus·ter [lʌ́stɚ] *s.* lustre, brillo.
lus·trous [lʌ́strəs] *adj.* lustroso.
lust·y [lʌ́stɪ] *adj.* vigoroso, fornido, robusto.
lute [lut] *s.* laúd.
lux·u·ri·ant [lʌgʒúrɪənt] *adj.* lozano, frondoso, exuberante.
lux·u·ri·ous [lʌgʒúrɪəs] *adj.* lujoso; dado al lujo; frondoso.
lux·u·ry [lʌ́kʃərɪ] *s.* lujo.
lye [laɪ] *s.* lejía.
ly·ing [láɪɪŋ] *ger. de* **to lie**; *adj.* mentiroso; **lying-in hospital** casa de maternidad.

lymph [lɪmpf] *s.* linfa.
lynch [lɪntʃ] *v.* linchar.
lynx [lɪŋks] *s.* lince.
lyre [laɪr] *s.* lira.
lyr·ic [lɪ́rɪk] *s.* poema lírico; *adj.* lírico.
lyr·i·cal [lɪ́rɪkl] *adj.* lírico.
lyr·i·cism [lɪ́rəsɪzəm] *s.* lirismo.

M:m

mac·a·ro·ni [mækərónɪ] *s.* macarrón o macarrones.
mac·a·roon [mækərún] *s.* macarrón, almendrado, bollito de almendra.
ma·chine [məʃín] *s.* máquina; automóvil; — **gun** ametralladora; — **made** hecho a máquina; **—pistol** metralleta; **political** — camarilla política; **sewing** — mácamarilla política; **sewing** — máquina para coser.
ma·chin·er·y [məʃínərɪ] *s.* maquinaria.
ma·chin·ist [məʃínɪst] *s.* mecánico, maquinista.
mack·er·el [mǽkərəl] *s.* escombro, caballa (*pez*).
mad [mæd] *adj.* loco; rabioso; furioso, enojado; **to drive** — enloquecer; volver loco; **to get** — encolerizarse; **to go** — volverse loco, enloquecerse; **-ly** *adv.* locamente.
mad·am, mad·ame [mǽdəm] *s.* madama, señora.
mad·cap [mǽdkæp] *s.* calavera (*m.*), *adj.* temerario; temerario; atolondrado.
mad·den [mǽdn] *v.* enloquecer(se).
made [med] *pret.* & *p.p. de* **to make**; **to be** — **of** estar hecho de; ser de; **to have something** — mandar hacer algo; **made-up** fingido, falso; artificial, pintado (*con afeites*).
made-to-or·der [medtuórdɚ] *adj.* hecho a la medida.
mad·man [mǽdmæn] *s.* loco.
mad·ness [mǽdnɪs] *s*— locura; rabia.
mag·a·zine [mǽgəzín] *s.* revista; almacén (*especialmente para provisiones militares*); **powder** — polvorín.
mag·ic [mǽdʒɪk] *s.* magia; *adj.* mágico.
ma·gi·cian [mədʒíʃən] *s.* mágico; prestidigitador; brujo.
mag·is·trate [mǽdʒɪstret] *s.* magistrado.
mag·nan·i·mous [mægnǽnəməs] *adj.* magnánimo.
mag·ne·sia [mægníʒə] *s.* magnesia.
mag·ne·si·um [mægnízɪəm] *s.* magnesio.
mag·net [mǽgnɪt] *s.* imán.
mag·net·ic [mægnétɪk] *adj.* magnético; — **pole** polo magnético; — **tape** cinta magnetofónica.
mag·net·ize [mǽgnətaɪz] *v.* magnetizar; imantar; cautivar.
mag·nif·i·cence [mægnífəsn̩s] *s.* magnificencia.
mag·nif·i·cent [mægnífəsn̩t] *adj.* magnífico.
mag·ni·fy [mǽgnəfaɪ] *v.* agrandar, engrandecer; amplificar; exagerar.
mag·ni·tude [mǽgnətjud] *s.* magnitud.
mag·pie [mǽgpaɪ] *s.* urraca; cotorra, hablador, habladora.
ma·hog·a·ny [məhǽgənɪ] *s.* caoba.
maid [med] *s.* criada, sirvienta, camarera, *Méx.* recamarera, *Ríopl., Andes* mucama; doncella; — **of honor** doncella de honor; **old** — solterona.
maid·en [médn̩] *s.* doncella; virgen; mozuela; soltera; — **lady** mujer soltera; — **voyage** primer viaje (*de un vapor*).
mail [mel] *s.* correo; correspondencia; **air** — correo aéreo; **coat of** — malla; **—bag** valija;

—**train** tren correo; *v.* echar al correo.
mail·box [mélbɑks] *s.* buzón.
mail·man [mélmæn] *s.* cartero.
maim [mem] *v.* mutilar, estropear.
main [men] *adj.* principal, mayor, de mayor importancia; *s.* tubería, cañería principal (*de agua o gas*); alta mar, océano; **in the** — en su mayor parte; en general, en conjunto; **-ly** *adv.* principalmente.
main·land [ménlænd] *s.* continente, tierra firme.
main·spring [ménsprɪŋ] *s.* muelle real; origen.
main·tain [mentén] *v.* mantener; sostener, afirmar; guardar.
main·te·nance [méntənəns] *s.* mantenimiento; sustento; manutención; sostén, sostenimiento.
maize [mez] *s.* maíz.
ma·jes·tic [mədʒéstɪk] *adj.* majestuoso.
maj·es·ty [mædʒɪstɪ] *s.* majestad.
ma·jor [médʒɚ] *adj.* (*greater*) mayor, más grande; (*principal*) principal; — **key** tono mayor; *s.* comandante; mayor, mayor de edad; curso o asignatura de especialización (*en la universidad*); — **league** liga mayor; *v.* especializarse (*en un curso de estudios*).
ma·jor·i·ty [mədʒɔ́rətɪ] *s.* mayoría; mayor edad.
make [mek] *v.* (*do*) hacer; (*create*) fabricar; formar; (*deliver*) pronunciar (*un discurso*); **to — a clean breast of** confesar; **to — a train** alcanzar un tren; **to — a turn** dar vuelta; **to — away with** llevarse, robar; matar; **to — fast** asegurar, afianzar; **to — headway** progresar, adelantar, avanzar; **to — much of** dar mucha importancia a; **to — neither head nor tail of** no comprender nada de; **to — nothing out of** no comprender nada de, no sacar nada en limpio; **to — out in the distance** distinguir a lo lejos; **to — over** rehacer, alterar (*un traje*); **to — sure** asegurarse; **to — toward** dirigirse a, encaminarse a; **to — up a story** inventar un cuento; **to — up after a quarrel** hacer las paces; **to — up for a loss** compensar por una pérdida; **to — up one's face** pintarse la cara; **to — up one's mind** resolverse, decidirse; *s.* hechura, forma; marca (*de fábrica*); manufactura.
mak·er [mékɚ] *s.* hacedor; fabricante; artífice.
make·shift [mékʃɪft] *adj.* provisional.
make-up [mékʌp] *s.* (*composition*) compostura, composición, hechura; (*character*) naturaleza, carácter; **facial** — afeite, cosmético; maquillaje.
mal·a·chite [mæləkaɪt] *s.* malaquita.
mal·a·dy [mælədɪ] *s.* mal, enfermedad.
ma·lar·i·a [məlérɪə] *s.* malaria, fiebre palúdica, paludismo.
mal·con·tent [mælkəntɛnt] *adj.* & *s.* malcontento.
male [mel] *adj.* macho; varón; masculino; varonil; de hombres, de varones; *s.* macho; varón; hombre.
mal·ice [mǽlɪs] *s.* malicia.
ma·li·cious [məlíʃəs] *adj.* malicioso, perverso, malévolo.
ma·lign [məláɪn] *v.* calumniar, difamar; *adj.* maligno; pernicioso.
ma·lig·nant [məlígnənt] *adj.* maligno; malévolo.
mal·le·a·ble [mǽlɪəbl] *adj.* maleable; manejable.
mal·let [mǽlɪt] *s.* mazo, maceta.
mal·nu·tri·tion [mælnutríʃən] *s.* desnutrición.
malt [mɔlt] *s.* malta; **-ed milk** leche malteada.
ma·ma, mam·ma [mámə] *s.* mamá.
mam·mal [mæml] *s.* mamífero.
mam·moth [mǽməθ] *adj.* gigantesco, enorme.
mam·my [mǽmɪ] *s.* mamita; niñera negra; criada

negra.
man [mæn] *s.* hombre; varón; pieza (*de ajedrez*); — **and wife** marido y mujer; **to a** — unánimente, todos a una; **officers and men** oficiales y soldados; **man-of-war** buque de guerra; — **cook** cocinero; *v.* armar, proveer de gente armada; guarnecer (*una fortaleza*); tripular (*una embarcación*).
man·age [mænɪdʒ] *v.* manejar; gobernar, dirigir; gestionar; **to — to do something** arreglárselas para hacer algo.
man·age·a·ble [mænɪdʒəbl] *adj.* manejable; domable, dócil.
man·age·ment [mænɪdʒmənt] *s.* manejo; dirección; gobierno, administración; gerencia.
man·ag·er [mænɪdʒɚ] *s.* gerente; director. administrador; empresario.
man·date [mændet] *s.* mandato; *v.* asignar por mandato.
man·do·lin [mændəlɪn] *s.* mandolina.
mane [men] *s.* melena (*del león*), crin (*del caballo*).
ma·neu·ver [mənúvɚ] *s.* maniobra; gestión; *v.* maniobrar; manipular, manejar.
man·ful [mænfəl] *adj.* varonil; viril.
man·ga·nese [mǽŋgənɪs] *s.* manganeso.
mange [mendʒ] *s.* sarna, roña.
man·ger [méndʒɚ] *s.* pesebre.
man·gle [mǽŋgl] *v.* magullar, mutilar, destrozar, estropear; planchar en máquina de planchar; *s.* planchadora (*máquina de planchar*).
man·grove [mæŋgrov] *s.* mangle.
man·gy [méndʒɪ] *adj.* sarnoso, *Am.* sarniento.
man·hood [mænhʊd] *s.* virilidad; edad viril; hombres.
ma·ni·a [ménɪə] *s.* manía.
man·i·cure [mænɪkjʊr] *v.* manicura; *v.* manicurar.
man·i·fest [mænəfest] *adj.* manifiesto; *s.* manifiesto (*lista de la carga de un buque*); *v.* manifestar; poner de manifiesto; declarar.
man·i·fes·ta·tion [mænəfestéʃən] *s.* manifestación.
man·i·fes·to [mænɪfésto] *s.* manifiesto, bando, proclama.
man·i·fold [mænəfold] *adj.* múltiple; numeroso, diverso.
man·i·kin [mænəkɪn] *s.* maniquí; muñeco; hombrecillo.
ma·nil·a [mənílə] *s.* abacá (*cáñamo de Manila*); — **paper** papel de Manila.
man·i·oc [mǽnɪak] *s.* mandioca.
ma·nip·u·late [mənípjəlet] *v.* manipular; manejar.
ma·nip·u·la·tion [mənɪpjəléʃən] *s.* manipulación.
man·kind [mænkáɪnd] *s.* humanidad, género humano; los hombres.
man·like [mænlaɪk] *adj.* hombruno; varonil; *s.* (*mujer*) marimacho.
man·ly [mænlɪ] *adj.* varonil; viril; *adv.* varonilmente.
man·ner [mænɚ] *s.* (*way*) manera; modo; género; (*air*) aire, ademán; **-s** manejas, modales; costumbres; **after the — of** a la manera de; **by no — of means** de ningún modo.
man·ner·ism [mænɚɪzm] *s.* costumbre; amaneramiento.
man·nish [mǽnɪʃ] *adj.* hombruno.
ma·noeu·vre = **maneuver.**
man·or [mænɚ] *s.* solar, casa solariega.
man·sion [mænʃən] *s.* mansión; palacio.
man·slaugh·ter [mænslɔtɚ] *s.* homicidio impremeditado o casual.
man·tel [mæntl] *s.* manto (*de una chimenea*); repisa de chimenea.

LO

man·tle [mǽntl] s. manto; capa.
man·u·al [mǽnjʊəl] adj. manual; — **training school** escuela de artes y oficios; s. manual; teclado de órgano.
man·u·fac·ture [mænjəfǽktʃɚ] s. fabricación; manufactura; v. fabricar, manufacturar.
man·u·fac·tur·er [mænjəfǽktʃərɚ] s. fabricante.
man·u·fac·tur·ing [mænjəfǽktʃərɪŋ] s. fabricación; adj. fabril, manufacturero.
ma·nure [mənʊ́r] s. estiércol, abono; v. estercolar, abonar (la tierra).
man·u·script [mǽnjəskrɪpt] adj. & s. manuscrito.
man·y [mɛ́nɪ] adj. muchos; — **a time** muchas veces; a **great** — muchísimos; **as** — **as** tantos como; cuantos; **as** — **as five** hasta cinco; **how** —? ¿cuántos?; **three books too** — tres libros de más; **too** — demasiados.
map [mǽp] s. mapa; v. trazar un mapa de; **to** — **out** proyectar, planear.
ma·ple [mépl] s. arce, Méx. meple; Riopl. maple.
mar [mɑr] v. desfigurar, estropear.
mar·ble [mɑ́rbl] s. mármol; canica (para jugar); **to play -s** jugar a las canicas; adj. de mármol; marmóreo.
march [mɑrtʃ] s. marcha; v. marchar, caminar; hacer marchar; **to** — **in** entrar marchando; **to** — **out** marcharse; salirse marchando.
March [mɑrtʃ] s. marzo.
mare [mɛr] s. yegua.
mar·ga·rine [mɑ́rdʒərɪn] s. margarina.
mar·gin [mɑ́rdʒɪn] s. margen; orilla; sobrante; reserva (fondos).
mar·gin·al [mɑ́rdʒɪnl] adj. marginal; — **note** nota marginal, acotación.
mar·i·gold [mǽrəgold] s. caléndula, maravilla.
ma·rine [mərín] adj. marino; marítimo; — **corps** cuerpo de marinos; s. marino; soldado de marina; **merchant** — marina mercante.
mar·i·ner [mǽrənɚ] s. marinero.
mar·i·time [mǽrətaɪm] adj. marítimo.
mark [mɑrk] s. marca; señal, seña; nota, calificación; **question** — punto de interrogación; **to come up to the** — alcanzar la norma requerida; **to hit the** — dar en el blanco; **to make one's** — distinguirse; **to miss one's** — fallar; errar el tiro; fracasar; v. marcar; señalar; notar; observar; calificar; — **my words!** ¡advierte lo que te digo!; **to** — **down** anotar, apuntar; rebajar el precio de.
mark·er [mɑ́rkɚ] s. marcador; marca, señal; jalón.
mar·ket [mɑ́rkɪt] s. mercado, plaza; — **place** mercado, plaza; — **price** precio corriente; **meat** — carnicería; **stock** — mercado de valores, bolsa; v. vender; vender o comprar en el mercado; **to go -ing** ir de compras.
mar·ma·lade [mɑ́rmled] s. mermelada.
ma·roon [mərún] s. & adj. rojo obscuro.
ma·rooned [mərúnd] adj. abandonado (en lugar desierto); aislado; **to get** — encontrarse aislado, perdido o incomunicado.
mar·quis [mɑ́rkwɪs] s. marqués.
mar·quise [mɑrkíz] s. marquesa.
mar·riage [mǽrɪdʒ] s. matrimonio; casamiento, boda; unión, enlace; — **license** licencia para casarse.
mar·riage·a·ble [mǽrɪdʒəbl] adj. casadero.
mar·ried [mǽrɪd] adj. casado; conyugal; — **couple** matrimonio, cónyuges; pareja de casados; **to get** — casarse.
mar·row [mǽro] s. meollo, tuétano, medula (de los huesos).

mar·ry [mǽrɪ] v. casar; casarse; casarse con.
marsh [mɑrʃ] s. pantano; ciénaga.
mar·shal [mɑ́rʃəl] s. mariscal; alguacil; jefe de policía (en ciertas regiones); maestro de ceremonia; **fire** — jefe de bomberos; v. ordenar, arreglar; guiar, conducir con ceremonia.
marsh·mal·low [mɑ́rʃmælo] s. pastilla o bombón de altea.
marsh·y [mɑ́rʃɪ] adj. pantanoso, cenagoso.
mart [mɑrt] s. mercado.
mar·tial [mɑ́rʃəl] adj. marcial; — **law** estado de sitio.
mar·tin [mɑ́rtɪn] s. avión pájaro).
mar·tyr [mɑ́rtɚ] s. mártir; v. martirizar, torturar, atormentar.
mar·tyr·dom [mɑ́rtɚdəm] s. martirio.
mar·vel [mɑ́rvl] s. maravilla; v. maravillarse.
mar·vel·ous [mɑ́rvləs] adj. maravilloso.
Marx·ism [mɑ́rksɪzəm] s. marxismo.
mas·cot [mǽskɑt] s. mascota.
mas·cu·line [mǽskjəlɪn] adj. masculino; varonil; hombruno.
mash [mǽʃ] v. majar, amasar; machacar, magullar; **-ed potatoes** puré de papas (o patatas); patatas majadas.
mask [mǽsk] s. máscara; disfraz; careta; v. disfrazar, enmascarar; encubrir; **-ed ball** baile de máscaras.
ma·son [mésn] s. albañil; **Mason** masón, francmasón.
ma·son·ry [mésnrɪ] s. albañilería; mampostería; **Masonry** masonería, francmasonería.
mas·quer·ade [mæskəréd] s. mascarada; disfraz, máscara; v. enmascararse, disfrazarse; andar disfrazado.
mass [mǽs] s. masa; montón; mole; mayoría, mayor parte; misa; — **meeting** mitin popular; — **communication** comunicación extensa; — **media** los medios de comunicarse con el público (radio, televisión, periódicos, etc.); **the -es** las masas, el pueblo; v. juntar(se) en masa.
mas·sa·cre [mǽsəkɚ] s. hecatombe, matanza, carnicería, destrozo; v. hacer matanza o hecatombe, destrozar.
mas·sage [məsáʒ] v. friccionar, dar masaje; s. masaje.
mas·sive [mǽsɪv] adj. sólido, macizo; voluminoso, imponente.
mast [mǽst] s. mástil, palo.
mas·ter [mǽstɚ] s. (head) amo, dueño, señor; maestro; patrón; (skilled) experto, perito; **band** — director de la banda; — **of arts** maestro en artes, licenciado; **-'s degree** licenciatura, grado de licenciado; adj. maestro; — **builder** maestro de obras; — **key** llave maestra; v. dominar; domar; gobernar; **to** — **a language** dominar un idioma.
mas·ter·ful [mǽstɚfəl] adj. magistral; dominante.
mas·ter·ly [mǽstɚlɪ] adj. magistral; adv. magistralmente.
mas·ter·piece [mǽstɚpis] s. obra maestra.
mas·ter·y [mǽstərɪ] s. maestría, arte, destreza; dominio.
mas·tiff [mǽstɪf] s. mastín, alano.
mat [mǽt] s. (covering) estera; esterilla, felpudo, tapete; (gymnasium) colchoncillo (de gimnasia); borde de cartón (para hacer resaltar una pintura).
match [mǽtʃ] s. (pair) pareja; (game) partida, contienda, juego; (light) fósforo, cerilla; Méx. cerillo; **he has no** — no tiene igual; **he is a**

good — es un buen partido; **the hat and coat are a good** — el abrigo y el sombrero hacen juego; *v.* igualar; aparear; hacer juego, armonizar; **to** — **one's strength** medir uno sus fuerzas; **these colors do not** — **well** estos colores no casan bien.

match·less [mǽtʃlɪs] *adj.* sin par, sin igual, incomparable.

mate [met] *s.* compañero, compañera; consorte; macho o hembra (*entre animales o aves*); piloto (*el segundo de un buque mercante*); oficial subalterno (*en la marina*); *v.* aparear(se).

ma·te·ri·al [mətírɪəl] *adj.* material; esencial; *s.* material; tejido, género; materia; **raw** — materia prima.

ma·ter·nal [mətɜ́nl] *adj.* maternal, materno.

ma·ter·ni·ty [mətɜ́ʒnətɪ] *s.* maternidad.

math·e·mat·i·cal [mæθəmǽtɪkl] *adj.* matemático.

math·e·mati·cian [mæθəmətíʃən] *s.* matemático.

math·e·mat·ics [mæθəmǽtɪks] *s.* matemáticas.

mat·i·née [mætɪné] *s.* función de la tarde, *Am.* matiné.

ma·tri·arch [métrɪark] *s.* matriarca.

ma·tric·u·late [mətríkjəlet] *v.* matricular(se).

ma·tric·u·la·tion [mətrɪkjəléʃən] *s.* matriculación, matrícula.

mat·ri·mo·ny [mǽtrəmonɪ] *s.* matrimonio, casamiento.

ma·trix [métrɪks] *s.* matriz; molde.

ma·tron [métrən] *s.* matrona, madre de familia; ama de llaves; vigilante, cuidadora (*de un asilo, cárcel par mujeres, etc.*).

mat·ter [mǽtɚ] *s.* (*substance*) material, materia; sustancia; (*affair*) asunto, cuestión; cosa; (*discharge*) pus; — **for complaint** motivo de queja; — **of two minutes** cosa de dos minutos; **as a** — **of fact** de hecho; en verdad, en realidad; **business -s** negocios; **printed** — impresos; **serious** — cosa seria; **it is of no** — no tiene importancia; **to do something as a** — **of course** hacer algo por rutina; **what is the** —? ¿qué tiene Vd.?; **matter-of-fact person** persona de poca imaginación; *v.* importar; supurar; **it does not** — no importa, no le hace.

mat·tress [mǽtrɪs] *s.* colchón; **spring** — colchón de muelles.

ma·ture [mətjúr] *adj.* maduro; **a** — **note** un pagaré vencido; *v.* madurar(se); vencerse, hacerse cobrable o pagadero (*un pagaré, una deuda*).

ma·tur·i·ty [mətjúrəɪ] *s.* madurez; vencimiento (*de una deuda u obligación*).

maul [mɔl] *v.* magullar; maltratar; manejar rudamente; golpear.

mav·er·ick [mǽvɚɪk] *s.* animal sin marca; becerro suelto.

max·im [mǽksɪm] *s.* máxima.

max·i·mum [mǽksəməm] *adj.* & *s.* máximo.

may [me] *v. irr. y. defect.* (*able*) poder; (*permitted*) tener permiso para, serle permitido a uno; (*possible*) ser posible; — **I sit down?** ¿puedo sentarme?; — **you have a good time** que se divierta Vd., **it** — **be that** puede ser que, tal vez sea que; **it** — **rain** puede (ser) que llueva, es posible que llueva; **she** — **be late** puede (ser) que llegue ella tarde.

May [me] *s.* mayo, mes de mayo; — **Day** primero de mayo; —**pole** mayo; — **Queen** maya (*reina de la fiesta del primero de mayo*).

may·be [mébɪ] *adv.* quizás, tal vez, acaso.

may·on·naise [meənéz] *s.* mayonesa.

may·or [méɚ] *s.* alcalde, alcalde mayor.

maze [mez] *s.* laberinto; confusión; **to be in a** — estar confuso o perplejo.

me [mi] *pron. pers.* me; mí (*después de preposición*); **give it to** — démelo (a mí); **for** — para mí; **with** — conmigo.

mead·ow [médo] *s.* pradera, prado; — **lark** alondra de los prados.

mea·ger [mígɚ] *adj.* escaso, insuficiente; magro, flaco.

meal [mil] *s.* comida; harina (*a medio moler*); **corn** — harina de maíz; —**time** hora de comer.

mean [min] *adj.* (*malicious*) ruin, bajo; vil; (*humble*) humilde; (*stingy*) mezquino, tacaño; (*difficult*) de mal genio; (*sick*) malo, indispuesto; (*middle*) mediano; medio; intermedio; — **distance** distancia media; *s.* medio; término medio; **-s** medios; recursos; **a man of -s** un hombre pudiente o rico; **by -s of** por medio de; **by all -s** de todos modos; a toda costa; por supuesto; **by no -s** de ningún modo; *v.* querer decir, significar; pensar, proponerse, tener la intención de; intentar; destinar; **he -s well** tiene buenas intenciones.

me·an·der [miǽndɚ] *v.* serpentear.

mean·ing [mínɪŋ] *s.* (*sense*) significado, sentido; significación; (*intent*) propósito, intención; *adj.* significativo; **well-meaning** bien intencionado.

mean·ing·less [mínɪŋlɪs] *adj.* sin sentido, vacío de sentido.

mean·ness [mínnɪs] *s.* ruindad, vileza, bajeza; mezquindad.

meant [mɛnt] *pret.* & *p.p.* de **to mean.**

mean·time [míntaɪm] *adv.* mientras tanto, entretanto; *s.* ínterin, entretanto; **in the** — en el ínterin, mientras tanto.

mean·while [mínhwaɪl] = **meantime.**

mea·sles [mízlz] *s.* sarampión.

mea·sur·a·ble [méʒrəbl] *adj.* medible, mensurable; **mea·sur·a·bly** *adv.* marcadamente.

mea·sure [méʒɚ] *s.* (*dimension*) medida; compás (*de música*); cadencia, ritmo; (*law*) proyecto de ley; ley; **beyond** — sobremanera; con exceso; **dry** — medida para áridos; **in large** — en gran parte, en gran manera; *v.* medir.

mea·sured [méʒɚd] *adj.* medido; moderado; acompasado.

mea·sure·ment [méʒɚmənt] *s.* medida; dimensión; tamaño; medición.

meat [mit] *s.* carne; meollo, sustancia; — **ball** albóndiga; — **market** carnicería; **cold** — fiambre.

meat·y [mítɪ] *adj.* carnoso; sustancioso.

me·chan·ic [məkǽnɪk] *adj.* & *s.* mecánico; **-s** *s.* mecánica.

me·chan·i·cal [məkǽnɪkl] *adj.* mecánico; maquinal.

mech·a·nism [mékənɪzəm] *s.* mecanismo.

med·al [médl] *s.* medalla.

med·dle [médl] *v.* entrometerse o entremeterse; meterse.

med·dler [médlɚ] *s.* entremetido.

med·dle·some [médlsəm] *adj.* entremetido.

me·di·an [mídɪən] *adj.* mediano, del medio; *s.* punto, línea o número del medio; mediana.

me·di·ate [mídɪet] *v.* mediar; intervenir; arbitrar.

me·di·a·tion [midɪéʃən] *s.* mediación, intervención, intercesión.

me·di·a·tor [mídɪətɚ] *s.* mediador, medianero, árbitro.

med·i·cal [médɪkl] *adj.* médico; — **school** escuela de medicina.

med·i·ca·tion [mɛdɪkéʃən] s. medicación.
med·i·cine [mɛ́dəsṇ] s. medicina; medicamento; — **ball** pelota grande de cuero; — **cabinet** botiquín; — **man** curandero indio.
me·di·e·val [midíívl] adj. medioeval o medieval.
me·di·o·cre [midɪó́kəˑ] adj. mediocre, mediano; ordinario.
me·di·oc·ri·ty [midɪákrətɪ] s. mediocridad, medianía.
med·i·tate [mɛ́dətet] v. meditar.
med·i·ta·tion [mɛdətéʃən] s. meditación.
me·di·um [mídɪəm] s. medio; medio ambiente; adj. mediano; intermedio; a medio cocer, a medio asar; — **of exchange** mediador de cambio.
med·ley [mɛ́dlɪ] s. baturrillo, mezcla, mezcolanza.
meek [mik] adj. manso, dócil, paciente, sufrido.
meek·ness [míknɪs] s. mansedumbre, docilidad.
meet [mit] v. encontrar(se); reunirse; conocer (*personalmente*), ser presentado a; ir a esperar (*un tren, vapor, o a alguien*); satisfacer (*deseos, requisitos, etc.*); pagar (*una deuda*); sufragar (*gastos*); responder a (*una acusación*); **to — in battle** trabar batalla; **to — with** encontrarse con; tropezar con; topar con; reunirse con; s. concurso; contienda (*tratándose de deportes*); **track** — competencia de atletas.
meet·ing [mítɪŋ] s. reunión; mitin; sesión; asamblea; encuentro.
meg·a·phone [mɛ́gəfon] s. megáfono, portavoz, bocina.
meg·a·ton [mɛ́gətʌn] s. megatón.
mel·an·chol·y [mɛ́lənkalɪ] s. melancolía; adj. melancólico.
me·lee [méle] s. reyerta; zafarrancho.
mel·low [mɛ́lo] adj. maduro, sazonado; dulce, blando, suave; v. madurar(se), sazonar(se); ablandar(se), suavizar(se).
me·lo·di·ous [məlódɪəs] adj. melodioso.
mel·o·dra·ma [mɛ́lodramə] s. melodrama.
mel·o·dy [mɛ́lədɪ] s. melodía.
mel·on [mɛ́lən] s. melón.
melt [mɛlt] v. derretir(se); disolver(se); fundir(se).
mem·ber [mɛ́mbəˑ] s. miembro; socio.
mem·ber·ship [mɛ́mbəˑʃɪp] s. número de miembros o socios; asociación; (*los*) miembros (*de un club o sociedad*).
mem·brane [mɛ́mbren] s. membrana.
me·men·to [mɪmɛ́nto] s. memento, memoria, recuerdo.
mem·oir [mɛ́mwɑr] s. memoria, apuntaciones; -**s** memorias; autobiografía.
mem·o·ra·ble [mɛ́mərəbl] adj. memorable.
mem·o·ran·dum [mɛmərǽndəm] s. memorándum; memoria, apunte; — **book** memorándum, librito de apuntes, memorial.
me·mo·ri·al [məmóriəl] s. (*monument*) monumento conmemorativo; (*occasion*) obra o fiesta conmemorativa; memorial, petición; adj. conmemorativo.
mem·o·rize [mɛ́məraɪz] v. aprender de memoria.
mem·o·ry [mɛ́mərɪ] s. memoria; recuerdo.
men [mɛn] pl. de **man.**
men·ace [mɛ́nɪs] s. amenaza; v. amenazar.
mend [mɛnd] v. remendar, reparar, componer; enmendar; **to — one's ways** enmendarse, reformarse; s. remiendo; reparación; **to be on the — ir** mejorando.
me·ni·al [mínɪəl] adj. servil, bajo.
men·stru·a·tion [mɛnstruéʃən] s. menstruo o menstruación.

men·tal [mɛ́ntl] adj. mental.
men·tal·i·ty [mɛntǽlətɪ] s. mentalidad, ingenio.
men·tion [mɛ́nʃən] s. mención; alusión; v. mencionar, mentar; **don't — it** no hay de qué (*contestación a* "thank you").
men·u [mɛ́nju] s. menú, lista de platos.
me·ow [mjaU] = **mew.**
mer·can·tile [mɝ́kəntɪl] adj. mercantil.
mer·ce·nar·y [mɝ́sṇɛrɪ] adj. mercenario.
mer·chan·dise [mɝ́tʃəndaɪz] s. mercancías, mercaderías; **piece of** — mercancía.
mer·chant [mɝ́tʃənt] s. comerciante; negociante; mercader; adj. mercante, mercantil; — **marine** marina mercante.
mer·ci·ful [mɝ́sɪfəl] adj. misericordioso, piadoso.
mer·ci·less [mɝ́sɪlɪs] adj. sin piedad, despiadado, incompasivo.
mer·cu·ry [mɝ́kjərɪ] s. mercurio; azogue.
mer·cy [mɝ́sɪ] s. (*favor*) merced; favor, gracia; (*compassion*) misericordia, piedad, compasión; **to be at the — of** estar a merced de.
mere [mɪr] adj. mero; simple, puro; **a — formality** una pura formalidad, no más que una formalidad, una formalidad no más; **a — trifle** una nonada; -**ly** adv. meramente; sólo, solamente; simplemente.
merge [mɝdʒ] v. combinar(se), unir(se); absorber(se); fundirse.
merg·er [mɝ́dʒəˑ] s. amalgamación comercial.
me·rid·i·an [mərídɪən] adj. & s. meridiano.
mer·it [mɛ́rɪt] s. mérito; v. merecer.
mer·i·to·ri·ous [mɛrətóriəs] adj. meritorio.
mer·maid [mɝ́med] s. ninfa marina.
mer·ri·ly [mɛ́rəlɪ] adv. alegremente, con regocijo.
mer·ri·ment [mɛ́rɪmənt] s. alegría, regocijo, júbilo.
mer·ry [mɛ́rɪ] adj. alegre; jovial; divertido; festivo; —**Christmas** Felices Navidades, Felices Pascuas; **to make** — divertirse.
mer·ry-go-round [mɛ́rɪgəraUnd] s. tío vivo, *Méx., C.A.* los caballitos; *Riopl.* calesita.
mer·ry-mak·er [mɛ́rɪmekəˑ] s. fiestero; juerguista.
mer·ry-mak·ing [mɛ́rɪmekɪŋ] s. regocijo; jaleo, juerga, jolgorio; adj. regocijado, alegre, festivo, fiestero.
mesh [mɛʃ] s. malla; red; -**es** red, redes; v. enredar, coger con red; **to — gears** engranar.
mess [mɛs] s. (*food*) rancho, comida (*en el ejército o la marina*); (*confusion*) lío, confusión; (*dirt*) suciedad; — **of fish** plato o ración de pescado; **to make a — of** revolver, confundir; ensuciar; echar a perder; v. revolver, confundir; ensuciar, echar a perder (*generalmente*: **to — up**); **to — around** revolver o mezclar las cosas; entrometerse; **mess·y** [mɛ́sɪ] adj. desordenado, desarreglado; sucio.
mes·sage [mɛ́sɪdʒ] s. mensaje; parte (*m.*), comunicación; recado.
mes·sen·ger [mɛ́sṇdʒəˑ] s. mensajero; mandadero.
met [mɛt] pret. & p.p. de **to meet.**
me·tab·o·lism [mətǽbəlɪzm] s. metabolismo.
met·al [mɛ́tl] s. metal; adj. de metal, metálico.
me·tal·lic [mətǽlɪk] adj. metálico.
met·al·lur·gy [mɛ́tl̩ɝdʒɪ] s. metalurgia.
met·a·mor·pho·sis [mɛtəmɔ́rfəsɪs] s. metamorfosis.
met·a·phor [mɛ́təfəˑ] s. metáfora.
me·tath·e·sis [mətǽθəsɪs] s. metátesis.
me·te·or [mítɪəˑ] s. meteoro; estrella fugaz.
me·te·or·ic [mítɪorɪt] s. meteorito.
me·te·or·ite [mítɪoraɪt] s. meteorito.
me·te·or·ol·o·gy [mitɪərálədʒɪ] s. meteorología.
me·ter [mítəˑ] s. metro; contador (*de gas, agua,*

electricidad, etc.); *Am.* medidor.
meth·od [méθəd] *s.* método; técnica.
me·thod·i·cal [məθádɪk̩l] *adj.* metódico.
me·tre = **meter.**
met·ric [métrɪk] *adj.* métrico; — **system** sistema métrico.
me·trop·o·lis [mətrápl̩ɪs] *s.* metrópoli.
met·ro·pol·i·tan [mɛtrəpálətn̩] *adj.* metropolitano.
met·tle [métl̩] *s.* temple, brío, ánimo, valor.
mew [mju] *s.* maullido, maúllo, miau; *v.* maullar.
Mex·i·can [mɛ́ksɪkən] *adj. & s.* mejicano o mexicano.
mez·za·nine [mézənɪn] *s.* entresuelo.
mice [maɪs] *pl. de* **mouse.**
mi·crobe [máɪkrob] *s.* microbio.
mi·cro·bus [máɪkrobʌs] *s.* microbús.
mi·cro·film [máɪkrəfɪlm] *s.* microfilm.
mi·cro·phone [máɪkrəfon] *s.* micrófono.
mi·cro·scope [máɪkrəskop] *s.* microscopio.
mi·cro·scop·ic [maɪkrəskápɪk] *adj.* microscópico.
mid [mɪd] *adj.* medio (*úsase por lo general en composición*); **in** — **air** en el aire; *prep.* en medij de, entre.
mid·day [mídde] *s.* mediodía; *adj.* del mediodía.
mid·dle [mídl̩] *adj.* medio; intermedio; **Middle Ages** Edad Media; — **finger** dedo de en medio, dedo del corazón; — **size** tamaño mediano; *s.* medio, centro, mitad; **in the** — **of** en medio de, a la mitad de **towards the** — **of the month** a mediados del mes; — **class** clase media.
mid·dle-aged [mídléʒd] *adj.* de edad mediana, de edad madura.
mid·dle·man [mídl̩mæn] *s.* revendedor; medianero, corredor, agente.
mid·dle-sized [mídl̩saɪzd] *adj.* de mediano tamaño, de mediana estatura.
mid·dy [mídɪ] *s.* guardiamarina (*m.*); — **blouse** blusa a la marinera.
midg·et [mídʒɪt] *s.* enanillo.
mid·night [mídnaɪt] *s.* medianoche; *adj.* de (la) medianoche; — **blue** azul oscuro; — **Mass** misa de gallo.
mid·riff [mídrɪf] *s.* diafragma.
mid·ship·man [mídʃɪpmən] *s.* guardiamarina (*m.*).
midst [mɪdst] *s.* medio, centro; **in the** — **of** en medio de, entre; **in our** — entre nosotros.
mid·stream [mídstrim] *s.* el medio (*o* el centro) de la corriente.
mid·sum·mer [mídsʌ́mɚ] *s.* pleno verano, solsticio estival, la mitad del verano.
mid·term [mídtɝm] *s.*; — **examination** examen a mitad del curso.
mid·way [mídwe] *adj.* situado a medio camino; equidistante; *adv.* a medio camino; en medio del camino.
mid·wife [mídwaɪf] *s.* partera, comadrona.
mien [min] *s.* facha, aspecto.
might [maɪt] *imperf. de* **may** podía; podría; pudiera, pudiese; *s.* poder, poderío, fuerza.
might·y [máɪtɪ] *adj.* poderoso, potente, fuerte; *adv.* muy, sumamente.
mi·grant [máɪgrənt] *adj.* migratorio.
mi·grate [máɪgret] *v.* emigrar.
mi·gra·tion [maɪgréʃən] *s.* migración.
mike [maɪk] = **microphone.**
mild [maɪld] *adj.* (*gentle*) suave; blando; apacible; (*moderate*) templado, moderado.
mil·dew [míldu] *s.* moho; enmohecimiento.
mild·ness [máɪldnɪs] *s.* suavidad; mansedumbre; apacibilidad; templanza, dulzura.
mile [maɪl] *s.* milla; —**stone** mojón.

mile·age [máɪlɪdʒ] *s.* millaje, número de millas; recorrido (*en millas*). *Compárese* kilometraje, número de kilómetros.
mil·i·tant [mílɪtənt] *s.* militante; belicoso.
mil·i·tar·y [mílətɛrɪ] *adj.* militar; de guerra; *s.* **the** — el ejército; los militares.
mi·li·tia [məlíʃə] *s.* milicia.
milk [mɪlk] *s.* leche; — **diet** régimen lácteo; *v.* ordeñar.
milk·maid [mílkmed] *s.* lechera.
milk·man [mílkmən] *s.* lechero, *Am.* vaquero.
milk·y [mílkɪ] *adj.* lácteo; lechoso; **Milky Way** Vía Láctea.
mill [mɪl] *s.* (*grinder*) molino; (*factory*) fábrica; (*money*) la milésima parte de un dólar; **saw** — aserradero; **spinning** — hilandería; **sugar** — ingenio de azúcar; **textile** — fábricar; acordonar (*el* moler; aserrar (*madera*); fabricar; acordonar (*el canto de la moneda*); **to** — **around** arremolinarse (*una muchedumbre*).
mill·er [mílɚ] *s.* molinero; mariposa nocturna.
mil·li·gram [míləgræm] *s.* miligramo.
mil·li·me·ter [míləmitɚ] *s.* milímetro.
mil·li·ner [mílənɚ] *s.* modista (*de sombreros para señoras*).
mil·li·ner·y [mílənɛrɪ] *s.* sombreros de señora; artículos para sombreros de señora; oficio de modista; — **shop** sombrerería.
mil·lion [míljən] *s.* millón; **a** — **dollars** un millón de dólares.
mil·lion·aire [mɪljənɛ́r] *adj. & s.* millonario.
mil·lionth [míljənθ] *adj. & s.* millonésimo.
mill·stone [mílston] *s.* muela o piedra de molino; carga pesada.
mim·ic [mímɪk] *adj.* mímico, imitativo; — **battle** simulacro; *s.* imitador, remedador; *v.* imitar, remedar.
mince [mɪns] *v.* picar, desmenuzar; **not to** — **words** hablar con toda franqueza.
mince·meat [mínsmit] *s.* picadillo (*especialmente el de carne, pasas, manzanas y especias*).
mind [maɪnd] *s.* (*brain*) mente; (*thought*) pensamiento; inteligencia; (*spirit*) ánimo, espíritu; (*purpose*) propósito, intención; (*opinion*) parecer, opinión; **to be out of one's** — estar loco, haber perdido el juicio; **to change one's** — cambiar de parecer; **to give someone a piece of one's** — cantarle a alguien la verdad; echarle a alguien un buen regaño; **to have a** — **to** estar por; sentir ganas de; **to make up one's** — decidirse, resolverse; **to my** — a mi modo de ver; **to speak one's** — **freely** hablar con toda franqueza; *v.* cuidar; atender a; hacer caso de; obedecer; **I don't** — no tengo inconveniente en ello; **never** — no importa; no se preocupe; no se moleste; no haga Vd. caso; **to** — **one's own business** atender a lo suyo, no meterse en lo ajeno.
mind·ful [máɪndfəl] *adj.* atento (a); cuidadoso (de).
mine [maɪn] *pron. pos.* mío (mía, míos, mías); **el** mío (la mía, los míos, las mías); **a book of** — un libro mío.
mine [maɪn] *s.* mina; — **sweeper** dragaminas; *v.* minar; explotar (*una mina*); extraer (*mineral*).
min·er [máɪnɚ] *s.* minero.
min·er·al [mínərəl] *adj. & s.* mineral.
min·gle [míŋgl̩] *v.* mezclar(se); entremezclar(se); confundir(se); juntarse.
min·i·a·ture [mínɪtʃɚ] *s.* miniatura; *adj.* en miniatura; diminuto.
min·i·mal [mínəml̩] *adj.* mínimo.

ME

min-mis   398

min·i·mize [mínəmaɪz] v. empequeñecer.
min·i·mum [mínəməm] adj. & s. mínimo.
min·ing [máɪnɪŋ] s. minería, explotación de minas;
adj. minero; — engineer ingeniero de minas.
min·i·skirt [mínɪskət] s. minifalda.
min·is·ter [mínɪstə] s. ministro; pastor, clérigo; v.
ministrar; atender; proveer, socorrer.
min·is·try [mínɪstrɪ] s. ministerio; socorro, ayuda.
mink [mɪŋk] s. visón.
min·now [míno] s. pececillo de río.
mi·nor [máɪnə] adj. (young) menor; de menor edad;
(secondary) secundario; — key tono menor; s.
menor de edad; premisa menor (de un silogismo);
tono menor; curso o asignatura menor.
mi·nor·i·ty [mənórətɪ] s. minoría; minoridad;
menor edad; menor parte.
min·strel [mínstrəl] s. trovador; bardo, vate; actor
cómico que remeda al negro norteamericano.
mint [mɪnt] s. (flavor) menta, hierbabuena
(yerbabuena); (candy) pastilla o bombón de
menta; (money) casa de moneda; a — of money
un montón de dinero, la mar de dinero; v.
acuñar.
mint·age [míntədʒ] s. acuñación; moneda acuñada.
min·u·et [mɪnjuét] s. minué.
mi·nus [máɪnəs] adj. negativo; sin, falto de; seven
— four siete menos cuatro; s. menos, signo
menos.
min·ute [mínɪt] s. minuto; -s acta (de una junta);
— hand minutero.
mi·nute [mənjút] adj. menudo, diminuto;
minucioso, detallado.
mir·a·cle [mírəkl] s. milagro.
mi·rac·u·lous [mərǽkjələs] adj. milagroso.
mi·rage [məráʒ] s. espejismo.
mire [maɪr] s. cieno, fango, lodo; v. atascar(se) en
el fango; enlodar(se).
mir·ror [mírə] s. espejo; v. reflejar.
mirth [mɜθ] s. júbilo, regocijo, alegría.
mirth·ful [mɜθfəl] adj. jubiloso, regocijado, gozoso,
alegre.
mir·y [máɪrɪ] adj. cenagoso, fangoso, lodoso.
mis·ad·ven·ture [mɪsədvéntʃə] s. desgracia;
contratiempo.
mis·be·have [mɪsbihév] v. portarse mal, obrar mal.
mis·car·riage [mɪskǽrɪdʒ] s. aborto, malparto; mal
éxito; extravío (de una carta, papel, etc.).
mis·car·ry [mɪskǽrɪ] v. (fail) malograrse,
frustrarse; extraviarse (una carta); (abort)
abortar.
mis·cel·la·ne·ous [mɪslénɪəs] adj. misceláneo,
diverso.
mis·chief [místʃɪf] s. travesura; diablura; mal,
daño; diablillo, persona traviesa.
mis·chie·vous [místʃɪvəs] adj. travieso; malicioso;
dañino; revoltoso.
mis·con·cep·tion [mɪskənsépʃən] s. concepto
erróneo.
mis·con·duct [mɪskándʌkt] s. mala conducta; mala
administración; [mɪskəndʌkt] v. maladministrar,
manejar mal; to — oneself portarse mal,
conducirse mal.
mis·cue [mɪskjú] s. pifia.
mis·deed [mɪsdíd] s. fechoría, mala acción.
mis·de·mean·or [mɪsdimínə] s. mal
comportamiento; fechoría.
mi·ser [máɪzə] s. avaro, avariento.
mis·er·a·ble [mízrəbl] adj. miserable; infeliz,
desdichado.
mi·ser·ly [máɪzəlɪ] adj. avariento, avaro; tacaño,
mezquino.

mis·er·y [mízrɪ] s. miseria, desgracia; estrechez,
pobreza; dolor.
mis·for·tune [mɪsfɔrtʃən] s. infortunio, desgracia,
desastre.
mis·giv·ing [mɪsgívɪŋ] s. mal presentimiento,
aprensión, recelo, temor.
mis·guid·ed [mɪsgáɪdəd] adj. mal aconsejado.
mis·hap [míshæp] s. desgracia, contratiempo,
accidente.
mis·judge [mɪsdʒʌ́dʒ] v. juzgar mal.
mis·laid [mɪsléd] pret. & p.p. de to mislay.
mis·lay [mɪslé] v. extraviar, perder; poner fuera de
su sitio, colocar mal; traspapelar (una carta,
documento, etc.).
mis·lead [mɪslíd] v. guiar por mal camino;
extraviar, descarriar; engañar.
mis·led [mɪsléd] pret. & p.p. de to mislead.
mis·man·age [mɪsmǽnɪdʒ] v. administrar mal.
mis·place [mɪsplés] v. extraviar, poner fuera de su
sitio, colocar mal; traspapelar (una carta,
documento, etc.).
mis·print [mɪsprínt] s. errata, error tipográfico,
error de imprenta.
mis·pro·nounce [mɪsprənɑuns] v. pronunciar mal.
mis·rep·re·sent [mɪsrɛprɪzént] v. falsear, falsificar;
tergiversar.
miss [mɪs] v. (not hit) errar, no acertar; fallar;
(omit) equivocar; perder; faltar a; (feel absence
of) echar de menos; Am. extrañar; he just -ed
being killed por poco lo matan; s. error; falla,
falta.
miss [mɪs] s. señorita; Miss Smith la señorita
Smith.
mis·sile [mísl] s. proyectil; arma arrojadiza; adj.
arrojadizo, que se puede arrojar o tirar.
miss·ing [mísɪŋ] adj. ausente; perdido; one book is
— falta un libro.
mis·sion [míʃən] s. misión.
mis·sion·ar·y [míʃənɛrɪ] adj. & s. misionero.
mis·spell [mɪsspél] v. escribir con mala ortografía,
deletrear mal.
mist [mɪst] s. neblina, niebla; llovizna, Ven., Col.,
Andes garúa; v. lloviznar; anublar.
mis·take [məsték] s. error, yerro, equivocación;
errata (de imprenta); to make a — equivocarse;
v. equivocar.
mis·tak·en [məstékən] p.p. de to mistake & adj.
equivocado; errado; erróneo, incorrecto; to be
— estar equivocado, equivocarse, errar.
mis·ter [místə] s. señor.
mis·took [mɪstúk] pret. de to mistake.
mis·treat [mɪstrít] v. maltratar.
mis·tress [místrɪs] s. señora; ama, dueña; querida,
amante; school— maestra.
mis·tri·al [mɪstráɪl] s. pleito viciado de nulidad.
mis·trust [mɪstrʌ́st] s. desconfianza; v. desconfiar
de.
mis·trust·ful [mɪstrʌ́stfəl] adj. desconfiado,
sospechoso, receloso.
mist·y [místɪ] adj. brumoso; nublado; empañado;
vago, indistinto.
mis·un·der·stand [mɪsʌndəstǽnd] v. comprender
mal; entender mal; interpretar mal; no
comprender.
mis·un·der·stand·ing [mɪsʌndəstǽndɪŋ] s.
equivocación; mala interpretación, mala
inteligencia; desavenencia.
mis·un·der·stood [mɪsʌndəstúd] pret. & p.p. de to
misunderstand.
mis·use [mɪsjús] s. abuso; mal uso; malversación
(de fondos); [mɪsjúz] v. abusar de; maltratar;

usar o emplear mal; malversar (*fondos*).
mite [maɪt] *s.* óbolo, friolera, pequeñez; criatura.
mi·ter [máɪtɚ] *s.* mitra; dignidad de obispo.
mit·i·gate [mítəget] *v.* mitigar.
mit·ten [mítṇ] *s.* mitón (*guante de una pieza y sin dedos*).
mix [mɪks] *v.* mezclar(se); unir(se), juntar(se), asociar(se); **to — someone up** confundir a uno; *s.* mezcla; confusión, lío.
mix·ture [míkstʃɚ] *s.* mezcla; mezcolanza.
mix·up [míksʌp] *s.* equívoco; enredo.
moan [mon] *s.* quejido, gemido; *v.* gemir; quejarse; lamentar(se).
moat [mot] *s.* foso.
mob [mɑb] *s.* populacho; muchedumbre, gentío, *Am.* bola (*de gente*); *v.* atropellar; apiñarse o agolparse alrededor de.
mo·bile [móbḷ] *adj.* móvil; movible; movedizo.
mo·bi·li·za·tion [mobḷəzéʃən] *s.* movilización.
mo·bi·lize [móbḷaɪz] *v.* movilizar.
moc·ca·sin [mákəsṇ] *s. Am.* mocasín (*zapato burdo de cuero*); *Am.* mocasín (*víbora venenosa*).
mock [mɑk] *v.* (*ridicule*) mofar, mofarse de; (*imitate*) remedar, imitar; **to — at** mofarse de; burlarse de; *s.* mofa, burla, escarnio; mímica; remedo; *adj.* falso, ficticio, imitado; **— battle** simulacro, batalla fingida.
mock·er·y [mɔ́kərɪ] *s.* burla, mofa, escarnio; remedo.
mock·up [mákʌp] *s.* maqueta; modelo.
mode [mod] *s.* modo, manera; moda.
mod·el [mádḷ] *s.* (*guide*) modelo; (*pattern*) patrón; (*figure*) figurín, maniquí; *adj.* ejemplar; modelo; **— school** escuela modelo; *v.* modelar; moldear, formar; posar, servir de modelo.
mod·er·ate [mádərɪt] *adj.* moderado; templado; módico; (mádəret] *v.* moderar(se); templar(se).
mod·er·a·tion [madəréʃən] *s.* moderación; templanza.
mod·ern [mádɚn] *adj.* moderno.
mod·ern·ize [mádɚnaɪz] *v.* modernizar.
mod·est [mádɪst] *adj.* modesto.
mod·es·ty [mádəstɪ] *s.* modestia.
mod·i·fi·ca·tion [madəfəkéʃən] *s.* modificación.
mod·i·fy [mádəfaɪ] *v.* modificar.
mod·u·late [mádʒəlet] *v.* modular.
mo·hair [móhɛr] *s.* moer.
Mo·ham·med·an [mohǽmədən] *adj. & s.* mahometano.
moist [mɔɪst] *adj.* húmedo; mojado.
mois·ten [mɔ́ɪsṇ] *v.* humedecer, mojar.
mois·ture [mɔ́ɪstʃɚ] *s.* humedad.
mo·lar [mólɚ] *adj.* molar; *s.* muela.
mo·las·ses [məlǽsɪz] *s.* melaza, miel de caña.
mold [mold] *s.* (*form*) molde, matriz; (*substance*) moho; tierra vegetal; *v.* moldear, amoldar; modelar; enmohecer(se), cubrir(se) de moho.
mold·er [móldɚ] *v.* desmoronarse.
mold·ing [móldɪŋ] *s.* moldura; moldeamiento.
mold·y [móldɪ] *adj.* mohoso.
mole [mol] *s.* lunar; topo (*animal*); dique, malecón, rompeolas.
mol·e·cule [máləkjul] *s.* molécula.
mo·lest [məlést] *v.* molestar.
mol·li·fy [máləfaɪ] *v.* apaciguar.
mol·ten [móltṇ] *adj.* derretido, fundido, en fusión.
mo·lyb·de·num [məlíbdənəm] *s.* molibdeno.
mo·ment [mómənt] *s.* momento; importancia, consecuencia.
mo·men·tar·y [mómənterɪ] *adj.* momentáneo.

mo·men·tous [moméntəs] *adj.* importante.
mo·men·tum [moméntəm] *s.* momento (*de una fuerza*); ímpetu.
mon·arch [mánɚk] *s.* monarca.
mon·ar·chy [mánɚkɪ] *s.* monarquía.
mon·as·ter·y [mánəsterɪ] *s.* monasterio.
Mon·day [mʌ́ndɪ] *s.* lunes.
mon·e·tar·y [mánətɛrɪ] *adj.* monetario.
mon·ey [mánɪ] *s.* dinero; **— changer** cambista; **— order** giro postal; **paper —** papel moneda; **silver —** moneda de plata; **money-making** lucrativo, provechoso, ganancioso.
mon·ger [máŋɡɚ] *s.* traficante; defensor.
mon·grel [máŋɡrəl] *adj. & s.* mestizo, mixto, cruzado, *Am.* chusco (*perro*).
monk [mʌŋk] *s.* monje.
mon·key [máŋkɪ] *s.* mono; **—shine** monada, monería; **— wrench** llave inglesa; *v.* juguetear; hacer monerías; payasear; entremeterse; **to — with** juguetear con; meterse con.
mon·o·gram [mánəɡræm] *s.* monograma.
mon·o·graph [mánəɡræf] *s.* monografía.
mon·o·logue [mánlɔɡ] *s.* monólogo, soliloquio.
mo·nop·o·lize [mənápḷaɪz] *v.* monopolizar, acaparar.
mo·nop·o·ly [mənápḷɪ] *s.* monopolio.
mon·o·syl·la·ble [mánəsɪləbḷ] *s.* monosílabo.
mon·o·tone [mánəton] *adj.* monótono.
mo·not·o·nous [mənátṇəs] *adj.* monótono.
mo·not·o·ny [mənátṇɪ] *s.* monotonía.
mon·ster [mánstɚ] *s.* monstruo; *adj.* enorme.
mon·stros·i·ty [manstrásətɪ] *s.* monstruosidad; monstruo.
mon·strous [mánstrəs] *adj.* monstruoso.
month [mʌnθ] *s.* mes.
month·ly [mʌ́nθlɪ] *adj.* mensual; *s.* publicación mensual; *adv.* mensualmente.
mon·u·ment [mánjəmənt] *s.* monumento.
mon·u·men·tal [manjəméntḷ] *adj.* monumental; colosal, grandioso.
moo [mu] *s.* mugido; *v.* mugir.
mood [mud] *s.* humor, disposición de ánimo; modo (*del verbo*); **to be in a good —** estar de buen humor; **to be in the — to** estar dispuesto a, tener gana de.
mood·y [múdɪ] *adj.* (*changing*) caprichoso, voluble, mudable; (*sad*) melancólico, mohíno.
moon [mun] *s.* luna; mes lunar; **once in a blue —** de Pascuas a San Juan, muy rara vez, *Am.* por campanada de vacante, *Am.* a cada muerte de (*o por la muerte de*) obispo.
moon·light [múnlaɪt] *s.* luz de la luna; **— dance** baile a la luz de la luna; **— night** noche de luna.
moor [mʊr] *v.* amarrar, atracar (*un buque*); anclar; estar anclado; *s.* terreno inculto o baldío.
Moor [mʊr] *s.* moro.
Moor·ish [múrɪʃ] *adj.* morisco, moro.
mop [map] *s. Am.* trapeador; **dust —** limpiapolvo; **— of hair** greñas, cabellera abundante; *v.* limpiar (*el suelo*), *Am.* trapear; **to — one's brow** limpiarse (*o secarse*) la frente; **to — up** limpiar; vencer; acabar con.
mope [mop] *v.* andar quejumbroso o abatido.
mor·al [mɔ́rəl] *adj.* moral; **— philosophy** ética, moral; *s.* moraleja; **-s** moral, ética.
mo·rale [mərǽl] *s.* moral, entereza de ánimo.
mor·al·ist [mɔ́rəlɪst] *s.* moralista.
mo·ral·i·ty [mərǽlɪtɪ] *s.* moralidad.
mor·al·ize [mɔ́rəlaɪz] *v.* moralizar.
mor·bid [mɔ́rbɪd] *adj.* mórbido, morboso: malsano.
mor·dant [mɔ́rdənt] *adj.* mordaz.

MI

more [mor] *adj.* & *adv.* más; — **and** — cada vez
más, más y más; — **or less** poco más o menos;
there is no — no hay más, ya no hay; se
acabó.
more·o·ver [moróvɚ] *adv.* además.
morn·ing [mɔ́rnɪŋ] *s.* mañana; **good** —! ¡buenos
días!; **tomorrow** — mañana por la mañana; *adj.*
de la mañana; matutino, matinal; **morning-glory**
dondiego de día; — **star** lucero del alba.
mor·phine [mɔ́rfin] *s.* morfina.
mor·phol·o·gy [mɔrfáləd ʒɪ] *s.* morfología.
mor·row [mɔ́ro]: **on the** — el día de mañana;
mañana.
mor·sel [mɔ́rsl] *s.* bocado; manjar sabroso.
mor·tal [mɔ́rtl] *adj.* & *s.* mortal.
mor·tal·i·ty [mɔrtǽlətɪ] *s.* mortalidad; mortandad.
mor·tar [mɔ́rtɚ] *s.* mortero; argamasa, mezcla;
metal — almirez.
mort·gage [mɔ́rgɪd ʒ] *s.* hipoteca, gravamen; *v.*
hipotecar; *adj.* hipotecario.
mor·ti·fy [mɔ́rtəfaɪ] *v.* mortificar; avergonzar.
mo·sa·ic [mozéɪk] *adj.* & *s.* mosaico.
Mos·lem [mázləm] *adj.* & *s.* musulmán.
mosque [mɔsk] *s.* mezquita.
mos·qui·to [məskíto] *s.* mosquito; — **net**
mosquitero.
moss [mɔs] *s.* musgo; **moss-grown** musgoso,
cubierto de musgo; anticuado.
moss·y [mɔ́sɪ] *adj.* musgoso.
most [most] *adv.* más; sumamente, muy; *s.* la
mayoría, la mayor parte, el mayor número o
cantidad; los más; — **people** la mayoría (*o* la
mayor parte) de la gente; **at the** — a lo más, a
lo sumo; **for the** — **part** por la mayor parte;
generalmente, mayormente; **the** — **that I can do**
lo más que puedo hacer; **the** — **votes** el mayor
número de votos, los más votos.
most·ly [móstlɪ] *adv.* por la mayor parte;
mayormente, principalmente.
moth [mɔθ] *s.* polilla; mariposa nocturna; —**ball**
bolita de naftalina; **moth-eaten** apolillado.
moth·er [mʌ́ðɚ] *s.* madre; **mother-of-pearl**
madreperla, nácar; *adj.* de madre; materno,
maternal; nativo, natal; — **country** madre
patria; país natal; — **Superior** superiora; —
tongue lengua materna; *v.* servir de madre a,
cuidar de.
moth·er·hood [mʌ́ðɚhʊd] *s.* maternidad.
moth·er-in-law [mʌ́ðɚrɪnlɔ] *s.* suegra.
moth·er·ly [mʌ́ðɚlɪ] *adj.* maternal, materno.
mo·tif [motíf] *s.* motivo, tema.
mo·tion [móʃən] *s.* (*movement*) moción;
movimiento; (*signal*) ademán; señal, seña; —
sickness mareo; *v.* hacer una seña o señas;
indicar.
mo·tion·less [móʃənlɪs] *adj.* inmóvil, inmoble.
mo·tion pic·ture [móʃənpíktʃɚ] *s.* cine o
cinematógrafo; película; fotografia
cinematográfica; **motion-picture** *adj.*
cinematográfico.
mo·tive [mótɪv] *s.* motivo; tema; *adj.* motriz.
mot·ley [mátlɪ] *adj.* abigarrado, multicolor, de
diversos colores; variado, mezclado; *s.* mezcla,
mezcolanza.
mo·tor [mótɚ] *s.* motor; automóvil; *v.* pasear o ir
en automóvil.
mo·tor·bike [mótɚbaɪk] *s.* motocicleta pequeña;
moto.
mo·tor·boat [mótɚbot] *s.* autobote, lancha de
gasolina, bote de motor.
mo·tor·car [mótɚkɑr] *s.* automóvil.

mo·tor·coach [mótɚkotʃ] *s.* autobús, ómnibus,
Méx. camión, *Carib.* guagua; *Ríopl., Ch.* micro;
C.A. bus.
mo·tor·cy·cle [mótɚsaɪkl] *s.* motocicleta.
mo·tor·ist [mótɚrɪst] *s.* motorista, automovilista.
mo·tor·man [mótɚmən] *s.* motorista.
mo·tor scoot·er [mótɚskutɚ] *s.* motoneta.
mot·tled [mátld] *adj.* moteado; jaspeado,
manchado.
mot·to [máto] *s.* mote, divisa, lema.
mould = **mold**.
mould·er = **molder**.
mould·ing = **molding**.
mould·y = **moldy**.
mound [maʊnd] *s.* montecillo, montículo, montón
de tierra.
mount [maʊnt] *s.* (*elevation*) monte; (*horse*)
montura, cabalgadura, caballo; *v.* montar;
montar a caballo; subir, ascender; armar (*una
máquina*); engastar (*joyas*).
moun·tain [máʊntn̩] *s.* montaña; *adj.* montañés; de
montaña; — **goat** cabra montés; — **lion** puma;
— **range** cordillera, cadena de montañas.
moun·tain climb·er [máʊntn̩klaɪmɚ] *s.* alpinista.
moun·tain·eer [maʊntn̩ír] *s.* montañés.
moun·tain·ous [máʊntn̩əs] *adj.* montañoso.
mourn [morn] *v.* lamentar; deplorar; **to** — **for**
llorar a; estar de duelo por.
mourn·ful [mórnfəl] *adj.* fúnebre; lúgubre;
lastimero; triste.
mourn·ing [mórnɪŋ] *s.* luto; duelo; lamentación; **to
be in** — estar de luto, estar de duelo; *adj.* de
luto.
mouse [maʊs] *s.* ratón; — **trap** ratonera.
mous·tache = **mustache**.
mouth [maʊθ] *s.* boca; abertura; desembocadura,
embocadura (*de un río*).
mouth·ful [máʊθfəl] *s.* bocado.
mouth·piece [máʊθpis] *s.* boquilla (*de un
instrumento de viento*); portavoz.
mov·a·ble [múvəbl] *adj.* movible, móvil, **-s** *s. pl.*
muebles, bienes muebles.
move [muv] *v.* (*motion*) mover(se); (*change*)
mudar(se), mudar de casa; (*propose*) proponer,
hacer la moción de; (*game*) hacer una jugada (*en
ajedrez o damas*); (*emotion*) conmover; inducir;
— **away** irse; alejarse; apartarse; **to** — **forward**
avanzar; **to** — **on** seguir adelante, caminar; **to** —
out irse, mudarse, mudar de casa; *s.* movimiento;
mudanza (*de una casa a otra*); paso, trámite
(*para conseguir algo*); jugada, turno (*en juegos*);
get a — **on there!** ¡ande! ¡dése prisa!; *Am.*
¡ándele!
move·ment [múvmənt] *s.* (*motion*) movimiento;
maniobra; meneo; acción; (*mechanism*)
mecanismo, movimiento (*de un reloj*); (*bowel*)
evacuación.
mov·ie [múvɪ] *s.* cine, película; **-s** cine.
mow [mo] *v.* segar; cortar (*césped*).
mow·er [móɚ] *s.* segador; segadora, cortadora
mecánica; máquina segadora.
mown [mon] *adj.* & *p.p.* segado.
Mr. [místɚ] Sr., señor; **Mrs.** [mísɪz] Sra., señora.
much [mʌtʃ] *adj.*, *adv.* & *s.* mucho; — **the same**
casi lo mismo; **as** — **as** tanto como; **how** —?
¿cuánto?; **not** — **of a book** un libro de poco
valor; **not** — **of a poet** un poetastro; **so** — **that**
tanto que; **too** — demasiado; **very** — muchísimo;
to make — **of** dar mucha importancia a.
muck [mʌk] *s.* (*manure*) estiércol húmedo; (*mire*)
cieno; (*filth*) porquería, suciedad.

mu·cous [mjúkəs] *adj.* mucoso; — **membrane** membrana mucosa.

mud [mʌd] *s.* lodo, fango, cieno; — **wall** tapia.

mud·dle [mʌdl] *v.* enturbiar; confundir; embrollar; *s.* confusión, embrollo, lío, desorden.

mud·dy [mʌdɪ] *adj.* fangoso, lodoso; turbio; confuso; *v.* enlodar, ensuciar; enturbiar.

muff [mʌf] *s.* manguito (*para las manos*); falla, error (*en ciertos juegos*); *v.* no coger, dejar escapar (*la pelota*).

muf·fin [mʌfɪn] *s.* bollo, panecillo.

muf·fle [mʌfl] *v.* embozar; tapar; apagar, amortiguar (*un sonido*).

muf·fler [mʌflə] *s.* bufanda; silenciador (*para maquinaria*); mofle.

mug [mʌg] *s.* pichel, vaso con asa.

mu·lat·to [məlǽto] *s.* mulato.

mul·ber·ry [mʌlbɛrɪ] *s.* mora; — **tree** moral.

mule [mjul] *s.* mulo, mula; **muleteer** [mjulətír] *s.* arriero.

mull [mʌl] *v.* meditar, ponderar, revolver en la mente; calentar (*vino, sidra, etc.*) con azúcar y especias.

mul·ti·ple [mʌltəpl] *s.* múltiplo; *adj.* múltiple.

mul·ti·pli·ca·tion [mʌltəpləkéʃən] *s.* multiplicación; — **table** tabla de multiplicar.

mul·ti·plic·i·ty [mʌltəplísətɪ] *s.* multiplicidad.

mul·ti·ply [mʌltəplaɪ] *v.* multiplicar(se).

mul·ti·tude [mʌltətjud] *s.* multitud.

mum [mʌm] *adj.* callado, silencioso; **to keep** — estarse (*o* quedarse) callado.

mum·ble [mʌmbl] *v.* murmurar, hablar entre dientes; mascullar; *s.* murmullo; **to talk in a** — mascullar las palabras, hablar entre dientes.

mum·my [mʌmɪ] *s.* momia.

mumps [mʌmps] *s.* parótidas, paperas.

munch [mʌntʃ] *v.* mascar ruidosamente, mascullar.

mun·dane [məndén] *adj.* mundano.

mu·nic·i·pal [mjunísəpl] *adj.* municipal.

mu·nic·i·pal·i·ty [mjunɪsəpǽlətɪ] *s.* municipio; municipalidad.

mu·ni·tion [mjuníʃən] *s.* munición; — **plant** fábrica de municiones, arsenal; *v.* guarnecer, abastecer de municiones.

mu·ral [mjúrəl] *adj. & s.* mural.

mur·der [mʒdə] *s.* asesinato, homicidio; *v.* asesinar.

mur·der·er [mʒdərə] *s.* asesino, homicida.

mur·der·ess [mʒdərɪs] *s.* asesina, homicida.

mur·der·ous [mʒdərəs] *adj.* asesino, homicida.

mur·mur [mʒmə] *s.* (*noise*) murmullo; susurro; (*complaint*) queja; *v.* murmurar; susurrar; quejarse.

mus·cle [mʌsl] *s.* músculo.

mus·cu·lar [mʌskjələ] *adj.* muscular; musculoso.

muse [mjuz] *v.* meditar; *s.* meditación; **Muse** musa.

mu·se·um [mjuzíəm] *s.* museo.

mush [mʌʃ] *s.* potaje espeso de maíz; masa de maíz; cualquier masa blanda; sentimentalismo.

mush·room [mʌʃrum] *s.* seta, hongo.

mu·sic [mjúzɪk] *s.* música; — **stand** atril.

mu·si·cal [mjúzɪkl] *adj.* musical, músico; melodioso; armonioso; aficionado a la música; — **comedy** zarzuela, comedia musical.

mu·si·cian [mjuzíʃən] *s.* músico.

musk·mel·on [mʌskmɛlən] *s.* melón.

musk·rat [mʌskræt] *s.* almizclera (*roedor semejante a la rata*).

mus·lin [mʌzlɪn] *s.* muselina.

muss [mʌs] *v.* desarreglar, desordenar; arrugar.

must [mʌst] *v. defect.* (*por lo general se usa sólo en*

el presente) deber; deber de, haber de; tener que.

mus·tache [mʌstæʃ] *s.* bigote, mostacho.

mus·tard [mʌstəd] *s.* mostaza; — **plaster** sinapismo.

mus·ter [mʌstə] *v.* pasar lista o revista; juntarse para una formación militar; reunir(se); **to** — **out** dar de baja; **to** — **up one's courage** cobrar valor o ánimo; *s.* revista (*de soldados o marinos*); **to pass** — pasar lista o revista; ser aceptable (*en una inspección*).

must·y [mʌstɪ] *adj.* mohoso; rancio, añejo.

mu·ta·tion [mjutéʃən] *s.* mutación.

mute [mjut] *adj.* mudo; *s.* mudo; letra muda; sordina (*de violín*).

mu·ti·late [mjútlet] *v.* mutilar.

mu·ti·ny [mjútnɪ] *s.* motín; *v.* amotinarse.

mut·ter [mʌtə] *v.* murmurar, refunfuñar; hablar entre dientes; *s.* murmullo, refunfuño.

mut·ton [mʌtn̩] *s.* carne de carnero; — **chop** chuleta de carnero.

mu·tu·al [mjútʃʊəl] *adj.* mutuo.

muz·zle [mʌzl] *s.* hocico; bozal (*para el hocico*); boca (*de arma de fuego*); *v.* abozalar, poner bozal a; amordazar; hacer callar.

my [maɪ] *adj.* mi (mis).

myr·i·ad [mírɪəd] *s.* miríada, diez mil; millares, gran cantidad.

myrrh [mʒ] *s.* mirra.

myr·tle [mʒtl] *s.* mirto, arrayán.

my·self [maɪsélf] *pron.* yo mismo; me (*como reflexivo*); a mí mismo; **by** — solo; **I** — **did it** yo mismo lo hice; **I talk to** — hablo conmigo mismo, hablo para mis adentros.

mys·te·ri·ous [mɪstírɪəs] *adj.* misterioso.

mys·ter·y [mɪstrɪ] *s.* misterio.

mys·tic [mɪstɪk] *adj. & s.* místico.

mys·ti·cal [mɪstɪkl] *adj.* místico.

myth [mɪθ] *s.* mito, fábula.

my·thol·o·gy [mɪθálədʒɪ] *s.* mitología.

N:n

nab [næb] *v.* agarrar, coger; arrestar.

nag [næg] *s.* rocín, caballejo, jaco; *v.* importunar, irritar (*con repetidos regaños*).

nail [nel] *s.* clavo; uña (*del dedo*); — **file** lima (*para las uñas*); *v.* clavar; clavear; agarrar, atrapar.

na·ive [naív] *adj.* simple, ingenuo, cándido.

na·ked [nékɪd] *adj.* desnudo.

na·ked·ness [nékɪdnɪs] *s.* desnudez.

name [nem] *s.* (*designation*) nombre; (*fame*) renombre, fama; —**sake** tocayo; **by the** — **of** nombrado, llamado; apellidado; **family** — apellido; **to call someone -s** motejar o decirle groserías a uno; ponerle apodos a uno; **to make a** — **for oneself** ganar fama; **what is your** — ? ¿cómo se llama Vd.?; *v.* nombrar; mentar, mencionar; llamar; *adj.* onomástico.

name·less [némlɪs] *adj.* sin nombre; anónimo.

name·ly [némlɪ] *adv.* a saber, esto es, es decir.

nap [næp] *s.* siesta; pelo (*de un tejido*); **to take a** — echar un sueño, echar una siesta; *v.* dormitar; echar un sueño; sestear.

nape [nep] *s.* nuca, cogote.

naph·tha [næfθə] *s.* nafta.

nap·kin [næpkɪn] *s.* servilleta.

nar·cis·sus [narsísəs] *s.* narciso.

nar·cot·ic [narkátɪk] *adj. & s.* narcótico.

nar·rate [nærét] v. narrar.
nar·ra·tion [næréʃən] s. narración.
nar·ra·tive [nǽrətɪv] adj. narrativo; s. narración; narrativa; relato.
nar·row [nǽro] adj. (cramped) estrecho; angosto; limitado (intolerant) intolerante; — escape trance difícil, escapada difícil; — search búsqueda esmerada; **narrow-minded** fanático, intolerante; -s s. pl. desfiladero, paso; estrecho o estrechos; v. angostar(se), estrechar(se); limitar, restringir, reducir; -ly adv. estrechamente; **he -ly escaped** por poco no se escapa.
nar·row·ness [nǽrənɪs] s. (cramped) estrechez, estrechura, angostura; limitación; (intolerance) intolerancia.
na·sal [nézl] adj. nasal.
nas·ti·ness [nǽstɪnɪs] s. suciedad, porquería; grosería.
na·stur·tium [næstɚʃəm] s. mastuerzo.
nas·ty [nǽstɪ] adj. (foul) sucio, asqueroso; feo (indecent) grosero; indecente; **a — fall** una caída terrible; **a — disposition** un genio horrible.
na·tal [nétl] adj. natal.
na·tion [néʃən] s. nación.
na·tion·al [nǽʃənl] adj. nacional; s. nacional, ciudadano.
na·tion·al·ism [nǽʃənəlɪzm] s. nacionalismo.
na·tion·al·i·ty [næʃənǽlətɪ] s. nacionalidad; **adjective of —** gentilicio.
na·tive [nétɪv] adj. nativo; natal; natural; indígena; del país, Am. criollo; — **of** oriundo de, natural de; s. nativo, natural, indígena; habitante.
na·tiv·i·ty [nətívətɪ] s. nacimiento; natividad (de la Virgen María); **the Nativity** la Navidad.
nat·u·ral [nǽtʃərəl] adj. natural; sencillo, sin afectación; s. becuadro (signo musical); **he is a — for that job** tiene aptitud natural para ese puesto; -ly adv. naturalmente; con naturalidad.
nat·u·ral·ism [nǽtʃərəlɪzm] s. naturalismo.
nat·u·ral·ist [nǽtʃərəlɪst] s. naturalista.
nat·u·ral·i·za·tion [nætʃərələzéʃən] s. naturalización.
nat·u·ral·ize [nǽtʃərəlaɪz] v. naturalizar.
nat·u·ral·ness [nǽtʃərəlnts] s. naturalidad.
na·ture [nétʃɚ] s. naturaleza; natural, genio, índole; instinto; especie; **to copy from —** copiar del natural.
naught [nɔt] s. cero; nada.
naugh·ty [nɔ́tɪ] adj. malo, desobediente; travieso; pícaro; malicioso.
nau·se·a [nɔ́zɪə] s. náusea.
nau·se·ate [nɔ́zɪet] v. dar náuseas, dar bascas, asquear, dar asco; sentir náusea; **to be -ed** tener náuseas.
nau·se·at·ing [nɔ́zɪetɪŋ] adj. nauseabundo, asqueroso.
nau·ti·cal [nɔ́tɪkl] adj. náutico, naval.
na·val [névl] adj. naval; — **officer** oficial de marina.
nave [nev] s. nave (de una iglesia).
na·vel [névl] s. ombligo; — **orange** naranja california (sin semillas).
nav·i·ga·ble [nǽvəgəbl] adj. navegable.
nav·i·gate [nǽvəget] v. navegar.
nav·i·ga·tion [nævəgéʃən] s. navegación; náutica.
nav·i·ga·tor [nǽvəgetɚ] s. navegador, navegante.
na·vy [névɪ] s. marina de guerra; armada; — **blue** azul marino; — **yard** astillero, arsenal.
nay [ne] adv. no; no sólo ... sino (que) también; s. no, voto negativo.
near [nɪr] adv. (space, time) cerca; (almost) casi; — **at hand** cerca, a la mano; **I came — forgetting**

to do it por poco se me olvida hacerlo; **to come (go, draw) —** acercarse; — **sighted** miope; prep. cerca de; — **the end of the month** hacia fines del mes; adj. cercano, próximo; estrecho, íntimo; — **silk** seda imitada; **I had a — accident** por poco me sucede un accidente; v. acercarse (a).
near·by [nírbáɪ] adv. cerca, a la mano; adj. cercano, próximo.
near·ly [nírlɪ] adv. casi, cerca de; aproximadamente, próximamente; **I — did it** estuve al punto de hacerlo, estuve para hacerlo.
near·ness [nírnɪs] s. cercanía, proximidad.
neat [nit] adj. pulcro, aseado, limpio; ordenado; esmerado; hábil, diestro; -ly adv. aseadamente; esmeradamente; ordenadamente; hábilmente.
neat·ness [nítnɪs] s. pulcritud, aseo; limpieza; esmero; claridad.
neb·u·lous [nébjʊləs] adj. nebuloso.
nec·es·sar·i·ly [nɛsəsérəlɪ] adv. necesariamente; forzosamente.
nec·es·sar·y [nɛ́səsɛrɪ] adj. necesario; forzoso; **nec·es·sar·ies** s. pl. necesidades, requisitos.
ne·ces·si·tate [nəsésətet] v. necesitar, precisar.
ne·ces·si·ty [nəsésətɪ] s. necesidad.
neck [nɛk] s. cuello; pescuezo; cerviz; garganta; — **of land** istmo; **low —** escote; — **and —** parejos (en una carrera).
neck·lace [néklɪs] s. collar; gargantilla.
neck·tie [néktaɪ] s. corbata.
ne·crol·o·gy [nɛkrálədʒɪ] s. necrología.
need [nid] s. (lack) necesidad; (poverty) pobreza; **for — of** por falta de; **if —** be si fuere menester, en caso de necesidad; v. necesitar; tener necesidad de; hacerle falta a uno; tener que.
need·ful [nídfəl] adj. necesario; necesitado.
nee·dle [nídl] s. aguja.
nee·dle·point [nídlpɔɪnt] s. encaje de mano.
need·less [nídlɪs] adj. innecesario, inútil.
nee·dle·work [nídlwɚk] s. labor, bordado; costura.
need·y [nídɪ] adj. necesitado, menesteroso.
ne'er [nɛr] adv. contr. de **never**; **ne'er-do-well** s. persona incompetente; haragán.
ne·ga·tion [nɪgéʃən] s. negación; negativa.
neg·a·tive [négətɪv] adj. negativo; s. negativa; negación, partícula o voz negativa; negativa (de una fotografía).
ne·glect [nɪglékt] s. negligencia; descuido; abandono; v. descuidar; desatender; abandonar; **to — to** dejar de, olvidar, olvidarse de.
ne·glect·ful [nɪgléktfəl] adj. negligente, descuidado.
neg·li·gence [néglədʒəns] s. negligencia.
neg·li·gent [néglədʒənt] adj. negligente, descuidado.
ne·go·ti·ate [nɪgóʃiet] v. negociar; agenciar; vencer (un obstáculo o dificultad), dar cima a.
ne·go·ti·a·tion [nɪgoʃiéʃən] s. negociación.
Ne·gro [nígro] s. & adj. negro.
Ne·groid [nígrɔɪd] adj. negroide.
neigh [ne] s. relincho; v. relinchar.
neigh·bor [nébɚ] s. vecino; prójimo; adj. vecino; cercano.
neigh·bor·hood [nébɚhʊd] s. vecindad; vecindario; inmediación; **in the — of a hundred dollars** cerca de cien dólares.
neigh·bor·ing [nébərɪŋ] adj. vecino; cercano; colindante.
nei·ther [níðɚ] pron. ninguno, ni (el) uno ni (el) otro; — **of the two** ninguno de los dos; adj. ninguno; — **one of us** ninguno de nosotros; conj. ni; — **...** — **nor** ni ... ni; — **will I** tampoco yo, ni yo tampoco.
ne·ol·o·gism [niálədʒɪzm] s. neologismo.

ne·on [nían] *s.* neón.
ne·o·phyte [níofaɪt] *s.* neófito.
neph·ew [néfju] *s.* sobrino.
ne·phri·tis [nəfráɪtɪs] *s.* nefritis.
nep·o·tism [népətɪzm] *s.* nepotismo.
nerve [nɜv] *s.* (*anatomy*) nervio; (*courage*) valor, ánimo; audacia; (*effrontery*) descaro; **-s** nervios; nerviosidad; **to strain every —** esforzarse hasta más no poder, poner el mayor empeño posible.
nerv·ous [nɜvəs] *adj.* nervioso.
nerv·ous·ness [nɜvəsnɪs] *s.* nerviosidad; agitación.
nest [nɛst] *s.* nido; nidada; **— egg** nidal; ahorros; **— of baskets (boxes, tables)** juego graduado de cestas (cajas, mesitas); **wasp's —** avispero; *v.* anidar.
nes·tle [nésl] *v.* acurrucarse; abrigar(se); anidar.
net [nɛt] *s.* red; malla; tejido de mallas; *adj.* de mallas, de punto de malla; *v.* redar, enredar, coger con red; cubrir con una red.
net [nɛt] *adj.* neto; **— price** precio neto; **— profit** ganancia neta o líquida; *v.* producir una ganancia neta o líquida; obtener una ganancia líquida.
net·tle [nétl] *s.* ortiga; *v.* picar, irritar, enfadar.
net·work [nétwɜk] *s.* red; malla; **radio —** red de estaciones radiofónicas.
neu·ral·gia [nuræ̃ldʒə] *s.* neuralgia.
neu·ras·the·ni·a [nurəsθíniə] *s.* neurastenia.
neu·rot·ic [njurátɪk] *adj.* & *s.* neurótico.
neu·ter [njútɚ] *adj.* neutro.
neu·tral [njútrəl] *adj.* neutral; neutro.
neu·tral·i·ty [njutræ̃ləti] *s.* neutralidad.
neu·tral·ize [njútrəlaɪz] *v.* neutralizar.
neu·tron [nútran] *s.* neutrón.
nev·er [névɚ] *adv.* nunca, jamás; **— mind** no importa; no haga Vd. caso; no se moleste Vd.; **never-ending** perpetuo, eterno; de nunca acabar.
nev·er·the·less [nevɚðəlés] *adv.* & *conj.* sin embargo, no obstante, con todo, empero.
new [nju] *adj.* (*not old*) nuevo; moderno; (*fresh*) fresco; reciente; *adv.* recién; **—born baby** criatura recién nacida.
new·com·er [njúkʌmɚ] *s.* recién llegado.
new·ly [njúlɪ] *adv.* nuevamente, recientemente; **— arrived** recién llegado; **— wed** recién casado.
new·ness [njúnɪs] *s.* novedad, calidad de nuevo.
news [njuz] *s.* noticias, nuevas; novedades; **piece of —** noticia, nueve; **—boy** vendedor de periódicos; **— reel** película noticiera; película de noticias mundiales; **—stand** puesto de periódicos.
news·mong·er [njúzmʌŋgɚ] *s.* chismoso, chismero, gacetilla.
news·pa·per [njúzpepɚ] *s.* periódico.
next [nɛkst] *adj.* (*future*) próximo; entrante, que viene; (*following*) siguiente; contiguo; **in the — life** en la otra vida; **to be — in turn** tocarle a uno, ser su turno; *adv.* después, luego; **— best** segundo en cualidad o importancia; *prep.*; **— to** junto a; al lado de; después de.
nib·ble [níbl] *s.* mordisco; *v.* mordiscar, mordisquear; picar, morder.
nice [naɪs] *adj.* (*attractive*) fino; bueno; amable, simpático; lindo; primoroso; (*refined*) refinado; esmerado; preciso, exacto; **-ly** *adv.* con esmero; con finura o primor; sutilmente, con delicadeza; amablemente; bien; **to get along -ly with** llevarse bien con.
ni·ce·ty [náɪsətɪ] *s.* fineza, finura; delicadeza; exactitud.
niche [nɪtʃ] *s.* nicho.
nick [nɪk] *s.* mella, desportilladura; **in the — of**

time en el momento crítico; *v.* mellar, desportillar.
nick·el [níkl] *s.* níquel; moneda de cinco centavos; **nickel-plated** niquelado.
nick·name [níknem] *s.* mote, apodo; *v.* apodar, poner apodo a.
nic·o·tine [níkətin] *s.* nicotina.
niece [nis] *s.* sobrina.
nig·gard·ly [nígədlɪ] *adj.* mezquino, ruin, tacaño; *adv.* mezquinamente, ruinmente.
night [naɪt] *s.* noche; **good —!** ¡buenas noches!; **tomorrow —** mañana por la noche; *adj.* nocturno; de noche; **— owl** buho; trasnochador; **— watchman** sereno, vigilante nocturno.
night·fall [náɪtfɔl] *s.* anochecer, caída de la tarde, anochecida.
night·gown [náɪtgaʊn] *s.* camisa de dormir, camisa de noche, *Am.* camisón.
night·in·gale [náɪtŋgel] *s.* ruiseñor.
night·ly [náɪtlɪ] *adv.* cada noche, todas las noches; *adj.* nocturno, de noche.
night·mare [náɪtmɛr] *s.* pesadilla.
ni·hil·ism [náɪɪlɪzm] *s.* nihilismo.
nim·ble [nímbl] *adj.* ágil, ligero; listo.
ni·o·bi·um [naɪóbiəm] *s.* niobio.
nip [nɪp] *v.* (*pinch*) pellizcar; (*bite*) mordiscar; (*frostbite*) marchitar, helar (*por la acción del frío*); **to — in the bud** cortar en germen, destruir al nacer; **to — off** despuntar; podar; *s.* pellizco; mordisco; trago.
nip·ple [nípl] *s.* teta, tetilla, pezón; pezón de goma.
ni·trate [náɪtret] *s.* nitrato.
ni·tric·a·cid [náɪtrɪkǽsɪd] *s.* ácido nítrico.
ni·tro·gen [náɪtrədʒən] *s.* nitrógeno.
ni·tro·glyc·er·in [naɪtroglísɜɪn] *s.* nitroglicerina.
no [no] *adv.* no; **— longer** ya no; **there is — more** no hay más; *adj.* ningun(o); **— matter how much** por mucho que; **— one** ninguno, nadie; **— smoking** se prohibe fumar; **I have — friend** no tengo ningún amigo; **of — use** inútil, sin provecho; *s.* no, voto negativo.
no·bil·i·ty [nobíləti] *s.* nobleza.
no·ble [nóbl] *s.* & *adj.* noble.
no·ble·man [nóblmən] *s.* noble.
no·ble·ness [nóblnɪs] *s.* nobleza.
no·bly [nóblɪ] *adv.* noblemente.
no·bod·y [nóbadɪ] *pron.* nadie, ninguno.
noc·tur·nal [naktɜnl] *adj.* nocturno.
nod [nad] *v.* inclinar la cabeza (*para hacer una seña, saludar, o asentir*); cabecear, dar cabezadas (*dormitando*); *s.* inclinación de cabeza, saludo; señal de asentimiento (*con la cabeza*).
noise [nɔɪz] *s.* ruido; barullo; sonido; *v.* divulgar; **it is being -d about that** corre el rumor que.
noise·less [nɔ́ɪzlɪs] *adj.* sin ruido, silencioso, quieto; **-ly** *adv.* sin ruido, silenciosamente.
nois·i·ly [nɔ́ɪzɪlɪ] *adv.* ruidosamente.
nois·y [nɔ́ɪzɪ] *adj.* ruidoso.
no·men·cla·ture [nómənklefɚ] *s.* nomenclatura.
nom·i·nal [námənl] *adj.* nominal.
nom·i·nate [námənet] *v.* nombrar, designar.
nom·i·na·tion [namənéfən] *s.* nombramiento, nominación.
non·con·form·ist [nankənfɔ́rmɪst] *adj.* & *s.* disidente.
none [nʌn] *pron.* ninguno; ningunos; nada; **I want — of that** no quiero nada de eso; **that is — of his business** no le importa a Vd. eso; *adv.* no, de ningún modo; **— the less** no menos; **to be — the happier for that** no estar por eso más contento.
non·en·ti·ty [nanéntəti] *s.* nulidad, persona o cosa

NA

inútil.

non·in·ter·ven·tion [nɑnɪntəvénʃən] *s.* no intervención.

non·par·ti·san [nɑnpártəzən] *adj.* imparcial; independiente.

non·sense [nánsɛns] *s.* tontería, necedad; disparate, desatino; **to talk** — pavear.

noo·dle [núdl] *s.* tallarín, fideo, pasta (*para sopa*).

nook [nʊk] *s.* rincón; **breakfast** — desayunador.

noon [nun] *s.* mediodía.

noon·day [núnde] *s.* mediodía; *adj.* meridiano, de mediodía; — **meal** comida de mediodía.

noon·tide [núntaɪd] *s.* mediodía.

noon·time [núntaɪm] *s.* mediodía.

noose [nus] *s.* dogal; lazo, nudo corredizo, *Am.* gaza; *v.* lazar, coger con lazo; hacer un lazo corredizo en.

nor [nɔr] *conj.* ni; **neither** ... — ni ... ni.

Nor·dic [nɔ́rdɪk] *adj.* nórdico.

norm [nɔrm] *s.* norma.

nor·mal [nɔ́ml] *adj.* normal; *s.* norma; normal, línea perpendicular.

north [nɔrθ] *s.* norte; *adj.* septentrional; norteño; del norte; — **pole** polo norte, polo ártico; — **wind** cierzo, norte; **North American** norteamericano; *adv.* al norte, hacia el norte.

north·east [nɔrθíst] *adj.* & *s.* nordeste; *adv.* hacia el nordeste, rumbo al nordeste.

north·east·ern [nɔrθístən] *adj.* del nordeste, nordeste.

north·ern [nɔ́rðən] *adj.* septentrional; norteño; del norte; hacia el norte; — **lights** aurora boreal.

north·ern·er [nɔ́rðənə] *s.* norteño, habitante del norte.

north·ward [nɔ́rθwəd] *adv.* hacia el norte, rumbo al norte.

north·west [nɔrθwést] *adj.* & *s.* noroeste; *adv.* hacia el noroeste.

north·west·ern [nɔrθwéstən] *adj.* noroeste, del noroeste.

Nor·we·gian [nɔrwídʒən] *adj.* & *s.* noruego.

nose [noz] *s.* nariz; proa (*de un barco*); — **dive** picada (*de un avión*); *v.* olfatear; **to** — **around** husmear, curiosear.

nos·tal·gi·a [nɑstældʒɪə] *s.* nostalgia, añoranza.

nos·trils [nástrəlz] *s. pl.* narices, ventanas de la nariz.

not [nɑt] *adv.* no; — **at all** de ningún modo; de nada (*contestación a* "thank you"); — **at all sure** nada seguro; — **even a word** ni siquiera una palabra.

no·ta·ble [nótəbl] *adj.* notable.

no·ta·ry [nótərɪ] *s.* notario.

no·ta·tion [notéʃən] *s.* notación; apunte; anotación.

notch [nɑtʃ] *s.* muesca, ranura; hendidura; *v.* ranurar, hacer una ranura en.

note [not] *s.* nota; apunte, apuntación; **bank** — billete de banco; **promissory** — pagaré, abonaré; *v.* notar, observar, reparar; **to** — **down** apuntar.

note·book [nótbʊk] *s.* libreta, cuaderno, libro de apuntes.

not·ed [nótɪd] *adj.* notable, célebre, famoso.

note·worth·y [nótwɜðɪ] *adj.* notable, célebre.

noth·ing [náθɪŋ] *s.* nada; cero; **for** — por nada; inútilmente; de balde, gratis.

no·tice [nótɪs] *s.* noticia; aviso; advertencia, anuncio; mención; **to give a short** — avisar a última hora; **to take** — **of** hacer caso de, prestar atención a; *v.* notar, observar; prestar atención a; hacer caso a (*o* de); notificar.

no·tice·a·ble [nótɪsəbl] *adj.* notable; conspicuo;

perceptible.

no·ti·fy [nótəfaɪ] *v.* notificar, avisar.

no·tion [nóʃən] *s.* noción; idea; capricho; **-s** mercería, artículos menudos (*como alfileres, botones, etc.*), chucherías.

no·to·ri·ous [notórɪəs] *adj.* notorio.

not·with·stand·ing [nɑtwɪθstǽndɪŋ] *prep.* a pesar de; *adv.* & *conj.* no obstante, sin embargo; — **that** a pesar (de) que.

nought = **naught.**

noun [naʊn] *s.* nombre, sustantivo.

nour·ish [nɜ́ɪʃ] *v.* nutrir, alimentar.

nour·ish·ing [nɜ́ɪʃɪŋ] *adj.* nutritivo, alimenticio.

nour·ish·ment [nɜ́ɪʃmənt] *s.* nutrimento, sustento, alimento; nutrición.

nov·el [návl] *s.* novela; *adj.* novel, nuevo; raro, original.

nov·el·ist [návlɪst] *s.* novelista.

nov·el·ty [návltɪ] *s.* novedad; innovación; **nov·el·ties** novedades.

No·vem·ber [novémbə] *s.* noviembre.

nov·ice [návɪs] *s.* novicio; novato, principiante.

now [naʊ] *adv.* ahora; ya; — ... — ya ... ya, ora ... ora; — **and than** de vez en cuando, de cuando en cuando; — **that** ahora que; — **then** ahora bien; **he left just** — salió hace poco, *Ríopl., Ch., Andes* recién salió.

now·a·days [náʊədez] *adv.* hoy día.

no·where [nóhwɛr] *adv.* en ninguna parte, a ninguna parte.

nox·ious [nákʃəs] *adj.* nocivo.

nu·cle·us [njúklɪəs] *s.* núcleo.

nude [njud] *adj.* desnudo.

nude [nʌdʒ] *v.* codear, tocar con el codo; *s.* codazo ligero.

nudge [nʌdʒ] *v.* codear, tocar con el codo; *s.* codzao ligero.

nug·get [nʌ́gɪt] *s.* pepita; pedazo.

nui·sance [njúsns] *s.* molestia; lata, fastidio; persona *o* cosa fastidiosa.

null [nʌl] *adj.* nulo; — **and void** nulo e inválido.

nul·li·fy [nʌ́lɪfaɪ] *v.* invalidar; anular.

numb [nʌm] *adj.* entumecido *o* entumido, aterido; **to become** — entumecerse, entumirse, aterirse; *v.* entumecer.

num·ber [nʌ́mbə] *s.* número; *v.* numerar; ascender a (*cierto número*); **to** — **him among one's friends** contarle entre sus amigos.

num·ber·less [nʌ́mbəlɪs] *adj.* innumerable, sin número.

nu·mer·al [njúmrəl] *s.* número, cifra; guarismo; *adj.* numeral.

nu·mer·i·cal [njumérɪk] *adj.* numérico.

nu·mer·ous [njúmrəs] *adj.* numeroso; numerosos, muchos.

nu·mis·mat·ics [numɪsmǽtɪks] *s.* numismática.

nun [nʌn] *s.* monja.

nuptial [nápʃəl] *adj.* nupcial; **-s** *s. pl.* nupcias, bodas.

nurse [nɜs] *s.* (*for the sick*) enfermera, enfermero; (*for children*) niñera, aya; *Méx., Ven., Col., Andes* nana, *Am.* manejadora, *Andes* pilmama; *C.A.* china; **wet** — nodriza, ama de cría; *v.* criar, amamantar, dar de mamar, lactar; mamar; cuidar (*un enfermo*); abrigar (*rencor*).

nurs·er·y [nɜ́srɪ] *s.* cuarto para niños; criadero, semillero (*de plantas*); **day** — sala donde se cuida y divierte a los niños.

nur·ture [nɜ́tʃə] *s.* crianza; nutrimento; *v.* criar; nutrir; cuidar; fomentar.

nut [nʌt] *s.* nuez (*nombre genérico de varias frutas como la almendra, la castaña, la avellana, etc.*);

tuerca; loco, tipo raro o extravagante.
nut·crack·er [nʌ́tkrækəˠ] *s.* cascanueces.
nut·meg [nʌ́tmɛg] *s.* nuez moscada.
nu·tri·ent [nútrɪənt] *s.* nutritivo.
nu·tri·tion [njurʃən] *s.* nutrición; nutrimento, alimento.
nu·tri·tious [njutríʃəs] *adj.* nutritivo, alimenticio.
nu·tri·tive [njútrɪtɪv] *adj.* nutritivo.
nut·shell [nʌ́tʃɛl] *s.* cáscara de nuez (*o de otro fruto semejante*); **in a — en** suma, en breve, en pocas palabras.
nymph [nɪmf] *s.* ninfa.

O:o

oak [ok] *s.* roble; encina; **— grove** robledo o robledal; **live —** encina siempreverde.
oar [or] *s.* remo; *v.* remar, bogar.
o·a·sis [oésɪs] *s.* oasis.
oat [ot] *s.* avena (*planta*); **-s** avena, granos de avena.
oath [oθ] *s.* juramento; blasfemia, reniego.
oat·meal [ótmɪl] *s.* harina de avena; gachas de avena.
o·be·di·ence [əbídɪəns] *s.* obediencia.
o·be·di·ent [əbídɪənt] *adj.* obediente.
ob·e·lisk [ábəlɪsk] *s.* obelisco.
o·be·si·ty [obisəti] *s.* obesidad, gordura.
o·bey [əbé] *v.* obedecer.
ob·ject [ábdʒɪkt] *s.* objeto; cosa; complemento (*del verbo*); [əbdʒékt] *v.* objetar; oponerse; tener inconveniente.
ob·jec·tion [əbdʒékʃən] *s.* objeción, reparo; inconveniente.
ob·jec·tive [əbdʒéktɪv] *adj.* objetivo; **— case** caso complementario; *s.* objetivo; fin, propósito.
ob·li·gate [ábləget] *v.* obligar, constreñir; comprometer.
ob·li·ga·tion [abləgéʃən] *s.* (*duty*) obligación; deber (*debt*) deuda; **to be under — to** estar obligado a; estar agradecido a, deber favores a.
o·blig·a·to·ry [əblígətorɪ] *adj.* obligatorio.
o·blige [əbláɪdʒ] *v.* obligar; complacer; **much -ed!** ¡muchas gracias! ¡muy agradecido!; **to be very much -ed to someone** quedar muy agradecido con alguien.
o·blig·ing [əbláɪdʒɪŋ] *adj.* complaciente, obsequioso, comedido, cortés.
o·blique [əblík] *adj.* oblicuo.
o·blit·er·ate [əblítəret] *v.* borrar; arrasar, destruir.
o·bliv·i·on [əblívɪən] *s.* olvido.
o·bliv·i·ous [əblívɪəs] *adj.* olvidado, abstraído.
ob·long [ábloŋ] *adj.* cuadrilongo; oblongo.
ob·nox·ious [əbnákʃəs] *adj.* ofensivo; molesto; odioso.
o·boe [óbo] *s.* oboe.
ob·scene [əbsín] *adj.* obsceno.
ob·scen·i·ty [əbsénətɪ] *s.* obscenidad, indecencia.
ob·scure [əbskjúr] *adj.* obscuro; *v.* obscurecer; ofuscar.
ob·scu·ri·ty [əbskjúrətɪ] *s.* obscuridad.
ob·se·quies [ábsɪkwɪz] *s.* exequias, honras, funerales.
ob·se·qui·ous [əbsíkwɪəs] *adj.* obsequioso; servil; zalamero.
ob·serv·a·ble [əbzɚvəbl] *adj.* observable.
ob·ser·vance [əbzɚvəns] *s.* observancia; ceremonia, rito.
ob·ser·vant [əbzɚvənt] *adj.* observador; observante.

ob·ser·va·tion [abzɚvéʃən] *s.* observación.
ob·ser·va·to·ry [əbzɚvətorɪ] *s.* observatorio; mirador.
ob·serve [əbzɚv] *v.* observar; guardar (*las fiestas religiosas*); celebrar (*una fiesta*).
ob·serv·er [əbzɚvəˠ] *s.* observador.
ob·sess [əbsés] *v.* obsesionar, causar obsesion.
ob·ses·sion [əbséʃən] *s.* obsesión; idea fija.
ob·so·lete [ábsəlit] *adj.* anticuado; desusado.
ob·sta·cle [ábstəkl] *s.* obstáculo.
ob·stet·rics [abstétrɪks] *s.* obstetricia.
ob·sti·na·cy [ábstənəsɪ] *s.* obstinación, terquedad, porfía.
ob·sti·nate [ábstənɪt] *adj.* obstinado, terco, porfiado.
ob·strep·er·ous [abstrépɚəs] *adj.* estrepitoso, turbulento.
ob·struct [əbstrʌ́kt] *v.* obstruir.
ob·struc·tion [əbstrʌ́kʃən] *s.* obstrucción; impedimento, estorbo.
ob·tain [əbtén] *v.* obtener, conseguir, alcanzar, adquirir.
ob·tain·a·ble [əbténəbl] *adj.* obtenible, asequible.
ob·tru·sive [əbtrúsɪv] *adj.* intruso, entremetido.
ob·vi·ate [ábvɪet] *v.* obviar; allanar (*una dificultad*).
ob·vi·ous [ábvɪəs] *adj.* obvio, evidente.
oc·ca·sion [əkéʒən] *s.* (*timely*) ocasión; (*chance*) oportunidad; (*cause*) motivo, causa; (*event*) acontecimiento; *v.* ocasionar, causar.
oc·ca·sion·al [əkéʒənl] *adj.* ocasional; infrecuente; poco frecuente; **-ly** *adv.* de vez en cuando, a veces.
oc·ci·den·tal [aksədéntl] *adj. & s.* occidental.
oc·clu·sive [oklúsɪv] *adj. & s.* oclusivo.
oc·cult [əkʌ́lt] *adj.* oculto, misterioso.
oc·cu·pant [ákjəpənt] *s.* ocupante; inquilino.
oc·cu·pa·tion [akjəpéʃən] *s.* ocupación; trabajo, empleo, oficio.
oc·cu·py [ákjəpaɪ] *v.* ocupar.
oc·cur [əkɚ́] *v.* ocurrir, suceder; **to — to one** ocurrírsele a uno, venirle a la mente.
oc·cur·rence [əkɚ́əns] *s.* ocurrencia, suceso, caso, acontecimiento.
o·cean [óʃən] *s.* océano.
o·cean·og·ra·phy [oʃənágrəfɪ] *s.* oceanografía.
o·cher [okəˠ] *s.* ocre.
o'clock [əklák] *contr. de* **of the clock; it is two —** son las dos.
oc·tave [áktɪv] *s.* octava.
Oc·to·ber [aktóbəˠ] *s.* octubre.
oc·u·list [ákəlɪst] *s.* oculista.
odd [ad] *adj.* (*rare*) extraño, singular, raro; (*not even*) non, impar; **— change** suelto, cambio sobrante; **— moments** momentos libres, momentos de ocio; **— shoe** zapato suelto (*sin compañero*); **— volume** tomo suelto (*sin compañero*); **— volume** tomo suelto; **thirty —** treinta y tantos, treinta y pico; **-ly** *adv.* extrañamente, de un modo raro.
odd·i·ty [ádətɪ] *s.* rareza.
odds [adz] *s. pl. o sing.* diferencia, disparidad (*en apuestas*); ventaja, puntos de ventaja (*en apuestas*); **— and ends** retazos, trozos sobrantes, pedacitos varios; **the — are against me** la suerte me es contraria, estoy de mala suerte; **to be at -s with** estar reñido o enemistado con.
ode [od] *s.* oda.
o·di·ous [ódɪəs] *adj.* odioso.
o·dor [ódəˠ] *s.* olor; **bad —** mal olor, hedor.
o·dor·ous [ódərəs] *adj.* oloroso.
o'er [or] *contr. de* **over.**
of [ɑv, ʌv] *prep.* de; **— course** por supuesto, claro,

ya se ve; — **late** últimamente; **a quarter — five** las cinco menos cuarto; **to smell** — oler a; **to taste** — saber a.

off [ɔf] *adv.* (*distant*) lejos, fuera, a distancia; (*not attached*) suelto; apagado (*la luz*); (*equivale al reflexivo se en ciertos verbos*: marcharse, irse, *etc.*); — **and on** de vez en cuando; a intervalos; **ten cents** — rebaja de diez centavos; **ten miles** — a una distancia de diez millas; **to take a day** — ausentarse por un día; descansar por un día; *adj.* ausente; distante, más remoto; quitado; **the** — **side** el lado más remoto; **with his hat** — con el sombrero quitado; **the electricity is** — está cortada la electricidad; **to be** — **in one's accounts** estar errado en sus cuentas; **to be** — **to war** haberse ido a la guerra; **to be well** — ser persona acomodada, estar en buenas circunstancias; *prep.* lejos de; **offcolor** de mal color; verde (*indecente*); — **shore** a vista de la costa; — **standard** de calidad inferior; — **the road** deviado, descarriado; a un lado del camino; **to be** — **duty** no estar de turno; estar libre.

of·fend [əfɛnd] *v.* ofender.

of·fend·er [əfɛndər] *s.* ofensor; transgresor, delincuente.

of·fense [əfɛns] *s.* ofensa; agravio; delito, culpa; **no** — **was meant** lo hice (*o* lo dije) sin malicia; **weapon of** — arma ofensiva.

of·fen·sive [əfɛnsɪv] *adj.* ofensivo; *s.* ofensiva.

of·fer [ɔfər] *v.* ofrecer; **to** — **to do it** ofrecerse a hacerlo; *s.* oferta; ofrecimiento; promesa; propuesta.

of·fer·ing [ɔfərɪŋ] *s.* ofrenda; oferta, ofrecimiento.

off·hand [ɔfhænd] *adv.* de improviso, por el momento, sin pensarlo, impensadamente; *adj.* impensado, hecho de improviso; **in an** — **manner** con indiferencia; descuidadamente; sin plan.

of·fice [ɔfɪs] *s.* (*function*) oficio; cargo; función; (*place*) oficina, despacho; — **building** edificio para oficinas; **post** — correo; **box** — taquilla, *Ch., Riopl.* boletería; **through the good -s of** por el intermedio de.

of·fi·cer [ɔfəsər] *s.* (*office holder*) oficial; funcionario; (*police*) policía, gendarme; agente de policía; *v.* comandar, dirigir (*como oficial*); proveer de oficiales.

of·fi·cial [əfíʃəl] *adj.* oficial; *s.* oficial, funcionario; empleado público.

of·fi·ci·ate [əfíʃɪet] *v.* oficiar.

of·fi·cious [əfíʃəs] *adj.* oficioso, intruso, entremetido.

off·set [ɔfsét] *v.* compensar por; contrapesar.

off·shore [ɔfʃór] *adj. & adv.* (*land*) terral; (*at sea*) lejos de la playa.

off·spring [ɔfsprɪŋ] *s.* prole, hijos, descendientes; hijo, vástago; resultado, consecuencia.

off·stage [ɔfstédʒ] *adv. & adj.* entre bastidores.

oft [ɔft] = **often.**

of·ten [ɔfən] *adv.* muchas veces, con frecuencia, frecuentemente, a menudo; **how** — **?** ¿cuántas veces?; ¿cada cuándo?

o·gre [ógər] *s.* ogro, gigante, monstruo.

oil [ɔɪl] *s.* aceite; óleo; petróleo; — **can** alcuza; — **painting** pintura al óleo; — **well** pozo de petróleo; **motor** — aceite para motores; *v.* aceitar, angrasar, lubricar; untar.

oil·cloth [ɔɪlklɔθ] *s.* hule, tela de hule.

oil·y [ɔɪlɪ] *adj.* aceitoso, oleoso; grasiento.

oint·ment [ɔɪntmənt] *s.* ungüento.

O.K. [óké] *adj.* bueno; corriente, convenido; *adv.*

bien; **it's** — está bien; **to give one's** — dar el V°. B°. (visto bueno); *v.* dar el V°. B°., aprobar.

old [old] *adj.* viejo; antiguo; añejo; — **maid** solterona; — **man** anciano, viejo; — **wine** vino añejo; **days of** — días de antaño; **how** — **are you?** ¿cuántos años tiene Vd.? ¿qué edad tiene Vd.?; **to be** — **enough to ...** tener bastante edad para ...; **to be an** — **hand at** ser ducho en, ser muy perito o experto en.

old·en [óldn] *adj.* viejo, antiguo, de antaño.

old-fash·ioned [óldfǽʃənd] *adj.* pasado de moda; anticuado; chapado a la antigua.

old-time [óldtáɪm] *adj.* vetusto, de tiempos antiguos; de antaño.

old-tim·er [óldtáɪmə] *s.* antiguo residente.

o·le·an·der [óliændə] *s.* adelfa.

ol·fac·to·ry [ɔlfǽktərɪ] *adj.* olfatorio.

ol·ive [álɪv] *s.* oliva, aceituna; — **grove** olivar; — **oil** aceite de oliva; — **tree** olivo; — **branch** ramo de olivo; *adj.* aceitunado, verde aceituna.

O·lym·pi·ad [olímpiæd] *s.* olimpiada.

O·lym·pic [olímpɪk] *adj.* olímpico.

om·e·let [ámlɪt] *s.* tortilla de huevos.

o·men [ómən] *s.* agüero, presagio.

om·i·nous [ámənəs] *adj.* siniestro, de mal agüero, amenazador.

o·mis·sion [omíʃən] *s.* omisión.

o·mit [omít] *v.* omitir; dejar de.

om·nip·o·tent [amnípətənt] *adj.* omnipotente, todopoderoso.

on [an] *prep.* en; a; sobre, encima de; — **all sides** por todos lados; — **arriving** al llegar; — **board** a bordo; en el tren; — **condition that** con la condición de que; — **credit** al fiado; — **foot** a pie; — **horseback** a caballo; — **Monday** el lunes; — **purpose** a propósito, adrede; — **sale** de venta; — **time** a tiempo; a plazo; *adv.* adelante; **farther** — más adelante; **later** — después; — **and** — sin parar, sin cesar, continuamente; *adj.* puesto; **his hat is** — lleva puesto el sombrero; **the light is** — está encendida la luz.

once [wʌns] *adv.* una vez; en otro tiempo; — **and for all** una vez por todas, definitivamente; — **in a while** de vez en cuando; — **upon a time** érase que se era; en otro tiempo; **at** — al punto; a un mismo tiempo; **just this** — siquiera esta vez, sólo esta vez; *conj.* una vez que, cuando; luego que.

one [wʌn] *adj.* un, uno; — **hundred** cien, ciento; — **thousand** mil; **his** — **chance** su única oportunidad; **the** — **and only** el único; **one-armed** manco; **one-eyed** tuerto; **one-sided** de un solo lado; unilateral; parcial; desigual; **one-way** de un sentido; *s. & pron.* uno; — **another** uno a otro; — **by** — uno a uno; uno por uno; **the** — **who** el que, la que; **the green** — el verde; **this** — éste, ésta.

one·self [wʌnsélf] *pron.* se (*reflexivo*); **to speak to** — hablar consigo mismo; **by** — solo; por sí, por sí solo.

on·go·ing [ángoɪŋ] *adj.* que está haciéndose; corriente; que cursa.

on·ion [ʌ́njən] *s.* cebolla; — **patch** cebollar.

on·look·er [ánlʊkə] *s.* espectador, mirón.

on·ly [ónlɪ] *adj.* solo, único; *adv.* sólo, solamente; *conj.* sólo que.

on·set [ánsɛt] *s.* embestida, ataque; impulso inicial; primer ímpetu; attanque.

on·to [ántu] *prep.* a; sobre.

on·ward [ánwəd] *adv.* adelante; hacia adelante.

on·yx [ánɪks] *s.* onix, ónice.

ooze [uz] v. rezumar(se), escurrir(se).
o·pal [ópl] s. ópalo.
o·paque [opék] adj. opaco; mate.
o·pen [ópən] v. abrir(se); **to — into** comunicarse con, tener paso a; **to — onto** dar a, caer a, mirar a; adj. abierto; franco, sincero; expuesto (a); **— country** campo raso, campo abierto; **— question** cuestión discutible; **— to temptation** expuesto a caer en la tentación; **— winter** invierno sin nieve; **in the — air** al (o en el) aire libre; **open-minded** receptivo; de amplias miras; **—mouthed** boquiabierto, con la boca abierta; **open-end** [ópənénd] sin límites; sin trabas; s. campo raso, aire libre.
o·pen·ing [ópənɪŋ] s. (hole) abertura; (beginning) apertura, comienzo; (clearing) claro (en un bosque); (vacancy) puesto vacante; oportunidad; adj. primero; **— night of a play** estreno de una comedia; **the — number** el primer número (de un programa).
op·er·a [ápərə] s. ópera; **— glasses** gemelos; **— house** ópera, teatro de la ópera; **comic —** ópera cómica, zarzuela.
op·er·ant [ápʒənt] adj. operante.
op·er·ate [ápəret] v. (function) operar; funcionar; obrar; (manage) maniobrar; manejar; **to — on a person** operar a una persona.
op·er·a·tion [apəréʃən] s. (function) operación; funcionamiento; (management) manipulación; manejo; maniobra; **to be in —** funcionar, estar funcionando.
op·er·a·tor [ápəretə] s. operador, cirujano; maquinista, mecánico, operario; especulador (en la Bolsa); **mine —** explotador de minas; **telegraph —** telegrafista; **telephone —** telefonista.
op·e·ret·ta [apərétə] s. opereta, zarzuela.
o·pin·ion [əpínjən] s. opinión, parecer.
o·pi·um [ópiəm] s. opio.
o·pos·sum [əpásəm] s. zarigüeya.
op·po·nent [əpónənt] s. contrario, adversario, antagonista.
op·por·tune [apətjún] adj. oportuno; a propósito.
op·por·tun·ist [apətúnɪst] s. oportunista.
op·por·tu·ni·ty [apətjúnətɪ] s. oportunidad; ocasión.
op·pose [əpóz] v. oponer(se); oponerse a.
op·pos·ing [əpózɪŋ] adj. opuesto, contrario.
op·po·site [ápəzɪt] adj. (contrary) opuesto; contrario; (facing) frontero, de enfrente; **— to** frente a; prep. frente a, en frente de; s. contrario; **the —** lo opuesto, lo contrario.
op·po·si·tion [apəzíʃən] s. oposición; resistencia.
op·press [əprɛs] v. oprimir; agobiar.
op·pres·sion [əpréʃən] s. opresión.
op·pres·sive [əprésɪv] adj. (harsh) opresivo; (distressing) abrumador; gravoso; bochornoso, sofocante.
op·pres·sor [əprésə] s. opresor.
op·tic [áptɪk] adj. óptico; **-s** s. óptica.
op·ti·cal [áptɪkl] adj. óptico.
op·ti·cian [aptíʃən] s. óptico.
op·ti·mism [áptəmɪzəm] s. optimismo.
op·ti·mist [áptəmɪst] s. optimista.
op·ti·mis·tic [aptəmístɪk] adj. optimista.
op·tion [ápʃən] s. opción, derecho de escoger; alternativa.
op·tion·al [ápʃənl] adj. discrecional.
op·u·lence [ápjələns] s. opulencia, riqueza, abundancia.
op·u·lent [ápjələnt] adj. opulento, rico; abundante.
or [ɔr] conj. o; u (delante de o, ho).

or·a·cle [ɔ́rəkl] s. oráculo.
o·ral [ɔ́rəl] adj. oral; bucal.
or·ange [ɔ́rɪndʒ] s. naranja; **— blossom** azahar; **— grove** naranjal; **— tree** naranjo; adj. de naranja; anaranjado.
or·ange·ade [ɔrɪndʒéd] s. naranjada.
o·ra·tion [oréʃən] s. discurso, peroración, arenga.
or·a·tor [ɔ́rətə] s. orador.
or·a·to·ry [ɔ́rətorɪ] s. oratoria, elocuencia; oratorio, capilla.
orb [ɔrb] s. orbe.
or·bit [ɔ́rbɪt] s. órbita; v. moverse en órbita.
or·bit·al [ɔ́rbɪtl] adj. orbital.
or·chard [ɔ́rtʃəd] s. huerto.
or·ches·tra [ɔ́rkɪstrə] s. orquesta; **— seat** butaca, luneta, Am. platea (de orquesta).
or·ches·trate [ɔ́rkɪstret] v. orquestar.
or·chid [ɔ́rkɪd] s. orquídea.
or·dain [ɔrdén] v. ordenar; decretar.
or·deal [ɔrdíl] s. prueba penosa.
or·der [ɔ́rdə] s. (request) orden (s.); pedido; (group) clase; orden; (arrangement) orden (m.); **holy -s** órdenes sagradas; **in —** en orden; en buen estado; en regla; **in — to** para, a fin de; **in — that** para que, a fin de que; **made to —** mandado hacer, hecho a la medida; **to be out of —** estar descompuesto; estar desordenado; no estar en regla; v. ordenar; mandar; arreglar; pedir (hacer un pedido); **to — away** echar, despedir, expulsar.
or·der·ly [ɔ́rdəlɪ] adj. ordenado; en orden, bien arreglado; bien disciplinado; s. ordenanza (soldado); asistente de hospital.
or·di·nal [ɔ́rdɪnl] adj. ordinal; **— number** número ordinal.
or·di·nance [ɔ́rdnəns] s. ordenanza, ley, reglamento.
or·di·nar·i·ly [ɔrdŋérəlɪ] adv. ordinariamente, por lo común.
or·di·nar·y [ɔ́rdŋerɪ] adj. ordinario.
ore [or] s. mineral.
or·gan [ɔ́rgən] s. órgano; **hand —** organillo.
or·gan·ic [ɔrgǽnɪk] adj. orgánico; constitutivo, fundamental.
or·gan·ism [ɔ́rgənɪzəm] s. organismo.
or·gan·ist [ɔ́rgənɪst] s. organista.
or·gan·i·za·tion [ɔrgənəzéʃən] s. organización; organismo; entidad; sociedad.
or·gan·ize [ɔ́rgənaɪz] v. organizar(se).
or·gan·iz·er [ɔ́rgənaɪzə] s. organizador.
or·gy [ɔ́rdʒɪ] s. orgía.
o·ri·ent [ɔ́rɪɛnt] s. oriente; v. orientar.
o·ri·en·tal [ɔrɪéntl] adj. & s. oriental.
o·ri·en·tate [ɔ́rɪɛntet] v. orientar.
o·ri·en·ta·tion [ɔrɪɛntéʃən] s. orientación.
or·i·fice [ɔ́rəfɪs] s. orificio.
or·i·gin [ɔ́rədʒɪn] s. origen; procedencia.
o·rig·i·nal [ərídʒənl] adj. & s. original; **-ly** adv. originalmente, originariamente; en el principio, al principio.
o·rig·i·nal·i·ty [ərídʒənǽlətɪ] s. originalidad.
o·rig·i·nate [ərídʒənet] v. originar(se).
o·ri·ole [ɔ́rɪol] s. oriol (pájaro).
Or·lon [ɔ́rlan] s. orlón.
or·na·ment [ɔ́rnəmənt] s. ornamento, adorno; [ɔ́rnəmɛnt] v. ornamentar, adornar, ornar.
or·na·men·tal [ɔrnəméntl] adj. ornamental, de adorno, decorativo.
or·nate [ɔrnét] adj. ornado, adornado en exceso; **— style** estilo florido.
or·ni·thol·o·gy [ɔrnəθálədʒɪ] s. ornitología.

or·phan [ɔ́rfən] *adj.* & *s.* huérfano; — **asylum** hospicio, orfanato, asilo de huérfanos; *v.* dejar huérfano a.

or·tho·dox [ɔ́rθədɑks] *adj.* ortodoxo.

or·thog·ra·phy [ɔrθágrəfɪ] *s.* ortografía.

os·cil·late [ásəlet] *v.* oscilar.

os·cil·la·to·ry [ásələtɔrɪ] *adj.* oscilatorio.

os·mi·um [ázmiəm] *s.* osmio.

os·ten·ta·tion [ɑstəntéʃən] *s.* ostentación, boato.

os·ten·ta·tious [ɑstəntéʃəs] *adj.* ostentoso.

os·trich [ɔ́strɪtʃ] *s.* avestruz.

oth·er [ʌ́ðɚ] *adj.* & *s.* otro; — **than** otra cosa que; más que; **every** — **day** cada dos días, un día sí y otro no; **some** — **day** otro día.

oth·er·wise [ʌ́ðɚwaɪz] *adv.* de otro modo; en otros respectos; *adj.* otro, diferente.

ot·ter [átɚ] *s.* nutria; piel de nutria.

ought [ɔt] *v. defect.* (*por lo general se traduce por el presente y el condicional de deber*) debo, debes, etc.; debería, deberías, etc.; debiera, debieras, etc.

ounce [aʊns] *s.* onza.

our [aʊr] *adj.* nuestro (nuestra, nuestros, nuestras).

ours [aʊrz] *pron. pos.* nuestro (nuestra, nuestros, nuestras); el nuestro (la nuestra, los nuestros, las nuestras); **a friend of** — un amigo nuestro.

our·selves [aʊrsélvz] *pron.* nosotros mismos; nos (*reflexivo*); a nosotros mismos; **we** — nosotros mismos; **by** — solos; por nosotros; *véase* **herself**.

oust [aʊst] *v.* echar, expulsar.

out [aʊt] *adv.* fuera; afuera; hacia fuera; — **of fear** por miedo, de miedo; — **of humor** malhumorado; — **of money** sin dinero; — **of print** agotado; — **of touch** fuera de aislado de, sin contacto con; — **of tune** desentonado; **made** — **of** hecho de; **to fight it** — decidirlo luchando; **to have it** — **with** habérselas con; **to speak** — hablar francamente; *adj.* ausente; apagado; — **and** — **criminal** criminal empedernido; — **and** — **refusal** una negativa redonda; — **size** tamaño poco común o extraordinario; **before the week is** — antes de que termine la semana; **the book is just** — acaba de publicarse el libro; **the secret is** — se ha divulgado el secreto.

out·break [áʊtbrek] *s.* (*eruption*) erupción; (*revolt*) motín, insurrección, tumulto; (*attack*) ataque, arranque (*de ira*); **at the** — **of the war** al estallar la guerra.

out·burst [áʊtbɝst] *s.* explosión; estallido; arranque (*de pasión*); erupción.

out·cast [áʊtkæst] *adj.* excluido, desechado; desterrado; *s.* paria (*persona excluida de la sociedad*).

out·come [áʊtkʌm] *s.* resultado, consecuencia.

out·cry [áʊtkraɪ] *s.* grito; clamor.

out·door [áʊtdor] *adj.* externo; fuera de la casa; — **games** juegos al aire libre.

out·doors [aʊtdórz] *adv.* puertas afuera, fuera de casa, al aire libre, al raso; *s.* aire libre, campo raso, campiña.

out·er [áʊtɚ] *adj.* exterior, externo.

out·fit [áʊtfɪt] *s.* equipo; pertrechos; *v.* equipar, habilitar, aviar.

out·go·ing [áʊtgoɪŋ] *adj.* (*leaving*) saliente; (*extrovert*) extrovertido.

out·guess [aʊtgés] *v.* anticipar; madrugar.

out·ing [áʊtɪŋ] *s.* excursión, gira (jira), caminata.

out·law [áʊtlɔ] *s.* forajido, bandido; prófugo, fugitivo; *v.* proscribir, declarar ilegal.

out·lay [áʊtle] *s.* gasto, desembolso; [áʊtlé] *v.* gastar, desembolsar.

out·let [áʊtlet] *s.* salida; desaguadero, desagüe; escurridero.

out·line [áʊtlaɪn] *s.* (*abstract*) bosquejo, esbozo; (*boundary*) contorno; *v.* bosquejar, esbozar; delinear.

out·live [aʊtlív] *v.* sobrevivir.

out·look [áʊtlʊk] *s.* vista; perspectiva.

out·ly·ing [áʊtlaɪɪŋ] *adj.* circundante, exterior, remoto (*del centro*).

out-of-date [áʊtəvdét] *adj.* fuera de moda, anticuado.

out·post [áʊtpost] *s.* avanzada.

out·put [áʊtpʊt] *s.* rendimiento; producción total.

out·rage [áʊtredʒ] *s.* ultraje; *v.* ultrajar.

out·ra·geous [aʊtrédʒəs] *adj.* afrentoso; atroz.

out·ran [aʊtrǽn] *pret. de* **to outrun**.

out·right [aʊtráɪt] *adv.* & *adj.* sin rodeo; cabal; completo.

out·run [aʊtrʌ́n] *v.* aventajar (*en una carrera*); dejar atrás; *p.p. de* **to outrun**.

out·set [áʊtset] *s.* comienzo, principio.

out·shine [aʊtʃáɪn] *v.* eclipsar, sobrepasar (*en brillo o lucidez*).

out·shone [aʊtʃón] *pret.* & *p.p. de* **to outshine**.

out·side [áʊtsáɪd] *adj.* (*external*) exterior; externo; (*foreign*) foráneo, extranjero; *adv.* fuera, afuera; fuera de casa; *prep.* fuera de; *s.* exterior, parte exterior; superficie; lado de afuera; **in a week, at the** — en una semana, a lo sumo; **to close on the** — cerrar por fuera.

out·sid·er [aʊtsáɪdɚ] *s.* foráneo, persona de fuera; extraño.

out·skirts [áʊtskɝts] *s. pl.* alrededores, arrabales, cercanías.

out·spo·ken [aʊtspókən] *adj.* franco, francote, *Ven.*, *Méx.*, *C.A.*, *Carib.* claridoso.

out·stand·ing [áʊtstǽndɪŋ] *adj.* sobresaliente; destacado, notable; — **bills** cuentas por cobrar; — **debts** deudas por pagar.

out·stretched [aʊtstrétʃt] *adj.* extendido; **with** — **arms** con los brazos abiertos.

out·ward [áʊtwəd] *adj.* (*external*) exterior, externo; (*apparent*) aparente; superficial; *adv.* fuera, hacia fuera; — **bound** que sale, de salida; para fuera, para el extranjero; **-ly** *adv.* exteriormente; por fuera; aparentemente.

out·weigh [aʊtwé] *v.* exceder en peso o valor; sobrepujar.

o·val [óvl] *adj.* oval, ovalado; *s.* óvalo.

o·va·ry [óvərɪ] *s.* ovario.

o·va·tion [ovéʃən] *s.* ovación.

ov·en [ʌ́vən] *s.* horno.

o·ver [óvɚ] *prep.* sobre; por; por encima de; encima de; a través de; al otro lado de; más de; — **night** por la noche, durante la noche; (*véase* **overnight**); — **to** a; **all** — **the city** por toda la cuidad; *adv.* encima; al otro lado; otra vez, de nuevo; — **again** otra vez, de nuevo; — **against** en contraste con; — **and** — una y otra vez, repetidas veces; — **curious** demasiado curioso; — **generous** demasiado generoso; — **here** acá, aquí; — **there** allá, allí; **two years and** — más de dos años; **to do it** — hacerlo otra vez, volver a hacerlo; *adj.* excesivo; **it is all** — ya se acabó, se ha acabado; ha pasado.

o·ver·alls [óvɚɔlz] *s. pl. Am.* overol, overoles (*pantalones de trabajo*).

o·ver·ate [ovɚét] *pret. de* **to overeat**.

o·ver·board [óvɚbord] *adv.* al mar, al agua.

o·ver·came [ovɚkém] *pret. de* **to overcome**.

o·ver·cast [óvɚkæst] *adj.* encapotado, nublado; **to become** — encapotarse, nublarse; [ovɚkǽst] *v.* nublar o anublar; sobrehilar (*dar puntadas sobre el borde de una tela*); *pret.* & *p.p. de* **to overcast**.

o·ver·charge [ovɚtʃárdʒ] *v.* cargar demasiado; cobrar demasiado.

o·ver·coat [óvɚkot] *s.* sobretodo, abrigo.

o·ver·come [óvɚkʌ́m] *v.* vencer; rendir; *p.p.* & *adj.* vencido; rendido; agobiado; **to be** — **by weariness** estar rendido de fatiga.

o·ver·due [ovɚdú] *adj.* atrasado; vencido sin pago.

o·ver·eat [ovɚít] *v.* hartarse.

o·ver·eat·en [ovɚítn̩] *p.p. de* **to overeat**.

o·ver·ex·cite [óvɚɪksáɪt] *v.* sobreexcitar.

o·ver·flow [óvɚflo] *s.* derrame, desbordamiento; inundación; superabundancia; [ovɚfló] *v.* derramarse, desbordarse; rebosar; inundar.

o·ver·grown [óvɚgrón] *adj.* denso, frondoso, poblado (*de follaje, herbaje, etc.*); — **boy** muchachón, muchacho demasiado crecido para su edad.

o·ver·hang [ovɚhǽŋ] *v.* colgar por encima de; proyectarse o sobresalir por encima de; adornar con colgaduras; amenazar (*dícese de un desastre o calamidad*).

o·ver·haul [ovɚhól] *v.* reparar (*de cabo a rabo*); remendar; alcanzar (*en una carrera*).

o·ver·head [óvɚhɛd] *s.* gastos generales (*renta, seguro, alumbrado, calefacción, etc.*); *adj.* de arriba; elevado; — **expenses** gastos generales; [óvɚhɛ́d] *adv.* encima de la cabeza, arriba; en lo alto.

over·hear [ovɚhír] *v.* oír por casualidad, alcanzar a oír, acertar a oír.

o·ver·heard [ovɚhɝd] *pret.* & *p.p. de* **to overhear**.

o·ver·heat [ovɚhít] *v.* recalentar(se); calentar(se) demasiado.

o·ver·hung [ovɚhʌ́ŋ] *pret.* & *p.p. de* **to overhang**.

o·ver·land [óvɚlænd] *adv.* & *adj.* por tierra.

o·ver·lap [óvɚlǽp] *v.* solapar.

o·ver·lay [ovɚlé] *v.* cubrir; incrustar.

o·ver·load [ovɚlód] *v.* sobrecargar; [óvɚlod] *s.* sobrecarga.

o·ver·look [ovɚlúk] *v.* mirar a (*desde lo alto*); dar a, tener vista a; pasar por alto, omitir; perdonar (*faltas*); descuidar, no notar; inspeccionar, examinar.

o·ver·ly [óvɚlɪ] *adv.* excesivamente.

o·ver·night [óvɚnáɪt] *adv.* durante la noche; toda la noche; *adj.* de noche; nocturno; — **bag** saco de noche; — **trip** viaje de una noche.

o·ver·pass [óvɚpǽs] *v.* viaducto.

o·ver·pow·er [ovɚpáʊɚ] *v.* subyugar, abrumar, vencer.

o·ver·ran [ovɚfǽn] *pret. de* **to overrun**.

o·ver·ride [ovɚráɪd] *v.* anular; invalidar.

o·ver·rule [ovɚrúl] *v.* anular.

o·ver·run [ovɚrʌ́n] *v.* desbordarse, mundar; sobrepasar; infestar, invadir; *p.p. de* **to overrun**.

o·ver·seas [óvɚsíz] *adv.* en ultramar, allende los mares; *adj.* de ultramar.

o·ver·see [ovɚsí] *v.* dirigir; vigilar.

o·ver·se·er [óvɚsır] *s.* sobrestante, capataz; inspector, superintendente.

o·ver·shoe [óvɚʃu] *s.* chanclo; zapato de goma, caucho o hule.

o·ver·sight [óvɚsaɪt] *s.* inadvertencia, negligencia, descuido.

o·ver·step [ovɚstép] *v.* sobrepasarse, propasarse; traspasar; **to** — **the bounds** traspasar los límites;

propasarse.

o·ver·take [ovɚték] *v.* alcanzar.

o·ver·tak·en [ovɚtékən] *p.p. de* **to overtake**.

o·ver·threw [ovɚθrú] *pret. de* **to overthrow**.

o·ver·throw [óvɚθro] *s.* (*overturn*) derrocamiento; (*defeat*) derrota, destrucción; caída; [ovɚθró] *v.* derrocar; derribar, echar abajo, volcar; destronar.

o·ver·thrown [ovɚθrón] *p.p. de* **to overthrow**.

o·ver·time [óvɚtaɪm] *adv.* & *adj.* en exceso de las horas estipuladas; — **pay** sobresueldo.

o·ver·took [ovɚtúk] *pret. de* **to overtake**.

o·ver·ture [óvɚtʃɚ] *s.* obertura, preludio; propuesta, proposición.

o·ver·turn [ovɚtɝn] *v.* volcar(se); trastornar; derribar; echar abajo.

o·ver·whelm [ovɚhwélm] *v.* abrumar, agobiar; oprimir; arrollar.

o·ver·whelm·ing [ovɚhwélmɪŋ] *adj.* abrumador; opresivo; arrollador, irresistible, poderoso.

o·ver·work [óvɚwɝk] *v.* atarearse, afanarse más de lo debido, trabajar demasiado; *s.* exceso de trabajo.

owe [o] *v.* deber, adeudar.

ow·ing [óɪŋ] *adj.* debido; — **to** debido a.

owl [aul] *s.* lechuza, buho, *Méx., C.A.* tecolote.

own [on] *adj.* propio; **a house of his** — una casa suya; **his** — **people** los suyos; **to be on one's** — no estar a merced ajena; trabajar por su propia cuenta; **to come into one's** — entrar en posesión de lo suyo; **to hold one's** — mantenerse firme; *v.* poseer, tener; admitir, reconocer; **to** — **to** confesar; **to** — **up** confesar.

own·er [ónɚ] *s.* dueño, amo; propietario; poseedor.

own·er·ship [ónɚʃɪp] *s.* posesión, propiedad.

ox [ɑks] (*pl* ox·en [áksn̩]) *s.* buey.

ox·ide [áksaɪd] *s.* óxido.

ox·i·dize [áksədaɪz] *v.* oxidar.

ox·y·gen [áksədʒən] *s.* oxígeno.

oys·ter [ɔ́ɪstɚ] *s.* ostra, ostión.

o·zone [ózon] *s.* ozono.

OR

P:p

pace [pes] *s.* paso; *v.* pasear, andar; andar al paso; marchar; medir a pasos.

pace·mak·er [pésmekɚ] *s.* marcapaso.

pa·cif·ic [pəsífɪk] *adj.* pacífico.

pac·i·fy [pǽsəfaɪ] *v.* pacificar, apaciguar; calmar.

pack [pæk] *s.* fardo, lío, carga; manada (*de lobos*); cuadrilla, pandilla (*de ladrones*); jauría (*de perros*); muchedumbre; baraja (*de naipes*); — **animal** acémila, bestia de carga; *v.* empacar, empaquetar; embalar; enfardar; envasar; apiñar(se); cargar (*una bestia*); hacer (*el baúl, la maleta*); **to** — **off** despedir de repente; echar a la calle; largarse, irse.

pack·age [pǽkɪdʒ] *s.* paquete; fardo, bulto; cajetilla (*de cigarrillos*).

pack·er [pǽkɚ] *s.* empacador; embalador, envasador.

pack·et [pǽkɪt] *s.* paquetillo; cajetilla.

pack·ing [pǽkɪŋ] *s.* (*covering*) embalaje; envase; (*filling*) relleno; — **box** caja para embalar o empacar; — **house** establecimiento frigorífico; fábrica para envasar o enlatar comestibles.

pact [pækt] *s.* pacto, convenio.

pad [pæd] *s.* almohadilla, cojincillo; tableta, block

de papel; *v.* rellenar; forrar; acolchar.

pad·ding [pǽdɪŋ] *s.* relleno (*de pelo, algodón, paja, etc.*), *Andes* guata; ripio, palabras o frases inútiles.

pad·dle [pǽdl] *s.* pala; remo de canoa; — **wheel** rueda de paleta; *v.* remar con pala; apalear; chapotear (*en el agua*).

pad·dock [pǽdǝk] *s.* dehesa.

pad·lock [pǽdlɑk] *s.* candado; *v.* cerrar con candado.

pa·gan [pégǝn] *s.* & *adj.* pagano.

pa·gan·ism [pégǝnɪzǝm] *s.* paganismo.

page [pedʒ] *s.* página; paje; "botones" (*de hotel*), mensajero; *v.* paginar; vocear, llamar a voces.

pag·eant [pǽdʒǝnt] *s.* (*parade*) manifestación, desfile, procesión, pompa; (*drama*) representación al aire libre.

paid [ped] *pret.* & *p.p. de* **to pay**.

pail [pel] *s.* balde, cubo, cubeta.

pain [pen] *s.* dolor; sufrimiento; **-s** esmero; **on (under)** — **of** so pena de; **to be in** — estar sufriendo, tener dolores; **to take -s** esmerarse, extremarse; *v.* doler; causar dolor; afligir.

pain·ful [pénfǝl] *adj.* doloroso; penoso; arduo.

pain·less [pénlɪs] *adj.* sin dolor; libre de dolor.

pains·tak·ing [pénztekɪŋ] *adj.* esmerado, cuidadoso; aplicado.

paint [pent] *s.* (*mixture*) pintura, color; (*rouge*) colorete; *v.* pintar; pintarse (*la cara*); **to** — **the town red** irse de juerga o de parranda, *Riopl.* irse de farra.

paint·brush [péntbrʌʃ] *s.* (*art*) pincel; (*house*) brocha.

paint·er [péntǝ] *s.* pintor.

paint·ing [péntɪŋ] *s.* pintura.

pair [pɛr] *s.* par; pareja; **a** — **of scissors** unas tijeras; *v.* aparear(se); hacer pareja, hacer pares; **to** — **off** aparear(se).

pa·jam·as [pǝdʒǽmǝz] *s. pl.* pijama.

pal [pæl] *s.* compañero, camarada.

pal·ace [pǽlɪs] *s.* palacio.

pal·ate [pǽlɪt] *s.* paladar.

pa·la·tial [pǝléʃl] *adj.* suntuoso.

pale [pel] *adj.* pálido; descolorido; *v.* palidecer, ponerse pálido o descolorido.

pale·ness [pélnɪs] *s.* palidez.

pal·i·sade [pælǝséd] *s.* palizada, estacada; **-s** riscos, acantilados.

pall [pɔl] *v.* empalagar; aburrir; **it -s on me** me empalaga; me aburre; *s.* paño de ataúd; palia (*lienzo que pone encima del cáliz*).

pal·la·di·um [pǝlédiǝm] *s.* paladio.

pal·li·a·tive [pǽljǝtɪv] *adj.* & *s.* paliativo.

pal·lid [pǽlɪd] *adj.* pálido.

pal·or [pǽlǝ] *s.* palidez.

palm [pɑm] *s.* palma; palmera; — **Sunday** Domingo de Ramos; — **tree** palma, palmera; *v.* **to** — **something off on someone** pasar o dar algo indeseable a una persona (*sin que se dé cuenta de ello*).

pal·pa·ble [pǽlpǝbl] *adj.* palpable, tangible; evidente.

pal·pi·tate [pǽlpǝtet] *v.* palpitar, latir.

pal·pi·ta·tion [pælpǝtéʃǝn] *s.* palpitación; latido.

pal·try [pɔ́ltrɪ] *adj.* mezquino, miserable, despreciable, insignificante.

pam·per [pǽmpǝ] *v.* mimar, consentir (*a un niño*).

pam·phlet [pǽmflɪt] *s.* folleto, *Am.* panfleto.

pan [pæn] *s.* cazuela, cacerola; cazo; platillo (*de balanza*); **dish** — cazo para lavar platos; **frying** — sartén; *v.* **to** — **out** (**well**) salir bien, dar buen resultado.

Pan-A·mer·i·can [pænǝmɛ́rǝkǝn] *adj.* panamericano.

pan·cake [pǽnkek] *s.* tortita de harina, *Ven., Col.* panqué; *Riopl.* panqueque.

pan·der [pǽndǝ] *s.* alcahuete, encubridor *v.* alcahuetear, servir de alcahuete.

pane [pen] *s.* vidrio, cristal (*de ventana o puerta*); cuadro (*de vidrio*).

pan·el [pǽnl] *s.* panel, tablero; cuarterón (*de puerta, ventana, etc.*); tabla (*doble pliegue de una falda o vestido*); **jury** — jurado; *v.* proveer de (*o adornar con*) paneles.

pang [pæŋ] *s.* dolor agudo; angustia, tormento.

pan·han·dle [pǽnhændl] *s.* mango de sartén; territorio en forma de mango; *v.* mendigar.

pan·ic [pǽnɪk] *adj.* & *s.* pánico; **pan·ic-strick·en** sobrecogido de pánico.

pan·o·ram·a [pænǝrǽmǝ] *s.* panorama.

pan·sy [pǽnzɪ] *s.* pensamiento (*flor*).

pant [pænt] *v.* jadear; palpitar; **to** — **for** anhelar, ansiar.

pan·ther [pǽnθǝ] *s.* pantera.

pant·ing [pǽntɪŋ] *s.* jadeo, palpitación; *adj.* jadeante.

pan·to·mime [pǽntǝmaɪm] *s.* pantomima.

pan·try [pǽntrɪ] *s.* despensa.

pants [pænts] *s. pl.* pantalones.

pa·pa [pɑ́pǝ] *s.* papá.

pa·pa·cy [pépǝsɪ] *s.* papado.

pa·pal [pépl] *adj.* papal.

pa·per [pépǝ] *s.* (*material*) papel; (*daily*) periódico; (*essay*) tema, ensayos; **-s** papeles, documentos, credenciales; **naturalization -s** carta de naturaleza, certificado de ciudadanía; **scholarly** — ponencia; **of pins** cartón de alfileres; **on** — escrito; por escrito; *adj.* de papel; para papel; — **doll** muñeca de papel; — **money** papel moneda; **—weight** pisapapeles; *v.* empapelar.

pa·per·back [pépǝbæk] *s.* & *adj.* libro en rústica.

pa·per·work [pépǝwǝk] *s.* preparación de escritos; papeleo.

pa·pri·ka [pǽpríkǝ] *s.* pimentón.

par [pɑr] *s.* (*equality*) paridad, igualdad; (*standard*) valor nominal; — **value** valor a la par; **above** — sobre par, a premio, con prima; **at** — a la par; **below** — bajo par, a descuento; **on a** — **with** al par de, al nivel de, igual a; **to feel above** — sentirse mejor que de ordinario; **to feel below** — sentirse menos bien que de ordinario.

par·a·ble [pǽrǝbl] *s.* parábola (*alegoría bíblica*).

par·a·chute [pǽrǝʃut] *s.* paracaídas.

par·a·chut·ist [pǽrǝʃutɪst] *s.* paracaidista.

pa·rade [pǝréd] *s.* (*procession*) desfile, procesión, manifestación; paseo; (*review*) parada; — **ground** campo de maniobras; **to make a** — **of** ostentar, hacer ostentación de; *v.* desfilar, pasar en desfile; marchar en parada; hacer ostentación de.

par·a·digm [pǽrǝdɪm], [pǽrǝdaɪm] *s.* paradigma.

par·a·dise [pǽrǝdaɪs] *s.* paraíso.

par·a·dox·i·cal [pærǝdáksɪkl] *adj.* paradójico.

par·a·dox [pǽrǝdɑks] *s.* paradoja.

par·af·fin [pǽrǝfɪn] *s.* parafina.

par·a·graph [pǽrǝgræf] *s.* párrafo; *v.* dividir en párrafos.

Par·a·guay·an [pærǝgwáɪǝn] *adj.* & *s.* paraguayo.

par·al·lel [pǽrǝlɛl] *adj.* & *s.* paralelo; *v.* ser (*o* correr) paralelo a; comparar, cotejar.

pa·ral·y·sis [pǝrǽlǝsɪs] *s.* parálisis.

par·a·lyt·ic [pærǝlítɪk] *adj.* paralítico.

par·a·lyze [pǽrǝlaɪz] *v.* paralizar.

pa·ram·e·ter [pərǽmətə·] *s.* parámetro.
par·a·mount [pǽrəmaʊnt] *adj.* importantísimo, superior, supremo, máximo.
par·a·noi·a [pærənɔ́jə] *s.* paranoia.
par·a·pet [pǽrəpɪt] *s.* parapeto.
par·a·phrase [pǽrəfrez] *v.* parafrasear.
par·a·site [pǽrəsaɪt] *s.* parásito.
par·a·sol [pǽrəsɔl] *s.* parasol, sombrilla.
par·a·troops [pǽrətrups] *s.* tropas paracaidistas.
par·cel [pársl] *s.* paquete; parcela, porción, lote (*de terreno*); — **post** paquete postal; *v.* parcelar, dividir en porciones o parcelas; hacer paquetes; **to** — **out** repartir.
parch [partʃ] *v.* resecar(se); tostar(se).
parch·ment [pártʃmənt] *s.* pergamino.
par·don [párdn̩] *s.* perdón; indulto; **I beg your** — perdone Vd.; dispense Vd.; *v.* perdonar; dispensar; indultar.
pare [pɛr] *v.* mondar, pelar (*manzanas, patatas, etc.*); cortar, recortar; **to** — **down expenditures** reducir gastos.
par·ent [pérənt] *s.* padre, madre; origen; **-s** padres.
par·ent·age [pérəntɪdʒ] *s.* linaje; padres.
pa·ren·tal [pərɛ́ntl] *adj.* parental.
pa·ren·the·sis [pərɛ́nθəsɪs] (*pl.* **pa·ren·the·ses** [pərɛ́nθəsiz]) *s.* paréntesis.
par·ish [pǽrɪʃ] *s.* parroquia.
par·ish [pərɪ́ʃənə·] *s.* parroquiano, feligrés; **-s** fieles, feligreses.
park [park] *s.* parque; *v.* estacionar, dejar (*un automóvil*); estacionarse; **-ing lot** *Ch., Ríopl.* playa de estacionamiento; *Mex., Ven.* estacionamiento; *Col.* parqueadero; **-ing space** sitio o lugar para estacionarse; **free -ing** estacionamiento gratis; **no -ing** se prohibe estacionarse; no estacionarse.
par·lance [párləns] *s.* lenguaje.
par·ley [párlɪ] *s.* parlamento, discusión, conferencia; *v.* parlamentar, discutir.
par·lia·ment [párləmənt] *s.* parlamento.
par·lia·men·ta·ry [parləméntərɪ] *adj.* parlamentario.
par·lor [párlə·] *s.* sala, salón; sala de recibo; — **car** coche salón; **beauty** — salón de belleza.
pa·ro·chi·al [pərókɪəl] *adj.* parroquial.
par·o·dy [pérədɪ] *s.* parodia; *v.* parodiar.
pa·role [pəról] *s.* palabra de honor; **to put on** — dejar libre (*a un prisionero*) bajo palabra de honor; *v.* dejar libre bajo palabra de honor.
par·rot [pǽrət] *s.* cotorra, loro, perico, papagayo; *v.* remedar, repetir como loro.
par·ry [pǽrɪ] *v.* parar, quitar o reparar (*un golpe*); *s.* quite, reparo.
pars·ley [párslɪ] *s.* perejil.
pars·nip [pársnəp] *s.* chirivía (*legumbre*).
par·son [pársn̩] *s.* pastor, clérigo.
part [part] *s.* parte (*f.*); papel (*dramático*); raya (*del cabello*); — **and parcel** parte esencial o inherente; — **owner** condueño, dueño en parte; — **time** parte del tiempo; **in foreign -s** en el extranjero, en países extranjeros; **spare -s** piezas accesorias, piezas de repuesto (*o de refacción*); **do your** — haga Vd. cuanto esté de su parte; *v.* partir(se); separar(se); **to** — **company** separarse; **to** — **from** separarse de, despedirse de; **to** — **one's hair** hacerse la raya; **to** — **with** separarse de, despedirse de, deshacerse de.
par·take [párték] *v.* tomar parte, tener parte, participar.
par·tak·en [partékən] *p.p. de* **to partake.**
par·tial [párʃəl] *adj.* parcial; **-ly** *adv.* parcialmente, en parte; con parcialidad.

par·ti·al·i·ty [parʃǽlətɪ] *s.* parcialidad.
par·tic·i·pant [pətísəpənt] *adj. & s.* participante, partícipe, copartícipe.
par·tic·i·pate [pətísəpet] *v.* participar.
par·tic·i·pa·tion [pətɪsəpéʃən] *s.* participación.
par·ti·ci·ple [pártəsɪpl] *s.* participio; **present** — gerundio.
par·ti·cle [pártɪl] *s.* partícula.
par·tic·u·lar [pətíkjələ·] *adj.* (*single*) particular; peculiar; (*special*) esmerado, exacto; escrupuloso; (*demanding*) quisquilloso; exigente; *s.* particular, detalle, circunstancia; **in** — en particular, especialmente; **-ly** *adv.* particularmente; en particular.
part·ing [pártɪŋ] (*departure*) despedida; (*division*) separación; bifurcación; **the** — **of the ways** encrujiada, bifurcación, cruce de caminos; *adj.* de despedida, último.
par·ti·san [pártəzn̩] *adj.* partidario; parcial; *s.* partidario; secuaz, seguidor.
par·ti·tion [pətíʃən] *s.* (*division*) partición; división, separación; (*wall*) tabique; *Am.* medianía; *v.* partir, dividir; repartir.
par·ti·tive [pártətɪv] *adj.* partitivo.
part·ner [pártnə·] *s.* socio, consocio; compañero; **dancing** — pareja de baile.
part·ner·ship [pártnə·ʃɪp] *s.* sociedad, compañía.
par·took [partúk] *pret. de* **to partake.**
par·tridge [pártrɪdʒ] *s.* perdiz.
par·ty [pártɪ] *s.* (*get-together*) tetulia, reunión, fiesta; (*group*) grupo, partida (*de gente*); (*legal*) parte; **hunting** — partida de caza; **political** — partido político.
pass [pæs] *s.* paso; pase, permiso de entrar; aprobación (*en un examen*); trance, situación; **key** llave maestra; **to come to** — suceder; *v.* pasar; pasar por; pronunciar (*sentencia*), dar (*un juicio o parecer*); aprobar (*a un estudiante*); adoptar (*una ley*); ser aprobado en (*un examen*); **to** — **away** pasar a mejor vida, morir; desaparecer; pasar (*el tiempo*).
pass·a·ble [pǽsəbl] *adj.* (*penetrable*) transitable; (*acceptable*) pasadero, regular, mediano.
pas·sage [pǽsɪdʒ] *s.* pasaje; paso, tránsito; transcurso (*del tiempo*); pasillo, pasadizo; travesía, viaje por mar; aprobación (*de un proyecto de ley*); adopción (*de una ley*).
pas·sage·way [pǽsədʒwe] *s.* corredor; pasaje.
pass·book [pǽsbʊk] *s.* libreta de banco.
pas·sen·ger [pǽsndʒə·] *s.* pasajero; **the -s** los pasajeros; el pasaje.
pas·ser·by [pǽsə·bái] *s.* transeúnte, viandante.
pas·sion [pǽʃən] *s.* pasión; **Passion play** drama de la Pasión; **to fly into a** — montar en cólera, encolerizarse.
pas·sion·ate [pǽʃənɪt] *adj.* apasionado.
pas·sive [pǽsɪv] *adj.* pasivo; *s.* voz pasiva.
pass·port [pǽsport] *s.* pasaporte.
pass·word [pǽswɜd] *s.* consigna, contraseña, santo y seña.
past [pæst] *adj.* pasado; último; — **master** perito; **the** — **president** el expresidente, el último presidente; — **tense** tiempo pasado; pretérito; **for some time** — desde hace algún tiempo, de poco tiempo a esta parte; *prep.* — **bearing** insoportable; — **understanding** incomprensible; **half** — **two** las dos y media; **woman** — **forty** cuarentona, mujer de más de cuarenta años; **to go** — **the house** pasar por (*o por enfrente de*) la casa; *s.* pasado; pretérito; pretérito imperfecto;

PA

man with a — hombre de dudosos antecedentes.

paste [pest] *s.* pasta; engrudo; *v.* pegar (*con engrudo*).

paste·board [péstbord] *s.* cartón; — **box** caja de cartón.

pas·teur·ize [pǽstəraɪz] *v.* pasterizar (*o* pasteurizar).

pas·time [pǽstaɪm] *s.* pasatiempo.

pas·tor [pǽstə·] *s.* pastor, clérigo, cura.

pas·tor·al [pǽstərəl] *adj.* pastoril; pastoral; *s.* pastoral, carta pastoral; écloga; pastorela, idilio.

pas·try [péstrɪ] *s.* pastelería, pasteles; — **cook** pastelero; — **shop** pastelería; repostería.

pas·ture [pǽstʃə·] *s.* pastura, pasto; dehesa; *v.* pastar, pacer; apacentar(se).

pat [pæt] *adj.* apto, oportuno; **to have a lesson** — saber al dedillo la lección; **to stand** — mantenerse firme; *adv.* a propósito; oportunamente; de molde; *s.* palmadita, caricia, golpecito; — **of butter** cuadrito de mantequilla; *v.* dar palmaditas a; acariciar; pasar la mano (*para alisar o acariciar*).

patch [pæt] *s.* (*repair*) remiendo; parche; mancha; (*plot*) pedazo (*de terreno*); sembrado; *v.* remendar; **to** — **up a quarrel** hacer las paces.

pate [pet] *s.* coronilla (*de la cabeza*); **bald** — calva.

pat·ent [pǽtnt] *adj.* patente, evidente, manifiesto; de patente; — **leather** charol; — **medicine** medicina de patente; — **right** patente; *s.* patente; *v.* patentar.

pa·ter·nal [pətǝ́nl] *adj.* paternal, paterno.

pa·ter·ni·ty [pətǝ́nətɪ] *s.* paternidad.

path [pæθ] *s.* senda, sendero; vereda; ruta; trayectoria (*de una bala*).

pa·thet·ic [pəθétɪk] *adj.* patético.

path·o·log·i·cal [pæθəládʒɪkl] *adj.* patalógico.

pa·thol·o·gy [pəθálədʒɪ] *s.* patología.

pa·thos [péθɑs] *s.* patetismo, cualidad patética.

path·way [pǽθwe] *s.* senda, vereda, vía.

pa·tience [péʃəns] *s.* paciencia.

pa·tient [péʃənt] *adj.* paciente; pacienzudo; *s.* paciente, enfermo.

pa·tri·arch [pétrɪɑrk] *s.* patriarca.

pa·tri·ar·chal [petrɪárkl] *adj.* patriarcal.

pa·tri·cian [pətríʃən] *s.* patricio.

pat·ri·mo·ny [pǽtrəmonɪ] *s.* patrimonio.

pa·tri·ot [pétrɪət] *s.* patriota.

pa·tri·ot·ic [petrɪátɪk] *adj.* patriótico.

pa·tri·ot·ism [pétrɪətɪzəm] *s.* patriotismo.

pa·trol [pətról] *s.* patrulla; ronda; *v.* patrullar, rondar.

pa·tron [pétrən] *s.* patrón, patrono; benefactor; cliente, parroquiano; — **saint** santo patrón.

pa·tron·age [pétrənɪdʒ] *s.* (*support*) patrocinio, amparo; (*clientele*) clientela; (*manner*) condescendencia; **political** — control de nombramientos políticos.

pa·tron·ess [pétrənɪs] *s.* patrona, protectora.

pa·tron·ize [pétrənaɪz] *v.* patrocinar, amparar; tratar con condescendencia; favorecer, ser parroquiano de.

pat·ter [pǽtə·] *v.* golpetear ligeramente; talonear; charlar, parlotear; *s.* golpeteo; golpecitos; taloneo; charla, parloteo.

pat·tern [pǽtə·n] *s.* (*model*) modelo; dechado; muestra; ejemplo; patrón, molde; (*design*) diseño, dibujo (*en tejidos, telas, etc.*); *v.* **to** — **oneself after** seguir el ejemplo de; **to** — **something after (on, upon)** forjar o modelar algo a imitación de.

pau·ci·ty [pɔ́sɪtɪ] *s.* escasez; falta.

paunch [pɔntʃ] *s.* panza, barriga.

pause [pɔz] *s.* pausa; *s.* pausar, hacer pausa; detenerse, parar.

pave [pev] *v.* pavimentar; **to** — **the way for** preparar o abrir el camino para; **to** — **with bricks** enladrillar; **to** — **with flagstones** enlosar.

pave·ment [pévmənt] *s.* pavimento; **brick** — enladrillado.

pa·vil·ion [pəvíljən] *s.* pabellón.

paw [pɔ] *s.* garra, zarpa; *v.* echar la zarpa; arañar; manosear; **to** — **the ground** patear la tierra (*dícese del caballo*).

pawn [pɔn] *s.* prenda, empeño; peón (*de ajedrez*); —**broker** prestamista, prendero; —**shop** empeño, casa de empeños, montepío; **in** — en prenda; *v.* empeñar, dejar en prenda.

pay [pe] *v.* (*remit*) pagar; (*pay for*) costear; (*profit*) ser provechoso; (*worthwhile*) valer la pena; **to** — **attention** prestar atención; **to** — **back** restituir, devolver; **to** — **court** hacer la corte; **to** — **down** pagar al contado; **to** — **homage** hacer o rendir homenaje; **to** — **one's respects** presentar sus respetos; **to** — **a visit** hacer una visita; *s.* pago; recompensa; paga; sueldo; — **day** día de pagos, *Am.* día de raya; — **master** pagador, *Am.* rayador; — **roll** nómina.

pay·a·ble [péəbl] *adj.* pagadero.

pay·ment [pémənt] *s.* pago; paga; **in full** pago total.

pay·off [péɔf] *s.* arreglo; pago.

pea [pi] *s.* guisante, chícharo; **sweet** — guisante de olor.

peace [pis] *s.* paz.

peace·a·ble [písəbl] *adj.* pacífico, tranquilo.

peace·ful [písfəl] *adj.* pacífico; tranquilo, quieto, sosegado.

peach [pitʃ] *s.* melocotón, durazno; persona bella o admirable; — **tree** durazno, duraznero, melocotonero.

pea·cock [píkɑk] *s.* pavón, pavo real; **to act like a** — pavonearse, hacer ostentación.

peak [pik] *s.* pico, cumbre, cima; cúspide; punto máximo.

peal [pil] *s.* repique (*de campanas*); — **of laughter** carcajada, risotada; — **of thunder** trueno; *v.* repicar (*las companas*).

pea·nut [pínət] *s.* cacahuate, *Carib., Ven., Col., Ch., Riopl., Andes* maní.

pear [pɛr] *s.* pera; — **tree** peral; **alligator** — aguacate, *Ch., Andes, Riopl.* palta (*variedad sudamericana*).

pearl [pɝl] *s.* perla; — **nucklace** collar de perlas; **mother-of-pearl** nácar, madreperla.

pear·ly [pɝlɪ] *adj.* perlino; nacarado; aperlado.

peas·ant [péznt] *adj.* & *s.* campesino, rústico, *P.R.* jíbaro, *Cuba* guajiro; *Col.* paisa; *Ch.* guaso; *Riopl.* gaucho.

peb·ble [pébl] *s.* guija, china, guijarro, piedrecilla.

pe·can [pikán] *s.* pacana.

peck [pɛk] *v.* picar, picotear; *s.* picotazo, picotada; medida de áridos (*aproximadamente 9 litros*); — **of trouble** la mar de disgustos o molestias.

pe·cu·liar [pɪkúljə·] *adj.* peculiar; raro, singular, extraño.

pe·cu·li·ar·i·ty [pɪkjulɪǽrətɪ] *s.* peculiaridad; particularidad; rareza.

ped·a·gogue [pédəgɑg] *s.* pedagogo, dómine.

ped·a·go·gy [pédəgodʒɪ] *s.* pedagogía.

ped·al [pédl] *s.* pedal; *v.* pedalear, mover los pedales.

ped·ant [pédn̩t] *s.* pedante.

pe·dan·tic [pɪdǽntɪk] *adj.* pedante, pedantesco.
ped·dle [pédl] *v.* ir vendiendo de puerta en puerta; **to — gossip** chismear.
ped·dler [pédlɚ] *s.* buhonero; vendedor ambulante.
ped·es·tal [pédɪstl] *s.* pedestal.
pe·des·tri·an [pədéstrɪən] *s.* peatón, transeúnte, viandante; *adj.* pedestre.
pe·di·at·rics [pidɪǽtrɪks] *s.* pediatría.
ped·i·gree [pédəgri] *s.* linaje, genealogía.
peek [pik] *v.* atisbar, espiar; *s.* atisbo.
peel [pil] *s.* corteza, cáscara (*de algunas frutas*); pellejo (*de patatas*); *v.* pelar(se), descortezar(se), deshollejar(se); **to keep one's eye -ed** tener los ojos muy abiertos, estar alerta.
peep [pip] *v.* atisbar, espiar; asomar(se); pipiar, piar; *s.* atisbo; ojeada; pío (*de pollo o ave*).
peer [pir] *s.* (*equal*) par, igual; (*noble*) noble; *v.* mirar con atención, atisbar; asomar; **to — into other people's business** fisgar, curiosear.
peer group [pírgrup] *s.* conjunto de personas de la misma edad y condiciones.
peer·less [pírlɛs] *adj.* incomparable; sin par.
peeve [piv] *v.* irritar, poner de mal humor; **to get -d** amoscarse, ponerse de mal humor.
pee·vish [pívɪʃ] *adj.* enojadizo; malhumorado.
peg [pɛg] *s.* espiga, clavo de madera, estaquilla; clavija (*de violín*); **to take a person down a —** rebajar o humillar a alguien; *v.* clavar, clavetear; poner estaquillas; **to — along** atarearse, trabajar con tesón.
pe·jor·a·tive [pədʒɔ́rətɪv] *adj.* peyorativo; despectivo.
pel·i·can [pélɪkən] *s.* pelícano.
pel·let [pélɪt] *s.* (*ball*) pelotilla; bola; (*pill*) píldora.
pell-mell [pélmél] *adj.* confuso, tumultuoso; *adv.* a trochemoche, atropelladamente, en tumulto.
pelt [pɛlt] *s.* zalea, cuero (*especialmente de oveja*); piel; *v.* golpear; **to — with stones** apedrear, arrojar piedras a.
pel·vis [pélvɪs] *s.* pelvis.
pen [pɛn] *s.* pluma (*para escribir*); corral; redil; **—holder** mango de pluma, portapluma; **—name** nombre de pluma; **fountain —** pluma fuente, pluma estilográfica; **ballpoint —** bolígrafo; **pig —** pocilga; *v.* escribir (*con pluma*); acorralar, encerrar.
pe·nal [pínl] *adj.* penal.
pe·nal·ize [pínəlaɪz] *v.* penar; aplicar sanción.
pen·al·ty [pénltɪ] *s.* pena, castigo; multa.
pen·ance [pénəns] *s.* penitencia.
pen·cil [pénsl] *s.* lápiz; lapicero; **— sharpener** tajalápiz.
pen·dant [péndənt] *s.* pendiente (*ardorno que cuelga*); *adj.* pendiente.
pend·ing [péndɪŋ] *adj.* pendiente; colgado; *prep.* durante.
pen·du·lum [péndʒələm] *s.* péndulo.
pen·e·trate [pénətret] *v.* penetrar.
pen·e·trat·ing [pénətretɪŋ] *adj.* penetrante.
pen·a·tra·tion [pɛnətréʃən] *s.* penetración.
pen·guin [péŋgwɪn] *s.* pingüino.
pen·i·cil·lin [pɛnəsílɪn] *s.* penicilina.
pen·in·su·la [pənínsələ] *s.* península.
pe·nis [pínɪs] *s.* pene.
pen·i·tent [pénətənt] *adj.* arrepentido, penitente; penitente.
pen·i·ten·tia·ry [pɛnətéʃərɪ] *s.* penitenciaría, presidio.
pen·knife [pénnaɪf] *s.* cortaplumas; navaja.
pen·man·ship [pénmənʃɪp] *s.* escritura, caligrafía.
pen·nant [pénənt] *s.* banderola, gallardete.

pen·ni·less [pénɪlɪs] *adj.* pobre, sin dinero.
pen·ny [pénɪ] *s.* centavo (*de dólar*); **to cost a pretty —** costar un ojo de la cara, costar un dineral.
pen·sion [pénʃən] *s.* pensión, retiro (*de un militar*); *v.* pensionar.
pen·sive [pénsɪv] *adj.* pensativo.
pent [pɛnt] *adj.* encerrado; acorralado; **pent-up emotions** sentimientos reprimidos.
pent·house [pénthaʊs] *s.* casa de azotea; colgadizo.
peo·ple [pípl] *s.* gente; pueblo *v.* poblar.
pep·per [pépɚ] *s.* pimienta; **— plant** pimentero; **— shaker** pimentero; **green -s** pimientos verdes; **red —** pimentón, chile, *Carib., Col., Ven., Andes, Ch., Ríopl.* ají; *v.* sazonar con pimienta; **to — with bullets** acribillar a balazos.
pep·per·mint [pépɚmɪnt] *s.* menta; pastilla o bombón de menta.
per [pɚ] *prep.* por; **— capita** por cabeza; **— cent** por ciento; **— year** al año; **ten cents — dozen** diez centavos por docena (*o diez centavos la docena*).
per·cale [pɚkél] *s.* percal.
per·ceive [pɚsív] *v.* percibir.
per·cent·age [pɚséntɪdʒ] *s.* porcentaje, tanto por ciento.
per·cep·ti·ble [pɚséptəbl] *adj.* perceptible.
per·cep·tion [pɚsépʃən] *s.* percepción.
per·cep·tive [pɚséptɪv] *adj.* perceptivo; sensible.
perch [pɚtʃ] *s.* percha (*para pájaros*); perca (*pez*); *v.* encaramar(se); posarse (*en una percha o rama*).
per·chance [pɚtʃǽns] *adv.* por ventura, acaso, quizás, tal vez.
per·co·late [pɝkəlet] *v.* filtrar(se), colar(se); rezumarse; penetrar.
per·cus·sion [pɚkʃən] *s.* percusión.
per·di·tion [pɚdíʃən] *s.* perdición.
per·en·ni·al [pərénɪəl] *adj.* perenne; continuo; perpetuo.
per·fect [pɝfɪkt] *adj.* perfecto; completo; *s.* tiempo perfecto (*del verbo*); [pɚfékt] *v.* perfeccionar.
per·fec·tion [pɚfékʃən] *s.* perfección.
per·fid·i·ous [pɚfídɪəs] *adj.* pérfido.
per·fi·dy [pɝfədɪ] *s.* perfidia.
per·fo·rate [pɝfəret] *v.* perforar.
per·force [pɚfɔ́rs] *adv.* necesariamente; por fuerza.
per·form [pɚfɔ́rm] *v.* ejecutar; llevar a cabo, cumplir, hacer; funcionar (*una máquina*); desempeñar o representar un papel.
per·form·ance [pɚfɔ́rməns] *s.* ejecución; desempeño; cumplimiento; funcionamiento (*de una máquina o motor*); función, representación; acto, acción.
per·fume [pɝfjum] *s.* perfume; [pɚfjúm] *v.* perfumar.
per·fum·er·y [pɚfjúmərɪ] *s.* perfumería; perfumes.
per·haps [pɚhǽps] *adv.* acaso, tal vez, quizá (*o quizás*), puede ser.
per·i·gee [pérədʒi] *s.* perigeo.
per·il [pérəl] *s.* peligro; riesgo; *v.* poner en peligro.
per·il·ous [pérələs] *adj.* peligroso.
pe·rim·e·ter [pərímətɚ] *s.* perímetro.
pe·ri·od [pírɪəd] *s.* período; punto final; fin, término.
pe·ri·od·ic [pɪrɪádɪk] *adj.* periódico.
pe·ri·od·i·cal [pɪrɪádɪkl] *adj.* periódico; *s.* revista, publicación periódica.
pe·riph·er·y [pərífərɪ] *s.* periferia.
per·ish [pérɪʃ] *v.* perecer.
per·ish·a·ble [pérɪʃəbl] *adj.* perecedero; deleznable.
per·i·to·ne·um [pɛrətəníəm] *s.* peritoneo.
per·i·to·ni·tis [pɛrətənáɪtɪs] *s.* peritonitis.
per·jure [pɝdʒɚ] *v.* **to — oneself** perjurar.

per·ju·ry [pɝ́dʒrɪ] *s.* perjurio, juramento falso.

per·ma·nence [pɝ́mənəns] *s.* permanencia.

per·ma·nent [pɝ́mənənt] *adj.* permanente; duradero.

per·me·ate [pɝ́mɪet] *v.* penetrar, saturar; difundirse por, filtrarse por.

per·mis·si·ble [pɚmísəbl] *adj.* lícito.

per·mis·sion [pɚmíʃən] *s.* permiso, licencia.

per·mis·sive [pɚmísɪv] *adj.* permisivo.

per·mit [pɝ́mɪt] *s.* permiso, pase; licencia; [pɚmít] *v.* permitir.

per·mu·ta·tion [pɚmjutéʃən] *s.* permutación.

per·ni·cious [pɚníʃəs] *adj.* pernicioso.

per·ox·ide [pɚráksaɪd] *s.* peróxido.

per·pen·dic·u·lar [pɝpəndíkjǝlɚ] *adj. & s.* perpendicular.

per·pe·trate [pɝ́pǝtret] *v.* perpetrar, cometer.

per·pet·u·al [pɚpétʃʊəl] *adj.* perpetuo.

per·pet·u·ate [pɚpétʃuet] *v.* perpetuar.

per·plex [pɚpléks] *v.* confundir, turbar, aturdir.

per·plexed [pɚplékst] *adj.* perplejo, confuso.

per·plex·i·ty [pɚpléksǝtɪ] *s.* perplejidad, confusión.

per·se·cute [pɝ́sɪkjut] *v.* perseguir, acosar.

per·se·cu·tion [pɝsɪkjúʃən] *s.* persecución.

per·se·cu·tor [pɝ́sɪkjutɚ] *s.* perseguidor.

per·se·ver·ance [pɝsəvírəns] *s.* perseverancia.

per·se·vere [pɝsəvír] *v.* perseverar; persistir.

per·sist [pɚzíst] *v.* persistir; porfiar.

per·sist·ence [pɚzístəns] *s.* persistencia; porfía.

per·sist·ent [pɚzístənt] *adj.* persistente; porfiado.

per·son [pɝ́sn̩] *s.* persona.

per·son·a·ble [pɝ́sənəbl] *adj.* presentable; bien parecido.

per·son·age [pɝ́snɪdʒ] *s.* personaje.

per·son·al [pɝ́sn̩l] *adj.* personal; en persona.

per·son·al·ism [pɝ́sənəlɪzm] *s.* personalismo.

per·son·al·i·ty [pɝsn̩ǽlǝtɪ] *s.* personalidad; persona, personaje; alusión personal.

per·son·nel [pɝsn̩él] *s.* personal.

per·spec·tive [pɚspéktɪv] *s.* perspectiva; — **drawing** dibujo en perspectiva.

per·spi·ca·cious [pɝspɪkéʃəs] *adj.* perspicaz.

per·spi·ra·tion [pɝspɚréʃən] *s.* sudor.

per·spire [pɚspáɪr] *v.* sudar.

per·suade [pɚswéd] *v.* persuadir.

per·sua·sion [pɚswéʒən] *s.* persuasión; creencia.

per·sua·sive [pɚswésɪv] *adj.* persuasivo.

pert [pɝt] *adj.* insolente, descarado, atrevido, *Am.* retobado.

per·tain [pɚtén] *v.* pertenecer; atañer.

per·ti·nent [pɝ́tn̩ənt] *adj.* pertinente, a propósito, al caso.

per·turb [pɚtɝ́b] *v.* perturbar.

pe·rus·al [pɚrúzl] *s.* lectura.

pe·ruse [pɚrúz] *v.* leer con cuidado.

Pe·ru·vi·an [pɚrúvɪən] *adj. & s.* peruano.

per·vade [pɚvéd] *v.* llenar, penetrar, difundirse por.

per·verse [pɚvɝ́s] *adj.* perverso; terco, obstinado.

per·vert [pɚvɝ́t] *v.* pervertir; falsear; [pɝ́vɝt] *s.* perverso.

pes·si·mism [pésəmɪzm] *s.* pesimismo.

pes·si·mist [pésəmɪst] *s.* pesimista; **-ic** *adj.* pesimista.

pest [pɛst] *s.* peste, plaga; pestilencia.

pes·ter [péstɚ] *v.* importunar, molestar.

pes·ti·cide [péstǝsaɪd] *s. & adj.* insecticida.

pes·ti·lence [péstlǝns] *s.* pestilencia.

pet [pɛt] *s.* animal mimado, animal casero o doméstico; niño mimado; favorito; *adj.* favorito; mimado; — **name** nombre de cariño (*por lo general diminutivo*); *v.* mimar, acariciar.

pet·al [pétl̩] *s.* pétalo.

pet·cock [pétkɑk] *s.* llave de desagüe (*purga*).

pe·ti·tion [pǝtíʃən] *s.* petición, súplica; instancia, memorial, solicitud, *Am.* ocurso; *v.* solicitar, pedir, dirigir una instancia o memorial a; suplicar, rogar.

pet·ri·fy [pétrɪfaɪ] *v.* petrificar.

pe·tro·le·um [pǝtrólɪəm] *s.* petróleo.

pet·ti·coat [pétɪkot] *s.* enaguas.

pet·ty [pétɪ] *adj.* insignificante, pequeño; nezquino, inferior, subordinado; — **cash** fondos para gastos menores; — **larceny** ratería; — **officer** oficial subordinado (*en la marina*); — **treason** traición menor.

pe·tu·nia [pǝtúnjǝ] *s.* petunia.

pew [pju] *s.* banco de iglesia.

pha·lanx [félæŋks] *s.* falanje.

phan·tom [fǽntəm] *s.* fantasma.

phar·ma·cist [fɑ́rməsɪst] *s.* farmacéutico, boticario.

phar·ma·cy [fɑ́rməsɪ] *s.* farmacia, botica.

phar·ynx [fǽrɪŋks] *s.* faringe.

phase [fez] *s.* fase.

pheas·ant [fézənt] *s.* faisán.

phe·nom·e·na [fǝnámǝnǝ] *pl. de* phenomenon.

phe·nom·e·non [fǝnámǝnɑn] *s.* fenómeno.

phi·lan·thro·py [fɪlǽnθrǝpɪ] *s.* filantropía.

phi·lat·e·ly [fɪlǽtlɪ] *s.* filatelia.

phil·har·mon·ic [fɪlhɑrmánɪk] *adj.* filarmónico.

phi·lol·o·gy [fɪláləʒɪ] *s.* filología.

phi·los·o·pher [fǝlásǝfɚ] *s.* filósofo.

phil·o·soph·i·cal [fɪlǝsáfɪk] *adj.* filosófico.

phi·los·o·phy [fǝlásǝfɪ] *s.* filosofía.

phlegm [flem] *s.* flema.

phone [fon] *s.* teléfono; *v.* telefonear.

pho·neme [fónim] *s.* fonema.

pho·net·ics [fǝnétɪks] *s.* fonética.

pho·no·graph [fónǝgræf] *s.* fonógrafo.

pho·nol·o·gy [fǝnálǝʒɪ] *s.* fonología.

phos·phate [fásfet] *s.* fosfato.

phos·pho·rous [fásfǝrǝs] *s.* fósforo (*elemento químico*).

pho·to [fóto] *s.* fotografía, retrato; foto.

pho·to·e·lec·tric [fotoléktrɪk] *s.* fotoeléctrico.

pho·to·graph [fótǝgræf] *s.* fotografía, retrato; *v.* fotografiar, retratar.

pho·tog·ra·pher [fǝtágrǝfɚ] *s.* fotógrafo.

pho·tog·ra·phy [fǝtágrǝfɪ] *s.* fotografía.

pho·to·syn·the·sis [fotosɪnθǝsɪs] *s.* fotosíntesis.

phrase [frez] *s.* frase; expresión, locución; *v.* frasear; espresar, formular.

phys·ic [fízɪk] *s.* purga, purgante; *v.* purgar.

phys·i·cal [fízɪk] *adj.* físico.

phy·si·cian [fǝzíʃən] *s.* médico.

phys·i·cist [fízǝsɪst] *s.* físico.

phys·ics [fízɪks] *s.* física.

phys·i·o·log·i·cal [fɪzɪǝládʒɪkl̩] *adj.* fisiológico.

phys·i·ol·o·gy [fɪzɪálǝdʒɪ] *s.* fisiología.

phy·sique [fɪzík] *s.* físico, constitución física, talle, cuerpo.

pi·an·o [pɪǽno] *s.* piano; — **bench** banqueta de piano; — **stool** taburete de piano; **grand** — piano de cola; **upright** — piano vertical.

pic·a·resque [pɪkǝrésk] *adj.* picaresco.

pick [pɪk] *v.* (*choose*) escoger; coger; (*break*) picar; (*clean*) mondarse, limpiarse (*los dientes*); desplumar (*un ave*); roer (*un hueso*); falsear (*una cerradura*); armar (*una pendencia*); **to — flaws** criticar, censurar; **to — out** escoger; **to — pockets** ratear; **to — up** recoger; **to — up speed** acelerar la marcha; *s.* pico (*herramienta*); selección; lo selecto, lo mejor; recolección,

cosecha; **ice** — punzón para romper hielo;
tooth— mondadientes, palillo de dientes.
pick·ax [píkæks] *s.* pico, zapapico.
pick·et [píkɪt] *s.* piquete (*estaca o palo clavado en
la tierra*); piquete (*vigilante huelguista*); piquete
de soldados; *v.* estacionar piquetes cerca de (*una
fábrica, campamento, etc.*); vigilar (*por medio de
piquetes*); estar de guardia.
pick·le [píkl] *s.* encurtido; **to be in a** — hallarse
en un aprieto; *v.* encurtir, escabechar; **-ed
cucumbers** pepinillos encurtidos; **-ed fish**
excabeche, pescado en escabeche.
pick·pock·et [píkpɑkɪt] *s.* rata (*m.*), ratero; *Méx.,
Ven., Col.* carterista.
pic·nic [píknɪk] *s.* partida de campo, día de campo,
comida campestre, *Am.* picnic; *v.* hacer una
comida campestre; ir a un picnic.
pic·ture [píktʃɚ] *s.* (*painting*) cuadro, pintura;
(*portrait*) retrato; (*photo*) fotografía; (*engraving*)
grabado; (*movie*) película; — **frame** marco; —
gallery museo o galería de pinturas; *v.* pintar,
dibujar; describir; imaginar(se).
pic·tur·esque [pɪktʃɚrésk] *adj.* pintoresco.
pie [paɪ] *s.* pastel; empanada.
piece [pis] *s.* (*section*) pieza; pedazo; parte;
sección; (*passage*) trozo; — **of advice** consejo;
— **of land** parcela; — **of money** moneda; — **of
news** noticia; — **of nonsense** tontería; —**meal** en
pedazos, a, pedazos, por partes; *v.* remendar;
to — **between meals** comer a deshoras; **to** — **on**
to juntar a, pegar a; **to** — **together** unir, pegar,
juntar.
pier [pɪr] *s.* muelle, embarcadero; rompeolas; pilar
(*de puente o arco*).
pierce [pɪrs] *v.* atravesar, traspasar; taladrar,
agujerar, perforar.
pi·e·ty [páɪətɪ] *s.* piedad, religiosidad.
pig [pɪg] *s.* puerco, cerdo, cochino; *S.A.* chancho;
C.A. tunco; cuchi; *adj.* porcino; — **iron** hierro
en lingotes; —**headed** cabezón, testarudo; **guinea**
— conejillo de Indias; **suckling** — gorrino.
pi·geon [pídʒən] *s.* pichón; paloma.
pi·geon·hole [pídʒənhol] *s.* casilla; *v.* encasillar.
pig·ment [pígmənt] *s.* pigmento, color.
pig·my [pígmɪ] *s.* pigmeo.
pike [paɪk] *s.* pica, lanza; lucio (*pez*).
pile [paɪl] *s.* pila, montón; pelo (*de ciertos tejidos*);
pilote; **-s** almorranas (*enfermedad*); — **driver**
martinete (*para clavar pilotes*); *v.* apilar(se),
amontonar(se); acumular(se).
pil·fer [pílfɚ] *v.* pillar, ratear, hurtar, sisar.
pil·grim [pílgrɪm] *s.* peregrino, romero.
pil·grim·age [pílgrəmɪdʒ] *s.* peregrinación, romería.
pill [pɪl] *s.* píldora; persona fastidiosa.
pil·lage [pílɪdʒ] *v.* pillar, saquear; *s.* pillaje, saqueo.
pil·lar [pílɚ] *s.* pilar, columna; **to go from** — **to
post** ir de Ceca en Meca.
pil·low [pílo] *s.* almohada; cojín.
pil·low·case [pílokes] *s.* funda de almohada.
pi·lot [páɪlət] *s.* piloto; guía; — **light** (*o* —
burner) mechero, encendedor (*de una cocina o
estufa de gas*); **harbor** — prático de puerto; *v.*
pilotar o pilotear; dirigir, guiar.
pim·ple [pímpl] *s.* grano, barro.
pin [pɪn] *s.* alfiler; prendedor; espiga; bolo (*del
juego de bolos*); — **money** dinero para alfileres;
— **wheel** molinete, *Am.* remolino; **breast** —
broche; **safety** — imperdible; *v.* prender (*con
alfiler*); asegurar, fijar, clavar; **to** — **down** fijar,
inmovilizar; hacer dar una contestación
definitiva; **to** — **one's hope to** poner toda su

esperanza en; **to** — **up** prender con alfileres;
colgar (*un dibujo o retrato*), fijar con tachuelas.
pin·cers [pínsɚz] *s. pl.* pinzas; tenazas; **small** —
tenacillas.
pinch [pɪntʃ] *v.* (*squeeze*) pellizcar; apretar;
(*economize*) economizar; (*arrest*) prender,
arrestar; **to** — **one's finger in the door**
machucarse el dedo en la puerta; *s.* pellizco;
pizca, porción pequeña; punzada, dolor agudo;
aprieto, apuro; — **hitter** suplente, sustituto.
pin·chers [píntʃɚz] = **pincers**.
pine [paɪn] *s.* pino; — **cone** piña; — **grove** pinar;
— **nut** piñón; *v.* languidecer; **to** — **away**
consumirse; **to** — **for** anhelar, suspirar por.
pine·ap·ple [páɪnæpl] *s.* piña, ananá o ananás.
pin·ion [pínjən] *s.* piñón.
pink [pɪŋk] *s.* clavel; color de rosa; **in the** — **of
condition** en la mejor condición; *adj.* rosado,
color de rosa.
pin·na·cle [pínəkl] *s.* pináculo, cumbre.
pint [paɪnt] *s.* pinta (*aproximadamente medio litro*).
pi·o·neer [paɪənír] *s.* explorador, colonizador;
fundador, iniciador, precursor; pionero; *v.*
explorar, colonizar; fundar, promover.
pi·ous [páɪəs] *adj.* pío, piadoso.
pipe [paɪp] *s.* pipa (*de fumar*); tubo, caño; cañón
(*de órgano*); caramillo, flauta; — **line** cañería,
tubería; oleoducto (*petróleo*); *v.* conducir por
cañerías; desaguar por cañería; proveer de
tuberías o cañerías; chillar; **to** — **down** bajar la
voz.
pip·er [páɪpɚ] *s.* gaitero, flautista.
pip·ing [páɪpɪŋ] *s.* cañería, tubería; cordoncillo (*de
adorno para costuras*); chillido, silbido; *adj.*
agudo, chillón; — **hot** muy caliente; hirviendo.
pip·pin [pípɪn] *s.* camuesa.
pique [pik] *s.* enojo, resentimiento; *v.* picar, excitar;
enojar, irritar; **to** — **oneself on** picarse de,
preciarse de.
pi·rate [páɪrət] *s.* pirata; *v.* piratear; plagiar.
pis·tol [pístl] *s.* pistola; revólver.
pis·ton [pístn] *s.* pistón, émbolo; — **ring** aro de
pistón; — **rod** vástago del émbolo.
pit [pɪt] *s.* hoyo; foso; hueso (*de ciertas frutas*);
— **of the stomach** boca del estómago.
pitch [pɪtʃ] *s.* (*throw*) tiro, lanzamiento (*de una
pelota*); cabezada (*de un barco*); (*music*)
diapasón, tono; (*inclination*) grado, declive,
grado de inclinación; pez (*f.*), brea; resina;
— **dark** oscurísimo; *v.* tirar, lanzar, arrojar;
cabecear (*un barco*); graduar el tono de (*un
instrumento o voz*); echarse de cabeza; inclinarse;
to — **a tent** armar una tienda de campaña;
acampar; **to** — **into** arremeter contra; reprender,
regañar; — **in!** ¡manos a la obra!
pitch·er [pítʃɚ] *s.* cántaro, jarro o jarra; tirador,
lanzador (*en béisbol*).
pitch·fork [pítʃfork] *s.* horca, horquilla (*para
hacinar* las mieses, levantar la paja, etc.).
pit·e·ous [pítɪəs] *adj.* lastimero, lastimoso.
pith [pɪθ] *s.* meollo, médula; esencia, sustancia.
pit·i·ful [pítɪfəl] *adj.* lastimoso; lamentable;
miserable.
pit·i·less [pítɪlɪs] *adj.* despiadado, incompasivo,
cruel.
pit·y [pítɪ] *s.* piedad; lástima; compasión; **for** -**'s
sake** por piedad, por Dios; **what a** —! ¡qué
lástima!; *v.* compadecer; tener lástima por;
apiadarse de, tener piedad de.
plac·ard [plækɑrd] *s.* letrero, cartel; *v.* fijar carteles.
place [ples] *s.* (*site*) lugar, sitio; localidad;

PE

(*position*) puesto; empleo; posición; *Col.* cupo; — **of business** oficina, despacho; — **of worship** templo, iglesia; **market** — plaza, mercado; **in** — **of** en lugar de, en vez de; **it is not my** — **to do it** no es mi deber hacerlo, no me toca a mí hacerlo; *v.* colocar; situar; poner; acomodar, dar empleo a.

plac·id [plǽsɪd] *adj.* plácido, apacible, sosegado.

pla·gia·rism [plédʒərɪzəm] *s.* plagio.

plague [pleg] *s.* plaga; peste, pestilencia; calamidad; *v.* plagar, infestar; importunar.

plaid [plæd] *s.* tartán, tela a cuadros; manta escocesa a cuadros; diseño a cuadros; *adj.* a cuadros.

plain [plen] *adj.* (*flat*) llano; (*simple*) sencillo; claro; franco; ordinario; — **fool** tonto de capriote; — **woman** mujer sin atractivo; **in** — **sight** en plena vista; **plain-clothes man** detectivo; *adv.* claramente; — **stupid** completamente estúpido; **plain-spoken** franco, francote, sincero; *s.* llano, llanura.

plain·tiff [pléntɪf] *s.* demandante.

plain·tive [pléntɪv] *adj.* lastimero, triste.

plan [plæn] *s.* plan; proyecto; plano (*dibujo o mapa*); *v.* planear; proyectar, idear; pensar, proponerse.

plane [plen] *s.* (*airplane*) avión; aeroplano; (*surface*) plano, superficie plana; cepillo (*de carpintero*); *adj.* plano, llano; — **tree** plátano falso; *v.* acepillar, alisar con cepillo (*la madera o los metales*).

plan·et [plǽnɪt] *s.* planeta.

plan·e·tar·i·um [plænətériəm] *s.* planetario.

plank [plæŋk] *s.* table, tablón; principio, base (*del programa de un partido político*); *v.* entablar, entarimar, cubrir con tablas; asar (*carne*) en una tabla.

plank·ton [plǽŋktən] *s.* plancton.

plant [plænt] *s.* (*vegetation*) planta; (*industry*) fábrica; taller; *v.* plantar; sembrar; implantar; establecer.

plan·ta·tion [plæntéʃən] *s.* plantación; haciendo; plantío; sembrado; **coffee** — cafetal; **cotton** — algodonal; **rubber** — cauchal; **sugar** — ingenio de azúcar.

plant·er [plǽntɚ] *s.* plantador, cultivador.

plaque [plæk] *s.* placa.

plas·ma [plǽzmə] *s.* plasma.

plas·ter [plǽstɚ] *s.* yeso; emplasto; — **of Paris** yeso, yeso mate; **court** — esparadrapo, tafetán inglés; **mustard** — sinapismo; *v.* enyesar; emplastar, poner emplastos a; pegar (*carteles, anuncios*); embarrar.

plas·tic [plǽstɪk] *adj.* plástico.

plat [plæt] *s.* plano; parcela; *v.* levantar o trazar un plano.

plate [plet] *s.* (*eating*) plato; (*metal*) placa; plancha; lámina; **dental** — dentadura postiza; *v.* platear; dorar; niquelar; blindar, proteger con planchas de metal; laminar.

pla·teau [plætó] *s.* antiplanicie, mesa, meseta.

plat·ed [plétəd] *adj.* chapeado; blindado.

plate·ful [plétfʊl] *s.* plato, plato lleno.

plat·form [plǽtfɔrm] *s.* plataforma; tablado; programa de un partido político; **railway** — andén.

plat·i·num [plǽtṇəm] *s.* platino.

plat·i·tude [plǽtətjud] *s.* lugar común, perogrullada.

plat·ter [plǽtɚ] *s.* platel, platón.

play [ple] *v.* (*game*) jugar; juguetear; (*instrument*)

tocar; (*drama*) representar; hacer, desempeñar (*un papel*); manipular (*un instrumento, radio, fonógrafo, etc.*); **to** — **a joke** hacer una broma, dar un chasco; **to** — **cards** jugar a los naipes, jugar a la baraja; **to** — **havoc** hacer estragos, causar daño; **to** — **tennis** jugar al tenis; **to** — **the fool** hacerse el tonto, fingirse tonto; **to be all -ed out** no poder más, estar agotado; *s.* juego; jugada (*acción, movimiento en un juego*); pieza, drama, comedia, representación; recreación, diversión; — **on words** juego de palabras, equívoco; **to give full** — **to** dar rienda suelta a.

play·er [pléɚ] *s.* (*games*) jugador; (*music*) músico; (*plays*) cómico, actor; artista; — **piano** piano mecánico, pianola; **piano** — pianista; **violin** — violinista.

play·ful [pléfəl] *adj.* juguetón, retozón; bromista.

play·ground [plégraʊnd] *s.* campo o patio de recreo.

play·mate [plémet] *s.* compañero de juego.

play·thing [pléθɪŋ] *s.* juguete.

play·wright [pléraɪt] *s.* dramático, dramaturgo.

plea [pli] *s.* súplica; ruego; alegato, defensa; pretexto; **on the** — **that** con el pretexto de que.

plead [plid] *v.* abogar; suplicar; argüir; alegar; defender (*una causa*); **to** — **guilty** declararse o confesarse culpable.

pleas·ant [plézṇt] *adj.* grato; agradable; simpático.

pleas·ant·ry [plézṇtrɪ] *s.* chanza, broma, chiste, humorada.

please [pliz] *v.* agradar, gustar, dar gusto a; complacer; — **do it** haga Vd. el favor de hacerlo, tenga Vd. la bondad de hacerlo, sírvase hacerlo; **as you** — como Vd. quiera, como Vd. guste; **if you** — si me hace Vd. (el) favor; **to be -ed to** complacerse en, tener gusto en; alegrarse de; **to be -ed with** gustarle a uno, estar satisfecho de (*o con*).

pleas·ing [plizɪŋ] *adj.* agradable.

pleas·ure [pléʒɚ] *s.* placer, gusto; deleite, alegría, gozo; — **trip** viaje de recreo; **what is your** —? ¿qué deseaba Vd.? ¿en qué puedo servirle?

pleat [plit] *s.* pliegue, doblez; *v.* plegar, hacer pliegues (en).

ple·be·ian [plɪbíən] *adj.* & *s.* plebeyo.

pledge [pledʒ] *s.* promesa; prenda (*garantía*); fianza; **as a** — **of** en prenda de; *v.* prometer; empeñar, dar en prenda; hacer firmar una promesa; **to** — **one's word** empeñar (*o dar*) su palabra; **to** — **to secrecy** exigir promesa de sigilo.

ple·na·ry [plénərɪ] *adj.* plenario.

plen·i·po·ten·ti·ar·y [plɛnəpəténʃərɪ] *adj.* & *s.* plenipotenciario.

plen·ti·ful [pléntɪfəl] *adj.* abundante, copioso.

plen·ty [pléntɪ] *s.* abundancia, copia; — **of time** bastante tiempo; **that is** — con eso basta, basta.

pleu·ri·sy [plúrəsɪ] *s.* pleuresía.

pli·a·ble [pláɪəbḷ] *adj.* flexible; manejable, dócil; transigente.

pli·ant [pláɪənt] *adj.* flexible; dócil, sumiso.

pli·ers [pláɪɚz] *s. pl.* alicates, tenazas.

plight [plaɪt] *s.* apuro, aprieto, situación difícil.

plod [plad] *v.* bregar, trafagar, afanarse, trabajar asiduamente.

plo·sive [plósɪv] *adj.* & *s.* oclusivo.

plot [plat] *s.* (*outline*) trama, enredo; argumento; (*conspiracy*) complot, conspiración; (*land*) parcela (*de tierra*), solar; (*plan*) plano, diagrama; *v.* tramar, urdir; maquinar, conspirar; hacer el

plano o diagrama de; **to — a curve** hacer una gráfica.
plot·ter [plátɚ] s. conspirador; tramador; conjurado.
plough = **plow.**
plow [plaʊ] s. arado; —**share** reja de arado; v. arar; surcar.
pluck [plʌk] v. coger; arrancar; desplumar (un ave); puntear (las cuerdas de una guitarra); **to — at** tirar de; **to — up** arrancar; cobrar ánimo; s. ánimo, valor; tirón.
pluck·y [plʌ́kɪ] adj. valeroso, animoso.
plug [plʌg] s. (stopper) taco, tapón; (horse) caballejo, penco; (boost) elogio incidental (de un producto comercial o de una persona); **— of tobacco** tableta de tabaco; **electric —** clavija de conexión; **fire —** boca de agua para incendios; **spark —** bujía; v. tapar; **to — along** afanarse, atarearse; **to — in** enchufar, conectar; **to — up** tapar, obstruir.
plum [plʌm] s. (fruit) ciruela; (prize) la cosa mejor; la mejor colocación; **— pudding** pudín inglés con pasas; **— tree** ciruelo.
plum·age [plúmɪdʒ] s. plumaje.
plumb [plʌm] s. plomo, pesa de plomo; sonda; **out of —** no vertical; adj. vertical, a plomo, recto; **— bob** plomo, plomada; adv. a plomo, verticalmente; **— crazy** completamente loco; v. sondear; aplomar (una pared).
plumb·er [plʌ́mɚ] s. plomero.
plumb·ing [plʌ́mɪŋ] s. plomería; cañerías (de un edificio); oficio de plomero.
plume [plum] s. pluma; plumaje; penacho; v. adornar con plumas; **to — its wing** alisarse o componerse el plumaje del ala.
plump [plʌmp] adj. rechoncho, regordete, rollizo; adv. de golpe; v. **to — down** dejar(se) caer; desplomarse, sentarse de golpe.
plun·der [plʌ́ndɚ] s. pillaje, saqueo; botín; v. pillar; saquear.
plunge [plʌndʒ] v. zambullir(se), sumergir(se); hundir(se); lanzar(se), arrojar(se), precipitar(se); **to — headlong** echarse de cabeza; s. zambullida; salto (de arriba abajo).
plunk [plʌŋk] v. (instrument) puntear; (place) arrojar.
plu·ral [plúrəl] adj. & s. plural.
plu·ral·i·ty [plʊrǽlɪtɪ] s. pluralidad.
plus [plʌs] s. más, signo más; **— quantity** cantidad positiva; **two — three** dos más tres.
plush [plʌʃ] s. felpa; velludo.
Plu·to [plúto] s. Plutón.
plu·ton·ic [plutánɪk] adj. plutónico.
ply [plaɪ] v. manejar con tesón (un instrumento o herramienta); importunar (con preguntas); hacer con regularidad un recorrido (entre dos puntos); **to — a trade** seguir o ejercer un oficio; **to — oneself with** saturarse de, rellenarse de; s. doblez, pliegue; capa (de tejido, goma, etc.).
pneu·mat·ic [njumǽtik] adj. neumático.
pneu·mo·nia [njumónjə] s. pulmonía.
poach [potʃ] v. escalfar (huevos); invadir (un vedado); cazar o pescar en vedado; robar caza o pesca (de un vedado).
pock·et [pákɪt] s. bolsillo, faltriquera, C.A. bolsa; tronera (de billar); cavidad; hoyo; v. embolsarse; apropiarse; ocultar (el orgullo o rencor); aguantar (un insulto).
pock·et·book [pákɪtbʊk] s. cartera; portamonedas; **woman's —** bolsa.
pock·et·knife [pákɪtnaɪf] s. navaja; cortaplumas.

pod [pɑd] s. vaina (de guisante, frijol, etc.).
po·di·um [pódɪəm] s. podio.
po·em [póɪm] s. poema, poesía.
po·et [pó̜ɪt] s. poeta; vate.
po·et·ess [póɪtɪs] s. poetisa.
po·et·ic [poétɪk] adj. poético; **-s** s. arte poética, poética.
po·et·i·cal [poétɪkl] adj. poético.
po·et·ry [póɪtrɪ] s. poesía.
poign·ant [póɪnjənt] adj. intenso; picante.
point [pɔɪnt] s. punto; punta (de lápiz, espada, tierra, etc.); **it is not to the —** no viene al caso; **not to see the —** no caer en la cuenta; no ver el chiste, propósito o intención; **on the — of a** punto de; v. apuntar; señalar; indicar; **to — out** señalar, mostrar, indicar.
point·blank [pɔɪntblǽŋk] adj. a quema ropa.
point·ed [pɔ́ɪntɪd] adj. puntiagudo, agudo; satírico; apto; a propósito, al caso; **— arch** arco apuntado, arco ojival.
point·er [pɔ́ɪntɚ] s. (indicator) puntero; indicador, señalador; (dog) perro de punta y vuelta; (advice) indicación, consejo.
poise [pɔɪz] s. equilibrio; porte, compostura; v. equilibrar(se); balancear(se).
poi·son [pɔ́ɪzn] s. veneno; ponzoña; v. envenenar, emponzoñar.
poi·son·ous [pɔ́ɪznəs] adj. venenoso, ponzoñoso.
poke [pok] v. atizar, remover (el fuego); picar (con el dedo o cualquier objeto puntiagudo); **to — along** andar perezosamente; **to — around** husmear, curiosear; **to — fun at** burlarse de; **to — into** meter en; **to — out** sacar; proyectarse; s. pinchazo; piquete; codazo; aguijonada; **slow —** tardón.
po·lar [pólɚ] adj. polar; **— bear** oso blanco.
po·lar·i·ty [polǽrɪtɪ] s. polaridad.
po·lar·i·za·tion [polərɪzéʃən] s. polarización.
pole [pol] s. poste; pértiga, palo largo; asta (de bandera); garrocha; polo; **Pole** polaco; **north —** polo norte, polo ártico; **south —** polo sur, polo antártico; **— vault** salto con garrocha (pértiga).
po·lem·ics [polémɪks] s. polémica.
po·lice [pəlís] s. policía; v. vigilar; guardar el orden; adj. policíaco.
po·lice·man [pəlísmən] s. policía (m.), guardia de policía, polizonte, Ven., Col. vigilante, Méx. gendarme, Ch. carabinero.
pol·i·cy [páləsɪ] s. política; **insurance —** póliza de seguro.
Po·lish [pólɪʃ] adj. polaco; s. polaco, idioma polaco.
pol·ish [pálɪʃ] s. pulimento; lustre, brillo; urbanidad, cultura; **shoe —** betún, bola; v. pulir, pulimentar; dar brillo o lustre a; embolar, dar bola o brillo a (zapatos); adj. pulidor.
po·lite [pəláɪt] adj. cortés, fino, urbano, político.
po·lite·ness [pəláɪtnɪs] s. cortesía; fineza, urbanidad.
pol·i·tic [pálətɪk] adj. político, prudente; conveniente.
po·lit·i·cal [pəlítɪkl] adj. político.
pol·i·ti·cian [palətíʃən] s. político; politicastro.
pol·i·tics [pálətɪks] s. política.
poll [pol] s. votación; lista electoral; **-s** comicios; urnas electorales; casilla (donde se vota); **— tax** impuesto (de tanto por cabeza); v. registrar los votos de; votar; recibir (votos).
pol·len [pálən] s. polen.
pol·li·nate [pálənet] v. polinizar.
po·lo [pólo] s. polo.

PL

po·lo·ni·um [pəlóniəm] s. polonio.
pol·y·glot [pálɪglɑt] s. políglota.
pome·gran·ate [pʌmgrǽnɪt] s. granada; — tree granado.
pomp [pɑmp] s. pompa, boato.
pom·pous [pámpəs] adj. pomposa, ostentoso.
pond [pɑnd] s. charca; estanque; fish — vivero.
pon·der [pándə·] v. ponderar, pesar, examinar; to — over reflexionar.
pon·der·ous [pándərɛs] adj. ponderoso; pesado.
pon·toon [pɑntún] s. pontón, chata, barco chato; flotador (de hidroavión); — bridge pontón, puente flotante.
po·ny [póni] s. caballito, potrillo; clave o traducción (usada ilícitamente en un examen).
poo·dle [púdl] s. perro de lanas.
pool [pul] s. charco; charca; trucos (juego parecido al billar); polla o puesta (en ciertos juegos); fondos en común, combinación de fondos (para una empresa o para especular); "trust"; swimming — piscina; v. formar una polla; combinar fondos.
poor [pUr] adj. pobre; malo; de mala calidad; — student estudiante pobre; mal estudiante; — little thing pobrecito; the — los pobres; -ly adv. pobremente; mal.
poor·house [púrhaUs] s. hospicio, casa de probes.
pop [pɑp] s. tronido, trueno, estallido; detonación; — of a cork taponazo; soda — gaseosa; v. reventar, estallar; detonar; saltar (un tapón); to — a question espetar una pregunta; to — corn hacer palomitas de maíz, hacer rosetas de maíz; to — in and out entrar y salir de sopetón; to — one's head out sacar o asomar de repente la cabeza.
pop·corn [pápkɔrn] s. rosetas, palomitas de maíz, Andes alborotos; Ch. cabritas; Méx. esquite.
Pope [pop] s. Papa.
pop·eyed [pápaɪd] adj. de ojos saltones, Am. desorbitado.
pop·lar [páplə·] s. álamo; black — chopo; — grove alameda.
pop·py [pápɪ] s. amapola.
pop·u·lace [pápjəlɪs] s. pueblo, populacho.
pop·u·lar [pápjələ·] adj. popular.
pop·u·lar·i·ty [pɑpjelǽrətɪ] s. popularidad.
pop·u·late [pápjələt] v. poblar.
pop·u·la·tion [pɑpjeléʃən] s. población.
pop·u·lous [pápjələs] adj. populoso.
por·ce·lain [pórslɪn] s. porcelana.
porch [pórtʃ] s. pórtico, porche; galería.
por·cu·pine [pɔ́rkjəpaɪn] s. puerco espín.
pore [por] s. poro; v. to — over a book engolfarse en la lectura.
pork [pɔrk] s. puerco, carne de puerco — chop chuleta de puerco; salt — tocino salado.
por·nog·ra·phy [pɔrnágrəfɪ] s. pornografía.
po·rous [pórəs] adj. poroso.
por·ridge [pórɪdʒ] s. potaje, gachas.
port [pɔrt] s. (harbor) puerto; (wine) oporto; (left side) babor (de un barco); —hole porta, portilla.
port·a·ble [pórtəbl] adj. portátil.
por·tal [pórtl] s. portal.
por·tent [pórtɛnt] s. portento, presagio, agüero.
por·ten·tous [pɔrtɛ́ntəs] adj. portentoso; prodigioso; de mal agüero.
por·ter [pórtə·] s. mozo de cordel, Méx., C.A. cargador; Ríopl. changador; camarero (en un coche-cama); portero.
port·fo·li·o [portfólɪo] s. portafolio, cartera; carpeta; ministerio.

por·tion [pórʃən] s. porción; v. repartir.
port·ly [pórtlɪ] adj. corpulento.
por·trait [pórtret] s. retrato.
por·tray [pɔrtré] v. retratar, pintar, dibujar, representar.
por·tray·al [pɔrtreəl] s. retrato, delineación, delineamiento, representación.
Por·tu·guese [pórtʃəgiz] adj. & s. portugués.
pose [poz] s. (posture) postura, actitud; (affected attitude) afectación; v. posar (como modelo); colocar(se) en cierta postura; afectar una actitud o postura; proponer, plantear (una cuestión o problema); to — as fingirse, hacerse pasar por.
po·si·tion [pəzíʃən] s. posición; postura; situación, empleo, puesto.
pos·i·tive [pázətɪv] adj. positivo; cierto, seguro; categórico; dogmático.
pos·sess [pəzɛ́s] v. poseer.
pos·ses·sion [pəzɛ́ʃən] s. posesión.
pos·ses·sive [pəzɛ́sɪv] adj. & s. posesivo.
pos·ses·sor [pəzɛ́sə·] s. poseedor, posesor, dueño.
pos·si·bil·i·ty [pɑsəbílətɪ] s. posibilidad.
pos·si·ble [pásəbl] adj. posible; possibly adv. posiblemente; acaso, tal vez.
post [post] s. (pole) poste, pilar; (position) puesto; empleo; army — guarnición militar; — haste por la posta, rápidamente; — office correo, casa de correos; post-office box apartado, casilla postal; —paid porte pagado, franco de porte; v. fijar (anuncios, carteles); anunciar; poner en lista; apostar, situar; echar al correo; to — an entry asentar o hacer un asiento (en teneduría); to be well -ed estar al corriente, estar bien enterado.
post·age [póstɪdʒ] s. porte, franqueo; — stamp sello de correo, Am. estampilla, Méx., Ríopl. timbre.
post·al [póstl] adj. postal; — card tarjeta postal; — money order giro postal.
post·card [póstkard] s. tarjeta postal.
post·er [póstə·] s. cartel, cartelón; fijador de carteles.
pos·te·ri·or [pastírɪə·] adj. posterior; trasero.
pos·ter·i·ty [pastérətɪ] s. posteridad.
post·hu·mous [póstʃUməs] adj. póstumo.
post·man [póstmən] s. cartero.
post·mas·ter [póstmæstə·] s. administrador de correos.
post·pone [postpón] v. posponer; aplazar, diferir; postergar.
post·pone·ment [postpónmənt] s. aplazamiento.
post·script [pósskrɪpt] s. posdata.
pos·ture [pástʃə·] s. postura, actitud; posición; v. adoptar una postura.
po·sy [pózɪ] s. flor.
pot [pɑt] s. pote; olla, puchero, cacharro (de cocina); bacín, bacinica (de cámara o recámara); flower — tiesto, maceta; —bellied panzudo, barrigón; — hole bache.
po·tas·si·um [pətǽsɪəm] s. potasio.
po·ta·to [pətéto] s. patata, papa; sweet — batata, Méx., C.A., Ch., Andes camote, Carib., Ríopl. boniato.
po·ten·cy [pótnsɪ] s. potencia, poder, fuerza.
po·tent [pótnt] adj. potente, poderoso, fuerte.
po·ten·tate [pótntet] s. potentado.
po·ten·tial [pəténʃəl] adj. & s. potencial.
pot·pour·ri [popurí] s. popurrí.
pot·tage [pátɪdʒ] s. potaje.
pot·ter [pátə·] s. alfarero, fabricante de vasijas o cacharros de barro; —'s field cementerio de

pobres y desconocidos.

pot·ter·y [pátərı] s. cerámica, alfarería; vasijas de barro.

pouch [pautʃ] s. bolsa, saquillo; **mail** — valija; **tobacco** — tabaquera, petaca.

poul·tice [póltıs] s. emplasto.

poul·try [póltrı] s. aves de corral.

pounce [pauns] s. salto (*para agarrar*); zarpada; *v.* **to** — **into** entrar de sopetón; **to** — **upon** abalanzarse sobre, saltar sobre, agarrar.

pound [paund] s. libra; golpazo; — **sterling** libra esterlina; *v.* golpear; machacar, martillar.

pour [por] *v.* vaciar, verter; servir (*una taza*); fluir; llover a cántaros, llover recio.

pout [paut] *v.* hacer pucheros, lloriquear; poner cara de enfado; s. puchero, pucherito.

pov·er·ty [pávətı] s. pobreza.

pow·der [páudɚ] s. polvo; pólvora (*explosivo*); polvos (*de tocador*); — **compact** polvera; — **magazine** polvorín; — **puff** polvera, borla, *Ríopl., Ch.* cisne, *Méx., Andes* mota; *v.* empolvar(se); polvorear, espolvorear; pulverizar(se); **to** — **one's face** empolvarse la cara, ponerse polvos.

pow·er [páuɚ] s. poder; poderío; potencia; fuerza; **motive** — fuerza motriz; — **of attorney** poder; — **plant** planta de fuerza motriz.

pow·er·ful [páuɚfəl] adj. poderoso.

pow·er·less [páuɚlıs] adj. impotente.

prac·ti·ca·ble [prǽktıkəbl] adj. practicable; factible, hacedero; práctico; — **road** camino transitable.

prac·ti·cal [prǽktıkl] adj. práctico; — **joke** chasco, burla pesada; **-ly** adv. casi, virtualmente; realmente, en realidad; prácticamente.

prac·tice [prǽktıs] s. práctica; ejercicio (*de una profesión*); método; regla, costumbre; clientela; *v.* practicar; ejercer (*una profesión*); ejercitarse.

prac·ticed [prǽktıst] adj. práctico, experimentado; experto, perito.

prac·ti·tion·er [prǽktıʃənɚ] s. profesional; práctico.

prai·rie [prérı] s. pradera, llanura.

praise [prez] s. alabanza; elogio; encomio; *v.* alabar; elogiar; encomiar.

praise·wor·thy [prézwɝ̌ðı] adj. laudable.

prance [præns] *v.* cabriolar, hacer cabriolas.

prank [præŋk] s. travesura, burla; **to play -s** hacer travesuras.

prate [pret] *v.* parlotear, charlar; s. parloteo, charla.

prat·tle [prǽtl] *v.* parlotear, charlar; s. parloteo, charla.

pray [pre] *v.* orar, rezar; rogar, suplicar; — **tell me** dígame por favor, le ruego que me diga.

prayer [prɛr] s. oración, rezo; ruego, súplica; — **book** devocionario; **Lord's** — Padre Nuestro.

preach [pritʃ] *v.* predicar; sermonear.

preach·er [pritʃɚ] s. predicador.

preach·ing [pritʃıŋ] s. predicación; sermón; sermoneo.

pre·am·ble [príæmbl] s. preámbulo.

pre·ar·ranged [priərǽndʒd] adj. arreglado de antemano.

pre·car·i·ous [prıkérıəs] adj. precario; inseguro.

pre·cau·tion [prıkóʃən] s. precaución.

pre·cede [prisíd] *v.* preceder.

pre·ce·dence [prısídns] s. precedencia; prioridad.

pre·ce·dent [présədənt] s. precedente.

pre·ced·ing [prisídıŋ] adj. precendente, anterior.

pre·cept [prisεpt] s. precepto.

pre·cinct [prísıŋkt] s. distrito; recinto; **-s** límites, inmediaciones.

pre·cious [préʃəs] adj. precioso; querido, amado,

caro; — **little** poquísimo, muy poco.

prec·i·pice [présəpıs] s. precipicio.

pre·cip·i·tate [prısípətet] *v.* precipitar(se); adj. precipitado, apresurado, atropellado; s. precipitado.

pre·cip·i·ta·tion [prısıpətéʃən] s. precipitación; lluvia (*o* nieve, rocío, granizo, *etc.*); cantidad de agua pluvial.

pre·cip·i·tous [prısípətəs] adj. precipitoso, excarpado; precipitado.

pre·cise [prısáıs] adj. preciso, exacto.

pre·ci·sion [prısíʒən] s. precisión, exactitud.

pre·clude [prıklúd] *v.* excluir; impedir.

pre·co·cious [prıkóʃəs] adj. precoz.

pre·cur·sor [prıkɚsɚ] s. precursor.

pred·e·ces·sor [prεdısέsɚ] s. predecesor.

pre·des·tine [prıdéstın] *v.* predestinar.

pre·dic·a·ment [prıdíkəmənt] s. aprieto, apuro, dificultad.

pred·i·cate [prédıkıt] adj. & s. predicado.

pre·dict [prıdíkt] *v.* predecir, vaticinar.

pre·dic·tion [prıdíkʃən] s. predicción, pronóstico, vaticinio.

pre·di·lec·tion [prıdļékʃən] s. predilección, preferencia.

pre·dis·pose [prıdıspóz] *v.* predisponer.

pre·dom·i·nance [prıdámənəns] s. predominio; ascendiente.

pre·dom·i·nant [prıdámənənt] adj. predominante.

pre·dom·i·nate [prıdámənet] *v.* predominar.

pref·ace [préfıs] s. prefacio; prólogo; *v.* prologar.

pre·fect [prifεkt] s. prefecto.

pre·fer [prıfɝ̌] *v.* preferir; **to** — **a claim** presentar una demanda.

pref·er·a·ble [préfrəbl] adj. preferible; preferente; **pref·er·a·bly** adv. preferiblemente; preferentemente, de preferencia.

pref·er·ence [préfrəns] s. preferencia.

pre·ferred [prıfɝ̌d] *p.p.* & adj. preferido; — **shares** acciones preferentes.

pre·fix [prifıks] s. prefijo; [prifíks] *v.* prefijar, anteponer.

preg·nan·cy [prέgnənsı] s. preñez, embarazo.

preg·nant [prέgnənt] adj. preñado; embarazada; encinta; lleno, repleto.

pre·hen·sile [prihέnsıl] adj. prensil.

pre·judge [prıdʒʌ́dʒ] *v.* prejuzgar.

prej·u·dice [prέdʒədıs] s. (*preconception*) prejuicio; prevención; (*harm*) daño; *v.* predisponer, prevenir; perjudicar.

prel·ate [prélıt] s. prelado.

pre·lim·i·nar·y [prılímənεrı] adj. & s. preliminar.

prel·ude [préljud] s. preludio; *v.* preludiar.

pre·ma·ture [primətjúr] adj. prematuro.

pre·med·i·tat·ed [primέdətetıd] adj. premeditado.

pre·mier [prímıɚ] s. primer ministro; adj. primero; principal.

prem·ise [prémıs] s. premisa; **-s** terrenos; local.

pre·mi·um [prímıəm] s. premio; **at a** — muy escaso, muy caro; **insurance** — prima de seguro.

pre·na·tal [prinétl] adj. prenatal.

pre·oc·cu·py [priákjəpaı] *v.* preocupar; ocupar de antemano.

pre·or·bit·al [prióɾbıtl] adj. preorbital.

pre·paid [pripéd] adj. pagado de antemano; **to send** — enviar porte pagado, enviar franco de porte.

prep·a·ra·tion [prεpəréʃən] s. preparación; preparativo.

pre·par·a·to·ry [prıpǽrətorı] adj. preparatorio.

pre·pare [prıpér] *v.* preparar(se).

pre·par·ed·ness [prıpérıdnıs] s. preparación,

prevención.
pre·pon·der·ance [pripándȝrəns] s. preponderancia.
pre·pon·der·ant [pripándrənt] adj. preponderante.
prep·o·si·tion [prɛpəzíʃən] s. preposición.
pre·pos·sess [pripozés] v. preocupar; predisponer.
pre·pos·ter·ous [pripástrəs] adj. absurdo, insensato.
pre·req·ui·site [prirékwəzit] s. requisito previo.
pre·rog·a·tive [prirágətiv] s. prerrogativa.
pres·age [présidȝ] s. presagio; [prisédȝ] v. presagiar.
pre·scribe [priskáib] v. prescribir; recetar.
pre·scrip·tion [priskrípʃən] s. recata; prescripción, precepto, mandato.
pres·ence [prézns] s. presencia; — of mind aplomo, serenidad.
pres·ent [préznt] s. (time) presente; (gift) regalo; at — al presente, ahora; for the — por ahora; adj. presente; corriente, actual; — company excepted mejorando lo presente; — participle gerundio; to be — asistir, estar presente; [prizént] v. presentar; regalar, obsequiar.
pres·en·ta·tion [prɛzn̩téʃən] s. presentación; regalo, obsequio.
pre·sen·ti·ment [prizéntəmənt] s. presentimiento; corazonada.
pres·ent·ly [prézn̩tlı] adv. luego, pronto, dentro de poco.
pres·er·va·tion [prɛzəvéʃən] s. preservación; conservación.
pre·serve [prizɝ́v] v. preservar, guardar; conservar; mantener; s. conserva, compota; forest — vedado.
pre·side [prizáid] v. presidir; to — at (— over) a meeting presidir una junta.
pres·i·den·cy [prézədənsı] s. presidencia.
pres·i·dent [prézədənt] s. presidente.
pres·i·den·tial [prɛzədénʃəl] adj. presidencial.
press [prɛs] v. (bear down) prensar; apretar; comprimir; planchar (ropa); (force) forzar; apremiar; urgir; empujar; to — forward empujar hacia adelante; avanzar, ganar terreno; to — one's point porfiar; insistir en su argumento; to — through the crowd abrirse paso por entre la multitud; to be hard -ed by work estar abrumado de trabajo; to be hard -ed for money estar escaso de fondos; s. prensa; imprenta.
press·ing [présıŋ] adj. apremiante, urgente.
pres·sure [préʃə] s. presión; apremio, urgencia; — cooker cocinilla de presión; — gauge manómetro.
pres·sur·ize [préʃəaız] v. sobrecargar.
pres·tige [prestíȝ] s. prestigio.
pre·sum·a·ble [prizúməbl] adj. presumible, probable.
pre·sume [prizúm] v. presumir; suponer; to — on (upon) abusar de; to — to atreverse a.
pre·sump·tion [prizámpʃən] s. presunción; pretensión; suposición.
pre·sump·tu·ous [prizámptʃuəs] adj. presuntuoso, pretencioso, presumido.
pre·sup·pose [prisəpóz] v. presuponer.
pre·tend [priténd] v. pretender; fingir.
pre·tense [priténs] s. pretensión; presunción; ostentación; apariencia; pretexto; under — of so pretexto de.
pre·ten·sion [priténʃən] s. pretensión; pretexto.
pre·ten·tious [priténʃəs] adj. pretencioso.
pre·text [prítɛkst] s. pretexto.
pret·ti·ly [prítılı] adv. lindamente; agradablemente.
pret·ti·ness [prítınıs] s. lindeza, gracia.
pret·ty [príti] adj. lindo, bonito, bello, Am. chulo; adv. medianamente; bastante; un poco, algo; —

well regular, así así; bastante bien, medianamente.
pre·vail [privél] v. prevalecer; to — on (upon) persuadir.
pre·vail·ing [privélıŋ] adj. predominante; en boga.
prev·a·lent [prévələnt] adj. prevaleciente; común, corriente.
pre·vent [privént] v. prevenir, evitar; impedir; estorbar.
pre·ven·tion [privénʃən] s. prevención; precaución.
pre·ven·tive [privéntıv] adj. impeditivo.
pre·view [prívju] s. vista previa (anticipada).
pre·vi·ous [prívıəs] adj. previo; -ly adv. previamente; antes; de antemano.
prey [pre] s. presa; victima; birds of — aves de rapiña; v. to — on cazar; rapiñar, pillar; robar; it -s upon my mind me tiene preocupado, me tiene en zozobra.
price [prais] s. precio; valor; costo (coste o costa); at any — a toda costa, a todo trance; v. apreciar, valuar, fijar el precio de; averiguar el precio de.
price·less [práislıs] adj. sin precio, inapreciable.
prick [prık] v. picar; pinchar; punzar; sentir comezón; sentir picazón; to — up one's ears aguzar las orejas; s. picadura; punzada; pinchazo; piquete; aguijón; púa.
prick·ly [príklı] adj. espinoso, lleno de espinas; lleno de púas; — heat picazón causada por el calor; — pear tuna (de nopal).
pride [praid] s. orgullo; soberbia; v. to — oneself on (upon) enorgullecerse de, preciarse de.
priest [prist] s. sacerdote.
priest·hood [prísthud] s. sacerdocio.
prim [prım] adj. remilgado; repulido; peripuesto; estirado.
pri·mar·i·ly [praimérəlı] adv. primariamente, principalmente; en primer lugar.
pri·ma·ry [práimɛrı] adj. (first) primario; primero; (basic) fundamental; principal; — colors colores elementales; — election elección primaria; — school escuela primaria.
prime [praim] adj. (main) principal; primario, primero; (select) selecto, de primera calidad; — minister primer ministro; — number número primo; s. flor (de la vida o de la edad); la flor y nata (lo mejor); plenitud; número primo; to be in one's — estar en la flor de la edad; v. preparar, informar, instruir de atemano; cebar (un carburador, bomba o arma de fuego).
prim·er [prímə] s. abecedario, cartilla de lectura; compendio.
pri·me·val [praimívl] adj. primitivo.
prim·i·tive [prímətıv] adj. primitivo.
prim·ness [prímnıs] s. remilgo, tiesura, demasiada formalidad; dengue, afectación.
primp [prımp] v. acicalar(se), adornar(se), arreglar(se).
prim·rose [prímroz] s. prímula o primavera (flor); color amarillo pálido.
prince [prıns] s. príncipe.
prince·ly [prínslı] adj. noble, regio, magnífico, propio de un príncipe.
prin·cess [prínsıs] s. princesa.
prin·ci·pal [prínsəpl] adj. principal; s. principal, capital; principal, jefe, director.
prin·ci·ple [prínsəpl] s. principio; regla, ley; fundamento, base.
print [prınt] s. (type) tipo, letra de molde; (art) lámina, grabado; estampado (tejido estampado); diseño (estampado); impresión; in — impreso,

publicado; **out of** — agotado; *v.* imprimir; estampar; escribir en letra de molde; **-ed fabric** estampado.

print·er [príntɚ] *s.* impresor.

print·ing [príntɪŋ] *s.* imprenta; impresión; tipografía; — **office** imprenta; — **press** prensa.

pri·or [práɪɚ] *adj.* previo, anterior, precedente; — **to** anterior a, con antelación a; *s.* prior (*de un monasterio*).

pri·or·i·ty [praɪɔ́rətɪ] *s.* prioridad, precedencia, antelación.

prism [prízəm] *s.* prisma.

pris·on [prízṇ] *s.* prisión, cárcel; *v.* encarcelar.

pris·on·er [prízṇɚ] *s.* prisionero, preso.

pri·va·cy [práɪvəsɪ] *s.* secreto, reserva; retiro; **to have no** — carecer de sitio privado; estar a la vista del público.

pri·vate [práɪvɪt] *adj.* privado; personal; particular; secreto; confidencial; **a** — **citizen** un particular; — **school** escuela particular; *s.* soldado raso; **in** — en secreto; a solas, privadamente.

pri·va·tion [praɪvéʃən] *s.* privación.

priv·i·lege [prívlɪdʒ] *s.* privilegio.

priv·i·leged [prívlɪdʒd] *adj.* privilegiado; **to be** — **to** tener el privilegio de.

priv·y [prívɪ] *adj.* privado; enterado de; *s.* excusado exterior.

prize [praɪz] *s.* (*reward*) premio, galardón; (*booty*) presa, botín de guerra; — **fight** boxeo público, pugilato; — **fighter** boxeador, pugilista; — **medal** medalla de premio; *v.* apreciar, estimar, tener en gran estima.

prob·a·bil·i·ty [prabəbílətɪ] *s.* probabilidad.

prob·a·ble [prábəbḷ] *adj.* probable; **prob·a·bly** *adv.* probablemente.

pro·ba·tion [probéʃən] *s.* probación; noviciado; prueba; **to put a prisoner on** — poner a un prisionero en libertad bajo la vigilancia de un juez.

probe [prob] *v.* tentar, reconocer, sondear (*una herida*); escudriñar, examinar a fondo; indagar; *s.* tienta (*instrumento de cirujano*); indagación.

prob·lem [prábləm] *s.* problema.

prob·lem·at·i·cal [prabləmǽtɪkḷ] *adj.* problemático.

pro·ce·dure [prəsídʒɚ] *s.* procedimiento; proceder.

pro·ceed [prəsíd] *v.* proceder; proseguir; seguir adelante; **to** — **to** proceder a, comenzar a, ponerse a.

pro·ceed·ing [prəsídɪŋ] *s.* procedimiento; transacción; **-s** transacciones; actas; proceso.

pro·ceeds [prósidz] *s. pl.* producto, ganancia.

proc·ess [prásɛs] *s.* (*series*) proceso; (*method*) procedimiento, método; **in** — **of time** con el transcurso del tiempo, con el tiempo, andando el tiempo; **in the** — **of being made** en vía de preparación; *v.* preparar mediante un procedimiento especial, someter a un procedimiento; procesar (*ante un juez*).

pro·ces·sion [prəséʃən] *s.* procesión; desfile; **funeral** — cortejo fúnebre.

pro·claim [proklém] *v.* proclamar; promulgar.

proc·la·ma·tion [prakləméʃən] *s.* proclamación; proclama.

pro·cliv·i·ty [proklívɪtɪ] *s.* inclinación.

pro·cure [prokjúr] *v.* procurar, conseguir, obtener.

prod [prad] *v.* aguijonear; picar.

prod·i·gal [prádɪgḷ] *adj. & s.* pródigo, gastador.

pro·di·gious [prədídʒəs] *adj.* prodigioso.

prod·i·gy [prádədʒɪ] *s.* prodigio.

pro·duce [prádjus] *s.* producto; productos agrícolas; [prədjús] *v.* producir.

pro·duc·er [prədjúsɚ] *s.* productor; **theatrical** — empresario.

prod·uct [prádəkt] *s.* producto.

pro·duc·tion [prədʌ́kʃən] *s.* producción; producto; obra, composición; representación teatral.

pro·duc·tive [prədʌ́ktɪv] *adj.* productivo.

pro·fa·na·tion [prafənéʃen] *s.* profanación, desacato.

pro·fane [prəfén] *adj.* profano; *v.* profanar.

pro·fess [prəfés] *v.* profesar; pretender.

pro·fes·sion [prəféʃən] *s.* profesión.

pro·fes·sion·al [prəféʃənḷ] *adj.* profesional; *s.* profesional, *Méx.* profesionista.

pro·fes·sor [prəfésɚ] *s.* profesor, catedrático.

prof·fer [práfɚ] *s.* oferta, propuesta; *v.* ofrecer, proponer.

pro·fi·cien·cy [prəfíʃənsɪ] *s.* pericia, destreza.

pro·fi·cient [prəfíʃənt] *adj.* proficiente, perito, experto.

pro·file [prófaɪl] *s.* perfil; contorno.

prof·it [práfɪt] *s.* (*gain*) ganancia; lucro; (*usefulness*) provecho, utilidad, beneficio; — **and loss** pérdidas y ganancias; **net** — ganancia neta o líquida; *v.* aprovechar; ganar, sacar provecho; **to** — **by** aprovecharse de, sacar provecho de.

prof·it·a·ble [práfɪtəbḷ] *adj.* provechoso; lucrativo.

prof·i·teer [prafətír] *s.* extorsionista, carero, explotador, logrero; *v.* extorsionar, explotar, cobrar más de lo justo.

pro·found [prəfáʊnd] *adj.* profundo.

pro·fuse [prəfjús] *adj.* profuso, abundante; pródigo.

prog·e·ny [prádʒenɪ] *s.* prole.

prog·no·sis [pragnósɪs] *s.* pronóstico.

pro·gram [prógræm] *s.* programa; plan.

prog·ress [prágrɛs] *s.* progreso; [prəgrɛ́s] *v.* progresar.

pro·gres·sive [prəgrésɪv] *adj.* progresivo; progresista; *s.* progresista.

pro·hib·it [prohíbɪt] *v.* prohibir; vedar.

pro·hi·bi·tion [proəbíʃən] *s.* prohibición.

proj·ect [prádʒɛkt] *s.* proyecto, plan; [prədʒɛ́kt] *v.* proyectar(se); extender(se) sobresalir.

pro·jec·tile [prədʒɛ́ktḷ] *s.* proyectil; *adj.* arrojadizo; — **weapon** arma arrojadiza.

pro·jec·tion [prədʒɛ́kʃən] *s.* proyección; saliente, salidizo.

pro·jec·tor [prədʒɛ́ktɚ] *s.* proyector.

pro·le·tar·i·an [prolətériən] *adj. & s.* proletario.

pro·le·tar·i·at [prolətériət] *s.* proletariado.

pro·lif·ic [prolífɪk] *adj.* prolífico.

pro·logue [prólɔg] *s.* prólogo.

pro·long [prəlɔ́ŋ] *v.* prolongar.

pro·lon·ga·tion [prolɔŋgéʃən] *s.* prolongación.

prom·e·nade [pramənéd] *s.* paseo; baile (*usualmente* **prom**); *v.* pasearse.

prom·i·nent [prámənənt] *adj.* prominente; notable; saliente; conspicuo.

pro·mis·cu·ous [prəmískjʊəs] *adj.* promiscuo.

prom·ise [prámɪs] *s.* promesa; *v.* prometer; **Promised Land** Tierra de Promisión.

prom·is·ing [prámɪsɪŋ] *adj.* prometedor.

prom·is·so·ry [práməsɔrɪ] *adj.* promisorio; — **note** pagaré.

prom·on·to·ry [práməntɔrɪ] *s.* promontorio.

pro·mote [prəmót] *v.* (*favor*) promover; fomentar; explotar; adelantar; (*raise*) ascender; elevar.

pro·mot·er [prəmótɚ] *s.* promotor, promovedor.

pro·mo·tion [prəmóʃən] *s.* promoción; ascenso; adelantamiento.

prompt [prampt] *adj.* pronto, puntual; listo, presto; *v.* mover, incitar, inducir; apuntar (*servir* de apuntador en el teatro); soplar (sugerir a otro lo que debe decir en una clase o junta).

prompt·ly [prámptlɪ] adv. pronto, prontamente, presto; puntualmente; con prontitud, con presteza.

prompt·ness [prámptnɪs] s. prontitud, presteza; puntualidad.

prom·ul·gate [prəmʌ́lget] v. promulgar.

prone [pron] adj. inclinado; propenso, dispuesto; boca abajo; postrado.

prong [prɔŋ] s. púa, punta.

pro·noun [prónaʊn] s. pronombre.

pro·nounce [prənáʊns] v. pronunciar; declarar.

pro·nounced [prənáʊnst] adj. pronunciado. marcado; — **opinions** opiniones decididas.

pro·nun·ci·a·tion [prənʌnsɪéʃən] s. pronunciación.

proof [pruf] s. prueba; comprobación; adj. impenetrable, resistente; — **against** a prueba de; —**reader** corrector de pruebas de imprenta; — **sheet** prueba, pliego de prueba; **galley** — galerada; **bomb**— a prueba de bomba; **fire** — a prueba de incendios; **water**— impermeable.

prop [prɑp] s. puntal; sostén, apoyo; v. apuntalar, sostener.

prop·a·gan·da [prɑpəgǽndə] s. propaganda.

prop·a·gate [prɑ́pəget] v. propagar(se).

prop·a·ga·tion [prɑpəgéʃen] s. propagación; diseminación.

pro·pel [prəpél] v. populsar, impeler.

pro·pel·ler [prəpélə·] s. hélice (de un buque o avión); propulsor, impulsor.

prop·er [prɑ́pə·] adj. propio; conveniente a propósito; justo; correcto; — **noun** nombre propio; **-ly** adv. propiamente; con propiedad, correctamente.

prop·er·ty [prɑ́pə·tɪ] s. propiedad; posesión; posesiones, bienes.

proph·e·cy [prɑ́fəsɪ] s. profecía.

proph·e·sy [prɑ́fəsaɪ] v. profetizar, predecir, pronosticar, augurar.

proph·et [prɑ́fɪt] s. profeta.

pro·phet·ic [prəfétɪk] adj. profético.

pro·pi·ti·ate [propíʃiet] v. propiciar.

pro·pi·tious [prəpíʃəs] adj. propicio, favorable.

pro·por·tion [prəpórʃən] s. proporción; **out of** — desproporcionado; v. proporcionar; **well -ed** bien proporcionado.

pro·pos·al [prəpózl] s. propuesta; proposición; declaración (de amor).

pro·pose [prəpóz] v. proponer; declararse, hacer propuesta de matrimonio; **to** — **to do something** proponerse hacer algo.

prop·o·si·tion [prɑpəzíʃən] s. proposición; propuesta; asunto.

pro·pri·e·tor [prəprɑ́ɪətə·] s. propietario, dueño.

pro·pri·e·ty [prəprɑ́ɪətɪ] s. propiedad, corrección; decoro.

pro·pul·sion [propʌ́lʃən] s. propulsión.

pro·rate [prorét] v. prorratear, repartir proporcionalmente.

pro·sa·ic [prozéɪk] adj. prosaico.

prose [proz] s. prosa; adj. prosaico.

pros·e·cute [prɑ́sɪkjut] v. procesar, enjuiciar, demandar ante un juez; llevar adelante (un negocio, empresa, demanda, etc.).

pros·e·cu·tion [prɑsɪkjúʃən] s. prosecución; seguimiento; parte acusadora (en un pleito).

pros·e·cu·tor [prɑ́sɪkjutə·] s. fiscal; acusador.

pros·e·lyte [prɑ́səlaɪt] s. prosélito.

pros·pect [prɑ́spɛkt] s. (hope) perspectiva, vista; esperanza; espectativa; (candidate) cliente;

(chances) probabilidad de éxito; v. explorar, andar en busca de.

pro·spec·tive [prəspéktɪv] adj. probable, posible, esperado; presunto.

pros·pec·tor [prəspéktə·] s. explorador, buscador (de minas, petróleo, etc.).

pros·per [prɑ́spə·] v. prosperar, medrar.

pros·per·i·ty [prɑspérətɪ] s. prosperidad.

pros·per·ous [prɑ́sprəs] adj. próspero.

pros·tate [prɑ́stet] s. próstata.

pros·ti·tute [prɑ́stətjut] s. ramera, prostituta; v. prostituir.

pros·trate [prɑ́stret] adj. postrado; abatido; v. postrar; abatir.

pro·tag·o·nist [protǽgənɪst] s. protagonista.

pro·tect [prətékt] v. proteger.

pro·tec·tion [prətékʃen] s. protección; amparo.

pro·tec·tive [prətéktɪv] adj. protector; — **tariff** tarifa proteccionista.

pro·tec·tor [prətéktə·] s. protector.

pro·tec·tor·ate [prətéktrɪt] s. protectorado.

pro·té·gé [prótəge] s. protegido.

pro·tein [prótiin] s. proteína.

pro·test [prótɛst] s. protesta, protestación; [prətést] v. protestar.

prot·es·tant [prɑ́tɪstənt] adj. & s. protestante.

prot·es·ta·tion [prɑtəstéʃən] s. protestación, protesta.

pro·to·col [prótəkɔl] s. protocol.

pro·to·plasm [prótəplæzəm] s. protoplasma.

pro·to·type [prótotaɪp] s. prototipo.

pro·tract [protrǽkt] v. alargar, extender, prolongar.

pro·trude [protrúd] v. sobresalir; resaltar; proyectar(se).

pro·tu·ber·ance [protjúbərəns] s. protuberancia.

proud [praʊd] adj. orgulloso; soberbio.

prove [pruv] v. probar; demostrar; comprobar; resultar.

prov·erb [prɑ́vɜb] s. proverbio; refrán.

pro·vide [prəváɪd] v. proveer; abastecer; suplir; estipular; **to** — **for** hacer provisión para; **to** — **with** proveer de.

pro·vid·ed [prəváɪdɪd] conj. con tal (de) que, a condición (de) que; — **that** con tal (de) que.

prov·i·dence [prɑ́vədəns] s. providencia.

prov·i·den·tial [prɑvədénʃəl] adj. providencial.

pro·vid·er [prəváɪdə·] s. proveedor.

prov·ince [prɑ́vɪns] s. provincia; jurisdicción; **it isn't within my** — no está dentro de mi jurisdicción; no es de mi incumbencia.

pro·vin·cial [prəvínʃəl] adj. provincial; s. provinciano.

pro·vi·sion [prəvíʒən] s. (goods) provision; abastecimiento; (plan) disposición; **-s** provisiones; víveres; **to make the necessary -s** tomar las medidas (o precauciones) necesarias.

pro·vi·so [prəvɑ́ɪzo] s. condición, estipulación.

prov·o·ca·tion [prɑvəkéʃən] s. provocación.

pro·voke [prəvók] v. provocar; irritar; enfadar.

prow [praʊ] s. proa.

prow·ess [práʊɪs] s. proeza.

prowl [praʊl] v. rondar en acecho; fisgonear.

prox·im·i·ty [prɑksímətɪ] s. proximidad.

prox·y [prɑ́ksɪ] s. apoderado, substituto, delegado; **by** — mediante apoderado.

prude [prud] s. mojigato, persona gazmoña.

pru·dence [prúdns] s. prudencia.

pru·dent [prúdņt] adj. prudente.

prud·er·y [prúdərɪ] s. mojigatería, gazmoñería, remilgo.

prud·ish [prúdɪʃ] *adj.* gazmoño, remilgado.
prune [prun] *s.* ciruela; ciruela pasa; *v.* podar, recortar.
pry [praɪ] *v.* atisbar, espiar; fisgar, fisgonear; curiosear; **to — a secret out** extraer (*o* arrancar) un secreto; **to — apart** separar por fuerza; **to — into other people's affairs** entremeterse en lo ajeno; **to — open** abrir a la fuerza; **to — up** levantar con una palanca.
psalm [sɑm] *s.* salmo.
pseu·do·nym [sjúdṇɪm] *s.* seudónimo.
psit·ta·co·sis [sɪtəkósɪs] *s.* psitacósis.
psy·chi·a·trist [saɪkáɪətrɪst] *s.* psiquiatra, alienista.
psy·chi·a·try [saɪkáɪətrɪ] *s.* psiquiatría.
psy·cho·log·i·cal [saɪkəládʒɪkḷ] *adj.* psicológico.
psy·chol·o·gist [saɪkálədʒɪst] *s.* psicólogo.
psy·chol·o·gy [saɪkálədʒɪ] *s.* psicología.
psy·cho·sis [saɪkósɪs] *s.* sicosis.
pto·maine [tómen] *s.* ptomaína.
pub·lic [pʌ́blɪk] *adj.* público; **— prosecutor** fiscal; *s.* público.
pub·li·ca·tion [pʌblɪkéʃən] *s.* publicación.
pub·lic·i·ty [pʌblísətɪ] *s.* publicidad, propaganda.
pub·lish [pʌ́blɪʃ] *v.* publicar; editar; **-ing house** editorial o editora.
pub·lish·er [pʌ́blɪʃɚ] *s.* publicador; editor.
puck·er [pʌ́kɚ] *v.* fruncir.
pud·ding [púdɪŋ] *s.* budín, pudín.
pud·dle [pʌ́dḷ] *s.* charco.
puff [pʌf] *s.* resoplido; bocanada (*de numo, vapor, etc.*); bullón (*de vestido*); **— of wind** ráfaga, soplo; **— paste** hojaldre; **cream —** bolo de crema; **powder —** polvera, borla, *Méx.* mota; *Riopl.* cisne; *v.* resoplar, jadear; echar bocanadas; **to — up** inflar(se); ahuecar(se); hinchar(se).
pug [pʌg] *s.* perro dogo; **— nose** nariz chata, ñata o respingada.
pull [pʊl] *v.* (*tug*) tirar de; jalar (halar); (*extract*) sacar; arrancar; (*stretch*) estirar; **to — apart** desgarrar; despedazar; descomponer; desmontar; **to — down the curtain** bajar la cortinilla; **to — oneself together** componerse, serenarse; **to — over to the right** hacerse a la derecha, desviarse hacia la derecha; **to — up** parar (*un caballo, un auto*); parar, hacer alto; **to — through** salir de un apuro; sacar (*a alguien*) de un apuro; **the train -ed into the station** el tren llegó a la estación; **to — out** desatascar; *s.* tirón; estirón; ascenso difícil; esfuerzo (*para subir*); **to have —** tener buenas aldabas, tener influencia (palanca).
pul·let [pʊ́lɪt] *s.* polla.
pul·ley [pʊ́lɪ] *s.* polea; garrucha.
pulp [pʌlp] *s.* pulpa.
pul·pit [pʊ́lpɪt] *s.* púlpito.
pul·sate [pʌ́lset] *v.* pulsar, latir.
pulse [pʌls] *s.* pulso; pulsación.
pul·ver·ize [pʌ́lvəraɪz] *v.* pulverizar.
pum·ice [pʌ́mɪs] *s.* piedra pómez.
pump [pʌmp] *s.* bomba (*para sacar agua*); zapatilla; **gasoline —** bomba de gasolina; **hand —** bomba de mano; **tire —** bomba para neumáticos; *v.* manejar la bomba, *Am.* bombear; inflar (*un neumático*); **to — someone** sacarle (*o* sonsacarle) a una persona la verdad o un secreto.
pump·kin [pʌ́mpkɪn] *s.* calabaza.
pun [pʌn] *s.* equívoco, retruécano, juego de palabras; *v.* decir retruécanos o equívocos, jugar del vocablo.
punch [pʌntʃ] *s.* (*blow*) puñetazo, puñada; (*drink*) ponche; (*drill*) punzón, sacabocados; (*vitality*)

fuerza, empuje; vitalidad; **— bowl** ponchera; *v.* dar un puñetazo, dar una puñada; punzar, horadar, perforar; **to — a hole** hacer un agujero o perforación.
punc·tu·al [pʌ́ŋktʃʊəl] *adj.* puntual.
punc·tu·al·i·ty [pʌŋktʃʊǽlətɪ] *s.* puntualidad.
punc·tu·ate [pʌ́ŋktʃʊet] *v.* puntuar.
punc·tu·a·tion [pʌŋktʃʊéʃən] *s.* puntuación.
punc·ture [pʌ́ŋktʃɚ] *v.* picar, punzar, pinchar; agujerear, perforar; **-d tire** neumático picado; *s.* picadura; pinchazo; perforación; **to have a tire —** tener un neumático picado, tener una llanta o goma picada.
pun·ish [pʌ́nɪʃ] *v.* castigar.
pun·ish·ment [pʌ́nɪʃmənt] *s.* castigo.
punt [pʌnt] *s.* puntapié, patada.
pu·ny [pjúnɪ] *adj.* endeble, débil, flaco, enfermizo; insignificante.
pup [pʌp] *s.* cachorro.
pu·pil [pjúpḷ] *s.* discípulo; **— of the eye** pupila, niña del ojo.
pup·pet [pʌ́pɪt] *s.* títere, muñeco, monigote; **— show** títeres.
pup·py [pʌ́pɪ] *s.* cachorrito.
pur·chase [pɝ́tʃəs] *v.* comprar; mercar; *s.* compra; merca; **to get a — upon** agarrarse fuerte a.
pur·chas·er [pɝ́tʃəsɚ] *s.* comprador, marchante.
pure [pjʊr] *adj.* puro; **-ly** *adv.* puramente; meramente.
pu·ree [pjʊré] *s.* puré.
pur·ga·tive [pɝ́gətɪv] *adj.* purgante; *s.* purga, purgante.
pur·ga·to·ry [pɝ́gətorɪ] *s.* purgatorio.
purge [pɝdʒ] *v.* purgar(se); limpiar; purificar(se); *s.* purga, purgante.
pu·ri·fy [pjúrəfaɪ] *v.* purificar(se); depurar.
pur·ist [pjúrɪst] *s.* purista.
pu·ri·ty [pjúrətɪ] *s.* pureza.
pur·ple [pɝ́pḷ] *s.* púrpura; *adj.* purpúreo, morado.
pur·port [pɝ́port] *s.* significado; tenor, sustancia; [pɚpórt] *v.* pretender, aparentar.
pur·pose [pɝ́pəs] *s.* (*intention*) propósito, intención; (*goal*) fin, objeto; **for no —** sin objeto, inútilmente, en vano, para nada; **on —** adrede, de propósito; *v.* proponerse.
purr [pɝ] *s.* ronroneo (*del gato*); zumbido (*del motor*); *v.* ronronear (*el gato*).
purse [pɝs] *s.* bolsillo, portamonedas, bolsa; *v.* to **— one's lips** fruncir los labios.
pur·su·ant [pɚsúənt] *adv.* conforme; de acuerdo con.
pur·sue [pɚsú] *v.* perseguir; seguir; dedicarse a (*una carrera, un estudio*).
pur·su·er [pɚsúɚ] *s.* perseguidor.
pur·suit [pɚsút] *s.* perseguimiento; busca; ocupación; ejercicio (*de una profesión, cargo, etc.*); **in — of** a caza de, en seguimiento de, en busca de.
pus [pʌs] *s.* pus, podre.
push [pʊʃ] *v.* (*shove*) empujar; (*promote*) fomentar, promover; (*hurry*) apresurar; **to — aside** hacer a un lado, rechazar, apartar; **to — forward** empujar, abrirse paso; avanzar; **to — through** encajar (*por un agujero o rendija*); abrirse paso a empujones; *s.* empuje; empujón, empellón; **— button** botón eléctrico.
push·cart [pʊ́ʃkart] *s.* carretilla de mano.
puss·y [pʊ́sɪ] *s.* minino, gatito; **— willow** especie de sauce americano.
put [pʊt] *v.* poner; colocar; **to — a question** hacer una pregunta; **to — across an idea** darse a

entender bien; hacer aceptar una idea; **to —
away** apartar; guardar; **to — before** poner
delante, anteponer; proponer ante; **to — by
money** ahorrar o guardar dinero; **to — down**
apuntar, anotar; sofocar (*una revolución*); rebajar
(*los precios*); **to — in words** expresar; **to — in
writing** poner por escrito; **to — off** aplazar,
posponer; diferir; **to — on** ponerse (*ropa*); **to —
on airs** darse tono o ínfulas; **to — on weight**
engordar; **to — out** apagar, extinguir; **to —
someone out** echar o expulsar a alguien;
molestar o incomodar a alguien; **to — to shame**
avergonzar; **to — up** enlatar, envasar (*frutas,
legumbres*); apostar (*dinero*); alojar(se); erigir; **to
— up for sale** poner de venta; **to — up with**
aguantar, tolerar; *pret. & p.p. de* **to put.**

pu·tre·fy [pjútrəfaɪ] *v.* podrir (*o* pudrir), corromper.

pu·trid [pjútrɪd] *adj.* putrefacto, podrido.

put·ter [pʌ́tɚ] *v.* trabajar sin orden ni sistema;
ocuparse en cosas de poca monta; malgastar el
tiempo.

put·ty [pʌ́tɪ] *s.* masilla; *v.* tapar o rellenar con
masilla.

puz·zle [pʌ́zl] *s.* rompecabezas, acertijo; enigma·
crossword — crucigrama; *v.* embrollar, poner
perplejo, confundir; **to — out** desenredar,
descifrar; **to — over** ponderar; tratar de resolver
o descifrar; **to be -d** estar perplejo.

pyr·a·mid [pírəmɪd] *s.* pirámide.

Q:q

quack [kwæk] *s.* graznido (*del
pato*); curandero, matasanos,
medicastro; charlatán; *adj.*
falso; *v.* graznar.

quag·mire [kwǽgmaɪr] *s.* tremedal, cenagal.

quail [kwel] *s.* codorniz.

quaint [kwent] *adj.* raro, extraño; pintoresco.

quake [kwek] *s.* temblor; terremoto; *v.* temblar.

qual·i·fi·ca·tion [kwɑləfəkéʃən] *s.* (*condition*)
calificación; cualidad, calidad; (*requirement*)
requisito; aptitud.

qual·i·fy [kwɑ́ləfaɪ] *v.* calificar; capacitar; **to — for
a position** estar capacitado para una posición;
his studies — him for the job sus estudios le
capacitan para el puesto.

qual·i·ty [kwɑ́lətɪ] *s.* cualidad; calidad.

qualm [kwɑm] *s.* escrúpulo.

quan·ti·fy [kwɑ́ntɪfaɪ] *v.* cuantificar.

quan·ti·ty [kwɑ́ntətɪ] *s.* cantidad.

quar·an·tine [kwɔ́rəntin] *s.* cuarentena; *v.* poner en
cuarentena, aislar.

quar·rel [kwɔ́rəl] *s.* riña, reyerta, pendencia;
querella; *v.* reñir; pelear, disputar.

quar·rel·some [kwɔ́rəlsəm] *adj.* reñidor,
pendenciero.

quar·ry [kwɔ́rɪ] *s.* cantera; presa, caza (*animal
perseguido*); *v.* explotar (*una cantera*); trabajar
en una cantera.

quart [kwɔrt] *s.* cuarto de galón (*0.9463 de un
litro*).

quar·ter [kwɔ́rtɚ] *s.* (*one-fourth*) cuarto, cuarta
parte; (*coin*) moneda de 25 centavos; (*district*)
barrio, distrito; **-s** morada, vivienda;
alojamiento; **from all —s** de todas partes; **to give
no — to the enemy** no dar cuartel al enemigo;
adj. cuarto; *v.* cuartear, dividir en cuartos;
descuartizar; acuartelar, acantonar, alojar
(*tropas*).

quar·ter·ly [kwɔ́rtəlɪ] *adv.* trimestralmente, por
trimestres; *adj.* trimestral; *s.* publicación
trimestral.

quar·tet [kwɔrtét] *s.* cuarteto.

quartz [kwɔrts] *s.* cuarzo.

qua·ver [kwévɚ] *v.* temblar; *s.* temblor; trémolo
(*de la voz*).

quay [ki] *s.* muelle, embarcadero.

queen [kwin] *s.* reina.

queer [kwɪr] *adj.* raro, extraño, singular; excéntrico;
to feel — sentirse raro, no sentirse bien; *v.* poner
en ridículo, comprometer; **to — oneself with**
quedar mal con, ponerse mal con.

quell [kwɛl] *v.* reprimir; sofocar (*una revuelta*);
calmar.

quench [kwɛntʃ] *v.* apagar (*el fuego, la sed*);
reprimir, sofocar, ahogar, templar el ardor de.

que·ry [kwírɪ] *s.* (*interrogation*) pregunta;
interrogación, signo de interrogación; (*doubt*)
duda; *v.* preguntar, expresar duda; marcar con
signo de interrogación.

quest [kwɛst] *s.* busca; pesquisa.

ques·tion [kwɛ́stʃən] *s.* (*interrogation*) pregunta;
(*issue*) cuestión; problema; duda; proposición;
— mark signo de interrogación; **beyond —** fuera
de duda; **that is out of the —** ¡imposible!; ¡ni
pensar en ello!; *v.* preguntar; interrogar; dudar.

ques·tion·a·ble [kwɛ́stʃənəbl] *adj.* dudoso;
discutible.

ques·tion·er [kwɛ́stʃənɚ] *s.* interrogador,
preguntador.

ques·tion·ing [kwɛ́stʃənɪŋ] *s.* interrogatorio; *adj.*
interrogador.

ques·tion·naire [kwɛstʃənér] *s.* cuestionario, lista de
preguntas, interrogatorio.

quib·ble [kwíbl] *v.* sutilizar, valerse de argucias o
sutilezas; andar en dimes y diretes; *s.* sutileza,
argucia.

quick [kwɪk] *adj.* (*soon*) pronto, presto; (*smart*)
listo; (*speedy*) rápido, veloz; agudo; **— temper**
genio violento; **— wit** mente aguda; *adv.*
rápidamente, de prisa, con prisa, pronto; *s.*
carne viva; **to cut to the —** herir en lo vivo,
herir en el alma.

quick·en [kwíkən] *v.* acelerar(se); avivar(se);
aguzar (*la mente, el entendimiento*).

quick·ly [kwíklɪ] *adv.* pronto, presto, de prisa,
aprisa, rápidamente.

quick·ness [kwíknɪs] *s.* (*speed*) rapidez; presteza,
prontitud; (*alertness*) vivezal; agudeza (*de
ingenio*).

quick·sand [kwíksænd] *s.* arena movediza.

quick·sil·ver [kwíksɪlvɚ] *s.* mercurio, azogue.

qui·et [kwáɪət] *adj.* quieto; callado; tranquilo; en
calma; reposado; *s.* quietud; sosiego, reposo;
calma; silencio; *v.* aquietar; sosegar; calmar,
tranquilizar; **to — down** aquietarse; calmarse;
-ly *adv.* quietamente, con quietud;
calladamente; tranquilamente.

qui·et·ness [kwáɪətnɪs] *s.* quietud; sosiego, calma.

quill [kwɪl] *s.* pluma; cañón (*de pluma de ave*);
púa (*de puerco espín*).

quilt [kwɪlt] *s.* colcha; *v.* acolchar.

quince [kwɪns] *s.* membrillo.

qui·nine [kwáɪnaɪn] *s.* quinina.

quip [kwɪp] *s.* pulla, dicharacho; agudeza.

quirk [kwɚk] *s.* chifladura, extravagancia,
capricho; peculiaridad mental.

quit [kwɪt] *v.* (*abandon*) dejar, abandonar; irse;
(*cease*) parar, cesar; **to — doing something** dejar
de hacer algo; **-s** *adj.* desquitado; **we are -s** no

nos debemos nada, estamos desquitados, *Am.*
estamos a mano; *pret. & p.p. de* to quit.
quite [kwaɪt] *adv.* bastante; del todo, enteramente;
— **a person** una persona admirable; — **so así es**,
en efecto; **it's** — **the fashion** está muy en boga.
quit·ter [kwítɚ] *s.* el que deja fácilmente lo
empezado, el que se da fácilmente por vencido;
evasor; desertor.
quiv·er [kwívɚ] *v.* temblar; estremecerse; *s.*
temblor; estremecimiento.
quix·ot·ic [kwiksátɪk] *adj.* quijotesco.
quiz [kwɪz] *s.* examen; interrogatorio; cuestionario;
v. examinar, interrogar, hacer preguntas.
quiz·zi·cal [kwízəkl̩] *adj.* curioso; burlón.
quo·ta [kwótə] *s.* cuota.
quo·ta·tion [kwotéʃən] *s.* citación, cita; cotización
(*de precios*); — **marks** comillas.
quote [kwot] *v.* citar; cotizar (*precios*); **to** — **from**
citar a, entresacar una cita de; *s.* cita, citación;
-s comillas; **in -s** entre comillas.
quo·tient [kwóʃənt] *s.* cociente.

R: r   **rab·bi** [rǽbaɪ] *s.* rabí, rabino.
      rab·bit [rǽbɪt] *s.* conejo.
      rab·ble [rǽbl̩] *s.* populacho, plebe;
canalla.
rab·id [rǽbəd] *adj.* rabioso.
ra·bies [rébiz] *s.* rabia, hidrofobia.
rac·coon [rækún] *s. Méx., C.A., Andes* mapache.
race [res] *s.* (*lineage*) raza; (*competition*) corrida,
carrera; contienda; —**track** (*o* —**course**) pista;
boat — regata; *v.* correr; competir en una
carrera; ir corriendo; regatear (*competir en una
regata*); acelerar (*un motor*).
rac·er [résɚ] *s.* corredor; caballo de carrera; auto
de carrera.
ra·cial [réʃəl] *adj.* racial.
ra·cism [résɪzm] *s.* racismo.
rack [ræk] *s.* (*framework*) percha, colgadero,
clavijero; (*torture*) potro de tormento; **baggage**
— red; **towel** — toallero; **to fall into** — **and
ruin** caer en un estado de ruina total; — **and
pinion** cremallera; *v.* atormentar; **to** — **one's
brain** devanarse los sesos, quebrarse uno la
cabeza.
rack·et [rǽkɪt] *s.* (*instrument*) raqueta (*de tenis*);
(*noise*) boruca, estrépito, baraúnda; bullicio;
trapacería.
rack·et·eer [rækɪtír] *s.* trapacista, trapacero,
extorsionista; *v.* trapacear, extorsionar.
ra·dar [rédɑr] *s.* radar.
ra·di·al [rédɪəl] *adj.* radial.
ra·di·ance [rédɪəns] *s.* resplandor, brillo.
ra·di·ant [rédɪənt] *adj.* radiante; resplandeciente,
brillante.
ra·di·ate [rédɪet] *v.* irradiar; radiar.
ra·di·a·tor [rédɪetɚ] *s.* radiador; calorífero.
rad·i·cal [rǽdɪkl̩] *adj. & s.* radical.
rad·i·cal·ism [rǽdɪkəlɪzm] *s.* extremismo.
ra·di·o [rédɪo] *s.* radio (*m. o f.*); radio-telefonía;
radiotelegrafía; — **commentator** comentarista
radial; — **listener** radioescucha, radioyente; —
program programa radiofónico; **by** — por radio;
v. radiar, emitir, transmitir, radioifundir o
difundir.
ra·di·o·ac·tive [redɪoǽktɪv] *adj.* radiactivo.
ra·di·ol·o·gy [redíálədʒɪ] *s.* radiología.
rad·ish [rǽdɪʃ] *s.* rábano.

ra·di·um [rédɪəm] *s.* radio (*elemento químico*).
ra·di·us [rédɪəs] *s.* radio (*de un círculo*).
ra·don [rédan] *s.* radón.
raf·fle [rǽfl̩] *s.* rifa, sorteo; tombola; *v.* rifar,
sortear.
raft [ræft] *s.* balsa; **a** — **of things** un montón (*o la
mar*) de cosas.
raft·er [rǽftɚ] *s.* viga (*del techo*).
rag [ræg] *s.* trapo; harapo, andrajo, *Am.* hilacho;
— **doll** muñeca de trapo; **to be in -s** estar
hecho andrajos, *Am.* estar hecho tiras.
rag·a·muf·fin [rǽgəmʌfɪn] *s.* pelagatos, golfo;
granuja, pilluelo.
rage [redʒ] *s.* rabia, furor; ira; **to be all the** — estar
en boga, estar de moda; *v.* rabiar; enfurecerse;
estar enfurecido; bramar; **to** — **with anger**
bramar de ira.
rag·ged [rǽgɪd] *adj.* andrajoso, haraposo,
harapiento, desharrapado, roto; — **edge** borde
radio o deshilachado; **to be on the** — **edge** estar
al borde del precipicio; estar muy nervioso.
raid [red] *s.* incursión, invasión repentina;
allanamiento (*de un local*); **air** — ataque aéreo,
bombardeo aéreo; *v.* hacer una incursión;
invadir de repente; caer sobre; allanar (*un local*),
entrar a la fuerza.
rail [rel] *s.* (*steel bar*) riel, carril; (*railroad*)
ferrocarril; (*railing*) barandal, barandilla; —
fence empalizada, estacada; **by** — por
ferrocarril.
rail·ing [rélɪŋ] *s.* baranda, barandilla; pasamano
(*de escalera*), balaustrada, barrera; rieles.
rail·road [rélrod] *s.* ferrocarril; *adj.* ferroviario; de
ferrocarril.
rail·way [rélwe] *s.* ferrocarril; *adj.* ferroviario; de
ferrocarril; — **crossing** cruce, crucero.
rai·ment [rémənt] *s.* vestidura, ropaje.
rain [ren] *s.* lluvia; — **water** agua llovediza; *v.*
llover; — **or shine** que llueva o no; llueva o
truene; a todo trance.
rain·bow [rénbo] *s.* arco iris.
rain·coat [rénkot] *s.* impermeable; *Ch.* capa de
agua, *Méx.* manga o capa de hule; *Ríopl.* piloto.
rain·drop [réndrɑp] *s.* gota de agua.
rain·fall [rénfɔl] *s.* lluvia, lluvias; cantidad de agua
pluvial; aguacero.
rain·y [rénɪ] *adj.* lluvioso.
raise [rez] *v.* (*lift*) levantar, alzar; subir; eregir;
(*cultivate*) criar; cultivar; (*collect*) reunir;
reclutar; **to** — **a question** hacer una observación
o suscitar una duda; **to** — **a racket** armar un
alboroto; *s.* aumento de sueldo.
rai·sin [rézn] *s.* pasa, uva seca.
ra·jah [rádʒə] *s.* rajá.
rake [rek] *s.* rastro, rastrillo, libertino, perdulario;
v. rastrear, rastrillar (*la tierra*); raspar; barrer
(*con rastrillo*); atizar (*el fuego*).
ral·ly [rǽlɪ] *v.* (*unite*) reunir(se); juntar(se);
(*improve*) recobrar(se); mejorar (*de salud*);
fortalecerse; revivir; tomar nueva vida; **to** — **to
the side of** acudir al lado de; *s.* junta
popular, junta libre; recuperación.
ram [ræm] *s.* (*animal*) carnero; (*tool*) ariete o
martillo hidráulico; espolón de buque; **battering**
— ariete; *v.* apisonar, aplanar a golpes; aplastar
de un choque; rellenar atestar; **to** — **a boat**
chocar con un barco; arremeter contra un
barco.
ram·ble [rǽmbl̩] *v.* vagar; divagar; callejear; *s.*
paseo, andanza.
ram·page [rǽmpedʒ] *s.* alboroto.

ram·pant [rǽmpɔnt] *adj.* extravagante; desenfrenado.

ram·part [rǽmpɑrt] *s.* baluarte, muralla.

ran [ræn] *pret. de* **to run.**

ranch [ræntʃ] *s.* hacienda, *Méx., C.A.* rancho; **cattle —** hacienda de ganado, *Méx., C.A.* rancho, *Ríopl.* estancia; *Ch.* fundo; *Ven., Col.* hato.

ran·cid [rǽnsɪd] *adj.* rancio, acedo.

ran·cor [rǽŋkɚ] *s.* rencor, encono.

ran·dom [rǽndɔm] *adj.* impensado; fortuito, al azar; **at —** al azar, a la ventura.

rang [ræŋ] *pret. de* **to ring.**

range [rendʒ] *v. (align)* alinear; poner en fila; arreglar; *(wander)* vagar por; rondar; fluctuar; **to — ten miles** tener un alcance de diez millas *(un arma de fuego)*; *s.* fila, hilera; alcance; extensión; fluctuación, variación *(dentro de ciertos límites)*; distancia; pastizal, *C.A.* pastal; estufa; **gas —** cocina de gas; **— of mountains** cordillera, cadena de montañas; **— of vision** campo de visión; **in — with** en línea con; **shooting —** campo de práctica para tirar.

range find·er [réndʒfaɪndɚ] *s.* telemetro.

rank [ræŋk] *s. (position)* rango, categoría; orden; calidad; grado; *(line)* fila; línea, hilera; **the — and file** el pueblo, la gente ordinaria; la tropa; *v.* poner en fila; ordenar, arreglar; clasificar; **to — above** sobrepasar a; ser de grado superior a; **to — high** tener un alto rango, categoría o renombre; ser tenido en alta estima; **to — second** tener el segundo lugar; **to — with** estar al nivel de, tener el mismo grado que; **he -s high in athletics** sobresale en los deportes.

ran·sack [rǽnsæk] *v.* escudriñar; saquear.

ran·som [rǽnsɔm] *s.* rescate; *v.* rescatar; redimir.

rant [rænt] *v.* desvariar; disparatar, gritar necedades.

rap [ræp] *v. (strike)* golpear, dar un golpe; *(censure)* criticar, censurar; **to — on the door** llamar o tocar a la puerta; *s.* golpe; **not to care a —** no importarle a uno un ardite.

ra·pa·cious [rɔpéʃɔs] *adj.* rapaz.

rape [rep] *s.* estupro, violación *(de una mujer)*; *v.* forzar, violar *(a una mujer)*.

rap·id [rǽpɪd] *adj.* rápido; **-s** *s. pl.* raudal, rápidos *(de un río).*

ra·pid·i·ty [rɔpídɔtɪ] *s.* rapidez, velocidad.

rap·port [rɔpɔ́r] *s.* relación de confianza mutua.

rapt [ræpt] *adj.* extasiado; absorto.

rap·ture [rǽptʃɚ] *s.* éxtasis, rapto.

rare [rɛr] *adj. (strange)* extraordinario, extraño; raro; *(precious)* raro; precioso; *(not well-done)* a medio asar, a medio freír, medio crudo; **-ly** *adv.* rara vez, raras veces; raramente; extraordinariamente.

rar·i·ty [rɛ́rɔtɪ] *s.* rareza; enrarecimiento *(de la atmósfera).*

ras·cal [rǽskl] *s.* bribón, bellaco, pícaro.

rash [ræʃ] *adj.* temerario, atrevido; precipitado; imprudente; *s.* salpullido, erupción *(de la piel).*

rash·ness [rǽʃnɪs] *s.* temeridad.

rasp [ræsp] *v.* chirriar; irritar; *s.* chirrido, sonido áspero; ronquera, carraspera.

rasp·ber·ry [rǽzbɛrɪ] *s.* frambuesa; **— bush** frambueso.

rasp·y [rǽspɪ] *adj.* ronco; áspero.

rat [ræt] *s.* rata; postizo *(para el pelo).*

rate [ret] *s.* proporción; porcentaje, tanto por ciento, *Am.* tipo *(de interés);* tarifa; precio; **— of exchange** cambio, *Am.* tipo de cambio; **— of**

increase incremento proporcional; **at any —** en todo caso, de todos modos; **at that —** a ese paso; en esa proporción; **at the — of** a razón de; **first —** de primera clase o calidad; *v.* calificar, clasificar, considerar; tasar; valuar; **he -s as the best** se le considera como el mejor; **he -s high** se le tiene en alta estima.

rath·er [rǽðɚ] *adv.* algo, un poco, un tanto; más bien; mejor; mejor dicho; **— than** más bien que; **I would — die than** prefiero antes la muerte que; **I would — not go** preferiría no ir.

rat·i·fy [rǽtɔfaɪ] *s.* ratificar.

rat·ing [rétɪŋ] *s.* clasificación; rango, grado; clase.

ra·tio [réʃo] *s.* razón, proporción; relación.

ra·tion [réʃɔn] *s.* ración; *v.* racionar.

ra·tio·nal [rǽʃɔnl] *adj.* racional.

ra·tio·nal·ize [rǽʃɔnlaɪz] *v.* buscar excusas.

ra·tion·ing [réʃɔnɪŋ] *s.* racionamiento.

rat·tle [rǽtl] *v.* traquetear; golpetear; sacudir ruidosamente; confundir, desconcertar; **to — off** decir de corrido *(o* decir muy aprisa); *s.* traqueteo; golpeteo; **child's —** sonaja, sonajero; **death —** estertor de la muerte.

rat·tle·snake [rǽtlsnek] *s.* culebra de cascabel, *Ríopl., Ch.* cascabel o cascabela.

rau·cous [rɔ́kɔs] *adj.* ronco; estentóreo.

rav·age [rǽvɪdʒ] *s.* estrago, ruina, destrucción; asolamiento; saqueo, pillaje; *v.* asolar, arruinar; pillar, saquear.

rave [rev] *v.* desvariar, delirar, disparatar; bramar; **to — about someone** deshacerse en elogios de alguien.

ra·ven [révɔn] *s.* cuervo; *adj.* negro lustroso.

rav·en·ous [rǽvɔnɔs] *adj.* voraz; devorador; **to be —** tener un hambre canina.

ra·vine [rɔvín] *s.* quebrada, hondonada, barranco *(o* barranca).

rav·ish [rǽvɪʃ] *v.* encantar; arrebatar; violar *(a una mujer).*

raw [rɔ] *adj. (crude)* crudo; áspero; pelado; descarnado; *(untrained)* inexperto, nuevo; **— material** materia prima; **— recruit** recluta nuevo; **— silk** seda en rama, seda cruda; **— sugar** azúcar bruto, azúcar crudo.

raw·hide [rɔ́haɪd] *s.* cuero crudo; **— whip** rebenque.

ray [re] *s.* rayo; raya *(especie de pez).*

ray·on [réɑn] *s.* rayón, seda artificial.

raze [rez] *v.* arrasar, asolar.

ra·zor [rézɚ] *s.* navaja de afeitar; **— blade** hoja de afeitar; **safety —** navaja de seguridad.

reach [ritʃ] *v. (go as far as)* llegar a; alcanzar; *(touch)* tocar; *(extend)* extenderse; **to — for** tratar de coger; echar mano a; **to — into** meter la mano en; penetrar en; **to — out one's hand** alargar o tender la mano; *s.* alcance; extensión; **beyond his —** fuera de su alcance; **within his —** a su alcance.

re·act [rɪǽkt] *v.* reaccionar.

re·ac·tion [rɪǽkʃɔn] *s.* reacción.

re·ac·tion·ar·y [rɪǽkʃɔnɛrɪ] *adj. & s.* reaccionario.

read [rid] *v.* leer; indicar *(dícese de un contador, termómetro, etc.);* **to — law** estudiar derecho; **it -s thus** dice así, reza así; **it -s easily** se lee fácilmente o sin esfuerzo.

read [rɛd] *pret. & p.p. de* **to read.**

read·er [rídɚ] *s.* lector; libro de lectura.

read·i·ly [rédlɪ] *adv.* pronto, con presteza; fácilmente, sin esfuerzo.

read·i·ness [rédɪnɪs] *s.* prontitud, presteza; facilidad; buena disposición; **to be in —** estar preparado, estar listo.

read·ing [rídɪŋ] *s.* lectura; indicación (*de un barómetro, termómetro, etc.*); — **room** sala o salón de lectura.

re·ad·just [riədʒʌ́st] *v.* reajustar, ajustar de nuevo; arreglar de nuevo; readaptar.

re·ad·just·ment [riədʒʌ́stmənt] *s.* reajuste; readaptación; nuevo arreglo.

read·y [rédɪ] *adj.* pronto, listo; preparado; propenso; dispuesto; — **cash** fondos disponibles; dinero a la mano.

read·y-made [rédɪméd] *adj.* hecho, ya hecho.

re·al [ríəl] *adj.* real, verdadero; — **estate** bienes raíces, bienes inmuebles; **-ly** *adv.* realmente, verdaderamente.

re·al·ism [ríəlɪzəm] *s.* realismo.

re·al·ist [ríəlɪst] *s.* realista; **-ic** *adj.* realista, vivo, natural.

re·al·i·ty [riǽlətɪ] *s.* realidad.

re·al·i·za·tion [riəlezéʃən] *s.* realización; comprensión.

re·al·ize [ríəlaɪz] *v.* (*comprehend*) darse cuenta de, hacerse cargo de; (*achieve*) realizar, efectuar; convertir en dinero.

realm [rɛlm] *s.* reino; dominio, región.

re·al·tor [ríəltɚ] *s.* corredor de bienes raíces.

reap [rip] *v.* segar; cosechar; recoger; obtener; sacar (*provecho, fruto, etc.*).

reap·er [rípɚ] *s.* segador; segadora, máquina segadora.

re·ap·pear [riəpír] *v.* reaparecer.

rear [rɪr] *adj.* trasero, posterior; de atráa; — **admiral** contraalmirante; — **guard** retaguardia; *s.* espalda, parte de atrás; trasero; fondo (*de una sala, salón, etc.*); cola (*de una fila*); **in the —** detrás, atrás, a la espalda; *v.* criar, educar; encabritarse, empinarse (*el caballo*).

rea·son [rízṇ] *s.* razón; causa, motivo; **by — of a** causa de; **it stands to —** es razonable; *v.* razonar; **to — out** discurrir, razonar.

rea·son·a·ble [ríznəbḷ] *adj.* razonable; justo; racional; módico, moderado; **rea·son·a·bly** *adv.* razonablemente; con razón; bastante.

rea·son·ing [ríznɪŋ] *s.* razonamiento, raciocinio.

re·as·sure [riəʃúr] *v.* tranquilizar, restaurar la confianza a; asegurar de nuevo.

re·bate [ríbet] *s.* rebaja (*de precio*); *v.* rebajar (*precio*).

reb·el [rébḷ] *s.* & *adj.* rebelde; [rɪbél] *v.* rebelarse.

re·bel·lion [rɪbéljən] *s.* rebelión.

re·bel·lious [rɪbéljəs] *adj.* rebelde.

re·birth [ribɝ́θ] *s.* renacimiento.

re·bound [rɪbáʊnd] *v.* rebotar; repercutir; [ríbaʊnd] *s.* rebote; **on the —** de rebote.

re·buff [rɪbʌ́f] *s.* desaire; repulsa; *v.* desairar; rechazar.

re·build [ribíld] *v.* reconstruir, reedificar.

re·built [ribílt] *pret.* & *p.p. de* **to rebuild.**

re·buke [rɪbjúk] *s.* reprensión, reproche, reprimenda, repulsa; *v.* reprender, reprochar.

re·call [rɪkɔ́l] *s.* llamada, aviso (*para hacer volver*); retirada (*de un diplomático*); revocación; [rɪkɔ́l] *v.* recordar; retirar; revocar.

re·ca·pit·u·late [rikəpítʃəlet] *v.* recapitular.

re·cede [rɪsíd] *v.* retroceder; retirarse.

re·ceipt [rɪsít] *s.* recibo; fórmula, receta; **-s** entradas, ingresos; **on — of** al recibo de; **we are in — of your kind letter . . .** obra en nuestro poder su grata . . .; *v.* sellar (*con el recibí*), dar recibo.

re·ceive [rɪsív] *v.* recibir.

re·ceiv·er [rɪsívɚ] *s.* receptor; recibidor, depositario, síndico; recipiente, receptáculo.

re·cent [rísṇt] *adj.* reciente; **-ly** *adv.* recientemente, *Ch., Ríopl.* recién (*como en* salió recién); **-ly married** recién casados.

re·cep·ta·cle [rɪséptəkḷ] *s.* receptáculo.

re·cep·tion [rɪsépʃən] *s.* recepción; recibimiento; acogida, acogimiento.

re·cess [rɪsés] *s.* (*niche*) nicho, hueco; (*cessation*) tregua, intermisión; (*period*) hora de recreo o asueto; **in the -es** of en lo más recóndito de; *v.* suspender el trabajo; levantar (*por corto tiempo*) una sesión; hacer un hueco o nicho en (*la pared*).

re·ces·sion [rɪséʃən] *s.* retroceso; contracción económica.

rec·i·pe [résəpɪ] *s.* receta, fórmula.

re·cip·i·ent [rɪsípɪənt] *s.* recipiente, recibidor; *adj.* receptivo.

re·cip·ro·cal [rɪsíprəkḷ] *adj.* recíproco, mutuo.

re·cip·ro·cate [rɪsíprəket] *v.* corresponder.

re·cit·al [rɪsáɪtḷ] *s.* recitación; relación; narración; recital (*músico*).

rec·i·ta·tion [rɛsətéʃən] *s.* recitación.

re·cite [rɪsáɪt] *v.* recitar; relatar; decir o dar la lección.

reck·less [réklɪs] *adj.* temerario, atrevido, precipitado; descuidado; — **with one's money** derrochador.

reck·less·ness [réklɪsnɪs] *s.* temeridad, osadía, descuido.

reck·on [rékən] *v.* contar, computar, calcular; juzgar; suponer; **to — on** contar con.

reck·on·ing [rékənɪŋ] *s.* cuenta; ajuste de cuentas; cálculo; **the day of —** el día del juicio.

re·claim [rɪklém] *v.* recobrar, aprovechar (*tierras baldías*); aprovechar o utilizar (*el hule usado*); pedir la devolución de, tratar de recobrar.

re·cline [rɪkláɪn] *v.* reclinar(se), recostar(se).

re·cluse [rɪklús] *adj.* recluso, solitario; *s.* recluso, solitario, ermitaño.

rec·og·ni·tion [rɛkəgníʃən] *s.* reconocimiento.

rec·og·nize [rékəgnaɪz] *v.* reconocer.

re·coil [rɪkɔ́ɪl] *v.* recular, *Am.* patear (*un arma de fuego*); retroceder, retirarse; *s.* reculada; rebote.

rec·ol·lect [rɛkəlékt] *v.* recordar; [rikəlékt] recobrar, volver a cobrar; recoger, reunir.

rec·ol·lec·tion [rɛkəlékʃən] *s.* recuerdo.

rec·om·mend [rɛkəménd] *v.* recomendar.

rec·om·men·da·tion [rɛkəmɛndéʃən] *s.* recomendación.

rec·om·pense [rékəmpɛns] *v.* recompensar; *s.* recompensa.

rec·on·cile [rékənsaɪl] *v.* reconciliar; ajustar, conciliar; **to — oneself to** resignarse a, conformarse con.

rec·on·cil·i·a·tion [rɛkənsɪlɪéʃən] *f.* reconciliación; ajuste, conciliación; conformidad, resignación.

re·con·noi·ter [rikənɔ́ɪtɚ] *v.* reconocer, explorar; hacer un reconocimiento o exploración.

re·con·sid·er [rikənsídɚ] *v.* reconsiderar.

re·con·struct [rikənstrʌ́kt] *v.* reconstruir, reedificar.

re·con·struc·tion [rikənstrʌ́kʃən] *s.* reconstrucción.

rec·ord [rékɚd] *s.* registro; copia oficial de un documento; memoria; historial (*de una persona*), hoja de servicios; disco (*fonográfico*); record (*en deportes*); **to break the speed —** batir el record de velocidad; **an off-the-record remark** una observación que no ha de constar en el acta; observación hecha en confianza; *adj.* notable, extraordinario; sobresaliente; [rɪkórd] *v.*

registrar; asentar, apuntar; inscribir; grabar en disco fonográfico.

re·cord·ing [rɪkɔ́rdɪŋ] *s.* grabación.

re·count [rikaʊnt] *s.* recuento, segunda cuenta; [rɪkáʊnt] *v.* contar, narrar, relatar, referir; [rikáʊnt] recontar, volver a contar.

re·course [rikors] *s.* recurso, refugio, auxilio; **to have — to** recurrir a.

re·cov·er [rɪkʌ́və·] *v.* recobrar(se), recuperar(se); recobrar la salud; reponerse; [rikʌ́və·] volver a cubrir.

re·cov·er·y [rɪkʌ́vrɪ] *s.* recobro; recuperación; cobranza; reivindicación.

rec·re·a·tion [rɛkrɪéʃən] *s.* recreación, recreo.

re·crim·i·nate [rɪkrímənet] *v.* recriminar.

re·cruit [rɪkrút] *v.* reclutar; alistar; *s.* recluta; novato, nuevo miembro (de una organización).

rec·tan·gle [rɛ́ktæŋgl] *s.* rectángulo.

rec·ti·fy [rɛ́ktəfaɪ] *v.* rectificar.

rec·tor [rɛ́ktə·] *s.* rector.

rec·tum [rɛ́ktəm] *s.* recto.

re·cu·per·ate [rɪkjúpəret] *v.* recuperar, recobrar; recobrar la salud.

re·cur [rɪkɚ́] *v.* volver a ocurrir; repetirse; **to — to a matter** volver a un asunto.

red [rɛd] *adj.* rojo; colorado, encarnado; **red-hot** candente; enfurecido, furioso; muy caliente; **— tape** formalismo, trámites enojosos; **— wine** vino tinto; **to see —** enfurecerse; *s.* color rojo; rojo.

red·den [rɛ́dn̩] *v.* enrojecer(se); ruborizarse, ponerse rojo; teñir de rojo.

red·dish [rɛ́dɪʃ] *adj.* rojizo.

re·deem [rɪdím] *v.* redimir; rescatar; desempeñar (una prenda); cumplir (una promesa).

re·deem·er [rɪdímə·] *s.* salvador, redentor; **the Redeemer** el Redentor.

re·demp·tion [rɪdɛmpʃən] *s.* redención; rescate; **— of a note** pago de una obligación.

red·ness [rɛ́dnɪs] *s.* rojez o rojura; inflamación.

re·dou·ble [ridʌ́bl] *v.* redoblar; repetir; repercutir.

re·dound [ridáʊnd] *v.* redundar.

re·dress [ridrɛs] *s.* reparación, enmienda; compensación; desagravio; [ridrɛ́s] *v.* enmendar, rectificar, remediar, reparar; desagraviar.

red snap·per [rɛdsnǽpə·] *s.* pargo; *Mex.* huachinango.

re·duce [rɪdjús] *v.* reducir; mermar; rebajar; adelgazar(se); subyugar.

re·duc·tion [rɪdʌ́kʃən] *s.* reducción; merma; rebaja.

re·dun·dant [ridʌ́ndənt] *adj.* redundante.

red·wood [rɛ́dwʊd] *s. Am.* secoya o secuoya (árbol gigantesco de California); madera roja de la secoya.

reed [rid] *s.* caña; junco, junquillo; lengüeta, boquilla (de ciertos instrumentos de viento); caramillo.

reef [rif] *s.* arrecife, escollo; banco de arena (en el mar).

reek [rik] *v.* (fume) exhalar, echar (vaho o vapor); (stink) heder, oler mal; *s.* hedor, mal olor.

reel [ril] *s.* (spool) carrete; carretel; (film) cinta cinematográfica; *v.* aspar, enredar (en carretel); bambolearse, tambalearse; **to — off stories** ensartar cuento tras cuento.

re·e·lect [riəlɛkt] *v.* reelegir.

re·e·lec·tion [riəlɛkʃən] *s.* reelección.

re·en·ter [riɛntə·] *v.* volver a entrar.

re·es·tab·lish [riəstǽblɪʃ] *v.* restablecer.

re·fer [rɪfɚ́] *v.* referir; transmitir, remitir; dejar

al juicio o decisión de; referirse, aludir; acudir, recurrir (a un tratado, diccionario, etc.).

ref·er·ee [rɛfərí] *s.* árbitro; *v.* arbitrar.

ref·er·ence [rɛ́frəns] *s.* (mention) referencia; mención, alusión; (sponsor) fiador, el que recomienda a otro; **— book** libro de referencia, libro de consulta; **commercial -s** fiadores, referencias comerciales; **letter of —** carta de recomendación; **with — to** con respecto a, respecto de, en cuanto a.

re·fill [rifɪl] *v.* rellenar.

re·fine [rɪfáɪn] *v.* refinar, purificar; pulir; perfeccionar.

re·fined [rɪfáɪnd] *adj.* refinado; pulido, fino, culto.

re·fine·ment [rɪfáɪnmənt] *s.* refinamiento, finura; buena crianza; refinación, purificación; perfeccionamiento.

re·fin·er·y [rɪfáɪnərɪ] *s.* refinería.

re·flect [rɪflɛkt] *v.* reflejar (luz, calor); reflexionar; meditar; **to — on one's character** desdecir del carácter de uno.

re·flec·tion [rɪflɛkʃən] *s.* reflexión; reflejo, imagen; tacha, descrédito; **on —** después de reflexionarlo.

re·flec·tive [rɪflɛktɪv] *adj.* reflexivo.

re·flex [rifłɛks] *adj.* reflejo; *s.* reflejo; acción refleja.

re·flex·ive [rɪflɛksɪv] *adj.* reflexivo.

re·form [rɪfɔrm] *v.* reformar(se); *s.* reforma.

ref·or·ma·tion [rɛfə·méʃən] *s.* reforma.

re·for·ma·to·ry [rɪfɔ́rmətorɪ] *adj.* reformatorio.

re·form·er [rɪfɔ́rmə·] *s.* reformador; reformista.

re·frac·tion [rɪfrǽkʃən] *s.* refracción.

re·frac·to·ry [rɪfrǽktərɪ] *adj.* refractario; terco, obstinado, rebelde.

re·frain [rɪfrén] *v.* refrenarse, abstenerse; *s.* estribillo.

re·fresh [rɪfrɛʃ] *v.* refrescar(se); renovar.

re·fresh·ing [rɪfrɛ́ʃɪʊ] *adj.* refrescante; renovador, que renueva; placentero.

re·fresh·ment [rɪfrɛ́ʃmənt] *s.* refresco.

re·frig·er·a·tion [rɪfrɪdʒəréʃən] *s.* refrigeración, enfriamiento.

re·frig·er·a·tor [rɪfrídʒəretə·] *s.* nevera, *Am.* refrigerador.

ref·uge [rɛ́fjudʒ] *s.* refugio, asilo, amparo.

ref·u·gee [rɛfjudʒí] *s.* refugiado.

re·fund [rifʌnd] *s.* reembolso, reintegro; [rɪfʌnd] *v.* reembolsar, restituir, reintegrar; [rifʌnd] consolidar (una deuda).

re·fur·bish [rifɚ·bɪʃ] *v.* retocar.

re·fus·al [rɪfjúzl] *s.* negativa; desaire; opción (derecho de recusar un convenio provisional).

re·fuse [rɪfjúz] *v.* rehusar; negar; desechar; rechazar; **to — to** rehusarse a, negarse a.

ref·use [rɛfjus] *s.* desechos, basura, sobras, desperdicios.

re·fute [rɪfjút] *v.* refutar.

re·gain [rɪgén] *v.* recobrar; ganar de nuevo.

re·gal [rigl] *adj.* regio, real.

re·gale [rɪgél] *v.* regalar, agasajar; recrear.

re·ga·lia [rɪgélɪə] *s. pl.* galas, decoraciones, insignias.

re·gard [rɪgárd] *v.* (look) mirar; (consider) considerar; juzgar; estimar; **as -s this** tocante a esto, en cuanto a esto; por lo que toca a esto; *s.* miramiento, consideración; respeto; estima; mirada, **-s** recuerdos, memorias; **in (o with) — to** con respecto a, tocante a, respecto de.

re·gard·ing [rɪgárdɪŋ] *prep.* tocante a, con respecto a, respecto de, relativo a.

re·gard·less [rɪgárdlɪs]: **— of** sin hacer caso de, prescindiendo de.

re·gen·cy [rídʒənsɪ] s. regencia.
re·gent [rídʒənt] s. regente.
re·gime [rɪʒím] s. régimen.
reg·i·ment [rédʒəmənt] s. regimiento.
re·gion [rídʒən] s. región.
reg·is·ter [rédʒɪstə] s. (recording) registro; matrícula; (entry) archivo; lista; (machine) contador; indicador; (voice) registro; **cash —** caja registradora; v. registrar; matricular(se); inscribir(se); marcar, indicar; mostrar, manifestar; certificar (una carta).
reg·is·trar [rédʒɪstrɑr] s. registrador, archivero.
reg·is·tra·tion [redʒɪstréʃən] s. registro; asiento (en un libro); matrícula; inscripción.
re·gret [rɪgrét] s. pesadumbre, dolor; sentimiento, remordimiento; **to send -s** enviar sus excusas (al rehusar una invitación); v. sentir, lamentar; arrenpentirse de.
re·gret·ful [rɪgrétfʊl] adj. deplorable.
re·gret·ta·ble [rɪgrétəbl] adj. lamentable.
reg·u·lar [régjələ] adj. regular; metódico, ordenado; **a — fool** un verdadero necio, un tonto de capirote; **— price** precio corriente; **— soldier** soldado de línea.
reg·u·lar·i·ty [regjəlǽrətɪ] s. regularidad.
reg·u·late [régjəlet] v. regular, regularizar.
reg·u·la·tion [regjəléʃən] s. regulación; regla, orden; **-s** reglamento; **— uniform** uniforme de regla, uniforme de ordenanza.
reg·u·la·tor [régjəletə] s. regulador; registro (de reloj).
re·ha·bil·i·tate [rihæbílətet] v. rehabilitar.
re·hears·al [rɪhɝsl] s. ensayo (de un drama; concierto, etc.); enumeración, repetición.
re·hearse [rɪhɝs] v. ensayar; repetir, repasar.
reign [ren] s. reino, reinado; v. reinar.
re·im·burse [riɪmbɝs] v. reembolsar.
re·im·burse·ment [riɪmbɝsmənt] s. reembolso, reintegro.
rein [ren] s. rienda; v. guiar, gobernar; refrenar (un caballo).
re·in·car·nate [riɪnkárnet] v. reencarnar.
rein·deer [réndɪr] s. reno (especie de ciervo).
re·in·force [riɪnfórs] v. reforzar.
re·in·force·ment [riɪnfórsmənt] s. refuerzo.
re·it·er·ate [riítəret] v. reiterar, repetir.
re·ject [rɪdʒékt] v. rechazar; desechar; descartar; rehusar.
re·joice [rɪdʒɔ́ɪs] v. regocijar(se).
re·joic·ing [rɪdʒɔ́ɪsɪŋ] s. regocijo, júbilo.
re·join [rɪdʒɔ́ɪn] v. reunirse con; volver(se) a unir; [rɪdʒɔ́ɪn] replicar.
re·ju·ve·nate [rɪdʒúvənet] v. rejuvenecer.
re·lapse [rɪlǽps] s. recaída; v. recaer, reincidir.
re·late [rɪlét] v. relatar, narrar; relacionar; **it -s to** se relaciona con, se refiere a.
re·lat·ed [rɪlétɪd] adj. relatado, narrado; relacionado; **to become — by marriage** emparentar; **we are —** somos parientes; estamos emparentados.
re·la·tion [rɪléʃən] s. (association) relación; (story) narración; (kinship) parentesco; pariente; **-s** parientes, parentela; **with — to** con relación a, con respecto a, tocante a.
re·la·tion·ship [rɪléʃənʃɪp] s. relación; parentesco.
rel·a·tive [rélətɪv] adj. relativo; s. relativo, pronombre relativo; pariente, deudo; **— to** relativo a; tocante a; referente a.
re·lax [rɪlǽks] v. relajar; aflojar; mitigar(se); esparcirse, recrearse.
re·lax·a·tion [rilækséʃən] s. (loosening) expansión, esparcimiento; aflojamento o relajamiento; (recreation) solaz, recreo; **— of discipline** relajación de la disciplina; **— of one's mind** esparcimiento del ánimo.
re·lay [ríle] s. relevo, remuda — **race** carrera de relevo; **electric —** relevador; [rɪlé] v. transmitir, despachar; hacer cundir (una noticia); **to — a broadcast** reemitir (o redifundir) un programa de radio.
re·lease [rɪlís] v. soltar; librar; poner en libertad; relevar, aliviar; **to — a piece of news** hacer pública una nueva; **to — from blame** exonerar; s. liberación; alivio; exoneración; escape.
rel·e·gate [réləget] v. relegar; **to — to a corner** arrinconar, arrumbar.
re·lent [rɪlént] v. mitigar(se); ceder; aplacarse.
re·lent·less [rɪléntlɪs] adj. implacable.
rel·e·vant [réləvənt] adj. pertinente; a propósito.
re·li·a·bil·i·ty [rɪlaɪəbílətɪ] s. formalidad; puntualidad; integridad.
re·li·a·ble [rɪláɪəbl] adj. formal; puntual; digno de confianza.
re·li·ance [rɪláɪəns] s. confianza; **self-reliance** confianza en sí, confianza en sus propias fuerzas.
rel·ic [rélɪk] s. reliquia.
re·lief [rɪlíf] s. (ease) alivio; descanso, consuelo; (help) ayuda, socorro; (projection) relieve, realce; **low —** bajo relieve; **to be on —** recibir manutención gratuita; **to put in —** realzar, poner en relieve.
re·lieve [rɪlív] v. relevar; librar; ayudar; aliviar; mitigar.
re·li·gion [rɪlídʒən] s. religión.
re·li·gious [rɪlídʒəs] adj. & s. religioso.
re·lin·quish [rɪlíŋkwɪʃ] v. abandonar, dejar.
rel·ish [rélɪʃ] s. (zest) buen sabor; gusto; apetito; goce; (condiment) condimento; entremés; v. saborear, paladear; gustarle a uno, agradarle a uno.
re·lo·cate [rilóket] v. restablecer.
re·luc·tance [rɪláktəns] s. repugnancia, renuencia, aversión, desgana.
re·luc·tant [rɪláktənt] adj. renuente, refractario, opuesto; **-ly** adv. renuentemente, con renuencia, de mala gana; a regañadientes.
re·ly [rɪláɪ] v. **to — on** contar con, confiar en, fiarse de.
re·main [rɪmén] v. quedar(se), permanecer, estarse; restar, faltar.
re·main·der [rɪméndə] s. resto; restante; residuo.
re·mains [rɪ ménz] s. pl. restos; reliquias; sobras.
re·make [rɪmék] v. rehacer, hacer de nuevo.
re·mark [rɪmárk] s. observación, nota, reparo; v. notar, observar; **to — on** comentar; aludir a.
re·mark·a·ble [rɪmárkəbl] adj. notable; extraordinario; **remarkably** adv. notablemente, extraordinariamente.
rem·e·dy [rémədɪ] s. remedio; cura; v. remediar; curar.
re·mem·ber [rɪmémbə] v. recordar; acordarse; **— me to him** déle Vd. recuerdos (o memorias) de mi parte.
re·mem·brance [rɪmémbrəns] s. recuerdo; recordación; memoria; **-s** recuerdos, saludos.
re·mind [rɪmáɪnd] v. recordar.
re·mind·er [rɪmáɪndə] s. recordatorio, recordativo, memorándum, memoria; advertencia.
rem·i·nis·cence [rɛmənísns] s. reminiscencia, memoria, recuerdo.
re·miss [rɪmís] adj. descuidado, negligente.
re·mis·sion [rɪmíʃən] s. remisión; perdón.

re·mit [rɪmít] *v.* remitir; remesar, enviar una remesa; perdonar, absolver.

re·mit·tance [rɪmítn̩s] *s.* remisión, envío, remesa (*de fondos*).

rem·nant [rémnənt] *s.* resto; residuo; retazo (*de tela, paño, etc.*); vestigio.

re·mod·el [rimádl̩] *v.* rehacer, reconstruir; modelar de nuevo.

re·morse [rɪmɔ́rs] *s.* remordimiento.

re·mote [rɪmót] *adj.* remoto; lejano; *s.* — **control** telecontrol; comando a distancia.

re·mov·al [rɪmúvl̩] *s.* mudanza, traslado; deposición (*de un empleo*); eliminación; extracción; alejamiento.

re·move [rɪmúv] *v.* remover; mudar(se), trasladar(se); quitar; eliminar; extirpar; sacar, extraer; deponer (*de un empleo*); apartar, alejar.

re·moved [rɪmúvd] *adj.* remoto, distante.

re·nais·sance [rɛnəsáns] *s.* renacimiento.

re·na·scence [rɪnǽsn̩s] *s.* renacimiento.

rend [rɛnd] *v.* desgarrar, rasgar; rajar.

ren·der [réndəˑ] *v.* dar; entregar; hacer; ejecutar, interpretar (*música o un papel dramático*); traducir; **to — an account of** rendir o dar cuenta de; **to — homage** rendir homenaje; **to — thanks** rendir gracias, dar las gracias; **to — useless** inutilizar, incapacitar.

ren·di·tion [rɛndíʃən] *s.* (*surrender*) rendición; (*version*) traducción, ejecución.

re·new [rɪnjú] *v.* renovar; restaurar; reanudar; prorrogar (*un préstamo*).

re·new·al [rɪnjúəl] *s.* renovación; reanudación; prórroga.

re·nounce [rɪnáuns] *v.* renunciar.

ren·o·vate [rénəvet] *v.* renovar.

re·nown [rɪnáun] *s.* renombre.

re·nowned [rɪnáund] *adj.* renombrado.

rent [rɛnt] *s.* alquiler; renta, arrendamiento; **it is for** — se alquila, se arrienda; *v.* alquilar, arrendar.

rent [rɛnt] *pret. & p.p.* de **to rend**; *s.* grieta, hendidura; rasgadura, rotura.

rent·al [réntl̩] *s.* renta, alquiler.

re·o·pen [riópən] *v.* reabrir(se), volver a abrir(se).

re·pair [rɪpér] *v.* reparar; remendar; componer; restaurar; **to — to** dirigirse a; *s.* reparo, reparación; remiendo; compostura; **in — en** buen estado; compuesto.

rep·a·ra·tion [rɛpəréʃən] *s.* reparación; desagravio.

rep·ar·tee [rɛpartí] *s.* respuesta viva; agudeza en el diálogo.

re·pay [rɪpé] *v.* resarcir; compensar; reembolsar; pagar.

re·pay·ment [rɪpémənt] *s.* reintegro, pago, devolución, restitución.

re·peal [rɪpíl] *v.* derogar, abrogar, revocar, abolir (*una ley*); *s.* abrogación, derogación, revocación, abolición (*de una ley*).

re·peat [rɪpít] *v.* repetir; *s.* repetición.

re·peat·ed [rɪpítɪd] *adj.* repetido; **-ly** *adv.* repetidamente; repetidas veces, una y otra vez.

re·pel [rɪpél] *v.* repeler; rechazar; repugnar; **that idea -s me** me repugna (*o* me es repugnante) esa idea.

re·pel·lent [rɪpélənt] *s.* repelente; (*water*) impermeable.

re·pent [rɪpént] *v.* arrepentirse (de).

re·pen·tance [rɪpéntəns] *s.* arrepentimiento.

re·pen·tant [rɪpéntənt] *adj.* arrepentido; penitente.

rep·er·toire [répəˑtwar] *s.* repertorio.

rep·e·ti·tion [rɛpɪtíʃən] *s.* repetición.

re·place [rɪplés] *v.* reponer, volver a colocar; reemplazar; restituir; remudar.

re·place·a·ble [rɪplésəbl̩] *adj.* reemplazable; substituible.

re·place·ment [rɪplésmənt] *s.* reposición; reemplazo; devolución, restitución; substitución.

re·plen·ish [rɪplénɪʃ] *v.* reabastecer; rellenar, llenar.

re·plete [rɪplít] *adj.* repleto, atestado.

rep·li·ca [réplɪkə] *s.* reproducción, copia exacta.

re·ply [rɪpláɪ] *v.* replicar, contestar, responder; *s.* réplica, contestación, respuesta.

re·port [rɪpórt] *v.* dar cuenta de; avisar; informar; presentar un informe; rendir informe; hacer un reportaje, *Am.* reportar; denunciar, delatar; presentarse; **to — for duty** presentarse; **it is -ed that** dizque, se dice que, corre la voz que; *s.* noticia, reporte; informe; memorial; relación; rumor; estallido, disparo; **news — reportaje**.

re·port·er [rɪpórtəˑ] *s.* reportero, repórter.

re·pose [rɪpóz] *v.* reposar, descansar; **to — one's confidence in** confiar en; depositar su confianza en; *s.* reposo.

re·pos·i·to·ry [rɪpázətorɪ] *s.* depósito; almacén.

rep·re·sent [rɛprɪzɛ́nt] *v.* representar.

rep·re·sen·ta·tion [rɛprɪzɛntéʃən] *s.* representación.

rep·re·sen·ta·tive [rɛprɪzɛ́ntətɪv] *adj.* representativo; representante; típico; *s.* representante; delegado; diputado.

re·press [rɪprés] *v.* reprimir; refrenar, restringir; cohibir.

re·pres·sion [rɪpréʃən] *s.* represión.

re·prieve [rɪpriv] *v.* suspensión temporal de pena; alivio.

rep·ri·mand [réprəmænd] *v.* reprender, regañar; *s.* reprimenda, represión, regaño.

re·pri·sal [rɪpráɪzl̩] *s.* represalia.

re·proach [rɪprótʃ] *v.* reprochar; censurar, criticar; echar en cara; *s.* reproche, reprimenda; censura.

re·pro·duce [riprədjús] *v.* reproducir.

re·pro·duc·tion [riprədʌ́kʃən] *s.* reproducción.

re·proof [rɪprúf] *s.* represión, reproche, regaño.

re·prove [rɪprúv] *v.* reprobar, reprender, censurar.

rep·tile [réptl̩] *s.* reptil.

re·pub·lic [rɪpʌ́blɪk] *s.* república.

re·pub·li·can [rɪpʌ́blɪkən] *adj. & s.* republicano.

re·pu·di·ate [rɪpjúdiet] *v.* repudiar.

re·pug·nance [rɪpʌ́gnəns] *s.* repugnancia; aversión.

re·pug·nant [rɪpʌ́gnənt] *adj.* repugnante; antipático.

re·pulse [rɪpʌ́ls] *v.* repulsar, repeler; rechazar; *s.* repulsa; desaire.

re·pul·sive [rɪpʌ́lsɪv] *adj.* repulsivo, repugnante.

rep·u·ta·ble [répjətəbl̩] *adj.* de buena reputación.

rep·u·ta·tion [rɛpjətéʃən] *s.* reputación, renombre.

re·pute [rɪpjút] *v.* reputar; estimar, considerar; *s.* reputación; renombre, fama; **of ill — de mala fama**.

re·quest [rɪkwést] *s.* solicitud, petición, demanda; súplica, ruego; **at the — of** a solicitud de, a instancias de; *v.* solicitar, pedir, rogar, suplicar.

re·quire [rɪkwáɪr] *v.* requerir; exigir, demandar.

re·quire·ment [rɪkwáɪrmənt] *s.* requerimiento, requisito; exigencia; necesidad.

req·ui·site [rékwəzɪt] *s.* requisito; *adj.* requerido, necesario.

req·ui·si·tion [rɛkwəzíʃən] *s.* requisición, demanda, orden; *v.* demandar, pedir, ordenar.

re·scind [rɪsínd] *v.* rescindir.

res·cue [réskju] *v.* rescatar; librar; salvar; *s.* rescate, salvamento, salvación, socorro; **to go to the — of** acudir al socorro de, ir a salvar a.

re·search [rísɜtʃ] *s.* rebusca, búsqueda,

investigación; [rɪsɜ́tʃ] v. rebuscar, investigar.
re·sem·blance [rɪzémbləns] s. semejanza, parecido.
re·sem·ble [rɪzémbl̩] v. asemejarse a, semejar, parecerse a.
re·sent [rɪzént] v. resentirse de, sentirse de, darse por agraviado de.
re·sent·ful [rɪzéntfəl] adj. resentido; rencoroso.
re·sent·ment [rɪzéntmənt] s. resentimiento.
res·er·va·tion [rɛzəvéʃən] s. reservación; reserva.
re·serve [rɪzɜ́v] v. reservar; s. reserva.
re·served [rɪzɜ́vd] adj. retraido.
res·er·voir [rézəvwɔr] s. depósito (de agua, aceite, gas, provisiones, etc.); receptáculo; **water —** alberca, aljibe, tanque, estanque.
re·side [rɪzáɪd] v. residir, vivir.
res·i·dence [rézədəns] s. residencia; domicilio.
res·i·dent [rézədənt] adj. & s. residente.
res·i·den·tial [rɛzɪdéntʃəl] adj. residencial.
res·i·due [rézədju] s. residuo; resto.
re·sign [rɪzáɪn] v. renunciar; dimitir; **to — oneself** to resignarse a.
res·ig·na·tion [rɛzɪgnéʃən] s. renuncia, dimisión; resignación.
re·sil·ience [rɪzíljəns] s. elasticidad.
res·in [rézn̩] s. resina.
re·sist [rɪzíst] v. resistir; oponerse, resistirse a.
re·sis·tance [rɪzístəns] s. resistencia.
re·sis·tant [rɪzístənt] adj. resistente.
res·o·lute [rézəlut] adj. resuelto.
res·o·lu·tion [rɛzəlúʃən] s. resolución; acuerdo.
re·solve [rɪzálv] v. resolver(se); **to — into** resolverse en, reducirse a, transformarse en; **to — to** acordar; proponerse, resolverse a.
res·o·nance [rézənəns] s. resonancia.
res·o·nant [rézənənt] adj. resonante.
re·sort [rɪzɔ́rt] v. recurrir, acudir; **to — to force** recurrir a la fuerza; s. refugio; morada; **as a last — como último recurso; summer —** lugar de veraneo; **vice —** garito; casa de mala fama; **to have — to** recurrir a.
re·sort·er [rɪzɔ́rtə] s. **summer —** veraneante.
re·sound [rɪzáʊnd] v. resonar; repercutir; retumbar.
re·source [rɪsɔ́rs] s. recurso; **natural -s** recursos o riquezas naturales.
re·spect [rɪspékt] v. respectar; **as -s** por lo que respecta a, por lo que toca a, tocante a; s. respeto; consideración; **with — to** (con) respecto a, respecto de; por lo que atañe a.
re·spect·a·ble [rɪspéktəbl̩] adj. respetable.
re·spect·ful [rɪspéktfəl] adj. respetuoso.
re·spect·ing [rɪspéktɪŋ] prep. con respecto a, tocante a.
re·spec·tive [rɪspéktɪv] adj. respectivo.
res·pi·ra·tion [rɛspəréʃən] s. respiración, respiro.
re·spite [réspɪt] s. tregua, pausa, descanso; intervalo; prórroga.
re·splen·dent [rɪspléndənt] adj. resplandeciente.
re·spond [rɪspánd] v. responder; corresponder; reaccionar.
re·sponse [rɪspáns] s. respuesta, contestación; reacción.
re·spon·si·bil·i·ty [rɪspɑnsəbílətɪ] s. responsabilidad.
re·spon·si·ble [rɪspánsəbl̩] adj. responsable; formal, digno de confianza.
rest [rɛst] s. (repose) descanso; reposo; quietud; tregua; pausa; (support) apoyo; **at — en** paz; en reposo; tranquilo; **the —** el resto; los demás; v. descansar; reposar; apoyar; **to — on** descansar sobre; apoyar(se) en; basar(se) en; contar con, confiar en, depender de.

res·tau·rant [réstərənt] s. restaurante. Am. restorán.
rest·ful [réstfəl] adj. reposado, sosegado, tranquilo.
res·ti·tu·tion [rɛstətjúʃən] s. restitución; devolución.
res·tive [réstɪv] adj. intranquilo.
rest·less [réstlɪs] adj. inquieto, intranquilo.
rest·less·ness [réstlɪsnɪs] s. inquietud, desasosiego, intranquilidad.
res·to·ra·tion [rɛstəréʃən] s. restauración; restitución; renovación.
re·store [rɪstór] v. restaurar; renovar; restituir; restablecer.
re·strain [rɪstrén] v. refrenar, contener, cohibir, reprimir, coartar; restringir.
re·straint [rɪstrént] s. restricción; reserva, circunspección; moderación; cohibición.
re·strict [rɪstríkt] v. restringir, limitar.
re·stric·tion [rɪstríkʃən] s. restricción.
re·sult [rɪzált] v. resultar; **to — from** resultar de; **to — in** parar en; causar; dar por resultado; s. resulta, resultado; **as a —** de resultas, como resultado.
re·sume [rɪzúm] v. reasumir, volver a tomar; recomenzar; reanudar, continuar.
ré·su·mé [rɛzʊmé] s. resumen, sumario.
re·sur·gent [rɪsɜ́dʒənt] adj. resurgente.
res·ur·rec·tion [rɛzərékʃən] s. resurrección.
re·sus·ci·tate [rɪsásətet] v. resucitar; revivir.
re·tail [rítel] s. venta al por menor; **at — al por menor; — merchant** detallista, comerciante al por menor; **— price** precio al por menor; v. detallar; vender al menudeo (o vender al por menor), Méx., C.A., Ven., Col. menudear.
re·tail·er [rítelə] s. detallista, revendedor, comerciante al por menor.
re·tain [rɪtén] v. retener; emplear.
re·tal·i·ate [rɪtǽliet] v. desquitarse, vengarse.
re·tal·i·a·tion [rɪtæliéʃən] s. desquite; desagravio; represalia, venganza.
re·tard [rɪtárd] v. retardar, retrasar, atrasar.
re·ten·tion [rɪténʃən] s. retención.
ret·i·cence [rétəsəns] s. reserva.
ret·i·nue [rétnju] s. comitiva, séquito, acompañamiento.
re·tire [rɪtáɪr] v. retirar(se); jubilar(se); acostarse; apartarse.
re·tire·ment [rɪtáɪrmənt] s. retiro; jubilación.
re·tort [rɪtɔ́rt] v. replicar; redargüir; s. réplica.
re·touch [ritátʃ] v. retocar; s. retoque.
re·trace [ritrés] v. repasar; volver a trazar; **to — one's steps** volver sobre sus pasos, retroceder.
re·tract [rɪtrǽkt] v. retractar, retractarse de; desdecirse (de); retraer.
re·treat [rɪtrít] s. retiro, refugio, asilo; retirada; retreta (toque de retirada); v. retirarse; retroceder.
re·trench [rɪtréntʃ] v. cercenar, reducir, disminuir; economizar.
re·trieve [rɪtrív] v. cobrar (la caza); recobrar, recuperar; reparar (una pérdida).
ret·ro·ac·tive [rɛtroǽktɪv] adj. retroactivo.
ret·ro·flex [rétrofleks] adj. retroflejo.
ret·ro·rock·et [rétrorakɪt] s. retrocohete.
ret·ro·spect [rétrospɛkt] s. retrospección; **in —** retrospectivamente.
re·turn [rɪtɜ́n] v. volver, regresar; retornar; devolver; replicar; redituar; producir; restar (la pelota en tenis); **to — a favor** corresponder a un favor; **to — a report** rendir un informe; s. vuelta, regreso; retorno; recompensa; restitución; devolución; réplica; resto (en un juego de pelota);

RE

rédito, ganancia; informe; — **game** desquite, juego de desquite; — **ticket** boleto de vuelta; **by** — **mail** a vuelta de correo; **election -s** reportaje de elecciones; **in** — en cambio; **in** — **for** a cambio de, a trueque de; **income tax** — declaración de rentas; **many happy -s** muchas felicidades (en su día).

re·un·ion [rijúnjən] s. reunión; junta.

re·u·nite [rijʊnáɪt] v. reunir(se), volver a unirse; reconciliar(se).

re·veal [rɪvíl] v. revelar.

rev·el [rɛ́vl] v. deleitarse, gozarse; parrandear, Am. farrear; andar de parranda, Ríopl. andar de farra; s. parranda, juerga, jarana.

rev·e·la·tion [rɛvɪléʃən] s. revelación; **Revelation(s)** Apocalipsis.

rev·el·ry [rɛ́vlrɪ] s. jaleo, juerga, jarana.

re·venge [rɪvɛ́ndʒ] v. vengar, vindicar; s. venganza; desquite.

re·venge·ful [rɪvɛ́ndʒfəl] adj. vengativo.

rev·e·nue [rɛ́vənju] s. renta; rédito; rentas públicas, ingresos.

re·vere [rɪvír] v. venerar.

rev·er·ence [rɛ́vrəns] s. reverencia; veneración; v. reverenciar, venerar.

rev·er·end [rɛ́vrənd] adj. reverendo; venerable.

rev·er·ent [rɛ́vrənt] adj. reverente.

rev·er·ie, rev·er·y [rɛ́vərɪ] s. ensueño; arrobamiento.

re·verse [rɪvɜ́s] adj. inverso, invertido; contrario, opuesto; s. revés; reverso, dorso; lo contrario; contratiempo; v. invertir; voltear; revocar (una sentencia).

re·vert [rɪvɜ́t] v. revertir, volver atrás, retroceder.

re·view [rɪvjú] v. (study) repasar, revisar; revistar; (inspect) pasar revista a (las tropas); (criticize) reseñar, hacer una reseña de (un libro); s. revista; repaso; reseña, crítica (de un libro, drama, etc.); revisión (de un caso jurídico, sentencia, etc.).

re·vile [rɪváɪl] v. vilipendiar, vituperar, denigrar.

re·vise [rɪváɪz] v. revisar, repasar, releer (para corregir); corregir, enmendar.

re·vi·sion [rɪvíʒən] s. revisión; enmienda; edición enmendada o mejorada.

re·viv·al [rɪváɪvl] s. (renewal) renovación; revivificación; (repeating) renacimiento; nueva presentación (teatral); — **meeting** junta para revivir el fervor religioso; **religious** — despertamiento (o nuevo fervor) religioso.

re·vive [rɪváɪv] v. revivir, resucitar; volver en sí; renacer; reavivar, reanimar(se); avivar.

re·voke [rɪvók] v. revocar, abrogar, anular; renunciar (en los juegos de naipes).

re·volt [rɪvólt] v. s. revuelta, rebelión, sublevación; v. rebelarse, sublevarse; **it -s me** me da asco, me repugna.

re·volt·ing [rɪvóltɪŋ] adj. repugnante; asqueroso.

rev·o·lu·tion [rɛvəlúʃən] s. revolución; vuelta (que da una rueda).

rev·o·lu·tion·ar·y [rɛvəlúʃənɛrɪ] adj. & s. revolucionario.

rev·o·lu·tion·ist [rɛvəlúʃənɪst] s. revolucionario.

re·volve [rɪválv] v. girar, dar vueltas; rodar; voltear, dar vueltas a; **to** — **in one's mind** revolver en la mente, ponderar, reflexionar.

re·volv·er [rɪválvɚ] s. revólver.

re·ward [rɪwɔ́rd] v. premiar; recompensar; s. premio, gratificación, recompensa, galardón; albricias (por haber hallado algún objeto perdido).

re·write [rɪráɪt] v. volver a escribir; refundir (un escrito).

rhap·so·dy [rǽpsədɪ] s. rapsodia.

rhe·ni·um [riniəm] s. renio.

rhet·o·ric [rɛ́tərɪk] s. retórica.

rheu·ma·tism [rúmətɪzəm] s. reumatismo, reuma.

rhi·noc·er·os [raɪnásərəs] s. rinoceronte.

rho·di·um [ródɪəm] s. rodio.

rho·do·den·dron [rodədɛ́ndrən] s. rododendro.

rhu·barb [rúbɑrb] s. ruibarbo.

rhyme [raɪm] s. rima; **without** — **or reason** sin ton ni son; v. rimar.

rhythm [rɪ́ðəm] s. ritmo.

rhyth·mi·cal [rɪ́ðmɪkl] adj. rítmico, acompasado, cadencioso.

rib [rɪb] s. costilla; varilla (de paraguas); cordoncillo (de ciertos tejidos).

rib·bon [rɪ́bən] s. cinta; listón, banda; moña; tira.

rice [raɪs] s. arroz; — **field** arrozal.

rich [rɪtʃ] adj. rico; costoso, suntuoso; sabroso; — **color** color vivo; — **food** alimento muy manteco o dulce.

rich·es [rɪ́tʃɪz] s. pl. riqueza, riquezas.

rick·et·y [rɪ́kɪtɪ] adj. desvencijado; raquítico.

rid [rɪd] v. librar, desembarazar; **to get** — **of** librarse de, deshacerse de, desembarazarse de; pret. & p.p. de **to rid**.

rid·den [rɪ́dn̩] p.p. de **to ride**.

rid·dle [rɪdl̩] acertijo, adivinanza, enigma; v. acribillar, perforar; **to** — **with bullets** acribillar a balazos.

ride [raɪd] v. (horse) cabalgar, montar; (vehicle) pasear; ir en (tranvía, tren); **to** — **a bicycle** andar o montar en bicicleta; **to** — **a horse** montar un caballo; **to** — **horseback** montar a caballo; **to** — **over a country** pasear o viajar por un país (en auto, a caballo o por tren); **to** — **someone** dominar a alguien; burlarse de alguien; s. paseo (a caballo o en automóvil); viaje (a caballo, en automóvil, por ferrocarril, etc.).

rid·er [ráɪdɚ] s. jinete; pasajero (de automóvil); biciclista; motociclista; aditamento, cláusula añadida (a un proyecto de ley).

ridge [rɪdʒ] s. espinazo; lomo (entre dos surcos); arista, intersección (de dos planos); cordillera; cerro; caballete (de tejado); cordoncillo (de ciertos tejidos).

rid·i·cule [rɪ́dɪkjul] s. ridículo; burla, mofa; v. ridiculizar, poner en ridículo.

ri·dic·u·lous [rɪdɪ́kjələs] adj. ridículo.

ri·fle [ráɪfl̩] s. rifle; v. pillar, robar; despojar.

rift [rɪft] s. (opening) raja; abertura; (disagreement) desacuerdo.

rig [rɪg] v. aparejar, equipar; enjarciar (un barco de vela); **to** — **oneself up** emperifollarse, ataviarse; s. aparejo, equipo; aparato; atavío, traje.

rig·ging [rɪ́gɪŋ] s— jarcia, aparejo.

right [raɪt] adj. (not left) derecho; diestro; (proper) recto; justo; propio; adecuado; correcto; — **angle** ángulo recto; — **side** lado derecho; derecho (de un tejido, traje, etc.); **it is** — **that** está bien que, es justo que; **to be** — tener razón; **to be all** — estar bien; estar bien de salud; **to be in one's** — **mind** estar en sus cabales; adv. derecho, directamente; rectamente; justamente; bien; correctamente; a la derecha; — **about-face** media vuelta; — **hungry** muy hambriento; — **now** ahora mismo, inmediatamente; — **there** allí mismo, Am. allí mero; **go** — **home!** ¡vete derechito a casa!; **it is** — **where you left it** está exactamente (o en el mero lugar) donde lo dejaste; **to to hit** — **in the eye** dar de lleno en el

ojo, *Am.* dar en el mero ojo; *s.* derecho; *s.* derecho; autoridad; privilegio; — **of way** derecho de vía; **by** — **(by -s)** justamente, con justicia; según la ley; **from** — **to left** de derecha a izquierda; **to the** — a la derecha; **to be in the** — tener razón; *v.* enderezar; corregir.

righ·teous [ráɪtʃəs] *adj.* recto, justo, virtuoso.

righ·teous·ness [ráɪtʃəsnɪs] *s.* rectitud, virtud.

right·ful [ráɪtfəl] *adj.* justo; legítimo.

right-hand [ráɪthǽnd] *adj.* derecho, de la mano derecha; — **man** brazo derecho.

right·ist [ráɪtɪst] *s.* derechista.

right·ly [ráɪtlɪ] *adv.* con razón; justamente, rectamente; propiamente, aptamente, debidamente.

right-wing [ráɪtwɪŋ] *adj.* derechista.

rig·id [rídʒɪd] *adj.* rígido.

ri·gid·i·ty [rɪdʒídətɪ] *s.* rigidez; tiesura.

rig·or [rígɚ] *s.* rigor; rigidez; severidad.

rig·or·ous [rígɚəs] *adj.* rigoroso (*o* riguroso), severo.

rim [rɪm] *s.* borde, orilla; aro.

rime = **rhyme.**

rind [raɪnd] *s.* corteza, cáscara; mondadura.

ring [rɪŋ] *s.* (*finger*) anillo, sortija; argolla; aro; (*circle*) arena; pista; (*sound*) toque; tañido; repique; (*telephone*) timbrazo; telefonazo; —**leader** cabecilla; — **of defiance** tono de reto; — **of shouts** gritería; — **of a telephone** llamada de teléfono; **ring-shaped** en forma de anillo, anular; **key**— llavero; **sarcastic** — retintín; *v.* tocar (*un timbre, una campanilla o campana*); sonar; tañer, repicar; resonar; zumbar (*los oídos*); **to** — **for something** llamar para pedir algo; **to** — **the nose of an animal** ponerle una argolla en la nariz a un animal; **to** — **up on the phone** llamar por teléfono.

ring·let [rínlɪt] *s.* rizo, bucle; pequeña sortija.

rink [rɪŋk] *s.* patinadero (*cancha para patinar*).

rinse [rɪns] *v.* enjuagar; lavar; aclarar (*la ropa*); *s.* enjuague.

ri·ot [ráɪət] *s.* motín, desorden, alboroto, tumulto; — **of color** riqueza o exceso de colores chillantes; *v.* amotinarse, alborotar, armar un tumulto.

ri·ot·ous [ráɪətəs] *adj.* revoltoso.

rip [rɪp] *v.* rasgar(se), romper(se); descoser(se); **to** — **off** rasgar, arrancar, cortar; **to** — **out a seam** descoser una costura; *s.* rasgón, rasgadura, rotura; descosido.

ripe [raɪp] *adj.* maduro, sazonado; en sazón; — **for** maduro para, sazonado para; bien preparado para, listo para.

rip·en [ráɪpən] *v.* madurar(se), sazonar(se).

ripe·ness [ráɪpnɪs] *s.* madurez, sazón.

rip·ple [rípl̩] *v.* rizar(se), agitar(se), ondear, temblar (*la superficie del agua*); murmurar (*un arroyo*); *s.* onda, temblor, ondulación (*en la superficie del agua*); murmullo (*de un arroyo*).

rise [raɪz] *v.* subir; ascender; alzarse, levantarse; elevarse; surgir; salir (*el sol, la luna, un astro*); hincharse (*la masa del pan*); **to** — **up in rebellion** sublevarse, levantarse, alzarse (en rebelión); *s.* subida; ascenso; pendiente; elevación; salida del sol, de la luna, etc.); subida, alza (*de precios*).

ris·en [rízn̩] *p.p. de* **to rise.**

risk [rɪsk] *s.* riesgo; *v.* arriesgar, aventurar, poner en peligro; exponerse a; **to** — **defeat** correr el riesgo de perder, exponerse a perder.

risk·y [rískɪ] *adj.* arriesgado, peligroso, aventurado.

ris·qué [rɪské] *adj.* escabroso.

rite [raɪt] *s.* rito, ceremonia.

rit·u·al [rítʃʊəl] *adj. & s.* ritual, ceremonial.

ri·val [ráɪvl̩] *s.* rival, competidor, émulo; *adj.* competidor; **the** — **party** el partido opuesto; *v.* rivalizar con, competir con.

ri·val·ry [ráɪvl̩rɪ] *s.* rivalidad.

riv·er [rívɚ] *s.* río.

riv·et [rívɪt] *s.* remache; *v.* remachar; fijar.

riv·u·let [rívjəlɪt] *s.* riachuelo, arroyuelo.

road [rod] *s.* camino; carretera; vía.

road·side [ródsaɪd] *s.* borde del camino.

road·way [ródwe] *s.* camino, carretera.

roam [rom] *v.* vagar, errar, andar errante.

roar [ror] *v.* rugir, bramar; **to** — **with laughter** reír a carcajadas; *s.* rugido, bramido; — **of laughter** risotada, carcajada.

roast [rost] *v.* asar(se); tostar (*café, maíz, etc.*); ridiculizar, criticar; *s.* asado, carne asada; *adj.* asado; — **beef** rosbif, rosbí.

rob [rɑb] *v.* robar, hurtar; **to** — **someone of something** robarle algo a alguien.

rob·ber [rábɚ] *s.* ladrón; **highway** — salteador.

rob·ber·y [rábrɪ] *s.* robo, hurto.

robe [rob] *s.* manto, traje talar, túnica, toga (*de un juez, letrado, etc.*); bata; **automobile** — manta de automóvil.

rob·in [rábɪn] *s.* petirrojo.

ro·bust [róbʌst] *adj.* robusto, fuerte.

rock [rɑk] *s.* roca, peña; peñasco; — **crystal** cristal de roca; — **salt** sal gema o sal mineral; **to go on the -s** tropezar en un escollo, *Am.* escollar; *v.* mecer(se), balancear(se); bambolear(se); estremecer; **to** — **to sleep** adormecer (*meciendo*), arrullar.

rock·er [rákɚ] *s.* mecedora; arco de una mecedora o cuna.

rock·et [rákɪt] *s.* cohete.

rock·et·ry [rákətrɪ] *s.* cohetería.

rock·ing [rákɪŋ] *s.* balanceo; *adj.* oscilante; — **chair** silla mecedora.

rock·y [rákɪ] *adj.* roqueño, rocoso, rocalloso; peñascoso; pedregoso; movedizo; tembloroso; débil, desvanecido.

rod [rɑd] *s.* vara, varilla; medida de longitud (*aproximadamente 5 metros*); **fishing** — caña de pescar.

rode [rod] *pret. de* **to ride.**

ro·dent [ródənt] *s.* roedor.

rogue [rog] *s.* pícaro, bribón, tunante, pillo; **-s' gallery** colección policíaca de retratos de criminales.

ro·guish [rógɪʃ] *adj.* pícaro, pillo, picaresco; travieso.

role [rol] *s.* papel, parte.

roll [rol] *v.* (*move*) rodar; girar; balancearse (*un barco*); bambolearse; ondular, retumbar (*el trueno, un cañón*); aplanar, alisar con rodillo; envolver; redoblar (*un tambor*); pronunciar (*la rr doble*); **to** — **over in the snow** revolverse o revolcarse en la nieve; **to** — **up** arrollar, enrollar, envolver; *s.* rollo (*de papel, paño, tela, etc.*); balanceo (*de un barco*); retumbo (*del trueno, de cañón*), redoble (*de un tambor*); lista ondulación; oleaje; bollo, rosca, panecillo; **to call the** — pasar lista.

roll·er [rólɚ] *s.* rodillo, cilindro (*para aplanar o alisar*); apisonadora; rollo (*rodillo de pastelero*); oleada; — **coaster** montaña rusa; — **skate** patín de ruedas.

Ro·man [rómən] *adj. & s.* romano; — **nose** nariz aguileña.

ro·mance [romǽns] *s.* (*literature*) romance; novela; cuento; fábula; (*affair*) aventura romántica; amorío, lance amoroso; *v.* contar o fingir fábulas; andar en amoríos o aventuras; **Ro·mance** *adj.* romance, románico, neolatino.

ro·man·tic [romǽntık] *adj.* romántico; novelesco.

ro·man·ti·cism [romǽntəsızəm] *s.* romanticismo.

ro·man·ti·cist [romǽntəsıst] *s.* romántico, escritor romántico.

romp [rɑmp] *v.* triscar, juguetear, retozar, travesear.

roof [ruf] *s.* techo, techumbre, techado; tejado; — **garden** azotea-jardín; — **of the mouth** paladar; **flat** — azotea; *v.* techar.

room [rum] *s.* (*in building*) cuarto, pieza, sala, habitación; (*space*) espacio; lugar, sitio; **there is no** — **for more** no cabe(n) más, no hay lugar o cabida para más; **to make** — hacer lugar; —**mate** compañero de cuarto; *v.* vivir, hospedarse, alojarse.

room·er [rúmɚ] *s.* inquilino.

room·i·ness [rúmınıs] *s.* holgura.

room·y [rúmı] *adj.* espacioso, amplio, holgado.

roost [rust] *s.* gallinero; peroha de gallinero; *v.* acurrucarse (*las aves en la percha*); pasar la noche.

roost·er [rústɚ] *s.* gallo.

root [rut] *s.* raíz; *v.* arraigar(se); echar raíces; hocicar, hozar (*dícese de los cerdos*); **to** — **for** vitorear, aclamar; **to** — **out** (*o* — **up**) desarraigar, arrancar de raíz; **to become -ed** arraigarse.

rope [rop] *s.* (*cord*) soga, cuerda; (*lasso*) reata, lazo; **to be at the end of one's** — haber agotado el último recurso; estar (*o* andar) en las últimas; no saber qué hacer; **to know the -s** saber todas las tretas de un asunto o negocio; *v.* amarrar, lazar, enlazar; **to** — **off** acordelar, poner cuerdas tirantes alrededor de (*un sitio*); **to** — **someone in** embaucar a alguien.

ro·sa·ry [rózərı] *s.* rosario.

rose [roz] *pret. de* **to rise.**

rose [roz] *s.* rosa; color de rosa; —**bush** rosal; — **window** rosetón.

rose·bud [rózbʌd] *s.* capullo o botón de rosa, yema, pimpollo.

ros·ette [rozét] *s.* roseta; rosetón.

ros·ter [rástɚ] *s.* registro; lista.

ros·trum [rástrəm] *s.* tribuna.

ros·y [rózı] *adj.* (*color*) rosado; color de rosa; (*condition*) alegre, risueño; — **future** porvenir risueño.

rot [rɑt] *v.* pudrir(se); corromperse; *s.* podre, podredumbre, putrefacción.

ro·ta·ry [rótərı] *adj.* rotatorio, giratorio, rotativo.

ro·tate [rótet] *v.* girar, dar vueltas; hacer girar; turnarse; cultivar en rotación.

ro·ta·tion [rotéʃən] *s.* rotación, vuelta; — **of crops** rotación de cultivos.

rote [rot] *s.* rutina, repetición maquinal; **by** — maquinalmente.

rot·ten [rátṇ] *adj.* podrido, putrefacto; hediondo; corrompido, corrupto.

rouge [ruʒ] *s.* colorete; *v.* pintar(se), poner(se) colorete.

rough [rʌf] *adj.* (*coarse*) áspero; tosco; fragoso; escabroso; (*rude*) brusco; grosero; (*stormy*) borrascoso, tempestuoso; — **diamond** diamante en bruto; — **draft** borrador; bosquejo; — **estimate** cálculo aproximativo, tanteo; — **ground** terreno escabroso; — **idea** idea aproximada; — **sea** mar picado; — **weather** tiempo borrascoso;

adv. véase **roughly**; *v.* **to** — **it** vivir sin lujos ni comodidades, hacer vida campestre.

rough·en [rʌfən] *v.* hacer o poner áspero; picar, rascar (*una superficie*); rajarse, agrietarse (*la piel*).

rough·ly [rʌflı] *adv.* ásperamente; groseramente, rudamente; aproximadamente; **to estimate** — tantear.

rough·ness [rʌfnıs] *s.* aspereza; escabrosidad; rudeza; tosquedad; **the** — **of the sea** lo picado del mar; **the** — **of the weather** lo borrascoso del tiempo.

round [raund] *adj.* redondo; rotundo; circular; — **trip** viaje redondo, viaje de ida y vuelta; **round-trip ticket** boleto (*o* billete) de ida y vuelta; *s.* vuelta, rotación, revolución; ronda; vuelta (*en el juego de naipes*); tanda, turno (*en ciertos deportes*); escalón, travesaño (*de escalera de mano*); danza en rueda; — **of ammunition** carga de municiones; descarga; — **of applause** explosión de aplausos; — **of pleasures** sucesión de placeres; **to make the -s** rondar; *prep. & adv. véase* **around**; — **about** a la redonda; por todos lados; **round-shouldered** cargado de espaldas; **to come** — **again** volver otra vez; **to go** — **a corner** doblar una esquina; *v.* redondear; dar vuelta a; **to** — **a corner** doblar una esquina; **to** — **out** redondear; completar; **to** — **up cattle** juntar el ganado, *Am.* rodear el ganado.

round·a·bout [ráundəbaut] *adj.* indirecto.

round·ness [ráundnıs] *s.* redondez.

round·up [ráundʌp] *s.* rodeo (*de ganado*); redada (*de criminales*); *v.* repuntar.

rouse [rauz] *v.* despertar(se), *Riopl.* recordar; excitar; incitar, provocar; levantar (*la caza*).

rout [raut] *s.* derrota, fuga desordenada; *v.* derrotar; poner en fuga; **to** — **out** echar, hacer salir a toda prisa.

route [rut] *s.* ruta, camino, vía; itinerario; *v.* dirigir o enviar por cierta ruta.

rou·tine [rutín] *s.* rutina.

rove [rov] *v.* vagar, errar, andar errante.

rov·er [róvɚ] *s.* vagabundo.

row [rau] *s.* riña, pelea, pelotera; *v.* pelearse, reñir; armar una riña o pelotera.

row [ro] *s.* fila, hilera; paseo en lancha; *v.* remar, bogar; llevar en lancha o bote.

row·boat [róbot] *s.* bote de remos, lancha.

reow·er [róɚ] *s.* remero.

roy·al [rɔ́ıəl] *adj.* real, regio.

roy·al·ist [rɔ́ıəlıst] *s.* realista.

roy·al·ty [rɔ́ıəltı] *s.* realeza, soberanía real; persona o personas reales; derechos (*pagados a un autor o inventor*).

rub [rʌb] *v.* (*apply friction*) frotar; restregar; fregar; (*scrape*) raspar; irritar; **to** — **out** borrar; **to** — **someone the wrong way** irritar, contrariar, llevarle a uno la contraria; *s.* fricción, friega, frotación; roce; sarcasmo; **there is the** — allí está la dificultad.

rub·ber [rʌbɚ] *s.* caucho, goma, *Méx.*, *C.A.* hule; goma elástica; goma de borrar; partida (*en ciertos juegos de naipes*); jugada decisiva (*en ciertos juegos de naipes*); **-s** chanclos, zapatos de goma o hule; *adj.* de caucho, de goma, *Méx.*, *C.A.* de hule; — **band** faja o banda de goma; — **plantation** cauchal; — **tree** *Am.* caucho, *Am.* gomero.

rub·bish [rʌbıʃ] *s.* basura, desechos, desperdicios; tonterías.

rub·ble [rʌbl] *s.* escombros; ripio, cascajo,

fragmentos de ladrillos o piedras; piedra en bruto, piedra sin labrar.

ru·bid·i·um [rubídiəm] *s.* rubidio.

ru·bric [rúbrɪk] *s.* rúbrica.

ru·by [rúbɪ] *s.* rubí.

rud·der [rʌ́də·] *s.* timón.

rud·dy [rʌ́dɪ] *adj.* rojo; rojizo; rubicundo.

rude [rud] *adj.* rudo; grosero; áspero; brusco; tosco.

rude·ness [rúdnɪs] *s.* rudeza; grosería, descortesía; tosquedad.

rue·ful [rúfəl] *adj.* triste; lastimoso, lamentable.

ruf·fi·an [rʌ́fɪən] *s.* rufián, hombre brutal.

ruf·fle [rʌ́fl] *v.* rizar, fruncir *(tela)*; arrugar; desarreglar; rizar *(la superficie del agua)*; perturbar; molestar; *s.* volante *(de un traje)*; frunce, pliegue; ondulación *(en al agua)*.

rug [rʌg] *s.* alfombra, tapete.

rug·ged [rʌ́gɪd] *adj.* escabroso, fragoso; áspero; recio, robusto; tosco; borrascoso, tempestuoso.

ru·in [rúɪn] *s.* ruina; **to go to —** arruinarse, caer en ruinas, venir a menos; *v.* arruinar; echar a perder; estropear.

ru·in·ous [rúɪnəs] *adj.* ruinoso; desastroso.

rule [rul] *s.* *(regulation)* regla; reglamento; precepto; *(control)* mando, gobierno; **as a —** por regla general; *v.* regir, gobernar; mandar; dirigir, guiar; dominar; fallar, decidir; rayar *(con regla)*; **to — out** excluir; **to — over** regir, gobernar.

rul·er [rúlə·] *s.* gobernante; soberano; regla *(para medir o trazar líneas)*.

rul·ing [rúlɪŋ] *s.* fallo, decisión; gobierno; *adj.* predominante, prevaleciente; principal.

rum [rʌm] *s.* ron.

rum·ble [rʌ́mbl] *v.* retumbar, hacer estruendo, rugir; *s.* retumbo, estruendo, rumor, ruido sordo; **— seat** asiento trasero *(de cupé)*.

ru·mi·nant [rúmənənt] *s.* rumiante.

ru·mi·nate [rúmənet] *v.* rumiar; reflexionar, meditar.

rum·mage [rʌ́mɪdʒ] *v.* escudriñar revolviéndolo todo; *s.* búsqueda desordenada; **— sale** venta de prendas usadas *(para beneficencia)*.

ru·mor [rúmə·] *s.* rumor; runrún; *v.* murmurar; **it is -ed that** corre la voz que.

rump [rʌmp] *s.* anca; trasero.

rum·ple [rʌ́mpl] *v.* estrujar, ajar; arrugar; *s.* arruga *(en un traje)*.

rum·pus [rʌ́mpəs] *s.* barullo, alharaca, boruca, batahola.

run [rʌn] *v.* *(on foot)* correr; *(function)* andar; marchar; funcionar; *(flow)* fluir; chorrear; *(go over)* recorrer; *(direct)* dirigir, gobernar; *(un negocio, empresa, máquina, casa, etc.)*; extenderse *(de un punto a otro)*; correrse *(los colores)*; ser candidato *(a un puesto político)*; **to — a fever** tener calentura; **to — away** huir; fugarse, escaparse; **to — across a person** encontrarse o tropezar con una persona; **to — down** dejar de funcionar *(una máquina, reloj, etc.)*; aprehender a *(un criminal)*; hablar mal de; atropellar; **to get — down in health** quebrantársele a uno la salud; **to — dry** secarse; **to — into** tropezar con, encontrarse con; chocar con; **to — around with** asociarse con; tener amores con; **to — into debt** adeudarse; **to — something into** meter algo en, clavar algo en; **to — out** salirse; **to — out of money** acabársele a uno el dinero; **to — over** derramarse *(un líquido)*; atropellar, pasar por encima de; repasar, echar un vistazo a *(la*

lección, un libro, etc.); **to — through a book** hojear un libro; **the play ran for three months** se dió la comedia durante tres meses; *s.* carrera, corrida; curso, marcha; recorrido; manejo; **— of good luck** serie de repetidos éxitos; **— of performances** serie de representaciones; **— on a bank** corrida, demanda extraordinaria de fondos bancarios; **in the long — a** la larga; **stocking —** carrera; **the common — of mankind** el común de las gentes; **to have the — of** tener el libre uso de; *p.p. de* **to run.**

run·a·way [rʌ́nəwe] *adj.* fugitivo; **— horse** caballo desbocado; **— marriage** casamiento de escapatoria; *s.* fugitivo; caballo desbocado; fuga.

rung [rʌŋ] *s.* barrote, travesaño *(de silla, escalera de mano, etc.)*; *pret. & p.p. de* **to ring.**

run·ner [rʌ́nə·] *s.* corredor; tapete *(para un pasillo o mesa)*, Riopl. pasillo; carrera *(en una media)*; cuchilla *(de patín o de trineo)*; contrabandista.

run·ning [rʌ́nɪŋ] *s.* *(race)* corrida, carrera; *(direction)* manejo, dirección; *(flow)* flujo; **to be out of the —** estar fuera de combate; *adj.* corriente; **— board** estribo; **— expenses** gastos corrientes; **— knot** nudo corredizo; **— water** agua corriente; **in — condition** en buen estado; **for ten days —** por diez días seguidos.

runt [rʌnt] *s.* enano; hombrecillo.

run·way [rʌ́nwe] *s.* senda; vía; pista *(de aterrizaje)*.

rup·ture [rʌ́ptʃə·] *s.* ruptura; rompimiento, rotura; hernia; *v.* romper(se); reventar.

ru·ral [rúrəl] *adj.* rural, campestre.

rush [rʌʃ] *v.* *(hurry)* apresurar(se); *Am.* apurarse; despachar con prisa; *(attack)* lanzar(se), precipitar(se); abalanzarse; acometer; **to — out** salir a todo correr; **to — past** pasar a toda prisa; *s.* precipitación, prisa; acometida; junco; **— chair** silla de junco; **— of business** gran movimiento comercial; **— of people** tropel de gente; **— order** pedido urgente.

Rus·sian [rʌ́ʃən] *adj. & s.* ruso.

rust [rʌst] *s.* moho, orín; herrumbre; tizón *(enfermedad de las plantas)*; **— color** color rojizo; *v.* enmohecer(se), oxidar(se).

rus·tic [rʌ́stɪk] *adj. & s.* rústico, campesino.

rus·tle [rʌ́sl] *v.* susurrar, crujir; menear; **to — cattle** robar ganado; *s.* susurro, crujido.

rust-proof [rʌ́stpruf] *adj.* inoxidable.

rust·y [rʌ́stɪ] *adj.* mohoso, cubierto de orín, oxidado; rojizo; entorpecido, falto de uso; falto de práctica.

rut [rʌt] *s.* rodada; rutina, método rutinario; **to be in a —** hacer una cosa por rutina, ser esclavo de la rutina.

ru·the·ni·um [ruθínɪəm] *s.* rutenio.

ruth·less [rúθlɪs] *adj.* despiadado, cruel, brutal.

ruth·less·ness [rúθlɪsnɪs] *s.* fiereza, falta de miramiento, truculencia, crueldad.

rye [raɪ] *s.* centeno.

S·s

sa·ber [sébə·] *s.* sable.

sab·o·tage [sǽbətɑʒ] *s.* sabotaje; *v.* sabotear.

sack [sæk] *s.* *(bag)* saco; costal; *(looting)* saqueo, pillaje; *v.* ensacar, meter en un saco; saquear, pillar.

sac·ra·ment [sǽkrəmənt] *s.* sacramento.

sa·cred [sékrɪd] *adj.* sagrado, sacro.

sa·cred·ness [sékrɪdnɪs] *s.* santidad; lo sagrado.

sac·ri·fice [sǽkrəfaɪs] s. sacrificio; **to sell at a —** vender con pérdida; v. sacrificar.
sac·ri·lege [sǽkrəlɪdʒ] s. sacrilegio.
sac·ri·le·gious [sækrɪlídʒəs] adj. sacrílego.
sac·ro·sanct [sǽkrosænkt] adj. sacrosanto.
sad [sæd] adj. triste.
sad·den [sǽdṇ] v. entristecer(se).
sad·dle [sǽdl] s. silla de montar; silla de bicicleta o motocicleta; —**bag** alforja; — **horse** caballo de silla —**tree** arzón; v. ensillar; **to — someone with responsibilities** cargar a alguien de responsabilidades.
sa·dis·tic [sədístɪk] adj. sádico, cruel.
sad·ness [sǽdnɪs] s. tristeza.
safe [sef] adj. (secure) seguro; salvo; sin riesgo, sin peligro; (trustworthy) digno de confianza; — **and sound** sano y salvo; **safe-conduct** salvo-conducto; **to be** — no correr peligro, estar a salvo; s. caja fuerte; -**ly** adv. seguramente; con seguridad; sin peligro; **to arrive -ly** llegar bien, llegar sin contratiempo alguno.
safe·guard [séfgɑrd] s. salvaguardia; resguardo, defensa; v. resguardar, proteger, salvaguardar.
safe·ty [séftɪ] s. seguridad; protección; **in** — con seguridad; sin peligro; adj. de seguridad; — **device** mecanismo de seguridad; — **pin** imperdible, alfiler de seguridad.
saf·fron [sǽfrən] s. azafrán; adj. azafranado, color de azafrán.
sag [sæg] v. combarse, pandearse; doblegarse; deprimirse, hundirse (en el centro); encorvarse; **his shoulders** — tiene las espaldas caídas; s. pandeo, flexión, depresión; concavidad.
sa·ga·cious [səgéʃəs] adj. sagaz, ladino, astuto.
sa·gac·i·ty [segǽsətɪ] s. sagacidad; astucia.
sage [sedʒ] adj. sabio; cuerdo, prudente; s. sabio; salvia (planta).
said [sɛd] pret. & p.p. de **to say.**
sail [sel] s. (canvas) vela (de barco); (trip) viaje o paseo en barco de vela; **under full** — a toda vela; **to set** — hacerse a la vela; v. navegar; hacerse a la vela; zarpar, salir (un buque); viajar, ir (en barco, bote, etc.); pasear en bote de vela; **to** — **a kite** volar una cometa o papalote; **to** — **along** deslizarse; navegar; ir bien; **to** — **along the coast** costear.
sail·boat [sélbot] s. bote o barco de vela.
sail·or [sélə] s. marinero; marino.
saint [sent] s. santo; adj. santo; san (delante de nombres masculinos excepto: Santo Tomás, Santo Domingo, Santo Toribio); v. canonizar.
saint·ly [séntlɪ] adj. santo; pío, devoto.
sake [sek]: **for the** — **of** por; por amor a; por consideración a; **for my** — por mí; **for pity's** — por piedad; ¡caramba!; **for the** — **of argument** por vía de argumento.
sa·la·cious [səléʃəs] adj. salaz.
sal·ad [sǽləd] s. ensalada; — **dressing** aderezo (para ensalada).
sal·a·ry [sǽlərɪ] s. salario, sueldo.
sale [sel] s. venta; saldo, Méx., C.A., Andes barata; Ríopl., Andes realización; — **by auction** almoneda, subasta; -**s tax** impuesto sobre ventas; **for (on)** — de venta.
sales·man [sélzmən] s. vendedor; dependiente (de tienda); **traveling** — agente viajero, viajante de comercio.
sales·wom·an [sélzwumən] s. vendedora; dependiente (de tienda).
sa·li·ent [sélɪənt] adj. saliente, sobresaliente; prominente.

sa·line [sélin] adj. salino.
sa·li·va [səláɪvə] s. saliva.
sal·low [sǽlo] adj. amarillento, pálido.
sal·ly [sǽlɪ] s. salida; agudeza, chiste agudo; v. salir, hacer una salida; **to** — **forth** salir.
salm·on [sǽmən] s. salmón.
sa·loon [səlún] s. salón (de un vapor); taberna, Am. cantina; Ríopl. bar; **dining** — **of a ship** salón-comedor de un vapor.
salt [sɔlt] s. (sodium chloride) sal; (wit) chiste, agudeza; **smelling -s** sales aromáticas; **the** — **of the earth** la flor y nata de la humanidad; adj. salado; salobre; —**cellar** salero; — **mine** salina; — **pork** tocino salado; — **shaker** salero; — **water** agua salada, agua de mar; v. salar; **to** — **one's money away** guardar o ahorrar su dinero.
salt·pe·ter [sɔ́ltpitə] s. salitre, nitro; — **mine** salitral, salitrera.
salt·y [sɔ́ltɪ] adj. salado; salobre.
sal·u·tar·y [sǽljutɛrɪ] adj. saludable.
sal·u·ta·tion [sæljətéʃən] s. salutación, saludo.
sa·lute [səlút] s. saludo; **gun** — salva; v. saludar; cuadrarse (militarmente).
sal·vage [sǽlvɪdʒ] s. salvamento.
sal·va·tion [sælvéʃən] s. salvación.
salve [sæv] s. untura, ungüento; alivio; v. aliviar, aquietar, calmar; untar.
sal·vo [sǽlvo] s. salva.
same [sem] adj. mismo; igual; idéntico; **it is all the** — **to me** me es igual, me da lo mismo; **the** — lo mismo; el mismo (la misma, los mismos, las mismas).
sam·ple [sǽmpl] s. muestra, prueba; **book of -s** muestrario; v. probar; calar.
san·a·to·ri·um [sænətorɪəm] s. sanatorio.
sanc·ti·fy [sǽŋktəfaɪ] v. santificar.
sanc·tion [sǽŋkʃən] s. sanción; aprobación; autorización;·v. sancionar; ratificar; aprobar, autorizar.
sanc·ti·ty [sǽŋktətɪ] s. santidad.
sanc·tu·ar·y [sǽŋktʃuɛrɪ] s. santuario; asilo.
sand [sænd] s. arena; — **pit** arenal; v. enarenar, cubrir de arena; mezclar con arena; refregar con arena.
san·dal [sǽndl] s. sandalia; alpargata; Méx. guarache (huarache); Andes ojota.
sand·pa·per [sǽndpepə] s. papel de lija; v. lijar, pulir o alisar con papel de lija.
sand·stone [sǽndston] s. piedra arenisca.
sand·wich [sǽndwɪtʃ] s. bocadillo, emparedado, sandwich; v. intercalar, meter (entre).
sand·y [sǽndɪ] adj. arenoso; arenisco; — **hair** pelo rojizo.
sane [sen] adj. sano, sensato; cuerdo.
sang [sæŋ] pret. de **to sing.**
san·i·tar·i·um [sænətérɪəm] s. sanatorio.
san·i·tar·y [sǽnətɛrɪ] adj. sanitario.
san·i·ta·tion [sænətéʃən] s. saneamiento; salubridad; sanidad.
san·i·ty [sǽnətɪ] s. cordura.
sank [sæŋk] pret. de **to sink.**
sap [sæp] s. savia; tonto, bobo; v. agotar, debilitar, minar.
sap·ling [sǽplɪŋ] s. vástago, renuevo; arbolillo.
sap·phire [sǽfaɪr] s. zafiro; color de zafiro.
sar·casm [sɑ́rkæzəm] s. sarcasmo.
sar·cas·tic [sɑrkǽstɪk] adj. sarcástico.
sar·coph·a·gus [sɑrkɔ́fəgəs] s. sarcófago.
sar·dine [sɑrdín] s. sardina.
sar·don·ic [sɑrdɑ́nɪk] adj. burlón; sarcástico.

sash [sæʃ] *s.* faja (*cinturón de lana, seda o algodón*); banda, cinta ancha; **window** — bastidor (*o marco*) de ventana.

sat [sæt] *pret. & p.p. de* **to sit.**

satch·el [sætʃəl] *s.* valija, maletín, maleta, saco.

sate [set] *v.* saciar.

sa·teen [sætin] *s.* satén o rasete (*raso de inferior calidad*).

sat·el·lite [sætlaɪt] *s.* satélite.

sa·ti·ate [séʃɪet] *v.* saciar, hartar.

sat·in [sætn] *s.* raso.

sat·ire [sætaɪr] *s.* sátira.

sa·tir·i·cal [sətírɪkl] *adj.* satírico.

sat·i·rize [sætəraɪz] *v.* satirizar.

sat·is·fac·tion [sætɪsfækʃən] *s.* satisfacción.

sat·is·fac·to·ri·ly [sætɪsfæktrəlɪ] *adv.* satisfactoriamente.

sat·is·fac·to·ry [sætɪsfæktrɪ] *adj.* satisfactorio.

sat·is·fied [sætɪsfaɪd] *adj.* satisfecho, contento.

sat·is·fy [sætɪsfaɪ] *v.* satisfacer.

sat·u·rate [sætʃəret] *v.* saturar, empapar.

Sat·ur·day [sætədɪ] *s.* sábado.

sauce [sɔs] *s.* salsa; — **dish** salsera; *v.* aderezar con salsa; sazonar, condimentar; insolentarse con.

sauce·pan [sɔ́spæn] *s.* cacerola.

sau·cer [sɔ́sə] *s.* platillo.

sau·ci·ness [sɔ́sɪnɪs] *s.* descaro, insolencia.

sau·cy [sɔ́sɪ] *adj.* descarado, respondón, insolente, *Am.* retobado.

saun·ter [sɔ́ntə] *v.* pasearse, vagar.

sau·sage [sɔ́sɪdʒ] *s.* salchicha, salchichón; longaniza; chorizo.

sav·age [sævɪdʒ] *adj.* salvaje; fiero; bárbaro, brutal, feroz; *s.* salvaje.

sav·age·ry [sævɪdʒrɪ] *s.* salvajismo; crueldad, fiereza.

sa·vant [səvánt] *s.* sabio.

save [sev] *v.* (*rescue*) salvar; (*hoard*) ahorrar; economizar; (*keep*) guardar; resguardar; **to** — **from** librar de; **to** — **one's eyes** cuidarse la vista; *prep.* salvo, menos, excepto.

sav·er [sévə] *s.* salvador; libertador; ahorrador; **life**— salvavidas.

sav·ing [sévɪŋ] *adj.* (*rescuer*) salvador; (*economizing*) ahorrativo, económico; frugal; *s.* ahorro, economía; **-s** ahorros; **-s bank** caja o banco de ahorros; *prep.* salvo, excepto, con excepción de.

sav·ior [sévjə] *s.* salvador.

sa·vor [sévə] *s.* sabor; dejo; *v.* saborear; sazonar; **to** — **of** saber a, tener el sabor de; **it -s of treason** huele a traición.

sa·vor·y [sévərɪ] *adj.* sabroso.

saw [sɔ] *s.* sierra; —**horse** caballete; *v.* aserrar, serrar; **it -s easily** es fácil de aserrar; *pret. de* **to see.**

saw·dust [sɔ́dʌst] *s.* aserrín, serrín.

saw·mill [sɔ́mɪl] *s.* aserradero.

sawn [sɔn] *p.p. de* **to saw.**

Sax·on [sæksn] *adj. & s.* sajón.

sax·o·phone [sæksəfon] *s.* saxófono; saxofón.

say [se] *v.* decir; declarar; —! ¡diga! ¡oiga usted!; **that is to** — es decir; **to** — **one's prayers** rezar, decir o recitar sus oraciones; **to** — **the least** por lo menos; **it is said that** dizque, se dice que, dicen que; *s.* afirmación, aserto; **the final** — la autoridad decisiva; **to have a** — **in a matter** tener voz y voto en un asunto; **to have one's** — expresarse, dar su opinión.

say·ing [séɪŋ] *s.* dicho, refrán; aserto; **as the** — **goes** como dice el refrán.

scab [skæb] *s.* costra (*de una herida*); roña;

esquirol (*obrero que sustituye a un huelguista*); obrero que acepta un jornal inferior; *v.* encostrarse (*una herida*), cubrirse de una costra.

scab·bard [skǽbəd] *s.* vaina, funda (*de espada, puñal, etc.*).

scab·by [skǽbɪ] *adj.* costroso; roñoso, sarnoso, tiñoso.

scab·rous [skébrəs] *adj.* escabroso.

scaf·fold [skǽfld] *s.* andamio, tablado; patíbulo, andamiaje, andamios.

scald [skɔld] *v.* escaldar; **to** — **milk** calentar la leche hasta que suelte el hervor; *s.* escaldadura, quemadura.

scale [skel] *s.* escala; platillo de balanza; balanza; escama (*de pez o de la piel*); costra; **pair of -s** balanza; **platform** — báscula; *v.* escalar; subir, trepar por; graduar (*a escala*); medir según escala; pesar; escamar, quitar las escamas a; pelarse, despellejarse; descostrar(se); **to** — **down prices** rebajar proporcionalmente los precios.

scal·lop [skáləp] *s.* onda, pico (*adorno*); molusco bivalvo; **-s** festón (*recortes en forma de ondas o picos*); *v.* festonear, recortar en forma de ondas o picos; asar con salsa o migas de pan.

scalp [skælp] *s.* cuero cabelludo; *v.* desollar el cráneo; revender (*boletos, billetes*) a precio subido.

scal·y [skélɪ] *adj.* escamoso, lleno de escamas; — **with rust** mohoso.

scamp [skæmp] *s.* pícaro, bribón, bellaco.

scam·per [skǽmpə] *v.* correr, escabullirse, escaparse; *s.* escabullida, carrera, corrida.

scan [skæn] *v.* escudriñar; examinar, mirar detenidamente; echar un vistazo a (*en el habla popular*); medir (*el verso*).

scan·dal [skǽndl] *s.* escándalo; maledicencia; murmuración.

scan·dal·ize [skǽndlaɪz] *v.* escandalizar, dar escándalo.

scan·dal·ous [skǽndləs] *adj.* escandaloso; difamatorio; vergonzoso.

scan·di·um [skǽndɪəm] *s.* escandio.

scant [skænt] *adj.* escaso; corto; insuficiente; *v.* escatimar, limitar.

scant·y [skǽntɪ] *adj.* escaso; insuficiente.

scar [skɑr] *s.* (*skin blemish*) cicatriz; costurón; (*mark*) raya, marca (*en una superficie pulida*); *v.* marcar, rayar; hacer o dejar una cicatriz en.

scarce [skɛrs] *adj.* escaso; raro; **-ly** *adv.* escasamente; apenas.

scar·ci·ty [skérsətɪ] *s.* escasez; carestía; insuficiencia.

scare [skɛr] *v.* espantar, asustar; alarmar; sobresaltar; **he -s easily** se asusta fácilmente; **to** — **away** ahuyentar, espantar; *s.* susto, sobresalto.

scare·crow [skérkro] *s.* espantajo; espantapájaros.

scarf [skɑrf] *s.* bufanda; mantilla; pañuelo (*para el cuello o la cabeza*); tapete (*para una mesa, tocador, etc.*).

scar·let [skárlɪt] *s.* escarlata; *adj.* de color escarlata; — **fever** escarlata, escarlatina.

scar·y [skérɪ] *adj.* espantadizo, asustadizo, miedoso.

scat [skæt] *interj.* ¡zape!

scat·ter [skǽtə] *v.* esparcir(se); desparramar(se); dispersar(se); —**brained** ligero de cascos, aturdido.

scene [sin] *s.* escena; escenario; decoración; vista; **to make a** — causar un escándalo.

SA

scen·er·y [sínərɪ] s. paisaje, vista; **stage —** decoraciones.

scent [sɛnt] s. (*odor*) olor; (*substance*) perfume; (*trace*) pista, rastro; **to be on the —** of seguir el rastro de; **to have a keen —** tener buen olfato; v. oler, olfatear, ventear, husmear; perfumar.

scep·ter [sɛ́ptə] s. cetro.

scep·tic [skɛ́ptɪk] *adj.* & s. escéptico.

scep·ti·cism [skɛ́ptəsɪzəm] s. escepticismo.

sched·ule [skɛ́dʒʊl] s. horario; itinerario (*de trenes*); lista, inventario (*adjunto a un documento*); v. fijar el día y la hora (*para una clase, conferencia, etc.*); establecer el itinerario para (*un tren o trenes*).

scheme [skim] s. (*plan*) esquema, plan, proyecto; empresa; (*plot*) ardid, trama, maquinación; **color — combinación** de colores; **metrical —** sistema de versificación; v. proyectar, urdir; maquinar, intrigar, tramar.

schem·er [skímə] s. maquinador, intrigante; proyectista.

schem·ing [skímɪŋ] *adj.* maquinador, intrigante; s. maquinación.

schism [sɪzəm] s. cisma.

schiz·o·phre·ni·a [skɪzofrínɪə] s. esquizofrenia.

schol·ar [skálə] s. escolar, estudiante; becario (*el que disfruta una beca*); erudito, docto.

schol·ar·ly [skálə lɪ] *adj.* erudito, sabio, docto; *adv.* eruditamente, doctamente.

schol·ar·ship [skálə ʃɪp] s. saber; erudición; beca; **to have a —** disfrutar una beca.

scho·las·tic [skolǽstɪk] *adj.* escolástico; escolar.

school [skul] s. escuela; **— of fish** banco de peces; *adj.* de escuela; **— day** día de escuela; **— board** consejo de enseñanza; v. enseñar, educar, instruir, aleccionar.

school·boy [skúlbɔɪ] s. muchacho de escuela.

school·girl [skúlgɜl] s. muchacha de escuela.

school·house [skúlhaʊs] s. escuela.

school·ing [skúlɪŋ] s. instrucción; enseñanza, educación.

school·mas·ter [skúlmæstə] s. maestro de escuela.

school·mate [skúlmet] s. condiscípulo, compañero de escuela.

school·room [skúlrum] s. clase, aula.

school·teach·er [skúltitʃə] s. maestro de escuela.

schoo·ner [skúnə] s. goleta; vaso grande para cerveza; **prairie —** galera con toldo.

sci·ence [sáɪəns] s. ciencia.

sci·en·tif·ic [saɪəntífɪk] *adj.* científico; **-ally** *adv.* científicamente.

sci·en·tist [sáɪəntɪst] s. científico, hombre de ciencia.

scin·til·late [síntəlet] v. centellear; chispear.

sci·on [sáɪən] s. vástago.

scis·sors [sízəz] s. *pl.* tijeras.

scle·ro·sis [skləósɪs] s. esclerosis.

scoff [skɔf] s. mofa, burla, befa, escarnio; v. escarnecer; mofarse; **to — at** mofarse de, burlarse de, escarnecer a.

scold [skold] v. reñir, reprender, regañar; s. regañón, persona regañona.

scold·ing [skóldɪŋ] s. regaño, reprensión; *adj.* regañón.

scoop [skup] s. (*tool*) cuchara, cucharón; pala; (*quantity*) palada, cucharada; (*winnings*) buena ganancia; **newspaper —** primera publicación de una noticia; v. cavar, excavar; ahuecar; cucharear, sacar con cucharón o pala; achicar (*agua*); **to — in a good profit** sacar buena ganancia.

scoot [skut] v. escabullirse, correr, irse a toda prisa; **—!** ¡largo de aquí!

scoot·er [skútə] s. motoneta (*de motor*); monopatín.

scope [skop] s. alcance, extensión; esfera, campo.

scorch [skɔrtʃ] v. chamuscar; resecar, agostar; s. chamusquina, *Am.* chamuscada o chamuscadura.

score [skor] s. cuenta; escor (*en el juego*); raya, línea; calificación (*expresada numéricamente*); veintena; **musical —** partitura; **on that —** a ese respecto; **on the —** of a causa de, con motivo de; **to keep the —** llevar el escor, llevar la cuenta; **to settle old -s** desquitarse; v. marcar el escor, señalar los tantos en un juego; calificar (*numéricamente*); instrumentar (*música*); rayar, marcar con rayas; **to — a point** ganar un punto o tanto; **to — a success** lograr éxito, obtener un triunfo.

scorn [skɔrn] s. desdén, menosprecio; v. desdeñar, menospreciar.

scorn·ful [skɔ́rnfəl] *adj.* desdeñoso.

scor·pi·on [skɔ́rpɪən] s. escorpión, alacrán.

Scotch [skɑtʃ] *adj.* escocés; **the —** los escoceses, el pueblo escocés.

scoun·drel [skáʊndrəl] s. bellaco, bribón, pícaro.

scour [skaʊr] v. fregar, restregar, limpiar; pulir; **to — the country** recorrer la comarca (*en busca de algo*).

scourge [skɜdʒ] s. azote; v. azotar; castigar.

scout [skaʊt] s. explorador (*usualmente militar*); **a good —** un buen explorador; una buena persona, un buen compañero; v. explorar; reconocer.

scowl [skaʊl] s. ceño; v. fruncir el ceño, mirar con ceño; poner mala cara.

scram·ble [skrǽmbl] v. (*move*) gatear; (*eggs*) hacer un revoltillo; (*mix up*) revolver, mezclar; **to — for something** forcejear por coger algo; pelearse por coger algo; **to — up** trepar o subir a gatas (*una cuesta*); **-d eggs** revoltillo, huevos, revueltos; s. revoltillo, confusión; pelea.

scrap [skræp] s. (*fragment*) fragmento, pedacito; migaja; (*fight*) riña, reyerta; **-s** sobras; desperdicios; desechos; retales; **—book** álbum de recortes; **— iron** recortes o desechos de hierro; v. desechar; tirar a la basura; descartar; pelear, reñir.

scrape [skrep] v. (*abrasively*) raspar; rasguñar; rascar; (*rub*) raer; rozar; **to — along** ir tirando, ir pasándola; **to — together** recoger o acumular poco a poco; **to bow and —** ser muy servil; s. raspadura; rasguño; aprieto, dificultad, lío.

scrap·er [skrépə] s. (*tool*) raspador; (*scrimping person*) tacaño.

scratch [skrætʃ] v. (*mark*) arañar, rasguñar; (*rub*) rascar; raspar; (*line*) rayar; escarbar; (*write badly*) hacer garabatos; **to — out** borrar, tachar; sacar (*los ojos*) con las uñas; s. arañazo, araño, rasguño; raya, marca; **to start from —** empezar sin nada; empezar desde el principio; empezar sin ventaja.

scrawl [skrɔl] s. garabato; v. hacer garabatos, escribir mal.

scraw·ny [skrɔ́nɪ] *adj.* huesudo, flaco.

scream [skrim] s. chillido, alarido, grito; **he's a —** es muy cómico o chistoso; v. chillar, gritar.

screech [skritʃ] s. chillido; **— owl** lechuza; v. chillar.

screen [skrin] s. (*projection*) pantalla; (*divider*) biombo; mampara; resguardo; (*sifter*) tamiz, cedazo; **—door** antepuerta de tela metálica;

motion-picture — pantalla de cinematógrafo;
wire — pantalla de tela metálica; *v.* tapar;
resguardar, proteger con una pantalla o
biombo; cerner; proyectar sobre la pantalla,
filmar; **to — windows** proteger las ventanas con tela
metálica.
screw [skru] *s.* tornillo; — **eye** armella; — **nut**
tuerca; — **propeller** hélice; — **thread** rosca; *v.*
atornillar; torcer, retorcer; **to — a lid on** atornillar
una tapa; **to — up one's courage** cobrar ánimo.
screw·driv·er [skrúdraɪvɚ] *s.* destornillador.
scrib·ble [skríbl] *v.* garrapatear, hacer garabatos,
borronear, escribir mal o de prisa; *s.* garabato.
script [skrɪpt] *s.* letra cursiva, escritura; manuscrito
(*de un drama, de una película*).
scrip·ture [skríptʃɚ] *s.* escritura sagrada; **the
Scriptures** la Sagrada Escritura, la Biblia.
scroll [skrol] *s.* rollo de pergamino o papel; voluta,
adorno en espiral; rúbrica (*de una firma*).
scrub [skrʌb] *v.* fregar; restregar; *s.* friega, fregado;
adj. achaparrado; bajo, inferior; — **oak**
chaparro; — **pine** pino achaparrado; — **team**
equipo de jugadores suplentes o menos bien
entrenados; — **woman** fregona.
scru·ple [skrúpl] *s.* escrúpulo; *v.* escrupulizar, tener
escrúpulos.
scru·pu·lous [skrúpjələs] *adj.* escrupuloso.
scru·ti·nize [skrútnaɪz] *v.* escudriñar, escrutar.
scru·ti·ny [skrútnɪ] *s.* escrutinio.
scuff [skʌf] *v.* raspar; arrastrar los pies.
scuf·fle [skʌfl] *s.* refriega, riña, pelea; *v.* forcejear;
luchar, pelear; arrastrar los pies.
sculp·tor [skʌlptɚ] *s.* escultor.
sculp·ture [skʌlptʃɚ] *s.* escultura; *v.* esculpir,
cincelar, tallar.
scum [skʌm] *s.* nata, capa, espuma; escoria;
residuo, desechos; canalla, gente baja; *v.*
espumar.
scur·ry [skɝɪ] *v.* escabullirse; echar a correr;
apresurarse; *s.* apresuramiento; corrida, carrera.
scut·tle [skʌtl] *v.* echar a correr; barrenar (*un
buque*); echar a pique; *s.* escotilla, escotillón;
balde (*para carbón*).
scythe [saɪð] *s.* guadaña.
sea [si] *s.* mar; **to be at** — estar en el mar; estar
perplejo o confuso; **to put to** — hacerse a la
mar; *adj.* marino, marítimo, de mar; — **biscuit**
galleta; — **green** verdemar; — **gull** gaviota; —
level nivel del mar; — **lion** léon marino, foca; —
power potencia naval.
sea·board [síbord] *s.* costa, litoral; *adj.* costanero,
litoral.
sea·coast [síkost] *s.* costa, litoral.
seal [sil] *s.* (*stamp*) sello; timbre; (*animal*) foca,
león marino; **to set one's** — **to** sellar; aprobar;
v. sellar; estampar; cerrar; tapar; **to** — **in**
encerrar, cerrar herméticamente; **to** — **with**
sealing wax lacrar.
seal·ing wax [sílɪŋ wæks] *s.* lacre.
seam [sim] *s.* costura; juntura; cicatriz; filón, veta;
v. echar una costura, coser.
sea·man [símən] *s.* marino, marinero.
seam·stress [símstrɪs] *s.* costurera.
sea·plane [síplen] *s.* hidroavión.
sea·port [síport] *s.* puerto de mar.
sear [sɪr] *v.* chamuscar(se), tostar(se); resecar(se);
herrar, marcar con hierro candente; *adj.* reseco,
marchito.
search [sɝtʃ] *v.* buscar; escudriñar; registrar;
examinar; **to** — **a prisoner** registrar a un
prisionero; **to** — **for something** buscar algo; **to**

— **into** investigar, indagar; *s.* busca, búsqueda;
registro, inspección; investigación, pesquisa,
indagación; — **warrant** mandato judicial de
practicar un registro; **in** — **of** en busca de.
search·light [sɝtʃlaɪt] *s.* reflector.
sea·shore [síʃor] *s.* costa, playa, orilla o ribera del
mar.
sea·sick [sísɪk] *adj.* mareado; **to get** — marearse.
sea·sick·ness [sísɪknɪs] *s.* mareo.
sea·side [sísaɪd] *s.* costa, litoral; playa.
sea·son [sízn] *s.* estación (*del año*); temporada;
sazón, ocasión, tiempo; — **ticket** billete de
abono; **Christmas** — navidades; **harvest** —
siega, tiempo de la cosecha; **opera** — temporada
de la ópera; **to arrive in good** — llegar en sazón,
llegar a tiempo; *v.* sazonar; condimentar;
aclimatar.
sea·son·ing [síznɪŋ] *s.* condimento; salsa;
desecación (*de la madera*).
seat [sit] *s.* (*furniture*) asiento; silla; (*site*) sitio;
(*headquarters*) residencia; sede (*episcopal, del
gobierno, etc.*); (*body*) nalgas; fondillos, parte
trasera (*de los pantalones o calzones*); — **of
learning** centro de estudios, centro de
erudición; *v.* sentar; asentar; dar asiento a; **to** —
oneself sentarse; **it -s a thousand people** tiene
cabida para mil personas.
sea·weed [síwid] *s.* alga marina.
se·cede [sisíd] *v.* separarse (*de una federación o
unión*).
se·clude [sɪklúd] *v.* recluir, apartar, aislar; **to** —
oneself from recluirse de, apartarse de.
se·clud·ed [sɪklúdɪd] *adj.* apartado, aislado;
solitario.
se·clu·sion [sɪklúʒən] *s.* apartamiento, soledad,
aislamiento; retiro.
sec·ond [sékənd] *adj.* segundo; inferior; — **hand**
segundero (*de reloj*); — **lieutenant** subteniente;
second-rate de segunda clase; mediocre, inferior;
on — **thought** después de pensarlo bien; *s.*
segundo; padrino (*en un desafío*); ayudante;
mercancía de segunda calidad; mercancía
defectuosa; — **child** segundón; *v.* secundar (*o
segundar*), apoyar; apadrinar.
sec·on·dar·y [sékəndɛrɪ] *adj.* secundario; —
education segunda enseñanza; — **school** escuela
secundaria, escuela de segunda enseñanza.
sec·ond-hand [sékəndhænd] *adj.* de segunda mano;
usado; de ocasión; indirecto, por intermedio de
otro.
sec·ond·ly [sékəndlɪ] *adv.* en segundo lugar.
se·cre·cy [síkrəsɪ] *s.* secreto, sigilo, reserva.
se·cret [síkrɪt] *s.* secreto; *adj.* secreto; escondido,
oculto; — **service** policía secreta; **-ly** *adv.*
secretamente, en secreto.
sec·re·tar·i·at [sɛkrətɛriət] *s.* secretaría.
sec·re·tar·y [sɛkrətɛrɪ] *s.* secretario; escritorio (*con
estantes para libros*).
se·crete [sɪkrít] *v.* secretar (*una secreción*);
esconder, ocultar.
se·cre·tion [sɪkríʃən] *s.* secreción.
se·cre·tive [sɪkrítɪv] *adj.* reservado, callado; —
gland glándula secretoria.
sect [sɛkt] *s.* secta.
sec·tion [sékʃən] *s.* sección; trozo; tajada; región;
barrio; *v.* seccionar, dividir en secciones.
sec·u·lar [sékjələ] *adj.* & *s.* secular.
se·cure [sɪkjúr] *adj.* seguro; firme; *v.* asegurar;
afianzar; obtener; resguardar; **-ly** *adv.*
seguramente, con seguridad; firmemente.
se·cu·ri·ty [sɪkjúrətɪ] *s.* seguridad; fianza, garantía,

SC

prenda; resguardo, protección; **securities** bonos, obligaciones, acciones, valores.
se·dan [sɪdǽn] s. sedán.
se·date [sɪdét] adj. sosegado; tranquilo, sereno; serio.
se·da·tion [sədéʃən] d. sedación.
sed·a·tive [sɛ́dətɪv] adj. & s. calmante, sedativo.
sed·en·tar·y [sɛ́dn̩tɛrɪ] adj. sedentario; inactivo.
sed·i·ment [sɛ́dəmənt] s. sedimento, heces, residuo.
se·di·tion [sɪdíʃən] s. sedición.
se·di·tious [sɪdíʃəs] adj. sedicioso.
se·duce [sɪdjús] v. seducir.
se·duc·tion [sɪdʌ́kʃən] s. seducción.
see [si] v. ver; — **that you do it** no deje Vd. de hacerlo; **tenga Vd. cuidado de hacerlo; I'll — to it** me encargaré de ello; **let me — a** ver; **to — a person home** acompañar a una persona a casa; **to — a person off** ir a la estación para despedir a una persona; **to — a person through a difficulty** ayudar a una persona a salir de un apuro; **to — through a person** adivinar lo que piensa una persona, darse cuenta de sus intenciones; **to — to one's affairs** atender a sus asuntos; **to have seen military service** haber servido en el ejército; s. sede, silla; **Holy See** Santa Sede.
seed [sid] s. (grains) semilla; (semen) simiente; (fruit) pepita; **to go to —** producir semillas; decaer, declinar; descuidar de su persona, andar desaseado; v. sembrar; despepitar, quitar las pepitas o semillas de; producir semillas.
seed·er [sidə-] s. sembradora.
seed·ling [sídlɪŋ] s. planta de semillero; arbolillo (de menos de tres pies de altura).
seed·y [sídɪ] adj. semilloso, lleno de semillas; raído; desaseado.
seek [sik] v. buscar; pedir, solicitar; **to — after** buscar; **to — to** tratar de, esforzarse por.
seem [sim] v. parecer; **it -s to me** me parece.
seem·ing·ly [símɪŋlɪ] adv. aparentemente, en apariencia, al parecer.
seem·ly [símlɪ] adj. propio, decente, decoroso.
seen [sin] p.p. de **to see.**
seep [sip] v. escurrirse, rezumarse, colarse, filtrarse.
seer [sɪr] s. vidente, adivino, profeta.
seethe [sið] v. bullir, hervir; burbujear.
seg·ment [sɛ́gmənt] s. segmento.
seg·re·gate [sɛ́grəget] v. segregar.
seize [siz] v. (grasp) asir, coger, agarrar; apoderarse de; (arrest) prender o aprehender; (take advantage of) aprovecharse de; (capture) embargar, secuestrar; **to — upon** asir; **to become -d with fear** sobrecogerse de miedo.
sei·zure [síʒə-] s. cogida; captura; aprehensión (de un criminal); secuestro, embargo (de bienes); ataque (de una enfermedad).
sel·dom [sɛ́ldəm] adv. rara vez, raras veces, raramente.
se·lect [səlɛ́kt] adj. selecto, escogido; v. elegir, escoger; entresacar.
se·lec·tion [səlɛ́kʃən] s. selección, elección.
se·le·ni·um [sɪlíniəm] s. selenio.
self [sɛlf]: **by one—** por sí, por sí mismo; **for one—** para sí; **one's other —** su otro yo; **his wife and —** su esposa y él (véase **herself, himself, ourselves, themselves,** etc.); **self-centered** egoísta, egocéntrico; **self-conscious** consciente de sí, cohibido, tímido; **self-control** dominio de sí mismo (o de sí propio); **self-defense** defensa propia; **self-denial** abnegación; **self-evident** patente, manifiesto; **self-esteem** respeto de sí mismo; amor propio; **self-government** gobierno

autónomo, autonomía; gobierno democrático; **self-interest** propio interés; egoísmo; **self-love** amor propio; **self-possessed** sereno, dueño de sí, tranquilo; **self-sacrifice** abnegación; **self-serv·ice** [sɛ́lfsɝ·vɪs] s. autoservicio; **self-satisfied** pagado de sí, satisfecho de sí.
self-ish [sɛ́lfɪʃ] adj. egoísta; **-ly** adv. con egoísmo, por egoísmo.
self·ish·ness [sɛ́lfɪʃnɪs] s. egoísmo.
self·same [sɛ́lfsém] adj. mismo, idéntico, mismísimo.
sell [sɛl] v. vender; venderse, estar de venta; **to — at auction** vender en almoneda o subasta, subastar; **to — out** venderlo todo.
sell·er [sɛ́lə-] s. vendedor.
selves [sɛlvz] pl. de **self.**
se·man·tics [səmǽntɪks] s. semántica.
sem·blance [sɛ́mbləns] s. semejanza; apariencia.
se·mes·ter [səmɛ́stə-] s. semestre.
sem·i·cir·cle [sɛ́məsə-kl] s. semicírculo.
sem·i·co·lon [sɛ́məkolən] s. punto y coma.
sem·i·nar·y [sɛ́mənɛrɪ] s. seminario.
Se·mit·ic [səmítɪk] adj. semítico.
sen·ate [sɛ́nɪt] s. senado.
sen·a·tor [sɛ́nɪtə-] s. senador.
send [sɛnd] v. enviar; mandar; despachar; remitir, expedir; lanzar (una flecha, pelota, etc.); **to — away** despedir, despachar; **to — forth** despachar, enviar; emitir; exhalar; echar; **to — someone up for 15 years** condenar a un reo a 15 años de prisión; **to — word** avisar, mandar decir, mandar recado.
send·er [sɛ́ndə-] s. remitente; transmisor.
se·nile [sínaɪl] adj. senil, caduco; chocho.
se·nil·i·ty [sənílətɪ] s. senectud; chochera o chochez.
sen·ior [sínjə-] adj. (older) mayor, de más edad; más antiguo; (superior) superior; — **class** clase del cuarto año; s. persona o socio más antiguo; estudiante del último año; **to be somebody's — by two years** ser dos años mayor que alguien.
sen·sa·tion [sɛnséʃən] s. sensación.
sen·sa·tion·al [sɛnséʃənl] adj. sensacional; emocionante.
sense [sɛns] s. (function) sentido; (sentiment) sentimiento; sensación; (judgment) juicio, sensatez; (meaning) significado; **common — sentido** común; **to make —** tener sentido; **to be out of one's —s** estar fuera de sí, estar loco; v. percibir, sentir; darse cuenta de.
sense·less [sɛ́nslɪs] adj. sin sentido; insensato, absurdo; insensible, privado de sentido.
sen·si·bil·i·ty [sɛnsəbílətɪ] s. sensibilidad.
sen·si·ble [sɛ́nsəbl] adj. (aware) sensato, razonable, cuerdo; (appreciable) sensible, perceptible; **sensibly** adv. sensatamente, con sensatez, con sentido común; sensiblemente, perceptiblemente.
sen·si·tive [sɛ́nsətɪv] adj. sensitivo; sensible; quisquilloso, susceptible.
sen·si·tive·ness [sɛ́nsətɪvnɪs] s. sensibilidad.
sen·si·tize [sɛ́nsətaɪz] v. sensibilizar.
sen·su·al [sɛ́nʃuəl] adj. sensual, carnal, lujurioso.
sen·su·al·i·ty [sɛnʃuǽlətɪ] s. sensualidad; lujuria.
sent [sɛnt] pret. & p.p. de **to send.**
sen·tence [sɛ́ntəns] s. sentencia, fallo, decisión; oración (grammatical); **death —** pena capital; v. sentenciar.
sen·ti·ment [sɛ́ntəmənt] s. sentimiento; sentido.
sen·ti·men·tal [sɛntəmɛ́ntl] adj. sentimental.
sen·ti·men·tal·i·ty [sɛntəmɛntǽlətɪ] s. sentimentalismo, sentimentalidad.

sen·ti·nel [séntənl] *s.* centinela.
sen·try [séntrɪ] *s.* centinela.
sep·a·rate [sέprɪt] *adj.* (*apart*) separado; apartado; solitario; (*different*) distinto, diferente; **-ly** *adv.* separadamente, por separado; aparte; [sέpəret] *v.* separar(se); apartar(se).
sep·a·ra·tion [sɛpəréʃən] *s.* separación.
Se·phar·dic [səfárdɪk] *adj.* sefardí, sefardita.
Sep·tem·ber [sɛptémbɚ] *s.* setiembre.
sep·ul·cher [sέplkɚ] *s.* sepulcro, sepultura.
se·quel [síkwəl] *s.* secuela; continuación, consecuencia; resultado.
se·quence [síkwəns] *s.* (*continuity*) secuencia, sucesión; serie, continuación; (*result*) consecuencia, resultado; runfla (*serie de tres o más naipes de un mismo palo*).
ser·e·nade [sɛrənéd] *s.* serenata; *v.* dar serenata a.
se·rene [sərín] *adj.* sereno; tranquilo; claro, despejado.
se·ren·i·ty [sərέnətɪ] *s.* serenidad; calma.
ser·geant [sárdʒənt] *s.* sargento; — **at arms** oficial que guarda el orden (*en un cuerpo legislativo*).
se·ri·al [sírɪəl] *s.* cuento o novela por entregas; *adj.* consecutivo, en serie; — **novel** novela por entregas.
se·ries [síriz] *s.* serie; series.
se·ri·ous [sírɪəs] *adj.* serio; grave; **-ly** *adv.* seriamente, con seriedad, en serio; gravemente.
se·ri·ous·ness [sírɪəsnɪs] *s.* seriedad; gravedad.
ser·mon [sɚmən] *s.* sermón.
ser·pent [sɚpənt] *s.* serpiente; sierpe.
se·rum [sírəm] *s.* suero.
ser·vant [sɚvənt] *s.* sirviente; criado; servidor; — **girl** criada, *Ríopl.* mucama; *Andes, Col., Ven.* muchacha de servicio.
serve [sɚv] *v.* (*wait on*) servir; (*supply*) surtir, abastecer; **to — a term in prison** cumplir una condena; **to — a warrant** entregar una citación; **to — as** servir de; **to — for** servir de, servir para; **to — notice on** notificar, avisar, advertir; **to — one's purpose** servir para el caso o propósito; **it -s me right** bien me lo merezco; *s.* saque (*de la pelota en tenis*).
serv·er [sɚvɚ] *s.* servidor; saque (*el que saca la pelota en el juego de tenis*); bandeja; mesa de servicio.
ser·vice [sɚvɪs] *s.* servicio; saque (*de la pelota en tenis*); entrega (*de una citación judicial*); **at your** — a la disposición de Vd., servidor de Vd.; **funeral** — honras fúnebres, funerales, exequias; **mail** — servicio de correos; **table** — servicio de mesa, vajilla; **tea** — juego o servicio de té; — **entrance** entrada para el servicio; — **man** militar; — **station** estación de servicio; *v.* servir; reparar; surtir (*una tienda*).
ser·vice·a·ble [sɚvɪsəbl] *adj.* servible; útil; duradero.
ser·vile [sɚvl] *adj.* servil.
ser·vi·tude [sɚvətjud] *s.* servidumbre; esclavitud.
ses·sion [séʃən] *s.* sesión.
set [sɛt] *v.* (*place*) poner; colocar, asentar; (*fix*) fijar; establecer; ajustar; engastar (*piedras preciosas*); solidificar(se), endurecer(se) (*el cemento, yeso, etc.*); ponerse (*el sol, la luna*); empollar; **to — a bone** componer un hueso dislocado; **to — a trap** armar una trampa; **to — about** ponerse a; **to — an example** dar ejemplo; **to — aside** poner a un lado, poner aparte; apartar; ahorrar; **to — back** retrasar, atrasar; **to — forth** exponer, expresar; manifestar; **to — forth on a journey** ponerse en camino; **to — off**

disparar, hacer estallar (*un explosivo*); hacer resaltar; salir; **to — on fire** pegar o poner fuego a, incendiar; **to — one's jaw** apretar las quijadas; **to — one's heart on** tener la esperanza puesta en; **to — one's mind on** resolverse a, aplicarse a; **to — out for** partir para, salir para; **to — out** to empezar a; **to — right** colocar bien; enderezar; rectificar; **to — sail** hacerse a la vela; **to — the brake** frenar, apretar el freno; **to — up** erigir, levantar; armar, montar (*una máquina*); parar (*tipo de imprenta*); establecer, poner (*una tienda, un negocio*); **to — upon** someone acometer, asaltar a alguien; *pret. & p.p.* de **to set**; *adj.* fijo; firme; sólido; resuelto; rígido; puesto; establecido; engastado; — **to go** listo para partir; *s.* juego, colección; serie; grupo, clase; partida (*de tenis*); — **of dishes** servicio de mesa, vajilla; — **of teeth** dentadura; **radio** — radio, radiorreceptor; **tea** — servicio para té.
set·back [sétbæk] *s.* atraso, revés, retroceso inesperado.
set·tee [sɛtí] *s.* canapé.
set·ting [sétɪŋ] *s.* engaste (*de una joya*); escena, escenario; puesta (*del sol, de un astro*); — **sun** sol poniente.
set·tle [sétl] *v.* (*colonize*) colonizar, poblar; establecer(se); fijar(se); asentar(se); (*solve*) arreglar, poner en orden, ajustar (*cuentas*); zanjar (*una disputa*); pagar, liquidar, saldar; **to — down** formalizarse; asentarse; calmarse; poner casa; **to — on a date** fijar o señalar una fecha; **to — property on (upon)** asignar bienes o propiedad a; **to — the matter** decidir el asunto, concluir con el asunto.
set·tle·ment [sétlmənt] *s.* (*community*) establecimiento; colonia; poblado; población; colonización; (*arrangement*) asignación o traspaso (*de propiedad*); ajuste, arreglo; pago; saldo, finiquito, liquidación; — **house** casa de beneficencia; **marriage** — dote.
set·tler [sétlɚ] *s.* colono, poblador; — **of disputes** zanjador de disputas.
set·up [sétəp] *s.* arreglo; organización.
sev·er [sévɚ] *v.* desunir(se), partir(se), dividir(se), separar(se); cortar, romper.
sev·er·al [sévrəl] *adj.* varios, diversos; distintos, diferentes.
se·vere [səvír] *adj.* severo; áspero; austero; rígido; riguroso; grave; recio, fuerte.
se·ver·i·ty [səvέrətɪ] *s.* severidad; austeridad; rigidez; gravedad; rigor.
sew [so] *v.* coser.
sew·er [sjúɚ] *s.* albañal, cloaca.
sew·ing [sóɪŋ] *s.* costura; modo de coser; — **machine** máquina de coser; — **room** cuarto de costura.
sewn [son] *p.p.* de **to sew.**
sex [sɛks] *s.* sexo; — **appeal** atracción sexual.
sex·tant [sékstənt] *s.* sextante.
sex·ton [sékstən] *s.* sacristán.
sex·u·al [sékʃʊəl] *adj.* sexual.
shab·by [ʃǽbɪ] *adj.* raído, gastado; andrajoso; mal vestido; vil, injusto; **to treat someone shabbily** tratar a alguien injustamente o con menosprecio.
shack [ʃæk] *s.* cabaña, choza, *Am.* bohío, *Am.* jacal.
shack·le [ʃǽkl] *v.* encadenar; trabar, echar trabas a, poner grillos a; estorbar; **-s** *s. pl.* cadenas, trabas, grillos, esposas; estorbo.
shad [ʃæd] *s.* sábalo.

shade [ʃed] *s.* (*shadow*) sombra; (*nuance*) tinte, matiz; (*cover*) visillo, cortinilla; pantalla (*de lámpara*); visera (*para los ojos*); **a — longer** un poco más largo; **— of meaning** matiz; **in the — of** a la sombra de; *v.* sombrear; dar sombra; resguardar de la luz; matizar.

shad·ow [ʃǽdo] *s.* (*darkness*) sombra; oscuridad; (*phantom*) espectro; **under the —** al abrigo de, a la sombra de; **without a — of doubt** sin sombra de duda; *v.* sombrear; obscurecer; **to — someone** espiarle a alguien los pasos, seguirle por todas partes.

shad·ow·y [ʃǽdəwɪ] *adj.* lleno de sombras, tenebroso; vago, indistinto.

shad·y [ʃédɪ] *adj.* sombrío, sombreado, umbrío; **— business** negocio sospechoso; **— character** persona de carácter dudoso, persona de mala fama.

shaft [ʃæft] *s.* pozo o tiro (*de mina, de elevador*); cañón de chimenea; columna; eje, árbol (*de maquinaria*); flecha.

shag·gy [ʃǽgɪ] *adj.* peludo, velludo; lanudo; desaseado; áspero.

shake [ʃek] *v.* menear(se); estremecer(se); temblar; sacudir(se); agitar(se); titubear, vacilar; hacer vacilar; dar, estrechar (*la mano*); **to — hands** dar un apretón de manos, darse la mano; **to — one's head** mover o menear la cabeza; cabecear; **to — with cold** tiritar de frío, estremecerse de frío; **to — with fear** temblar de miedo, estremecerse de miedo; *s.* sacudida; sacudimiento; estremecimiento, temblor; apretón (*de manos*); **hand—** apretón de manos.

shak·en [ʃékən] *p.p. de* **to shake.**

shake-up [ʃékəp] *s.* reorganización.

shak·y [ʃékɪ] *adj.* tembloroso; vacilante.

shall [ʃæl] *v. aux. del futuro del indicativo en las primeras personas* (**I, we**); *en las demás expresa mayor énfasis, mandato u obligación*; **he — not do it** no lo hará, no ha de hacerlo; **thou shalt not steal** no hurtarás.

shal·low [ʃǽlo] *adj.* bajo, poco profundo; superficial; ligero de cascos.

shal·low·ness [ʃǽlonɪs] *s.* poca hondura, poca profundidad; superficialidad; ligereza de juicio.

sham [ʃæm] *s.* fingimiento, falsedad, farsa; *adj.* fingido, simulado; falso; **— battle** simulacro, batalla fingida; *v.* fingir, simular.

sham·bles [ʃǽmblz] *s.* desorden.

shame [ʃem] *s.* vergüenza; deshonra; **— on you!** ¡qué vergüenza!; **it is a —** es una vergüenza; es una lástima; **to bring — upon** deshonrar; *v.* avergonzar; deshonrar.

shame·ful [ʃémfəl] *adj.* vergonzoso.

shame·less [ʃémlɪs] *adj.* desvergonzado, descarado.

shame·less·ness [ʃémlɪsnɪs] *s.* desvergüenza; descaro, desfachatez.

sham·poo [ʃæmpú] *s.* champú, lavado de la cabeza; *v.* dar un champú, lavar (*la cabeza*).

sham·rock [ʃǽmrak] *s.* trébol.

shank [ʃæŋk] *s.* canilla (*parte inferior de la pierna*); zanca.

shan·ty [ʃǽntɪ] *s.* choza, cabaña, casucha.

shape [ʃep] *s.* (*form*) forma; (*figure*) figura; (*condition*) estado, condición; **to be in a bad —** estar mal; **to put into —** arreglar, poner en orden, ordenar; *v.* formar, dar forma a; tomar forma; **to — one's life** dar forma a, ajustar o disponer su vida; **his plan is shaping well** va desarrollándose bien su plan.

shape·less [ʃéplɪs] *adj.* informe, sin forma.

share [ʃɛr] *s.* (*portion*) proción, parte; (*participation*) participación; acción (*participación en el capital de una compañía*); *v.* compartir; repartir; participar; **to — in** participar en, tener parte en; **to — a thing with** compartir una cosa con.

share·hold·er [ʃɛrholdə] *s.* accionista.

shark [ʃark] *s.* (*fish*) tiburón; (*usurer*) estafador; (*expert*) perito, experto; **loan —** usurero; **to be a —** at ser un águila (*o* ser muy listo) para.

sharp [ʃarp] *adj.* (*acute*) agudo, puntiagudo; cortante; punzante; (*biting*) mordaz; picante; (*bright*) astuto; (*clear*) claro, distinto, bien marcado; (*sudden*) repentino; **— curve** curva abrupta, curva pronunciada o muy cerrada; **— ear** oídofino; **— features** facciones bien marcadas; **— struggle** lucha violenta; **— taste** sabor acre; **— temper** genio áspero; **— turn** vuelta repentina; *s.* sostenido (*en música*); **card—** tahur, fullero; *adv. véase* **sharply; at ten o'clock —** a las diez en punto.

sharp·en [ʃárpən] *v.* afilar(se); sacar punta a; aguzar(se); amolar.

sharp·ly [ʃárplɪ] *adv.* agudamente; mordazmente, ásperamente; repentinamente; claramente; **to arrive —** llegar en punto.

sharp·ness [ʃárpnɪs] *s.* agudeza; sutileza; mordacidad; rigor; aspereza; acidez.

shat·ter [ʃǽtə] *v.* estrellar(se), astillar(se), hacer(se) añicos; quebrar(se), romper(se); **to — one's hopes** frustrar sus esperanzas; **his health was -ed** se le quebrantó la salud; **-s** *s. pl.* pedazos, trozos, añicos, fragmentos; **to break into —** hacer(se) añicos.

shave [ʃev] *v.* afeitar(se), rasurar(se); rapar(se); acepillar (*madera*); *s.* rasura, *Am.* afeitada; **he had a close —** por poco no se escapa; se salvó por milagro.

shav·en [ʃévən] *p.p. de* **to shave; clean-shaven** bien afeitado.

shav·ing [ʃévɪŋ] *s.* rasura, *Am.* afeitada; **wood -s** virutas; **— brush** brocha de afeitar; **— soap** jabón de afeitar.

shawl [ʃɔl] *s.* mantón, chal.

she [ʃi] *pron. pers.* ella; **— who** la que; *s.* hembra; **she-bear** osa; **she-goat** cabra.

sheaf [ʃif] *s.* haz, gavilla, manojo; lío; *v.* hacer gavillas.

shear [ʃɪr] *v.* trasquilar, esquilar (*las ovejas*); cortar (*con tijeras grandes*).

shear·ing [ʃɪrɪŋ] *s.* tonsura.

shears [ʃɪrz] *s. pl.* tijeras grandes.

sheath [ʃiθ] *s.* vaina; funda, envoltura.

sheathe [ʃið] *v.* envainar.

sheaves [ʃivz] *pl. de* **sheaf.**

shed [ʃed] *s.* cobertizo; tejadillo; tinglado; *Riopl., Andes* galpón (*de una estancia*); *v.* derramar; difundir; esparcir; mudar (*de piel plumas, etc.*); ser impermeable (*un paño, abrigo, sombrero, etc.*); **to — leaves** deshojarse; *pret. & p.p. de* **to shed.**

sheen [ʃin] *s.* lustre, viso.

sheep [ʃip] *s.* oveja; carnero; ovejas; **— dog** perro de pastor; **—fold** redil; **—skin** zalea; badana; pergamino; diploma (*de pergamino*).

sheep·ish [ʃipɪʃ] *adj.* vergonzoso, encogido, tímido.

sheer [ʃɪr] *adj.* (*pure*) pure; completo; (*thin*) fino, delgado, transparente, diáfano; (*steep*) escarpado; **by — force** a pura fuerza.

sheet [ʃit] *s.* (*bed*) sábana; (*paper*) hoja, pliego (*de papel*); lámina (*de metal*); extensión (*de agua, hielo*); **— lightning** relampagueo.

shelf [ʃɛlf] *s.* estante, anaquel; repisa; saliente de roca.

shell [ʃɛl] *s.* concha; cáscara (*de huevo, nuez, etc.*); vaina (*de guisantes, frijoles, garbanzos, etc.*); casco (*de una embarcación*); armazón (*de un edificio*); granada, bomba; cápsula (*para cartuchos*); *v.* cascar (*nueces*); desvainar, quitar la vaina a, pelar; desgranar (*maíz, trigo, etc.*); bombardear.

shel·lac [ʃəlæk] *s.* laca; *v.* barnizar con laca.

shell·fish [ʃɛlfɪʃ] *s.* marisco; mariscos.

shel·ter [ʃɛltɚ] *s.* abrigo, refugio, asilo; resguardo, protección; **to take** — refugiarse, abrigarse; *v.* abrigar, refugiar, guarecer; proteger, amparar.

shelve [ʃɛlv] *v.* poner o guardar en un estante; poner a un lado, arrinconar, arrumbar.

shelves [ʃɛlvz] *s. pl.* estantes, anaqueles; estantería.

shep·herd [ʃɛpɚd] *s.* pastor; zagal; — **dog** perro de pastor.

sher·bet [ʃɚbɪt] *s.* sorbete.

sher·iff [ʃɛrɪf] *s.* alguacil mayor (*de un condado en los Estados Unidos*).

sher·ry [ʃɛrɪ] *s.* jerez, vino de Jerez.

shield [ʃild] *s.* escudo, rodela, broquel; resguardo, defensa; *v.* escudar, resguardar, proteger.

shift [ʃɪft] *v.* (*change*) cambiar; mudar(se); alternar(se); variar; desviar(se); (*transfer*) trasladar, transferir; **to** — **for oneself** valerse o mirar por sí mismo; **to** — **gears** cambiar de marcha; **to** — **the blame** echar a otro su propio culpa; *s.* cambio; desvío, desviación; tanda, grupo de obreros; turno; **gear**— cambio de marcha.

shift·less [ʃɪftlɪs] *adj.* negligente; holgazán.

shil·ling [ʃɪlɪŋ] *s.* chelín.

shim·my [ʃɪmɪ] *s.* (*dance*) shimmy; (*vibration*) abaniqueo.

shin [ʃɪn] *s.* espinilla (*de la pierna*); *v.* **to** — **up** trepar.

shine [ʃaɪn] *v.* (*beam*) brillar, resplandecer, lucir; (*polish*) pulir; dar brillo, lustre o bola, embolar (*zapatos*); *s.* brillo, lustre, resplandor; **rain or** — llueva o truene; **to give a shoe** — dar bola (brillo *o* lustre) a los zapatos; embolar o embetunar los zapatos; limpiar el calzado.

shin·gle [ʃɪŋgl] *s.* ripia, tabla delgada, *Méx.* tejamanil o tejamaní; pelo corto escalonado; letrero de oficina; **-s** zona (*erupcion de la piel*); *v.* cubrir con tejamaniles; techar con tejamaniles.

shin·ing [ʃaɪnɪŋ] *adj.* brillante; resplandeciente.

shin·y [ʃaɪnɪ] *adj.* brillante; lustroso.

ship [ʃɪp] *s.* (*naval*) buque, barco, navío, nave; (*air*) aeronave, avión; —**builder** ingeniero naval, constructor de buques; —**mate** camarada de a bordo; —**yard** astillero; **on** —**board** a bordo; *v.* embarcar(se); despachar, enviar, remesar; transportar; alistarse como marino.

ship·ment [ʃɪpmənt] *s.* embarque; cargamento; despacho, envío; remesa.

ship·per [ʃɪpɚ] *s.* embarcador; remitente.

ship·ping [ʃɪpɪŋ] *s.* embarque; despacho, envío; — **charges** gastos de embarque; — **clerk** dependiente de muelle; dependiente encargado de embarques.

ship·wreck [ʃɪprɛk] *s.* naufragio; *v.* echar a pique, hacer naufragar; naufragar, irse a pique.

ship·yard [ʃɪpyɑrd] *s.* astillero.

shirk [ʃɚk] *v.* evadir, evitar.

shirt [ʃɚt] *s.* camisa; *C.A.* cotón; —**waist** blusa; **in** — **sleeves** en camisa, en mangas de camisa.

shiv·er [ʃɪvɚ] *v.* tiritar; temblar; estremecerse; *s.* escalofrío, temblor, estremecimiento.

shoal [ʃol] *s.* bajío, banco de arena; banco (*de peces*).

shock [ʃɑk] *s.* (*blow*) choque; sacudida; **Dn** < sacudimiento; golpe; (*surprise*) sobresalto; — **absorber** amortiguador; — **of grain** hacina o gavilla de mieses; — **of hair** guedeja, greña; — **troops** tropas de asalto; *v.* chocar, ofender; escandalizar; causar fuerte impresión; horrorizar; sacudir; conmover; hacinar, hacer gavillas de (*mieses*).

shock·ing [ʃɑkɪŋ] *adj.* chocante, ofensivo, repugnante; espantoso, escandaloso.

shod [ʃɑd] *pret.* & *p.p. de* **to shoe.**

shoe [ʃu] *s.* zapato; botín; **brake** — zapata de freno; **horse**— herradura; — **blacking** betún, bola; — **polish** brillo, lustre, bola; — **store** zapatería; *v.* calzar; herrar (*un caballo*).

shoe·black [ʃublæk] *s.* limpiabotas.

shoe·horn [ʃuhɔrn] *s.* calzador.

shoe·lace [ʃules] *s.* lazo, cinta, cordón de zapato.

shoe·mak·er [ʃumekɚ] *s.* zapatero.

shoe·string [ʃustrɪŋ] *s.* lazo, cinta, cordón de zapato.

shone [ʃon] *pret.* & *p.p. de* **to shine.**

shook [ʃʊk] *pret. de* **to shake.**

shoot [ʃut] *v.* (*firearm*) tirar, disparar, descargar; hacer fuego; fusilar; dar un balazo; (*throw*) lanzar, disparar (*una instantánea*); fotografiar, filmar (*una escena*); echar (*los dados*); brotar (*las plantas*); **to** — **by** pasar rápidamente; **to** — **forth** brotar, salir; germinar; lanzarse; **to** — **it out with someone** pelearse a balazos; **to** — **up a place** entrarse a balazos por un lugar; *s.* vástago, retoño, renuevo; **to go out for a** — salir a tirar; ir de caza.

shoot·er [ʃutɚ] *s.* tirador.

shoot·ing [ʃutɪŋ] *s.* tiroteo; — **match** certamen de tiradores (*o de tiro al blanco*); — **pain** punzada, dolor agudo; — **star** estrella fugaz.

shop [ʃɑp] *s.* tienda; taller; — **window** escaparate, vitrina, aparador, *Riopl., Andes* vidriera; **barber**— barbería; **beauty** — salón de belleza; **to talk** — hablar uno de su oficio o profesión; *v.* ir de tiendas; ir de compras, comprar.

shop·keep·er [ʃɑpkipɚ] *s.* tendero.

shop·per [ʃɑpɚ] *s.* comprador.

shop·ping [ʃɑpɪŋ] *s.* compra, compras; **to go** — ir de compras, ir de tiendas.

shore [ʃor] *s.* costa, playa, orilla, ribera; puntal; **ten miles off** — a diez millas de la costa; *v.* **to** — **up** apuntalar, poner puntales.

shorn [ʃorn] *p.p. de* **to shear.**

short [ʃɔrt] *adj.* (*duration*) corto; breve; (*height*) bajo; *Méx.* chaparro; escaso; brusco; — **cut** atajo; — **circuit** cortocircuito; — **wave** onda corta; método corto; **short-legged** de piernas cortas; — **loan** préstamo a corto plazo; **for** — para abreviar; **in** — en resumen, en suma, en conclusión; **in** — **order** rápidamente, prontamente; **in a** — **time** en poco tiempo; al poco tiempo; **to be** — **of** estar falto o escaso de; **to cut** — acortar, abreviar; terminar de repente; **to run** — **of something** acabársele (írsele acabando) a uno algo; **to stop** — parar de repente, parar en seco.

short·age [ʃɔrtɪdʒ] *s.* escasez, carestía; déficit; falta.

short·com·ing [ʃɔrtkʌmɪŋ] *s.* falta, defecto.

short·en [ʃɔrtn] *v.* acortar(se), abreviar(se), disminuir(se).

short·en·ing [ʃɔrtnɪŋ] *s.* manteca, grasa (*para hacer pasteles*); acortamiento; abreviación.

SH

short·hand [ʃɔ́rthænd] *s.* taquigrafía.
short·ly [ʃɔ́rtlɪ] *adj.* brevemente; en breve; al instante, pronto, luego; bruscamente, secamente.
short·ness [ʃɔ́rtnɪs] *s.* cortedad; brevedad; pequeñez; escasez, deficiencia.
shorts [ʃɔrts] *s. pl.* calzoncillos, calzones cortos.
short·sight·ed [ʃɔ́rtsáɪtɪd] *adj.* miope; corto de vista.
shot [ʃɑt] *pret. & p.p. de* **to shoot**; *s.* (*discharge*) tiro; disparo; balazo; cañonazo; (*pellet*) bala; balas; (*injection*) inyección; (*throw*) tirada; — **of liquor** trago de aguardiente; **buck**— municiones, postas; **not by a long** — ni con mucho, ni por pienso, nada de eso; **he is a good** — es buen tirador, tiene buen tino; **to take a** — **at** disparar un tiro a; hacer una tentativa de; **within rifle** — a tiro de rifle.
shot·gun [ʃátɡʌn] *s.* escopeta.
should [ʃʊd] *v. aux. del condicional en las primeras personas* (**I, we**): **I said that I** — **go** dije que iría; *equivale al imperfecto de subjuntivo;* **if it** — **rain** si lloviera; *se usa con la significación de deber:* **you** — **not do it** no debiera (*o* no debería) hacerlo.
shoul·der [ʃóldɚ] *s.* (*person*) hombro; (*animal*) lomo, pernil (*de puerco, cordero*); borde, saliente (*de un camino*); **-s** espalda, espaldas; — **blade** espaldilla, paletilla; **straight from the** — con toda franqueza; **to turn a cold** — **to** volver las espaldas a, tratar fríamente; *v.* cargar al hombro, echarse sobre las espaldas; cargar con, asumir; empujar con el hombro.
shout [ʃaʊt] *v.* gritar; vocear; *s.* grito.
shove [ʃʌv] *v.* empujar, dar empellones; **to** — **aside** echar a un lado, rechazar; **to** — **off** partir, zarpar (*un buque*); salir, irse; *s.* empujón, empellón; empuje.
shov·el [ʃʌ́vl] *s.* pala; *v.* traspalar.
show [ʃo] *v.* (*exhibit*) mostrar, enseñar; exhibir; (*prove*) probar, demostrar; indicar; (*appear*) verse; asomarse; — **him in** que pase, hágale entrar; **to** — **off** alardear, hacer ostentación de; lucirse; **to** — **up** aparecer, presentarse; **to** — **someone up** hacer subir a alguien; mostrarle el camino (*para subir*); desenmascarar a alguien, poner a alguien en la evidencia; *s.* exhibición; demostración; ostentación; espectáculo; representación, función; apariencia; — **window** escaparate, vitrina, aparador, *Am.* vidriera; **to go to the** — ir al teatro, ir al cine; **to make a** — **of oneself** exhibirse, hacer ostentación.
show·case [ʃókes] *s.* vitrina, aparador.
show·down [ʃódaʊn] *s.* arreglo terminante.
show·er [ʃáʊɚ] *s.* aguacero, chubasco, chaparrón, lluvia; ducha, baño de ducha; *Méx.* regadera; **bridal** — tertulia para obsequiar a una novia; *v.* llover; caer un aguacero.
shown [ʃon] *p.p. de* **to show**.
show·y [ʃóɪ] *adj.* ostentoso; vistoso, chillón.
shrank [ʃræŋk] *pret. de* **to shrink**.
shred [ʃrɛd] *s.* tira, triza; andrajo; fragmento; pizca; **to be in -s** estar raído; estar andrajoso; estar hecho trizas; **to tear to -s** hacer trizas; *v.* desmenuzar; hacer trizas, hacer tiras; *pret. & p.p. de* **to shred**.
shrew [ʃru] *s.* arpía, mujer brava, mujer de mal genio.
shrewd [ʃrud] *adj.* astuto, sagaz, agudo.
shriek [ʃrik] *v.* chillar, gritar; *s.* chillido, grito.
shrill [ʃrɪl] *adj.* agudo, penetrante, chillón; *v.* chillar.

shrimp [ʃrɪmp] *s.* camarón; *Esp.* gamba; hombrecillo insignificante.
shrine [ʃraɪn] *s.* santuario; altar; lugar venerado.
shrink [ʃrɪŋk] *v.* encoger(se); contraer(se); disminuir; **to** — **back** retroceder; **to** — **from** retroceder ante, apartarse de; huir de, rehuir.
shrink·age [ʃrínkɪdʒ] *s.* encogimiento; contracción; merma.
shriv·el [ʃrívl] *v.* encoger(se); fruncir(se), marchitar(se); disminuir(se).
shroud [ʃraʊd] *s.* mortaja; *v.* amortajar; cubrir, ocultar.
shrub [ʃrʌb] *s.* arbusto.
shrub·ber·y [ʃrʌ́bərɪ] *s.* arbustos.
shrug [ʃrʌɡ] *v.* encogerse de hombros; *s.* encogimiento de hombros.
shrunk [ʃrʌŋk] *pret. & p.p. de* **to shrink**.
shrunk·en [ʃrʌ́ŋkən] *p.p. de* **to shrink**.
shuck [ʃʌk] *s.* hollejo; cáscara.
shud·der [ʃʌ́dɚ] *v.* temblar, estremecerse; *s.* temblor, estremecimiento.
shuf·fle [ʃʌ́fl] *v.* barajar; revolver, mezclar; arrastrar (*los pies*); **to** — **along** ir arrastrando los pies; *s.* mezcla, confusión; evasiva; — **of feet** arrastramiento de pies; **it is your** — a Vd. le toca barajar.
shun [ʃʌn] *v.* esquivar, evadir, rehuir, evitar.
shut [ʃʌt] *v.* cerrar(se); *to* — **down** parar el trabajo; cerrar (*una fábrica*); **to** — **in** encerrar; **to** — **off** cortar (*el gas, la electricidad, el agua, etc.*); **to** — **off from** incomunicar, aislar de, cortar la comunicación con; excluir; **to** — **out** impedir la entrada de; cerrar la puerta a; **to** — **up** cerrar bien; tapar; encerrar; tapar la boca, hacer callar; callarse; *pret. & p.p. de* **to shut**; *adj.* cerrado.
shut·ter [ʃʌ́tɚ] *s.* contraventana; postigo (*de ventana*); cerrador; obturador (*de una cámara fotográfica*).
shut·tle [ʃʌ́tl] *s.* lanzadera; *v.* ir y venir acompasadamente (*como una lanzadera*).
shy [ʃaɪ] *adj.* tímido, apocado, retraído; vergonzoso; asustadizo; esquivo; **to be** — **on** estar escaso de; **to be** — **two cents** faltarle a uno dos centavos; *v.* esquivarse, hacerse a un lado; asustarse; **to** — **at something** retroceder ante algo; respingar (*un caballo*) al ver algo; espantarse con algo; **to** — **away** esquivarse de repente; respingar (*un caballo*); desviarse, apartarse.
shy·ness [ʃáɪnɪs] *s.* apocamiento, timidez, vergüenza.
shy·ster [ʃáɪstɚ] *s.* leguleyo, abogadillo tramposo, picapleitos.
sib·i·lant [síbələnt] *s.* sibilante.
sick [sɪk] *adj.* enfermo, malo; nauseado; angustiado; — **leave** licencia por enfermedad; **to be** — **for** languidecer por, suspirar por; **to be** — **of** estar cansado de; estar harto de; **to be** — **to** (*o* **at**) **one's stomach** tener náuseas; **to make** — enfermar; dar pena, dar lástima; **s. the** — los enfermos; *v.* incitar, azuzar (*a un perro*) — **him** ¡síguele!
sick·en [síkən] *v.* enfermar(se), poner(se) enfermo; dar asco; tener asco; sentir náuseas.
sick·en·ing [síknɪŋ] *adj.* nauseabundo, repugnante; lastimoso.
sick·le [síkl] *s.* hoz.
sick·ly [síklɪ] *adj.* enfermizo; achacoso, enclenque; malsano.
sick·ness [síknɪs] *s.* enfermedad; malestar; náusea.

side [saɪd] s. (*surface*) lado; cara; costado; ladera; falda (*de una colina*); (*faction*) partido, facción; — **by** — lado a lado; **by his** — a su lado; **by the** — **of** al lado de; **on all -s** por todos lados; **to take -s with** ser partidario de, ponerse al lado de; *adj.* lateral; de lado; oblicuo; incidental; secundario, de menos importancia; — **glance** mirada de soslayo, de través o de reojo; — **issue** cuestión secundaria; — **light** luz lateral; noticia, detalle o ilustración incidental; *v.* **to** — **with** estar por, ser partidario de, apoyar a, opinar con.
side·board [sáɪdbord] s. aparador; *Col., Ven.* seibó.
side·slip [sáɪdslɪp] s. deslizamiento.
side·track [sáɪdtræk] *v.* desviar; echar a un lado.
side·walk [sáɪdwɔk] s. acera, *Méx.* banqueta, *Ríopl., Ch., Andes* vereda; *C.A., Col.,* andén.
side·ways [sáɪdwez] *adv.* de lado, de costado; oblicuamente; hacia un lado; *adj.* lateral, de lado, oblicuo.
siege [sidʒ] s. cerco, sitio, asedio; **to lay** — **to** sitiar, cercar.
sieve [sɪv] s. tamiz, cedazo; criba; *v. véase* **sift.**
sift [sɪft] *v.* cerner, tamizar; cribar.
sigh [saɪ] *v.* suspirar; s. suspiro.
sight [saɪt] s. (*sense*) vista; (*view*) visión; espectáculo, escena; (*gun*) mira (*de un arma de fuego*); **in** — **of** a vista de; **payable at** — pagadero a la vista; **he is a** — es un adefesio o mamarracho; **this room is a** — este cuarto es un horror; **to catch** — **of** vislumbrar, avistar; **to know by** — conocer de vista; **to lose** — **of** perder de vista; **to see the -s** ver of visitar los puntos de interés; *v.* avistar; ver.
sight·see·ing [sáɪtsiɪŋ] s. turismo; — **tour** paseo en auto para ver puntos de interés.
sign [saɪn] s. (*signal*) signo; seña, señal; (*indication*) muestra; (*placard*) letrero; —**board** cartel; tablero (*para fijar anuncios*); *v.* firmar; contratar, hacer firmar; **to** — **over property** ceder una propiedad mediante escritura, hacer cesión legal de propiedad; **to** — **up for a job** firmar el contrato para un empleo; contratar para un empleo.
sig·nal [sɪgnl] s. señal, seña; *v.* señalar, indicar, hacer seña, dar la señal; *adj.* señalado, notable; extraordinario; — **beacon** faro; — **code** código de señales.
sig·na·ture [sɪgnətʃɚ] s. firma.
sign·er [sáɪnɚ] s. firmante.
sig·nif·i·cance [sɪgnífəkəns] s. significación; significado.
sig·nif·i·cant [sɪgnífəkənt] *adj.* significativo.
sig·ni·fy [sɪgnəfaɪ] *v.* significar.
si·lence [sáɪləns] s. silencio; *v.* acallar; apagar (*un sonido*); aquietar, sosegar.
si·lent [sáɪlənt] *adj.* silencioso; callado; tácito; — **partner** socio comanditario (*que no tiene voz ni voto*).
sil·hou·ette [sɪluét] s. silueta; *v.* perfilar; **to be -d against** perfilarse contra.
sil·i·con [sílǝkən] s. silicio.
silk [sɪlk] s. seda; *adj.* de seda; — **industry** industria sedera; — **ribbon** cinta de seda.
silk·en [sílkən] *adj.* sedoso; de seda.
silk·worm [sílkwɝm] s. gusano de seda.
silk·y [sílkɪ] *adj.* sedoso, sedeño; de seda.
sill [sɪl] s. umbral; **window** — antepecho de ventana.
sil·ly [sílɪ] *adj.* necio, tonto, bobo, simple; absurdo, insensato.

si·lo [sáɪlo] s. silo.
silt [sɪlt] s. cieno.
sil·ver [sílvɚ] s. (*metal*) plata; (*tableware*) cubierto; (*dishes*) vajilla de plata; (*color*) color de plata; *adj.* de plata; plateado; argentino; — **wedding** bodas de plata; *v.* platear; argentar; **to** — **a mirror** azogar un espejo.
sil·ver·smith [sílvɚsmɪθ] s. platero.
sil·ver·ware [sílvɚwɛr] s. vajilla de plata, vajilla plateada; cuchillos, cucharas y tenedores (*por lo general de plata o plateados*).
sil·ver·y [sílvərɪ] *adj.* plateado; argentino.
sim·i·lar [síməlɚ] *adj.* semejante; similar; -**ly** *adv.* semejantemente; de la misma manera.
sim·i·lar·i·ty [sɪmǝlærǝtɪ] s. semejanza, parecido.
sim·i·le [símǝlɪ] s. símil.
sim·mer [símɚ] *v.* hervir a fuego lento.
sim·ple [símpl] *adj.* simple; sencillo; llano; tonto, mentecato; **simpleminded** ingenuo, simple, simplón; s. simple.
sim·ple·ton [símpltǝn] s. simplón, papanatas, papamoscas.
sim·plic·i·ty [sɪmplísǝtɪ] s. sencillez; simplicidad; simpleza; ingenuidad.
sim·pli·fy [símplǝfaɪ] *v.* simplificar.
sim·ply [símplɪ] *adv.* simplemente; sencillamente; solamente.
sim·u·late [símjǝlet] *v.* simular.
si·mul·ta·ne·ous [saɪmlténɪǝs] *adj.* simultáneo.
sin [sɪn] s. pecado, culpa; *v.* pecar.
since [sɪns] *conj.* desde que; después (de) que; puesto que, como, visto que; dado que; *prep.* desde, despues de; *adv.* desde entonces; **ever** — desde entonces; **he died long** — murió hace mucho tiempo; **we have been here** — **five** estamos aquí desde las cinco.
sin·cere [sɪnsír] *adj.* sincero.
sin·cer·i·ty [sɪnsérǝtɪ] s. sinceridad.
si·ne·cure [sínɪkjur] s. sinecura (*trabajo fácil y bien pagado*).
sin·ew [sínju] s. tendón; fibra, vigor.
sin·ew·y [sínjawɪ] *adj.* nervudo, nervioso o nervioso; fuerte, vigoroso.
sin·ful [sínfǝl] *adj.* pecaminoso; pecador.
sing [sɪŋ] *v.* cantar; **to** — **out of tune** desentonar(se), desafinar; **to** — **to sleep** arrullar.
singe [sɪndʒ] *v.* chamuscar; s. chamusquina, *Am.* chamuscada, *Am.* chamuscadura.
sing·er [síŋɚ] s. cantor, cantora, cantatriz.
sin·gle [síŋgl] *adj.* (*unique*) solo; (*distinct*) individual; particular; (*unmarried*) soltero; — **entry bookkeeping** teneduría por partida simple; — **room** cuarto para uno; — **woman** mujer soltera; **not a** — **word** ni una sola palabra; s. billete de un dólar; *v.* **to** — **out** singularizar, distinguir, escoger; entresacar.
sin·gle·handed [síŋglhændɪd] *adj.* solo, sin ayuda.
sing·song [síŋsɔŋ] s. sonsonete; cadencia monótona.
sin·gu·lar [síŋgjǝlɚ] *adj.* singular; raro, extraordinario; s. singular, número singular.
sin·is·ter [sínɪstɚ] *adj.* siniestro, aciago, funesto.
sink [sɪŋk] *v.* hundir(se); sumir(se), sumergir(se); echar a pique; irse a pique, naufragar; cavar (*un pozo*); enterrar, clavar (*un puntal o poste*); **to** — **into one's mind** grabarse en la memoria; **to** — **one's teeth into** clavar el diente en; **to** — **to sleep** caer en el sueño; s. sumidero; fregadero.
sin·ner [sínɚ] s. pecador.
sin·u·ous [sínjuǝs] *adj.* sinuoso, tortuoso; con vueltas y rodeos.

SH

si·nus [sáɪnəs] s. seno, cavidad (en un hueso); **frontal** — seno frontal.

sip [sɪp] v. sorber; chupar; s. sorbo.

si·phon [sáɪfən] s. sifón; v. sacar (agua) con sifón.

sir [sɝ] s. señor.

si·ren [sáɪrən] s. sirena.

sir·loin [sɝ́lɔɪn] s. solomillo, solomo.

sir·up [sɪrəp] s. jarabe.

sis·sy [sísɪ] adj. & s. afeminado, maricón.

sis·ter [sístɚ] s. hermana; **Sister Mary Sor** María.

sis·ter-in-law [sístɚɪnlɔ] s. cuñada, hermana política.

sit [sɪt] v. sentar(se); colocar, asentar; posarse (un pájaro); estar sentado; estar situado; empollar (las gallinas); apoyarse; reunirse, celebrar sesión (un cuerpo legislativo, un tribunal); sentar, venir o caer (bien o mal un traje); **to** — **down** sentarse; **to** — **out a dance** quedarse sentado durante una pieza de baile; **to** — **still** estarse quieto; **to** — **tight** mantenerse firme en su puesto; **to** — **up** incorporarse; **to** — **up all night** velar toda la noche; **to** — **up and take notice** despabilarse.

site [saɪt] s. sitio, local, situación.

sit·ting [sɪtɪŋ] s. sesión (de un cuerpo legislativo, tribunal, etc.); sentada; **at one** — de una sentada; adj. sentado; — **hen** gallina ponedora; — **room** sala (de descanso); sala de espera; antesala.

sit·u·at·ed [sɪtʃʊetɪd] adj. situado, sito, ubicado, colocado.

sit·u·a·tion [sɪtʃʊéʃən] s. (location) situación, colocación; (employment) empleo; posición; (status) situación.

size [saɪz] s. tamaño; medida; talla; v. clasificar según el tamaño; **to** — **up** tantear, formarse una idea de, juzgar.

siz·zle [sízl] v. chirriar (aplícase al sonido que hace la carne al freírse); s. chirrido (de la carne al freírse).

skate [sket] s. patín; **ice** — patín de hielo, patín de cuchilla; **roller** — patín de ruedas; v. patinar.

skein [sken] s. madeja.

skel·e·ton [skélətn] s. esqueleto; osamenta; armazón; — **key** llave maestra.

skep·tic = **sceptic**.

sketch [skɛtʃ] s. (drawing) boceto; diseño; croquis; (outline) esbozo; bosquejo; v. bosquejar; delinear; esbozar, dibujar.

ski [ski] s. esquí; v. esquiar, patinar con esquís.

skid [skɪd] v. patinar, resbalar(se); patinar (una rueda); deslizarse.

skill [skɪl] s. destreza, maña, habilidad, pericia.

skilled [skɪld] adj. experto, práctico, experimentado, hábil.

skil·let [skílɪt] s. sartén; cacerola.

skill·ful, skil·ful [skílfəl] adj. experto, diestro, ducho, hábil, perito.

skim [skɪm] v. (remove layer) desnatar, quitar la nata a; espumar, quitar la espuma a; (read) leer superficialmente; **to** — **over the surface** rozar la superficie.

skimp [skɪmp] v. escatimar; economizar; ser tacaño; hacer (las cosas) con descuido.

skimp·y [skímpɪ] adj. escaso; tacaño.

skin [skɪn] s. piel; cutis; pellejo; cuero, cáscara, hollejo; **to save one's** — salvar el pellejo; **skin-deep** superficial; v. desollar; pelar; **to** — **someone (out of his money)** desplumar a una persona, quitarle a uno el dinero.

skin·ny [skínɪ] adj. flaco; descarnado.

skip [skɪp] v. saltar; brincar; saltarse (unos renglones, un párrafo, etc.), omitir; saltar por encima de, salvar de un brinco; **to** — **out** salir a escape, escabullirse, escaparse, s. salto, brinco; omisión.

skip·per [skípɚ] s. patrón (de barco); capitán; saltador, brincador.

skir·mish [skɝ́mɪʃ] s. escaramuza; v. escaramuzar, sostener una escaramuza.

skirt [skɝt] s. falda, Riopl. pollera; orilla, borde; **under**— enaguas; v. bordear, orillar, ir por la orilla de; circundar; **to** — **along a coast** costear.

skit [skɪt] s. parodia, juguete o paso cómico; boceto satírico o burlesco.

skull [skʌl] s. cráneo; calavera.

skunk [skʌŋk] s. C.A., Méx., Riopl. zorrillo o zorrino, Ven., Col. mapurite.

sky [skaɪ] s. cielo; — **blue** azul celeste.

sky·lark [skáɪlɑrk] s. alondra, calandria.

sky·light [skáɪlaɪt] s. claraboya, tragaluz.

sky·rock·et [skáɪrɑkɪt] s. cohete.

sky·scrap·er [skáɪskrepɚ] s. rascacielos.

slab [slæb] s. tabla, plancha, losa; tajada gruesa; **marble** — losa de mármol.

slack [slæk] adj. (not taut) flojo; (sluggish) tardo, lento; inactivo; — **season** temporada inactiva; s. flojedad, flojera; inactividad; **to take up the** — apretar, estirar; **-s** pantalones anchos con pliegues, v. véase **slacken**.

slack·en [slǽkən] v. aflojar(se); flojear; retardar(se); disminuir.

slag [slæg] s. escoria.

slain [slen] p.p. de **to slay.**

slam [slæm] v. cerrar(se) de golpe; dejar caer de golpe; **to** — **someone** decirle a alguien una claridad o grosería; **to** — **the door** dar un portazo; s. golpazo; claridad, grosería; — **of a door** portazo; **to make a grand** — ganar todas las bazas (en el juego de bridge).

slan·der [slǽndɚ] s. calumnia, maledicencia; v. calumniar.

slan·der·ous [slǽndərəs] adj. calumnioso; maldiciente.

slang [slæŋ] s. jerga, jerigonza; vulgarismo.

slant [slænt] s. sesgo; inclinación; punto de vista; adj. sesgado; inclinado; oblicuo; v. sesgar; inclinar(se); ladear.

slap [slæp] s. palmada, manazo, manotada; insulto, desaire; v. dar una palmada a, dar un manazo a.

slap·stick [slǽpstɪk] adj. de golpe y porrazo.

slash [slæʃ] v. acuchillar; dar cuchilladas o tajos; cortar; truncar; hacer fuerte rebaja de (precios, sueldos); s. cuchillada; tajo, tajada, cortadura.

slat [slæt] s. tabla, tablilla.

slate [slet] s. pizarra; color de pizarra; lista de candidatos; — **pencil** pizarrín.

slaugh·ter [slɔ́tɚ] s. carnicería, matanza, Riopl. carneada; —**house** matadero, Méx., C.A. rastro; v. matar; Riopl. carnear; hacer una matanza; destrozar.

slave [slev] s. esclavo; — **driver** capataz de esclavos; persona que agobia de trabajo a otra; — **labor** trabajo de esclavos; trabajadores forzados; — **dealer** negrero; v. trabajar como esclavo.

slav·er [slǽvɚ] s. baba; v. babosear, babear.

slav·er·y [slévɪ] s. esclavitud.

slav·ish [slévɪʃ] adj. servil.

slay [sle] v. matar.

sled [slɛd] s. trineo, rastra.

sleek [slik] adj. liso; pulido; resbaloso; suave;

artero, mañoso; *v.* alisar; pulir.

sleep [slip] *v.* dormir; **to — it off** dormir la mona; **to — off a headache** curarse con sueño un dolor de cabeza; **to — on it** consultarlo con la almohada; *s.* sueño; — **walker** sonámbulo; **to go to** — dormirse, quedarse dormido; **to put to** — adormecer; arrullar (*al nene*).

sleep·er [slípɚ] *s.* durmiente; cochecama, coche-dormitorio.

sleep·i·ly [slípɪlɪ] *adv.* con somnolencia.

sleep·i·ness [slípɪnɪs] *s.* sueño, modorra, somnolencia.

sleep·ing [slípɪŋ] *adj.* durmiente; dormido; — **car** coche-cama, coche-dormitorio; — **pills** píldoras para dormir; — **sickness** encefalitis letárgica.

sleep·less [slíplɪs] *adj.* desvelado, insomne, sin sueño.

sleep·y [slípɪ] *adj.* soñoliento; amodorrado; **to be — tener sueño.**

sleet [slit] *s.* cellisca; *v.* cellisquear.

sleeve [sliv] *s.* manga.

sleigh [sle] *s.* trineo; — **bell** cascabel; *v.* pasearse en trineo.

sleight [slait]: — **of hand** juego de manos; prestidigitación, escamoteo.

slen·der [slénda] *adj.* delgado; tenue; escaso, insuficiente.

slept [slɛpt] *pret. & p.p. de* **to sleep.**

sleuth [sluθ] *s.* detective (*o* detectivo).

slew [slu] *pret. de* **to slay.**

slice [slais] *s.* rebanada, tajada; lonja; *v.* rebanar, tajar; cortar.

slick [slɪk] *v.* alisar; pulir; **to — up** alisar bien, pulir bien; pulirse, acicalarse, componerse; *adj.* liso; meloso, suave; aceitoso; astuto, mañoso.

slick·er [slíkɚ] *s.* impermeable de hule (*o* de caucho); embaucador.

slid [slɪd] *pret. & p.p. de* **to slide.**

slid·den [slɪdn̩] *p.p. de* **to slide.**

slide [slaid] *v.* resbalar(se); deslizar(se); hacer resbalar; patinar; **to — into** meter(se) en; **to — out** (*o* — **away**) deslizarse, colarse, escabullirse, escaparse; **to let something** — dejar pasar algo; no hacer caso de algo; *s.* resbalón; resbaladero, lugar resbaladizo; ligado (*en música*); *véase* **landslide;** — **cover** tapa corrediza; — **rule** regla de cálculo; **microscope** — platina.

slight [slait] *s.* desaire, menosprecio, desdén; desatención; *v.* desairar, menospreciar; descuidar, desatender; *adj.* delgado; delicado; leve, ligero; pequeño; insignificante; escaso; **-ly** *adv.* escasamente; ligeramente; un poco, apenas.

slim [slɪm] *adj.* delgado; esbelto; escaso.

slime [slaim] *s.* limo, cieno, fango; baba, secreción viscosa.

slim·y [sláimɪ] *adj.* viscoso, mucoso, fangoso; baboso.

sling [slɪŋ] *s.* honda (*para tirar piedras*); cabestrillo (*para sostener el brazo*); eslinga (*maroma provista de ganchos para levantar pesos*); —**shot** tirador de goma o hule; *v.* tirar, arrojar; **to — a rifle over one's shoulder** echarse el rifle al hombro.

slink [slɪŋk] *v.* andar furtivamente; **to — away** escurrirse, escabullirse, deslizarse.

slip [slɪp] *v.* (*slide*) deslizar(se); resbalar(se); (*err*) cometer un desliz; equivocarse; **to — away** escaparse, escabullirse, escurrirse; **to — in** meter(se); **to — one's dress** on ponerse de prisa el vestido; **to — out** salirse; sacar a hurtadillas; **to — out of joint** dislocarse, *Am.* zafarse (*un hueso*); **to — something off** quitar(se) algo; **to let**

an opportunity — dejar pasar una oportunidad; **it slipped my mind** se me olvidó, se me pasó, **it slipped off** se zafó; *s.* desliz; resbalón; error, equivocación; funda (*de muebles, de almohada*); combinación-enagua; pedazo (*de papel*), papeleta; embarcadero; guía, sarmiento (*para transplantar*); — **knot** nudo corredizo.

slip·per [slípɚ] *s.* zapatilla; babucha; pantufla.

slip·per·y [slípɚɪ] *adj.* resbaloso, resbaladizo; evasivo.

slit [slɪt] *v.* cortar, hacer una rendija, abertura o incisión; **to — into strips** cortar en tiras; *pret. & p.p. de* **to slit;** *s.* abertura, hendedura, rendija; cortada, incisión.

slob·ber [slábɚ] *s.* baba; *v.* babosear, babear.

slob·ber·ing [slábɚɪŋ] *adj.* baboso.

slo·gan [slógən] *s.* lema, mote.

sloop [slup] *s.* balandra.

slop [slɑp] *v.* (*soil*) ensuciar; (*splash*) salpicar; (*spill*) derramar(se); *s.* fango suciedad; **-s** lavazas, agua sucia; desperdicios.

slope [slop] *v.* inclinar(se); *s.* inclinación; declive; falda, ladera; cuesta, bajada; vertiente.

slop·py [slápɪ] *adj.* puerco, sucio, cochino; desaseado; mal hecho.

slot [slɑt] *s.* (*opening*) abertura, hendedura; (*groove for coins*) ranura (*en que se introduce una moneda*); — **machine** máquina automática que funciona por medio de una moneda «traganíqueles,» «tragamonedas»; *v.* hacer una abertura o hendedura.

sloth [slɔθ] *s.* pereza; perezoso (*cuadrúpedo*).

slouch [slautʃ] *s.* (*posture*) postura muy relajada o floja; (*person*) persona perezosa o desaseada; — **hat** sombrero gacho; **to walk with a** — andar con los hombros caídos y la cabeza inclinada; *v.* andar agachado; andar caído de hombros; andar alicaído; arrellanarse, repantigarse (*en una silla*).

slov·en·li·ness [slávənlɪnɪs] *s.* desaseo, desaliño; suciedad.

slov·en·ly [slávənlɪ] *adj.* desaseado, desaliñado; desarreglado.

slow [slo] *adj.* (*low speed*) lento, despacio; (*late*) tardo; atrasado; (*sluggish*) lerdo; torpe; *adv.* lentamente, despacio; *v.* **to — down** (*o* — **up**) retardar disminuir (*el paso, la marcha, la velocidad*); aflojar el paso; **-ly** *adv.* despacio, lentamente.

slow·ness [slónɪs] *s.* lentitud; torpeza; cachaza.

slug [slʌg] *s.* bala; porrazo, puñetazo; babosa (*molusco sin concha*); haragán; trago (*de aguardiente*); lingote (*de imprenta*); *c.* aporrear, abofetear, dar puñetazos.

slug·gard [slágəd] *s.* holgazán, haragán.

slug·gish [slágɪʃ] *adj.* tardo; inactivo.

sluice [slus] *s.* compuerta; caño, canal; —**gate** compuerta.

slum [slʌm] *s.* barrio bajo; *v.* visitar los barrios bajos.

slum·ber [slámbɚ] *v.* dormitar; dormir; *s.* sueño, sueño ligero.

slump [slʌmp] *v.* hundirse; desplomarse; bajar repentinamente (*los precios o valores*); *s.* desplome, hundimiento, bajón, baja repentina (*de precios, valores, etc.*).

slung [slʌŋ] *pret. & p.p. de* **to sling.**

slunk [slʌŋk] *pret. & p.p. de* **to slink.**

slush [slʌʃ] *s.* (*snow*) nieve a medio derretir; (*mud*) lodazal, fango; (*refuse*) desperdicios; (*drivel*) sentimentalismo.

SI

sly [slaɪ] *adj.* astuto, socarrón, zorro, taimado; **on the —** a hurtadillas, a escondidas.

sly·ness [sláɪnɪs] *s.* disimulo, astucia.

smack [smæk] *s.* (*taste*) sabor, dejo; (*kiss*) beso ruidoso; (*crack*) chasquido (*de látigo*); (*slap*) palmada, manotada; **a — of something** una pizca de algo; *v.* dar un beso ruidoso; chasquear (*un látigo*); dar un manazo; **to — of** saber a, tener el sabor de; oler a; **to — one's lips** chuparse los labios, saborearse, rechuparse, relamerse.

small [smɔl] *adj.* (*size*) pequeño, chico; bajo; (*insignificant*) insignificante; mezquino; **— change** dinero menudo, suelto; **— hours** primeras horas de la mañana; **— letters** letras minúsculas; **— talk** conversación insubstancial, charladuría; **— voice** vocecita; **to feel —** sentirse pequeño o insignificante.

small·ness [smɔ́lnɪs] *s.* pequeñez; bajeza.

small·pox [smɔ́lpaks] *s.* viruelas.

smart [smart] *adj.* (*intelligent*) listo, inteligente; (*astute*) ladino; astuto; agudo; (*stylish*) elegante; **— remark** observación aguda o penetrante; **— set** gente de buen tono; *s.* escozor, *Ríopl.*, *C.A.*, *Méx.* ardor; *v.* picar, escocer, *Ríopl.*, *C.A.*, *Méx.* arder.

smash [smæʃ] *v.* quebrantar, quebrar, romper; destrozar; aplastar; **to — into** chocar con; topar con, darse un tope contra; *s.* quebrazón, quiebra; fracaso; choque o tope violento; derrota completa.

smat·ter·ing [smǽtərɪŋ] *s.* conocimiento superficial y rudimental.

smear [smɪr] *v.* embarrar, untar, manchar; **to — with paint** pintorrear, pintarrajear; *s.* mancha.

smell [smɛl] *v.* oler; **to — of** oler a; *s.* olor; olfato; **— of** olor a; **to take a —** oler.

smell·y [smɛ́lɪ] *adj.* oloroso; hediondo.

smelt [smɛlt] *v.* fundir (*metales*); *pret. & p.p. de* **to smell.**

smile [smaɪl] *v.* sonreír(se); *s.* sonrisa.

smil·ing [smáɪlɪŋ] *adj.* risueño, sonriente; **-ly** *adv.* sonriendo, con cara risueña.

smite [smaɪt] *v.* golpear; herir; castigar; afligir; *véase* **smitten.**

smith [smɪθ] *s.* forjador; *véase* **blacksmith, goldsmith, silversmith.**

smith·y [smíθɪ] *s.* herrería, fragua, forja.

smit·ten [smítn̩] *p.p. de* **to smite** & *adj.* afligido; castigado; enamorado; **to be — with a disease** darle a uno una enfermedad.

smock [smak] *s.* bata corta, batín.

smoke [smok] *s.* humo; **— screen** cortina de humo; **cloud of —** humareda; **to have a —** dar una fumada, fumar; *v.* fumar, *Am.* chupar (*un cigarro*); humear; ahumar; **to — out** ahuyentar o echar fuera con humo.

smok·er [smóka-] *s.* fumador; vagón de fumar; reunión o tertulia de fumadores.

smoke·stack [smókstæk] *s.* chimenea.

smok·ing [smókɪŋ] *adj.* humeante; de fumar; para fumadores; **— car** vagón de fumar; **— room** fumadero, cuarto de fumar.

smok·y [smókɪ] *adj.* humeante; humoso, lleno de humo; ahumado.

smooth [smuð] *adj.* (*even*) liso; terso; igual, parejo; plano, llano; (*serene*) tranquilo; (*pleasant*) suave; (*wise*) sagaz; **— disposition** genio afable; **— manners** maneras o modales afables; **— style** estilo flúido y fácil; **— talker** hablador melifluo y sagaz; *v.* alisar; allanar; pulir; emparejar; **to**

— over allanar, alisar, arreglar; **-ly** *adv.* suavemente; blandamente; fácilmente, con facilidad.

smooth·ness [smúðnɪs] *s.* (*evenness*) lisura; igualdad, uniformidad; (*pleasantness*) suavidad; afabilidad; tranquilidad; facilidad, fluidez.

smote [smot] *pret. de* **to smite.**

smoth·er [smʌ́ðɚ] *v.* ahogar(se); sofocar(se); asfixiar(se).

smudge [smʌdʒ] *v.* tiznar, manchar o ensuciar con tizne; ahumar; *s.* tiznón, mancha (*hecha con tizne*); humareda, nube espesa de humo.

smug·gle [smʌ́gl̩] *v.* contrabandear, hacer contrabando; **to — in** meter de contrabando; **to — out** sacar de contrabando.

smug·gler [smʌ́glɚ] *s.* contrabandista.

smut [smʌt] *s.* (*smudge*) tizne; suciedad, mancha; (*obscenity*) obscenidad, dicho obseno o indecente; tizón (*enfermedad de ciertas plantas*); *v.* tiznar; ensuciar, manchar.

smut·ty [smʌ́tɪ] *adj.* tiznado, manchado de tizne; sucio.

snack [snæk] *s.* bocado, bocadillo, tentempié, bocadito; merienda, comida ligera.

snag [snæg] *s.* (*protuberance*) tocón; raigón; (*obstacle*) tropiezo, obstáculo; **to hit a —** tropezar con un obstáculo; *v.* rasgar; enredar.

snail [snel] *s.* caracol.

snake [snek] *s.* culebra, víbora; *v.* culebrear.

snap [snæp] *v.* (*make sound*) chasquear, dar un chasquido; estallar; (*break*) quebrar(se); (*photograph*) fotografiar instantáneamente; **his eyes —** le chispean los ojos; **to — at** echar una mordida o mordisco a; dar una tarascada a, morder; asir (*una oportunidad*); **to — back at** tirar una mordida a; dar una respuesta grosera a; **to — off** soltarse, saltar; quebrar(se); **to — one's fingers** tronar los dedos, castañetear con los dedos; **to — shut** cerrar(se) de golpe; **to — together** apretar, abrochar; **to — up** agarrar, asir; morder; *s.* chasquido; estallido; mordida, mordisco, dentellada; broche de presión; energía, vigor; galleta; cosa fácil, ganga; **cold —** nortazo, repentino descenso de temperatura; **not to care a —** no importarle a uno un ardite o un comino; *adj.* hecho de prisa, impensado; instantáneo; **— fastener** broche de presión; **— judgment** decisión atolondrada; **— lock** cerradura de golpe.

snap·py [snǽpɪ] *adj.* mordedor, *Ven.*, *C.A.*, *Andes* mordelón; enojadizo, *Méx.* enojón; violento, vivo; elegante; **— cheese** queso acre o picante; **— eyes** ojos chispeantes.

snap·shot [snǽpʃat] *s.* instantánea, fotografía instantánea; *v.* sacar una instantánea.

snare [snɛr] *s.* (*trap*) trampa, lazo; (*ambush*) acechanza; red; *v.* enredar; atrapar, coger con trampa; tender lazos a.

snarl [snarl] *v.* gruñir; enmarañar(se), enredar(se); *s.* gruñido; maraña, enredo; pelo enmarañado.

snatch [snætʃ] *v.* arrebatar; agarrar; **to — at** tratar de asir o agarrar; *s.* arrebatiña, arrebatamiento; trozo, pedacito; **to make a — at** tratar de arrebatar, tratar de agarrarse a.

sneak [snek] *v.* andar furtivamente; obrar solapadamente; **to — in** meter(se) a escondidas; colarse; **to — out** escurrirse, salirse a hurtadillas; sacar, llevarse (*algo*) a escondidas; *s.* persona solapada.

sneer [snɪr] *v.* (*smile*) sonreír con sorna; (*gesture*) hacer un gesto de desdén; (*ridicule*) mofarse; **to — at** mofarse de; *s.* sorna, mofa, rechifla; gesto desdeñoso.

sneeze [sniz] *v.* estornudar; *s.* estornudo.

sniff [snɪf] *v.* husmear, olfatear; sorber (*por las narices*); resollar para adentro; **to — at** husmear; menospreciar; *s.* husmeo, olfateo; sorbo (*por las narices*).

snif·fle [snɪfl] *v.* sorber por las narices.

snip [snɪp] *v.* tijeretear; **to — off** cortar de un tijeretazo, recortar; *s.* tijeretada, tijeretazo; pedacito, recorte.

snipe [snaɪp] *v.* tirar, disparar desde un escondite.

snip·er [snáɪpɚ] *s.* francotirador; tirador emboscado.

snitch [snɪtʃ] *v.* arrebatar; ratear, hurtar.

sniv·el [snɪvl] *v.* moquear; gimotear.

snob [snab] *s.* esnob.

snoop [snup] *v.* fisgar, fisgonear, curiosear; *s.* curioso, fisgón.

snooze [snuz] *v.* dormitar, sestear; *s.* siestecita, siestita; **to take a —** echar un sueñecito o siestita; descabezar el sueño.

snore [snor] *v.* roncar; *s.* ronquido.

snor·kel [snɔrkl] *s.* tubo esnorkel.

snort [snɔrt] *v.* resoplar; bufar; *s.* resoplido, bufido.

snout [snaʊt] *s.* hocico, jeta.

snow [sno] *s.* nieve; *v.* nevar; **to be -ed under** estar totalmente cubierto por la nevada.

snow·ball [snóbɔl] *s.* bola de nieve; *v.* tirar bolas de nieve.

snow-drift [snódrɪft] *s.* ventisca, ventisquero, montón de nieve.

snow·fall [snófɔl] *s.* nevada.

snow·flake [snóflek] *s.* copo de nieve.

snow·storm [snóstɔrm] *s.* fuerte nevada, nevasca.

snow·y [snóɪ] *adj.* nevado; níveo, blanco como la nieve.

snub [snʌb] *v.* desairar, menospreciar; *s.* desaire; **snub-nosed** chato, *Am.* ñato.

snuff [snʌf] *v.* olfatear, husmear, ventear; aspirar (*por la nariz*); despabilar (*una candela*); **to — at** olfatear, ventear; **to — out** apagar, extinguir; **to — up** sorber (*por las narices*); *s.* sorbo (*por la nariz*); rapé, tabaco en polvo; pabilo, mecha quemada (*de una vela*).

snuf·fle [snʌfl] *v.* ganguear; husmear.

snug [snʌg] *adj.* (*squeezed*) apretado; ajustado; compacto; (*comfortable*) abrigado; cómodo.

so [so] *adv.* así; tan, muy; tanto; **so-so** regular; **so-and-so** Fulano (de tal); **— as to** para; **— far** tan lejos; hasta ahora, hasta aquí; **— many** tantos; **— much** tanto; **— much for that** basta por ese lado; **— much the better** tanto mejor; **— that** de modo que; para que; a fin de que; de suerte que; **— then** conque, pues bien, así pues; **— long!** ¡hasta luego!; **and — forth** etcétera; y así sucesivamente; **I believe —** así lo creo; **is that —?** ¿de veras? ¿de verdad?; ¡no diga!; **ten minutes or —** poco más o menos diez minutos, como diez minutos.

soak [sok] *v.* remojar(se); empapar(se); **to — up** absorber, embeber; chupar; **— in grease** pringar; **to be -ed through** estar empapado; estar calado hasta los huesos; *s.* remojo, mojada; borrachín; golpe, puñetazo.

soap [sop] *s.* jabón; **— bubble** pompa de jabón, *Ven., Col.* bombita; *Andes, Méx.* burbuja de jabón; **— dish** jabonera; **— soft** jabón blando; lisonja, adulación; *v.* enjabonar.

soap·y [sópɪ] *adj.* lleno de jabón.

soar [sor] *v.* remontarse; encumbrarse; subir muy alto; remontar el vuelo.

sob [sab] *v.* sollozar; *s.* sollozo.

so·ber [sóbɚ] *adj.* (*temperate*) sobrio; moderado, templado; (*serious*) serio, grave; (*sane*) cuerdo, sensato; (*calm*) tranquilo, sereno; **to be —** estar en su juicio; no estar borracho; *v.* **to — down** sosegar(se), calmar(se); formalizarse; **to — up** desembriagarse, desemborracharse; bajársele a uno la borrachera.

so·ber·ly [sóbɚlɪ] *adv.* sobriamente; cuerdamente, con sensatez; seriamente.

so·ber·ness [sóbɚnɪs] *s.* sobriedad; seriedad.

so·bri·e·ty [səbráɪətɪ] *s.* sobriedad; cordura.

so-called [sókóld] *adj.* así llamado, llamado.

soc·cer [sákɚ] *s.* fútbol.

so·cia·ble [sóʃəbl] *adj.* sociable, social, tratable.

so·cial [sóʃəl] *adj.* social; sociable; tratable, de buen trato; *s.* reunión social; tertulia.

so·cial·ism [sóʃəlɪzəm] *s.* socialismo.

so·cial·ist [sóʃəlɪst] *adj. & s.* socialista.

so·cial·ize [sóʃəlaɪz] *v.* socializar.

so·ci·e·ty [səsáɪətɪ] *s.* sociedad; compañía.

so·ci·ol·o·gy [soʃɪálədʒɪ] *s.* sociología.

sock [sak] *s.* (*garment*) calcetín; (*blow*) porrazo, golpe, puñetazo; *v.* pegar, apalear, golpear; *Am.* batear (*una pelota*).

sock·et [sákɪt] *s.* cuenca (*del ojo*); portalámparas, enchufe, *Carib.* sóquet.

sod [sad] *s.* césped; terrón (*de tierra sembrada de céaped*); *v.* cubrir de césped.

so·da [sódə] *s.* soda, sosa; **— fountain** *Am.* fuente de soda; **— water** agua gaseosa; **baking —** bicarbonato de soda.

so·di·um [sódɪəm] *s.* sodio.

sod·om·y [sádəmɪ] *s.* sodomia.

so·fa [sófə] *s.* sofá.

soft [sɔft] *adj.* (*bland*) blando; muelle; suave; (*gentle*) tierno; dulce; **soft-boiled eggs** huevos pasados por agua; **— coal** carbón bituminoso; **— drink** bebida no alcohólica; **— metal** metal dulce, metal maleable; **— soap** jabón blando; adulación; **— water** agua dulce; *adv. véase* **softly.**

sof·ten [sɔfən] *v.* ablandar(se); suavizar(se); enternecer(se); templar(se); **to — one's voice** bajar la voz, hablar quedo (*o* quedito).

soft-heart·ed [sɔfthártəd] *adj.* de buen corazón.

soft·ly [sɔftlɪ] *adv.* blandamente; suavemente; quedo, quedito.

soft·ness [sɔftnɪs] *s.* blandura; molicie; suavidad; ternura; dulzura.

sog·gy [ságɪ] *adj.* remojado; empapado.

soil [sɔɪl] *s.* suelo, terreno, tierra; mancha; **native —** terruño; *v.* ensuciar(se); manchar(se).

so·journ [sódʒɜ̃n] *s.* estada, estancia, permanencia, *Andes, Méx., Riopl.* estadía; [sodʒɜ̃n] *v.* permanecer; estarse, residir por una temporada.

sol·ace [sálɪs] *s.* solaz; *v.* solazar.

so·lar [sólɚ] *adj.* solar, del sol; **— plexis** plexo solar.

sold [sold] *pret. & p.p. de* **to sell; to be — on an idea** estar bien convencido de una idea.

sol·der [sádɚ] *v.* soldar; *s.* soldadura.

sol·dier [sóldʒɚ] *s.* soldado.

sole [sol] *adj.* solo, único; exclusivo; *s.* suela (*del zapato*); planta (*del pie*); lenguado (*pez*); *v.* solar, echar suelas a; **to half-sole** echar o poner medias suelas a.

sole·ly [sóllɪ] *adv.* sólamente, únicamente.

sol·emn [sáləm] *adj.* solemne.

so·lem·ni·ty [səlémnətɪ] *s.* solemnidad.

sol-fa·ing [solfáɪŋ] *s.* solfeo.

so·lic·it [səlísɪt] *v.* solicitar.
so·lic·i·tor [səlísətə·] *s.* solicitador, agente.
so·lic·i·tous [səlísɪtəs] *adj.* solícito.
so·lic·i·tude [səlísətjud] *s.* solicitud, cuidado.
sol·id [sálɪd] *s.* sólido; *adj.* sólido; firme; macizo; sensato; unánime; — **blue** todo azul; — **gold** oro puro; **for one** — **hour** por una hora entera, por una hora sin parar; **the country is** — **for** el país está firmemente unido en favor de.
sol·i·dar·ty [saɫədǽrətɪ] *s.* solidaridad.
so·lid·i·fy [səlídəfaɪ] *v.* solidificar(se).
so·lid·i·ty [səlídətɪ] *s.* solidez.
sol·id-state [saɫədstét] *adj.* física del estado sólido.
so·lil·o·quy [səlíləkwɪ] *s.* soliloquio.
sol·i·tar·y [sáɫətɛrɪ] *adj.* solitario; solo; *s.* solitario, ermitaño.
sol·i·tude [sáɫətjud] *s.* soledad.
so·lo [sólo] *s.* solo.
so·lo·ist [sóloɪst] *s.* solista.
sol·stice [sálstəs] *s.* solsticio.
sol·u·ble [sáljəbɫ] *adj.* soluble, que se disuelve fácilmente.
so·lu·tion [səlúʃən] *s.* solución.
solve [salv] *v.* resolver; explicar, aclarar, desenredar; solucionar.
som·ber [sámbə·] *adj.* sombrío.
some [sʌm] *adj.* algún, alguno; algunos, unos; algo de, un poco de; —**one** alguien, alguno; — **twenty people** unas veinte personas; *pron.* algunos, unos; algo, un poco; una parte.
some·bod·y [sʌ́mbadɪ] *pron.* alguien; **a** — un personaje de importancia.
some·how [sʌ́mhaʊ] *adv.* de algún modo, de alguna manera; — **or other** de una manera u otra; por alguna razón.
some·one [sʌ́mwʌn] *pron.* alguno, alguien.
som·er·sault [sʌ́mərsɔlt] *s.* voltereta; *v.* dar una voltereta.
some·thing [sʌ́mθɪŋ] *s.* algo, alguna cosa; un poco; — **else** alguna otra cosa, otra cosa.
some·time [sʌ́mtaɪm] *adv.* algún día; alguna vez; en algún tiempo; **-s** *adv.* a veces, algunas veces, de vez en cuando.
some·what [sʌ́mhwat] *s.* algo, alguna cosa, un poco; *adv.* algo, un tanto.
some·where [sʌ́mhwɛr] *adv.* en alguna parte; — **else** en alguna otra parte.
son [sʌn] *s.* hijo.
song [sɔŋ] *s.* canción; canto; **the Song of Songs** el Cantar de los Cantares; — **bird** ave canora, pájaro cantor; **to buy something for a** — comprar algo muy barato.
son·ic bar·ri·er [sɑnɪkbǽrɪə·] *s.* barrera sónica.
son-in-law [sʌ́nɪnlɔ] *s.* yerno, hijo político.
son·net [sánɪt] *s.* soneto.
so·no·rous [sənórəs] *adj.* sonoro.
soon [sun] *adv.* pronto, presto; luego; — **after** poco después (de); al poco tiempo; **as** — **as** tan pronto como; luego que, así que; **how** —? ¿cuándo?
soot [sʊt] *s.* hollín; tizne.
soothe [suð] *v.* calmar, sosegar; aliviar.
sooth·say·er [súðseə·] *s.* adivino.
soot·y [sútɪ] *adj.* tiznado, cubierto de hollín.
sop [sap] *v.* empapar; **to** — **up** absorber; **to be sopping wet** estar hecho una sopa, estar mojado hasta los huesos; *s.* sopa (*pan u otra cosa empapada en leche, agua, etc.*); soborno, regalo (*para acallar, conciliar, o sobornar*).
so·phis·ti·cat·ed [səfístəkətəd] *adj.* mundano; exento de simplicidad.

soph·o·more [sáfəmor] *s.* estudiante de segundo año.
so·pran·o [səprǽno] *s.* soprano; **high** — tiple; — **voice** voz de soprano.
sor·cer·er [sɔ́rsərə·] *s.* brujo, hechicero.
sor·did [sɔ́rdɪd] *adj.* sórdido; vil, indecente; mezquino.
sore [sor] *adj.* (*painful*) dolorido; inflamado, enconado; (*grevious*) afligido, apenado; (*injured*) lastimado; picado; (*offended*) ofendido; — **eyes** mal de ojos; **to be** — **at** estar enojado con; **to have a** — **throat** tener mal de garganta, dolerle a uno la garganta; *s.* úlcera, llaga; inflamación; lastimadura; pena, aflicción; **-ly** *adv.* dolorosamente, penosamente; **to be -ly in need of** necesitar con urgencia.
sore·ness [sórnɪs] *s.* dolor, dolencia; inflamación.
sor·rel [sɔ́rəl] *adj.* alazán (*rojo canela*); *s.* color alazán; caballo alazán.
sor·row [sáro] *s.* (*sadness*) dolor, pena, pesar; (*grieving*) pesadumbre; (*repentance*) arrepentimiento; *v.* apenarse, afligirse, sentir pena.
sor·row·ful [sárəfəl] *adj.* pesaroso, doloroso, lastimoso, afligido; **-ly** *adv.* tristemente, dolorosamente, con pena, desconsoladamente.
sor·ry [sɔ́rɪ] *adj.* triste, pesaroso, afligido, arrepentido; lastimoso; **I am** — lo siento; me pesa; **I am** — **for her** la compadezco.
sort [sɔrt] *s.* suerte, clase, especie; — **of tired** algo cansado, un tanto cansado; **all -s of** de toda suerte de, de toda clase de; **out of -s** de mal humor, malhumorado; indispuesto; *v.* clasificar, ordenar, arreglar; **to** — **out** separar, clasificar; entresacar; escoger.
sought [sɔt] *pret. & p.p. de* **to seek**.
soul [sol] *s.* alma; **not a** — nadie, ni un alma.
sound [saʊnd] *adj.* (*healthy*) sano; cuerdo; sensato; (*firm*) firme, sólido; ileso; **a** — **beating** una buena zurra o tunda; — **business** buen negocio, negocio bien oganizado; — **reasoning** raciocinio sólido; — **sleep** sueño profundo; — **title** título válido o legal; **of** — **mind** en su juicio cabal; **safe and** — sano y salvo; **to sleep** — dormir profundamente; *s.* son, sonido; tono; brazo de mar; — **wave** onda sonora; *v.* sonar, tocar; sondear; tantear; auscultar (*el pecho, los pulmones*); cantar, entonar (*alabanzas*); **to** — **out** tantear, sondear.
sound·ness [sáʊndnɪs] *s.* (*firmness*) solidez; (*healthiness*) cordura, buen juicio; (*validity*) rectitud; validez; — **of body** buena salud corporal.
soup [sup] *s.* sopa; **cold vegetable** — gazpacho; — **tureen** sopera; — **dish** sopero.
sour [saʊr] *adj.* (*acid-like*) agrio; acre; ácido; desabrido; rancio; (*peevish*) malhumorado; — **milk** leche cortada; *v.* agriar(se); cortarse (*la leche*); fermentar; poner(se) de mal humor.
source [sors] *s.* origen; manantial, fuente.
sour·ness [sáʊrnɪs] *s.* acidez, agrura, desabrimiento.
souse [saʊs] *v.* zambullir; chapuzar.
south [saʊθ] *s.* sur, sud; *adj.* meridional; del sur; austral; **South American** sudamericano, suramericano; — **pole** polo sur, polo antártico; *adv.* hacia el sur.
south·east [saʊθíst] *s. & adj.* sudeste; *adv.* hacia el sudeste.
south·east·ern [saʊθístə·n] *adj.* del sudeste, sudeste.
south·ern [sʌ́ðə·n] *adj.* meridional, del sur, austral; sureño; — **Cross** Cruz del Sur.

south·ern·er [sʌ́ðənɚ] *s.* sureño, meridional, habitante del sur.

south·ward [sáʊθwəd] *adv.* hacia el sur, rumbo al sur.

south·west [saʊθwést] *s. & adj.* sudoeste (*o* suroeste); *adv.* hacia el sudoeste.

south·west·ern [saʊθwéstən] *adj.* sudoeste (*o* suroeste), del sudoeste.

sou·ve·nir [suvənír] *s.* recuerdo, memoria.

sov·er·eign [sávrɪn] *s. & adj.* soberano.

sov·er·eign·ty [sávrɪntɪ] *s.* soberanía.

so·vi·et [sóvɪɪt] *s.* sóviet; *adj.* soviético.

sow [saʊ] *s.* puerca.

sow [so] *v.* sembrar.

sown [son] *p.p. de* **to sow.**

space [spes] *s.* espacio; — **science** ciencia del espacio; ciencia espacial; — **station** estación espacial; — **suit** traje espacial; *v.* espaciar.

space·craft [spéskræft] *s.* nave espacial; astronave.

space·man [spésmæn] *s.* astronauta.

spa·cious [spéʃəs] *adj.* espacioso; dilatado, vasto.

spade [sped] *s.* azada, azadón; espada (*del juego de naipes*); *v.* cavar con la azada.

span [spæn] *s.* palmo; espacio; tramo; arco u ojo (*de puente*); envergadura (*de un aeroplano*); — **of life** longevidad; *v.* medir a palmos; atravesar.

span·gle [spǽŋgl] *s.* lentejuela; *v.* adornar con lentejuelas; brillar, centellear; **-d with stars** estrellado, sembrado (*o* tachonado) de estrellas.

Span·iard [spǽnjəd] *s.* español.

span·iel [spǽnjəl] *s.* perro de aguas.

Span·ish [spǽnɪʃ] *adj.* español; *s.* español, idioma español.

spank [spæŋk] *v.* zurrar, dar una tunda, dar nalgadas; *s.* palmada, nalgada.

spank·ing [spǽŋkɪŋ] *s.* zurra, tunda, nalgadas.

spar [spɑr] *v.* boxear, pelear.

spare [spɛr] *v.* ahorrar; evitar (*molestias, trabajo, etc.*); perdonar; **I cannot — another dollar** no dispongo de otro dólar, no tengo más dinero disponible; **I cannot — the car today** no puedo pasarme hoy sin el automóvil; **to — no expense** no escatimar gastos; **to — the enemy** usar de clemencia con el enemigo; **to have time to —** tener tiempo de sobra; *adj.* flaco, descarnado; escaso, frugal; mezquino; sobrante; de sobra; de repuesto; — **cash** dinero disponible o de sobra; — **time** tiempo libre, tiempo disponible; — **tire** neumático de repuesto.

spark [spɑrk] *s.* chispa; — **plug** bujía; *v.* chispear, echar chispas, chisporrotear.

spar·kle [spárkl] *s.* (*flash*) chispa, centella; brillo, centelleo; (*spirit*) viveza, animación; *v.* centellear; chispear; relucir, brillar.

spark·ling [spárklɪŋ] *adj.* centelleante; reluciente; chispeante; — **wine** vino espumoso.

spar·row [spǽro] *s.* gorrión, pardal.

sparse [spɑrs] *adj.* escaso; esparcido; poco denso, poco poblado; — **hair** pelo ralo.

spasm [spǽzəm] *s.* espasmo.

spas·tic [spǽstɪk] *adj.* espástico.

spat [spæt] *pret. & p.p. de* **to spit**; *v.* reñir, disputar; dar un manazo o sopapo; *s.* sopapo, manotada; riña, desavenencia; **-s** polainas cortas.

speak [spik] *v.* hablar; decir; recitar; — **to the point!** ¡vamos al grano!; **so to —** por decirlo así; **to — for** hablar por, hablar en nombre o en favor de; pedir, solicitar; apalabrar, reservar; **to**

— one's mind hablar sin rodeos, decir claramente lo que se piensa; **to — out** (*o* — **up**) hablar claro; hablar con toda franqueza; hablar en voz alta.

speak·er [spínkɚ] *s.* orador; conferenciante, conferencista; el que habla; — **of the House** presidente de la cámara de representantes; **loud-speaker** altavoz, altoparlante.

spear [spɪr] *s.* lanza; arpón (*para pescar*); brote, retoño, hoja (*de hierba*); *v.* alancear, lancear, herir con lanza.

spear·mint [spírmɪnt] *s.* yerbabuena (hierbabuena), menta.

spe·cial [spéʃəl] *adj.* especial; particular; — **delivery** entrega especial de correo; *s.* tren o autobús especial; carta urgente, entrega especial; **-ly** *adv.* especialmente; en especial; sobre todo.

spe·cial·ist [spéʃəlɪst] *s.* especialista.

spe·cial·i·za·tion [spɛʃəlɪzéʃən] *s.* especialización.

spe·cial·ize [spéʃəlaɪz] *v.* especializarse.

spe·cial·ty [spéʃəltɪ] *s.* especialidad.

spe·cies [spíʃɪz] *s.* especie; especies.

spe·cif·ic [spɪsífɪk] *adj.* específico; peculiar, característico; — **gravity** peso específico; *s.* específico; **-ally** *adv.* específicamente; especificadamente; particularmente, en particular.

spec·i·fy [spésəfaɪ] *v.* especificar; estipular.

spec·i·men [spésəmən] *s.* espécimen, muestra, ejemplar.

speck [spɛk] *s.* mota; manchita; partícula; **not a —** ni pizca; *v. véase* **speckle.**

speck·le [spékl] *s.* manchita; mota; *v.* motear, salpicar de motas o manchas; manchar.

speck·led [spékld] *adj.* moteado; — **with freckles** pecoso.

spec·ta·cle [spéktəkl] *s.* espectáculo; **-s** gafas, anteojos; **to make a — of oneself** ponerse en la evidencia, ponerse en ridículo.

spec·tac·u·lar [spɛktǽkjələ] *adj.* espectacular, ostentoso, aparatoso.

spec·ta·tor [spéktetə] *s.* espectador.

spec·ter [spéktə] *s.* espectro, fantasma, aparecido.

spec·tro·graph [spéktrogræf] *s.* espectrógrafo.

spec·trum [spéktrəm] *s.* espectro.

spec·u·late [spékjəlet] *v.* especular; reflexionar.

spec·u·la·tion [spɛkjəléʃən] *s.* especulación; reflexión.

spec·u·la·tive [spékjələtɪv] *adj.* especulativo; teórico.

spec·u·la·tor [spékjəletə] *s.* especulador.

sped [spɛd] *pret. & p.p. de* **to speed.**

speech [spitʃ] *s.* habla; lenguaje, idioma; discurso, arenga; conferencia; parlamento (*de un actor*); **to make a —** pronunciar un discurso, hacer una perorata.

speech·less [spítʃlɪs] *adj.* sin habla; mudo; estupefacto.

speed [spid] *s.* velocidad; rapidez; presteza, prontitud; — **limit** velocidad máxima; **at full —** a toda velocidad; *v.* apresurar(se), acelerar(se), dar(se) prisa; correr; ir con exceso de velocidad; despachar.

speed·i·ly [spídɪlɪ] *adv.* velozmente, rápidamente; a todo correr; de prisa, con prontitud.

speed·om·e·ter [spidámətə] *s.* velocímetro.

speed·y [spídɪ] *adj.* veloz, rápido.

spell [spɛl] *s.* (*charm*) hechizo, encanto; (*period*) temporada, corto período; (*sickness*) ataque (*de una enfermedad*); **to put under a —** aojar; hechizar, encantar; *v.* deletrear; significar,

SO

indicar; **how is it -ed?** ¿cómo se escribe?
spell·er [spélə] s. silabario; deletreador.
spell·ing [spélɪŋ] s. ortografía; deletreo; — **book** silabario.
spelt [spɛlt] *pret. & p.p. de* to spell.
spend [spɛnd] v. gastar; usar, agotar, consumir; **to — a day** pasar un día.
spend·thrift [spéndθrɪft] s. derrochador, gastador, pródigo.
spent [spɛnt] *pret. & p.p. de* to spend.
sperm [spəm] s. esperma.
sphere [sfɪr] s. esfera; globo, orbe.
spher·i·cal [sfɛrɪkl̩] adj. esférico.
sphynx [sfɪŋks] s. esfinge.
spice [spaɪs] s. especia; picante; aroma; v. condimentar, sazonar con especias.
spic·y [spáɪsɪ] adj. sazonado con especias; picante; aromático.
spi·der [spáɪdə] s. araña; sartén; — **web** telaraña.
spig·ot [spígət] s. espita, grifo, canilla.
spike [spaɪk] s. espiga; perno; clavo largo; alcayata; pico; v. clavar; clavetear.
spill [spɪl] v. verter; derramar(se); desparramar(se); hacer caer (*de un caballo*); revelar (*una noticia, un secreto*); s. derrame, derramamiento; vuelco; caída (*de un caballo*).
spilt [spɪlt] *pret. & p.p. de* to spill.
spin [spɪn] v. hilar; girar, dar vueltas, rodar; bailar (*un trompo*); **to — out** prolongar, alargar; **to — yarns** contar cuentos; s. giro, vuelta; paseo (*en automóvil, bicicleta, etc.*); barrena (*hablando de aeroplanos*).
spin·ach [spínɪtʃ] s. espinaca.
spi·nal [spáɪnl̩] adj. espinal; — **column** columna vertebral, espina dorsal.
spin·dle [spíndl̩] s. huso; eje.
spine [spaɪn] s. espina; espinazo, espina dorsal, columna vertebral.
spin·ner [spínə] s. hilandero, hilandera; máquina de hilar.
spin·ning [spínɪŋ] s. hilandería, arte de hilar; — **machine** aparato para hilar, máquina de hilar; — **mill** hilandería; — **top** trompo; — **wheel** torno de hilar.
spin·ster [spínstə] s. soltera; solterona.
spi·ral [spáɪrəl] adj. espiral; — **staircase** caracol, escalera espiral; s. espiral.
spire [spaɪr] s. aguja, chapitel de torre; cúspide, ápice; punto más alto; — **of grass** brizna de hierba.
spir·it [spírɪt] s. (*essence*) espíritu; temple; (*animation*) viveza, animación; ánimo; **low -s** abatimiento; **to be in good -s** estar de buen humor; **to be out of -s** estar triste o abatido; v. **to — away** llevarse misteriosamente.
spir·it·ed [spírɪtɪd] adj. vivo, brioso, fogoso.
spir·i·tu·al [spírɪtʃʊəl] adj. espiritual; s. espiritual (*tonada religiosa de los negros del sur de los Estados Unidos*).
spit [spɪt] v. escupir; expectorar; *pret. & p.p. de* to spit; s. esputo, saliva; asador.
spite [spaɪt] s. despecho, rencor, inquina, ojeriza; **in — of** a despecho de; a pesar de; **out of — por** despecho; v. picar, irritar, hacer rabiar.
spite·ful [spáɪtfəl] adj. rencoroso.
splash [splæʃ] v. salpicar; rociar; enlodar, manchar; chapotear (*en el agua*); s. salpicadura; rociada; chapoteo.
spleen [splin] s. bazo; mal humor, rencor.
splen·did [spléndɪd] adj. espléndido.
splen·dor [spléndə] s. esplendor; esplendidez.

splice [splaɪs] v. empalmar, unir, juntar; s. empalme; junta.
splint [splɪnt] s. tablilla; astilla; v. entablillar.
splin·ter [splíntə] s. astilla; raja; v. astillar(se), hacer(se) astillas; romper(se) en astillas.
split [splɪt] v. hender(se), rajar(se); resquebrajar(se); partir(se), dividir(se); **to — hairs** pararse en pelillos; **to — one's dies with laughter** desternillarse de risa, reventar de risa; **to — the difference** partir la diferencia; *pret. & p.p. de* to split; adj. partido, hendido, rajado; dividido; resquebrajado; s. raja, hendedura, grieta; cisma, rompimiento.
splurge [spləd͡ʒ] s. ostentación; fachenda.
spoil [spɔɪl] v. (*decay*) dañar(se); echar(se) a perder, podrir(se), corromper(se); (*harm*) estropear(se); arruinar; (*overindulge*) consentir, mimar; s. botín, presa; **-s of war** botín o despojos de guerra.
spoke [spok] s. rayo (*de rueda*); *pret. de* to speak.
spo·ken [spókən] *p.p. de* to speak.
spokes·man [spóksmən] s. portavoz, vocero.
sponge [spʌnd͡ʒ] s. (*absorbent*) esponja; (*dependent person*) gorrón, parásito; v. lavar o limpiar con esponja; vivir de gorra, vivir a costa ajena; **to — up** chupar, absorber.
sponge·cake [spʌnd͡ʒkek] s. bizcocho esponjoso.
spong·er [spʌnd͡ʒə] s. esponja, gorrón, pegote, parásito, Am. pavo.
spon·gy [spʌnd͡ʒɪ] adj. esponjoso, esponjado.
spon·sor [spɑnsə] s. padrino, madrina; patrón (*el que patrocina una empresa*); defensor; fiador; fomentador, promovedor; v. apadrinar; promover, fomentar; patrocinar; ser fiador de.
spon·ta·ne·i·ty [spɑntəníətɪ] s. espontaneidad.
spon·ta·ne·ous [spɑnténɪəs] adj. espontáneo.
spook [spuk] s. espectro, fantasma, aparecido.
spool [spul] s. carrete, carretel; v. devanar, enredar (*hilo*) en carrete.
spoon [spun] s. cuchara; v. cucharear, sacar con cuchara.
spoon·ful [spúnfəl] s. cucharada.
sport [sport] s. deporte; **in —** en broma, de burla; **to make — of** reírse de, burlarse de; **to be a good —** ser buen perdedor (*en el juego*); ser un buen compañero; v. jugar; divertirse; bromear, chancearse; **to — a new dress** lucir un traje nuevo; **-s** adj. deportivo; — **clothes** trajes deportivos.
sports car [spórtskar] s. coche (*carro*) deportivo.
sports·man [spórtsmən] s. deportista; jugador generoso, buen perdedor (*en deportes*).
spot [spɑt] s. (*blemish*) mancha, mota; (*place*) sitio, lugar; **in -s** aquí y allí; aquí y allá; **on the —** allí mismo; al punto; **to pay — cash** pagar al contado; v. manchar, ensuciar; motear; echar de ver, distinguir; avistar; localizar.
spot·less [spátlɪs] adj. sin mancha, limpio.
spot·light [spátlaɪt] s. faro giratorio.
spot·ted [spátɪd] adj. manchado; moteado.
spouse [spauz] s. esposo, esposa.
spout [spaut] v. chorrear; brotar; salir en chorro; emitir; declamar, perorar; hablar mucho; s. chorro; surtidor; pico (*de tetera, cafetera, jarra, etc.*); espita.
sprain [spren] v. torcer (*una coyuntura o músculo*); **to — one's ankle** torcerse el tobillo; s. torsión, torcedura.
sprang [spræŋ] *pret. de* to spring.
sprawl [sprɔl] v. despatarrarse; estar despatarrado; tenderse; **to — one's legs** abrir las piernas; s.

postura floja (*abiertos los brazos y piernas*).

spray [spre] *s.* (*liquid*) rocío, rociada; líquido para rociar; (*branch*) ramita; **sea —** espuma del mar; *v.* rociar.

spread [sprɛd] *v.* extender(se); desparramar(se); esparcir(se); difundir(se), diseminar(se), dispersar(se); propalar(se) (*noticias, rumores, etc.*), propagar(se); **to — apart** abrir(se), separar(se); **to — butter on** poner mantequilla en; **to — out the tablecloth** tender el mantel; **to — paint on** dar una mano de pintura a; **to — with** cubrir de; untar con; *s.* extensión; amplitud, anchura; envergadura (*de un aeroplano*); difusión; diseminación; propagación; cubierta, sobrecama; comilitona, festín; mantequilla, queso, etc., que se le unta al pan; *pret. & p.p. de* **to spread.**

spree [spri] *s.* juerga, parranda, holgorio; **to go on a —** andar (*o* ir) de parranda o juerga, *Riopl.* ir de farra.

sprig [sprɪg] *s.* ramita.

spright·ly [spráɪtlɪ] *adj.* vivo, animado, brioso; alegre.

spring [sprɪŋ] *v.* saltar; brincar; hacer saltar; **to — a leak** hacer agua (*un barco*); comenzar a gotearse (*la cañería, el techo, etc.*); formarse una gotera; **to — a trap** hacer saltar una trampa; **to — at** abalanzarse sobre; **to — from** salir de, nacer de, brotar de; **to — news of a surprise** dar de sopetón una noticia o sorpresa; **to — something open** abrir algo a la fuerza; **to — to one's feet** levantarse de un salto; **to — up** brotar; surgir; crecer; levantarse de un salto; *s.* primavera; muelle (*de metal*); resorte; elasticidad; salto, brinco; manantial, fuente; origen; *adj.* primaveral; **— board** trampolín; **— mattress** colchón de muelles; **— water** agua de manantial.

spring·time [sprɪ́ŋtaɪm] *s.* primavera.

sprink·le [sprɪ́ŋkl̩] *v.* (*scatter*) rociar; regar; espolvorear; salpicar; (*rain*) lloviznar; *s.* rociada, rocío; llovizna; **— of salt** pizca de sal.

sprint [sprɪnt] *v.* echar una carrera; *s.* carrera, carrerilla, corrida corta.

sprout [spraʊt] *v.* brotar; retoñar, germinar; hacer germinar o brotar; *s.* retoño, renuevo; **Brussels -s** bretones, coles de Bruselas.

spruce [sprus] *s.* abeto; *adj.* pulcro, aseado, pulido; elegante; *v.* **to — up** asearse, componerse, emperifollarse.

sprung [sprʌŋ] *pret. & p.p. de* **to spring.**

spun [spʌn] *pret. & p.p. de* **to spin.**

spur [spɝ] *s.* espuela; acicate; aguijón, estímulo; espolón (*del gallo*); estirbación (*de una montaña*); **— track** ramal corto (*de ferrocarril*); **on the — of the moment** impensadamente, sin la reflexión debida; por el momento; *v.* espolear, aguijar, picar, incitar; **to — on** animar, incitar a obrar o a seguir adelante.

spu·ri·ous [spúrɪəs] *adj.* espurio.

spurn [spɝn] *v.* rechazar, desdeñar, menospreciar.

spurt [spɝt] *v.* salir a borbotones; chorrear; echar chorros; hacer un repentino esfuerzo (*para ganar una carrera*); *s.* borbotón, chorrazo, chorro repentino; esfuerzo repentino; **— of anger** arranque de ira; **-s of flame** llamaradas.

sput·ter [spʌ́tɚ] *v.* chisporrotear; refunfuñar; *s.* chisporroteo; refunfuño.

spu·tum [spjútəm] *s.* esputo.

spy [spaɪ] *s.* espía; *v.* espiar; acechar; atisbar; **to — on** espiar, atisbar.

spy·glass [spáɪglæs] *s.* anteojo de larga vista.

squab [skwɑb] *s.* pichón.

squab·ble [skwɑ́bl̩] *s.* reyerta; *v.* reñir, disputar.

squad [skwɑd] *s.* escuadra, patrulla, partida.

squad·ron [skwɑ́drən] *s.* escuadra; escuadrón.

squal·id [skwɑ́lɪd] *adj.* escuálido.

squall [skwɔl] *s.* chubasco; chillido; *v.* chillar.

squan·der [skwɑ́ndɚ] *v.* despilfarrar, derrochar, malgastar, disipar.

square [skwɛr] *s.* (*rectangle*) cuadro; cuadrado; (*central park*) plaza; (*block*) manzana de casas; *Am.* cuadra; escuadra (*de carpintero*); casilla (*de tablero de ajedrez, damas, etc.*); **he is on the —** obra de buena fe; *v.* cuadrar; ajustar, arreglar, saldar (*cuentas*); justificar; cuadricular; **to — one's shoulders** enderezar los hombros; cuadrarse; **to — oneself with** sincerarse con, justificarse ante; **to — a person with another** poner bien a una persona con otra; *adj.* cuadrado, en cuadro, a escuadra, en ángulo recto; saldado; justo, recto, equitativo; franco; **— corner** esquina en ángulo recto; **— meal** comida completa, comida en regla; **— mile** milla cuadrada; **— root** raíz cuadrada; **— dance** danza de figuras; cuadrilla; **to be — with someone** estar en paz con alguien, no deberle nada, *Am.* estar a mano; *adv.* véase **squarely.**

square·ly [skwɛ́rlɪ] *adv.* equitativamente, honradamente; firmemente; de buena fe; derecho, derechamente; **to hit the target — in the middle** pegar de lleno en el blanco.

squash [skwɑʃ] *s.* calabaza; *v.* aplastar, despachurrar o apachurrar.

squat [skwɑt] *v.* agazaparse, sentarse en cuclillas; agacharse; ocupar tierras baldías para ganar título de propietario; *adj.* agazapado, sentado en cuclillas; (*short*) rechoncho, achaparrado, *Méx., C.A., Andes* chaparro.

squawk [skwɔk] *v.* (*noise*) graznar; chillar; (*complain*) quejarse; *s.* graznido; chillido; queja.

squeak [skwik] *v.* rechinar, chirriar; chillar; *s.* rechinamiento; chirrido, chillico.

squeal [skwil] *v.* chillar; quejarse, protestar; soplar, delatar; *s.* chillido.

squea·mish [skwímɪʃ] escrupuloso; delicado; remilgado.

squeeze [skwiz] *v.* estrujar; despachurrar o apachurrar; exprimir; prensar; apretar; **to — into** meter(se) a estrujones, encajar(se) en; **to — out the juice** exprimir el jugo; **to — through a crowd** abrirse paso a estrujones por entre la muchedumbre; *s.* estrujón; apretón; abrazo fuerte; apretura.

squelch [skwɛltʃ] *v.* aplastar; acallar, imponer silencio; presionar; **to — a revolt** sofocar o apagar una revuelta.

squid [skwɪd] *s.* calamar.

squint [skwɪnt] *v.* mirar de través; mirar de soslayo; mirar achicando los ojos; mirar furtivamente; bizquear (*mirar bizco*); *s.* mirada de soslayo; mirada bizca; mirada furtiva; **squint-eyed** *adj.* bisojo o bizco.

squire [skwaɪr] *s.* escudero; *v.* acompañar, escoltar.

squirm [skwɝm] *v.* retorcerse; **to — out of a difficulty** forcejear para salir de un aprieto.

squir·rel [skwɝ́əl] *s.* ardilla.

squirt [skwɝt] *v.* jeringar; echar un chisguete; salir a chorritos (*o* a chisguetes); *s.* jeringazo; chisguete.

stab [stæb] *v.* apuñalar, dar una puñalada, dar de puñalada, acuchillar; pinchar; *s.* puñalada,

SP

cuchillada, estocada; pinchazo.

sta·bil·i·ty [stəbíləti] *s.* estabilidad.

sta·ble [stébl] *adj.* estable; *s..* establo, cuadra; caballeriza; *v.* poner (*los animales*) en la caballeriza.

stack [stæk] *s.* pila, montón, rimero; hacina (*de paja o heno*); chimenea, cañón de chimenea; **library -s** estanterías o anaqueles de biblioteca; *v.* amontonar, apilar.

sta·di·um [stédɪəm] *s.* estadio.

staff [stæf] *s.* (*stick*) báculo, cayado, bastón, vara; (*pole*) asta (*de bandera, de lanza*); (*group*) cuerpo, consejo administrativo; **— of life** sostén de la vida; **— officer** oficial de estado mayor; **army —** estado mayor; **editorial —** redacción; **musical —** pentagrama; **teaching —** cuerpo docente; *v.* proveer de funcionarios y empleados (*una organización*).

stag [stæg] *s.* venado, ciervo; macho, hombre; **— dinner** banquete exclusivo para hombres.

stage [stedʒ] *s.* (*platform*) tablado; tablas, escenario; escena; (*theater*) teatro; (*period*) etapa, tramo; período; (*stop*) parada; **—coach** ómnibus, autobús; **— hand** tramoyista; **by easy -s** por grados, gradualmente; *v.* representar, poner en escena; **to — a hold-up** hacer un asalto, atracar; **to — a surprise** dar una sorpresa.

stag·ger [stǽgɚ] *v.* (*totter*) tambalearse, tratabillar, bambolearse; hacer tambalear; (*overwhelm*) azorar, asombrar; **to — working hours** escalonar las horas de trabajo; *s.* tambaleo, bamboleo.

stag·nant [stǽgnənt] *adj.* estancado; **to become —** estancarse.

staid [sted] *adj.* grave, serio.

stain [sten] *v.* manchar; teñir; colorar; **stained-glass window** vidriera de colores; *s.* mancha, mancilla; tinte, tintura; materia colorante.

stain·less [sténlɪs] *adj.* sin mancha, inmaculado, limpio; **— steel** acero inempañable o inoxidable.

stair [stɛr] *s.* peldaño, escalón; **-s** escalera.

stair·case [stérkes] *s.* escalera.

stair·way [stérwe] *s.* escalera.

stake [stek] *s.* estaca; puesta, apuesta; **his future is at —** su porvenir está en peligro o riesgo; **to die at the —** morir en la hoguera; **to have a — in the future of** tener interés en el porvenir de; **to have much at —** irle a uno mucho en una cosa; haber aventurado mucho; *v.* estacar; atar a una estaca; apostar; arriesgar, aventurar; **to — off** señalar con estacas (*un perímetro*).

sta·lac·tite [stəlǽktaɪt] *s.* estalactita.

sta·lag·mite [stəlǽgmaɪt] *s.* estalagmita.

stale [stel] *adj.* viejo; rancio; gastado, improductivo.

stale·mate [stélmet] *s.* punto muerto; estancación.

stalk [stɔk] *s.* tallo; caña.

stall [stɔl] *s.* casilla, puesto (*de un mercado o feria*); casilla o sección de un establo; *v.* encasillar, meter en casilla; atascarse (*un auto*); pararse (*el motor*); **he is -ing** está haciendo la pala; **to be -ed in the mud** estar atascado en el lodo.

stal·lion [stǽljən] *s.* caballo de cría, caballo padre, *Ven., Col., Riopl.* padrillo; *Méx., C.A.* garañón.

stam·mer [stǽmɚ] *v.* tartamudear, balbucear; *s.* tartamudeo, balbuceo.

stam·mer·er [stǽmərɚ] *s.* tartamundo.

stam·mer·ing [stǽmərɪŋ] *s.* tartamudeo; *adj.* tartamudo.

stamp [stæmp] *v.* (*affix*) sellar; timbrar; poner un sello a; estampar; (*mark*) marcar, imprimir, señalar; (*with foot*) patear, patalear; **to — one's**

foot dar patadas en el suelo; **to — out** extirpar, borrar; *s.* sello; timbre, estampilla; estampa; marca, impresión; patada (*en el suelo*); **postage —** sello, *Am.* estampilla, *Am.* timbre; **revenue —** timbre.

stam·pede [stæmpíd] *s.* estampida; huída en desorden; tropel; éxodo repentino; *v.* arrancar, huir en tropel; ir en tropel; ahuyentar, hacer huir en desorden.

stanch [stɑntʃ] *v.* restañar, estancar; *adj.* fuerte, firme; leal, constante, fiel.

stand [stænd] *v.* poner derecho, colocar verticalmente; (*rise*) ponerse de pie, levantarse; *Am.* parar(se); (*be erect*) estar de pie; *Am.* estar parado; (*withstand*) augantar, sufrir, tolerar; **to — a chance of** tener probabilidad de; **to — an expense** sufragar un gasto; **to — aside** apartarse; mantenerse apartado; **to — back of** colocarse detrás de; salir fiador de, garantizar a, respaldar a; **to — by** mantenerse a corta distancia; apoyar, defender; estar alerta; **to — for** significar; estar por, apoyar; tolerar; **to — in the way** estorbar; **to — on end** poner(se) de punta; erizarse (*el pelo*); **to — one's ground** mantenerse firme; **to — out** resaltar, destacarse; sobre-salir; **to — six feet** tener seis pies de altura; **to — up for** apoyar, defender; **it -s to reason** es razonable, es lógico; *s.* puesto; mesilla; pedestal; posición; actitud; alto, parada (*para resistir*); quiosco; **grand—** andanada, gradería cubierta (*para espectadores*); **music —** atril; **umbrella —** paragüero.

stan·dard [stǽndɚd] *s.* (*norm*) norma; nivel normal; criterio; (*model*) modelo, patrón; *Am.* estándar; (*base*) base, pedestal; (*banner*) estandarte; **gold —** patrón de oro; **to be up to —** satisfacer las normas requeridas; *adj.* normal, que sirve de norma; de uso general; corriente; **standard-bearer** portaestandarte.

stan·dard·i·za·tion [stændɚdəzéʃən] *s.* normalización, uniformación, igualación.

stan·dard·ize [stǽndɚdaɪz] *v.* normalizar, uniformar, *Méx., C.A., Carib.* estandardizar.

stand·by [stǽndbaɪ] *s.* sustituto.

stand·ing [stǽndɪŋ] *s.* (*position*) posición; (*fame*) fama, reputación; **of long —** que ha prevalecido largo tiempo; muy antiguo; *adj.* derecho, en pie; de pie; establecido, permanente; **water —** agua estancada; **there is — room only** no quedan asientos.

stand·point [stǽndpɔɪnt] *s.* punto de vista.

stand·still [stǽndstɪl] *s.* alto; pausa; **to come to a —** pararse; hacer alto.

stank [stæŋk] *pret. de to* **stink.**

stan·za [stǽnzə] *s.* estrofa.

sta·ple [stépl] *s.* broche de alambre (*para sujetar papeles*); grapa, argolla, armella; artículo principal; **-s** artículos de necesidad prima; *adj.* principal; de uso corriente; indispensable; *v.* asegurar (*papeles*) con broche de alambre; sujetar con armellas.

star [stɑr] *s.* estrella; asterisco; **star-spangled** estrellado; *adj.* sobresaliente, excelente; *v.* estrellar, adornar o señalar con estrellas; marcar con asterisco; presentar como estrella (*a un actor*); lucir(se) en las tablas o el cine, hacer el papel principal

star·board [stárbord] *s.* estribor; *adj.* de estribor; **— side** banda de estribor; *adv.* a estribor.

starch [stɑrtʃ] *s.* almidón; fécula; *v.* almidonar.

stare [stɛr] *v.* mirar, mirar con fijeza o curiosidad;

mirar azorado; clavar la mirada, fijar la vista; *s.* mirada fija, mirada persistente.

star·fish [stárfiʃ] *s.* estrella de mar.

stark [stɑrk] *adj.* (*utter*) tieso; (*grim*) escueto; — **folly** pura tontería; — **in death** tieso, muerto; — **narrative** narración escueta, sin adornos; *adv.* completamente, totalmente; — **mad** loco de remate; — **naked** enteramente desnudo, en cueros, *Am.* encuerado.

star·light [stárlaɪt] *s.* luz estelar, luz de las estrellas.

star·ry [stárɪ] *adj.* estrellado, sembrado de estrellas; como estrellas, brillante.

start [stɑrt] *v.* comenzar, empezar, principiar; poner(se) en marcha; partir, salir; dar un salto, sobresaltarse; **the motor -s** el motor arranca; **to** — **after someone** salir en busca de alguien; **to** — **off** salir, partir; dar principio a; **to** — **out on a trip** empezar una jornada, emprender un viaje; **to** — **the motor** hacer arrancar el motor; *s.* comienzo, empiezo, principio; sobresalto; respingo (*de un caballo*); arranque; ventaja (*en una carrera*).

start·er [stártɚ] *s.* (*automobile*) arranque; (*person*) arrancador; iniciador; (*first*) primero de la serie; **self-starter** arranque automático.

star·tle [stártl̩] *v.* asustar(se), sobresaltar(se), espantar(se).

start·ling [stártlɪŋ] *adj.* sobresaltante, pasmoso, asombroso, sorprendente.

star·va·tion [stɑrvéʃən] *s.* inanición, hambre.

starve [stɑrv] *v.* morir(se) de hambre; hambrear; matar de hambre.

state [stet] *s.* estado; condición, situación; **in great** — con gran pompa; *adj.* de estado; del estado; de ceremonia; *v.* declarar, decir; expresar, exponer.

state·ly [stétlɪ] *adj.* majestuoso, imponente.

state·ment [stétmənt] *s.* (*declaration*) declaración; exposición; (*information*) informe, relato; (*bill*) cuenta, estado de cuentas.

state·room [stétrum] *s.* camarote (*de un buque*).

states·man [stétsmən] *s.* estadista, hombre de estado.

stat·ic [stǽtɪk] *adj.* estático; *s.* estática.

sta·tion [stéʃən] *s.* (*operations point*) estación; (*post*) paradero; puesto; (*condition*) estado, posición social; **broadcasting** — transmisora o emisora; *v.* estacionar, colocar, apostar; — **wagon** *Esp.* rubia; *Méx.* camioneta, huayin; *C.A.* camionetilla.

sta·tion·ar·y [stéʃənɛrɪ] *adj.* estacionario; fijo.

sta·tion·er·y [stéʃənɛrɪ] *s.* papelería.

sta·tis·tics [stətístɪks] *s.* estadística; datos estadísticos.

stat·u·ar·y [stǽtʃʊɛrɪ] *s.* estatuaria, arte de hacer estatuas; colección de estatuas.

stat·ue [stǽtʃʊ] *s.* estatua.

stat·ure [stǽtʃɚ] *s.* estatura.

stat·us [stétəs] *s.* estado, condición; posición social o profesional.

stat·ute [stǽtʃʊt] *s.* estatuto, ordenanza.

staunch = stanch.

stave [stev] *s.* duela de barril; *v.* poner duelas (*a un barril*); **to** — **off** mantener a distancia; evitar; rechazar.

stay [ste] *v.* (*remain*) quedarse, permanecer; parar(se); detener(se); (*sojourn*) hospedarse, alojarse; (*check*) resistir; **to** — **an execution** diferir o aplazar una ejecución; **to** — **one's hunger** engañar el hambre; **to** — **up all night** velar toda la noche; *s.* estada, estancia,

permanencia; suspensión; sostén, apoyo; varilla o ballena de corsé; **to grant a** — conceder una prórroga.

stead [stɛd]: **in her** (**his**) — en su lugar; **to stand one in good** — servirle a uno, ser de provecho para uno.

stead·fast [stédfæst] *adj.* fijo, firme; constante.

stead·i·ly [stédɪlɪ] *adv.* constantemente; firmemente; sin parar, de continuo; sin vacilar.

stead·i·ness [stédɪnɪs] *s.* firmeza; constancia; estabilidad.

stead·y [stédɪ] *adj.* firme; estable; invariable, constante; continuo; *v.* afianzar, mantener firme, asegurar; calmar (*los nervios*).

steak [stek] *s.* bistec o bisté; tajada (*para asar o freír*).

steal [stil] *v.* (*rob*) robar, hurtar; (*move*) andar furtivamente; **to** — **away** colarse, escabullirse, escaparse; **to** — **into a room** meterse a hurtadillas en un cuarto; **to** — **out of a room** salirse a escondidas de un cuarto, colarse, escabullirse; *s.* robo, hurto.

stealth [stɛlθ]: **by** — a hurtadillas, a escondidas, con cautela.

stealth·y [stɛlθɪ] *adj.* cauteloso, furtivo, secreto.

steam [stim] *s.* vapor; vaho; *adj.* de vapor; por vapor; — **engine** máquina de vapor; — **heat** calefacción por vapor; — **shovel** excavadora; *v.* cocer al vapor; dar un baño de vapor; saturar de vapor; echar vapor; **to** — **into port** llegar a puerto (*un vapor*).

steam·boat [stímbot] *s.* buque de vapor.

steam·er [stímɚ] *s.* vapor, buque de vapor.

steam·ship [stímʃɪp] *s.* vapor, buque de vapor.

steed [stid] *s.* corcel, caballo de combate; caballo brioso.

steel [stil] *s.* acero; — **industry** siderurgía; *adj.* acerado, de acero; *v.* acerar, revestir de acero; **to** — **oneself against** fortalecerse contra.

steep [stip] *adj.* empinado, escarpado, pendiente; muy alto; — **price** precio alto o excesivo; *v.* remojar, empapar; saturar; poner o estar en infusión.

stee·ple [stípl̩] *s.* aguja, chapitel; cúspide.

steep·ness [stípnɪs] *s.* inclinación abrupta; lo empinado, lo escarpado; altura (*de precios*).

steer [stɪr] *s.* novillo; buey; *v.* guiar, conducir, manejar, gobernar; timonear; **to** — **a course** seguir un rumbo; **the car -s easily** se maneja fácilmente el auto, es de fácil manejo.

steer·ing wheel [stírɪnhwil] *s.* volante; *Col.* timón.

stel·lar [stélə] *adj.* estelar.

stem [stɛm] *s.* tallo; tronco; pedúnculo (*de hoja, flor o fruto*); raíz (*de una palabra*); pie (*de copa*); cañón (*de pipa de fumar*); proa; *v.* estancar, represar; resistir, refrenar; contraponerse a; **to** — **from** provenir de.

stench [stɛntʃ] *s.* hedor, hediondez.

sten·cil [stɛnsl̩] *s.* patrón picado; esténcil.

ste·nog·ra·pher [stənágrəfə] *s.* estenógrafo, taquígrafo, mecanógrafo.

step [stɛp] *s.* (*walking*) paso; pisada; (*staircase*) peldaño, escalón, grada; (*degree*) grado; (*effort*) gestión; — **by** — paso a paso; **to be in** — **with** marchar a compás con; estar de acuerdo con; **to take -s** dar pasos; tomar medidas; gestionar; *v.* andar, caminar; dar un paso; **to** — **aside** hacerse a un lado, apartarse; **to** — **back** dar un paso o pasos atrás; retroceder; **to** — **down** bajar; **to** — **off a distance** medir a pasos una distancia; **to** — **on** pisar, pisotear; **to** — **on the**

gas pisar el acelerador; darse prisa; **to — out** salir; **to — up** subir; acelerar.

step·fa·ther [stépfɑðɚ] s. padrastro.

step·mo·ther [stépmʌðɚ] s. madrastra.

steppe [stɛp] s. estepa.

ster·e·o·type [stíriotaip] s. estéreotipo.

ster·ile [stérəl] adj. estéril.

ste·ril·i·ty [stəríləti] s. esterilidad.

ster·il·ize [stérəlaiz] v. esterilizar.

ster·ling [stɝlɪŋ] s. vajilla de plata esterlina; adj. genuino; de ley; **— silver** plata de ley, plata esterlina; **pound —** libra esterlina.

stern [stɝn] adj. austero, severo; firme; s. popa.

stern·ness [stɝnnɪs] s. austeridad, severidad; firmeza.

steth·o·scope [stéθəskop] s. estetoscopio.

ste·ve·dore [stívədor] s. estibador, cargador.

stew [stju] v. estofar; preocuparse, apurarse; s. estofado, guisado; cocido, puchero, sancocho; **to be in a —** estar preocupado o apurado.

stew·ard [stjúwɚd] s. mayordomo; camarero (de buque o avión).

stew·ard·ess [stjúwɚdɪs] s. camarera (de buque o avión); Esp. azafata.

stick [stɪk] s. palo; vara; garrote; raja de leña; **— of dynamite** barra de dinamita; **control —** palanca (de aeroplano); **walking —** bastón; chuzo (de sereno); **stick-up** atraco (para robar), asalto; v. pegar(se), adherir(se); permanecer; estar pegado; picar, pinchar; herir (con cuchillo, puñal, etc.); fijar (con clavos, alfileres, tachuelas, etc.); atascarse (en el fango un carro, auto, etc.); **to — something in** (o into) clavar o meter algo en; encajar en; **to — out** salir, sobresalir; proyectarse; **to — out one's head** asomar la cabeza; **to — out one's tongue** sacar la lengua; **to — to a job** perseverar (o persistir) en una tarea; **to — up** sobresalir, destacarse; estar de punta (el pelo); **to — one's hands up** alzar las manos; **to — someone up** asaltar o atracar a alguien (para robar); véase **stuck**.

stick·er [stíkɚ] s. marbete engomado; etiqueta.

stick·y [stíkɪ] adj. pegajoso.

stiff [stɪf] adj. tieso; rígido; entumido; duro; terco; fuerte; **— climb** subida ardua o difícil; **— price** precio alto o subido; **stiff-necked** terco, obstinado; **scared —** yerto, muerto de miedo; s. cadáver.

stiff·en [stífən] v. atiesar(se), poner(se) tieso; entumir(se); endurecer(se); espesar(se); subir de punto, aumentar (la resistencia).

stiff·ness [stífnɪs] s. tiesura; rigidez; dureza; rigor; terquedad.

sti·fle [stáɪfl] v. ahogar(se), asfixiar(se), sofocar(se); apagar, extinguir.

stig·ma [stígmə] s. estigma; baldón.

stig·ma·tize [stígmətaiz] v. estigmatizar.

still [stɪl] adj. (quiet) quieto; callado, silencioso; (at ease) tranquilo; inmóvil; **—born** nacido muerto; **— life** naturaleza muerta; v. aquietar; calmar; acallar; adv. todavía, aún; conj. empero, no obstante, sin embargo; s. destiladera, alambique; silencio.

still·ness [stílnɪs] s. quietud, calma, silencio.

stilt [stɪlt] s. zanco; pilote, puntal, soporte.

stilt·ed [stíltɪd] adj. tieso, afectado, pomposo.

stim·u·lant [stímjələnt] adj. & s. estimulante.

stim·u·late [stímjəlet] v. estimular.

stim·u·la·tion [stɪmjəléʃən] s. estimulación, estímulo.

stim·u·lus [stímjələs] s. estímulo.

sting [stɪŋ] v. (pierce) picar; pinchar, aguijonear; (irritate) escocer; Am. arder; (cheat) embaucar; estafar; s. picadura, piquete, mordedura, picazón; aguijón; escozor; **— of remorse** remordimiento.

stin·gi·ness [stíndʒɪnɪs] s. tacañería, mezquindad.

stin·gy [stíndʒɪ] adj. mezquino, ruin, tacaño; escaso; Riopl., Méx. codo.

stink [stɪŋk] v. heder, oler mal; apestar; s. hedor, mal olor, hediondez.

stint [stɪnt] v. escatimar; ser frugal o económico; **to — oneself** privarse de lo necesario, economizar demasiado; s. tarea, faena; **without — sin** límite; sin escatimar; generosamente.

stip·u·late [stípjəlet] v. estipular.

stip·u·la·tion [stɪpjəléʃən] s. estipulación, condición.

stir [stɝ] v. menear(se); mover(se), bullir(se); atizar (el fuego); incitar; conmover; perturbar; revolver; **to — up** incitar; conmover; revolver; suscitar (un argumento, pelea, etc.); s. meneo, agitación, movimiento; alboroto.

stir·ring [stɝɪŋ] adj. conmovedor.

stir·rup [stírəp] s. estribo.

stitch [stɪtʃ] v. coser; dar puntadas; s. puntada; punzada; **to be in -es** desternillarse de risa.

stock [stɑk] s. (supply) surtido; existencias, provisión; (cattle) ganado; (lineage) cepa, linaje, estirpe; (shares) acciones, valores; **in — en** existencia; **live—** ganado; **meat —** caldo de carne; adj. en existencia, esistente, disponible; común, trivial; **— answer** contestación corriente, común o trivial; **— company** sociedad anónima; compañía teatral; **— exchange** bolsa; **— farm** hacienda de ganado, Am. rancho, Am. estancia; **— market** mercado de valores, bolsa; **— room** almacén; **— size** tamaño ordinario (regularmente en existencia); **— yard** matadero; v. surtir, abastecer; tener en existencia (para vender); **to — a farm** surtir o proveer de ganado un rancho; **to — up** with surtirse de, acumular.

stock·ade [stɑkéd] s. estacada, empalizada; vallado; v. empalizar, rodear de empalizadas.

stock·bro·ker [stɑkbrokɚ] s. bolsista, corredor de bolsa.

stock·hold·er [stɑkholdɚ] s. accionista.

stock·ing [stɑkɪŋ] s. media.

sto·ic [stóɪk] adj. & s. estoico.

stoke [stok] v. atizar (el fuego); cebar, alimentar (un horno).

stole [stol] pret. de to **steal.**

sto·len [stólən] p.p. de to **steal.**

stol·id [stálɪd] adj. estólido, insensible.

stom·ach [stʌmək] s. estómago; v. aguantar, tolerar.

stomp [stɑmp] v. pisar violentamente.

stone [ston] s. piedra; hueso (de las frutas); **within a -'s throw** a tiro de piedra; adj. pétreo, de piedra; **Stone Age** Edad de Piedra; **stone-deaf** totalmente sordo, sordo como una tapia; v. apedrear; deshuesar (las frutas).

ston·y [stónɪ] adj. pedregoso; pétreo, de piedra; duro.

stood [stʊd] pret. & p.p. de to **stand.**

stool [stul] s. (furniture) taburete; C.A. banquillo; (toilet) bacín, bacinica; (excrement) excremento; **— pigeon** soplón (el que delata a otro).

stoop [stup] v. agacharse; doblarse, inclinarse; encorvarse; andar encorvado o caído de hombros; rebajarse, humillarse, abajarse; s. encorvamiento, inclinación (de espaldas); **to walk**

with a — andar encorvado o caído de hombros; **stoop-shouldered** cargado de espaldas encorvado.

stop [stɑp] v. (*pause*) parar(se), hacer alto, detener(se); (*cease*) acabar(se); cesar; parar de, dejar de; (*block*) atajar; reprimir; suspender; obstruir, tapar; **to** — **at a hotel** hospedarse o alojarse en un hotel; **to** — **at nothing** no pararse en escrúpulos; **to** — **from** impedir; **to** — **over at** hacer escala en; **to** — **short** parar(se) de sopetón, parar(se) en seco; **to** — **up** tapar, obstruir; atascar; s. parada; alto, pausa; estada, estancia; detención; suspensión; llave (*de instrumento de viento*); traste (*de guitarra*); registro (*de órgano*); — **consonant** consonante explosiva.

stop·o·ver [stɑ́povɚ] s. parada, escala; **to make a** — **in** hacer escala en.

stop·page [stɑ́pidʒ] s. detención; obstrucción; **work** — paro.

stop·per [stɑ́pɚ] s. tapón.

stor·age [stórɪdʒ] s. almacenaje; — **battery** acumulador; **to keep in** — almacenar.

store [stor] s. (*shop*) tienda; almacén; (*supply*) depósito; acopio; -**s** provisiones; bastimentos; víveres; **department** — almacén; **dry-goods** — lencería, *Méx., Ríopl., Andes* mercería, *Am.* cajón de ropa; **fruit** — frutería; **hat** — sombrerería; **grocery** — abacería, tienda de comestibles, *Méx., C.A.* tienda de abarrotes, *Carib.* bodega; **shoe** — zapatería; **to have in** — tener guardado; v. almacenar; guardar; abastecer; **to** — **up** acumular.

store·house [stórhaʊs] s. almacén, depósito.

store·keep·er [stórkipɚ] s. tendero; almacenista; guardalmacén.

store·room [stórrum] s. almacén; bodega; despensa.

stork [stɔrk] s. cigüeña.

storm [stɔrm] s. (*weather*) tormenta, tempestad, borrasca, temporal; (*disturbance*) tumulto; asalto; — **troops** tropas de asalto; **hail** — granizada; **snow**— nevasca; **wind**— vendaval; v. asaltar, atacar; rabiar; **it is -ing** hay tormenta, hay tempestad.

storm·y [stórmɪ] adj. tempestuoso, borrascoso; turbulento.

sto·ry [stórɪ] s. (*tale*) cuento, historia, historieta; relato; (*gossip*) chisme; rumor; bola; (*plot*) argumento, trama; (*floor*) piso (*de un edificio*); **newspaper** — artículo de periódico, gacetilla.

stout [staʊt] adj. corpulento, robusto, fornido; fuerte; firme; leal; valiente.

stove [stov] s. estufa; concina de gas, cocina eléctrica; *pret. & p.p.* de **to stave.**

stow [sto] v. meter, guardar; esconder; estibar, acomodar la carga de un barco; rellenar; **to** — **away on a ship** embarcarse clandestinamente, esconderse en un barco.

strad·dle [strǽdl] v. ponerse o estar a horcajadas; ponerse a caballo, cabalgar; favorecer ambos lados (*de un pleito, controversia, etc.*).

strafe [stref] v. ametrallar; *Am.* abalear.

strag·gle [strǽgl] v. vagar, desviarse; extraviarse; andar perdido; dispersarse; **to** — **behind** rezagarse.

straight [stret] adj. (*direction*) recto; derecho; directo; (*proper*) honrado; franco; erguido; correcto; en orden; — **face** cara seria; — **hair** pelo lacio; — **hand of five cards** runfla de cinco naipes del mismo palo; — **rum** ron puro, sin mezcla; **for two hours** — por dos horas seguidas, por dos horas sin parar; **to set a person** — dar

consejo a una persona; mostrarle el camino, modo o manera de hacer algo; *adv.* directamente, derecho, en línea recta; francamente; honradamente; —**away** (*o* — **off**) en seguida, al punto; **to talk** — **from the shoulder** hablar con toda franqueza o sinceridad.

straight·en [strétn̩] v. enderezar(se); arreglar; poner en orden.

straight·for·ward [stretfɔ́rwɚd] adj. derecho, recto; honrado; franco, sincero; *adv.* directamente, en línea recta.

straight·ness [strétnɪs] s. derechura; rectitud; honradez.

straight·way [strétwe] adv. luego, inmediatamente, en seguida.

strain [stren] v. (*force*) estirar demasiado, hacer fuerza; poner tirante; violentar, forzar (*los músculos, los nervios, la vista, etc.*); (*sift*) colar, tamizar; **to** — **one's wrist** torcerse la muñeca; s. tensión excesiva; tirantez; torcedura; esfuerzo excesivo; linaje, rasgo racial; aire, tonada.

strain·er [strénɚ] s. coladera; cedazo.

strait [stret] s. estrecho; -**s** estrecho; aprieto, apuro; —**jacket** camisa de fuerza.

strait·laced [strétlest] adj. estricto.

strand [strænd] v. encallar; dejar perdido (*sin medios de salir*), dejar aislado, extraviar; **to be** -**ed** estar encallado; estar extraviado (*sin medios de salir*), estar aislado, andar perdido; s. ribera, playa; ramal (*de cuerda, cable, etc.*); hebra, hilo; — **of hair** guedeja; trenza; — **of pearls** hilera de perlas.

strange [strendʒ] adj. extraño; raro, singular; desconocido.

strange·ness [stréndʒnɪs] s. extrañeza, rareza.

stran·ger [stréndʒɚ] s. extraño, desconocido; forastero.

stran·gle [strǽŋgl] v. estrangular(se).

strap [stræp] s. correa; tira de cuero o de tela; correón; tirante; **metal** — banda de metal; v. amarrar o atar con correas; azotar (*con correa*); *véase* **strop.**

strat·a·gem [strǽtədʒəm] s. estratagema.

stra·te·gic [strətídʒɪk] adj. estratégico.

strat·e·gy [strǽtədʒɪ] s. estrategia.

strat·o·sphere [strǽtəsfɪr] s. estratosfera.

straw [strɔ] s. paja; **I don't care a** — no me importa un comino; adj. de paja; pajizo; **straw-colored** pajizo, color de paja; — **hat** sombrero de paja; — **vote** voto no oficial (*para averiguar la opinion pública*).

straw·ber·ry [strɔ́bɛrɪ] s. fresa.

stray [stre] v. extraviarse, descarriarse, desviarse; perderse, errar el camino; vagar; adj. extraviado, perdido; — **remark** observación aislada; s. animal perdido o extraviado.

streak [strik] s. (*line*) raya, línea, lista; (*vein*) vena; (*trace*) rasgo; (*beam*) rayo (*de luz*); — **of lightning** relámpago, rayo; v. rayar, *Am.* listar, hacer rayas o listas en.

stream [strim] s. corriente; chorro; río, arroyo, arroyuelo; — **of cars** desfile de autos; **down**— río abajo, agua abajo, con la corriente; **up**— río arriba, agua arriba, contra la corriente; v. correr (*el agua*), fluir; brotar, manar; derramarse; flotar (*en el viento*), ondear; **to** — **out of** salir a torrentes de.

stream·er [strímɚ] s. banderola; gallardete; listón, cinta (*que flota en el aire*).

stream·lined [strímlaɪnd] adj. aerodinámico.

street [strit] s. calle.

ST

street·car [strítkɑr] *s.* tranvía.
strength [strɛŋkθ] *s.* fuerza; poder; potencia; fortaleza; **on the — of his promise** fundado en su promesa.
strength·en [strɛ́ŋkθən] *v.* fortalecer(se); reforzar(se).
stren·u·ous [strɛ́njʊəs] *adj.* arduo; enérgico, vigoroso.
strep·to·my·cin [strɛptomáɪsɪn] *s.* estreptomicina.
stress [strɛs] *s.* (*force*) fuerza, esfuerzo; tensión, torsión, compresión; (*importance*) urgencia; énfasis; (*intensity*) acento; *v.* acentuar; recalcar, dar énfasis a, hacer hincapié en.
stretch [strɛtʃ] *v.* estirar(se); alargar(se); tender(se); ensanchar; **to — oneself** estirarse, desperezarse; **to — out one's hand** tender o alargar la mano; *s.* trecho, distancia; extension; período de tiempo; elasticidad; tensión; esfuerzo (*de la imaginación*); estirón; **home — último** trecho (*de una carrera*).
stretch·er [strɛ́tʃɚ] *s.* estirador, ensanchador, dilatador; camilla (*para los heridos*).
strew [stru] *v.* regar, esparcir.
strewn [strun] *p.p. de* **to strew; — with** regado de, cubierto de.
strick·en [stríkən] *p.p. de* **to strike;** *adj.* herido; afligido; agobiado; atacado.
strict [strɪkt] *adj.* estricto; **in — confidence** en absoluta confianza, con toda reserva.
strid·den [strídn] *p.p. de* **to stride.**
stride [straɪd] *v.* tranquear, caminar a paso largo, dar zancadas, andar a trancos; *s.* zancada, tranco, paso largo.
strife [straɪf] *s.* refriega, contienda, pleito.
strike [straɪk] *v.* (*hit*) dar, golpear, pegar; azotar; herir; atacar; (*collide with*) chocar con; dar con, encontrar (*oro, petróleo, etc.*); ocurrírsele a uno (*una idea*); asumir, afectar (*una postura, una actitud*); dar (*la hora un reloj*); encender (*un fósforo*); acuñar (*moneda*); declararse o estar en huelga; **to — at** amagar; acometer; **to — off** borrar, tachar; cortar; **to — one's attention** atraer o llamar la atención; **to — one's fancy** antojársele a uno; **to — one's head against** darse un cabezazo contra; **to — out in a certain direction** tomar cierto rumbo, encaminarse o irse en cierta dirección; **to — someone for a loan** darle un sablazo a alguien; **to — up a friendship** trabar amistad; **to — with terror** sobrecoger de terror; **how does she — you?** ¿qué tal le parece?; ¿qué piensa Vd. de ella;? *s.* golpe; huelga; descubrimiento repentino (*de petróleo, de una mina, etc*); —**breaker** esquirol (*obrero que sustituye a un huelguista*).
strik·er [stráɪkɚ] *s.* (*person on strike*) huelguista; (*device*) golpeador.
strik·ing [stráɪkɪŋ] *adj.* notable; llamativo; conspicuo, manifiesto; sorprendente; extraordinario; (*on strike*) que está de huelga; que está en huelga.
string [strɪŋ] *s.* cuerda; cordel, cinta, cordón; sarta (*de perlas, cuentas, etc.*); fibra (*de habichuelas, porotos, etc.*); fila, hilera; **— bean** habichuela, judía verde, *Méx.* ejote, *Ch., Ríopl.* poroto; **— of lies** sarta de mentiras; *v.* ensartar; tender (*un cable, un alambre*); desfibrar, quitar las fibras a; encordar (*una raqueta, un violín*); encordelar, atar con cordeles, lazos o cuerdas; tomar el pelo, engañar; **to — out** extender(se), prolongar(se); **to — up** colgar.
strip [strɪp] *v.* despojar; robar; desnudar(se); desvestir(se), desmantelar; **to — the gears**

estropear el engranaje; **to — the skin from** desollar, pelar; *s.* tira, lista, listón; **— of land** faja de tierra.
stripe [straɪp] *s.* (*band*) franja, raya, lista, tira; banda, galón; (*kind*) tipo, índole; *v.* rayar, *Am.* listar, adornar con listas.
striped [straɪpt, stráɪpɪd] *adj.* listado.
strive [straɪv] *v.* esforzarse; luchar, forcejear; hacer lo posible; **to — to** esforzarse por.
striv·en [strívən] *p.p. de* **to strive.**
strode [strod] *pret. de* **to stride.**
stroke [strok] *s.* golpe; ataque, apoplejía; **— of a bell** campanada; **— of a painter's brush** pincelada; **— of lightning** rayo; **— of the hand** caricia; **— of the pen** plumada; **at the — of ten** al dar las diez; *v.* frotar suavemente, pasar suavemente la mano, acacriciar; alisar.
stroll [strol] *v.* dar un paseo, pasearse; vagar; **to — the streets** callejear; *s.* paseo, paseíto.
strong [strɔŋ] *adj.* fuerte; forzudo, fornido; vigoroso; recio; enérgico; firme; bien marcado; acérrimo; **— chance** buena probabilidad; **— coffee** café cargado; **— market** mercado firme; **strong-willed** de voluntad fuerte, decidido; **strong-arm** violento; *adv.* fuertemente; firmemente.
strong·hold [strɔ́ŋhold] *s.* fuerte, plaza fuerte.
stron·ti·um [stránt∫iəm] *s.* estroncio.
strop [strɑp] *v.* asentar (*navajas de afeitar*); *s.* asentador de navajas.
strove [strov] *pret. de* **to strive.**
struck [strʌk] *pret. & p.p. de* **to strike; to be — with a disease** darle a uno una enfermedad; **to be — with terror** estar o quedar sobrecogido de terror.
struc·tu·ral [strʌ́ktʃərəl] *adj.* estructural, relativo a la estructura.
struc·ture [strʌ́ktʃɚ] *s.* estructura; construcción; edificio.
strug·gle [strʌ́gl] *v.* bregar, luchar, pugnar; forcejear; esforzarse; *s.* esfuerzo; contienda; lucha, pugna.
strung [strʌŋ] *pret. & p.p. de* **to string.**
strut [strʌt] *v.* pavonearse, contonearse; *s.* contoneo; tirante, puntal.
stub [stʌb] *s.* trozo, fragmento, pedazo mochado; tocón (*de árbol*); talón (*de libro talonario, boleto, etc.*); **— book** libro talonario; **— pen** pluma de punta mocha; *v.* **to — one's foot** dar(se) un tropezón.
stub·ble [stʌ́bl] *s.* rastrojo; cañones (*de la barba*).
stub·born [stʌ́bɚn] *adj.* terco, testarudo, obstinado, porfiado, cabezón.
stub·born·ness [stʌ́bɚnnɪs] *s.* terquedad, testarudez, porfía, obstinación.
stuc·co [stʌ́ko] *s.* estuco; *v.* estucar, cubrir de estuco.
stuck [stʌk] *pret. & p.p. de* **to stick** pegado; atorado; atascado; **— full of holes** agujereado; **stuck-up** tieso, estirado, orgulloso.
stud [stʌd] *s.* (*knob*) tachón, tachuela de adorno; (*button*) botón postizo para camisa; (*bolt*) perno; —**horse** caballo padre; *v.* tachonar; clavetear.
stu·dent [stjúdn̩t] *s.* estudiante; *adj.* estudiantil.
stud·ied [stʌ́dɪd] *adj.* estudiado.
stu·di·o [stjúdɪo] *s.* estudio, taller.
stu·di·ous [stjúdɪəs] *adj.* estudioso; aplicado; estudiado.
stud·y [stʌ́dɪ] *s.* estudio; cuidado, solicitud; gabinete de estudio; *v.* estudiar.

stuff [stʌf] *s. (material)* materia; material; *(cloth)* género, tela; *(thing)* cosa; *(medicine)* menjurje, medicina; *(junk)* cachivaches, baratijas; **of good** — de buena estofa; *v.* rellenar; henchir; hartar(se), atracar(se), atiborrar(se).
stuf·fing [stʌfɪŋ] *s.* relleno; material para rellenar.
stum·ble [stʌmbl] *v.* tropezar, dar(se) un tropezón; dar un traspié; hablar o recitar equivocándose a cada paso; **to** — **upon** tropezar con; *s.* tropiezo, tropezón, traspié.
stump [stʌmp] *s.* tocón *(tronco que queda de un árbol)*; raigón *(de muela)*; muñón *(de brazo o pierna cortada)*; — **of a tail** rabo; **to be up a** — hallarse en un apuro, estar perplejo; *v.* trozar el tronco de *(un árbol)*; renquear, cojear; dejar confuso, confundir; **to** — **the country** recorrer el país pronunciando discursos políticos.
stump·y [stʌmpɪ] *adj.* rechoncho, *Am.* chaparro; lleno de tocones.
stun [stʌn] *v.* aturdir, pasmar; atolondrar.
stung [stʌŋ] *pret. & p.p. de* **to sting.**
stunk [stʌŋk] *pret. & p.p. de* **to stink.**
stun·ning [stʌnɪŋ] *adj.* aplastante; elegante, bellísimo.
stunt [stʌnt] *v.* achaparrar, impedir el desarrollo de, no dejar crecer; hacer suertes; hacer piruetas; *s.* suerte; pirueta, suerte acrobática, maniobra gimnástica; hazaña sensacional.
stu·pe·fy [stjúpəfaɪ] *v.* atontar; entorpecer; aturdir, atolondrar, pasmar, dejar estupefacto.
stu·pen·dous [stjupéndəs] *adj.* estupendo.
stu·pid [stjúpɪd] *adj.* estúpido; atontado.
stu·pid·i·ty [stjupídətɪ] *s.* estupidez.
stu·por [stjúpə] *s.* letargo, modorra; sopor; aturdimiento; **in a** — aletargado.
stur·dy [stɝdɪ] *adj.* fornido, fuerte, robusto; firme.
stut·ter [stʌtə] *v.* tartamudear; *s.* tartamudeo; tartamudez.
stut·er·er [stʌtərə] *s.* tartamudo.
stut·ter·ing [stʌtərɪŋ] *adj.* tartamudo; *s.* tartamudeo.
sty [staɪ] *s.* pocilga; orzuelo *(en el párpado), Méx.* perilla; *Ríopl.* chiquero.
style [staɪl] *s.* estilo; moda; **to be in** — estar de moda, estilarse; *v.* intitular, nombrar; **to** — **a dress** cortar un vestido a la moda.
styl·ish [stáɪlɪʃ] *adj.* elegante; a la moda.
styl·ize [stáɪlaɪz] *v.* estilizar.
sub·con·scious [sʌbkánʃəs] *adj.* subconsciente.
sub·di·vi·sion [sʌbdəvíʒən] *s.* subdivisión; parcelación de terrenos.
sub·due [səbdjú] *v.* subyugar, someter; sujetar; dominar; amansar, domar.
sub·dued [səbdjúd] *p.p. de* **to subdue;** *adj.* sumiso; sujeto; manso; suave; tenue; — **light** luz tenue.
sub·ject [sʌbdʒɪkt] *s.* súbdito; sujeto; asunto, tema, materia; *adj.* sujeto; sometido; inclinado, propenso; expuesto; [səbdʒékt] *v.* sujetar; someter; subyugar, sojuzgar.
sub·jec·tion [səbdʒékʃən] *s.* sujeción; dominación; sumisión.
sub·jec·tive [səbdʒéktɪv] *adj.* subjetivo.
sub·ju·gate [sʌbdʒəget] *v.* subyugar, sojuzgar.
sub·li·mate [sʌbləmet] *v.* sublimar.
sub·lime [səbláɪm] *adj.* sublime.
sub·ma·rine [sʌbmərín] *adj.* submarino; [sʌbmərin] *s.* submarino.
sub·merge [səbmɝdʒ] *v.* sumergir(se), hundir(se), sumir(se).
sub·mis·sion [səbmíʃən] *s.* sumisión, sometimiento.
sub·mis·sive [səbmísɪv] *adj.* sumiso.

sub·mit [səbmít] *v.* someter; **to** — **a report** someter (presentar o rendir) un informe; **to** — **to punishment** someterse a un castigo.
sub·or·di·nate [səbɔ́rdnɪt] *adj. & s.* subordinado; subalterno; dependiente; [səbɔ́rdnet] *v.* subordinar.
sub·scribe [səbskráɪb] *v.* subscribir(se); firmar; **to** — **five dollars** prometer una cuota o subscripción de cinco dólares; **to** — **for** subscribirse a, abonarse a; **to** — **to a plan** subscribirse a *(o aprobar)* un plan.
sub·scrib·er [səbskráɪbə] *s.* suscritor, abonado; infrascrito *(que firma un documento),* firmante.
sub·scrip·tion [səbskrípʃən] *s.* subscripción, abono.
sub·se·quent [sʌbsɪkwent] *adj.* subsiguiente, subsecuente, posterior; **-ly** *adv.* después, posteriormente, subsiguientemente.
sub·ser·vi·ent [səbsɝvɪənt] *adj.* servil, servilón.
sub·side [səbsáɪd] *v.* menguar, disminuir; bajar *(de nivel)*; calmarse, aquietarse.
sub·sid·i·ar·y [səbsídɪerɪ] *s.* subsidiario; sucursal.
sub·si·dize [sʌbsədaɪz] *v.* subvencionar.
sub·si·dy [sʌbsədɪ] *s.* subvención.
sub·sist [səbsíst] *v.* subsistir.
sub·stance [sʌbstəns] *s.* substancia (sustancia).
sub·stan·tial [səbstǽnʃəl] *adj.* substancial, substancioso; sólido; considerable; importante; **to be in** — **agreement** estar en substancia de acuerdo.
sub·stan·ti·ate [səbstǽnʃɪet] *v.* comprobar; verificar.
sub·stan·tive [sʌbstəntɪv] *adj. & s.* sustantivo.
sub·sti·tute [sʌbstətjut] *v.* sustituir (substituir); reemplazar; *s.* sustituto, suplente; reemplazo.
sub·sti·tu·tion [sʌbstətjúʃən] *s.* sustitución (substitución); reemplazo.
sub·stra·tum [sʌbstrætəm] *s.* sustrato.
sub·ter·fuge [sʌbtəfjudʒ] *s.* escapatoria; subterfugio.
sub·ter·ra·ne·an [sʌbtərénɪən] *adj.* subterráneo.
sub·tle [sʌtl] *adj.* sutil.
sub·tle·ty [sʌtltɪ] *s.* sutileza; agudeza.
sub·tract [səbtrǽkt] *v.* sustraer (substraer); restar.
sub·trac·tion [səbtrǽkʃən] *s.* sustracción (substracción), resta.
sub·urb [sʌbɝb] *s.* suberbio, arrabal.
sub·ur·ban [səbɝbən] *adj. & s.* suburbano.
sub·ver·sive [səbvɝsɪv] *adj.* subversivo *(en contra de la autoridad constituida)*; trastornador, destructivo.
sub·way [sʌbwe] *s.* subterráneo, túnel; metro, ferrocarril subterráneo.
suc·ceed [səksíd] *v.* suceder a; medrar, tener buen éxito, salir bien.
suc·cess [səksés] *s.* éxito, buen éxito; triunfo.
suc·cess·ful [səksésfəl] *adj.* afortunado; próspero; **to be** — tener buen éxito; **-ly** *adv.* con buen éxito, prósperamente.
suc·ces·sion [səkséʃən] *s.* sucesión.
suc·ces·sive [səksésɪv] *adj.* sucesivo.
suc·ces·sor [səksésə] *s.* sucesor; heredero.
suc·cor [sʌkə] *s.* socorro; *v.* socorrer.
suc·cumb [səkʌ́m] *v.* sucumbir.
such [sʌtʃ] *adj.* tal; semejante; — **a** tal, semejante; — **a good man** un hombre tan bueno; — **as** tal como, tales como; **at** — **an hour** a tal hora; **at** — **and** — **a place** en tal o cual lugar.
suck [sʌk] *v.* chupar; mamar; **to** — **up** chupar; sorber; *s.* chupada; mamada.
suck·er [sʌkə] *s.* chupador; mamón, mamantón; dulce *(que se chupa)*; primo *(persona demasiado*

ST

crédula).

suck·le [sʌ́kl] v. mamar; amamantar, dar de mamar.

suc·tion [sʌ́kʃən] s. succión; chupada, aspiración.

sud·den [sʌ́dn] adj. súbito, repentino; precipitado; inesperado; **all of a —** de súbito, de repente, de sopetón; **-ly** adv. de súbito, de repente, de sopetón.

sud·den·ness [sʌ́dnnɪs] s. precipitación; rapidez.

suds [sʌdz] s. espuma, jabonadura.

sue [su] v. demandar; **to — for damages** demandar por daños y perjuicios; **to — for peace** pedir la paz.

su·et [súɪt] s. sebo, gordo, grasa.

suf·fer [sʌ́fɚ] v. sufrir; padecer.

suf·fer·er [sʌ́fɚrɚ] s. sufridor.

suf·fer·ing [sʌ́fərɪŋ] s. sufrimiento, padecimiento; adj. doliente; sufrido, paciente.

suf·fice [səfáɪs] v. bastar, ser bastante o suficiente.

suf·fi·cient [səfíʃənt] adj. suficiente, bastante; **-ly** adv. suficientemente, bastante.

suf·fix [sʌ́fɪks] s. sufijo.

suf·fo·cate [sʌ́fəket] v. sofocar(se), ahogar(se), asfixiar(se).

suf·fo·ca·tion [sʌfəkéʃən] s. asfixia, sofoco.

suf·frage [sʌ́frɪdʒ] s. sufragio; voto.

sug·ar [ʃúgɚ] s. azúcar; **— bowl** azucarera; **— cane** caña de azúcar; **lump of —** terrón de azúcar; v. azucarar; cristalizarse (el almíbar), Am. azucararse.

sug·gest [səgdʒést] v. sugerir, indicar.

sug·ges·tion [səgdʒéstʃən] s. sugestión, Am. sugerencia; indicación.

sug·ges·tive [səgdʒéstɪv] adj. sugestivo.

su·i·cide [súəsaɪd] s. suicidio; suicida; **to commit —** suicidarse.

suit [sut] s. traje, terno, Carib., Ven. flux (o flus); palo (de la baraja); demanda, pleito; petición; galanteo; v. adaptar, acomodar; agradar; satisfacer; sentar bien, venir bien; caer bien; convenir; set a propósito; **— yourself** haz lo que quieras, haga Vd. lo que guste.

suit·a·ble [sútəbl] adj. propio, conveniente, debido, a propósito, apropiado, adecuado.

suit·a·bly [sútəblɪ] adv. propiamente, adecuadamente, convenientemente.

suit·case [sútkes] s. maleta, valija.

suite [swit] s. serie; comitiva, acompañamiento; **— of rooms** vivienda, apartamento, habitación; **bedroom —** juego de muebles para alcoba.

suit·or [sútɚ] s. pretendiente, galán; demandante (en un pleito).

sulk [sʌlk] v. tener murria; estar hosco o malhumorado; s. murria.

sulk·y [sʌ́lkɪ] adj. malcontento, hosco, malhumorado; **to be —** tener murria.

sul·len [sʌ́lɪn] adj. hosco, sombrío, tétrico; malhumorado, taciturno.

sul·ly [sʌ́lɪ] v. manchar, ensuciar; empañar.

sul·phate [sʌ́lfet] s. sulfato.

sul·phide [sʌ́lfaɪd] s. sulfuro.

sul·phur [sʌ́lfɚ] s. azufre.

sul·phur·ic [sʌlfjúrɪk] adj. sulfúrico.

sul·tan [sʌ́ltn] s. sultán.

sul·try [sʌ́ltrɪ] adj. bochornoso, sofocante; **— heat** bochorno, calor sofocante.

sum [sʌm] s. suma; cantidad; esencia, substancia; **— total** total; v. sumar; **to — up** resumir, recapitular.

sum·ma·rize [sʌ́məraɪz] v. resumir, compendiar.

sum·ma·ry [sʌ́mərɪ] s. sumario, resumen;

compendio; adj. sumario; breve.

sum·mer [sʌ́mɚ] s. verano; estío; adj. veraniego, estival de verano; **— resort** balneario, lugar de veraneo; v. veranear.

sum·mit [sʌ́mɪt] s. cima, cúspide, cumbre.

sum·mon [sʌ́mən] v. citar; convocar, llamar; **-s** s. notificación; cita judicial, citación, emplazamiento.

sump·tu·ous [sʌ́mptʃuəs] adj. suntuoso.

sun [sʌn] s. sol; **— bath** baño de sol; **— lamp** lámpara de rayos ultravioletas; **— porch** solana; v. asolear; **to — oneself** asolearse, tomar el sol.

sun·beam [sʌ́nbim] s. rayo de sol.

sun·burn [sʌ́nbɚn] s. quemadura de sol; v. asolear(se); quemar(se) al sol, tostar(se) al sol.

Sun·day [sʌ́ndɪ] s. domingo.

sun·di·al [sʌ́ndaɪəl] s. cuadrante solar, reloj de sol.

sun·down [sʌ́ndaʊn] s. puesta del sol.

sun·dry [sʌ́ndrɪ] adj. varios, diversos.

sun·flow·er [sʌ́nflaʊɚ] s. girasol; tornasol.

sung [sʌŋ] pret. & p.p. de to sing.

sun·glass·es [sʌ́nglæsəz] s. gafas (anteojos) de sol.

sunk [sʌŋk] pret. & p.p. de to sink.

sunk·en [sʌ́ŋkən] adj. hundido, sumido.

sun·light [sʌ́nlaɪt] s. luz del sol, luz solar.

sun·ny [sʌ́nɪ] adj. asoleado o soleado; alegre, risueño, resplandeciente; **— day** día de sol.

sun·rise [sʌ́nraɪz] s. salida del sol, amanecer, amanecida.

sun·set [sʌ́nsɛt] s. puesta del sol.

sun·shine [sʌ́nʃaɪn] s. luz del sol, solana.

sun·stroke [sʌ́nstrok] s. insolación.

sup [sʌp] v. cenar.

su·perb [supɚ́b] adj. soberbio.

su·per·fi·cial [supɚfíʃəl] adj. superficial.

su·per·flu·ous [supɚ́fluəs] adj. superfluo.

su·per·hu·man [supɚhjúmən] adj. sobrehumano.

su·per·in·tend [suprɪnténd] v. dirigir, inspeccionar, vigilar.

su·per·in·ten·dent [suprɪnténdənt] s. superintendente; inspector; capataz.

su·pe·ri·or [səpírɪɚ] adj. & s. superior; **— letter** volado.

su·pe·ri·or·i·ty [səpɪriɔ́rətɪ] s. superioridad.

su·per·la·tive [supɚ́lətɪv] adj. & s. superlativo.

su·per·mar·ket [súpɚmarkət] s. supermercado.

su·per·nat·u·ral [supɚnǽtʃrəl] adj. sobrenatural; **the —** lo sobrenatural.

su·per·sede [supɚsíd] v. reemplazar.

su·per·sti·tion [supɚstíʃən] s. superstición.

su·per·sti·tious [supɚstíʃəs] adj. supersticioso.

su·per·vise [supɚváɪz] v. dirigir, inspeccionar, vigilar.

su·per·vi·sion [supɚvíʒən] s. inspección, vigilancia.

su·per·vi·sor [supɚváɪzɚ] s. superintendente, inspector; interventor.

sup·per [sʌ́pɚ] s. cena.

sup·plant [səplǽnt] v. suplantar; reemplazar.

sup·ple [sʌ́pl] adj. flexible; dócil.

sup·ple·ment [sʌ́pləmənt] s. suplemento; apéndice; [sʌ́pləmɛnt] v. suplementar, completar.

sup·pli·ant [sʌ́plɪənt] adj. & s. suplicante.

sup·pli·ca·tion [sʌplɪkéʃən] s. súplica, plegaria; ruego.

sup·ply [səpláɪ] v. proveer; abastecer, surtir; suplir; dar, suministrar; s. provisión, abastecimiento; bastimento; abasto; surtido; **supplies** provisiones; materiales; víveres; pertrechos; **— pipe** cañería o caño de abastecimiento, tubería o tubo de suministro.

sup·port [səpórt] v. (keep from falling) sostener;

apoyar; (*provide for*) mantener; sustentar; (*bear*) soportar, aguantar; *s.* apoyo; sostén, soporte, puntal; sustento, manutención; amparo.

sup·port·er [səpórtɚ] *s.* defensor; partidario; mantenedor; sostén, apoyo; tirante (*para medias*).

sup·pose [səpóz] *v.* suponer.

sup·posed [səpózd] *adj.* supuesto; presunto; -ly *adv.* supuestamente.

sup·po·si·tion [sʌpəzíʃən] *s.* suposición.

sup·press [səprés] *v.* suprimir; reprimir; parar, suspender; **to — a revolt** sofocar una revuelta o motín.

sup·pres·sion [səpréʃən] *s.* supresión; represión.

su·prem·a·cy [səprémɔsɪ] *s.* supremacía.

su·preme [səprím] *adj.* supremo.

sure [ʃur] *adj.* seguro; cierto; estable; *adv. véase* **surely; be — to do it** hágalo sin falta, no deje Vd. de hacerlo; -ly *adv.* seguramente; ciertamente; con toda seguridad; sin falta.

sure·ty [ʃúrtɪ] *s.* seguridad; garantía, fianza; fiador.

surf [sɚf] *s.* oleaje, rompientes; resaca.

sur·face [sɚfɪs] *s.* superficie; cara; *v.* alisar, allanar; poner superficie a.

surf·board [sɚfbord] *s.* patín de mar.

sur·feit [sɚfɪt] *s.* hastío, exceso; *v.* hastiar; empalagar.

surge [sɚdʒ] *s.* oleada, oleaje; *v.* agitarse, hinchar(se) (*el mar*); surgir.

sur·geon [sɚdʒən] *s.* cirujano.

sur·ger·y [sɚdʒərɪ] *s.* cirujía.

sur·gi·cal [sɚdʒɪkl] *adj.* quirúrgico.

sur·ly [sɚlɪ] *adj.* rudo, hosco, malhumorado.

sur·mise [səmáɪz] *v.* conjeturar, suponer, presumir; *s.* conjetura, suposición.

sur·mount [səmáunt] *v.* superar, vencer; coronar.

sur·name [sɚnem] *s.* sobrenombre, apellido; *v.* apellidar, llamar.

sur·pass [səpǽs] *v.* sobrepasar, superar, sobrepujar, exceder, aventajar.

sur·pass·ing [səpǽsɪŋ] *adj.* sobresaliente, excelente.

sur·plus [sɚplʌs] *s.* sobra, sobrante, exceso, excedente; superávit; *adj.* sobrante, excedente, de sobra.

sur·prise [səpráɪz] *s.* sorpresa; *v.* sorprender.

sur·pris·ing [səpráɪzɪŋ] *adj.* sorprendente.

sur·ren·der [sɚrɛ́ndə] *v.* rendir(se), entregar(se), darse; ceder; *s.* rendición; entrega; cesión; sumisión.

sur·round [səráund] *v.* rodear, cercar, circundar.

sur·round·ing [səráundɪŋ] *adj.* circundante, circunvecino, circunstante.

sur·round·ings [səráundɪŋz] *s. pl.* alrededores, inmediaciones, cercanías; ambiente.

sur·vey [sɚve] *s.* (*inspection*) examen, reconocimiento, enspección, estudio; (*measure*) medición agrimensura (*de un terreno*); plano (*de un terreno*); bosquejo o esbozo general (*de historia, literatura, etc.*); — **course** curso general o comprensivo; [səvé] *v.* examinar, inspeccionar, reconocer medir (*un terreno*), levantar un plano (*el agrimensor*).

sur·vey·or [səvéɚ] *s.* agrimensor.

sur·viv·al [səváɪvl] *s.* supervivencia; sobreviviente; resto.

sur·vive [səváɪv] *c.* sobrevivir; quedar vivo, salvarse.

sur·vi·vor [səváɪvə] *s.* sobreviviente.

sus·cep·ti·ble [səséptəbl] *adj.* susceptible; — **of proof** capaz de probarse; — **to** propenso a.

sus·pect [sʌ́spɛkt] *s.* sospechoso; [səspɛ́kt] *v.*

sospechar.

sus·pend [səspénd] *v.* suspender.

sus·pend·ers [səspéndɚz] *s.* tirantes (*de pantalón*).

sus·pense [səspéns] *s.* (*uncertainty*) suspensión, incertidumbre; (*anxiety*) ansiedad; **to keep in —** tener en suspenso, tener en duda.

sus·pen·sion [səspénʃən] *s.* suspensión; — **bridge** puente colgante.

sus·pi·cion [səspíʃən] *s.* sospecha.

sus·pi·cious [səspíʃəs] *adj.* sospechoso; suspicaz.

sus·tain [səstén] *v.* (*prolong*) sostener; mantener; (*support*) sustentar; (*bear, endure*) aguantar; (*defend*) apoyar, defender; (*undergo*) sufrir (*un daño o pérdida*).

sus·te·nance [sʌ́stənəns] *s.* sustento; subsistencia; alimentos; mantenimiento.

swab [swab] *s.* escobillón.

swag·ger [swǽgɚ] *v.* pavonearse, contonearse; fanfarronear; *s.* pavoneo, contoneo; fanfarronada.

swain [swen] *s.* galán.

swal·low [swálo] *s.* golondrina; trago; *v.* tragar; deglutir.

swam [swæm] *pret. de* **to swim.**

swamp [swamp] *s.* pantano; ciénaga; — **land** cenagal, terreno pantanoso; *v.* inundar(se); sumergir(se); **to be -ed with work** estar abrumado de trabajo.

swamp·y [swámpɪ] *adj.* pantanoso, cenagoso, fangoso.

swan [swɑn] *s.* cisne.

swap [swap] *v.* cambalachear, cambiar, trocar; *s.* cambalache, cambio, trueque.

swarm [swɔrm] *s.* enjambre; *v.* pulular; bullir, hervir, hormiguear.

swarth·y [swórðɪ] *adj.* trigueño, moreno, *Am.* prieto.

swat [swat] *v.* pegar, aporrear; aplastar de un golpe (*una mosca*); *s.* golpe.

sway [swe] *v.* mecer(se); cimbrar(se); balancearse; ladear(se); oscilar; tambalear; influir; *s.* oscilación; vaivén; balanceo; influjo, influencia; mando; predominio.

swear [swɛr] *v.* jurar; renegar, blasfemar, echar maldiciones; juramentar, tomar juramento; **to — by** jurar por; poner toda su confianza en; **to — in** juramentar; **to — off smoking** jurar no fumar más, renunciar al tabaco.

sweat [swɛt] *v.* sudar; trasudar; hacer sudar; *s.* sudor; trasudor.

sweat·er [swétɚ] *s.* suéter; sudador, el que suda.

sweat·y [swétɪ] *adj.* sudoroso.

Swede [swid] *s.* sueco.

Swed·ish [swídɪʃ] *adj.* sueco; *s.* sueco, idioma sueco.

sweep [swip] *v.* barrer; dragar (*puertos, rios, etc.*); extenderse; **to — down upon** caer sobre; asolar; **to — everything away** barrer con todo; **she swept into the room** entró garbosamente en la sala; *s.* barrida; extensión; soplo (*del viento*).

sweep·er [swípɚ] *s.* barrendero; **carpet —** escoba mecánica.

sweep·ing [swípɪŋ] *adj.* barrido; -s basura; *adj.* abarcador, que lo abarca todo, vasto; asolador; — **victory** victoria completa.

sweet [swit] *adj.* dulce; oloroso; fresco; — **butter** mantequilla sin sal; — **corn** maíz tierno; — **milk** leche fresca; — **pea** guisante de olor; — **potato** batata, *Mex. C.A.* camote, *Carib.* boniato; **to have a — tooth** ser goloso, gustarle a uno los dulces; *s.* dulce, golosina; **my** — mi vida, mi alma.

sweet·en [swítɳ] *v.* endulzar(se), dulcificar(se); suavizar.

sweet·heart [swíthɑrt] *s.* querida, novia, prometida; amante, querido, galán, novio.

sweet·meat [swítmit] *s.* confite, confitura dulce, golosina.

sweet·ness [swítnɪs] *s.* dulzura; melosidad; suavidad.

swell [swɛl] *v.* hinchar(se), henchir(se), inflar(se); dilatar(se), abultar(se); acrecentar;.*s.* hinchazón; protuberancia; oleaje; *adj.* elegante; muy bueno, excelente, magnífico; **to have a — head** creerse gran cosa; ser vanidoso.

swel·ling [swélɪŋ] *s.* hinchazón; chichón, bulto; protuberancia.

swel·ter [swéltɚ] *v.* sofocarse de calor.

swept [swɛpt] *pret. & p.p. de* **to sweep.**

swerve [swɝv] *v.* desviar(se); torcer; cambiar repentinamente de rumbo; *s.* desvío brusco, cambio repentino de dirección; **to make a — to the right** torcer a la derecha.

swift [swɪft] *adj.* veloz, rápido.

swift·ness [swíftnɪs] *s.* velocidad, rapidez, presteza, prontitud.

swim [swɪm] *v.* nadar; flotar; **to — across** pasar a nado, atravesar nadando; **my head is swimming** tengo vértigo, se me va la cabeza, estoy desvanecido; *s.* nadada; — **suit** traje de baño o natación.

swim·mer [swímɚ] *s.* nadador.

swin·dle [swíndl] *v.* estafar; *s.* estafa.

swine [swaɪn] *s.* marrano, puerco, cerdo, cochino; marranos, puercos, cerdos.

swing [swɪŋ] *v.* columpiar(se), mecer(se), balancear(se); oscilar; hacer oscilar; blandir (*un bastón, espada, etc.*); colgar; girar; hacer girar; **to — a deal** llevar a cabo un negocio; **to — around** dar vuelta, girar; **to — one's arms** girar o menear los brazos; **to — open** abrirse de pronto (*una puerta*); *s.* columpio; hamaca; balanceo; vaivén; compás, ritmo; golpe, guantada, puñetazo; — **door** puerta giratoria; — **shift** turno de trabajo desde las dieciséis hasta medianoche; **in full** — en su apogeo, en pleno movimiento; **to give someone full** — darle a alguien completa libertad de acción.

swipe [swaɪp] *v.* hurtar, sisar.

swirl [swɝl] *v.* arremolinarse; girar, dar vueltas; *s.* remolino; torbellino; vuelta, movimiento giratorio.

Swiss [swɪs] *adj. & s.* suizo.

switch [swɪtʃ] *s.* (*change*) mudanza; (*whip*) látigo, (*blow*) azote; *Méx., Andes* chicote, *Riopl.* rebenque; *Méx., Andes* fuete; latigazo; pelo postizo; cambio; **electric** — interruptor, conmutador; **railway** — aguja, cambio; —**man** guardagujas, *Andes, Riopl.* cambiavía; *Méx.* guardavía; *v.* azotar; desviar(se); cambiar(se); **to — off** cortar (*la comunicación o la corriente eléctrica*); apagar (*la luz eléctrica*); **to — on the** encender la luz.

switch·board [swítʃbɔrd] *s.* cuadro o tablero de distribución; cuadro conmutador.

swiv·el [swívl] *adj.* giratorio.

swol·len [swólən] *p.p. de* **to swell.**

swoon [swun] *v.* desvanecerse, desmayarse; *s.* desmayo.

swoop [swup] *v.* **to — down upon** caer de súbito sobre; abalanzarse sobre; acometer; **to —**

off cortar de un golpe; **to — up** agarrar, arrebatar; *s.* descenso súbito; arremetida; **at one** — de un golpe.

sword [sord] *s.* espada; — **belt** talabarte.

swore [swor] *pret. de* **to swear.**

sworn [sworn] *p.p. de* **to swear.**

swum [swʌm] *p.p. de* **to swim.**

swung [swʌŋ] *pret. & p.p. de* **to swing.**

syl·lab·i·cate [sɪlǽbəket] *v.* silabear.

syl·la·ble [síləbl] *s.* sílaba.

syl·la·bus [síləbəs] *s.* sílabo.

syl·lo·gism [sílədʒɪzəm] *s.* silogismo.

sym·bol [símbl] *s.* símbolo.

sym·bol·ic [sɪmbálɪk] *adj.* simbólico.

sym·bol·ism [símbḷɪzəm] *s.* simbolismo.

sym·met·ri·cal [sɪmétrɪkḷ] *adj.* simétrico.

sym·me·try [símɪtrɪ] *s.* simetría.

sym·pa·thet·ic [sɪmpəθétɪk] *adj.* compasivo; favorablemente dispuesto; que compadece; — **towards** favorablemente dispuesto a (*o* hacia).

sym·pa·thize [símpəθaɪz] *v.* compadecer(se); condolerse.

sym·pa·thy [símpəθɪ] *s.* compasión, lástima; armonía; **to extend one's** — dar el pésame.

sym·pho·ny [símfənɪ] *s.* sinfonía; — **orchestra** orquesta sinfónica.

sym·po·si·um [sɪmpósɪəm] *s.* coloquio; simposio.

symp·tom [símptəm] *s.* síntoma.

syn·a·gogue [sínəgag] *s.* sinagoga.

syn·chro·nize [sínkənaɪz] *v.* sincronizar.

syn·di·cate [síndɪkɪt] *s.* sindicato; **newspaper** — sindicato periodístico; [síndɪket] *v.* sindicar, formar un sindicato; sindicarse, combinarse para formar un sindicato; vender (*un cuento, caricatura, serie de artículos, etc.*) a un sindicato.

syn·drome [síndrom] *s.* síndrome.

syn·o·nym [sínənɪm] *s.* sinónimo.

syn·on·y·mous [sɪnánəmes] *adj.* sinónimo.

syn·op·sis [sɪnápsɪs] *s.* sinopsis.

syn·tax [síntæks] *s.* sintaxis.

syn·the·sis [sínθəsɪs] *s.* síntesis.

syn·the·size [sínθəsaɪz] *v.* sintetizar.

syn·thet·ic [sɪnθétɪk] *adj.* sintético.

syr·inge [sírɪndʒ] *s.* jeringa.

syr·up = **sirup.**

sys·tem [sístəm] *s.* sistema.

sys·tem·at·ic [sɪstəmǽtɪk] *adj.* sistemático

sys·tem·ic [sɪstémɪk] *adj.* sistemático.

T:t

tab [tæb] *s.* (*flap*) lengüeta; (*bill*) cuenta.

tab·er·na·cle [tǽbɚnækl] *s.* tabernáculo.

ta·ble [tébl] *s.* mesa; tabla (*de materias, de multiplicar, etc.*); — **cover** tapete, cubremesa; —**land** mesa, meseta; *v.* poner sobre la mesa; formar tabla o índice; **to — a motion** dar carpetazo a una moción, aplazar la discusión de una moción.

ta·ble·cloth [téblklɔθ] *s.* mantel.

ta·ble·spoon [téblspun] *s.* cuchara grande.

ta·ble·spoon·ful [téblspunfʊl] *s.* cucharada.

tab·let [tǽblɪt] *s.* tableta; tablilla, pastilla; comprimido; bloc de papel; lápida, placa.

ta·ble·ware [téblwɛr] *s.* vajilla, servicio de mesa.

ta·boo [tæbú] *s.* tabú.

tab·u·late [tǽbjəlet] *v.* formar tablas o listas.

tac·it [tǽsɪt] *adj.* tácito.

tac·i·turn [tǽsətɜrn] *adj.* taciturno, silencioso.

tack [tæk] *s.* tachuela; hilván; virada o cambio de rumbo (*de una embarcación*); amura, jarcia (*para sostener el ángulo de una vela*); **to change —** cambiar de amura, cambiar de rumbo; *v.* clavetear con tachuelas; coser, hilvanar; pegar, clavar; juntar, unir; virar, cambiar de rumbo; zigzaguear (*un barco de vela*).

tack·le [tækl] *s.* aparejo, equipo, enseres, avíos; agarrada (*en fútbol*); atajador (*en fútbol*); **fishing —** avíos de pescar; *v.* agarrar, asir, atajar (*en futbol*); atacar (*un problema*); acometer (*una empresa*).

tact [tækt] *s.* tacto, tino, tiento.

tact·ful [tæktfəl] *adj.* cauto, prudente, diplomático.

tac·tics [tæktɪks] *s.* táctica.

tact·less [tæktlɪs] *adj.* falto de tacto o de tino; imprudente, incauto.

taf·fe·ta [tæfɪtə] *s.* tafetán.

tag [tæg] *s.* (*label*) marbete, etiqueta; cartela; (*loose end*) pingajo, rabito, cabo; **to play —** jugar al tócame tú, jugar a la pega; *v.* pegar un marbete a, marcar; **to — after** seguir de cerca a, pisar los talones a; **to — something on to** juntar, añadir o agregar algo a.

tail [tel] *s.* (*animal*) cola, rabo; (*object*) cabo, extremo, extremidad; **— light** farol trasero, farol de cola; **— spin** barrena.

tai·lor [télɚ] *s.* sastre; **— shop** sastrería.

taint [tent] *s.* tacha, mancha, corrupción; *v.* manchar; corromper(se), inficionar(se).

take [tek] *v.* tomar; coger; llevar; conducir; dar (*un paseo, vuelta, paso, salto*); hacer (*un viaje*); asumir; sacar o tomar (*una fotografía*); **to — a chance** aventurarse, correr un riesgo; **to — a fancy to** caerle en gracia a uno; aficionarse a; antojársele a uno; **to — a look at** mirar a, echar una mirada a; **to — a notion to** antojársele a uno; **to — after** salir a, parecerse a; seguir el ejemplo de; **to — amiss** interpretar mal, echar a mala parte; **to — an oath** prestar juramento; **to — apart** desarmar, desmontar; **to — away** llevarse; **to — back one's words** desdecirse, retractarse; **to — back to** devolver (*algo*) a; **to — by surprise** coger desprevenido, coger de sorpresa; **to — care of** cuidar de, atender a; **to — charge of** encargarse de; **to — cold** resfriarse, acatarrarse; **to — down in writing** poner por escrito, apuntar; **to — effect** surtir efecto, dar resultado; entrar en vigencia (*una ley*); **to — exercise** hacer ejercicio; hacer gimnasia; **to — from** quitar a; sustraer de, restar de; **to — in** meter en; recibir; abarcar; embaucar; reducir; achicar (*un vestido*); **to — leave** decir adiós, despedirse; **to — off** quitar; descontar, rebajar; despegar (*un aeroplano*); remedar, parodiar (*a alguien*); **to — offense** ofenderse, darse por ofendido; **to — on a responsibility** asumir una responsabilidad; **to — out** sacar; **to — place** tener lugar, suceder, ocurrir; **to — stock** hacer inventario; **to — stock in** creer, tener confianza en; **to — the floor** tomar la palabra; **to — to** heart tomar a pechos, tomar en serio; **to — to one's heels** poner pies en polvorosa; **to — to task** reprender, regañar; **to — up a matter** tratar un asunto; **to — up space** ocupar espacio; **I — it that** supongo que; *s.* toma; **take-off** despegue (*de un aeroplano*); remedo, parodia.

tak·en [tékən] *p.p. de* **to take**; **to be — ill** caer enfermo.

tal·cum [tælkəm] *s.* talco; **— powder** talco en polvo.

tale [tel] *s.* (*story*) cuento, relato, fábula; (*gossip*) chisme; **to tell -s** contar cuentos o chismes; chismear, murmurar.

tale·bear·er [télbɛrɚ] *s.* soplón, chismoso.

tal·ent [tælənt] *s.* talento.

tal·ent·ed [tæləntɪd] *adj.* talentoso.

talk [tɔk] *v.* hablar; charlar, platicar, conversar; **to — into** inducir o persuadir a; **to — nonsense** decir tonterías, hablar disparates; **to — out of** disuadir de; **to — over** discutir; **to — up** alabar; hablar claro o recio, hablar en voz alta; *s.* charla, conversación, plática; habla; discurso; conferencia; rumor; **— of the town** comidilla, tema de murmuración.

talk·a·tive [tɔkətɪv] *adj.* hablador, locuaz, platicador.

talk·er [tɔkɚ] *s.* hablador; conversador; platicador; orador.

tall [tɔl] *adj.* alto; **— tale** cuento exagerado o increíble; **six feet —** seis pies de altura o de alto.

tal·low [tælo] *s.* sebo.

tal·low·y [tælowɪ] *adj.* seboso.

tal·ly [tælɪ] *s.* cuenta; **— sheet** plana para llevar la cuenta; *v.* llevar la cuenta; **to — up** contar, sumar; **to — with** corresponder con, concordar con.

tam·a·rind [tæmərɪnd] *s.* tamarindo.

tame [tem] *adj.* manso; dócil; **— amusement** diversión poco animada o desabrida; *v.* amansar, domar, domeñar; domesticar; desbravar.

tam·per [tæmpɚ] *v.* **to — with** meterse con, juguetear con; falsificar (*un documento*); **to — with a lock** tratar de forzar una cerradura.

tan [tæn] *v.* (*cure*) curtir, adobar (*pieles*); (*punish*) zurrar, azotar; (*sunburn*) tostar(se), requemar(se); *adj.* tostado, requemado; color de canela; bayo, amarillento; *s.* color moreno, de canela o café con leche.

tang [tæŋ] *s.* sabor u olor picante.

tangent [tændʒənt] *adj. & s.* tangente; **to go off at a —** salirse por la tangente.

tan·ger·ine [tændʒərin] *s.* naranja tangerina o mandarina.

tan·gi·ble [tændʒəbl] *adj.* tangible, palpable; corpóreo.

tan·gle [tæŋgl] *v.* enredar(se), enmarañar(se); confundir(se), embrollar(se); *s.* enredo, maraña, embrollo; confusión.

tank [tæŋk] *s.* tanque; depósito; **swimming —** piscina.

tan·ner [tænɚ] *s.* curtidor.

tan·ner·y [tænərɪ] *s.* curtiduría, tenería.

tan·nic ac·id [tænɪkæsəd] *s.* ácido tánico.

tan·ta·lize [tæntlaɪz] *v.* molestar; hacer desesperar; exasperar.

tan·ta·lum [tæntələm] *s.* tantalio.

tan·ta·mount [tæntəmaʊnt] *adj.* equivalente.

tan·trum [tæntrəm] *s.* berrinche.

tap [tæp] *s.* (*blow*) palmadita; golpecito; (*faucet*) espita, grifo, llave; **— dance** zapateado, *Andes, Ríopl.* zapateo; **—room** bar; **beer on —** cerveza del barril, cerveza de sifón; *v.* tocar, golpear ligeramente; dar una palmadita o golpecito; taladrar; extraer; **to — a tree** sangrar un árbol.

tape [tep] *s.* cinta, cintilla; **— measure** cinta para medir; **— recorder** magnetófono; grabadora; **adhesive —** tela adhesiva, esparadrapo; *v.* atar o vendar con cinta; medir con cinta.

ta·per [tépɚ] *s.* (*candle*) velita, candela; (*diminished* *size*) adelgazamiento paulatino; *v.* adelgazar, disminuir gradualmente; **to — off** ahusar(se), ir disminuyendo (*hasta rematar en punta*).

tap·es·try [tǽpɪstrɪ] *s.* tapiz, colgadura; tapicería; tela (*para forrar muebles*).

tape·worm [tépwəm] *s.* tenîa, solitaria.

tap·i·o·ca [tæpɪókə] *s.* tapioca.

tar [tɑr] *s.* alquitrán, brea, pez (*f.*); *Am.* chapapote; *v.* alquitranar, embrear, poner brea o alquitrán.

tar·dy [tárdɪ] *adj.* tardo, tardío; **to be — llegar** tarde o retrasado.

tar·get [tárgɪt] *s.* blanco; — **practice** tiro al blanco.

tar·iff [tǽrɪf] *s.* tarifa; arancel, impuesto.

tar·nish [tárnɪʃ] *v.* empañar(se); manchar; perder el lustre; *s.* deslustre, falta de lustre, empañamiento; mancha.

tar·ry [tǽrɪ] *v.* demorarse, tardar(se).

tart [tɑrt] *adj.* acre, agridulce; agrio; picante; — **reply** respuesta mordaz o agria; *s.* tarta, torta rellena con dulce de frutas.

tar·tar [tártə] *s.* tártaro.

task [tæsk] *s.* faena, tarea, quehacer; **to take to — reprender, regañar.**

task force [tǽskfɔrs] *s.* agrupación de fuerzas militares para cierta misión.

tas·sel [tǽsl] *s.* borla.

taste [test] *v.* gustar; probar; saborear, paladear; **to — of onion** saber a cebolla; **it -s sour** sabe agrio, tiene un sabor o gusto agrio; *s.* gusto; sabor; prueba; afición; **after —** dejo; **in good —** de buen gusto; **to take a — of** probar.

taste·less [téstlɪs] *adj.* insípido; desabrido; de mal gusto.

tast·y [téstɪ] *adj.* sabroso, gustoso; de buen gusto.

tat·ter [tǽtə] *s.* harapo, *Carib.* hilacho.

tat·ter·ed [tǽtəd] *adj.* roto, harapiento, andrajoso.

tat·tle [tǽtl] *v.* chismear, murmurar; *s.* habladuría, murmuración, hablilla; —**tale** chismoso, soplón.

tat·too [tætú] *s.* tatuaje; *v.* tatuar.

taught [tɔt] *pret. & p.p. de* **to teach.**

taunt [tɔnt] *v.* mofarse de, echar pullas; reprochar; *s.* mofa, pulla.

tav·ern [tǽvən] *s.* taberna; posada.

tax [tæks] *s.* impuesto, contribución; esfuerzo; *v.* imponer contribuciones a; tasar; abrumar; reprender, reprobar; cobrar (*un precio*); **to — one's patience** abusar de la paciencia.

tax·a·tion [tækséʃən] *s.* impuestos, contribuciones; imposición de contribuciones.

tax·i [tǽksɪ] *s.* taxímetro, taxi, automóvil de alquiler; *v.* ir en taxímetro; taxear (*un aeroplano*).

tax·i·cab [tǽksɪkæb] = **taxi.**

tax·i·der·my [tǽksɪdəmɪ] *s.* taxidermia.

tax·on·o·my [tæksánəmɪ] *s.* taxonomía.

tax·pay·er [tǽkspeə] *s.* contribuyente.

tea [ti] *s.* té; **linden—** tila.

teach [titʃ] *v.* enseñar; instruir.

teach·er [títʃə] *s.* maestro, maestra.

teach·ing [títʃɪŋ] *s.* enseñanza; instrucción; doctrina.

tea·cup [tíkʌp] *s.* taza para té.

tea·ket·tle [tíketl] *s.* marmita, tetera, *Ríopl.* pava (*para el mate*).

team [tim] *s.* equipo (*de jugadores*); partido, grupo; tronco (*de caballos, mulas, etc.*); yunta (*de bueyes*): — **work** cooperación; *v.* uncir, enganchar; formar pareja; acarrear, transportar; **to — up** unirse, formar un equipo.

team·ster [tímstə] *s.* carretero.

tea·pot [típɑt] *s.* tetera.

tear [tɪr] *s.* lágrima; — **gas** gas lacrimógeno o lacrimante; **to burst into -s** romper a llorar; deshacerse en lágrimas.

tear [tɛr] *v.* rasgar(se); desgarrar, romper; **to — along** ir a toda velocidad; andar aprisa, correr; **to — apart** desarmar, desmontar; separar, apartar; **to — away** arrancar; irse; **to — down** demoler, derribar (*un edificio*); desarmar, desmontar (*una máquina*); **to — off in a hurry** salir corriendo, salir a la carrera; **to — one's hair** mesarse los cabellos; *s.* desgarradura, rasgadura; rasgón, rotura; prisa; **wear and —** desgaste.

tear·ful [tírfəl] *adj.* lloroso.

tease [tiz] *v.* embromar; molestar; importunar.

tea·spoon [tíspun] *s.* cucharilla, cucharita.

tea·spoon·ful [tíspunfʊl] *s.* cucharadita.

teat [tit] *s.* teta.

tech·ne·ti·um [tɛkníʃəm] *s.* tecnecio.

tech·ni·cal [tɛknɪkl] *adj.* técnico.

tech·ni·cian [tɛkníʃən] *s.* técnico.

tech·nique [tɛkník] *s.* técnica.

tech·nol·o·gy [tɛknálədʒɪ] *s.* tecnología.

te·di·ous [tídɪəs] *adj.* tedioso, pesado, aburrido, fastidioso.

te·di·ous·ness [tídɪəsnɪs] *s.* tedio.

teem [tim] *v.* **to — with** abundar en, estar lleno de.

teen·ag·er [tínedʒə] *s.* joven de le edad de 13 a 19 años; *Col.* cocacolo.

teens [tinz] *s. pl.* edad de trece a diecinueve años; números de trece a diecinueve; **to be in one's —** tener de trece a diecinueve años.

teeth [tiθ] *s. pl. de* **tooth; he escaped by the skin of his —** por poco no se escapa, se escapó por milagro.

tel·e·cast [téləkæst] *s.* teledifusión.

tel·e·gram [téləgræm] *s.* telegrama.

tel·e·graph [téləgræf] *s.* telégrafo; *v.* telegrafiar.

tel·e·graph·ic [tɛləgrǽfɪk] *adj.* telegráfico.

te·leg·ra·phy [təlégrəfɪ] *s.* telegrafía.

te·lep·a·thy [təlépəθɪ] *s.* telepatía.

tel·e·phone [téləfon] *s.* teléfono; — **booth** casilla de teléfono; — **operator** telefonista; — **receiver** receptor telefónico; *v.* telefonear, llamar por teléfono.

tel·e·scope [téləskop] *s.* telescopio; *v.* enchufar(se), encajar(se) un objeto en otro.

tel·e·vi·sion [téləvɪʒən] *s.* televisión; — **viewer** televidente.

tell [tɛl] *v.* (*recount*) decir; contar; expresar; explicar; (*identify*) adivinar; **to — on someone** delatar a alguien, contar chismes de alguien; **to — someone off** decirle a alguien cuatro verdades; **his age is beginning to —** ya comienza a notársele la edad.

tell·er [télə] *s.* narrador, relator; pagador o recibidor (*de un banco*); escrutador de votos.

tel·lu·ri·um [təlúrɪəm] *s.* telurio.

te·mer·i·ty [təmérətɪ] *s.* temeridad.

tem·per [tempə] *v.* templar; *s.* temple (*de un metal*); genio, temple, humor; mal genio; **to keep one's —** contenerse, dominarse; **to lose one's —** perder la calma, encolerizarse.

tem·per·a·ment [témprəmənt] *s.* temperamento; disposición; temple.

tem·per·ance [témprəns] *s.* templanza, sobriedad.

tem·per·ate [témprɪt] *adj.* templado, moderado; sobrio.

tem·per·a·ture [témprətʃə] *s.* temperatura; **to have a — tener calentura o fiebre.**

tem·pest [témpɪst] *s.* tempestad.

tem·pes·tu·ous [tɛmpéstʃ∪əs] *adj.* tempestuoso. borrascoso.

tem·ple [témpl] *s.* templo; sien.

tem·po·ral [témpərəl] *adj.* temporal.

tem·po·rar·i·ly [témpərɛrəlɪ] *adv.* temporalmente.

tem·po·rar·y [témpərɛrɪ] *adj.* temporal, transitorio, provisorio; interino.

tempt [tɛmpt] *v.* tentar; incitar; provocar; atraer.

temp·ta·tion [tɛmptéʃən] *s.* tentación.

tempt·er [témptə] *s.* tentador.

tempt·ing [témptɪŋ] *adj.* tentador, atractivo.

ten·a·ble [ténəbl] *adj.* defendible.

te·na·cious [tɪnéʃəs] *adj.* tenaz, aferrado.

te·nac·i·ty [tɪnǽsətɪ] *s.* tenacidad; aferramiento; tesón.

ten·ant [ténənt] *s.* inquilino, arrendatario.

tend [tɛnd] *v.* cuidar, vigilar, guardar; atender; tender, inclinarse.

ten·den·cy [téndənsɪ] *s.* tendencia; propensión.

ten·der [téndə] *adj.* tierno; delicado; sensible; **tender-hearted** de corazón tierno; *s.* oferta, ofrecimiento; ténder (*de un tren*); lancha (*de auxilio*); cuidador, vigilante; **legal —** moneda corriente; *v.* ofrecer.

ten·der·loin [téndəlɔɪn] *s.* filete.

ten·der·ness [téndənɪs] *s.* ternura, terneza; delicadeza.

ten·don [téndən] *s.* tendón.

ten·dril [téndrɪl] *s.* zarcillo (*tallito de una planta trepadora*).

ten·e·ment [ténəmənt] *s.* casa de vecindad.

ten·nis [ténɪs] *s.* tenis; — **court** cancha de tenis.

ten·or [ténə] *s.* tenor; significado; — **voice** voz de tenor.

tense [tɛns] *adj.* tenso; tirante; *s.* tiempo (*del verbo*).

ten·sion [ténʃən] *s.* tensión; tirantez.

tent [tɛnt] *s.* tienda de campaña; pabellón; *v.* acampar.

ten·ta·cle [téntəkl] *s.* tentáculo.

ten·ta·tive [téntətɪv] *adj.* tentativo.

ten·u·ous [ténjʊəs] *adj.* tenue.

ten·ure [ténjʊr] *s.* tenencia.

tep·id [tépɪd] *adj.* tibio.

term [tɜm] *s.* término; período; plazo; sesión; **-s** términos, expresiones, palabras; condiciones; **to be on good -s** estar en buenas relaciones; **not to be on speaking -s** no hablarse, no dirigirse la palabra; **to come to -s** ajustarse, ponerse de acuerdo; *v.* nombrar, llamar, denominar.

ter·mi·na·ble [tɜmɪnəbl] *adj.* terminable.

ter·mi·nal [tɜmən̩l] *adj.* terminal, final, último; *s.* término, fin; estación terminal; **electric —** toma de corriente; borne (*de aparato eléctrico*).

ter·mi·nate [tɜmənet] *v.* terminar, acabar.

ter·mi·na·tion [tɜmənéʃən] *s.* terminación, fin; desinencia (*gramatical*).

ter·mite [tɜmaɪt] *s.* termita.

ter·race [térɪs] *s.* terraplén; terraza, terrado; *v.* terraplenar.

ter·res·tri·al [təréstrɪəl] *adj.* terrestre, terreno, terrenal.

ter·ri·ble [térəbl] *adj.* terrible; **terribly** *adv.* terriblemente.

ter·ri·er [térɪə] *s.* perro de busca.

ter·ri·fic [tərɪfɪk] *adj.* terrífico.

ter·ri·fy [térəfaɪ] *v.* aterrar, aterrorizar.

ter·ri·to·ry [térətorɪ] *s.* territorio.

ter·ror [térə] *s.* terror, espanto.

ter·ror·ist [térərɪst] *s.* terrorista.

test [tɛst] *s.* prueba, ensayo, experimento; comprobación; examen; — **tube** probeta, tubo

de ensayo; **to undergo a —** sufrir una prueba; *v.* probar, ensayar, comprobar, experimentar; poner a prueba; examinar.

tes·ta·ment [tɛstəmənt] *s.* testamento.

tes·ti·cle [téstɪk] *s.* testículo.

tes·ti·fy [téstəfaɪ] *v.* atestiguar, atestar.

tes·ti·mo·ny [téstəmonɪ] *s.* testimonio.

tet·a·nus [tétənəs] *s.* tétanos.

Teu·ton·ic [tutánɪk] *adj.* teutónico.

text [tɛkst] *s.* texto.

text·book [tékstbʊk] *s.* texto, libro de texto.

tex·tile [tékstl] *adj.* textil; de tejidos; — **mill** fábrica de tejidos; *s.* tejido, materia textil.

tex·ture [tékstʃə] *s.* textura, contextura; tejido.

thal·li·um [θǽlɪəm] *s.* talio.

than [ðæn] *conj.* que; **more —** once más de una vez; **more —** he knows más de lo que él sabe.

thank [θæŋk] *v.* dar gracias, agradecer; — **heaven!** ¡gracias a Dios!; — **you** gracias; **to have oneself to —** for tener la culpa de; ser responsable de; **-s** *s. pl.* gracias.

thank·ful [θǽŋkfəl] *adj.* agradecido; **-ly** *adv.* agradecidamente, con agradecimiento, con gratitud.

thank·ful·ness [θǽŋkfəlnɪs] *s.* gratitud, agradecimiento.

thank·less [θǽŋklɪs] *adj.* ingrato; — **task** tarea ingrata o infructuosa.

thanks·giv·ing [θæŋksgɪ́vɪŋ] *s.* acción de gracias; — **Day** día de acción de gracias.

that [ðæt] *adj.* ese, esa, aquel, aquella; — **one** ése, ésa, aquél, aquélla; *pron.* ése, esa, aquel, aquélla, aquello; *pron. rel.* que; — **is** es decir; — **of** el de, la de, lo de; — **which** el que, la que, lo que; *conj.* que; para que, a fin de que; **so —** para que; de modo que, a fin de que, de suerte que, de tal manera que; *adv.* tan; — **far** tan lejos; hasta allí; hasta allí; — **long** así de largo; de este tamaño; tanto tiempo.

thatch [θætʃ] *s.* paja (*para techar*); *v.* techar con paja; **-ed roof** techumbre o techo de paja.

thaw [θɔ] *v.* deshelar(se), derretir(se); volverse más tratable o amistoso; *s.* deshielo, derretimiento.

the [*delante de consonante* ðə; *delante de vocal* ðɪ] *art.* el, la; lo; los, las; *adv.* — **more ... — less** cuanto más ... tanto menos; mientras más ... tanto menos.

the·a·ter [θíətə] *s.* teatro.

the·at·ri·cal [θɪǽtrɪkl] *adj.* teatral.

thee [ðɪ] *pron.* te.

theft [θɛft] *s.* hurto, robo.

their [ðɛr] *adj.* su (sus), de ellos, de ellas.

theirs [ðɛrz] *pron. pos.* suyo (suya, suyos, suyas), de ellos, de ellas; el suyo (la suya, los suyos, las suyas); el (la, los, las) de ellos; **a friend of —** un amigo suyo, un amigo de ellos.

them [ðɛm] *pron.* los, las; les; ellos, ellas (*con preposición*).

the·mat·ic [θɪmǽtɪk] *adj.* temático.

theme [θim] *s.* tema; ensayo; — **song** tema central.

them·selves [ðəmsélvz] *pron.* ellos mismos, ellas mismas; se (*como reflexivo*); **to —** a sí mismos; *véase* **herself.**

then [ðɛn] *adv.* entonces; en aquel tiempo; en aquella ocasión; después, luego, en seguida; *conj.* pues, en tal caso; **now —** ahora bien; **now and —** de vez en cuando, de cuando en cuando; **now ...** — ora ... ora; **ya ...** ya; **well —** conque, pues entonces; ahora bien.

thence [ðɛns] *adv.* desde allí, de allí; desde entonces, desde aquel tiempo; por seo, por esa razón;

—forth de allí en adelante, desde entonces.
the·o·log·i·cal [θiəlάdʒɪkl̩] *adj.* teológico; teologal.
the·ol·o·gy [θiάlədʒɪ] *s.* teología.
the·o·ret·i·cal [θiərɛ́tɪkl̩] *adj.* teórico.
the·o·ry [θíərɪ] *s.* teoría.
ther·a·peu·tic [θɛrəpjútɪk] *adj.* terapéutico.
ther·a·py [θɛ́rəpɪ] *s.* terapia.
there [δɛr] *adv.* allí, allá, ahí; **— is, — are** hay; **— followed an argument** siguió una disputa.
there·a·bouts [δɛrəbáʊts] *adv.* por allí, por ahí; aproximadamente.
there·af·ter [δɛrǽftɚ] *adv.* después de eso, de allí en adelante.
there·by [δɛrbáɪ] *adv.* en relación con eso; así, de ese modo; por allí cerca.
there·fore [δɛ́rfor] *adv.* por eso, por consiguiente, por lo tanto.
there·in [δɛrín] *adv.* en eso, en ello; allí dentro.
there·of [δɛráv] *adv.* de eso, de ello.
there·on [δɛrάn] *adv.* encima; encima de (*o* sobre) él, ella, ello, etc.
there·up·on [δɛrəpán] *adv.* luego, después, en eso, en esto; por consiguiente, por eso, por lo tanto; encima de (*o* sobre) él, ella, ello, etc.
there·with [δɛrwíθ] *adv.* con eso, con ello, con esto; luego, en seguida.
ther·mal [θɚ́ml̩] *adj.* termal.
ther·mom·e·ter [θɚmάmətɚ] *s.* termómetro.
ther·mo·nu·cle·ar [θɚmonúkljɚ] *adj.* termonuclear.
ther·mos [θɚ́məs] (*marca de fábrica*): **— bottle** termos.
ther·mo·stat [θɚ́məstæt] *s.* termóstato.
these [δiz] *adj.* estos, estas; *pron.* éstos, éstas.
the·sis [θísɪs] *s.* tesis.
they [δe] *pron.* ellos, ellas.
thick [θɪk] *adj.* (*not thin*) espeso; grueso; (*dense*) denso; tupido; (*slow*) torpe, estúpido; **— voice** voz ronca; **one inch —** una pulgada de espesor; *adv. véase* **thickly; thick-headed** cabezudo; testarudo; estúpido; **thick-set** grueso, rechoncho; **thick-skinned** insensible; que no se avergüenza fácilmente; *s.* espesor; densidad, lo más denso; **the — of the crowd** lo más denso de la muchedumbre; **the — of the fight** lo más reñido del combate; **through — and thin** por toda suerte de penalidades.
thick·en [θíkən] *v.* espesar(se); engrosar; **the plot -s** se complica el enredo.
thick·et [θíkɪt] *s.* espesura, maleza, matorral, *Am.* manigua.
thick·ly [θíklɪ] *adv.* espesamente; densamente.
thick·ness [θíknɪs] *s.* espesor; espesura, grueso, grosor; densidad.
thief [θif] *s.* ladrón.
thieve [θiv] *v.* hurtar, robar.
thieves [θivz] *pl. de* **thief.**
thigh [θaɪ] *s.* muslo.
thim·ble [θímbl̩] *s.* dedal.
thin [θɪn] *adj.* (*slim*) delgado; flaco; (*sparse*) ralo; escaso; (*fine*) tenue, fino; transparente; (*weak*) débil; aguado; **— broth** caldo aguado; **— hair** pelo ralo; *v.* adelgazar(se); enflaquecer; aguar (*el caldo*); **to — out** ralear (*el pelo*); ralear *o* aclarar (*un bosque*).
thine [δaɪn] *pron. pos.* tuyo (tuya, tuyos, tuyas); el tuyo (la tuya, los tuyos, las tuyas); *adj.* tu, tus.
thing [θɪŋ] *s.* cosa; **no such —** nada de eso; **that is the — to do** eso es lo que debe hacerse; eso es lo debido.
think [θɪŋk] *v.* (*cerebrate*) pensar; (*believe*) creer, juzgar; opinar; **to — it over** pensarlo; **to — of**

pensar en; pensar de; **to — up an excuse** urdir una excusa; **to — well of** tener buena opinión de; **— nothing of it** no haga Vd. caso de ello, no le dé Vd. importancia; **what do you — of her?** ¿qué piensa Vd. de ella?; **to my way of -ing** a mi modo de ver.
think·er [θíŋkɚ] *s.* pensador.
thin·ly [θínlɪ] *adv.* delgadamente; escasamente.
thin·ness [θínnɪs] *s.* delgadez; flacura; raleza (*del cabello*); enrarecimiento (*del aire*).
third [θɚd] *adj.* tercero; *s.* tercio, tercera parte.
thirst [θɚst] *s.* sed; anhelo, ansia; *v.* tener sed; **to — for** tener sed de; anhelar, ansiar.
thirst·y [θɚ́stɪ] *adj.* sediento; **to be —** tener sed.
this [δɪs] *adj.* este, esta; *pron.* éste, esto.
this·tle [θísl̩] *s.* abrojo; cardo.
thith·er [θíδɚ] *adv.* allá, hacia allá, para allá.
tho [δo] = **though.**
thong [θɔŋ] *s.* correa, tira de cuero, *Am.* guasca.
tho·rax [θóræks] *s.* tórax.
thorn [θɔrn] *s.* espina, púa; espino; abrojo.
thorn·y [θɔ́rnɪ] *adj.* espinoso; arduo, difícil.
thor·ough [θɚ́o] *adj.* (*finished*) completo, entero, cabal, cumplido, acabado; (*careful*) esmerado.
thor·ough·bred [θɚ́obrɛd] *adj.* de casta pura, de raza pura; bien nacido; *s.* animal o persona de casta; caballo de casta.
thor·ough·fare [θɚ́ofer] *s.* vía pública, carretera, camino real; pasaje.
thor·ough·ly [θɚ́olɪ] *adj.* completamente, enteramente, cabalmente; a fondo.
those [δoz] *adj.* esos, esas, aquellos, aquellas; *pron.* ésos, ésas, aquéllos, aquéllas; **— of** los de, las de; **— which** los que, las que; aquellos que; **— who** los que, las que, quienes.
thou [δaʊ] *pron.* tú.
though [δo] *conj.* aunque, si bien, bien que; aun cuando; sin embargo; **as —** como si.
thought [θɔt] *s.* (*cogitation*) pensamiento; (*idea*) idea, intención; reflexión, meditación; (*concern*) consideración; cuidado; **to be lost in —** estar abstraído; **to give it no —** no pensar en ello, no darle importancia, no hacerle caso; *pret. & p.p. de* **to think.**
thought·ful [θɔ́tfəl] *adj.* pensativo; considerado; atento, solícito, cuidadoso; **to be — of others** pensar en los demás, tener consideración o solicitud por los demás; **-ly** *adv.* con reflexión; consideradamente, con consideración; con solicitud.
thought·ful·ness [θɔ́tfəlnɪs] *s.* consideración, atención, cuidado, solicitud.
thought·less [θɔ́tlɪs] *adj.* inconsiderado; descuidado; irreflexivo, atolondrado; **-ly** *adv.* inconsideradamente, sin consideración; sin reflexión; sin pensar; descuidadamente, irreflexivamente, atolondradamente.
thought·less·ness [θɔ́tlɪsnɪs] *s.* irreflexión, inadvertencia, descuido; atolondramiento.
thrash [θræʃ] *v.* trillar, desgranar (*las mieses*); zurrar, azotar; to revolcarse, agitarse, menearse; **to — out a matter** ventilar un asunto.
thread [θrɛd] *s.* hilo; hebra, fibra; **screw —** rosca de tornillo; *v.* ensartar, enhebrar; **to — a screw** roscar un tornillo; **to — one's way through a crowd** colarse por entre la muchedumbre.
thread·bare [θrɛ́dbɚ] *adj.* raído, gastado.
threat [θrɛt] *s.* amenaza; amago.
threat·en [θrɛ́tn̩] *v.* amenazar; amagar.
threat·en·ing [θrɛ́tnɪŋ] *adj.* amenazante, amenazador.

thresh [θrɛ] *véase* **thrash.**
thresh·old [θrɛ́ʃold] *s.* umbral, entrada.
threw [θru] *pret. de* **to throw.**
thrice [θraɪs] *adv.* tres veces.
thrift [θrɪft] *s.* economía, frugalidad.
thrift·y [θrɪ́ftɪ] *adj.* económico, frugal; próspero.
thrill [θrɪl] *v.* emocionar(se), conmover(se); estremecerse de emoción, sobreexcitarse; *s.* emoción viva, estremecimiento emotivo, sobreexcitación.
thrive [θraɪv] *v.* medrar, prosperar; florecer.
thriv·en [θrɪ́vən] *p.p. de* **to thrive.**
throat [θrot] *s.* garganta.
throb [θrɑb] *v.* latir, pulsar, palpitar; *s.* latido, palpitación.
throe [θro] *s.* agonía; congoja.
throne [θron] *s.* trono.
throng [θrɔŋ] *s.* muchedumbre, multitud, tropel, gentío; *v.* agolparse, apiñarse; atestar.
throt·tle [θrɑ́tl] *s.* válvula reguladora, obturador, regulador; — **lever** palanca del obturador o regulador; *v.* ahogar; estrangular; **to — down** disminuir o reducir la velocidad.
through [θru] *prep.* por; a través de; por medio de; por conducto de; por entre; *adv.* de un lado a otro; de parte a parte, a través; de cabo a baco; desde el principio hasta el fin; completamente, enteramente; **loyal — and —** leal a toda prueba; **to be wet —** estar empapado; estar mojado hasta los tuétanos; **to carry a plan —** llevar a cabo un plan; *adj.* directo, continuo; — **ticket** billete (*Am.* boleto) directo; — **train** tren rápido, tren de servicio directo; **to be — with** haber acabado con; no querer ocuparse más de.
through·out [θruáʊt] *prep.* (*all through*) por todo; por todas partes de; (*during*) desde el principio; hasta el fin de; — **the year** durante todo el año; *adv.* por todas partes; en todas partes; en todo, en todos respetos; desde el principio hasta el fin.
throve [θrov] *pret. de* **to thrive.**
throw [θro] *v.* tirar, arrojar, lanzar; echar; **to — away** tirar, arrojar; malgastar; **to — down** arrojar, echar por tierra, derribar; **to — in gear** engranar; **to — in the clutch** embragar; **to — off a burden** librarse o deshacerse de una carga; **to — out** echar fuera; expeler; **to — out of gear** desengranar; **to — out of work** privar de trabajo, quitar el empleo a; **to — out the clutch** desembragar; **to — overboard** echar al agua; **to — up** vomitar; *s.* tiro, tirada.
thrown [θron] *p.p. de* **to throw.**
thrush [θrʌʃ] *s.* tordo, zorzal.
thrust [θrʌst] *v.* (*push into*) meter; hincar, clavar; encajar; (*shove*) empujar; **to — a task upon someone** imponer una tarea a una persona, obligar a alguien a desempeñar un quehacer; **to — aside** echar o empujar a un lado; rechazar; **to — in** (*o* **into**) meter en, encafar en, intercalar en; **to — out** sacar; echar fuera; **to — someone through with a sword** atravesar a alguien de parte a parte con la espada; *pret. & p.p. de* **to thrust;** *s.* estocada, cuchillada, puñalada, lanzada; empuje, empujón o empellón; arremetida, acometida.
thud [θʌd] *s.* porrazo, golpazo, golpe sordo.
thug [θʌg] *s.* ladrón, salteador.
thumb [θʌm] *s.* pulgar; **under the — of** bajo el poder o influencia de; *v.* hojear (*con el pulgar*).
thumb·tack [θʌ́mtæk] *s.* chinche.
thump [θʌmp] *s.* golpazo, porrazo, trastazo; golpe sordo; *v.* golpear, golpetear, aporrear, dar un

porrazo.
thun·der [θʌ́ndɚ] *s.* trueno; tronido; estruendo; *v.* tronar.
thun·der·bolt [θʌ́ndɚbolt] *s.* rayo.
thun·der·ing [θʌ́ndərɪŋ] *adj.* atronador.
thun·der·ous [θʌ́ndərəs] *adj.* atronador, estruendoso.
thun·der·storm [θʌ́ndɚstɔrm] *s.* tronada, tormenta o tempestad de truenos.
Thurs·day [θɝ́zdɪ] *s.* jueves.
thus [θʌs] *adv.* así; — **far** hasta aquí, hasta ahora, hasta hoy.
thwart [θwɔrt] *v.* frustrar; estorbar; impedir.
thy [ðaɪ] *adj.* tu, tus.
thyme [taɪm] *s.* tomillo.
thy·roid [θáɪɔɪd] *s.* tiroides.
thy·self [ðaɪsɛ́lf] *pron.* tú mismo; a tí mismo; te (*como reflexivo*); *véase* **herself.**
tick [tɪk] *s.* tic tac; funda (*de colchón o almohada*); garrapata (*insecto parásito*); *v.* hacer tic tac (*como un reloj*); latir (*el corazón*); **to — off** marcar.
tick·et [tɪ́kɪt] *s.* billete, *Am.* boleto; lista de candidatos (*de un partido*); balota (*para votar*); — **office** taquilla; despacho de boletos, *Am.* boletería.
tick·le [tɪ́kl] *v.* (*touch*) cosquillear, hacer cosquillas; (*feel*) sentir o tener cosquillas; (*please*) halagar, gustarle a uno; **to be -d to death** morirse de gusto, estar muy contento; *s.* cosquilleo, cosquillas.
tick·lish [tɪ́klɪʃ] *adj.* cosquilloso; delicado, arriesgado, difícil.
tid·bit [tɪ́dbɪt] *s.* bocado, bocadito, golosina.
tide [taɪd] *s.* marea; corriente; **Christmas —** navidades, temporada de navidad; *v.* **to — someone over a difficulty** ayudar a alguien durante una crisis o dificultad.
tide·wa·ter [táɪdwɔtɚ] *adj.* costanero.
tid·ings [táɪdɪŋz] *s. pl.* noticias, nuevas.
ti·dy [táɪdɪ] *adj.* aseado, limpio, ordenado; **a — sum** una suma considerable; *v.* asear, arreglar, poner en orden; **to — oneself up** asearse.
tie [taɪ] *v.* (*fasten*) atar, liar, ligar; *Am.* amarrar; (*unite*) enlazar, vincular; (*equal*) empatar (*en juegos, etc.*); **to — tight** amarrar bien, apretar fuerte; **to — up the traffic** obstruir el tráfico; *s.* lazo, ligadura, atadura; enlace, vínculo; corbata; empate (*en carreras, juegos, etc.*); **railway —** traviesa, *Andes, C.A., Méx.* durmiente; *Ríopl., Ch.* travesaño.
tier [tɪr] *s.* fila, hilera, ringlera.
ti·ger [táɪgɚ] *s.* tigre; — **cat** gato montés.
tight [taɪt] *adj.* (*squeezed*) apretado, ajustado, estrecho; (*sealed*) hermético; (*firm*) firme, tieso; (*stingy*) tacaño, mezquino; (*drunk*) borracho; **to be in a — spot** estar en un aprieto; **to close —** apretar, cerrar herméticamente; **to hold on —** agarrarse bien; **it fits —** está muy estrecho o ajustado.
tight·en [táɪtṇ] *v.* apretar; estrechar; estirar, poner tirante.
tight·ness [táɪtnɪs] *s.* estrechez; tirantez, tensión; mezquindad, tacañería.
tight·wad [táɪtwɑd] *s.* tacaño; cicatero.
ti·gress [táɪgrɪs] *s.* tigre hembra; *Am.* tigra.
tile [taɪl] *s.* teja; baldosa, azulejo; — **roof** tejado; *v.* tejar, cubrir con tejas; cubrir con azulejos; embaldosar.
till [tɪl] *prep.* hasta; *conj.* hasta que; *v.* cultivar, labrar, arar; *s.* gaveta o cajón para el dinero.
till·age [tɪ́ladʒ] *s.* labranza, cultivo, labor.

TH

tilt [tɪlt] *s.* ladeo, inclinación; declive; altercación disputa; **at full** — a toda velocidad; *v.* ladear(se), inclinar(se).

tim·ber [tímbɚ] *s.* madera de construcción; maderaje; madero; viga.

time [taɪm] *s.* tiempo; hora; vez; plazo; **at -s** a veces; **at one and the same** — a la vez; **at this** — ahora, al presente; **behind** — atrasado, retrasado; **from** — **to** — de vez en cuando; **in** — a tiempo; andando el tiempo; **on** — puntual; con puntualidad; a tiempo; a la hora debida; **several -s** varias veces; **to beat** — marcar el compás; **to buy on** — comprar a plazo; **to have a good** — divertirse, pasar un buen rato; **what** — **is it?** ¿qué hora es?; *v.* cronometrar, medir el tiempo de; regular, poner en punto (*el reloj, el motor*); escoger el momento oportuno para; — **zone** zona horaria; huso horario.

time·less [táɪmlɛs] *adj.* eterno, infinito.

time·ly [táɪmlɪ] *adj.* oportuno.

time·piece [tátmpis] *s.* reloj; cronómetro.

time·ta·ble [táɪmtebl] *s.* itinerario, horario.

tim·id [tímɪd] *adj.* tímido.

ti·mid·i·ty [tɪmídətɪ] *s.* timidez.

tim·ing [táɪmɪŋ] *s.* medida del tiempo; cronometraje; (*pace*) selección del momento oportuno; sincronización.

tim·or·ous [tímərəs] *adj.* timorato, tímido, miedoso.

tin [tɪn] *s.* estaño; hojalata, lata; cosa de hojalata; — **can** lata; — **foil** hoja de estaño; *v.* estañar, cubrir con estaño; enlatar.

tinc·ture [tíŋktʃɚ] *s.* tintura; tinte; — **of iodine** tintura de yodo; *v.* tinturar, teñir.

tin·der [tíndɚ] *s.* yesca.

tinge [tɪndʒ] *v.* teñir; matizar; *s.* tinte, matiz; dejo, saborcillo.

tin·gle [tíŋgl] *v.* hormiguear, sentir hormigueo; **to** — **with excitement** estremecerse de entusiasmo; *s.* hormigueo, picazón, comezón.

tin·ker [tíŋkɚ] *v.* ocuparse vanamente.

tin·kle [tíŋkl] *v.* tintinear; hacer retintín; *s.* tintineo; retintín.

tin·sel [tínsl] *s.* oropel; *adj.* de oropel.

tint [tɪnt] *s.* tinte, matiz; *v.* teñir, matizar.

ti·ny [táɪnɪ] *adj.* diminuto, menudo, chiquitico, chiquitín.

tip [tɪp] *s.* (*point*) punta, extremo, extremidad; (*money*) propina; (*hint*) noticia o aviso secreto; *v.* ladear(se), inclinar(se); dar propina (a); **to** — **a person off** dar aviso secreto a; **to** — **one's hat** tocarse el sombrero; **to** — **over** volcar(se), voltear(se).

tip·sy [típsɪ] *adj.* alumbrado, algo borracho; ladeado.

tip·toe [típto] *s.* punta del pie; **on** — de puntillas; *v.* andar de puntillas.

ti·rade [táɪred] *s.* invectiva.

tire [taɪr] *s.* llanta, neumático, goma; **flat** — llanta o goma reventada; *v.* cansar(se), fatigar(se).

tired [taɪrd] *adj.* cansado, fatigado; — **out** extenuado de fatiga, rendido.

tire·less [táɪrlɪs] *adj.* incansable, infatigable.

tire·some [táɪrsəm] *adj.* cansado, aburrido, pesado.

tis·sue [tíʃU] *s.* tejido; — **paper** papel de seda.

ti·tan·ic [taɪtǽnɪk] *adj.* titánico.

ti·ta·ni·um [taɪténɪəm] *s.* titanio.

tithe [taɪð] *s.* diezmo.

ti·tle [táɪtl] *s.* título; — **holder** titulado; — **page** portada.

to [tu] *prep.* a; hasta; hacia; para; — **try** — tratar de; esforzarse por; **a quarter** — **five** las cinco

menos cuarto; **bills** — **be paid** cuentas por pagar; **frightened** — **death** muerto de susto; **from house** — **house** de casa en casa; **he has** — **go** tiene que ir; **near** — cerca de; **not** — **my knowledge** no que yo sepa; *adv.* — **and fro** de acá para allá; **to come** — volver en si.

toad [tod] *s.* sapo o escuerzo.

toast [tost] *v.* tostar(se); brindar por, beber a la salud de; *s.* tostada; brindis.

toast·er [tóstɚ] *s.* tostador.

to·bac·co [təbǽko] *s.* tabaco.

to·day [tədé] *adv.* hoy; hoy día.

toe [to] *s.* dedo del pie; punta (*de la media, del zapato, etc.*); *v.* **to** — **in** andar con la punta de los pies para dentro.

toe·nail [tónel] *s.* uña del dedo del pie.

to·geth·er [təgéðɚ] *adv.* juntamente; a un mismo tiempo, a la vez; juntos; — **with** junto con; **all** — juntos; en junto; **to call** — convocar; juntar; **to come** — juntarse, unirse; ponerse de acuerdo; **to walk** — andar juntos.

toil [tɔɪl] *v.* afanarse, trafagar atearearse; *s.* esfuerzo, trabajo, faena, fatiga.

toi·let [tɔ́ɪLɪt] *s.* retrete, excusado, común, *Am.* inodoro; — **articles** artículos de tocador; — **case** neceser; — **paper** papel de excusado, papel higiénico.

to·ken [tókən] *s.* señal, símbolo; prenda; recuerdo; prueba, muestra; ficha (*de metal*); — **payment** pago nominal.

told [told] *pret. & p.p.* de **to tell.**

tol·er·ance [tálərəns] *s.* tolerancia.

tol·er·ant [tálərənt] *adj.* tolerante.

tol·er·ate [táləret] *v.* tolerar.

tol·er·a·tion [taləréʃan] *s.* tolerancia.

toll [tol] *s.* doble, tañido (*de las companas*); peaje; portazgo; — **bridge** puente de peaje; — **gate** barrera de peaje; — **call** llamada por cobrar; **to pay** — pagar peaje o portazgo; *v.* tañer, doblar (*las campanas*).

to·ma·to [təméto] *s.* tomate, *Méx.* jitomate.

tomb [tum] *s.* tumba.

tomb·stone [túmston] *s.* lápida sepulcral.

tom·cat [támkæt] *s.* gato.

tome [tom] *s.* tomo.

to·mor·row [təmóro] *adv.* mañana; — **morning** mañana por la mañana; — **noon** mañana al mediodía; **day after** — pasado mañana.

ton [tʌn] *s.* tonelada.

tone [ton] *s.* (*pitch*) tono; timbre; (*sound*) sonido; *v.* dar tono a, modificar el tono de; **to** — **down** bajar de tono; suavizar; **to** — **down one's voice** moderar la voz; **to** — **in well with** armonizar con, entonar bien con; **to** — **up** subir de tono; tonificar, vigorizar.

tongs [tɔŋz] *s. pl.* tenazas.

tongue [tʌŋ] *s.* lengua; idioma; **to be tongue-tied** tener trabada la lengua.

ton·ic [tánɪk] *s. & adj.* tónico.

to·night [tənáɪt] *adv.* esta noche, a la noche.

ton·nage [tánɪdʒ] *s.* tonelaje.

ton·sil [tánsl] *s.* amígdala.

ton·sil·li·tis [tansəláɪtɪs] *s.* amigdalitis.

too [tu] *adv.* también; demasiado; — **many** demasiados; — **much** demasiado; **it is** — **bad!** ¡es una lástima!

took [tʊk] *pret.* de **to take.**

tool [tul] *s.* instrumento; herramienta; — **box** caja de herramientas.

toot [tut] *v.* tocar o sonar la bocina; pitar; tocar (*un cuerno, trompa o trompeta*); **to** — **one's own**

horn alabarse, cantar sus propias alabanzas; *s.* toque o sonido (*de bocina, trompeta, etc.*); silbido, pitido; pitazo (*de locomotora*).

tooth [tuθ] *s.* diente; muela; — **mark** dentellada; **to fight — and nail** luchar a brazo partido; **to have a sweet —** ser amigo de golosinas.

tooth·ache [túθek] *s.* dolor de muelas.

tooth·brush [túθbrʌʃ] *s.* cepillo de dientes.

toothed [tuθt] *adj.* dentado.

tooth·less [túθlɪs] *adj.* desdentado.

tooth·paste [túθpest] *s.* pasta para los dientes, pasta dentífrica.

tooth·pick [túθpɪk] *s.* mondadientes, palillo de dientes.

top [tɑp] *s.* (*peak*) cumbre, cima; cúspide; tope; pináculo; remate; cabeza; (*surface*) superficie; copa (*de árbol*); (*cover*) tapa, cubierta; (*toy*) trompo; peonza; **at the — of his class** a la cabeza de su clase; **at the — of one's voice** a voz en cuello; **filled up to the —** lleno hasta el tope; **from — to bottom** de arriba abajo; **from — to toe** de pies a cabeza; **on — of** encima de, sobre; *adj.* superior; más alto; —**coat** abrigo, sobretodo; **at — speed** a velocidad máxima; *v.* coronar; exceder; sobresalir, sobrepujar; rematar; **to — off** rematar; terminar.

to·paz [tópæz] *s.* topacio.

top·er [tópɚ] *s.* bebedor, borrachín.

top-heav·y [tɑphévɪ] *adj.* más pesado arriba que abajo.

top·ic [tápɪk] *s.* tema, asunto, materia, topico.

top·most [tápmost] *adj.* más alto; superior.

to·pog·ra·phy [təpágrəfɪ] *s.* topografía.

to·pon·y·my [təpánəmɪ] *s.* toponimia.

top·ple [tápl] *v.* echar abajo, derribar; volcar; **to — over** venirse abajo; volcarse.

top·sy-tur·vy [tápsɪtɚvɪ] *adj. & adv.* patas arriba; en confusión; trastornado; enrevesado, al revés.

torch [tɔrtʃ] *s.* antorcha; **blow —** soplete.

tore [tor] *pret. de* **to tear.**

tor·ment [tɔrmɛnt] *s.* tormento; [tɔrmént] *v.* atormentar; afligir.

torn [torn] *p.p. de* **to tear** roto, rompido, rasgado.

tor·na·do [tɔrnédo] *s.* tornado.

tor·pe·do [tɔrpído] *s.* torpedo; — **boat** torpedero; *v.* torpedear.

torque [tɔrk] *s.* fuerza rotatoria.

tor·rent [tɔrənt] *s.* torrente.

tor·rid [tɔrɪd] *adj.* tórrido.

tor·sion [tɔrʃən] *s.* torsión.

tor·toise [tɔrtəs] *s.* tortuga.

tor·tu·ous [tɔrtʃʊəs] *adj.* tortuoso.

tor·ture [tɔrtʃɚ] *s.* tortura, tormento; *v.* torturar, atormentar.

toss [tɔs] *v.* tirar, echar, arrojar, lanzar; menear(se); cabecear (*un buque*); **to — aside** echar a un lado; desechar; **to — up** echar para arriba; aventar; *s.* tiro, tirada; meneo, sacudida.

tot [tɑt] *s.* chiquitín, chiquitina, chiquitico, chiquitica, niñito, niñita, nene, nena.

to·tal [tótl] *adj. & s.* total.

to·tal·i·tar·i·an [totælətériən] *adj.* totalitario.

tot·ter [tátɚ] *v.* tambalear(se), bambolear(se); estar para desplomarse.

touch [tʌtʃ] *v.* tocar; palpar, tentar; conmover, enternecer; compararse con, igualar; **to — at a port** hacer escala en un puerto; **to — off an explosive** prender la mecha de un explosivo; **to — up** retocar; *s.* toque; tacto, sentido del tacto; tiento; —**stone** piedra de toque; **a — of fever** algo de calentura; **to keep in — with**

mantener(se) en comunicación con.

touch-and-go [tʌtʃəndgó] *adj.* arriesgado.

touch·ing [tʌtʃɪŋ] *adj.* conmovedor, enternecedor.

touch·y [tʌtʃɪ] *adj.* quisquilloso, susceptible, sensible, sensitivo.

tough [tʌf] *adj.* correoso; fuerte; firme; duro; arduo, difícil; terco; empedernido, malvado.

tough·en [tʌfn] *v.* curtir(se); endurecer(se), empedernir(se); hacer(se) correoso.

tough·ness [tʌfnɪs] *s.* dureza; correosidad; flexibilidad; tenacidad; resistencia; dificultad.

tou·pee [tupé] *s.* peluca.

tour [tur] *s.* viaje, excursión; vuelta; jira; *v.* viajar por; recorrer; hacer una jira; hacer un viaje de turismo.

tour·ism [túrɪzəm] *s.* turismo.

tour·ist [túrɪst] *s.* turista.

tour·na·ment [tɚnəmənt] *s.* torneo; certamen, concurso.

tow [to] *v.* remolcar; *s.* remolque; —**boat** remolcador; —**rope** cuerda de remolque; **to take in —** remolcar, llevar a remolque.

to·ward [tord] *prep.* hacia; rumbo a; alrededor de; para, para con; — **four o'clock** a eso de las cuatro.

to·wards [tordz] = **toward.**

tow·el [taʊl] *s.* toalla.

tow·er [táʊɚ] *s.* torre; torreón; **bell —** campanario; *v.* sobresalir, sobrepujar; destacarse, descollar; elevarse.

tow·er·ing [táʊrɪŋ] *adj.* encumbrado; elevado, muy alto; sobresaliente.

town [taʊn] *s.* (*center*) población, ciudad, pueblo, aldea; (*administration*) municipio; — **hall** ayuntamiento.

town·ship [táʊnʃɪp] *s.* unidad primaria de gobierno local; sección de seis millas cuadradas (*en terrenos públicos*).

tox·in [táksɪn] *s.* toxina.

toy [tɔɪ] *s.* juguete; *adj.* de juego, de juguete; pequeñito; *v.* jugar, juguetear.

trace [tres] *s.* señal, indicio, vestigio; huella, rastro; tirante (*de una guarnición*); *v.* trazar; calcar; rastrear, seguir la huella de; rebuscar, investigar; **to — the source of** remontarse al origen de, buscar el origen de.

tra·che·a [trékɪə] *s.* tráquea.

tra·cho·ma [trəkomə] *s.* tracoma.

track [træk] *s.* pista, huella, rastro; pisada; vereda, senda; vía; — **sports** deportes de pista; **race —** pista; **railroad —** rieles, vía del tren, vía férrea o ferrovía; **to be off the —** estar extraviado, estar descarrilado; **to be on the — of** rastrear, ir siguiendo la pista de; **to keep — of** llevar la cuenta de; no perder de vista; *v.* rastrear, seguir la huella de; **to — down** coger, atrapar; descubrir; **to — in mud** traer lodo en los pies, entrar con los pies enlodados.

tract [trækt] *s.* área; terreno; folleto; **digestive —** canal digestivo.

trac·tion [trækʃən] *s.* tracción.

trac·tor [træktɚ] *s.* tractor.

trade [tred] *s.* (*business*) comercio; trato, negocio; (*swap*) trueque, cambio; (*occupation*) oficio; (*customers*) clientela, parroquianos; — **school** escuela de artes y oficios; — **union** gremio obrero o de obreros; *v.* comerciar, negociar, traficar, tratar; trocar, cambiar; feriar, mercar.

trade·mark [trédmɑrk] *s.* marca de fábrica.

trad·er [trédɚ] *s.* mercader, comerciante, negociante, traficante.

trades·man [trédzmən] *s.* mercader, comerciante, traficante; tendero.

tra·di·tion [trədíʃən] *s.* tradición.

tra·di·tion·al [trədíʃənl] *adj.* tradicional.

traf·fic [træfɪk] *s.* tráfico; tráfago; tránsito; circulación; *v.* traficar, comerciar, negociar.

trag·e·dy [trædʒədɪ] *s.* tragedia.

trag·ic [trædʒɪk] *adj.* trágico.

trail [trel] *s.* (*trace*) pista, rastro, huella; (*path*) senda, sendero, trocha, vereda; cola (*de vestido*); *v.* arrastrar(se); rastrear, seguir la pista de; andar detrás de; **to — behind** ir rezagado, rezagarse.

train [tren] *s.* (*railroad*) tren; (*dress*) cola (*de vestido*); (*retinue*) séquito, comitiva; *v.* amaestrar(se), ejercitar(se); adiestrar(se) o adestrar(se), *Am.* entrenar(se); educar; disciplinar (*tropas*); apuntar (*un cañón*).

train·er [trénɚ] *s.* amaestrador; *Méx., C.A., Andes, Ven., Col., Carib.* entrenador.

train·ing [trénɪŋ] *s.* adiestramiento, disciplina, *Méx., C.A., Andes, Ven., Col., Carib.,* entrenamiento; educación; **— camp** campo de entrenamiento o práctica.

trait [tret] *s.* rasgo, característica; cualidad.

trai·tor [trétɚ] *s.* traidor.

tram [træm] *s.* vagoneta (*de una mina de carbón*).

tramp [træmp] *v.* pisotear; andar a pie; vagabundear; *s.* vago, vagabundo; caminata, marcha; pisadas.

tram·ple [træmpl] *v.* pisar, hollar, pisotear; **to — on** pisotear, hollar; *s.* pisadas.

trance [træns] *s.* rapto, arrobamiento, enajenamiento, éxtasis; **to be in a —** estar arrobado, estar enajenado; estar distraído o ensimismado.

tran·quil [trǽnkwɪl] *adj.* tranquilo.

tran·quil·iz·er [trǽŋkwəlaɪzɚ] *s.* tranquilizador.

tran·quil·li·ty [trænkwíləɪti] *s.* tranquilidad.

trans·act [trænsǽkt] *v.* tramitar, despachar, llevar a cabo.

trans·ac·tion [trænsǽkʃən] *s.* transacción, trato, negocio; trámite; negociación; **-s** actas; memorias.

trans·at·lan·tic [trænsətlǽntɪk] *adj.* transatlántico.

tran·scend [trænsénd] *v.* trascender, ir más allá de.

trans·con·ti·nen·tal [trænskɑntənéntl] *adj.* transcontinental.

tran·scribe [trænskráɪb] *v.* transcribir.

tran·script [trænskrɪpt] *s.* transcripción, copia.

trans·fer [trænsfɚ] *s.* transferencia; traslado; traspaso; trasbordo; **— of ownership** cesión o traspaso de propiedad; **streetcar —** transferencia, contraseña, cupón de trasbordo; [trænsfɚ] *v.* transferir; trasbordar (*de un tren a otro*), cambiar (*de tren, de tranvía*); traspasar (*propiedad*), trasladar.

trans·fer·a·ble [trænsfɚəbl] *adj.* transferible.

trans·fig·ure [trænsfígjɚ] *v.* transfigurar.

trans·form [trænsfɔrm] *v.* transformar(se).

trans·for·ma·tion [trænsfɚméʃən] *s.* transformación.

trans·gress [trænsgrés] *v.* transgredir, violar, quebrantar (*una ley*); pecar; **to — the bounds of** traspasar los límites de.

trans·gres·sion [trænsgréʃən] *s.* transgresión; violación de una ley; pecado.

trans·gres·sor [trænsgrésɚ] *s.* transgresor.

tran·sient [trǽnʃənt] *s.* transeúnte; *adj.* transeúnte; transitorio, pasajero.

tran·sis·tor [trænzístɚ] *s.* transistor.

tran·sit [trǽnsɪt] *s.* tránsito; **in —** en tránsito, de paso.

tran·si·tion [trænzíʃən] *s.* transición; tránsito, paso.

tran·si·tive [trǽnsətɪv] *adj.* transitivo.

tran·si·to·ry [trǽnsətorɪ] *adj.* transitorio, pasajero.

trans·late [trænslét] *v.* traducir, verter; trasladar.

trans·la·tion [trænsléʃən] *s.* traducción, versión; translación (*de un lugar a otro*).

trans·la·tor [trænslétɚ] *s.* traductor.

trans·lu·cent [trænslúsn̩t] *adj.* translúcido; **to be —** traslucirse.

trans·mis·sion [trænsmíʃən] *s.* transmisión; caja de velocidades.

trans·mit [trænsmít] *v.* transmitir; emitir.

trans·mit·ter [trænsmítɚ] *s.* transmisor; emisor.

tran·som [trǽnsəm] *s.* montante.

trans·par·ent [trænspérənt] *adj.* transparente.

trans·plant [trænsplǽnt] *v.* trasplantar.

trans·port [trænsport] *s.* (*moving*) transporte; acarreo; (*rapture*) éxtasis; **— plane** aeroplano de transporte; [trænspórt] *v.* transportar; acarrear; **to be -ed with joy** estar enajenado de placer.

trans·por·ta·tion [trænspɚtéʃən] *s.* transportación, transporte; boleto, pasaje.

trans·pose [trænspóz] *v.* transponer.

trans·verse [trænsvɚ́s] *adj.* transverso, transversal; puesto de través.

trap [træp] *s.* trampa, lazo, red; **— door** trampa; **mouse —** ratonera; *v.* entrampar, coger con trampa; atrapar.

tra·peze [træpíz] *s.* trapecio.

trap·e·zoid [trǽpəzɔɪd] *s.* trapezoide; trapecio.

trap·pings [trǽpɪŋz] *s. pl.* arreos, jaeces, guarniciones.

trash [træʃ] *s.* basura; hojarasca; cachivaches; gentuza, plebe.

trau·ma [trómə] *s.* traumatismo.

trau·mat·ic [trɔmǽtɪk] *adj.* traumático.

trav·el [trǽvl] *v.* viajar; viajar por; recorrer; *s.* viaje; tráfico.

trav·el·er [trǽvlɚ] *s.* viajero; **—'s check** cheque de viajero.

trav·el·ing [trǽvlɪŋ] *adj.* de viaje, para viaje; **— expenses** gastos de viaje; **— salesman** agente viajero, viajante de comercio.

trav·e·logue [trǽvəlɔg] *s.* conferencia sobre viajes.

trav·erse [trǽvɚs] *v.* atravesar, cruzar; recorrer; *s.* travesaño.

trav·es·ty [trǽvɪstɪ] *s.* parodia; *v.* parodiar, falsear.

tray [tre] *s.* bandeja; batea; *Mex.* charola.

treach·er·ous [trétʃərəs] *adj.* traicionero, traidor, alevoso.

treach·er·y [trétʃərɪ] *s.* traición, perfidia, alevosía.

tread [trɛd] *v.* (*trample*) pisar, hollar; pisotear; (*walk*) andar a pie, caminar; *s.* paso; pisada, huella; *Am.* pise (*de una rueda*); **tire —** rodadura del neumático, *Am.* banda rodante.

tread·mill [trédmɪl] *s.* noria; rueda de andar.

trea·son [trízn̩] *s.* traición.

trea·son·a·ble [tríznəbl] *adj.* traidor, traicionero.

treas·ure [tréʒɚ] *s.* tesoro; *v.* atesorar.

treas·ur·er [tréʒərɚ] *s.* tesorero.

treas·ur·y [tréʒərɪ] *s.* tesorería; tesoro, erario; **Secretary of the Treasury** ministro de hacienda.

treat [trit] *v.* tratar; curar; convidar, invitar; *s.* obsequio, agasajo, convite; placer, gusto.

trea·tise [trítɪs] *s.* tratado.

treat·ment [trítmənt] *s.* trato; **medical —** tratamiento médico.

trea·ty [trítɪ] *s.* tratado, pacto, convenio.

treb·le [trébl̩] *adj.* triple; **— voice** voz atiplada;

s. tiple; v. triplicar.

tree [tri] s. árbol; **apple** — manzano; **family** — árbol genealógico; **shoe** — horma de zapato; **to be up a** — estar subido a un árbol; estar en un gran aprieto; estar perplejo.

tree·less [trílɪs] adj. pelado, sin árboles, despoblado de árboles.

tree·top [trítɑp] s. copa de árbol.

trel·lis [trélɪs] s. emparrado, enrejado.

trem·ble [trémbl] v. temblar; estremecerse; s. temblor; estremecimiento.

tre·men·dous [trɪméndəs] adj. tremendo.

trem·or [trémə˞] s. temblor.

trem·u·lous [trémjələs] adj. trémulo; tembloroso.

trench [trɛntʃ] s. trinchera; zanja, foso.

trend [trɛnd] s. tendencia; rumbo, dirección.

tres·pass [tréspəs] v. invadir, traspasar; violar, infringir; pecar; **to** — **on property** meterse sin derecho en la propiedad ajena; **no -ing** prohibida la entrada; s. transgresión; pecado.

tress [trɛs] s. trenza; bucle.

tres·tle [trɛsl] s. caballete; puente de caballetes.

tri·al [tráɪəl] s. ensayo, prueba; tentativa; aflicción; juicio, proceso; — **flight** vuelo de prueba.

tri·an·gle [tráɪæŋgl] s. triángulo.

tri·an·gu·lar [traɪæŋgjələ˞] adj. triangular.

tribe [traɪb] s. tribu.

trib·u·la·tion [trɪbəléʃən] s. tribulación.

tri·bu·nal [trɪbjún̩l] s. tribunal, juzgado.

trib·u·tar·y [tríbjətɛrɪ] adj. & s. tributario.

trib·ute [tríbjut] s. tributo; homenaje.

trich·i·no·sis [trɪkənósɪs] s. triquinosis.

trick [trɪk] s. treta; suerte; truco, artificio; maña, ardid, trampa; travesura; baza (en el juego de naipes); **to be up to one's old -s** hacer de las suyas; v. embaucar, trampear, hacer trampa; burlar; **to** — **oneself up** componerse, emperifollarse.

trick·er·y [tríkərɪ] s. engaños, malas mañas, astucia.

trick·le [tríkl] v. gotear; escurrir; s. goteo.

trick·y [tríkɪ] adj. tramposo, Am. mañero; intrincado, complicado.

tri·cy·cle [tráɪsɪkl] s. triciclo.

tried [traɪd] p.p. de **to try** & adj. probado.

tri·fle [tráɪfl] s. fruslería, friolera, nadería, nonada; bagatela; v. chancear(se), bromear; jugar, juguetear.

trig·ger [trígə˞] s. gatillo (de pistola, rifle, etc).

trill [trɪl] v. trinar; **to** — **the r** pronunciar la erre doble; s. trino.

tril·o·gy [trílədʒɪ] s. trilogía.

trim [trɪm] v. guarnecer, adornar; atusar; recortar; podar, mondar; despabilar (una vela); ganarle a uno (en el juego); **to** — **up** adornar, componer; adj. aseado, limpio, pulcro, acicalado; s. adorno, franja, ribete, guarnición; **to be in** — **for** estar en buena salud para; estar bien entrenado para.

trim·ming [trímɪŋ] s. adorno, aderezo, guarnición; orla, ribete, franja; paliza, zurra; **-s** adornos; accesorios; recortes.

trin·i·ty [trínətɪ] s. trinidad.

trin·ket [tríŋkɪt] s. chuchería, baratija; miriñaque.

trip [trɪp] s. viaje; travesía; recorrido, jira; tropezón; v. tropezar; dar un traspié; equivocarse; hacer tropezar, hacer caer; saltar; brincar, corretear.

triph·thong [trífθɔŋ] s. triptongo.

trip·le [trípl] adj. & s. triple; v. triplicar.

trip·li·cate [trípləkət] adj. triplicado.

tri·pod [tráɪpɑd] s. trípode.

trite [traɪt] adj. trillado, trivial, vulgar.

tri·umph [tráɪəmf] s. triunfo; v. triunfar.

tri·um·phal [traɪʌmfl] adj. triunfal.

tri·um·phant [traɪʌmfənt] adj. triunfante; **-ly** adv. triunfantemente, en triunfo.

triv·i·al [trívjəl] adj. trivial, insignificante.

trod [trɑd] pret. & p.p. de **to tread**.

trod·den [trɑdn̩] p.p. de **to tread**.

trol·ley [trɑlɪ] s. trole; tranvía de trole; — **bus** trolebús.

trom·bone [trámbon] s. trombón.

troop [trup] s. tropa; cuadrilla.

tro·phy [trófɪ] s. trofeo.

trop·ic [trápɪk] s. trópico; — **of Cancer** trópico de Cáncer; — **of Capricorn** trópico de Capricornio; adj. tropical.

trop·i·cal [trápɪkl] adj. tropical.

trot [trɑt] v. trotar; hacer trotar; s. trote.

trou·ba·dour [trúbədɔr] s. trovador.

trou·ble [trʌbl] v. perturbar, turbar; molestar, incomodar; afligir; preocupar(se); **don't** — **to come** no se moleste Vd. en venir; s. pena, aflicción; inquietud, perturbación; dificultad; molestia; panne, avería, accidente (a un mecanismo); **heart** — enfermedad del corazón; **to be in** — estar en un aprieto o apuro; **it is not worth the** — no vale la pena; — **shooter** investigador de fallas o averías.

trou·ble·mak·er [trʌblmekə˞] s. agitador, alborotador, malcontento.

trou·ble·some [trʌblsəm] adj. molesto, fastidioso, enfadoso, dificultoso; penoso.

trough [trɔf] s. comedero; artesa; batea; **eaves** — canal, gotera del tejado; **drinking** — abrevadero.

trou·sers [tráʊzə˞z] s. pl. pantalones.

trous·seau [trúso] s. ajuar de novia.

trout [traʊt] s. trucha.

trow·el [tráʊəl] s. llana, Am. cuchara (de albañil); desplantador (de jardín).

tru·ant [trúənt] s. novillero, holgazán (que se ausenta de una escuela); **to play** — hacer novillos, Am. capear la escuela, Mex. pintar venado, Am. jubilarse; adj. vago, perezoso.

truce [trus] s. tregua.

truck [trʌk] s. camión; carretón; carreta; basura; baratijas; **garden** — hortalizas, legumbres y verduras; — **garden** hortaliza, huerta de legumbres; v. acarrear, transportar en camión o carretón.

trudge [trʌdʒ] v. caminar, caminar con esfuerzo; s. caminata.

true [tru] adj. (not false) verdadero; cierto; verídico, fiel; (exact) exacto, preciso; legítimo.

tru·ly [trúlɪ] adv. (not falsely) verdaderamente, en verdad; (in reality) (exactly) exactamente, correctamente; fielmente; **very** — **yours** su seguro servidor.

trump [trʌmp] s. triunfo (en el juego de naipes); v. matar con un triunfo (en el juego de naipes); **to** — **up an excuse** forjar o inventar una excusa.

trum·pet [trʌmpɪt] s. trompeta; clarín; **ear** — trompetilla acústica; v. trompetear; tocar la trompeta; pregonar, divulgar.

trunk [trʌŋk] s. tronco; baúl; trompa (de elefante); **-s** calzones cortos (para deportes); — **line** línea principal.

trust [trʌst] s. (reliance) confianza, fe; (credit) crédito; (charge) cargo; custodia; depósito; (firms) trust, sindicato monopolista; v. confiar; fiar en, tener confianza en, fiarse de; esperar;

TR

dar crédito a.

trus·tee [trʌstí] *s.* fideicomisario, depositario; **university -s** regentes universitarios; **board of -s** patronato; consejo.

trust·ful [trʌstfəl] *adj.* confiado.

trust·ing [trʌstɪŋ] *adj.* confiado.

trust·wor·thy [trʌstwɝ̃ðɪ] *adj.* fidedigno, digno de confianza.

trust·y [trʌstɪ] *adj.* fidedigno; honrado, leal; *s.* presidiario fidedigno (*a quien se le conceden ciertos privilegios*).

truth [truθ] *s.* verdad.

truth·ful [trúθfəl] *adj.* verdadero; verídico; veraz.

truth·ful·ness [trúθfəlnɪs] *s.* veracidad.

try [traɪ] *v.* probar, ensayar; hacer la prueba; poner a prueba; intentar, procurar; procesar, enjuiciar, formar causa (*a un acusado*); ver (*una causa*); **to — on a suit** probarse un traje; **to — one's luck** probar fortuna; **to — someone's patience** poner a prueba la paciencia de alguien; **to — to** tratar de, procurar, intentar; *s.* prueba, tentativa, ensayo.

try·ing [tráɪŋ] *adj.* molesto; penoso, irritante.

tub [tʌb] *s.* tina; bañera; baño; batea, cuba; *v.* lavar en tina o cuba.

tu·ba [túbə] *s.* tuba.

tube [tjub] *s.* tubo; **inner —** cámara (*de un neumático*); **radio —** lámpara o tubo de radio.

tu·ber·cu·lar [tjubɝ̃kjələ˞] *adj.* tuberculoso, tísico.

tu·ber·cu·lo·sis [tjubɝ̃kjəlósɪs] *s.* tuberculosis.

tuck [tʌk] *v.* alforzar, hacer o echar alforzas; **to — in** meter en; **to — in bed** arropar; **to — under one's arm** meter bajo el brazo; **to — up** arremanger, recoger; **to — up one's sleeves** arremangarse; *s.* alforza.

Tues·day [tjúzdɪ] *s.* martes.

tuft [tʌft] *s.* (*cluster*) penacho, copete; borla; (*clump*) macizo (*de plantas*).

tug [tʌg] *v.* remoclar; jalar (halar); arrastrar; trabajar con esfuerzo; **to — at** tirar de, jalar; *s.* tirón, estirón, *Am.* jalón; remolcador; **—boat** remolcador; **— of war** lucha a tirones de cuerda.

tu·i·tion [tjuíʃən] *s.* derechos de enseñanza; matrícula, *Am.* colegiatura.

tu·lip [tjúləp] *s.* tulipán.

tum·ble [tʌmbl] *v.* caer(se); voltear; dar volteretas; **to — down** caerse; desplomarse; **to — down** caerse; desplomarse; **to — into someone** tropezar con alguien; **to — over** volcar, tumbar, derribar; venirse abajo; *s.* caída, tumbo, vuelco, voltereta, *Am.* rodada; desorden.

tum·bler [tʌmblə˞] *s.* vaso (*de mesa*); acróbata.

tu·mor [tjúmə˞] *s.* tumor.

tu·mult [tjúmʌlt] *s.* tumulto.

tu·mul·tu·ous [tjumʌltʃúəs] *adj.* tumultuoso.

tu·na [túnə] *s.* atún (*pez*).

tune [tjun] *s.* (*melody*) tonada; (*pitch*) tono; armonía; **to be in —** estar a tono, estar afinado o templado; estar entonado; **to be out of —** estar desentonado o desafinado; desentonar; *v.* afinar, templar; armonizar; **to — in** sintonizar; **to — up the motor** poner al punto el motor.

tung·sten [tʌ́ŋstən] *s.* tungsteno.

tu·nic [tjúnɪk] *s.* túnica.

tun·nel [tʌnl] *s.* túnel; socavón; *v.* socavar; abrir un túnel.

tur·ban [tɝ̃bən] *s.* turbante.

tur·bine [tɝ̃baɪn], [tɝ̃bɪn] *s.* turbina.

tur·bo·prop [tɝ̃boprap] *s.* turbopropulsor.

tur·bu·lent [tɝ̃bjələnt] *adj.* turbulento; revoltoso.

turf [tɝf] *s.* césped; terrón de tierra (*con césped*);

hipódromo, pista (*para carreras*).

Turk [tɝk] *s.* turco.

tur·key [tɝ̃kɪ] *s.* pavo, *Méx.* guajolote (*o guajalote*); *C.A.* jolote, chumpe, chompipe; *Col.* pisco.

Turk·ish [tɝ̃kɪʃ] *adj.* turco; *s.* turco, idioma turco.

tur·moil [tɝ̃mɔɪl] *s.* alboroto; confusión.

turn [tɝn] *v.* (*rotate*) volver(se); voltear(se); girar, dar vueltas, rodar; virar; (*shape*) tornear, labrar al torno; (*become*) ponerse (*pálido, rojo, etc.*); **to — back** volver atrás; volverse, retroceder; devolver; **to — down an offer** rechazar una oferta; **to — in** entregar; recogerse, acostarse; **to — inside out** volver o volver al revés; **to — into** convertir(se) en; **to — off** apagar (*la luz*); cortar (*el agua, el gas, etc.*); **to — off the main road** salirse o desviarse de la carretera; **to — on** encender (*la luz*); abrir la llave (*del gas, del agua*); **to — on someone** volverse contra, acometer o caer sobre alguien; **to — out** apagar (*la luz*); echar, expulsar, arrojar; producir; **to — out well** salir o resultar bien; **to — over** volcar(se), voltear(se); doblar; revolver (*en la mente*); entregar; **to — over and over** dar repetidas vueltas; **to — sour** agriarse, fermentarse; **to — the corner** doblar la esquina; **to — to** acudir a; volverse a; dirigirse a; convertir(se) en; **to — to the left** doblar o torcer a la izquierda; **to — up** aparecer; **to — up one's nose** at desdeñar; hacer ascos a; **to — up one's sleeves** arremangarse; **to — upside down** trastornar; volcar; **it -s my stomach** me da asco o náusea; *s.* vuelta, revolución; giro; recodo (*del camino*); turno; virada, cambio de rumbo; **— of mind** actitud mental; **at every —** a cada paso; **to be one's —** tocarle a uno; **to do one a good —** hacerle a uno un favor; **to take -s** turnarse.

tur·nip [tɝ̃nəp] *s.* nabo.

turn·o·ver [tɝ̃novə˞] *s.* vuelco (*de un coche*); cambio (*de empleados*); **business —** movimiento de mercancías, número de transacciones; **labor —** movimiento de obreros, cambio frecuente de trabajadores; **apple —** pastel de manzana; **— collar** cuello doblado.

turn·stile [tɝ̃nstaɪl] *s.* torniquete.

turn·ta·ble [tɝ̃ntebl] *s.* plato giratorio.

tur·pen·tine [tɝ̃pəntaɪn] *s.* trementina; aguarrás.

tur·pi·tude [tɝ̃pətjud] *s.* torpeza, vileza.

tur·quoise [tɝ̃kwɔɪz] *s.* turquesa.

tur·ret [tɝ̃ɪt] *s.* torrecilla; torre blindada; alminar.

tur·tle [tɝ̃tl] *s.* tortuga; **—dove** tórtola.

tusk [tʌsk] *s.* colmillo.

tu·tor [tútə˞] *s.* tutor, maestro particular; *v.* enseñar, instruir.

tux·e·do [tʌksído] *s.* esmoquin.

twang [twæŋ] *s.* tañido (*de una cuerda de guitarra*); nasalidad, tonillo gangoso; *v.* puntear, tañer (*una cuerda*); hablar con voz nasal, hablar con tonillo gangoso.

twang·y [twæŋɪ] *adj.* gangoso, nasal.

tweed [twid] *s.* mezclilla de lana; **— suit** traje de mezclilla.

tweez·ers [twízə˞z] *s. pl.* pinzas, tenacillas.

twice [twaɪs] *adv.* dos veces.

twig [twɪg] *s.* ramita; varita.

twi·light [twáɪlaɪt] *s.* crepúsculo; **at —** entre dos luces; *adj.* crepuscular.

twin [twɪn] *adj.* & *s.* gemelo, mellizo, *Méx.* cuate.

twine [twaɪn] *s.* cuerda, cordel; *v.* enroscar(se), torcer(se), retorcer(se); entrelazar.

twinge [twɪndʒ] *s.* punzada (*dolor agudo*); *v.*

punzar.

twin·kle [twíŋkl] v. titilar, parpadear, pestañear; chispear; s. titilación; parpadeo; pestañeo; guiño, guiñada; **in the — of an eye** en un abrir y cerrar de ojos.

twirl [twɜ́l] v. girar; dar vueltas; s. giro, vuelta; molinete, floreo.

twist [twɪst] v. (turn) torcer(se); retorcer(se); (coil) enroscar(se); s. torsión, torcedura; torzal, cordoncillo (hecho de varias hebras torcidas); curva, recodo, vuelta; rosca (de pan); **mental —** sesgo de la mente, sesgo mental.

twitch [twɪtʃ] v. crisparse, contraerse, torcerse convulsivamente (un músculo); temblar (los párpados); dar un tirón; s. temblor, ligera, convulsión, contracción nerviosa; tirón.

twit·ter [twítə] v. gorjear (los pájaros); temblar; agitarse; s. gorjeo; agitación, estremecimiento nervioso.

two-faced [túfest] adj. de dos caras.

two-fist·ed [túfɪstəd] adj. vigoroso; de dos puños.

two·fold [túfold] adj. doble.

two-way [túwe] adj. de dos sentidos.

type [taɪp] s. tipo; v. escribir a máquina.

type·write [táɪpraɪt] v. escribir a máquina.

type·writ·er [táɪpraɪtə] s. máquina de escribir.

type·writ·ing [táɪpraɪtɪŋ] s. mecanografía; trabajo de mecanógrafo.

type·writ·ten [táɪprɪtn̩] adj. escrito a máquina.

ty·phoid [táɪfɔɪd] s. tifoidea, fiebre tifoidea.

ty·phus [táɪfəs] s. tifo.

typ·i·cal [típɪkl] adj. típico.

typ·ist [táɪpɪst] s. mecanógrafo; mecanógrafa.

typ·o·graph·i·cal [taɪpográfɪkl] adj. tipográfico; **— error** error de máquina.

ty·ran·ni·cal [tɪrǽnɪkl] adj. tiránico, tirano.

tyr·an·ny [tírəni] s. tiranía.

ty·rant [táɪrənt] s. tirano.

U:u

u·big·ui·tous [jubíkwɪtəs] adj. ubicuo.

ud·der [Ʌ́də] s. ubre.

ug·li·ness [Ʌ́glɪnɪs] s. fealdad; fiereza.

ug·ly [Ʌ́glɪ] adj. feo; fiero; repugnante; de mal genio; desagradable.

ul·cer [Ʌ́lsə] s. úlcera.

ul·te·ri·or [Ʌltírɪə] adj. ulterior.

ul·ti·mate [Ʌ́ltəmɪt] adj. último; final; fundamental; **-ly** adv. finalmente, a la larga.

ul·tra·mod·ern [Ʌltrəmádə̩n] adj. ultramoderno.

ul·tra·vi·o·let [Ʌltrəvaɪəlɛt] adj. ultravioleta.

um·bil·i·cal cord [ʌmbíləklkord] s. cordón umbilical.

um·brel·la [Ʌmbrélə] s. paraguas; sombrilla.

um·pire [Ʌ́mpaɪr] s. árbitro, arbitrador; v. arbitrar.

un [Ʌn-] prefijo negativo equivalente a: sin, no, in-, des-.

un·a·ble [Ʌnébl] adj. incapaz, inhábil; **to be —, to come** no poder venir.

un·ac·cent·ed [Ʌnǽksɛntəd] adj. inacentuado.

un·ac·cus·tomed [Ʌnəkʌ́stəmd] adj. desacostumbrado; insólito, inusitado.

un·af·fect·ed [Ʌnəfɛ́ktɪd] adj. inafectado, sin afectación, natural, sincero.

un·al·ter·a·ble [Ʌnɔ́ltərəbl] adj. inalterable.

u·na·nim·i·ty [junənímətɪ] s. unanimidad.

u·nan·i·mous [jʊnǽnəməs] adj. unánime.

un·armed [Ʌnármd] adj. desarmado.

un·at·tached [Ʌnətǽtʃt] adj. suelto; libre; (law) no embargado.

un·a·void·a·ble [Ʌnəvɔ́ɪdəbl] adj. inevitable, ineludible; forzoso.

un·a·ware [Ʌnəwɛ́r] adj. desprevenido; inadvertido; ignorante; incauto; **-s** adv. inesperadamente, inopinadamente; impensadamente.

un·bal·anced [Ʌnbǽlənst] adj. desequilibrado; **— account** cuenta no saldada.

un·bear·a·ble [Ʌnbɛ́rəbl] adj. inaguantable, insoportable.

un·be·com·ing [Ʌnbɪkʌ́mɪŋ] adj. impropio; **an — dress** un vestido que no siente bien o que cae mal.

un·be·lief [Ʌnbəlíf] s. incredulidad.

un·be·liev·a·ble [Ʌnbəlívəbl] adj. increible.

un·be·liev·er [Ʌnbəlívə] s. descreído, incrédulo.

un·be·liev·ing [Ʌnbəlívɪŋ] adj. descreído, incrédulo.

un·bend·ing [Ʌnbɛ́ndɪŋ] adj. inflexible.

un·bi·ased [Ʌnbáɪəst] adj. imparcial, libre de prejuicio.

un·bos·om [Ʌnbúzəm] v. revelar, confesar, descubrir (secretos); **to — oneself** desahogarse con alguien, revelarle sus más íntimos secretos.

un·bound [Ʌnbáund] adj. desencuadernado, no encuadernado; suelto, desatado.

un·bro·ken [Ʌnbrókən] adj. intacto, entero; indómito; ininterrumpido, continuo.

un·but·ton [Ʌnbʌ́tn̩] v. desabotonar, desabrochar.

un·can·ny [Ʌnkǽnɪ] adj. extraño, raro, misterioso.

un·ceas·ing [Ʌnsísɪŋ] adj. incesante.

un·cer·tain [Ʌnsɜ́tn̩] adj. incierto; dudoso; indeciso.

un·cer·tain·ty [Ʌnsɜ́ɪntɪ] s. incertidumbre; falta de certeza.

un·change·a·ble [Ʌntʃéndʒəbl] adj. inmutable, inalterable, invariable.

un·changed [Ʌntʃéndʒd] adj. inalterado, igual.

un·char·i·ta·ble [Ʌntʃǽrətəbl] adj. duro falto de caridad.

un·cle [Ʌ́ŋkl] s. tío.

un·clean [Ʌnklín] adj. inmundo, sucio; impuro.

un·com·fort·a·ble [Ʌnkʌ́mfətəbl] adj. incómodo; molesto.

un·com·mon [Ʌnkámən] adj. poco común, insólito, raro.

un·com·pro·mis·ing [Ʌnkámprəmaɪzɪŋ] adj. intransigente; inflexible.

un·con·cern [Ʌnkənsɜ́n] s. indiferencia.

un·con·di·tion·al [Ʌnkəndíʃənl] adj. incondicional, absoluto.

un·con·ge·ni·al [Ʌnkəndʒínjəl] adj. que no congenia, incompatible.

un·con·quer·a·ble [Ʌnkáŋkərəbl] adj. invencible, inconquistable.

un·con·quered [Ʌnkáŋkəd] adj. no conquistado, no vencido.

un·con·scious [Ʌnkánʃəs] adj. inconsciente; privado.

un·con·scious·ness [Ʌnkánʃəsnɪs] s. inconsciencia; insensibilidad.

un·con·sti·tu·tion·al [Ʌnkánstɪtuʃənl] adj. inconstitucional.

un·con·trol·la·ble [Ʌnkəntróləbl] adj. irrefrenable, ingobernable.

un·con·ven·tion·al [Ʌnkənvénʃənl] adj. despreocupado, libre de trabas o reglas.

un·coup·le [Ʌnkʌ́pl] v. desacoplar.

un·couth [Ʌnkúθ] adj. rudo, tosco, inculto, grosero; desmañado.

un·cov·er [ʌnkʌ́vɚ] v. descubrir(se); revelar; destapar(se); desabrigar(se).

unc·tion [ʌ́ŋkʃən] s. unción; fervor; **Extreme Unction** Extremaunción.

unc·tu·ous [ʌ́ŋkʃəs] adj. untuoso.

un·cul·ti·vat·ed [ʌnkʌ́ltəvetɪd] adj. inculto; baldío.

un·cul·tured [ʌnkʌ́ltʃɚd] adj. inculto; grosero.

un·daunt·ed [ʌndɔ́ntəd] adj. impávido.

un·de·cid·ed [ʌndɪsáɪdɪd] adj. indeciso.

un·de·ni·a·ble [ʌndɪnáɪəbl] adj. innegable.

un·der [ʌ́ndɚ] prep. (beneath) bajo; debajo de; (less) menos de; — **age** menor de edad; — **cover** a cubierto; — **the cover of** al abrigo de, al amparo de; — **pretense of** so pretexto de; — **twelve** menos de doce; **to be** — **obligation to** deber favores a; adv. debajo; abajo; menos; adj. inferior, de abajo (en ciertas combinaciones); — **dose** dosis escasa o corta; — **secretary** subsecretario; — **side** lado de abajo, lado inferior; **the** — **dogs** los de abajo.

un·der·brush [ʌ́ndɚbrʌʃ] s. maleza.

un·der·clothes [ʌ́ndɚkloz] s. pl. ropa interior.

un·der·de·vel·oped [ʌndɚdɪvéləpt] adj. subdesarrollado.

un·der·dog [ʌ́ndɚdɔg] s. perdidoso, víctima.

un·der·es·ti·mate [ʌ́ndɚéstəmet] v. menospreciar, apreciar en menos de lo justo; salir corto en un cálculo.

un·der·fed [ʌ́ndɚféd] adj. malnutrido.

un·der·go [ʌndɚgó] v. sufrir, aguantar, padecer.

un·der·gone [ʌndɚgón] p.p. de to **undergo**.

un·der·grad·u·ate [ʌndɚgrǽdʒuɪt] s. estudiante del bachillerato; — **course** cursos o asignaturas para el bachillerato.

un·der·ground [ʌ́ndɚgraʊnd] adj. subterráneo; s. subterráneo; adv. bajo tierra; en secreto; ocultamente.

un·der·hand·ed [ʌ́ndɚhǽndɪd] adj. socarrón, secreto, disimulado, clandestino.

un·der·line [ʌ́ndɚlaɪn] v. subrayar.

un·der·ly·ing [ʌndɚláɪɪŋ] adj. fundamental.

un·der·mine [ʌndɚmáɪn] v. minar, socavar.

un·der·neath [ʌndɚníθ] prep. bajo, debajo de; adv. debajo.

un·der·pay [ʌ́ndɚpé] v. malpagar; escatimar la paga.

un·der·pin·ning [ʌ́ndɚpɪnɪŋ] s. apuntalamiento.

un·der·score [ʌ́ndɚskor] v. subrayar.

un·der·sell [ʌ́ndɚsél] v. malbaratar; vender a menos precio que.

un·der·shirt [ʌ́ndɚʃɝt] s. camiseta.

un·der·signed [ʌ́ndɚsáɪnd] s. firmante, infrascrito; **the** — el infrascrito, los infrascritos; el que suscribe.

un·der·sized [ʌ́ndɚsáɪzd] adj. achaparrado, de tamaño inferior al normal.

un·der·skirt [ʌ́ndɚskɝt] s. enaguas, refajo.

un·der·staffed [ʌndɚstǽft] adj. de personal insuficiente.

un·der·stand [ʌndɚstǽnd] v. entender; comprender; sobrentender.

un·der·stand·a·ble [ʌndɚstǽndəbl] adj. comprensible.

un·der·stand·ing [ʌndɚstǽndɪŋ] s. comprensión; entendimiento, inteligencia; acuerdo; adj. comprensivo.

un·der·stood [ʌndɚstúd] pret. & p.p. de to **understand**; adj. entendido; convenido; sobrentendido.

un·der·stud·y [ʌ́ndɚstʌdɪ] s. sobresaliente, actor suplente; v. servir de sobresaliente o actor suplente.

un·der·take [ʌndɚték] v. emprender; tratar de, intentar; comprometerse a.

un·der·tak·en [ʌndɚtékən] p.p. de to **undertake**.

un·der·tak·er [ʌ́ndɚtekɚ] s. director de funeraria; embalsamador.

un·der·tak·ing [ʌndɚtékɪŋ] s. empresa.

un·der·took [ʌndɚtúk] pret. de to **undertake**.

un·der·tow [ʌ́ndɚto] s. resaca.

un·der·wa·ter [ʌ́ndɚwɔtɚ] adj. submarino; subacuático.

un·der·wear [ʌ́ndɚwɛr] s. ropa interior.

un·der·went [ʌ́ndɚwént] pret. de to **undergo**.

un·der·world [ʌ́ndɚwɝld] s. hampa, bajos fondos de la sociedad; clase criminal; — jargon caló.

un·der·write [ʌ́ndɚraɪt] v. asegurar; subscribir.

un·de·sir·a·ble [ʌndɪzáɪrəbl] adj. indeseable; inconveniente.

un·did [ʌndíd] pret. de to **undo**.

un·dis·turbed [ʌndɪstɝ́bd] adj. impasible; sereno, tranquilo; intacto.

un·do [ʌndú] v. deshacer; desatar; desabrochar; desenredar; anular; **to** — **one's hair** soltarse el cabello.

un·do·ing [ʌndúɪŋ] s. destrucción; pérdida.

un·done [ʌndʌ́n] p.p. de to **undo**; inacabado, sin hacer; sin terminar; **it is still** — está todavía por hacer, está inacabado; **to come** — desatarse.

un·doubt·ed·ly [ʌndáʊtɪdlɪ] adv. indudablemente, sin duda.

un·dress [ʌndrés] v. desnudar(se), desvestir(se).

un·due [ʌndjú] adj. indebido; impropio; excesivo.

un·du·late [ʌ́ndjəlet] v. ondular, ondear.

un·du·ly [ʌndjúlɪ] adv. indebidamente.

un·dy·ing [ʌndáɪɪŋ] adj. imperecedero, eterno.

un·earth [ʌnɝ́θ] v. desenterrar.

un·eas·i·ly [ʌnízlɪ] adv. intranquilamente, inquietamente, con inquietud; incómodamente.

un·eas·i·ness [ʌnízɪnɪs] s. malestar, inquietud, intranquilidad, desasosiego.

un·eas·y [ʌnízɪ] adj. ansioso, inquieto, intranquilo; cohibido; incómodo.

un·ed·u·cat·ed [ʌnédʒəketɪd] adj. inculto, indocto, falto de instrucción, ignorante.

un·em·ployed [ʌnɪmplɔ́ɪd] adj. desocupado, desempleado, cesante; ocioso; — **funds** fondos no invertidos o inactivos.

un·em·ploy·ment [ʌnɪmplɔ́ɪmənt] s. desempleo, cesantía, falta de empleo, desocupación.

un·end·ing [ʌnéndɪŋ] adj. inacabable, interminable.

un·e·qual [ʌníkwəl] adj. desigual; insuficiente, ineficaz.

un·e·quiv·o·cal [ʌnɪkwívəkl] adj. inequívoco.

un·err·ing [ʌnérɪŋ] adj. infalible.

un·es·sen·tial [ʌnɪsénʃl] adj. no esencial.

un·e·ven [ʌnívən] adj. desigual, desparejo; irregular, accidentado; — **numbers** números impares o nones.

un·e·ven·ness [ʌnívənnɪs] s. desigualdad; desnivel; irregularidad, escabrosidad (del terreno).

un·e·vent·ful [ʌnɪvéntfl] adj. sin novedad.

un·ex·pect·ed [ʌnɪkspéktɪd] adj. inesperado; -ly adv. de improviso, inesperadamente.

un·ex·pres·sive [ʌnɪksprésɪv] adj. sin emoción.

un·fail·ing [ʌnfélɪŋ] adj. que nunca falta, constante, indefectible; infalible.

un·fair [ʌnfér] adj. injusto; tramposo; **to act -ly** obrar de mala fe.

un·faith·ful [ʌnféθfʊl] adj. infiel; desleal.

un·fa·mil·iar [ʌnfəmɪljɚ] adj. poco familiar; desconocido; **to be** — **with** no tener conocimiento de; no estar al tanto de, ignorar; no conocer bien.

un·fas·ten [ʌnfǽsn̩] *v.* desabrochar; desatar; aflojar.

un·fa·vor·a·ble [ʌnfévrəbl̩] *adj.* desfavorable, contrario, adverso.

un·feel·ing [ʌnfílɪŋ] *adj.* insensible; incompasivo.

un·fin·ished [ʌnfínɪʃt] *adj.* inacabado, inconcluso; sin terminar, sin acabar; sin barnizar, sin pulir.

un·fit [ʌnfít] *adj.* incompetente, inepto, incapaz; inservible; impropio; *v.* incapacitar.

un·fold [ʌnfóld] *v.* desenvolver(se), desarrollar(se); desdoblar; revelar.

un·fore·seen [ʌnforsín] *adj.* imprevisto.

un·for·get·ta·ble [ʌnfəgétəbl̩] *adj.* inolvidable.

un·for·tu·nate [ʌnfɔ́rtʃənɪt] *adj.* desventurado, infeliz, desgraciado, desdichado; **-ly** *adv.* desgraciadamente, por desgracia.

un·found·ed [ʌnfáʊndəd] *adj.* infundado.

un·fre·quent·ed [ʌnfríkwəntəd] *adj.* poco frecuentado.

un·friend·ly [ʌnfréndlɪ] *adj.* hostil, enemigo; poco amistoso; *adv.* hostilmente.

un·fruit·ful [ʌnfrútfl̩] *adj.* infructuoso.

un·furl [ʌnfɝ́l] *v.* desplegar.

un·fur·nished [ʌnfɝ́nɪʃt] *adj.* desamueblado.

un·gain·ly [ʌngénlɪ] *adj.* desgarbado, torpe.

un·grate·ful [ʌngrétfəl] *adj.* ingrato, desagradecido.

un·guard·ed [ʌngárdəd] *adj.* desprevenido; descuidado.

un·hap·py [ʌnhǽpɪ] *adj.* infeliz; desgraciado, desventurado, desdichado.

un·harmed [ʌnhármd] *adj.* sin daño, ileso.

un·health·y [ʌnhélθɪ] *adj.* malsano; insalubre; enfermizo.

un·heard-of [ʌnhɝ́dav] *adj.* inaudito; desconocido.

un·hinge [ʌnhíndʒ] *v.* desquiciar.

un·hitch [ʌnhítʃ] *v.* desenganchar; desatar; desacoplar.

un·ho·ly [ʌnhólɪ] *adj.* impío, malo.

un·hook [ʌnhúk] *v.* desenganchar; desabrochar.

un·hurt [ʌnhɝ́t] *adj.* ileso.

u·ni·form [júnəfɔrm] *adj. & s.* uniforme.

u·ni·for·mi·ty [junəfɔ́rmətɪ] *s.* uniformidad.

u·ni·fy [júnəfaɪ] *v.* unificar, unir.

u·ni·lat·er·al [junɪlǽtəˌl] *adj.* unilateral.

un·im·port·ant [ʌnɪmpórtn̩t] *adj.* insignificante, poco importante.

un·im·prov·a·ble [ʌnɪmprúvəbl̩] *adj.* inmejorable.

un·in·hib·i·ted [ʌnɪnhíbətəd] *adj.* sin inhibición.

un·ion [júnjən] *s.* unión; **labor — sindicato; — leader** jefe de un gremio obrero; **trade-union** gremio obrero; **— shop** obreros sindicados o agremiados; *adj.* gremial.

u·nique [juník] *adj.* único, singular; señero.

u·ni·son [júnəzn̩]: **in —** al unísono (*en el mismo tono*); **al compás.**

u·nit [júnɪt] *s.* unidad.

u·nite [junáɪt] *v.* unir(se).

u·ni·ty [júnətɪ] *s.* unidad; unión.

u·ni·ver·sal [junəvɝ́sl̩] *adj.* universal; **— joint** cruceta.

u·ni·verse [júnəvɝs] *s.* universo.

u·ni·ver·si·ty [junəvɝ́sətɪ] *s.* universidad.

un·just [ʌndʒʌ́st] *adj.* injusto.

un·just·i·fi·a·ble [ʌndʒʌ́stəfaɪəbl̩] *adj.* injustificable, injustificado.

un·kempt [ʌnkémpt] *adj.* desaseado, desaliñado; desgreñado.

un·kind [ʌnkáɪnd] *adj.* falto de bondad; descortés; cruel.

un·known [ʌnnón] *adj.* desconocido; no sabido;

ignoto; **— quality** incógnita; **it is —** se ignora, no se sabe, se desconoce.

un·law·ful [ʌnlɔ́fəl] *adj.* ilegal, ilícito.

un·leash [ʌnlíʃ] *v.* soltar.

un·less [ʌnlés] *conj.* a menos que, a no ser que.

un·li·censed [ʌnláɪsənzd] *adj.* sin autorización.

un·like [ʌnláɪk] *adj.* desemejante, distinto, diferente; *prep.* a diferencia de.

un·like·ly [ʌnláɪklɪ] *adj.* improbable, inverosímil.

un·lim·it·ed [ʌnlímɪtɪd] *adj.* ilimitado.

un·load [ʌnlód] *v.* descargar; vaciar; deshacerse de (*acciones, mercancías*).

un·lock [ʌnlák] *v.* abrir (*con llave*); soltar, destrabar; revelar, penetrar (*secretos*).

un·loose [ʌnlús] *v.* soltar.

un·luck·y [ʌnlʌ́kɪ] *adj.* (*unfortunate*) desdichado, desventurado, desgraciado, desafortunado; (*of bad omen*) aciago, de mal agüero, funesto; **an — number** un número de mala suerte.

un·man·age·a·ble [ʌnmǽnɪdʒəbl̩] *adj.* inmanejable, ingobernable, intratable, indomable.

un·manned [ʌnmǽnd] *adj.* desguarnecido; sin tripulación.

un·marked [ʌnmárkt] *adj.* sin identificación.

un·mar·ried [ʌnmǽrɪd] *adj.* soltero.

un·mask [ʌnmǽsk] *v.* desenvascar(se).

un·mer·ci·ful [ʌnmɝ́sɪfəl] *adj.* despiadado, inclemente.

un·mis·tak·a·ble [ʌnməstékəbl̩] *adj.* inequívoco, claro, inconfundible.

un·moved [ʌnmúvd] *adj.* fijo; inmutable, impasible; indiferente.

un·nat·u·ral [ʌnnǽtʃərəl] *adj.* afectado, artificial; anormal; **an — mother** una madre desnaturalizada.

un·nec·es·sar·y [ʌnnésəsɛrɪ] *adj.* innecesario.

un·not·iced [ʌnnótɪst] *adj.* inadvertido.

un·o·blig·ing [ʌnəbláɪdʒɪŋ] *adj.* poco complaciente, descortés, descomedido.

un·ob·served [ʌnəbzɝ́vd] *adj.* inadvertido; sin ser visto.

un·ob·tain·a·ble [ʌnəbténəbl̩] *adj.* inobtenible, inasequible, inaccesible.

un·ob·tru·sive [ʌnəbtrusɪv] *adj.* discreto; sin ser visto.

un·oc·cu·pied [ʌnákjəpaɪd] *adj.* desocupado; vacío; desalquilado.

un·of·fi·cial [ʌnəfíʃl] *adj.* extraoficial.

un·or·gan·ized [ʌnɔ́rgənaɪzd] *adj.* sin organización; inorganizado.

un·o·rig·i·nal [ʌnərídʒənl] *adj.* trivial; ordinario.

un·or·tho·dox [ʌnɔ́rθədaks] *adj.* heterodoxo.

un·pack [ʌnpǽk] *v.* desempacar; desembalar.

un·paid [ʌnpéd] *adj.* no pagado; sin pagar; **— bills** cuentas por pagar.

un·pleas·ant [ʌnpléznt] *adj.* desagradable.

un·pleas·ant·ness [ʌnplézntnɪs] *s.* manera desagradable; desazón; desavenencia; **the — of a situation** lo desagradable de una situación; **to have an — with** tener una desavenencia con.

un·prec·e·dent·ed [ʌnprésədɛntɪd] *adj.* sin precedente; inaudito.

un·pre·med·i·tat·ed [ʌnprimédətetəd] *adj.* impremeditado.

un·pre·pared [ʌnprɪpérd] *adj.* desprevenido; no preparado; no listo.

un·pre·ten·tious [ʌnpriténʃəs] *adj.* modesto; sin pretenciones.

un·print·a·ble [ʌnpríntəbl̩] *adj.* que no puede imprimirse.

un·pro·duc·tive [ʌnprədʌ́ktɪv] *adj.* improductivo.

un·pro·fes·sion·al [ʌnprəféʃənl] *adj.* no profesional.
un·prof·it·a·ble [ʌnpráfɪtəbl] *adj.* infructuoso.
un·pub·lished [ʌnpʌ́blɪʃt] *adj.* inédito, no publicado.
un·qual·i·fied [ʌnkwáləfaɪd] *adj.* incompetente; inepto.
un·quench·a·ble [ʌnkwéntʃəbl] *adj.* inapagable, inextinguible.
un·ques·tion·a·ble [ʌnkwéstʃənəbl] *adj.* indisputable, indudable; irreprochable.
un·rav·el [ʌnrǽvl] *v.* desenredar; desenmarañar; deshilachar(se); deshilar.
un·real [ʌnríəl] *adj.* irreal; ilusorio, imaginario.
un·rea·son·a·ble [ʌnrízənəbl] *adj.* desrazonable, fuera de razón; irracional.
un·rec·og·niz·a·ble [ʌnrékəgnaɪzəbl] *adj.* irreconocible, no conocible, incapaz de reconocerse; desconocido.
un·re·fined [ʌnrɪfáɪnd] *adj.* no refinado; inculto, grosero.
un·re·li·a·ble [ʌnrɪlaiəbl] *adj.* informal; indigno de confianza.
un·rest [ʌnrést] *s.* inquietud, desasosiego.
un·roll [ʌnról] *v.* desenrollar(se), desenvolver(se).
un·ru·ly [ʌnrúlɪ] *adj.* indómito; indócil; desobediente.
un·safe [ʌnséf] *adj.* inseguro, peligroso.
un·sal·a·ble [ʌnséləbl] *adj.* invendible.
un·sat·is·fac·to·ry [ʌnsætɪsfǽktrɪ] *adj.* no satisfactorio, inaceptable.
un·scru·pu·lous [ʌnskrúpjʊləs] *adj.* poco escrupuloso.
un·sea·son·a·ble [ʌnsízənəbl] *adj.* intempestivo.
un·seat [ʌnsít] *v.* destituir.
un·seen [ʌnsín] *adj.* no visto, oculto; invisible.
un·self·ish [ʌnsélfɪʃ] *adj.* desinteresado.
un·self·ish·ness [ʌnsélfɪʃnɪs] *s.* desinterés, abnegación.
un·set·tled [ʌnsétld] *adj.* (*disturbed*) desordenado, en desorden; turbio; inestable; (*uncertain*) incierto; indeciso; (*unpopulated*) deshabitado; no establecido; — **bills** cuentas no liquidadas, cuentas pendientes; — **weather** tiempo variable; **an** — **liquid** un líquido revuelto o turbio.
un·shak·en [ʌnʃékən] *adj.* inmóvil, inmovible, firme.
un·sight·ly [ʌnsáɪtlɪ] *adj.* feo, desagradable a la vista.
un·skilled [ʌnskíld] *adj.* inexperto.
un·skill·ful [ʌnskílfəl] *adj.* inhábil, desmañado, inexperto.
un·so·cia·ble [ʌnsóʃəbl] *adj.* insociable, huraño, intratable, arisco.
un·so·phis·ti·cat·ed [ʌnsəfístəketəd] *adj.* cándido, sencillo.
un·sound [ʌnsáʊnd] *adj.* erróneo, falso.
un·speak·a·ble [ʌnspíkəbl] *adj.* indecible; inefable; atroz.
un·sta·ble [ʌnstébl] *adj.* inestable.
un·stead·y [ʌnstédɪ] *adj.* inseguro, inestable; movedizo; variable, inconstante.
un·suc·cess·ful [ʌnsəksésfəl] *adj.* sin éxito; desafortunado; **to be** — no tener éxito.
un·suit·a·ble [ʌnsútəbl] *adj.* impropio, inapropiado; inepto; inconveniente; incongruente; incompatible.
un·sus·pect·ed [ʌnsəspéktɪd] *adj.* insospechado.
un·ten·a·ble [ʌnténəbl] *adj.* insostenible.
un·think·a·ble [ʌnθíŋkəbl] *adj.* impensable.
un·ti·dy [ʌntáɪdɪ] *adj.* desaliñado, desaseado; desarreglado, en desorden.
un·tie [ʌntáɪ] *v.* desatar(se); desamarrar; deshacer

(un nudo o lazo).
un·til [ʌntíl] *prep.* hasta; *conj.* hasta que.
un·time·ly [ʌntáɪmlɪ] *adj.* inoportuno; prematuro; *adv.* inoportunamente; fuera de sazón; demasiado pronto.
un·tir·ing [ʌntáɪrɪŋ] *adj.* incansable.
un·told [ʌntóld] *adj.* indecible, innumerable, incalculable, inestimable.
un·touched [ʌntʌ́ʃt] *adj.* (*unscathed*) intacto, no tocado, integro; (*impassive*) impasible, no conmovido; **to leave** — no tocar, dejar intacto; dejar impasible, no conmover.
un·trained [ʌntrénd] *adj.* indisciplinado, falto de disciplina; sin educación; inexperto.
un·tried [ʌntráɪd] *adj.* no probado, no ensayado, no experimentado; — **law case** causa todavía no vista.
un·troub·led [ʌntrʌ́bld] *adj.* sosegado, tranquilo, quieto.
un·true [ʌntrú] *adj.* falso; infiel; desleal; mentiroso.
un·truth [ʌntrúθ] *s.* falsedad; mentira.
un·tu·tored [ʌntútəd] *adj.* sin instrucción; ingenuo.
un·twist [ʌntwíst] *v.* destorcer.
un·used [ʌnjúzd] *adj.* no usado; desacostumbrado; — **to** no hecho a, desacostumbrado a.
un·u·su·al [ʌnjúʒʊəl] *adj.* inusitado, insólito; desusado; raro, extraño; extraordinario.
un·var·nished [ʌnvárnɪʃt] *adj.* sin barnizar; sin adornos.
un·veil [ʌnvél] *v.* quitar el velo a; revelar, descubrir.
un·war·rant·ed [ʌnwɔ́rəntəd] *adj.* no justificado.
un·war·y [ʌnwérɪ] *adj.* incauto.
un·washed [ʌnwɔ́ʃt] *adj.* no lavado, sin lavar; sucio.
un·wel·come [ʌnwélkəm] *adj.* indeseable, no deseado; mal acogido, mal recibido, mal quisto.
un·whole·some [ʌnhólsəm] *adj.* malsano; insalubre, dañino.
un·wield·y [ʌnwíldɪ] *adj.* inmanejable, difícil de manejar, embarazoso, engorroso.
un·will·ing [ʌnwílɪŋ] *adj.* renuente, maldispuesto, reacio; **to be** — **to** no querer, no estar dispuesto a; **-ly** *adv.* de mala gana, sin querer.
un·will·ing·ness [ʌnwílɪŋnɪs] *s.* renuencia, falta de voluntad; mala gana.
un·wise [ʌnwáɪz] *adj.* imprudente, indiscreto; necio.
un·wont·ed [ʌnwʌ́ntəd] *adj.* inusitado, inacostumbrado; inédito.
un·wor·thy [ʌnwɔ́ðɪ] *adj.* indigno.
un·wrap [ʌnrǽp] *v.* desenvolver.
un·writ·ten [ʌnrítən] *adj.* no escrito.
up [ʌp] *adv.* (*above*) arriba, hacia arriba; en lo alto; (*standing*) de pie; *adj.* levantado, derecho, erecto; (*finished*) terminado, concluido; — **and down** de arriba abajo; de acá para allá; **-s and downs** altibajos; fluctuaciones, vaivenes; — **the river** río arriba; — **to now** hasta ahora; **his time is** — ha expirado su tiempo; se ha cumplido su plazo; **prices are** — los precios han subido; **that is** — **to you** queda a la discreción de Vd.; eso es cosa suya; **to be** — **against it** estar perplejo, no saber qué hacer; estar en un aprieto; **to be** — **on the news** estar al corriente (o al tanto) de las noticias; **to be** — **to one's old tricks** hacer de las suyas; **to eat it** — comérselo; **what's** — ? ¿qué pasa?; *v.* levantar, alzar.
up·braid [ʌpbréd] *v.* reprender, regañar.
up·date [ʌpdét] *v.* poner al día.
up·grade [ʌpgréd] *v.* adelantar; mejorar.

up·heav·al [ʌphívl] s. trastorno.
up·held [ʌphéld] pret. & p.p. de to uphold.
up·hill [ʌphíl] adv. cuesta arriba; adj. ascendente; trabajoso, arduo.
up·hold [ʌphóld] v. sostener; apoyar.
up·hol·ster [ʌphólstɚ] v. entapizar y rellenar (muebles).
up·hol·ster·y [ʌphólstrɪ] s. tapicería.
up·keep [ʌpkip] s. manutención.
up·land [ʌplənd] s. altiplanicie, tierra alta.
up·lift [ʌplíft] s. elevación; edificación (espiritual); [ʌplíft] v. elevar; edificar (espiritualmente).
up·on [əpán] prep. en, sobre, encima de; — arriving al llegar.
up·per [ʌpɚ] adj. superior; alto; — berth litera alta, cama alta (de un coche dormitorio); to have the — hand ejercer dominio o mando; llevar la ventaja; s. litera alta, cama alta; pala (parte superior del calzado).
up·right [ʌpraɪt] adj. recto; derecho; vertical; justo, honrado; — piano piano vertical; s. poste; puntal; piano vertical.
up·right·ness [ʌpraɪtnɪs] s. rectitud.
up·ris·ing [ʌpráɪzɪŋ] s. alzamiento, levantamiento; revuelta.
up·roar [ʌpror] s. tumulto, alboroto, bulla, gritería.
up·roar·i·ous [ʌprórɪəs] adj. estruendoso, bullicioso, tumultuoso.
up·root [ʌprút] v. desarraigar, arrancar de raíz.
up·set [ʌpsét] v. (capsize) volcar, tumbar; (distress) trastornar; perturbar, turbar; desquiciar; to become — volcarse; turbarse; trastornársele a uno el estómago; pret. & p.p. de to upset; adj. indispuesto, descompuesto; desarreglado, trastornado; [ʌpsɛt] s. vuelco; trastorno; desorden; indisposición.
up·shot [ʌpʃat] s. resultado, fin.
up·side [ʌpsaid] s. lado o parte superior; — down al revés; patas arriba; en desorden.
up·stage [ʌpstédʒ] v. quitarle la escena a uno.
up·stairs [ʌpstérz] adv. arriba, en el piso de arriba; adj. de arriba; s. piso (o pisos) de arriba.
up·start [ʌpstart] s. advenedizo, principiante presuntuoso.
up-to-date [ʌptədét] adj. moderno; al corriente, al tanto.
up·turn [ʌptɜ̇n] s. alza, subida (de precios); mejora.
up·ward [ʌpwɚd] adv. arriba, para arriba, hacia arriba; más; — of más de; adj. ascendente, hacia arriba, para arriba.
up·wards [ʌpwɚdz] adv. – upward.
u·ra·ni·um [juréniəm] s. uranio.
ur·ban [ɝ́bən] adj. urbano.
ur·chin [ɝ́tʃɪn] s. granuja, pilluelo; sea — erizo de mar.
u·re·thra [juríθrə] s. uretra.
urge [ɝdʒ] v. urgir, instar; exhortar; recomendar o solicitar con instancia; apremiar, incitar, estimular; s. impulso; gana, ganas; estímulo.
ur·gen·cy [ɝ́dʒənsɪ] s. urgencia; apremio.
ur·gent [ɝ́dʒənt] adj. urgente, apremiante.
u·ric [júrɪk] adj. úrico.
u·ri·nal [júrɪnl] s. urinario.
u·ri·nate [júrənet] v. orinar.
u·rine [júrɪn] s. orina, (los) orines.
urn [ɝn] s. urna; coffee — cafetera.
us [ʌs] pron. nos; nosotros (con preposición).
us·age [júsɪdʒ] s. usanza; uso; hard — uso constante.
use [jus] s. (application) uso; empleo; (goal) utilidad; it is of no — es inútil; no sirve; out of

— desusado, ya no usado; pasado de moda; to have no further — for ya no necesitar, ya no tener necesidad de; what is the — of it? ¿para qué sirve?; ¿qué ventaja tiene?; ¿qué objeto tiene?; [juz] v. usar; emplear; servirse de, hacer uso de; acostumbrar, soler, Am. saber; — your judgment haz lo que te parezca; to — up gastar, agotar; consumir; to be -d to estar hecho, acostumbrado o habituado a; he -d to do it solía hacerlo, lo hacía.
use·ful [júsfəl] adj. útil.
use·ful·ness [júsfəlnɪs] s. utilidad.
use·less [júslɪs] adj. inútil; inservible.
use·less·ness [júslɪsnɪs] s. inutilidad.
ush·er [ʌʃɚ] s. acomodador (en un teatro o iglesia); ujier; v. conducir, llevar, acompañar; introducir.
u·su·al [júʒuəl] adj. usual; corriente, común, general; -ly adv. usualmente, usualmente, por lo general.
u·su·rer [júʒɚɚ] s. usurero.
u·surp [juzɝ́p] v. usurpar.
u·su·ry [júʒɚɪ] s. usura.
u·ten·sil [juténsl] s. utensilio.
u·ter·us [jútərəs] s. útero.
u·til·i·tar·i·an [jutɪlətérɪən] adj. utilitario.
u·til·i·ty [jutíloti] s. utilidad; servicio.
u·til·ize [jútlaɪz] v. utilizar; aprovechar.
ut·most [ʌtmost] adj. (extreme) sumo, extremo; más distante; más grande, mayor; más alto; (last) último; he did his — hizo cuanto pudo; to the — hasta más no poder.
u·to·pi·a [jutópjə] s. utopía.
ut·ter [ʌtɚ] v. proferir; decir, expresar; to — a cry dar un grito; adj. completo, total; absoluto.
ut·ter·ance [ʌtɚəns] s. declaración; expresión; modo de hablar.
ut·ter·most [ʌtɚmost] = utmost.
u·vu·la [júvjələ] s. campanilla, galillo de la garganta; úvula.
u·vu·lar [júvjUlɚ] adj. uvular.

V:v

va·can·cy [vékənsɪ] s. vacante, empleo vacante; vacío; habitación o apartamento desocupado.
va·cant [vékənt] adj. vacante; vacío; desocupado; libre.
va·cate [véket] v. desocupar, dejar vacío; dejar vacante.
va·ca·tion [vekéʃən] s. vacación; vacaciones.
vac·ci·nate [væksn̩et] v. vacunar.
vac·ci·na·tion [væksnéʃən] s. vacunación.
vac·cine [væksin] s. vacuna.
vac·il·late [væslet] v. vacilar.
vac·u·um [vækjuəm] s. vacío; — cleaner escoba eléctrica.
vag·a·bond [vægəbɑnd] adj. & s. vagabundo.
va·gi·na [vədʒaɪnə] s. vagina.
va·gran·cy [végrənsɪ] s. vagancia.
va·grant [végrənt] adj. vago, vagabundo, errante; s. vago, vagabundo.
vague [veg] adj. vago.
vain [ven] adj. vano; vanidoso; in — en vano.
vain·glor·y [venglórɪ] s. vanagloria.
vale [vel] s. valle; cañada.
val·en·tine [vǽləntaɪn] s. tarjeta o regalo del día de San Valentín (el día de los enamorados); to my — a mi querido, a mi querida.

UN

478

val·et [vǽlɪt] s. criado, camarero; planchador de trajes.
val·iant [vǽljənt] adj. valiente, valeroso.
val·id [vǽlɪd] adj. válido; valedero.
va·lid·i·ty [vəlídətɪ] s. validez.
va·lise [vəlís] s. valija, maleta, Méx. velís, Méx. petaca.
val·ley [vǽlɪ] s. valle.
val·or [vǽlə] s. valor, ánimo, valentía.
val·or·ous [vǽlərəs] adj. valeroso, valiente.
val·u·a·ble [vǽljəbl] adj. valioso; precioso; preciado; -s s. pl. objetos de valor, hoyas, alhajas.
val·u·a·tion [væljʊéʃən] s. valuación, valoración; avalúo; tasa.
val·ue [vǽljʊ] s. (price) valor; precio; (merit) mérito; (consideration) estimación, aprecio; v. valorar, avaluar, valuar; apreciar, estimar.
val·ue·less [vǽljʊlɪs] adj. sin valor.
valve [vælv] s. válvula; valva (de los moluscos); safety — válvula de seguridad.
vam·pire [vǽmpaɪr] s. vampiro.
van [væn] s. camión (para transportar muebles); —guard vanguardia.
va·na·di·um [vənédiəm] s. vanadio.
van·dal [vǽndl] s. vándalo.
vane [ven] s. veleta; aspa (de molino de viento); paleta (de hélice).
van·guard [vǽngɑrd] s. vanguardia.
va·nil·la [vənílə] s. vainilla.
van·ish [vǽnɪʃ] v. desvanecerse, desaparecer(se).
van·i·ty [vǽnətɪ] s. vanidad; — case neceser; — table tocador.
van·quish [vǽnkwɪʃ] v. vencer.
van·tage [vǽntɪdʒ] s. ventaja; point of — lugar estratégico.
va·por [vépə] s. vapor; vaho.
va·por·ize [vépəaɪz] v. vaporizar.
var·i·a·ble [vérɪəbl] adj. & s. variable.
var·i·ance [vérɪəns] s. variación, cambio; desavenencia; to be at — estar desavenidos; no estar de acuerdo.
var·i·ant [vérɪənt] s. variante.
var·i·a·tion [verɪéʃən] s. variación; variedad.
var·ied [vérɪd] adj. variado, vario.
var·i·e·gat·ed [vérɪgetɪd] adj. abigarrado.
va·ri·e·ty [vəráɪətɪ] s. variedad.
var·i·ous [vérɪəs] adj. varios; diferentes, distintos.
var·nish [vɑrnɪʃ] s. barniz; v. barnizar.
var·y [vérɪ] v. variar; cambiar.
vase [ves] s. vaso, jarrón.
Vas·e·line [vǽsəlin] s. vaselina.
vas·sal [vǽsl] adj. & s. vasallo.
vast [væst] adj. vasto; inmenso; anchuroso; -ly adv. vastamente, sumamente, muy.
vast·ness [vǽstnɪs] s. inmensidad.
vat [væt] s. tina, tanque.
vaude·ville [vódəvɪl] s. vodevil, función de variedades.
vault [vɔlt] s. bóveda; tumba; bank — caja fuerte; depósito; pole — salto con garrocha; v. abovedar, edificar una bóveda; dar figura de bóveda; saltar con garrocha; saltar por encima de.
vaunt [vɔnt] v. jactarse; ostentar, alardear; s. jactancia.
veal [vil] s. carne de ternera; — cutlet chuleta de ternera.
veer [vɪr] v. virar; s. virada.
veg·e·ta·ble [védʒtəbl] s. (plant) vegetal, planta; (food) legumbre; -s hortaliza, legumbres; green

-s verduras; adj. vegetal; de legumbres, de hortaliza; — garden hortaliza.
veg·e·tar·i·an [vɛdʒətérɪən] s. vegetariano.
veg·e·tate [védʒətet] v. vegetar.
veg·e·ta·tion [vɛdʒətéʃən] s. vegetación.
ve·he·mence [víəməns] s. vehemencia.
ve·he·ment [víəmənt] adj. vehemente.
ve·hi·cle [víɪkl] s. vehículo.
veil [vel] s. velo; v. velar; tapar, encubrir.
vein [ven] s. vena; veta, filón.
veined [vend] adj. veteado, jaspeado; venoso.
ve·loc·i·ty [vəlásətɪ] s. velocidad.
vel·vet [vélvɪt] s. terciopelo; velludo; adj. de terciopelo; aterciopelado.
vel·vet·y [vélvɪtɪ] adj. aterciopelado.
ven·dor [véndə] s. vendedor; buhonero, vendedor ambulante.
ve·neer [vənír] s. chapa; v. chapar o chapear, Am. enchapar.
ven·er·a·ble [vénərəbl] adj. venerable; venerando.
ven·er·ate [vénəret] v. venerar.
ven·er·a·tion [venəréʃən] s. veneración.
ve·ne·re·al [vənírɪəl] adj. venéreo.
Ven·e·zue·lan [venəzwilən] adj. & s. venezolano.
ven·geance [véndʒəns] s. venganza; with a — con furia; con violencia.
ven·i·son [vénəzṇ] s. venado, carne de venado.
ven·om [vénəm] s. veneno, ponzoña.
ven·om·ous [vénəməs] adj. venenoso, ponzoñoso.
vent [vɛnt] s. (opening) abertura; (escape) escape; (utterance) desahogo; fogón (de arma de fuego); to give — to anger desahogar la ira, dar desahogo a la cólera; v. dar salida o desahogo; desahogar, descargar.
ven·ti·late [véntlet] v. ventilar.
ven·ti·la·tion [ventléʃən] s. ventilación.
ven·ti·la·tor [véntletə] s. ventilador.
ven·ture [véntʃə] s. ventura, riesgo; business — especulación; empresa o negocio arriesgado; v. aventurar, arriesgar; to — outside aventurarse a salir; to — to aventurarse a, atreverse a, osar.
ven·tur·ous [véntʃərəs] adj. aventurado.
ve·ran·da [vərǽndə] s. galería; terraza; balcón corrido.
verb [vɝb] s. verbo.
ver·bal [vɝbl] adj. verbal; oral.
ver·bal·ize [vɝbəlaɪz] v. expresar por medio de palabras.
ver·bose [vəbós] adj. verboso; palabrero.
ver·dict [vɝdɪkt] s. veredicto; fallo, decisión, sentencia; — of "not guilty" veredicto de inculpabilidad.
ver·dure [vɝdʒə] s. verdura, verdor, verde.
verge [vɝdʒ] s. borde, margen, orilla; on the — of al borde de; a punto de; v. to — on rayar en, estar al margen de; to — toward tender a, inclinarse a.
ver·i·fy [vérəfaɪ] v. verificar; comprobar.
ver·i·ly [vérəlɪ] adv. en verdad.
ver·i·ta·ble [vérətəbl] adj. verdadero.
ver·mil·lion [vəmíljən] adj. bermejo.
ver·nac·u·lar [vənǽkjʊlə] adj. vernáculo; s. idioma corriente.
ver·sa·tile [vɝsətl] adj. hábil para muchas cosas; flexible; versátil.
verse [vɝs] s. verso.
versed [vɝst] adj. versado, experto, perito.
ver·sion [vɝʒən] s. versión.
ver·te·brate [vɝtəbrɪt] adj. vertebrado.
ver·ti·cal [vɝtɪkl] adj. vertical.
ver·y [vérɪ] adv. muy; — much muchísimo; —

many muchísimos; **it is — cold today** hace
mucho frío hoy; *adj.* mismo; mismísimo; mero;
the — man el mismísimo hombre; **the — thought
of** la mera idea de.

ves·pers [véspɚz] *s. pl.* vísperas.

ves·sel [vésl] *s.* vasija; vaso; barco, embarcación;
blood — vaso, vena, arteria.

vest [vɛst] *s.* chaleco; *v.* conferir; **to — with
power** revestir de autoridad, conferir poder a.

ves·ti·bule [véstəbjul] *s.* vestíbulo; zaguán.

ves·tige [véstɪdӡ] *s.* vestigio.

vest·ment [véstmənt] *s.* vestidura.

vet·er·an [vétərən] *adj. & s.* veterano.

vet·er·i·nar·y [vétrənɛrɪ] *s.* veterinario o albéitar.

ve·to [víto] *s.* veto; prohibición; *v.* vedar, prohibir;
poner el veto a; negarse a aprobar.

vex [vɛks] *v.* molestar, hostigar; incomodar,
enfadar; perturbar.

vex·a·tion [vɛkséʃən] *s.* molestia, incomodidad;
enojo; vejamen.

vi·a [váiə] *prep.* por, por la vía de.

vi·a·ble [váiəbl] *adj.* viable.

vi·a·duct [váiədʌkt] *s.* viaducto.

vi·al [váiəl] *s.* frasco, redoma; **small —** ampolleta.

vi·ands [váiəndz] *s. pl.* vianda, alimentos,
comida.

vi·brate [váibret] *v.* vibrar.

vi·bra·tion [vaibréʃən] *s.* vibración.

vi·car·i·ous [vaikériəs] *adj.* vicario.

vice [vais] *s.* vicio; falta, defecto.

vice-pres·i·dent [váisprézədənt] *s.* vice-presidente.

vice·re·gal [vaisrígl] *adj.* virreinal.

vice·roy [váisrɔi] *s.* virrey.

vice ver·sa [váisivӡsə] viceversa.

vi·cin·i·ty [vəsínəti] *s.* vecindad; cercanía;
inmediaciones.

vi·cious [víʃəs] *adj.* vicioso; malo; maligno;
malicioso; **— dog** perro mordedor, perro bravo.

vi·cis·si·tude [vəsísətjud] *s.* vicisitud, peripecia.

vic·tim [víktɪm] *s.* víctima.

vic·tim·ize [víktimaiz] *v.* inmolar; engañar.

vic·tor [víktɚ] *s.* vencedor.

vic·to·ri·ous [viktóriəs] *adj.* victorioso.

vic·to·ry [víktri] *s.* victoria.

vic·tuals [vítlz] *s. pl.* vituallas, víveres.

vie [vai] *v.* competir.

view [vju] *s.* (*field of vision*) vista; paisaje; (*opinion*)
parecer, opinión; (*inspection*) inspección; (*aim*)
mira, propósito; **in — of** en vista de; **to be
within —** estar al alcance de la vista; **with a —
to** con el propósito de; con la esperanza o
expectación de; con la mira puesta en; *v.* mirar;
examinar.

view·point [vjúpɔint] *s.* punto de vista.

vig·il [vídӡəl] *s.* vigilia, velada; **to keep —** velar.

vig·i·lance [vídӡələns] *s.* vigilancia, desvelo.

vig·i·lant [vídӡələnt] *adj.* vigilante.

vig·or [vígɚ] *s.* vigor.

vig·or·ous [vígərəs] *adj.* vigoroso.

vile [vail] *adj.* vil, bajo, ruin; pésimo.

vil·la [vílə] *s.* quinta, casa de campo.

vil·lage [vílidӡ] *s.* villa, aldea.

vil·lag·er [vílidӡɚ] *s.* aldeano.

vil·lain [vílən] *s.* vilano, malvado, bellaco.

vil·lain·ous [vílənəs] *adj.* villano, ruin, vil, bellaco.

vil·lain·y [víləni] *s.* villanía, vileza.

vim [vim] *s.* vigor, fuerza, energía.

vin·di·cate [víndəket] *v.* vindicar, vengar.

vin·dic·tive [vindíktiv] *adj.* vengativo.

vine [vain] *s.* vid, parra; enredadera.

vin·e·gar [vínigɚ] *s.* vinagre.

vine·yard [vínjɚd] *s.* viña, viñedo.

vin·tage [víntidӡ] *s.* vendimia; edad, época.

vi·o·late [váiəlet] *v.* violar; infringir.

vi·o·la·tion [vaiəléʃən] *s.* violación; infracción.

vi·o·lence [váiələns] *s.* violencia.

vi·o·lent [váiələnt] *adj.* violento.

vi·o·let [váiəlit] *s.* violeta; violado, color de
violeta; *adj.* violado.

vi·o·lin [vaiəlín] *s.* violín.

vi·o·lin·ist [vaiəlínist] *s.* violinista.

vi·o·lon·cel·lo [vaiələntʃélo] *s.* violonchelo.

vi·per [váipɚ] *s.* víbora.

vir·gin [vӡ́dӡin] *adj. & s.* virgen.

vir·gin·al [vӡ́dӡinl] *adj.* virginal.

vir·ile [vírl] *adj.* viril.

vir·tu·al [vӡ́tʃuəl] *adj.* virtual; **-ly** *adv.*
virtualmente.

vir·tue [vӡ́tʃu] *s.* virtud.

vir·tu·ous [vӡ́tʃuəs] *adj.* virtuoso.

vi·sa [vízə] *s.* visa, visado; *v.* visar, refrendar.

vis·cer·al [vísɚl] *adj.* visceral.

vi·sé = visa.

vise [vais] *s.* tornillo de banco.

vis·i·ble [vízəbl] *adj.* visible.

Vis·i·goth [vízəgɵ] *s.* visigodo.

vi·sion [vídӡən] *s.* visión; vista.

vi·sion·ar·y [vídӡənɛri] *adj.* visionario; imaginario;
s. visionario, iluso, soñador.

vis·it [vízit] *v.* visitar; **to — punishment upon**
mandar un castigo a, castigar a; *s.* visita.

vis·i·ta·tion [vizətéʃən] *s.* visitación, visita; castigo,
calamidad.

vis·i·tor [vízitɚ] *s.* visita; visitador.

vi·sor [váizɚ] *s.* visera.

vis·ta [vístə] *s.* vista, paisaje.

vis·u·al [vízjul] *adj.* visual; visible.

vis·u·al·ize [vízjuəlaiz] *v.* representarse en la
mente.

vi·tal [váitl] *adj.* vital.

vi·tal·i·ty [vaitǽləti] *s.* vitalidad.

vi·tal·ize [váitəlaiz] *v.* vitalizar.

vi·ta·min [váitəmin] *s.* vitamina.

vi·ta·min·ized [váitəmənaizd] *adj.* vitaminado.

vi·va·cious [vaivéʃəs] *adj.* vivaz, vivaracho, vivo,
alegre, animado.

vi·vac·i·ty [vaivǽsəti] *s.* viveza, vivacidad.

viv·id [vívid] *adj.* vívido, vivo; animado.

viv·i·fy [vívəfai] *v.* vivificar.

vo·cab·u·lar·y [vəkǽbjələri] *s.* vocabulario.

vo·cal [vókl] *adj.* vocal; oral; **— cords** cuerdas
vocales; **to be —** hablar, expresarse.

vo·ca·tion [vokéʃən] *s.* vocación.

vogue [vog] *s.* boga, moda; **in —** en boga, de
moda.

voice [vɔis] *s.* (*vocalization*) voz; (*speech*) habla;
(*opinion*) voto; *v.* expresar, decir; **-d consonant**
consonante sonora.

voice·less [vɔíslis] *adj.* mudo; sin voz; **— consonant**
consonante sorda.

void [vɔid] *adj.* vació; nulo, inválido; **— of** falto de,
desprovisto de; *s.* vacío; *v.* vaciar, evacuar;
anular, invalidar.

vol·a·tile [válətl] *adj.* volátil; inconstante.

vol·can·ic [valkǽnik] *adj.* volcánico.

vol·ca·no [valkéno] *s.* volcán.

vo·li·tion [volíʃən] *s.* volición; voluntad.

vol·ley [váli] *s.* descarga, lluvia (*de piedras, flechas,
balas, etc.*); voleo (*de la pelota*); *v.* descargar una
lluvia de proyectiles; volear una pelota.

volt [volt] *s.* voltio.

volt·age [vóltidӡ] *s.* voltaje.

VA

vol·u·ble [váljəbl] *adj.* facundo.
vol·ume [váljəm] *s.* volumen; tomo; bulto; suma, cantidad.
vo·lu·mi·nous [vəlúmənəs] *adj.* voluminoso.
vol·un·tar·y [váləntɛrɪ] *adj.* voluntario.
vol·un·teer [valəntír] *s.* voluntario; *adj.* voluntario; de voluntarios; *v.* ofrecer, dar voluntariamente; ofrecerse.
vo·lup·tu·ous [vəlʌ́ptʃʊəs] *adj.* voluptuoso.
vom·it [vámɪt] *s.* vómito; *v.* vomitar, *Méx.* deponer.
vo·ra·cious [voréʃəs] *adj.* voraz.
vor·tex [vɔ́rteks] *s.* vórtice; vorágine.
vote [vot] *s.* voto; votación; *v.* votar; votar por.
vot·er [vótə·] *s.* votante, elector.
vouch [vaʊtʃ] *v.* **to — for** dar fe de; garantizar, responder de; salir fiador de.
vouch·er [váʊtʃə·] *s.* comprobante, justificante; recibo; fiador.
vouch·safe [vaʊtʃséf] *v.* otorgar, conceder.
vow [vaʊ] *s.* voto; juramente; *v.* votar, jurar, hacer voto de.
vow·el [váʊəl] *s.* & *adj.* vocal.
voy·age [vɔɪɪdʒ] *s.* viaje; travesía; *v.* viajar.
vul·gar [vʌ́lgə·] *adj.* soez, ordinario, grosero; vulgar.
vul·ner·a·ble [vʌ́nə·əbl] *adj.* vulnerable.
vul·ture [vʌ́ltʃə·] *s.* buitre, *Andes, Ríopl.* cóndor.
vul·va [vʌ́lvə] *s.* vulva.

W:w

wab·ble [wábl] *v.* tambalear(se), bambolear(se); vacilar; temblar; *s.* tambaleo, bamboleo; balanceo.
wad [wad] *s.* taco; bodoque; pelotilla, bolita, rollo; **— of money** rollo de billetes (*de banco*); dinero; *v.* atacar (*un arma de fuego*); rellenar; hacer una pelotilla de.
wad·dle [wádl] *v.* anadear; contonearse, zarandearse (*al andar*); *s.* anadeo; zarandeo, contoneo.
wade [wed] *v.* vadear; chapotear; andar descalzo por la orilla del agua; **to — through a book** leer con dificultad un libro.
wa·fer [wéfə·] *s.* oblea; hostia (*consagrada*).
waft [wæft] *v.* llevar en vilo, llevar por el aire; llevar a flote; *s.* ráfaga de aire; movimiento (*de la mano*).
wag [wæg] *v.* menear; sacudir; **to — the tail** colear, menear la cola; *s.* meneo; bromista, farsante.
wage [wedʒ] *v.* hacer (*guerra*); dar (*batalla*); *s.* (*usualmente* **wages**) paga, jornal; **— earner** jornalero, obrero; trabajador; **— scale** escala de salarios (*sueldos*).
wa·ger [wédʒə·] *s.* apuesta; *v.* apostar.
wag·gle [wǽgl] *s.* meneo rápido.
wag·on [wǽgən] *s.* carro, carreta; carretón.
wail [wel] *v.* gemir, lamentar; *s.* gemido, lamento.
waist [west] *s.* cintura; talle; blusa; **—band** pretina.
waist·coat [wéstkot] *s.* chaleco.
waist·line [wéstlaɪn] *s.* talle.
wait [wet] *v.* (*stay*) esperar, aguardar; (*serve*) servir; **to — for** esperar, aguardar; **to — on (upon)** servir a; atender a; **to — table** servir la mesa, servir de mozo o camarero (*en un restaurante*); *s.* espera; **to lie in — for** estar en

acecho de. .
wait·er [wétə·] *s.* mozo, camarero, sirviente, *Méx., C.A.* mesero.
wait·ing [wétɪŋ] *s.* espera; **— room** sala de espera.
wait·ress [wétrɪs] *s.* camarera, moza, *Mex.* mesera.
waive [wev] *v.* renunciar a; **to — one's right** renunciar voluntariamente a sus derechos.
waiv·er [wévə·] *s.* renuncia.
wake [wek] *v.* despertar(se); **to — up** despertar(se); despabilarse; *s.* velatorio (*acto de velar a un muerto*), *Am.* velorio; estela (*huella que deja un barco en el agua*); **in the — of** después de, detrás de.
wake·ful [wékfəl] *adj.* desvelado, despierto; insomne.
wak·en [wékən] *v.* despertar(se); *Ríopl.* recordar (*a una persona que está dormida*).
walk [wɔk] *v.* andar, caminar, ir a pie; recorrer a pie; pasear; **to — away** irse, marcharse; **to — back home** volverse a casa (a pie); **to — down** bajar; **to — in** entrar; **to — out** salirse, irse; parar el trabajo, declararse en huelga; **to — the streets** callejear; **to — up** subir; *s.* paseo; senda, vereda; acera; paso (*del caballo*); manera de andar; **— of life** vocación; **a ten minutes' —** una caminata de diez minutos.
wall [wɔl] *s.* (*interior*) pared; (*garden*) muro; (*fort*) muralla; **execution —** paredón; **low mud —** tapia; **to drive to the —** poner entre la espada y la pared, poner en un aprieto.
wal·let [wálɪt] *s.* cartera.
wall·flow·er [wɔ́lflaʊə·] *s.* aleli; **to be a — at a dance** comer pavo, *Andes, Méx.* planchar el asiento.
wal·lop [wáləp] *v.* pegar, zurrar, golpear; *s.* guantada, bofetón, golpazo.
wal·low [wálo] *v.* revolcarse; chapalear o chapotear (*en el lodo*).
wall·pa·per [wɔ́lpepə·] *s.* papel (de empapelar).
wal·nut [wɔ́lnət] *s.* nuez de nogal; nogal; **— tree** nogal.
waltz [wɔlts] *s.* vals; *s.* valsar, bailar el vals.
wan [wɑn] *adj.* pálido, enfermizo, enclenque; lánguido.
wand [wɑnd] *s.* vara, varita; **magic —** varita de virtud.
wan·der [wándə·] *v.* vagar, errar; **to — away** extraviarse; **to — away from** apartarse de, desviarse de; **my mind -s easily** me distraigo fácilmente.
wan·der·er [wándərə·] *s.* vago, vagabundo.
wane [wen] *v.* menguar; decaer; *s.* mengua; diminución; **to be on the —** ir menguando; ir desapareciendo.
want [wɑnt] *v.* (*desire*) querer, desear; (*lack*) necesitar; *s.* falta; necesidad; escasez, carencia; **to be in —** estar necesitado.
want·ing [wántɪŋ] *adj.* falto; deficiente; necesitado.
wan·ton [wántən] *adj.* desenfrenado, libre; licencioso; inconsiderado; temerario.
war [wɔr] *s.* guerra; *v.* guerrear, hacer guerra; **to — on** guerrear con.
war·ble [wɔ́rbl] *v.* gorjear; trinar; *s.* gorjeo; trino.
war·bler [wɔ́rblə·] *s.* cantor; pájaro gorjeador.
ward [wɔrd] *s.* pupilo, menor o huérfano (*bajo tutela*); cuadra (*de hospital, prisión, etc.*); distrito (*de una ciudad*); *v.* **to — off** resguardarse de; evitar; parar (*un golpe*).
war·den [wɔ́rdn] *s.* guardián; alcaide; **prison —** alcaide de una prisión.
ward·robe [wɔ́rdrob] *s.* (*closet*) guardarropa,

ropero, armario; (*garments*) vestuario; ropa.
ware·house [wέrhaʊs] *s.* almacén, depósito.
wares [wɛrz] *s. pl.* artículos, mercancías,
mercaderías, efectos.
war·fare [wɔ́rfɛr] *s.* guerra.
war·head [wɔ́rhɛd] *s.* punta de combate.
war·like [wɔ́rlaɪk] *adj.* guerrero, bélico.
warm [wɔrm] *adj.* (*temperature*) caliente, cálido,
caluroso; (*enthusiastic*) acalorado; (*fresh*)
reciente; — **hearted** de buen corazón; — **blooded**
apasionado; ardiente; **he is** — tiene calor; **it is**
— **today** hace calor hoy; *v.* calentar(se); **to** —
over recalentar; **to** — **up** calentar(se); acalorarse;
entusiasmarse.
warmth [wɔrmpθ] *s.* (*heat*) calor; (*friendship*)
cordialidad.
warn [wɔrn] *v.* avisar, advertir, amonestar;
prevenir, precaver.
warn·ing [wɔ́rnɪŋ] *s.* aviso, advertencia,
amonestación; escarmiento; **let that be a** — **to**
you que te sirva de escarmiento.
warp [wɔrp] *s.* urdimbre (*de un tejido*); torcedura,
deformación; comba; *v.* combar(se),
deformar(se), torcer(se); urdir (*los hilos de un*
telar).
war·rant [wɔ́rənt] *s.* (*sanction*) autorización; (*right*)
garantía, justificación; (*writ*) comprobante;
orden, mandato, citación (*ante un juez*); *v.*
autorizar; garantizar; justificar.
war·ri·or [wɔ́rɪɚ] *s.* guerrero.
war·ship [wɔ́rʃɪp] *s.* buque de guerra, acorazado.
wart [wɔrt] *s.* verruga.
war·y [wέrɪ] *adj.* cauteloso, cauto, precavido,
prevenido; **to be** — **of** desconfiar de.
was [wɑz] *pret. de* **to be** (*primera y tercera persona*
del singular).
wash [waʃ] *v.* lavar(se); **to** — **away** deslavar(se);
to be -ed away by the waves ser arrastrado por
las olas; *s.* lavado; lavadura; lavatorio; lavazas,
agua sucia; **mouth** — enjuague o enjuagatorio;
—**bowl** lavabo, palangana, lavamanos; —**cloth**
paño para lavarse; — **dress** vestido lavable;
— **room** lavabo, lavatorio.
wash·a·ble [wɑ́ʃəbl] *adj.* lavable.
wash-and-wear [wɑ́ʃændwέr] *adj.* de lava y pon.
washed·out [wɑ́ʃtáʊt] *adj.* desteñido; agotado, sin
fuerzas.
washed-up [waʃtʌ́p] *adj.* fracasado.
wash·er [wɑ́ʃɚ] *s.* lavador; máquina de lavar;
arandela (*para una tuerca*); —**woman** lavandera.
wash·ing [wɑ́ʃɪŋ] *s.* lavado; ropa sucia o para
lavar; ropa lavada; — **machine** lavadora,
máquina de lavar.
wash·out [wɑ́ʃaʊt] *s.* derrubio; fracaso.
wasp [wɑsp] *s.* avispa.
waste [west] *v.* gastar; desgastar; malgastar,
desperdiciar, derrochar; disipar; **to** — **away**
gastarse, consumirse; desgastarse; *s.* desperdicio;
gasto inútil; desgaste; desechos, desperdicios;
terreno baldío, desierto; *adj.* inútil, desechado;
desierto; baldío; — **of time** pérdida de tiempo;
— **basket** cesto para papeles; — **land** terreno
baldío; — **paper** papeles inútiles, papel de
desecho; **to go to** — gastarse, perderse;
malgastarse, desperdiciarse; **to lay** — asolar,
arruinar.
waste·ful [wéstfəl] *adj.* despilfarrado, gastador;
desperdiciado; ineconómico.
watch [watʃ] *v.* (*look*) mirar; observar; (*be alert*)
vigilar; velar; cuidar; — **out!** ¡cuidado!; **to** —
out for tener cuidado con; cuidar; vigilar; *s.*

reloj (de bolsillo); vela, vigilia; guardia;
centinela, vigilante; — **chain** cadena de reloj,
Ven., Méx. leontina; — **charm** dije; **wrist**— reloj
de pulsera; **to be on the** — tener cuidado;
estar alerta; **to keep** — **over** vigilar a.
watch·ful [wátʃfəl] *adj.* alerto, vigilante, despertio,
atento.
watch·mak·er [wátʃmekɚ] *s.* relojero.
watch·man [wátʃmən] *s.* vigilante, guardia, sereno.
watch·tow·er [wátʃtaʊɚ] *s.* atalaya, mirador.
watch·word [wátʃwɝd] *s.* contraseña, santo y seña,
consigna; lema.
wa·ter [wɔ́tɚ] *s.* agua; — **color** acuarela; color
para acuarela; — **power** fuerza hidráulica;
—**shed** vertiente; — **sports** deportes acuáticos;
— **supply** abastecimiento de agua; *v.* regar;
aguar, diluir con agua; abrevar, dar de beber
(*al ganado*); beber agua (*el ganado*); tomar agua
(*un barco, locomotora, etc.*); **my eyes** — me
lloran los ojos; **my mouth -s** se me hace agua
la boca.
wa·ter·cress [wɔ́tɚkrɛs] *s.* berro.
wa·ter·fall [wɔ́tɚfɔl] *s.* cascada, catarata, caída de
agua.
wa·ter·front [wɔ́tɚfrʌnt] *s.* terreno ribereño.
wa·ter·mel·on [wɔ́tɚmɛlən] *s.* sandía.
wa·ter·pow·er [wɔ́tɚpaʊɚ] *s.* fuerza hidráulica.
wa·ter·proof [wɔ́tɚpruf] *adj. & s.* impermeable; *v.*
hacer impermeable.
wa·ter·ski [wɔ́tɚski] *s.* esqui acuático
wa·ter·spout [wɔ́tɚspaʊt] *s.* surtidor; tromba;
manga de agua.
wa·ter·way [wɔ́tɚwe] *s.* vía de agua, río navegable,
canal.
wa·ter·y [wɔ́tɚɪ] *adj.* aguado; acuoso; mojado,
húmedo.
wave [wev] *v.* ondear; ondular; agitar; blandir (*una*
espada, bastón, etc.); **to** — **aside** apartar,
rechazar; **to** — **good-bye** hacer una seña o
ademán de despedida; **to** — **hair** ondular el
pelo; **to** — **one's hand** hacer una seña o señas
con la mano; mover la mano; *s.* onda; ola;
ondulación; — **of the hand** ademán, movimiento
de la mano; **permanent** — ondulación
permanente.
wave·length [wévlɛŋθ] *s.* longitud de onda.
wa·ver [wévɚ] *v.* oscilar; vacilar, titubear;
tambalear(se); *s.* vacilación, titubeo.
wa·vy [wévɪ] *adj.* rizado, ondulado; ondulante.
wax [wæks] *s.* cera; — **candle** vela de cera; —
paper papel encerado; *v.* encerar; pulir con cera;
hacerse, ponerse; crecer (*la luna*).
way [we] *s.* (*road*) camino; ruta; senda; (*manner*)
modo, manera; — **in** entrada; — **out** salida;
— **through** paso, pasaje; **a long** — **off** muy lejos,
a una larga distancia; **by** — **of** por, por vía de;
by — **of comparison** a modo de comparación;
by the — de paso; **in no** — de ningún modo;
on the — camino de, rumbo a; **out of the** —
fuera del camino; apartado; a un lado;
impropio; extraordinario; **to be in a bad** —
hallarse en mal estado; **to be well under** —
estar (*un trabajo*) ya bastante avanzado; **to give**
— ceder; quebrarse; **to have one's** — hacer su
capricho, salirse con la suya; **to make** — **for**
abrir paso para.
way·far·er [wéfɛrɚ] *s.* caminante.
way·lay [welé] *v.* estar en acecho de (*alguien*);
asaltar; detener (*a una persona*).
way·side [wésaɪd] *s.* borde del camino; — **inn**
posada al borde del camino.

VO

way·ward [wéwəd] *adj. adj.* voluntarioso, desobediente.

we [wi] *pron.* nosotros, nosotras.

weak [wik] *adj.* débil; flaco; endeble; — **market** mercado flojo; **weak-minded** de voluntad débil; simple; — **tea** té claro o suave.

weak·en [wikən] *v.* debilitar(se); desmayar, flaquear, perder ánimo.

weak·ly [wíklɪ] *adv.* débilmente; *adj.* enfermizo, débil, enclenque.

weak·ness [wíknɪs] *s.* debilidad; flaqueza.

wealth [wɛlθ] *s.* riqueza; copia, abundancia.

wealth·y [wélθɪ] *adj.* rico; acaudalado.

wean [win] *v.* destetar; apartar gradualmente (*de un hábito, de una amistad*).

weap·on [wépən] *s.* arma.

wear [wɛr] *v.* (*have on*) llevar, tener o traer puesto; usar; (*waste away*) gastar, desgastar; **to** — **away** gastar(se), degastar(se); consumir(se); **to** — **off** degastar(se), gastar(se); borrarse; **to** — **out** gastar(se); desgastar(se); consumir(se); agotar; cansar; **it -s well** es duradero; dura mucho; **as the day wore on** a medida que pasaba el día; *s.* uso, gasto; durabilidad; — **and tear** desgaste; uso; **men's** — ropa para hombres; **clothes for summer** — ropa de verano.

wea·ri·ly [wírlɪ] *adv.* penosamente, con cansancio, con fatiga, fatigadamente.

wea·ri·ness [wírnɪs] *s.* cansancio, fatiga.

wear·ing [wérɪŋ] *adj.* cansado, aburrido, fastidioso.

wea·ri·some [wírɪsəm] *adj.* fatigoso, molesto, fastidioso.

wea·ry [wírɪ] *adj.* cansado, fatigado; aburrido; *v.* cansar(se), fatigar(se).

wea·sel [wízl] *s.* comadreja.

weath·er [wéðəʳ] *s.* tiempo; **weather-beaten** desgastado o curtido por la intemperie; — **bureau** oficina meteorológica; — **conditions** condiciones atmosféricas; —**vane** veleta; **it is fine** — hace buen tiempo; **to be under the** — estar enfermo; estar indispuesto; *v.* exponer a la intemperie; orear, secar al aire; **to** — **a storm** aguantar un chubasco; salir ileso de una tormenta.

weave [wiv] *v.* (*cloth*) tejer, entretejer; (*to plan*) urdir; **to** — **together** entretejer, entrelazar; combinar; *s.* tejido.

weav·er [wívəʳ] *s.* tejedor.

web [wɛb] *s.* tela; membrana (*entre los dedos de los pájaros acuáticos*); **spider's** —telaraña.

wed [wɛd] *v.* casarse; casarse con; casar; *p.p. de* **to wed**.

wed·ded [wédɪd] *p.p. & adj.* casado; unido; — **to an idea** aferrado a una idea.

wed·ding [wédɪŋ] *s.* boda, casamiento, nupcias, enlace; — **day** día de bodas; — **trip** viaje de novios; **silver** — bodas de plata.

wedge [wɛdʒ] *s.* cuña; **entering** —cuña, entrada, medio de entrar, modo de penetrar; *v.* acuñar, meter cuñas; **to be -d between** estar encajado entre.

Wednes·day [wénzdɪ] *s.* miércoles.

wee [wi] *adj.* diminuto, chiquitico, pequeñito.

weed [wid] *s.* cizaña, mala hierba; *v.* desherbar (*o* desyerbar), quitar o arrancar la mala hierba; **to** — **a garden** desherbar un huerto; **to** — **out** escardar; eliminar, arrancar, entresacar.

weed·y [wídɪ] *adj.* herboso, lleno de malas hierbas.

week [wik] *s.* semana; —**day** día de trabajo, día laborable, día hábil; — **end** fin de semana; **a** — **from today** de hoy en ocho días.

week·ly [wíklɪ] *adj.* semanal, semanario; *adv.* semanalmente, por semana; *s.* semanario, periódico o revista semanal.

weep [wip] *v.* llorar.

weep·ing [wípɪŋ] *adj.* llorón; lloroso; — **willow** sauce llorón; *s.* llanto, lloro, lágrimas.

wee·vil [wívl] *s.* gorgojo.

weigh [we] *v.* pesar; ponderar, considerar; **to** — **anchor** zarpar, levar el ancla; **to** — **down** agobiar; abrumar; **to** — **on one's conscience** serle a uno gravoso, pesarle a uno.

weight [wet] *s.* peso; pesa (*de reloj o medida para pesar*); carga; **paper** — pisapapeles; *v.* cargar, sobrecargar; añadir peso a; asignar un peso o valor relativo a.

weight·y [wétɪ] *adj.* grave, ponderoso; de mucho peso; importante.

weird [wɪrd] *adj.* extraño, raro, misterioso, fantástico.

wel·come [wélkəm] *s.* bienvenida; buena acogida; *adj.* grato, agradable; bien acogido, bien quisto; bien-venido; bien recibido; — **home!** ¡bienvenido!; — **rest** grato reposo o descanso; **you are** — no hay de qué, de nada (*para contestar a* "thank you"); **you are** — **here** está Vd. en su casa; **you are** — **to use it** se lo presto con todo gusto; está a su disposición; *v.* dar la bienvenida a; acoger o recibir con gusto.

weld [wɛld] *v.* soldar(se); *s.* soldadura.

wel·fare [wélfɛr] *s.* bienestar; bien; felicidad; — **work** labor social o de beneficencia.

well [wɛl] *adv.* bien; **he is** — **over fifty** tiene mucho más de cincuenta años; — **then** pues bien, ahora bien, conque; **well-being** bienestar; **well-bred** bien criado; bien educado; **well-done** bien cocido; **well-fixed** acomodado; **well-groomed** acicalado; **well-meaning** bien intencionado; **well-nigh** casi, muy cerca de; *adj.* bueno; bien de salud, sano; conveniente; — **and good** santo y muy bueno; **well-off** acomodado, adinerado; en buenas condiciones; **well-to-do** próspero, acomodado; adinerado; **all is** — no hay novedad, todo va bien; **it is** — **to do it** conviene hacerlo, es conveniente hacerlo.

well [wɛl] *s.* (*shaft*) pozo; (*cistern*) cisterna; (*spring*) manantial; **artesian** — pozo artesiano; *v.* manar; **tears -ed up in her eyes** se le arrasaron los ojos de lágrimas.

welt [wɛlt] *s.* verdugo, verdugón, roncha.

went [wɛnt] *pret. de* **to go**.

wept [wɛpt] *pret. & p.p. de* **to weep**.

were [wɜ] *pret. de* **to be** (*en el plural y en la segunda persona del singular del indicativo*); *es además el imperfecto del subjuntivo*); **if I** — **you** si yo fuera Vd.; **there** — había, hubo.

west [wɛst] *s.* oeste, occidente, ocaso; *adj.* occidental, del oeste; **West Indies** Antillas; *adv.* hacia el oeste, al oeste; en el oeste.

west·ern [wéstən] *adj.* occidental, del oeste.

west·ern·er [wéstənə] *s.* natural del oeste, habitante del oeste, occidental.

west·ward [wéstwəd] *adv.* hacia el oeste; *adj.* occidental, oeste.

wet [wɛt] *adj.* húmedo; mojado; — **nurse** nodriza, ama de leche; *s.* humedad; antiprohibicionista (*el que favorece la venta de bebidas alcohólicas*); *v.* mojar; humedecer; *pret. & p.p. de* **to wet**.

wet-back [wétbæk] *s.* panza mojada.

wet·ness [wétnɪs] *s.* humedad.

whack [hwæk] *v.* golpear, pegar; *s.* golpe; golpazo; tentativa, prueba.

whale [hwel] *s.* ballena; *v.* pescar ballenas.

wharf [hwɔrf] s. muelle, embarcadero.
what [hwɑt] pron. interr. qué; qué cosa; cuál; pron. rel. lo que; — **for?** ¿para qué? adj. qué; — **book?** ¿qué libro? — **a man!** ¡qué hombre!; — **happy children!** ¡qué niños más (o tan) felices!; **take** — **books you need** tome Vd. los libros que necesite.
what·ev·er [hwɑtévɚ] pron. cualquiera cosa que, lo que, cuanto, todo lo que; — **do you mean?** ¿qué quiere Vd. decir?; **do it,** — **happens** hágalo suceda lo que suceda; adj. cualquiera; **any person** — una persona cualquiera; **no money** — nada de dinero.
what·so·ev·er [hwɑtsoévɚ] = **whatever.**
wheat [hwit] s. trigo; **cream of** — crema de trigo.
whee·dle [hwídl̩] v. engatusar.
wheel [hwil] s. (disc) rueda; rodaja; disco; (bike) bicicleta; — **chair** silla rodante, silla de ruedas; **steering** — volante (de automóvil); rueda del timón; v. rodar; hacer rodar; girar; acarrear; andar en bicicleta; **to** — **around** dar una vuelta; girar sobre los talones; **to** — **the baby** pasear al bebé en su cochecito.
wheel·bar·row [hwílbæro] s. carretilla.
wheeze [hwiz] s. resuello ruidoso.
when [hwɛn] adv. & conj. cuando; adv. interr. ¿cuándo?
whence [hwɛns] adv. de donde; de que.
when·ev·er [hwɛnévɚ] adj. & conj. cuando, siempre que, cada vez que.
where [hwɛr] adv. donde; adonde; en donde; por donde; —? ¿dónde?; ¿adónde?
where·a·bouts [hwɛrəbaʊts] s. paradero; adv. interr. ¿dónde?
where·as [hwɛræz] conj. mientras que; puesto que, visto que, considerando que.
where·by [hwɛrbái] adv. por donde, por lo cual; con lo cual.
where·fore [hwɛrfor] adv. por lo que; por lo cual; por eso, por lo tanto.
where·in [hwɛrín] adv. en que; en donde; en lo cual.
where·of [hwɛráv] adv. de que; de donde; de quien, de quienes.
where·up·on [hwɛrəpán] adv. después de lo cual; entonces.
where·ev·er [hwɛrévɚ] adv. dondequiera que, adondequiera que, por dondequiera que.
where·with·al [hwɛrwiðɔl] s. medios, fondos; dinero.
whet [hwɛt] v. amolar, afilar; aguzar, estimular.
wheth·er [hwɛðɚ] conj. si; ya sea que, sea que; — **we escape or not** ya sea que escapemos o no; **I doubt** — dudo (de) que.
which [hwɪtʃ] pron. interr. ¿cuál?; ¿cuáles?; pron. rel. que; el cual, la cual, los cuales, las cuales; el que, la que, los que, las que; adj. interr. ¿qué?; — **boy has it?** ¿cuál de los muchachos lo tiene? ¿qué muchacho lo tiene?; — **way did he go?** ¿por qué camino se fue?; ¿por dónde se fue?; **during** — **time** tiempo durante el cual.
which·ev·er [hwɪtʃévɚ] pron. & adj. cualquiera (que), cualesquiera (que); el que, la que; — **road you take** cualquier camino que tome Vd. siga.
whiff [hwɪf] s. (waft) soplo; fumada, bocanada; (odor) repentino olor o hedor; v. soplar; echar bocanadas.
while [hwaɪl] s. rato; tiempo, temporada; **a short** — un ratito; **a short** — **ago** hace poco, hace poco rato; **to be worth** — valer la pena; conj. mientras, mientras que; v. **to** — **away the time**

pasar el tiempo.
whilst [hwaɪlst] conj. mientras, mientras que.
whim [hwɪm] s. capricho, antojo.
whim·per [hwímpɚ] v. lloriquear, gimotear; quejarse; s. lloriqueo, gimoteo; quejido.
whim·si·cal [hwímzɪk]̩ adj. caprichoso.
whine [hwaɪn] v. lloriquear; quejarse; s. gemido, quejido.
whin·er [hwáɪnɚ] s. llorón, persona quejosa, Méx. quejumbres; Andes quejumbroso; Ríopl. rezongón.
whip [hwɪp] v. azotar, fustigar; zurrar, dar una paliza a, dar latigazos a; batir (crema, huevos); vencer; **to** — **up** batir, coger o asir de repente; hacer de prisa; s. azote, látigo, fuete; batido.
whip·ping [hwípɪŋ] s. tunda, zurra, paliza; — **cream** crema para batir.
whir [hwɝ] v. zumbar; s. zumbido.
whirl [hwɝl] v. girar, dar vueltas; arremolinarse; **my head -s** siento vértigo, estoy desvanecido; s. giro, vuelta; remolino; espiral (de humo); confusión.
whirl·pool [hwɝlpul] s. remolino, vorágine, vórtice.
whirl·wind [hwɝlwɪnd] s. remolino, torbellino.
whisk [hwɪsk] v. barrer; desempolvar (con escobilla); batir (huevos); **to** — **away** barrer de prisa; llevarse de prisa, arrebatar; irse de prisa, escaparse; **to** — **something out of sight** escamotear algo, esconder algo de prisa; s. — **broom** escobilla; **with a** — **of the broom** de un escobillazo.
whis·ker [hwískɚ] s. pelo de la barba; **-s** barbas; patillas; bigotes (del gato).
whis·key [hwískɪ] s. whisky (aguardiente de maíz, centeno, etc.).
whis·per [hwíspɚ] v. cuchichear, hablar en secreto; soplar, decir al oído; susurrar; secretearse; **it is -ed that** corre la voz que; dizque, dicen que; s. cuchicheo, secreteo; susurro; murmullo; **to talk in a** — hablar en secreto; susurrar.
whis·tle [hwísl̩] v. silbar; chiflar; pitar; **to** — **for someone** llamar a uno con un silbido; s. silbido, chiflido; silbato, pito.
whit [hwɪt] s. jota, pizca.
white [hwaɪt] adj. (color) blanco; (pure) puro; inocente; (honorable) honrado, recto; —**caps** cabrillas o palomas (olas con crestas blancas); — **lead** albayalde; — **lie** mentirilla, mentira venial; **white-livered** cobarde; **white-collar** de oficina; **to show the** — **feather** mostrar cobardía, portarse como cobarde; s. blanco; clara (del huevo).
whit·en [hwáɪtn̩] v. blanquear; emblanquecer(se), poner(se) blanco.
white·ness [hwáɪtnɪs] s. blancura; palidez; pureza.
white·wash [hwáɪtwɑʃ] v. (paint) blanquear, enjalbegar; (gloss over) encubrir, disimular (faltas, errores); absolver (sin justicia); s. lechada.
whith·er [hwíðɚ] adv. adonde; —? ¿adónde?
whit·ish [hwáɪtɪʃ] adj. blancuzco, blancuzco, blanquizco.
whit·tle [hwítl̩] v. cortar, mondar, tallar; tajar; sacar punta a (un lápiz); **to** — **down expenses** cercenar o reducir los gastos.
whiz [hwɪz] v. zumbar; s. zumbido, silbido; **to be a** — ser un águila, ser muy listo.
who [hu] pron. rel. quien, quienes, que, el que, la que, los que, las que; **he** — el que, quien; pron. interr. ¿quién?; ¿quiénes?; — **is it?** ¿quién es?
who·ev·er [huévɚ] pron. quienquiera que,

WA

cualquiera que; el que.

whole [hol] *adj.* todo; entero; íntegro; **the — day** todo el día; **—hearted** sincero, cordial; **—heartedly** de todo corazón; con todo ánimo; *s.* todo, total, totalidad; **as a** — en conjunto; **on the** — en general, en conjunto.

whole·sale [hólsel] *s.* venta al por mayor, *Am.* mayoreo; **by** — al por mayor; *adj.* al por mayor; en grandes cantidades; — **dealer** comerciante al por mayor; *Am.* mayorista; — **slaughter** matanza; gran hecatombe; — **trade** comercio al por mayor, *Am.* comercio mayorista; *adv.* al por mayor, por mayor; *v.* vender al por mayor, *Am.* mayorear.

whole·some [hólsəm] *adj.* saludable, sano; salubre; — **man** hombre normalmente bueno o de buena índole.

whol·ly [hólı] *adv.* enteramente, completamente, totalmente.

whom [hum] *pron. pers.* a quien, a quienes; que; al que (a la que, a los que, *etc.*); al cual (a la cual, a los cuales, *etc.*); **for** — para quien; — **did you see?** ¿a quién vió Vd.?

whoop [hup] *s.* grito, chillido, alarido; respiro convulsivo (*que acompaña a la tos ferina*); *v.* gritar, vocear, echar gritos; respirar convulsivamente (*al toser*); **to** — **it up** armar una gritería, gritar; **whooping cough** tos ferina.

whore [hor] *s.* ramera, puta, prostituta.

whose [huz] *pron.* cuyo, cuya, cuyos, cuyas; *pron. interr.* ¿de quién?; ¿de quiénes?; — **book is this?** ¿de quién es este libro?

why [hwaɪ] *adv.* ¿por qué?; **the reason** — la razón por la que (*o* la cual); —, **of course!** ¡sí, por supuesto!; ¡claro que sí!; —, **that is not true!** ¡sí eso no es verdad! *s.* porqué, causa, razón, motivo.

wick [wɪk] *s.* mecha, pabilo.

wick·ed [wíkɪd] *adj.* malvado, malo, inicuo; nefasto.

wick·ed·ness [wíkɪdnɪs] *s.* maldad, iniquidad, perversidad.

wick·er [wíkɚ] *s.* mimbre; — **chair** silla de mimbre.

wick·et [wíkɪt] *s.* postigo; ventanilla.

wide [waɪd] *adj.* ancho; amplio; vasto; extenso; — **apart** muy apartados; **wide-awake** muy despierto; alerta, vigilante; — **eyed** ojoso; — **of the mark** muy lejos del blanco; — **open** muy abierto; abierto de par en par; **far and** — por todas partes, extensamente; **to open** — abrir mucho; abrir (*la puerta*) de par en par; **two feet** — dos pies de ancho (*o* de anchura).

wide·ly [wáɪdlɪ] *adv.* ampliamente; extensamente; muy; mucho.

wid·en [wáɪdn] *v.* ensanchar(se), ampliar(se), dilatar(se).

wide·spread [wáɪdspréd] *adj.* muy esparcido, muy extensivo; bien difundido; extendido; general, extendido por todas partes.

wid·ow [wído] *s.* viuda.

wid·ow·er [wídəwɚ] *s.* viudo.

width [wɪdθ] *s.* ancho, anchura.

wield [wild] *v.* manejar; esgrimir (*la espada o la pluma*); ejercer (*el poder*).

wife [waɪf] *s.* esposa.

wig [wɪg] *s.* peluca.

wig·gle [wígl] *v.* menear(se); *s.* meneo.

wig·wam [wígwam] *s.* choza de los indios norteños.

wild [waɪld] *adj.* salvaje; (*animal*) feroz, fiero; indómito; montaraz; (*plant*) silvestre; *Ven.*,

Méx. cimarrón; impetuoso, desenfrenado; bullicioso; violento; loco; enojado; desatinado; ansioso; **to talk** — disparatar, desatinar; *s.* yermo, desierto, monte.

wild·cat [wáɪldkæt] *s.* gato montés; — **scheme** empresa arriesgada.

wil·der·ness [wíldɚnɪs] *s.* yermo, desierto, monte; inmensidad.

wild-eyed [wáɪldaɪd] *adj.* de ojos huraños.

wild·ness [wáɪldnɪs] *s.* salvajez; ferocidad, fiereza; locura.

wile [waɪl] *s.* ardid, engaño; astucia.

will [wɪl] *v.* (*desire*) querer, decidir; (*order*) ordenar, mandar; (*dispose of legally*) legar; *v. defect. y aux.* querer; *rigurosamente debe usarse para formar el futuro en las segundas y terceras personas*: **she** — **go** ella irá; *en las primeras personas indica voluntad o determinación*: **I** — **not do it** no lo haré, no quiero hacerlo.

will [wɪl] *s.* (*wish*) voluntad; albedrío; (*legal disposition*) testamento; **free** — libre albedrío; **ill** — mala voluntad, malquerencia.

will·ful, wil·ful [wílfəl] *adj.* voluntarioso, testarudo, caprichudo; intencional.

will·ing [wílɪŋ] *adj.* bien dispuesto, deseoso, complaciente; voluntario; **-ly** *adv.* con gusto, de buena gana, de buena voluntad; voluntariamente.

will·ing·ness [wílɪŋnɪs] *s.* buena voluntad, buena gana.

wil·low [wílo] *s.* sauce; mimbrera; **weeping** — sauce llorón.

wilt [wɪlt] *v.* marchitar(se); ajar(se); desmayar; languidecer.

wi·ly [wáɪlɪ] *adj.* astuto, artero.

win [wɪn] (*achieve*) ganar; lograr, obtener; alcanzar; (*persuade*) persuadir; **to** — **out** ganar, triunfar; salirse con la suya; **to** — **over** persuadir; atraer; alcanzar o ganar el favor de.

wince [wɪns] *v.* cejar (*ante una dificultad o peligro*); encogerse (*de dolor, susto, etc.*).

winch [wɪntʃ] *s.* malacate.

wind [wɪnd] *s.* viento, aire; resuello; — **instrument** instrumento de viento; **to get** — **of** barruntar; tener noticia de.

wind [waɪnd] *v.* enredar; devanar, ovillar; dar cuerda a (*un reloj*); serpentear (*un camino*); dar vueltas; **to** — **someone around one's finger** manejar fácilmente a alguien, gobernarle; **to** — **up one's affairs** terminar o concluir uno sus negocios; *s.* vuelta; recodo.

wind·bag [wíndbœg] *s.* (*instrument*) fuelle; (*person*) parlanchín, hablador.

wind·fall [wíndfɔl] *s.* golpe de fortuna, ganancia repentina, herencia inesperada.

wind·ing [wáɪndɪŋ] *adj.* sinuoso, tortuoso, que da vueltas; — **staircase** escalera de caracol.

wind·mill [wíndmɪl] *s.* molino de viento.

win·dow [wíndo] *s.* ventana; **show** — escaparate, vitrina, aparador, *Am.* vidriera; — **shade** visillo, cortinilla; — **sill** antepecho, repisa de ventana.

win·dow·pane [wíndopen] *s.* cristal de ventana, vidriera.

wind·pipe [wíndpaɪp] *s.* tráquea, gaznate.

wind·shield [wíndʃild] *s.* parabrisa, guardabrisa; — **wiper** limpiaparabrisas.

wind tunnel [wíndtʌnl] *s.* túnel aerodinámico.

wind·ward [wíndwəd] *s.* barlovento.

wind·y [wíndɪ] *adj.* airoso; ventoso; **it is** — hace aire, ventea, sopla el viento.

wine [waɪn] *s.* vino; *adj.* vinícola; — **cellar** bodega.

wing [wɪŋ] *s.* ala; bastidor (*de escenario*); **under the — of** bajo la tutela de; **to take — ** leventar el vuelo.

winged, wing·ed [wɪŋd, wɪŋɪd] *adj.* alado.

wing·spread [wɪ́ŋsprɛd] *s.* envergadura.

wink [wɪŋk] *v.* guiñar; pestanear, parpadear; *s.* guiño, guiñada; **I didn't sleep a —** no pegué los ojos en toda la noche.

win·ner [wɪ́nə] *s.* ganador; vencedor; **— of a prize** agraciado, premiado.

win·ning [wɪ́nɪŋ] *adj.* (*successful*) ganancioso; triunfante, victorioso; (*charming*) atractivo, encantador; **-s** *s. pl.* ganancias.

win·some [wɪ́nsəm] *adj.* simpático, atractivo, gracioso.

win·ter [wɪ́ntə] *s.* invierno; **— clothes** ropa de invierno; *v.* invernar, pasar el invierno.

win·try [wɪ́ntrɪ] *adj.* invernal, de invierno; frío, helado.

wipe [waɪp] *v.* secar; enjugar; limpiar; **to — away one's tears** limpiarse las lágrimas; **to — off** borrar; limpiar; **to — out a regiment** destruir o aniquilar un regimiento.

wire [waɪr] *s.* (*strand*) alambre; (*telegram*) telegrama; **by —** por telégrafo; **— entanglement** alambrada; **— fence** alambrado; **— netting** tela metálica, alambrado; **to pull -s** mover los hilos; *v.* poner alambrado, instalar alambrado eléctrico; atar con alambre; telegrafiar.

wire·less [wáɪrlɪs] *adj.* inalámbrico, sin hilos; **— telegraphy** radiotelegrafía; *s.* radio, radiotelegrafía; telegrafía sin hilos; radiotelefonía; radiograma.

wire tap·ping [wáɪrtæpɪŋ] *s.* secreta conexión interceptora de teléfono.

wir·y [wáɪrɪ] *adj.* de alambre; como alambre; nervudo.

wis·dom [wízdəm] *s.* sabiduría, saber; cordura; prudencia; **— tooth** muela del juicio.

wise [waɪz] *adj.* (*judicious*) sabio, cuerdo, sensato; (*prudent*) discreto, prudente; **the Three Wise Men** los Tres Reyes Magos; **to get —** to darse cuenta de; *s.* modo, manera; **in no —** de ningún modo.

wise·crack [wáɪzkræk] *s.* bufonada, dicho agudo o chocarrero, dicharacho.

wish [wɪʃ] *v.* desear, querer; **to — for** desear; anhelar; **I — it were true!** ¡ojalá (que) fuera verdad!; *s.* deseo.

wish·ful think·ing [wíʃfʊl θɪ́ŋkɪŋ] *s.* optimismo ilusorio.

wist·ful [wístfəl] *adj.* anhelante, anheloso, ansioso; tristón, melancólico.

wit [wɪt] *s.* agudeza, sal, chiste; ingenio; hombre agudo o de ingenio; **to be at one's wit's end** haber agotado todo su ingenio; **to be out of one's -s** estar fuera de sí, estar loco; **to lose one's -s** perder el juicio; **to use one's -s** valerse de su industria o ingenio.

witch [wɪtʃ] *s.* hechicera; bruja.

witch·craft [wítʃkræft] *s.* hechicería.

with [wɪð, wɪθ] *prep.* con; para con; en compañía de; **filled —** lleno de; **ill —** enfermo de; **the one — the black hat** el del (*o* la del) sombrero negro.

with·draw [wɪðdrɔ́] *v.* retirar(se); apartar(se); separar(se); **to — a statement** retractarse.

with·draw·al [wɪðdrɔ́əl] *s.* retirada, retiro.

with·drawn [wɪðdrɔ́n] *p.p. de* **to withdraw.**

with·drew [wɪðdrú] *pret. de* **to withdraw.**

with·er [wíðə] *v.* marchitar(se); ajar(se); secar(se).

with·held [wɪθhɛ́ld] *pret. & p.p. de* **to withhold.**

with·hold [wɪθhóld] *v.* retener; detener; **to — one's consent** negarse a dar su consentimiento.

with·in [wɪðín] *prep.* dentro de; **— call** al alcance de la voz; **— five miles** a poco menos de cinco millas; **it is — my power** está en mi mano; *adv.* dentro, adentro.

with·out [wɪðáʊt] *prep.* sin; **— my seeing him** sin que yo le viera; *adv.* fuera, afuera.

with·stand [wɪθstǽnd] *v.* resistir; aguantar, padecer.

with·stood [wɪθstúd] *pret. & p.p. de* **to withstand.**

wit·ness [wítnɪs] *s.* testigo; testimonio; *v.* ver, presenciar; ser testigo de; atestiguar, dar fe de.

wit·ti·cism [wítəsɪzəm] *s.* ocurrencia, agudeza, dicho agudo.

wit·ty [wítɪ] *adj.* agudo, ocurrente, gracioso; divertido, chistoso; **— remark** dicho agudo, agudeza, ocurrencia.

wives [waɪvz] *s. pl. de* **wife.**

wiz·ard [wízəd] *s.* genio, hombre de ingenio; mago, mágico.

wob·ble [wábl] *s.* bamboleo.

woe [wo] *s.* miseria, aflicción, infortunio; **— is me!** ¡miserable de mi!

woe·ful [wófʊl] *adj.* miserable; abatido.

woke [wok] *pret. de* **to wake.**

wolf [wʊlf] (*pl.* **wolves** [wʊlvz]) *s.* lobo.

wom·an [wúmən] (*pl.* **women** [wímɪn]) *s.* mujer; **— writer** escritora; **— chaser** mujeriego, faldero.

wom·an·hood [wúmənhʊd] *s.* estado de mujer; la mujer (las mujeres); integridad femenil; feminidad.

wom·an·kind [wúmənkaɪnd] *s.* la mujer, las mujeres, el sexo femenino.

wom·an·ly [wúmənlɪ] *adj.* femenil, mujeril, femenino; *adv.* femenilmente, como mujer.

womb [wum] *s.* vientre, entrañas; útero, matriz.

won [wʌn] *pret. & p.p. de* **to win.**

won·der [wʌ́ndə] *s.* (*marvel*) maravilla; prodigio; (*emotion*) admiración; **in —** maravillado; **no — that** no es mucho que; no es extraño que; *v.* asombrarse, maravillarse, pasmarse, admirarse; **to — at** admirarse de, maravillarse de; **I — what time it is** ¿qué hora será? **I — when he came** ¿cuándo vendría? **I should not — if** no me extrañaría que.

won·der·ful [wʌ́ndəfəl] *adj.* maravilloso, admirable; **-ly** *adv.* maravillosamente, admirablemente, a las mil maravillas; **-ly well** sumamente bien.

won·drous [wʌ́ndrəs] *adj.* maravilloso, pasmoso, extraño.

wont [wʌnt] *adj.* acostumbrado; **to be —** to soler, acostumbrar, *C.A.* saber; *s.* costumbre, hábito, uso.

woo [wu] *v.* cortejar, enamorar, galantear.

wood [wʊd] *s.* (*material*) madera; (*stick*) palo; (*firewood*) leña, **-s** bosque; selva; **— engraving** grabado en madera; **—shed** leñera, cobertizo par leña; **fire—** leña; **piece of fire—** leño.

wood·cut [wúdkʌt] *s.* grabado en madera.

wood·cut·ter [wúdkʌtə] *s.* leñador.

wood·ed [wúdɪd] *adj.* arbolado, poblado de árboles.

wood·en [wúdn] *adj.* de madera, de palo; tieso.

wood·land [wúdlænd] *s.* monte, bosque, selva.

wood·man [wúdmən] *s.* (*vendor*) leñador; (*dweller*) habitante del bosque.

wood·peck·er [wúdpɛkə] *s.* pájaro carpintero.

wood·work [wúdwɜk] *s.* maderamen; labrado en madera; obra de carpintería.

woof [wʊf] *s.* trama (*de un tejido*); tejido.

wool [wʊl] *s.* lana; *adj.* de lana; lanar; **wool-**

WH

bearing lanar; — **dress** vestido de lana.
wool·en [wúlın] *adj.* de lana; lanudo; — **mill** fábrica de tejidos de lana; *s.* tejido de lana; género o paño de lana.
wool·ly [wúlı] *adj.* lanudo; de lana.
word [wɜ́d] *s.* (*vocable*) palabra; vocablo, voz; (*news*) noticia, aviso; (*order*) mandato, orden; **pass**— contraseña; **by** — **of mouth** de palabra, verbalmente; *v.* expresar; redactar, formular.
word·y [wɜ́dı] *adj.* palabrero, verboso, ampuloso.
wore [wor] *pret. de* **to wear.**
work [wɜ́k] *s.* (*effort*) trabajo; (*masterpiece*) obra maestra (*task*) tarea; faena; (*employment*) empleo, ocupación; oficio; (*accomplishment*) labor; **-s** taller, fábrica; maquinaria, mecanismo; **at** — trabajando; ocupado; *v.* trabajar; funcionar; obrar; surtir efecto; manejar, manipular; resolver (*un problema*); explotar (*una mina*); hacer trabajar; **to** — **havoc** hacer estropicios, causar daño; **to** — **loose** soltarse, aflojarse; **to** — **one's way through college** sufragar los gastos universitarios con su trabajo; **to** — **one's way up** subir por sus propios esfuerzos; **to** — **out a plan** urdir un plan; **to be all -ed up** estar sobreexcitado; **it didn't** — **out** no dió resultado; **the plan -ed well** tuvo buen éxito el plan.
work·a·ble [wɚkəbl] *adj.* practicable; explotable.
work·er [wɜ́kɚ] *s.* trabajador; obrero; operario.
work·ing [wɜ́kıŋ] *s.* funcionamiento, operación; cálculo (*de un problema*); explotación (*de una mina*); *adj.* obrero, trabajador; — **class** clase obrera o trabajadora; — **hours** horas de trabajo; **a hard-working man** un hombre muy trabajador.
work·ing·man [wɜ́kıŋmæn] *s.* trabajador; obrero.
work·man [wɜ́kmən] *s.* trabajador, obrero, operario.
work·man·ship [wɜ́kmənʃɪp] *s.* hechura; trabajo; mano de obra.
work·shop [wɜ́kʃɑp] *s.* taller.
world [wɜ́ld] *s.* mundo; **the World War** la Guerra Mundial; **world-shaking** de gran importancia.
world·ly [wɜ́ldlı] *adj.* mundano, mundanal, terreno, terrenal.
worm [wɜ́m] *s.* gusano; lombriz; **worm-eaten** comido de gusanos; carcomido, apolillado; *v.* **to** — **a secret out of someone** extraerle o sonsacarle un secreto a una persona; **to** — **oneself into** insinuarse en, meterse en.
worn [worn] *p.p. de* **to wear; worn-out** gastado, roto; rendido de fatiga.
wor·ry [wɜ́ı] *s.* inquietud, ansiedad, cuidado, preocupación, apuro, apuración; *v.* inquietar(se), preocupar(se), afligir(se), apurar(se).
worse [wɜ́s] *adj.* peor; más malo; *adv.* peor; — **and** — cada vez peor; — **than ever** peor que nunca; **from bad to** — de mal en peor; **so much the** — tanto peor; **to be** — **off** estar peor que antes; **to change for the** — empeorar(se); **to get** — empeorar(se).
wor·ship [wɜ́ʃəp] *s.* adoración, culto; veneración; *v.* adorar; reverenciar.
wor·ship·er [wɜ́ʃəpɚ] *s.* adorador; **the -s** los fieles.
worst [wɜ́st] *adj.* peor; *adv.* peor; **the** — el peor; la peor; lo peor; *v.* derrotar.
worth [wɜ́θ] *s.* valor, valía, mérito; precio; **ten cent's** — of diez centavos de; **to get one's money's** — **out** sacar todo el provecho posible del dinero gastado en; *adj.* digno de; — **hearing** digno de oirso; **to be** — valer; **to be** — **doing** valer la pena de hacerse; **to be** — **while** valer la

pena.
worth·less [wɜ́θlıs] *adj.* sin valor; inútil; despreciable.
wor·thy [wɜ́ðı] *adj.* digno; valioso, apreciable; meritorio, merecedor; *s.* benemérito, hombre ilustre.
would [wud] *imperf. de indic. y de subj. del verbo* defect. **will: she** — **come every day** solía venir (o venía) todos los días; **if you** — **do it** si lo hiciera Vd.; *expresa a veces deseo:* — **that I knew it!** ¡quién lo supiera!; ¡ojalá que yo lo supiera!; *v. aux. del condicional:* **she said she** — **go** dijo que iría.
wound [wund] *s.* herida; llaga, lesión; *v.* herir; lastimar; agraviar.
wound [waund] *pret. & p.p. de* **to wind.**
wove [wov] *pret. de* **to weave.**
wo·ven [wóvən] *p.p. de* **to weave.**
wow [wau] *v.* entusiasmar.
wran·gle [ræŋgl] *v.* (*quarrel*) altercar, disputar; reñir; (*herd*) juntar; *Am.* rodear (*el ganado*); *s.* riña, pendencia.
wrap [ræp] *v.* envolver; enrollar, arrollar; **to** — **up** envolver(se); abrigar(se), tapar(se); **to be wrapped up in** estar envuelto en; estar absorto en; *s.* abrigo, manto.
wrap·per [ræpɚ] *s.* envoltura, cubierta; **woman's** — bata.
wrap·ping [ræpıŋ] *s.* envoltura; — **paper** papel de envolver.
wrath [ræθ] *s.* ira, cólera, rabia.
wrath·ful [ræθfəl] *adj.* colérico, rabioso, iracundo.
wreath [riθ] *s.* guirnalda, corona; — **of smoke** espiral de humo.
wreathe [rið] *v.* hacer guirnaldas; adornar con guirnaldas; **-d in smiles** sonriente.
wreck [rεk] *s.* (*destruction*) ruina; destrucción; (*shipwreck*) naufragio; (*accident*) accidente; (*wreckage*) destrozos, despojos (*de un naufragio*); *v.* arruinar; naufragar; echar a pique; destrozar, demoler; **to** — **a train** descarrilar un tren.
wrench [rεntʃ] *v.* torcer, retorcer; arrancar, arrebatar; *s.* torcedura, torsión; tirón, arranque, *Andes, Méx., C.A.* jalón; llave de tuercas; **monkey** — llave inglesa.
wrest [rεst] *v.* arrebatar, arrancar; usurpar.
wres·tle [rέsl] *v.* luchar a brazo partido; luchar; *s.* lucha a brazo partido.
wres·tler [rέslɚ] *s.* luchador (*a brazo partido*).
wretch [rεtʃ] *s.* miserable, infeliz; villano.
wretch·ed [rέtʃɪd] *adj.* (*miserable*) miserable; afligido; (*unfortunate*) desdichado, infeliz; (*bad*) bajo, vil; malísimo; **a** — **piece of work** un trabajo pésimo o malísimo.
wrig·gle [rɪgl] *v.* menear(se); retorcer(se); **to** — **out** of salirse, escaparse de; escabullirse de.
wring [rɪŋ] *v.* torcer, retorcer; exprimir, estrujar; **to** — **money from someone** arrancar dinero a alguien; **to** — **out** exprimir (*la ropa*).
wrin·kle [rɪŋkl] *s.* arruga; surco; **the latest** — **in style** la última novedad; *v.* arrugar(se).
wrist [rɪst] *s.* muñeca; — **watch** reloj de pulsera.
writ [rɪt] *s.* auto, orden judicial, mandato jurídico; **the Holy Writ** la Sagrada Escritura.
write [raɪt] *v.* escribir; **to** — **back** contestar por carta; **to** — **down** apuntar, poner por escrito; **to** — **off** cancelar (*una deuda*); **to** — **out** poner por escrito; escribir por entero; **to** — **up** relatar, describir; redactar.
writ·er [ráɪtɚ] *s.* escritor; autor.
writhe [raɪð] *v.* retorcerse.

writ·ing [ráıtıŋ] s. escritura; escrito; composición literaria; forma o estilo literario; **hand—** letra; **— desk** escritorio; **— paper** papel de escribir; **to put in —** poner por escrito.

writ·ten [rítŋ] p.p. *de* to write.

wrong [rɔŋ] adj. (*incorrect*) falso, incorrecto; equivocado; (*wicked*) malo; injusto; mal hecho; (*improper*) inoportuno; inconveniente; **the — side of a fabric** el envés o el revés de un tejido; **the — side of the road** el lado izquierdo o contrario del camino; **that is the — book** ése no es el libro; **it is in the — place** no está en su sitio, está mal colocado; *adv.* mal; al revés; **to go —** extraviarse, descaminarse; resultar mal; s. mal, daño perjuicio; injusticia; agravio; **to be in the —** no tener razón, estar equivocado; **to do —** hacer mal; v. perjudicar; agraviar; hacer mal a.

wrote [rot] pret. *de* to write.

wrought [rɔt] pret. & p.p. irr. *de* to work; adj. labrado; forjado; **— iron** hierro forjado; **— silver** plata labrada; **to be wrought-up** estar sobreexcitado.

wrung [rʌŋ] pret. & p.p. *de* to wring.

wry [raɪ] adj. torcido; **to make a — face** hacer una mueca.

X:x

xe·non [zinɑn] s. xenón.

Y:y

yacht [jɑt] s. yate; v. navegar en yate.

Yan·kee [jǽŋkɪ] adj. & s. yanqui.

yard [jɑrd] s. (*measure*) yarda (*medida*); (*enclosure*) patio; cercado; terreno (*adyacente a una casa*); **back —** corral; **barn—** corral; **navy —** arsenal; **ship—** astillero.

yard·stick [jɑ́rdstɪk] s. yarda (*de medir*); medida (*metro, vara, etc.*); patrón, norma.

yarn [jɑrn] s. estambre; hilado, hilaza; cuento enredado y poco probable.

yawn [jɔn] v. bostezar; s. bostezo.

year [jɪr] s. año; **—book** anuario; **-'s income** renta anual; **by the —** por año; **leap —** año bisiesto.

year·ling [jírlɪŋ] s. primal; becerro.

year·ly [jírlɪ] adj. anual; adv. anualmente; una vez al año, cada año.

yearn [jɝn] v. anhelar; **to — for** anhelar; suspirar por.

yearn·ing [jɝ́nɪŋ] s. anhelo.

yeast [jist] s. levadura, fermento.

yell [jɛl] v. gritar, dar gritos, vociferar; s. grito, alarido.

yel·low [jɛ́lo] adj. amarillo; cobarde; **— fever** fiebre amarilla; s. amarillo; v. poner(se) amarillo.

yel·low·ish [jɛ́loɪʃ] adj. amarillento.

yelp [jɛlp] v. aullar, ladrar; s. aullido, ladrido.

yes [jɛs] adv. sí.

yes·ter·day [jɛ́stɚdɪ] adv. & s. ayer; **day before —** anteayer o antier.

yet [jɛt] adv. & conj. todavía, aún; con todo, sin embargo; no obstante; **as —** todavía, aún; **not —** todavía no.

yield [jild] v. (*surrender*) ceder; rendir; someterse; (*produce*) producir; **to — five percent** redituar el cinco por ciento; s. rendimiento, rendición; rédito.

yod [jod] s. yod.

yo·del [jódl] s. canto en que la voz fluctúa entre natural y falsete.

yo·ga [jógə] s. yoga.

yo·gurt [jógɚt] s. yogur.

yoke [jok] s. yugo; yunta (*de bueyes, mulas, etc.*); v. uncir; unir.

yolk [jok] s. yema (*de huevo*).

yon·der [jándɚ] adj. aquel, aquella, aquellos, aquellas; adv. allá, allí, más allá, acullá.

yore [jor]: **in days of —** antaño, en días de antaño.

you [ju] pron. pers. tú, usted, vosotros, ustedes; te, le, lo, la, os, las, los; **to —** a tí, a usted, a vosotros, a ustedes; te, le, les; pron. impers. se, uno.

young [jʌŋ] adj. joven; nuevo; **— leaves** hojas tiernas; **— man** joven; **her — ones** sus niños, sus hijitos; **the — people** la gente joven, los jóvenes, la juventud; s. jóvenes; cría, hijuelos (*de los animales*).

young·ster [jʌ́ŋstɚ] s. muchacho, niño, jovencito, chiquillo.

your [jʊr] adj. tu (tus), vuestro (vuestra, vuestros, vuestras), su (sus), de usted, de ustedes.

yours [jʊrz] pron. pos. tuyo (tuya, tuyos, tuyas); vuestro (vuestra, vuestros, vuestras); suyo (suya, suyos, suyas), de usted, de ustedes; el tuyo (la tuya, los tuyos, las tuyas); el suyo (la suya, los suyos, las suyas); el (la, los, las) de usted; el (la, los, las) de ustedes; **a friend of —** un amigo tuyo, un amigo vuestro; un amigo suyo, un amigo de usted o ustedes.

your·self [jʊrsélf] pron. te, se (*como reflexivo*); **to — ** a tí mismo; a usted mismo; **you —** tú mismo; usted mismo; *véase* herself.

your·selves [jʊrsélvz] pron. os, se (*como reflexivo*); **to —** a vosotros mismos; a ustedes mismos; **you —** vosotros mismos; ustedes mismos.

youth [juθ] s. joven; juventud; jóvenes.

youth·ful [júθfəl] adj. joven; juvenil.

yt·tri·um [ítrıəm] s. itrio.

yuc·ca [jʌ́kə] s. yuca.

Yule·tide [júltaɪd] s. Pascua de Navidad; Navidades.

Z:z

zeal [zil] s. celo, fervor, ardor, entusiasmo.

zeal·ot [zélət] s. fanático.

zeal·ous [zéləs] adj. celoso, ardiente, fervoroso.

ze·nith [zínɪθ] s. cenit, cumbre.

zeph·yr [zéfɚ] s. céfiro.

ze·ro [zíro] s. cero.

zest [zɛst] s. entusiasmo; buen sabor.

zig·zag [zígzæg] s. zigzag; adj. & adv. en zigzag; v. zigzaguear, culebrear, andar en zigzag, serpentear.

zinc [zɪŋk] s. cinc (zinc).
zip code [zíp kod] s. sistema de cifras norteamericano, establecido para facilitar la entrega de cartas.
zip·per [zipɚ] s. cierre relámpago, abrochador corredizo o de corredera, *Am.* riqui.

zir·co·ni·um [zɪrkóniəm] s. circonio.
zo·di·ac [zódɪæk] s. zodíaco.
zone [zon] s. zona; *v.* dividir en zonas.
zoo [zu] s. jardín zoológico.
zo·o·log·i·cal [zoəládʒɪkl̩] *adj.* zoológico.
zo·ol·o·gy [zoáìədʒɪ] s. zoología.